Mastering™

Praise for the Previous Edition of *Mastering Delphi*

"Weighing in at a whopping 1,100 pages, this comprehensive, thorough, and skillfully written book makes the strong claim that it is the most comprehensive resource available for Delphi 5. Whether you are a beginner or an expert, this text offers exemplary coverage of this powerful programming tool. *Mastering Delphi 5* does a great job of explaining the new and exciting features of Delphi 5...."

—*Richard Dragan, Amazon.com Official Review*

"Another great catch-all of knowledge from Marco Cantù. This is a great book for up-and-coming developers and provides good examples for the seasoned folks as well."

—*www.delphiworld.com*

"Marco is one of the best-known members of the Delphi programming community.... [the] book offers the most complete coverage of Delphi programming available anywhere. No matter what your level of experience, you'll find expert instructions."

—*Zarko Gaijic, About.com's Delphi expert*

"Like its predecessors, *Mastering Delphi 5* covers the Delphi landscape remarkably well. Its comprehensiveness and attention to detail set it apart from many other general introductory texts. The newest edition continues this excellent tradition, and provides valuable information on the new features in Delphi 5. My opinion of Marco Cantù's excellent book has not changed with this latest edition; it's been strengthened....packed with useful tips, excellent information about new Delphi 5 features, and many practical programming examples.... I recommend it highly."

—*Alan C. Moore, Ph.D, Delphi Informant Magazine*

SYBEX®

www.sybex.com

MASTERING DELPHI 6

MASTERING™ DELPHI™ 6

Marco Cantù

SYBEX®

San Francisco • Paris • Düsseldorf • Soest • London

Associate Publisher: Richard Mills
Acquisitions Editor: Denise Santoro Lincoln
Developmental Editors: Diane Lowery and Denise Santoro Lincoln
Editor: Pete Gaughan
Production Editor: Leslie E. H. Light
Technical Editors: Danny Thorpe, Nando Dessena, and
Eddie Churchill
Graphic Illustrator: Tony Jonick
Electronic Publishing Specialist: Kris Warrenburg, Cyan Design
Proofreaders: Nanette Duffy, Amey Garber, Jennifer Greiman,
Emily Hsuan, Laurie O'Connell, Nancy Riddiough
Indexer: Ted Laux
CD Coordinator: Christine Harris
CD Technician: Kevin Ly
Book Designer: Robin Kibby
Cover Designer: Design Site
Cover Illustrator/Photographer: Sergie Loobkoff

Library of Congress Card Number: 2001088115
ISBN: 0-7821-2874-2

To Lella, the love of my life,
and Benedetta, our love come to life.

ACKNOWLEDGMENTS

This edition of *Mastering Delphi* marks the seventh year of the Delphi era, as it took Borland two years to release the latest incarnation of Delphi (along with its Linux twin, Kylix). As it has for many other programmers, Delphi has been my primary interest throughout these years; and writing, consulting, teaching, and speaking at conferences about Delphi have absorbed more and more of my time, leaving other languages and programming tools in the dust of my office. Because my work and my life are quite intertwined, many people have been involved in both, and I wish I had enough space and time to thank them all as they deserve. Instead, I'll just mention a few particular people and say a warm "Thank You" to the entire Delphi community (especially for the Spirit of Delphi 1999 Award I've been happy to share with Bob Swart).

The first official thanks are for the Borland programmers and managers who made Delphi possible and continue to improve it: Chuck Jazdzewski, Danny Thorpe, Eddie Churchill, Allen Bauer, Steve Todd, Mark Edington, Jim Tierney, Ravi Kumar, Jörg Weingarten, Anders Ohlsson, and all the others I have not had a chance to meet. I'd also like to give particular mention to my friends Ben Riga (the current Delphi product manager), John Kaster and David Intersimone (at Borland's Developer Relations), and others who have worked at Borland, including Charlie Calvert, Zack Urlocker, and Nan Borreson.

The next thanks are for the Sybex editorial and production crew, many of whom I don't even know. Special thanks go to Pete Gaughan, Leslie Light, Denise Santoro Lincoln, and Diane Lowery; I'd also like to thank Richard Mills, Kristine O'Callaghan, and Kris Warrenburg.

This edition of *Mastering Delphi* has once again had an incredibly picky and detailed review from Delphi R&D team member Danny Thorpe. His highlights and comments in this and past editions have improved the book in all areas: technical content, accuracy, examples, and even readability. Thanks a lot. Previous editions also had special contributions: Tim Gooch worked on Part V for *Mastering Delphi 4*, and Giuseppe Madaffari contributed database material for the Delphi 5 edition. For this edition, Guy Smith-Ferrier rewrote the chapter on ADO, and Nando Dessena helped me with the InterBase chapter. Many improvements to the text and sample programs were suggested by technical reviewers of past editions (Juancarlo Añez, Ralph Friedman, Tim Gooch, and Alain Tadros) and in other reviews over the years by Bob Swart, Giuseppe Madaffari, and Steve Tendon.

Special thanks go to my friends Bruce Eckel, Andrea Provaglio, Norm McIntosh, Johanna and Phil of the BUG-UK, Ray Konopka, Mark Miller, Cary Jensen, Chris Frizelle of *The Delphi Magazine*, Foo Say How, John Howe, Mike Orriss, Chad "Kudzu" Hower, Dan Miser, Marco Miotti, and the entire D&D Team (Paolo, Andrea, Uberto, Nando, Giuseppe, and Mr. Coke). Also, a very big "Thank You" to all the attendees of my Delphi programming courses, seminars, and conferences in Italy, the United States, France, the United Kingdom, Singapore, the Netherlands, Germany, Sweden....

My biggest thanks go to my wife Lella who had to endure yet another many-months-long book-writing session and too many late nights (after spending the evenings with our daughter, Benedetta—I'll thank her with a hug, as Daddy's book looks quite boring to her). Many of our friends (and their kids) provided healthy breaks in the work: Sandro and Monica with Luca, Stefano and Elena, Marco and Laura with Matteo and Filippo, Bianca, Luca and Elena with Tommaso, Chiara and Daniele with Leonardo, Laura, Vito and Marika with Sofia. Our parents, brothers, sisters, and their families were very supportive, too. It was nice to spend some of our free time with them and our six nephews—Matteo, Andrea, Giacomo, Stefano, Andrea, and Pietro.

Finally, I would like to thank all of the people, many of them unknown, who enjoy life and help to build a better world. If I never stop believing in the future and in peace, it is also because of them.

Contents at a Glance

CONTENTS

INTRODUCTION

The first time Zack Urlocker showed me a yet-to-be-released product code-named Delphi, I realized that it would change my work—and the work of many other software developers. I used to struggle with C++ libraries for Windows, and Delphi was and still is the best combination of object-oriented programming and visual programming for Windows.

Delphi 6 simply builds on this tradition and on the solid foundations of the VCL to deliver another astonishing and all-encompassing software development tool. Looking for database, client/server, multitier, intranet, or Internet solutions? Looking for control and power? Looking for fast productivity? With Delphi 6 and the plethora of techniques and tips presented in this book, you'll be able to accomplish all this.

Six Versions and Counting

Some of the original Delphi features that attracted me were its form-based and object-oriented approach, its extremely fast compiler, its great database support, its close integration with Windows programming, and its component technology. But the most important element was the Object Pascal language, which is the foundation of everything else.

Delphi 2 was even better! Among its most important additions were these: the Multi-Record Object and the improved database grid, OLE Automation support and the variant data type, full Windows 95 support and integration, the long string data type, and Visual Form Inheritance. Delphi 3 added to this the code insight technology, DLL debugging support, component templates, the TeeChart, the Decision Cube, the WebBroker technology, component packages, ActiveForms, and an astonishing integration with COM, thanks to interfaces.

Delphi 4 gave us the AppBrowser editor, new Windows 98 features, improved OLE and COM support, extended database components, and many additions to the core VCL classes, including support for docking, constraining, and anchoring controls. Delphi 5 added to the picture many more improvements of the IDE (too many to list here), extended database support (with specific ADO and InterBase datasets), an improved version of MIDAS with Internet support, the TeamSource version-control tool, translation capabilities, the concept of frames, and new components.

Now Delphi 6 adds to all these features support for cross-platform development with the new Component Library for Cross-Platform (CLX), an extended run-time library, the new dbExpress database engine, Web services and exceptional XML support, a powerful Web development framework, more IDE enhancements, and a plethora of new components and classes, as you'll see in the following pages.

Delphi is a great tool, but it is also a complex programming environment that involves many elements. This book will help you master Delphi programming, including the Object Pascal language, Delphi components (both using the existing ones and developing your own), database and client/server support, the key elements of Windows and COM programming, and Internet and Web development.

You do not need in-depth knowledge of any of these topics to read this book, but you do need to know the basics of Pascal programming. Having some familiarity with Delphi will help you considerably, particularly after the introductory chapters. The book starts covering its topics in depth immediately; much of the introductory material from previous editions has been removed. Some of this material and an introduction to Pascal is available on the companion CD-ROM and on my Web site and can be a starting point if you are not confident with Delphi basics. Each new Delphi 6 feature is covered in the relevant chapters throughout the book.

The Structure of the Book

The book is divided into four parts:

- Part I, "Foundations," introduces new features of the Delphi 6 Integrated Development Environment (IDE) in Chapter 1, then moves to the Object Pascal language and to the run-time library (RTL) and Visual Component Library (VCL), providing both foundations and advanced tips.

- Part II, "Visual Programming," covers standard components, Windows common controls, graphics, menus, dialogs, scrolling, docking, multipage controls, Multiple Document Interface, the Action List and Action Manager architectures, and many other topics. The focus is on both the VCL and CLX libraries. The final chapters discuss the development of custom components and the use of libraries and packages.

- Part III, "Database Programming," covers plain database access, in-depth coverage of the data-aware controls, client/server programming, dbExpress, InterBase, ADO and dbGo, DataSnap (or MIDAS), and the development of custom data-aware controls and data sets.

- Part IV, "Beyond Delphi: Connecting with the World," first discusses COM, OLE Automation, and COM+. Then it moves to Internet programming, covering TCP/IP sockets, Internet protocols and Indy, Web server-side extensions (with WebBroker and WebSnap), XML, and the development of Web services.

As this brief summary suggests, the book covers topics of interest to Delphi users at nearly all levels of programming expertise, from "advanced beginners" to component developers.

In this book, I've tried to skip reference material almost completely and focus instead on techniques for using Delphi effectively. Because Delphi provides extensive online documentation, to include lists of methods and properties of components in the book would not only be superfluous, it would also make it obsolete as soon as the software changes slightly. I suggest that you read this book with the Delphi Help files at hand, to have reference material readily available.

However, I've done my best to allow you to read the book away from a computer if you prefer. Screen images and the key portions of the listings should help in this direction. The book uses just a few conventions to make it more readable. All the source code elements, such as keywords, properties, classes, and functions, appear in `this font`, and code excerpts are formatted as they appear in the Delphi editor, with boldfaced keywords and italic comments and strings.

Free Source Code on CD (and the Web)

This book focuses on examples. After the presentation of each concept or Delphi component, you'll find a working program example (sometimes more than one) that demonstrates how the feature can be used. All told, there are about 300 examples presented in the book. These programs are directly available on the companion CD-ROM. The same material is also available on my Web site (`www.marcocantu.com`), where you'll also find updates and examples from past editions. Inside the back cover of the book, you'll find more information about the CD. Most of the examples are quite simple and focus on a single feature. More complex examples are often built step-by-step, with intermediate steps including partial solutions and incremental improvements.

NOTE   Some of the database examples also require you to have the Delphi sample database DBDEMOS installed; it is part of the default Delphi installation. Others require the InterBase EMPLOYEE sample database.

Beside the source code files, the CD hosts the ready-to-use compiled programs. There is also an HTML version of the source code, with full syntax highlighting, along with a complete cross-reference of keywords and identifiers (class, function, method, and property names, among others). The cross-reference is an HTML file, so you'll be able to use your browser to easily find all the programs that use a Delphi keyword or identifier you're looking for (not a full search engine, but close enough).

The directory structure of the sample code is quite simple. Basically, each chapter of the book has its own folder, with a subfolder for each example (e.g., 06\Borders). In the text, the examples are simply referenced by name (e.g., Borders).

TIP To change an example, first copy it (or the entire md6code folder) to your hard disk, but before opening it remember to set the read-only flag to False (it is True by default on the read-only media). You can also unzip the md6code.zip file, as suggested on the inside back cover of the book.

NOTE Be sure to read the source code archive's Readme file, which contains important information about using the software legally and effectively.

How to Reach the Author

If you find any problems in the text or examples in this book, both the publisher and I would be happy to hear from you. Besides reporting errors and problems, please give us your unbiased opinion of the book and tell us which examples you found most useful and which you liked least. There are several ways you can provide this feedback:

- On the Sybex Web site (www.sybex.com), you'll find updates to the text or code as necessary. To comment on this book, click the Contact Sybex link and then choose Book Content Issues. This link displays a form where you can enter your comments.

- My own Web site (www.marcocantu.com) hosts further information about the book and about Delphi, where you might find answers to your questions. The site has news and tips, technical articles, free online books, white papers, Delphi links, and my collection of Delphi components and tools.

- I have also set up a newsgroup section specifically devoted to my books and to general Delphi Q&A. Refer to my Web site for a list of the newsgroup areas and for the instructions to subscribe to them. (In fact, these newsgroups are totally free but require a login password.) The newsgroups can also be accessed via a Web interface you can find on my site.

- Finally, you can reach me via e-mail at marco@marcocantu.com. For technical questions, please try using the newsgroups first, as you might get answers earlier and from multiple people. My mailbox is usually quite full and, regretfully, I cannot reply promptly to every request. (Please write to me in English or Italian.)

PART I

Foundations

CHAPTER 1

The Delphi 6 IDE

- Object TreeView and Designer view

- The AppBrowser editor

- The code insight technology

- Designing forms

- The Project Manager

- Delphi files

In a visual programming tool such as Delphi, the role of the environment is at times even more important than the programming language. Delphi 6 provides many new features in its visual development environment, and this chapter covers them in detail. This chapter isn't a complete tutorial but mainly a collection of tips and suggestions aimed at the average Delphi user. In other words, it's not for newcomers. I'll be covering the new features of the Delphi 6 Integrated Development Environment (IDE) and some of the advanced and little-known features of previous versions as well, but in this chapter I won't provide a step-by-step introduction. Throughout this book, I'll assume you already know how to carry out the basic hands-on operations of the IDE, and all the chapters after this one focus on programming issues and techniques.

If you *are* a beginning programmer, don't be afraid. The Delphi Integrated Development Environment is quite intuitive to use. Delphi itself includes a manual (available in Acrobat format on the Delphi CD) with a tutorial that introduces the development of Delphi applications. You can also find a step-by-step introduction to the Delphi IDE on my Web site, `http://www.marcocantu.com`. The short online book *Essential Delphi* is based on material from the first chapters of earlier editions of *Mastering Delphi*.

Editions of Delphi 6

Before delving into the details of the Delphi programming environment, let's take a side step to underline two key ideas. First, there isn't a single edition of Delphi; there are many of them. Second, any Delphi environment can be customized. For these reasons, Delphi screens you see illustrated in this chapter may differ from those on your own computer. Here are the current editions of Delphi:

- The "Personal" edition is aimed at Delphi newcomers and casual programmers and has support for neither database programming nor any of the other advanced features of Delphi 6.

- The "Professional" edition is aimed at professional developers. It includes all the basic features, plus database programming support (including ADO support), basic Web server support (WebBroker), and some of the external tools. This book generally assumes you are working with at least the Professional edition.

- The "Enterprise" edition is aimed at developers building enterprise applications. It includes all the new XML and advanced Web services technologies, internationalization, three-tier architecture, and many other tools. Some chapters of this book cover features included only in Delphi Enterprise; these sections are specifically identified.

In the past, some of the features of Delphi Enterprise have been available as an "up-sell" to owners of Delphi Professional. This might also happen for this version.

Besides the different editions available, there are ways to customize the Delphi environment. In the screen illustrations throughout the book, I've tried to use a standard user interface (as it comes out of the box); however, I have my preferences, of course, and I generally install many add-ons, which might be reflected in some of the screen shots.

The Delphi 6 IDE

The Delphi 6 IDE includes large and small changes that will really improve a programmer's productivity. Among the key features are the introduction of the Object TreeView for every designer, an improved Object Inspector, extended code completion, and loadable views, including diagrams and HTML.

Most of the features are quite easy to grasp, but it's worth examining them with some care so that you can start using Delphi 6 at its full potential right away. You can see an overall image of Delphi 6 IDE, highlighting some of the new features, in Figure 1.1.

FIGURE 1.1:

The Delphi 6 IDE: Notice the Object TreeView and the Diagram view.

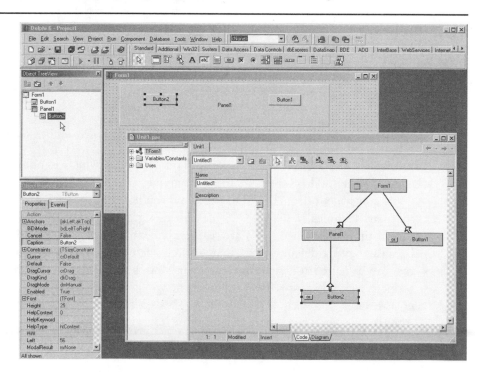

The Object TreeView

Delphi 5 introduced a TreeView for data modules, where you could see the relations among nonvisual components, such as datasets, fields, actions, and so on. Delphi 6 extends the idea by providing an Object TreeView for every designer, including plain forms. The Object TreeView is placed by default above the Object Inspector; use the View ➣ Object TreeView command in case it is hidden.

The Object TreeView shows all of the components and objects on the form in a tree, representing their relations. The most obvious is the parent/child relation: Place a panel on a form, a button inside it and one outside of the panel. The tree will show the two buttons, one under the form and the other under the panel, as in Figure 1.1. Notice that the TreeView is synchronized with the Object Inspector and Form Designer, so as you select an item and change the focus in any one of these three tools, the focus changes in the other two tools.

Besides parent/child, the Object TreeView shows also other relations, such as owner/owned, component/subobject, collection/item, plus various specific ones, including dataset/connection and data source/dataset relations. Here, you can see an example of the structure of a menu in the tree.

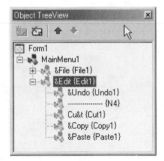

At times, the TreeView also displays "dummy" nodes, which do not correspond to an actual object but do correspond to a predefined one. As an example of this behavior, drop a Table component (from the BDE page) and you'll see two grayed icons for the session and the alias. Technically, the Object TreeView uses gray icons for components that do not have design-time persistence. They are real components (at design time and at run time), but because they are default objects that are constructed at run time and have no persistent data that can be edited at design time, the Data Module Designer does not allow you to edit their properties. If you drop a Table on the form, you'll also see items with a red question mark enclosed in a yellow circle next to them. This symbol indicates partially undefined items (there used to be a red square around those items in Delphi 5).

The Object TreeView supports multiple types of *dragging*:

- You can select a component from the palette (by clicking it, not actually dragging it), move the mouse over the tree, and click a component to drop it there. This allows you to drop a component in the proper container (form, panel, and others) regardless of the fact that its surface might be totally covered by other components, something that prevents you from dropping the component in the designer without first rearranging those components.

- You can drag components within the TreeView—for example, moving a component from one container to another—something that, with the Form Designer, you can do only with cut and paste techniques. Moving instead of cutting provides the advantage that if you have connections among components, these are not lost, as happens when you delete the component during the cut operation.

- You can drag components from the TreeView to the Diagram view, as we'll see later.

Right-clicking any element of the TreeView displays a shortcut menu similar to the component menu you get when the component is in a form (and in both cases, the shortcut menu may include items related to the custom component editors). You can even delete items from the tree.

The TreeView doubles also as a collection editor, as you can see here for the Columns property of a ListView control. In this case, you can not only rearrange and delete items, but also add new items to the collection.

TIP   You can print the contents of the Object TreeView for documentation purposes. Simply select the window and use the File ➤ Print command, as there is no Print command in the shortcut menu.

Loadable Views

Another important change has taken place in the Code Editor window. For any single file loaded in the IDE, the editor can now show multiple views, and these views can be defined programmatically and added to the system, then loaded for given files—hence the name *loadable* views.

The most frequently used view is the Diagram page, which was already available in Delphi 5 data modules, although it was less powerful. Another set of views is available in Web applications, including an HTML Script view, an HTML Result preview, and many others discussed in Chapter 22.

The Diagram View

Along with the TreeView, another feature originally introduced in Delphi 5 Data Modules and now available for every designer is the Diagram view. This view shows dependencies among components, including parent/child relations, ownership, linked properties, and generic relations. For dataset components, it also supports master/detail relations and lookup connections. You can even add your comments in text blocks linked to specific components.

The Diagram is not built automatically. You must drag components from the TreeView to the diagram, which will automatically display the existing relations among the components you drop there. In Delphi 6, you can now select multiple items from the Object TreeView and drag them all at once to the Diagram page.

What's nice is that you can set properties by simply drawing arrows between the components. For example, after moving an edit and a label to Diagram, you can select the Property Connector icon, click the label, and drag the mouse cursor over the edit. When you release the mouse button, the Diagram will set up a property relation based on the `FocusControl` property, which is the only property of the label referring to an edit control. This situation is depicted in Figure 1.2.

As you can see, setting properties is *directional*: If you drag the property relation line from the edit to the label, you end up trying to use the label as the value of a property of the edit box. Because this isn't possible, you'll see an error message indicating the problem and offering to connect the components in the opposite way.

In Delphi 6, the Diagram view allows you to create multiple diagrams for each Delphi unit—that is, for each form or data module. Simply give a name to the diagram and possibly add a description, click the New Diagram button, prepare another diagram, and you'll be able to switch back and forth between diagrams using the combo box available in the toolbar of the Diagram view.

FIGURE 1.2:

The Diagram view allows you to connect components using the Property connector.

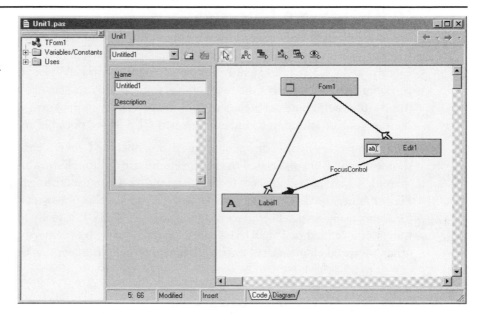

Although you can use the Diagram view to set up relations, its main role is to document your design. For this reason, it is important to be able to print the content of this view. Using the standard File ➤ Print command while the Diagram is active, Delphi prompts you for options, as you can see in Figure 1.3, allowing you to customize the output in many ways.

FIGURE 1.3:

The Print Options for the Diagram view

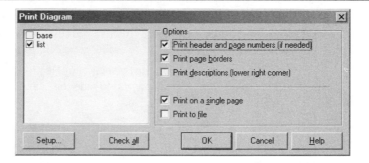

The information in the Data Diagram view is saved in a separate file, not as part of the DFM file. Delphi 5 used design-time information (DTI) files, which had a structure similar to INI files. Delphi 6 can still read the older .DTI format, but uses the new Delphi Diagram Portfolio format (.DDP). These files apparently use the DFM binary format (or a similar one), so they are not editable as text. All of these files are obviously useless at run time (it makes no sense to include them in the compilation of the executable file).

An IDE for Two Libraries

Another very important change I just want to introduce here is the fact that Delphi 6, for the first time, allows you to use to different component libraries, VCL (Visual Components Library) and CLX (Component Library for Cross-Platform). When you create a new project, you simply choose which of the two libraries you want to use, starting with the File ➤ New ➤ Application command for a classic VCL-based Windows program and with the File ➤ New ➤ CLX Application command for a new CLX-based portable application.

Creating a new project or opening an existing one, the Component Palette is rearranged to show only the controls related to the current library (although most of them are actually shared). This topic is fully covered in Chapter 6, so I don't want to get into the details here; I'll just underline that you can use Delphi 6 to build applications you can compile right away for Linux using Kylix. The effect of this change on the IDE is really quite large, as many things "under the hood" had to be reengineered. Only programmers using the ToolsAPI and other advanced elements will notice all these internal differences, as they are mostly transparent to most users.

Smaller Enhancements

Besides this important change and others I'll discuss in later sections, such as the update of the Object Inspector and of code completion, there are small (but still quite important) changes in the Delphi 6 IDE. Here is a list of these changes:

- There is a new Window menu in the IDE. This menu lists the open windows, something you could obtain in the past using the Alt+0 keys. This is really very handy, as windows often end up behind others and are hard to find. (Thanks, Borland, for listening to this and other simple but effective requests from users.)

TIP   Two entries of the Main Window registry section of Delphi (under `\Software\Borland\Delphi\6.0` for the current user) allow you to hide this menu and disable its alphabetic sort order. This registry keys use strings (in place of Boolean values) where "-1" indicates true and "0" false.

- The File menu doesn't include specific items for creating new forms or applications. These commands have been increased in number and grouped under the File ➤ New secondary menu. The Other command of this menu opens the New Item dialog box (the Object Repository) as the File ➤ New command did in the past.
- The Component Palette local menu has a submenu listing all of the palette pages in alphabetic order. You can use it to change the active page, particularly when it is not visible on the screen.

TIP   The order of the entries in the Tabs submenu of the Component Palette local menu can be set in the same order as the palette itself, and not sorted alphabetically. This is accomplished by setting to "0" (false) the value of the Sort Palette Tabs Menu key of the Main Window registry section of Delphi (under `\Software\Borland\Delphi\6.0` for the current user).

- There is a new toolbar, the Internet toolbar, which is initially disabled. This toolbar supports WebSnap applications.

Updated Environment Options Dialog Box

Quite a few small changes relate to the commonly used Environment Options dialog box. The pages of this dialog box have been rearranged, moving the Form Designer options from the Preferences page to the new Designer page. There are also a few new options and pages:

- The Preferences page of the Environment Options dialog box has a new check box that prevents Delphi windows from automatically docking with each other. This is a very welcome addition!

- A new page, Environment Variables, allows you to see system environment variables (such as the standard path names and OS settings) and set user-defined variables. The nice point is that you can use both system- and user-defined environment variables in each of the dialog boxes of the IDE—for example, you can avoid hard-coding commonly used path names, replacing them with a variable. In other words, the environment variables work similarly to the $DELPHI variable, referring to Delphi's base directory, but can be defined by the user.

- Another new page is called Internet. In this page, you can choose the default file extensions used for HTML and XML files (mainly by the WebSnap framework) and also associate an external editor with each extension.

Delphi Extreme Toys

At times, the Delphi team comes up with small enhancements of the IDE that aren't included in the product because they either aren't of general use or will require time to be improved in quality, user interface, or robustness. Some of these internal wizards and IDE extensions have now been made available, with the collective name of Delphi Extreme Toys, to registered Delphi 6 users. You should automatically get this add-on as you register your copy of the product (online or through a Borland office).

There isn't an official list of the content of the Extreme Toys, as Borland plans to keep extending them. The initial release includes an IDE-based search engine for seeking answers on Delphi across the Internet, a wizard for turning on and off specific compiler warnings, and an "invokamatic" wizard for accelerating the creation of Web services. The Extreme Toys will, in essence, be *unofficial* wizards, code utilities, and components from the Delphi team—or useful stuff from various people.

Recent IDE Additions

Delphi 5 provided a huge number of new features to the IDE. In case you've only used versions of Delphi prior to 5, or need to brush up on some useful added information, this is a short summary of the most important of the features introduced in Delphi 5.

Saving the Desktop Settings

The Delphi IDE allows programmers to customize it in various ways—typically, opening many windows, arranging them, and docking them to each other. However, programmers often need to open one set of windows at design time and a different set at debug time. Similarly, programmers might need one layout when working with forms and a completely different layout when writing components or low-level code using only the editor. Rearranging the IDE for each of these needs is a tedious task.

For this reason, Delphi allows you to save a given arrangement of IDE windows (called a *desktop*) with a name and restore it easily. Also, you can make one of these groupings your default debugging setting, so that it will be restored automatically when you start the debugger. All these features are available in the Desktops toolbar. You can also work with desktop settings using the View ➢ Desktops menu.

Desktop setting information is saved in DST files, which are INI files in disguise. The saved settings include the position of the main window, the Project Manager, the Alignment Palette, the Object Inspector (including its new property category settings), the editor windows (with the status of the Code Explorer and the Message View), and many others, plus the docking status of the various windows.

Here is a small excerpt from a DST file, which should be easily readable:

```
[Main Window]
Create=1
Visible=1
State=0
Left=0
Top=0
Width=1024
Height=105
ClientWidth=1016
ClientHeight=78
```

```
[ProjectManager]
Create=1
Visible=0
State=0
...
Dockable=1

[AlignmentPalette]
Create=1
Visible=0
...
```

Desktop settings override project settings. This helps eliminate the problem of moving a project between machines (or between developers) and having to rearrange the windows to your liking. Delphi 5 separates per-user and per-machine preferences from the project settings, to better support team development.

If you open Delphi and cannot see the form or other windows, I suggest you try checking (or deleting) the desktop settings. If the project desktop was last saved on a system running in a high-resolution video mode (or a multimonitor configuration) and opened on a different system with lower screen resolution or fewer monitors, some of the windows in the project might be located off-screen on the lower-resolution system. The simplest ways to fix that are either to load your own named desktop configuration after opening the project, thus overriding the project desktop settings, or just delete the DST file that came with the project files.

The To-Do List

Another feature added in Delphi 5 was the to-do list. This is a list of tasks you still have to do to complete a project, a collection of notes for the programmer (or programmers, as this tool can be very handy in a team). While the idea is not new, the key concept of the to-do list in Delphi is that it works as a two-way tool.

In fact, you can add or modify to-do items by adding special TODO comments to the source code of any file of a project; you'll then see the corresponding entries in the list. But you can also visually edit the items in the list to modify the corresponding source code comment. For example, here is how a to-do list item might look like in the source code:

```
procedure TForm1.FormCreate(Sender: TObject);
begin
  // TODO -oMarco: Add creation code
end;
```

The same item can be visually edited in the window shown in Figure 1.4.

FIGURE 1.4:

The Edit To-Do Item window can be used to modify a to-do item, an operation you can also do directly in the source code.

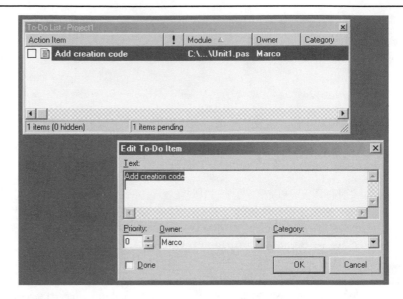

The exception to this two-way rule is the definition of project-wide to-do items. You must add these items directly to the list. To do that, you can either use the Ctrl+A key combination in the To-Do List window or right-click in the window and select Add from the shortcut menu. These items are saved in a special file with the .TODO extension.

You can use multiple options with a TODO comment. You can use –o (as in the code excerpt above) to indicate the owner, the programmer who entered the comment; the –c option to indicate a category; or simply a number from 1 to 5 to indicate the priority (0, or no number, indicates that no priority level is set). For example, using the Add To-Do Item command on the editor's shortcut menu (or the Ctrl+Shift+T shortcut) generated this comment:

```
{ TODO 2 -oMarco : Button pressed }
```

Delphi treats everything after the colon, up to the end of line or the closing brace, depending on the type of comment, as the text of the to-do item. Finally, in the To-Do List window you can check off an item to indicate that it has been done. The source code comment will change from TODO to DONE. You can also change the comment in the source code manually to see the check mark appear in the To-Do List window.

One of the most powerful elements of this architecture is the main To-Do List window, which can automatically collect to-do information from the source code files as you type them, sort and filter them, and export them to the Clipboard as plain text or an HTML table.

The AppBrowser Editor

The editor included with Delphi hasn't changed recently, but it has many features that many Delphi programmers don't know and use. It's worth briefly examining this tool. The Delphi editor allows you to work on several files at once, using a "notebook with tabs" metaphor, and you can also open multiple editor windows. You can jump from one page of the editor to the next by pressing Ctrl+Tab (or Shift+Ctrl+Tab to move in the opposite direction).

TIP   In Delphi 6, you can drag-and-drop the tabs with the unit names in the upper portion of the editor to change their order, so that you can use a single Ctrl+Tab to move between the units you are mostly interested in. The local menu of the editor has also a Pages command, which lists all of the available pages in a submenu, a handy feature when many units are loaded.

Several options affect the editor, located in the new Editor Properties dialog box. You have to go to the Preferences page of the Environment Options dialog box, however, to set the editor's AutoSave feature, which saves the source code files each time you run the program (preventing data loss in case the program crashes badly).

I won't discuss the various settings of the editor, as they are quite intuitive and are described in the online Help. A tip to remember is that using the Cut and Paste commands is not the only way to move source code. You can also select and drag words, expressions, or entire lines of code. You can also copy text instead of moving it, by pressing the Ctrl key while dragging.

The Code Explorer

The Code Explorer window, which is generally docked on the side of the editor, simply lists all of the types, variables, and routines defined in a unit, plus other units appearing in uses statements. For complex types, such as classes, the Code Explorer can list detailed information, including a list of fields, properties, and methods. All the information is updated as soon as you start typing in the editor. You can use the Code Explorer to navigate in the editor. If you double-click one of the entries in the Code Explorer, the editor jumps to the corresponding declaration.

TIP   In Delphi 6 you can modify variables, properties, and method names directly in the Code Explorer.

While all that is quite obvious after you've used Delphi for a few minutes, some features of the Code Explorer are not so intuitive. One important point is that you have full control of the layout of the information, and you can reduce the depth of the tree usually displayed in this window by customizing the Code Explorer. Collapsing the tree can help you make your selections more quickly. You can configure the Code Explorer by using the corresponding page of the Environment Options, as shown in Figure 1.5.

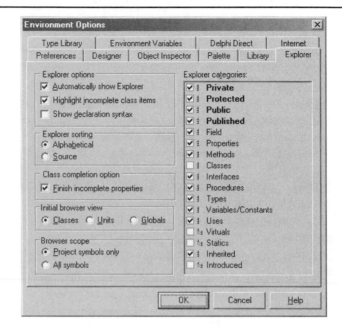

Notice that when you deselect one of the Explorer Categories items on the right side of this page of the dialog box, the Explorer doesn't remove the corresponding elements from view—it simply adds the node in the tree. For example, if you deselect the Uses check box, Delphi doesn't hide the list of the used units from the Code Explorer. On the contrary, the used units are listed as main nodes instead of being kept in the Uses folder. I generally disable the Types, Classes, and Variables selections.

Because each item of the Code Explorer tree has an icon marking its type, arranging by field and method seems less important than arranging by access specifier. My preference is to show all items in a single group, as this requires the fewest mouse clicks to reach each item. Selecting items in the Code Explorer, in fact, provides a very handy way of navigating the source code of a large unit. When you double-click a method in the Code Explorer, the focus moves to the definition in the class declaration (in the interface portion of the unit). You can use the Ctrl+Shift combination with the Up or Down arrow keys to jump from the definition of a method or procedure in the interface portion of a unit to its complete definition in the implementation portion (or back again).

NOTE   Some of the Explorer Categories shown in Figure 1.5 are used by the Project Explorer, rather than by the Code Explorer. These include, among others, the Virtuals, Statics, Inherited, and Introduced grouping options.

Browsing in the Editor

Another feature of the AppBrowser editor is *Tooltip symbol insight*. Move the mouse over a symbol in the editor, and a Tooltip will show you where the identifier is declared. This feature can be particularly important for tracking identifiers, classes, and functions within an application you are writing, and also for referring to the source code of the Visual Component Library (VCL).

WARNING   Although it may seem a good idea at first, you cannot use Tooltip symbol insight to find out which unit declares an identifier you want to use. If the corresponding unit is not already included, in fact, the Tooltip won't appear.

The real bonus of this feature, however, is that you can turn it into a navigational aid. When you hold down the Ctrl key and move the mouse over the identifier, Delphi creates an active link to the definition instead of showing the Tooltip. These links are displayed with the blue color and underline style that are typical of Web browsers, and the pointer changes to a hand whenever it's positioned on the link.

For example, you can Ctrl+click the TLabel identifier to open its definition in the VCL source code. As you select references, the editor keeps track of the various positions you've jumped to, and you can move backward and forward among them—again as in a Web browser. You can also click the drop-down arrows near the Back and Forward buttons to view a detailed list of the lines of the source code files you've already jumped to, for more control over the backward and forward movement.

How can you jump directly to the VCL source code if it is not part of your project? The AppBrowser editor can find not only the units in the Search path (which are compiled as part of the project), but also those in Delphi's Debug Source, Browsing, and Library paths. These directories are searched in the order I've just listed, and you can set them in the Directories/ Conditionals page of the Project Options dialog box and in the Library page of the Environment Options dialog box. By default, Delphi adds the VCL source code directories in the Browsing path of the environment.

Class Completion

The third important feature of Delphi's AppBrowser editor is *class completion*, activated by pressing the Ctrl+Shift+C key combination. Adding an event handler to an application is a fast operation, as Delphi automatically adds the declaration of a new method to handle the event in the class and provides you with the skeleton of the method in the implementation portion of the unit. This is part of Delphi's support for visual programming.

Newer versions of Delphi also simplify life in a similar way for programmers who write a little extra code behind event handlers. The new code-generation feature, in fact, applies to general methods, message-handling methods, and properties. For example, if you type the following code in the class declaration:

```
public
  procedure Hello (MessageText: string);
```

and then press Ctrl+Shift+C, Delphi will provide you with the definition of the method in the implementation section of the unit, generating the following lines of code:

```
{ TForm1 }
procedure TForm1.Hello(MessageText: string);
begin
end;
```

This is really handy, compared with the traditional approach of many Delphi programmers, which is to copy and paste one or more declarations, add the class names, and finally duplicate the begin...end code for every method copied.

Class completion can also work the other way around. You can write the implementation of the method with its code directly, and then press Ctrl+Shift+C to generate the required entry in the class declaration.

Code Insight

Besides the Code Explorer, class completion, and the navigational features, the Delphi editor supports the *code insight* technology. Collectively, the code insight techniques are based on a constant background parsing, both of the source code you write and of the source code of the system units your source code refers to.

Code insight comprises five capabilities: code completion, code templates, code parameters, Tooltip expression evaluation, and Tooltip symbol insight. This last feature was already covered in the section "Browsing in the Editor"; the other four will be discussed in the following subsections. You can enable, disable, and configure each of these features in the Code Insight page of the Editor Options dialog box.

Code Completion

Code completion allows you to choose the property or method of an object simply by looking it up on a list or by typing its initial letters. To activate this list, you just type the name of an object, such as `Button1`, then add the dot, and wait. To force the display of the list, press Ctrl+spacebar; to remove it when you don't want it, press Esc. Code completion also lets you look for a proper value in an assignment statement.

In Delphi 6, as you start typing, the list filters its content according to the initial portion of the element you've inserted. The code completion list uses colors and shows more details to help you distinguish different items. Another new feature is that in the case of functions with parameters, parentheses are included in the generated code, and the parameters list hint is displayed immediately.

As you type `:=` after a variable or property, Delphi will list all the other variables or objects of the same type, plus the objects having properties of that type. While the list is visible, you can right-click it to change the order of the items, sorting either by scope or by name, and you can also resize the window.

In Delphi 6, code completion also works in the interface section of a unit. If you press Ctrl+spacebar while the cursor is inside the class definition, you'll get a list of: virtual methods you can override (including abstract methods), the methods of implemented interfaces, the base class properties, and eventually system messages you can handle. Simply selecting one of them will add the proper method to the class declaration. In this particular case, the code completion list allows multiple selection.

TIP   When the code you've written is incorrect, code insight won't work, and you may see just a generic error message indicating the situation. It is possible to display specific code insight errors in the Message pane (which must already be open; it doesn't open automatically to display compilation errors). To activate this feature, you need to set an undocumented registry entry, setting the string key `\Delphi\6.0\Compiling\ShowCodeInsiteErrors` to the value '1'.

There are advanced features of Delphi 6 code completion that aren't easy to spot. One that I found particularly useful relates to the discovery of symbols in units not used by your project. As you invoke it (with Ctrl+spacebar) over a blank line, the list also includes symbols from common units (such as Math, StrUtils, and DateUtils) not already included in the `uses` statement of the current one. By selecting one of these *external* symbols, Delphi adds the unit to the `uses` statement for you. This feature (which doesn't work inside expressions) is driven by a customizable list of extra units, stored in the registry key `\Delphi\6.0\CodeCompletion\ExtraUnits`.

Code Templates

Code templates allow you to insert one of the predefined code templates, such as a complex statement with an inner `begin...end` block. Code templates must be activated manually, by typing Ctrl+J to show a list of all of the templates. If you type a few letters (such as a keyword) before pressing Ctrl+J, Delphi will list only the templates starting with those letters.

You can add your own custom code templates, so that you can build your own shortcuts for commonly used blocks of code. For example, if you use the `MessageDlg` function often, you might want to add a template for it. In the Code Insight page of the Environment Options dialog box, click the Add button in the Code Template area, type in a new template name (for example, **mess**), type a description, and then add the following text to the template body in the Code memo control:

```
MessageDlg ('|', mtInformation, [mbOK], 0);
```

Now every time you need to create a message dialog box, you simply type **mess** and then press Ctrl+J, and you get the full text. The vertical line (or pipe) character indicates the position within the source code where the cursor will be in the editor after expanding the template. You should choose the position where you want to start typing to complete the code generated by the template.

Although code templates might seem at first sight to correspond to language keywords, they are in fact a more general mechanism. They are saved in the `DELPHI32.DCI` file, so it should be possible to copy this file to make your templates available on different machines. Merging two code template files is not documented, though.

Code Parameters

Code parameters display, in a hint or Tooltip window, the data type of a function's or method's parameters while you are typing it. Simply type the function or method name and the open (left) parenthesis, and the parameter names and types appear immediately in a pop-up hint window. To force the display of code parameters, you can press Ctrl+Shift+spacebar. As a further help, the current parameter appears in bold type.

Tooltip Expression Evaluation

Tooltip expression evaluation is a debug-time feature. It shows you the value of the identifier, property, or expression that is under the mouse cursor.

More Editor Shortcut Keys

The editor has many more shortcut keys that depend on the editor style you've selected. Here are a few of the less-known shortcuts, most of which are useful:

- Ctrl+Shift plus a number key from 0 to 9 activates a bookmark, indicated in a "gutter" margin on the side of the editor. To jump back to the bookmark, press the Ctrl key plus the number key. The usefulness of bookmarks in the editor is limited by the facts that a new bookmark can override an existing one and that bookmarks are not persistent; they are lost when you close the file.

- Ctrl+E activates the incremental search. You can press Ctrl+E and then directly type the word you want to search for, without the need to go through a special dialog box and click the Enter key to do the actual search.

- Ctrl+Shift+I indents multiple lines of code at once. The number of spaces used is the one set by the Block Indent option in the Editor page of the Environment Options dialog box. Ctrl+Shift+U is the corresponding key for unindenting the code.

- Ctrl+O+U toggles the case of the selected code; you can also use Ctrl+K+E to switch to lowercase and Ctrl+K+F to switch to uppercase.

- Ctrl+Shift+R starts recording a macro, which you can later play by using the Ctrl+Shift+P shortcut. The macro records all the typing, moving, and deleting operations done in the source code file. Playing the macro simply repeats the sequence—an operation that might have little meaning once you've moved on to a different source code file. Editor macros are quite useful for performing multistep operations over and over again, such as reformatting source code or arranging data more legibly in source code.

- Holding down the Alt key, you can drag the mouse to select rectangular areas of the editor, not just consecutive lines and words.

The Form Designer

Another Delphi window you'll interact with very often is the Form Designer, a visual tool for placing components on forms. In the Form Designer, you can select a component directly with the mouse or through the Object Inspector, a handy feature when a control is behind another one or is very small. If one control covers another completely, you can use the Esc key to select the parent control of the current one. You can press Esc one or more times to select the form, or press and hold Shift while you click the selected component. This will deselect the current component and select the form by default.

There are two alternatives to using the mouse to set the position of a component. You can either set values for the Left and Top properties, or you can use the arrow keys while holding down Ctrl. Using arrow keys is particularly useful for fine-tuning an element's position. (The Snap To Grid option works only for mouse operations.) Similarly, by pressing the arrow keys while you hold down Shift, you can fine-tune the size of a component. (If you press Shift+Ctrl along with an arrow key, the component will be moved only at grid intervals.) Unfortunately, during these fine-tuning operations, the component hints with the position and size are not displayed.

To align multiple components or make them the same size, you can select several components and set the Top, Left, Width, or Height property for all of them at the same time. To select several components, you can click them with the mouse while holding down the Shift key, or, if all the components fall into a rectangular area, you can drag the mouse to "draw" a rectangle surrounding them. When you've selected multiple components, you can also set their relative position using the Alignment dialog box (with the Align command of the form's shortcut menu) or the Alignment Palette (accessible through the View ➢ Alignment Palette menu command).

When you've finished designing a form, you can use the Lock Controls command of the Edit menu to avoid accidentally changing the position of a component in a form. This is particularly helpful, as Undo operations on forms are limited (only an Undelete one), but the setting is not persistent.

Among its other features, the Form Designer offers several Tooltip hints:

- As you move the pointer over a component, the hint shows you the name and type of the component. Delphi 6 offers extended hints, with details on the control position, size, tab order, and more. This is an addition to the Show Component Captions environment setting, which I keep active.

- As you resize a control, the hint shows the current size (the Width and Height properties). Of course, this feature is available only for controls, not for nonvisual components (which are indicated in the Form Designer by icons).

- As you move a component, the hint indicates the current position (the Left and Top properties).

Finally, you can save DFM (Delphi Form Module) files in plain text instead of the traditional binary resource format. You can toggle this option for an individual form with the Form Designer's shortcut menu, or you can set a default value for newly created forms in the

Designer page of the Environment Options dialog box. In the same page, you can also specify whether the secondary forms of a program will be automatically created at startup, a decision you can always reverse for each individual form (using the Forms page of the Project Options dialog box).

Having DFM files stored as text was a welcome addition in Delphi 5; it lets you operate more effectively with version-control systems. Programmers won't get a real advantage from this feature, as you could already open the binary DFM files in the Delphi editor with a specific command of the shortcut menu of the designer. Version-control systems, on the other hand, need to store the textual version of the DFM files to be able to compare them and capture the differences between two versions of the same file.

In any case, note that if you use DFM files as text, Delphi will still convert them into a binary resource format before including them in the executable file of your programs. DFMs are linked into your executable in binary format to reduce the executable size (although they are not really compressed) and to improve run-time performance (they can be loaded faster).

> **NOTE**   Text DFM files are more portable between versions of Delphi than their binary version. While an older version of Delphi might not accept a new property of a control in a DFM created by a newer version of Delphi, the older Delphis will still be able to read the rest of the text DFM file. If the newer version of Delphi adds a new data type, though, older Delphis will be unable to read the newer Delphi's binary DFMs at all. Even if this doesn't sound likely, remember that 64-bit operating systems are just around the corner. When in doubt, save in text DFM format. Also note that all versions of Delphi support text DFMs, using the command-line tool Convert in the `bin` directory.

The Object Inspector in Delphi 6

Delphi 5 provided new features to the Object Inspector, and Delphi 6 includes even more additions to it. As this is a tool programmers use all the time, along with the editor and the Form Designer, its improvements are really significant.

The most important change in Delphi 6 is the ability of the Object Inspector to expand component references in-place. Properties referring to other components are now displayed in a different color and can be expanded by selecting the + symbol on the left, as it happens with internal subcomponents. You can then modify the properties of that other component without having to select it. See Figure 1.6 for an example.

> **NOTE**   This interface-expansion feature also supports subcomponents, as demonstrated by the new LabeledEdit control.

FIGURE 1.6:

A connected component (a pop-up menu) expanded in the Object Inspector while working on another component (a list box)

TIP   A related feature of the Object Inspector is the ability to select the component referenced by a property. To do this, double-click the property value with the left mouse button while keeping the Ctrl key pressed. For example, if you have a MainMenu component in a form and you are looking at the properties of the form in the Object Inspector, you can select the MainMenu component by moving to the MainMenu property of the form and Ctrl+double-clicking the value of this property. This selects the main menu indicated as the value of the property in the Object Inspector.

Here are some other relevant changes of the Object Inspector:

- The list at the top of the Object Inspector shows the type of the object and can be removed to save some space (and considering the presence of the Object TreeView).

- The properties that reference an object are now a different color and may be expanded without changing the selection.

- You can optionally also view read-only properties in the Object Inspector. Of course, they are grayed out.

- The Object Inspector has a new Properties dialog box (see Figure 1.7), which allows you to customize the colors of the various types of properties and the overall behavior of this window.

The new Object Inspector
Properties dialog box

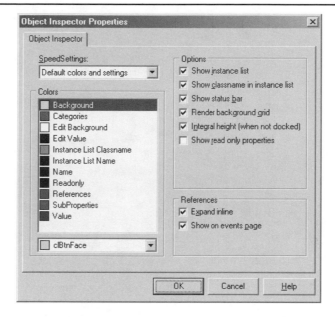

- Since Delphi 5, the drop-down list for a property can include graphical elements. This is used for properties such as Color and Cursor, and is particularly useful for the ImageIndex property of components connected with an ImageList.

NOTE   Interface properties can now be configured at design time using the Object Inspector. This makes use of the Interfaced Component Reference model introduced in Kylix/Delphi 6, where components may implement and hold references to interfaces as long as the interfaces are implemented by components. Interfaced Component References work like plain old component references, except that interface properties can be bound to any component that implements the necessary interface. Unlike component properties, interface properties are not limited to a specific component type (a class or its derived classes). When you click the drop-down list in the Object Inspector editor for an interface property, all components on the current form (and linked forms) that implement the interface are shown.

Drop-Down Fonts in the Object Inspector

The Delphi Object Inspector has graphical drop-down lists for several properties. You might want to add one showing the actual image of the font you are selecting, corresponding to the Name subproperty of the Font property. This capability is actually built into Delphi, but it has been disabled because most computers have a large number of fonts installed and rendering

Continued on next page

them can really slow down the computer. If you want to enable this feature, you have to install in Delphi a package that enables the `FontNamePropertyDisplayFontNames` global variable of the new VCLEditors unit. I've done this in the OiFontPk package, which you can find among the program examples for this chapter on the companion CD-ROM.

Once this package is installed, you can move to the `Font` property of any component and use the graphical Name drop-down menu, as displayed here:

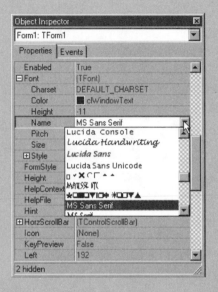

There is a second, more complex customization of the Object Inspector that I like and use frequently: a custom font for the entire Object Inspector, to make its text more visible. This feature is particularly useful for public presentations. You can find the package to install custom fonts in the Object Inspector on my Web site, `www.marcocantu.com`.

Property Categories

Delphi 5 also introduced the idea of property categories, activated by the Arrange option of the local menu of the Object Inspector. If you set it, properties won't be listed alphabetically but arranged by group, with each property possibly appearing in multiple groups.

Categories have the benefit of reducing the complexity of the Object Inspector. You can use the View submenu from the shortcut menu to hide properties of given categories, regardless of the way they are displayed (that is, even if you prefer the traditional arrangement by name, you can still hide the properties of some categories).

Secrets of the Component Palette

The Component Palette is very simple to use, but there are a few things you might not know. There are four simple ways to place a component on a form:

- After selecting a control in the palette, click within the form to set the position for the control, and press-and-drag the mouse to size it.

- After selecting any component, simply click within the form to place it with the default height and width.

- Double-click the icon in the palette to add a component of that type in the center of the form.

- Shift-click the component icon to place several components of the same kind in the form. To stop this operation, simply click the standard selector (the arrow icon) on the left side of the Component Palette.

You can select the Properties command on the shortcut menu of the palette to completely rearrange the components in the various pages, possibly adding new elements or just moving them from page to page. In the resulting Properties page, you can simply drag a component from the Components list box to the Pages list box to move that component to a different page.

TIP   When you have too many pages in the Component Palette, you'll need to scroll them to reach a component. There is a simple trick you can use in this case: Rename the pages with shorter names, so that all the pages will fit on the screen. Obvious—once you've thought about it.

The real undocumented feature of the Component Palette is the "hot-track" activation. By setting special keys of the Registry, you can simply select a page of the palette by moving over the tab, without any mouse click. The same feature can be applied to the component scrollers on both sides of the palette, which show up when a page has too many components. To activate this hidden feature, you must add an Extras key under HKEY_CURRENT_USER\Software\ Borland\Delphi\6.0. Under this key enter two string values, AutoPaletteSelect and AutoPaletteScroll, and set each value to the string '1'.

Defining Event Handlers

There are several techniques you can use to define a handler for an event of a component:

- Select the component, move to the Events page, and either double-click in the white area on the right side of the event or type a name in that area and press the Enter key.

- For many controls, you can double-click them to perform the default action, which is to add a handler for the OnClick, OnChange, or OnCreate events.

When you want to remove an event handler you have written from the source code of a Delphi application, you could delete all of the references to it. However, a better way is to delete all of the code from the corresponding procedure, leaving only the declaration and the begin and end keywords. The text should be the same as what Delphi automatically generated when you first decided to handle the event. When you save or compile a project, Delphi removes any empty methods from the source code and from the form description (including the reference to them in the Events page of the Object Inspector). Conversely, to keep an event handler that is still empty, consider adding a comment to it (even just the // characters), so that it will not be removed.

Copying and Pasting Components

An interesting feature of the Form Designer is the ability to copy and paste components from one form to another or to duplicate the component in the form. During this operation, Delphi duplicates all the properties, keeps the connected event handlers, and, if necessary, changes the name of the control (which must be unique in each form).

It is also possible to copy components from the Form Designer to the editor and vice versa. When you copy a component to the Clipboard, Delphi also places the textual description there. You can even edit the text version of a component, copy the text to the Clipboard, and then paste it back into the form as a new component. For example, if you place a button on a form, copy it, and then paste it into an editor (which can be Delphi's own source-code editor or any word processor), you'll get the following description:

```
object Button1: TButton
  Left = 152
  Top = 104
  Width = 75
  Height = 25
  Caption = 'Button1'
  TabOrder = 0
end
```

Now, if you change the name of the object, its caption, or its position, for example, or add a new property, these changes can be copied and pasted back to a form. Here are some sample changes:

```
object Button1: TButton
  Left = 152
  Top = 104
  Width = 75
  Height = 25
  Caption = 'My Button'
  TabOrder = 0
  Font.Name = 'Arial'
end
```

Copying this description and pasting it into the form will create a button in the specified position with the caption *My Button* in an Arial font.

To make use of this technique, you need to know how to edit the textual representation of a component, what properties are valid for that particular component, and how to write the values for string properties, set properties, and other special properties. When Delphi interprets the textual description of a component or form, it might also change the values of other properties related to those you've changed, and it might change the position of the component so that it doesn't overlap a previous copy. Of course, if you write something completely wrong and try to paste it into a form, Delphi will display an error message indicating what has gone wrong.

You can also select several components and copy them all at once, either to another form or to a text editor. This might be useful when you need to work on a series of similar components. You can copy one to the editor, replicate it a number of times, make the proper changes, and then paste the whole group into the form again.

From Component Templates to Frames

When you copy one or more components from one form to another, you simply copy all of their properties. A more powerful approach is to create a *component template*, which makes a copy of both the properties and the source code of the event handlers. As you paste the template into a new form, by selecting the pseudo-component from the palette, Delphi will replicate the source code of the event handlers in the new form.

To create a component template, select one or more components and issue the Component ≻ Create Component Template menu command. This opens the Component Template Information dialog box, where you enter the name of the template, the page of the Component Palette where it should appear, and an icon.

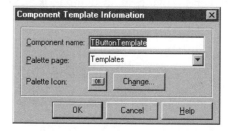

By default, the template name is the name of the first component you've selected followed by the word *Template*. The default template icon is the icon of the first component you've selected, but you can replace it with an icon file. The name you give to the component template will be used to describe it in the Component Palette (when Delphi displays the pop-up hint).

All the information about component templates is stored in a single file, DELPHI32.DCT, but there is apparently no way to retrieve this information and edit a template. What you can do, however, is place the component template in a brand-new form, edit it, and install it again as a component template *using the same name*. This way you can overwrite the previous definition.

Component templates are handy when different forms need the same group of components and associated event handlers. The problem is that once you place an instance of the template in a form, Delphi makes a copy of the components and their code, which is no longer related to the template. There is no way to modify the template definition itself, and it is certainly not possible to make the same change effective in all the forms that use the template. Am I asking too much? Not at all. This is what the *frames* technology in Delphi does.

A frame is a sort of panel you can work with at design time in a way similar to a form. You simply create a new frame, place some controls in it, and add code to the event handlers. After the frame is ready, you can open a form, select the Frame pseudo-component from the Standard page of the Component Palette, and choose one of the available frames (of the current project). After placing the frame in a form, you'll see it as if the components were copied to it. If you modify the original frame (in its own designer), the changes will be reflected in each of the instances of the frame.

You can see a simple example, called Frames1, in Figure 1.8 (its code is available on the companion CD). A screen snapshot doesn't really mean much; you should open the program or rebuild a similar one if you want to start playing with frames. Like forms, frames define classes, so they fit within the VCL object-oriented model much more easily than component templates. Chapter 4 provides an in-depth look at VCL and includes a more detailed description of frames. As you might imagine from this short introduction, frames are a powerful new technique.

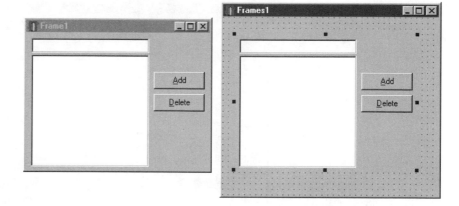

FIGURE 1.8:

The Frames1 example demonstrates the use of frames. The frame (on the left) and its instance inside a form (on the right) are kept in synch.

Managing Projects

Delphi's multitarget Project Manager (View ➤ Project Manager) works on a project *group*, which can have one or more projects under it. For example, a project group can include a DLL and an executable file, or multiple executable files.

> **TIP**   In Delphi 6, all open packages will show up as projects in the Project Manager view, even if they haven't been added to the project group.

In Figure 1.9, you can see the Project Manager with the project group for the current chapter. As you can see, the Project Manager is based on a tree view, which shows the hierarchical structure of the project group, the projects, and all of the forms and units that make up each project. You can use the simple toolbar and the more complex shortcut menus of the Project Manager to operate on it. The shortcut menu is context-sensitive; its options depend on the selected item. There are menu items to add a new or existing project to a project group, to compile or build a specific project, or to open a unit.

Of all the projects in the group, only one is active, and this is the project you operate upon when you select a command such as Project ➤ Compile. The Project pull-down of the main menu has two commands you can use to compile or build all the projects of the group. (Strangely enough, these commands are not available in the shortcut menu of the Project Manager for the project group.) When you have multiple projects to build, you can set a relative order by using the Build Sooner and Build Later commands. These two commands basically rearrange the projects in the list.

FIGURE 1.9:

Delphi's multitarget Project
Manager

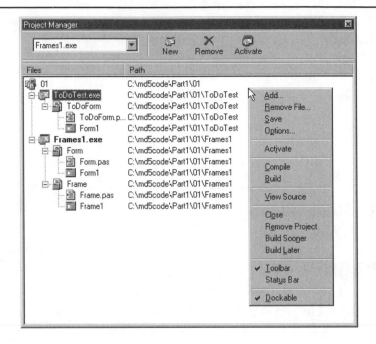

Among its advanced features, you can drag source code files from Windows folders or Windows Explorer onto a project in the Project Manager window to add them to that project.

The Project Manager automatically selects as the current project the one you are working with—for example, opening a file. You can easily see which project is selected and change it by using the combo box on the top of the form.

TIP   Besides adding Pascal files and projects, you can add Windows resource files to the Project Manager; they are compiled along with the project. Simply move to a project, select the Add shortcut menu, and choose Resource File (*.rc) as the file type. This resource file will be automatically bound to the project, even without a corresponding $R directive.

Delphi saves the project groups with the new .BPG extension, which stands for Borland Project Group. This feature comes from C++Builder and from past Borland C++ compilers, a history that is clearly visible as you open the source code of a project group, which is basically that of a makefile in a C/C++ development environment. Here is a simple example:

```
#————————————————————————
VERSION = BWS.01
#————————————————————————
!ifndef ROOT
ROOT = $(MAKEDIR)\..
```

```
!endif
#------------------------------
MAKE = $(ROOT)\bin\make.exe -$(MAKEFLAGS) -f$**
DCC = $(ROOT)\bin\dcc32.exe $**
BRCC = $(ROOT)\bin\brcc32.exe $**
#------------------------------
PROJECTS = Project1.exe
#------------------------------
default: $(PROJECTS)
#------------------------------
Project1.exe: Project1.dpr
  $(DCC)
```

Project Options

The Project Manager doesn't provide a way to set the options of two different projects at one time. What you can do instead is invoke the Project Options dialog from the Project Manager for each project. The first page of Project Options (Forms) lists the forms that should be created automatically at program startup and the forms that are created manually by the program. The next page (Application) is used to set the name of the application and the name of its Help file, and to choose its icon. Other Project Options choices relate to the Delphi compiler and linker, version information, and the use of run-time packages.

There are two ways to set compiler options. One is to use the Compiler page of the Project Options dialog. The other is to set or remove individual options in the source code with the {$X+} or {$X-} commands, where you'd replace X with the option you want to set. This second approach is more flexible, since it allows you to change an option only for a specific source-code file, or even for just a few lines of code. The source-level options override the compile-level options.

All project options are saved automatically with the project, but in a separate file with a .DOF extension. This is a text file you can easily edit. You should not delete this file if you have changed any of the default options. Delphi also saves the compiler options in another format in a CFG file, for command-line compilation. The two files have similar content but a different format: The *dcc* command-line compiler, in fact, cannot use .DOF files, but needs the .CFG format.

Another alternative for saving compiler options is to press Ctrl+O+O (press the O key twice while keeping Ctrl pressed). This inserts, at the top of the current unit, compiler directives that correspond to the current project options, as in the following listing:

```
{$A+,B-,C+,D+,E-,F-,G+,H+,I+,J+,K-,L+,M-,N+,O+,P+,Q-,R-,S-,T-,U-,V+,
W-,X+,Y+,Z1}

{$MINSTACKSIZE $00004000}
```

```
{$MAXSTACKSIZE $00100000}

{$IMAGEBASE $00400000}

{$APPTYPE GUI}
```

Compiling and Building Projects

There are several ways to compile a project. If you run it (by pressing F9 or clicking the Run toolbar icon), Delphi will compile it first. When Delphi compiles a project, it compiles only the files that have changed.

If you select Compile ➢ Build All instead, every file is compiled, even if it has not changed. You should only need this second command infrequently, since Delphi can usually determine which files have changed and compile them as required. The only exception is when you change some project options, in which case you have to use the Build All command to put the new options into effect.

To build a project, Delphi first compiles each source code file, generating a Delphi compiled unit (DCU). (This step is performed only if the DCU file is not already up-to-date.) The second step, performed by the linker, is to merge all the DCU files into the executable file, optionally with compiled code from the VCL library (if you haven't decided to use packages at run time). The third step is binding into the executable file any optional resource files, such as the RES file of the project, which hosts its main icon, and the DFM files of the forms. You can better understand the compilation steps and follow what happens during this operation if you enable the Show Compiler Progress option (in the Preferences page of the Environment Options dialog box).

WARNING   Delphi doesn't always properly keep track of when to rebuild units based on other units you've modified. This is particularly true for the cases (and there are many) in which user intervention confuses the compiler logic. For example, renaming files, modifying source files outside the IDE, copying older source files or DCU files to disk, or having multiple copies of a unit source file in your search path can break the compilation. Every time the compiler shows some strange error message, the first thing you should try is the Build All command to resynchronize the make feature with the current files on disk.

The Compile command can be used only when you have loaded a project in the editor. If no project is active and you load a Pascal source file, you cannot compile it. However, if you load the source file *as if it were a project*, that will do the trick and you'll be able to compile the file. To do this, simply select the Open Project toolbar button and load a PAS file. Now you can check its syntax or compile it, building a DCU.

I've mentioned before that Delphi allows you to use run-time packages, which affect the distribution of the program more than the compilation process. Delphi packages are dynamic link libraries (DLLs) containing Delphi components. By using packages, you can make an executable file much smaller. However, the program won't run unless the proper dynamic link libraries (such as vc150.bpl, which is quite large) are available on the computer where you want to run the program.

If you add the size of this dynamic library to that of the small executable file, the total amount of disk space required by the apparently smaller program built with run-time packages is much larger than the space required by the apparently bigger stand-alone executable file. Of course, if you have multiple applications on a single system, you'll end up saving a lot, both in disk space and memory consumption at run time. The use of packages is often but not always recommended. I'll discuss all the implications of packages in detail in Chapter 12.

In both cases, Delphi executables are extremely fast to compile, and the speed of the resulting application is comparable to that of a C or C++ program. Delphi compiled code runs at least five times faster than the equivalent code in interpreted or "semicompiled" tools.

Exploring a Project

Past versions of Delphi included an Object Browser, which you could use when a project was compiled to see a hierarchical structure of its classes and to look for its symbols and the source-code lines where they are referenced. Delphi now includes a similar but enhanced tool, called Project Explorer. Like the Code Explorer, it is updated automatically as you type, without recompiling the project.

The Project Explorer allows you to list Classes, Units, and Globals, and lets you choose whether to look only for symbols defined within your project or for those from both your project and VCL. You can see an example with only project symbols in Figure 1.10.

FIGURE 1.10:

The Project Explorer

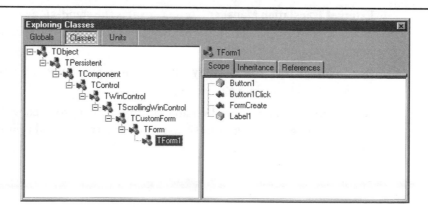

You can change the settings of this Explorer and those of the Code Explorer in the Explorer page of the Environment Options or by selecting the Properties command in the shortcut menu of the Project Explorer. Some of the Explorer categories you see in this window are specific to the Project Explorer; others relate to both tools.

Additional and External Delphi Tools

Besides the IDE, when you install Delphi you get other, external tools. Some of them, such as the Database Desktop, the Package Collection Editor (PCE.exe), and the Image Editor (ImagEdit.exe), are available from Tools menu of the IDE. In addition, the Enterprise edition has a link to the SQL Monitor (SqlMon.exe).

Other tools that are not directly accessible from the IDE include many command-line tools you can find in the bin directory of Delphi. For example, there is a command-line Delphi compiler (DCC.exe), a Borland resource compiler (BRC32.exe and BRCC32.exe), and an executable viewer (TDump.exe).

Finally, some of the sample programs that ship with Delphi are actually useful tools that you can compile and keep at hand. I'll discuss some of these tools in the book, as needed. Here are a few of the useful and higher-level tools, mostly available in the \Delphi6\bin folder and in the Tools menu:

Web App Debugger (WebAppDbg.exe) is the debugging Web server introduced in Delphi 6. It is used to keep track of the requests send to your applications and debug them. I'll discuss this tool in Chapter 21.

XML Mapper (XmlMapper.exe), again new in Delphi 6, is a tool for creating XML transformations to be applied to the format produced by the ClientDataSet component. More on this topic in Chapter 22.

External Translation Manager (etm60.exe) is the stand-alone version of the Integrated Translation Manager. This external tool can be given to external translators and is available for the first time in Delphi 6.

Borland Registry Cleanup Utility (D6RegClean.exe) helps you remove all of the Registry entries added by Delphi 6 to a computer.

TeamSource is an advanced version-control system provided with Delphi, starting with version 5. The tool is very similar to its past incarnation and is installed separately from Delphi.

WinSight   (Ws.exe) is a Windows "message spy" program available in the bin directory.

Database Explorer   can be activated from the Delphi IDE or as a stand-alone tool, using the DBExplor.exe program of the bin directory.

OpenHelp   (oh.exe) is the tool you can use to manage the structure of Delphi's own Help files, integrating third-party files into the help system.

Convert   (Convert.exe) is a command-line tool you can use to convert DFM files into the equivalent textual description and vice versa.

Turbo Grep   (Grep.exe) is a command-line search utility, much faster than the embedded Find In Files mechanism but not so easy to use.

Turbo Register Server   (TRegSvr.exe) is a tool you can use to register ActiveX libraries and COM servers. The source code of this tool is available under \Demos\ActiveX\ TRegSvr.

Resource Explorer   is a powerful resource viewer (but not a full-blown resource editor) you can find under \Demos\ResXplor.

Resource Workshop   The Delphi 5 CD also includes a separate installation for Resource Workshop. This is an old 16-bit resource editor that can also manage Win32 resource files. It was formerly included in Borland C++ and Pascal compilers for Windows and was much better than the standard Microsoft resource editors then available. Although its user interface hasn't been updated and it doesn't handle long filenames, this tool can still be very useful for building custom or special resources. It also lets you explore the resources of existing executable files.

The Files Produced by the System

Delphi produces various files for each project, and you should know what they are and how they are named. Basically, two elements have an impact on how files are named: the names you give to a project and its units, and the predefined file extensions used by Delphi. Table 1.1 lists the extensions of the files you'll find in the directory where a Delphi project resides. The table also shows when or under what circumstances these files are created and their importance for future compilations.

TABLE 1.1: Delphi Project File Extensions

Extension	File Type and Description	Creation Time	Required to Compile?
.BMP, .ICO, .CUR	Bitmap, icon, and cursor files: standard Windows files used to store bitmapped images.	Development: Image Editor	Usually not, but they might be needed at run time and for further editing.
.BPG	Borland Project Group: the files used by the new multiple-target Project Manager. It is a sort of makefile.	Development	Required to recompile all the projects of the group at once.
.BPL	Borland Package Library: a DLL including VCL components to be used by the Delphi environment at design time or by applications at run time. (These files used a .DPL extension in Delphi 3.)	Compilation: Linking	You'll distribute packages to other Delphi developers and, optionally, to end-users.
.CAB	The Microsoft Cabinet compressed-file format used for Web deployment by Delphi. A CAB file can store multiple compressed files.	Compilation	Distributed to users.
.CFG	Configuration file with project options. Similar to the DOF files.	Development	Required only if special compiler options have been set.
.DCP	Delphi Component Package: a file with symbol information for the code that was compiled into the package. It doesn't include compiled code, which is stored in DCU files.	Compilation	Required when you use packages. You'll distribute it only to other developers along with DPL files.
.DCU	Delphi Compiled Unit: the result of the compilation of a Pascal file.	Compilation	Only if the source code is not available. DCU files for the units you write are an intermediate step, so they make compilation faster.
.DDP	The new Delphi Diagram Portfolio, used by the Diagram view of the editor (was .DTI in Delphi 5)	Development	No. This file stores "design-time only" information, not required by the resulting program but very important for the programmer.

TABLE 1.1 continued: Delphi Project File Extensions

Extension	File Type and Description	Creation Time	Required to Compile?
.DFM	Delphi Form File: a binary file with the description of the properties of a form (or a data module) and of the components it contains.	Development	Yes. Every form is stored in both a PAS and a DFM file.
.~DF	Backup of Delphi Form File (DFM).	Development	No. This file is produced when you save a new version of the unit related to the form and the form file along with it.
.DFN	Support file for the Integrated Translation Environment (there is one DFN file for each form and each target language).	Development (ITE)	Yes (for ITE). These files contain the translated strings that you edit in the Translation Manager.
.DLL	Dynamic Link Library: another version of an executable file.	Compilation: Linking	See .EXE.
.DOF	Delphi Option File: a text file with the current settings for the project options.	Development	Required only if special compiler options have been set.
.DPK	Delphi Package: the project source code file of a package.	Development	Yes.
.DPR	Delphi Project file. (This file actually contains Pascal source code.)	Development	Yes.
.~DP	Backup of the Delphi Project file (.DPR).	Development	No. This file is generated automatically when you save a new version of a project file.
.DSK	Desktop file: contains information about the position of the Delphi windows, the files open in the editor, and other Desktop settings.	Development	No. You should actually delete it if you copy the project to a new directory.

TABLE 1.1 continued: Delphi Project File Extensions

Extension	File Type and Description	Creation Time	Required to Compile?
.DSM	Delphi Symbol Module: stores all the browser symbol information.	Compilation (but only if the Save Symbols option is set)	No. Object Browser uses this file, instead of the data in memory, when you cannot recompile a project.
.EXE	Executable file: the Windows application you've produced.	Compilation: Linking	No. This is the file you'll distribute. It includes all of the compiled units, forms, and resources.
.HTM	Or .HTML, for Hypertext Markup Language: the file format used for Internet Web pages.	Web deployment of an ActiveForm	No. This is not involved in the project compilation.
.LIC	The license files related to an OCX file.	ActiveX Wizard and other tools	No. It is required to use the control in another development environment.
.OBJ	Object (compiled) file, typical of the C/C++ world.	Intermediate compilation step, generally not used in Delphi	It might be required to merge Delphi with C++ compiled code in a single project.
OCX	OLE Control Extension: a special version of a DLL, containing ActiveX controls or forms.	Compilation: Linking	See .EXE.
.PAS	Pascal file: the source code of a Pascal unit, either a unit related to a form or a stand-alone unit.	Development	Yes.
.~PA	Backup of the Pascal file (.PAS).	Development	No. This file is generated automatically by Delphi when you save a new version of the source code.
.RES, .RC	Resource file: the binary file associated with the project and usually containing its icon. You can add other files of this type to a project. When you create custom resource files you might use also the textual format, .RC.	Development Options dialog box. The ITE (Integrated Translation Environment) generates resource files with special comments.	Yes. The main RES file of an application is rebuilt by Delphi according to the information in the Application page of the Project Options dialog box.

TABLE 1.1 continued: Delphi Project File Extensions

Extension	File Type and Description	Creation Time	Required to Compile?
.RPS	Translation Repository (part of the Integrated Translation Environment).	Development (ITE)	No. Required to manage the translations.
.TLB	Type Library: a file built automatically or by the Type Library Editor for OLE server applications.	Development	This is a file other OLE programs might need.
TODO	To-do list file, holding the items related to the entire project.	Development	No. This file hosts notes for the programmers.
.UDL	Microsoft Data Link.	Development	Used by ADO to refer to a data provider. Similar to an alias in the BDE world (see Chapter 12).

Besides the files generated during the development of a project in Delphi, there are many others generated and used by the IDE itself. In Table 1.2, I've provided a short list of extensions worth knowing about. Most of these files are in proprietary and undocumented formats, so there is little you can do with them.

TABLE 1.2: Selected Delphi IDE Customization File Extensions

Extension	File Type
.DCI	Delphi code templates
.DRO	Delphi's Object Repository (The repository should be modified with the Tools ➢ Repository command.)
.DMT	Delphi menu templates
.DBI	Database Explorer information
.DEM	Delphi edit mask (files with country-specific formats for edit masks)
.DCT	Delphi component templates
.DST	Desktop settings file (one for each desktop setting you've defined)

Looking at Source Code Files

I've just listed some files related to the development of a Delphi application, but I want to spend a little time covering their actual format. The fundamental Delphi files are Pascal source code files, which are plain ASCII text files. The bold, italic, and colored text you see in the editor depends on syntax highlighting, but it isn't saved with the file. It is worth noting that there is one single file for the whole code of the form, not just small code fragments.

TIP   In the listings in this book, I've matched the bold syntax highlighting of the editor for keywords and the italic for strings and comments.

For a form, the Pascal file contains the form class declaration and the source code of the event handlers. The values of the properties you set in the Object Inspector are stored in a separate form description file (with a .DFM extension). The only exception is the Name property, which is used in the form declaration to refer to the components of the form.

The DFM file is a binary and, in Delphi, can be saved either as a plain-text file or in the traditional Windows Resource format. You can set the default format you want to use for new projects in the Preferences page of the Environment Options dialog box, and you can toggle the format of individual forms with the Text DFM command of a form's shortcut menu. A plain-text editor can read only the text version. However, you can load DFM files of both types in the Delphi editor, which will, if necessary, first convert them into a textual description. The simplest way to open the textual description of a form (whatever the format) is to select the View As Text command on the shortcut menu in the Form Designer. This closes the form, saving it if necessary, and opens the DFM file in the editor. You can later go back to the form using the View As Form command on the shortcut menu in the editor window.

You can actually edit the textual description of a form, although this should be done with extreme care. As soon as you save the file, it will be turned back into a binary file. If you've made incorrect changes, compilation will stop with an error message and you'll need to correct the contents of your DFM file before you can reopen the form. For this reason, you shouldn't try to change the textual description of a form manually until you have good knowledge of Delphi programming.

TIP   In the book, I often show you excerpts of DFM files. In most of these excerpts, I only show the most relevant components or properties; generally, I have removed the positional properties, the binary values, and other lines providing little useful information.

In addition to the two files describing the form (PAS and DFM), a third file is vital for rebuilding the application. This is the Delphi project file (DPR), which is another Pascal source code file. This file is built automatically, and you seldom need to change it manually. You can see this file with the View ➤ Project Source menu command.

Some of the other, less relevant files produced by the IDE use the structure of Windows INI files, in which each section is indicated by a name enclosed in square brackets. For example, this is a fragment of an option file (DOF):

```
[Compiler]
A=1
B=0
ShowHints=1
ShowWarnings=1

[Linker]
MinStackSize=16384
MaxStackSize=1048576
ImageBase=4194304

[Parameters]
RunParams=
HostApplication=
```

The same structure is used by the Desktop files (DSK), which store the status of the Delphi IDE for the specific project, listing the position of each window. Here is a small excerpt:

```
[MainWindow]
Create=1
Visible=1
State=0
Left=2
Top=0
Width=800
Height=97
```

NOTE   A lot of information related to the status of the Delphi environment is saved in the Windows Registry, as well as in DSK and other files. I've already indicated a few special undocumented entries of the Registry you can use to activate specific features. You should explore the HKEY_CURRENT_USER\Software\Borland\Delphi\6.0 section of the Registry to examine all the settings of the Delphi IDE (including all those you can modify with the Project Options and the Environment Options dialog boxes, as well as many others).

The Object Repository

Delphi has menu commands you can use to create a new form, a new application, a new data module, a new component, and so on. These commands are located in the File ≻ New menu and in other pull-down menus. What happens if you simply select File ≻ New ≻ Other? Delphi opens the Object Repository, which is used to create new elements of any kind: forms, applications, data modules, thread objects, libraries, components, automation objects, and more.

The New dialog box (shown in Figure 1.11) has several pages, hosting all the new elements you can create, existing forms and projects stored in the Repository, Delphi wizards, and the forms of the current project (for visual form inheritance). The pages and the entries in this tabbed dialog box depend on the specific version of Delphi, so I won't list them here.

FIGURE 1.11:

The first page of the New dialog box, generally known as the "Object Repository"

> **TIP**
> The Object Repository has a shortcut menu that allows you to sort its items in different ways (by name, by author, by date, or by description) and to show different views (large icons, small icons, lists, and details). The Details view gives you the description, the author, and the date of the tool, information that is particularly important when looking at wizards, projects, or forms that you've added to the Repository.

The simplest way to customize the Object Repository is to add new projects, forms, and data modules as templates. You can also add new pages and arrange the items on some of them (not including the New and "current project" pages). Adding a new template to Delphi's Object Repository is as simple as using an existing template to build an application. When you have a working application you want to use as a starting point for further development of similar programs, you can save the current status to a template, ready to use later on. Simply use the Project ➢ Add To Repository command, and fill in its dialog box.

Just as you can add new project templates to the Object Repository, you can also add new form templates. Simply move to the form that you want to add and select the Add To Repository command of its shortcut menu. Then indicate the title, description, author, page, and icon in its dialog box.

You might want to keep in mind that as you copy a project or form template to the repository and then copy it back to another directory, you are simply doing a copy and paste operation. This isn't much different than copying the files manually.

The Empty Project Template

When you start a new project, it automatically opens a blank form, too. If you want to base a new project on one of the form objects or Wizards, this is not what you want, however. To solve this problem, you can add an Empty Project template to the Gallery.

The steps required to accomplish this are simple:

1. Create a new project as usual.

2. Remove its only form from the project.

3. Add this project to the templates, naming it *Empty Project*.

When you select this project from the Object Repository, you gain two advantages: You have your project without a form, and you can pick a directory where the project template's files will be copied. There is also a disadvantage—you have to remember to use the File ➢ Save Project As command to give a new name to the project, because saving the project any other way automatically uses the default name in the template.

To further customize the Repository, you can use the Tools ➢ Repository command. This opens the Object Repository dialog box, which you can use to move items to different pages, to add new elements, or to delete existing ones. You can even add new pages, rename or delete them, and change their order. An important element of the Object Repository setup is the use of defaults:

- Use the New Form check box below the list of objects to designate a form as the one to be used when a new form is created (File ➢ New Form).

- The Main Form check box indicates which type of form to use when creating the main form of a new application (File ➢ New Application) when no special New Project is selected.

- The New Project check box, available when you select a project, marks the default project that Delphi will use when you issue the File ➢ New Application command.

Only one form and only one project in the Object Repository can have each of these three settings marked with a special symbol placed over its icon. If no project is selected as New Project, Delphi creates a default project based on the form marked as Main Form. If no form is marked as the main form, Delphi creates a default project with an empty form.

When you work on the Object Repository, you work with forms and modules saved in the OBJREPOS subdirectory of the Delphi main directory. At the same time, if you use a form or any other object directly without copying it, then you end up having some files of your project in this directory. It is important to realize how the Repository works, because if you want to modify a project or an object saved in the Repository, the best approach is to operate on the original files, without copying data back and forth to the Repository.

Installing New DLL Wizards

Technically, new wizards come in two different forms: They may be part of components or packages, or they may be distributed as stand-alone DLLs. In the first case, they would be installed the same way you install a component or a package. When you've received a stand-alone DLL, you should add the name of the DLL in the Windows Registry under the key \Software\Borland\ Delphi\6.0\Experts. Simply add a new string key under this key, choose a name you like (it doesn't really matter what it is), and use as text the path and filename of the wizard DLL. You can look at the entries already present under the Experts key to see how the path should be entered.

What's Next?

This chapter has presented an overview of the new and more advanced features of the Delphi 6 programming environment, including tips and suggestions about some lesser-known features that were already available in previous Delphi versions. I didn't provide a step-by-step description of the IDE, partly because it is generally simpler to start *using* Delphi than it is to read about how to use it. Moreover, there is a detailed Help file describing the environment and the development of a new simple project; and you might already have some exposure to one of the past versions of Delphi or a similar development environment.

Now we are ready to spend the next two chapters looking into the Object Pascal language and then proceed by studying the RTL and the class library included in Delphi 6.

CHAPTER 2

The Object Pascal Language: Classes and Objects

- The Pascal language

- New conditional compilation and hint directives

- Classes and objects

- The *Self* keyword

- Class methods and overloading

- Encapsulation: *private* and *public*

- Using properties

- Constructors

- Objects and memory

Most modern programming languages support *object-oriented programming* (OOP). OOP languages are based on three fundamental concepts: encapsulation (usually implemented with classes), inheritance, and polymorphism (or late binding).

You can write Delphi applications even without knowing the details of Object Pascal. As you create a new form, add new components, and handle events, Delphi prepares most of the related code for you automatically. But knowing the details of the language and its implementation will help you to understand precisely what Delphi is doing and to master the language completely.

A single chapter doesn't allow space for a full introduction to the principles of object-oriented programming and the Object Pascal language. Instead, I will outline the key OOP features of the language and show how they relate to everyday Delphi programming. Even if you don't have a precise knowledge of OOP, the chapter will introduce each of the key concepts so that you won't need to refer to other sources.

The Pascal Language

The Object Pascal language used by Delphi is an OOP extension of the classic Pascal language, which Borland pushed forward for many years with its Turbo Pascal compilers. The syntax of the Pascal language is known to be quite verbose and more readable than, for example, the C language. Its OOP extension follows the same approach, delivering the same power of the recent breed of OOP languages, from Java to C#.

In this chapter, I'll discuss only the object-oriented extensions of the Pascal language available in Delphi. However, I'll highlight recent additions Borland has done to the core language. These features have been introduced in Delphi 6 and are, at least partially, related to the Linux version of Delphi.

New Pascal features include the $IF and $ELSEIF directives for conditional compilation, the $WARN and $MESSAGE directives, and the platform, library, and deprecated hint directives. These topics are discussed in the following sections. Changes to the assembler (with new directives, support for MMX and Pentium Pro instructions, and many more features) are really beyond the scope of this book.

Other relatively minor changes in the language include a change in the default value for the $WRITEABLECONST compiler switch, which is now disabled. This option allows programs to modify the value of typed constants and should generally be left disabled, using variables instead of constants for modifyable values. Another change is the support for the Int64 data type in variants. Finally, you can assign specific values to the elements of an enumeration (as in the C/C++ language), instead of using the default sequence of values.

The New *$IF* Compiler Directive

Delphi has always had a $IFDEF directive you could use to test whether a specific symbol was defined. (Delphi also has a $IFNDEF directive, with the opposite test.) This is used to obtain conditional compilation, as in

```
{$IFDEF DEBUG}
  // executes only if the DEBUG directive is set
  ShowMessage ('Executing critical code');
{$ENDIF}
```

By setting or not setting the DEBUG directive and recompiling, the extra line of code will be included or skipped by the compiler.

This code directive is powerful, but checking for multiple versions of Delphi and operating systems can force you to use multiple-nested $IFDEF directives, making the code totally unreadable. For this reason, Borland has introduced a new and more powerful directive for conditional compilation, $IF. Inside the directive you can use the Defined function to check whether a conditional symbol is defined, or use the Declared function to see whether a language constant is defined and use these constants within a constant Boolean expression. Here is some code that shows how to use a constant within the $IF directive (you can find this and other code excerpts of this and the next section in the IfDirective example on the companion CD):

```
const
  DebugControl = 2;

{$IF Defined(DEBUG) and (DebugControl > 3)}
  ShowMessage ('Executing critical code');
{$IFEND}
```

Notice that the statement is closed by a $IFEND and that you can also have an optional $ELSE branch. You can also concatenate conditions with the $ELSEIF directive, followed by another condition and evaluated only as an alternative to the $IF directive it refers to:

```
{$IF one}
  ...
{$ELSEIF two}
  ...
{$ELSE}
  ...
{$IFEND}
```

Within the expressions of the $IF directive, you can use only untyped constants, which are really and invariably treated as constants by the compiler. You can follow the general rules of Pascal constant expressions. You can use all the language operators, the and, or, xor, and not Boolean operators, and mathematical ones including div, mod, +, -, *, /, > and <, to mention just a few common ones. You can also use predefined functions such as SizeOf, High, Low,

Prev, Succ, and others listed in the Delphi Help page "Constant expressions." The expression can use constant symbols of any type, including floats and strings, so long as the expression itself ultimately evaluates to a True or False value.

WARNING   In these constant expressions, it is not possible to use type constants, which can be optionally modified in the code depending on the status of the writeable-typed constants directive (**$J** or $WRITEABLECONST). In any case, using constants you can modify is quite a bad idea in the first place.

Delphi provides a few predefined conditional symbols, including compiler version, the operating system, the GUI environment, and so on. I've listed the most important ones in Table 2.1. You can also use the RTLVersion constant defined in the System unit to test which version of Delphi (and its run-time library) you are compiling on. The predefined symbol ConditionalExpressions can be used to shield the new directives from older versions of Delphi:

```
{$IFDEF ConditionalExpressions}
  {$IF System.RTLVersion > 14.0}
    // do something
  {$IFEND}
{$ENDIF}
```

TABLE 2.1: Commonly Used Predefined Conditional Symbols

Symbol	Description
VER140	Compiling with Delphi 6, which is the 14.0 version of the Borland Pascal compiler; Delphi 5 used **VER130**, with lower numbers for past versions.
MSWINDOWS	Compiling on the Windows platform (new in Delphi 6).
LINUX	Compiling on the Linux platform. On Kylix, there are also the **LINUX32**, **POSIX**, and **ELF** predefined symbols.
WIN32	Compiling only on the 32-bit Windows platform. This symbol was introduced in Delphi 2 to distinguish from 16-bit Windows compilations (Delphi 1 defined the **WINDOWS** symbol). You should use **WIN32** only to mark code specifically for Win32, not Win16 or future Win64 platforms (for which the **WIN64** symbol has been reserved). Use **MSWINDOWS**, instead, to distinguish between Windows and other operating systems.
CONSOLE	Compiling a console application, and not a GUI one. This symbol is meaningful only under Windows, as all Linux applications are console applications.
BCB	Defined when the C++Builder IDE invokes the Pascal compiler.
ConditionalExpressions	Indicates that the **$IF** directive is available. It is defined in Kylix and Delphi 6, but not in earlier versions.

TIP   I recommend using conditional compilation sparingly and only when it is really required. It is generally better, whenever possible, to write code that can adapt to different situations—for example, adding different versions of the same class (or different inherited classes) to the same program. Excessive use of conditional compilation makes a program hard to read and to debug.

WARNING   Remember to issue a Build All command when you change a conditional symbol or a constant, which can affect a conditional compilation; otherwise the affected units won't be recompiled unless their source code changes.

New Hint Directives

Supporting multiple operating systems within the same source code base implies a number of compatibility issues. Besides a modified run-time library and a wholly new component library (discussed in Chapter 4, "The Run-Time Library," and Chapter 5, "Core Library Classes"), Delphi 6 includes special directives Borland uses to mark special portions of the code. As they introduced the idea of custom warnings and messages (described in the previous section), they've added a few special predefined ones.

The *platform* Directive

The first directive of this group is the platform directive, used to mark nonportable code. This directive can be used to mark procedures, variables, types, and almost any defined symbol. Borland uses platform in its libraries, so that when you use a platform-specific capability (for example, calling the IncludeTrailingBackslash function of the SysUtils unit), you'll receive a warning message, such as:

```
Symbol 'IncludeTrailingBackslash' is specific to a platform.
```

This warning is a hint for developers who plan to port their code between the Linux and Windows platforms, even in the future. In many cases, you'll be able to find an alternative approach that is fully platform independent. Check the help file (or eventually the library source code) for hints in this direction. In the case of the IncludeTrailingBackslash function, there is now a new version, called IncludeTrailingDelimiter, that is also portable to a Unix-based file system.

Of course you can use the platform directive to mark your code, for example, if you write a component or library that has platform-specific features. Here are a few examples:

```
var
   windowsversion: Integer = 2000 platform;
```

```
procedure Test; platform;
begin
  Beep;
end;

type
  TWinClass = class
    x: Integer;
  end platform;
```

The code fragments of this section are available, for your experiments, in the IfDirective example on the companion CD.

NOTE　The position of semicolons for hint directives can be quite confusing at first. The rule is that a hint directive must appear before the semicolon following the symbol it modifies. But a procedure, function, or unit header declaration can be followed only by reserved words, so its hint directive can appear following the semicolon. A type, variable, or constant declaration can be followed by another identifier, so the hint directive must come before the semicolon closing its declaration. Part of the rationale behind this is that the hint directives are not reserved words, so they can be used as the name of an identifier.

The *deprecated* Directive

The deprecated directive works in a similar way to the platform directive; the only real differences are that it is used in a different context and produces a different compiler warning. The role of deprecated is to mark identifiers that are still part of the system for compatibility reasons, but either are going to be removed in the future or expose you to risks of incompatibility. This symbol is used sparingly in the Delphi library.

The *library* Directive

The library directive works in a similar way to deprecated and platform; its role is to mark out code or components that are specific to a library (either VCL or CLX) and are not portable among them. However, apparently this symbol is never used within the Delphi library.

The *$WARN* Directive

The $WARNINGS directive (and the corresponding compiler option) allows you to turn off all the warning messages. Most programmers like to keep the messages on and tend to work with programs that compile with no hints and warnings. With the advent of the three hint directives discussed in the last section, however, there are programs specifically aimed for a platform, which cannot compile without compatibility warnings.

To overcome this situation, Delphi 6 introduces the $WARN directive, specifically aimed at disabling hint directives. As an example, you'll disable platform hints by writing this code:

```
{$WARN SYMBOL_PLATFORM OFF}
```

The $WARN directive has five different parameters, related to the three hint directives, and can use the ON and OFF values for each:

- SYMBOL_PLATFORM and UNIT_PLATFORM can be used to disable the platform directive in the current unit or in the unit where the directive is specified. The warning, in fact, is issued while compiling the code that uses the symbol, not while compiling the code with the definition.

- SYMBOL_LIBRARY and UNIT_LIBRARY work on the library directive in the same manner as the platform-related parameters above.

- SYMBOL_DEPRECATED can be used to disable the deprecated directive.

The *$MESSAGE* Directive

The compiler has now the ability to generate warnings in many different situations, so that the developer of a library or a portion of a program can let other programmers know of a given problem or risk in using a given feature, when the program can still legally compile. An extension to this idea is to let programmers insert custom warning messages in the code, with this syntax:

```
{$MESSAGE 'Old version of the unit: consider using the updated version'}
```

Compiling this code will issue a hint message with the text provided. This feature can be used to indicate possible problems, suggest alternative approaches, mark unfinished code, and more. This is probably more reliable than using a TODO item (discussed in the preceding chapter), because a programmer might not open the To-Do List window but the compiler will remind him of the pending problem. However, it is the compiler that issues the message, so you'll see it even if the given portion of the code is not really used by the program because the linker will remove it from the executable file.

These type of free messages, like the hint directives, become very useful to let the developer of a component communicate with the programmers using it, warning of potential pitfalls.

Introducing Classes and Objects

The cornerstone of the OOP extensions available in Object Pascal is represented by the class keyword, which is used inside type declarations. Classes define the blueprint of the objects you create in Delphi. As the terms *class* and *object* are commonly used and often misused, let's be sure we agree on their definitions.

A *class* is a user-defined data type, which has a state (its representation) and some operations (its behavior). A class has some internal data and some methods, in the form of procedures or functions, and usually describes the generic characteristics and behavior of some similar objects.

An *object* is an instance of a class, or a variable of the data type defined by the class. Objects are *actual* entities. When the program runs, objects take up some memory for their internal representation. The relationship between object and class is the same as the one between variable and type.

To declare a new class data type in Object Pascal, with some local data fields and some methods, use the following syntax:

```
type
  TDate = class
    Month, Day, Year: Integer;
    procedure SetValue (m, d, y: Integer);
    function LeapYear: Boolean;
  end;
```

NOTE   The convention in Delphi is to use the letter *T* as a prefix for the name of every class you write and every other type (*T* stands for *Type*). This is just a convention—to the compiler, *T* is just a letter like any other—but it is so common that following it will make your code easier to understand.

The following is a complete class definition, with two methods declared and not yet fully defined. The definition of these two methods (the `LeapYear` function and the `SetValue` procedure) must be present in the same unit of the class declaration and are written with this syntax:

```
procedure TDate.SetValue (m, d, y: Integer);
begin
  Month := m;
  Day := d;
  Year := y;
end;

function TDate.LeapYear: Boolean;
begin
  // call IsLeapYear in SysUtils.pas
  Result := IsLeapYear (Year);
end;
```

The method names are prefixed with the class name (using the dot-notation), because a unit can hold multiple classes, possibly with methods having the same names. You can actually avoid retyping the method names and parameter list by using the class completion feature of the editor. Simply type or modify the class definition and press Ctrl+Shift+C while the cursor is within the class definition itself; this will allow Delphi to generate a skeleton of the definition of the methods, including the begin and end statements.

Once the class has been defined, we can create an object and use it as follows:

```
var
  ADay: TDate;
begin
  // create an object
  ADay := TDate.Create;
  // use the object
  ADay.SetValue (1, 1, 2000);
  if ADay.LeapYear then
    ShowMessage ('Leap year: ' + IntToStr (ADay.Year));
  // destroy the object
  ADay.Free;
end;
```

Notice that ADay.LeapYear is an expression similar to ADay.Year, although the first is a function call and the second a direct data access. You can optionally add parentheses after the call of a function with no parameters. You can find the code snippets above in the source code of the Date1 example; the only difference is that the program creates a date based on the year provided in an edit box.

Classes, Objects, and Visual Programming

When I teach classes about OOP in Delphi, I always tell my students that regardless of how much OOP you know and how much you use it, Delphi forces you in the OOP direction. Even if you simply create a new application with a form and place a button over it to execute some code when the button is pressed, you are building an object-oriented application. In fact, the form is an object of a new class (by default TForm1, which inherits from the base TForm class provided by Borland), and the button is an instance of the TButton class, provided by Borland, as you can see in the following code snippet:

```
type
  TForm1 = class(TForm)
    Button1: TButton;
  end;
```

Given these premises, it would be very hard to build a Delphi application without using classes and objects. Yes, I know it is technically possible, but I doubt it would make a lot of sense. Not using objects and classes with Delphi would probably be more difficult than using them, as you have to give up all of the design-time tools for visual programming.

In any case, the real challenge is using OOP properly, something I'll try to teach you in this chapter (and in the rest of the book), along with an introduction to the key elements of the Object Pascal language.

The *Self* Keyword

Methods are very similar to procedures and functions. The real difference is that methods have an implicit parameter, which is a reference to the current object. Within a method you can refer to this parameter—the current object—using the Self keyword. This extra hidden parameter is needed when you create several objects of the same class, so that each time you apply a method to one of the objects, the method will operate only on its own data and not affect sibling objects.

For example, in the SetValue method of the TDate class, listed earlier, we simply use Month, Year, and Day to refer to the fields of the current object, something you might express as

```
Self.Month := m;
Self.Day := d;
```

This is actually how the Delphi compiler translates the code, *not* how you are supposed to write it. The Self keyword is a fundamental language construct used by the compiler, but at times it is used by programmers to resolve name conflicts and to make tricky code more readable.

NOTE   The C++ and Java languages have a similar feature based on the keyword this.

All you really need to know about Self is that the technical implementation of a call to a method differs from that of a call to a generic subroutine. Methods have an extra hidden parameter, Self. Because all this happens behind the scenes, you do not need to know how Self works at this time.

If you look at the definition of the TMethod data type in the System unit, you'll see that it is a record with a Code field and a Data field. The first is a pointer to the function's address in memory; the second the value of the Self parameter to use when calling that function address. We'll discuss method pointers in Chapter 5.

Overloaded Methods

Object Pascal supports overloaded functions and methods: you can have multiple methods with the same name, provided that the parameters are different. By checking the parameters, the compiler can determine which of the versions of the routine you want to call.

There are two basic rules:

- Each version of the method must be followed by the overload keyword.

- The differences must be in the number or type of the parameters or both. The return type cannot be used to distinguish between two methods.

Overloading can be applied to global functions and procedures and to methods of a class. As an example of overloading, I've added to the TDate class two different versions of the SetValue method:

```
type
  TDate = class
  public
    procedure SetValue (y, m, d: Integer); overload;
    procedure SetValue (NewDate: TDateTime); overload;
...//the rest of the class declaration

procedure TDate.SetValue (y, m, d: Integer);
begin
  fDate := EncodeDate (y, m, d);
end;

procedure TDate.SetValue(NewDate: TDateTime);
begin
  fDate := NewDate;
end;
```

NOTE   In Delphi 6, the compiler has been enhanced to improve the resolution of overloaded methods, allowing the compilation of calls that were considered ambiguous. In particular, the compiler handles the difference between **AnsiString** and **WideString** types. The overload resolution also has better support for variant-type parameters (which will provide matches in case there is no exact match for another overloaded version) and interfaces (which are given precedence to object types). Finally, the compiler allows the **nil** value to match an interface-type parameter. Some of these improvements were already introduced in the Kylix compiler.

Creating Components Dynamically

In Delphi, the Self keyword is often used when you need to refer to the current form explicitly in one of its methods. The typical example is the creation of a component at run time, where you must pass the owner of the component to its Create constructor and assign the same value to its Parent property. (The difference between Owner and Parent properties is discussed in the next chapter.) In both cases, you have to supply the current form as parameter or value, and the best way to do this is to use the Self keyword.

To demonstrate this kind of code, I've written the CreateC example (the name stands for *Create Component*) included on the companion CD. This program has a simple form with no components and a handler for its OnMouseDown event. I've used OnMouseDown because it receives as its parameter the position of the mouse click (unlike the OnClick event). I need this information to create a button component in that position. Here is the code of the method:

```
procedure TForm1.FormMouseDown (Sender: TObject;
  Button: TMouseButton; Shift: TShiftState; X, Y: Integer);
var
  Btn: TButton;
begin
  Btn := TButton.Create (Self);
  Btn.Parent := Self;
  Btn.Left := X;
  Btn.Top := Y;
  Btn.Width := Btn.Width + 50;
  Btn.Caption := Format ('Button at %d, %d', [X, Y]);
end;
```

The effect of this code is to create buttons at mouse-click positions, with a caption indicating the exact location, as you can see in Figure 2.1. In the code above, notice in particular the use of the Self keyword, as the parameter of the Create method and as the value of the Parent property. I'll discuss these two elements (ownership and the Parent property) in Chapter 5.

FIGURE 2.1:

The output of the CreateC example, which creates Button components at run time

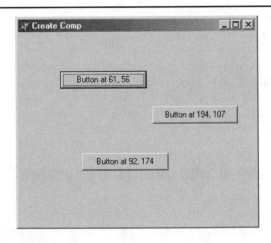

It is very common to write code like the above method using a with statement, as in the following listing:

```
procedure TForm1.FormMouseDown (Sender: TObject;
  Button: TMouseButton; Shift: TShiftState; X, Y: Integer);
```

```
begin
  with TButton.Create (Self) do
  begin
    Parent := Self;
    Left := X;
    Top := Y;
    Width := Width + 50;
    Caption := Format ('Button in %d, %d', [X, Y]);
  end;
end;
```

TIP   When writing a procedure like the code you've just seen, you might be tempted to use the Form1 variable instead of Self. In this specific example, that change wouldn't make any practical difference, but if there are multiple instances of a form, using Form1 would be an error. In fact, if the Form1 variable refers to the first form of that type being created, by clicking in another form of the same type, the new button will always be displayed in the first form. Its Owner and Parent will be Form1 and not the form the user has clicked. In general, referring to a particular instance of a class when the current object is required is bad OOP practice.

Class Methods and Class Data

When you define a field in a class, you actually specify that the field should be added to each object of that class. Each instance has its own independent representation (referred to by the Self pointer). In some cases, however, it might be useful to have a field that is shared by all the objects of a class.

Other object-oriented programming languages have formal constructs to express this, while in Object Pascal we can simulate this feature using the encapsulation provided at the unit level. You can simply add a variable in the implementation portion of a unit, to obtain a class variable—a single memory location shared by all of the objects of a class.

If you need to access this value from outside the unit, you might use a method of the class. However, this forces you to apply this method to one of the instances of the class. An alternative solution is to declare a *class method*. A class method cannot access the data of any single object but can be applied to a class as a whole rather than to a particular instance.

To declare a class method in Object Pascal, you simply add the class keyword in front of it:

```
type
  MyClass = class
    class function ClassMeanValue: Integer;
```

The use of class methods is not very common in Object Pascal, because you can obtain the same effect by adding a procedure or function to a unit declaring a class. Object-oriented purists, however, will definitely prefer the use of a class method over a routine unrelated to a class. For example, an OOP purist would add a class method for getting the current date to a TDate class instead of using a global function (also because some OOP languages, including Java, don't have the notion of global functions).

We'll see several class methods in the next chapter, when we'll examine the structure of the TObject class.

TIP   Contrary to other OOP languages, Delphi class methods can also be virtual, so they can be overridden and used to obtain polymorphism (a technique discussed later in this chapter).

Encapsulation

A class can have any amount of data and any number of methods. However, for a good object-oriented approach, data should be hidden, or *encapsulated*, inside the class using it. When you access a date, for example, it makes no sense to change the value of the day by itself. In fact, changing the value of the day might result in an invalid date, such as February 30. Using methods to access the internal representation of an object limits the risk of generating erroneous situations, as the methods can check whether the date is valid and refuse to modify the new value if it is not. Encapsulation is important because it allows the class writer to modify the internal representation in a future version.

The concept of encapsulation is often indicated by the idea of a "black box," where you don't know about the internals: You only know how to interface with it or how to use it regardless of its internal structure. The "how to use" portion, called the *class interface*, allows other parts of a program to access and use the objects of that class. However, when you use the objects, most of their code is hidden. You seldom know what internal data the object has, and you usually have no way to access the data directly. Of course, you are supposed to use methods to access the data, which is shielded from unauthorized access. This is the object-oriented approach to a classical programming concept known as *information hiding*.

Delphi implements this class-based encapsulation but still supports the classic module-based encapsulation using the structure of units. Because the two are strictly related, let me recap the traditional approach first.

Encapsulation and Units

A unit in Object Pascal is a secondary source-code file, with the main source-code file being represented by the project source code. Every unit has two main sections, called interface and implementation, as well as two optional ones for initialization and finalization code. I want to focus here on the information hiding implemented by units.

In short, every identifier (type, routine, variable, and so on) that you declare in the interface portion of a unit becomes visible to any other unit of the program, provided there is a `uses` statement referring back to the unit that defines the identifier. All the routines and methods you declare in the interface portion of the unit must later be fully defined in the implemented portion of the same unit. In the interface section of a unit, however, you cannot write any actual statements to execute.

On the other hand, any identifier you declare in the implementation portion of the unit is local to the unit and is not visible outside it. A unit can have local data, local support functions, and even local types that the rest of the program is not allowed to access. This provides a direct way to hide the implementation details of an abstraction from its users, so you can later change your code without affecting other units of the program (and without even having to notify the changes to other programmers writing those units).

When you write classes in a unit, you'll generally define them in the interface portion of a unit, but some special keywords allow you to hide portions of this class interface.

Private, Protected, and Public

For class-based encapsulation, the Object Pascal language has three access specifiers: `private`, `protected`, and `public`. A fourth, `published`, controls RTTI and design time information and will be discussed in more detail in Chapter 5. Here are the three *classic* access specifiers:

- The `private` directive denotes fields and methods of a class that are not accessible outside the unit (the source code file) that declares the class.

- The `protected` directive is used to indicate methods and fields with limited visibility. Only the current class and its subclasses can access `protected` elements. We'll discuss this keyword again in the "Protected Fields and Encapsulation" section.

- The `public` directive denotes fields and methods that are freely accessible from any other portion of a program as well as in the unit in which they are defined.

Generally, the fields of a class should be `private`; the methods are usually `public`. However, this is not always the case. Methods can be `private` or `protected` if they are needed only internally to perform some partial computation. Fields can be `protected` so that you can manipulate them in subclasses, but only if you are fairly sure that their type definition is not going to change. Access specifiers only restrict code outside your unit from accessing certain members of classes declared in the interface section of your unit. This means that if two classes are in the same unit, there is no protection for their private fields. Only by placing a class in the interface portion of a unit will you limit the visibility from classes and functions in other units to the public method and fields of the class.

As an example, consider this new version of the `TDate` class:

```
type
  TDate = class
  private
    Month, Day, Year: Integer;
  public
    procedure SetValue (y, m, d: Integer); overload;
    procedure SetValue (NewDate: TDateTime); overload;
    function LeapYear: Boolean;
    function GetText: string;
    procedure Increase;
  end;
```

In this version, the fields are now declared to be `private`, and there are some new methods. The first, `GetText`, is a function that returns a string with the date. You might think of adding other functions, such as `GetDay`, `GetMonth`, and `GetYear`, which simply return the corresponding `private` data, but similar direct data-access functions are not always needed. Providing access functions for each and every field might reduce the encapsulation and make it harder to modify the internal implementation of a class. Access functions should be provided only if they are part of the logical interface of the class you are implementing.

Another new method is the `Increase` procedure, which increases the date by one day. This is far from simple, because you need to consider the different lengths of the various months as well as leap and non–leap years. What I'll do to make it easier to write the code is change the internal implementation of the class to Delphi's `TDateTime` type for the internal implementation. The class definition will change to (the complete code will be in the next example, DateProp):

```
type
  TDate = class
  private
    fDate: TDateTime;
  public
    procedure SetValue (y, m, d: Integer); overload;
    procedure SetValue (NewDate: TDateTime); overload;
    function LeapYear: Boolean;
    function GetText: string;
    procedure Increase;
  end;
```

Notice that because the only change is in the `private` portion of the class, you won't have to modify any of your existing programs that use it. This is the advantage of encapsulation!

NOTE   The TDateTime type is actually a floating-point number. The integral portion of the number indicates the date since 12/30/1899, the same base date used by OLE Automation and Microsoft applications. (Use negative values to express previous years.) The decimal portion indicates the time as a fraction. For example, a value of 3.75 stands for the second of January 1900, at 6:00 A.M. (three-quarters of a day). To add or subtract dates, you can add or subtract the number of days, which is much simpler than adding days with a day/month/year representation.

Encapsulating with Properties

Properties are a very sound OOP mechanism, or a very well thought out application of the idea of encapsulation. Essentially, you have a name that completely hides its implementation details. This allows you to modify the class extensively without affecting the code using it. A good definition of properties is that of *virtual fields*. From the perspective of the user of the class that defines them, properties look exactly like fields, as you can generally read or write their value. For example, you can read the value of the Caption property of a button and assign it to the Text property of an edit box with the following code:

```
Edit1.Text := Button1.Caption;
```

This looks like we are reading and writing fields. However, properties can be directly mapped to data, as well as to access methods, for reading and writing the value. When properties are mapped to methods, the data they access can be part of the object or outside of it, and they can produce side effects, such as repainting a control after you change one of its values. Technically, a property is an identifier that is mapped to data or methods using a read and a write clause. For example, here is the definition of a Month property for a date class:

```
property Month: Integer read FMonth write SetMonth;
```

To access the value of the Month property, the program reads the value of the private field FMonth, while to change the property value it calls the method SetMonth (which must be defined inside the class, of course). Different combinations are possible (for example, we could also use a method to read the value or directly change a field in the write directive), but the use of a method to change the value of a property is very common. Here are two alternative definitions for the property, mapped to two access methods or mapped directly to data in both directions:

```
property Month: Integer read GetMonth write SetMonth;
property Month: Integer read FMonth write FMonth;
```

TIP   When you write code that accesses a property, it is important to realize that a method might be called. The issue is that some of these methods take some time to execute; they can also produce side effects, often including a (slow) repainting of the component on the screen. Although side effects of properties are seldom documented, you should be aware that they exist, particularly when you are trying to optimize your code.

Often, the actual data and access methods are private (or protected) while the property is public. This means you must use the property to have access to those methods or data, a technique that provides both an extended and a simplified version of encapsulation. It is an *extended* encapsulation because not only can you change the representation of the data and its access functions, but you can also add or remove access functions without changing the calling code at all. A user only needs to recompile the program using the property.

Class Completion for Properties

Properties provide a *simplified* encapsulation because when extra code is not required, you map the properties directly to fields, without writing tedious and useless access methods. And even when you want to write those methods, the IDE can use class completion (the Ctrl+Shift+C key combination) to generate the skeleton of the access methods of the properties for you. If you simply type in a class (say TMyClass),

```
property X: Integer;
```

and activate class completion, Delphi generates a SetX method for the property and adds the FX field to the class. The resulting code looks like this:

```
type
  TMyClass = class(TForm)
  private
    FX: Integer;
    procedure SetX(const Value: Integer);
  public
    property X: Integer read FX write SetX;
  end;

implementation

procedure TMyClass.SetX(const Value: Integer);
begin
  FX := Value;
end;
```

This really saves a lot of typing. You can even partially control how class completion generates Set and Get methods for the property. In fact, if you first type the property declaration including the read and write directives, as in

```
property X: Integer read GetX write SetX;
```

Class completion will generate the requested methods or add the field definition. If you want both the field and the methods, type in only the property name and its data type (as in the first example above), and let Delphi expand the declaration. At this point, fix the expanded declaration by replacing the FX field with a GetX method in the read portion, and invoke class completion a second time.

Properties for the *TDate* Class

As an example, I've added properties for accessing the year, the month, and the day to an object of the TDate class discussed earlier. These properties are not mapped to specific fields, but they all map to the single fDate field storing the entire date information. This is the new definition of the class:

```
type
  TDate = class
  private
    fDate: TDateTime;
    procedure SetDay(const Value: Integer);
    procedure SetMonth(const Value: Integer);
    procedure SetYear(const Value: Integer);
    function GetDay: Integer;
    function GetMonth: Integer;
    function GetYear: Integer;
  public
    procedure SetValue (y, m, d: Integer); overload;
    procedure SetValue (NewDate: TDateTime); overload;
    function LeapYear: Boolean;
    function GetText: string;
    procedure Increase;
    property Year: Integer read GetYear write SetYear;
    property Month: Integer read GetMonth write SetMonth;
    property Day: Integer read GetDay write SetDay;
  end;
```

Each of the Get and Set methods is easily implemented using functions available in the new DateUtils unit (discuss in more detail in Chapter 4). Here is the code for two of them (the others are very similar):

```
function TDate.GetYear: Integer;
begin
  Result := YearOf (fDate);
end;

procedure TDate.SetYear(const Value: Integer);
begin
  fDate := RecodeYear (fDate, Value);
end;
```

The code for this class is available in the DateProp example. The program uses a secondary unit for the definition of the TDate class to enforce encapsulation and creates a single-date object stored in a form variable and kept in memory for the entire execution of the program. Using a standard approach, the object is created in the form OnCreate event handler and destroyed in the form OnDestroy event handler.

The form of the program (see Figure 2.2) has three edit boxes and buttons to copy the values of these edit boxes to and from the properties of the date object:

FIGURE 2.2:

The form of the DateProp example

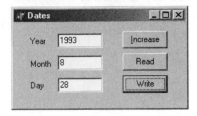

```
procedure TDateForm.BtnReadClick(Sender: TObject);
begin
  EditYear.Text := IntToStr (TheDay.Year);
  EditMonth.Text := IntToStr (TheDay.Month);
  EditDay.Text := IntToStr (TheDay.Day);
end;
```

WARNING When writing the values, the program uses the SetValue method instead of setting each of the properties. In fact, assigning the month and the day separately can cause you trouble when the month is not valid for the current day. For example, the day is currently January 31, and you want to assign to it February 20. If you assign the month first, this part of the assignment will fail, as February 31 does not exist. If you assign the day first, the problem will arise when doing the reverse assignment. Due to the validity rules for dates, it is better to assign everything at once.

Advanced Features of Properties

Properties have several advanced features I'll focus on in future chapters, specifically the introduction to the base classes of the library in Chapter 5 and writing custom Delphi components in Chapter 11, "Creating Components." This is a short summary of these more advanced features:

- The write directive of a property can be omitted, making it a *read-only* property. The compiler will issue an error if you try to change it. You can also omit the read directive and define a *write-only* property, but that doesn't make much sense and is used infrequently.

- The Delphi IDE gives special treatment to *design-time* properties, declared with the published access specifier and generally displayed in the Object Inspector for the selected component. More on the published keyword and its effect is in Chapter 5.

- The other properties, often called *run-time only* properties, are those declared with the public access specifier. These properties can be used in the program code.

- You can define *array-based* properties, which use the typical notation with square brackets to access an element of a list. The *string list–based* properties, such as the `Lines` of a list box, are a typical example of this group.

- Properties have special directives, including `stored` and `default`, which control the *component streaming system*, introduced in Chapter 5 and detailed in Chapter 11.

NOTE   You can usually assign a value to a property or read it, and you can even use properties in expressions, but you cannot always pass a property as a parameter to a procedure or method. This is because a property is not a memory location, so it cannot be used as a `var` parameter; it cannot be passed by reference.

Encapsulation and Forms

One of the key ideas of encapsulation is to reduce the number of global variables used by a program. A global variable can be accessed from every portion of a program. For this reason, a change in a global variable affects the whole program. On the other hand, when you change the representation of a class's field, you only need to change the code of some methods of that class and nothing else. Therefore, we can say that information hiding refers to *encapsulating changes*.

Let me clarify this idea with an example. When you have a program with multiple forms, you can make some data available to every form by declaring it as a global variable in the interface portion of the unit of one of the forms:

```
var
  Form1: TForm1;
  nClicks: Integer;
```

This works but has two problems. First, the data is not connected to a specific instance of the form, but to the entire program. If you create two forms of the same type, they'll share the data. If you want every form of the same type to have its own copy of the data, the only solution is to add it to the form class:

```
type
  TForm1 = class(TForm)
  public
    nClicks: Integer;
  end;
```

The second problem is that if you define the data as a global variable or as a public field of a form, you won't be able to modify its implementation in the future without affecting the code that uses the data. For example, if you only have to read the current value from other forms, you can declare the data as private and provide a method to read the value:

```
type
  TForm1 = class(TForm)
  public
    function GetClicks: Integer;
  private
    nClicks: Integer;
  end;

function TForm1.GetClicks: Integer;
begin
  Result := nClicks;
end;
```

Adding Properties to Forms

An even better solution is to add a property to the form. Every time you want to make some information of a form available to other forms, you should really use a property, for all the reasons discussed in the previous section. Simply change the field declaration of the form, shown in the preceding listing, by adding the keyword property in front of it and then press Ctrl+Shift+C to activate code completion. Delphi will automatically generate all of the extra code you need. In the form, you also need to handle the OnClick event, increasing the value of the property (and showing it in the form caption):

```
procedure TForm1.FormClick(Sender: TObject);
begin
  Inc (FClicks);
  Caption := 'Clicks: ' + IntToStr (FClicks);
end;
```

The complete code for this form class is available in the FormProp example and illustrated in Figure 2.3. The program can create multi-instances of the form (that is, multiple objects based on the same form class), each with its own click count. Clicking the Create Form button creates the secondary forms, using the following code:

```
procedure TForm1.btnCreateFormClick(Sender: TObject);
begin
  with TForm1.Create (Self) do
    Show;
end;
```

Two forms of the FormProp example at run time

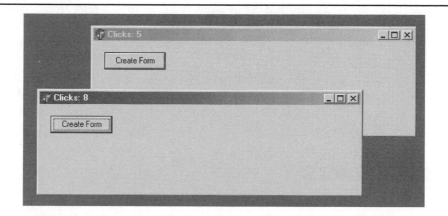

> **NOTE** Notice that adding a property to a form doesn't add to the list of the form properties in the Object Inspector.

In my opinion, properties should also be used in the form classes to encapsulate the access to the components of a form. For example, if you have a main form with a status bar used to display some information (and with the SimplePanel property set to True) and you want to modify the text from a secondary form, you might be tempted to write:

```
Form1.StatusBar1.SimpleText := 'new text';
```

This is a standard practice in Delphi, but it's not a good one, because it doesn't provide any encapsulation of the form structure or components. If you have similar code in many places throughout an application, and you later decide to modify the user interface of the form (replacing StatusBar with another control or activating multiple panels), you'll have to fix the code in many places. The alternative is to use a method or, even better, a property to hide the specific control. Simply type

```
property StatusText: string read GetText write SetText;
```

and press the Ctrl+Shift+C combination again, to let Delphi add the definition of both methods for reading and writing the property:

```
function TForm1.GetText: string;
begin
  Result := StatusBar1.SimpleText;
end;

procedure TForm1.SetText(const Value: string);
begin
  StatusBar1.SimpleText := Value;
end;
```

In the other forms of the program, you can simply refer to the StatusText property of the form, and if the user interface changes, only the Set and Get methods of the property are affected.

NOTE   See Chapter 5 for a detailed discussion of how you can avoid having published form fields for components, which will improve encapsulation. But don't rush there: the description requires a good knowledge of Delphi, and the technique discussed has a few drawbacks!

Constructors

As I've mentioned, to allocate the memory for the object, we call the Create method. This is a *constructor*, a special method that you can apply to a class to allocate memory for an instance of that class. The instance is returned by the constructor and can be assigned to a variable for storing the object and using it later on. The default TObject.Create constructor initializes all the data of the new instance to zero.

If you want your instance data to start out with a nonzero value, then you need to write a custom constructor to do that. The new constructor can be called Create, or it can have any other name; use the constructor keyword in front of it. Notice that you don't need to call TObject.Create: it is Delphi that allocates the memory for the new object, not the class constructor. All you have to do is to initialize the class base.

If you create objects without initializing them, calling methods later may result in odd behavior or even a run-time error. A consistent use of constructors to initialize objects' data is an important *preventive* technique to avoid these errors in the first place. For example, we must call the SetValue procedure of the TDate class after we've created the object. As an alternative, we can provide a customized constructor, which creates the object and gives it an initial value.

Although you can use any name for a constructor, you should stick to the standard name, Create. If you use a name other than Create, the Create constructor of the base TObject class will still be available, but a programmer calling this default constructor might bypass the initialization code you've provided because they don't recognize the name.

By defining a Create constructor with some parameters, you replace the default definition with a new one and make its use compulsory. For example, after you define

```
type
  TDate = class
  public
    constructor Create (y, m, d: Integer);
```

```
constructor TDate.Create (y, m, d: Integer);
begin
  fDate := EncodeDate (y, m, d);
end;
```

you'll be able to call this constructor and not the standard `Create`:

```
var
  ADay: TDate;
begin
  // Error, does not compile:
  ADay := TDate.Create;
  // OK:
  ADay := TDate.Create (1, 1, 2000);
```

The rules for writing constructors for custom components are different, as we'll see in Chapter 11. In short, when you inherit from TComponent, you should override the default `Create` constructor with one parameter and avoid disabling it.

Overloaded Constructors

Overloading is particularly relevant for constructors, because we can add to a class multiple constructors and call them all `Create`, which makes them easy to remember.

NOTE   Historically, overloading was added to C++ to allow the use of multiple constructors that have the same name (the name of the class). In Object Pascal, this feature was considered unnecessary because multiple constructors can have different specific names. The increased integration of Delphi with C++Builder has motivated Borland to make this feature available in both languages, starting with Delphi 4. Technically, when C++Builder constructs an instance of a Delphi VCL class, it looks for a Delphi constructor named **Create** and nothing but **Create**. If the Delphi class has constructors by other names, they cannot be used from C++Builder code. Therefore, when creating classes and components you intend to share with C++Builder programmers, you should be careful to name all your constructors **Create** and distinguish between them by their parameter lists (using **overload**). Delphi does not require this, but it is required for C++Builder to use your Delphi classes.

As an example, I've added to the class two separate `Create` constructors: one with no parameters, which hides the default constructor, and one with the initialization values. The constructor with no parameter uses as the default value today's date:

```
type
  TDate = class
  public
    constructor Create; overload;
    constructor Create (y, m, d: Integer); overload;
```

```
constructor TDate.Create (y, m, d: Integer);
begin
  fDate := EncodeDate (y, m, d);
end;

constructor TDate.Create;
begin
  fDate := Date;
end;
```

Having these two constructors makes it possible to define a new TDate object in two different ways:

```
var
  Day1, Day2: TDate;
begin
  Day1 := TDate.Create (2001, 12, 25);
  Day2 := TDate.Create; // today
```

See the section "The Complete *TDate* Class" later in this chapter for the DateView example, which includes the code of these constructors.

Destructors

In the same way that a class can have a custom constructor, it can have a custom destructor, a method declared with the destructor keyword and called Destroy, which can perform some resource cleanup before an object is destroyed. Just as a constructor call allocates memory for the object, a destructor call frees the memory.

We can write code for a destructor, generally overriding the default Destroy destructor, to let the object execute some code before it is destroyed. Destructors are needed only for objects that acquire resources in their constructors or during their lifetime. In your code, of course, you don't have to handle memory de-allocation—this is something Delphi does for you.

Destroy is a virtual destructor of the TObject class. Most of the classes that require custom clean-up code when the objects are destroyed override this virtual method. The reason you should never define a new destructor is that objects are usually destroyed by calling the Free method, and this method calls the Destroy virtual destructor of the specific class (virtual methods will be discussed later in this chapter).

Free (and *nil*)

Free is a method of the TObject class, inherited by all other classes. The Free method basically checks whether the current object (Self) is not nil before calling the Destroy virtual destructor. Here is its pseudocode (the actual Delphi code is written in assembler):

```
procedure TObject.Free;
begin
  if Self <> nil then
    Destroy;
end;
```

By looking at this code, you can see that calling Free doesn't set the object to nil automatically; this is something you should do yourself! The reason is that the object doesn't know which variables may be referring to it, so it has no way to set them all to nil.

NOTE   Automatically setting an object to nil is not possible. You might have several references to the same object, and Delphi doesn't track them. At the same time, within a method (such as Free) we can operate on the object, but we know nothing about the object reference—the memory address of the variable we've used to call the method. In other words, inside the Free method or any other method of a class, we know the memory address of the object (Self), but we don't know the memory location of the variable referring to the object.

Delphi 5 introduced a FreeAndNil procedure you can use to free an object and set its reference to nil at the same time. Simply call

```
FreeAndNil (Obj1)
```

instead of writing

```
Obj1.Free;
Obj1 := nil;
```

The FreeAndNil procedure knows about the object reference, passed as a parameter, and can act on it. Here is Delphi code for FreeAndNil:

```
procedure FreeAndNil(var Obj);
var
  P: TObject;
begin
  P := TObject(Obj);
  // clear the reference before destroying the object
  TObject(Obj) := nil;
  P.Free;
end;
```

NOTE   There's more on this topic in the section "Destroying Objects Only Once" later in this chapter.

The Complete *TDate* Class

In the initial portion of this chapter, I've shown you bits and pieces of the source code for different versions of a TDate class. In Listing 2.1 is the complete interface portion of the unit that defines the TDate class.

Listing 2.1:   **The *TDate* class, from the ViewDate example**

```
unit Dates;

interface

type
  TDate = class
  private
    fDate: TDateTime;
    procedure SetDay(const Value: Integer);
    procedure SetMonth(const Value: Integer);
    procedure SetYear(const Value: Integer);
    function GetDay: Integer;
    function GetMonth: Integer;
    function GetYear: Integer;
  public
    constructor Create; overload;
    constructor Create (y, m, d: Integer); overload;
    procedure SetValue (y, m, d: Integer); overload;
    procedure SetValue (NewDate: TDateTime); overload;
    function LeapYear: Boolean;
    procedure Increase (NumberOfDays: Integer = 1);
    procedure Decrease (NumberOfDays: Integer = 1);
    function GetText: string;
    property Year: Integer read GetYear write SetYear;
    property Month: Integer read GetMonth write SetMonth;
    property Day: Integer read GetDay write SetDay;
  end;

implementation

uses
  SysUtils, DateUtils;

procedure TDate.SetValue (y, m, d: Integer);
begin
  fDate := EncodeDate (y, m, d);
end;

function TDate.LeapYear: Boolean;
begin
  Result := IsInLeapYear(fDate);
end;
```

```pascal
procedure TDate.Increase (NumberOfDays: Integer = 1);
begin
  fDate := fDate + NumberOfDays;
end;

function TDate.GetText: string;
begin
  GetText := DateToStr (fDate);
end;

procedure TDate.Decrease (NumberOfDays: Integer = 1);
begin
  fDate := fDate - NumberOfDays;
end;

constructor TDate.Create (y, m, d: Integer);
begin
  fDate := EncodeDate (y, m, d);
end;

constructor TDate.Create;
begin
  fDate := Date;
end;

procedure TDate.SetValue(NewDate: TDateTime);
begin
  fDate := NewDate;
end;

procedure TDate.SetDay(const Value: Integer);
begin
  fDate := RecodeDay (fDate, Value);
end;

procedure TDate.SetMonth(const Value: Integer);
begin
  fDate := RecodeMonth (fDate, Value);
end;

procedure TDate.SetYear(const Value: Integer);
begin
  fDate := RecodeYear (fDate, Value);
end;

function TDate.GetDay: Integer;
begin
  Result := DayOf (fDate);
end;
```

```
function TDate.GetMonth: Integer;
begin
  Result := MonthOf (fDate);
end;

function TDate.GetYear: Integer;
begin
  Result := YearOf (fDate);
end;

end.
```

The aim of the Increase and Decrease methods, which have a default value for their parameter, is quite easy to understand. If called with no parameter, they change the value of the date to the next or previous day. If a NumberOfDays parameter is part of the call, they add or subtract that number.

GetText returns a string with the formatted date, using the DateToStr function.

The form of the example I've built to show you how to use the TDate class, as illustrated in Figure 2.4, has a caption to display a date and six buttons, which can be used to modify the date. To make the label component look nice, I've given it a big font, made it as wide as the form, set its Alignment property to taCenter, and set its AutoSize property to False.

FIGURE 2.4:

The output of the ViewDate example at startup

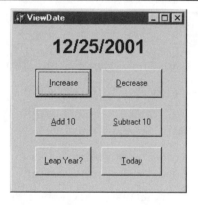

The startup code of this program is in the OnCreate event handler. In the corresponding method, we create an instance of the TDate class, initialize this object, and then show its textual description in the Caption of the label.

```
procedure TDateForm.FormCreate(Sender: TObject);
begin
  TheDay := TDate.Create (2001, 12, 25);
  LabelDate.Caption := TheDay.GetText;
end;
```

TheDay is a private field of the class of the form, TDateForm. (By the way, the name for the form class is automatically chosen by Delphi when we change the Name property of the form to DateForm.) The object is then destroyed along with the form:

```
procedure TDateForm.FormDestroy(Sender: TObject);
begin
  TheDay.Free;
end;
```

When the user clicks one of the six buttons, we need to apply the corresponding method to the TheDay object and then display the new value of the date in the label:

```
procedure TDateForm.BtnTodayClick(Sender: TObject);
begin
  TheDay.SetValue (Date);
  LabelDate.Caption := TheDay.GetText;
end;
```

Notice that in this code we reuse an existing object, assigning a new date to it. We could also create a new object and assign it to the existing TheDate variable, but this can lead to confusing situations, as explained in the next section.

Delphi's Object Reference Model

In some OOP languages, declaring a variable of a class type creates an instance of that class. Object Pascal, instead, is based on an *object reference model*. The idea is that a variable of a class type, such as the TheDay variable in the preceding ViewDate example, does not hold the value of the object. Rather, it contains a reference, or a *pointer*, to indicate the memory location where the object has been stored. You can see this structure depicted in Figure 2.5.

FIGURE 2.5:

A representation of the structure of an object in memory, with a variable referring to it

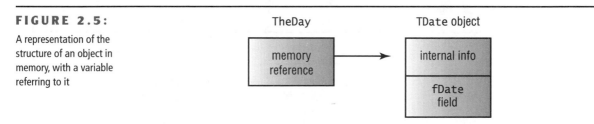

The only problem with this approach is that when you declare a variable, you don't create an object in memory; you only reserve the memory location for a reference to an object. Object instances must be created manually, at least for the objects of the classes you define. Instances of the components you place on a form are built automatically by Delphi.

You've seen how to create an instance of an object by applying a constructor to its class. Once you have created an object and you've finished using it, you need to dispose of it (to avoid filling up memory you don't need any more, which causes what is known as a *memory leak*). This can be accomplished by calling the Free method. As long as you create objects when you need them and free them when you're finished with them, the object reference model works without a glitch. The object reference model has many consequences on assigning object and on managing memory, as we'll see in the next two sections.

Assigning Objects

If a variable holding an object only contains a reference to the object in memory, what happens if you copy the value of that variable? Suppose we write the BtnTodayClick method of the ViewDate example in the following way:

```
procedure TDateForm.BtnTodayClick(Sender: TObject);
var
  NewDay: TDate;
begin
  NewDay := TDate.Create;
  TheDay := NewDay;
  LabelDate.Caption := TheDay.GetText;
end;
```

This code copies the memory address of the NewDay object to the TheDay variable (as shown in Figure 2.6); it doesn't copy the data of an object into the other. In this particular circumstance, this is not a very good approach, as we keep allocating memory for a new object every time the button is pressed, but we never release the memory of the object the TheDay variable was previously pointing to. This specific issue can be solved by freeing the old object, as in the following code (which is also simplified, without the use of an explicit variable for the newly created object):

FIGURE 2.6:

A representation of the operation of assigning an object reference to another one. This is different from copying the actual content of an object to another.

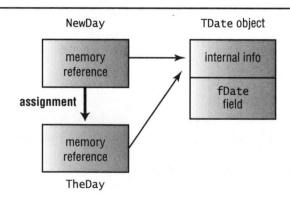

```
procedure TDateForm.BtnTodayClick(Sender: TObject);
begin
  TheDay.Free;
  TheDay := TDate.Create;
```

The important thing to keep in mind is that, when you assign an object to another object, Delphi copies the reference to the object in memory to the new object/reference. You should not consider this a negative: In many cases, being able to define a variable referring to an existing object can be a plus. For example, you can store the object returned by calling a function or accessing a property and use it in subsequent statements, as this code snippet indicates:

```
var
  ADay: TDate;
begin
  ADay: UserInformation.GetBirthDate;
  // use a ADay
```

The same happens if you pass an object as a parameter to a function: You don't create a new object, but you refer to the same one in two different places of the code. For example, by writing this procedure and calling it as follows, you'll modify the Caption property of the Button1 object, not of a copy of its data in memory (which would be totally useless):

```
procedure CaptionPlus (Button: TButton);
begin
  Button.Caption := Button.Caption + '+';
end;

// call...
CaptionPlus (Button1)
```

What if you really want to change the data inside an existing object, so that it matches the data of another object? You have to copy each field of the object, which is possible only if they are all public, or provide a specific method to copy the internal data. Some classes of the VCL have an Assign method, which does this copy operation. To be more precise, most of the VCL classes inheriting from TPersistent, but not inheriting from TComponent, have the Assign method. Other TComponent-derived classes have this method but raise an exception when it is called.

In the DateCopy example, slightly modified from the ViewDate program, I've added an Assign method to the TDate class, and I've called it from the Today button, with the following code:

```
procedure TDate.Assign (Source: TDate);
begin
  fDate := Source.fDate;
end;
```

```
procedure TDateForm.BtnTodayClick(Sender: TObject);
var
  NewDay: TDate;
begin
  NewDay := TDate.Create;
  TheDay.Assign(NewDay);
  LabelDate.Caption := TheDay.GetText;
  NewDay.Free;
end;
```

Objects and Memory

Memory management in Delphi is subject to three rules: Every object must be created before it can be used; every object must be destroyed after it has been used; and every object must be destroyed only once. Whether you have to do these operations in your code, or you can let Delphi handle memory management for you, depends on the model you choose among the different approaches provided by Delphi.

Delphi supports three types of memory management for dynamic elements (that is, elements not in the stack and the global memory area):

- Every time you create an object explicitly, in the code of your application, you should also free it. If you fail to do so, the memory used by that object won't be released for other objects until the program terminates.

- When you create a component, you can specify an owner component, passing the owner to the component constructor. The owner component (often a form) becomes responsible for destroying all the objects it owns. In other words, when you free the form, it frees all the components it owns. So, if you create a component and give it an owner, you don't have to remember to destroy it. This is the standard behavior of the components you create at design time by placing them on a form or data module.

- When you allocate memory for strings, dynamic arrays, and objects referenced by interface variables (discussed in Chapter 3), Delphi automatically frees the memory when the reference goes out of scope. You don't need to free a string: when it becomes unreachable, its memory is released.

Destroying Objects Only Once

Another problem is that if you call the Destroy destructor of an object twice, you get an error. If you remember to set the object to nil, you can call Free twice with no problem.

NOTE   You might wonder why you can safely call `Free` if the object reference is `nil`, but you can't call `Destroy`. The reason is that `Free` is a known method at a given memory location, whereas the virtual function `Destroy` is determined at run time by looking at the type of the object, a very dangerous operation if the object doesn't exist any more.

To sum things up, here are a couple of guidelines:

- Always call `Free` to destroy objects, instead of calling the `Destroy` destructor.

- Use `FreeAndNil`, or set object references to `nil` after calling `Free`, unless the reference is going out of scope immediately afterward.

In general, you can also check whether an object is `nil` by using the `Assigned` function. So the following two statements are equivalent, at least in most cases:

```
if Assigned (ADate) then ...
if ADate <> nil then ...
```

Notice that these statements test only whether the pointer is not `nil`; they do not check whether it is a valid pointer. If you write the following code, the test will be satisfied, and you'll get an error on the line with the call to the method of the object:

```
ToDestroy.Free;
if ToDestroy <> nil then
  ToDestroy.DoSomething;
```

It is important to realize that calling `Free` doesn't set the object to `nil`.

What's Next?

In this chapter, we have discussed the foundations of object-oriented programming (OOP) in Object Pascal. We have considered the definition of classes, the use of methods, encapsulation, and memory management, but also some more advanced concepts such as properties and the dynamic creation of components.

This is certainly a lot of information if you are a newcomer, but if you are fluent in another OOP language or if you've already used past versions of Delphi, you should be able to apply the topics covered in this chapter to your programming.

The next chapter continues on the same line, highlighting inheritance in particular, along with virtual functions and interfaces. It also includes a discussion on exception handling and class references, so that at the end you'll have a complete overview of the language. At that point, you'll be ready to start focusing on the libraries the compiler relies on, and we'll get back to see how properties are used by Delphi and its IDE (in Chapter 5). Other chapters will provide further information on applying the OOP concepts to Delphi programming. You'll find OOP tips throughout the entire book, but particularly in Chapter 11, devoted to writing custom Delphi components.

CHAPTER 3

The Object Pascal Language: Inheritance and Polymorphism

- Inheritance

- Virtual methods

- Polymorphism

- Type-safe down-casting (run-time type information)

- Interfaces

- Working with exceptions

- Class references

After the introduction to classes and objects we've seen over the last chapter, let's move on to another key element of the language, *inheritance*. Deriving a class from an existing one is the real revolutionary idea of object-oriented programming, and it goes along with polymorphism, virtual functions, abstract functions, and many other topics discussed in this chapter.

We'll focus also on interfaces, another intriguing idea of the most recent OOP languages, and we'll cover a few more elements of Object Pascal, such as exception handling and class references. Together with the previous chapter, this will provide an almost complete roundup of the language.

Inheriting from Existing Types

We often need to use a slightly different version of an existing class that we have written or that someone has given to us. For example, you might need to add a new method or slightly change an existing one. You can do this easily by modifying the original code, unless you want to be able to use the two different versions of the class in different circumstances. Also, if the class was originally written by someone else (including Borland), you might want to keep your changes separate.

A typical alternative is to make a copy of the original type definition, change its code to support the new features, and give a new name to the resulting class. This might work, but it also might create problems: In duplicating the code you also duplicate the bugs; and if you want to add a new feature, you'll need to add it two or more times, depending on the number of copies of the original code you've made. This approach results in two completely different data types, so the compiler cannot help you take advantage of the similarities between the two types.

To solve these kinds of problems in expressing similarities between classes, Object Pascal allows you to define a new class directly from an existing one. This technique is known as *inheritance* (or *subclassing*) and is one of the fundamental elements of object-oriented programming languages. To inherit from an existing class, you only need to indicate that class at the beginning of the declaration of the subclass. For example, Delphi does this automatically each time you create a new form:

```
type
  TForm1 = class(TForm)
  end;
```

This simple definition indicates that the TForm1 class inherits all the methods, fields, properties, and events of the TForm class. You can apply any public method of the TForm class to an object of the TForm1 type. TForm, in turn, inherits some of its methods from another class, and so on, up to the TObject base class.

As an example of inheritance, we can change the ViewDate program, deriving a new class from TDate and modifying its GetText function. You can find this code in the DATES.PAS file of the NewDate example on the companion CD.

```
type
  TNewDate = class (TDate)
  public
    function GetText: string;
  end;
```

In this example, the TNewDate class is derived from TDate. It is common to say that TDate is an *ancestor* class or *parent* class of TNewDate and that TNewDate is a *subclass*, *descendant* class, or *child* class of TDate.

To implement the new version of the GetText function, I used the FormatDateTime function, which uses (among other features) the predefined month names available in Windows; these names depend on the user's regional and language settings. Many of these regional settings are actually copied by Delphi into constants defined in the library, such as LongMonthNames, ShortMonthNames, and many others you can find under the "Currency and date/time formatting variables" topic in the Delphi Help file. Here is the GetText method, where '*dddddd*' stands for the long date format:

```
function TNewDate.GetText: string;
begin
  GetText := FormatDateTime ('dddddd', fDate);
end;
```

TIP   Using regional information, the NewDate program automatically adapts itself to different Windows user settings. If you run this same program on a computer with regional settings referring to a language other than English, it will automatically show month names in that language. To test this behavior, you just need to change the regional settings; you don't need a new version of Windows. Notice that regional-setting changes immediately affect the running programs.

Once we have defined the new class, we need to use this new data type in the code of the form of the NewDate example. Simply define the TheDay object of type TNewDate, and call its constructor in the FormCreate method:

```
type
  TDateForm = class(TForm)
    ...
  private
    TheDay: TNewDate; // updated declaration
  end;
```

```
procedure TDateForm.FormCreate(Sender: TObject);
begin
  TheDay := TNewDate.Create (2001, 12, 25); // updated
  DateLabel.Caption := TheDay.GetText;
end;
```

Without any other changes, the new NewDate example will work properly. The TNewDate class inherits the methods to increase the date, add a number of days, and so on. In addition, the older code calling these methods still works. Actually, to call the new version of the GetText method, we don't need to change the source code! The Delphi compiler will automatically bind that call to a new method. The source code of all the other event handlers remains exactly the same, although its meaning changes considerably, as the new output demonstrates (see Figure 3.1).

FIGURE 3.1:

The output of the NewDate program, with the name of the month and of the day depending on Windows regional settings

Protected Fields and Encapsulation

The code of the GetText method of the TNewDate class compiles only if it is written in the same unit as the TDate class. In fact, it accesses the fDate private field of the ancestor class. If we want to place the descendant class in a new unit, we must either declare the fDate field as protected or add a protected access method in the ancestor class to read the value of the private field.

Many developers believe that the first solution is always the best, because declaring most of the fields as protected will make a class more extensible and will make it easier to write sub-classes. However, this violates the idea of encapsulation. In a large hierarchy of classes, changing the definition of some protected fields of the base classes becomes as difficult as changing some global data structures. If ten derived classes are accessing this data, changing its definition means potentially modifying the code in each of the ten classes.

In other words, flexibility, extension, and encapsulation often become conflicting objectives. When this happens, you should try to favor encapsulation. If you can do so without sacrificing flexibility, that will be even better. Often this intermediate solution can be obtained by using a virtual method, a topic I'll discuss in detail later in the section "Late Binding and Polymorphism." If you choose not to use encapsulation in order to obtain faster coding of the subclasses, then your design might not follow the object-oriented principles.

Accessing Protected Data of Other Classes

We've seen that in Delphi, the `private` and `protected` data of a class is accessible to any functions or methods that appear *in the same unit as the class*. For example, consider this class (part of the Protection example on the companion CD):

```
type
  TTest = class
  protected
    ProtectedData: Integer;
  public
    PublicData: Integer;
    function GetValue: string;
  end;
```

The `GetValue` method simply returns a string with the two integer values:

```
function TTest.GetValue: string;
begin
  Result := Format ('Public: %d, Protected: %d',
    [PublicData, ProtectedData]);
end;
```

Once you place this class in its own unit, you won't be able to access its protected portion from other units directly. Accordingly, if you write the following code,

```
procedure TForm1.Button1Click(Sender: TObject);
var
  Obj: TTest;
begin
  Obj := TTest.Create;
  Obj.PublicData := 10;
  Obj.ProtectedData := 20;  // won't compile
  ShowMessage (Obj.GetValue);
  Obj.Free;
end;
```

the compiler will issue an error message, "Undeclared identifier: 'ProtectedData.'"

Continued on next page

At this point, you might think there is no way to access the protected data of a class defined in a different unit. (This is what Delphi manuals and most Delphi books say.) However, there is a way around it. Consider what happens if you create an apparently useless derived class, such as

```
type
  TFake = class (TTest);
```

Now, if you make a direct cast of the object to the new class and access the protected data through it, this is how the code will look:

```
procedure TForm1.Button2Click(Sender: TObject);
var
  Obj: TTest;
begin
  Obj := TTest.Create;
  Obj.PublicData := 10;
  TFake (Obj).ProtectedData := 20; // compiles!
  ShowMessage (Obj.GetValue);
  Obj.Free;
end;
```

This code compiles and works properly, as you can see by running the Protection program. How is it possible for this approach to work? Well, if you think about it, the **TFake** class automatically inherits the protected fields of the **TTest** base class, and because the **TFake** class is in the same unit as the code that tries to access the data in the inherited fields, the protected data is accessible. As you would expect, if you move the declaration of the **TFake** class to a secondary unit, the program won't compile any more.

Now that I've shown you how to do this, I must warn you that violating the class-protection mechanism this way is likely to cause errors in your program (from accessing data that you really shouldn't), and it runs counter to good OOP technique. However, there are times when using this technique is the best solution, as you'll see by looking at the VCL source code and the code of many Delphi components. Two examples that come to mind are accessing the Text property of the TControl class and the Row and Col positions of the DBGrid control. These two ideas are demonstrated by the TextProp and DBGridCol examples, respectively. (These examples are quite advanced, so I suggest that only programmers with a good background of Delphi programming read them at this point in the text—other readers might come back later.) Although the first example shows a reasonable example of using the typecast *cracker*, the DBGrid example of Row and Col is actually a counterexample, one that illustrates the risks of accessing bits that the class writer chose not to expose. The row and column of a DBGrid do not mean the same thing as they do in a DrawGrid or StringGrid (the base classes). First, DBGrid does not count the fixed cells as actual cells (it distinguishes data cells

Continued on next page

from decoration), so your row and column indexes will have to be adjusted by whatever decorations are currently in effect on the grid (and those can change on the fly). Second, the DBGrid is a virtual view of the data. When you scroll up in a DBGrid, the data may move underneath it, but the currently selected row might not change.

This technique—declaring a local type only so that you can access protected data members of a class—is often described as a *hack*, and it should be avoided whenever possible. The problem is not accessing protected data of a class in the same unit but declaring a class for the sole purpose of accessing protected data of an existing object of a different class! The danger of this technique is in the hard-coded typecast of an object from a class to a different one.

Inheritance and Type Compatibility

Pascal is a strictly typed language. This means that you cannot, for example, assign an integer value to a Boolean variable, unless you use an explicit typecast. The rule is that two values are type-compatible only if they are of the same data type, or (to be more precise) if their data type refers to a single type definition.

WARNING   If you redefine the same data type in two different units, they won't be compatible, even if their name is identical. A program using two equally named types of two different units will be a nightmare to compile and debug.

There is an important exception to this rule in the case of class types. If you declare a class, such as TAnimal, and derive from it a new class, say TDog, you can then assign an object of type TDog to a variable of type TAnimal. That is because a dog is an animal! So, although this might surprise you, the following constructor calls are both legal:

```
var
  MyAnimal1, MyAnimal2: TAnimal;
begin
  MyAnimal1 := TAnimal.Create;
  MyAnimal2 := TDog.Create;
```

As a general rule, you can use an object of a descendant class any time an object of an ancestor class is expected. However, the reverse is not legal; you cannot use an object of an ancestor class when an object of a descendant class is expected. To simplify the explanation, here it is again in code terms:

```
type
  TDog = class (TAnimal)
    ...
  end;
```

```pascal
var
  MyAnimal: TAnimal;
  MyDog: TDog;

begin
  MyAnimal := MyDog;  // This is OK
  MyDog := MyAnimal;  // This is an error!!!
```

Before we look at the implications of this important feature of the language, you can try out the Animals1 example from the companion CD, which defines the two TAnimal and TDog classes:

```pascal
type
  TAnimal = class
  public
    constructor Create;
    function GetKind: string;
  private
    Kind: string;
  end;

  TDog = class (TAnimal)
  public
    constructor Create;
  end;
```

The two Create methods set the value of Kind, which is returned by the GetKind function. The form displayed by this example, shown in Figure 3.2, has a private field MyAnimal of type TAnimal. An instance of this class is created and initialized when the form is created and each time one of the radio buttons is selected:

```pascal
procedure TFormAnimals.FormCreate(Sender: TObject);
begin
  MyAnimal := TAnimal.Create;
end;

procedure TFormAnimals.RadioDogClick(Sender: TObject);
begin
  MyAnimal.Free;
  MyAnimal := TDog.Create;
end;
```

FIGURE 3.2:

The form of the Animals1 example

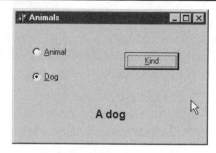

Finally, the Kind button calls the GetKind method for the current animal and displays the result in the label:

```
procedure TFormAnimals.BtnKindClick(Sender: TObject);
begin
  KindLabel.Caption := MyAnimal.GetKind;
end;
```

Late Binding and Polymorphism

Pascal functions and procedures are usually based on *static* or *early binding*. This means that a method call is resolved by the compiler and linker, which replace the request with a call to the specific memory location where the function or procedure resides. (This is known as the *address* of the function.) OOP languages allow the use of another form of binding, known as *dynamic* or *late binding*. In this case, the actual address of the method to be called is determined at run time based on the type of the instance used to make the call.

The advantage of this technique is known as *polymorphism*. Polymorphism means you can write a call to a method, applying it to a variable, but which method Delphi actually calls depends on the type of the object the variable relates to. Delphi cannot determine until run time the actual class of the object the variable refers to, because of the type-compatibility rule discussed in the previous section.

NOTE   The term *polymorphism* is quite a mouthful. A glance at the dictionary tells us that in a general sense, it refers to something having more than one form. In the OOP sense, then, it refers to the facts that there may be several versions of a given method across several related classes and that a single method call on an object instance of a particular class type can refer to one of these versions. Which version of the method gets called depends on the type of the object instance used to make the call at run time.

For example, suppose that a class and its subclass (let's say TAnimal and TDog) both define a method, and this method has late binding. Now you can apply this method to a generic variable, such as MyAnimal, which at run time can refer either to an object of class TAnimal or to an object of class TDog. The actual method to call is determined at run time, depending on the class of the current object.

The Animals2 example extends the Animals1 program to demonstrate this technique. In the new version, the TAnimal and the TDog classes have a new method: Voice, which means to output the sound made by the selected animal, both as text and as sound. This method is defined as virtual in the TAnimal class and is later overridden when we define the TDog class, by the use of the virtual and override keywords:

```
type
  TAnimal = class
  public
    function Voice: string; virtual;

  TDog = class (TAnimal)
  public
    function Voice: string; override;
```

Of course, the two methods also need to be implemented. Here is a simple approach:

```
uses
  MMSystem;

function TAnimal.Voice: string;
begin
  Voice := 'Voice of the animal';
  PlaySound ('Anim.wav', 0, snd_Async);
end;

function TDog.Voice: string;
begin
  Voice := 'Arf Arf';
  PlaySound ('dog.wav', 0, snd_Async);
end;
```

TIP   This example uses a call to the **PlaySound** API function, defined in the MMSystem unit. The first parameter of this function is the name of the WAV sound file or the system sound you want to execute. The second parameter indicates an optional resource file containing the sound. The third parameter indicates (among other options) whether the call should be synchronous or asynchronous; that is, whether the program should wait for the sound to finish before continuing with the following statements.

Now what is the effect of the call MyAnimal.Voice? It depends. If the MyAnimal variable currently refers to an object of the TAnimal class, it will call the method TAnimal.Voice. If it refers to an object of the TDog class, it will call the method TDog.Voice instead. This happens only because the function is virtual (as you can experiment by removing this keyword and recompiling).

The call to MyAnimal.Voice will work for an object that is an instance of any descendant of the TAnimal class, even classes that are defined in other units—or that haven't been written yet! The compiler doesn't need to know about all the descendants in order to make the call compatible with them; only the ancestor class is needed. In other words, this call to MyAnimal.Voice is compatible with all future TAnimal subclasses.

NOTE   This is the key technical reason why object-oriented programming languages favor reusability. You can write code that uses classes within a hierarchy without any knowledge of the specific classes that are part of that hierarchy. In other words, the hierarchy—and the program—is still extensible, even when you've written thousands of lines of code using it. Of course, there is one condition: the ancestor classes of the hierarchy need to be designed very carefully.

The Animals2 program demonstrates the use of these new classes and has a form similar to that of the previous example. This code is executed by clicking the button:

```
procedure TFormAnimals.BtnVerseClick(Sender: TObject);
begin
  LabelVoice.Caption := MyAnimal.Voice;
end;
```

In Figure 3.3, you can see an example of the output of this program. By running it, you'll also hear the corresponding sounds produced by the PlaySound API call.

FIGURE 3.3:

The output of the Animals2 example

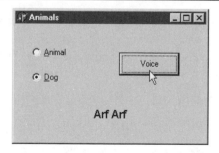

Overriding and Redefining Methods

As we have just seen, to override a late-bound method in a descendant class, you need to use the override keyword. Note that this can take place only if the method was defined as virtual in the ancestor class. Otherwise, if it was a static method, there is no way to activate late binding, other than by changing the code of the ancestor class.

The rules are simple: A method defined as static remains static in every subclass, unless you hide it with a new virtual method having the same name. A method defined as virtual remains late-bound in every subclass. There is no way to change this, because of the way the compiler generates different code for late-bound methods.

NOTE   The new C# programming language proposed by Microsoft (which is in essence a clone of Java) has the same notion as the Object Pascal language of marking the overridden version of a method with a specific keyword.

To redefine a static method, you add a method to a subclass having the same parameters or different parameters than the original one, without any further specifications. To override a virtual method, you must specify the same parameters and use the override keyword:

```
type
  MyClass = class
    procedure One; virtual;
    procedure Two; {static method}
  end;

  MySubClass = class (MyClass)
    procedure One; override;
    procedure Two;
  end;
```

There are typically two ways to override a method. One is to replace the method of the ancestor class with a new version. The other is to add some more code to the existing method. This can be accomplished by using the inherited keyword to call the same method of the ancestor class. For example, you can write

```
procedure MySubClass.One;
begin
  // new code
  ...
  // call inherited procedure MyClass.One
  inherited One;
end;
```

You might wonder why you need to use the override keyword. In other languages, when you redefine a method in a subclass, you automatically override the original one. However, having a specific keyword allows the compiler to check the correspondence between the names of the methods of the ancestor class and the subclass (misspelling a redefined function is a common error in other OOP languages), check that the method was virtual in the ancestor class, and so on.

When you override an existing virtual method of a base class, you must use the same parameters. When you introduce a new version of a method in a descendent class, you can declare it with the parameters you want. In fact, this will be a new method unrelated to the ancestor method of the same name. They only happen to use the same name. Here is an example:

```
type
  TMyClass = class
    procedure One;
  end;

  TMySubClass = class (TMyClass)
    procedure One (S: string);
  end;
```

Using the class definitions above, when you create an object of the TMySubClass class, you can apply to it the One method with the string parameter, but not the parameter-less version defined in the base class. If this is what you need, it can be accomplished by marking the re-declared method (the one in the derived class) with the overload keyword. If the method has different parameters than the version in the base class, it becomes effectively an overloaded method; otherwise it replaces the base class method. Notice that the method doesn't need to be marked as overload in the base class. However, if the method in the base class is virtual, the compiler issues the warning "Method 'One' hides virtual method of base type 'TMyClass.'" To avoid this message and to instruct the compiler more precisely on your intentions, you can use the reintroduce directive. If you are interested in this advanced topic, you can find this code in the Reintr example on the companion CD and experiment with it further.

Virtual versus Dynamic Methods

In Delphi, there are two different ways to activate late binding. You can declare the method as virtual, as we have seen before, or declare it as dynamic. The syntax of these two keywords is exactly the same, and the result of their use is also the same. What is different is the internal mechanism used by the compiler to implement late binding.

virtual methods are based on a *virtual method table* (VMT, also known as a *vtable*), which is an array of method addresses. For a call to a virtual method, the compiler generates code to jump to an address stored in the nth slot in the object's virtual method table.

Virtual method tables allow fast execution of the method calls. Their main drawback is that they require an entry for each `virtual` method for each descendant class, even if the method is not overridden in the subclass. At times, this has the effect of propagating VMT entries throughout a class hierarchy (even for methods that aren't redefined). This might require a lot of memory just to store the same method address multiple times.

`Dynamic` method calls, on the other hand, are dispatched using a unique number indicating the method. The search for the corresponding function is generally slower than the one-step table lookup for `virtual` methods. The advantage is that dynamic method entries only propagate in descendants when the descendants override the method. For large or deep object hierarchies, using `dynamic` methods instead of `virtual` methods can result in significant memory savings with only a minimal speed penalty.

From a programmer's perspective, the difference between these two approaches lies only in a different internal representation and slightly different speed or memory usage. Apart from this, `virtual` and `dynamic` methods are the same.

Message Handlers

A late-bound method can be used to handle a Windows message, too, although the technique is somewhat different. For this purpose Delphi provides yet another directive, `message`, to define message-handling methods, which must be procedures with a single `var` parameter. The `message` directive is followed by the number of the Windows message the method wants to handle.

> **WARNING** The `message` directive is also available in Delphi for Linux and is fully supported by the language and the RTL. However, the visual portion of the CLX application framework does not use message methods to dispatch notifications to controls. For this reason, whenever possible, you should use a virtual method provided by the library rather than handle a Windows message directly. Of course, this matters only if you want your code to be more portable.

For example, the following code allows you to handle a user-defined message, with the numeric value indicated by the `wm_User` Windows constant:

```
type
  TForm1 = class(TForm)
    ...
    procedure WmUser (var Msg: TMessage);
      message wm_User;
  end;
```

The name of the procedure and the actual type of the parameters are up to you, although there are several predefined record types for the various Windows messages. You could later send this message, invoking the corresponding method, by writing:

```
PostMessage (Form1.Handle, wm_User, 0, 0);
```

This technique can be extremely useful for veteran Windows programmers, who know all about Windows messages and API functions. You can also dispatch a message to an object by calling the TObject.Dispatch method on the object. This will be a synchronous message call, not asynchronous like PostMessage. TObject.Dispatch is fully platform independent.

The ability to handle Windows messages and call API functions as you do when you are programming Windows with the C language may horrify some programmers and delight others. But in Delphi, when writing Windows applications, you will seldom need to use message methods or call Windows APIs directly. Obviously, these techniques will also affect the portability of your code to other platforms.

Abstract Methods

The abstract keyword is used to declare methods that will be defined only in subclasses of the current class. The abstract directive fully defines the method; it is not a forward declaration. If you try to provide a definition for the method, the compiler will complain. In Object Pascal, you can create instances of classes that have abstract methods. However, when you try to do so, Delphi's 32-bit compiler issues the warning message "Constructing instance of <class name> containing abstract methods." If you happen to call an abstract method at run time, Delphi will raise an exception, as demonstrated by the following Animals3 example.

NOTE   C++ and Java use a more strict approach: in these languages, you cannot create instances of classes containing abstract methods.

You might wonder why you would want to use abstract methods. The reason lies in the use of polymorphism. If class TAnimal has the abstract method Voice, every subclass can redefine it. The advantage is that you can now use the generic MyAnimal object to refer to each animal defined by a subclass and invoke this method. If this method was not present in the interface of the TAnimal class, the call would not have been allowed by the compiler, which performs static type checking. Using a generic MyAnimal object, you can call only the method defined by its own class, TAnimal.

You cannot call methods provided by subclasses, unless the parent class has at least the declaration of this method—in the form of an abstract method. The next example, Animals3, demonstrates the use of abstract methods and the abstract call error. In Listing 3.1, you can see the interfaces of the classes of this new example. (Here TAnimal is an abstract class.)

Listing 3.1:   Declaration of the three classes of the Animals3 example

```
type
  TAnimal = class
  public
    constructor Create;
    function GetKind: string;
    function Voice: string; virtual; abstract;
  private
    Kind: string;
  end;

  TDog = class (TAnimal)
  public
    constructor Create;
    function Voice: string; override;
    function Eat: string; virtual;
  end;

  TCat = class (TAnimal)
  public
    constructor Create;
    function Voice: string; override;
    function Eat: string; virtual;
  end;
```

The most interesting portion of Listing 3.1 is the definition of the class TAnimal, which includes a virtual abstract method: Voice. It is also important to notice that each derived class overrides this definition and adds a new virtual method, Eat. What are the implications of these two different approaches? To call the Voice function, we can write the same code as in the previous version of the program:

```
LabelVoice.Caption := MyAnimal.Voice;
```

How can we call the Eat method? We cannot apply it to an object of the TAnimal class. The statement

```
LabelVoice.Caption := MyAnimal.Eat;
```

generates the compiler error "Field identifier expected."

To solve this problem, you can use run-time type information (RTTI) to cast the TAnimal object to a TCat or TDog object; but without the proper cast, the program will raise an exception. You will see an example of this approach in the next section. Adding the method definition to the TAnimal class is a typical solution to the problem, and the presence of the abstract keyword favors this choice.

What happens if a method overriding an abstract method calls `inherited`? In past versions of Delphi, this resulted in an abstract method call. In Delphi 6, the compiler has been enhanced to notice the presence of the abstract method and simply skip the `inherited` call. This means you can safely always use `inherited` in every overridden method, unless you specifically want to disable executing some code of the base class.

Type-Safe Down-Casting

The Object Pascal type-compatibility rule for descendant classes allows you to use a descendant class where an ancestor class is expected. As I mentioned earlier, the reverse is not possible.

Now suppose that the TDog class has an Eat method, which is not present in the TAnimal class. If the variable MyAnimal refers to a dog, it should be possible to call the function. But if you try, and the variable is referring to another class, the result is an error. By making an explicit typecast, we could cause a nasty run-time error (or worse, a subtle memory overwrite problem), because the compiler cannot determine whether the type of the object is correct and the methods we are calling actually exist.

To solve the problem, we can use techniques based on *run-time type information* (RTTI, for short). Essentially, because each object "knows" its type and its parent class, and we can ask for this information with the is operator or using the InheritsFrom method of the TObject class. The parameters of the is operator are an object and a class type, and the return value is a Boolean:

```
if MyAnimal is TDog then ...
```

The is expression evaluates as True only if the MyAnimal object is currently referring to an object of class TDog or a type descendant from TDog. This means that if you test whether a TDog object is of type TAnimal, the test will succeed. In other words, this expression evaluates as True if you can safely assign the object (MyAnimal) to a variable of the data type (TDog).

Now that you know for sure that the animal is a dog, you can make a safe typecast (or type conversion). You can accomplish this direct cast by writing the following code:

```
var
  MyDog: TDog;
begin
  if MyAnimal is TDog then
  begin
    MyDog := TDog (MyAnimal);
    Text := MyDog.Eat;
  end;
```

This same operation can be accomplished directly by the second RTTI operator, as, which converts the object only if the requested class is compatible with the actual one. The parameters of the as operator are an object and a class type, and the result is an object converted to the new class type. We can write the following snippet:

```
MyDog := MyAnimal as TDog;
Text := MyDog.Eat;
```

If we only want to call the Eat function, we might also use an even shorter notation:

```
(MyAnimal as TDog).Eat;
```

The result of this expression is an object of the TDog class data type, so you can apply to it any method of that class. The difference between the traditional cast and the use of the as cast is that the second raises an exception if the type of the object is incompatible with the type you are trying to cast it to. The exception raised is EInvalidCast (exceptions are described at the end of this chapter).

To avoid this exception, use the is operator and, if it succeeds, make a plain typecast (in fact, there is no reason to use is and as in sequence, doing the type check twice):

```
if MyAnimal is TDog then
  TDog(MyAnimal).Eat;
```

Both RTTI operators are very useful in Delphi because you often want to write generic code that can be used with several components of the same type or even of different types. When a component is passed as a parameter to an event-response method, a generic data type is used (TObject), so you often need to cast it back to the original component type:

```
procedure TForm1.Button1Click(Sender: TObject);
begin
  if Sender is TButton then
    ...
end;
```

This is a common technique in Delphi, and I'll use it in examples throughout the book. The two RTTI operators, is and as, are extremely powerful, and you might be tempted to consider them as standard programming constructs. Although they are indeed powerful, you should probably limit their use to special cases. When you need to solve a complex problem involving several classes, try using polymorphism first. Only in special cases, where polymorphism alone cannot be applied, should you try using the RTTI operators to complement it. *Do not use RTTI instead of polymorphism.* This is bad programming practice, and it results in slower programs. RTTI, in fact, has a negative impact on performance, because it must walk the hierarchy of classes to see whether the typecast is correct. As we have seen, virtual method calls require just a memory lookup, which is much faster.

NOTE   There is actually more to run-time type information (RTTI) than the `is` and `as` operators. You can access to detailed class and type information at run time, particularly for published properties, events, and methods. More on this topic in Chapter 5.

Using Interfaces

When you define an abstract class to represent the base class of a hierarchy, you can come to a point in which the abstract class is so abstract that it only lists a series of virtual functions without providing any actual implementation. This kind of *purely abstract class* can also be defined using a specific technique, an `interface`. For this reason, we refer to these classes as *interfaces*.

Technically, an interface is not a class, although it may resemble one. Interfaces are not classes, because they are considered a totally separate element with distinctive features:

- Interface type objects are reference-counted and automatically destroyed when there are no more references to the object. This mechanism is similar to how Delphi manages long strings and makes memory management almost automatic.

- A class can inherit from a single base class, but it can implement multiple interfaces.

- As all classes descend from `TObject`, all interfaces descend from `IInterface`, forming a totally separate hierarchy.

The base interface class used to be `IUnknown` until Delphi 5, but Delphi 6 introduces a new name for it, `IInterface`, to mark even more clearly the fact that this language feature is separate from Microsoft's COM. In fact, Delphi interfaces are available also in the Linux version of the product.

You can use this rule: Interface types describing things that relate to COM and the related operating-system services should inherit from `IUnknown`. Interface types that describe things that do not necessarily require COM (for example, interfaces used for the internal application structure) should inherit from `IInterface`. Doing this consistently in your applications will make it easier to identify which portions of your application probably assume or require the Windows operating system and which portions are probably OS-independent.

NOTE   Borland introduced interfaces in Delphi 3 along with the support COM programming. Though the interface language syntax may have been created to support COM, interfaces do not require COM. You can use interfaces to implement abstraction layers within your applications, without building COM server objects. For example, the Delphi IDE uses interfaces extensively in its internal architecture. COM is discussed in Chapter 19.

From a more general point of view, interfaces support a slightly different object-oriented programming model than classes. Objects implementing interfaces are subject to polymorphism for each of the interfaces they support. Indeed, the interface-based model is powerful. But having said that, I'm not interested in trying to assess which approach is better in each case. Certainly, interfaces favor encapsulation and provide a looser connection between classes than inheritance. Notice that the most recent OOP languages, from Java to C#, have the notion of interfaces.

Here is the syntax of the declaration of an interface (which, by convention, starts with the letter *I*):

```
type
  ICanFly = interface
    ['{EAD9C4B4-E1C5-4CF4-9FA0-3B812C880A21}']
    function Fly: string;
  end;
```

The above interface has a GUID, a numeric ID following its declaration and based on Windows conventions. You can generate these identifiers (called GUIDs in jargon) by pressing Ctrl+Shift+G in the Delphi editor.

Although you can compile and use interfaces even without specifying a GUID (as in the code above) for them, you'll generally want to do it, as this is required to perform QueryInterface or dynamic as typecasts using that interface type. Since the whole point of interfaces is (usually) to take advantage of greatly extended type flexibility at run time, if compared with class types, interfaces without GUIDs are not very useful.

Once you've declared an interface, you can define a class to implement it, as in:

```
type
  TAirplane = class (TInterfacedObject, ICanFly)
    function Fly: string;
  end;
```

The RTL already provides a few base classes to implement the basic behavior required by the IInterface interface. The simplest one is the TInterfacedObject class I've used in this code.

You can implement interface methods with static methods (as in the code above) or with virtual methods. You can override virtual methods in subclasses by using the override directive. If you don't use virtual methods, you can still provide a new implementation in a subclass by redeclaring the interface type in the subclass, rebinding the interface methods to new versions of the static methods. At first sight, using virtual methods to implement interfaces seems to allow for smoother coding in subclasses, but both approaches are equally powerful and flexible. However, the use of virtual methods affects code size and memory.

NOTE The compiler has to generate stub routines to fix up the interface call entry points to the matching method of the implementing class, and adjust the `self` pointer. The interface method stubs for static methods are very simple: adjust `self` and jump to the real method in the class. The interface method stubs for virtual methods are much more complicated, requiring about four times more code (20 to 30 bytes) in each stub than the static case. Also, adding more virtual methods to the implementing class just bloats the virtual method table (VMT) that much more in the implementing class and all its descendents. Interfaces already have their own VMT, and redeclaring interfaces in descendents to rebind the interface to new methods in the descendent is just as polymorphic as using virtual methods, but much smaller in code size.

Now that we have defined an implementation of the interface, we can write some code to use an object of this class, as usual:

```
var
  Airplane1: TAirplane;
begin
  Airplane1 := TAirplane.Create;
  Airplane1.Fly;
  Airplane1.Free;
end;
```

But we can also use an interface-type variable:

```
var
  Flyer1: ICanFly;
begin
  Flyer1 := TAirplane.Create;
  Flyer1.Fly;
end;
```

As soon as you assign an object to an interface-type variable, Delphi automatically checks to see whether the object implements that interface, using the **as** operator. You can explicitly express this operation as follows:

```
Flyer1 := TAirplane.Create as ICanFly;
```

NOTE   The compiler generates different code for the **as** operator when used with interfaces or with classes. With classes, the compiler introduces run-time checks to verify that the object is effectively "type-compatible" with the given. With interfaces, the compiler sees at compile time that it can extract the necessary interface from the available class type, so it does. This operation is like a "compile-time **as**," not something that exists at run time.

Whether we use the direct assignment or the **as** statement, Delphi does one extra thing: it calls the _AddRef method of the object (defined by IInterface and implemented by TInterfacedObject), increasing its reference count. At the same time, as soon as the

Flyer1 variable goes out of scope, Delphi calls the _Release method (again part of IInterface), which decreases the reference count, checks whether the reference count is zero, and if necessary, destroys the object. For this reason in the listing above, there is no code to free the object we've created.

In other words, in Delphi, objects referenced by interface variables are reference-counted, and they are automatically de-allocated when no interface variable refers to them any more.

WARNING   When using interface-based objects, you should generally access them only with object variables or only with interface variables. Mixing the two approaches breaks the reference counting scheme provided by Delphi and can cause memory errors that are extremely difficult to track. In practice, if you've decided to use interfaces, you should probably use exclusively interface-based variables.

Interface Properties, Delegation, Redefinitions, Aggregation, and Reference Counting Blues

To demonstrate a few technical elements related to interfaces, I've written the IntfDemo example. This example is based on two different interfaces, IWalker and IJumper, defined as follows:

```
IWalker = interface
  ['{0876F200-AAD3-11D2-8551-CCA30C584521}']
  function Walk: string;
  function Run: string;
  procedure SetPos (Value: Integer);
  function GetPos: Integer;
property Position: Integer read GetPos write SetPos;
end;

IJumper = interface
  ['{0876F201-AAD3-11D2-8551-CCA30C584521}']
  function Jump: string;
  function Walk: string;
  procedure SetPos (Value: Integer);
  function GetPos: Integer;
property Position: Integer read GetPos write SetPos;
end;
```

Notice that the first interface also defines a property. An interface property is just a name mapped to a read and a write method. You cannot map an interface property to a field, simply because an interface cannot have a data field.

Here comes a sample implementation of the IWalker interface. Notice that you don't have to define the property, only its access methods:

```
TRunner = class (TInterfacedObject, IWalker)
private
  Pos: Integer;
public
  function Walk: string;
  function Run: string;
  procedure SetPos (Value: Integer);
  function GetPos: Integer;
end;
```

The code is trivial, so I'm going to skip it (you can find it in the IntfDemo example, where there is also a destructor showing a message, used to verify that reference counting works properly). I've implemented the same interface also in another class, TAthlete, that I'll discuss in a second.

As I want to implement also the IJumper interface in two different classes, I've followed a different approach. Delphi allows you to delegate the implementation of an interface inside a class to an object exposed with a property. In other words, I want to share the actual implementation code for an interface implemented by several unrelated classes.

To support this technique, Delphi has a special keyword, implements. For example, you can write:

```
TMyJumper = class (TInterfacedObject, IJumper)
private
  fJumpImpl: IJumper;
public
  constructor Create;
  property Jumper: IJumper read fJumpImpl implements IJumper;
end;
```

In this case the property refers to an interface variable, but you can also use a plain object variable (my preferred approach). The constructor is required for initializing the internal *implementation* object:

```
constructor TMyJumper.Create;
begin
  fJumpImpl := TJumperImpl.Create;
end;
```

As a first attempt (and in the last edition of the book), I defined the implementation class as follows:

```
TJumperImpl = class (TInterfacedObject, IJumper)
private
  Pos: Integer;
public
  function Jump: string;
```

```
  function Walk: string;
  procedure SetPos (Value: Integer);
  function GetPos: Integer;
end;
```

If you try this code, the program will compile and everything will run smoothly, until you try to check out what happens with reference counting. It won't work, period. The problem lies in the fact that when the program extracts the IJumper interface from the TMyJumper object, it actually increases and decreases the reference counting of the inner object, instead of the external one. In other words, you have a single compound object and two separate reference counts going on. This can lead to objects being both kept in memory and released too soon.

The solution to this problem is to have a single reference count, by redirecting the _AddRef and _Release calls of the internal object to the external one (actually we need to do the same also for QueryInterface). In the example, I've used the TAggregatedObject provided in Delphi 6 by the system unit; refer to the sidebar "Implementing Aggregates" for more details.

As a result of this approach, the implementation class is now defined as follows:

```
TJumperImpl = class (TAggregatedObject, IJumper)
private
  Pos: Integer;
public
  function Jump: string;
  function Walk: string;
  procedure SetPos (Value: Integer);
  function GetPos: Integer;

  property Position: Integer read GetPos write SetPos;
end;
```

An object using this class for implementing the IJumper interface must have a Create constructor, to create the internal object, and a destructor, to destroy it. The constructor of the aggregate object requires the container object as parameter, so that it can redirect back the IInterface calls. The key element, of course, is the property mapped to the interface with the implements keyword:

```
TMyJumper = class (TInterfacedObject, IJumper)
private
  fJumpImpl: TJumperImpl;
public
  constructor Create;
  property Jumper: TJumperImpl read fJumpImpl implements IJumper;
  destructor Destroy; override;
end;

constructor TMyJumper.Create;
begin
  fJumpImpl := TJumperImpl.Create (self);
end;
```

This example is simple, but in general, things get more complex as you start to modify some of the methods or add other methods that still operate on the data of the internal fJumpImpl object. This final step is demonstrated, along with other features, by the TAthlete class, which implements both the IWalker and IJumper interfaces:

```
TAthlete = class (TInterfacedObject, IWalker, IJumper)
private
  fJumpImpl: TJumperImpl;
public
  constructor Create;
  destructor Destroy; override;
  function Run: string; virtual;
  function Walk1: string; virtual;
  function IWalker.Walk = Walk1;
  procedure SetPos (Value: Integer);
  function GetPos: Integer;

  property Jumper: TJumperImpl read fJumpImpl implements IJumper;
end;
```

One of the interfaces is implemented directly, whereas the other is delegated to the internal fJumpImpl object. Notice also that by implementing two interfaces that have a method in common, we end up with a name clash. The solution is to rename one of the methods, with the statement

```
function IWalker.Walk = Walk1;
```

This declaration indicates that the class implements the Walk method of the IWalker interface with a method called Walk1 (instead of with a method having the same name). Finally, in the implementation of all of the methods of this class, we need to refer to the Position property of the fJumpImpl internal object. By declaring a new implementation for the Position property, we'll end up with two positions for a single athlete, a rather odd situation. Here are a couple of examples:

```
function TAthlete.GetPos: Integer;
begin
  Result := fJumpImpl.Position;
end;

function TAthlete.Run: string;
begin
  fJumpImpl.Position := fJumpImpl.Position + 2;
  Result := IntToStr (fJumpImpl.Position) + ': Run';
end;
```

You can further experiment with the IntfDemo example, which has a simple form with buttons to create and call methods of the various objects. Nothing fancy, though, as you can see in Figure 3.4. Simply keep in mind that each call returns the position after the requested movement and a description of the movement itself. Also, each object notifies with a message when it is destroyed.

FIGURE 3.4:

The IntfDemo example

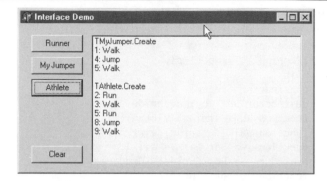

Implementing Aggregates

As mentioned, when you want to use an internal object to implement an interface, you are faced with reference counting problems. Of course, you can provide your own version of the _AddRef and _Release methods of IInterface, but having a ready-to-use solution might help. In fact, QueryInterface on the internal object must also be reflected to the outer object. The user of the interface (whether it works on the outer object or the internal one) should never be able to discern any difference in behavior between _AddRef, _Release, and QueryInterface calls on the aggregated interface and any other interface obtained from the implementing class.

Borland provides a solution to this problem with the TAggregatedObject class. In past version of Delphi, this was defined in the ComObj unit, but now it has been moved into the System unit, to make this feature also available to Linux and to separate it completely from COM support.

The TAggregatedObject class keeps a reference to the controller, the external object, passed as parameter in the constructor. This *weak reference* is kept using a pointer type variable to avoid artificially increasing the reference count of the controller from the aggregated object, something that will prevent the object's reference count from reaching zero. You create an object of this type (used as internal object) passing the reference to the controller (the external object), and all of the IInterface methods are passed back to the controller. A similar class, TContainedObject, lets the controller resolve reference counting, but handles the QueryInterface call internally, limiting the type resolution only to interfaces supported by the internal object.

Working with Exceptions

Another key feature of Object Pascal I'll cover in this chapter is the support for *exceptions*. The idea of exceptions is to make programs more robust by adding the capability of handling software or hardware errors in a uniform way. A program can survive such errors or terminate gracefully, allowing the user to save data before exiting. Exceptions allow you to separate the error-handling code from your normal code, instead of intertwining the two. You end up writing code that is more compact and less cluttered by maintenance chores unrelated to the actual programming objective.

Another benefit is that exceptions define a uniform and universal error-reporting mechanism, which is also used by Delphi components. At run time, Delphi raises exceptions when something goes wrong (in the run-time code, in a component, in the operating system). From the point of the code in which it is raised, the exception is passed to its calling code, and so on. Ultimately, if no part of your code handles the exception, Delphi handles it, by displaying a standard error message and trying to continue the program, by handing the next system message or user request.

The whole mechanism is based on four keywords:

try   delimits the beginning of a protected block of code.

except   delimits the end of a protected block of code and introduces the exception-handling statements, with this syntax form:

> on *exception-type* **do** *statement*

finally   is used to specify blocks of code that must always be executed, even when exceptions occur. This block is generally used to perform cleanup operations that should always be executed, such as closing files or database tables, freeing objects, and releasing memory and other resources acquired in the same program block.

raise   is the statement used to generate an exception. Most exceptions you'll encounter in your Delphi programming will be generated by the system, but you can also raise exceptions in your own code when it discovers invalid or inconsistent data at run time. The raise keyword can also be used inside a handler to *re-raise* an exception; that is, to propagate it to the next handler.

The most important element to notice up front is that exception handling is no substitute for if statements or for tests on input parameters of functions. So *in theory* we could write this code:

```
function DivideTwicePlusOne (A, B: Integer): Integer;
begin
  try
    // error if B equals 0
    Result := A div B;
```

```
    // do something else... skip if exception is raised
    Result := Result div B;
    Result := Result + 1;
  except
    on EDivByZero do
      Result := 0;
  end;
end;
```

In practice, however, this is certainly not a good way of writing your programs. The except block above, like most of the except blocks of the simple examples presented here, has almost no sense at all. In the code above, you should probably not handle the exception but let the program display the error message to the user. An algorithm calling this DivideTwicePlusOne function should not continue (with a meaningless zero value) when this internal error is encountered.

Program Flow and the *finally* Block

But how do we stop the algorithm? The power of exceptions in Delphi relates to the fact that they are "passed" from a routine or method to the calling one, up to a global handler (if the program provides one, as Delphi applications generally do). So the real problem you might have is not how to stop an exception but how to execute some code when an exception is raised.

Consider this method (part of the TryFinally example from the CD), which performs some time-consuming operations and uses the hourglass cursor to show the user that it's doing something:

```
procedure TForm1.BtnWrongClick(Sender: TObject);
var
  I, J: Integer;
begin
  Screen.Cursor := crHourglass;
  J := 0;
  // long (and wrong) computation...
  for I := 1000 downto 0 do
    J := J + J div I;
  MessageDlg ('Total: ' + IntToStr (J), mtInformation, [mbOK], 0);
  Screen.Cursor := crDefault;
end;
```

Because there is an error in the algorithm (as the variable I can reach a value of 0 and is also used in a division), the program will break, but it won't reset the default cursor. This is what a try/finally block is for:

```
procedure TForm1.BtnTryFinallyClick(Sender: TObject);
var
  I, J: Integer;
begin
```

```
    Screen.Cursor := crHourglass;
    J := 0;
    try
      // long (and wrong) computation...
      for I := 1000 downto 0 do
        J := J + J div I;
      MessageDlg ('Total: ' + IntToStr (J), mtInformation, [mbOK], 0);
    finally
      Screen.Cursor := crDefault;
    end;
  end;
```

When the program executes this function, it always resets the cursor, whether an exception (of any sort) occurs or not.

This code doesn't handle the exception; it merely makes the program robust in case an exception is raised. As a `try` block can be followed by either an `except` or a `finally` statement, but not both of them at the same time, the typical solution if you want to also handle the exception is to use two nested `try` blocks. In this case, you associate the internal one with a `finally` statement and the external one with an `except` statement, or vice versa as the situation requires. Here is the code of this third button of the TryFinally example:

```
procedure TForm1.BtnTryTryClick(Sender: TObject);
var
  I, J: Integer;
begin
  Screen.Cursor := crHourglass;
  J := 0;
  try try
    // long (and wrong) computation...
    for I := 1000 downto 0 do
      J := J + J div I;
    MessageDlg ('Total: ' + IntToStr (J), mtInformation, [mbOK], 0);
  finally
    Screen.Cursor := crDefault;
  end;
  except
    on E: EDivByZero do
    begin
      // re-raise the exception with a new message
      raise Exception.Create ('Error in Algorithm');
    end;
  end;
end;
```

Every time you have some finalization code at the end of a method, you should place this code in a `finally` block. You should always, invariably, and continuously (how can I stress this more?) protect your code with `finally` statements, to avoid resource or memory leaks in case an exception is raised.

TIP   Handling the exception is generally much less important than using `finally` blocks, since Delphi can survive most of them. And too many exception-handling blocks in your code probably indicate errors in the program flow and possibly a misunderstanding of the role of exceptions in the language. In the examples in the rest of the book you'll see many `try`/`finally` blocks, a few `raise` statements, and almost no `try`/`except` blocks.

Exception Classes

In exception-handling statements shown earlier, we caught the `EDivByZero` exception, which is defined by Delphi's RTL. Other such exceptions refer to run-time problems (such as a wrong dynamic cast), Windows resource problems (such as out-of-memory errors), or component errors (such as a wrong index). Programmers can also define their own exceptions; you can create a new subclass of the default exception class or one of its subclasses:

```
type
  EArrayFull = class (Exception);
```

When you add a new element to an array that is already full (probably because of an error in the logic of the program), you can raise the corresponding exception by creating an object of this class:

```
if MyArray.Full then
  raise EArrayFull.Create ('Array full');
```

This `Create` method (inherited from the `Exception` class) has a string parameter to describe the exception to the user. You don't need to worry about destroying the object you have created for the exception, because it will be deleted automatically by the exception-handler mechanism.

The code presented in the previous excerpts is part of a sample program, called Exception1. Some of the routines have actually been slightly modified, as in the following `DivideTwicePlusOne` function:

```
function DivideTwicePlusOne (A, B: Integer): Integer;
begin
  try
    // error if B equals 0
    Result := A div B;
    // do something else... skip if exception is raised
    Result := Result div B;
    Result := Result + 1;
  except
    on EDivByZero do
    begin
      Result := 0;
      MessageDlg ('Divide by zero corrected.', mtError, [mbOK], 0);
    end;
    on E: Exception do
    begin
      Result := 0;
```

```
        MessageDlg (E.Message, mtError, [mbOK], 0);
    end;
  end; // end except
end;
```

Debugging and Exceptions

When you start a program from the Delphi environment (for example, by pressing the F9 key), you'll generally run it within the debugger. When an exception is encountered, the debugger will stop the program by default. This is normally what you want, of course, because you'll know where the exception took place and can see the call of the handler step-by-step. You can also use the Stack Trace feature of Delphi to see the sequence of function and method calls, which caused the program to raise an exception.

In the case of the Exception1 test program, however, this behavior will confuse the program's execution. In fact, even if the code is prepared to properly handle the exception, the debugger will stop the program execution at the source code line closest to where the exception was raised. Then, moving step-by-step through the code, you can see how it is handled.

If you just want to let the program run when the exception is properly handled, run the program from Windows Explorer, or temporarily disable the Stop on Delphi Exceptions options in the Language Exceptions page of the Debugger Options dialog box (activated by the Tools ➤ Debugger Options command), shown in the Language Exceptions page of the Debugger Options dialog box shown here.

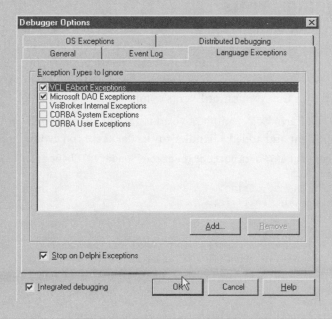

In the Exception1 code there are two different exception handlers after the same `try` block. You can have any number of these handlers, which are evaluated in sequence. For this reason, you need to place the broader handlers (the handlers of the ancestor `Exception` classes) at the end.

In fact, using a hierarchy of exceptions, a handler is also called for the subclasses of the type it refers to, as any procedure will do. This is polymorphism in action again. But keep in mind that using a handler for every exception, such as the one above, is not usually a good choice. It is better to leave unknown exceptions to Delphi. The default exception handler in the VCL displays the error message of the exception class in a message box, and then resumes normal operation of the program. You can actually modify the normal exception handler with the `Application.OnException` event, as demonstrated in the ErrorLog example later in this chapter.

Another important element of the code above is the use of the exception object in the handler (see `on E: Exception do`). The object E of class `Exception` receives the value of the exception object passed by the `raise` statement. When you work with exceptions, remember this rule: You raise an exception by creating an object and handle it by indicating its type. This has an important benefit, because as we have seen, when you handle a type of exception, you are really handling exceptions of the type you specify as well as any descendant type.

Delphi defines a hierarchy of exceptions, and you can choose to handle each specific type of exception in a different way or handle groups of them together.

Logging Errors

Most of the time, you don't know which operation is going to `raise` an exception, and you cannot (and should not) wrap each and every piece of code in a `try/except` block. The general approach is to let Delphi handle all the exceptions and eventually pass them all to you, by handling the `OnException` event of the global `Application` object. This can be done rather easily with the ApplicationEvents component.

In the ErrorLog example, I've added to the main form a copy of the ApplicationEvents component and added a handler for its `OnException` event:

```
procedure TFormLog.LogException(Sender: TObject; E: Exception);
var
  Filename: string;
  LogFile: TextFile;
begin
  // prepares log file
  Filename := ChangeFileExt (Application.Exename, '.log');
  AssignFile (LogFile, Filename);
  if FileExists (FileName) then
    Append (LogFile) // open existing file
  else
    Rewrite (LogFile); // create a new one
  // write to the file and show error
```

```
    Writeln (LogFile, DateTimeToStr (Now) + ':' + E.Message);
    if not CheckBoxSilent.Checked then
      Application.ShowException (E);
    // close the file
    CloseFile (LogFile);
  end;
```

NOTE   The ErrorLog example uses the text file support provided by the traditional Turbo Pascal TextFile data type. You can assign a text file variable to an actual file and then read or write it. You can find more on TextFile operations in Chapter 12 of *Essential Pascal,* available on the companion CD.

In the global exceptions handler, you can write to the log, for example, the date and time of the event, and also decide whether to show the exception as Delphi usually does (executing the ShowException method of the TApplication class). In fact, Delphi by default executes ShowException only if there is no OnException handler installed.

Finally, remember to close the file, flushing the buffers, every time the exception is handled or when the program terminates. I've chosen the first approach to avoid keeping the log file open for the lifetime of the application, potentially making it difficult to work on it. You can accomplish this in the OnDestroy event handler of the form:

```
procedure TFormLog.FormDestroy(Sender: TObject);
begin
  CloseFile (LogFile);
end;
```

The form of the program includes a check box to determine its behavior and two buttons generating exceptions. In Figure 3.5, you can see the ErrorLog program running and a sample exceptions log open in Notepad.

FIGURE 3.5:

The ErrorLog example and the log it produces

Class References

The final language feature I want to discuss in this chapter is *class references*, which implies the idea of manipulating classes themselves (not just class instances) within your code. The first point to keep in mind is that a class reference isn't a class, it isn't an object, and it isn't a reference to an object; it is simply a reference to a class type.

A class reference type determines the type of a class reference variable. Sounds confusing? A few lines of code might make this a little clearer. Suppose you have defined the class TMy-Class. You can now define a new class reference type, related to that class:

```
type
    TMyClassRef = class of TMyClass;
```

Now you can declare variables of both types. The first variable refers to an object, the second to a class:

```
var
    AClassRef: TMyClassRef;
    AnObject: TMyClass;
begin
    AClassRef := TMyClass;
    AnObject := TMyClass.Create;
```

You may wonder what class references are used for. In general, class references allow you to manipulate a class data type at run time. You can use a class reference in any expression where the use of a data type is legal. Actually, there are not many such expressions, but the few cases are interesting. The simplest case is the creation of an object. We can rewrite the two lines above as follows:

```
AClassRef := TMyClass;
AnObject := AClassRef.Create;
```

This time I've applied the Create constructor to the class reference instead of to an actual class; I've used a class reference to create an object of that class.

NOTE   Class references remind us of the concept of *metaclass* available in other OOP languages. In Object Pascal, however, a class reference is not itself a class but only a type pointer. Therefore, the analogy with metaclasses (classes describing other classes) is a little misleading. Actually, TMetaclass is also the term used in Borland C++Builder.

Class reference types wouldn't be as useful if they didn't support the same type-compatibility rule that applies to class types. When you declare a class reference variable, such as MyClassRef above, you can then assign to it that specific class and any subclass. So if MyNewClass is a subclass of my class, you can also write

```
AClassRef := MyNewClass;
```

Delphi declares a lot of class references in the run-time library and the VCL, including the following:

```
TClass = class of TObject;
ExceptClass = class of Exception;
TComponentClass = class of TComponent;
TControlClass = class of TControl;
TFormClass = class of TForm;
```

In particular, the TClass class reference type can be used to store a reference to any class you write in Delphi, because every class is ultimately derived from TObject. The TFormClass reference, instead, is used in the source code of most Delphi projects. The CreateForm method of the Application object, in fact, requires as parameter the class of the form to create:

```
Application.CreateForm(TForm1, Form1);
```

The first parameter is a class reference; the second is a variable that stores a reference to the created object instance.

Finally, when you have a class reference you can apply to it the class methods of the related class. Considering that each class inherits from TObject, you can apply to each class reference some of the methods of TObject, as we'll see in the next chapter.

Creating Components Using Class References

What is the *practical* use of class references in Delphi? Being able to manipulate a data type at run time is a fundamental element of the Delphi environment. When you add a new component to a form by selecting it from the Component Palette, you select a data type and create an object of that data type. (Actually, that is what Delphi does for you behind the scenes.) In other words, class references give you polymorphism for object construction.

To give you a better idea of how class references work, I've built an example named ClassRef. The form displayed by this example is quite simple. It has three radio buttons, placed inside a panel in the upper portion of the form. When you select one of these radio buttons and click the form, you'll be able to create new components of the three types indicated by the button labels: radio buttons, push buttons, and edit boxes.

To make this program run properly, you need to change the names of the three components. The form must also have a class reference field:

```
private
  ClassRef: TControlClass;
  Counter: Integer;
```

The first field stores a new data type every time the user clicks one of the three radio buttons. Here is one of the three methods:

```
procedure TForm1.RadioButtonRadioClick(Sender: TObject);
begin
  ClassRef := TRadioButton;
end;
```

The other two radio buttons have OnClick event handlers similar to this one, assigning the value TEdit or TButton to the ClassRef field. A similar assignment is also present in the handler of the OnCreate event of the form, used as an initialization method.

The interesting part of the code is executed when the user clicks the form. Again, I've chosen the OnMouseDown event of the form to hold the position of the mouse click:

```
procedure TForm1.FormMouseDown(Sender: TObject; Button: TMouseButton;
  Shift: TShiftState; X, Y: Integer);
var
  NewCtrl: TControl;
  MyName: String;
begin
  // create the control
  NewCtrl := ClassRef.Create (Self);
  // hide it temporarily, to avoid flickering
  NewCtrl.Visible := False;
  // set parent and position
  NewCtrl.Parent := Self;
  NewCtrl.Left := X;
  NewCtrl.Top := Y;
  // compute the unique name (and caption)
  Inc (Counter);
  MyName := ClassRef.ClassName + IntToStr (Counter);
  Delete (MyName, 1, 1);
  NewCtrl.Name := MyName;
  // now show it
  NewCtrl.Visible := True;
end;
```

The first line of the code for this method is the key. It creates a new object of the class data type stored in the ClassRef field. We accomplish this simply by applying the Create constructor to the class reference. Now you can set the value of the Parent property, set the position of the new component, give it a name (which is automatically used also as Caption or Text), and make it visible.

Notice in particular the code used to build the name; to mimic Delphi's default naming convention, I've taken the name of the class with the expression ClassRef.ClassName, using a class method of the TObject class. Then I've added a number at the end of the name and removed the initial letter of the string. For the first radio button, the basic string is TRadioButton, plus the *1* at the end, and minus the *T* at the beginning of the class name—RadioButton1. Sound familiar?

You can see an example of the output of this program in Figure 3.6. Notice that the naming is not exactly the same as used by Delphi. Delphi uses a separate counter for each type of control; I've used a single counter for all of the components. If you place a radio button, a push button, and an edit box in a form of the ClassRef example, their names will be RadioButton1, Button2, and Edit3.

NOTE   For polymorphic construction to work, the base class type of the class reference must have a virtual constructor. If you use a virtual constructor (as in the example), the constructor call applied to the class reference will call the constructor of the type that the class reference variable *currently refers to*. But without a virtual constructor, your code will call the constructor of *fixed class type* indicated in the class reference declaration. Virtual constructors are required for polymorphic construction in the same way that virtual methods are required for polymorphism.

FIGURE 3.6:

An example of the output of the ClassRef example

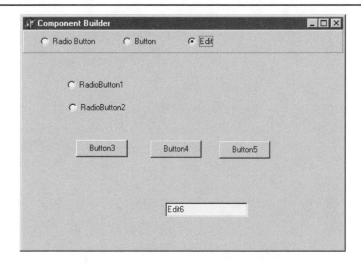

What's Next?

In this chapter, we have discussed the more advanced elements of object-oriented programming in Object Pascal. We have considered inheritance, virtual and abstract methods, polymorphism, safe typecasting, interfaces, exceptions, and class references.

Understanding the secrets of Object Pascal and the structure of the Delphi library is vital for becoming an expert Delphi programmer. These topics form the foundation of working with the VCL and CLX class libraries; after exploring them in the next two chapters, we'll *finally* go on in Part II of the book to explore the development of real applications using all the various components provided by Delphi.

In the meantime, the next chapter will give you an over view of the Delphi run-time library, mainly a collection of functions with little OOP involved. The RTL is an assorted collection of routines and tasks for performing basic tasks with Delphi, and it has been largely extended in Delphi 6.

Chapter 5 will give you more information about the Object Pascal language, discussing features related to the structure of the Delphi class library, such as the effect of the `published` keyword and the role of events. The chapter, as a whole, will discuss the overall architecture of the component library.

CHAPTER 4

The Run-Time Library

- Overview of the RTL

- New Delphi 6 RTL functions

- The conversion engine

- Dates, strings, and other new RTL units

- The *TObject* class

- Showing class information at run time

Delphi uses Object Pascal as its programming language and favors an object-oriented approach, tied with a visual development style. This is where Delphi shines, and we will cover component-based and visual development in this book; however, I want to underline the fact that a lot of ready-to-use features of Delphi come from its run-time library, or RTL for short. This is a large collection of functions you can use to perform simple tasks, as well as some complex ones, within your Pascal code. (I use "Pascal" here, because the run-time library mainly contains procedures and functions and not classes and objects.)

There is actually a second reason to devote this chapter of the book to the run-time library: Delphi 6 sees a large number of enhancements to this area. There are new groups of functions, functions have been moved to new units, and other elements have changed, creating a few incompatibilities with existing code. So even if you've used past versions of Delphi and feel confident with the RTL, you should still read at least portions of this chapter.

The Units of the RTL

As I mentioned above, in Delphi 6 the RTL (run-time library) has a new structure and several new units. The reason for adding new units is that many new functions were added. In most cases, you'll find the existing functions in the units where they used to be, but the new functions will appear in specific units. For example, new functions related to dates are now in the DateUtils unit, but existing date functions have not been moved away from SysUtils in order to avoid incompatibilities with existing code.

The exception to this rule relates to some of the variant support functions, which were moved out of the System unit to avoid unwanted linkage of specific Windows libraries, even in programs that didn't use those features. These variant functions are now part of the new Variants unit, described later in the chapter.

WARNING   Some of your existing Delphi code might need to use this new Variants unit to recompile. Delphi 6 is smart enough to acknowledge this and auto-include the Variants unit in projects that use the `Variant` type, issuing only a warning.

A little bit of fine-tuning has also been applied to reduce the minimum size of an executable file, at times enlarged by the unwanted inclusion of global variables or initialization code.

Executable Size under the Microscope

While touching up the RTL, Borland engineers have been able to trim a little "fat" out of each and every Delphi application. Reducing the minimum program size of a few KB seems quite odd, with all the bloated applications you find around these days, but it is a good service to developers. There are cases in which even few KB (multiplied by many applications) can reduce size and eventually download time.

Continued on next page

As a simple test, I've built the MiniSize program, which is not an attempt to build the smallest possible program, but rather an attempt to build a very small program that does something interesting: It reports the size of its own executable file. All of the code of this example is in the source code on the companion CD:

```
program MiniSize;

uses
  Windows;

{$R *.RES}

var
  nSize: Integer;
  hFile: THandle;
  strSize: String;

begin
  // open the current file and read the size
  hFile := CreateFile (PChar (ParamStr (0)),
    0, FILE_SHARE_READ, nil, OPEN_EXISTING, 0, 0);
  nSize := GetFileSize (hFile, nil);
  CloseHandle (hFile);

  // copy the size to a string and show it
  SetLength (strSize, 20);
  Str (nSize, strSize);
  MessageBox (0, PChar (strSize),
    'Mini Program', MB_OK);
end.
```

The program opens its own executable file, after retrieving its name from the first command-line parameter (ParamStr (0)), extracts the size, converts it into a string using the simple Str function, and shows the result in a message. The program does not have top-level windows. Moreover, I use the Str function for the integer-to-string conversion to avoid including SysUtils, which defines all the more complex formatting routines and would impose a little extra overhead.

If you compile this program with Delphi 5, you obtain an executable size of 18,432 bytes. Delphi 6 reduces this size to only 15,360 bytes, trimming about 3 KB. Replacing the long string with a short string, and modifying the code a little, you can trim down the program further, up to 9,216 bytes. This is because you'll end up removing the string support routines and also the memory allocator, something possible only in programs using exclusively low-level calls. You can find both versions in the source code of the example.

Continued on next page

Notice, anyway, that decisions of this type always imply a few trade-offs. In eliminating the overhead of variants from Delphi applications that don't use them, for example, Borland added a little extra burden to applications that do. The real advantage of this operation, though, is in the reduced memory footprint of Delphi applications that do not use variants, as a result of not having to bring in several megabytes of the Ole2 system libraries.

What is really important, in my opinion, is the size of full-blown Delphi applications based on run-time packages. A simple test with a do-nothing program, the MimiPack example, shows an executable size of 15,972 bytes.

In the following sections is a list of the RTL units in Delphi 6, including all the units available (with the complete source code) in the Source\Rtl\Sys subfolder of the Delphi directory and some of those available in the new subfolder Source\Rtl\Common. This new directory hosts the source code of units that make up the new RTL package, which comprises both the function-based library and the core classes, discussed in the next chapter.

NOTE   The VCL50 package has now been split into the VCL and RTL packages, so that nonvisual applications using run-time packages don't have the overhead of also deploying visual portions of the VCL. Also, this change helps with Linux compatibility, as the new package is shared between the VCL and CLX libraries. Notice also that the package names in Delphi 6 don't have the version number in their name anymore. When they are compiled, though, the BPL does have the version in its file name, as discussed in more detail in Chapter 12.

I'll give a short overview of the role of each unit and an overview of the groups of functions included. I'll also devote more space to the new Delphi 6 units. I won't provide a detailed list of the functions included, because the online help includes similar reference material. However, I've tried to pick a few interesting or little-known functions, and I will discuss them shortly.

The System and SysInit Units

System is the core unit of the RTL and is automatically included in any compilation (considering an automatic and implicit uses statement referring to it). Actually, if you try adding the unit to the uses statement of a program, you'll get the compile-time error:

```
[Error] Identifier redeclared: System
```

The System unit includes, among other things:

- The TObject class, the base class of any class defined in the Object Pascal language, including all the classes of the VCL. (This class is discussed later in this chapter.)

- The IUnknown and IDispatch interfaces as well as the simple implementation class TInterfacedObject. There are also the new IInterface and IInvokable interfaces. IInterface was added to underscore the point that the interface type in Delphi's Object Pascal language definition is in no way dependent on the Windows operating system (and never has been). IInvokable was added to support SOAP-based invocation. (Interfaces and related classes were introduced in the last chapter and will be discussed further in multiple sections of the book.)

- Some variant support code, including the variant type constants, the TVarData record type and the new TVariantManager type, a large number of variant conversion routines, and also variant records and dynamic arrays support. This area sees a lot of changes compared to Delphi 5. The basic information on variants is provided in Chapter 10 of *Essential Pascal* (available on the companion CD), while an introduction to custom variants is available later in this chapter.

- Many base data types, including pointer and array types and the TDateTime type I've already described in the last chapter.

- Memory allocation routines, such as GetMem and FreeMem, and the actual memory manager, defined by the TMemoryManager record and accessed by the GetMemoryManager and SetMemoryManager functions. For information, the GetHeapStatus function returns a THeapStatus data structure. Two new global variables (AllocMemCount and AllocMemSize) hold the number and total size of allocated memory blocks. There is more on memory and the use of these functions in Chapter 10.

- Package and module support code, including the PackageInfo pointer type, the GetPackageInfoTable global function, and the EnumModules procedure (packages internals are discussed in Chapter 12).

- A rather long list of global variables, including the Windows application instance Main-Instance; IsLibrary, indicating whether the executable file is a library or a stand-alone program; IsConsole, indicating console applications; IsMultiThread, indicating whether there are secondary threads; and the command-line string CmdLine. (The unit includes also the ParamCount and ParamStr for an easy access to command-line parameters.) Some of these variables are specific to the Windows platform.

- Thread-support code, with the BeginThread and EndThread functions; file support records and file-related routines; wide string and OLE string conversion routines; and many other low-level and system routines (including a number of automatic conversion functions).

The companion unit of System, called SysInit, includes the system initialization code, with functions you'll seldom use directly. This is another unit that is always implicitly included, as it is used by the System unit.

New in System Unit

I've already described some interesting new features of the System unit in the list above, and most of the changes relate to making the core Delphi RTL more cross-platform portable, replacing Windows-specific features with generic implementations. Along this line, there are new names for interface types, totally revised support for variants, new pointer types, dynamic array support, and functions to customize the management of exception objects.

Another addition for compatibility with Linux relates to line breaks in text files. There is a new DefaultTextLineBreakStyle variable, which can be set to either tlbsLF or tlbsCRLF, and a new sLineBreak string constant, which has the value #13#10 in the Windows version of Delphi and the value #10 in the Linux version. The line break style can also be set on a file-by-file basis with SetTextLineBreakStyle function.

Finally, the System unit now includes the TFileRec and TTextRec structures, which were defined in the SysUtils unit in earlier versions of Delphi.

The SysUtils and SysConst Units

The SysConst unit defines a few constant strings used by the other RTL units for displaying messages. These strings are declared with the resourcestring keyword and saved in the program resources. As other resources, they can be translated by means of the Integrated Translation Manager or the External Translation Manager.

The SysUtils unit is a collection of system utility functions of various types. Different from other RTL units, it is in large part an operating system–dependent unit. The SysUtils unit has no specific focus, but it includes a bit of everything, from string management to locale and multibyte-characters support, from the Exception class and several other derived exception classes to a plethora of string-formatting constants and routines.

Some of the features of SysUtils are used every day by every programmer as the IntToStr or Format string-formatting functions; other features are lesser known, as they are the Windows version information global variables. These indicate the Windows platform (Window 9x or NT/2000), the operating system version and build number, and the eventual service pack installed on NT. They can be used as in the following code, extracted from the WinVersion example on the companion CD:

```
case Win32Platform of
  VER_PLATFORM_WIN32_WINDOWS:  ShowMessage ('Windows 9x');
  VER_PLATFORM_WIN32_NT:       ShowMessage ('Windows NT');
end;

ShowMessage ('Running on Windows: ' + IntToStr (Win32MajorVersion) + '.' +
  IntToStr (Win32MinorVersion) + ' (Build ' + IntToStr (Win32BuildNumber) +
  ') ' + #10#13 + 'Update: ' + Win32CSDVersion);
```

The second code fragment produces a message like the one in Figure 4.1, depending, of course, on the operating-system version you have installed.

FIGURE 4.1:

The version information
displayed by the WinVer-
sion example

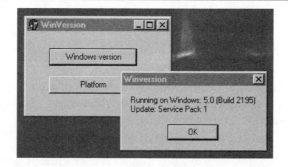

Another little-known feature, but one with a rather long name, is a class that supports multithreading: TMultiReadExclusiveWriteSynchronizer. This class allows you to work with resources that can be used by multiple threads at the same time for reading (multiread) but must be used by one single thread when writing (exclusive-write). This means that the writing cannot start until all the reading threads have terminated.

NOTE   The multi-read synchronizer is unique in that it supports recursive locks and promotion of read locks to write locks. The main purpose of the class is to allow multiple threads easy, fast access to read from a shared resource, but still allow one thread to gain exclusive control of the resource for relatively infrequent updates. There are other synchronization classes in Delphi, declared in the SyncObjs unit and closely mapped to operating-system synchronization objects (such as events and critical sections in Windows).

New SysUtils Functions

Delphi 6 has some new functions within the SysUtils unit. One of the new areas relates to Boolean to string conversion. The BoolToStr function generally returns '-1' and '0' for true and false values. If the second optional parameter is specified, the function returns the first string in the TrueBoolStrs and FalseBoolStrs arrays (by default 'TRUE' and 'FALSE'):

```
BoolToStr (True) // returns '-1'
BoolToStr (False, True) // returns 'FALSE' by default
```

The reverse function is StrToBool, which can convert a string containing either one of the values of two Boolean arrays mentioned above or a numeric value. In the latter case, the result will be true unless the numeric value is zero. You can see a simple demo of the use of the Boolean conversion functions in the StrDemo example, later in this chapter.

Other new functions of SysUtils relate to floating-point conversions to currency and date time types: `FloatToCurr` and `FloatToDateTime` can be used to avoid an explicit type cast. The `TryStrToFloat` and `TryStrToCurr` functions try to convert a string into a floating point or currency value and will return False in case of error instead of generating an exception (as the classic `StrToFloat` and `StrToCurr` functions do).

There is an `AnsiDequotedStr` function, which removes quotes from a string, matching the `AnsiQuoteStr` function added in Delphi 5. Speaking of strings, Delphi 6 has much-improved support for wide strings, with a series of new routines, including `WideUpperCase`, `WideLowerCase`, `WideCompareStr`, `WideSameStr`, `WideCompareText`, `WideSameText`, and `WideFormat`. All of these functions work like their `AnsiString` counterparts.

Three functions (`TryStrToDate`, `TryEncodeDate`, and `TryEncodeTime`) try to convert a string to a date or to encode a date or time, without raising an exception, similarly to the `Try` functions previously mentioned. In addition, the `DecodeDateFully` function returns more detailed information, such as the day of the week, and the `CurrentYear` function returns the year of today's date.

There is a portable, friendly, overloaded version of the `GetEnvironmentVariable` function. This new version uses string parameters instead of PChar parameters and is definitely easier to use:

```
function GetEnvironmentVariable(Name: string): string;
```

Other new functions relate to interface support. Two new overloaded versions of the little-known `Support` function allow you to check whether an object or a class supports a given interface. The function corresponds to the behavior of the `is` operator for classes and is mapped to the `QueryInterface` method. Here's an example in the code of the IntfDemo program from Chapter 3:

```
var
  W1: IWalker;
  J1: IJumper;
begin
  W1 := TAthlete.Create;
  // more code...
  if Supports (w1, IJumper) then
  begin
    J1 := W1 as IJumper;
    Log (J1.Walk);
  end;
```

There are also an `IsEqualGUID` function and two functions for converting strings to GUIDs and vice versa. The function `CreateGUID` has been moved to SysUtils, as well, to make it also available on Linux (with a custom implementation, of course).

Finally, Delphi 6 has some more Linux-compatibility functions. The `AdjustLineBreaks` function can now do different types of *adjustments* to carriage-return and line-feed sequences, along with the introduction of new global variables for text files in the System unit, as described earlier. The `FileCreate` function has an overloaded version in which you can specify file-access rights *the Unix way*. The `ExpandFileName` function can locate files (on case-sensitive file systems) even when their cases don't exactly correspond. The functions related to path delimiters (backslash or slash) have been made more generic and renamed accordingly. (For example, the `IncludeTralingBackslash` function is now better known as `IncludingTrailingPathDelimiter`.)

The Math Unit

The Math unit hosts a collection of mathematical functions: about forty trigonometric functions, logarithmic and exponential functions, rounding functions, polynomial evaluations, almost thirty statistical functions, and a dozen financial functions.

Describing all of the functions of this unit would be rather tedious, although some readers are probably very interested in the mathematical capabilities of Delphi. Here are some of the newer math functions.

New Math Functions

Delphi 6 adds to the Math unit quite a number of new features. There is support for infinite constants (`Infinity` and `NegInfinity`) and related comparison functions (`IsInfinite` and `IsNan`). There are new trigonometric functions for cosecants and cotangents and new angle-conversion functions.

A handy feature is the availability of an overloaded `IfThen` function, which returns one of two possible values depending on a Boolean expression. (A similar function is now available also for strings.) You can use it, for example, to compute the minimum of two values:

```
nMin := IfThen (nA < nB, na, nB);
```

NOTE   The `IfThen` function is similar to the `?:` operator of the C/C++ language, which I find very handy because you can replace a complete `if/then/else` statement with a much shorter expression, writing less code and often declaring fewer temporary variables.

The `RandomRange` and `RandomFrom` can be used instead of the traditional `Random` function to have more control on the random values produced by the RTL. The first function returns a number within two extremes you specify, while the second selects a random value from an array of possible numbers you pass to it as a parameter.

The `InRange` Boolean function can be used to check whether a number is within two other values. The `EnsureRange` function, instead, forces the value to be within the specified range.

The return value is the number itself or the lower limit or upper limit, in the event the number is out of range. Here is an example:

```
// do something only if value is within min and max
if InRange (value, min, max) then
  ...

// make sure the value is between min and max
value := EnsureRange (value, min, max);
  ...
```

Another set of very useful functions relates to comparisons. Floating-point numbers are fundamentally inexact; a floating-point number is an approximation of a theoretical real value. When you do mathematical operations on floating-point numbers, the inexactness of the original values accumulates in the results. Multiplying and dividing by the same number might not return exactly the original number but one that is very close to it. The SameValue function allows you to check whether two values are close enough in value to be considered equal. You can specify how close the two numbers should be or let Delphi compute a reasonable error range for the representation you are using. (This is why the function is overloaded.) Similarly, the IsZero function compares a number to zero, with the same "fuzzy logic."

The CompareValue function uses the same rule for floating-point numbers but is available also for integers; it returns one of the three constants LessThanValue, EqualsValue, and GreaterThanValue (corresponding to –1, 0, and 1). Similarly, the new Sign function returns –1, 0, and 1 to indicate a negative value, zero, or a positive value.

The DivMod function is equivalent to both div and mod operations, returning the result of the integer division and the remainder (or modulus) at once. The RoundTo function allows you to specify the rounding digit—allowing, for example, rounding to the nearest thousand or to two decimals:

```
RoundTo (123827, 3);   // result is 124,000
RoundTo (12.3827, -2); // result is 12.38
```

WARNING Notice that the RoundTo function uses a positive number to indicate the power of ten to round to (for example, 2 for hundreds) or a negative number for the number of decimal places. This is exactly the opposite of the **Round** function used by spreadsheets such as Excel.

There are also some changes to the standard rounding operations provided by the Round function: You can now control how the FPU (the floating-point unit of the CPU) does the rounding by calling the SetRoundMode function. There are also functions to control the FPU precision mode and its exceptions.

The New ConvUtils and StdConvs Units

The new ConvUtils unit contains the core of the conversion engine. It uses the conversion constants defined by a second unit, StdConvs. I'll cover these two units later in this chapter, showing you also how to extend them with new measurement units.

The New DateUtils Unit

The DateUtils unit is a new collection of date and time-related functions. It includes new functions for picking values from a TDateTime variable or counting values from a given interval, such as

```
// pick value
function DayOf(const AValue: TDateTime): Word;
function HourOf(const AValue: TDateTime): Word;
// value in range
function WeekOfYear(const AValue: TDateTime): Integer;
function HourOfWeek(const AValue: TDateTime): Integer;
function SecondOfHour(const AValue: TDateTime): Integer;
```

Some of these functions are actually quite odd, such as MilliSecondOfMonth or SecondOfWeek, but Borland developers have decided to provide a complete set of functions, no matter how impractical they sound. I actually used some of these functions in Chapter 2, to build the TDate class.

There are functions for computing the initial or final value of a given time interval (day, week, month, year) including the current date, and for range checking and querying; for example:

```
function DaysBetween(const ANow, AThen: TDateTime): Integer;
function WithinPastDays(const ANow, AThen: TDateTime;
  const ADays: Integer): Boolean;
```

Other functions cover incrementing and decrementing by each of the possible time intervals, encoding and "recoding" (replacing one element of the TDateTime value, such as the day, with a new one), and doing "fuzzy" comparisons (approximate comparisons where a difference of a millisecond will still make two dates equal). Overall, DateUtils is quite interesting and not terribly difficult to use.

The New StrUtils Unit

The StrUtils unit is a new unit with some new string-related functions. One of the key features of this unit is the availability of many new string comparison functions. There are functions based on a "soundex" algorithm (AnsiResembleText), some providing lookup in arrays of strings (AnsiMatchText and AnsiIndexText), sub-string location, and replacement (including AnsiContainsText and AnsiReplaceText).

NOTE   *Soundex* is an algorithm to compare names based on how they sound rather then how they are spelled. The algorithm computes a number for each word sound, so that comparing two such numbers you can determine whether two names sound similar. The system was first applied 1880 by the U.S. Bureau of the Census, patented in 1918, and is now in the public domain. The soundex code is an indexing system that translates names into a four-character code consisting of one letter and three numbers. More information is at `www.nara.gov/genealogy/coding.html`.

Beside comparisons, other functions provide a two-way test (the nice `IfThen` function, similar to the one we've already seen for numbers), duplicate and reverse strings, and replace sub-strings. Most of these string functions were added as a convenience to Visual Basic programmers migrating to Delphi.

I've used some of these functions in the StrDemo example on the companion CD, which uses also some of the new Boolean-to-string conversions defined within the SysUtils unit. The program is actually a little more than a test for a few of these functions. For example, it uses the "soundex" comparison between the strings entered in two edit boxes, converting the resulting Boolean into a string and showing it:

```
ShowMessage (BoolToStr (AnsiResemblesText
  (EditResemble1.Text, EditResemble2.Text), True));
```

The program also showcases the `AnsiMatchText` and `AnsiIndexText` functions, after filling a dynamic array of strings (called `strArray`) with the values of the strings inside a list box. I could have used the simpler `IndexOf` method of the `TStrings` class, but this would have defeated the purpose of the example. The two list comparisons are done as follows:

```
procedure TForm1.ButtonMatchesClick(Sender: TObject);
begin
  ShowMessage (BoolToStr (AnsiMatchText(EditMatch.Text, strArray), True));
end;

procedure TForm1.ButtonIndexClick(Sender: TObject);
var
  nMatch: Integer;
begin
  nMatch := AnsiIndexText(EditMatch.Text, strArray);
  ShowMessage (IfThen (nMatch >= 0, 'Matches the string number ' +
    IntToStr (nMatch), 'No match'));
end;
```

Notice the use of the `IfThen` function in the last few lines of code, with two alternative output strings, depending on the result of the initial test (nMatch <= 0).

Three more buttons do simple calls to three other new functions, with the following lines of code (one for each):

```
// duplicate (3 times) a string
ShowMessage (DupeString (EditSample.Text, 3));
// reverse the string
ShowMessage (ReverseString (EditSample.Text));
// choose a random string
ShowMessage (RandomFrom (strArray));
```

The New Types Unit

The Types unit is a new Pascal file holding data types common to multiple operating systems. In past versions of Delphi, the same types were defined by the Windows unit; now they've been moved to this common unit, shared by Delphi and Kylix. The types defined here are simple ones and include, among others, the TPoint, TRect, and TSmallPoint record structures plus their related pointer types.

The New Variants and VarUtils Units

Variants and VarUtils are two new variant-related units. The Variants unit contains generic code for variants. As mentioned earlier, some of the routines in this unit have been moved here from the System unit. Functions include generic variant support, variant arrays, variant copying, and dynamic array to variant array conversions. There is also the TCustomVariantType class, which defines customizable variant data types.

The Variants unit is totally platform independent and uses the VarUtils unit, which contains OS-dependent code. In Delphi, this unit uses the system APIs to manipulate variant data, while in Kylix it uses some custom code provided by the RTL library.

Custom Variants and Complex Numbers

The possibility to extend the type system with custom variants is brand new in Delphi 6. It allows you to define a new data type that, contrary to a class, overloads standard arithmetic operators.

In fact, a variant is a type holding both type specification and the actual value. A variant can contain a string, another can contain a number. The system defines automatic conversions among variant types, allowing you to mix them inside operations (including custom variants). This flexibility comes at a high cost: operations on variants are much slower than on native types, and variants use extra memory.

As an example of a custom variant type, Delphi 6 ships with an interesting definition for complex numbers, found in the VarCmplx unit (available in source-code format in the

Rtl\Common folder). You can create complex variants by using one of the overloaded `VarComplex-Create` functions and use them in any expression, as the following code fragment demonstrates:

```
var
  v1, v2: Variant;
begin
  v1 := VarComplexCreate (10, 12);
  v2 := VarComplexCreate (10, 1);
  ShowMessage (v1 + v2 + 5);
```

The complex numbers are actually defined using classes, but they are surfaced as variants by inheriting a new class from the `TCustomVariantType` class (defined in the Variants unit), overriding a few virtual abstract functions, and creating a global object that takes care of the registration within the system.

Beside these internal definitions, the unit includes a long list of routines for operating on variant, including mathematical and trigonometric operations. I'll leave them to your study, as not all readers may be interested in complex numbers for their programs.

WARNING   Building a custom variant is certainly not an easy task, and I can hardly find reasons for using them instead of objects and classes. In fact, with a custom variant you gain the advantage of using operator overloading on your own data structures, but you lose compile-time checking, make the code much slower, miss several OOP features, and have to write a lot of rather complex code.

The DelphiMM and ShareMem Units

The DelphiMM and ShareMem units relate to memory management. The actual Delphi memory manager is declared in the System unit. The DelphiMM unit defines an alternative memory manager library to be used when passing strings from an executable to a DLL (a Windows dynamic linking library), both built with Delphi.

The interface to this memory manager is defined in the ShareMem unit. This is the unit you must include (compulsory as first unit) in the projects of both your executable and library (or libraries). Then, you'll also need to distribute and install the `Borlndmm.dll` library file along with your program.

COM-Related Units

ComConts, ComObj, and ComServ provide low-level COM support. As these units are not really part of the RTL, from my point of view, I won't discuss them here in any detail. You can refer to Chapter 20 for all the related information. In any case, these units have not changed a lot since the last version of Delphi.

Converting Data

Delphi 6 includes a new conversion engine, defined in the ConvUtils unit. The engine by itself doesn't include any definition of actual measurement units; instead, it has a series of core functions for end users.

The key function is the actual conversion call, the Convert function. You simply provide the amount, the units it is expressed in, and the units you want it converted into. The following would convert a temperature of 31 degrees Celsius to Fahrenheit:

```
Convert (31, tuCelsius, tuFahrenheit)
```

An overloaded version of the Convert function allows converting values that have two units, such as speed (which has both a length and a time unit). For example, you can convert miles per hours to meters per second with this call:

```
Convert (20, duMiles, tuHours, duMeters, tuSeconds)
```

Other functions in the unit allow you to convert the result of an addition or a difference, check if conversions are applicable, and even list the available conversion families and units.

A predefined set of measurement units is provided in the StdConvs unit. This unit has conversion families and an impressive number of actual values, as in the following reduced excerpt:

```
// Distance Conversion Units
// basic unit of measurement is meters
cbDistance: TConvFamily;

duAngstroms: TConvType;
duMicrons: TConvType;
duMillimeters: TConvType;
duMeters: TConvType;
duKilometers: TConvType;
duInches: TConvType;
duMiles: TConvType;
duLightYears: TConvType;
duFurlongs: TConvType;
duHands: TConvType;
duPicas: TConvType;
```

This family and the various units are registered in the conversion engine in the initialization section of the unit, providing the conversion ratios (saved in a series of constants, as MetersPerInch in the code below):

```
cbDistance := RegisterConversionFamily('Distance');
duAngstroms := RegisterConversionType(cbDistance, 'Angstroms', 1E-10);
duMillimeters := RegisterConversionType(cbDistance, 'Millimeters', 0.001);
duInches := RegisterConversionType(cbDistance, 'Inches', MetersPerInch);
```

To test the conversion engine, I built a generic example (ConvDemo on the companion CD) that allows you to work with the entire set of available conversions. The program fills a combo box with the available conversion families and a list box with the available units of the active family. This is the code:

```
procedure TForm1.FormCreate(Sender: TObject);
var
  i: Integer;
begin
  GetConvFamilies (aFamilies);
  for i := Low(aFamilies) to High(aFamilies) do
    ComboFamilies.Items.Add (ConvFamilyToDescription (aFamilies[i]));
  // get the first and fire event
  ComboFamilies.ItemIndex := 0;
  ChangeFamily (self);
end;

procedure TForm1.ChangeFamily(Sender: TObject);
var
  aTypes: TConvTypeArray;
  i: Integer;
begin
  ListTypes.Clear;
  CurrFamily := aFamilies [ComboFamilies.ItemIndex];
  GetConvTypes (CurrFamily, aTypes);
  for i := Low(aTypes) to High(aTypes) do
    ListTypes.Items.Add (ConvTypeToDescription (aTypes[i]));
end;
```

The aFamilies and CurrFamily variables are declared in the private section of the form as follows:

```
aFamilies: TConvFamilyArray;
CurrFamily: TConvFamily;
```

At this point, a user can enter two measurement units and an amount in the corresponding edit boxes of the form, as you can see in Figure 4.2. To make the operation faster, it is actually possible to select a value in the list and drag it to one of the two Type edit boxes. The dragging support is described in the sidebar "Simple Dragging in Delphi."

FIGURE 4.2:

The ConvDemo example
at run time

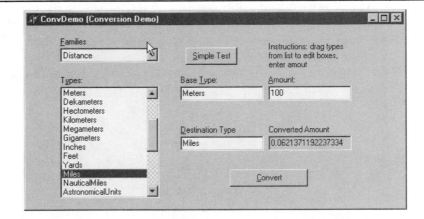

Simple Dragging in Delphi

The ConvDemo example I've built to show how to use the new conversion engine of Delphi 6 uses an interesting technique: dragging. In fact, you can move the mouse over the list box, select an item, and then keep the left mouse button pressed and drag the item over one of the edit boxes in the center of the form.

To accomplish this, I had to set the DragMode property of the list box (the source component) to dmAutomatic and implement the OnDragOver and OnDragDrop events of the target edit boxes (the two edit boxes are connected to the same event handlers, sharing the same code). In the first method, the program indicates that the edit boxes always accept the dragging operation, regardless of the source. In the second method, the program copies the text selected in the list box (the Source control of the dragging operation) to the edit box that fired the event (the Sender object). Here is the code for the two methods:

```
procedure TForm1.EditTypeDragOver(Sender, Source: TObject;
  X, Y: Integer; State: TDragState; var Accept: Boolean);
begin
  Accept := True;
end;


procedure TForm1.EditTypeDragDrop(Sender, Source: TObject;
  X, Y: Integer);
begin
  (Sender as TEdit).Text := (Source as TListBox).Items
    [(Source as TListBox).ItemIndex];
end;
```

The units must match those available in the current family. In case of error, the text of the Type edit boxes is shown in red. This is the effect of the first part of the DoConvert method of the form, which is activated as soon as the value of one of the edit boxes for the units or the amount changes. After checking the types in the edit boxes, the DoConvert method does the actual conversion, displaying the result in the fourth, grayed edit box. In case of errors, you'll get a proper message in the same box. Here is the code:

```
procedure TForm1.DoConvert(Sender: TObject);
var
  BaseType, DestType: TConvType;
begin
  // get and check base type
  if not DescriptionToConvType(CurrFamily, EditType.Text, BaseType) then
    EditType.Font.Color := clRed
  else
    EditType.Font.Color := clBlack;

  // get and check destination type
  if not DescriptionToConvType(CurrFamily, EditDestination.Text,
      DestType) then
    EditDestination.Font.Color := clRed
  else
    EditDestination.Font.Color := clBlack;

  if (DestType = 0) or (BaseType = 0) then
    EditConverted.Text := 'Invalid type'
  else
    EditConverted.Text := FloatToStr (Convert (
      StrToFloat (EditAmount.Text), BaseType, DestType));
end;
```

If all this is not interesting enough for you, consider that the conversion types provided serve only as a demo: You can fully customize the engine, by providing the measurement units you are interested in, as described in the next section.

What About Currency Conversions?

Converting currencies is not exactly the same as converting measurement units, as currency rates change at very high speed. In theory, you can register a conversion rate with Delphi's conversion engine. From time to time, you check the new rate exchange, unregister the existing conversion, and register a new one. However, keeping up with the actual rate means changing the conversion so often that the operation might not make a lot of sense. Also, you'll have to triangulate conversions: you have to define a base unit (probably the U.S. dollar if you live in America) and convert to and from this currency even for converting between two different ones.

What's more interesting is to use the engine for converting member currencies of the euro, for two reasons. First, conversion rates are fixed (until the single euro currency actually takes over). Second, the conversion among euro currencies is legally done by converting a currency to euros first and then from the euro amount to the other currency, the exact behavior of Delphi's conversion engine. There is only a small problem, as you should apply a rounding algorithm at every step of the conversion. I'll consider this problem after I've provided the base code for integrating euro currencies with Delphi 6 conversion engine.

NOTE   The ConvertIt demo of Delphi 6 provides support for euro conversions, using a slightly different rounding approach (which might be more correct or not, I'm not really sure). I've decided to keep this example anyway, as it is instructive in showing how to create a new measurement system (and I lacked another example as good).

The example, called EuroConv, is actually meant to teach how to register any new measurement unit with the engine. Following the template provided by the StdConvs unit, I've created a new unit (called EuroConvConst) and in the interface portion I've declared variables for the family and the specific units, as follows:

```
interface

var
  // Euro Currency Conversion Units
  cbEuroCurrency: TConvFamily;

  cuEUR: TConvType;
  cuDEM: TConvType; // Germany
  cuESP: TConvType; // Spain
  cuFRF: TConvType; // France
  cuIEP: TConvType; // Ireland
  cuITL: TConvType; // Italy
  // and so on...
```

In the implementation portion of the unit, I've defined constants for the various official conversion rates:

```
implementation

const
  DEMPerEuros = 1.95583;
  ESPPerEuros = 166.386;
  FRFPerEuros = 6.55957;
  IEPPerEuros =  0.787564;
  ITLPerEuros =  1936.27;
  // and so on...
```

Finally, in the unit initialization code I've registered the family and the various currencies, each with its own conversion rate and a readable name:

```
initialization
  // Euro Currency's family type
  cbEuroCurrency := RegisterConversionFamily('EuroCurrency');

  cuEUR := RegisterConversionType(
    cbEuroCurrency, 'EUR', 1);
  cuDEM := RegisterConversionType(
    cbEuroCurrency, 'DEM', 1 / DEMPerEuros);
  cuESP := RegisterConversionType(
    cbEuroCurrency, 'ESP', 1 / ESPPerEuros);
  cuFRF := RegisterConversionType(
    cbEuroCurrency, 'FRF', 1 / FRFPerEuros);
  cuIEP := RegisterConversionType(
    cbEuroCurrency, 'IEP', 1 / IEPPerEuros);
  cuITL := RegisterConversionType(
    cbEuroCurrency, 'ITL', 1 / ITLPerEuros);
```

NOTE   The engine uses as a conversion factor the amount of the base unit to obtain the secondary ones, with a constant like `MetersPerInch`, for example. The standard rate of euro currencies is defined in the opposite way. For this reason, I've decided to keep the conversion constants with the official values (as `DEMPerEuros above`) and pass them to the engine as fractions (`1/DEMPerEuros`).

Having registered this unit, we can now convert 120 German marks to Italian liras by writing:

```
Convert (120, cuDEM, cuITL)
```

The demo program actually does a little more, providing two list boxes with the available currencies, extracted as in the previous example, and edit boxes for the input value and final result. You can see the form at run time in Figure 4.3.

FIGURE 4.3:

The output of the EuroConv unit, showing the use of Delphi's conversion engine with a custom measurement unit

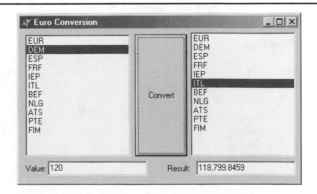

The program works nicely but is not perfect, as the proper rounding is not applied. In fact, you should round not only the final result of the conversion but also the intermediate value. Using the conversion engine to accomplish this directly is not easy. The engine allows you to provide either a custom conversion function or a conversion rate. But writing identical conversion functions for the all the various currencies seems a bad idea, so I've decided to go a different path. (You can see examples of custom conversion functions in the StdConvs unit, in the portion related to temperatures.)

In the EuroConv example, I've added to the unit with the conversion rates a custom function, called EuroConv, that does the proper conversion. Simply calling this function instead of the standard Convert function does the trick (and I really see no drawback to this approach, because in programs like this, you'll hardly mix currencies with meters or temperatures). As an alternative, I could inherit a new class from TConvTypeFactor, providing a new version of the FromCommon and ToCommon methods, or I could have called the overloaded versions of the RegisterConversionType that accepts these two functions as parameters. None of these techniques, however, would have allowed me to handle special cases, such as the conversion of a currency to itself.

This is the code of the EuroConv function, which uses the internal EuroRound function for rounding to the number of digits specified in the Decimals parameter (which must be between 3 and 6, according with the official rules):

```
type
  TEuroDecimals = 3..6;

function EuroConvert (const AValue: Double;
  const AFrom, ATo: TConvType;
  const Decimals: TEuroDecimals = 3): Double;

  function EuroRound (const AValue: Double): Double;
  begin
    Result := AValue * Power (10, Decimals);
    Result := Round (Result);
    Result := Result / Power (10, Decimals);
  end;

begin
  // check special case: no conversion
  if AFrom = ATo then
    Result := AValue
  else
  begin
    // convert to Euro, then round
    Result := ConvertFrom (AFrom, AValue);
    Result := EuroRound (Result);
```

```
      // convert to currency then round again
      Result := ConvertTo (Result, ATo);
      Result := EuroRound (Result);
   end;
 end;
```

Of course, you might want to extend the example by providing conversion to other non-euro currencies, eventually picking the values automatically from a Web site. I'll leave this as a rather complex exercise.

The *TObject* Class

As mentioned earlier, a key element of the System unit is the definition of the TObject class, the *mother of all Delphi classes*. Every class in the system is a subclass of the TObject class, either directly (for example, if you indicate no base class) or indirectly. The whole hierarchy of the classes of an Object Pascal program has a single root. This allows you to use the TObject data type as a replacement for the data type of any class type in the system.

For example, event handlers of components usually have a Sender parameter of type TObject. This simply means that the Sender object can be of any class, since every class is ultimately derived from TObject. The typical drawback of such an approach is that to work on the object, you need to know its data type. In fact, when you have a variable or a parameter of the TObject type, you can apply to it only the methods and properties defined by the TObject class itself. If this variable or parameter happens to refer to an object of the TButton type, for example, you cannot directly access its Caption property. The solution to this problem lies in the use of the safe down-casting or run-time type information (RTTI) operators (is and as) discussed in Chapter 3.

There is another approach. For any object, you can call the methods defined in the TObject class itself. For example, the ClassName method returns a string with the name of the class. Because it is a class method (see Chapter 2 for details), you can actually apply it both to an object and to a class. Suppose you have defined a TButton class and a Button1 object of that class. Then the following statements have the same effect:

```
 Text := Button1.ClassName;
 Text := TButton.ClassName;
```

There are occasions when you need to use the name of a class, but it can also be useful to retrieve a class reference to the class itself or to its base class. The class reference, in fact, allows you to operate on the class at run time (as we've seen in the preceding chapter), while the class name is just a string. We can get these class references with the ClassType and ClassParent methods. The first returns a class reference to the class of the object, the second to its base class. Once you have a class reference, you can apply to it any class methods of TObject—for example, to call the ClassName method.

Another method that might be useful is InstanceSize, which returns the run-time size of an object. Although you might think that the SizeOf global function provides this information, that function actually returns the size of an object reference—a pointer, which is invariably four bytes—instead of the size of the object itself.

In Listing 4.1, you can find the complete definition of the TObject class, extracted from the System unit. Beside the methods I've already mentioned, notice InheritsFrom, which provides a test very similar to the is operator but that can be applied also to classes and class references (while the first argument of is must be an object).

Listing 4.1:   The definition of the *TObject* class (in the System RTL unit)

```
type
  TObject = class
    constructor Create;
    procedure Free;
    class function InitInstance(Instance: Pointer): TObject;
    procedure CleanupInstance;
    function ClassType: TClass;
    class function ClassName: ShortString;
    class function ClassNameIs(
      const Name: string): Boolean;
    class function ClassParent: TClass;
    class function ClassInfo: Pointer;
    class function InstanceSize: Longint;
    class function InheritsFrom(AClass: TClass): Boolean;
    class function MethodAddress(const Name: ShortString): Pointer;
    class function MethodName(Address: Pointer): ShortString;
    function FieldAddress(const Name: ShortString): Pointer;
    function GetInterface(const IID: TGUID;out Obj): Boolean;
    class function GetInterfaceEntry(
      const IID: TGUID): PInterfaceEntry;
    class function GetInterfaceTable: PInterfaceTable;
    function SafeCallException(ExceptObject: TObject;
      ExceptAddr: Pointer): HResult; virtual;
    procedure AfterConstruction; virtual;
    procedure BeforeDestruction; virtual;
    procedure Dispatch(var Message); virtual;
    procedure DefaultHandler(var Message); virtual;
    class function NewInstance: TObject; virtual;
    procedure FreeInstance; virtual;
    destructor Destroy; virtual;
  end;
```

NOTE   The `ClassInfo` method returns a pointer to the internal run-time type information (RTTI) of the class, introduced in the next chapter.

These methods of `TObject` are available for objects of every class, since `TObject` is the common ancestor class of every class. Here is how we can use these methods to access class information:

```
procedure TSenderForm.ShowSender(Sender: TObject);
begin
  Memo1.Lines.Add ('Class Name: ' + Sender.ClassName);

  if Sender.ClassParent <> nil then
    Memo1.Lines.Add ('Parent Class: ' + Sender.ClassParent.ClassName);

  Memo1.Lines.Add ('Instance Size: ' + IntToStr (Sender.InstanceSize));
end;
```

The code checks to see whether the `ClassParent` is `nil` in case you are actually using an instance of the `TObject` type, which has no base type. This `ShowSender` method is part of the IfSender example on the companion CD. The method is connected with the `OnClick` event of several controls: three buttons, a check box, and an edit box. When you click each control, the `ShowSender` method is invoked with the corresponding control as sender (more on events in the next chapter). One of the buttons is actually a Bitmap button, an object of a `TButton` subclass. You can see an example of the output of this program at run time in Figure 4.4.

FIGURE 4.4:

The output of the IfSender example

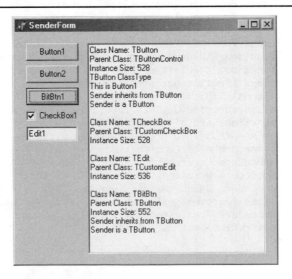

You can use other methods to perform tests. For example, you can check whether the Sender object is of a specific type with the following code:

```
if Sender.ClassType = TButton then ...
```

You can also check whether the Sender parameter corresponds to a given object, with this test:

```
if Sender = Button1 then...
```

Instead of checking for a particular class or object, you'll generally need to test the type compatibility of an object with a given class; that is, you'll need to check whether the class of the object is a given class *or* one of its subclasses. This lets you know whether you can operate on the object with the methods defined for the class. This test can be accomplished using the InheritsFrom method, which is also called when you use the is operator. The following two tests are equivalent:

```
if Sender.InheritsFrom (TButton) then ...
if Sender is TButton then ...
```

Showing Class Information

I've extended the IfSender example to show a complete list of base classes of a given object or class. Once you have a class reference, in fact, you can add all of its base classes to the List-Parent list box with the following code:

```
with ListParent.Items do
begin
  Clear;
  while MyClass.ClassParent <> nil do
  begin
    MyClass := MyClass.ClassParent;
    Add (MyClass.ClassName);
  end;
end;
```

You'll notice that we use a class reference at the heart of the while loop, which tests for the absence of a parent class (so that the current class is TObject). Alternatively, we could have written the while statement in either of the following ways:

```
while not MyClass.ClassNameIs ('TObject') do...
while MyClass <> TObject do...
```

The code in the with statement referring to the ListParent list box is part of the ClassInfo example (see the companion CD), which displays the list of parent classes and some other information about a few components of the VCL, basically those on the Standard page of the Component Palette. These components are manually added to a dynamic array holding classes and declared as

```
private
  ClassArray: array of TClass;
```

When the program starts, the array is used to show all the class names in a list box. Selecting an item from the list box triggers the visual presentation of its details and its base classes, as you can see in the output of the program, in Figure 4.5.

FIGURE 4.5:

The output of the ClassInfo
example

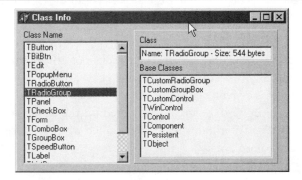

NOTE   As a further extension to this example, it is possible to create a tree with all of the base classes of the various components in a hierarchy. To do that, I've created the VclHierarchy program, which you can find on my Web site, `www.marcocantu.com`, in the CanTools section.

What's Next?

In this chapter I've focused my attention on new features of the Delphi 6 function-based run-time library. I have provided only a summary of the entire RTL, not a complete overview, as this would have taken too much space. You can find more examples of the basic RTL functions of Delphi in my free electronic book *Essential Pascal*, which is featured on the companion CD.

In the next chapter, we'll start moving from the function-based RTL to the class-based RTL, which is the core of Delphi's class library. I won't debate whether the core classes common to the VCL and CLX, such as TObject, actually belong to the RTL or the class library. I've covered everything defined in System, SysUtils, and other units hosting functions and procedures in this chapter, while the next chapter focuses on the Classes unit and other core units defining classes.

Along with the preceding two chapters on the Object Pascal language, this will provide a foundation for discussing visual- and database-oriented classes, or components, if you prefer. Looking to the various library units, we'll find many more global functions, which don't belong to the core RTL but are still quite useful!

CHAPTER 5

Core Library Classes

- The RTL package, CLX, and VCL

- *TPersistent* and *published*

- The *TComponent* base class and its properties

- Components and ownership

- Events

- Lists, container classes, and collections

- Streaming

- Summarizing the units of the RTL package

We saw in the preceding chapter that Delphi includes a large number of functions and procedures, but the real power of Delphi's visual programming lies in the huge class library it comes with. Delphi's standard class library contains hundreds of classes, with thousands of methods, and it is so large that I certainly cannot provide a detailed reference in this book. What I'll do, instead, is explore various areas of this library starting with this chapter and continuing through the following ones.

This first chapter is devoted to the core classes of the library as well as to some standard programming techniques, such as the definition of events. We'll explore some commonly used classes, such as lists, string lists, collections, and streams. We'll devote most of our time to exploring the content of the Classes unit, but we'll devote time also to other core units of the library.

Delphi classes can be used either entirely in code or within the visual form designer. Some of them are component classes, which show up in the Component Palette, while others are more general-purpose. The terms *class* and *component* can be used almost as synonyms in Delphi. Components are the central elements of Delphi applications. When you write a program, you basically choose a number of components and define their interactions. That's all there is to Delphi visual programming.

Before reading this chapter, you need to have a good understanding of the Object Pascal programming language, including inheritance, properties, virtual methods, class references, and so on, as discussed in Chapters 2 and 3 of this book.

The RTL Package, VCL, and CLX

Until version 5, Delphi's class library was known as VCL, which stands for Visual Components Library. Kylix, the Delphi version for Linux, introduced a new component library, called CLX (pronounced "clicks" and standing for Component Library for X-Platform or Cross Platform). Delphi 6 includes both the VCL and CLX libraries. For visual components, the two class libraries are alternative one to the other. However, the core classes and the database and Internet portions of the two libraries are basically shared.

VCL was considered as a single large library, although programmers used to refer to different parts of it (components, controls, nonvisual components, data sets, data-aware controls, Internet components, and so on). CLX introduces a distinction in four parts: BaseCLX, VisualCLX, DataCLX, and NetCLX. Only in VisualCLX does the library use a totally different approach between the two platforms, with the rest of the code being inherently portable to Linux. In the following section, I discuss the sections of these two libraries, while the rest of the chapter focuses on the common core classes.

In Delphi 6, this distinction is underlined by the fact that the core non-visual components and classes of the library are part of the new RTL package, which is used by both VCL and CLX. Moreover, using this package in non-visual applications (for example, Web server programs) allows you to reduce the size of the files to deploy and load in memory considerably.

Traditional Sections of VCL

Delphi programmers use to refer to different sections of VCL with names Borland originally suggested in its documentation, and names that became common afterwards for different groups of components. Technically, components are subclasses of the TComponent class, which is one of the root classes of the hierarchy, as you can see in Figure 5.1. Actually the TComponent class inherits from the TPersistent class; the role of these two classes will be explained in the next section.

FIGURE 5.1:

A graphical representation of the main groups of components of VCL

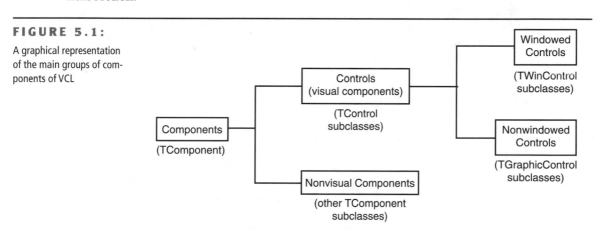

Besides components, the library includes classes that inherit directly from TObject and from TPersistent. These classes are collectively known as *Objects* in portions of the documentation, a rather confusing name for me. These noncomponent classes are often used for values of properties or as utility classes used in code; not inheriting from TComponent, these classes cannot be used directly in visual programming.

NOTE   To be more precise, noncomponent classes cannot be made available in the Component Palette and cannot be dropped directly into a form, but they can be visually managed with the Object Inspector, as subproperties of other properties or items of collections of various types. So even noncomponent classes are often easily used when interacting with the Form Designer.

The component classes can be further divided into two main groups: controls and nonvisual components. Controls groups all the classes that descend from TControl.

Controls   have a position and a size on the screen and show up in the form at design time in the same position they'll have at run time. Controls have two different subspecifications, window-based or graphical, but I'll discuss them in more detail in the next chapter.

Nonvisual components   are all the components that are not controls—all the classes that descend from TComponent but not from TControl. At design time, a nonvisual component appears on the form as an icon (optionally with a caption below it). At run time, some of these components may be visible (for example, the standard dialog boxes), and others are always invisible (for example, the database table component).

TIP   You can simply move the mouse cursor over a control or component in the Form Designer to see a Tooltip with its name and class type (and, in Delphi 6, some extended information). You can also use an environment option, Show Component Captions, to see the name of a nonvisual component right under its icon.

The Structure of CLX

This is the traditional subdivision of VCL, which is very common for Delphi programmers. Even with the introduction of CLX and some new naming schemes, the traditional names will probably survive and merge into Delphi programmers' jargon.

Borland now refers to different portions of the CLX library using one terminology under Linux and a slightly different (and less clear) naming structure in Delphi. This is the subdivision of the Linux-compatible library:

BaseCLX   forms the core of the class library, the topmost classes (such as TComponent), and several general utility classes (including lists, containers, collections, and streams). Compared to the corresponding classes of VCL, BaseCLX is largely unchanged and is highly portable between the Windows and Linux platforms. This chapter is largely devoted to exploring BaseCLX and the common VCL core classes.

VisualCLX   is the collection of visual components, generally indicated as controls. This is the portion of the library that is more tightly related to the operating system: VisualCLX is implemented on top of the Qt library, available both on Windows and on Linux. Using VisualCLX allows for full portability of the visual portion of your application between Delphi on Windows and Kylix on Linux. However, most of the VisualCLX components have corresponding VCL controls, so that you can also easily move your code from one library to the other. I'll discuss VisualCLX and the controls of VCL in the next chapter.

DataCLX   comprises all the database-related components of the library. Actually, DataCLX is the front end of the new dbExpress database engine included in Delphi 6 and Kylix. Delphi includes also the traditional BDE front end, dbGo, and InterBase Express (IBX). If we can consider all these components as part of DataCLX, only the dbExpress front end and IBX are portable between Windows and Linux. DataCLX includes also the ClientDataSet component, now indicated as MyBase, and other related classes. Delphi's data access components are discussed in Part III of the book.

NetCLX   includes the Internet-related components, from the WebBroker framework, to the HTML producer components, from Indy (Internet Direct) to Internet Express, from the new Site Express to XML support. This part of the library is, again, highly portable between Windows and Linux. Internet support is discussed in the last part of the book.

VCL-Specific Sections of the Library

The preceding areas of the library are available, with the differences I've mentioned, on both Delphi and Kylix. In Delphi 6, however, there are other sections of VCL, which for one reason or another are specific to Windows only:

- The Delphi ActiveX (DAX) framework provides support for COM, OLE Automation, ActiveX, and other COM-related technologies. See Chapter 16 for more information on this area of Delphi.

- The Decision Cube components provide OLAP support but have ties with the BDE and haven't been updated recently. Decision Cube is not discussed in the book.

Finally, the default Delphi 6 installation includes some third party components, such as TeeChart for business graphics and QuickReport for reporting. These components will be mentioned in the book but are not discussed in detail.

The *TPersistent* Class

The first core class of the Delphi library we'll look at is the TPersistent class, which is quite a strange one: it has very little code and almost no direct use, but it provides a foundation for the entire idea of visual programming. You can see the definition of the class in Listing 5.1.

Listing 5.1:   **The definition of the *TPersistent* class, from the Classes unit**

```
{$M+}
TPersistent = class(TObject)
  private
    procedure AssignError(Source: TPersistent);
```

```
protected
  procedure AssignTo(Dest: TPersistent); virtual;
  procedure DefineProperties(Filer: TFiler); virtual;
  function  GetOwner: TPersistent; dynamic;
public
  destructor Destroy; override;
  procedure Assign(Source: TPersistent); virtual;
  function  GetNamePath: string; dynamic;
end;
```

As the name implies, this class handles persistency—that is, saving the value of an object to a file to be used later to re-create the object in the same state and with the same data. Persistency is a key element of visual programming. In fact (as we saw in Chapter 1) at design time in Delphi you manipulate actual objects, which are saved to DFM files and re-created at run time when the specific component container—form or data module—is created.

The streaming support, though, is not embedded in the TPersistent class but is provided by other classes, which target TPersistent and its descendants. In other words, you can "persist" with Delphi default streaming-only objects of classes inheriting from TPersistent. One of the reasons for this behavior lies in the fact that the class is compiled with a special option turned on, {$M+}. This flag activates the generation of extended RTTI information for the published portion of the class.

Delphi's streaming system, in fact, doesn't try to save the in-memory data of an object, which would be complex because of the many pointers to other memory locations, totally meaningless when the object would be reloaded. Instead, Delphi saves objects by listing the value of all of properties marked with a special keyword, published. When a property refers to another object, Delphi saves the name of the object or the entire object (with the same mechanism) depending on its type and relationship with the main object.

Of the methods of the TPersistent class, the only one you'll generally use is the Assign procedure, which can be used for copying the actual value of an object. In the library, this method is implemented by many noncomponent classes but by very few components. Actually, most subclasses reimplement the virtual protected AssignTo method, called by the default implementation of Assign.

NOTE   Other methods include DefineProperties, used for customizing the streaming system and adding extra information (pseudo-properties), and the GetOwner and GetNamePath methods used by collections and other special classes to identify themselves to the Object Inspector.

The *published* Keyword

Along with the public, protected, and private access directives, you can use a fourth one, called published. For any published field, property, or method, the compiler generates extended RTTI information, so that Delphi's run time environment or a program can query a class for its published interface. For example, every Delphi component has a published interface that is used by the IDE, in particular the Object Inspector. A regular use of published fields is important when you write components. Usually, the published part of a component contains no fields or methods but properties and events.

When Delphi generates a form or data module, it places the definitions of its components and methods (the event handlers) in the first portion of its definition, before the public and private keywords. These fields and methods of the initial portion of the class are published. The default is published when no special keyword is added before an element of a component class.

To be more precise, published is the default keyword only if the class was compiled with the $M+ compiler directive or is descended from a class compiled with $M+. As this directive is used in the TPersistent class, most classes of VCL and all of the component classes default to published. However, noncomponent classes in Delphi (such as TStream and TList) are compiled with $M- and default to public visibility.

The methods assigned to any event should be published methods, and the fields corresponding to your components in the form should be published to be automatically connected with the objects described in the DFM file and created along with the form. (We'll see later in this chapter the details of this situation and the problems it generates.)

Accessing Published Fields and Methods

As I've mentioned, there are three different declarations that make sense in the published section of a class: fields, methods, and properties. I'll discuss properties in the section "Accessing Properties by Name," while here I'll introduce possible ways of interacting with fields and methods first. The TObject class, in fact, has three interesting methods for this area: MethodAddress, MethodName, and FieldAddress.

The first function, MethodAddress, returns the memory address of the compiled code (a sort of function pointer) of the method passed as parameter in a string. By assigning this method address to the Code field of a TMethod structure and assigning an object to the Data field, you can obtain a complete method pointer. At this point, to call the method you'll need to cast it to

Continued on next page

the proper method pointer type. This is a code fragment highlighting the key points of this technique:

```
var
  Method: TMethod;
  Evt: TNotifyEvent;
begin
  Method.Code := MethodAddress ('Button1Click');
  Method.Data := Self;
  Evt := TNotifyEvent(Method);
  Evt (Sender); // call the method
end;
```

Delphi uses similar code to assign an event handler when it loads a DFM file, as these files store the name of the methods used to handle the events, while the components actually store the method pointer. The second method, `MethodName`, does the opposite transformation, returning the name of the method at a given memory address. This can be used to obtain the name of an event handler, given its value, something Delphi does when streaming a component into a DFM file.

Finally, the `FieldAddress` method of `TObject` returns the memory location of a published field, given its name. This is used by Delphi to connect components created from the DFM files with the fields of their owner (for example, a form) having the same name.

Notice that these three methods are seldom used in "normal" programs but play a key role to make Delphi work as it actually does and are strictly related to the streaming system. You'll need to use these methods only when writing extremely dynamic programs or special-purpose wizards or other Delphi extensions.

Accessing Properties by Name

The Object Inspector displays a list of an object's published properties, even for components you've written. To do this, it relies on the RTTI information generated for published properties. Using some advanced techniques, an application can retrieve a list of the published properties of an object and use them.

Although this capability is not very well known, in Delphi it is possible to access properties by name simply by using the string with the name of the property and then retrieving its value. Access to the RTTI information of properties is provided through a group of undocumented subroutines, part of the TypInfo unit.

These subroutines have always been undocumented in past versions of Delphi, so that Borland remained free to change them. However, from Delphi 1 to Delphi 5, changes were actually very limited and related only to the data structures declared in TypInfo, not the functions provided by the unit. In Delphi 5 Borland actually added many more goodies, and a few "helper" routines, that are officially promoted (even if still not fully documented in the help file but only with comments provided in the unit).

Rather than explore the entire TypInfo unit here, we will look at only the minimal code required to access properties by name. Prior to Delphi 5 it was necessary to use the GetPropInfo function to retrieve a pointer to some internal property information and then apply one of the access functions, such as GetStrProp, to this pointer. You also had to check for the existence and the type of the property.

Delphi 5 introduced a new set of TypInfo routines, including the handy GetPropValue, which returns a variant with the value of the property or varNULL if the property doesn't exist. You simply pass to this function the object and a string with the property name. A further optional parameter allows you to choose the format for returning values of properties of the set type.

For example, we can call

```
ShowMessage (GetPropValue (Button1, 'Caption'));
```

This call has the same effect as calling ShowMessage, passing as parameter Button1.Caption. The only real difference is that this version of the code is much slower, since the compiler generally resolves normal access to properties in a more efficient way. The advantage of the run-time access is that you can make it very flexible, as in the following RunProp example (also available on the companion CD).

This program displays in a list box the value of a property of any type for each component of a form. The name of the property we are looking for is provided in an edit box. This makes the program very flexible. Besides the edit box and the list box, the form has a button to generate the output and some other components added only to test their properties. When you click the button, the following code is executed:

```
uses
  TypInfo;

procedure TForm1.Button1Click(Sender: TObject);
var
  I: Integer;
  Value: Variant;
begin
  ListBox1.Clear;
```

```
for I := 0 to ComponentCount -1 do
begin
  Value := GetPropValue (Components[I], Edit1.Text);
  if Value <> varNULL then
    ListBox1.Items.Add (Components[I].Name + '.' + Edit1.Text + ' = ' +
      string (Value))
  else
    ListBox1.Items.Add ('No ' + Components[I].Name + '.' +
      Edit1.Text);
end;
end;
```

You can see the effect of pressing the Fill List button while using the default *Caption* value in the edit box in Figure 5.2. You can try with any other property name. Numbers will be converted to strings by the variant conversion. Objects (such as the value of the Font property) will be displayed as memory addresses.

FIGURE 5.2:

The output of the RunProp example, which accesses properties by name at run time

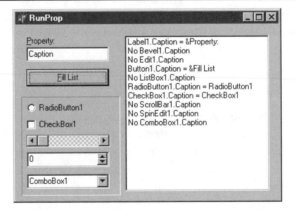

WARNING　Do not use regularly the TypInfo unit instead of polymorphism and other property-access techniques. Use base-class property access first, or use the safe **as** typecast when required, and reserve RTTI access to properties as a very last resort. Using TypInfo techniques makes your code slower, more complex, and more prone to human error; in fact, it skips the compile-time type-checking.

The *TComponent* Class

If the TPersistent class is really more important than it seems at first sight, the key class at the heart of Delphi's component-based class library is TComponent, which inherits from

`TPersistent` (and from `TObject`). The `TComponent` class defines many core elements of components, but it is not as complex as you might think, as the base classes and the language already provide most of what's actually needed.

I won't explore all of the details of the `TComponent` class, some of which are more important for component designers than they are for component users. I'll just discuss ownership (which accounts for some public properties of the class) and the two published properties of the class, `Name` and `Tag`.

Ownership

One of the core features of the `TComponent` class is the definition of ownership. When a component is created, it can be assigned an owner component, which will be responsible for destroying it. So every component can have an owner and can also be the owner of other components. Several public methods and properties of the class are actually devoted to handling the *two sides* of ownership. Here is a list, extracted from the class declaration (in the Classes unit of VCL):

```
type
  TComponent = class(TPersistent, IInterface, IInterfaceComponentReference)
  public
    constructor Create(AOwner: TComponent); virtual;
    procedure DestroyComponents;
    function FindComponent(const AName: string): TComponent;
    procedure InsertComponent(AComponent: TComponent);
    procedure RemoveComponent(AComponent: TComponent);

    property Components[Index: Integer]: TComponent read GetComponent;
    property ComponentCount: Integer read GetComponentCount;
    property ComponentIndex: Integer
      read GetComponentIndex write SetComponentIndex;
    property Owner: TComponent read FOwner;
```

If you create a component giving it an owner, this will be added to the list of components (`InsertComponent`), which is accessible using the `Components` array property. The specific component has an `Owner` and knows its position in the owner components list, with the `ComponentIndex` property. Finally, the destructor of the owner will take care of the destruction of the object it owns, calling `DestroyComponents`. There are a few more protected methods involved, but this should give you the overall picture.

What is important to emphasize is that component ownership can solve a large part of the memory management problems of your applications, if used properly. If you always create components with an owner—the default operation if you use the visual designers of the IDE—you only need to remember to destroy these component containers when they are not needed anymore, and you can forget about the components they contain. For example, you delete a form to destroy all of the components it contains at once, which is a large simplification compared to having to remember to free each and every object individually.

The Components Array

The Components property can also be used to access one component owned by another—let's say, a form. This can be very handy (compared to using directly a specific component) for writing generic code, acting on all or many components at a time. For example, you can use the following code to add to a list box the names of all the components of a form (this code is actually part of the ChangeOwner example, presented in the next section):

```
procedure TForm1.Button1Click(Sender: TObject);
var
  I: Integer;
begin
  ListBox1.Items.Clear;
  for I := 0 to ComponentCount - 1 do
    ListBox1.Items.Add (Components [I].Name);
end;
```

This code uses the ComponentCount property, which holds the total number of components owned by the current form, and the Components property, which is actually the list of the owned components. When you access a value from this list you get a value of the TComponent type. For this reason you can directly use only the properties common to all components, such as the Name property. To use properties specific to particular components, you have to use the proper type-downcast (as).

NOTE   In Delphi, some components are also component containers: the GroupBox, Panel, PageControl, and, of course, Form components. When you use these controls, you can add other components inside them. In this case, the container is the parent of the components (as indicated by the **Parent** property), while the form is their owner (as indicated by the **Owner** property). You can use the **Controls** property of a form or group box to navigate the child controls, and you can use the **Components** property of the form to navigate all the owned components, regardless of their parent.

Using the Components property, we can always access each component of a form. If you need access to a specific component, however, instead of comparing each name with the name of the component you are looking for, you can let Delphi do this work, by using the FindComponent method of the form. This method simply scans the Components array looking for a name match. More information about the role of the Name property for a component is in a later section.

Changing the Owner

We have seen that almost every component has an owner. When a component is created at design time (or from the resulting DFM file), its owner will invariably be its form. When you create a component at run time, the owner is passed as a parameter to the Create constructor.

Owner is a read-only property, so you cannot change it. The owner is set at creation time and should generally not change during the lifetime of a component. To understand why you should not change the owner of a component at design time nor freely change its name, read the following discussion. Be warned, that the topic covered is not simple, so if you're only starting with Delphi, you might want to come back to this section at a later time.

To change the owner of a component, you can call the InsertComponent and RemoveComponent methods of the owner itself, passing the current component as parameter. Using these methods you can change a component's owner. However, you cannot apply them directly in an event handler of a form, as we attempt to do here:

```
procedure TForm1.Button1Click(Sender: TObject);
begin
  RemoveComponent (Button1);
  Form2.InsertComponent (Button1);
end;
```

This code produces a memory access violation, because when you call RemoveComponent, Delphi disconnects the component from the form field (Button1), setting it to nil. The solution is to write a procedure like this:

```
procedure ChangeOwner (Component, NewOwner: TComponent);
begin
  Component.Owner.RemoveComponent (Component);
  NewOwner.InsertComponent (Component);
end;
```

This method (extracted from the ChangeOwner example) changes the owner of the component. It is called along with the simpler code used to change the parent component; the two commands combined move the button *completely* to another form, changing its owner:

```
procedure TForm1.ButtonChangeClick(Sender: TObject);
begin
  if Assigned (Button1) then
  begin
    // change parent
    Button1.Parent := Form2;
    // change owner
    ChangeOwner (Button1, Form2);
  end;
end;
```

The method checks whether the Button1 field still refers to the control, because while moving the component, Delphi will set Button1 to nil. You can see the effect of this code in Figure 5.3.

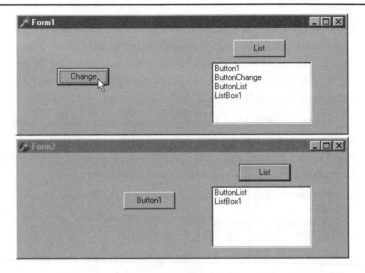

To demonstrate that the Owner of the Button1 component actually changes, I've added another feature to both forms. The List button fills the list box with the names of the components each form owns, using the procedure shown in the previous section. Click the two List buttons before and after moving the component, and you'll see what happens behind the scenes. As a final feature, the Button1 component has a simple handler for its OnClick event, to display the caption of the owner form:

```
procedure TForm1.Button1Click(Sender: TObject);
begin
  ShowMessage ('My owner is ' + ((Sender as TButton).Owner as TForm).Caption);
end;
```

The *Name* Property

Every component in Delphi should have a name. The name must be unique within the owner component, which is generally the form into which you place the component. This means that an application can have two different forms, each with a component with the same name, although you might want to avoid this practice to prevent confusion. It is generally better to keep component names unique throughout an application.

Setting a proper value for the Name property is very important: If it's too long, you'll need to type a lot of code to use the object; if it's too short, you may confuse different objects.

Usually the name of a component has a prefix with the component type; this makes the code more readable and allows Delphi to group components in the combo box of the Object Inspector, where they are sorted by name. There are three important elements related to the Name property of the components:

- First, the value of the Name property is used to define the name of the object in the declaration of the form class. This is the name you're generally going to use in the code to refer to the object. For this reason, the value of the name property must be a legal Pascal identifier (it has to be without spaces and must start with a letter, not a number).

- Second, if you set the Name property of a control before changing its Caption or Text property, the new name is often copied to the caption. That is, if the name and the caption are identical, then changing the name will also change the caption.

- Third, Delphi uses the name of the component to create the default name of the methods related to its events. If you have a Button1 component, its default OnClick event handler will be called Button1Click, unless you specify a different name. If you later change the name of the component, Delphi will modify the names of the related methods accordingly. For example, if you change the name of the button to MyButton, the Button1Click method automatically becomes MyButtonClick.

As mentioned earlier, if you have a string with the name of a component, you can get its instance by calling the FindComponent of its owner, which returns nil in case the component is not found. For example, you can write

```
var
  Comp: TComponent;
begin
  Comp := FindComponent ('Button1');
  if Assigned (Comp) then
    with Comp as TButton do
      // some code...
```

NOTE   Delphi includes also a FindGlobalComponent function, which finds a top-level component, basically a form or data module, that has a given name. To be precise, the FindGlobalComponent function calls one or more installed functions, so in theory you can modify the way the function works. However, as FindGlobalComponent is used by the streaming system, I strongly recommend against installing your own replacement functions. If you want to have a customized way to search for components on other containers, simply write a new function with a custom name.

Removing Form Fields

Every time you add a component to a form, Delphi adds an entry for it, along with some of its properties, to the DFM file. To the Pascal file, Delphi adds the corresponding field in the form class declaration. When the form is created, Delphi loads the DFM file and uses it to re-create all the components and set their properties back. Then it hooks the new object with the form field corresponding to its Name property.

For this reason, it is certainly possible to have a component without a name. If your application will not manipulate the component or modify it at run time, you can remove the component name from the Object Inspector. Examples are a static label with fixed text, or a menu item, or even more obviously, menu item separators. By blanking out the name, you'll remove the corresponding element from the form class declaration. This reduces the size of the form object (by only four bytes, the size of the object reference) and it reduces the DFM file by not including a useless string (the component name). Reducing the DFM also implies reducing the final EXE file size, even if only slightly.

WARNING   If you blank out component names, just make sure to leave at least one named component of each class used on the form so that the smart linker will link in the required code for the class. If, as an example, you remove from a form all the fields referring to TLabel components, the Delphi linker will remove the implementation of the TLabel class from the executable file. The effect is that when the system loads the form at run time, it is unable to create an object of an unknown class and issues an error indicating that the class is not available.

You can also keep the component name and manually remove the corresponding field of the form class. Even if the component has no corresponding form field, it is created anyway, although using it (through the FindComponent method, for example) will be a little more difficult.

Hiding Form Fields

Many OOP purists complain that Delphi doesn't really follow the encapsulation rules, because all of the components of a form are mapped to public fields and can be accessed from other forms and units. Fields for components, in fact, are listed in the first unnamed section of a class declaration, which has a default visibility of published. However, Delphi does that only as a default to help beginners learn to use the Delphi visual development environment quickly. A programmer can follow a different approach and use properties and methods to operate on forms. The risk, however, is that another programmer of the same team might inadvertently bypass this approach, directly accessing the components if they are left in the published section. The solution, which many programmers don't know about, is to move the components to the private portion of the class declaration.

As an example, I've taken a very simple form with an edit box, a button, and a list box. When the edit box contains text and the user presses the button, the text is added to the list box. When the edit box is empty, the button is disabled. This is the simple code of the HideComp example:

```
procedure TForm1.Button1Click(Sender: TObject);
begin
  ListBox1.Items.Add (Edit1.Text);
end;

procedure TForm1.Edit1Change(Sender: TObject);
begin
  Button1.Enabled := Length (Edit1.Text) <> 0;
end;
```

I've listed these methods only to show you that in the code of a form we usually refer to the available components, defining their interactions. For this reason it seems impossible to get rid of the fields corresponding to the component. However, what we can do is hide them, moving them from the default published section to the private section of the form class declaration:

```
TForm1 = class(TForm)
  procedure Button1Click(Sender: TObject);
  procedure Edit1Change(Sender: TObject);
  procedure FormCreate(Sender: TObject);
private
  Button1: TButton;
  Edit1: TEdit;
  ListBox1: TListBox;
end;
```

Now if you run the program you'll get in trouble: The form will load fine, but because the private fields are not initialized, the events above will use nil object references. Delphi usually initializes the published fields of the form using the components created from the DFM file. What if we do it ourselves, with the following code?

```
procedure TForm1.FormCreate(Sender: TObject);
begin
  Button1 := FindComponent ('Button1') as TButton;
  Edit1 := FindComponent ('Edit1') as TEdit;
  ListBox1 := FindComponent ('ListBox1') as TListBox;
end;
```

It will *almost* work, but it generates a system error, similar to the one we discussed in the previous section. This time, the private declarations will cause the linker to link in the implementations of those classes, but the problem is that the streaming system needs to know the names of the classes in order to locate the class reference needed to construct the components while loading the DFM file.

The final touch we need is some registration code to tell Delphi at run time about the existence of the component classes we want to use. We should do this before the form is created, so I generally place this code in the initialization section of the unit:

```
initialization
  RegisterClasses ([TButton, TEdit, TListBox]);
```

Now the question is, is this really worth the effort? What we obtain is a higher degree of encapsulation, protecting the components of a form from other forms (and other programmers writing them). I have to say that replicating these steps for each and every form can be tedious, so I ended up writing a wizard to generate this code for me on the fly. The wizard is far from perfect, as it doesn't handle changes automatically, but it is usable. You can find it on my Web site, www.marcocantu.com, under the CanTools section. My simple wizard apart, for a large project built according to the principles of object-oriented programming, I recommend you consider this or a similar technique.

The Customizable Tag Property

The Tag property is a strange one, because it has no effect at all. It is merely an extra memory location, present in each component class, where you can store custom values. The kind of information stored and the way it is used are completely up to you.

It is often useful to have an extra memory location to attach information to a component without needing to define your component class. Technically, the Tag property stores a long integer so that, for example, you can store the entry number of an array or list that corresponds to an object. Using typecasting, you can store in the Tag property a pointer, an object, or anything else that is four bytes wide. This allows a programmer to associate virtually anything with a component using its tag. We'll see how to use this property in several examples in future chapters, including the ODMenu examples in Chapter 5.

Events

Now that I've introduced the TComponent class, there is one more element of Delphi we have to introduce. Delphi components, in fact, are programmed using "PME," properties, methods, and events. If methods and properties should be clear by now, events have not been fully introduced yet. The reason is that events don't imply a new language feature but are simply a standard coding technique. An event, in fact, is technically a property, with the only difference being that it refers to a method (a method pointer type, to be precise) instead of other types of data.

Events in Delphi

When a user does something with a component, such as clicking it, the component generates an event. Other events are generated by the system, in response to a method call or a change to one of that component's properties (or even a different component's). For example, if you set the focus on a component, the component currently having the focus loses it, triggering the corresponding event.

Technically, most Delphi events are triggered when a corresponding operating system message is received, although the events do not match the messages on a one-to-one basis. Delphi events tend to be higher-level than operating system messages, and Delphi provides a number of extra inter-component messages.

From a theoretical point of view, an event is the result of a request sent to a component or control, which can respond to the message. Following this approach, to handle the click event of a button, we would need to subclass the TButton class and add the new event handler code inside the new class.

In practice, creating a new class for every component you want to use is too complex to be a reasonable solution. In Delphi, the event handler of a component usually is a method of the form that holds the component, not of the component itself. In other words, the component relies on its owner, the form, to handle its events. This technique is called *delegation*, and it is fundamental to the Delphi component-based model. This way, you don't have to modify the TButton class, unless you want to define a new type of component, but simply customize its owner to modify the behavior of the button.

Method Pointers

Events rely on a specific feature of the Object Pascal language: *method pointers*. A method pointer type is like a procedural type, but one that refers to a method. Technically, a method pointer type is a procedural type that has an implicit Self parameter. In other words, a variable of a procedural type stores the address of a function to call, provided it has a given set of parameters. A method pointer variable stores two addresses: the address of the method code and the address of an object instance (data). The address of the object instance will show up as Self inside the method body when the method code is called using this method pointer.

NOTE   This explains the definition of Delphi's generic TMethod type, a record with a Code field and a Data field.

The declaration of a method pointer type is similar to that of a procedural type, except that it has the keywords of object at the end of the declaration:

```
type
  IntProceduralType = procedure (Num: Integer);
  IntMethodPointerType = procedure (Num: Integer) of object;
```

When you have declared a method pointer, such as the one above, you can declare a variable of this type and assign to it a compatible method—a method that has the same parameters—of another object.

When you add an OnClick event handler for a button, Delphi does exactly that. The button has a method pointer type property, named OnClick, and you can directly or indirectly assign to it a method of another object, such as a form. When a user clicks the button, this method is executed, even if you have defined it inside another class.

What follows is a sketch of the code actually used by Delphi to define the event handler of a button component and the related method of a form:

```
type
  TNotifyEvent = procedure (Sender: TObject) of object;

  MyButton = class
    OnClick: TNotifyEvent;
  end;

  TForm1 = class (TForm)
    procedure Button1Click (Sender: TObject);
    Button1: MyButton;
  end;

var
  Form1: TForm1;
```

Now inside a procedure, you can write

```
MyButton.OnClick := Form1.Button1Click;
```

The only real difference between this code fragment and the code of VCL is that OnClick is a property name, and the actual data it refers to is called FOnClick. An event that shows up in the Events page of the Object Inspector, in fact, is nothing more than a property of a method pointer type. This means, for example, that you can dynamically modify the event handler attached to a component at design time or even build a new component at run time and assign an event handler to it.

Events Are Properties

Another important concept I've already mentioned is that events are properties. This means that to handle an event of a component, you assign a method to the corresponding event property. When you double-click an event in the Object Inspector, a new method is added to the owner form and assigned to the proper event property of the component.

This is why it is possible for several events to share the same event handler or change an event handler at run time. To use this feature, you don't need much knowledge of the language. In fact, when you select an event in the Object Inspector, you can press the arrow button on the right of the event name to see a drop-down list of "compatible" methods—a list of methods having the same method pointer type. Using the Object Inspector, it is easy to select the same method for the same event of different components or for different, compatible events of the same component.

As we've added some properties to the TDate class in Chapter 3, we can add one event. The event is going to be very simple. It will be called OnChange, and it can be used to warn the user of the component that the value of the date has changed. To define an event, we simply define a property corresponding to it, and we add some data to store the actual method pointer the event refers to. These are the new definitions added to the class, available in the DateEvt example:

```
type
  TDate = class
  private
    FOnChange: TNotifyEvent;
    ...
  protected
    procedure DoChange; dynamic;
    ...
  public
    property OnChange: TNotifyEvent
      read FonChange write FOnChange;
    ...
  end;
```

The property definition is actually very simple. A user of this class can assign a new value to the property and, hence, to the FOnChange private field. The class doesn't assign a value to this FOnChange field; it is the user of the component who does the assignment. The TDate class simply calls the method stored in the FOnChange field when the value of the date changes. Of course, the call takes place only if the event property has been assigned. The DoChange method (declared as a dynamic method as it is traditional with event firing methods) makes the test and the method call:

```
procedure TDate.DoChange;
begin
  if Assigned (FOnChange) then
    FOnChange (Self);
end;
```

The DoChange method in turn is called every time one of the values changes, as in the following method:

```
procedure TDate.SetValue (y, m, d: Integer);
begin
  fDate := EncodeDate (y, m, d);
  // fire the event
  DoChange;
```

Now if we look at the program that uses this class, we can simplify its code considerably. First, we add a new custom method to the form class:

```
type
  TDateForm = class(TForm)
    ...
    procedure DateChange(Sender: TObject);
```

The code of this method simply updates the label with the current value of the Text property of the TDate object:

```
procedure TDateForm.DateChange;
begin
  LabelDate.Caption := TheDay.Text;
end;
```

This event handler is then installed in the FormCreate method:

```
procedure TDateForm.FormCreate(Sender: TObject);
begin
  TheDay := TDate.Init (2001, 7, 4);
  LabelDate.Caption := TheDay.Text;
  // assign the event handler for future changes
  TheDay.OnChange := DateChange;
end;
```

Well, this seems like a lot of work. Was I lying when I told you that the event handler would save us some coding? No. Now, after we've added some code, we can completely forget about updating the label when we change some of the data of the object. Here, as an example, is the handler of the OnClick event of one of the buttons:

```
procedure TDateForm.BtnIncreaseClick(Sender: TObject);
begin
  TheDay.Increase;
end;
```

The same simplified code is present in many other event handlers. Once we have installed the event handler, we don't have to remember to update the label continually. That eliminates a significant potential source of errors in the program. Also note that we had to write some code at the beginning because this is not a component installed in Delphi but simply a class. With a component, you simply select the event handler in the Object Inspector and write a single line of code to update the label. That's all.

NOTE   This is meant to be just a short introduction to defining events. A basic understanding of these features is important for every Delphi programmer. If your aim is to write new components, with complex events, you'll find a lot more information on all these topics in Chapter 11.

Lists and Container Classes

It is often important to handle groups of components or objects. Besides using standard arrays and dynamic arrays, there are a few classes of VCL that represent lists of other objects. These classes can be divided into three groups: simple lists, collections, and containers. The last group was introduced in Delphi 5 and has been further expanded in Delphi 6.

Lists and String Lists

Lists are represented by the generic list of objects, TList, and by the two lists of strings, TStrings and TStringList:

- TList defines a list of pointers, which can be used to store objects of any class. A TList is more flexible than a dynamic array, because it is expanded automatically, simply by adding new items to it. The advantage of dynamic arrays over a TList, instead, is that dynamic arrays allow you to indicate a specific type for contained objects and perform the proper compile-time type checking.

- TStrings is an abstract class to represent all forms of string lists, regardless of their storage implementations. This class defines an abstract list of strings. For this reason, TStrings objects are used only as properties of components capable of storing the strings themselves, such as a list box.

- TStringList, a subclass of TStrings, defines a list of strings with their own storage. You can use this class to define a list of strings in a program.

TStringList and TStrings objects have both a list of strings and a list of objects associated with the strings. This opens up a number of different uses for these classes. For example, you can use them for dictionaries of associated objects or to store bitmaps or other elements to be used in a list box.

The two classes of lists of strings also have ready-to-use methods to store or load their contents to or from a text file, SaveToFile and LoadFromFile. To loop through a list, you can use a simple for statement based on its index, as if the list were an array. All these lists have a number of methods and properties. You can operate on lists using the array notation ("[" and "]") both to read and to change elements. There is a Count property, as well as typical access methods, such as Add, Insert, Delete, Remove, and search methods (for example, IndexOf). In Delphi 6, the TList class has an Assign method that, besides copying the source data, can perform set operations on the two lists, including *and*, *or*, and *xor*.

To fill a string list with items and later check whether one is present, you can write code like this:

```
var
  sl: TStringList;
  idx: Integer;
begin
  sl := TStringList.Create;
  try
    sl.Add ('one');
    sl.Add ('two');
    sl.Add ('three');
    // later
    idx := sl.IndexOf ('two');
    if idx >= 0 then
      ShowMessage ('String found');
  finally
    sl.Free;
  end;
end;
```

Using Lists of Objects

We can write an example focusing on the use of the generic TList class. When you need a list of any kind of data, you can generally declare a TList object, fill it with the data, and then access the data while casting it to the proper type. The ListDemo example demonstrates just this. It also shows the pitfalls of this approach. Its form has a private variable, holding a list of dates:

```
private
  ListDate: TList;
```

This list object is created when the form itself is created:

```
procedure TForm1.FormCreate(Sender: TObject);
begin
  Randomize;
  ListDate := TList.Create;
end;
```

A button of the form adds a random date to the list (of course, I've included in the project the unit containing the date component built in the previous chapter):

```
procedure TForm1.ButtonAddClick(Sender: TObject);
begin
  ListDate.Add (TDate.Create (1900 + Random (200), 1 + Random (12),
    1 + Random (30)));
end;
```

When you extract the items from the list, you have to cast them back to the proper type, as in the following method, which is connected to the List button (you can see its effect in Figure 5.4):

```
procedure TForm1.ButtonListDateClick(Sender: TObject);
var
  I: Integer;
begin
  ListBox1.Clear;
  for I := 0 to ListDate.Count - 1 do
    Listbox1.Items.Add ((TObject(ListDate [I]) as TDate).Text);
end;
```

FIGURE 5.4:

The list of dates shown by the ListDemo example

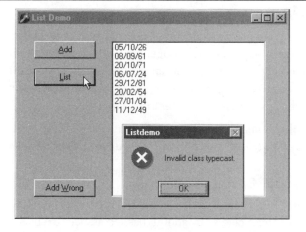

At the end of the code above, before we can do an **as** downcast, we first need to hard-cast the pointer returned by the TList into a TObject reference. This kind of expression can result in an invalid typecast exception, or it can generate a memory error when the pointer is not a reference to an object.

To demonstrate that things can indeed go wrong, I've added one more button, which adds a TButton object to the list:

```
procedure TForm1.ButtonWrongClick(Sender: TObject);
begin
  // add a button to the list
  ListDate.Add (Sender);
end;
```

If you click this button and then update one of the lists, you'll get an error. Finally, remember that when you destroy a list of objects, you should remember to destroy all of the objects of the list first. The ListDemo program does this in the FormDestroy method of the form:

```
procedure TForm1.FormDestroy(Sender: TObject);
var
  I: Integer;
begin
  for I := 0 to ListDate.Count - 1 do
    TObject(ListDate [I]).Free;
  ListDate.Free;
end;
```

Collections

The second group, collections, contains only two classes, TCollection and TCollectionItem. TCollection defines a homogeneous list of objects, which are owned by the collection class. The objects in the collection must be descendants of the TCollectionItem class. If you need a collection storing specific objects, you have to create both a subclass of TCollection and a matching subclass of TCollectionItem.

Collections are used to specify values of properties of components. It is very unusual to work with collections for storing your own objects, so I won't discuss them here.

Container Classes

Delphi 5 introduced a new series of container classes, defined in the Contnrs unit. Delphi 6 extends these classes by adding hashed associative lists, as discussed in the following section. The container classes extend the TList classes by adding the idea of ownership and by defining specific extraction rules (mimicking stacks and queues) or sorting capabilities.

The basic difference between TList and the new TObjectList class, for example, is that the latter is defined as a list of TObject objects, not a list of pointers. Even more important, however, is the fact that if the object list has the OwnsObjects property set to True, it automatically deletes an object when it is replaced by another one and deletes each object when the list itself is destroyed. Here's a list of all the new container classes:

- The TObjectList class I've already described represents a list of objects, eventually owned by the list itself.

- The inherited class TComponentList represents a list of components, with full support for destruction notification (an important safety feature when two components are connected using their properties; that is, when a component is the value of a property of another component).

- The TClassList class is a list of class references. It inherits from TList and requires no destruction.

- The classes TStack and TObjectStack represent lists of pointers and objects, from which you can only extract elements starting from the last one you've inserted. A stack follows the LIFO order (Last In, First Out). The typical methods of a stack are Push for insertion, Pop for extraction, and Peek to preview the first item without removing it. You can still use all the methods of the base class, TList.

- The classes TQueue and TObjectQueue represent lists of pointers and objects, from which you always remove the *first* item you've inserted (FIFO: first in, first out). The methods of these classes are the same as those of the stack classes but behave differently.

WARNING   Unlike the TObjectList, the TObjectStack and the TObjectQueue do not own the inserted objects and will not destroy those objects left in the data structure when it is destroyed. You can simply **Pop** all the items, destroy them once you're finished using them, and then destroy the container.

To demonstrate the use of these classes, I've modified the earlier ListDate example into the new Contain example on the CD. First, I changed the type of the ListDate variable to TObjectList. In the FormCreate method, I've modified the list creation to the following code, which activates the list ownership:

```
ListDate := TObjectList.Create (True);
```

At this point, we can simplify the destruction code, as applying Free to the list will automatically free the dates it holds.

I've also added to the program a stack and a queue object, filling each of them with numbers. One of the form's two buttons displays a list of the numbers in each container, and the other removes the last item (displayed in a message box):

```
procedure TForm1.btnQueueClick(Sender: TObject);
var
  I: Integer;
```

```
begin
  ListBox1.Clear;
  for I := 0 to Stack.Count - 1 do begin
    ListBox1.Items.Add (IntToStr (Integer (Queue.Peek)));
    Queue.Push(Queue.Pop);
  end;
  ShowMessage ('Removed: ' + IntToStr (Integer (Stack.Pop)));
end;
```

By pressing the two buttons, you can see that calling Pop for each container returns the last item. The difference is that the TQueue class inserts elements at the beginning, and the TStack class inserts them at the end.

Hashed Associative Lists

After whetting our appetite in Delphi 5, Borland has pushed the idea of container classes a little further in Delphi 6, introducing a new set of lists, particularly TBucketList and TObjectBucketList. These two lists are associative, which means they have a key and an actual entry. The key is used to identify the items and search for them. To add an item, you call the Add method, with two parameters, the key and the actual data. When you use the Find method, you pass the key and retrieve the data. The same effect is achieved by using the Data array property, passing the key as parameter.

These lists are also based on a hash system. The lists create an internal array of items, called buckets, each having a sub-list of actual elements of the list. As you add an item, its key value is used to compute the *hash* value, which determines the bucket to add the item to. When searching the item, the hash is computed again, and the list immediately grabs the sublist containing the item, searching for it there. This makes for very fast insertion and searches, but only if the hash algorithm distributes the items evenly among the various buckets and if there are enough different entries in the array. In fact, when many elements can be in the same bucket, searching gets slower.

For this reason, as you create the TObjectBucketList you can specify the number of entries for the list, using the parameter of the constructor, choosing a value between 2 and 256. The value of the bucket is determined by taking the first byte of the pointer (or number) passed as key and doing an and operation with a number corresponding to the entries.

NOTE   I don't find this algorithm very convincing for a hash system, but replacing it with your own implies only overriding the BucketFor virtual function and eventually changing the number of entries in the array, by setting a different value for the BucketCount property.

Another interesting feature, not available for lists, is the ForEach method, which allows you to execute a given function on each item contained in the list. You pass to the ForEach method a pointer to data of your own and a procedure, which receives four parameters, including your custom pointer, each key and object of the list, and a Boolean parameter you can set to False to stop the execution. In other words, these are the two signatures:

```
type
  TBucketProc = procedure(AInfo, AItem, AData: Pointer;
    out AContinue: Boolean);

function TCustomBucketList.ForEach(AProc: TBucketProc;
  AInfo: Pointer): Boolean;
```

NOTE   Besides these containers, Delphi includes also a THashedStringList class, which inherits from TStringList. This class has no direct relationship with the hashed lists and is even defined in a different unit, IniFile. The hashed string list has two associated hash tables (of type TStringHash), which are completely refreshed every time the content of the string list changes. So this class is useful only for reading a large set of fixed strings, not for handling a list of strings changing often over time. On the other hand, the TStringHash support class seems to be quite useful in general cases, and has a good algorithm for computing the hash value of a string.

Type-Safe Containers and Lists

Containers and lists have a problem: They are not type-safe, as I've shown in both examples by adding a button object to a list of dates. To ensure that the data in a list is homogenous, you can check the type of the data you extract before you insert it, but as an extra safety measure you might also want to check the type of the data while extracting it. However, adding run-time type checking slows down a program and is risky—a programmer might fail to check the type in some cases.

To solve both problems, you can create specific list classes for given data types and fashion the code from the existing TList or TObjectList classes (or another container class). There are two approaches to accomplish this:

- Derive a new class from the list class and customize the Add method and the access methods, which relate to the Items property. This is also the approach used by Borland for the container classes, which all derive from TList.

NOTE   Delphi container classes use static overrides to perform simple type conveniences (parameters and function results of the desired type). Static overrides are not the same as polymorphism; someone using a container class via a TList variable will not be calling the container's specialized functions. Static override is a simple and effective technique, but it has one very important restriction: The methods in the descendent should not do anything beyond simple type-casting, because you aren't guaranteed that the descendent methods will be called. The list might be accessed and manipulated using the ancestor methods as much as by the descendent methods, so their actual operations must be identical. The only difference is the type used in the descendent methods, which allows you to avoid extra typecasting.

- Create a brand-new class that contains a TList object, and map the methods of the new class to the internal list using proper type checking. This approach defines a wrapper class, a class that "wraps" around an existing one to provide a different or limited access to its methods (in our case, to perform a type conversion).

I've implemented both solutions in the DateList example, which defines lists of TDate objects. In the code that follows, you'll find the declaration of the two classes, the inheritance-based TDateListI class and the wrapper class TDateListW.

```
type
// inheritance-based
TDateListI = class (TObjectList)
protected
  procedure SetObject (Index: Integer; Item: TDate);
  function GetObject (Index: Integer): TDate;
public
  function Add (Obj: TDate): Integer;
  procedure Insert (Index: Integer; Obj: TDate);
  property Objects [Index: Integer]: TDate
    read GetObject write SetObject; default;
end;

// wrapper based
TDateListW = class(TObject)
private
  FList: TObjectList;
  function GetObject (Index: Integer): TDate;
    procedure SetObject (Index: Integer; Obj: TDate);
  function GetCount: Integer;
public
  constructor Create;
  destructor Destroy; override;
  function Add (Obj: TDate): Integer;
  function Remove (Obj: TDate): Integer;
  function IndexOf (Obj: TDate): Integer;
  property Count: Integer read GetCount;
  property Objects [Index: Integer]: TDate
    read GetObject write SetObject; default;
end;
```

Obviously, the first class is simpler to write—it has fewer methods, and they simply call the inherited ones. The good thing is that a TDateListI object can be passed to parameters expecting a TList. The problem is that the code that manipulates an instance of this list via a generic TList variable will not be calling the specialized methods, because they are not virtual and might end up adding to the list objects of other data types.

Instead, if you decide not to use inheritance, you end up writing a lot of code, because you need to reproduce each and every one of the original TList methods, simply calling the methods of the internal FList object. The drawback is that the TDateListW class is not type compatible with TList, which limits its usefulness. It can't be passed as parameter to methods expecting a TList.

Both of these approaches provide good type checking. After you've created an instance of one of these list classes, you can add only objects of the appropriate type, and the objects you extract will naturally be of the correct type. This is demonstrated by the DateList example. This program has a few buttons, a combo box to let a user choose which of the lists to show, and a list box to show the actual values of the list. The program stretches the lists by trying to add a button to the list of TDate objects. To add an object of a different type to the TDateListI list, we can simply convert the list to its base class, TList. This might accidentally happen if you pass the list as a parameter to a method that expects a base class object. In contrast, for the TDateListW list to fail we must explicitly cast the object to TDate before inserting it, something a programmer should never do:

```
procedure TForm1.ButtonAddButtonClick(Sender: TObject);
begin
  ListW.Add (TDate(TButton.Create (nil)));
  TList(ListI).Add (TButton.Create (nil));
  UpdateList;
end;
```

The UpdateList call triggers an exception, displayed directly in the list box, because I've used an as typecast in the custom list classes. A wise programmer should never write the above code. To summarize, writing a custom list for a specific type makes a program much more robust. Writing a wrapper list instead of one that's based on inheritance tends to be a little safer, although it requires more coding.

NOTE   Instead of rewriting wrapper-style list classes for different types, you can use my List Template Wizard, available on my Web site, **www.marcocantu.com**.

Streaming

Another core area of the Delphi class library is its support for streaming, which includes file management, memory, sockets, and other sources of information arranged in a sequence. The idea of streaming is that you move along the data while reading it, much like the traditional read and write functions used by the Pascal language (and discussed in Chapter 12 of *Essential Pascal*, available on the companion CD).

The *TStream* Class

The VCL defines the abstract TStream class and several subclasses. The parent class, TStream, has just a few properties, and you'll never create an instance of it, but it has an interesting list of methods you'll generally use when working with derived stream classes.

The TStream class defines two properties, Size and Position. All stream objects have a specific size (which generally grows if you write something after the end of the stream), and you must specify a position within the stream where you want to either read or write information.

Reading and writing bytes depends on the actual stream class you are using, but in both cases you don't need to know much more than the size of the stream and your relative position in the stream to read or write data. In fact, that's one of the advantages of using streams. The basic interface remains the same whether you're manipulating a disk file, a binary large object (BLOB) field, or a long sequence of bytes in memory.

In addition to the Size and Position properties, the TStream class also defines several important methods, most of which are virtual and abstract. (In other words, the TStream class doesn't define what these methods do; therefore, derived classes are responsible for implementing them.) Some of these methods are important only in the context of reading or writing components within a stream (for instance, ReadComponent and WriteComponent), but some are useful in other contexts, too. In Listing 5.2, you can find the declaration of the TStream class, extracted from the Classes unit.

Listing 5.2:   The public portion of the definition of the *TStream* class

```
TStream = class(TObject)
public
  // read and write a buffer
  function Read(var Buffer; Count: Longint): Longint; virtual; abstract;
  function Write(const Buffer; Count: Longint): Longint; virtual; abstract;
  procedure ReadBuffer(var Buffer; Count: Longint);
  procedure WriteBuffer(const Buffer; Count: Longint);

  // move to a specific position
  function Seek(Offset: Longint; Origin: Word): Longint; overload; virtual;
  function Seek(const Offset: Int64; Origin: TSeekOrigin): Int64;
    overload; virtual;

  // copy the stream
  function CopyFrom(Source: TStream; Count: Int64): Int64;

  // read or write a component
  function ReadComponent(Instance: TComponent): TComponent;
  function ReadComponentRes(Instance: TComponent): TComponent;
  procedure WriteComponent(Instance: TComponent);
  procedure WriteComponentRes(const ResName: string; Instance: TComponent);
```

```
procedure WriteDescendent(Instance, Ancestor: TComponent);
procedure WriteDescendentRes(
  const ResName: string; Instance, Ancestor: TComponent);
procedure WriteResourceHeader(const ResName: string; out FixupInfo: Integer);
procedure FixupResourceHeader(FixupInfo: Integer);
procedure ReadResHeader;

// properties
property Position: Int64 read GetPosition write SetPosition;
property Size: Int64 read GetSize write SetSize64;
end;
```

The basic use of a string involves calling the ReadBuffer and WriteBuffer methods, which are very powerful but not terribly easy to use. The first parameter, in fact, is an untyped buffer in which you can pass the variable to save from or load to. For example, you can save into a file a number (in binary format) and a string, with this code:

```
var
  stream: TStream;
  n: integer;
  str: string;
begin
  n := 10;
  str := 'test string';
  stream := TFileStream.Create ('c:\tmp\test', fmCreate);
  stream.WriteBuffer (n, sizeOf(integer));
  stream.WriteBuffer (str[1], Length (str));
  stream.Free;
```

A totally alternative approach is to let specific components save or load data to and from streams. Many VCL classes define a LoadFromStream or a SaveToStream method, including TStrings, TStringList, TBlobField, TMemoField, TIcon, and TBitmap.

Specific Stream Classes

Creating a TStream instance makes no sense, because this class is abstract and provides no direct support for saving data. Instead, you can use one of the derived classes to load data from or store it to an actual file, a BLOB field, a socket, or a memory block. Use TFileStream when you want to work with a file, passing the filename and some file access options to the Create method. Use TMemoryStream to manipulate a stream in memory and not an actual file.

Several units define TStream-derived classes. In the Classes unit are the following classes:

- THandleStream defines a stream that manipulates a disk file represented by a Windows file handle.

- TFileStream defines a stream that manipulates a disk file (a file that exists on a local or network disk) represented by a filename. It inherits from THandleStream.

- TCustomMemoryStream is the base class for streams stored in memory but is not used directly.

- TMemoryStream defines a stream that manipulates a sequence of bytes in memory. It inherits from TCustomMemoryStream.

- TStringStream provides a simple way for associating a stream to a string in memory, so that you can access the string with the TStream interface and also copy the string to and from another stream.

- TResourceStream defines a stream that manipulates a sequence of bytes in memory, and provides read-only access to resource data linked into the executable file of an application (an example of these resource data are the DFM files). It inherits from TCustomMemoryStream.

Stream classes defined in other units include

- TBlobStream defines a stream that provides simple access to database BLOB fields. There are similar BLOB streams for other database access technologies rather than the BDE.

- TOleStream defines a stream for reading and writing information over the interface for streaming provided by an OLE object.

- TWinSocketStream provides streaming support for a socket connection.

Using File Streams

Creating and using a file stream can be as simple as creating a variable of a type that descends from TStream and calling components methods to load content from the file:

```
var
  S: TFileStream;
begin
  if OpenDialog1.Execute then
  begin
    S := TFileStream.Create (OpenDialog1.FileName, fmOpenRead);
    try
      Memo1.Lines.LoadFromStream (S);
    finally
      S.Free;
    end;
  end;
end;
```

As you can see in this code, the Create method for file streams has two parameters: the name of the file and a flag indicating the requested access mode. In this case, we want to read the file, so we used the fmOpenRead flag (other available flags are documented in the Delphi help).

Of the different modes, the most important are fmShareDenyWrite, which you'll use when you're simply reading data from a shared file, and fmShareExclusive, which you'll use when you're writing data to a shared file.

A big advantage of streams over other file access techniques is that they're very interchangeable, so you can work with memory streams and then save them to a file, or you can perform the opposite operations. This might be a way to improve the speed of a file-intensive program. Here is a snippet of code, a file-copying function, to give you another idea of how you can use streams:

```
procedure CopyFile (SourceName, TargetName: String);
var
  Stream1, Stream2: TFileStream;
begin
  Stream1 := TFileStream.Create (SourceName, fmOpenRead);
  try
    Stream2 := TFileStream.Create (TargetName, fmOpenWrite or fmCreate);
    try
      Stream2.CopyFrom (Stream1, Stream1.Size);
    finally
      Stream2.Free;
    end
  finally
    Stream1.Free;
  end
end;
```

Another important use of streams is to handle database BLOB fields or other large fields directly. In fact, you can export such data to a stream or read it from one by simply calling the SaveToStream and LoadFromStream methods of the TBlobField class.

The *TReader* and *TWriter* Classes

By themselves, the stream classes of VCL don't provide much support for reading or writing data. In fact, stream classes don't implement much beyond simply reading and writing blocks of data. If you want to load or save specific data types in a stream (and don't want to perform a great deal of typecasting), you can use the TReader and TWriter classes, which derive from the generic TFiler class.

Basically, the TReader and TWriter classes exist to simplify loading and saving stream data according to its type, and not just as a sequence of bytes. To do this, TWriter embeds special signatures into the stream that specify the type for each object's data. Conversely, the TReader class reads these signatures from the stream, creates the appropriate objects, and then initializes those objects using the subsequent data from the stream.

For example, I could have written out a number and a string to a stream by writing:

```
var
  stream: TStream;
  n: integer;
  str: string;
  w: TWriter;
begin
  n := 10;
  str := 'test string';
  stream := TFileStream.Create ('c:\tmp\test.txt', fmCreate);
  w := TWriter.Create (stream, 1024);
  w.WriteInteger (n);
  w.WriteString (str);
  w.Free;
  stream.Free;
```

This time the actual file will include also the extra signature characters, so that I can read back this file only by using a TReader object. For this reason, using the TReader and TWriter is generally confined to components streaming and is seldom applied in general file management.

Streams and Persistency

In Delphi, streams play a considerable role for persistency. For this reason, many methods of TStream relate to saving and loading a component and its subcomponents. For example, you can store a form in a stream by writing

```
stream.WriteComponent(Form1);
```

If you examine the structure of a Delphi DFM file, you'll discover that it's really just a resource file that contains a custom format resource. Inside this resource, you'll find the component information for the form or data module and for each of the components it contains. As you would expect, the stream classes provide two methods to read and write this custom resource data for components: WriteComponentRes to store the data, and ReadComponentRes to load it.

For your experiment in memory (not involving actual DFM files), though, using WriteComponent is generally better suited. After you create a memory stream and save the current form to it, the problem is how to display it. This can be accomplished by transforming the binary representation of forms to a textual representation. Even though the Delphi

IDE, since version 5, can save DFM files in text format, the representation used internally for the compiled code is invariably a binary format.

The form conversion can be accomplished by the IDE, generally with the View as Text command of the form designer, and in other ways. There is also a command-line utility, CONVERT.EXE, found in the Delphi Bin directory. Within your own code, the standard way to obtain a conversion is to call the specific methods of VCL. There are four functions for converting to and from the internal object format obtained by the WriteComponent method:

```
procedure ObjectBinaryToText(Input, Output: TStream); overload;
procedure ObjectBinaryToText(Input, Output: TStream;
  var OriginalFormat: TStreamOriginalFormat); overload;
procedure ObjectTextToBinary(Input, Output: TStream); overload;
procedure ObjectTextToBinary(Input, Output: TStream;
  var OriginalFormat: TStreamOriginalFormat); overload;
```

Four different functions, with the same parameters and names containing the name *Resource* instead of *Binary* (as in ObjectResourceToText), convert the resource format obtained by WriteComponentRes. A final method, TestStreamFormat, indicates whether a DFM is storing a binary or textual representation.

In the FormToText program, I've used the ObjectBinaryToText method to copy the binary definition of a form into another stream, and then I've displayed the resulting stream in a memo, as you can see in Figure 5.5. This is the code of the two methods involved:

FIGURE 5.5:

The textual description of a form component, displayed inside itself by the FormTo-Text example

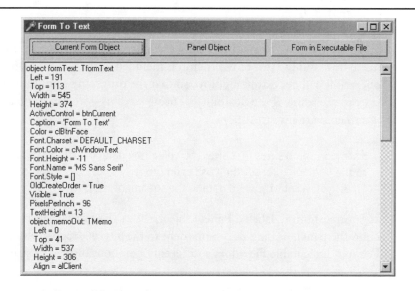

```
procedure TformText.btnCurrentClick(Sender: TObject);
var
  MemStr: TStream;
begin
  MemStr := TMemoryStream.Create;
  try
    MemStr.WriteComponent (Self);
    ConvertAndShow (MemStr);
  finally
    MemStr.Free
  end;
end;

procedure TformText.ConvertAndShow (aStream: TStream);
var
  ConvStream: TStream;
begin
  aStream.Position := 0;
  ConvStream := TMemoryStream.Create;
  try
    ObjectBinaryToText (aStream, ConvStream);
    ConvStream.Position := 0;
    MemoOut.Lines.LoadFromStream (ConvStream);
  finally
    ConvStream.Free
  end;
end;
```

Notice that by repeatedly clicking the Current Form Object button you'll get more and more text, and the text of the memo is included in the stream. After a few times, the entire operation will get extremely slow, so that the program seems to be hung up. In this code, we start to see some of the flexibility of using streams—we can write a generic procedure we can use to convert any stream.

NOTE   It's important to stress that after you've written data to a stream, you must explicitly seek back to the beginning (or set the **Position** property to 0) before you can use the stream further, unless you want to append data to the stream, of course.

Another button, labeled Panel Object, shows the textual representation of a specific component, the panel, passing the component to the WriteComponent method. The third button, Form in Executable File, does a different operation. Instead of streaming an existing object in memory, it loads in a TResourceStream object the design-time representation of the form—that is, its DFM file—from the corresponding resource embedded in the executable file:

```
procedure TformText.btnResourceClick(Sender: TObject);
var
  ResStr: TResourceStream;
begin
  ResStr := TResourceStream.Create(hInstance, 'TFORMTEXT', RT_RCDATA);
  try
    ConvertAndShow (ResStr);
  finally
    ResStr.Free
  end;
end;
```

By clicking the buttons in sequence (or modifying the form of the program) you can compare the form saved in the DFM file to the current run-time object.

Writing a Custom Stream Class

Besides using the existing stream classes, Delphi programmers can write their own stream classes, and use them in place of the existing ones. To accomplish this, you need only specify how a generic block of raw data is saved and loaded, and VCL will be able to use your new class wherever you call for it. You may not need to create a brand-new stream class for working with a new type of media, but only need to customize an existing stream. In that case, all you have to do is write the proper read and write methods.

As an example, I created a class to encode and decode a generic file stream. Although this example is limited by its use of a totally dumb encoding mechanism, it fully integrates with VCL and works properly. The new stream class simply declares the two core reading and writing methods and has a property that stores a key.

```
type
  TEncodedStream = class (TFileStream)
  private
    FKey: Char;
  public
    constructor Create(const FileName: string; Mode: Word);
    function Read(var Buffer; Count: Longint): Longint; override;
    function Write(const Buffer; Count: Longint): Longint; override;
    property Key: Char read FKey write FKey;
  end;
```

Continued on next page

The value of the key is simply added to each of the bytes saved to a file, and subtracted when the data is read. Here is the complete code of the Write and Read methods, which uses pointers quite heavily:

```
constructor TEncodedStream.Create( const FileName: string; Mode: Word);
begin
  inherited Create (FileName, Mode);
  FKey := 'A'; // default
end;

function TEncodedStream.Write(const Buffer; Count: Longint): Longint;
var
  pBuf, pEnc: PChar;
  I, EncVal: Integer;
begin
  // allocate memory for the encoded buffer
  GetMem (pEnc, Count);
  try
    // use the buffer as an array of characters
    pBuf := PChar (@Buffer);
    // for every character of the buffer
    for I := 0 to Count - 1 do
    begin
      // encode the value and store it
      EncVal := ( Ord (pBuf[I]) + Ord(Key) ) mod 256;
      pEnc [I] := Chr (EncVal);
    end;
    // write the encoded buffer to the file
    Result := inherited Write (pEnc^, Count);
  finally
    FreeMem (pEnc, Count);
  end;
end;

function TEncodedStream.Read(var Buffer; Count: Longint): Longint;
var
  pBuf, pEnc: PChar;
  I, CountRead, EncVal: Integer;
begin
  // allocate memory for the encoded buffer
  GetMem (pEnc, Count);
  try
```

Continued on next page

```
    // read the encoded buffer from the file
    CountRead := inherited Read (pEnc^, Count);
    // use the output buffer as a string
    pBuf := PChar (@Buffer);
    // for every character actually read
    for I := 0 to CountRead - 1 do
    begin
      // decode the value and store it
      EncVal := ( Ord (pEnc[I]) - Ord(Key) ) mod 256;
      pBuf [I] := Chr (EncVal);
    end;
  finally
    FreeMem (pEnc, Count);
  end;
  // return the number of characters read
  Result := CountRead;
end;
```

The comments in this rather complex code should help you understand the details. Now that we have an encoded stream, we can try to use it in a demo program, which is called EncDemo. The form of this program has two memo components and three buttons, as you can see in the graphic below. The first button loads a plain text file in the first memo; the second button saves the text of this first memo in an encoded file; and the last button reloads the encoded file into the second memo, decoding it. In this example, after encoding the file, I've reloaded it in the first memo as a plain text file on the left, which of course is unreadable.

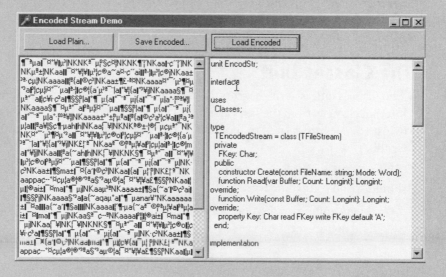

Continued on next page

Since we have the encoded stream class available, the code of this program is very similar to that of any other program using streams. For example, here is the method used to save the encoded file (you can compare its code to that of earlier examples based on streams):

```
procedure TFormEncode.BtnSaveEncodedClick(Sender: TObject);
var
  EncStr: TEncodedStream;
begin
  if SaveDialog1.Execute then
  begin
    EncStr := TEncodedStream.Create(SaveDialog1.Filename, fmCreate);
    try
      Memo1.Lines.SaveToStream (EncStr);
    finally
      EncStr.Free;
    end;
  end;
end;
```

Summarizing the Core VCL and BaseCLX Units

We've spent most of the space of this chapter discussing the classes of a single unit of the library, Classes. This unit is certainly important, but it is not the only core unit of the library (although there aren't many others). In this section, I'm providing an overview of these units and their content.

The Classes Unit

The Classes unit is at the heart of both VCL and CLX libraries, and though it sees many internal changes from the last version of Delphi, there is little new for the average users. (Most changes are related to modified IDE integration and are meant for expert component writers.)

Here is a list of what you can find in the Classes unit, a unit that every Delphi programmer should spend some time with:

- Many enumerated types, the standard method pointer types (including TNotifyEvent), and many exception classes.

- Core library classes, including TPersistent and TComponent but also TBasicAction and TBasicActionLink.

- List classes, including TList, TThreadList (a thread-safe version of the list), TInterfaceList (a list of interfaces, used internally), TCollection, TCollectionItem, TOwnedCollection (which is simply a collection with an owner), TStrings, and TStringList.

- All the stream classes I discussed in the previous section but won't list here again. There are also the TFiler, TReader, and TWriter classes and a TParser class used internally for DFM parsing.

- Utility classes, such as TBits for binary manipulation and a few utility routines (for example, point and rectangle constructors, and string list manipulation routines such as LineStart and ExtractStrings). There are also many registration classes, to notify the system of the existence of components, classes, special utility functions you can replace, and much more.

- The TDataModule class, a simple object container alternative to a form. Data modules can contain only nonvisual components and are generally used in database and Web applications.

NOTE In past versions of Delphi, the TDataModule class was defined in the Forms unit; now it has been moved to the Classes unit. This was done to eliminate the code overhead of the GUI classes from non-visual applications (for example, Web server modules) and to better separate non-portable Windows code from OS-independent classes, such as TDataModule. Other changes relate to the data modules, for example, to allow the creation of Web applications with multiple data modules, something not possible in Delphi 5.

- New interface-related classes, such as TInterfacedPersistent, aimed at providing further support for interfaces. This particular class allows Delphi code to hold onto a reference to a TPersistent object or any descendent implementing interfaces, and is a core element of the new support for interfaced objects in the Object Inspector (see Chapter 11 for an example).

- The new TRecall class, used to maintain a temporary copy of an object, particularly useful for graphical-based resources.

- The new TClassFinder class used for finding a registered class instead of the FindClass method.

- The TThread class, which provides the core to operating system–independent support for multithreaded applications.

Other Core Units

Other units that are part of the RTL package are not directly used by typical Delphi programmers as often as Classes. Here is a list:

- The TypInfo unit includes support for Accessing RTTI information for published properties, as we've seen in the section "Accessing Properties by Name."

- The SyncObjs unit contains a few generic classes for thread synchronization.

Of course, the RTL package also includes the units with functions and procedures discussed in the preceding chapter, such as Math, SysUtils, Variants, VarUtils, StrUtils, DateUtils, and so on.

What's Next?

As we have seen in this chapter, the Delphi class library has a few root classes that play a considerable role and that you should learn to leverage to the maximum possible extent. Some programmers tend to become expert on the components they use every day, and this is important, but without understanding the core classes (and ideas such as ownership and streaming), you'll have a tough time grasping the full power of Delphi.

Of course, in this book, we also need to discuss visual and database classes, which I will do in the next chapter. Now that we've seen all the base elements of Delphi (language, RTL, core classes), we are ready to discuss the development of real applications with this tool.

Part II of the book, which starts with the next chapter, is fully devoted to examples of the use of the various components, particularly visual components with the development of the user interface. We'll start with the advanced use of traditional controls and menus, discuss the actions architecture, cover the TForm class, and then examine toolbars, status bars, dialog boxes, and MDI applications in later chapters. Then we'll move to the development of database applications in Part III of the book.

PART II

Visual Programming

CHAPTER 6

Controls: VCL Versus VisualCLX

- VCL versus VisualCLX

- TControl, TWinControl, and TWidgetControl

- An overview of the standard components

- Basic and advanced menu construction

- Modifying the system menu

- Graphics in menus and list boxes

- OwnerDraw and styles

Now that you've been introduced to the Delphi environment and have seen an overview of the Object Pascal language and the base elements of component library, we are ready to delve into the second part of the book: the use of components and the development of the user interface of applications. This is really what Delphi is about. Visual programming using components is the key feature of this development environment.

Delphi comes with a large number of ready-to-use components. I won't describe every component in detail, examining each of its properties and methods; if you need this information, you can find it in the Help system. The aim of Part II of this book is to show you how to use some of the advanced features offered by the Delphi predefined components to build applications and to discuss specific programming techniques.

I'll start with a comparison of the VCL and VisualCLX libraries available in Delphi 6 and a coverage of the core classes (particularly TControl). Then I'll try to list all the various visual components you have, because choosing the right basic controls is often a way to get into a project faster.

VCL versus VisualCLX

As we've seen in the last chapter, Delphi 6 introduces the new CLX library alongside the traditional VCL library. There are certainly many differences, even in the use of the RTL and code library classes, between developing programs specifically for Windows or with a cross-platform attitude, but the user interface portion is where differences are most striking.

The visual portion of VCL is a wrapper of the Window API. It includes wrappers of the native Windows controls (like buttons and edit boxes), of the common controls (like tree views and list views), plus a bunch of native Delphi controls bound to the Windows concept of a window. There is also a TCanvas class that wraps the basic graphic calls, so you can easily paint on the surface of a window.

VisualCLX, the visual portion of CLX, is a wrapper of the Qt (pronounced "cute") library. It includes wrappers of the native Qt widgets, which range from basic to advanced controls, very similar to Windows' own standard and common controls. It includes also painting support using another, similar, TCanvas class. Qt is a C++ class library, developed by Trolltech (www.trolltech.com), a Norwegian company with a strong relationship with Borland.

On Linux, Qt is one of the de facto standard user-interface libraries and is the basis of the KDE desktop environment. On Windows, Qt provides an alternative to the use of the native APIs. In fact, unlike VCL, which provides a wrapper to the native controls, Qt provides an alternate implementation to those controls. This allows programs to be truly portable, as there are no hidden differences created by the operating system (and that the operating system vendor can introduce behind the scenes). It also allows us to avoid an extra layer; CLX on top of Qt on top of Windows native controls suggests three layers, but in fact there are two layers in each solution (CLX controls on top of Qt, VCL controls on top of Windows).

NOTE   Distributing Qt applications on Windows implies the distribution of the Qt library itself (something you can generally take for granted on the Linux platform). Distributing the Qt libraries with a professional application (as opposed to an open source project) generally implies paying a license to Trolltech. If you use Delphi or Kylix to build Qt applications, however, Borland has already paid the license to Trolltech for you. However, you must use the CLX classes wrapping Qt: If you use the Qt classes directly, you apparently still owe the license to Qt, even when using Delphi or Kylix.

Technically, there are huge differences behind the scenes between a native Windows application built with VCL and a portable Qt program developed with VisualCLX. Suffice to say that at the low level, Windows uses API function calls and messages to communicate with controls, while Qt uses class methods and direct method callbacks and has no internal messages. Technically, the Qt classes offer a high-level object-oriented architecture, while the Windows API is still bound to its C legacy and a message-based system dated 1985 (when Windows was released). VCL offers an object-oriented abstraction on top of a low-level API, while VisualCLX remaps an already high-level interface into a more *familiar* class library.

NOTE   To be honest, Microsoft has apparently reached the point of starting to abandon the traditional low-level Windows API for a native high-level class library, part of the dotNet architecture. Of course, this change won't happen overnight, but new high-level user-interface technologies might be introduced only in dotNet. Actually, dotNet consists of multiple technologies, including a virtual machine or runtime interpreter, a low-level nonvisual RTL, and a class framework for visual stuff (partially overlapping with VCL. If having a new visual class library on top of the Windows API might be of little use to programmers already using a modern class library (like VCL) other areas of dotNet would be of interest to Delphi programmers. So far, Borland has released no official statement regarding possible support for the dotNet byte code and virtual machine, or other areas of the future Microsoft operating system offering.

Having a familiar class library on top of a totally new platform is the advantage for Delphi programmers of using VisualCLX on Linux. This implies that the two class libraries, CLX and VCL, are very similar for their users, even if they are very different internally, as I mentioned. From the outside, a button is an object of the TButton class for both libraries, and it has more or less the same set of methods, properties, and events. In many occasions, you can recompile your existing programs for the new class library in a matter of minutes, if they don't map directly to low-level APIs.

Delphi 6 Dual Libraries Support

Delphi 6 has full support for both libraries at design time and at run time. As you start developing a new application, you can use the File ➤ New Application command to create a new VCL-based program and File ➤ New CLX Application for a new CLX-based program. After giving one of these two commands, Delphi's IDE will create a VCL or CLX design-time form and update the Component Palette so that it displays only the visual components compatible with the type of application you've selected (see Figure 6.1 for a comparison). In fact, you cannot place a VCL button into a CLX form, and you cannot even mix forms of the libraries within a single executable file. In other words, the user interface of every application must be built using exclusively one of the two libraries, which (aside from the technical implications) actually makes a lot of sense to me.

FIGURE 6.1:

A comparison of the first three pages of the Component Palette for a CXL-based application (above) and a VCL-based application (below)

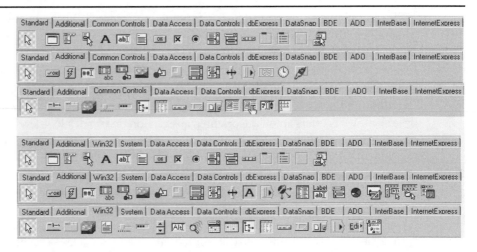

If you haven't already done so, I suggest you to try experimenting with the creation of a CLX application, looking at the available controls and trying to use them. You'll find very few differences in the use of the components, and if you have been using Delphi for some time, you'll probably be immediately adept with CLX.

Same Classes, Different Units

One of the cornerstones of the source-code compatibility between CLX and VCL code is that fact that similar classes in the two libraries have exactly the same class name. Each library has a class called TButton representing a push button; the methods and properties are so similar, this code will work with both libraries:

```
with TButton.Create (Self) do
begin
  SetBounds (20, 20, 80, 35);
```

```
    Caption := 'New';
    Parent := Self;
  end;
```

The two TButton classes have the same name, and this is possible because they are saved in two different units, called StdCtrls and QStdCtrls. Of course, you cannot have the two components available at design time in the palette, as the Delphi IDE can register only components with unique names. The entire VisualCLX library is defined by units corresponding to the VCL units, but with the letter *Q* as a prefix—so there is a QForms unit, a QDialogs unit, a QGraphics unit, and so on. There are also a few peculiar ones, such as the QStyle unit, that have no correspondence in VCL.

Notice that there are no compile settings or other hidden techniques to distinguish between the two libraries; what matters is the set of units referenced in the code. Remember that these references must be consistent, as you cannot mix visual controls of the two libraries in a single form and not even in a single program.

DFM and XFM

As you create a form at design time, this is saved to a form definition file. Traditional VCL applications use the DFM extension, which stands for Delphi form module. CLX applications use the XFM extension, which stands for cross-platform (i.e., *X*) form modules. The actual format of DFM or XFM files, which can be based on a textual or binary representation, is identical. A form module is the result of streaming the form and its components, and the two libraries share the streaming code, so they produce a fairly similar effect.

So the reason for having two different extensions doesn't lie in internal compiler tricks or incompatible formats. It is merely an indication to programmers and to the IDE of the type of components you should expect to find within that definition (as this indication is *not* included in the file itself).

If you want to convert a DFM file into an XFM file, you can simply rename the file. However, expect to find some differences in the properties, events, and available components, so that reopening the form definition for a different library will probably cause quite a few warnings.

TIP   Apparently Delphi's IDE chooses the active library only by looking at the extension of the form module, ignoring the references in the **uses** statements. For this reason, do change the extension if you plan using CLX. On Kylix, a different extension is pretty useless, because any form is opened in the IDE as a CLX form, regardless of the extension. On Linux, there is only the Qt-based CLX library, which is both the cross-platform *and* the native library.

As an example, I've built two simple identical applications, LibComp and QLibComp (available on this book's CD-ROM), with only a few components and a single event handler. Listing 6.1 presents the textual form definitions for two applications, built using the same steps in the Delphi 6 IDE, after choosing a CLX or VCL application. I've marked out differences in bold; as you can see, there are very few, most relating to the form and its font. The OldCreateOrder is a legacy property, used for compatibility with Delphi 3 and older code; standard colors have different names; and CLX saves the scrollbars' ranges.

Listing 6.1:   **An XFM file (left) and an equivalent DFM file (right)**

```
object Form1: TForm1                object Form1: TForm1
  Left = 192                          Left = 192
  Top = 107                           Top = 107
  Width = 350                         Width = 350
  Height = 210                        Height = 210
  Caption = 'QLibComp'                Caption = 'LibComp'
  Color = clBackground                Color = clBtnFace
  VertScrollBar.Range = 161           Font.Charset = DEFAULT_CHARSET
  HorzScrollBar.Range = 297           Font.Color = clWindowText
                                      Font.Height = -11
                                      Font.Name = 'MS Sans Serif'
                                      Font.Style = []
  TextHeight = 13                     TextHeight = 13
  TextWidth = 6                       OldCreateOrder = False
  PixelsPerInch = 96                  PixelsPerInch = 96
  object Button1: TButton             object Button1: TButton
    Left = 56                           Left = 56
    Top = 64                            Top = 64
    Width = 75                          Width = 75
    Height = 25                         Height = 25
    Caption = 'Add'                     Caption = 'Add'
    TabOrder = 0                        TabOrder = 0
    OnClick = Button1Click              OnClick = Button1Click
  end                                 end
  object Edit1: TEdit                 object Edit1: TEdit
    Left = 40                           Left = 40
    Top = 32                            Top = 32
    Width = 105                          Width = 105
    Height = 21                         Height = 21
    TabOrder = 1                        TabOrder = 1
    Text = 'my name'                    Text = 'my name'
  end                                 end
  object ListBox1: TListBox           object ListBox1: TListBox
    Left = 176                          Left = 176
    Top = 32                            Top = 32
    Width = 121                          Width = 121
    Height = 129                        Height = 129
    Rows = 3                            ItemHeight = 13
    Items.Strings = (                   Items.Strings = (
```

```
        'marco'                        'marco'
        'john'                         'john'
        'helen')                       'helen')
      TabOrder = 2                   TabOrder = 2
    end                            end
  end                            end
```

uses Statements

By looking at the source code of the two examples, the differences are even less relevant, as they simply relate to the uses statements. The form of the CLX application has the following initial code:

```
unit QLibCompForm;
interface
uses
  SysUtils, Types, Classes, QGraphics, QControls, QForms, QDialogs, QStdCtrls;
```

The form of the VCL program has the traditional uses statement:

```
unit LibCompForm;
interface
uses
  Windows, Messages, SysUtils, Variants, Classes, Graphics, Controls, Forms,
  Dialogs, StdCtrls;
```

The code of the class and of the only event handler is absolutely identical. Of course, the classic compiler directive {$R *.dfm} is replaced by {$R *.xfm} in the CLX version of the program.

Disabling the Dual Library Help Support

In Delphi 6, when you press the F1 key in the editor asking for help on a routine, class, or method of the Delphi library, you'll usually get a choice between the VCL and CLX declarations of the same feature. You'll need to make a choice to proceed to the related help page, which can be quite annoying after a while (especially as the two pages are often identical).

If you don't care about CLX and are planning to use only VCL (or vice versa), you can disable this alternative by choosing the Help ➤ Customize command, removing everything with *CLX* in the name from Contents, Index, and Link, and saving the project. Then restart the Delphi IDE, and the Help engine won't bother asking you about CLX any more. Of course, don't forget to add those help files again in case you decide to start using CLX.

Choosing a Visual Library

Because you have two different user interface libraries available in Delphi 6, you'll have to choose one for each *visual* application. You must evaluate multiple criteria to come to the proper decision, which isn't always easy.

The first criterion is portability. If running your program on Windows and on Linux, with the same user interface, is a major concern to you, using CLX will probably make your life simpler and let you keep a single source code file with very limited IFDEFs. The same applies if you consider Linux to be (or possibly become) your key platform. Instead, if most of your users are on Windows and you just want to extend your offering with a Linux version, you might want to keep a dual VCL/CLX system. This probably implies two different sets of source code files, or too many for IFDEFs.

In fact, another criterion is the native look-and-feel. By using CLX on Windows, some of the controls will behave slightly differently than users will expect—at least expert users. For a simple user interface (edits, buttons, grids), this probably won't matter much, but if you have many tree view and list view controls, the differences will be quite clear. On the other hand, with CLX you'll be able to let your users select a look-and-feel of their choice, different from the basic Windows look, and use it consistently across platforms.

Using native controls implies also that as soon as you get a new version of the Windows operating system, your application will (probably) adapt to it. This is good for the user, but might cause you a lot of headaches in case of incompatibilities. Differences in the Microsoft common controls library over the last few years have been a major source of frustration for Windows programmers in general, including Delphi programmers.

Another criterion is the deployment: If you use CLX, you'll have to ship your Windows program with the Qt libraries, which are not commonly available on Windows systems.

Finally, I've done a little testing, and it seems that the speed of VCL and CLX applications is similar. I've tried creating a thousand components, showing them on screen, and the speed differences are few, with a slight advantage for the VCL-based solution. You can try them out with the LibSpeed and QLibSpeed applications on the companion CD.

Running It on Linux

So the real issue of choosing the library resolves to the importance of Linux for you and your users. What is very important to notice is that, if you create a CLX application, you'll be able to recompile it unchanged (with the exact source code) with Kylix producing a native Linux application.

As an example, I've recompiled the QLibComp example introduced earlier, and you can see it running in Figure 6.2, where you can also see the Kylix IDE in action on a KDE 2 SuSE system.

FIGURE 6.2:

An application written with CLX can be directly recompiled under Linux with Kylix (displayed in the background).

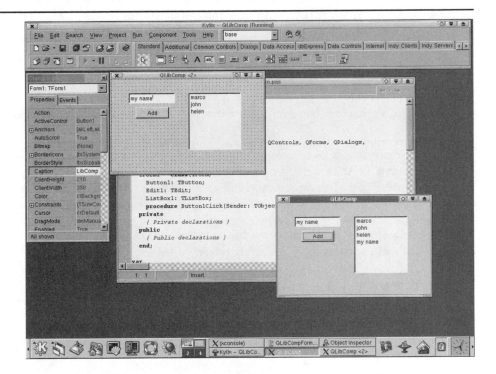

Conditional Compilation for Libraries

If you want to keep a single source code file but compile with VCL on Windows and CXL on Linux, you can use platform-specific symbols (such as $IFDEF LINUX) to distinguish the two situations in case of conditional compilation. But what if you want to be able to compile a portion of code for both libraries on Windows?

You can either define a symbol of your own, and use conditional compilation, or (at times) test for the presence of identifiers that exist only in VCL or CLX only, as in:

```
{$IF Declared(QForms)}
  ...CLX-specific code
{$IFEND}
```

Converting Existing Applications

Besides starting with new CLX applications, you might want to convert some of your existing VCL applications to the new class library. There are a series of operations you have to do, without any specific help from the Delphi IDE:

- You'll have to rename the DFM file as XFM and update all of the {$R *.DFM} statements as {$R *.XFM}.

- You'll have to update all of the uses statements of your program (in the units and project files) to refer to the CLX units instead of the VCL units. Notice that by missing even a few, you'll bump into trouble when running your application.

TIP   To prevent a CLX application from compiling if it contains references to VCL units, you can move the VCL units to a different directory under lib and avoid including this folder in your search path. This way, eventual leftover references to VCL units will cause a "Unit not found" error.

Table 6.1 is a comparison of the names of the visual VCL and CLX units, excluding the database portion and some rarely referenced units:

TABLE 6.1: Names of Equivalent VCL and CLX Units

VCL	CLX
ActnList	QActnList
Buttons	QButtons
Clipbrd	QClipbrd
ComCtrls	QComCtrls
Consts	QConsts
Controls	QControls
Dialogs	QDialogs
ExtCtrls	QExtCtrls
Forms	QForms
Graphics	QGraphics
Grids	QGrids
ImgList	QImgList
Menus	QMenus
Printers	QPrinters
Search	QSearch
StdCtrls	QStdCtrls

You might also convert references to Windows and Messages into references to the Qt unit. Some Windows data structures are now also available in the Types unit (see Chapter 4, "The Run-Time Library," for details), so you might have to add it to your CLX programs. Notice, however, that the QTypes unit is not the CLX version of VCL's Types unit; these two units are totally unrelated.

WARNING   Watch out for your **uses** statements! If you happen to compile a project that includes a CLX form, but fail to update the project unit, leaving a reference to the VCL Forms unit there, your program will run but stop immediately. The reason is that no VCL form was created, so the program terminated right away. In other cases, trying to create a CLX form within a VCL application will cause run-time errors. Finally, the Delphi IDE might inappropriately add references to **uses** statements of the wrong library, so you end up with a single **uses** statement referring to the same unit for both, but only the second of the two will be effective. This rarely prevents the program from compiling, but you won't be able to run it.

The VclToClx Helper Tool

As a helper in converting some of my own programs, I've written a simple unit-replacement tool, called VclToClx and available with its complete source code in the `Tools` folder of the book CD and on my Web site.

The program converts unit names, based on a configuration file, and fixes the DFM issue, by renaming the DFM files to XFM and fixing the references in the source code. The program is quite naive, as it doesn't really parse the source code, but simply looks for the occurrences of the unit names followed by a comma or semicolon, as happens in a uses statement. It also requires that the unit name is preceded by a space, but of course you can modify the program to look for a comma. Don't skip this extra test; otherwise the Forms unit will be turned to QForms, but the QForms unit will be converted again to QQForms!

TControl and Derived Classes

In the preceding chapter, I discussed the base classes of the Delphi library, focusing particularly on the TComponent class. One of the most important subclasses of TComponent is TControl, which corresponds to visual components. This base class is available both in CLX and VCL and defines general concepts, such as the position and the size of the control, the parent control hosting it, and more. For an actual implementation, though, you have to refer to its two subclasses. In VCL these are TWinControl and TGraphicControl; in CLX they are TWidget-Control and TGraphicControl. Here are their key features:

- *Window-based controls* (also called *windowed controls*) are visual components based on an operating-system window. A TWinControl in VCL has a window handle, a number referring to an internal Windows structure. A TWidgetControl in CLX has a Qt handle, a reference to the internal Qt object. From a user perspective, windowed controls can receive the input focus, and some of them can contain other controls. This is the biggest group of components in the Delphi library. We can further divide windowed controls in two groups: wrappers of native controls of Windows or Qt, and custom controls, which generally inherit from TCustomControl.

- *Graphical controls* (also called *nonwindowed controls*) are visual components that are not based on an operating-system window. Therefore, they have no handle, cannot receive the focus, and cannot contain other controls. These controls inherit from TGraphicControl and are painted by their parent form, which sends them mouse-related and other events. Examples of nonwindowed controls are the Label and SpeedButton components. There are just a few controls in this group, which were critical to minimizing the use of system resources in the early days of Delphi (on 16-bit Windows). Using graphical controls to save Windows resources is still quite useful on Win9*x*/Me, which has pushed the system limits higher but hasn't fully gotten rid of them (unlike Windows NT/2000).

A Short History of Windows Controls

You might have asked yourself where the idea of using components for Windows programming came from. The answer is simple: Windows itself has some components, usually called controls. A *control* is technically a predefined window that has a specific behavior and some styles and is capable of responding to specific messages. These controls were the first step in the direction of component development. The second step was probably Visual Basic controls, and the third step is Delphi components. (Actually, Microsoft's third step was its ActiveX technology, which is now followed by the dotNet framework, which is more or less at the level of the VCL controls.)

Windows 3.1 had six kinds of predefined controls, which were generally used in dialog boxes. Still used in Win32, they are buttons (push buttons, check boxes, and radio buttons), static labels, edit fields, list boxes, combo boxes, and scroll bars. Windows 95 added new predefined components, such as the list view, the status bar, the spin button, the progress bar, the tab control, and many others. Win32 developers can use the standard common controls provided by the system, and Delphi developers have the further advantage of having corresponding easy-to-use components.

As we have seen, Qt offers to CLX comparable basic and common controls, and even if there are internal differences, the Delphi libraries exposing those controls provide wrappers that can minimize those differences. VCL, in fact, literally wraps Windows predefined controls in some of its basic components. A Delphi wrapper class—for example, TEdit—simply surfaces the capabilities of the underlying Windows control, making it easier to use. However, Delphi adds nothing to the capabilities of this control. In Windows 95/98, an edit or memo control has a physical limit of 32 KB of text, and this limit is retained by the Delphi component.

Continued on next page

Why hasn't Borland overcome this limit? Why can't we change the color of a button? Simply because by replacing a Windows control with a custom version, we would lose the close connection with the operating system. Suppose Microsoft improves some of the controls in the next version of Windows. If we use our own version of the component, the application we build won't have the new features. By using controls that are based on the operating-system capabilities, instead, our programs have the opportunity to migrate through different versions of the OS and retain all the features provided by the specific version. This doesn't apply to the use of Qt, of course, but you have the advantage of being able to have an identical application based on the same source code running on Linux.

Note that wrapping an existing Windows or Qt control is an effective way of reusing code and also helps reduce the size of your compiled program. Implementing yet another button control from scratch requires custom code in your application, while a wrapper around the OS-supplied button control requires less code and makes use of system code shared by many applications.

Parent and Controls

The Parent property of a control indicates which other control is responsible for displaying it. When you drop a component into a form in the Form Designer, the form will become both parent and owner of the new control. But if you drop the component inside a Panel, ScrollBox, or any other *container* component, this will become its parent, while the form will still be the owner of the control.

When you create the control at run time, you'll need to set the owner (using the Create constructor parameter); but you must also set the Parent property, or the control won't be visible.

Like the Owner property, the Parent property has an inverse. The Controls array, in fact, lists all of the controls parented by the current one, numbered from 0 to ControlsCount - 1. You can scan this property to operate on all of the controls hosted by another one, eventually using a recursive method that operates on the controls parented by each subcontrol.

Properties Related to Control Size and Position

Some of the properties introduced by TControl and common to all controls are those related to size and position. The position of a control is determined by its Left and Top properties, its size by the Height and Width properties. Technically, all components have a position, because when you reopen an existing form at design time, you want to be able to see the icons for the nonvisual components in exactly the position where you've placed them. This position is visible in the form file.

As you change any of the positional or size properties, you end up calling the single `Set-Bounds` method. So any time you need to change two or more of these properties at once, calling `SetBounds` directly will speed up the program. Another method, `BoundsRect`, returns the rectangle bounding of the control and corresponds to accessing those four properties.

An important feature of the position of a component is that, like any other coordinate, it always relates to the client area of its parent component (indicated by its `Parent` property). For a form, the client area is the surface included within its borders (excluding the borders themselves). It would have been messy to work in screen coordinates, although there are some ready-to-use methods that convert the coordinates between the form and the screen and vice versa.

Note, however, that the coordinates of a control are always relative to the parent control, such as a form or another *container* component. If you place a panel in a form, and a button in a panel, the coordinates of the button relate to the panel and not to the form containing the panel. In fact, in this case, the parent component of the button is the panel.

Activation and Visibility Properties

There are two basic properties you can use to let the user activate or hide a component. The simpler is the `Enabled` property. When a component is disabled (when `Enabled` is set to False), usually some visual hint indicates this state to the user. At design time, the "disabled" property does not always have an effect, but at run time, disabled components are generally grayed.

For a more radical approach, you can completely hide a component, either by using the corresponding `Hide` method or by setting its `Visible` property to False. Be aware, however, that reading the status of the `Visible` property does not tell you whether the control is actually visible. In fact, if the container of a control is hidden, even if the control is set to `Visible`, you cannot see it. For this reason, there is another property, `Showing`, which is a run-time and read-only property. You can read the value of `Showing` to know whether the control is really visible to the user; that is, if it is visible, its parent control is also visible, the parent control of the parent control is also visible, and so on.

Fonts

Two properties often used to customize the user interface of a component are `Color` and `Font`. Several properties are related to the color. The `Color` property itself usually refers to the background color of the component. Also, there is a `Color` property for fonts and many other graphic elements. Many components also have a `ParentColor` and a `ParentFont` property, indicating whether the control should use the same font and color as its parent component, which is usually the form. You can use these properties to change the font of each control on a form by setting only the `Font` property of the form itself.

When you set a font, either by entering values for the attributes of the property in the Object Inspector or by using the standard font selection dialog box, you can choose one of the fonts installed in the system. The fact that Delphi allows you to use all the fonts installed on your system has both advantages and drawbacks. The main advantage is that if you have a number of nice fonts installed, your program can use any of them. The drawback is that if you distribute your application, these fonts might not be available on your users' computers.

If your program uses a font that your user doesn't have, Windows will select some other font to use in its place. A program's carefully formatted output can be ruined by the font substitution. For this reason, you should probably rely only on standard Windows fonts (such as MS Sans Serif, System, Arial, Times New Roman, and so on).

Colors

There are various ways to set the value of a color. The type of this property is TColor. For properties of this type, you can choose a value from a series of predefined name constants or enter a value directly. The constants for colors include clBlue, clSilver, clWhite, clGreen, clRed, and many others.

TIP   Delphi 6 adds four new standard colors: clMoneyGreen, clSkyBlue, clCream, and clMedGray.

As a better alternative, you can use one of the colors used by the system to denote the status of given elements. These sets of colors are different in VCL and CLX. VCL includes predefined Windows colors such as the background of a window (clWindow), the color of the text of a highlighted menu (clHightlightText), the active caption (clActiveCaption), and the ubiquitous button face color (clBtnFace).

CLX includes a different and incompatible set of system colors, including clBackground, which is the standard color of a form; clBase, used by edit boxes and other visual controls; clActiveForeground, the foreground color for active controls; and clDisabledBase, the background color for disabled text controls. All the color constants mentioned here are listed in VCL and CLX Help files under the "TColor type" topic.

Another option is to specify a TColor as a number (a 4-byte hexadecimal value) instead of using a predefined value. If you use this approach, you should know that the low three bytes of this number represent RGB color intensities for blue, green, and red, respectively. For example, the value $00FF0000 corresponds to a pure blue color, the value $0000FF00 to green, the value $000000FF to red, the value $00000000 to black, and the value $00FFFFFF to white. By specifying intermediate values, you can obtain any of 16 million possible colors.

Instead of specifying these hexadecimal values directly, you should use the Windows RGB function, which has three parameters, all ranging from 0 to 255. The first indicates the amount of red, the second the amount of green, and the last the amount of blue. Using the RGB function makes programs generally more readable than using a single hexadecimal constant. Actually, RGB is *almost* a Windows API function. It is defined by the Windows-related units and not by Delphi units, but a similar function does not exist in the Windows API. In C, there is a macro that has the same name and effect, so this is a welcome addition to the Pascal interface to Windows. RGB is not available on CLX, so I've written my own version as:

```
function RGB (red, green, blue: Byte): Cardinal;
begin
  Result := blue + green * 256 + red * 256 * 256;
end;
```

The highest-order byte of the TColor type is used to indicate which palette should be searched for the closest matching color, but palettes are too advanced a topic to discuss here. (Sophisticated imaging programs also use this byte to carry transparency information for each display element on the screen.) Regarding palettes and color matching, note that Windows sometimes replaces an arbitrary color with the closest available solid color, at least in video modes that use a palette. This is always the case with fonts, lines, and so on. At other times, Windows uses a dithering technique to mimic the requested color by drawing a tight pattern of pixels with the available colors. In 16-color (VGA) adapters and at higher resolutions, you often end up seeing strange patterns of pixels of different colors and not the color you had in mind.

The *TWinControl* Class (VCL)

In Windows, most elements of the user interface are windows. From a user standpoint, a window is a portion of the screen surrounded by a border, having a caption and usually a system menu. But technically speaking, a window is an entry in an internal system table, often corresponding to an element visible on the screen that has some associated code. Most of these windows have the role of controls; others are temporarily created by the system (for example, to show a pull-down menu). Still other windows are created by the application but remain hidden from the user and are used only as a way to receive a message (for example, nonblocking sockets use windows to communicate with the system).

The common denominator of all windows is that they are known by the Windows system and refer to a function for their behavior; each time something happens in the system, a notification message is sent to the proper window, which responds by executing some code. Each window of the system, in fact, has an associated function (generally called its *window procedure*), which handles the various messages the window is interested in.

In Delphi, any TWinControl class can override the WndProc method or define a new value for the WindowProc property. Interesting Windows messages, however, can be better tracked by providing specific message handlers. Even better, VCL converts these lower-level messages into events. In short, Delphi allows us to work at a high level, making application development easier, but still allows us to go low-level when this is required.

Notice also that creating a WinControl doesn't automatically create its corresponding Window handle. Delphi, in fact, uses a lazy initialization technique, so that the low control is only created when this is required, generally as soon as a method accesses the Handle property. The get method for this property the first time calls HandleNeeded, which eventually calls CreateHandle... and so on reaching CreateWnd, CreateParams, and CreateWindowHandle (the sequence is rather complex, and I don't think it is necessary to know it in detail). At the opposite end, you can keep an existing (perhaps invisible) control in memory but destroy its window handle, to save system resources.

The *TWidgetControl* Class (CLX)

In CLX, every TWidgetControl has an internal Qt object, referenced using the Handle property. This property has the same name as the corresponding Windows property, but it is totally different behind the scenes.

The Qt object is generally owned by the TWidgetControl, which automatically frees the object when it is destroyed. The class also uses delayed construction, as you can see in the InitWidget method, similar to CreateWindow. However it is also possible to create a widget around an existing Qt object: in this case, the widget won't own the Qt object and won't destroy it. The behavior is indicated by the OwnHandle property.

Actually each VisualCLX component has two associated C++ objects, the Qt Handle and the Qt Hook, which is the object receiving the system events. With the current Qt design, this has to be a C++ object, which acts as an intermediary to the event handlers of the Object Pascal control. The HookEvents method associates the hook object to the CLX control.

Differently from Windows, Qt defines two different types of events:

- *Events* are the translation of input or system events (such as key press, mouse move, and paint).

- *Signals* are internal component events (corresponding to VCL internal or abstract operations, such as OnClick and OnChange)

NOTE   In CLX there is a seldom-used EventHandler method, which corresponds more or less to the WndProc method of VCL.

Opening the Component Tool Box

So you want to write a Delphi application. You open a new Delphi project and find yourself faced with a large number of components. The problem is that for every operation, there are multiple alternatives. For example, you can show a list of values using a list box, a combo box, a radio group, a string grid, a list view, or even a tree view if there is a hierarchical order. Which should you use? That's difficult to say. There are many considerations, depending on what you want your application to do. For this reason, I've provided a highly condensed summary of alternative options for a few common tasks.

NOTE   For some of the controls described in the following sections, Delphi also includes a data-aware version, usually indicated by the *DB* prefix. As you'll see in Chapter 13, "Delphi's Database Architecture," the DB version of a control typically serves a role similar to that of its "standard" equivalent; but the properties and the ways you use it are often quite different. For example, in an Edit control you use the `Text` property, while in a DBEdit component you access the `Value` of the related field object.

The Text Input Components

Although a form or component can handle keyboard input directly, using the `OnKeyPress` event, this isn't a common operation. Windows provides ready-to-use controls you can use to get string input and even build a simple text editor. Delphi has several slightly different components in this area.

The Edit Component

The Edit component allows the user to enter a single line of text. You can also display a single line of text with a Label or a StaticText control, but these components are generally used only for fixed text or program-generated output, not for input. In CLX, there is also a native LCD digit control you can use to display numbers.

The Edit component uses the `Text` property, whereas many other controls use the `Caption` property to refer to the text they display. The only condition you can impose on user input is the number of characters to accept. If you want to accept only specific characters, you can handle the `OnKeyPress` event of the edit box. For example, we can write a method that tests whether the character is a number or the Backspace key (which has a numerical value of 8). If it's not, we change the value of the key to the null character (#0), so that it won't be processed by the edit control and will produce a warning beep:

```
procedure TForm1.Edit1KeyPress(
  Sender: TObject; var Key: Char);
begin
  // check if the key is a number or backspace
  if not (Key in ['0'..'9', #8]) then
  begin
    Key := #0;
    Beep;
  end;
end;
```

A minor difference of CLX is that the Edit control has no Undo mechanism built in. Another is that the `PasswordChar` property is *replaced* by the `EchoMode` property. You don't determine the character to display, but whether to echo the entered text or display an asterisk instead.

The New LabeledEdit Control

Delphi 6 adds a very nice control, called LabeledEdit, which is an Edit control with a label attached to it. The Label appears as a property of the compound control, which inherits from `TCustomEdit`.

I have to say this component is very handy, because it allows you to reduce the number of components on your forms, move them around more easily, and have a more standard layout for labels, particularly when they are placed above the edit box. The `EditLabel` property is connected with the subcomponent, which has the usual properties and events. Two more properties, `LabelPosition` and `LabelSpacing`, allow you to configure the relative positions of the two controls.

This component has been added to the ExtCtrls unit to demonstrate the use of subcomponents in the Object Inspector, which is a new feature of Delphi 6. I'll discuss the development of these components in Chapter 11, "Creating Components." Notice also that this component, along with all of the other new Delphi 6 components, is not (yet) available on CLX and on the first release of Kylix. However, we can expect all non–Windows-specific additions to VCL, including subcomponents in general and the LabeledEdit control in particular, to be available in the next release of Kylix.

The MaskEdit Component

To customize the input of an edit box further, you can use the MaskEdit component, which has an `EditMask` property. This is a string indicating for each character whether it should be uppercase, lowercase, or a number, and other similar conditions. You can see the editor of the `EditMask` property in Figure 6.3.

FIGURE 6.3:

The MaskEdit component's EditMask property editor

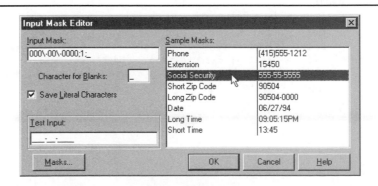

You can display any property's editor by selecting the property in the Object Inspector and clicking the ellipsis (…) button.

The Input Mask editor allows you to enter a mask, but it also asks you to indicate a character to be used as a placeholder for the input and to decide whether to save the *literals* present in the mask, together with the final string. For example, you can choose to display the parentheses around the area code of a phone number only as an input hint or to save them with the string holding the resulting number. These two entries in the Input Mask editor correspond to the last two fields of the mask (separated by semicolons).

Clicking the Masks button of the Mask Editor lets you choose predefined input masks for different countries.

The Memo and RichEdit Components

Both of the controls discussed so far allow a single line of input. The Memo component, by contrast, can host several lines of text but (on the Win95/98 platforms) still retains the 16-bit Windows text limit (32 KB) and allows only a single font for the entire text. You can work on the text of the memo line by line (using the Lines string list) or access the entire text at once (using the Text property).

If you want to host a large amount of text or change fonts and paragraph alignments, in VCL you should use the RichEdit control, a Win32 common control based on the RTF document format. You can find an example of a complete editor based on the RichEdit component among the sample programs that ship with Delphi. (The example is named RichEdit, too.)

The RichEdit component has a DefAttributes property indicating the default styles and a SelAttributes property indicating the style of the current selection. These two properties are not of the TFont type, but they are compatible with fonts, so we can use the Assign method to copy the value, as in the following code fragment:

```
procedure TForm1.Button1Click(Sender: TObject);
begin
  if RichEdit1.SelLength > 0 then
  begin
    FontDialog1.Font.Assign (RichEdit1.DefAttributes);
    if FontDialog1.Execute then
      RichEdit1.SelAttributes.Assign (FontDialog1.Font);
  end;
end;
```

The TextViewer CLX Control

Among all of the common controls, CLX and Qt lack a RichEdit control. However, they provide a full-blown HTML viewer, which is very powerful for displaying formatted text but not for typing it. This HTML viewer is embedded in two different controls, the single-page TextViewer control or the TextBrowser control with active links.

As a simple demo, I've added a memo and a text viewer to a CLX form and connected them so that everything you type on the memo is immediately displayed in the viewer. I've called the example HtmlEdit not because this is a real HTML editor, but because this is the simplest way I know of to build an HTML preview inside a program. The form of the program is visible at run time in Figure 6.4, while typing some text inside a cell of the table.

FIGURE 6.4:

The HtmlEdit example at run time: when you add new HTML text to the memo, you get an immediate preview.

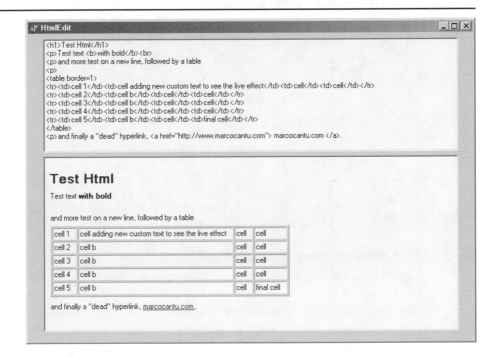

TIP   I originally built this example with Kylix on Linux. To port it to Windows and Delphi 6, all I had to do was to copy the files and recompile.

Selecting Options

There are two standard Windows controls that allow the user to choose different options, as well as controls for grouping sets of options.

The CheckBox and RadioButton Components

The first standard option-selecting control is the *check box*, which corresponds to an option that can be selected regardless of the status of other check boxes. Setting the `AllowGrayed` property of the check box allows you to display three different states (selected, not selected, and grayed), which alternate as a user clicks the check box.

The second type of control is the *radio button*, which corresponds to an exclusive selection. Two radio buttons on the same form or inside the same radio group container cannot be selected at the same time, and one of them should always be selected (as programmer, you are responsible for selecting one of the radio buttons at design time).

The GroupBox Components

To host several groups of radio buttons, you can use a GroupBox control to hold them together, both functionally and visually. To build a group box with radio buttons, simply place the GroupBox component on a form and then add the radio buttons to the group box.

You can handle the radio buttons individually, but it's easier to navigate through the array of controls owned by the group box, as discussed in the previous chapter. Here is a small code excerpt used to get the text of the selected radio button of a group:

```
var
  I: Integer;
  Text: string;
begin
  for I := 0 to GroupBox1.ControlCount - 1 do
    if (GroupBox1.Controls[I] as TRadioButton).Checked then
      Text := (GroupBox1.Controls[I] as TRadioButton).Caption;
```

The RadioGroup Component

Delphi has a similar component that can be used specifically for radio buttons: the RadioGroup component. A RadioGroup is a group box with some radio button *clones* painted inside it. The term *clone* in this context refers to the fact that the RadioGroup component is a single control, a single window, with elements similar to radio buttons painted on its surface.

Using the radio group is generally easier than using the group box, since the various items are part of a list, as in a list box. This is how you can get the text of the selected item:

```
Text := RadioGroup1.Items [RadioGroup1.ItemIndex];
```

Technically, a RadioGroup uses fewer resources and less memory, and it should be faster to create and paint. Also, the RadioGroup component can automatically align its radio buttons in one or more columns (as indicated by the `Columns` property), and you can easily add new choices at run time, by adding strings to the `Items` string list. By contrast, adding new radio buttons to a group box would be quite complex.

Lists

When you have many selections, radio buttons are not appropriate. The usual number of radio buttons is no more than five or six, to avoid cluttering the user interface; when you have more choices, you can use a list box or one of the other controls that display lists of items and allow the selection of one of them.

The ListBox Component

The selection of an item in a list box uses the `Items` and `ItemIndex` properties as in the code shown above for the RadioGroup control. If you need access to the text of selected list box items often, you can write a small wrapper function like this:

```
function SelText (List: TListBox): string;
var
  nItem: Integer;
begin
  nItem := List.ItemIndex;
  if nItem >= 0 then
    Result := List.Items [nItem]
  else
    Result := '';
end;
```

Another important feature is that by using the ListBox component, you can choose between allowing only a single selection, as in a group of radio buttons, and allowing multiple selections, as in a group of check boxes. You make this choice by specifying the value of the `MultiSelect` property. There are two kinds of multiple selections in Windows and in Delphi list boxes: *multiple selection* and *extended selection*. In the first case, a user selects multiple items simply by clicking them, while in the second case the user can use the Shift and Ctrl keys to select multiple consecutive or nonconsecutive items, respectively. This second choice is determined by the `ExtendedSelect` property.

For a multiple-selection list box, a program can retrieve information about the number of selected items by using the `SelCount` property, and it can determine which items are selected by examining the `Selected` array. This array of Boolean values has the same number of entries as the list box. For example, to concatenate all the selected items into a string, you can scan the `Selected` array as follows:

```
var
  SelItems: string;
  nItem: Integer;
begin
  SelItems := '';
  for nItem := 0 to ListBox1.Items.Count - 1 do
    if ListBox1.Selected [nItem] then
      SelItems := SelItems + ListBox1.Items[nItem] + ' ';
```

In CLX the ListBox can be configured to use a fixed number of columns and rows, using the `Columns`, `Row`, `ColumnLayout` and `RowLayout` properties. Of these, the VCL ListBox has only the `Columns` property.

The ComboBox Component

List boxes take up a lot of screen space, and they offer a fixed selection—that is, a user can choose only among the items in the list box and cannot enter any choice that the programmer did not specifically foresee.

You can solve both problems by using a ComboBox control, which combines an edit box and a drop-down list. The behavior of a ComboBox component changes a lot depending on the value of its `Style` property:

- The csDropDown style defines a typical combo box, which allows direct editing and displays a list box on request.

- The csDropDownList style defines a combo box that does not allow editing (but uses the keystrokes to select an item).

- The csSimple style defines a combo box that always displays the list box below it.

Note also that accessing the text of the selected value of a ComboBox is easier than doing the same operation for a list box, since you can simply use the `Text` property. A useful and common trick for combo boxes is to add a new element to the list when a user enters some text and presses the Enter key. The following method first tests whether the user has pressed that key, by looking for the character with the numeric (ASCII) value of 13. It then tests to make sure the text of the combo box is not empty and is not already in the list—if its position in the list is less than zero. Here is the code:

```
procedure TForm1.ComboBox1KeyPress(
  Sender: TObject; var Key: Char);
begin
  // if the user presses the Enter key
  if Key = Chr (13) then
    with ComboBox3 do
      if (Text <> '') and (Items.IndexOf (Text) < 0) then
        Items.Add (Text);
end;
```

NOTE   In CLX, the combo box can automatically add the text typed into the edit to the drop-down list, when the user presses the Enter key. Also, some events fire at different times than in VCL.

Delphi 6 includes two new events for the combo box. The OnCloseUp event corresponds to the closing of the drop-down list and complements the preexisting OnDropDown event. The OnSelect event fires only when the user selects something in the drop-down list, as opposed to typing in the edit portion.

Another very nice addition is the AutoComplete property. When it is set, the ComboBox component (and the ListBox, as well) automatically locates the string nearest to the one the user is entering, suggesting the final part of the text. The core of this feature, available also in CLX, is implemented in the TCustomListBox.KeyPress method.

The CheckListBox Component

Another extension of the list box control is represented by the CheckListBox component, a list box with each item preceded by a check box (as you can see in Figure 6.5). A user can select a single item of the list, but can also click the check boxes to toggle their status. This makes the CheckListBox a very good component for multiple selections or for highlighting the status of a series of independent items (as in a series of check boxes).

To check the current status of each item, you can use the Checked and the State array properties (use the latter if the check boxes can be grayed). Delphi 5 introduced the Item-Enabled array property, which you can use to enable or disable each item of the list. We'll use the CheckListBox in the DragList example, later in this chapter.

FIGURE 6.5:

The user interface of the CheckListBox control, basically a list of check boxes

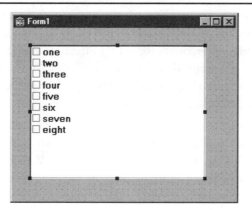

TIP Most of the list-based controls share a common and important feature. Each item of the list has an associated 32-bit value, usually indicated by the **TObject** type. This value can be used as a tag for each list item, and it's very useful for storing additional information along with each item. This approach is connected to a specific feature of the native Windows list box control, which offers four bytes of extra storage for each list box item. We'll use this feature in the ODList example later on in this chapter.

New Combo Boxes: ComboBoxEx and ColorBox

The ComboBoxEx (where *ex* stands for extended) is the wrapper of a new Win32 common controls, which extends the traditional combo box by allowing images to appear next to the items in the list. You attach an image list to the combo, and then select an image index for each item to display. The effect of this change is that the simple `Items` string list is replaced by a more complex collection, the `ItemsEx` property.

The ColorBox control is a new version of the combo box specifically aimed at selecting colors. You can use its `Style` property for choosing which groups of colors you want to see in the list (standard color, extended colors, system colors, and so on).

The ListView and TreeView Components

If you want an even more sophisticated list, you can use the ListView common control, which will make the user interface of your application look very modern. This component is slightly more complex to use, as described at the beginning of the next chapter, "Advanced VCL Controls." Other alternatives for listing values are the TreeView common control, which shows items in a hierarchical output, and the StringGrid control, which shows multiple elements for each line. The string grid control is described in the "Graphics in Delphi" bonus chapter, available on the companion CD.

If you use the common controls in your application, users will already know how to interact with them, and they will regard the user interface of your program as up to date. TreeView and ListView are the two key components of Windows Explorer, and you can assume that many users will be familiar with them, even more than with the traditional Windows controls. CLX adds also an IconView control, which parallels part of the features of the VCL ListView.

The New ValueListEditor Component

Delphi applications often use the name/value structure natively offered by string lists, which I discussed in the last chapter. Delphi 6 introduces a version of the StringGrid component specifically geared towards this type of string lists. The ValueListEditor has two columns where you can display and let the user edit the contents of a string list with name/value pairs, as you can see in Figure 6.6. This string list is indicated in the `Strings` property of the control.

FIGURE 6.6:

The NameValues example
has the new ValueListEditor
component, which shows
the name/value or key/
value pairs of a string list,
visible also in a plain memo.

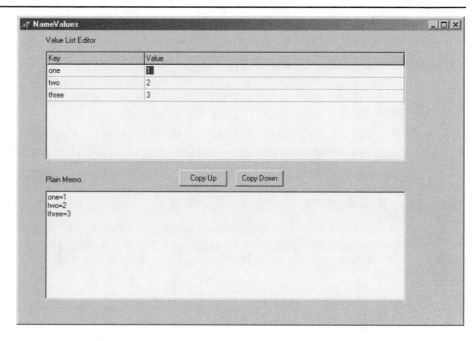

The power of this control lies in the fact you can customize the editing options for each position of the grid or for each key value, using the run-time-only `ItemProps` array property. For each item, you can indicate:

- Whether it is read-only
- The maximum number of characters of the string
- An edit mask (eventually requested in the `OnGetEditMask` event)
- The items of a drop-down pick list (eventually requested in the `OnGetPickList` event)
- The display of a button for showing an editing dialog (in the `OnEditButtonClick` event)

Needless to say, this behavior resembles what is available generally for string grids and the DBGrid control, but also the behavior of the Object Inspector.

The `ItemProps` property has to be set up at run time, by creating an object of the `TItemProp` class and assigning it to an index or a key of the string list. To have a default editor for each line, you can assign the same item property object multiple times. In the example, this shared editor sets an edit mask for up to three numbers:

```
procedure TForm1.FormCreate(Sender: TObject);
var
  I: Integer;
```

```
begin
  SharedItemProp := TItemProp.Create (ValueListEditor1);
  SharedItemProp.EditMask := '999;0; ';

  Memo1.Lines := ValueListEditor1.Strings;
  for I := 0 to ValueListEditor1.Strings.Count - 1 do
    ValueListEditor1.ItemProps [I] := SharedItemProp;
end;
```

Similar code has to be repeated in case the number of lines changes—for example, by adding new elements in the memo and copying them up to the value list:

```
procedure TForm1.ValueListEditor1StringsChange(Sender: TObject);
var
  I: Integer;
begin
  for I := 0 to ValueListEditor1.Strings.Count - 1 do
    if not Assigned (ValueListEditor1.ItemProps [I]) then
      ValueListEditor1.ItemProps [I] := SharedItemProp;
end;
```

NOTE   Apparently reassigning the same editor twice causes some trouble, so I've assigned the editor only to the lines not having already one.

Another property, KeyOptions, allows you to let the user also edit the keys (the names), add new entries, delete existing ones, and allow for duplicated names in the first portion of the string. Oddly enough, you cannot add new keys unless you also activate the edit options, which makes it hard to let the user add extra entries while preserving the names of the basic ones.

Ranges

Finally, there are a few components you can use to select values in a range. Ranges can be used for numeric input and for selecting an element in a list.

The ScrollBar Component

The stand-alone ScrollBar control is the original component of this group, but it is seldom used by itself. Scroll bars are usually associated with other components, such as list boxes and memo fields, or are associated directly with forms. In all these cases, the scroll bar can be considered part of the surface of the other components. For example, a form with a scroll bar is actually a form that has an area resembling a scroll bar painted on its border, a feature governed by a specific Windows style of the form window. By *resembling*, I mean that it is not technically a separate window of the ScrollBar component type. These "fake" scroll bars are usually controlled in Delphi using specific properties of the form and the other components hosting them.

The TrackBar and ProgressBar Components

Direct use of the ScrollBar component is quite rare, especially with the TrackBar component introduced with Windows 95, which is used to let a user select a value in a range. Among Win32 common controls is the companion ProgressBar control, which allows the program to output a value in a range, showing the progress of a lengthy operation.

The UpDown Component

Another related control is the UpDown component, which is usually connected to an edit box so that the user can either type a number in it or increase and decrease the number using the two small arrow buttons. To connect the two controls, you set the `Associate` property of the UpDown component. Nothing prevents you from using the UpDown component as a stand-alone control, displaying the current value in a label or in some other way.

> **NOTE** In CLX there is no UpDown control, but a SpinEdit that bundles an Edit with the UpDown in a single control.

The PageScroller Component

The Win32 PageScroller control is a container allowing you to scroll the internal control. For example, if you place a toolbar in the page scroller and the toolbar is larger than the available area, the PageScroller will display two small arrows on the side. Clicking these arrows will scroll the internal area. This component can be used as a scrollbar, but it also partially replaces the ScrollBox control.

The ScrollBox Component

The ScrollBox control represents a region of a form that can scroll independently from the rest of the surface. For this reason, the ScrollBox has two scrollbars used to move the embedded components. You can easily place other components inside a ScrollBox, as you do with a panel. In fact, a ScrollBox is basically a panel with scroll bars to move its internal surface, an interface element used in many Windows applications. When you have a form with many controls and a toolbar or status bar, you might use a ScrollBox to cover the central area of the form, leaving its toolbars and status bars outside of the scrolling region. By relying on the scrollbars of the form, in fact, you might allow the user to move the toolbar or status bar out of view, a very odd situation.

Handling the Input Focus

Using the `TabStop` and `TabOrder` properties available in most controls, you can specify the order in which controls will receive the input focus when the user presses the Tab key.

Instead of setting the tab order property of each component of a form manually, you can use the shortcut menu of the Form Designer to activate the Edit Tab Order dialog box, as shown in Figure 6.7.

FIGURE 6.7:

The Edit Tab Order
dialog box

Besides these basics settings, it is important to know that each time a component receives or loses the input focus, it receives a corresponding OnEnter or OnExit event. This allows you to fine-tune and customize the order of the user operations. Some of these techniques are demonstrated by the InFocus example, which creates a fairly typical password-login window. Its form has three edit boxes with labels indicating their meaning, as shown in Figure 6.8. At the bottom of the window is a status area with prompts guiding the user. Each item needs to be entered in sequence.

FIGURE 6.8:

The InFocus example at
run time

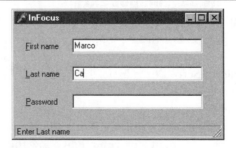

For the output of the status information, I've used the StatusBar component, with a single output area (obtained by setting its SimplePanel property to True). Here is a summary of the properties for this example. Notice the & character in the labels, indicating a shortcut key, and the connection of these labels with corresponding edit boxes (using the FocusControl property):

```
object FocusForm: TFocusForm
  ActiveControl = EditFirstName
  Caption = 'InFocus'
  object Label1: TLabel
    Caption = '&First name'
    FocusControl = EditFirstName
  end
  object EditFirstName: TEdit
    OnEnter = GlobalEnter
    OnExit = EditFirstNameExit
  end
  object Label2: TLabel
    Caption = '&Last name'
    FocusControl = EditLastName
  end
  object EditLastName: TEdit
    OnEnter = GlobalEnter
  end
  object Label3: TLabel
    Caption = '&Password'
    FocusControl = EditPassword
  end
  object EditPassword: TEdit
    PasswordChar = '*'
    OnEnter = GlobalEnter
  end
  object StatusBar1: TStatusBar
    SimplePanel = True
  end
end
```

The program is very simple and does only two operations. The first is to identify, in the status bar, the edit control that has the focus. It does this by handling the controls' OnEnter event, possibly using a single generic event handler to avoid repetitive code. In the example, instead of storing some extra information for each edit box, I've checked each control of the form to determine which label is connected to the current edit box (indicated by the Sender parameter):

```
procedure TFocusForm.GlobalEnter(Sender: TObject);
var
  I: Integer;
begin
  for I := 0 to ControlCount - 1 do
    // if the control is a label
```

```
    if (Controls [I] is TLabel) and
      // and the label is connected to the current edit box
      (TLabel(Controls[I]).FocusControl = Sender) then
    // copy the text, leaving off the initial & character
    StatusBar1.SimpleText := 'Enter ' +
      Copy (TLabel(Controls[I]).Caption, 2, 1000);
  end;
```

The second event handler of the form relates to the OnExit event of the first edit box. If the control is left empty, it refuses to release the input focus and sets it back before showing a message to the user. The methods also look for a given input value, automatically filling the second edit box and moving the focus directly to the third one:

```
procedure TFocusForm.EditFirstNameExit(Sender: TObject);
begin
  if EditFirstName.Text = '' then
  begin
    // don't let the user get out
    EditFirstName.SetFocus;
    MessageDlg ('First name is required', mtError, [mbOK], 0);
  end
  else if EditFirstName.Text = 'Admin' then
  begin
    // fill the second edit and jump to the third
    EditLastName.Text := 'Admin';
    EditPassword.SetFocus;
  end;
end;
```

TIP   The CLX version of this example has exactly the same code and is available as the QInFocus program. The same happens for most of the other examples of this chapter. Notice that some of the examples are quite complex, but I rarely had to touch the code at all.

Working with Menus

Working with menus and menu items is generally quite simple. This section offers only some very brief notes and a few more advanced examples. The first thing to keep in mind about menu items is that they can serve different purposes:

Commands   are menu items used to execute an action.

State-setters   are menu items used to toggle an option on and off, to change the state of a particular element. These commands usually have a check mark on the left to indicate they are active. In Delphi 6 you can automatically obtain this behavior using the handy AutoCheck property.

Radio items   have a round check mark and are grouped to represent alternative selections, like radio buttons. To obtain radio menu items, simply set the RadioItem property to True and set the GroupIndex property for the alternative menu items to the same value.

Dialog menu items   cause a dialog box to appear and are usually indicated by an ellipsis (three dots) after the text.

As you enter new elements in the Menu Designer, Delphi creates a new component for each menu item and lists it in the Object Inspector (although nothing is added to the form). To name each component, Delphi uses the caption you enter and appends a number (so that *Open* becomes Open1). Because Delphi removes spaces and other special characters in the caption when it creates the name, and the menu item separators are set up using a hyphen as caption, these items would have an empty name. For this reason Delphi adds the letter *N* to the name, appending the number and generating items called N1, N2, and so on.

> **WARNING**   Do not use the Break property, which is used to lay out a pull-down menu on multiple columns. The mbMenuBarBreak value indicates that this item will be displayed in a second or subsequent line; the mbMenuBreak value that this item will be added to a second or subsequent column of the pull-down.

Accelerator Keys

Since Delphi 5, you don't need to enter the & character in the Caption of a menu item; it provides an automatic accelerator key if you omit one. Delphi's automatic accelerator-key system can also figure out if you have entered conflicting accelerator keys and fix them on-the-fly. This doesn't mean you should stop adding custom accelerator keys with the & character, because the automatic system simply uses the first available letter, and it doesn't follow the default standards. You might also find better mnemonic keys than those chosen by the automatic system.

This feature is controlled by the AutoHotkeys property, which is available in the main menu component and in each of the pull-down menus and menu items. In the main menu, this property defaults to maAutomatic, while in the pull-downs and menu items it defaults to maParent, so that the value you set for the main menu component will be used automatically by all the subitems, unless they have a specific value of maAutomatic or maManual.

The engine behind this system is the RethinkHotkeys method of the TMenuItem class, and the companion InternalRethinkHotkeys. There is also a RethinkLines method, which checks whether a pull-down has two consecutive separators or begins or ends with a separator. In all these cases, the separator is automatically removed.

One of the reasons Delphi includes this feature is the Integrated Translation Environment (ITE). When you need to translate the menu of an application, it is convenient if you don't have to deal with the accelerator keys, or at least if you don't have to worry about whether two items on the same menu conflict. Having a system that can automatically resolve similar problems is definitely an advantage. Another motivation was Delphi's IDE itself. With all the dynamically loaded packages that install menu items in the IDE main menu or in pop-up menus, and with different packages loaded in different versions of the product, it's next to impossible to get nonconflicting accelerator-key selections in each menu. That is why this mechanism isn't a wizard that does static analysis of your menus at design time; it was created to deal with the real problem of managing menus created dynamically at run time.

WARNING This feature is certainly very handy, but because it is active by default, it can break existing code. I had to modify two of this chapter's program examples, between the Delphi 4 and Delphi 5 edition of the book, just to avoid run-time errors caused by this change. The problem is that I use the caption in the code, and the extra & broke my code. The change was quite simple, though: All I had to do was to set the `AutoHotkeys` property of the main menu component to maManual.

Pop-Up Menus and the *OnContextPopup* Event

Besides the MainMenu component, you can use the similar PopupMenu component. This is typically displayed when the user right-clicks a component that uses the given pop-up menu as the value for its `PopupMenu` property.

However, besides connecting the pop-up menu to a component with the corresponding property, you can call its `Popup` method, which requires the position of the pop-up in screen coordinates. The proper values can be obtained by converting a local point to a screen point with the `ClientToScreen` method of the local component, in this code fragment a label:

```
procedure TForm1.Label3MouseDown(Sender: TObject;
  Button: TMouseButton; Shift: TShiftState; X, Y: Integer);
var
  ScreenPoint: TPoint;
begin
  // if some condition applies...
  if Button = mbRight then
  begin
    ScreenPoint := Label3.ClientToScreen (Point (X, Y));
    PopupMenu1.Popup (ScreenPoint.X, ScreenPoint.Y)
  end;
end;
```

An alternative approach is the use of the OnContextMenu event. This event, introduced in Delphi 5, fires when a user right-clicks a component—exactly what we've traced above with the test if Button = mbRight. The advantage is that the same event is also fired in response to a Shift+F10 key combination, as well as by any other user-input methods defined by Windows Accessibility options or hardware (including the shortcut-menu key of some Windows-compatible keyboards). We can use this event to fire a pop-up menu with little code:

```
procedure TFormPopup.Label1ContextPopup(Sender: TObject;
  MousePos: TPoint; var Handled: Boolean);
var
  ScreenPoint: TPoint;
begin
  // add dynamic items
  PopupMenu2.Items.Add (NewLine);
  PopupMenu2.Items.Add (NewItem (TimeToStr (Now), 0, False, True, nil, 0, ''));
  // show popup
  ScreenPoint := ClientToScreen (MousePos);
  PopupMenu2.Popup (ScreenPoint.X, ScreenPoint.Y);
  Handled := True;
  // remove dynamic items
  PopupMenu2.Items [4].Free;
  PopupMenu2.Items [3].Free;
end;
```

This example adds some dynamic behavior to the shortcut menu, adding a temporary item indicating when the pop-up menu is displayed. This is not particularly useful, but I've done it to highlight that if you need to display a plain pop-up menu, you can easily use the PopupMenu property of the control in question or one of its parent controls. Handling the OnContextMenu event makes sense only when you want to do some extra processing.

The Handled parameter is preinitialized to False, so that if you do nothing in the event handler, the normal pop-up menu processing will occur. If you do something in your event handler to replace the normal pop-up menu processing (such as popping up a dialog or a customized menu, as in this case), you should set Handled to True and the system will stop processing the message. Setting Handled to True should be fairly rare, as you'll generally handle the OnContextPopup to dynamically create or customize the pop-up menu, but then you can let the default handler actually show the menu.

The handler of an OnContextPopup event isn't limited to displaying a pop-up menu. It can do any other operation, such as directly display a dialog box. Here is an example of a right-click operation used to change the color of the control:

```
procedure TFormPopup.Label2ContextPopup(Sender: TObject;
  MousePos: TPoint; var Handled: Boolean);
begin
```

```
    ColorDialog1.Color := Label2.Color;
    if ColorDialog1.Execute then
      Label2.Color := ColorDialog1.Color;
    Handled := True;
  end;
```

All the code snippets of this section are available in the simple CustPop example for VCL and QCustPop for CLX, on the book's companion CD.

Creating Menu Items Dynamically

Besides defining the structure of a menu with the Menu Designer and modifying the status of the items using the Checked, Visible, and Caption properties, you can create an entire menu or portions of one at run time. This makes sense, for example, when you have many repetitive items, or when the menu items depend on some system configuration or user permissions.

The basic idea is that each object of the TMenuItem class—which Delphi uses for both menu items and pull-down menus—contains a list of menu items. Each of these items has the same structure, in a kind of recursive way. A pull-down menu has a list of submenus, and each submenu has a list of submenus, each with its own list of submenus, and so on. The properties you can use to explore the structure of an existing menu are Items, which contains the actual list of menu items, and Count, which contains the number of subitems. Adding new menu items or entire pull-down menus to an existing menu is fairly easy, particularly if you can write a single event handler for all of them.

This is demonstrated by the DynaMenu example (and its QDynaMenu counterpart), which also illustrates the use of menu check marks, radio items, and many other features of menus that aren't described in detail in the text. As soon as you start this program, it creates a new pull-down with menu items used to change the font size of a big label hosted by the form. Instead of creating a bunch of menu items with captions indicating sizes ranging from 8 to 48, you can let the program do this repetitive work for you.

The new pull-down menu should be inserted in the Items property of the MainMenu1 component. You can calculate the position by asking the MainMenu component for the previous pull-down menu:

```
procedure TFormColorText.FormCreate(Sender: TObject);
var
  PullDown, Item: TMenuItem;
  Position, I: Integer;
begin
  // create the new pull-down menu
  PullDown := TMenuItem.Create (Self);
  PullDown.AutoHotkeys := maManual;
  PullDown.Caption := '&Size';
  PullDown.OnClick := SizeClick;
  // compute the position and add it
```

```
Position := MainMenu1.Items.IndexOf (Options1);
MainMenu1.Items.Insert (Position + 1, PullDown);
// create menu items for various sizes
I := 8;
while I <= 48 do
begin
  // create the new item
  Item := TMenuItem.Create (Self);
  Item.Caption := IntToStr (I);
  // make it a radio item
  Item.GroupIndex := 1;
  Item.RadioItem := True;
  // handle click and insert
  Item.OnClick := SizeItemClick;
  PullDown.Insert (PullDown.Count, Item);
  I := I + 4;
end;
// add extra item at the end
Item := TMenuItem.Create (Self);
Item.Caption := 'More...';
// make it a radio item
Item.GroupIndex := 1;
Item.RadioItem := True;
// handle it by showing the font selection dialog
Item.OnClick := Font1Click;
PullDown.Insert (PullDown.Count, Item);
end;
```

As you can see in the preceding code, the menu items are created in a while loop, setting the radio item style and calling the Insert method with the number of items as a parameter to add each item at the end of the pull-down. At the end, the program adds one extra item, which is used to set a different size than those listed. The OnClick event of this last menu item is handled by the Font1Click method (also connected to a specific menu item), which displays the font selection dialog box. You can see the dynamic menu in Figure 6.9.

FIGURE 6.9:

The Size pull-down menu of the DynaMenu example is created at run time, along with all of its menu items.

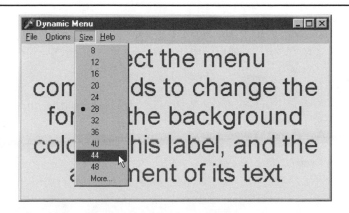

Because the program uses the `Caption` of the new items dynamically, we should either disable the `AutoHotkeys` property of the main menu component, or disable this feature for the pull-down menu we are going to add (and thus automatically disable it for the menu items). This is what I've done in the code above by setting the `AutoHotkeys` property of the dynamically created pull-down component to maManual. An alternative approach is to let the menu display the automatic captions and then call the new `StripHotkeys` function before converting the caption to a number. There is also a new `GetHotkey` function, which returns the *active* character of the caption.

The handler for the `OnClick` event of these dynamically created menu items uses the caption of the `Sender` menu item to set the size of the font:

```
procedure TFormColorText.SizeItemClick(Sender: TObject);
begin
  with Sender as TMenuItem do
    Label1.Font.Size := StrToInt (Caption);
end;
```

This code doesn't set the proper radio-item mark next to the selected item, because the user can select a new size also by changing the font. The proper radio item is checked in the `OnClick` event handler of the entire pull-down menu, which is connected just after the pull-down is created and activated just before showing the pull-down. The code scans the items of the pull-down menu (the `Sender` object) and checks whether the caption matches the current `Size` of the font. If no match is found, the program checks the last menu item, to indicate that a different size is active:

```
procedure TFormColorText.SizeClick (Sender: TObject);
var
  I: Integer;
  Found: Boolean;
begin
  Found := False;
  with Sender as TMenuItem do
  begin
    // look for a match, skipping the last item
    for I := 0 to Count - 2 do
      if StrToInt (Items [I].Caption) = Label1.Font.Size then
      begin
        Items [I].Checked := True;
        Found := True;
        System.Break; // skip the rest of the loop
      end;
    if not Found then
      Items [Count - 1].Checked := True;
  end;
end;
```

When you want to create a menu or a menu item dynamically, you can use the corresponding components, as I've done in the DynaMenu and QDynaMenu examples. As an alternative, you can also use some global functions available in the Menus unit: `NewMenu`, `NewPopupMenu`, `NewSubMenu`, `NewItem`, and `NewLine`.

Using Menu Images

In Delphi it is very easy to improve a program's user interface by adding images to menu items. This is becoming common in Windows applications, and it's very nice that Borland has added all the required support, making the development of graphical menu items trivial.

All you have to do is add an image list control to the form, add a series of bitmaps to the image list, connect the image list to the menu using its `Images` property, and set the proper `ImageIndex` property for the menu items. You can see the effect of these simple operations in Figure 6.10. (You can also associate a bitmap with the menu item directly, using the `Bitmap` property.)

FIGURE 6.10:

The simple graphical menu of the MenuImg example

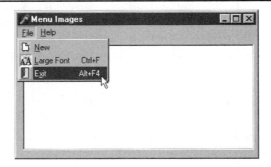

TIP   The definition of images for menus is quite flexible, as it allows you to associate an image list with any specific pull-down menu (and even a specific menu item) using the `SubMenuImages` property. Having a specific and smaller image list for each pull-down menu, instead of one single huge image list for the entire menu, allows for more run-time customization of an application.

To create the image list, double-click the component, activating the corresponding editor (shown in Figure 6.11), then import existing bitmap or icon files. You can actually prepare a single large bitmap and let the image editor divide it according to the `Height` and `Width` properties of the ImageList component, which refer to the size of the individual bitmaps in the list.

FIGURE 6.11:

The Image List editor, with
the bitmaps of the
MenuImg example

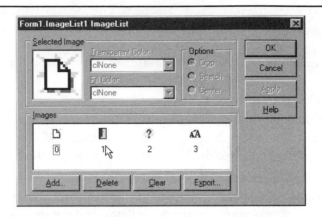

> **TIP**   As an alternative, you can use the series of images that ship with Delphi and are stored by
> default in the `\Program Files\Common Files\Borland Shared\Images\Buttons` direc-
> tory. Each bitmap contains both an "enabled" and a "disabled" image. As you import them,
> the Image List editor will ask you whether to split them in two, a suggestion you should
> accept. This operation adds to the image list a normal image and a disabled one, which is not
> generally used (as it can be built automatically when needed). For this reason I generally delete
> the disabled part of the bitmap from the image list.

The program's code is very simple. The only element I want to emphasize is that if you set
the Checked property of a menu item with an image instead of displaying a check mark, the
item paints its image as "sunken" or "recessed." You can see this in the Large Font menu of
the MenuImg example in Figure 6.10. Here is the code for that menu item selection:

```
procedure TForm1.LargeFont1Click(Sender: TObject);
begin
  if Memo1.Font.Size = 8 then
    Memo1.Font.Size := 12
  else
    Memo1.Font.Size := 8;
  // changes the image style near the item
  LargeFont1.Checked := not LargeFont1.Checked;
end;
```

> **WARNING**   To make the CLX version of the program, QMenuImg, display the bitmaps properly, I had to
> reimport them. Simply converting the Image List component data didn't work.

Customizing the System Menu

In some circumstances, it is interesting to add menu commands to the system menu itself, instead of (or besides) having a menu bar. This might be useful for secondary windows, toolboxes, windows requiring a large area on the screen, and "quick-and-dirty" applications. Adding a single menu item to the system menu is straightforward:

```
AppendMenu (GetSystemMenu (Handle, FALSE), MF_SEPARATOR, 0, '');
AppendMenu (GetSystemMenu (Handle, FALSE), MF_STRING, idSysAbout, '&About...');
```

This code fragment (extracted from the OnCreate event handler of the SysMenu example) adds a separator and a new item to the system menu item. The GetSystemMenu API function, which requires as a parameter the handle of the form, returns a handle to the system menu. The AppendMenu API function is a general-purpose function you can use to add menu items or complete pull-down menus to any menu (the menu bar, the system menu, or an existing pull-down menu). When adding a menu item, you have to specify its text and a numeric identifier. In the example I've defined this identifier as:

```
const idSysAbout = 100;
```

Adding a menu item to the system menu is easy, but how can we handle its selection? Selecting a normal menu generates the wm_Command Windows message. This is handled internally by Delphi, which activates the OnClick event of the corresponding menu item component. The selection of system menu commands, instead, generates a wm_SysCommand message, which is passed by Delphi to the default handler. Windows usually needs to do something in response to a system menu command.

We can intercept this command and check to see whether the command identifier (passed in the CmdType field of the TWmSysCommand parameter) of the menu item is idSysAbout. Since there isn't a corresponding event in Delphi, we have to define a new message-response method for the form class:

```
public
  procedure WMSysCommand (var Msg: TMessage);
    message wm_SysCommand;
```

The code of this procedure is not very complex. We just need to check whether the command is our own and call the default handler:

```
procedure TForm1.WMSysCommand (var Msg: TWMSysCommand);
begin
  if Msg.CmdType = idSysAbout then
    ShowMessage ('Mastering Delphi: SysMenu example');
  inherited;
end;
```

To build a more complex system menu, instead of adding and handling each menu item as we have just done, we can follow a different approach. Just add a MainMenu component to the form, create its structure (any structure will do), and write the proper event handlers. Then reset the value of the Menu property of the form, removing the menu bar.

Now we can add some code to the SysMenu example to add each of the items from the hidden menu to the system menu. This operation takes place when the button of the form is clicked. The corresponding handler uses generic code that doesn't depend on the structure of the menu we are appending to the system menu:

```
procedure TForm1.Button1Click(Sender: TObject);
var
  I: Integer;
begin
  // add a separator
  AppendMenu (GetSystemMenu (Handle, FALSE), MF_SEPARATOR, 0, '');
  // add the main menu to the system menu
  with MainMenu1 do
    for I := 0 to Items.Count - 1 do
      AppendMenu (GetSystemMenu (Self.Handle, FALSE),
        mf_Popup, Items[I].Handle, PChar (Items[I].Caption));
  // disable the button
  Button1.Enabled := False;
end;
```

TIP   This code uses the expression Self.Handle to access the handle of the form. This is required because we are currently working on the MainMenu1 component, as specified by the with statement.

The menu flag used in this case, mf_Popup, indicates that we are adding a pull-down menu. In this function call, the fourth parameter is interpreted as the handle of the pull-down menu we are adding (in the previous example, we passed the identifier of the menu, instead). Since we are adding to the system menu items with submenus, the final structure of the system menu will have two levels, as you can see in Figure 6.12.

FIGURE 6.12:

The second-level system menu items of the SysMenu example are the result of copying a complete main menu to the system menu.

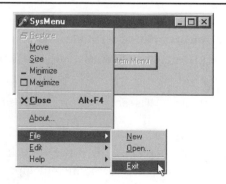

WARNING The Windows API uses the terms *pop-up menu* and *pull-down menu* interchangeably. This is really odd, because most of us use the terms to mean different things. Pop-up menus are shortcut menus, and pull-down menus are the secondary menus of the menu bar. Apparently, Microsoft uses the terms in this way because the two elements are implemented with the same kind of internal windows; the fact that they are two distinct user-interface elements is probably something that was later conceptually built over a single basic internal structure.

Once you have added the menu items to the system menu, you need to handle them. Of course, you can check for each menu item in the WMSysCommand method, or you can try building a smarter approach. Since in Delphi it is easier to write a handler for the OnClick event of each item, we can look for the item corresponding to the given identifier in the menu structure. Delphi helps us by providing a FindItem method.

When (and if) we have found a main menu item that corresponds to the item selected in the system menu, we can call its Click method (which invokes the OnClick handler). Here is the code I've added to the WMSysCommand method:

```
var
  Item: TMenuItem;
begin
  ...
  Item := MainMenu1.FindItem (Msg.CmdType, fkCommand);
  if Item <> nil then
    Item.Click;
```

In this code, the CmdType field of the message structure that is passed to the WMSysCommand procedure holds the command of the menu item being called.

You can also use a simple if or case statement to handle one of the system menu's predefined menu items that have special codes for this identifier, such as sc_Close, sc_Minimize, sc_Maximize, and so on. For more information, you can see the description of the wm_SysCommand message in the Windows API Help file.

This application works but has one glitch. If you click the right mouse button over the Taskbar icon representing the application, you get a plain system menu (actually different from the default one). The reason is that this system menu belongs to a different window, the window of the Application global object. I'll discuss the Application object, and update this example to make it work with the Taskbar button, in Chapter 9, "Working with Forms."

NOTE Because this program uses low-level Windows features (API calls and messages), it is not possible to compile it with CLX, so there is no Qt version of this example.

Owner-Draw Controls and Styles

Let's return briefly to menu graphics. Besides using an ImageList to add glyphs to the menu items, you can turn a menu into a completely graphical element, using the owner-draw technique. The same technique also works for other controls, such as list boxes. In Windows, the system is usually responsible for painting buttons, list boxes, edit boxes, menu items, and similar elements. Basically, these controls know how to paint themselves. As an alternative, however, the system allows the owner of these controls, generally a form, to paint them. This technique, available for buttons, list boxes, combo boxes, and menu items, is called *owner-draw*.

In VCL, the situation is slightly more complex. The components can take care of painting themselves in this case (as in the TBitBtn class for bitmap buttons) and possibly activate corresponding events. The system sends the request for painting to the owner (usually the form), and the form forwards the event back to the proper control, firing its event handlers.

In CLX, some of the controls, such as ListBoxes and ComboBoxes, surface events very similar to Windows owner-draw, but menus lack them. The native approach of Qt is to use styles to determine the graphical behavior of all of the controls in the system, of a specific application, or of a given control. I'll introduce styles shortly, later in this section.

NOTE   Most of the Win32 common controls have support for the owner-draw technique, generally called *custom drawing*. You can fully customize the appearance of a ListView, TreeView, TabControl, PageControl, HeaderControl, StatusBar, and ToolBar. The ToolBar, ListView, and TreeView controls also support *advanced* custom drawing, a more fine-tuned drawing capability introduced by Microsoft in the latest versions of the Win32 common controls library. The downside to owner-draw is that when the Windows user interface style changes in the future (and it always does), your owner-draw controls that fit in perfectly with the current user interface styles will look outdated and out of place. Since you are creating a custom user interface, you'll need to keep it updated yourself. By contrast, if you use the standard output of the controls, your applications will automatically adapt to a new version of such controls.

Owner-Draw Menu Items

VCL makes the development of graphical menu items quite simple compared to the traditional approach of the Windows API: You set the OwnerDraw property of a menu item component to True and handle its OnMeasureItem and OnDrawItem events. This same feature is not available on CLX.

In the OnMeasureItem event, you can determine the size of the menu items. This event handler is activated once for each menu item when the pull-down menu is displayed and has two reference parameters you can set:

```
procedure ColorMeasureItem (Sender: TObject; ACanvas: TCanvas;
  var Width, Height: Integer);
```

The other parameter, ACanvas, is typically used to determine the height of the current font.

In the OnDrawItem event, you paint the actual image. This event handler is activated every time the item has to be repainted. This happens when Windows first displays the items and each time the status changes; for example, when the mouse moves over an item, it should become highlighted. In fact, to paint the menu items, we have to consider all the possibilities, including drawing the highlighted items with specific colors, drawing the check mark if required, and so on. Luckily enough, the Delphi event passes to the handler the Canvas where it should paint, the output rectangle, and the status of the item (selected or not):

```
procedure ColorDrawItem(Sender: TObject; ACanvas: TCanvas; ARect: TRect;
  Selected: Boolean);
```

In the ODMenu example, I'll handle the highlighted color, but skip other advanced aspects (such as the check marks). I've set the OwnerDraw property of the menu and written handlers for some of the menu items. To write a single handler for each event of the three color-related menu items, I've set their Tag property to the value of the actual color in the OnCreate event handler of the form. This makes the handler of the actual OnClick event of the items quite straightforward:

```
procedure TForm1.ColorClick(Sender: TObject);
begin
  ShapeDemo.Brush.Color := (Sender as TComponent).Tag
end;
```

The handler of the OnMeasureItem event doesn't depend on the actual items, but uses fixed values (different from the handler of the other pull-down). The most important portion of the code is in the handlers of the OnDrawItem events. For the color, we use the value of the tag to paint a rectangle of the given color, as you can see in Figure 6.13. Before doing this, however, we have to fill the background of the menu items (the rectangular area passed as a parameter) with the standard color for the menu (clMenu) or the selected menu items (clHighlight):

```
procedure TForm1.ColorDrawItem(Sender: TObject; ACanvas: TCanvas;
  ARect: TRect; Selected: Boolean);
begin
  // set the background color and draw it
  if Selected then
    ACanvas.Brush.Color := clHighlight
  else
    ACanvas.Brush.Color := clMenu;
  ACanvas.FillRect (ARect);
  // show the color
  ACanvas.Brush.Color := (Sender as TComponent).Tag;
  InflateRect (ARect, -5, -5);
  ACanvas.Rectangle (ARect.Left, ARect.Top, ARect.Right, ARect.Bottom);
end;
```

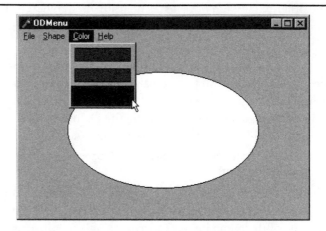

The three handlers for this event of the Shape pull-down menu items are all different,
although they use similar code:

```
procedure TForm1.Ellipse1DrawItem(Sender: TObject; ACanvas: TCanvas;
  ARect: TRect; Selected: Boolean);
begin
  // set the background color and draw it
  if Selected then
    ACanvas.Brush.Color := clHighlight
  else
    ACanvas.Brush.Color := clMenu;
  ACanvas.FillRect (ARect);
  // draw the ellipse
  ACanvas.Brush.Color := clWhite;
  InflateRect (ARect, -5, -5);
  ACanvas.Ellipse (ARect.Left, ARect.Top, ARect.Right, ARect.Bottom);
end;
```

NOTE   To accommodate the increasing number of states in the Windows 2000 user interface style,
since version 5, Delphi has included the `OnAdvancedDrawItem` event for menus.

A ListBox of Colors

As we have just seen for menus, list boxes have an owner-draw capability, which means a program can paint the items of a list box. The same support is provided for combo boxes and is
also available on CLX. To create an owner-draw list box, we set its `Style` property to lbOwn-
erDrawFixed or lbOwnerDrawVariable. The first value indicates that we are going to set the
height of the items of the list box by specifying the `ItemHeight` property and that this will be

the height of each and every item. The second owner-draw style indicates a list box with items of different heights; in this case, the component will trigger the `OnMeasureItem` event for each item, to ask the program for their heights.

In the ODList example (and its QODList version), I'll stick with the first, simpler, approach. The example stores color information along with the items of the list box and then draws the items in colors (instead of using a single color for the whole list).

The DFM or XFM file of every form, including this one, has a `TextHeight` attribute, which indicates the number of pixels required to display text. This is the value we should use for the `ItemHeight` property of the list box. An alternative solution is to compute this value at run time, so that if we later change the font at design time, we don't have to remember to set the height of the items accordingly.

NOTE   I've just described `TextHeight` as an *attribute* of the form, not a property. And in fact it isn't a property but a local value of the form. If it is not a property, you might ask, how does Delphi save it in the DFM file? Well, the answer is that Delphi's streaming mechanism is based on properties plus special *property clones* created by the `DefineProperties` method.

Since `TextHeight` is *not* a property, although it is listed in the form description, we cannot access it directly. Studying the VCL source code, I found that this value is computed by calling a private method of the form: `GetTextHeight`. Since it is private, we cannot call this function. What we can do is duplicate its code (which is actually quite simple) in the `FormCreate` method of the form, after selecting the font of the list box:

```
Canvas.Font := ListBox1.Font;
ListBox1.ItemHeight := Canvas.TextHeight('0');
```

The next thing we have to do is add some items to the list box. Since this is a list box of colors, we want to add color names to the `Items` of the list box and the corresponding color values to the `Objects` data storage related to each item of the list. Instead of adding the two values separately, I've written a procedure to add new items to the list:

```
procedure TODListForm.AddColors (Colors: array of TColor);
var
  I: Integer;
begin
  for I := Low (Colors) to High (Colors) do
    ListBox1.Items.AddObject (ColorToString (Colors[I]), TObject(Colors[I]));
end;
```

This method uses an open-array parameter, an array of an undetermined number of elements of the same type. For each item passed as a parameter, we add the name of the color to the list, and we add its value to the related data, by calling the AddObject method. To obtain the string corresponding to the color, we call the Delphi ColorToString function. This returns a string containing either the corresponding color constant, if any, or the hexadecimal value of the color. The color data is added to the list box after casting its value to the `TObject` data type (a four-byte reference), as required by the `AddObject` method.

> **TIP** Besides `ColorToString`, which converts a color value into the corresponding string with the identifier or the hexadecimal value, there is also a Delphi function to convert a properly formatted string into a color, `StringToColor`.

In the ODList example, this method is called in the `OnCreate` event handler of the form (after previously setting the height of the items):

```
AddColors ([clRed, clBlue, clYellow, clGreen, clFuchsia, clLime, clPurple,
   clGray, RGB (213, 23, 123), RGB (0, 0, 0), clAqua, clNavy, clOlive, clTeal]);
```

To compile the CLX version of this code, I've added to it the RGB function described earlier in the section "Colors." The code used to draw the items is not particularly complex. We simply retrieve the color associated with the item, set it as the color of the font, and then draw the text:

```
procedure TODListForm.ListBox1DrawItem(Control: TWinControl; Index: Integer;
  Rect: TRect; State: TOwnerDrawState);
begin
  with Control as TListbox do
  begin
    // erase
    Canvas.FillRect(Rect);
    // draw item
    Canvas.Font.Color := TColor (Items.Objects [Index]);
    Canvas.TextOut(Rect.Left, Rect.Top, Listbox1.Items[Index]);
  end;
end;
```

The system already sets the proper background color, so the selected item is displayed properly even without any extra code on our part. You can see an example of the output of this program at startup in Figure 6.14.

The example also allows you to add new items, by double-clicking the list box:

```
procedure TODListForm.ListBox1DblClick(Sender: TObject);
begin
  if ColorDialog1.Execute then
    AddColors ([ColorDialog1.Color]);
end;
```

If you try using this capability, you'll notice that some colors you add are turned into color names (one of the Delphi color constants) while others are converted into hexadecimal numbers.

The output of the ODList example, with a colored owner-draw list box

CLX Styles

In Windows, the system has full control of the user interface of the controls, unless the program takes over using owner-draw or other advanced techniques. In Qt (and in Linux in general), the user chooses the user interface style of the controls. A system will generally offer a few basic styles, such as the Windows look-and-feel, the Motif one, and others. A user can add also install new styles in the system and make them available to applications.

NOTE   The styles I'm discussing here refer to the user interface of the controls, not of the forms and their borders. This is generally configurable on Linux systems but is technically a separate element of the user interface.

Because this technique is embedded in Qt, it is also available on the Windows version of the library, and CLX makes it available to Delphi developers. The Application global object of CLX has a Style property, which can be used to set a custom style or a default one, indicated by the DefaultStyle subproperty. For example, you can select a Motif look-and-feel with this code:

```
Application.Style.DefaultStyle := dsMotif;
```

In the StylesDemo program, I've added, among various sample controls, a list box with the names of the default styles, as indicated in the TDefaultStyle enumeration, and this code for its OnDblClick event:

```
procedure TForm1.ListBox1DblClick(Sender: TObject);
begin
  Application.Style.DefaultStyle := TDefaultStyle (ListBox1.ItemIndex);
end;
```

The effect is that, by double-clicking the list box, you can change the current application style and immediately see its effect on screen, as demonstrated in Figure 6.15.

FIGURE 6.15:

The StylesDemo program, a Windows application currently with an unusual Motif layout

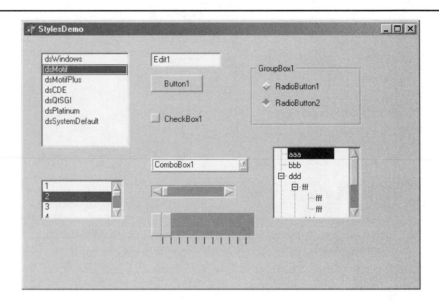

What's Next?

In this chapter, we have explored the foundations of the libraries available in Delphi for building user interfaces, the native-Windows VCL and the Qt-based CLX. We've discussed the TControl class, its properties, and its most important derived classes.

Then we've started to explore some of the basic components available in Delphi, looking at both libraries. These components correspond to the standard Windows controls and some of the common controls, and they are extremely common in applications. You've also seen how to create main menus and pop-up menus and how to add extra graphics to some of these controls.

The next step, however, is to explore in depth the elements of a complete user interface, discussing other common controls, multipage forms, action lists, and the new Delphi 6 Action Manager, to end up discussing technical details of forms. All of these topics will be covered in the next three chapters.

CHAPTER **7**

Advanced VCL Controls

- ListView and TreeView controls

- Multipage forms

- Pages and tabs

- Form-splitting techniques

- Control anchors

- A ToolBar and a StatusBar for the RichEdit control

- Customizing hints

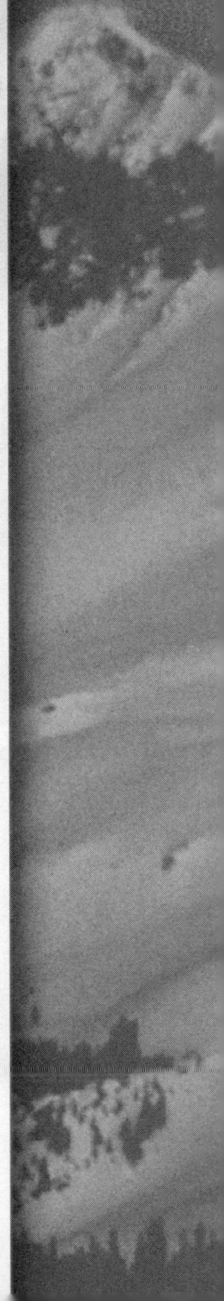

In the preceding chapter, I discussed the core concepts of the TControl class and its derived classes in the VCL and VisualCLX libraries. After that, I provided a sort of rapid tour of the key controls you can use to build a user interface, including editing components, lists, range selectors, and more.

This chapter provides more details on some of these components (such as the ListView and TreeView) and then discusses other controls used to define the overall design of a form, such as the PageControl, TabControl, and Splitter. The chapter also presents examples of splitting forms and resizing controls dynamically. These topics are not particularly complex, but it is worth examining their key concepts briefly.

After these components, I'll introduce toolbars and status bars, including the customization of hints and other slightly more advanced features. This will give us all the foundation material for the following chapter, which covers actions and the new action manager architecture of Delphi 6.

ListView and TreeView Controls

In Chapter 6, I introduced all the various visual controls you can use to display lists of values. The standard list box and combo box components are still very common, but they are often replaced by the more powerful ListView and TreeView controls. Again, these two controls are part of the Win32 common controls, stored in the ComCtl32.DLL library. Similar controls are available in Qt and VisualCLX.

A Graphical Reference List

When you use a ListView component, you can provide bitmaps both indicating the status of the element (for example, the selected item) and describing the contents of the item in a graphical way.

How do we connect the images to a list or tree? We need to refer to the ImageList component we've already used for the images of the menu. A ListView can actually have three image lists: one for the large icons (the LargeImages property), one for the small icons (the SmallImages property), and one used for the state of the items (the StateImages property). In the RefList example on the companion CD, I've set the first two properties using two different ImageList components.

Each of the items of the ListView has an ImageIndex, which refers to its image in the list. For this to work properly, the elements in the two image lists should follow the same order. When you have a fixed image list, you can add items to it using Delphi's ListView Item Editor, which is connected to the Items property. In this editor, you can define items and so-called subitems. The subitems are displayed only in the detailed view (when you set the vsReport value of the ViewStyle property) and are connected with the titles set in the Columns property.

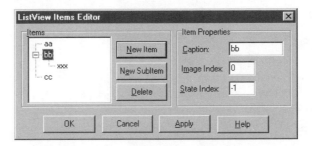

In my RefList example (a simple list of references to books, magazines, CD-ROMs, and Web sites), the items are stored to a file, since users of the program can edit the contents of the list, which are automatically saved as the program exits. This way, edits made by the user become persistent. Saving and loading the contents of a ListView is not trivial, since the TListItems type doesn't have an automatic mechanism to save the data. As an alternative simple approach, I've copied the data to and from a string list, using a custom format. The string list can then be saved to a file and reloaded with a single command.

The file format is simple, as you can see in the following saving code. For each item of the list, the program saves the caption on one line, the image index on another line (prefixed by the @ character), and the subitems on the following lines, indented with a tab character:

```
procedure TForm1.FormDestroy(Sender: TObject);
var
  I, J: Integer;
  List: TStringList;
begin
  // store the items
  List := TStringList.Create;
  try
    for I := 0 to ListView1.Items.Count - 1 do
    begin
      // save the caption
      List.Add (ListView1.Items[I].Caption);
      // save the index
      List.Add ('@' + IntToStr (ListView1.Items[I].ImageIndex));
      // save the subitems (indented)
      for J := 0 to ListView1.Items[I].SubItems.Count - 1 do
        List.Add (#9 + ListView1.Items[I].SubItems [J]);
    end;
    List.SaveToFile (ExtractFilePath (Application.ExeName) + 'Items.txt');
  finally
```

```
      List.Free;
    end;
  end;
```

The items are then reloaded in the FormCreate method:

```
procedure TForm1.FormCreate(Sender: TObject);
var
  List: TStringList;
  NewItem: TListItem;
  I: Integer;
begin
  // stops warning message
  NewItem := nil;
  // load the items
  ListView1.Items.Clear;
  List := TStringList.Create;
  try
    List.LoadFromFile (
      ExtractFilePath (Application.ExeName) + 'Items.txt');
    for I := 0 to List.Count - 1 do
      if List [I][1] = #9 then
        NewItem.SubItems.Add (Trim (List [I]))
      else if List [I][1] = '@' then
        NewItem.ImageIndex := StrToIntDef (List [I][2], 0)
      else
      begin
        // a new item
        NewItem := ListView1.Items.Add;
        NewItem.Caption := List [I];
      end;
  finally
    List.Free;
  end;
end;
```

The program has a menu you can use to choose one of the different views supported by the ListView control, and to add check boxes to the items, as in a CheckListBox. You can see some of the various combinations of these styles in Figure 7.1.

FIGURE 7.1:

Different examples of the output of a ListView component of the RefList program, obtained by changing the ViewStyle property and adding the check boxes

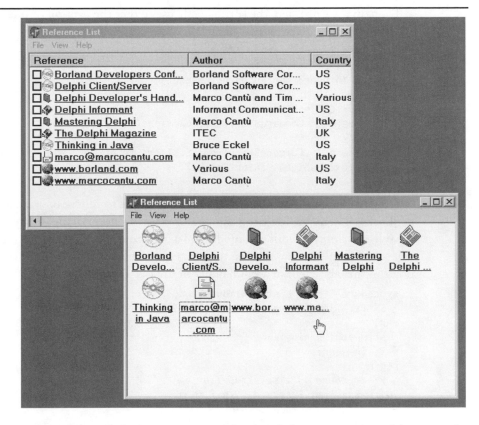

Another important feature, which is common in the detailed or report view of the control, is to let a user sort the items on one of the columns. To accomplish this requires three operations. The first is to set the SortType property of the ListView to stBoth or stData. In this way, the ListView will operate the sorting not based on the captions, but by calling the OnCompare event for each two items it has to sort. Since we want to do the sorting on each of the columns of the detailed view, we also handle the OnColumnClick event (which takes place when the user clicks the column titles in the detailed view, but only if the ShowColumnHeaders property is set to True). Each time a column is clicked, the program saves the number of that column in the nSortCol private field of the form class:

```
procedure TForm1.ListView1ColumnClick(Sender: TObject;
  Column: TListColumn);
begin
  nSortCol := Column.Index;
  ListView1.AlphaSort;
end;
```

Then, in the third step, the sorting code uses either the caption or one of the subitems according to the current sort column:

```
procedure TForm1.ListView1Compare(Sender: TObject;
  Item1, Item2: TListItem;
  Data: Integer; var Compare: Integer);
begin
  if nSortCol = 0 then
    Compare := CompareStr (Item1.Caption, Item2.Caption)
  else
    Compare := CompareStr (Item1.SubItems [nSortCol - 1],
      Item2.SubItems [nSortCol - 1]);
end;
```

The final features I've added to the program relate to mouse operations. When the user left-clicks an item, the RefList program shows a description of the selected item. Right-clicking the selected item sets it in edit mode, and a user can change it (keep in mind that the changes will automatically be saved when the program terminates). Here is the code for both operations, in the OnMouseDown event handler of the ListView control:

```
procedure TForm1.ListView1MouseDown(Sender: TObject; Button: TMouseButton;
  Shift: TShiftState; X, Y: Integer);
var
  strDescr: string;
  I: Integer;
begin
  // if there is a selected item
  if ListView1.Selected <> nil then
    if Button = mbLeft then
    begin
      // create and show a description
      strDescr := ListView1.Columns [0].Caption + #9 +
        ListView1.Selected.Caption + #13;
      for I := 1 to ListView1.Selected.SubItems.Count do
        strDescr := strDescr + ListView1.Columns [I].Caption + #9 +
          ListView1.Selected.SubItems [I-1] + #13;
      ShowMessage (strDescr);
    end
    else if Button = mbRight then
      // edit the caption
      ListView1.Selected.EditCaption;
end;
```

Although it is not feature-complete, this example shows some of the potential of the ListView control. I've also activated the "hot-tracking" feature, which lets the list view highlight and underline the item under the mouse. The relevant properties of the ListView can be seen in its textual description:

```
object ListView1: TListView
  Align = alClient
  Columns = <
    item
      Caption = 'Reference'
      Width = 230
    end
    item
      Caption = 'Author'
      Width = 180
    end
    item
      Caption = 'Country'
      Width = 80
    end>
  Font.Height = -13
  Font.Name = 'MS Sans Serif'
  Font.Style = [fsBold]
  FullDrag = True
  HideSelection = False
  HotTrack = True
  HotTrackStyles = [htHandPoint, htUnderlineHot]
  SortType = stBoth
  ViewStyle = vsList
  OnColumnClick = ListView1ColumnClick
  OnCompare = ListView1Compare
  OnMouseDown = ListView1MouseDown
end
```

This program is actually quite interesting, and I'll further extend it in Chapter 9, adding a dialog box to it.

To build its CLX version, QRefList, I had to use only one of the image lists, and disable the small images and large images menus, as a ListView is limited to the list and report view styles. Large and small icons are available in a different control, called IconView.

A Tree of Data

Now that we've seen an example based on the ListView, we can examine the TreeView control. The TreeView has a user interface that is flexible and powerful (with support for editing and dragging elements). It is also standard, because it is the user interface of the Windows Explorer. There are properties and various ways to customize the bitmap of each line or of each type of line.

To define the structure of the nodes of the TreeView at design time, you can use the Tree-View Items property editor. In this case, however, I've decided to load it in the TreeView data at startup, in a way similar to the last example.

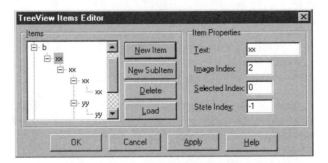

The Items property of the TreeView component has many member functions you can use to alter the hierarchy of strings. For example, we can build a two-level tree with the following lines:

```
var
  Node: TTreeNode;
begin
  Node := TreeView1.Items.Add (nil, 'First level');
  TreeView1.Items.AddChild (Node, 'Second level');
```

Using these two methods (Add and AddChild), we can build a complex structure at run time. But how do we load the information? Again, you can use a StringList at run time, load a text file with the information, and parse it.

However, since the TreeView control has a LoadFromFile method, the DragTree and QDragTree examples use the following simpler code:

```
procedure TForm1.FormCreate(Sender: TObject);
begin
  TreeView1.LoadFromFile (ExtractFilePath (Application.ExeName) +
    'TreeText.txt');
end;
```

The LoadFromFile method loads the data in a string list and checks the level of each item by looking at the number of tab characters. (If you are curious, see the TTreeStrings.Get-BufStart method, which you can find in the ComCtrls unit in the VCL source code included in Delphi.) By the way, the data I've prepared for the TreeView is the organizational chart of a multinational company.

Besides loading the data, the program saves it when it terminates, making the changes persistent. It also has a few menu items to customize the font of the TreeView control and change some other simple settings. The specific feature I've implemented in this example is support for dragging items and entire subtrees. I've set the DragMode property of the component to dmAutomatic and written the event handlers for the OnDragOver and OnDragDrop events.

In the first of the two handlers, the program makes sure the user is not trying to drag an item over a child item (which would be moved along with the item, leading to an infinite recursion):

```
procedure TForm1.TreeView1DragOver(Sender, Source: TObject;
  X, Y: Integer; State: TDragState; var Accept: Boolean);
var
  TargetNode, SourceNode: TTreeNode;
begin
  TargetNode := TreeView1.GetNodeAt (X, Y);
  // accept dragging from itself
  if (Source = Sender) and (TargetNode <> nil) then
  begin
    Accept := True;
    // determines source and target
    SourceNode := TreeView1.Selected;
    // look up the target parent chain
    while (TargetNode.Parent <> nil) and (TargetNode <> SourceNode) do
      TargetNode := TargetNode.Parent;
    // if source is found
    if TargetNode = SourceNode then
      // do not allow dragging over a child
      Accept := False;
  end
  else
    Accept := False;
end;
```

The effect of this code is that (except for the particular case we need to disallow) a user can drag an item of the TreeView over another one, as shown in Figure 7.2. Writing the actual code for moving the items is simple, because the TreeView control provides the support for this operation, through the MoveTo method of the TTreeNode class.

The DragTree example during a dragging operation

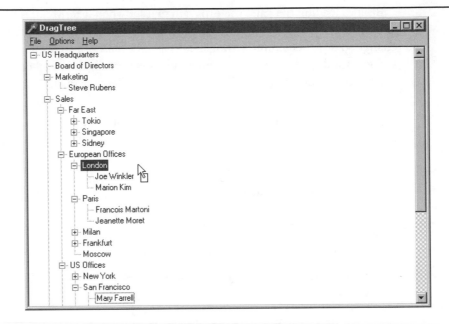

```
procedure TForm1.TreeView1DragDrop(Sender, Source: TObject; X, Y: Integer);
var
  TargetNode, SourceNode: TTreeNode;
begin
  TargetNode := TreeView1.GetNodeAt (X, Y);
  if TargetNode <> nil then
  begin
    SourceNode := TreeView1.Selected;
    SourceNode.MoveTo (TargetNode, naAddChildFirst);
    TargetNode.Expand (False);
    TreeView1.Selected := TargetNode;
  end;
end;
```

NOTE   Among the demos shipping with Delphi is an interesting one showing a custom-draw Tree-View control. The example is in the `CustomDraw` subdirectory.

Custom Tree Nodes

Delphi 6 adds a few new features to the TreeView controls, including multiple selection (see the `MultiSelect` and `MultiSelectStyle` properties and the `Selections` array), improved sorting, and several new events.

Another improved area relates to the creation of custom tree node items, which is useful to add extra custom information to each node and possibly create nodes of different classes. To support this technique, there is a new AddNode method for the TTreeItems class and a new specific event, OnCreateNodesClass. In the handler of this event, you return the class of the object to be created, which must inherit from TTreeNode.

As this is a very common technique, I've built an example to discuss it in detail. The CustomNodes example on the CD doesn't focus on a real-world case, but it shows a rather complex situation, in which there are two different custom tree node classes, derived one from the other. The base class adds an ExtraCode property, mapped to virtual methods, and the subclass overrides one of these methods. For the base class the GetExtraCode function simply returns the value, while for the derived class the value is multiplied to the parent node value. Here are the classes and this second method:

```
type
  TMyNode = class (TTreeNode)
  private
    FExtraCode: Integer;
  protected
    procedure SetExtraCode(const Value: Integer); virtual;
    function GetExtraCode: Integer; virtual;
  public
    property ExtraCode: Integer read GetExtraCode write SetExtraCode;
  end;

  TMySubNode = class (TMyNode)
  protected
    function GetExtraCode: Integer; override;
  end;

function TMySubNode.GetExtraCode: Integer;
begin
  Result := fExtraCode * (Parent as TMyNode).ExtraCode;
end;
```

With these custom tree node classes available, the program creates a tree of items, using the first type for the first-level nodes and the second class for the other nodes. As we have only one OnCreateNodeClass event handler, it uses the class reference stored in a private field of the form (CurrentNodeClass of type TTreeNodeClass):

```
procedure TForm1.TreeView1CreateNodeClass(Sender: TCustomTreeView;
  var NodeClass: TTreeNodeClass);
begin
  NodeClass := CurrentNodeClass;
end;
```

The program sets this class reference before creating nodes of each type—for example, with code like

```
var
  MyNode: TMyNode;
begin
  CurrentNodeClass := TMyNode;
  MyNode := TreeView1.Items.AddChild (nil, 'item' + IntToStr (nValue))
    as TMyNode;
  MyNode.ExtraCode := nValue;
```

Once the entire tree has been created, as the user selects an item, you can cast its type to TMyNode and access to the extra properties (but also methods and data):

```
procedure TForm1.TreeView1Click(Sender: TObject);
var
  MyNode: TMyNode;
begin
  MyNode := TreeView1.Selected as TMyNode;
  Label1.Caption := MyNode.Text + ' [' + MyNode.ClassName + '] = ' +
    IntToStr (MyNode.ExtraCode);
end;
```

This is the code used by the CustomNodes example to display the description of the selected node into a label, as you can see in Figure 7.3. Note that when you select an item down into the tree, its value is multiplied for that of each of the parent nodes. Though there are certainly easier ways to obtain this effect, having a tree view with item objects created from different classes of a hierarchy provides an object-oriented structure upon which you can base some very complex code.

FIGURE 7.3:

The CustomNodes example has a tree view with node objects based on different custom classes, thanks to the new OnCreateNodesClass event.

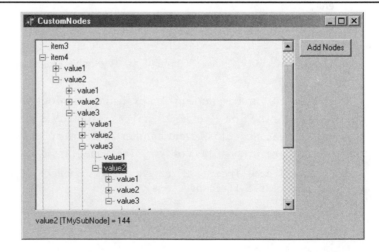

Multiple-Page Forms

When you have a lot of information and controls to display in a dialog box or a form, you can use multiple pages. The metaphor is that of a notebook: Using tabs, a user can select one of the possible pages.

There are two controls you can use to build a multiple-page application in Delphi:

- You can use the PageControl component, which has tabs on one of the sides and multiple pages (similar to panels) covering the rest of its surface. As there is one page per tab, you can simply place components on each page to obtain the proper effect both at design time and at run time.

- You can use the TabControl, which has only the tab portion but offers no pages to host the information. In this case, you'll want to use one or more components to mimic the *page change* operation.

A third related class, the TabSheet, represents a single page of the PageControl. This is not a stand-alone component and is not available on the Component Palette. You create a TabSheet at design time by using the local menu of the PageControl or at run time by using methods of the same control.

NOTE   Delphi still includes the Notebook, TabSet, and TabbedNotebook components introduced in early versions. Use these components only if you need to create a 16-bit version of an application. For any other purpose, the PageControl and TabControl components, which encapsulate Win32 common controls, provide a more modern user interface. Actually, in 32-bit versions of Delphi, the TabbedNotebook component was reimplemented using the Win32 PageControl internally, to reduce the code size and update the look.

PageControls and TabSheets

As usual, instead of duplicating the Help system's list of properties and methods of the Page-Control component, I've built an example that stretches its capabilities and allows you to change its behavior at run time. The example, called Pages, has a PageControl with three pages. The structure of the PageControl and of the other key components is listed here:

```
object Form1: TForm1
  BorderIcons = [biSystemMenu, biMinimize]
  BorderStyle = bsSingle
  Caption = 'Pages Test'
  OnCreate = FormCreate
  object PageControl1: TPageControl
    ActivePage = TabSheet1
    Align = alClient
```

```
      HotTrack = True
      Images = ImageList1
      MultiLine = True
      object TabSheet1: TTabSheet
        Caption = 'Pages'
        object Label3: TLabel
        object ListBox1: TListBox
      end
      object TabSheet2: TTabSheet
        Caption = 'Tabs Size'
        ImageIndex = 1
        object Label1: TLabel
        // other controls
      end
      object TabSheet3: TTabSheet
        Caption = 'Tabs Text'
        ImageIndex = 2
        object Memo1: TMemo
          Anchors = [akLeft, akTop, akRight, akBottom]
          OnChange = Memo1Change
        end
        object BitBtnChange: TBitBtn
          Anchors = [akTop, akRight]
          Caption = '&Change'
        end
      end
    end
    object BitBtnPrevious: TBitBtn
      Anchors = [akRight, akBottom]
      Caption = '&Previous'
      OnClick = BitBtnPreviousClick
    end
    object BitBtnNext: TBitBtn
      Anchors = [akRight, akBottom]
      Caption = '&Next'
      OnClick = BitBtnNextClick
    end
    object ImageList1: TImageList
      Bitmap = {...}
    end
  end
```

Notice that the tabs are connected to the bitmaps provided by an ImageList control and that some controls use the Anchors property to remain at a fixed distance from the right or bottom borders of the form. Even if the form doesn't support resizing (this would have been far too complex to set up with so many controls), the positions can change when the tabs are displayed on multiple lines (simply increase the length of the captions) or on the left side of the form.

Each TabSheet object has its own Caption, which is displayed as the sheet's tab. At design time, you can use the local menu to create new pages and to move between pages. You can see the local menu of the PageControl component in Figure 7.4, together with the first page. This page holds a list box and a small caption, and it shares two buttons with the other pages.

FIGURE 7.4:

The first sheet of the
PageControl of the
Pages example, with
its local menu

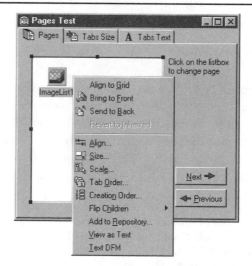

If you place a component on a page, it is available only in that page. How can you have the same component (in this case, two bitmap buttons) in each of the pages, without duplicating it? Simply place the component on the form, outside of the PageControl (or before aligning it to the client area) and then move it in front of the pages, calling the Bring To Front command of the form's local menu. The two buttons I've placed in each page can be used to move back and forth between the pages and are an alternative to using the tabs. Here is the code associated with one of them:

```
procedure TForm1.BitBtnNextClick(Sender: TObject);
begin
  PageControl1.SelectNextPage (True);
end;
```

The other button calls the same procedure, passing False as its parameter to select the previous page. Notice that there is no need to check whether we are on the first or last page, because the SelectNextPage method considers the last page to be the one before the first and will move you directly between those two pages.

Now we can focus on the first page again. It has a list box, which at run time will hold the names of the tabs. If a user clicks an item of this list box, the current page changes. This is the third method available to change pages (after the tabs and the Next and Previous buttons). The list box is filled in the FormCreate method, which is associated with the OnCreate event of the form and copies the caption of each page (the Page property stores a list of Tab-Sheet objects):

```
for I := 0 to PageControl1.PageCount - 1 do
  ListBox1.Items.Add (PageControl1.Pages.Caption);
```

When you click a list item, you can select the corresponding page:

```
procedure TForm1.ListBox1Click(Sender: TObject);
begin
  PageControl1.ActivePage := PageControl1.Pages [ListBox1.ItemIndex];
end;
```

The second page hosts two edit boxes (connected with two UpDown components), two check boxes, and two radio buttons, as you can see in Figure 7.5. The user can input a number (or choose it by clicking the up or down buttons with the mouse or pressing the Up or Down arrow key while the corresponding edit box has the focus), check the boxes and the radio buttons, and then click the Apply button to make the changes:

```
procedure TForm1.BitBtnApplyClick(Sender: TObject);
begin
  // set tab width, height, and lines
  PageControl1.TabWidth := StrToInt (EditWidth.Text);
  PageControl1.TabHeight := StrToInt (EditHeight.Text);
  PageControl1.MultiLine := CheckBoxMultiLine.Checked;
  // show or hide the last tab
  TabSheet3.TabVisible := CheckBoxVisible.Checked;
  // set the tab position
  if RadioButton1.Checked then
    PageControl1.TabPosition := tpTop
  else
    PageControl1.TabPosition := tpLeft;
end;
```

FIGURE 7.5:

The second page of the example can be used to size and position the tabs. Here you can see the tabs on the left of the page control.

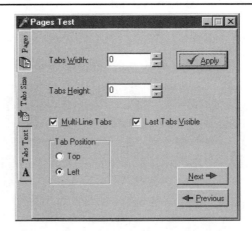

With this code, we can change the width and height of each tab (remember that 0 means the size is computed automatically from the space taken by each string). We can choose to have either multiple lines of tabs or two small arrows to scroll the tab area, and move them to the left side. The control also allows tabs to be placed on the bottom or on the right, but our program doesn't allow that, because it would make the placement of the other controls quite complex.

You can also hide the last tab on the PageControl, which corresponds to the TabSheet3 component. If you hide one of the tabs by setting its TabVisible property to False, you cannot reach that tab by clicking on the Next and Previous buttons, which are based on the SelectNextPage method. Instead, you should use the FindNextPage function, as shown below in this new version of the Next button's OnClick event handler:

```
procedure TForm1.BitBtnNextClick(Sender: TObject);
begin
  PageControl1.ActivePage := PageControl1.FindNextPage (
    PageControl1.ActivePage, True, False);
end;
```

The last page has a memo component, again with the names of the pages (added in the FormCreate method). You can edit the names of the pages and click the Change button to change the text of the tabs, but only if the number of strings matches the number of tabs:

```
procedure TForm1.BitBtnChangeClick(Sender: TObject);
var
  I: Integer;
begin
  if Memo1.Lines.Count <> PageControl1.PageCount then
    MessageDlg ('One line per tab, please', mtError, [mbOK], 0)
  else
    for I := 0 to PageControl1.PageCount -1 do
      PageControl1.Pages [I].Caption := Memo1.Lines [I];
  BitBtnChange.Enabled := False;
end;
```

Finally the last button, Add Page, allows you to add a new tab sheet to the page control, although the program doesn't add any components to it. The (empty) tab sheet object is created using the page control as its owner, but it won't work unless you also set the PageControl property. Before doing this, however, you should make the new tab sheet visible. Here is the code:

```
procedure TForm1.BitBtnAddClick(Sender: TObject);
var
  strCaption: string;
  NewTabSheet: TTabSheet;
begin
  strCaption := 'New Tab';
  if InputQuery ('New Tab', 'Tab Caption', strCaption) then
```

```
begin
  // add a new empty page to the control
  NewTabSheet := TTabSheet.Create (PageControl1);
  NewTabSheet.Visible := True;
  NewTabSheet.Caption := strCaption;
  NewTabSheet.PageControl := PageControl1;
  PageControl1.ActivePage := NewTabSheet;
  // add it to both lists
  Memo1.Lines.Add (strCaption);
  ListBox1.Items.Add (strCaption);
  end;
end;
```

TIP   Whenever you write a form based on a PageControl, remember that the first page displayed at run time is the page you were in before the code was compiled. This means that if you are working on the third page and then compile and run the program, it will start with that page. A common way to solve this problem is to add a line of code in the **FormCreate** method to set the PageControl or notebook to the first page. This way, the current page at design time doesn't determine the initial page at run time.

An Image Viewer with Owner-Draw Tabs

The use of the TabControl and of a dynamic approach, as described in the last example, can also be applied in more general (and simpler) cases. Every time you need multiple pages that all have the same type of content, instead of replicating the controls in each page, you can use a TabControl and change its contents when a new tab is selected.

This is what I'll do in the multiple-page bitmap viewer example, called BmpViewer. The image that appears in the TabControl of this form, aligned to the whole client area, depends on the selection in the tab above it (as you can see in Figure 7.6).

FIGURE 7.6:

The interface of the bitmap viewer in the BmpViewer example. Notice the owner-draw tabs.

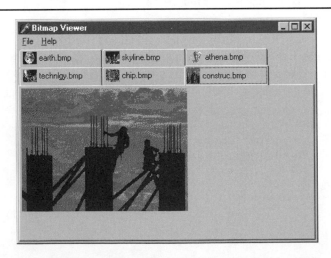

At the beginning, the TabControl is empty. After selecting File ➤ Open, the user can choose various files in the File Open dialog box, and the array of strings with the names of the files (the `Files` property of the `OpenDialog1` component) is added to the tabs (the `Tabs` property of `TabControl1`):

```
procedure TFormBmpViewer.Open1Click(Sender: TObject);
begin
  if OpenDialog1.Execute then
  begin
    TabControl1.Tabs.AddStrings (OpenDialog1.Files);
    TabControl1.TabIndex := 0;
    TabControl1Change (TabControl1);
  end;
end;
```

After we display the new tabs, we have to update the image so that it matches the first tab. To accomplish this, the program calls the method connected with the `OnChange` event of the TabControl, which loads the file corresponding to the current tab in the image component:

```
procedure TFormBmpViewer.TabControl1Change(Sender: TObject);
begin
  Image1.Picture.LoadFromFile (TabControl1.Tabs [TabControl1.TabIndex]);
end;
```

This example works, unless you select a file that doesn't contain a bitmap. The program will warn the user with a standard exception, ignore the file, and continue its execution.

The program also allows pasting the bitmap on the clipboard (without actually copying it, though) and copying the current bitmap to it. Clipboard support is available in Delphi via the global `Clipboard` object defined in the ClipBrd unit. For copying or pasting bitmaps, you can use the `Assign` method of the `TClipboard` and `TBitmap` classes. When you select the Edit ➤ Paste command of the example, a new tab named Clipboard is added to the tab set (unless it is already present). Then the number of the new tab is used to change the active tab:

```
procedure TFormBmpViewer.Paste1Click(Sender: TObject);
var
  TabNum: Integer;
begin
  // try to locate the page
  TabNum := TabControl1.Tabs.IndexOf ('Clipboard');
  if TabNum < 0 then
    // create a new page for the Clipboard
    TabNum := TabControl1.Tabs.Add ('Clipboard');
  // go to the Clipboard page and force repaint
  TabControl1.TabIndex := TabNum;
  TabControl1Change (Self);
end;
```

The Edit ➢ Copy operation, instead, is as simple as copying the bitmap currently in the image control:

```
Clipboard.Assign (Image1.Picture.Graphic);
```

To account for the possible presence of the Clipboard tab, the code of the TabControl1Change method becomes:

```
procedure TFormBmpViewer.TabControl1Change(Sender: TObject);
var
  TabText: string;
begin
  Image1.Visible := True;
  TabText := TabControl1.Tabs [TabControl1.TabIndex];
  if TabText <> 'Clipboard' then
    // load the file indicated in the tab
    Image1.Picture.LoadFromFile (TabText)
  else
    {if the tab is 'Clipboard' and a bitmap
    is available in the clipboard}
    if Clipboard.HasFormat (cf_Bitmap) then
      Image1.Picture.Assign (Clipboard)
    else
    begin
      // else remove the clipboard tab
      TabControl1.Tabs.Delete (TabControl1.TabIndex);
      if TabControl1.Tabs.Count = 0 then
        Image1.Visible := False;
    end;
```

This program pastes the bitmap from the Clipboard each time you change the tab. The program stores only one image at a time, and it has no way to store the Clipboard bitmap. However, if the Clipboard content changes and the bitmap format is no longer available, the Clipboard tab is automatically deleted (as you can see in the listing above). If no more tabs are left, the Image component is hidden.

An image can also be removed using either of two menu commands: Cut or Delete. Cut removes the tab after making a copy of the bitmap to the Clipboard. In practice, the Cut1Click method does nothing besides calling the Copy1Click and Delete1Click methods. The Copy1Click method is responsible for copying the current image to the Clipboard, Delete1Click simply removes the current tab. Here is their code:

```
procedure TFormBmpViewer.Copy1Click(Sender: TObject);
begin
  Clipboard.Assign (Image1.Picture.Graphic);
end;
```

```
procedure TFormBmpViewer.Delete1Click(Sender: TObject);
begin
  with TabControl1 do
  begin
    if TabIndex >= 0 then
      Tabs.Delete (TabIndex);
    if Tabs.Count = 0 then
      Image1.Visible := False;
  end;
end;
```

One of the special features of the example is that the TabControl has the OwnerDraw property set to True. This means that the control won't paint the tabs (which will be empty at design time) but will have the application do this, by calling the OnDrawTab event. In its code, the program displays the text vertically centered, using the DrawText API function. The text displayed is not the entire file path but only the filename. Then, if the text is not *None*, the program reads the bitmap the tab refers to and paints a small version of it in the tab itself. To accomplish this, the program uses the TabBmp object, which is of type TBitmap and is created and destroyed along with the form. The program also uses the BmpSide constant to position the bitmap and the text properly:

```
procedure TFormBmpViewer.TabControl1DrawTab(Control: TCustomTabControl;
  TabIndex: Integer; const Rect: TRect; Active: Boolean);
var
 TabText: string;
 OutRect: TRect;
begin
  TabText := TabControl1.Tabs [TabIndex];
  OutRect := Rect;
  InflateRect (OutRect, -3, -3);
  OutRect.Left := OutRect.Left + BmpSide + 3;
  DrawText (Control.Canvas.Handle, PChar (ExtractFileName (TabText)),
    Length (ExtractFileName (TabText)), OutRect,
    dt_Left or dt_SingleLine or dt_VCenter);
  if TabText = 'Clipboard' then
    if Clipboard.HasFormat (cf_Bitmap) then
      TabBmp.Assign (Clipboard)
    else
      TabBmp.FreeImage
  else
    TabBmp.LoadFromFile (TabText);
  OutRect.Left := OutRect.Left - BmpSide - 3;
  OutRect.Right := OutRect.Left + BmpSide;
  Control.Canvas.StretchDraw (OutRect, TabBmp);
end;
```

The program has also support for printing the current bitmap, after showing a page preview form in which the user can select the proper scaling. This extra portion of the program I built for earlier editions of the book is not discussed in detail, but I've left the code in the program so that you can have a look at its code anyway.

The User Interface of a Wizard

Just as you can use a TabControl without pages, you can also take the opposite approach and use a PageControl without tabs. What I want to focus on now is the development of the user interface of a wizard. In a wizard, you are directing the user through a sequence of steps, one screen at a time, and at each step you typically want to offer the choice of proceeding to the next step or going back to correct input entered in a previous step. So instead of tabs that can be selected in any order, wizards typically offer Next and Back buttons to navigate. This won't be a complex example; its purpose is just to give you a few guidelines. The example is called WizardUI.

The starting point is to create a series of pages in a PageControl and set the TabVisible property of each TabSheet to False (while keeping the Visible property set to True). Unlike past versions, since Delphi 5 you can also hide the tabs at design time. In this case, you'll need to use the shortcut menu of the page control or the combo box of the Object Inspector to move to another page, instead of the tabs. But why don't you want to see the tabs at design time? You can place controls on the pages and then place extra controls in front of the pages (as I've done in the example), without seeing their relative positions change at run time. You might also want to remove the useless captions of the tabs, which take up space in memory and in the resources of the application.

In the first page, I've placed on one side an image and a bevel control and on the other side some text, a check box, and two buttons. Actually, the Next button is inside the page, while the Back button is over it (and is shared by all the pages). You can see this first page at design time in Figure 7.7. The following pages look similar, with a label, check boxes, and buttons on the right side and nothing on the left.

When you click the Next button on the first page, the program looks at the status of the check box and decides which page is the following one. I could have written the code like this:

```
procedure TForm1.btnNext1Click(Sender: TObject);
begin
  BtnBack.Enabled := True;
  if CheckInprise.Checked then
    PageControl1.ActivePage := TabSheet2
  else
    PageControl1.ActivePage := TabSheet3;
  // move image and bevel
  Bevel1.Parent := PageControl1.ActivePage;
  Image1.Parent := PageControl1.ActivePage;
end;
```

FIGURE 7.7:

The first page of the
WizardUI example at
design time

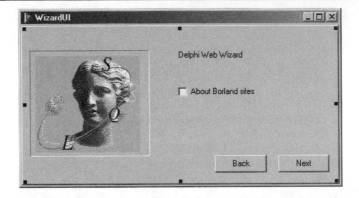

After enabling the common Back button, the program changes the active page and finally moves the graphical portion to the new page. Because this code has to be repeated for each button, I've placed it in a method after adding a couple of extra features. This is the actual code:

```
procedure TForm1.btnNext1Click(Sender: TObject);
begin
  if CheckInprise.Checked then
    MoveTo (TabSheet2)
  else
    MoveTo (TabSheet3);
end;

procedure TForm1.MoveTo(TabSheet: TTabSheet);
begin
  // add the last page to the list
  BackPages.Add (PageControl1.ActivePage);
  BtnBack.Enabled := True;
  // change page
  PageControl1.ActivePage := TabSheet;
  // move image and bevel
  Bevel1.Parent := PageControl1.ActivePage;
  Image1.Parent := PageControl1.ActivePage;
end;
```

Besides the code I've already explained, the MoveTo method adds the last page (the one before the page change) to a list of visited pages, which behaves like a stack. In fact, the BackPages object of the TList class is created as the program starts and the last page is always added to the end. When the user clicks the Back button, which is not dependent on the page, the program extracts the last page from the list, deletes its entry, and moves to that page:

```
procedure TForm1.btnBackClick(Sender: TObject);
var
```

```
    LastPage: TTabSheet;
begin
  // get the last page and jump to it
  LastPage := TTabSheet (BackPages [BackPages.Count - 1]);
  PageControl1.ActivePage := LastPage;
  // delete the last page from the list
  BackPages.Delete (BackPages.Count - 1);
  // eventually disable the back button
  BtnBack.Enabled := not (BackPages.Count = 0);
  // move image and bevel
  Bevel1.Parent := PageControl1.ActivePage;
  Image1.Parent := PageControl1.ActivePage;
end;
```

With this code, the user can move back several pages until the list is empty, at which point we disable the Back button. The complication we need to deal with is that while moving from a particular page, we know which pages are its "next" and "previous," but we don't know which page we came from, because there can be multiple paths to reach a page. Only by keeping track of the movements with a list can we reliably go back.

The rest of the code of the program, which simply shows some Web site addresses, is very simple. The good news is that you can reuse the navigational structure of this example in your own programs and modify only the graphical portion and the content of the pages. Actually, as most of the labels of the programs show HTTP addresses, a user can click those labels to open the default browser showing that page. This is accomplished by extracting the HTTP address from the label and calling the `ShellExecute` function.

```
procedure TForm1.LabelLinkClick(Sender: TObject);
var
  Caption, StrUrl: string;
begin
  Caption := (Sender as TLabel).Caption;
  StrUrl := Copy (Caption, Pos ('http://', Caption), 1000);
  ShellExecute (Handle, 'open', PChar (StrUrl), '', '', sw_Show);
end;
```

The method above is hooked to the `OnClick` event of many labels of the form, which have been turned into *links* by setting its `Cursor` to a hand. This is one of the labels:

```
object Label2: TLabel
  Cursor = crHandPoint
  Caption = 'Main site: http://www.borland.com'
  OnClick = LabelLinkClick
end
```

Form-Splitting Techniques

There are several ways to implement form-splitting techniques in Delphi, but the simplest approach is to use the Splitter component, found in the Additional page of the Component Palette. To make it more effective, the splitter can be used in combination with the Constraints property of the controls it relates to. As we'll see in the Split1 example, this allows us to define maximum and minimum positions of the splitter and of the form.

To build this example, simply place a ListBox component in a form; then add a Splitter component, a second ListBox, another Splitter, and finally a third ListBox component. The form also has a simple toolbar based on a panel.

By simply placing these two splitter components, you give your form the complete functionality of moving and sizing the controls it hosts at run time. The Width, Beveled, and Color properties of the splitter components determine their appearance, and in the Split1 example you can use the toolbar controls to change them. Another relevant property is MinSize, which determines the minimum size of the components of the form. During the splitting operation (see Figure 7.8), a line marks the final position of the splitter, but you cannot drag this line beyond a certain limit. The behavior of the Split1 program is not to let controls become too small. An alternative technique is to set the new AutoSnap property of the splitter to True. This property will make the splitter hide the control when its size goes below the MinSize limit.

FIGURE 7.8:

The splitter component of the Split1 example determines the minimum size for each control on the form, even those not adjacent to the splitter itself.

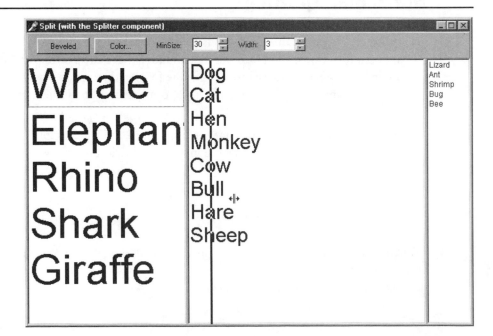

I suggest you try using the Split1 program, so that you'll fully understand how the splitter affects its adjacent controls and the other controls of the form. Even if we set the MinSize property, a user of this program can reduce the size of its entire form to a minimum, hiding some of the list boxes. If you test the Split2 version of the example, instead, you'll get better behavior. In Split2, I've set some Constraints for the ListBox controls—for example,

```
object ListBox1: TListBox
  Constraints.MaxHeight = 400
  Constraints.MinHeight = 200
  Constraints.MinWidth = 150
```

The size constraints are applied only as you actually resize the controls, so to make this program work in a satisfactory way, you have to set the ResizeStyle property of the two splitters to rsUpdate. This value indicates that the position of the controls is updated for every movement of the splitter, not only at the end of the operation. If you select the rsLine or the new rsPattern values, instead, the splitter simply draws a line in the required position, checking the MinSize property but not the constraints of the controls.

TIP   When you set the Splitter component's AutoSnap property to True, the splitter will completely hide the neighboring control when the size of that control is below the minimum set for it in the Splitter component.

Horizontal Splitting

The Splitter component can also be used for horizontal splitting, instead of the default vertical splitting. However, this approach is a little more complicated. Basically you can place a component on a form, align it to the top, and then place the splitter on the form. By default, it will be left aligned. Choose the alTop value for the Align property, and then resize the component manually, by changing the Height property in the Object Inspector (or by resizing the component).

You can see a form with a horizontal splitter in the SplitH example. This program has two memo components you can open a file into, and it has a splitter dividing them, defined as:

```
object Splitter1: TSplitter
  Cursor = crVSplit
  Align = alTop
  OnMoved = Splitter1Moved
end
```

When you double-click a memo, the program loads a text file into it (notice the structure of the with statement):

```
procedure TForm1.MemoDblClick(Sender: TObject);
begin
```

```
  with Sender as TMemo, OpenDialog1 do
    if Execute then
      Lines.LoadFromFile (FileName);
end;
```

The program features a status bar, which keeps track of the current height of the two memo components. It handles the OnMoved event of the splitter (the only event of this component) to update the text of the status bar. The same code is executed whenever the form is resized:

```
procedure TForm1.Splitter1Moved(Sender: TObject);
begin
  StatusBar1.Panels[0].Text := Format ('Upper Memo: %d - Lower Memo: %d',
    [MemoUp.Height, MemoDown.Height]);
end;
```

You can see the effect of this code by looking at Figure 7.9, or by running the SplitH example.

FIGURE 7.9:

The status bar of the
SplitH example indicates
the position of the
horizontal splitter
component.

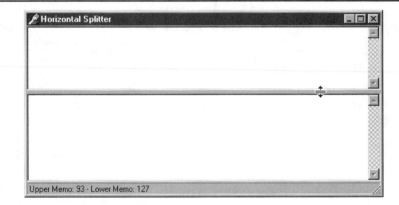

Splitting with a Header

An alternative to using splitters is to use the standard HeaderControl component. If you place this control on a form, it will be automatically aligned with the top of the form. Then you can add the three list boxes to the rest of the client area of the form. The first list box can be aligned on the left, but this time you cannot align the second and third list box as well. The problem is that the sections of the header can be dragged outside the visible surface of the form. If the list boxes use automatic alignment, they cannot move outside the visible surface of the form, as the program requires.

The solution is to define the sections of the header, using the specific editor of the Sections property. This property editor allows you to access the various subobjects of the collection, changing various settings. You can set the caption and alignment of the text; the current, minimum, and maximum size of the header; and so on. Setting the limit values is a powerful tool,

and it replaces the MinSize property of the splitter or the constraints of the list boxes we've used in past examples. You can see the output of this program, named HdrSplit, in Figure 7.10.

FIGURE 7.10:

The output of the HdrSplit example

We need to handle two events: OnSectionResize and OnSectionClick. The first handler simply resizes the list box connected with the modified section (determined by associating numbers with the ImageIndex property of each section and using it to determine the name of the list box control):

```
procedure TForm1.HeaderControl1SectionResize(
    HeaderControl: THeaderControl; Section: THeaderSection);
var
    List: TListBox;
begin
    List := FindComponent ('ListBox' + IntToStr (Section.ImageIndex))
        as TListBox;
    List.Width := Section.Width;
end;
```

Along with this event, we need to handle the resizing of the form, using it to synchronize the list boxes with the sections, which are all resized by default:

```
procedure TForm1.FormResize(Sender: TObject);
var
    I: Integer;
    List: TListBox;
begin
    for I := 0 to 2 do
    begin
        List := FindComponent ('ListBox' + IntToStr (
            HeaderControl1.Sections[I].ImageIndex)) as TListBox;
```

```
      List.Left := HeaderControl1.Sections[I].Left;
      List.Width := HeaderControl1.Sections[I].Width;
    end;
  end;
```

After setting the height of the list boxes, this method simply calls the previous one, passing parameters that we won't use in this example. The second method of the HeaderControl, called in response to a click on one of the sections, is used to sort the contents of the corresponding list box:

```
procedure TForm1.HeaderControl1SectionClick(
  HeaderControl: THeaderControl; Section: THeaderSection);
var
  List: TListBox;
begin
  List := FindComponent ('ListBox' + IntToStr (Section.ImageIndex))
    as TListBox;
  List.Sorted := not List.Sorted;
end;
```

Of course, this code doesn't provide the common behavior of sorting the elements when you click the header and then sorting them in the reverse order if you click again. To implement this, you should write your own sorting algorithm.

Finally, the HdrSplit example uses a new feature for the header control. It sets the DragReorder property to enable dragging operations to reorder the header sections. When this operation is performed, the control fires the OnSectionDrag event, where you can exchange the positions of the list boxes. This event fires before the sections are actually moved, so I have to use the coordinates of the other section:

```
procedure TForm1.HeaderControl1SectionDrag(Sender: TObject; FromSection,
  ToSection: THeaderSection; var AllowDrag: Boolean);
var
  List: TListBox;
begin
  List := FindComponent ('ListBox' + IntToStr (FromSection.ImageIndex))
    as TListBox;
  List.Left := ToSection.Left;
  List.Width := ToSection.Width;

  List := FindComponent ('ListBox' + IntToStr (ToSection.ImageIndex))
    as TListBox;
  List.Left := FromSection.Left;
  List.Width :=fromSection.Width
end;
```

Control Anchors

In this chapter, I've described how you can use alignment and splitters to create nice, flexible user interfaces, that adapt to the current size of the form, giving users maximum freedom. Delphi also supports right and bottom anchors. Before this feature was introduced in Delphi 4, every control placed a form had coordinates relative to the top and bottom, unless it was aligned to the bottom or right sides. Aligning is good for some controls but not all of them, particularly buttons.

By using anchors, you can make the position of a control relative to any side of the form. For example, to have a button anchored to the bottom-right corner of the form, place the button in the required position and set its Anchors property to [akRight, akBottom]. When the form size changes, the distance of the button from the anchored sides is kept fixed. In other words, if you set these two anchors and remove the two defaults, the button will remain in the bottom-right corner.

On the other hand, if you place a large component such as a Memo or a ListBox in the middle of a form, you can set its Anchors property to include all four sides. This way the control will behave as an aligned control, growing and shrinking with the size of the form, but there will be some margin between it and the form sides.

TIP   Anchors, like constraints, work both at design time and at run time, so you should set them up as early as possible, to benefit from this feature while you're designing the form as well as at run time.

As an example of both approaches, you can try out the Anchors application, which has two buttons on the bottom-right corner and a list box in the middle. As shown in Figure 7.11, the controls automatically move and stretch as the form size changes. To make this form work properly, you must also set its Constraints property; otherwise, as the form becomes too small the controls can overlap or disappear.

TIP   If you remove all of the anchors, or two opposite ones (for example, left and right), the resize operations will cause the control to float. The control keeps its current size, and the system adds or removes the same number of pixels on each side of it. This can be defined as a centered anchor, because if the component is initially in the middle of the form it will keep that position. In any case, if you want a centered control, you should generally use both opposite anchors, so that if the user makes the form larger, the control size will grow as well. In the case just presented, in fact, making the form larger leaves a small control in its center.

FIGURE 7.11:

The controls of the Anchors example move and stretch automatically as the user changes the size of the form. No code is needed to move the controls, only a proper use of the Anchors property.

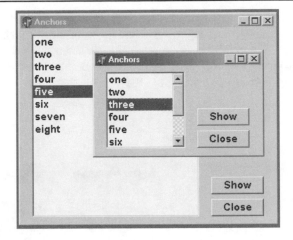

The ToolBar Control

In early versions of Delphi, toolbars had to be created using panels and speed buttons. Starting with version 3, Delphi introduced a specific ToolBar component, which encapsulates the corresponding Win32 common control or the corresponding Qt widget in VisualCLX. This component provides a toolbar, with its own buttons, and it has many advanced capabilities. To use this component, you place it on a form and then use the component editor (the shortcut menu activated by a right mouse button click) to create a few buttons and separators.

Building a Toolbar with a Panel

Before the toolbar control was available in Delphi, the standard approach for building a toolbar was to use a panel aligned to the top of the form and place SpeedButton components inside it. A *speed button* is a lightweight graphical control (consuming no Windows resources); it cannot receive the input focus, it has no tab order, and it is faster to create and paint than a bitmap button.

Speed buttons can behave like push buttons, check boxes, or radio buttons, and they can have different bitmaps depending on their status. To make a group of speed buttons work like radio buttons, just place some speed buttons on the panel, select all of them, and give the same value to each one's `GroupIndex` property. All the buttons having the same `GroupIndex` become mutually exclusive selections. One of these buttons should always be selected, so remember to set the **Down** property to True for one of them at design time or as soon as the program starts.

Continued on next page

By setting the `AllowAllUp` property, you can create a group of mutually exclusive buttons, each of which can be *up*—that is, a group from which the user can select one option or leave them all unselected. As a special case, you can make a speed button work as a check box, simply by defining a group (the `GroupIndex` property) that has only one button and that allows it to be deselected (the `AllowAllUp` property).

Finally, you can set the `Flat` property of all the SpeedButton components to True, obtaining a more modern user interface. If you are interested in this approach, you can look at the Panel-Bar example, illustrated here:

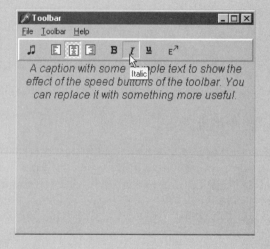

The use of SpeedButton controls is becoming less common. Besides the fact that the ToolBar control is very handy and definitely more standard, speed buttons have two big problems. First, each of them requires a specific bitmap and cannot use one from an image list (unless you write some complex code). Second, speed buttons don't work very well with actions, because some properties, such as the Down state, do not map directly.

The toolbar is populated with objects of the TToolButton class. These objects have a fundamental property, Style, which determines their behavior:

- The tbsButton style indicates a standard push button.
- The tbsCheck style indicates a button with the behavior of a check box, or that of a radio button if the button is Grouped with the others in its block (determined by the presence of separators).

- The tbsDropDown style indicates a drop-down button, a sort of combo box. The drop-down portion can be easily implemented in Delphi by connecting a PopupMenu control to the `DropdownMenu` property of the control.

- The tbsSeparator and tbsDivider styles indicate separators with no or different vertical lines (depending on the `Flat` property of the toolbar).

To create a graphic toolbar, you can add an ImageList component to the form, load some bitmaps into it, and then connect the ImageList with the `Images` property of the toolbar. By default, the images will be assigned to the buttons in the order they appear, but you can change this quite easily by setting the `ImageIndex` property of each toolbar button. You can prepare further ImageLists for special conditions of the buttons and assign them to the `DisabledImages` and `HotImages` properties of the toolbar. The first group is used for the disabled buttons; the second for the button currently under the mouse.

NOTE   In a nontrivial application, you would generally create toolbars using an ActionList or the new Action Manager architecture, both discussed in the next chapter. In this case, you'll attach very little behavior to the toolbar buttons, as their properties and events will be managed by the action components.

The RichBar Example

As an example of the use of a toolbar, I've built the RichBar application, which has a RichEdit component you can operate by using the toolbar. The program has buttons for loading and saving files, for copy and paste operations, and to change some of the attributes of the current font.

I don't want to cover the details of the features of the RichEdit control, which are many, nor discuss the details of this application, which has quite a lot of code. All I want to do is to focus on features specific to the ToolBar used by the example and visible in Figure 7.12. This toolbar has buttons, separators, and even a drop-down menu and two combo boxes discussed in the next section.

The various buttons implement features, one of them being a complete scheme for opening and saving the text files, including the ability to ask the user to save any modified file before opening a new one, to avoid losing any changes. The file-handling portion of the program is quite complex, but it is worth exploring, as many file-based applications will use similar code. I've made more details available in the bonus chapter "The RichBar Example" on the companion CD.

Besides file operations, the program supports copy and paste operations and font management. The copy and paste operations don't require an actual interaction with the clipboard, as the component can handle them with simple commands, such as:

```
RichEdit.CutToClipboard;
RichEdit.CopyToClipboard;
RichEdit.PasteFromClipboard;
RichEdit.Undo;
```

FIGURE 7.12:

The toolbar of the RichBar example. Notice the drop-down menu.

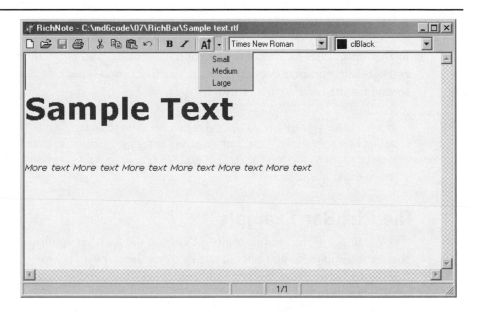

It is a little more advanced to know when these operations (and the corresponding buttons) should be enabled. We can enable Copy and Cut buttons when some text is selected, in the OnSelectionChange event of the RichEdit control:

```
procedure TFormRichNote.RichEditSelectionChange(Sender: TObject);
begin
  tbtnCut.Enabled := RichEdit.SelLength > 0;
  tbtnCopy.Enabled := tbtnCut.Enabled;
end;
```

The Copy operation, instead, cannot be determined by an action of the user, as it depends on the content of the Clipboard, influenced also by other applications. One approach is to use a timer and check the clipboard content from time to time. A better approach is to use the OnIdle event of the Application object (or the ApplicationEvents component). As the

RichEdit supports multiple clipboard formats, the code cannot simply look at those, but should ask the component itself, using a low-level feature not surfaced by the Delphi control:

```
procedure TFormRichNote.ApplicationEvents1Idle(Sender: TObject;
  var Done: Boolean);
begin
  // update toolbar buttons
  tbtnPaste.Enabled := SendMessage (RichEdit.Handle, em_CanPaste, 0, 0) <> 0;
end;
```

Basic font management is given by the Bold and Italic buttons, which have similar code. The Bold button toggles the relative attribute from the selected text (or changes the style at the current edit position):

```
procedure TFormRichNote.BoldExecute(Sender: TObject);
begin
  with RichEdit.SelAttributes do
    if fsBold in Style then
      Style := Style - [fsBold]
    else
      Style := Style + [fsBold];
end;
```

Again, the current status of the button is determined by the current selection, so we'll need to add the following line to the RichEditSelectionChange method:

```
tbtnBold.Down := fsBold in RichEdit.SelAttributes.Style;
```

A Menu and a Combo Box in a Toolbar

Besides a series of buttons, the RichBar example has a drop-down menu and a couple of combo boxes, a feature shared by many common applications. The drop-down button allows selection of the font size, while the combo boxes allow rapid selection of the font family and the font color. This second combo is actually built using a ColorBox control.

The Size button is connected to a PopupMenu component (called SizeMenu) using the DropdownMenu property. A user can press the button, firing its OnClick event as usual, or select the drop-down arrow, open the pop-up menu (see again Figure 7.12), and choose one of its options. This case has three possible font sizes, per the menu definition:

```
object SizeMenu: TPopupMenu
  object Small1: TMenuItem
    Tag = 10
    Caption = 'Small'
    OnClick = SetFontSize
  end
  object Medium1: TMenuItem
    Tag = 16
```

```
      Caption = 'Medium'
      OnClick = SetFontSize
   end
   object Large1: TMenuItem
     Tag = 32
     Caption = 'Large'
     OnClick = SetFontSize
   end
end
```

Each menu item has a tag indicating the actual size of the font, activated by a shared event handler:

```
procedure TFormRichNote.SetFontSize(Sender: TObject);
begin
  RichEdit.SelAttributes.Size := (Sender as TMenuItem).Tag;
end;
```

As the ToolBar control is a full-featured control container, you can directly take an edit box, a combo box, and other controls and place them inside the toolbar. The combo box in the toolbar is initialized in the FormCreate method, which extracts the screen fonts available in the system:

```
ComboFont.Items := Screen.Fonts;
ComboFont.ItemIndex := ComboFont.Items.IndexOf (RichEdit.Font.Name)
```

The combo box initially displays the name of the default font used in the RichEdit control, which is set at design time. This value is recomputed each time the current selection changes, using the font of the selected text, along with the current color for the ColorBox:

```
procedure TFormRichNote.RichEditSelectionChange(Sender: TObject);
begin
  ComboFont.ItemIndex :=
    ComboFont.Items.IndexOf (RichEdit.SelAttributes.Name);
  ColorBox1.Selected := RichEdit.SelAttributes.Color;
end;
```

When a new font is selected from the combo box, the reverse action takes place. The text of the current combo box item is assigned as the name of the font for any text selected in the RichEdit control:

```
RichEdit.SelAttributes.Name := ComboFont.Text;
```

The selection of a color in the ColorBox activates similar code.

Toolbar Hints

Another common element in toolbars is the *fly-by hint*, also called *balloon help*—some text that briefly describes the button currently under the cursor. This text is usually displayed in a yellow box after the mouse cursor has remained steady over a button for a set amount of time. To add hints to an application's toolbar, simply set its ShowHints property to True and enter some text for the Hint property of each button (more on hints text in the next section, "A Simple Status Bar").

If you want to have more control on how hints are displayed, you can use some of the properties and events of the Application object. This global object has, among others, the following properties:

Property	Defines
HintColor	The background color of the hint window
HintPause	How long the cursor should remain on a component before hints are displayed
HintHidePause	How long the hint will be displayed
HintShortPause	How long the system should wait to display a hint if another hint has just been displayed

A program, for example, might allow a user to customize the hint background color by selecting a specific with the following code:

```
ColorDialog.Color := Application.HintColor;
if ColorDialog.Execute then
  Application.HintColor := ColorDialog.Color;
```

NOTE   As an alternative, you can change the hint color by handling the OnShowHint property of the Application object. This handler can change the color of the hint just for specific controls. The OnShowHint event is used in the CustHint example described later in this chapter.

A Simple Status Bar

Building a status bar is even simpler than building a toolbar. Delphi includes a specific StatusBar component, based on the corresponding Windows common control (a similar control is available also in VisualCLX). This component can be used almost as a panel when its SimplePanel property is set to True. In this case, you can use the SimpleText property to output some text. The real advantage of this component, however, is that it allows you to define a number of subpanels just by activating the editor of its Panels property. (You can also display this property editor by double-clicking the status bar control.) Each subpanel has its own graphical attributes, which you can customize using the editor. Another feature of the status bar component is the "size grip" area added to the lower-right corner of the bar, which is useful for resizing the form itself. This is a typical element of the Windows user interface, and you can control it with the SizeGrip property.

There are various uses for a status bar. The most common is to display information about the menu item currently selected by the user. Besides this, a status bar often displays other information about the status of a program: the position of the cursor in a graphical application, the current line of text in a word processor, the status of the lock keys, the time and date, and so on. To show information on a panel, you simply use its Text property, generally using an expression like this:

```
StatusBar1.Panels[1].Text := 'message';
```

In the RichBar example, I've built a status bar with three panels, for command hints, the status of the Caps Lock key, and the current editing position. The StatusBar component of the example actually has four panels; we need to define the fourth in order to delimit the area of the third panel. The last panel, in fact, is always large enough to cover the remaining surface of the status bar.

TIP   Again, for more detail on the RichBar program, see the bonus chapter "The RichBar Example" on the companion CD.

The panels are not independent components, so you cannot access them by name, only by position as in the preceding code snippet. A good solution to improve the readability of a program is to define a constant for each panel you want to use, and then use these constants when referring to the panels. This is my sample code:

```
const
  sbpMessage = 0;
  sbpCaps = 1;
  sbpPosition = 2;
```

In the first panel of the status bar, I want to display the hint message of the toolbar button. The program obtains this effect by handling the application's OnHint event, again using the ApplicationEvents component, and copying the current value of the application's Hint property to the status bar:

```
procedure TFormRichNote.ApplicationEvents1Hint (Sender: TObject);
begin
  StatusBar1.Panels[sbpMessage].Text := Application.Hint;
end;
```

By default, this code displays in the status bar the same text of the fly-by hints. Actually, we can use the Hint property to specify different strings for the two cases, by writing a string divided into two portions by a separator, the pipe (|) character. For example, you might enter the following as the value of the Hint property:

```
'New|Create a new document'
```

The first portion of the string, *New*, is used by fly-by hints, and the second portion, *Create a new document*, by the status bar. You can see an example in Figure 7.13.

FIGURE 7.13:

The StatusBar of the RichBar example displays a more detailed description than the fly-by hint.

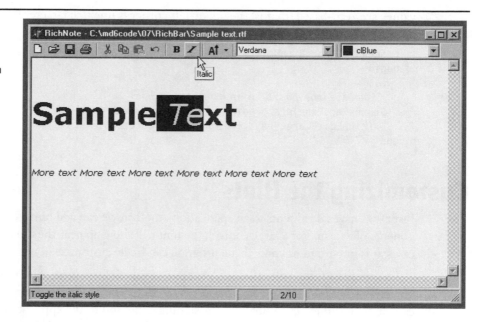

When the hint for a control is made up of two strings, you can use the `GetShortHint` and `GetLongHint` methods to extract the first (short) and second (long) substrings from the string you pass as a parameter, which is usually the value of the `Hint` property.

The second panel displays the status of the Caps Lock key, obtained by calling the `GetKeyState` API function, which returns a state number. If the low-order bit of this number is set (that is, if the number is odd), then the key is pressed. When do we check this state? I've decided to do this when the application is idle, so that this test is executed every time a key is pressed, but also as soon as a message reaches the window (in case the user changes this setting while working with another program). I've added to the `ApplicationEvents1Idle` handler a call to the custom `CheckCapslock` method, implemented as follows:

```
procedure TFormRichNote.CheckCapslock;
begin
  if Odd (GetKeyState (VK_CAPITAL)) then
    StatusBar1.Panels[sbpCaps].Text := 'CAPS'
  else
    StatusBar1.Panels[sbpCaps].Text := '';
end;
```

Finally, the program uses the third panel to display the current cursor position (measured in lines and characters per line) every time the selection changes. Because the `CaretPos` values are zero-based (that is, the upper-left corner is line 0, character 0), I've decided to add one to each value, to make them more reasonable for a casual user:

```
procedure TFormRichNote.RichEditSelectionChange(Sender: TObject);
begin
  ...
  // update the position in the status bar
  StatusBar.Panels[sbpPosition].Text := Format ('%d/%d',
    [RichEdit.CaretPos.Y + 1, RichEdit.CaretPos.X + 1]);
end;
```

Customizing the Hints

Just as we have added hints to an application's toolbar, we can add hints to forms or to the components of a form. For a large control, the hint will show up near the mouse cursor. In some cases, it is important to know that a program can freely customize how hints are displayed.

The simplest thing you can do is, change the value of the properties of the Application object as I mentioned at the end of the last section. To obtain more control over hints, you can customize them even further by assigning a method to the application's OnShowHint event. You need to either hook them up manually or—better—add an ApplicationEvents component to the form and handle its OnShowHint event.

The method you have to define has some interesting parameters, such as a string with the text of the hint, a Boolean flag for its activation, and a THintInfo structure with further information, including the control, the hint position, and its color. Each of the parameters is passed by reference, so you have a chance to change them and also modify the values of the THintInfo structure; for example, you can change the position of the hint window before it is displayed.

This is what I've done in the CustHint example, which shows the hint of the label at the center of its area. Here is what you can write to show the hint for the big label in the center of its surface:

```
procedure TForm1.ShowHint (var HintStr: string; var CanShow: Boolean;
  var HintInfo: THintInfo);
begin
  with HintInfo do
    if HintControl = Label1 then
      HintPos := HintControl.ClientToScreen (Point (
        HintControl.Width div 2, HintControl.Height div 2));
end;
```

The code has to retrieve the center of the generic control (the HintInfo.HintControl) and then convert its coordinates to screen coordinates, applying the ClientToScreen method to the control itself. We can further update the CustHint example in a different way. The RadioGroup control in the form has three radio buttons. However, these are not stand-alone components, but simply radio button clones painted on the surface of the radio group. What if we want to add a hint for each of them?

The `CursorRect` field of the `THintInfo` record can be used for this purpose. It indicates the area of the component that the cursor can move over without disabling the hint. When the cursor moves outside this area, Delphi hides the hint window. If we specify a different text for the hint and a different area for each of the radio buttons, we can in practice provide three different hints. Because computing the actual position of each radio button isn't easy, I've simply divided the surface of the radio group into as many equal parts as there are radio buttons. The text of the radio button (not the selected item, but the item under the cursor) is then added to the text of the hint:

```
procedure TForm1.ShowHint (var HintStr: string;
  var CanShow: Boolean; var HintInfo: THintInfo);
var
  RadioItem, RadioHeight: Integer;
  RadioRect: TRect;
begin
  with HintInfo do
    if HintControl = Label1 ... // as before
    else
    if HintControl = RadioGroup1 then
    begin
      RadioHeight := (RadioGroup1.Height) div RadioGroup1.Items.Count;
      RadioItem := CursorPos.Y div RadioHeight;
      HintStr := 'Choose the ' + RadioGroup1.Items [RadioItem] + ' button';
      RadioRect := RadioGroup1.ClientRect;
      RadioRect.Top := RadioRect.Top + RadioHeight * RadioItem;
      RadioRect.Bottom := RadioRect.Top + RadioHeight;
      // assign the hints rect and pos
      CursorRect := RadioRect;
    end;
end;
```

The final part of the code builds the rectangle for the hint, starting with the rectangle corresponding to the client area of the component and moving its `Top` and `Bottom` values to the proper section of the `RadioGroup1` component. The resulting effect is that each radio button of the radio group appears to have a specific hint, as shown in Figure 7.14.

FIGURE 7.14:

The RadioGroup control of the CustHint example shows a different hint, depending on which radio button the mouse is over.

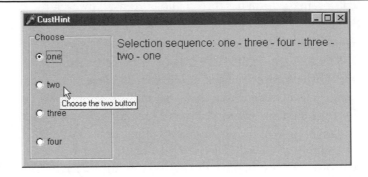

What's Next?

In this chapter I've discussed the use of some Delphi common controls, including the ListView, TreeView, PageControl, TabControl, ToolBar, StatusBar, and RichEdit. For each of these controls, I've built one example, trying to discuss it in the context of an actual application, even if most of the programs have been quite simple. I've also covered the Splitter component and various form-splitting techniques, the anchors for control positioning, and the customization of hints.

What is still missing is the development of an application with a complete user interface, including a menu and one or more toolbars. The reason I haven't covered this topic in the current chapter is that Delphi 6 adds quite a lot to VCL in this respect, including a complete architecture for letting the end users configure menus and toolbars based on a number of predefined actions. As this topic and related ones, such as docking toolbars, are complex, I've devoted the entire next chapter to them.

After this step, we'll move to the development of applications with multiple forms, including advanced dialog boxes, MDI, visual form inheritance, and the use of frames. All these topics are covered in Chapters 9 and 10.

CHAPTER 8

Building the User Interface

- Actions and ActionList

- Predefined actions in Delphi 6

- The ControlBar and CoolBar components

- Docking toolbars and other controls

- The Action Manager architecture

Modern Windows applications usually have multiple ways of giving a command, including menu items, toolbar buttons, shortcut menus, and so on. To separate the actual commands a user can give from their multiple representations in the user interface, Delphi has the idea of actions. In Delphi 6 this architecture has been largely extended to make the construction of the user interface on top of actions totally visual. You can now also easily let the user of your programs customize this interface, as happens in many professional programs.

This chapter focuses on actions, action lists and action managers, and the related components. It also covers a few related topics, such as toolbar container controls and toolbar docking, and docking in general.

The ActionList Component

Delphi's event architecture is very open: You can write a single event handler and connect it to the OnClick events of a toolbar button and a menu. You can also connect the same event handler to different buttons or menu items, as the event handler can use the Sender parameter to refer to the object that fired the event. It's a little more difficult to synchronize the status of toolbar buttons and menu items. If you have a menu item and a toolbar button that both toggle the same option, every time the option is toggled, you must both add the check mark to the menu item and change the status of the button to show it pressed.

To overcome this problem, Delphi 4 introduced an event-handling architecture based on actions. An *action* (or command) both indicates the operation to do when a menu item or button is clicked and determines the status of all the elements connected to the action. The connection of the action with the user interface of the linked controls is very important and should not be underestimated, because it is where you can get the real advantages of this architecture.

NOTE   If you have ever written code using the MFC class library of Visual C++, you'll recognize that a Delphi action maps to both a command and a CCommandUpdateUI object. The Delphi architecture is more flexible, though, because it can be extended by subclassing the action classes.

There are many players in this event-handling architecture. The central role is certainly played by the action objects. An action object has a name, like any other component, and other properties that will be applied to the linked controls (called action clients). These properties include the Caption, the graphical representation (ImageIndex), the status (Checked, Enabled, and Visible), and the user feedback (Hint and HelpContext). There is also the ShortCut and a list of SecondaryShortCuts, the AutoCheck property for two-state actions, the help support, and a Category property used to arrange actions in logical groups.

The base class for an all action object is TBasicAction, which introduces the abstract core behavior of an action, without any specific binding or correction (not even to menu items or controls). The derived TContainedAction class introduces properties and methods that enable actions to appear in an action list or action manager. The further-derived TCustomAction class introduces support for the properties and methods of menu items and controls that are linked to action objects. Finally, there is the derived ready-to-use TAction class.

Each action object is connected to one or more client objects through an ActionLink object. Multiple controls, possibly of different types, can share the same action object, as indicated by their Action property. Technically, the ActionLink objects maintain a bidirectional connection between the client object and the action. The ActionLink object is required because the connection works in both directions. An operation on the object (such as a click) is forwarded to the action object and results in a call to its OnExecute event; an update to the status of the action object is reflected in the connected client controls. In other words, one or more client controls can create an ActionLink, which registers itself with the action object.

You should not set the properties of the client controls you connect with an action, because the action will override the property values of the client controls. For this reason, you should generally write the actions first and then create the menu items and buttons you want to connect with them. Note also that when an action has no OnExecute handler, the client control is automatically disabled (or grayed), unless the DisableIfNoHandler property is set to False.

The client controls connected to actions are usually menu items and various types of buttons (push buttons, check boxes, radio buttons, speed buttons, toolbar buttons, and the like), but nothing prevents you from creating new components that hook into this architecture. Component writers can even define new actions, as we'll do in Chapter 11, and new link action objects.

Besides a client control, some actions can also have a target component. Some predefined actions hook to a specific target component (for examples, see the coverage of the DataSet components in the Chapter 13 section "Looking for Records in a Table"). Other actions automatically look for a target component in the form that supports the given action, starting with the active control.

Finally, the action objects are held by an ActionList component, the only class of the basic architecture that shows up on the Component Palette. The action list receives the execute actions that aren't handled by the specific action objects, firing the OnExecuteAction. If even the action list doesn't handle the action, Delphi calls the OnExecuteAction event of the Application object. The ActionList component has a special editor you can use to create several actions, as you can see in Figure 8.1.

FIGURE 8.1:

The ActionList component
editor, with a list of predefined actions you can use

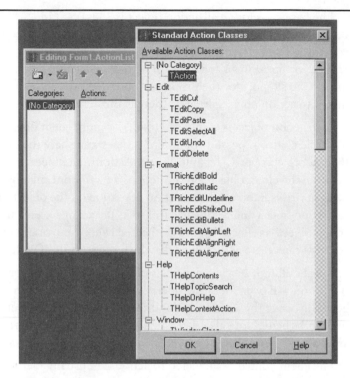

In the editor, actions are displayed in groups, as indicated by their Category property. By
simply setting this property to a brand-new value, you instruct the editor to introduce a new
category. These categories are basically logical groups, although in some cases a group of
actions can work only on a specific type of target component. You might want to define a category for every pull-down menu or group them in some other logical way.

Predefined Actions in Delphi 6

With the action list editor, you can create a brand new action or choose one of the existing
actions registered in the system. These are listed in a secondary dialog box, as shown in Figure 8.1. There are many predefined actions, which can be divided into logical groups:

File actions   include open, save as, open with, run, print setup, and exit.

Edit actions   are illustrated in the next example. They include cut, copy, paste, select all,
undo, and delete.

RichEdit actions   complement the edit actions for RichEdit controls and include bold,
italic, underline, strikeout, bullets, and various alignment actions.

MDI window actions   will be demonstrated in Chapter 10, as we examine the Multiple Document Interface approach. They include all the most common MDI operations: arrange, cascade, close, tile (horizontally or vertically), and minimize all.

Dataset actions   relate to database tables and queries and will be discussed in Chapter 13. There are many dataset actions, representing all the main operations you can perform on a dataset.

Help actions   allow you to activate the contents page or index of the Help file attached to the application.

Search actions   include find, find first, find next, and replace.

Tab and Page control actions   include previous page and next page navigation.

Dialog actions   activate color, font, open, save, and print dialogs.

List actions   include clear, copy, move, delete, and select all. These actions let you interact with a list control. Another group of actions, including static list, virtual list, and some support classes, allow the definition of lists that can be connected to a user interface. More on this topic is in the section "Using List Actions" toward the end of this chapter.

Web actions   include browse URL, download URL, and send mail actions.

Tools actions   include only the dialog to customize the action bars.

NOTE   You can also define new custom actions and register them in Delphi's IDE, as we'll see in Chapter 11.

Besides handling the OnExecute event of the action and changing the status of the action to affect the user interface of the client controls, an action can also handle the OnUpdate event, which is activated when the application is idle. This gives you the opportunity to check the status of the application or the system and change the user interface of the controls accordingly. For example, the standard PasteEdit action enables the client controls only when there is some text in the Clipboard.

Actions in Practice

Now that you understand the main ideas behind this very important Delphi feature, let's try out an example from the companion CD. The program is called Actions and demonstrates a number of features of the action architecture. I began building it by placing a new ActionList component in its form and adding the three standard edit actions and a few custom ones. The form also has a panel with some speed buttons, a main menu, and a Memo control (the automatic target of the edit actions). Listing 8.1 is the list of the actions, extracted from the DFM file.

Listing 8.1:   The actions of the Actions example

```
object ActionList1: TActionList
  Images = ImageList1
  object ActionCopy: TEditCopy
    Category = 'Edit'
    Caption = '&Copy'
    ShortCut = <Ctrl+C>
  end
  object ActionCut: TEditCut
    Category = 'Edit'
    Caption = 'Cu&t'
    ShortCut = <Ctrl+X>
  end
  object ActionPaste: TEditPaste
    Category = 'Edit'
    Caption = '&Paste'
    ShortCut = <Ctrl+V>
  end
  object ActionNew: TAction
    Category = 'File'
    Caption = '&New'
    ShortCut = <Ctrl+N>
    OnExecute = ActionNewExecute
  end
  object ActionExit: TAction
    Category = 'File'
    Caption = 'E&xit'
    ShortCut = <Alt+F4>
    OnExecute = ActionExitExecute
  end
  object NoAction: TAction
    Category = 'Test'
    Caption = '&No Action'
  end
  object ActionCount: TAction
    Category = 'Test'
    Caption = '&Count Chars'
    OnExecute = ActionCountExecute
    OnUpdate = ActionCountUpdate
  end
  object ActionBold: TAction
    Category = 'Edit'
    Caption = '&Bold'
    ShortCut = <Ctrl+B>
    OnExecute = ActionBoldExecute
  end
  object ActionEnable: TAction
    Category = 'Test'
    Caption = '&Enable NoAction'
```

```
    OnExecute = ActionEnableExecute
  end
  object ActionSender: TAction
    Category = 'Test'
    Caption = 'Test &Sender'
    OnExecute = ActionSenderExecute
  end
end
```

NOTE   The shortcut keys are stored in the DFM files using virtual key numbers, which also include
values for the Ctrl and Alt keys. In this and other listings throughout the book, I've replaced
the numbers with the literal values, enclosing them in angle brackets.

All of these actions are connected to the items of a MainMenu component and some of
them also to the buttons of a Toolbar control. Notice that the images selected in the Action-
List control affect the actions in the editor only, as you can see in Figure 8.2. For the images
of the ImageList to show up also in the menu items and in the toolbar buttons, you must also
select the image list in the MainMenu and in the Toolbar components.

FIGURE 8.2:

The ActionList editor of the
Actions example

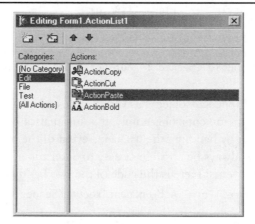

The three predefined actions for the Edit menu don't have associated handlers, but these
special objects have internal code to perform the related action on the active edit or memo
control. These actions also enable and disable themselves, depending on the content of the
Clipboard and on the existence of selected text in the active edit control. Most other actions
have custom code, except for the NoAction object. Having no code, the menu item and the
button connected with this command are disabled, even if the Enabled property of the action
is set to True.

I've added to the example, and to the Test menu, another action that enables the menu item connected to the `NoAction` object:

```
procedure TForm1.ActionEnableExecute(Sender: TObject);
begin
  NoAction.DisableIfNoHandler := False;
  NoAction.Enabled := True;
  ActionEnable.Enabled := False;
end;
```

Simply setting `Enabled` to True will produce the effect for only a very short time, unless you set the `DisableIfNoHandler` property, as discussed in the previous section. Once this operation is done, I disable the current action, since there is no need to issue the same command again.

This is different from an action you can toggle, such as the Edit ➢ Bold menu item and the corresponding speed button. Here is the code of the Bold action:

```
procedure TForm1.ActionBoldExecute(Sender: TObject);
begin
  with Memo1.Font do
    if fsBold in Style then
      Style := Style - [fsBold]
    else
      Style := Style + [fsBold];
  // toggle status
  ActionBold.Checked := not ActionBold.Checked;
end;
```

The `ActionCount` object has very simple code, but it demonstrates an `OnUpdate` handler; when the memo control is empty, it is automatically disabled. We could have obtained the same effect by handling the `OnChange` event of the memo control itself, but in general it might not always be possible or easy to determine the status of a control simply by handling one of its events. Here is the code of the two handlers of this action:

```
procedure TForm1.ActionCountExecute(Sender: TObject);
begin
  ShowMessage ('Characters: ' + IntToStr (Length (Memo1.Text)));
end;

procedure TForm1.ActionCountUpdate(Sender: TObject);
begin
  ActionCount.Enabled := Memo1.Text <> '';
end;
```

Finally, I've added a special action to test the sender object of the action event handler and get some other system information. Besides showing the object class and name, I've added code that accesses the action list object. I've done this mainly to show that you can access this information and how to do it:

```
procedure TForm1.ActionSenderExecute(Sender: TObject);
begin
  Memo1.Lines.Add ('Sender class: ' + Sender.ClassName);
  Memo1.Lines.Add ('Sender name: ' + (Sender as TComponent).Name);
  Memo1.Lines.Add ('Category: ' + (Sender as TAction).Category);
  Memo1.Lines.Add (
    'Action list name: ' + (Sender as TAction).ActionList.Name);
end;
```

You can see the output of this code in Figure 8.3, along with the user interface of the example. Notice that the Sender is not the menu item you've selected, even if the event handler is connected to it. The Sender object, which fires the event, is the action, which intercepts the user operation.

FIGURE 8.3:

The Actions example, with a detailed description of the Sender of an Action object's OnExecute event

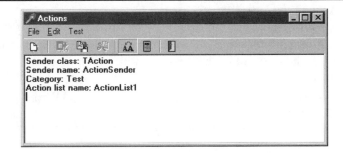

Finally, keep in mind that you can also write handlers for the events of the ActionList object itself, which play the role of global handlers for all the actions of the list, and for the Application global object, which fires for all the actions of the application. Before calling the action's OnExecute event, in fact, Delphi activates the OnExecute event of the ActionList and the OnActionExecute event of the Application global object. These events can have a look at the action, eventually execute some shared code, and then stop the execution (using the Handled parameter) or let it reach the next level.

If no event handler is assigned to respond to the action, either at the action list, application, or action level, then the application tries to identify a target object to which the action can apply itself.

NOTE   When an action is executed, it searches for a control to play the role of the action target, by looking at the active control, the active form, and other controls on the form. For example, edit actions refer to the currently active control (if they inherit from TCustomEdit), while dataset controls look for the dataset connected with the data source of the data-aware control having the input focus. Other actions follow different approaches to find a target component, but the overall idea is shared by most standard actions.

The Toolbar and the ActionList of an Editor

In the previous chapter, I built the RichBar example to demonstrate the development of an editor with a toolbar and a status bar. Of course, I should have also added a menu bar to the form, but this would have created quite a few troubles in synchronizing the status of the toolbar buttons with those of the menu items. A very good solution to this problem is to use actions, which is what I've done in the MdEdit example, discussed in this section and available on the CD.

The application is based on an ActionList component, which includes actions for file handling and Clipboard support, with code similar to the RichBar version. The Font type and color selection is still based on combo boxes, so this doesn't involve action—same for the drop-down menu of the Size button. The menu, however, has a few extra commands, including one for character counting and one for changing the background color. These are based on actions, and the same happens for the three new paragraph justification buttons (and menu commands).

One of the key differences in this new version is that the code never refers to the status of the toolbar buttons, but eventually modifies the status of the actions. In other cases I've used the actions OnUpdate events. For example, the RichEditSelectionChange method doesn't update the status of the bold button, which is connected to an action with the following OnUpdate handler:

```
procedure TFormRichNote.acBoldUpdate(Sender: TObject);
begin
  acBold.Checked := fsBold in RichEdit.SelAttributes.Style;
end;
```

Similar OnUpdate event handlers are available for most actions, including the counting operations (available only if there is some text in the RichEdit control), the Save operation (available if the text has been modified), and the Cut and Copy operations (available only if some text is selected):

```
procedure TFormRichNote.acCountcharsUpdate(Sender: TObject);
begin
  acCountChars.Enabled := RichEdit.GetTextLen > 0;
end;


procedure TFormRichNote.acSaveUpdate(Sender: TObject);
begin
  acSave.Enabled := Modified;
end;


procedure TFormRichNote.acCutUpdate(Sender: TObject);
begin
  acCut.Enabled := RichEdit.SelLength > 0;
  acCopy.Enabled := acCut.Enabled;
end;
```

In the older example, the status of the Paste button was updated in the OnIdle event of the Application object. Now that we use actions we can convert it into yet another OnUpdate handler (see the preceding chapter for details on this code):

```
procedure TFormRichNote.acPasteUpdate(Sender: TObject);
begin
  acPaste.Enabled := SendMessage (RichEdit.Handle, em_CanPaste, 0, 0) <> 0;
end;
```

Finally, the program has an addition compared to the last version: the three paragraph-alignment buttons. These toolbar buttons and the related menu items should work like radio buttons, being mutually exclusive with one of the three options always selected. For this reason the actions have the GroupIndex set to 1, the corresponding menu items have the RadioItem property set to True, and the three toolbar buttons have their Grouped property set to True and the AllowAllUp property set to False. (They are also visually enclosed between two separators.)

This is required so that the program can set the Checked property for the action corresponding to the current style, which avoids unchecking the other two actions directly. This code is part of the OnUpdate event of the action list, as it applies to multiple actions:

```
procedure TFormRichNote.ActionListUpdate(Action: TBasicAction;
  var Handled: Boolean);
begin
  // check the proper paragraph alignment
  case RichEdit.Paragraph.Alignment of
    taLeftJustify: acLeftAligned.Checked := True;
    taRightJustify: acRightAligned.Checked := True;
    taCenter: acCentered.Checked := True;
  end;
  // checks the caps lock status
  CheckCapslock;
end;
```

Finally, when one of these buttons is selected, the shared event handler uses the value of the Tag, set to the corresponding value of the TAlignment enumeration, to determine the proper alignment:

```
procedure TFormRichNote.ChangeAlignment(Sender: TObject);
begin
  RichEdit.Paragraph.Alignment := TAlignment ((Sender as TAction).Tag);
end;
```

Toolbar Containers

Most modern applications have multiple toolbars, generally hosted by a specific container. Microsoft Internet Explorer, the various standard business applications, and the Delphi IDE all use this general approach. However, they each implement this differently. Delphi has two ready-to-use toolbar containers, the CoolBar and the ControlBar components. They have differences in their user interface, but the biggest one is that the CoolBar is a Win32 common control, part of the operating system, while the ControlBar is a VCL-based component.

Both components can host toolbar controls as well as some extra elements such as combo boxes and other controls. Actually, a toolbar can also replace the menu of an application, as we'll see later on.

We'll investigate the two components in the next two sections, but I want to emphasize here (without getting too far ahead of myself) that I generally favor the use of the ControlBar. It is based on VCL (and not subject to upgrade along with each minor release of Microsoft Internet Explorer), and its user interface is nicer and more similar to that of common office applications.

A Really Cool Toolbar

The CoolBar component is basically a collection of TCoolBand objects that you can activate by selecting the Band Editor item of the CoolBar shortcut menu, the Bands property, or the Object TreeView. You can customize the CoolBar component in many ways: You can set a bitmap for its background, add some bands to the Bands collection, and then assign to each band an existing component or component container. You can use any window-based control (not graphic controls), but only some of them will show up properly. If you want to have a bitmap on the background of the CoolBar, for example, you need to use partially transparent controls.

The typical component used in a CoolBar is the Toolbar (which can be made completely transparent), but combo boxes, edit boxes, and animation controls are also quite common. This is often inspired by the user interface of Internet Explorer, the first Microsoft application featuring the CoolBar component.

You can place one band on each line or all of them on the same line. Each would use a part of the available surface, and it would be automatically enlarged when the user clicks on its title. It is easier to use this new component than to explain it. Try it yourself or follow the description below, in which we build a new version of our continuing toolbar example based on a CoolBar control. You can see the form displayed by this application at run time in Figure 8.4.

The CoolBar example has a TCoolBar component with four bands, two for each of the two lines. The first band includes a subset of the toolbar of the previous example, this time adding an ImageList for the highlighted images. The second has an edit box used to set the font of the text; the third has a ColorGrid component, used to choose the font color and that of the background. The last band has a ComboBox control with the available fonts.

FIGURE 8.4:

The form of the CoolBar example at run time

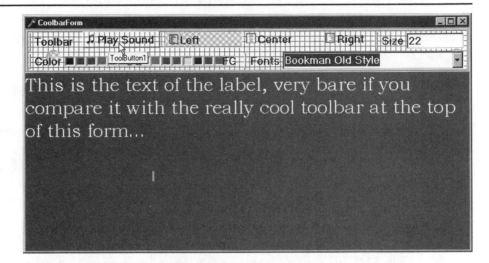

The user interface of the CoolBar component is really very nice, and Microsoft is increasingly using it in its applications. However, the Windows CoolBar control has had many different and incompatible versions, as Microsoft has released different versions of the common control library with different versions of the Internet Explorer. Some of these versions "broke" existing programs built with Delphi.

NOTE   It is interesting to note that Microsoft applications generally don't use the common control libraries. Word and Excel use their own internal versions of the common controls, and VB uses an OCX, not the common controls directly. Part of the reason that Borland had so much trouble with the common controls is that it uses them more (and in more ways) than even Microsoft does.

For this reason, Borland introduced (in Delphi 4) a toolbar container called the Control-Bar. A control bar hosts several controls, as a CoolBar does, and offers a similar user interface that lets a user drag items and reorganize the toolbar at run time. A good example of the use of the ControlBar control is Delphi's own toolbar, but Microsoft applications use a very similar user interface.

The ControlBar

The ControlBar is a control container, and you build it just by placing other controls inside it, as you do with a panel (there is no list of Bands in it). Every control placed in the bar gets its own dragging area (a small panel with two vertical lines, on the left of the control), as you can see in Figure 8.5. For this reason, you should generally avoid placing specific buttons inside the ControlBar, but rather add containers with buttons inside them. Rather than using a panel, you should generally use one ToolBar control for every section of the ControlBar.

FIGURE 8.5:

The ControlBar is a container that allows a user to drag all the elements, using the special drag bar on the side. Notice that each button gets a separate drag bar, something you'll generally try to avoid.

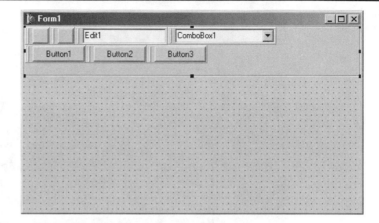

The MdEdit2 example is another version of the demo we've developed throughout the last and this chapter. I've basically grouped the buttons into three toolbars (instead of a single one) and left the two combo boxes as stand-alone controls. All these components are inside a ControlBar, so that a user can arrange them at runtime, as you can see in Figure 8.6.

FIGURE 8.6:

The MdEdit2 example at run time, while a user is rearranging the toolbars in the control bar

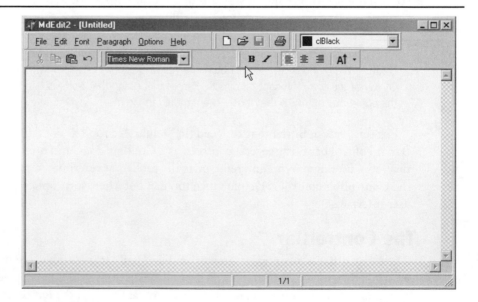

The following snippet of the DFM listing of the MdEdit2 example shows how the various toolbars and controls are embedded in the ControlBar component:

```
object ControlBar1: TControlBar
  Align = alTop
  AutoSize = True
  ShowHint = True
  PopupMenu = BarMenu
  object ToolBarFile: TToolBar
    Flat = True
    Images = Images
    Wrapable = False
    object ToolButton1: TToolButton
      Action = acNew
    end
    // more buttons...
  end
  object ToolBarEdit: TToolBar...
  object ToolBarFont: TToolBar...
  object ToolBarMenu: TToolBar
    AutoSize = True
    Flat = True
    Menu = MainMenu
  end
  object ComboFont: TComboBox
    Hint = 'Font Family'
    Style = csDropDownList
    OnClick = ComboFontClick
  end
  object ColorBox1: TColorBox...
end
```

To obtain the standard effect, you have to disable the edges of the toolbar controls and set their style to flat. Sizing all the controls alike, so that you obtain one or two rows of elements of the same height, is not as easy as it might seem at first. Some controls have automatic sizing or various constraints. In particular, to make the combo box the same height as the toolbars, you have to tweak the type and size of its font. Resizing the control itself has no effect.

The ControlBar also has a shortcut menu that allows you to show or hide each of the controls currently inside it. Instead of writing code specific to this example, I've implemented a more generic (and reusable) solution. The shortcut menu, called BarMenu, is empty at design time and is populated when the program starts:

```
procedure TFormRichNote.FormCreate(Sender: TObject);
var
  I: Integer;
  mItem: TMenuItem;
```

```
begin
  ...
  // populate the control bar menu
  for I := 0 to ControlBar.ControlCount - 1 do
  begin
    mItem := TMenuItem.Create (Self);
    mItem.Caption := ControlBar.Controls [I].Name;
    mItem.Tag := Integer (ControlBar.Controls [I]);
    mItem.OnClick := BarMenuClick;
    BarMenu.Items.Add (mItem);
  end;
```

The BarMenuClick procedure is a single event handler that is used by all of the items of the menu and uses the Tag property of the Sender menu item to refer to the element of the ControlBar associated with the item in the FormCreate method:

```
procedure TFormRichNote.BarMenuClick(Sender: TObject);
var
  aCtrl: TControl;
begin
  aCtrl := TControl ((Sender as TComponent).Tag);
  aCtrl.Visible := not aCtrl.Visible;
end;
```

Finally, the OnPopup event of the menu is used to refresh the check mark of the menu items:

```
procedure TFormRichNote.BarMenuPopup(Sender: TObject);
var
  I: Integer;
begin
  // update the menu checkmarks
  for I := 0 to BarMenu.Items.Count - 1 do
    BarMenu.Items [I].Checked := TControl (BarMenu.Items [I].Tag).Visible;
end;
```

A Menu in a Control Bar

If you look at the user interface of the MdEdit2 application, in Figure 8.6, you'll notice that the menu of the form actually shows up inside a toolbar, hosted by the control bar, and below the application caption. In prior versions of Delphi, this required writing some custom code. In Delphi 6, instead, all you have to do is to set the Menu property of the toolbar. You must also remove the main menu from the Menu property of the form, to avoid having two menus.

Delphi's Docking Support

Another feature added in Delphi 4 was support for *dockable* toolbars and controls. In other words, you can create a toolbar and move it to any of the sides of a form, or even move it freely on the screen, undocking it. However, setting up a program properly to obtain this effect is not as easy as it sounds.

First of all, Delphi's docking support is connected with container controls, not with forms. A panel, a ControlBar, and other containers (technically, any control derived from TWinControl) can be set up as dock targets by enabling their DockSite property. You can also set the Auto-Size property of these containers, so that they'll show up only if they actually hold a control.

To be able to drag a control (an object of any TControl-derived class) into the dock site, simply set its DragKind property to dkDock and its DragMode property to dmAutomatic. This way, the control can be dragged away from its current position into a new docking container. To undock a component and move it to a special form, you can set its FloatingDockSiteClass property to TCustomDockForm (to use a predefined stand-alone form with a small caption).

All the docking and undocking operations can be tracked by using special events of the component being dragged (OnStartDock and OnEndDock) and the component that will receive the docked control (OnDragOver and OnDragDrop). These docking events are very similar to the dragging events available in earlier versions of Delphi.

There are also commands you can use to accomplish docking operations in code and to explore the status of a docking container. Every control can be moved to a different location using the Dock, ManualDock, and ManualFloat methods. A container has a DockClientCount property, indicating the number of docked controls, and a DockClients property, with the array of these controls.

Moreover, if the dock container has the UseDockManager property set to True, you'll be able to use the DockManager property, which implements the IDockManager interface. This interface has many features you can use to customize the behavior of a dock container, even including support for streaming its status.

As you can see from this brief description, docking support in Delphi is based on a large number of properties, events, methods and objects (such as dock zones and dock trees)—more features than we have room to explore in detail. The next example introduces the main features you'll generally need.

NOTE   Docking support in not currently available in VisualCLX on either platform.

Docking Toolbars in ControlBars

In the MdEdit2 example, already discussed, I've included docking support. The program has a second ControlBar at the bottom of the form, which accepts dragging one of the toolbars in the ControlBar at the top. Since both toolbar containers have the AutoSize property set to True, they are automatically removed when the host contains no controls. I've also set to True the AutoDrag and AutoDock properties of both ControlBars.

Actually, I had to place the bottom ControlBar inside a panel, together with the RichEdit control. Without this trick, the ControlBar, when activated and automatically resized, kept moving below the status bar, which I don't think is the correct behavior. Because, in the example, the ControlBar is the only control of the panel aligned to the bottom, there is no possible confusion.

To let users drag the toolbars out of the original container, all you have to do is, once again (as stated previously), set their DragKind property to dkDock and their DragMode property to dmAutomatic. The only two exceptions are the menu toolbar, which I decided to keep close to the typical position of a menu bar, and the ColorBox control, as unlike the combo box this component doesn't expose the DragMode and DragKind properties. (Actually, in the FormCreate method of the example, you'll find code you can use to activate docking for the component, based on the "protected hack" discussed in Chapter 3.) The Fonts combo box can be dragged, but I don't want to let a user dock it in the lower control bar. To implement this constraint, I've used the control bar's OnDockOver event handler, by accepting the docking operation only for toolbars:

```
procedure TFormRichNote.ControlBarLowerDockOver(Sender: TObject;
  Source: TDragDockObject; X, Y: Integer; State: TDragState;
  var Accept: Boolean);
begin
  Accept := Source.Control is TToolbar;
end;
```

When you move one of the toolbars outside of any container, Delphi automatically creates a floating form; you might be tempted to set it back by closing the floating form. This doesn't work, as the floating form is removed along with the toolbar it contains. However, you can use the shortcut menu of the topmost ControlBar, attached also to the other ControlBar, to show this hidden toolbar.

The floating form created by Delphi to host undocked controls has a thin caption, the so-called *toolbar caption*, which by default has no text. For this reason, I've added some code to the OnEndDock event of each dockable control, to set the caption of the newly created form into which the control is docked. To avoid a custom data structure for this information, I've used the text of the Hint property of these controls, which is basically not used, to provide a suitable caption:

```
procedure TFormRichNote.EndDock(Sender, Target: TObject; X, Y: Integer);
begin
  if Target is TCustomForm then
    TCustomForm(Target).Caption := GetShortHint((Sender as TControl).Hint);
end;
```

You can see an example of this effect in the MdEdit2 program in Figure 8.7. Another extension of the example, one which I haven't done, could be the addition of dock areas on the two sides of the form. The only extra effort this requires would be a routine to turn the toolbars vertically, instead of horizontally. This basically implies switching the Left and Top properties of each button, after disabling the automatic sizing.

FIGURE 8.7:

The MdEdit2 example allows you to dock the toolbars (but not the menu) at the top or bottom of the form or to leave them floating.

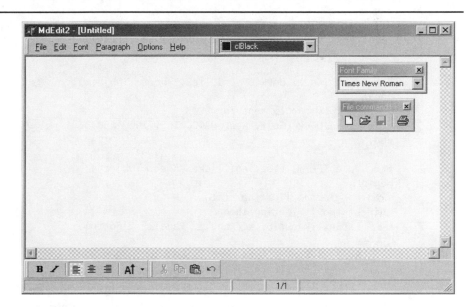

Controlling Docking Operations

Delphi provides many events and methods that give you a lot of control over docking operations, including a dock manager. To explore some of these features, try out the DockTest example, a test bed for docking operations. The program assigns the FloatingDockSiteClass property of a Memo component to TForm2, so that you can design specific features and add them to the floating frame that will host the control when it is floating, instead of using an instance of the default TCustomDockForm class.

Another feature of the program is that it handles the OnDockOver and OnDockDrop events of a dock host panel to display messages to the user, such as the number of controls currently docked:

```
procedure TForm1.Panel1DockDrop(Sender: TObject; Source: TDragDockObject;
  X, Y: Integer);
begin
  Caption := 'Docked: ' + IntToStr (Panel1.DockClientCount);
end;
```

In the same way, the program also handles the main form's docking events. Another control, a list box, has a shortcut menu you can invoke to perform docking and undocking operations in code, without the usual mouse dragging:

```
procedure TForm1.DocktoPanel1Click(Sender: TObject);
begin
  // dock to the panel
  ListBox1.ManualDock (Panel1, Panel1, alBottom);
end;

procedure TForm1.DocktoForm1Click(Sender: TObject);
begin
  // dock to the current form
  ListBox1.Dock (Self, Rect (200, 100, 100, 100));
end;

procedure TForm1.Floating1Click(Sender: TObject);
begin
  // toggle the floating status
  if ListBox1.Floating then
    ListBox1.ManualDock (Panel1, Panel1, alBottom)
  else
    ListBox1.ManualFloat (Rect (100, 100, 200, 300));
  Floating1.Checked := ListBox1.Floating;
end;
```

The final feature of the example is probably the most interesting one: Every time the program closes, it saves the current docking status of the panel, using the dock manager support. When the program is reopened, it reapplies the docking information, restoring the previous configuration of the windows. The program does this only with the panel, so the other floating windows will be displayed in their original positions. Here is the code for saving and loading:

```
procedure TForm1.FormDestroy(Sender: TObject);
var
  FileStr: TFileStream;
begin
```

```
  if Panel1.DockClientCount > 0 then
  begin
    FileStr := TFileStream.Create (DockFileName, fmCreate or fmOpenWrite);
    try
      Panel1.DockManager.SaveToStream (FileStr);
    finally
      FileStr.Free;
    end;
  end
  else
    // remove the file
    DeleteFile (DockFileName);
end;

procedure TForm1.FormCreate(Sender: TObject);
var
  FileStr: TFileStream;
begin
  // reload the settings
  DockFileName := ExtractFilePath (Application.Exename) + 'dock.dck';
  if FileExists (DockFileName) then
  begin
    FileStr := TFileStream.Create (DockFileName, fmOpenRead);
    try
      Panel1.DockManager.LoadFromStream (FileStr);
    finally
      FileStr.Free;
    end;
  end;
  Panel1.DockManager.ResetBounds (True);
end;
```

There are more features one might theoretically add to a docking program, but to add those you should remove other features, as some of them might conflict. For example, automatic alignments don't work terribly well with the docking manager's code for restoring. I suggest you take this program and explore its behavior, extending it to support the type of user interface you prefer.

NOTE   Remember that although docking panels make an application look nice, some users get confused by the fact that their toolbars might disappear or be in a different position than they are used to. Don't overuse the docking features, or some of your inexperienced users may get lost.

Docking to a PageControl

Another interesting feature of page controls is the specific support for docking. As you dock a new control over a PageControl, a new page is automatically added to host it, as you can easily see in the Delphi environment. To accomplish this, you simply set the PageControl as a dock host and activate docking for the client controls. This works best when you have secondary forms you want to host. Moreover, if you want to be able to move the entire Page-Control into a floating window and then dock it back, you'll need a docking panel in the main form.

This is exactly what I've done in the DockPage example, which has a main form with the following settings:

```
object Form1: TForm1
  Caption = 'Docking Pages'
  object Panel1: TPanel
    Align = alLeft
    DockSite = True
    OnMouseDown = Panel1MouseDown
    object PageControl1: TPageControl
      ActivePage = TabSheet1
      Align = alClient
      DockSite = True
      DragKind = dkDock
      object TabSheet1: TTabSheet
        Caption = 'List'
        object ListBox1: TListBox
          Align = alClient
        end
      end
    end
  end
  object Splitter1: TSplitter
    Cursor = crHSplit
  end
  object Memo1: TMemo
    Align = alClient
  end
end
```

Notice that the Panel has the UseDockManager property set to True and that the PageControl invariably hosts a page with a list box, as when you remove all of the pages, the code used for automatic sizing of dock containers might cause you some trouble. Now the program has two other forms, with similar settings (although they host different controls):

```
object Form2: TForm2
  Caption = 'Small Editor'
```

```
    DragKind = dkDock
    DragMode = dmAutomatic
    object Memo1: TMemo
      Align = alClient
    end
  end
```

You can drag these forms onto the page control to add new pages to it, with captions corresponding with the form titles. You can also undock each of these controls and even the entire PageControl. To do this, the program doesn't enable automatic dragging, which would make it impossible to switch pages anymore. Instead, the feature is activated when the user clicks on the area of the PageControl that has no tabs—that is, on the underlying panel:

```
procedure TForm1.Panel1MouseDown(Sender: TObject; Button: TMouseButton;
  Shift: TShiftState; X, Y: Integer);
begin
  PageControl1.BeginDrag (False, 10);
end;
```

You can test this behavior by running the DockPage example, although Figure 8.8 tries to depict it. Notice that when you remove the PageControl from the main form, you can directly dock the other forms to the panel and then split the area with other controls. This is the situation captured by the figure.

FIGURE 8.8:

The main form of the Dock-Page example after a form has been docked to the page control on the left. Notice that another form uses part of the area of a hosting panel.

The ActionManager Architecture

We have seen that actions and the ActionManager component can play a central role in the development of Delphi applications, since they allow a much better separation of the user interface from the actual code of the application. The user interface, in fact, can now easily change without impacting the code too much. The drawback of this approach is that a programmer has more work to do. To have a new menu item, you need to add the corresponding action first, than move to the menu, add the menu item, and connect it to the action.

To solve this issue, and to provider developers and end users with some advanced features, Delphi 6 introduces a brand new architecture, based on the ActionManager component, which largely extends the role of actions. The ActionManager, in fact, has a collection of actions but also a collection of toolbars and menus tied to them. The development of these toolbars and menus is completely visual: you drag actions from a special component editor of the ActionManager to the toolbars to have the buttons you need. Moreover, you can let the end user of your programs do the same operation, and rearrange their own toolbars and menus starting with the actions you provide them.

In other words, using this architecture allows you to build applications with a modern user interface, customizable by the user. The menu can show only the recently used items (as many Microsoft programs do, nowadays), allows for animation, and more.

This architecture is centered on the ActionManager component, but includes also a few others components found at the end of the Additional page of the palette:

- The ActionManager component is a replacement of the ActionList (but can also use one or more existing ActionLists) adding to the architecture visual containers of actions.

- The ActionMainMenuBar control is a toolbar used to display the menu of an application based on the actions of an ActionManager component.

- The ActionToolBar control is a toolbar used to host buttons based on the actions of an ActionManager component.

- The CustomizeDlg component includes the dialog box you can use to let users customize the user interface of an application based on the ActionManager component.

Building a Simple Demo

As this architecture is mostly a visual architecture, a demo is probably worth more than a general discussion (although a printed book is not the best way to discuss a highly visual series of operations). To create a sample program based on this architecture, first drop an ActionManager component on a form, then double click it to open its component editor, shown in Figure 8.9. Notice that this editor is not modal, so you can keep it open while doing other operations in Delphi. Consider also that this same dialog box is displayed by the CustomizeDlg component, although with some limited features (for example, adding new actions is disabled).

FIGURE 8.9:

The three pages of the ActionManager editor dialog box

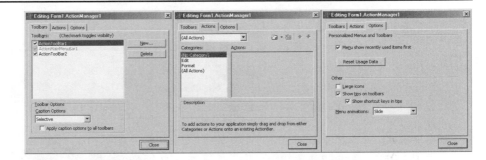

- The first page of this editor provides a list of visual containers of actions (toolbars or menus). You add new toolbars by clicking the New button. To add new menus, you have to add the corresponding component to the form, then open the `ActionBars` collection of the ActionManager, select an action bar or add a new one, and hook the menu to it using the `ActionBar` property. These are the same steps you could follow to connect a new toolbar to this architecture at run time.

- The second page of the ActionManager editor is very similar to the ActionList editor, providing a way to add new standard or custom action, arrange them in categories, and change their order. The new feature of this page, though, is that fact you can drag a category or a single action from it and drop it onto an action bar control. If you drag a category to a menu, you obtain a pull-down menu with all of the items of the category; if you drag it to a toolbar, each of the actions of the category gets a button on the toolbar. If you drag a single action to a toolbar, you get the corresponding button; if you drag it to the menu, you get a direct menu command, which is something you should generally avoid.

- The last page of the ActionManager editor allows you (and optionally an end user) to activate the display of recently used menu items and to modify some of the visual properties of the toolbars.

The AcManTest program is an example that uses some of the standard actions and a RichEdit control to showcase the use of this architecture (I haven't actually written any custom code to make the actions work better, as I wanted to focus only on the action manager for this example). You can experiment with it at design time or run it, click the Customize button, and see what an end user can do to customize the application (see Figure 8.10).

FIGURE 8.10:

Using the CustomizeDlg component, you can let a user customize the toolbars and the menu of an application, simply by dragging items from the dialog box or moving them around in the actions bars themselves.

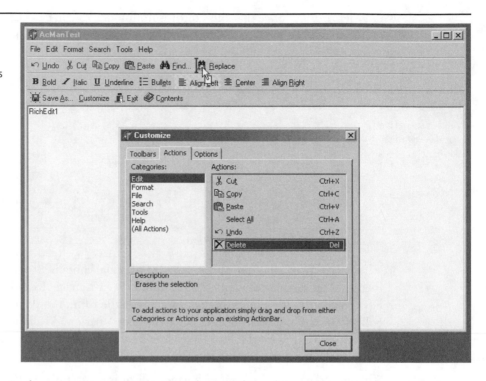

Actually, in the program you can prevent the user from doing some operations on actions. Any specific element of the user interface (a TActionClient object) has a ChangedAllowed property that you can use to disable modify, move, and delete operations. Any action client container (the visual bars) has a property to disable hiding itself (AllowHiding by default is set to True). Each ActionBar Items collection has a Customizable option you can turn off to disable all user changes to the entire bar.

TIP   When I say "ActionBar" I don't mean the visual toolbars containing action items, but the items of the ActionBars collection of the ActionManager component, which in turn has an Items collection. The best way to understand this structure is to look at the sub-tree displayed by the Object TreeView for an ActionManager component. Each TActionBar collection item has an actual TCustomActionBar visual component connected, but not the reverse (so, for example, you cannot reach this Customizable property if you start by selecting the visual toolbar). Due to the similarity of the two names, it can take a while to understand what the Delphi help actually means.

To make user settings persistent, I've connected a file (called settings) to the FileName property of the ActionManager component. When you assign this property, you should enter a name of the file you want to use; when you start the program, the file will be created for you by the ActionManager.

The persistency is accomplished by streaming each ActionClientItem connected with the action manager. As these action client items are based on the user settings and maintain state information, a single file collects both user changes to the interface and usage data.

Since Delphi stores user setting and status information in a file you provide, you can make your application support multiple users on a single computer. Simply use a file of settings for each of them and connect it to the action manager as the program starts (using the current user of the computer or after some custom login). Another possibility is to store these settings over the network, so that even when a user moves to a different computer, the current personal settings will move along.

Least-Recently Used Menu Items

Once a file for the user settings is available, the ActionManager will save into it the user preferences and also use it to track the user activity. This is essential to let the system remove menu items which haven't been used for some time, making them available in an extended menu, using the same user interface adopted by Microsoft (see Figure 8.11 for an actual example).

FIGURE 8.11:

The ActionManager disables least recently used menu items that you can still see by selecting the menu extension command.

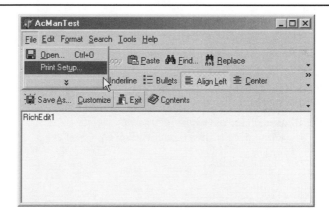

The ActionManager doesn't simply show the least recently used items: it allows you to customize this behavior in a very precise way. Each action bar has a SessionCount property that keeps track of the number of times the application has been executed. Each ActionClientItem has a LastSession property and a UsageCount property used to track user operations. Notice, by the way, that a user can reset all this dynamic information by using the Reset Usage Data button of the customization dialog.

The system calculates the number of sessions the action has gone unused, by computing the difference between the number of times the application has been executed (SessionCount) and the last session in which the action has been used (LastSession). The value of UsageCount is used to look up in the PrioritySchedule how many sessions the items can go unused before it is removed. In other words, the PrioritySchedule maps each the usage count with a number of *unused* sessions. By modifying the PrioritySchedule, you can determine how fast the items are removed in case they are not used.

You can also prevent this system to be activated for specific actions or groups of actions. The Items property of the ActionBars of the ActionManager has a HideUnused property you can toggle to disable this feature for an entire menu. To make a specific item always visible, regardless of the actual usage, you can also set its UsageCount property to –1. However, the user settings might override this value.

To understand a little better how this system works, I've added a custom action (Action-ShowStatus) to the AcManTest example. The action has the following code that saves the current action manager settings to a memory stream, converts it to text, and shows it inside the memo (refer to Chapter 5 for more information about streaming):

```
procedure TForm1.ActionShowStatusExecute(Sender: TObject);
var
  memStr, memStr2: TMemoryStream;
begin
  memStr := TMemoryStream.Create;
  try
    memStr2 := TMemoryStream.Create;
    try
      ActionManager1.SaveToStream(memStr);
      memStr.Position := 0;
      ObjectBinaryToText(memStr, memStr2);
      memStr2.Position := 0;
      RichEdit1.Lines.LoadFromStream(memStr2);
    finally
      memStr2.Free;
    end;
  finally
    memStr.Free;
  end;
end;
```

The output you obtain is the textual version of the settings file automatically updated at each execution of the program. Here a small portion of this file, with the details of one of pull-down menus and plenty of extra comments:

```
item // File pulldown of the main menu action bar
  Items = <
```

```
item
  Action = Form1.FileOpen1
  LastSession = 19 // was used in the last session
  UsageCount = 4 // was used four times
end
item
  Action = Form1.FileSaveAs1 // never used
end
item
  Action = Form1.FilePrintSetup1
  LastSession = 7 // used some time ago
  UsageCount = 1 // only once
end
item
  Action = Form1.FileRun1 // never used
end
item
  Action = Form1.FileExit1 // never used
end>
Caption = '&File'
LastSession = 19
UsageCount = 5 // the sum of the usage count of the items
end
```

Porting an Existing Program

If this architecture is nice, you'll probably need to redo most of your applications to take advantage of it. However, if you're already using actions (with the ActionList component), this conversion will be much simpler. In fact, the ActionManager has its own set of actions but can also use actions from another ActionManager or ActionList. The LinkedActionLists property of the ActionManager is a collection of other containers of actions (ActionLists or ActionManagers), which can be associated with the current one. Associating all the various groups of action is useful to let a user customize the entire user interface with a single dialog box.

If you hook external actions and open the ActionManager editor, you'll see in the Actions page a combo box listing the current ActionManager plus the other action containers linked to it. You can choose one of these containers to see its set of actions and change their properties. The All Action option of this combo box allows you to work on all of the actions from the various containers at once, but I've noticed that at startup it is selected but not always *effective*. Reselect it to actually see all of the actions.

As an example of porting an existing application, I've extended the program built throughout this chapter, into the MdEdit3 example. This example uses the same action list of the previous version hooked to an ActionManager that has the extra customize property, to let users rearrange the user interface. Differently from the earlier AcManDemo program, the MdEdit3 example uses a ControlBar as a container for the action bars (a menu, three toolbars, and the usual combo boxes) and has full support for dragging them outside of the container as floating bars and dropping them into the lower ControlBar.

To accomplish this, I only had to modify the source code slightly to refer to the new classes for the containers (that is, `TCustomActionToolBar` instead of `TToolBar`) in the `ControlBarLowerDockOver` method. I also found out that the `OnEndDock` event of the ActionToolBar component passes as parameter an empty target when the system creates a floating form to host the control, so that I couldn't easily give to this forms a new custom caption (see the `EndDock` method of the form).

Using List Actions

We'll see more examples of the use of this architecture in the chapters devoted to MDI and database programming. For the moment, I just want to add an extra example showing how to use a rather complex group of standard actions introduced in Delphi 6, the list actions. List actions, in fact, comprise two different groups. Some of them (such as the Move, Copy, Delete, Clear, and Select All) actions are normal actions working on list boxes or other lists. The VirtualListAction and StaticListAction elements, instead, define actions based multiple choices, which are going to be displayed in a toolbar as a combo box.

The ListActions demo highlights both groups of list actions, as its ActionManager has five of them, displayed on two separate toolbars. This is a summary of the actions of the actions manager (I've omitted the action bars portion of the component's DFM file):

```
object ActionManager1: TActionManager
  ActionBars.SessionCount = 1
  ActionBars = <...>
  object StaticListAction1: TStaticListAction
    Caption = 'Numbers'
    Items.CaseSensitive = False
    Items.SortType = stNone
    Items = <
      item
        Caption = 'one'
      end
      item
        Caption = 'two'
      end
      ...>
    OnItemSelected = ListActionItemSelected
  end
  object VirtualListAction1: TVirtualListAction
    Caption = 'Items'
```

```
      OnGetItem = VirtualListAction1GetItem
      OnGetItemCount = VirtualListAction1GetItemCount
      OnItemSelected = ListActionItemSelected
    end
    object ListControlCopySelection1: TListControlCopySelection
      Caption = 'Copy'
      Destination = ListBox2
      ListControl = ListBox1
    end
    object ListControlDeleteSelection1: TListControlDeleteSelection
      Caption = 'Delete'
    end
    object ListControlMoveSelection2: TListControlMoveSelection
      Caption = 'Move'
      Destination = ListBox2
      ListControl = ListBox1
    end
  end
```

The program has also two list boxes in its form, used as action targets. The Copy and Move actions are tied to these two list boxes by their ListControl and Destination properties. The Delete action, instead, automatically works with the list box having the input focus.

The StaticListAction defines a series of alternative items, in its Items collection. This is not a plain string list, as any item has also an ImageIndex, which allows turning the combo box in graphical selection. You can, of course, add more items to this list programmatically. However, in case of a highly dynamic list, you can also use the VirtualListAction. This component doesn't define a list of items but has two events you can use to provide strings and images for the list. The OnGetItemCount event allows you to indicate the number of items to display; the OnGetItem event is then called for each specific item.

In the ListActions demo, the VirtualListAction has the following event handlers for its definition, producing the list you can see in the active combo box of Figure 8.12:

```
procedure TForm1.VirtualListAction1GetItemCount(Sender: TCustomListAction;
  var Count: Integer);
begin
  Count := 100;
end;

procedure TForm1.VirtualListAction1GetItem(Sender: TCustomListAction;
  const Index: Integer; var Value: String;
  var ImageIndex: Integer; var Data: Pointer);
begin
  Value := 'Item' + IntToStr (Index);
end;
```

FIGURE 8.12:

The ListActions application has a toolbar hosting a static list and a virtual one.

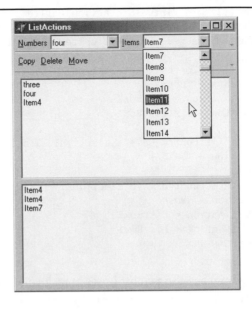

I thought that the virtual action items were actually requested only when needed to display them, making this actually a virtual list. Instead, all the items are created right away, as you can prove by enabling the commented code of the `VirtualListAction1GetItem` method (not in the listing above), which adds to each item the time its string is requested.

Both the static and the virtual list have an `OnItemSelected` event. In the shared event handler, I've written the following code, to add the current item to the first list box of the form:

```
procedure TForm1.ListActionItemSelected(Sender: TCustomListAction;
  Control: TControl);
begin
  ListBox1.Items.Add ((Control as TCustomActionCombo).SelText);
end;
```

In this case, the sender is the custom action list, but the `ItemIndex` property of this list is not updated with the selected item. However, accessing the visual control that displays the list, we can obtain the value of the selected item.

What's Next?

In this chapter, I've introduced the use of actions, the actions list, and action manager architectures. As you've seen, this is an extremely powerful architecture to separate the user interface from the actual code of your applications, which uses and refers to the actions and not the menu items or toolbar button related to them. The Delphi 6 extension of this architecture allows users of your programs to have a lot of control, and makes your applications resemble high-end programs without much effort on your part. The same architecture is also very handy to let you design the user interface of your program, regardless of whether you give this ability to users.

I've also covered other user-interface techniques, such as docking toolbars and other controls. You can consider this chapter the first step toward building professional applications. We will take other steps in the following chapters; but you already know enough to make your programs similar to some best-selling Windows applications, which may be very important for your clients.

Now that the elements of the main form of our programs are properly set up, we can consider adding secondary forms and dialog boxes. This is the topic of the next chapter, along with a general introduction to forms. The following chapter will then cover the overall structure of a Delphi application.

CHAPTER 9

Working with Forms

- Form styles, border styles, and border icons

- Mouse and keyboard input

- Painting and special effects

- Positioning, scaling, and scrolling forms

- Creating and closing forms

- Modal and modeless dialog boxes and forms

- Creating secondary forms dynamically

- Predefined dialog boxes

- Building a splash screen

If you've read the previous chapters, you should now be able to use Delphi's visual components to create the user interface of your applications. So let's turn our attention to another central element of development in Delphi: forms. We have used forms since the initial chapters, but I've never described in detail what you can do with a form, which properties you can use, or which methods of the TForm class are particularly interesting.

This chapter looks at some of the properties and styles of forms and at sizing and positioning them. I'll also introduce applications with multiple forms, the use of dialog boxes (custom and predefined ones), frames, and visual form inheritance. I'll also devote some time to input on a form, both from the keyboard and the mouse.

The *TForm* Class

Forms in Delphi are defined by the TForm class, included in the Forms unit of VCL. Of course, there is now a second definition of forms inside VisualCLX. Although I'll mainly refer to the VCL class in this chapter, I'll also try to highlight differences with the cross-platform version provided in CLX.

The TForm class is part of the windowed-controls hierarchy, which starts with the TWinControl (or TWidgetControl) class. Actually, TForm inherits from the *almost complete* TCustomForm, which in turn inherits from TScrollingWinControl (or TScrollingWidget). Having all of the features of their many base classes, forms have a long series of methods, properties, and events. For this reason, I won't try to list them here, but I'd rather present some interesting techniques related to forms throughout this chapter. I'll start by presenting a technique for *not* defining the form of a program at design time, using the TForm class directly, and then explore a few interesting properties of the form class.

Throughout the chapter, I'll point out a few differences between VCL forms and CLX forms. I've actually built a CLX version for most of the examples of this chapter, so you can immediately start experimenting with forms and dialog boxes in CLX, as well as VCL. As in past chapters, the CLX version of each example is prefixed by the letter *Q*.

Using Plain Forms

Generally, Delphi developers tend to create forms at design time, which implies deriving a new class from the base one, and build the content of the form visually. This is certainly a reasonable standard practice, but it is not compulsory to create a descendant of the TForm class to show a form, particularly if it is a simple one.

Consider this case: you have to show a rather long message (based on a string) to a user, and you don't want to use the simple predefined message box, as it will show up too large and not provide scroll bars. You can create a form with a memo component in it, and display the string inside it. Nothing prevents you from creating this form in the standard visual way, but you might consider doing this in code, particularly if you need a large degree of flexibility.

The DynaForm and QDynaForm examples (both on the companion CD), which are somewhat extreme, have no form defined at design time but include a unit with this function:

```
procedure ShowStringForm (str: string);
var
  form: TForm;
begin
  Application.CreateForm (TForm, form);
  form.caption := 'DynaForm';
  form.Position := poScreenCenter;
  with TMemo.Create (form) do
  begin
    Parent := form;
    Align := alClient;
    Scrollbars := ssVertical;
    ReadOnly := True;
    Color := form.Color;
    BorderStyle := bsNone;
    WordWrap := True;
    Text := str;
  end;
  form.Show;
end;
```

Besides the fact I had to create the form using the Application global object, a feature required by Delphi applications and discussed in the next chapter, this code simply does dynamically what you generally do with the form designer. Writing this code is undoubtedly more tedious, but it allows also a greater deal of flexibility, because any parameter can depend on external settings.

The ShowStringForm function above is not executed by an event of another form, as there are no traditional forms in this program. Instead, I've modified the project's source code to the following:

```
program DynaForm;

uses
  Forms,
  DynaMemo in 'DynaMemo.pas';

{$R *.RES}

var
```

```
  str: string;

begin
  str := '';
  Randomize;
  while Length (str) < 2000 do
    str := str + Char (32 + Random (94));
  ShowStringForm (str);

  Application.Run;
end.
```

The effect of running the DynaForm program is a strange-looking form filled with random characters (as you can see in Figure 9.1), not terribly useful in itself but for the idea it underscores.

FIGURE 9.1:

The dynamic form generated by the DynaForm example is completely created at run time, with no design-time support.

TIP   An indirect advantage of this approach, compared to the use of DFM files for design-time forms, is that it would be much more difficult for an external programmer to grab information about the structure of the application. In Chapter 5 we saw that you can extract the DFM from the current Delphi executable file, but the same can be easily accomplished for any executable file compiled with Delphi for which you don't have the source code. If it is really important for you to keep to yourself a specific set of components you are using (maybe those in a specific form), and the default values of their properties, writing the extra code might be worth the effort.

The Form Style

The FormStyle property allows you to choose between a normal form (fsNormal) and the windows that make up a Multiple Document Interface (MDI) application. In this case, you'll use the fsMDIForm style for the MDI parent window—that is, the frame window of the MDI application—and the fsMDIChild style for the MDI child window. To know more about the development of an MDI application, look at Chapter 10.

A fourth option is the fsStayOnTop style, which determines whether the form has to always remain on top of all other windows, except for any that also happen to be "stay-on-top" windows.

To create a top-most form (a form whose window is always on top), you need only set the FormStyle property, as indicated above. This property has two different effects, depending on the kind of form you apply it to:

- The main form of an application will remain in front of every other application (unless other applications have the same top-most style, too). At times, this generates a rather ugly visual effect, so this makes sense only for special-purpose alert programs.

- A secondary form will remain in front of any other form of the application it belongs to. The windows of other applications are not affected, though. This is often used for floating toolbars and other forms that should stay in front of the main window.

The Border Style

Another important property of a form is its BorderStyle. This property refers to a visual element of the form, but it has a much more profound influence on the *behavior* of the window, as you can see in Figure 9.2.

FIGURE 9.2:

Sample forms with the various border styles, created by the Borders example

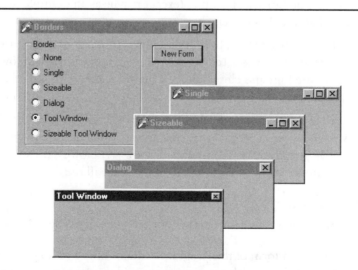

At design time, the form is always shown using the default value of the BorderStyle property, bsSizeable. This corresponds to a Windows style known as *thick frame*. When a main window has a thick frame around it, a user can resize it by dragging its border. This is made clear by the special *resize* cursors (with the shape of a double-pointer arrow) displayed when the user moves the mouse onto this thick window border.

A second important choice for this property is bsDialog. If you select it, the form uses as its border the typical dialog-box frame—a thick frame that doesn't allow resizing. In addition to this graphical element, note that if you select the bsDialog value, the form becomes a dialog box. This involves several changes. For example, the items on its system menu are different, and the form will ignore some of the elements of the `BorderIcons` set property.

WARNING Setting the `BorderStyle` property at design time produces no visible effect. In fact, several component properties do not take effect at design time, because they would prevent you from working on the component while developing the program. For example, how could you resize the form with the mouse if it were turned into a dialog box? When you run the application, though, the form will have the border you requested.

There are four more values we can assign to the `BorderStyle` property. The style bsSingle can be used to create a main window that's not resizable. Many games and applications based on windows with controls (such as data-entry forms) use this value, simply because resizing these forms makes no sense. Enlarging a form to see an empty area or reducing its size to make some components less visible often doesn't help a program's user (although Delphi's automatic scroll bars partially solve the last problem). The value bsNone is used only in very special situations and inside other forms. You'll never see an application with a main window that has no border or caption (except maybe as an example in a programming book to show you that it makes no sense).

The last two values, bsToolWindow and bsSizeToolWin, are related to the specific Win32 extended style `ws_ex_ToolWindow`. This style turns the window into a floating toolbox, with a small title font and close button. This style should not be used for the main window of an application.

To test the effect and behavior of the different values of the `BorderStyle` property, I've written a simple program called Borders, available also as QBorders in the CLX version. You've already seen its output, in Figure 9.2. However, I suggest you run this example and experiment with it for a while to understand all the differences in the forms.

WARNING In CLX, the enumeration for the `BorderStyle` property uses slightly different values, prefixed by the letters *fbs* (form border style). So we have fbsSingle, fbsDialog, and so on.

The main form of this program contains only a radio group and a button. There is also a secondary form, with no components and the `Position` property set to poDefaultPosOnly. This affects the initial position of the secondary form we'll create by clicking the button. (I'll discuss the `Position` property later in this chapter.)

The code of the program is very simple. When you click the button, a new form is dynamically created, depending on the selected item of the radio group:

```
procedure TForm1.BtnNewFormClick(Sender: TObject);
var
  NewForm: TForm2;
begin
  NewForm := TForm2.Create (Application);
  NewForm.BorderStyle := TFormBorderStyle (BorderRadioGroup.ItemIndex);
  NewForm.Caption := BorderRadioGroup.Items[BorderRadioGroup.ItemIndex];
  NewForm.Show;
end;
```

This code actually uses a trick: it casts the number of the selected item into the TFormBorder-Style enumeration. This works because I've given the radio buttons the same order as the values of this enumeration:

```
type
  TFormBorderStyle = (bsNone, bsSingle, bsSizeable, bsDialog, bsTolWindow,
    bsSizeToolWin);
```

The BtnNewFormClick method then copies the text of the radio button to the caption of the secondary form. This program refers to TForm2, the secondary form defined in a secondary unit of the program, saved as SECOND.PAS. For this reason, to compile the example, you must add the following lines to the implementation section of the unit of the main form:

```
uses
  Second;
```

TIP   Whenever you need to refer to another unit of a program, place the corresponding **uses** statement in the **implementation** portion instead of the **interface** portion if possible. This speeds up the compilation process, results in cleaner code (because the units you include are separate from those included by Delphi), and prevents circular unit compilation errors. To accomplish this, you can also use the File ➤ Use Unit menu command.

The Border Icons

Another important element of a form is the presence of icons on its border. By default, a window has a small icon connected to the system menu, a Minimize button, a Maximize button, and a Close button on the far right. You can set different options using the BorderIcons property, a set with four possible values: biSystemMenu, biMinimize, biMaximize, and biHelp.

NOTE The biHelp border icon enables the "What's this?" Help. When this style is included and the biMinimize and biMaximize styles are excluded, a question mark appears in the form's title bar. If you click this question mark and then click a component inside the form (but not the form itself!), Delphi activates the Help about that object inside a pop-up window. This is demonstrated by the BIcons example, which has a simple Help file with a page connected to the `HelpContext` property of the button in the middle of the form.

The BIcons example demonstrates the behavior of a form with different border icons and shows how to change this property at run time. The form of this example is very simple: It has only a menu, with a pull-down containing four menu items, one for each of the possible elements of the set of border icons. I've written a single method, connected with the four commands, that reads the check marks on the menu items to determine the value of the `BorderIcons` property. This code is therefore also a good exercise in working with sets:

```
procedure TForm1.SetIcons(Sender: TObject);
var
  BorIco: TBorderIcons;
begin
  (Sender as TMenuItem).Checked := not (Sender as TMenuItem).Checked;
  if SystemMenu1.Checked then
    BorIco := [biSystemMenu]
  else
    BorIco := [];
  if MaximizeBox1.Checked then
    Include (BorIco, biMaximize);
  if MinimizeBox1.Checked then
    Include (BorIco, biMinimize);
  if Help1.Checked then
    Include (BorIco, biHelp);
  BorderIcons := BorIco;
end;
```

While running the BIcons example, you can easily set and remove the various visual elements of the form's border. You'll immediately see that some of these elements are closely related: if you remove the system menu, all of the border icons will disappear; if you remove either the Minimize or Maximize button, it will be grayed; if you remove both these buttons, they will disappear. Notice also that in these last two cases, the corresponding items of the system menu are automatically disabled. This is the standard behavior for any Windows application. When the Maximize and Minimize buttons have been disabled, you can activate the Help button. As a shortcut to obtain this effect, you can click the button inside the form. Also, you can click the button after clicking the Help Menu icon to see a Help message, as you can see in Figure 9.3.

FIGURE 9.3:

The BIcons example. By selecting the help border icon and clicking over the button, you get the help displayed in the figure.

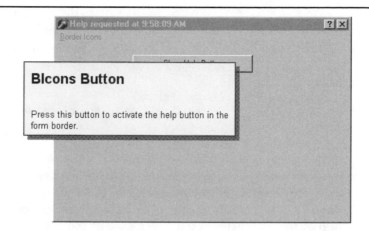

As an extra feature, the program also displays the time that the Help was invoked in the caption, by handling the OnHelp event of the form. This effect is visible in the figure.

WARNING By looking at the QBIcons version, built with CLX, you can clearly notice that a bug in the library prevents you from changing the border icons at run time, while the different design-time settings fully work.

Setting More Window Styles

The border style and border icons are indicated by two different Delphi properties, which can be used to set the initial value of the corresponding user interface elements. We have seen that besides changing the user interface, these properties affect the behavior of a window. It is important to know that in VCL (and obviously not in CLX), these border-related properties and the FormStyle property mainly correspond to different settings in the *style* and *extended style* of a window. These two terms reflect two parameters of the CreateWindowEx API function Delphi uses to create forms.

It is important to acknowledge this, because Delphi allows you to modify these two parameters freely by overriding the CreateParams virtual method:

```
public
  procedure CreateParams (var Params: TCreateParams); override;
```

This is the only way to use some of the peculiar window styles that are not directly available through form properties. For a list of window styles and extended styles, see the API Help under the topics "CreateWindow" and "CreateWindowEx." You'll notice that the Win32 API has styles for these functions, including those related to tool windows.

To show how to use this approach, I've written the NoTitle example on the companion CD, which lets you create a program with a custom caption. First we have to remove the standard caption but keep the resizing frame by setting the corresponding styles:

```
procedure TForm1.CreateParams (var Params: TCreateParams);
begin
  inherited CreateParams (Params);
  Params.Style := (Params.Style or ws_Popup) and not ws_Caption;
end;
```

NOTE   Besides changing the style and other features of a window when it is created, you can change them at run time, although some of the settings do not take effect. To change most of the creation parameters at run time, you can use the SetWindowLong API function, which allows you to change the internal information of a window. The companion GetWindowLong function can be used to read the current status. Two more functions, GetClassLong and SetClassLong, can be used to read and modify class styles (the information of the WindowClass structure of TCreateParams). You'll seldom need to use these low-level Windows API functions in Delphi, unless you write advanced components.

To remove the caption, we need to change the overlapped style to a pop-up style; otherwise, the caption will simply stick. Now how do we add a custom caption? I've placed a label aligned to the upper border of the form and a small button on the far end. You can see this effect at run time in Figure 9.4.

FIGURE 9.4:

The NoTitle example has no real caption but a fake one made with a label.

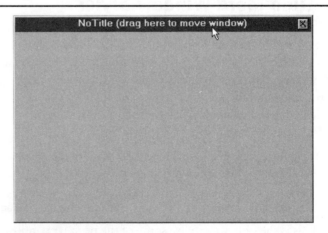

To make the fake caption work, we have to tell the system that a mouse operation on this area corresponds to a mouse operation on the caption. This can be done by intercepting the wm_NCHitTest Windows message, which is frequently sent to Windows to determine where the mouse currently is. When the hit is in the client area and on the label, we can pretend the mouse is on the caption by setting the proper result:

```
procedure TForm1.HitTest (var Msg: TWmNCHitTest);
  // message wm_NcHitTest
begin
  inherited;
  if (Msg.Result = htClient) and
    (Msg.YPos < Label1.Height + Top + GetSystemMetrics (sm_cyFrame)) then
    Msg.Result := htCaption;
end;
```

The GetSystemMetrics API function used in the listing above is used to query the operating system about the size of the various visual elements. It is important to make this request every time (and not cache the result) because users can customize most of these elements by using the Appearance page of the Desktop options (in Control Panel) and other Windows settings. The small button, instead, has a call to the Close method in its OnClick event handler. The button is kept in its position even when the window is resized by using the [akTop,akRight] value for the Anchors property. The form also has size constraints, so that a user cannot make it too small, as described in the "Form Constraints" section later in this chapter.

Direct Form Input

Having discussed some special capabilities of forms, I'll now move to a very important topic: user input in a form. If you decide to make limited use of components, you might write complex programs as well, receiving input from the mouse and the keyboard. In this chapter, I'll only introduce this topic.

Supervising Keyboard Input

Generally, forms don't handle keyboard input directly. If a user has to type something, your form should include an edit component or one of the other input components. If you want to handle keyboard shortcuts, you can use those connected with menus (possibly using a hidden pop-up menu).

At other times, however, you might want to handle keyboard input in particular ways for a specific purpose. What you can do in these cases is turn on the KeyPreview property of the form. Then, even if you have some input controls, the form's OnKeyPress event will always be activated for any keyboard-input operation. The keyboard input will then reach the destination component, unless you stop it in the form by setting the character value to zero (not the character *0*, but the value 0 of the character set, indicated as #0).

The example I've built to demonstrate this, KPreview, has a form with no special properties (not even `KeyPreview`), a radio group with four options, and some edit boxes, as you can see in Figure 9.5.

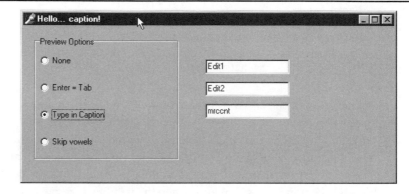

By default the program does nothing special, except when the various radio buttons are used to enable the key preview:

```
procedure TForm1.RadioPreviewClick(Sender: TObject);
begin
  KeyPreview := RadioPreview.ItemIndex <> 0;
end;
```

Now we'll start receiving the `OnKeyPress` events, and we can do one of the three actions requested by the three special buttons of the radio group. The action depends on the value of the `ItemIndex` property of the radio group component. This is the reason the event handler is based on a `case` statement:

```
procedure TForm1.FormKeyPress(Sender: TObject; var Key: Char);
begin
  case RadioPreview.ItemIndex of
    ...
```

In the first case, if the value of the `Key` parameter is #13, which corresponds to the Enter key, we disable the operation (setting `Key` to zero) and then mimic the activation of the Tab key. There are many ways to accomplish this, but the one I've chosen is quite particular. I send the `CM_DialogKey` message to the form, passing the code for the Tab key (`VK_TAB`):

```
1: // Enter = Tab
  if Key = #13 then
  begin
    Key := #0;
    Perform (CM_DialogKey, VK_TAB, 0);
  end;
```

The CM_DialogKey message is an internal, undocumented Delphi message. There are a few of them, actually quite interesting to build advanced components for and for some special coding, but Borland never described those. For more information on this topic, refer to the sidebar "Component Messages and Notifications" in Chapter 11. Notice also that this exact message-based coding style is not available under CLX.

To type in the caption of the form, the program simply adds the character to the current Caption. There are two special cases. When the Backspace key is pressed, the last character of the string is removed (by copying to the Caption all the characters of the current Caption but the last one). When the Enter key is pressed, the program stops the operation, by resetting the ItemIndex property of the radio group control. Here is the code:

```
2: // type in caption
begin
  if Key = #8 then // backspace: remove last char
    Caption := Copy (Caption, 1, Length (Caption) - 1)
  else if Key = #13 then // enter: stop operation
    RadioPreview.ItemIndex := 0
  else // anything else: add character
    Caption := Caption + Key;
  Key := #0;
end;
```

Finally, if the last radio item is selected, the code checks whether the character is a vowel (by testing for its inclusion in a constant "vowel set"). In this case, the character is skipped altogether:

```
3: // skip vowels
  if Key in ['a', 'e', 'i', 'o', 'u', 'A', 'E', 'I', 'O', 'U'] then
    Key := #0;
```

Getting Mouse Input

When a user clicks one of the mouse buttons over a form (or over a component, by the way), Windows sends the application some messages. Delphi defines some events you can use to write code that responds to these messages. The two basic events are OnMouseDown, received when a mouse button is clicked, and OnMouseUp, received when the button is released. Another fundamental system message is related to mouse movement; the event is OnMouseMove. Although it should be easy to understand the meaning of the three messages—down, up, and move— the question that might arise is, how do they relate to the OnClick event we have often used up to now?

We have used the OnClick event for components, but it is also available for the form. Its general meaning is that the left mouse button has been clicked and released on the same window or component. However, between these two actions, the cursor might have been moved outside the area of the window or component, while the left mouse button was held down.

Another difference between the OnMouseXX and OnClick events is that the latter relates only to the *left* mouse button. Most of the mouse types connected to a Windows PC have two mouse buttons, and some even have three. Usually we refer to these buttons as the left mouse button, generally used for selection; the right mouse button, for local menus; and the middle mouse button, seldom used. Nowadays most new mouse devices have a "button wheel" instead of the middle button. Users typically use the wheel for scrolling (causing an OnMouseWheel event), but they can also press it (generating the OnMouseWheelDown and OnMouseWheelUp events). Mouse wheel events are automatically converted into scrolling events.

Using Windows without a Mouse

A user should always be able to use any Windows application without the mouse. This is not an option; it is a Windows programming rule. Of course, an application might be easier to use with a mouse, but that should never be mandatory. In fact, there are users who for various reasons might not have a mouse connected, such as travelers with a small laptop and no space, workers in industrial environments, and bank clerks with other peripherals around.

There is another reason to support the keyboard: Using the mouse is nice, but it tends to be slower. If you are a skilled touch typist, you won't use the mouse to drag a word of text; you'll use shortcut keys to copy and paste it, without moving your hands from the keyboard.

For all these reasons, you should always set up a proper tab order for a form's components, remember to add keys for buttons and menu items for keyboard selection, use shortcut keys on menu commands, and so on.

The Parameters of the Mouse Events

All of the lower-level mouse events have the same parameters: the usual Sender parameter; a Button parameter indicating which of the three mouse buttons has been clicked (mbRight, mbLeft, or mbCenter); the Shift parameter indicating which of the *mouse-related keys* (Alt, Ctrl, and Shift, plus the three mouse buttons themselves) were pressed when the event occurred; and the x and y coordinates of the position of the mouse, in *client area* coordinates of the current window.

Using this information, it is very simple to draw a small circle in the position of a left mouse button–down event:

```
procedure TForm1.FormMouseDown(
  Sender: TObject; Button: TMouseButton;
```

```
    Shift: TShiftState; X, Y: Integer);
begin
  if Button = mbLeft then
    Canvas.Ellipse (X-10, Y-10, X+10, Y+10);
end;
```

NOTE To draw on the form, we use a very special property: Canvas. A TCanvas object has two distinctive features: it holds a collection of drawing tools (such as a pen, a brush, and a font) and it has some drawing methods, which use the current tools. The kind of direct drawing code in this example is not correct, because the on-screen image is not persistent: moving another window over the current one will clear its output. The next example demonstrates the Windows "store-and-draw" approach.

Dragging and Drawing with the Mouse

To demonstrate a few of the mouse techniques discussed so far, I've built a simple example based on a form without any component and called MouseOne in the VCL version and QMouseOne in the CLX version. The first feature of this program is that it displays in the Caption of the form the current position of the mouse:

```
procedure TMouseForm.FormMouseMove(Sender: TObject; Shift: TShiftState;
  X, Y: Integer);
begin
  // display the position of the mouse in the caption
  Caption := Format ('Mouse in x=%d, y=%d', [X, Y]);
end;
```

You can use this simple feature of the program to better understand how the mouse works. Make this test: run the program (this simple version or the complete one) and resize the windows on the desktop so that the form of the MouseOne or QMouseOne program is behind another window and inactive but with the title visible. Now move the mouse over the form, and you'll see that the coordinates change. This means that the OnMouseMove event is sent to the application even if its window is not active, and it proves what I have already mentioned: Mouse messages are always directed to the window under the mouse. The only exception is the mouse capture operation I'll discuss in this same example.

Besides showing the position in the title of the window, the MouseOne/QMouseOne example can track mouse movements by painting small pixels on the form if the user keeps the Shift key pressed. (Again this direct painting code produces non-persistent output.)

```
procedure TMouseForm.FormMouseMove(Sender: TObject; Shift: TShiftState;
  X, Y: Integer);
begin
  // display the position of the mouse in the caption
  Caption := Format ('Mouse in x=%d, y=%d', [X, Y]);
```

```
    if ssShift in Shift then
      // mark points in yellow
      Canvas.Pixels [X, Y] := clYellow;
  end;
```

TIP   The TCanvas class of the CLX library doesn't include a Pixels array. Instead, you can call the DrawPoint method after setting a proper color for the pen, as I've done in the QMouseOne example.

The real feature of this example, however, is the direct mouse-dragging support. Contrary to what you might think, Windows has no system support for dragging, which is implemented in VCL by means of lower-level mouse events and operations. (An example of dragging from one control to another was discussed in the last chapter.) In VCL, forms cannot originate dragging operations, so in this case we are obliged to use the low-level approach. The aim of this example is to draw a rectangle from the initial position of the dragging operation to the final one, giving the users some visual clue of the operation they are doing.

The idea behind dragging is quite simple. The program receives a sequence of button-down, mouse-move, and button-up messages. When the button is clicked, dragging begins, although the real actions take place only when the user moves the mouse (without releasing the mouse button) and when dragging terminates (when the button-up message arrives). The problem with this basic approach is that it is not reliable. A window usually receives mouse events only when the mouse is over its client area; so if the user clicks the mouse button, moves the mouse onto another window, and then releases the button, the second window will receive the button-up message.

There are two solutions to this problem. One (seldom used) is mouse clipping. Using a Windows API function (namely ClipCursor), you can force the mouse not to leave a certain area of the screen. When you try to move it outside the specified area, it stumbles against an invisible barrier. The second and more common solution is to capture the mouse. When a window captures the mouse, all the subsequent mouse input is sent to that window. This is the approach we will use for the MouseOne/QMouseOne example.

The code of the example is built around three methods: FormMouseDown, FormMouseMove, and FormMouseUp. Clicking the left mouse button over the form starts the process, setting the fDragging Boolean field of the form (which indicates that dragging is in action in the other two methods). The method also uses a TRect variable used to keep track of the initial and current position of the dragging. Here is the code:

```
procedure TMouseForm.FormMouseDown(Sender: TObject; Button: TMouseButton;
  Shift: TShiftState; X, Y: Integer);
begin
  if Button = mbLeft then
```

```
  begin
    fDragging := True;
    Mouse.Capture := Handle;
    fRect.Left := X;
    fRect.Top := Y;
    fRect.BottomRight := fRect.TopLeft;
    Canvas.DrawFocusRect (fRect);
  end;
end;
```

An important action of this method is the call to the SetCapture API function, obtained by setting the Capture property of the global object Mouse. Now even if a user moves the mouse outside of the client area, the form still receives all mouse-related messages. You can see that for yourself by moving the mouse toward the upper-left corner of the screen; the program shows negative coordinates in the caption.

When dragging is active and the user moves the mouse, the program draws a dotted rectangle corresponding to the actual position. Actually, the program calls the DrawFocusRect method twice. The first time this method is called, it deletes the current image, thanks to the fact that two consecutive calls to DrawFocusRect simply reset the original situation. After updating the position of the rectangle, the program calls the method a second time:

```
procedure TMouseForm.FormMouseMove(Sender: TObject; Shift: TShiftState;
  X, Y: Integer);
begin
  // display the position of the mouse in the caption
  Caption := Format ('Mouse in x=%d, y=%d', [X, Y]);
  if fDragging then
  begin
    // remove and redraw the dragging rectangle
    Canvas.DrawFocusRect (fRect);
    fRect.Right := X;
    fRect.Bottom := Y;
    Canvas.DrawFocusRect (fRect);
  end
  else
    if ssShift in Shift then
      // mark points in yellow
      Canvas.Pixels [X, Y] := clYellow;
end;
```

When the mouse button is released, the program terminates the dragging operation by resetting the `Capture` property of the `Mouse` object, which internally calls the `ReleaseCapture` API function, and by setting the value of the `fDragging` field to False:

```
procedure TMouseForm.FormMouseUp(Sender: TObject; Button: TMouseButton;
  Shift: TShiftState; X, Y: Integer);
begin
  if fDragging then
  begin
    Mouse.Capture := 0; // calls ReleaseCapture
    fDragging := False;
    Invalidate;
  end;
end;
```

The final call, `Invalidate`, triggers a painting operation and executes the following `OnPaint` event handler:

```
procedure TMouseForm.FormPaint(Sender: TObject);
begin
  Canvas.Rectangle (fRect.Left, fRect.Top, fRect.Right, fRect.Bottom);
end;
```

This makes the output of the form persistent, even if you hide it behind another form. Figure 9.6 shows a previous version of the rectangle and a dragging operation in action.

FIGURE 9.6:

The MouseOne example uses a dotted line to indicate, during a dragging operation, the final area of a rectangle.

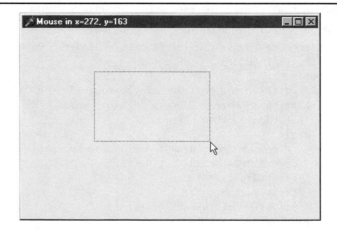

TIP   Under Qt, there are no Windows handles, but the `Capture` property of the mouse is still available. You assign to it, however, the object of the component that has to capture the mouse (for example, `Self` to indicate the form), or set the property to `nil` to release it. You can see this code in the QMouseOne example.

Painting in Windows

Why do we need to handle the OnPaint event to produce a proper output, and why can't we paint directly over the form canvas? It depends on Windows' default behavior. As you draw on a window, Windows does *not* store the resulting image. When the window is covered, its contents are usually lost.

The reason for this behavior is simple: to save memory. Windows assumes it's "cheaper" in the long run to redraw the screen using code than to dedicate system memory to preserving the display state of a window. It's a classic memory-versus-CPU-cycles trade-off. A color bitmap for a 300×400 image at 256 colors requires about 120 KB. By increasing the color count or the number of pixels, you can easily have full-screen bitmaps of about 1 MB and reach 4 MB of memory for a 1280×1024 resolution at 16 million colors. If storing the bitmap was the default choice, running half a dozen simple applications would require at least 8 MB of memory, if not 16 MB, just for remembering their current output.

In the event that you want to have a consistent output for your applications, there are two techniques you can use. The general solution is to store enough data about the output to be able to reproduce it when the system sends a *painting* requested. An alternative approach is to save the output of the form in a bitmap while you produce it, by placing an Image component over the form and drawing on the canvas of this image component.

The first technique, painting, is the common approach to handling output in Windows, aside from particular graphics-oriented programs that store the form's whole image in a bitmap. The approach used to implement painting has a very descriptive name: *store and paint*. In fact, when the user clicks a mouse button or performs any other operation, we need to store the position and other elements; then, in the painting method, we use this information to actually paint the corresponding image.

The idea of this approach is to let the application repaint its whole surface under any of the possible conditions. If we provide a method to redraw the contents of the form, and if this method is automatically called when a portion of the form has been hidden and needs repainting, we will be able to re-create the output properly.

Since this approach takes two steps, we must be able to execute these two operations in a row, asking the system to repaint the window—without waiting for the system to ask for this. You can use several methods to invoke repainting: Invalidate, Update, Repaint, and Refresh. The first two correspond to the Windows API functions, while the latter two have been introduced by Delphi.

- The Invalidate method informs Windows that the entire surface of the form should be repainted. The most important thing is that Invalidate does *not* enforce a painting operation immediately. Windows simply stores the request and will respond to it only after the current procedure has been completely executed and as soon as there are no other events pending in the system. Windows deliberately delays the painting operation because it is one of the most time-consuming operations. At times, with this delay, it is possible to paint the form only after multiple changes have taken place, avoiding multiple consecutive calls to the (slow) paint method.

- The `Update` method asks Windows to update the contents of the form, repainting it immediately. However, remember that this operation will take place only if there is an *invalid area*. This happens if the `Invalidate` method has just been called or as the result of an operation by the user. If there is no invalid area, a call to `Update` has no effect at all. For this reason, it is common to see a call to `Update` just after a call to `Invalidate`. This is exactly what is done by the two Delphi methods, `Repaint` and `Refresh`.

- The `Repaint` method calls `Invalidate` and `Update` in sequence. As a result, it activates the `OnPaint` event immediately. There is a slightly different version of this method called `Refresh`. For a form the effect is the same; for components it might be slightly different.

When you need to ask the form for a repaint operation, you should generally call `Invalidate`, following the standard Windows approach. This is particularly important when you need to request this operation frequently, because if Windows takes too much time to update the screen, the requests for repainting can be accumulated into a simple repaint action. The `wm_Paint` message in Windows is a sort of low-priority message. To be more precise, if a request for repainting is pending but other messages are waiting, the other messages are handled before the system actually performs the paint action.

On the other hand, if you call `Repaint` several times, the screen must be repainted each time before Windows can process other messages, and because paint operations are computationally intensive, this can actually make your application less responsive. There are times, however, when you want the application to repaint a surface as quickly as possible. In these less-frequent cases, calling `Repaint` is the way to go.

NOTE   Another important consideration is that during a paint operation Windows redraws only the so-called *update region*, to speed up the operation. For this reason if you invalidate only a portion of a window, only that area will be repainted. To accomplish this you can use the `InvalidateRect` and `InvalidateRegion` functions. Actually, this feature is a double-edged sword. It is a very powerful technique, which can improve speed and reduce the flickering caused by frequent repaint operations. On the other hand, it can also produce incorrect output. A typical problem is when only some of the areas affected by the user operations are actually modified, while others remain as they were even if the system executes the source code that is supposed to update them. In fact, if a painting operation falls outside the update region, the system ignores it, as if it were outside the visible area of a window.

Unusual Techniques: Alpha Blending, Color Key, and the Animate API

One of the few new features of Delphi 6 related to forms is support for some new Windows APIs regarding the way forms are displayed (not available under Qt/CLX). For a form, *alpha blending* allows you to merge the content of a form with what's behind it on the screen, something you'll rarely need, at least in a business application. The technique is certainly more interesting when applied to bitmap (with the new `AlphaBlend` and `AlphaDIBBlend` API functions) than to a form itself. In any case, by setting the `AlphaBlend` property of a form to True and giving to the `AlphaBlendValue` property a value lower than 255, you'll be able to see, in transparency, what's behind the form. The lower the `AlphaBlendValue`, the more the form will *fade*. You can see an example of alpha blending in Figure 9.7, taken from the CkKeyHole example

FIGURE 9.7:

The output of the CkKeyHole, showing the effect of the new `TransparentColor` and `AlphaBlend` properties, and also the AnimateWindow API.

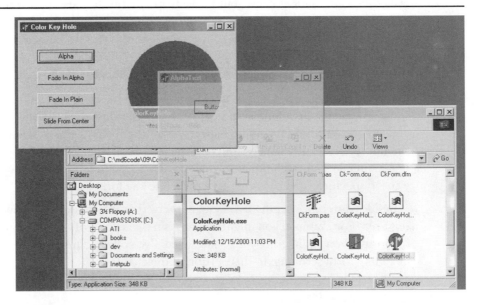

This is not the only new Delphi feature in the area of what I can only call *unusual*. The second is the new `TransparentColor` property, which allows you to indicate a transparent color, which will be replaced by the background, creating a sort of hole in a form. The transparent color is indicated by the `TransparentColorValue` property. Again, you can see an example of this effect in Figure 9.7.

Finally, you can use a native Windows technique, animated display, which is not directly supported by Delphi (beyond the display of hints). For example, instead of calling the Show method of a form, you can write:

```
Form3.Hide;
AnimateWindow (Form3.Handle, 2000, AW_BLEND);
Form3.Show;
```

Notice you have to call the Show method at the end for the form to behave properly. A similar animation effect can also be obtained by changing the AlphaBlendValue in a loop. The AnimateWindow API can also be used to obtain the display of the form starting from the center (with the AW_CENTER flag) or from one of its sides (AW_HOR_POSITIVE, AW_HOR_NEGATIVE, AW_VER_POSITIVE, or AW_VER_NEGATIVE), as is common for slide shows.

This same function can also be applied to windowed controls, obtaining a fade-in effect instead of the usual direct appearance. I keep having serious doubts about the waste of CPU cycles these animations cause, but I have to say that if they are applied properly and in the right program, they can improve the user interface.

Position, Size, Scrolling, and Scaling

Once you have designed a form in Delphi, you run the program, and you expect the form to show up exactly as you prepared it. However, a user of your application might have a different screen resolution or might want to resize the form (if this is possible, depending on the border style), eventually affecting the user interface. We've already discussed (mainly in Chapter 7) some techniques related to controls, such as alignment and anchors. Here I want to specifically address elements related to the form as a whole.

Besides differences in the user system, there are many reasons to change Delphi defaults in this area. For example, you might want to run two copies of the program and avoid having all the forms show up in exactly the same place. I've collected many other related elements, including form scrolling, in this portion of the chapter.

The Form Position

There are a few properties you can use to set the position of a form. The Position property indicates how Delphi determines the initial position of the form. The default poDesigned value indicates that the form will appear where you designed it and where you use the positional (Left and Top) and size (Width and Height) properties of the form.

Some of the other choices (poDefault, poDefaultPosOnly, and poDefaultSizeOnly) depend on a feature of the operating system: using a specific flag, Windows can position and/or size new windows using a cascade layout. In this way, the positional and size properties you set at design time will be ignored, but running the application twice you won't get overlapping windows. The default positions are ignored when the form has a dialog border style.

Finally, with the poScreenCenter value, the form is displayed in the center of the screen, with the size you set at design time. This is a very common setting for dialog boxes and other secondary forms.

Another property that affects the initial size and position of a window is its *state*. You can use the `WindowState` property at design time to display a maximized or minimized window at startup. This property, in fact, can have only three values: wsNormal, wsMinimized, and wsMaximized. The meaning of this property is intuitive. If you set a minimized window state, at startup the form will be displayed in the Windows Taskbar. For the main form of an application, this property can be automatically set by specifying the corresponding attributes in a shortcut referring to the application.

Of course, you can maximize or minimize a window at run time, too. Simply changing the value of the `WindowState` property to wsMaximized or to wsNormal produces the expected effect. Setting the property to wsMinimized, however, creates a minimized window that is placed over the Taskbar, not within it. This is not the expected action for a main form, but for a secondary form! The simple solution to this problem is to call the `Minimize` method of the `Application` object. There is also a `Restore` method in the `TApplication` class that you can use when you need to restore a form, although most often the user will do this operation using the Restore command of the system menu.

The Size of a Form and Its Client Area

At design time, there are two ways to set the size of a form: by setting the value of the `Width` and `Height` properties or by dragging its borders. At run time, if the form has a resizable border, the user can resize it (producing the `OnResize` event, where you can perform custom actions to adapt the user interface to the new size of the form).

However, if you look at a form's properties in source code or in the online Help, you can see that there are two properties referring to its width and two referring to its height. `Height` and `Width` refer to the size of the form, including the borders; `ClientHeight` and `ClientWidth` refer to the size of the internal area of the form, excluding the borders, caption, scroll bars (if any), and menu bar. The client area of the form is the surface you can use to place components on the form, to create output, and to receive user input.

Since you might be interested in having a certain available area for your components, it often makes more sense to set the client size of a form instead of its global size. This is straightforward, because as you set one of the two client properties, the corresponding form property changes accordingly.

TIP   In Windows, it is also possible to create output and receive input from the nonclient area of the form—that is, its border. Painting on the border and getting input when you click it are complex issues. If you are interested, look in the Help file at the description of such Windows messages as wm_NCPaint, wm_NCCalcSize, and wm_NCHitTest and the series of nonclient messages related to the mouse input, such as wm_NCLButtonDown. The difficulty of this approach is in combining your code with the default Windows behavior.

Form Constraints

When you choose a resizable border for a form, users can generally resize the form as they like and also maximize it to full screen. Windows informs you that the form's size has changed with the wm_Size message, which generates the OnResize event. OnResize takes place after the size of the form has already been changed. Modifying the size again in this event (if the user has reduced or enlarged the form too much) would be silly. A preventive approach is better suited to this problem.

Delphi provides a specific property for forms and also for all controls: the Constraints property. Simply setting the subproperties of the Constraints property to the proper maximum and minimum values creates a form that cannot be resized beyond those limits. Here is an example:

```
object Form1: TForm1
  Constraints.MaxHeight = 300
  Constraints.MaxWidth = 300
  Constraints.MinHeight = 150
  Constraints.MinWidth = 150
end
```

Notice that as you set up the Constraints property, it has an immediate effect even at design time, changing the size of the form if it is outside the permitted area.

Delphi also uses the maximum constraints for maximized windows, producing an awkward effect. For this reason, you should generally disable the Maximize button of a window that has a maximum size. There are cases in which maximized windows with a limited size make sense—this is the behavior of Delphi's main window. In case you need to change constraints at run time, you can also consider using two specific events, OnCanResize and OnConstrainedResize. The first of the two can also be used to disable resizing a form or control in given circumstances.

Scrolling a Form

When you build a simple application, a single form might hold all of the components you need. As the application grows, however, you may need to squeeze in the components, increase the size of the form, or add new forms. If you reduce the space occupied by the components, you might add some capability to resize them at run time, possibly splitting the form into different areas. If you choose to increase the size of the form, you might use scroll bars to let the user move around in a form that is bigger than the screen (or at least bigger than its visible portion on the screen).

Adding a scroll bar to a form is simple. In fact, you don't need to do anything. If you place several components in a big form and then reduce its size, a scroll bar will be added to the form automatically, as long as you haven't changed the value of the `AutoScroll` property from its default of True.

Along with `AutoScroll`, forms have two properties, `HorzScrollBar` and `VertScrollBar`, which can be used to set several properties of the two `TFormScrollBar` objects associated with the form. The `Visible` property indicates whether the scroll bar is present, the `Position` property determines the initial status of the scroll thumb, and the `Increment` property determines the effect of clicking one of the arrows at the ends of the scroll bar. The most important property, however, is `Range`.

The `Range` property of a scroll bar determines the virtual size of the form, not the actual range of values of the scroll bar. Suppose you need a form that will host several components and will therefore need to be 1000 pixels wide. We can use this value to set the "virtual range" of the form, changing the `Range` of the horizontal scroll bar.

The `Position` property of the scroll bar will range from 0 to 1000 minus the current size of the client area. For example, if the client area of the form is 300 pixels wide, you can scroll 700 pixels to see the far end of the form (the thousandth pixel).

A Scroll Testing Example

To demonstrate the specific case I've just discussed, I've built the Scroll1 example, which has a virtual form 1000 pixels wide. To accomplish this, I've set the range of the horizontal scroll bar to 1000:

```
object Form1: TForm1
  Width = 458
  Height = 368
  HorzScrollBar.Range = 1000
  VertScrollBar.Range = 305
  AutoScroll = False
  Caption = 'Scrolling Form'
  OnResize = FormResize
  ...
```

The form of this example has been filled with meaningless list boxes, and I could have obtained the same scroll-bar range by placing the right-most list box so that its position (`Left`) plus its size (`Width`) would equal 1000.

The interesting part of the example is the presence of a toolbox window displaying the status of the form and of its horizontal scroll bar. This second form has four labels; two with fixed text and two with the actual output. Besides this, the secondary form (called `Status`) has a bsToolWindow border style and is a top-most window. You should also set its `Visible` property to True, to have its window automatically displayed at startup:

```
object Status: TStatus
  BorderIcons = [biSystemMenu]
  BorderStyle = bsToolWindow
  Caption = 'Status'
  FormStyle = fsStayOnTop
  Visible = True
  object Label1: TLabel...
  ...
```

There isn't much code in this program. Its aim is to update the values in the toolbox each time the form is resized or scrolled (as you can see in Figure 9.8). The first part is extremely simple. You can handle the `OnResize` event of the form and simply copy a couple of values to the two labels. The labels are part of another form, so you need to prefix them with the name of the form instance, `Status`:

```
procedure TForm1.FormResize(Sender: TObject);
begin
  Status.Label3.Caption := IntToStr(ClientWidth);
  Status.Label4.Caption := IntToStr(HorzScrollBar.Position);
end;
```

FIGURE 9.8:

The output of the Scroll1 example

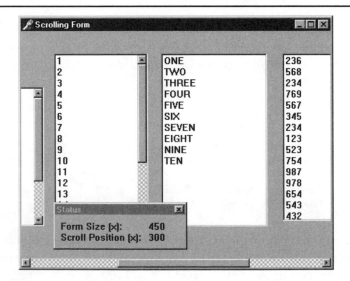

If we wanted to change the output each time the user scrolls the contents of the form, we could not use a Delphi event handler, because there isn't an OnScroll event for forms (although there is one for stand-alone ScrollBar components). Omitting this event makes sense, because Delphi forms handle scroll bars automatically in a powerful way. In Windows, by contrast, scroll bars are extremely low-level elements, requiring a lot of coding. Handling the scroll event makes sense only in special cases, such as when you want to keep track precisely of the scrolling operations made by a user.

Here is the code we need to write. First, add a method declaration to the class and associate it with the Windows horizontal scroll message (wm_HScroll):

```
public
  procedure FormScroll (var ScrollData: TWMScroll);
    message wm_HScroll;
```

Then write the code of this procedure, which is almost the same as the code of the FormResize method we've seen before:

```
procedure TForm1.FormScroll (var ScrollData: TWMScroll);
begin
  inherited;
  Status.Label3.Caption := IntToStr(ClientWidth);
  Status.Label4.Caption := IntToStr(HorzScrollBar.Position);
end;
```

It's important to add the call to inherited, which activates the method related to the same message in the base class form. The inherited keyword in Windows message handlers calls the method of the base class we are overriding, which is the one associated with the corresponding Windows message (even if the procedure name is different). Without this call, the form won't have its default scrolling behavior; that is, it won't scroll at all.

NOTE Because in CLX you cannot handle the low-level scroll messages, there seems to be no easy way to create a program similar to Scroll1. This isn't terribly important in real-world applications, as the scrolling system is automatic, and can probably be accomplished by hooking in the CLX library at a lower level.

Automatic Scrolling

The scroll bar's Range property can seem strange until you start to use it consistently. When you think about it a little, you'll start to understand the advantages of the "virtual range" approach. First of all, the scroll bar is automatically removed from the form when the client area of the form is big enough to accommodate the virtual size; and when you reduce the size of the form, the scroll bar is added again.

This feature becomes particularly interesting when the AutoScroll property of the form is set to True. In this case, the extreme positions of the right-most and lower controls are automatically copied into the Range properties of the form's two scroll bars. Automatic scrolling works well in Delphi. In the last example, the virtual size of the form would be set to the right border of the last list box. This was defined with the following attributes:

```
object ListBox6: TListBox
  Left = 832
  Width = 145
end
```

Therefore, the horizontal virtual size of the form would be 977 (the sum of the two preceding values). This number is automatically copied into the Range field of the HorzScrollBar property of the form, unless you change it manually to have a bigger form (as I've done for the Scroll1 example, setting it to 1000 to leave some space between the last list box and the border of the form). You can see this value in the Object Inspector, or make the following test: run the program, size the form as you like, and move the scroll thumb to the right-most position. When you add the size of the form and the position of the thumb, you'll always get 1000, the virtual coordinate of the right-most pixel of the form, whatever the size.

Scrolling and Form Coordinates

We have just seen that forms can automatically scroll their components. But what happens if you paint directly on the surface of the form? Some problems arise, but their solution is at hand. Suppose that we want to draw some lines on the virtual surface of a form, as shown in Figure 9.9.

Since you probably do not own a monitor capable of displaying 2000 pixels on each axis, you can create a smaller form, add two scroll bars, and set their Range property, as I've done in the Scroll2 example. Here is the textual description of the form:

```
object Form1: TForm1
  HorzScrollBar.Range = 2000
  VertScrollBar.Range = 2000
  ClientHeight = 336
  ClientWidth = 472
  OnPaint = FormPaint
end
```

FIGURE 9.9:

The lines to draw on the virtual surface of the form

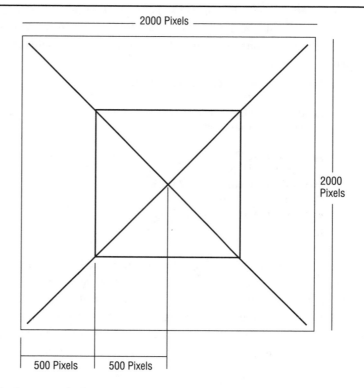

2000 Pixels

2000 Pixels

500 Pixels   500 Pixels

If we simply draw the lines using the virtual coordinates of the form, the image won't display properly. In fact, in the OnPaint response method, we need to compute the virtual coordinates ourselves. Fortunately, this is easy, since we know that the virtual X1 and Y1 coordinates of the upper-left corner of the client area correspond to the current positions of the two scroll bars:

```
procedure TForm1.FormPaint(Sender: TObject);
var
  X1, Y1: Integer;
begin
  X1 := HorzScrollBar.Position;
  Y1 := VertScrollBar.Position;

  // draw a yellow line
  Canvas.Pen.Width := 30;
  Canvas.Pen.Color := clYellow;
  Canvas.MoveTo (30-X1, 30-Y1);
  Canvas.LineTo (1970-X1, 1970-Y1);
  // and so on ...
```

As a better alternative, instead of computing the proper coordinate for each output operation, we can call the `SetWindowOrgEx` API to move the origin of the coordinates of the `Canvas` itself. This way, our drawing code will directly refer to virtual coordinates but will be displayed properly:

```
procedure TForm2.FormPaint(Sender: TObject);
begin
  SetWindowOrgEx (Canvas.Handle, HorzScrollbar.Position,
    VertScrollbar.Position, nil);

  // draw a yellow line
  Canvas.Pen.Width := 30;
  Canvas.Pen.Color := clYellow;
  Canvas.MoveTo (30, 30);
  Canvas.LineTo (1970, 1970);

  // and so on ...
```

This is the version of the program you'll find in the source code on the CD. Try using the program and commenting out the `SetWindowOrgEx` call to see what happens if you don't use virtual coordinates: You'll find that the output of the program is not correct—it won't scroll, and the same image will always remain in the same position, regardless of scrolling operations. Notice also that the Qt/CLX version of the program, called QScroll2, doesn't use virtual coordinates but simply subtracts the scroll positions from each of the hard-coded coordinates.

Scaling Forms

When you create a form with multiple components, you can select a fixed size border or let the user resize the form and automatically add scroll bars to reach the components falling outside the visible portion of the form, as we've just seen. This might also happen because a user of your application has a display driver with a much smaller number of pixels than yours.

Instead of simply reducing the form size and scrolling the content, you might want to reduce the size of each of the components at the same time. This automatically happens also if the user has a system font with a different pixel-per-inch ratio than the one you used for development. To address these problems, Delphi has some nice scaling features, but they aren't fully intuitive.

The form's `ScaleBy` method allows you to scale the form and each of its components. The `PixelsPerInch` and `Scaled` properties allow Delphi to resize an application automatically when the application is run with a different system font size, often because of a different screen resolution. In both cases, to make the form scale its window, be sure to also set the

`AutoScroll` property to False. Otherwise, the contents of the form will be scaled, but the form border itself will not. These two approaches are discussed in the next two sections.

> **NOTE**   Form scaling is calculated based on the difference between the font height at run time and the font height at design time. Scaling ensures that edit and other controls are large enough to display their text using the user's font preferences without clipping the text. The form scales as well, as we will see later on, but the main point is to make edit and other controls readable.

Manual Form Scaling

Any time you want to scale a form, including its components, you can use the `ScaleBy` method, which has two integer parameters, a multiplier and a divisor—it's a fraction. For example, with this statement the size of the current form is reduced to three-quarters of its original size:

```
ScaleBy (3, 4);
```

Generally, it is easier to use percentage values. The same effect can be obtained by using:

```
ScaleBy (75, 100);
```

When you scale a form, all the proportions are maintained, but if you go below or above certain limits, the text strings can alter their proportions slightly. The problem is that in Windows, components can be placed and sized only in whole pixels, while scaling almost always involves multiplying by fractional numbers. So any fractional portion of a component's origin or size will be truncated.

I've built a simple example, Scale or QScale, to show how you can scale a form manually, responding to a request by the user. The form of this application (see Figure 9.10) has two buttons, a label, an edit box, and an UpDown control connected to it (via its `Associate` property). With this setting, a user can type numbers in the edit box or click the two small arrows to increase or decrease the value (by the amount indicated by the `Increment` property). To extract the input value, you can use the `Text` property of the edit box or the `Position` of the UpDown control.

When you click the Do Scale button, the current input value is used to determine the scaling percentage of the form:

```
procedure TForm1.ScaleButtonClick(Sender: TObject);
begin
  AmountScaled := UpDown1.Position;
  ScaleBy (AmountScaled, 100);
  UpDown1.Height := Edit1.Height;
  ScaleButton.Enabled := False;
  RestoreButton.Enabled := True;
end;
```

The form of the Scale
example after a scaling
with 50 and 200

This method stores the current input value in the form's AmountScaled private field and enables the Restore button, disabling the one that was clicked. Later, when the user clicks the Restore button, the opposite scaling takes place. By having to restore the form before another scaling operation takes place, I avoid an accumulation of round-off errors. I've added also a line to set the Height of the UpDown component to the same Height as the edit box it is attached to. This prevents small differences between the two, due to scaling problems of the UpDown control.

NOTE   If you want to scale the text of the form properly, including the captions of components, the items in list boxes, and so on, you should use TrueType fonts exclusively. The system font (MS Sans Serif) doesn't scale well. The font issue is important because the size of many components depends on the text height of their captions, and if the caption does not scale well, the component might not work properly. For this reason, in the Scale example I've used an Arial font.

Exactly the same scaling technique also works in CLX, as you can see by running the QScale example. The only real difference is that I have to replace the UpDown component (and the related Edit box) with a SpinEdit control, as the former is not available in Qt.

Automatic Form Scaling

Instead of playing with the ScaleBy method, you can ask Delphi to do the work for you. When Delphi starts, it asks the system for the display configuration and stores the value in the PixelsPerInch property of the Screen object, a special global object of VCL, available in any application.

`PixelsPerInch` sounds like it has something to do with the pixel resolution of the screen, but unfortunately, it doesn't. If you change your screen resolution from 640×480 to 800×600 to 1024×768 or even 1600×1280, you will find that Windows reports the same `PixelsPerInch` value in all cases, unless you change the system font. What `PixelsPerInch` really refers to is the screen pixel resolution that the currently installed system font was designed for. When a user changes the system font scale, usually to make menus and other text easier to read, the user will expect all applications to honor those settings. An application that does not reflect user desktop preferences will look out of place and, in extreme cases, may be unusable to visually impaired users who rely on very large fonts and high-contrast color schemes.

The most common `PixelPerInch` values are 96 (small fonts) and 120 (large fonts), but other values are possible. Newer versions of Windows even allow the user to set the system font size to an arbitrary scale. At design time, the `PixelsPerInch` value of the screen, which is a read-only property, is copied to every form of the application. Delphi then uses the value of `PixelsPerInch`, if the `Scaled` property is set to True, to resize the form when the application starts.

As I've already mentioned, both automatic scaling and the scaling performed by the `ScaleBy` method operate on components by changing the size of the font. The size of each control, in fact, depends on the font it uses. With automatic scaling, the value of the form's `PixelsPerInch` property (the design-time value) is compared to the current system value (indicated by the corresponding property of the `Screen` object), and the result is used to change the font of the components on the form. Actually, to improve the accuracy of this code, the final height of the text is compared to the design-time height of the text, and its size is adjusted if they do not match.

Thanks to Delphi automatic support, the same application running on a system with a different system font size automatically scales itself, without any specific code. The application's edit controls will be the correct size to display their text in the user's preferred font size, and the form will be the correct size to contain those controls. Although automatic scaling has problems in some special cases, if you comply with the following rules, you should get good results:

- Set the `Scaled` property of forms to True. (This is the default.)
- Use only TrueType fonts.
- Use Windows small fonts (96 dpi) on the computer you use to develop the forms.
- Set the `AutoScroll` property to False, if you want to scale the form and not just the controls inside it. (AutoScroll defaults to True, so don't forget to do this step.)
- Set the form position either near the upper-left corner or in the center of the screen (with the poScreenCenter value) to avoid having an out-of-screen form. Form position is discussed in the next section.

Creating and Closing Forms

Up to now we have ignored the issue of form creation. We know that when the form is created, we receive the OnCreate event and can change or test some of the initial form's properties or fields. The statement responsible for creating the form is in this project's source file:

```
begin
  Application.Initialize;
  Application.CreateForm(TForm1, Form1);
  Application.Run;
end.
```

To skip the automatic form creation, you can either modify this code or use the Forms page of the Project Options dialog box (see Figure 9.11). In this dialog box, you can decide whether the form should be automatically created. If you disable the automatic creation, the project's initialization code becomes the following:

```
begin
  Applications.Initialize;
  Application.Run;
end.
```

FIGURE 9.11:

The Forms page of the
Delphi Project Options
dialog box

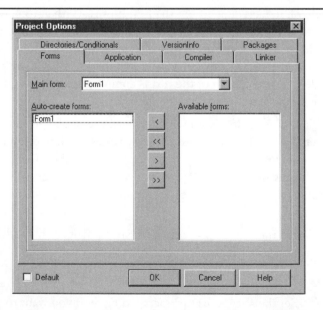

If you now run this program, nothing happens. It terminates immediately because no main window is created. So what is the effect of the call to the application's CreateForm method? It creates a new instance of the form class passed as the first parameter and assigns it to the variable passed as the second parameter.

Something else happens behind the scenes. When CreateForm is called, if there is currently no main form, the current form is assigned to the application's MainForm property. For this reason, the form indicated as Main Form in the dialog box shown in Figure 9.11 corresponds to the first call to the application's CreateForm method (that is, when several forms are created at start-up).

The same holds for closing the application. Closing the main form terminates the application, regardless of the other forms. If you want to perform this operation from the program's code, simply call the Close method of the main form, as we've done several times in past examples.

TIP   You can control the automatic creation of secondary forms by using the Auto Create Forms check box on the Preferences page of the Environment Options dialog box.

Form Creation Events

Regardless of the manual or automatic creation of forms, when a form is created, there are many events you can intercept. Form-creation events are fired in the following order:

1. OnCreate indicates that the form is being created.

2. OnShow indicates that the form is being displayed. Besides main forms, this event happens after you set the Visible property of the form to True or call the Show or ShowModal methods. This event is fired again if the form is hidden and then displayed again.

3. OnActivate indicates that the form becomes the active form within the application. This event is fired every time you move from another form of the application to the current one.

4. Other events, including OnResize and OnPaint, indicate operations always done at start-up but then repeated many times.

As you can see in the list above, every event has a specific role apart from form initialization, except for the OnCreate event, which is guaranteed to be called only once as the form is created.

However, there is an alternative approach to adding initialization code to a form: overriding the constructor. This is usually done as follows:

```
constructor TForm1.Create(AOwner: TComponent);
begin
  inherited Create (AOwner);
  // extra initialization code
end;
```

Before the call to the Create method of the base class, the properties of the form are still not loaded and the internal components are not available. For this reason the standard approach is to call the base class constructor first and then do the custom operations.

Old and New Creation Orders

Now the question is whether these custom operations are executed before or after the OnCreate event is fired. The answer depends on the value of the OldCreateOrder property of the form, introduced in Delphi 4 for backward compatibility with earlier versions of Delphi. By default, for a new project, all of the code in the constructor is executed before the OnCreate event handler. In fact, this event handler is not activated by the base class constructor but by its AfterConstruction method, a sort of constructor introduced for compatibility with C++Builder.

To study the creation order and the potential problems, you can examine the CreatOrd program. This program has an OnCreate event handler, which creates a list box control dynamically. The constructor of the form can access this list box or not, depending on the value of the OldCreateOrder property.

Closing a Form

When you close the form using the Close method or by the usual means (Alt+F4, the system menu, or the Close button), the OnCloseQuery event is called. In this event, you can ask the user to confirm the action, particularly if there is unsaved data in the form. Here is a simple scheme of the code you can write:

```
procedure TForm1.FormCloseQuery(Sender: TObject; var CanClose: Boolean);
begin
  if MessageDlg ('Are you sure you want to exit?', mtConfirmation,
      [mbYes, mbNo], 0) = idNo then
    CanClose := False;
end;
```

If OnCloseQuery indicates that the form should still be closed, the OnClose event is called. The third step is to call the OnDestroy event, which is the opposite of the OnCreate event and is generally used to de-allocate objects related to the form and free the corresponding memory.

NOTE   To be more precise, the BeforeDestruction method generates an OnDestroy event before the Destroy destructor is called. That is, unless you have set the OldCreateOrder property to True, in which case Delphi uses a different closing sequence.

So what is the use of the intermediate OnClose event? In this method, you have another chance to avoid closing the application, or you can specify alternative "close actions." The method, in fact, has an Action parameter passed by reference. You can assign the following values to this parameter:

caNone   The form is not allowed to close. This corresponds to setting the CanClose parameter of the OnCloseQuery method to False.

caHide   The form is not closed, just hidden. This makes sense if there are other forms in the application; otherwise, the program terminates. This is the default for secondary forms, and it's the reason I had to handle the OnClose event in the previous example to actually close the secondary forms.

caFree   The form is closed, freeing its memory, and the application eventually terminates if this was the main form. This is the default action for the main form and the action you should use when you create multiple forms dynamically (if you want to remove the Windows and destroy the corresponding Delphi object as the form closes).

caMinimize   The form is not closed but only minimized. This is the default action for MDI child forms.

> **NOTE**   When a user shuts down Windows, the OnCloseQuery event is activated, and a program can use it to stop the shut-down process. In this case, the OnClose event is not called even if OnCloseQuery sets the CanClose parameter to True.

Dialog Boxes and Other Secondary Forms

When you write a program, there is really no big difference between a dialog box and another secondary form, aside from the border, the border icons, and similar user-interface elements you can customize.

What users associate with a dialog box is the concept of a *modal window*—a window that takes the focus and must be closed before the user can move back to the main window. This is true for message boxes and usually for dialog boxes, as well. However, you can also have non-modal—or *modeless*—dialog boxes. So if you think that dialog boxes are just modal forms, you are on the right track, but your description is not precise. In Delphi (as in Windows), you can have modeless dialog boxes and modal forms. We have to consider two different elements:

- The form's border and its user interface determine whether it looks like a dialog box.

- The use of two different methods (Show or ShowModal) to display the secondary form determines its behavior (modeless or modal).

Adding a Second Form to a Program

To add a second form to an application, you simply click on the New Form button on the Delphi toolbar or use the File ➤ New Form menu command. As an alternative you can select File ➤ New, move to the Forms or Dialogs page, and choose one of the available form templates or form wizards.

If you have two forms in a project, you can use the Select Form or Select Unit button of the Delphi toolbar to navigate through them at design time. You can also choose which form is the main one and which forms should be automatically created at start-up using the Forms page of the Project Options dialog box. This information is reflected in the source code of the project file.

TIP Secondary forms are automatically created in the project source-code file depending on a new Delphi 5 setting, which is the Auto Create Forms check box of the Preferences page of the Environment Options dialog box. Although automatic creation is the simplest and most reliable approach for novice developers and quick-and-dirty projects, I suggest that you disable this check box for any serious development. When your application contains hundreds of forms, you really shouldn't have them all created at application start-up. Create instances of secondary forms when and where you need them, and free them when you're done.

Once you have prepared the secondary form, you can simply set its Visible property to True, and both forms will show up as the program starts. In general, the secondary forms of an application are left "invisible" and are then displayed by calling the Show method (or setting the Visible property at run time). If you use the Show function, the second form will be displayed as modeless, so you can move back to the first one while the second is still visible. To close the second form, you might use its system menu or click a button or menu item that calls the Close method. As we've just seen, the default close action (see the OnClose event) for a secondary form is simply to hide it, so the secondary form is not destroyed when it is closed. It is kept in memory (again, not always the best approach) and is available if you want to show it again.

Creating Secondary Forms at Run Time

Unless you create all the forms when the program starts, you'll need to check whether a form exists and create it if necessary. The simplest case is when you want to create multiple copies of the same form at run time. In the MultiWin/QMultiWin example, I've done this by writing the following code:

```
procedure TForm1.btnMultipleClick(Sender: TObject);
begin
  with TForm3.Create (Application) do
    Show;
end;
```

Every time you click the button, a new copy of the form is created. Notice that I don't use the `Form3` global variable, because it doesn't make much sense to assign this variable a new value every time you create a new form object. The important thing, however, is not to refer to the global `Form3` object in the code of the form itself or in other portions of the application. The `Form3` variable, in fact, will invariably be a pointer to `nil`. My suggestion, in such a case, is to actually remove it from the unit to avoid any confusion.

TIP   In the code of a form, you should never explicitly refer to the form by using the global variable that Delphi sets up for it. For example, suppose that in the code of **TForm3** you refer to `Form3.Caption`. If you create a second object of the same type (the class **TForm3**), the expression `Form3.Caption` will invariably refer to the caption of the form object referenced by the `Form3` variable, which might not be the current object executing the code. To avoid this problem, refer to the `Caption` property in the form's method to indicate the caption of the current form object, and use the `Self` keyword when you need a specific reference to the object of the current form. To avoid any problem when creating multiple copies of a form, I suggest removing the global form object from the interface portion of the unit declaring the form. This global variable is required only for the automatic form creation.

When you create multiple copies of a form dynamically, remember to destroy each form object as is it closed, by handling the corresponding event:

```
procedure TForm3.FormClose(Sender: TObject; var Action: TCloseAction);
begin
  Action := caFree;
end;
```

Failing to do so will result in a lot of memory consumption, because all the forms you create (both the windows and the Delphi objects) will be kept in memory and simply hidden from view.

Creating Single-Instance Secondary Forms

Now let us focus on the dynamic creation of a form, in a program that accounts for only one copy of the form at a time. Creating a modal form is quite simple, because the dialog box can be destroyed when it is closed, with code like this:

```
procedure TForm1.btnModalClick(Sender: TObject);
var
  Modal: TForm4;
begin
  Modal := TForm4.Create (Application);
  try
    Modal.ShowModal;
  finally
    Modal.Free;
  end;
end;
```

Because the ShowModal call can raise an exception, you should write it in a finally block to make sure the object will be de-allocated. Usually this block also includes code that initializes the dialog box before displaying it and code that extracts the values set by the user before destroying the form. The final values are read-only if the result of the ShowModal function is mrOK, as we'll see in the next example.

The situation is a little more complex when you want to display only one copy of a modeless form. In fact, you have to create the form, if it is not already available, and then show it:

```
procedure TForm1.btnSingleClick(Sender: TObject);
begin
  if not Assigned (Form2) then
    Form2 := TForm2.Create (Application);
  Form2.Show;
end;
```

With this code, the form is created the first time it is required and then is kept in memory, visible on the screen or hidden from view. To avoid using up memory and system resources unnecessarily, you'll want to destroy the secondary form when it is closed. You can do that by writing a handler for the OnClose event:

```
procedure TForm2.FormClose(Sender: TObject; var Action: TCloseAction);
begin
  Action := caFree;
  // important: set pointer to nil!
  Form2 := nil;
end;
```

Notice that after we destroy the form, the global Form2 variable is set to nil. Without this code, closing the form would destroy its object, but the Form2 variable would still refer to the original memory location. At this point, if you try to show the form once more with the btnSingleClick method shown earlier, the if not Assigned test will succeed, as it simply checks whether the Form2 variable is nil. The code fails to create a new object, and the Show method, invoked on a nonexistent object, will result in a system memory error.

As an experiment, you can generate this error by removing the last line of the listing above. As we have seen, the solution is to set the Form2 object to nil when the object is destroyed, so that properly written code will "see" that a new form has to be created before using it. Again, experimenting with the MultiWin/QMultiWin example can prove useful to test various conditions. I haven't illustrated any screens from this example because the forms it displays are quite bare (totally empty except for the main form, which has three buttons).

NOTE   Setting the form variable to nil makes sense—and works—if there is to be only one instance of the form present at any given instant. If you want to create multiple copies of a form, you'll have to use other techniques to keep track of them. Also keep in mind that in this case we cannot use the **FreeAndNil** procedure, because we cannot call Free on **Form2**. The reason is that we cannot destroy the form before its event handlers have finished executing.

Creating a Dialog Box

I stated earlier in this chapter that a dialog box is not very different from other forms. To build a dialog box instead of a form, you just select the bsDialog value for the BorderStyle property. With this simple change, the interface of the form becomes like that of a dialog box, with no system icon, and no Minimize or Maximize boxes. Of course, such a form has the typical thick dialog box border, which is non-resizable.

Once you have built a dialog box form, you can display it as a modal or modeless window using the two usual show methods (Show and ShowModal). Modal dialog boxes, however, are more common than modeless ones. This is exactly the reverse of forms; modal forms should generally be avoided, because a user won't expect them.

The Dialog Box of the RefList Example

In Chapter 6 we explored the RefList/QRefList program, which used a ListView control to display references to books, magazines, Web sites, and more. In the RefList2 version on the CD (and its QRefLsit2 CLX counterpart), I'll simply add to the basic version of that program a dialog box, used in two different circumstances: adding new items to the list and editing existing items. You can see the form of the dialog box in Figure 9.12 and its textual description in the following listing (detailed because it has many interesting features, so I suggest you read this code with care).

FIGURE 9.12:

The form of the dialog box of the RefList2 example at design time

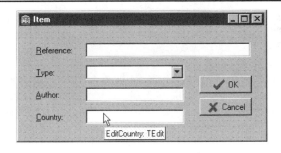

```
object FormItem: TFormItem
  Caption = 'Item'
  Color = clBtnFace
  Position = poScreenCenter
  object Label1: TLabel
    Caption = '&Reference:'
    FocusControl = EditReference
  end
  object EditReference: TEdit...
  object Label2: TLabel
```

```
    Caption = '&Type:'
    FocusControl = ComboType
  end
  object ComboType: TComboBox
    Style = csDropDownList
    Items.Strings = (
      'Book'
      'CD'
      'Magazine'
      'Mail Address'
      'Web Site')
  end
  object Label3: TLabel
    Caption = '&Author:'
    FocusControl = EditAuthor
  end
  object EditAuthor: TEdit...
  object Label4: TLabel
    Caption = '&Country:'
    FocusControl = EditCountry
  end
  object EditCountry: TEdit...
  object BitBtn1: TBitBtn
    Kind = bkOK
  end
  object BitBtn2: TBitBtn
    Kind = bkCancel
  end
end
```

TIP   The items of the combo box in this dialog describe the available images of the image list so that a user can select the type of the item and the system will show the corresponding glyph. An even better option would have been to show those glyphs in a graphical combo box, along with their descriptions.

As I mentioned, this dialog box is used in two different cases. The first takes place as the user selects File ➢ Add Items from the menu:

```
procedure TForm1.AddItems1Click(Sender: TObject);
var
  NewItem: TListItem;
begin
  FormItem.Caption := 'New Item';
  FormItem.Clear;
  if FormItem.ShowModal = mrOK then
  begin
```

```
  NewItem := ListView1.Items.Add;
  NewItem.Caption := FormItem.EditReference.Text;
  NewItem.ImageIndex := FormItem.ComboType.ItemIndex;
  NewItem.SubItems.Add (FormItem.EditAuthor.Text);
  NewItem.SubItems.Add (FormItem.EditCountry.Text);
  end;
end;
```

Besides setting the proper caption of the form, this procedure needs to initialize the dialog box, as we are entering a brand-new value. If the user clicks OK, however, the program adds a new item to the list view and sets all its values. To empty the edit boxes of the dialog, the program calls the custom Clear method, which resets the text of each edit box control:

```
procedure TFormItem.Clear;
var
  I: Integer;
begin
  // clear each edit box
  for I := 0 to ControlCount - 1 do
    if Controls [I] is TEdit then
      TEdit (Controls[I]).Text := '';
end;
```

Editing an existing item requires a slightly different approach. First, the current values are moved to the dialog box before it is displayed. Second, if the user clicks OK, the program modifies the current list item instead of creating a new one. Here is the code:

```
procedure TForm1.ListView1DblClick(Sender: TObject);
begin
  if ListView1.Selected <> nil then
  begin
    // dialog initialization
    FormItem.Caption := 'Edit Item';
    FormItem.EditReference.Text := ListView1.Selected.Caption;
    FormItem.ComboType.ItemIndex := ListView1.Selected.ImageIndex;
    FormItem.EditAuthor.Text := ListView1.Selected.SubItems [0];
    FormItem.EditCountry.Text := ListView1.Selected.SubItems [1];

    // show it
    if FormItem.ShowModal = mrOK then
    begin
      // read the new values
      ListView1.Selected.Caption := FormItem.EditReference.Text;
      ListView1.Selected.ImageIndex := FormItem.ComboType.ItemIndex;
      ListView1.Selected.SubItems [0] := FormItem.EditAuthor.Text;
      ListView1.Selected.SubItems [1] := FormItem.EditCountry.Text;
    end;
  end;
end;
```

You can see the effect of this code in Figure 9.13. Notice that the code used to read the value of a new item or modified one is similar. In general, you should try to avoid this type of duplicated code and possibly place the shared code statements in a method added to the dialog box. In this case, the method could receive as parameter a TListItem object and copy the proper values into it.

FIGURE 9.13:

The dialog box of the RefList2 example used in edit mode

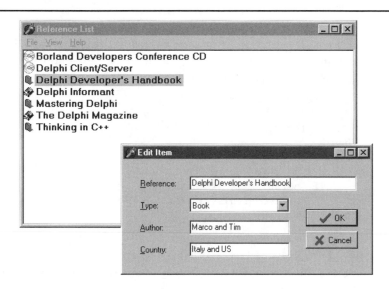

NOTE   What happens internally when the user clicks the OK or Cancel button of the dialog box? A modal dialog box is closed by setting its ModalResult property, and it returns the value of this property. You can indicate the return value by setting the ModalResult property of the button. When the user clicks on the button, its ModalResult value is copied to the form, which closes the form and returns the value as the result of the ShowModal function.

A Modeless Dialog Box

The second example of dialog boxes shows a more complex modal dialog box that uses the standard approach as well as a modeless dialog box. The main form of the DlgApply example (and of the identical CLX-based QDlgApply demo) has five labels with names, as you can see in Figure 9.14 and by viewing the source code on the companion CD.

FIGURE 9.14:

The three forms (a main form and two dialog boxes) of the DlgApply example at run time

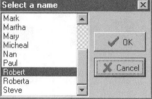
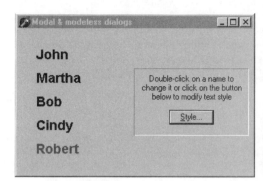

If the user clicks a name, its color turns to red; if the user double-clicks it, the program displays a modal dialog box with a list of names to choose from. If the user clicks the Style button, a modeless dialog box appears, allowing the user to change the font style of the main form's labels. The five labels of the main form are connected to two methods, one for the OnClick event and the second for the OnDoubleClick event. The first method turns the last label a user has clicked to red, resetting to black all the others (which have the Tag property set to 1, as a sort of group index). Notice that the same method is associated with all of the labels:

```
procedure TForm1.LabelClick(Sender: TObject);
var
  I: Integer;
begin
  for I := 0 to ComponentCount - 1 do
   if (Components[I] is TLabel) and (Components[I].Tag = 1) then
     TLabel (Components[I]).Font.Color := clBlack;
  // set the color of the clicked label to red
  (Sender as TLabel).Font.Color := clRed;
end;
```

The second method common to all of the labels is the handler of the OnDoubleClick event. The LabelDoubleClick method selects the Caption of the current label (indicated by the Sender parameter) in the list box of the dialog and then shows the modal dialog box. If the user closes the dialog box by clicking OK and an item of the list is selected, the selection is copied back to the label's caption:

```
procedure TForm1.LabelDoubleClick(Sender: TObject);
begin
  with ListDial.Listbox1 do
```

```
begin
  // select the current name in the list box
  ItemIndex := Items.IndexOf (Sender as TLabel).Caption);
  // show the modal dialog box, checking the return value
  if (ListDial.ShowModal = mrOk) and (ItemIndex >= 0) then
    // copy the selected item to the label
    (Sender as TLabel).Caption := Items [ItemIndex];
  end;
end;
```

TIP   Notice that all the code used to customize the modal dialog box is in the `LabelDoubleClick` method of the main form. The form of this dialog box has no added code.

The modeless dialog box, by contrast, has a lot of coding behind it. The main form simply displays the dialog box when the Style button is clicked (notice that the button caption ends with three dots to indicate that it leads to a dialog box), by calling its Show method. You can see the dialog box running in Figure 9.14 above.

Two buttons, Apply and Close, replace the OK and Cancel buttons in a modeless dialog box. (The fastest way to obtain these buttons is to select the bkOK or bkCancel value for the Kind property and then edit the Caption.) At times, you may see a Cancel button that works as a Close button, but the OK button in a modeless dialog box usually has no meaning. Instead, there might be one or more buttons that perform specific actions on the main window, such as Apply, Change Style, Replace, Delete, and so on.

If the user clicks one of the check boxes of this modeless dialog box, the style of the sample label's text at the bottom changes accordingly. You accomplish this by adding or removing the specific flag that indicates the style, as in the following OnClick event handler:

```
procedure TStyleDial.ItalicCheckBoxClick(Sender: TObject);
begin
  if ItalicCheckBox.Checked then
    LabelSample.Font.Style := LabelSample.Font.Style + [fsItalic]
  else
    LabelSample.Font.Style := LabelSample.Font.Style - [fsItalic];
end;
```

When the user selects the Apply button, the program copies the style of the sample label to each of the form's labels, rather than considering the values of the check boxes:

```
procedure TStyleDial.ApplyBitBtnClick(Sender: TObject);
begin
  Form1.Label1.Font.Style := LabelSample.Font.Style;
  Form1.Label2.Font.Style := LabelSample.Font.Style;
  ...
```

As an alternative, instead of referring to each label directly, you can look for it by calling the FindComponent method of the form, passing the label name as a parameter, and then casting the result to the TLabel type. The advantage of this approach is that we can create the names of the various labels with a for loop:

```
procedure TStyleDial.ApplyBitBtnClick(Sender: TObject);
var
  I: Integer;
begin
  for I := 1 to 5 do
    (Form1.FindComponent ('Label' + IntToStr (I)) as TLabel).Font.Style :=
      LabelSample.Font.Style;
end;
```

TIP   The ApplyBitBtnClick method could also be written by scanning the Controls array in a loop, as I've already done in other examples. I decided to use the FindComponent method, instead, to demonstrate a different technique.

This second version of the code is certainly slower, because it has more operations to do, but you won't notice the difference, because it is very fast anyway. Of course, this second approach is also more flexible; if you add a new label, you only need to fix the higher limit of the for loop, provided all the labels have consecutive numbers. Notice that when the user clicks the Apply button, the dialog box does not close. Only the Close button has this effect. Consider also that this dialog box needs no initialization code because the form is not destroyed, and its components maintain their status each time the dialog box is displayed.

Predefined Dialog Boxes

Besides building your own dialog boxes, Delphi allows you to use some default dialog boxes of various kinds. Some are predefined by Windows; others are simple dialog boxes (such as message boxes) displayed by a Delphi routine. The Delphi Component Palette contains a page of dialog box components. Each of these dialog boxes—known as *Windows common dialogs*—is defined in the system library ComDlg32.DLL.

Windows Common Dialogs

I have already used some of these dialog boxes in several examples in the previous chapters, so you are probably familiar with them. Basically, you need to put the corresponding component on a form, set some of its properties, run the dialog box (with the Execute method, returning a Boolean value), and retrieve the properties that have been set while running it. To help you experiment with these dialog boxes, I've built the CommDlg test program.

What I want to do is simply highlight some key and nonobvious features of the common dialog boxes, and let you study the source code of the example for the details:

- The Open Dialog Component can be customized by setting different file extensions filters, using the `Filter` property, which has a handy editor and can be assigned directly with a string like `Text File (*.txt)|*.txt`. Another handy feature is to let the dialog check whether the extension of the selected file matches the default extension, by checking the ofExtensionDifferent flag of the `Options` property after executing the dialog. Finally, this dialog allows multiple selections by setting its ofAllowMultiSelect option. In this case you can get the list of the selected files by looking at the `Files` string list property.

- The SaveDialog component is used in similar ways and has similar properties, although you cannot select multiple files, of course.

- The OpenPictureDialog and SavePictureDialog components provide similar features but have a customized form, which shows a preview of an image. Of course, it makes sense to use them only for opening or saving graphical files.

- The FontDialog component can be used to show and select from all types of fonts, fonts useable on both the screen and a selected printer (WYSIWYG), or only TrueType fonts. You can show or hide the portion related to the special effects, and obtain other different versions by setting its `Options` property. You can also activate an Apply button simply by providing an event handler for its `OnApply` event and using the fdApplyButton option. A Font dialog box with an Apply button (see Figure 9.15) behaves almost like a modeless dialog box (but isn't one).

FIGURE 9.15:

The Font selection dialog box with an Apply button

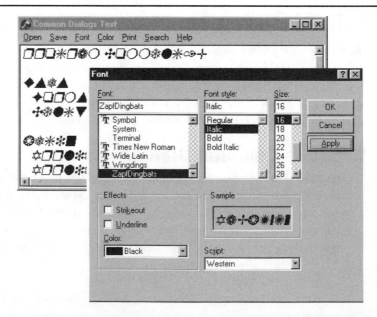

- The ColorDialog component is used with different options, to show the dialog fully open at first or to prevent it from opening fully. These settings are the cdFullOpen or cdPreventFullOpen values of the Options property.

- The Find and Replace dialog boxes are truly modeless dialogs, but you have to implement the find and replace functionality yourself, as I've partially done in the CommDlg example. The custom code is connected to the buttons of the two dialog boxes by providing the OnFind and OnReplace events.

NOTE   Qt offers a similar set of predefined dialog boxes, only the set of options is often more limited. I've created the QCommDlg version of the example you can use to experiment with these settings. The CLX program has fewer menu items, as some of the options are not available and there are other minimal changes in the source code.

A Parade of Message Boxes

The Delphi message boxes and input boxes are another set of predefined dialog boxes. There are many Delphi procedures and functions you can use to display simple dialog boxes:

- The MessageDlg function shows a customizable message box, with one or more buttons and usually a bitmap. The MessageDlgPos function is similar to the MessageDlg function, but the message box is displayed in a given position, not in the center of the screen.

- The ShowMessage procedure displays a simpler message box, with the application name as the caption and just an OK button. The ShowMessagePos procedure does the same, but you also indicate the position of the message box. The ShowMessageFmt procedure is a variation of ShowMessage, which has the same parameters as the Format function. It corresponds to calling Format inside a call to ShowMessage.

- The MessageBox method of the Application object allows you to specify both the message and the caption; you can also provide various buttons and features. This is a simple and direct encapsulation of the MessageBox function of the Windows API, which passes as a main window parameter the handle of the Application object. This handle is required to make the message box behave like a modal window.

- The InputBox function asks the user to input a string. You provide the caption, the query, and a default string. The InputQuery function asks the user to input a string, too. The only difference between this and the InputBox function is in the syntax. The InputQuery function has a Boolean return value that indicates whether the user has clicked OK or Cancel.

To demonstrate some of the message boxes available in Delphi, I've written another sample program, with a similar approach to the preceding CommDlg example. In the MBParade example, you have a high number of choices (radio buttons, check boxes, edit boxes, and spin edit controls) to set before you click one of the buttons that displays a message box. The similar QMbParade example misses only the possibility of the help button, not available in the CLX message boxes.

About Boxes and Splash Screens

Applications usually have an About box, where you can display information, such as the version of the product, a copyright notice, and so on. The simplest way to build an About box is to use the MessageDlg function. With this method, you can show only a limited amount of text and no special graphics.

Therefore, the usual method for creating an About box is to use a dialog box, such as the one generated with one of the Delphi default templates. In this about box you might want to add some code to display system information, such as the version of Windows or the amount of free memory, or some user information, such as the registered user name.

Building a Splash Screen

Another typical technique used in applications is to display an initial screen before the main form is shown. This makes the application seem more responsive, because you show something to the user while the program is loading, but it also makes a nice visual effect. Sometimes, this same window is displayed as the application's About box.

For an example in which a splash screen is particularly useful, I've built a program displaying a list box filled with prime numbers. The prime numbers are computed on program startup, so that they are displayed as soon as the form becomes visible:

```
procedure TForm1.FormCreate(Sender: TObject);
var
  I: Integer;
begin
  for I := 1 to 30000 do
    if IsPrime (I) then
      ListBox1.Items.Add (IntToStr (I));
end;
```

This method calls an IsPrime function I've added to the program. This function, which you can find in the source code, computes prime numbers in a terribly slow way; but I needed a slow form creation to demonstrate my point. The numbers are added to a list box that covers the full client area of the form and allows multiple columns to be displayed, as you can see in Figure 9.16.

FIGURE 9.16:

The main form of the Splash example, with the About box activated from the menu

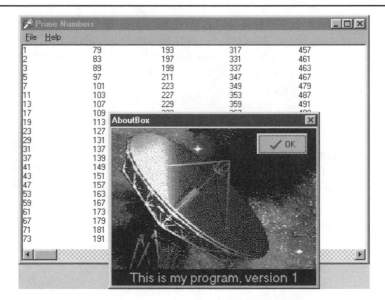

There are three versions of the Splash program (plus the three corresponding CLX versions). As you can see by running the Splash0 example, the problem with this program is that the initial operation, which takes place in the FormCreate method, takes a lot of time. When you start the program, it takes several seconds to display the main form. If your computer is very fast or very slow, you can change the upper limit of the for loop of the FormCreate method to make the program faster or slower.

This program has a simple dialog box with an image component, a simple caption, and a bitmap button, all placed inside a panel taking up the whole surface of the About box. This form is displayed when you select the Help ➢ About menu item. But what we really want is to display this About box while the program starts. You can see this effect by running the Splash1 and Splash2 examples, which show a splash screen using two different techniques.

First of all, I've added a method to the TAboutBox class. This method, called MakeSplash, changes some properties of the form to make it suitable for a splash form. Basically it removes the border and caption, hides the OK button, makes the border of the panel thick (to replace the border of the form), and then shows the form, repainting it immediately:

```
procedure TAboutBox.MakeSplash;
begin
  BorderStyle := bsNone;
  BitBtn1.Visible := False;
  Panel1.BorderWidth := 3;
```

```
    Show;
    Update;
  end;
```

This method is called after creating the form in the project file of the Splash1 example. This code is executed before creating the other forms (in this case only the main form), and the splash screen is then removed before running the application. These operations take place within a try/finally block. Here is the source code of the main block of the project file for the Splash2 example:

```
var
  SplashAbout: TAboutBox;

begin
  Application.Initialize;

  // create and show the splash form
  SplashAbout := TAboutBox.Create (Application);
  try
    SplashAbout.MakeSplash;
    // standard code...
    Application.CreateForm(TForm1, Form1);
    // get rid of the splash form
    SplashAbout.Close;
  finally
    SplashAbout.Free;
  end;

  Application.Run;
end.
```

This approach makes sense only if your application's main form takes a while to create, to execute its startup code (as in this case), or to open database tables. Notice that the splash screen is the first form created, but because the program doesn't use the CreateForm method of the Application object, this doesn't become the main form of the application. In this case, in fact, closing the splash screen would terminate the program!

An alternative approach is to keep the splash form on the screen a little longer and use a timer to get rid of it after a while. I've implemented this second technique in the Splash2 example. This example also uses a different approach for creating the splash form: instead of creating it in the project source code, it creates the form at the very beginning of the FormCreate method of the main form.

```
procedure TForm1.FormCreate(Sender: TObject);
var
  I: Integer;
  SplashAbout: TAboutBox;
```

```
begin
  // create and show the splash form
  SplashAbout := TAboutBox.Create (Application);
  SplashAbout.MakeSplash;
  // standard code...
  for I := 1 to 30000 do
    if IsPrime (I) then
      ListBox1.Items.Add (IntToStr (I));
  // get rid of the splash form, after a while
  SplashAbout.Timer1.Enabled := True;
end;
```

The timer is enabled just before terminating the method. After its interval has elapsed (in the example, 3 seconds) the OnTimer event is activated, and the splash form handles it by closing and destroying itself:

```
procedure TAboutBox.Timer1Timer(Sender: TObject);
begin
  Close;
  Release;
end;
```

NOTE　The Release method of a form is similar to the Free method of objects, only the destruction of the form is delayed until all event handlers have completed execution. Using Free inside a form might cause an access violation, as the internal code, which fired the event handler, might refer again to the form object.

There is one more thing to fix. The main form will be displayed later and in front of the splash form, unless you make this a top-most form. For this reason I've added one line to the MakeSplash method of the About box in the Splash2 example:

```
FormStyle := fsStayOnTop;
```

What's Next?

In this chapter we've explored some important form properties. Now you know how to handle the size and position of a form, how to resize it, and how to get mouse input and paint over it. You know more about dialog boxes, modal forms, predefined dialogs, splash screens, and many other techniques, including the funny effect of alpha blending. Understanding the details of working with forms is critical to a proper use of Delphi, particularly for building complex applications (unless, of course, you're building services or Web applications with no user interface).

In the next chapter we'll continue by exploring the overall structure of a Delphi application, with coverage of the role of two global objects, Application and Screen. I'll also discuss MDI development as you learn some more advanced features of forms, such as visual form inheritance. I'll also discuss frames, visual component containers similar to forms.

In this chapter, I've also provided a short introduction to direct painting and to the use of the TCanvas class. More about graphics in Delphi forms can also be found in the bonus chapter "Graphics in Delphi" on the companion CD.

CHAPTER 10

The Architecture of Delphi Applications

- The *Application* and *Screen* global objects

- Messages and multitasking in Windows

- Finding the previous instance of an application

- MDI applications

- Visual form inheritance

- Frames

- Base forms and interfaces

Although together we've built Delphi applications since the beginning of the book, we've never really focused on the structure and the architecture of an application built with Delphi's class library. For example, there hasn't been much coverage about the global Application object, about techniques for keeping tracks of the forms we've created, about the flow of messages in the system, and other such elements.

In the last chapter you saw how to create applications with multiple forms and dialog boxes, but we haven't discussed how these forms can be related one to the other, how can you share similar features of forms, and how you can operate on multiple similar forms in a coherent way. All of this is the ambitious goal of this chapter, which covers both basic and advanced techniques, including visual form inheritance, the use of frames, and MDI development, but also the use of interfaces for building complex hierarchies of form classes.

The *Application* Object

I've already mentioned the Application global object on multiple occasions, but as in this chapter we are focusing on the structure of Delphi applications, it is time to delve into some more details of this global object and its corresponding class. Application is a global object of the TApplication class, defined in the Forms unit and created in the Controls unit.

The TApplication class is a component, but you cannot use it at design time. Some of its properties can be directly set in the Application page of the Project Options dialog box; others must be assigned in code.

To handle its events, instead, Delphi includes a handy ApplicationEvents component. Besides allowing you to assign handlers at design time, the advantage of this component is that it allows for multiple handlers. If you simply place two instances of the ApplicationEvents component in two different forms, each of them can handle the same event, and both event handlers will be executed. In other words, multiple ApplicationEvents components can chain the handlers.

Some of these application-wide events, including OnActivate, OnDeactivate, OnMinimize, and OnRestore, allow you to keep track of the status of the application. Other events are forwarded to the application by the controls receiving them, as in OnActionExecute, OnAction-Update, OnHelp, OnHint, OnShortCut, and OnShowHint. Finally, there is the OnException global exception handler we used in Chapter 3, the OnIdle event used for background computing, and the OnMessage event, which fires whenever a message is posted to any of the windows or windowed controls of the application.

Although its class inherits directly from TComponent, the Application object has a window associated with it. The application window is hidden from sight but appears on the Taskbar. This is why Delphi names the window *Form1* and the corresponding Taskbar icon *Project1*.

The window related to the `Application` object—the application window—serves to keep together all the windows of an application. The fact that all the top-level forms of a program have this invisible owner window, for example, is fundamental when the application is activated. In fact, when the windows of your program are behind those of other programs, clicking one window in your application will bring all of that application's windows to the front. In other words, the unseen application window is used to connect the various forms of the application. Actually the application window is not *hidden*, because that would affect its behavior; it simply has zero height and width, and therefore it is not visible.

TIP   In Windows, the Minimize and Maximize operations are associated by default with system sounds and a visual animated effect. Applications built with Delphi (starting with version 5) produce the sound and display the visual effect by default.

When you create a new, blank application, Delphi generates a code for the project file, which includes the following:

```
begin
  Application.Initialize;
  Application.CreateForm(TForm1, Form1);
  Application.Run;
end.
```

As you can see in this standard code, the `Application` object can create forms, setting the first one as the `MainForm` (one of the `Application` properties) and closing the entire application when this main form is destroyed. Moreover, it contains the Windows message loop (started by the `Run` method) that delivers the system messages to the proper windows of the application. A message loop is required by any Windows application, but you don't need to write one in Delphi because the `Application` object provides a default one.

If this is the main role of the `Application` object, it manages few other interesting areas as well:

- Hints (discussed at the end of Chapter 7)

- The help system, which in Delphi 6 includes the ability to define the type of help viewer (something not covered in detail in this book)

- Application activation, minimize, and restore

- A global exceptions handler, as discussed in Chapter 3 in the ErrorLog example

- General application information, including the `MainForm`, executable file name and path (`ExeName`), the `Icon`, and the `Title` displayed in the Windows taskbar and when you scan the running applications with the Alt+Tab keys

   To avoid a discrepancy between the two titles, you can change the application's title at design time. As an alternative, at run time, you can copy the form's caption to the title of the application with this code: `Application.Title := Form1.Caption`.

In most applications, you don't care about the application window, apart from setting its `Title` and icon and handling some of its events. There are some simple operations you can do anyway. Setting the `ShowMainForm` property to False in the project source code indicates that the main form should not be displayed at startup. Inside a program, instead, you can use the `MainForm` property of the `Application` object to access the main form, which is the first form created in the program.

Displaying the Application Window

There is no better proof that a window indeed exists for the `Application` object than to display it. Actually, we don't need to show it—we just need to resize it and set a couple of window attributes, such as the presence of a caption and a border. We can perform these operations by using Windows API functions on the window indicated by the `Handle` property of the `Application` object:

```
procedure TForm1.Button1Click(Sender: TObject);
var
  OldStyle: Integer;
begin
  // add border and caption to the app window
  OldStyle := GetWindowLong (Application.Handle, gwl_Style);
  SetWindowLong (Application.Handle, gwl_Style,
    OldStyle or ws_ThickFrame or ws_Caption);
  // set the size of the app window
  SetWindowPos (Application.Handle, 0, 0, 0, 200, 100,
    swp_NoMove or swp_NoZOrder);
end;
```

The two `GetWindowLong` and `SetWindowLong` API functions are used to access the system information related to the window. In this case, we are using the `gwl_Style` parameter to read or write the styles of the window, which include its border, title, system menu, border icons, and so on. The code above gets the current styles and adds (using an `or` statement) a standard border and a caption to the form. As we'll see later in this chapter, you seldom need to use these low-level API functions in Delphi, because there are properties of the `TForm` class that have the same effect. We need this code here because the application window is not a form.

Executing this code displays the project window, as you can see in Figure 10.1. Although there's no need to implement something like this in your own programs, running this program will reveal the relation between the application window and the main window of a Delphi program. This is a very important starting point if you want to understand the internal structure of Delphi applications.

FIGURE 10.1:

The hidden application window revealed by the
ShowApp program

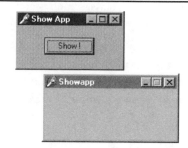

The Application System Menu

Unless you write a very odd program like the example we've just looked at, users will only see
the application window in the Taskbar. There, they can activate the window's system menu by
right-clicking it. As I mentioned in the SysMenu example in Chapter 6, when discussing the
system menu, an application's menu is not the same as that of the main form. In that example,
I added custom items to the system menu of the main form. Now in the SysMenu2 example, I
want to customize the system menu of the application window in the Taskbar.

First we have to add the new items to the system menu of the application window when the
program starts. Here is the updated code of the FormCreate method:

```
procedure TForm1.FormCreate(Sender: TObject);
begin
  // add a separator and a menu item to the system menu
  AppendMenu (GetSystemMenu (Handle, FALSE), MF_SEPARATOR, 0, '');
  AppendMenu (GetSystemMenu (Handle, FALSE), MF_STRING, idSysAbout,
    '&About...');
  // add the same items to the application system menu
  AppendMenu (GetSystemMenu (Application.Handle, FALSE), MF_SEPARATOR, 0, '');
  AppendMenu (GetSystemMenu (Application.Handle, FALSE), MF_STRING, idSysAbout,
    '&About...');
end;
```

The first part of the code adds the new separator and item to the system menu of the main
form. The other two calls add the same two items to the application's system menu, simply
by referring to Application.Handle. This is enough to display the updated system menu, as
you can see by running this program. The next step is to handle the selection of the new
menu item.

To handle form messages, we can simply write new event handlers or message-handling
methods. We cannot do the same with the application window, simply because inheriting
from the TApplication class is quite a complex issue. Most of the time we can just handle

the OnMessage event of this class, which is activated for every message the application retrieves from the message queue.

To handle the OnMessage event of the global Application object, simply add an Application-Events component to the main form, and define a handler for the OnMessage event of this component. In this case, we only need to handle the wm_SysCommand message, and we only need to do that if the wParam parameter indicates that the user has selected the menu item we've just added, idSysAbout:

```
procedure TForm1.ApplicationEvents1Message(var Msg: tagMSG;
  var Handled: Boolean);
begin
  if (Msg.Message = wm_SysCommand) and (Msg.wParam = idSysAbout) then
  begin
    ShowMessage ('Mastering Delphi: SysMenu2 example');
    Handled := True;
  end;
end;
```

This method is very similar to the one used to handle the corresponding system menu item of the main form:

```
procedure WMSysCommand (var Msg: TWMSysCommand);
  message wm_SysCommand;
...
procedure TForm1.WMSysCommand (var Msg: TWMSysCommand);
begin
  // handle a specific command
  if Msg.CmdType = idSysAbout then
    ShowMessage ('Mastering Delphi: SysMenu2 example');
  inherited;
end;
```

Activating Applications and Forms

To show how the activation of forms and applications works, I've written a simple, self-explanatory example, available on the companion CD, called ActivApp. This example has two forms. Each form has a Label component (LabelForm) used to display the status of the form. The program uses text and color for this, as the handlers of the OnActivate and OnDeactivate events of the first form demonstrate:

```
procedure TForm1.FormActivate(Sender: TObject);
begin
  LabelForm.Caption := 'Form2 Active';
  LabelForm.Color := clRed;
end;

procedure TForm1.FormDeactivate(Sender: TObject);
begin
  LabelForm.Caption := 'Form2 Not Active';
```

```
    LabelForm.Color := clBtnFace;
  end;
```

The second form has a similar label and similar code. The main form also displays the status of the entire application. It uses an ApplicationEvents component to handle the OnActivate and OnDeactivate events of the Application object. These two event handlers are similar to the two listed previously, with the only difference being that they modify the text and color of a second label of the form.

If you try running this program, you'll see whether this application is the active one and, if so, which of its forms is the active one. By looking at the output (see Figure 10.2) and listening for the beep, you can understand how each of the activation events is triggered by Delphi. Run this program and play with it for a while to understand how it works. We'll get back to other events related to the activation of forms in a while.

FIGURE 10.2:

The ActivApp example shows whether the application is active and which of the application's forms is active.

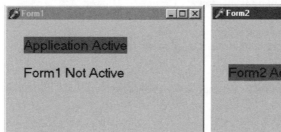 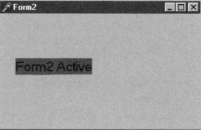

Tracking Forms with the *Screen* Object

We have already explored some of the properties and events of the Application object. Other interesting global information about an application is available through the Screen object, whose base class is TScreen. This object holds information about the system display (the screen size and the screen fonts) and also about the current set of forms in a running application. For example, you can display the screen size and the list of fonts by writing:

```
Label1.Caption := IntToStr (Screen.Width) + 'x' + IntToStr (Screen.Height);
ListBox1.Items := Screen.Fonts;
```

TScreen also reports the number and resolution of monitors in a multimonitor system. What I want to focus on now, however, is the list of forms held by the Forms property of the Screen object, the top-most form indicated by the ActiveForm property, and the related OnActiveFormChange event. Note that the forms the Screen object references are the forms of the application and not those of the system.

These features are demonstrated by the Screen example on the CD, which maintains a list of the current forms in a list box. This list must be updated each time a new form is created, an existing form is destroyed, or the active form of the program changes. To see how this works, you can create secondary forms by clicking the button labeled New:

```
procedure TMainForm.NewButtonClick(Sender: TObject);
var
  NewForm: TSecondForm;
begin
  // create a new form, set its caption, and run it
  NewForm := TSecondForm.Create (Self);
  Inc (nForms);
  NewForm.Caption := 'Second ' + IntToStr (nForms);
  NewForm.Show;
end;
```

One of the key portions of the program is the OnCreate event handler of the form, which fills the list a first time and then connects a handler to the OnActiveFormChange event:

```
procedure TMainForm.FormCreate(Sender: TObject);
begin
  FillFormsList (Self);
  // set the secondary forms counter to 0
  nForms := 0;
  // set an event handler on the screen object
  Screen.OnActiveFormChange := FillFormsList;
end;
```

The code used to fill the Forms list box is inside a second procedure, FillFormsList, which is also installed as an event handler for the OnActiveFormChange event of the Screen object:

```
procedure TMainForm.FillFormsList (Sender: TObject);
var
  I: Integer;
begin
  // skip code in destruction phase
  if Assigned (FormsListBox) then
  begin
    FormsLabel.Caption := 'Forms: ' + IntToStr (Screen.FormCount);
    FormsListBox.Clear;
    // write class name and form title to the list box
    for I := 0 to Screen.FormCount - 1 do
      FormsListBox.Items.Add (Screen.Forms[I].ClassName + ' - ' +
        Screen.Forms[I].Caption);
    ActiveLabel.Caption := 'Active Form : ' + Screen.ActiveForm.Caption;
  end;
end;
```

It is very important not to execute this code while the main form is being destroyed. As an alternative to testing for the listbox not to be set to `nil`, you could as well test the form's `ComponentState` for the csDestroying flag. Another approach would be to remove the `OnActiveFormChange` event handler before exiting the application; that is, handle the `OnClose` event of the main form and assign `nil` to `Screen.OnActiveFormChange`.

The `FillFormsList` method fills the list box and sets a value for the two labels above it to show the number of forms and the name of the active one. When you click the New button, the program creates an instance of the secondary form, gives it a new title, and displays it. The Forms list box is updated automatically because of the handler we have installed for the `OnActiveFormChange` event. Figure 10.3 shows the output of this program when some secondary windows have been created.

FIGURE 10.3:

The output of the Screen example with some secondary forms

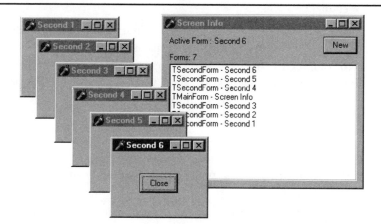

TIP   The program always updates the text of the `ActiveLabel` above the list box to show the currently active form, which is always the same as the first one in the list box.

The secondary forms each have a Close button you can click to remove them. The program handles the `OnClose` event, setting the `Action` parameter to caFree, so that the form is actually destroyed when it is closed. This code closes the form, but it doesn't update the list of the windows properly. The system moves the focus to another window first, firing the event that updates the list, and destroys the old form only after this operation.

The first idea I had to update the windows list properly is to introduce a delay, posting a user-defined Windows message. Because the posted message is queued and not handled immediately, if we send it at the last possible moment of life of the secondary form, the main form will receive it when the other form is destroyed.

The trick is to post the message in the OnDestroy event handler of the secondary form. To accomplish this, we need to refer to the MainForm object, by adding a uses statement in the implementation portion of this unit. I've posted a wm_User message, which is handled by a specific message method of the main form, as shown here:

```
public
  procedure ChildClosed (var Message: TMessage);
    message wm_User;
```

Here is the code for this method:

```
procedure TMainForm.ChildClosed (var Message: TMessage);
begin
  FillFormsList (Self);
end;
```

The problem here is that if you close the main window before closing the secondary forms, the main form exists, but its code cannot be executed anymore. To avoid another system error (an Access Violation Fault), you need to post the message only if the main form is not closing. But how do you know that? One way is to add a flag to the TMainForm class and change its value when the main form is closing, so that you can test the flag from the code of the secondary window.

This is a good solution—so good that the VCL already provides something similar. There is a barely documented ComponentState property. It is a Pascal set that includes (among other flags) a csDestroying flag, which is set when the form is closing. Therefore, we can write the following code:

```
procedure TSecondForm.FormDestroy(Sender: TObject);
begin
  if not (csDestroying in MainForm.ComponentState) then
    PostMessage (MainForm.Handle, wm_User, 0, 0);
end;
```

With this code, the list box always lists all of the forms in the application. Note that you need to disable the automatic creation of the secondary form by using the Forms page of the Project Options dialog box.

After giving it some thought, however, I found an alternative and much more Delphi-oriented solution. Every time a component is destroyed, it tells its owner about the event by calling the Notification method defined in the TComponent class. Because the secondary forms are owned by the main one, as specified in the code of the NewButtonClick method, we can override this method and simplify the code. In the form class, simply write

```
protected
  procedure Notification(AComponent: TComponent;
    Operation: TOperation); override;
```

Here is the code of the method:

```
procedure TMainForm.Notification(AComponent: TComponent;
  Operation: TOperation);
begin
  inherited Notification(AComponent, Operation);
  if (Operation = opRemove) and Showing and (AComponent is TForm) then
    FillFormsList;
end;
```

You'll find the complete code of this version in the Screen2 directory on the CD.

NOTE   In case the secondary forms were not owned by the main one, we could have used the **FreeNotification** method to get the secondary form to notify the main form when they are destroyed. **FreeNotification** receives as parameter the component to notify when the current component is destroyed. The effect is a call to the **Notification** method coming from a component other than the owned ones. **FreeNotification** is generally used by component writers to safely connect components on different forms or data modules.

The last feature I've added to both versions of the program is a simple one. When you click an item in the list box, the corresponding form is activated, using the BringToFront method:

```
procedure TMainForm.FormsListBoxClick(Sender: TObject);
begin
  Screen.Forms [FormsListBox.ItemIndex].BringToFront;
end;
```

Nice—well, almost nice. If you click the list box of an inactive form, the main form is activated first, and the list box is rearranged, so you might end up selecting a different form than you were expecting. If you experiment with the program, you'll soon realize what I mean. This minor glitch in the program is an example of the risks you face when you dynamically update some information and let the user work on it at the same time.

Events, Messages, and Multitasking in Windows

To understand how Windows applications work internally, we need to spend a minute discussing how multitasking is supported in this environment. We also need to understand the role of timers (and the Timer component) and of background (or *idle*) computing.

In short, we need to delve deeper into the event-driven structure of Windows and its multitasking support. Because this is a book about *Delphi* programming, I won't discuss this topic in detail, but I will provide an overview for readers who have limited experience with Windows API programming.

Event-Driven Programming

The basic idea behind event-driven programming is that specific events determine the control flow of the application. A program spends most of its time waiting for these events and provides code to respond to them. For example, when a user clicks one of the mouse buttons, an event occurs. A message describing this event is sent to the window currently under the mouse cursor. The program code that responds to events for that window will receive the event, process it, and respond accordingly. When the program has finished responding to the event, it returns to a waiting or "idle" state.

As this explanation shows, events are serialized; each event is handled only after the previous one is completed. When an application is executing event-handling code (that is, when it is not waiting for an event), other events for that application have to wait in a message queue reserved for that application (unless the application uses multiple threads). When an application has responded to a message and returned to a waiting state, it becomes the last in the list of programs waiting to handle additional messages. In every version of Win32 (9*x*, NT, Me, and 2000), after a fixed amount of time has elapsed, the system interrupts the current application and immediately gives control to the next one in the list. The first program is resumed only after each application has had a turn. This is called preemptive multitasking.

So, an application performing a time-consuming operation in an event handler doesn't prevent the system from working properly, but is generally unable even to repaint its own windows properly, with a very nasty effect. If you've never experienced this problem, try for yourself: Write a time-consuming loop executed when a button is pressed, and try to move the form or move another window on top of it. The effect is really annoying. Now try adding the call `Application.ProcessMessages` within the loop, and you'll see that the operation becomes much slower, but the form will be immediately refreshed.

If an application has responded to its events and is waiting for its turn to process messages, it has no chance to regain control until it receives another message (unless it uses multithreading). This is a reason to use timers, a system component that will send a message to your application every time a time interval elapses.

One final note—when you think about events, remember that input events (using the mouse or the keyboard) account for only a small percentage of the total message flow in a Windows application. Most of the messages are the system's internal messages or messages exchanged between different controls and windows. Even a familiar input operation such as clicking a mouse button can result in a huge number of messages, most of which are internal Windows messages. You can test this yourself by using the WinSight utility included in Delphi. In WinSight, choose to view the Message Trace, and select the messages for all of the windows. Select Start, and then perform some normal operations with the mouse. You'll see hundreds of messages in a few seconds.

Windows Message Delivery

Before looking at some real examples, we need to consider another key element of message handling. Windows has two different ways to send a message to a window:

- The `PostMessage` API function is used to place a message in the application's message queue. The message will be handled only when the application has a chance to access its message queue (that is, when it receives control from the system), and only after earlier messages have been processed. This is an asynchronous call, since you do not know when the message will actually be received.

- The `SendMessage` API function is used to execute message-handler code immediately. `SendMessage` bypasses the application's message queue and sends the message directly to a target window or control. This is a synchronous call. This function even has a return value, which is passed back by the message-handling code. Calling `SendMessage` is no different than directly calling another method or function of the program.

The difference between these two ways of sending messages is similar to that between mailing a letter, which will reach its destination sooner or later, and sending a fax, which goes immediately to the recipient. Although you will rarely need to use these low-level functions in Delphi, this description should help you determine which one to use if you do need to write this type of code.

Background Processing and Multitasking

Suppose that you need to implement a time-consuming algorithm. If you write the algorithm as a response to an event, your application will be stopped completely during all the time it takes to process that algorithm. To let the user know that something is being processed, you can display the hourglass cursor, but this is not a user-friendly solution. Win32 allows other programs to continue their execution, but the program in question will freeze; it won't even update its own user interface if a repaint is requested. In fact, while the algorithm is executing, the application won't be able to receive and process any other messages, including the paint messages.

The simplest solution to this problem is to call the `ProcessMessages` method of the `Application` object many times within the algorithm, usually inside an internal loop. This call stops the execution, allows the program to receive and handle a message, and then resumes execution. The problem with this approach, however, is that while the program is paused to accept messages, the user is free to do any operation and might again click the button or press the keystrokes that started the algorithm. To fix this, you can disable the buttons and commands you don't want the user to select, and you can display the hourglass cursor (which technically doesn't prevent a mouse click event, but it does suggest that the user should wait before doing any other operation). An alternative solution is to split the algorithm into smaller pieces and execute each of them in turn, letting the application respond to pending messages in between processing the pieces. We can use a timer to let the system notify us once a time interval has elapsed. Although you can use timers to implement some form of background computing, this is far from a good solution. A slightly better technique would be to execute each step of the program when the Application object receives the OnIdle event.

The difference between calling ProcessMessages and using the OnIdle events is that by calling ProcessMessages, you will give your code more processing time than with the OnIdle approach. Calling ProcessMessages is a way to let the system perform other operations while your program is computing; using the OnIdle event is a way to let your application perform background tasks when it doesn't have pending requests from the user.

> **NOTE**   All these techniques for background computing were necessary in 16-bit Windows days. In Win32, you should generally use secondary threads to perform lengthy or background operations.

Checking for a Previous Instance of an Application

One form of multitasking is the execution of two or more instances of the same application. Any application can generally be executed by a user in more than one instance, and it needs to be able to check for a previous instance already running, in order to disable this default behavior and allow for one instance at most. This section demonstrates several ways of implementing such a check, allowing me to discuss some interesting Windows programming techniques.

Looking for a Copy of the Main Window

To find a copy of the main window of a previous instance, use the FindWindow API function and pass it the name of the window class (the name used to register the form's window type, or WNDCLASS, in the system) and the caption of the window for which you are looking. In a Delphi application, the name of the WNDCLASS window class is the same as the Object Pascal name for the form's class (for example, TForm1). The result of the FindWindow function is either a handle to the window or zero (if no matching window was found).

The main code of your Delphi application should be written so that it will execute only if the FindWindow result is zero:

```
var
  Hwnd: THandle;
begin
  Hwnd := FindWindow ('TForm1', nil);
  if Hwnd = 0 then
```

```
  begin
    Application.Initialize;
    Application.CreateForm(TForm1, Form1);
    Application.Run;
  end
  else
    SetForegroundWindow (Hwnd)
end.
```

To activate the window of the previous instance of the application, you can use the
SetForegroundWindow function, which works for windows owned by other processes. This
call produces its effect only if the window passed as parameter hasn't been minimized. When
the main form of a Delphi application is minimized, in fact, it is hidden, and for this reason
the activation code has no effect.

Unfortunately, if you run a program that uses the FindWindow call just shown from within
the Delphi IDE, a window with that caption and class may already exist: the design-time
form. Thus, the program won't start even once. However, it will run if you close the form
and its corresponding source code file (closing only the form, in fact, simply hides the window), or if you close the project and run the program from the Windows Explorer.

Using a Mutex

A completely different approach is to use a *mutex*, or mutual exclusion object. This is a typical Win32 approach, commonly used for synchronizing threads, as we'll see later in this
chapter. Here we are going to use a mutex for synchronizing two different applications, or
(to be more precise) two instances of the same application.

Once an application has created a mutex with a given name, it can test whether this object
is already owned by another application, calling the WaitForSingleObject Windows API
function. If the mutex has no owner, the application calling this function becomes the owner.
If the mutex is already owned, the application waits until the time-out (the second parameter
of the function) elapses. It then returns an error code.

To implement this technique, you can use the following project source code, which you'll
find in the OneCopy example:

```
var
  hMutex: THandle;
begin
  HMutex := CreateMutex (nil, False, 'OneCopyMutex');
  if WaitForSingleObject (hMutex, 0) <> wait_TimeOut then
  begin
    Application.Initialize;
    Application.CreateForm(TForm1, Form1);
    Application.Run;
```

```
      end;
   end.
```

If you run this example twice, you'll see that it creates a new, temporary copy of the application (the icon appears in the Taskbar) and then destroys it when the time-out elapses. This approach is certainly more robust than the previous one, but it lacks a feature: how do we enable the existing instance of the application? We still need to find its form, but we can use a better approach.

Searching the Window List

When you want to search for a specific main window in the system, you can use the EnumWindows API functions. Enumeration functions are quite peculiar in Windows, because they usually require another function as a parameter. These enumeration functions require a pointer to a function (often described as a *callback* function) as parameter. The idea is that this function is applied to each element of the list (in this case, the list of main windows), until the list ends or the function returns False. Here is the enumeration function from the OneCopy example:

```
function EnumWndProc (hwnd: THandle;
  Param: Cardinal): Bool; stdcall;
var
  ClassName, WinModuleName: string;
  WinInstance: THandle;
begin
  Result := True;
  SetLength (ClassName, 100);
  GetClassName (hwnd, PChar (ClassName), Length (ClassName));
  ClassName := PChar (ClassName);
  if ClassName = TForm1.ClassName then
  begin
    // get the module name of the target window
    SetLength (WinModuleName, 200);
    WinInstance := GetWindowLong (hwnd, GWL_HINSTANCE);
    GetModuleFileName (WinInstance,
      PChar (WinModuleName), Length (WinModuleName));
    WinModuleName := PChar(WinModuleName); // adjust length
    // compare module names
    if WinModuleName = ModuleName then
    begin
      FoundWnd := Hwnd;
      Result := False; // stop enumeration
    end;
  end;
end;
```

This function, called for each nonchild window of the system, checks the name of each window's class, looking for the name of the TForm1 class. When it finds a window with this string in its class name, it uses GetModuleFilename to extract the name of the executable file of the application that owns the matching form. If the module name matches that of the current program (which was extracted previously with similar code), you can be quite sure that you have found a previous instance of the same program. Here is how you can call the enumerated function:

```
var
  FoundWnd: THandle;
  ModuleName: string;
begin
  if WaitForSingleObject (hMutex, 0) <> wait_TimeOut then
    ...
  else
  begin
    // get the current module name
    SetLength (ModuleName, 200);
    GetModuleFileName (HInstance, PChar (ModuleName), Length (ModuleName));
    ModuleName := PChar (ModuleName); // adjust length
    // find window of previous instance
    EnumWindows (@EnumWndProc, 0);
```

Handling User-Defined Window Messages

I've mentioned earlier that the SetForegroundWindow call doesn't work if the main form of the program has been minimized. Now we can solve this problem. You can ask the form of another application—the previous instance of the same program in this case—to restore its main form by sending it a user-defined window message. You can then test whether the form is minimized and post a new user-defined message to the old window. Here is the code; in the OneCopy program, it follows the last fragment shown in the preceding section:

```
  if FoundWnd <> 0 then
  begin
    // show the window, eventually
    if not IsWindowVisible (FoundWnd) then
      PostMessage (FoundWnd, wm_User, 0, 0);
    SetForegroundWindow (FoundWnd);
  end;
```

Again, the PostMessage API function sends a message to the message queue of the application that owns the destination window. In the code of the form, you can add a special function to handle this message:

```
public
  procedure WMUser (var msg: TMessage);
    message wm_User;
```

Now you can write the code of this method, which is simple:

```
procedure TForm1.WMUser (var msg: TMessage);
begin
  Application.Restore;
end;
```

Creating MDI Applications

A common approach for the structure of an application is MDI (Multiple Document Interface). An MDI application is made up of several forms that appear inside a single main form. If you use Windows Notepad, you can open only one text document, because Notepad isn't an MDI application. But with your favorite word processor, you can probably open several different documents, each in its own child window, because they are MDI applications. All these document windows are usually held by a *frame*, or *application*, window.

NOTE   Microsoft is departing more and more from the MDI model stressed in Windows 3 days. Starting with Resource Explorer in Windows 95 and even more with Office 2000, Microsoft tends to use a specific main window for every document, the classic SDI (Single Document Interface) approach. In any case, MDI isn't dead and can sometimes be a useful structure.

MDI in Windows: A Technical Overview

The MDI structure gives programmers several benefits automatically. For example, Windows handles a list of the child windows in one of the pull-down menus of an MDI application, and there are specific Delphi methods that activate the corresponding MDI functionality, to tile or cascade the child windows. The following is the technical structure of an MDI application in Windows:

- The main window of the application acts as a frame or a container.

- A special window, known as the *MDI client*, covers the whole client area of the frame window. This MDI client is one of the Windows predefined controls, just like an edit box or a list box. The MDI client window lacks any specific user-interface element, but it is visible. In fact, you can change the standard system color of the MDI work area (called the Application Background) in the Appearance page of the Display Properties dialog box in Windows.

- There are multiple child windows, of the same kind or of different kinds. These child windows are not placed in the frame window directly, but each is defined as a child of the MDI client window, which in turn is a child of the frame window.

Frame and Child Windows in Delphi

Delphi makes the development of MDI applications easy, even without using the MDI Application template available in Delphi (see the Applications page of the File ≻ New dialog box). You only need to build at least two forms, one with the FormStyle property set to fsMDIForm and the other with the same property set to fsMDIChild. Set these two properties in a simple program and run it, and you'll see the two forms nested in the typical MDI style.

Generally, however, the child form is not created at startup, and you need to provide a way to create one or more child windows. This can be done by adding a menu with a New menu item and writing the following code:

```
var
   ChildForm: TChildForm;
begin
   ChildForm := TChildForm.Create (Application);
   ChildForm.Show;
```

Another important feature is to add a "Window" pull-down menu and use it as the value of the WindowMenu property of the form. This pull-down menu will automatically list all the available child windows. Of course, you can choose any other name for the pull-down menu, but Window is the standard.

To make this program work properly, we can add a number to the title of any child window when it is created:

```
procedure TMainForm.New1Click(Sender: TObject);
var
   ChildForm: TChildForm;
begin
   WindowMenu := Window1;
   Inc (Counter);
   ChildForm := TChildForm.Create (Self);
   ChildForm.Caption := ChildForm.Caption + ' ' + IntToStr (Counter);
   ChildForm.Show;
end;
```

You can also open child windows, minimize or maximize each of them, close them, and use the Window pull-down menu to navigate among them. Now suppose that we want to close some of these child windows, to unclutter the client area of our program. Click the Close boxes of some of the child windows and they are minimized! What is happening here? Remember that when you close a window, you generally hide it from view. The closed forms in Delphi still exist, although they are not visible. In the case of child windows, hiding them won't work, because the MDI Window menu and the list of windows will still list existing child windows, even if they are hidden. For this reason, Delphi minimizes the MDI child windows when you try to close them. To solve this problem, we need to delete the child windows when they are closed, setting the `Action` reference parameter of the `OnClose` event to caFree.

Building a Complete Window Menu

Our first task is to define a better menu structure for the example. Typically the Window pull-down menu has at least three items, titled Cascade, Tile, and Arrange Icons. To handle the menu commands, we can use some of the predefined methods of `TForm` that can be used only for MDI frames:

- The `Cascade` method cascades the open MDI child windows. The windows overlap each other. Iconized child windows are also arranged (see `ArrangeIcons` below).

- The `Tile` method tiles the open MDI child windows; the child forms are arranged so that they do not overlap. The default behavior is horizontal tiling, although if you have several child windows, they will be arranged in several columns. This default can be changed by using the `TileMode` property (either tbHorizontal or tbVertical).

- The `ArrangeIcons` procedure arranges all the iconized child windows. Open forms are not moved.

As a better alternative to calling these methods, you can place an ActionList in the form and add to it a series of predefined MDI actions. The related classes are `TWindowArrange`, `TWindowCascade`, `TWindowClose`, `TWindowTileHorizontal`, `TWindowTileVertical`, and `TWindowMinimizeAll`. The connected menu items will perform the corresponding actions and will be disabled if no child window is available. The MdiDemo example, which we'll look at next, demonstrates the use of the MDI actions, among other things.

There are also some other interesting methods and properties related strictly to MDI in Delphi:

- `ActiveMDIChild` is a run-time and read-only property of the MDI frame form, and it holds the active child window. The user can change this value by selecting a new child window, or the program can change it using the `Next` and `Previous` procedures, which activate the child window following or preceding the currently active one.

- The `ClientHandle` property holds the Windows handle of the MDI client window, which covers the client area of the main form.

- The `MDIChildren` property is an array of child windows. You can use this and the `MDIChildCount` property to cycle among all of the child windows. This can be useful for finding a particular child window or to operate on each of them.

Note that the internal order of the child windows is the reverse order of activation. This means that the last child window selected is the active window (the first in the internal list), the second-to-last child window selected is the second, and the first child window selected is the last. This order determines how the windows are arranged on the screen. The first window in the list is the one above all others, while the last window is below all others, and probably hidden away. You can imagine an axis (the *z* axis) coming out of the screen toward you. The active window has a higher value for the *z* coordinate and, thus, covers other windows. For this reason, the Windows ordering schema is known as the *z-order*.

The MdiDemo Example

I've built a first example to demonstrate most of the features of a simple MDI application. MdiDemo is actually a full-blown MDI text editor, because each child window hosts a Memo component and can open and save text files. The child form has a Modified property used to indicate whether the text of the memo has changed (it is set to True in the handler of the memo's OnChange event). Modified is set to False in the Save and Load custom methods and checked when the form is closed (prompting to save the file).

As I've already mentioned, the main form of this example is based on an ActionList component. The actions are available through some menu items and a toolbar, as you can see in Figure 10.4. You can see the details of the ActionList in the source code of the example. Next, I want to focus on the code of the custom actions. Once more, this example demonstrates that using actions makes it very simple to modify the user interface of the program, without writing any extra code. In fact, there is no code directly tied to the user interface.

One of the simplest actions is the ActionFont object, which has both an OnExecute handler, which uses a FontDialog component, and an OnUpdate handler, which disables the action (and hence the associated menu item and toolbar button) when there are no child forms:

```
procedure TMainForm.ActionFontExecute(Sender: TObject);
begin
  if FontDialog1.Execute then
    (ActiveMDIChild as TChildForm).Memo1.Font := FontDialog1.Font;
end;

procedure TMainForm.ActionFontUpdate(Sender: TObject);
begin
  ActionFont.Enabled := MDIChildCount > 0;
end;
```

The MdiDemo program uses a series of predefined Delphi actions connected to a menu and a toolbar.

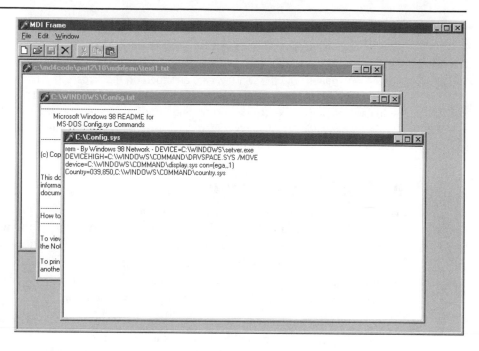

The action named New creates the child form and sets a default filename. The Open action calls the ActionNewExcecute method prior to loading the file:

```
procedure TMainForm.ActionNewExecute(Sender: TObject);
var
  ChildForm: TChildForm;
begin
  Inc (Counter);
  ChildForm := TChildForm.Create (Self);
  ChildForm.Caption :=
    LowerCase (ExtractFilePath (Application.Exename)) + 'text' +
    IntToStr (Counter) + '.txt';
  ChildForm.Show;
end;

procedure TMainForm.ActionOpenExecute(Sender: TObject);
begin
  if OpenDialog1.Execute then
  begin
    ActionNewExecute (Self);
    (ActiveMDIChild as TChildForm).Load (OpenDialog1.FileName);
  end;
end;
```

The actual file loading is performed by the Load method of the form. Likewise, the Save method of the child form is used by the Save and Save As actions. Notice the OnUpdate handler of the Save action, which enables the action only if the user has changed the text of the memo:

```
procedure TMainForm.ActionSaveAsExecute(Sender: TObject);
begin
  // suggest the current file name
  SaveDialog1.FileName := ActiveMDIChild.Caption;
  if SaveDialog1.Execute then
  begin
    // modify the file name and save
    ActiveMDIChild.Caption := SaveDialog1.FileName;
    (ActiveMDIChild as TChildForm).Save;
  end;
end;

procedure TMainForm.ActionSaveUpdate(Sender: TObject);
begin
  ActionSave.Enabled := (MDIChildCount > 0) and
    (ActiveMDIChild as TChildForm).Modified;
end;

procedure TMainForm.ActionSaveExecute(Sender: TObject);
begin
  (ActiveMDIChild as TChildForm).Save;
end;
```

MDI Applications with Different Child Windows

A common approach in complex MDI applications is to include child windows of different kinds (that is, based on different child forms). I will build a new example, called MdiMulti, to highlight some problems you may encounter with this approach. This example has two different types of child forms. The first type will host a circle drawn in the position of the last mouse click, while the second will contain a bouncing square. Another feature I'll add to the main form is a custom background obtained by painting a tiled image in it.

Child Forms and Merging Menus

The first type of child form can display a circle in the position where the user clicked one of the mouse buttons. Figure 10.5 shows an example of the output of the MdiMulti program. The program includes a Circle menu, which allows the user to change the color of the surface of the circle as well as the color and size of its border. What is interesting here is that to program the child form, we do not need to consider the existence of other forms or of the frame window. We simply write the code of the form, and that's all. The only special care required is for the menus of the two forms.

FIGURE 10.5:

The output of the MdiMulti example, with a child window that displays circles

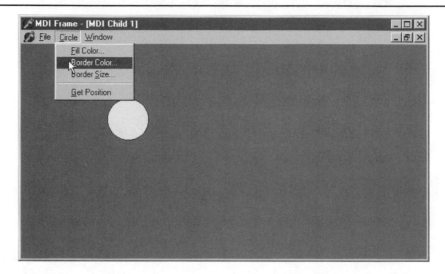

If we prepare a main menu for the child form, it will replace the main menu of the frame window when the child form is activated. An MDI child window, in fact, cannot have a menu of its own. But the fact that a child window can't have any menus should not bother you, because this is the standard behavior of MDI applications. You can use the menu bar of the frame window to display the menus of the child window. Even better, you can merge the menu bar of the frame window and that of the child form. For example, in this program, the menu of the child form can be placed between the frame window's File and Window pull-down menus. You can accomplish this using the following GroupIndex values:

- File pull-down menu, main form: 1
- Window pull-down menu, main form: 3
- Circle pull-down menu, child form: 2

Using these settings for the menu group indexes, the menu bar of the frame window will have either two or three pull-down menus. At startup, the menu bar has two menus. As soon as you create a child window, there are three menus, and when the last child window is closed (destroyed), the Circle pull-down menu disappears. You should also spend some time testing this behavior by running the program.

The second type of child form shows a moving image. The square, a Shape component, moves around the client area of the form at fixed time intervals, using a Timer component, and bounces on the edges of the form, changing its direction. This turning process is determined by a fairly complex algorithm, which we don't have space to examine. The main point of the example, instead, is to show you how menu merging behaves when you have an MDI frame with child forms of different types. (You can study the source code on the companion CD to see how it works.)

The Main Form

Now we need to integrate the two child forms into an MDI application. The File pull-down menu here has two separate New menu items, which are used to create a child window of either kind. The code uses a single child window counter. As an alternative, you could use two different counters for the two kinds of child windows. The Window menu uses the predefined MDI actions.

As soon as a form of this kind is displayed on the screen, its menu bar is automatically merged with the main menu bar. When you select a child form of one of the two kinds, the menu bar changes accordingly. Once all the child windows are closed, the original menu bar of the main form is reset. By using the proper menu group indexes, we let Delphi accomplish everything automatically, as you can see in Figure 10.6.

FIGURE 10.6:

The menu bar of the Mdi-Multi Demo4 application changes automatically to reflect the currently selected child window, as you can see by comparing the menu bar with that of Figure 10.5.

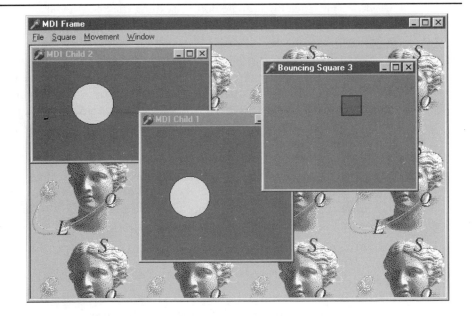

I've added a few other menu items in the main form, to close every child window and show some statistics about them. The method related to the Count command scans the MDIChildren array property to count the number of child windows of each kind (using the RTTI operator is):

```
for I := 0 to MDIChildCount - 1 do
  if MDIChildren is TBounceChildForm then
    Inc (NBounce)
  else
    Inc (NCircle);
```

Subclassing the MdiClient Window

Finally, the program includes support for a background-tiled image. The bitmap is taken from an Image component and should be painted on the form in the wm_EraseBkgnd Windows message's handler. The problem is that we cannot simply connect the code to the main form, as a separate window, the MdiClient, covers its surface.

We have no corresponding Delphi form for this window, so how can we handle its messages? We have to resort to a low-level Windows programming technique known as *subclassing*. (In spite of the name, this has little to do with OOP inheritance.) The basic idea is that we can replace the window procedure, which receives all the messages of the window, with a new one we provide. This can be done by calling the SetWindowLong API function and providing the memory address of the procedure, the function pointer.

NOTE   A window procedure is a function receiving all the messages for a window. Every window must have a window procedure and can have only one. Even Delphi forms have a window procedure; although this is hidden in the system, it calls the **WndProc** virtual function, which you can use. But the VCL has a predefined handling of the messages, which are then forwarded to the message-handling methods of a form after some preprocessing. With all this support, you need to handle window procedures explicitly only when working with non-Delphi windows, as in this case.

Unless we have some reason to change the default behavior of this system window, we can simply store the original procedure and call it to obtain a default processing. The two function pointers referring to the two procedures (the old and the new one) are stored in two local fields of the form:

```
private
  OldWinProc, NewWinProc: Pointer;
  procedure NewWinProcedure (var Msg: TMessage);
```

The form also has a method we'll use as a new window procedure, with the actual code used to paint on the background of the window. Because this is a method and not a plain window procedure, the program has to call the MakeObjectInstance method to add a prefix to the method and let the system use it as if it were a function. All this description is summarized by just two complex statements:

```
procedure TMainForm.FormCreate(Sender: TObject);
begin
  NewWinProc := MakeObjectInstance (NewWinProcedure);
  OldWinProc := Pointer (SetWindowLong (ClientHandle, gwl_WndProc, Cardinal
    (NewWinProc)));
  OutCanvas := TCanvas.Create;
end;
```

The window procedure we install calls the default one. Then, if the message is wm_EraseBkgnd and the image is not empty, we draw it on the screen many times using the Draw method of a temporary canvas. This canvas object is created when the program starts (see the code above) and connected to the handle passed as wParam parameter by the message. With this approach, we don't have to create a new TCanvas object for every background painting operation requested, thus saving a little time in the frequent operation. Here is the code, which produces the output already seen in Figure 10.6:

```
procedure TMainForm.NewWinProcedure (var Msg: TMessage);
var
  BmpWidth, BmpHeight: Integer;
  I, J: Integer;
begin
  // default processing first
  Msg.Result := CallWindowProc (OldWinProc, ClientHandle, Msg.Msg, Msg.wParam,
    Msg.lParam);

  // handle background repaint
  if Msg.Msg = wm_EraseBkgnd then
  begin
    BmpWidth := MainForm.Image1.Width;
    BmpHeight := MainForm.Image1.Height;
    if (BmpWidth <> 0) and (BmpHeight <> 0) then
    begin
      OutCanvas.Handle := Msg.wParam;
      for I := 0 to MainForm.ClientWidth div BmpWidth do
        for J := 0 to MainForm.ClientHeight div BmpHeight do
          OutCanvas.Draw (I * BmpWidth, J * BmpHeight,
            MainForm.Image1.Picture.Graphic);
    end;
  end;
end;
```

Visual Form Inheritance

When you need to build two or more similar forms, possibly with different event handlers, you can use dynamic techniques, hide or create new components at run time, change event handlers, and use if or case statements. Or you can apply the object-oriented techniques, thanks to visual form inheritance. In short, instead of creating a form based on TForm, you can inherit a form from an existing one, adding new components or altering the properties of the existing ones. But what is the real advantage of visual form inheritance?

Well, this mostly depends on the kind of application you are building. If it has multiple forms, some of which are very similar to each other or simply include common elements, then you can place the common components and the common event handlers in the base form and add the specific behavior and components to the subclasses. For example, if you prepare a standard parent form with a toolbar, a logo, default sizing and closing code, and the handlers of some Windows messages, you can then use it as the parent class for each of the forms of an application.

You can also use visual form inheritance to customize an application for different clients, without duplicating any source code or form definition code; just inherit the specific versions for a client from the standard forms. Remember that the main advantage of visual inheritance is that you can later change the original form and automatically update all the derived forms. This is a well-known advantage of inheritance in object-oriented programming languages. But there is a beneficial side effect: polymorphism. You can add a virtual method in a base form and override it in a subclassed form. Then you can refer to both forms and call this method for each of them.

NOTE   Delphi includes another feature, frames, which resembles visual form inheritance. In both cases, you can work at design time on two versions of a form/frame. However, in visual form inheritance, you are defining two different classes (parent and derived), whereas with frames, you work on a class and an instance. Frames will be discussed in detail later in this chapter.

Inheriting from a Base Form

The rules governing visual form inheritance are quite simple, once you have a clear idea of what inheritance is. Basically, a subclass form has the same components as the parent form as well as some new components. You cannot remove a component of the base class, although (if it is a visual control) you can make it invisible. What's important is that you can easily change properties of the components you inherit.

Notice that if you change a property of a component in the inherited form, any modification of the same property in the parent form will have no effect. Changing other properties of the component will affect the inherited versions, as well. You can resynchronize the two property values by using the Revert to Inherited local menu command of the Object Inspector. The same thing is accomplished by setting the two properties to the same value and recompiling the code. After modifying multiple properties, you can resynchronize them all to the base version by applying the Revert to Inherited command of the component's local menu.

Besides inheriting components, the new form inherits all the methods of the base form, including the event handlers. You can add new handlers in the inherited form and also override existing handlers.

To describe how visual form inheritance works, I've built a very simple example, called VFI. I'll describe step-by-step how to build it. First, start a new project, and add four buttons to its main form. Then select File ➤ New ➤ Other, and choose the page with the name of the project in the New Items dialog box (see Figure 10.7).

FIGURE 10.7:

The New Items dialog box allows you to create an inherited form.

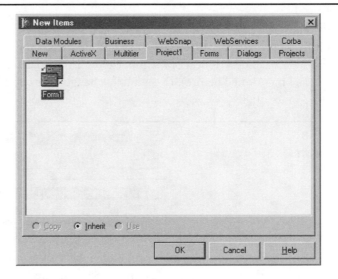

In the New Items dialog, you can choose the form from which you want to inherit. The new form has the same four buttons. Here is the initial textual description of the new form:

```
inherited Form2: TForm2
  Caption = 'Form2'
end
```

And here is its initial class declaration, where you can see that the base class is not the usual TForm but the actual base class form:

```
type
  TForm2 = class(TForm1)
  private
    { Private declarations }
```

```
public
  { Public declarations }
end;
```

Notice the presence of the `inherited` keyword in the textual description; also notice that the form indeed has some components, although they are defined in the base class form. If you move the form and add the caption of one of the buttons, the textual description will change accordingly:

```
inherited Form2: TForm2
  Left = 313
  Top = 202
  Caption = 'Form2'
  inherited Button2: TButton
    Caption = 'Beep...'
  end
end
```

Only the properties with a different value are listed (and by removing these properties from the textual description of the inherited form, you can reset them to the value of the base form, as I mentioned before). I've actually changed the captions of most buttons, as you can see in Figure 10.8.

FIGURE 10.8:

The two forms of the VFI example at run time

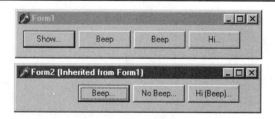

Each of the buttons of the first form has an `OnClick` handler, with simple code. The first button shows the inherited form calling its `Show` method; the second and the third buttons call the `Beep` procedure; and the last button displays a simple message.

What happens in the inherited form? First we should remove the Show button, because the secondary form is already visible. However, we cannot delete a component from an inherited form. An alternative solution is to leave the component there but set its `Visible` property to False. The button will still be there but not visible (as you can guess from Figure 10.8). The other three buttons will be visible but with different handlers. This is simple to accomplish. If you select the `OnClick` event of a button in the inherited form (by double-clicking it), you'll get an empty method slightly different from the default one:

```
procedure TForm2.Button2Click(Sender: TObject);
begin
  inherited;
end;
```

The `inherited` keyword stands for a call to the corresponding event handler of the base form. This keyword is always added by Delphi, even if the handler is not defined in the parent class (and this is reasonable, because it might be defined later) or if the component is not present in the parent class (which doesn't seem like a great idea to me). It is very simple to execute the code of the base form and perform some other operations:

```
procedure TForm2.Button2Click(Sender: TObject);
begin
  inherited;
  ShowMessage ('Hi');
end;
```

This is not the only choice. An alternative approach is to write a brand-new event handler and not execute the code of the base class, as I've done for the third button of the VFI example: To accomplish this, simply remove the `inherited` keyword. Still another choice includes calling a base-class method after some custom code has been executed, calling it when a condition is met, or calling the handler of a different event of the base class, as I've done for the fourth button:

```
procedure TForm2.Button4Click(Sender: TObject);
begin
  inherited Button3Click (Sender);
  inherited;
end;
```

You probably won't do this very often, but you must be aware that you can. Of course, you can consider each method of the base form as a method of your form, and call it freely. This example allows you to explore some features of visual form inheritance, but to see its true power you'll need to look at real-world examples more complex than this book has room to explore. There is something else I want to show you here: *visual form polymorphism*.

Polymorphic Forms

The problem is simple. If you add an event handler to a form and then change it in an inherited form, there is no way to refer to the two methods using a common variable of the base class, because the event handlers use static binding by default.

Confusing? Here is an example, which is intended for experienced Delphi programmers. Suppose you want to build a bitmap viewer form and a text viewer form in the same program. The two forms have similar elements, a similar toolbar, a similar menu, an OpenDialog component, and different components for viewing the data. So you decide to build a base-class form containing the common elements and inherit the two forms from it. You can see the three forms at design time in Figure 10.9.

FIGURE 10.9:

The base-class form and
the two inherited forms of
the PoliForm example at
design time

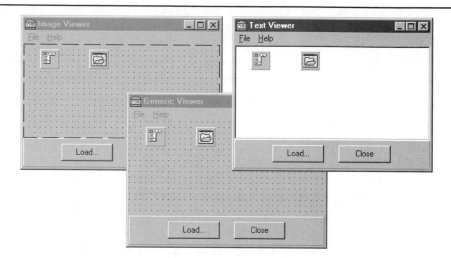

The main form contains a toolbar panel with a few buttons (real toolbars apparently have a few problems with visual form inheritance), a menu, and an open dialog component. The two inherited forms have only minor differences, but they feature a new component, either an image viewer (TImage) or a text viewer (TMemo). They also modify the settings of the OpenDialog component, to refer to different types of files.

The main form includes some common code. The Close button and the File ➤ Close command call the `Close` method of the form. The Help ➤ About command shows a simple message box. The Load button of the base form has the following code:

```
procedure TViewerForm.ButtonLoadClick(Sender: TObject);
begin
  ShowMessage ('Error: File-loading code missing');
end;
```

The File ➤ Load command, instead, calls another method:

```
procedure TViewerForm.Load1Click(Sender: TObject);
begin
  LoadFile;
end;
```

This method is defined in the TViewerForm class as a virtual abstract method (so that the class of the base form is actually an abstract class). Because this is an abstract method, we will need to redefine it (and override it) in the inherited forms. The code of this `LoadFile` method simply uses the `OpenDialog1` component to ask the user to select an input file and loads it into the image component:

```
procedure TImageViewerForm.LoadFile;
begin
```

```
  if OpenDialog1.Execute then
    Image1.Picture.LoadFromFile (OpenDialog1.Filename);
end;
```

The other inherited class has similar code, loading the text into the memo component. The project has one more form, a main form with two buttons, used to reload the files in each of the viewer forms. The main form is the only form created by the project when it starts. The generic viewer form is never created: it is only a generic base class, containing common code and components of the two subclasses. The forms of the two subclasses are created in the OnCreate event handler of the main form:

```
procedure TMainForm.FormCreate(Sender: TObject);
var
  I: Integer;
begin
  FormList [1] := TTextViewerForm.Create (Application);
  FormList [2] := TImageViewerForm.Create (Application);
  for I := 1 to 2 do
    FormList[I].Show;
end;
```

See Figure 10.10 for the resulting forms (with text and image already loaded in the viewers). FormList is a *polymorphic* array of generic TViewerForm objects, declared in the TMainForm class.

FIGURE 10.10:

The PoliForm example at
run time

Note that to make this declaration in the class, you need to add the Viewer unit (but not the specific forms) in the uses clause of the interface portion of the main form. The array of forms is used to load a new file in each viewer form when one of the two buttons is pressed. The handlers of the two buttons' OnClick events use different approaches:

```
procedure TMainForm.ReloadButton1Click(Sender: TObject);
var
  I: Integer;
begin
  for I := 1 to 2 do
    FormList [I].ButtonLoadClick (Self);
end;

procedure TMainForm.ReloadButton2Click(Sender: TObject);
var
  I: Integer;
begin
  for I := 1 to 2 do
    FormList [I].LoadFile;
end;
```

The second button simply calls a virtual method, and it will work without any problem. The first button calls an event handler and will always reach the generic TFormView class (displaying the error message of its ButtonLoadClick method). This happens because the method is static, not virtual.

Is there a way to make this approach work? Sure. Declare the ButtonLoadClick method of the TFormView class as virtual, and declare it as overridden in each of the inherited form classes, as we do for any other virtual method:

```
type
  TViewerForm = class(TForm)
    // components and plain methods...
    procedure ButtonLoadClick(Sender: TObject); virtual;
  public
    procedure LoadFile; virtual; abstract;
  end;
...
type
  TImageViewerForm = class(TViewerForm)
    Image1: TImage;
    procedure ButtonLoadClick(Sender: TObject); override;
  public
    procedure LoadFile; override;
  end;
```

This trick really works, although it is never mentioned in the Delphi documentation. This ability to use virtual event handlers is what I actually mean by visual form polymorphism. In other (more technical) words, you can assign a virtual method to an event property, which will take the address of the method according to the instance available at run time.

Understanding Frames

Chapter 1 briefly discussed frames, which were introduced in Delphi 5. We've seen that you can create a new frame, place some components in it, write some event handlers for the components, and then add the frame to a form. In other words, a frame is similar to a form, but it defines only a portion of a window, not a complete window. This is certainly not a feature worth a new construct. The totally new element of frames is that you can create multiple instances of a frame at design time, and you can modify the class and the instance at the same time. This makes frames an effective tool for creating customizable composite controls at design time, something close to a visual component-building tool.

In visual form inheritance you can work on both a base form and a derived form at design time, and any changes you make to the base form are propagated to the derived one, unless this overrides some property or event. With frames, you work on a class (as usual in Delphi), but the difference is that you can also customize one or more instances of the class at design time. When you work on a form, you cannot change a property of the TForm1 class for the Form1 object at design time. With frames, you can.

Once you realize you are working with a class and one or more of its instances at design time, there is nothing more to understand about frames. In practice, frames are useful when you want to use the same group of components in multiple forms within an application. In this case, in fact, you can customize each of the instances at design time. Wasn't this already possible with component templates? It was, but component templates were based on the concept of copying and pasting some components and their code. There was no way to change the original definition of the template and see the effect in every place it was used. That is what happens with frames (and in a different way with visual form inheritance); changes to the original version (the class) are reflected in the copies (the instances).

Let's discuss a few more elements of frames with an example from the CD, called Frames2. This program has a frame with a list box, an edit box, and three buttons with simple code operating on the components. The frame also has a bevel aligned to its client area, because frames have no border. Of course, the frame has also a corresponding class, which looks like a form class:

```
type
  TFrameList = class(TFrame)
    ListBox: TListBox;
    Edit: TEdit;
    btnAdd: TButton;
    btnRemove: TButton;
    btnClear: TButton;
    Bevel: TBevel;
    procedure btnAddClick(Sender: TObject);
```

```
    procedure btnRemoveClick(Sender: TObject);
    procedure btnClearClick(Sender: TObject);
  private
    { Private declarations }
  public
    { Public declarations }
  end;
```

What is different is that you can add the frame to a form. I've used two instances of the frame in the example (as you can see in Figure 10.11) and modified the behavior slightly. The first instance of the frame has the list box items sorted. When you change a property of a component of a frame, the DFM file of the hosting form will list the differences, as it does with visual form inheritance:

FIGURE 10.11:

A frame and two instances of it at design time, in the Frames2 example

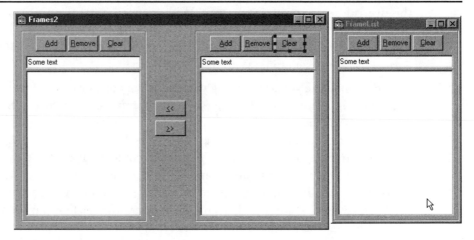

```
object FormFrames: TFormFrames
  Caption = 'Frames2'
  inline FrameList1: TFrameList
    Left = 8
    Top = 8
    inherited ListBox: TListBox
      Sorted = True
    end
  end
  inline FrameList2: TFrameList
    Left = 232
    Top = 8
    inherited btnClear: TButton
      OnClick = FrameList2btnClearClick
    end
  end
end
```

As you can see from the listing, the DFM file for a form that has frames uses a new DFM keyword, inline. The references to the modified components of the frame, instead, use the inherited keyword, although this term is used with an extended meaning. inherited here doesn't refer to a base class we are inheriting from, but to the class we are instancing (or inheriting) an object from. It was probably a good idea, though, to use an existing feature of visual form inheritance and apply it to the new context. The effect of this approach, in fact, is that you can use the Revert to Inherited command of the Object Inspector or of the form to cancel the changes and get back to the default value of properties.

Notice also that unmodified components of the frame class are not listed in the DFM file of the form using the frame, and that the form has two frames with different names, but the components on the two frames have the same name. In fact, these components are not owned by the form, but are owned by the frame. This implies that the form has to reference those components through the frame, as you can see in the code for the buttons that copy items from one list box to the other:

```
procedure TFormFrames.btnLeftClick(Sender: TObject);
begin
  FrameList1.ListBox.Items.AddStrings (FrameList2.ListBox.Items);
end;
```

Finally, besides modifying properties of any instance of a frame, you can change the code of any of its event handlers. If you double-click one of the buttons of a frame while working on the form (not on the stand-alone frame), Delphi will generate this code for you:

```
procedure TFormFrames.FrameList2btnClearClick(Sender: TObject);
begin
  FrameList2.btnClearClick(Sender);
end;
```

The line of code automatically added by Delphi corresponds to a call to the inherited event handler of the base class in visual form inheritance. This time, however, to get the default behavior of the frame we need to call an event handler and apply it to a specific instance—the frame object itself. The current form, in fact, doesn't include this event handler and knows nothing about it.

Whether you leave this call in place or remove it depends on the effect you are looking for. In the example I've decided to conditionally execute the default code, depending on the user confirmation:

```
procedure TFormFrames.FrameList2btnClearClick(Sender: TObject);
begin
  if MessageDlg ('OK to empty the list box?', mtConfirmation,
      [mbYes, mbNo], 0) = idYes then
    // execute standard frame code
    FrameList2.btnClearClick(Sender);
end;
```

TIP   By the way, note that because the event handler has some code, leaving it empty and saving the form won't remove it as usual: in fact, it isn't empty! Instead, if you simply want to omit the default code for an event, you need to add at least a comment to it, to avoid it being automatically removed by the system!

Frames and Pages

When you have a dialog box with many pages full of controls, the code underlying the form becomes very complex because all the controls and methods are declared in a single form. Also, creating all these components (and initializing them) might result in a delay in the display of the dialog box. Frames actually don't reduce the construction and initialization time of equivalently loaded forms; quite the contrary, as loading frames is more complicated for the streaming system than loading simple components. However, using frames you can load only the visible pages of a multipage dialog box, reducing the *initial* load time, which is what the user perceives.

Frames can solve both of these issues. First, you can easily divide the code of a single complex form into one frame per page. The form will simply host all of the frames in a PageControl. This certainly helps you to have simpler and more focused units and makes it simpler to reuse a specific page in a different dialog box or application. Reusing a single page of a Page-Control without using a frame or an embedded form, in fact, is far from simple.

As an example of this approach I've built the FramePag example, which has some frames placed inside the three pages of a PageControl, as you can see in Figure 10.12. All of the frames are aligned to the client area, using the entire surface of the tab sheet (the page) hosting them. Actually two of the pages have the same frame, but the two instances of the frame have some differences at design time. The frame, called Frame3 in the example, has a list box that is populated with a text file at startup, and has buttons to modify the items in the list and saves them to a file. The filename is placed inside a label, so that you can easily select a file for the frame at design time by changing the Caption of the label.

TIP   Being able to use multiple instances of a frame is one of the reasons this technique was introduced, and customizing the frame at design time is even more important. Because adding properties to a frame and making them available at design time requires some customized and complex code, it is nice to use a component to host these custom values. You have the option of hiding these components (such as the label in our example) if they don't pertain to the user interface.

FIGURE 10.12:

Each page of the FramePag example contains a frame, thus separating the code of this complex form into more manageable chunks.

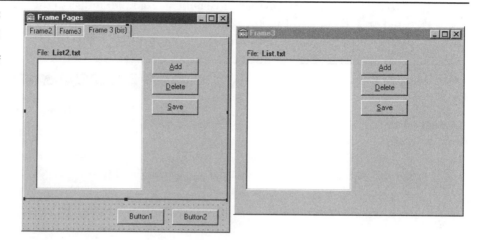

In the example, we need to load the file when the frame instance is created. Because frames have no OnCreate event, our best choice is probably to override the CreateWnd method. Writing a custom constructor, in fact, doesn't work as it is executed too early—before the specific label text is available. Here is the frame class code:

```
type
  TFrame3 = class(TFrame)
    ...
  public
    procedure CreateWnd; override;
```

Within the CreateWnd method, we simply load the list box content from a file.

Multiple Frames with No Pages

Another approach is to avoid creating all of the pages along with the form hosting them. This can be accomplished by leaving the PageControl empty and creating the frames only when a page is displayed. Actually, when you have frames on multiple pages of a PageControl, the windows for the frames are created only when they are first displayed, as you can find out by placing a breakpoint in the creation code of the last example.

As an even more radical approach, you can get rid of the page controls and use a TabControl. Used this way, the tab has no connected tab sheets (or pages) but can display only one set of information at a time. For this reason, we'll need to create the current frame and destroy the previous one or simply hide it by setting its Visible property to False or by calling the BringToFront of the new frame. Although this sounds like a lot of work, in a large application this technique can be worth it for the reduced resource and memory usage you can obtain by applying it.

To demonstrate this approach, I've built an example similar to the previous one, this time based on a TabControl and dynamically created frames. The main form, visible at run time in Figure 10.13, has only a TabControl with one page for each frame:

FIGURE 10.13:

The first page of the Frame-
Tab example at run time.
The frame inside the tab is
created at run time.

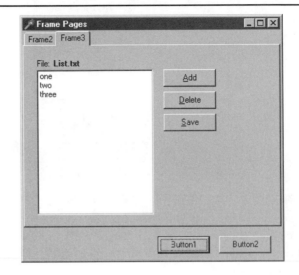

```
object Form1: TForm1
  Caption = 'Frame Pages'
  OnCreate = FormCreate
  object Button1: TButton...
  object Button2: TButton...
  object Tab: TTabControl
    Anchors = [akLeft, akTop, akRight, akBottom]
    Tabs.Strings = ( 'Frame2' 'Frame3' )
    OnChange = TabChange
  end
end
```

I've given each tab a caption corresponding to the name of the frame, because I'm going to use this information to create the new pages. When the form is created, and whenever the user changes the active tab, the program gets the current caption of the tab and passes it to the custom ShowFrame method. The code of this method, listed below, checks whether the requested frame already exists (frame names in this example follow the Delphi standard of having a number appended to the class name), and then brings it to the front. If the frame doesn't exist, it uses the frame name to find the related frame class, creates an object of that class, and assigns a few properties to it. The code makes extensive use of class references and dynamic creation techniques:

```
type
  TFrameClass = class of TFrame;

procedure TForm1.ShowFrame(FrameName: string);
var
  Frame: TFrame;
  FrameClass: TFrameClass;
begin
  Frame := FindComponent (FrameName + '1') as TFrame;
  if not Assigned (Frame) then
  begin
    FrameClass := TFrameClass (FindClass ('T' + FrameName));
    Frame := FrameClass.Create (Self);
    Frame.Parent := Tab;
    Frame.Visible := True;
    Frame.Name := FrameName + '1';
  end;
  Frame.BringToFront;
end;
```

To make this code work, you have to remember to add a call to `RegisterClass` in the initialization section of each unit defining a frame.

Base Forms and Interfaces

We have seen that when you need two similar forms inside an application, you can use visual form inheritance to inherit one from the other or both of them from a common ancestor. The advantage of visual form inheritance is that you can use it to inherit the visual definition, the DFM. However, this is not always requested.

At times, you might want several forms to exhibit a common behavior, or respond to the same commands, without having any shared component or user interface elements. Using visual form inheritance with a base form that has no extra components makes little sense to me. I rather prefer defining my own custom form class, inherited from TForm, and then manually editing the form class declarations to inherit from this custom base form class instead of the standard one. If all you need is to define some shared methods, or override TForm virtual methods in a consistent way, defining custom form classes can be a very good idea.

Using a Base Form Class

A simple demonstration of this technique is available in the FormIntf demo, showcasing also the use of interfaces for forms. In a new unit, called SaveStatusForm, I've defined the following form class (with no related DFM file—don't use the New Form command, but create a new unit and type the code in it):

```
type
  TSaveStatusForm = class (TForm)
  protected
    procedure DoCreate; override;
    procedure DoDestroy; override;
  end;
```

The two overridden methods are called at the same time of the event handler, so that I can attach extra code (allowing the event handler to be defined as usual). Inside the two methods I simply load or save the form position inside an INI file of the application, in a section marked with the form caption. Here is the code of the two methods:

```
procedure TSaveStatusForm.DoCreate;
var
  Ini: TIniFile;
begin
  inherited;
  Ini := TIniFile.Create (ExtractFileName (Application.ExeName));
  Left := Ini.ReadInteger(Caption, 'Left', Left);
  Top := Ini.ReadInteger(Caption, 'Top', Top);
  Width := Ini.ReadInteger(Caption, 'Width', Width);
  Height := Ini.ReadInteger(Caption, 'Height', Height);
  Ini.Free;
end;

procedure TSaveStatusForm.DoDestroy;
var
  Ini: TIniFile;
begin
  Ini := TIniFile.Create (ExtractFileName (Application.ExeName));
  Ini.WriteInteger(Caption, 'Left', Left);
  Ini.WriteInteger(Caption, 'Top', Top);
  Ini.WriteInteger(Caption, 'Width', Width);
  Ini.WriteInteger(Caption, 'Height', Height);
  Ini.Free;
  inherited;
end;
```

Again, this is a simple common behavior for your forms, but you can define a very complex class here. To use this as a base class of the forms you create, simply let Delphi create the forms as usual (with no inheritance) and then update the form declaration to something like:

```
type
  TFormBitmap = class(TSaveStatusForm)
    Image1: TImage;
    OpenPictureDialog1: TOpenPictureDialog;
    ...
```

Simple as it seems, this is a very powerful technique, as all you need to do is change the definition of the forms of your application to refer to this base class. If even this is too tedious, as you might want to change this base class in the life of your program, you can use an extra trick, "interposer" classes.

INI Files and the Registry in Delphi

If you want to save information about the status of an application in order to restore it the next time the program is executed, you can use the explicit support that Windows provides for storing this kind of information. INI files, the old Windows standard, are once again the preferred way to save application data. The alternative is the Registry, which is still quite popular. Delphi provides ready-to-use classes to manipulate both.

The *TIniFile* Class

For INI files, Delphi has a `TIniFile` class. Once you have created an object of this class and connected it to a file, you can read and write information to it. To create the object, you need to call the constructor, passing a filename to it, as in the following code:

```
var
  IniFile: TIniFile;
begin
  IniFile := TIniFile.Create ('myprogram.ini');
```

There are two choices for the location of the INI file. The code just listed will store the file in the Windows directory or a user folder for settings in Windows 2000. To store data locally to the application (as opposed to local to the current user), you should provide a full path to the constructor.

INI files are divided into sections, each indicated by a name enclosed in square brackets. Each section can contain multiple items of three possible kinds: strings, integers, or Booleans. The `TIniFile` class has three Read methods, one for each kind of data: `ReadBool`, `ReadInteger`, and `ReadString`. There are also three corresponding methods to write the data: `WriteBool`, `WriteInteger`, and `WriteString`. Other methods allow you to read or erase a whole section. In the Read methods, you can also specify a default value to be used if the corresponding entry doesn't exist in the INI file.

Continued on next page

By the way, notice that Delphi uses INI files quite often, but they are disguised with different names. For example, the desktop (.dsk) and options (.dof) files are structured as INI files.

The *TRegistry* and *TRegIniFile* classes

The Registry is a hierarchical database of information about the computer, the software configuration, and the user preferences. Windows has a set of API functions to interact with the Registry; you basically open a key (or folder) and then work with subkeys (or subfolders) and with values (or items), but you must be aware of the structure and the details of the Registry.

Delphi provides basically two approaches to the use of the Registry. The TRegistry class provides a generic encapsulation of the Registry API, while the TRegIniFile class provides the interface of the TIniFile class but saves the data in the Registry. This class is the natural choice for portability between INI-based and Registry-based versions of the same program. When you create a TRegIniFile object, your data ends up in the current user information, so you'll generally use a constructor like this:

```
IniFile := TRegIniFile.Create ('Software\MyCompany\MyProgram');
```

By using the TIniFile and the TRegistryIniFile classes offered by the VCL, you can move from one model of local and per-user storage to the other. Not that I think you should use the Registry a lot, as the idea of having a centralized repository for the settings of each application was a architectural error. Even Microsoft acknowledges this (without really admitting the error) by suggesting, in the Windows 2000 Compatibility Requirements, that you not use the Registry anymore for applications settings, but go back to the use of INI files.

An Extra Trick: Interposer Classes

In contrast with Delphi VCL components, which must have unique names, Delphi classes in general must be unique only within their unit. This means you can have two different units defining a class with the same name. This looks really weird, at first sight, but can be useful. For example, Borland is using this technique to provide compatibility between VCL and VisualCLX classes. Both have a TForm class, one defined in the Forms unit and the other in the QForms unit. How can this be interesting for the topic discussed here?

NOTE   This technique is actually much older than CLX/VCL. For example, the service and control panel applet units define their own TApplication object, which is not related to the TApplication used by VCL visual GUI applications and defined in the Forms unit.

There is a technique that I've seen mentioned with the name "interposer classes" in an old issue of *The Delphi Magazine*, which suggested replacing standard Delphi class names with your own versions, having the same class name. This way you can use Delphi designer referring to Delphi standard components at design time, but using your own classes at run time.

The idea is simple. In the SaveStatusForm unit, I could have defined the new form class as follows:

```
type
  TForm = class (Forms.TForm)
  protected
    procedure DoCreate; override;
    procedure DoDestroy; override;
  end;
```

This class is called TForm, and inherits from TForm of the Forms unit (this last reference is compulsory to avoid a kind of recursive definition). In the rest of the program, at this point, you don't need to change the class definition for your form, but simply add the unit defining the interposer class (the SaveStatusForm unit in this case) in the uses statement *after* the unit defining the Delphi class. The order of the unit in the uses statement is important here, and the reason some people criticize this technique, as it is hard to know what is going on. I have to agree: I find interposer classes handy at times (more for components than for forms, I have to say), but their use makes programs less readable and at times even harder to debug.

Using Interfaces

Another technique, which is slightly more complex but even more powerful than the definition of a common base form class, is to have forms that implement specific interfaces. This way you can have forms implementing one or more of these interfaces, query each form for the interfaces it implements, and call the supported methods.

As an example (available in the same FormIntf program I began discussing in the last section), I've defined a simple interface for loading and storing:

```
type
  IFormOperations = interface
    ['{DACFDB76-0703-4A40-A951-10D140B4A2A0}']
    procedure Load;
    procedure Save;
  end;
```

Each form can optionally implement this interface, as the following TFormBitmap class:

```
type
  TFormBitmap = class(TForm, IFormOperations)
    Image1: TImage;
    OpenPictureDialog1: TOpenPictureDialog;
    SavePictureDialog1: TSavePictureDialog;
  public
    procedure Load;
    procedure Save;
  end;
```

You can see the actual code of the example for the code of the Load and Save methods, which use the standard dialog boxes to load or save the image. (In the example's code, the form also inherits from the TSaveStatusForm class.)

When an application has one or more forms implementing interfaces, you can apply a given interface method to all the forms supporting it, with code like this (extracted from the main form of the IntfForm example):

```
procedure TFormMain.btnLoadClick(Sender: TObject);
var
  i: Integer;
begin
  for i := 0 to Screen.FormCount - 1 do
    if Supports (Screen.Forms [i], IFormOperations) then
      (Screen.Forms [i] as IFormOperations).Load;
end;
```

Consider a business application when you can synchronize all of the forms to the data of a specific company, or a specific business event. And consider also that, unlike inheritance, you can have several forms each implementing multiple interfaces, with unlimited combinations. This is why using an architecture like this can improve a complex Delphi application a great deal, making it much more flexible and easier to adapt to implementation changes.

What's Next?

After the detailed description of forms and secondary forms in the previous chapters, I have focused on the architecture of applications, discussing both how Delphi's Application object works and how we can structure applications with multiple forms.

In particular, I've discussed MDI, visual form inheritance, and frames. Toward the end I also discussed custom architectures, with form inheritance and interfaces. Now we can move forward to another key element of non-trivial Delphi applications: building custom components to use within your programs. It is possible to write a specific book about this, so the description won't be exhaustive, but you should be able to get a comprehensive overview.

Another element related to the architecture of Delphi applications is the use of packages, which I'll introduce as a technology related to components but which really goes beyond this. In fact, you can structure the code of a large application in multiple packages, containing forms and other units. The development of programs based on multiple executable files, libraries, and packages, is discussed in Chapter 12.

After this further step, I will start delving into Delphi database programming, certainly another key element of the Borland development environment.

CHAPTER 11

Creating Components

- Extending the Delphi library

- Writing packages

- Customizing existing components

- Building graphical components

- Defining custom events

- Using array properties

- Placing a dialog box in a component

- Writing property and component editors

While most Delphi programmers are probably familiar with using existing components, at times it can also be useful to write our own components or to customize existing ones. One of the most interesting aspects of Delphi is that creating components is simple. For this reason, even though this book is intended for Delphi application programmers and not Delphi tool writers, this chapter will cover the topic of creating components and introduce Delphi add-ins, such as component and property editors.

This chapter gives an overview of writing Delphi components and presents some simple examples. There is not enough space to present very complex components, but the ideas in this chapter will cover all the basics to get you started.

> **NOTE**   You'll find a more information about writing components in Chapter 18, "Writing Database Components," including how to build data-aware components.

Extending the Delphi Library

Delphi components are classes, and the Visual Components Library (VCL) is the collection of all the classes defining Delphi components. Each time you add a new package with some components to Delphi, you actually extend VCL with a new class. This new class will be derived from one of the existing component-related classes or the generic TComponent class, adding new capabilities to those it inherits.

You can derive a new component from an existing component or from an *abstract component class*—one that does not correspond to a usable component. The VCL hierarchy includes many of these intermediate classes (often indicated with the TCustom prefix in their name) to let you choose a default behavior for your new component and to change its properties.

Component Packages

Components are added to component packages. Each component package is basically a DLL (a dynamic link library) with a BPL extension (which stands for Borland Package Library).

Packages come in two flavors: design-time packages used by the Delphi IDE and run-time packages optionally used by applications. The design-only or run-only package option determines the package's type. When you attempt to install a package, the IDE checks whether it has the design-only or run-only flags, and decides whether to let the user install the package and whether it should be added to the list of run-time packages. Since there are two nonexclusive options, each with two possible states, there are four different kinds of component packages—two main variations and two special cases:

- Design-only component packages can be installed in the Delphi environment. These packages usually contain the design-time parts of a component, such as its property editors and the registration code. Often they can also contain the components themselves, although this is not the most professional approach. The code of the components of a design-only package is usually statically linked into the executable file, using the code of the corresponding Delphi Compiled Unit (DCU) files. Keep in mind, however, that it is also technically possible to use a design-only package as a run-time package.

- Run-only component packages are used by Delphi applications at run time. They cannot be installed in the Delphi environment, but they are automatically added to the list of run-time packages when they are required by a design-only package you install. Run-only packages usually contain the code of the component classes, but no design-time support (this is done to minimize the size of the component libraries you ship along with your executable file). Run-time packages are important because they can be freely distributed along with applications, but other Delphi programmers won't be able to install them in the environment to build new programs.

- Plain component packages (having neither the design-only nor the run-only option set) cannot be installed and will not be added to the list of run-time packages automatically. This might make sense for utility packages used by other packages, but they are certainly rare.

- Packages with both flags set can be installed and are automatically added to the list of run-time packages. Usually these packages contain components requiring little or no design-time support (apart from the limited component registration code). Keep in mind, however, that users of applications built with these packages can use them for their own development.

TIP   The filenames of Delphi's own design-only packages start with the letters *DCL* (for example, DCLSTD60.BPL); filenames of run-only packages start with the letters VCL (for example, VCL60.BPL). You can follow the same approach for your own packages, if you want.

In Chapter 1, "The Delphi 6 IDE," we discussed the effect of packages on the size of a program's executable file. Now we'll focus on building packages, since this is a required step in creating or installing components in Delphi.

When you compile a run-time package, you produce both a dynamic link library with the compiled code (the BPL file) and a file with only symbol information (a DCP file), including no compiled machine code. The latter file is used by the Delphi compiler to gather symbol information about the units that are part of the package without having access to the unit (DCU) files, which contain both the symbol information and the compiled machine code. This reduces compilation time and allows you to distribute just the packages without the precompiled unit files. The precompiled units are still required to statically link the components into an application. Distribution of precompiled DCU files (or source code) may make sense depending on the kind of components you develop. We'll see how to create a package after we've discussed some general guidelines and built our very first component.

NOTE   DLLs are executable files containing collections of functions and classes, which can be used by an application or another DLL at run time. The typical advantage is that if many applications use the same DLL, only one copy needs to be on the disk or loaded in memory, and the size of each executable file will be much smaller. This is what happens with Delphi packages, as well. Chapter 12, "Libraries and Packages," looks at DLLs and packages in more detail.

Rules for Writing Components

Some general rules govern the writing of components. You can find a detailed description of most of them in the *Delphi Component Writer's Guide* Help file, which is required reading for Delphi component writers.

Here is my own summary of the rules for component writers:

- Study the Object Pascal language with care. Particularly important concepts are inheritance, method overriding and overloading, the difference between public and published sections of a class, and the definition of properties and events. If you don't feel confident with the Object Pascal language or the basic ideas about VCL, you can refer to the overall description of the language and library presented in Part I of the book, particularly Chapters 3 ("The Object Pascal Language: Inheritance and Polymorphism") and 5 ("Core Library Classes").

- Study the structure of the VCL class hierarchy and keep a graph of the classes at hand (such as the one included with Delphi).

- Follow the standard Delphi naming conventions. There are several of them for components, as we will see, and following these rules makes it easier for other programmers to interact with your components and further extend them.

- Keep components simple, mimic other components, and avoid dependencies. These three rules basically mean that a programmer using your components should be able to use them as easily as preinstalled Delphi components. Use similar property, method, and event names whenever possible. If users don't need to learn complex rules about the use of your component (that is, if the dependencies between methods or properties are limited) and can simply access properties with meaningful names, they'll be happy.

- Use exceptions. When something goes wrong, the component should raise an exception. When you are allocating resources of any kind, you must protect them with `try/finally` blocks and destructor calls.

- To complete a component, add a bitmap to it, to be used by Delphi's Component Palette. If you intend your component to be used by more than a few people, consider adding a Help file as well.

- Be ready to write *real* code and forget about the visual aspects of Delphi. Writing components generally means writing code without visual support (although Class Completion can speed up the coding of plain classes quite a lot). The exception to this rule is that you can use frames to write components visually.

> **NOTE** You can also use a third-party component writing tool to build your component or to speed up its development. The most powerful third-party tool for creating Delphi components I know of is the Component Development Kit (CDK) from Eagle Software (`www.eagle-software.com`), but many others are available.

The Base Component Classes

To build a new component you generally start from an existing one, or from one of the base classes of VCL. In both cases your component is in one of three broad categories of components (introduced in Chapter 5), set by the three basic classes of the component hierarchy:

- `TWinControl` is the parent class of any component based on a window. Components that descend from this class can receive the input focus and get Windows messages from the system. You can also use their window handle when calling API functions. When creating a brand-new window control, you'll generally inherit from the derived class `TCustomControl`, which has a few extra useful features (particularly some support for painting the control).

- `TGraphicControl` is the parent class of visible components that have no Windows handle (which saves some Windows resources). These components cannot receive the input focus or respond to Windows messages directly. When creating a brand-new graphical control, you'll inherit directly from this class (which has a set of features very similar to `TCustomControl`).

- `TComponent` is the parent class of all components (including the controls) and can be used as a direct parent class for nonvisual components.

In the rest of the chapter, we will build some components using various parent classes, and we'll look at the differences among them. We'll start with components inheriting from existing components or classes at a low level of the hierarchy, and then we'll see examples of classes inheriting directly from the ancestor classes mentioned above.

Building Your First Component

Building components is an important activity for Delphi programmers. The basic idea is that any time you need the same behavior in two different places in an application, or in two different applications, you can place the shared code inside a class—or, even better, a component.

In this section I'll just introduce a couple of simple components, to give you an idea of the steps required to build one and to show you different things you can do to customize an existing component with a limited amount of code.

The Fonts Combo Box

Many applications have a toolbar with a combo box you can use to select a font. If you often use a customized combo box like this, why not turn it into a component? It would probably take less than a minute. To begin, close any active projects in the Delphi environment and start the Component Wizard, either by choosing Component ➢ New Component or by selecting File ➢ New to open the Object Repository and then choosing the Component in the New page. As you can see in Figure 11.1, the Component Wizard requires the following information:

FIGURE 11.1:

Defining the new TMdFont-Combo component with the Component Wizard

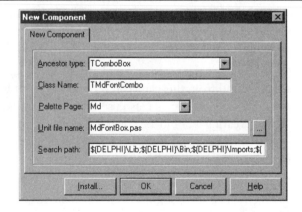

- The name of the ancestor type: the component class you want to inherit from. In this case we can use TComboBox.

- The name of the class of the new component you are building; we can use TMdFontCombo.

- The page of the Component Palette where you want to display the new component, which can be a new or an existing page. We can create a new page, called *Md*.

- The filename of the Pascal unit where Delphi will place the source code of the new component; we can type MdFontBox.

- The current search path (which should be set up automatically).

Click the OK button, and the Component Wizard will generate the following simple Pascal source file with the structure of your component. The Install button can be used to install the component in a package immediately. Let's look at the code first, Listing 11.1, and then discuss the installation.

Listing 11.1:   **Code of the TMdFontCombo, generated by the Component Wizard**

```pascal
unit MdFontBox;

interface

uses
  Windows, Messages, SysUtils, Classes, Graphics, Controls, Forms, Dialogs,
  StdCtrls;

type
  TMdFontCombo = class (TComboBox)
  private
    { Private declarations }
  protected
    { Protected declarations }
  public
    { Public declarations }
  published
    { Published declarations }
  end;

procedure Register;

implementation

procedure Register;
begin
  RegisterComponents('Md', [TMdFontCombo]);
end;

end.
```

One of the key elements of this listing is the class definition, which begins by indicating the parent class. The only other relevant portion is the Register procedure. In fact, you can see that the Component Wizard does very little work.

WARNING Starting with Delphi 4, the `Register` procedure *must* be written with an uppercase *R*. This requirement is apparently imposed for C++Builder compatibility (identifiers in C++ are case-sensitive).

TIP Use a naming convention when building components. All the components installed in Delphi should have different class names. For this reason most Delphi component developers have chosen to add a two- or three-letter signature prefix to the names of their components. I've done the same, using *Md* (for *Mastering Delphi*) to identify components built in this book. The advantage of this approach is that you can install my **TMdFontCombo** component even if you've already installed a component named **TFontCombo**. Notice that the unit names must also be unique for all the components installed in the system, so I've applied the same prefix to the unit names.

That's all it takes to build a component. Of course, in this example there isn't a lot of code. We need only copy all the system fonts to the `Items` property of the combo box at startup. To accomplish this, we might try to override the `Create` method in the class declaration, adding the statement `Items := Screen.Fonts`. However, this is not the correct approach. The problem is that we cannot access the combo box's `Items` property before the window handle of the component is available; the component cannot have a window handle until its `Parent` property is set; and that property isn't set in the constructor, but later on.

For this reason, instead of assigning the new strings in the `Create` constructor, we must perform this operation in the `CreateWnd` procedure, which is called to create the window control after the component is constructed, its `Parent` property is set, and its window handle is available. Again, we execute the default behavior, and then we can write our custom code. I could have skipped the `Create` constructor and written all the code in `CreateWnd`, but I decided to use both startup methods to demonstrate the difference between them. Here is the declaration of the component class:

```
type
  TMdFontCombo = class (TComboBox)
  private
    FChangeFormFont: Boolean;
    procedure SetChangeFormFont(const Value: Boolean);
  public
    constructor Create (AOwner: TComponent); override;
    procedure CreateWnd; override;
    procedure Change; override;
  published
    property Style default csDropDownList;
    property Items stored False;
```

```
    property ChangeFormFont: Boolean
      read FChangeFormFont write SetChangeFormFont default True;
  end;
```

And here is the source code of its two methods executed at startup:

```
constructor TMdFontCombo.Create (AOwner: TComponent);
begin
  inherited Create (AOwner);
  Style := csDropDownList;
  FChangeFormFont := True;
end;

procedure TMdFontCombo.CreateWnd;
begin
  inherited CreateWnd;
  Items.Assign (Screen.Fonts);

  // grab the default font of the owner form
  if FChangeFormFont and Assigned (Owner) and (Owner is TForm) then
    ItemIndex := Items.IndexOf ((Owner as TForm).Font.Name);
end;
```

Notice that besides giving a new value to the component's Style property, in the Create method, I've redefined this property by setting a value with the default keyword. We have to do both operations because adding the default keyword to a property declaration has no direct effect on the property's initial value. Why specify a property's default value then? Because properties that have a value equal to the default are not streamed with the form definition (and they don't appear in the textual description of the form, the DFM file). The default keyword tells the streaming code that the component initialization code will set the value of that property.

The other redefined property, Items, is set as a property that should not be saved to the DFM file at all, regardless of the actual value. This is obtained with the stored directive followed by the value False. The component and its window are going to be created again when the program starts, so it doesn't make any sense to save in the DFM file information that will be discarded later on (to be replaced with the new list of fonts).

The third property, ChangeFormFont, is not inherited but introduced by the component. It is used to determine whether the current font selection of the combo box should determine the font of the form hosting the component. Again this property is declared with a default value, set in the constructor. The ChangeFormFont property is used in the code of the CreateWnd method, shown before, to set up the initial selection of the combo depending on the font of the form hosting the component. This is generally the Owner of the component, although I could have also walked the Parent tree looking for a form component. This code isn't perfect, but the Assigned and is tests provide some extra safety.

The ChangeFormFont property and the same if test play a key role in the Changed method, which in the base class triggers the OnChange event. By overriding this method we provide a default behavior, which can be disabled by toggling the value of the property, but also allow the execution of the OnChange event, so that users of this class can fully customize its behavior. The final method, SetChangeFormFont, has been modified to refresh the form's font in case the property is being turned on. This is the complete code:

```
procedure TMdFontCombo.Change;
begin
  // assign the font to the owner form
  if FChangeFormFont and Assigned (Owner) and (Owner is TForm) then
    TForm (Owner).Font.Name := Text;
  inherited;
end;

procedure TMdFontCombo.SetChangeFormFont(const Value: Boolean);
begin
  FChangeFormFont := Value;
  // refresh font
  if FChangeFormFont then
    Change;
end;
```

Creating a Package

Now we have to install the component in the environment, using a package. For this example, we can either create a new package or use an existing one, like the default user's package.

In each case, choose the Component ➤ Install Component menu command. The resulting dialog box has a page to install the component into an existing package, and a page to create a new package. In this last case, simply type in a filename and a description for the package. Clicking OK opens the Package Editor (see Figure 11.2), which has two parts:

- The Contains list indicates the components included in the package (or, to be more precise, the units defining those components).

- The Requires list indicates the packages required by this package. Your package will generally require the rtl and vcl packages (the main run-time library package and core VCL package), but it might also need the vcldb package (which includes most of the database-related classes) if the components of the new package do any database-related operations.

FIGURE 11.2:

The Package Editor

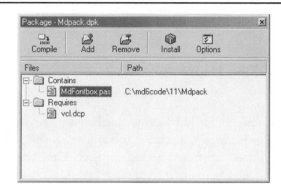

NOTE   Package names in Delphi 6 aren't version specific any more, even if the compiled packages still have a version number in the filename. See the section "Project and Library Names in Delphi 6" in Chapter 12, "Libraries and Packages," for more details on how this is technically achieved.

If you add the component to the new package we've just defined, and then simply compile the package and install it (using the two corresponding toolbar buttons of the package editor), you'll immediately see the new component show up in the Md page of the Component Palette. The Register procedure of the component unit file told Delphi where to install the new component. By default, the bitmap used will be the same as the parent class, because we haven't provided a custom bitmap (we will do this in later examples). Notice also that if you move the mouse over the new component, Delphi will display as a hint the name of the class without the initial letter *T*.

What's Behind a Package?

What is behind the package we've just built? The Package Editor basically generates the source code for the package project: a special kind of DLL built in Delphi. The package project is saved in a file with the DPK (for Delphi PacKage) extension. A typical package project looks like this:

```
package MdPack;

{$R *.RES}
```

```
{$ALIGN ON}
{$BOOLEVAL OFF}
{$DEBUGINFO ON}
...
{$DESCRIPTION 'Mastering Delphi Package'}
{$IMPLICITBUILD ON}

requires
  vcl;

contains
  MdFontBox in 'MdFontBox.pas';

end.
```

As you can see, Delphi uses specific language keywords for packages: the first is the package keyword (which is similar to the library keyword I'll discuss in the next chapter). This keyword introduces a new package project. Then comes a list with all the compiler options, some of which I've omitted from the listing. Usually the options for a Delphi project are stored in a separate file; packages, by contrast, include all the compiler options directly in their source code. Among the compiler options there is a DESCRIPTION compiler directive, used to make the package description available to the Delphi environment. In fact, after you've installed a new package, its description will be shown in the Packages page of the Project Options dialog box, a page you can also activate by selecting the Component ➢ Install Packages menu item. This dialog box is shown in Figure 11.3.

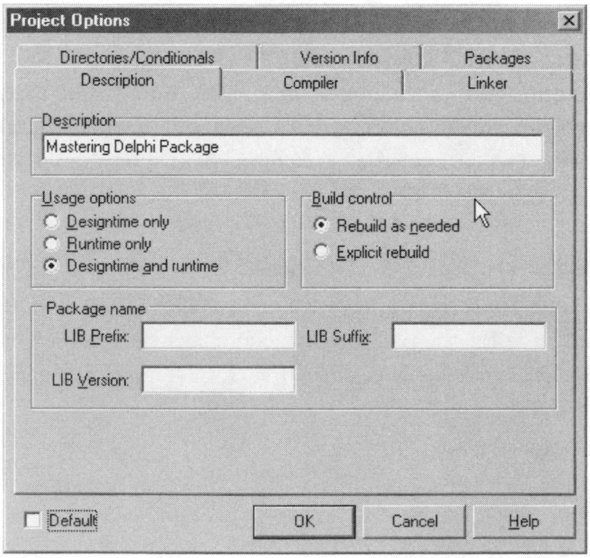

FIGURE 11.3:

The Project Options for packages. You can see the new package we've just created.

Besides common directives like the DESCRIPTION one, there are other compiler directives specific to packages. The most common of these options are easily accessible through the Options button of the Package Editor. After this list of options come the requires and contains keywords, which list the items displayed visually in the two pages of the Package Editor. Again, the first is the list of packages required by the current one, and the second is a list of the units installed by this package.

What is the technical effect of building a package? Besides the DPK file with the source code, Delphi generates a BPL file with the dynamic link version of the package and a DCP file with the symbol information. In practice, this DCP file is the sum of the symbol information of the DCU files of the units contained in the package.

At design time, Delphi requires both the BPL and DCP files, because the first has the actual code of the components created on the design form and the symbol information required by the code insight technology. If you link the package dynamically (using it as a run-time package), the DCP file will also be used by the linker, and the BPL file should be shipped along with the main executable file of the application. If you instead link the package statically, the linker refers to the DCU files, and you'll need to distribute only the final executable file.

For this reason, as a component designer, you should generally distribute at least the BPL file, the DCP file, and the DCU files of the units contained in the package and any corresponding DFM files, plus a Help file. As an option, of course, you might also make available the source code files of the package units (the PAS files) and of the package itself (the DPK file).

WARNING Delphi, by default, will place all the compiled package files (BPL and DCP) not in the folder of the package source code but under the \Projects\BPL folder. This is done so that the IDE can easily locate them, and creates no particular problem. When you have to compile a project using components declared on those packages, though, Delphi might complain that it cannot find the corresponding DCU files, which are stored in the package source code folder. This problem can be solved by indicating the package source code folder in the Library Path (in the Environment Options, which affect all projects) or by indicating it in the Search Path of the current project (in the Project Options). If you choose the first approach, placing different components and packages in a single folder might result in a real time-saver.

Installing the Components of This Chapter

Having built our first package, we can now start using the component we've added to it. Before we do so, however, I should mention that I've extended the MdPack package to include all of the components we are going to build in this chapter, including different versions of the same component. I suggest you install this package. The best approach is to copy it into a directory of your path, so that it will be available both to the Delphi environment and to the programs you build with it. I've collected all the component source code files and the package definition in a single subdirectory, called MdPack. This allows the Delphi environment, or a specific project, to refer only to one directory when looking for the DCU files of this package. As suggested in the warning above, I could have collected all of the components presented in the book in a single folder on the companion CD, but I decided that keeping the chapter-based organization was actually more understandable for readers.

Remember, anyway, that if you compile an application using the packages as run-time DLLs, you'll need to install these new libraries on your clients' computers. If you instead compile the programs by statically linking the package, the DLL will be required only by the development environment and not by the users of your applications.

Using the Font Combo Box

Now you can create a new Delphi program to test the Font combo box. Move to the Component Palette, select the new component, and add it to a new form. A traditional-looking combo box will appear. However, if you open the Items property editor, you'll see a list of the fonts installed on your computer. To build a simple example, I've added a Memo component to the form with some text inside it. By leaving the ChangeFormFont property on, you don't need to write any other code to the program, as you'll see in the example. As an alternative I could have turned off the property and handled the OnChange event of the component, with code like this:

```
Memo1.Font.Name := MdFontCombo1.Text;
```

The aim of this simple program is only to test the behavior of the new component we have built. The component is still not very useful—we could have added a couple of lines of code to a form to obtain the same effect—but looking at a couple of simple components should help you get an idea of what is involved in component building.

Creating Compound Components

The next component I want to focus on is a digital clock. This example has some interesting features. First, it embeds a component (a Timer) in another component; second, it shows the live-data approach.

NOTE   The first feature has become even more relevant in Delphi 6, as the Object Inspector of the latest version of Delphi allows you to expose properties of subcomponents directly. As an effect, the example presented in this section has been modified (and simplified) compared to the previous edition of the book. I'll actually mention the differences, when relevant.

Since the digital clock will provide some text output, I considered inheriting from the TLabel class. However, this would allow a user to change the label's caption—that is, the text of the clock. To avoid this problem, I simply used the TCustomLabel component as the parent class.

A TCustomLabel object has the same capabilities as a TLabel object, but few published properties. In other words, a TCustomLabel subclass can decide which properties should be available and which should remain hidden.

NOTE Most of the Delphi components, particularly the Windows-based ones, have a TCustomXxx base class, which implements the entire functionality but exposes only a limited set of properties. Inheriting from these base classes is the standard way to expose only some of the properties of a component in a customized version. In fact, you cannot hide public or published properties of a base class.

With past versions of Delphi, the component had to define a new property, Active, wrapping the Enabled property of the Timer. A *wrapper* property means that the get and set methods of this property read and write the value of the *wrapped* property, which belongs to an internal component (a wrapper property generally has no local data). In this specific case, the code looked like this:

```
function TMdClock.GetActive: Boolean;
begin
  Result := FTimer.Enabled;
end;

procedure TMdClock.SetActive (Value: Boolean);
begin
  FTimer.Enabled := Value;
end;
```

Publishing Subcomponents in Delphi 6

With Delphi 6 we can simply expose the entire subcomponent, the timer, in a property of its own, that will be regularly expanded by the Object Inspector, allowing a user to set each and every of its subproperties, and even to handle its events.

Here is the full type declaration for the TMdClock component, with the subcomponent declared in the private data and exposed as a published property (in the last line):

```
type
  TMdClock = class (TCustomLabel)
  private
    FTimer: TTimer;
  protected
    procedure UpdateClock (Sender: TObject);
  public
    constructor Create (AOwner: TComponent); override;
  published
    property Align;
```

```
    property Alignment;
    property Color;
    property Font;
    property ParentColor;
    property ParentFont;
    property ParentShowHint;
    property PopupMenu;
    property ShowHint;
    property Transparent;
    property Visible;
    property Timer: TTimer read FTimer;
  end;
```

The Timer property is read-only, as I don't want users to select another value for this component in the Object Inspector (or detach the component by clearing the value of this property). Developing sets of subcomponents that can be used alternately is certainly possible, but adding write support for this property in a safe way is far from trivial (considering that the users of your component might not be very expert Delphi programmers). So I suggest you to stick with read-only properties for subcomponents.

To create the Timer, we must override the constructor of the clock component. The Create method calls the corresponding method of the base class and creates the Timer object, installing a handler for its OnTimer event:

```
constructor TMdClock.Create (AOwner: TComponent);
begin
  inherited Create (AOwner);
  // create the internal timer object
  FTimer := TTimer.Create (Self);

  FTimer.Name := 'ClockTimer';
  FTimer.OnTimer := UpdateClock;
  FTimer.Enabled := True;
  FTimer.SetSubComponent (True);
end;
```

The code gives the component a name, for display in the Object Inspector (see Figure 11.4), and calls the specific SetSubComponent method. We don't need a destructor, simply because the FTimer object has our TMDClock component as owner (as indicated by the parameter of its Create constructor), so it will be destroyed automatically when the clock component is destroyed.

NOTE   What is the actual effect of the call to the SetSubComponent method in the code above? This call sets an internal flag, saved in the ComponentStyle property set. The flag (csSubComponent) affects the streaming system, allowing the subcomponent and its properties to be saved in the DFM file. In fact, the streaming system by default ignores components that are not owned by the form.

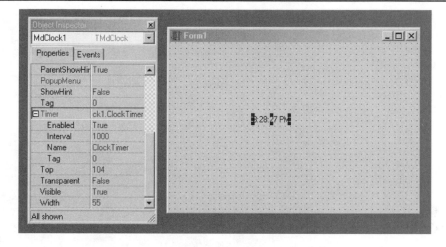

The key piece of the component's code is the UpdateClock procedure, which is just one statement:

```
procedure TMdLabelClock.UpdateClock (Sender: TObject);
begin
  // set the current time as caption
  Caption := TimeToStr (Time);
end;
```

This method uses Caption, which is an unpublished property, so that a user of the component cannot modify it in the Object Inspector. The result of this statement is to display the current time. This happens continuously, because the method is connected to the Timer's OnTimer event.

The Component Palette Bitmaps

Before installing this second component, we can take one further step: define a bitmap for the Component Palette. If we fail to do so, the Palette uses the bitmap of the parent class, or a default object's bitmap if the parent class is not an installed component (as is the case of the TCustomLabel). Defining a new bitmap for the component is easy, once you know the rules. You can create one with the Image Editor (as shown in Figure 11.5), starting a new project and selecting the Delphi Component Resource (DCR) project type.

TIP   DCR files are simply standard RES files with a different extension. If you prefer, you can create them with any resource editor, including the Borland Resource Workshop, which is certainly a more powerful tool than the Delphi Image editor. When you finish creating the resource file, simply rename the RES file to use a DCR extension.

The definition of a
Component Palette
bitmap in Delphi's
Image Editor

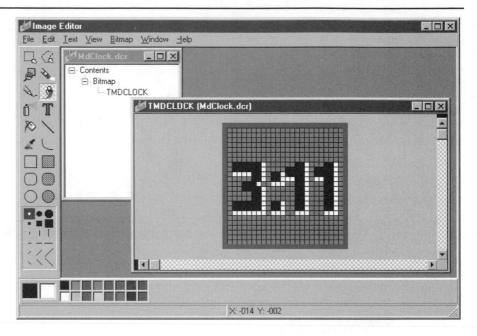

Now we can add a new bitmap to the resource, choosing a size of 24×24 pixels, and we are ready to draw the bitmap. The other important rules refer to naming. In this case, the naming rule is not just a convention; it is a requirement so that the IDE can find the image for a given component class:

- The name of the bitmap resource must match the name of the component, including the initial *T*. In this case, the name of the bitmap resource should be TMDCLOCK. The name of the bitmap resource must be uppercase—this is mandatory.

- If you want the Package Editor to recognize and include the resource file, the name of the DCR file must match the name of the compiled unit that defines the component. In this case, the filename should be MdClock.DCR. If you manually include the resource file, via a $R directive, you can give it the name you like, and also use a RES or DCR file with multiple palette icons.

When the bitmap for the component is ready, you can install the component in Delphi, by using the Package Editor's Install Package toolbar button. After this operation, the Contains section of the editor should list both the PAS file of the component and the corresponding DCR file. In Figure 11.6 you can see all the files (including the DCR files) of the final version of the MdPack package. If the DCR installation doesn't work properly, you can manually add the {$R unitname.dcr} statement in the package source code.

FIGURE 11.6:

The Contains section of the Package Editor shows both the units that are included in the package and the component resource files.

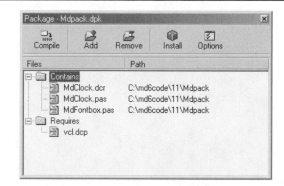

Building Compound Components with Frames

Instead of building the compound component in code and hooking up the timer event manually, we could have obtained a similar effect by using a frame. Frames make the development of compound components with custom event handlers a visual operation, and thus simpler. You can share this frame by adding it to the Repository or by creating a template using the Add to Palette command of the frame's shortcut menu.

As an alternative, you might want to share the frame by placing it in a package and registering it as a component. Technically, this is not difficult. You add a `Register` procedure to the frame's unit, add the unit to a package, and build it. The new component/frame will be in the Component Palette, like any other component. In Delphi 6, when you place this component/frame on a form, you'll see its subcomponents. You cannot select these subcomponents with a mouse click in the Form Designer, but can do it in the Object TreeView. However, any change you make to these components at design time will inevitably get lost when you run the program or save and reload the form, because the changes to those subcomponents won't be streamed, contrary to what happened with standard frames you place inside a form.

If this is not what you might expect, I've found a *reasonable* way to use frames in packages, demonstrated by the MdFramedClock component, part of the examples on the CD for this chapter. The idea is to turn the components owned by the form into actual subcomponents, by calling the new `SetSubComponent` method. As I was up to it, I've also exposed the internal components with properties, even if this isn't compulsory as they can be selected in the Object TreeView anyway. This is the declaration of the component and the code of its methods:

```
type
  TMdFramedClock = class(TFrame)
    Label1: TLabel;
    Timer1: TTimer;
    Bevel1: TBevel;
```

Continued on next page

```
      procedure Timer1Timer(Sender: TObject);
  public
    constructor Create(AOnwer: TComponent); override;
  published
    property SubLabel: TLabel read Label1;
    property SubTimer: TTimer read Timer1;
  end;


constructor TMdFramedClock.Create(AOnwer: TComponent);
begin
  inherited;
  Timer1.SetSubComponent (true);
  Label1.SetSubComponent (true);
end;


procedure TMdFramedClock.Timer1Timer(Sender: TObject);
begin
  Label1.Caption := TimeToStr (Time);
end;
```

In contrast to the clock component built earlier, there is no need to set up the properties of the timer, or to connect the timer event to its handler function manually, as this is done visually and saved in the DFM file of the frame. Notice also that I haven't exposed the Bevel component—I haven't called SetSubComponent on it—so that you can try editing it at design time and see that all the changes get lost, as I mentioned above.

After you install this frame/component, you can use it inside any application. In this particular case, as soon as you drop the frame on the form, the timer will start to update the label with the current time. However, you can still handle its OnTimer event, and the Delphi IDE (recognizing that the component is inside a frame) will define a method with this predefined code:

```
procedure TForm1.MdFramedClock1Timer1Timer(Sender: TObject);
begin
  MdFramedClock1.Timer1Timer(Sender);
end;
```

As soon as this timer is connected, even at design time, the live clock will stop, as its original event handler is disconnected. After compiling and running the program, however, the original behavior will be restored (at least if you don't delete the line above) and your extra custom code will be executed as well. This is exactly what you'll expect from frames. You can find a complete demo of the use of this frame/component in the FrameClock example.

Continued on next page

As a short conclusion of this digression on frames compiled inside packages, I can certainly say that this approach is still far from linear. It is certainly much better than in Delphi 5, where frames inside packages were really unusable. The question is, is it worth the effort? In short, I'd say no. If you work alone or with a small team, it's better to use plain frames stored in the Repository. In larger organizations and for distributing your frames to a larger audience, I bet most people will rather build their components in the traditional way, without trying to use frames. In other words, I'm still hoping that Borland will address more complete support to the visual development of packaged components based on frames.

A Complex Graphical Component

The graphical component I want to build is an arrow component. You can use such a component to indicate a flow of information, or an action, for example. This component is quite complex, so I'll show you the various steps instead of looking directly at the complete source code. The component I've added to the MdPack package on the CD is only the final version of this process, which will demonstrate several important concepts:

- The definition of new enumerated properties, based on custom enumerated data types.

- The use of properties of TPersistent-derived classes, such as TPen and TBrush, and the issues related to their creation and destruction, and to handling their OnChange events internally in our component.

- The implementation of the Paint method of the component, which provides its user interface and should be generic enough to accommodate all the possible values of the various properties, including its Width and Height. The Paint method plays a substantial role in this graphical component.

- The definition of a custom event handler for the component, responding to user input (in this case, a double-click on the point of the arrow). This will require direct handling of Windows messages and the use of the Windows API for graphic regions.

- The registration of properties in Object Inspector categories and the definition of a custom category.

Defining an Enumerated Property

After generating the new component with the Component Wizard and choosing TGraphicControl as the parent class, we can start to customize the component. The arrow can point in any of four directions: up, down, left, or right. An enumerated type expresses these choices:

```
type
    TMdArrowDir = (adUp, adRight, adDown, adLeft);
```

This enumerated type defines a private data member of the component, a parameter of the procedure used to change it, and the type of the corresponding property. Two more simple properties are ArrowHeight and Filled, the first determining the size of the arrowhead and the second whether to fill the arrowhead with color:

```
type
  TMdArrow = class (TGraphicControl)
  private
    fDirection: TMdArrowDir;
    fArrowHeight: Integer;
    fFilled: Boolean;
    procedure SetDirection (Value: TMd4ArrowDir);
    procedure SetArrowHeight (Value: Integer);
    procedure SetFilled (Value: Boolean);
  published
    property Width default 50;
    property Height default 20;
    property Direction: TMd4ArrowDir
      read fDirection write SetDirection default adRight;
    property ArrowHeight: Integer
      read fArrowHeight write SetArrowHeight default 10;
    property Filled: Boolean read fFilled write SetFilled default False;
```

NOTE   A graphic control has no default size, so when you place it in a form, its size will be a single pixel. For this reason it is important to add a default value for the Width and Height properties and set the class fields to the default property values in the constructor of the class.

The three custom properties are read directly from the corresponding field and are written using three Set methods, all having the same standard structure:

```
procedure TMdArrow.SetDirection (Value: TMdArrowDir);
begin
  if fDirection <> Value then
  begin
    fDirection := Value;
    ComputePoints;
    Invalidate;
  end;
end;
```

Notice that we ask the system to repaint the component (by calling Invalidate) only if the property is really changing its value and after calling the ComputePoints method, which computes the triangle delimiting the arrowhead. Otherwise, the code is skipped and the method ends immediately. This code structure is very common, and we will use it for most of the Set procedures of properties.

We must also remember to set the default values of the properties in the component's constructor:

```
constructor TMdArrow.Create (AOwner: TComponent);
begin
  // call the parent constructor
  inherited Create (AOwner);
  // set the default values
  fDirection := adRight;
  Width := 50;
  Height := 20;
  fArrowHeight := 10;
  fFilled := False;
```

In fact, as mentioned before, the default value specified in the property declaration is used only to determine whether to save the property's value to disk. The Create constructor is defined in the public section of the type definition of the new component, and it is indicated by the override keyword. It is fundamental to remember this keyword; otherwise, when Delphi creates a new component of this class, it will call the constructor of the base class, rather than the one you've written for your derived class.

Property-Naming Conventions

In the definition of the Arrow component, notice the use of several naming conventions for properties, access methods, and fields. Here is a summary:

- A property should have a meaningful and readable name.

- When a private data field is used to hold the value of a property, the field should be named with an *f* (field) at the beginning, followed by the name of the corresponding property.

- When a function is used to change the value of the property, the function should have the word *Set* at the beginning, followed by the name of the corresponding property.

- A corresponding function used to read the property should have the word *Get* at the beginning, again followed by the property name.

These are just guidelines to make programs more readable. The compiler doesn't enforce them. These conventions are described in the *Delphi Component Writers' Guide* and are followed by the Delphi's class completion mechanism.

Writing the *Paint* Method

Drawing the arrow in the various directions and with the various styles requires a fair amount of code. To perform custom painting, you override the Paint method and use the protected Canvas property.

Instead of computing the position of the arrowhead points in drawing code that will be executed often, I've written a separate function to compute the arrowhead area and store it in an array of points defined among the private fields of the component as:

```
fArrowPoints: array [0..3] of TPoint;
```

These points are determined by the ComputePoints private method, which is called every time some of the component properties change. Here is an excerpt of its code:

```
procedure TMdArrow.ComputePoints;
var
  XCenter, YCenter: Integer;
begin
  // compute the points of the arrowhead
  YCenter := (Height - 1) div 2;
  XCenter := (Width - 1) div 2;
  case FDirection of
    adUp: begin
      fArrowPoints [0] := Point (0, FArrowHeight);
      fArrowPoints [1] := Point (XCenter, 0);
      fArrowPoints [2] := Point (Width-1, FArrowHeight);
    end;
  // and so on for the other directions
```

The code computes the center of the component area (simply dividing the Height and Width properties by two) and then uses it to determine the position of the arrowhead. Besides changing the direction or other properties, we need to refresh the position of the arrowhead when the size of the component changes. What we can do is to override the SetBounds method of the component, which is called by VCL every time the Left, Top, Width, and Height properties of a component change:

```
procedure TMdArrow.SetBounds(ALeft, ATop, AWidth, AHeight: Integer);
begin
  inherited SetBounds (ALeft, ATop, AWidth, AHeight);
  ComputePoints;
end;
```

Once the component knows the position of the arrowhead, its painting code becomes simpler. Here is an excerpt of the Paint method:

```
procedure TMdArrow.Paint;
var
  XCenter, YCenter: Integer;
```

```
begin
  // compute the center
  YCenter := (Height - 1) div 2;
  XCenter := (Width - 1) div 2;

  // draw the arrow line
  case FDirection of
    adUp: begin
      Canvas.MoveTo (XCenter, Height-1);
      Canvas.LineTo (XCenter, FArrowHeight);
    end;
    // and so on for the other directions
  end;

  // draw the arrow point, eventually filling it
  if FFilled then
    Canvas.Polygon (fArrowPoints)
  else
    Canvas.PolyLine (fArrowPoints);
end;
```

You can see an example of the output of this component in Figure 11.7.

FIGURE 11.7:

The output of the Arrow component

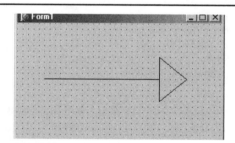

Adding *TPersistent* Properties

To make the output of the component more flexible, I've added to it two new properties, defined with a class type (specifically, a TPersistent data type, which defines objects that can be automatically streamed by Delphi). These properties are a little more complex to handle, because the component now has to create and destroy these internal objects (as we did with the internal Timer of the clock component). This time, however, we also export the internal objects using some properties, so that users can directly change them from the Object Inspector. To update the component when these subobjects change, we'll also need to handle their internal OnChange property. Here is the definition of the two new TPersistent-type properties and the other changes to the definition of the component class:

```
type
  TMdArrow = class (TGraphicControl)
  private
    FPen: TPen;
    FBrush: TBrush;
    ...
    procedure SetPen (Value: TPen);
    procedure SetBrush (Value: TBrush);
    procedure RepaintRequest (Sender: TObject);
  published
    property Pen: TPen read FPen write SetPen;
    property Brush: TBrush read FBrush write SetBrush;
  end;
```

The first thing to do is to create the objects in the constructor and set their OnChange event handler:

```
constructor TMdArrow.Create (AOwner: TComponent);
begin
  ...
  // create the pen and the brush
  FPen := TPen.Create;
  FBrush := TBrush.Create;
  // set a handler for the OnChange event
  FPen.OnChange := RepaintRequest;
  FBrush.OnChange := RepaintRequest;
end;
```

These OnChange events are fired when one of the properties of these subobjects changes; all we have to do is to ask the system to repaint our component:

```
procedure TMdArrow.RepaintRequest (Sender: TObject);
begin
  Invalidate;
end;
```

You must also add to the component a destructor, to remove the two graphical objects from memory (and free their system resources):

```
destructor TMdArrow.Destroy;
begin
  FPen.Free;
  FBrush.Free;
  inherited Destroy;
end;
```

The properties related to these two components require some special handling: instead of copying the pointer to the objects, we should copy the internal data of the object passed as parameter. The standard := operation copies the pointers, so in this case we have to use the Assign method instead. Here is one of the two Set procedures:

```
procedure TMdArrow.SetPen (Value: TPen);
begin
  FPen.Assign(Value);
  Invalidate;
end;
```

Many TPersistent classes have an Assign method that should be used when we need to update the data of these objects. Now, to actually use the pen and brush for the drawing, you have to modify the Paint method, setting the Pen and the Brush properties of the component Canvas to the value of the internal objects before drawing any line:

```
procedure TMdArrow.Paint;
begin
  // use the current pen and brush
  Canvas.Pen := FPen;
  Canvas.Brush := FBrush;
```

You can see an example of the new output of the component in Figure 11.8.

FIGURE 11.8:

The output of the Arrow component with a thick pen and a special hatch brush

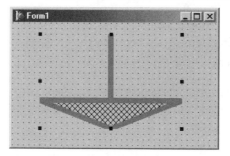

Defining a New Custom Event

To complete the development of the Arrow component, let's add a custom event. Most of the time, new components use the events of their parent classes. For example, in this component, I've made some standard events available simply by redeclaring them in the published section of the class:

```
type
  TMdArrow = class (TGraphicControl)
  published
    property OnClick;
```

```
property OnDragDrop;
property OnDragOver;
property OnEndDrag;
property OnMouseDown;
property OnMouseMove;
property OnMouseUp;
```

Thanks to this declaration, the above events (originally declared in a parent class) will now be available in the Object Inspector when the component is installed.

Sometimes, however, a component requires a custom event. To define a brand-new event, you first need to add to the class a field of the type of the event. This type is actually a method pointer type (see Chapter 5 for details). Here is the definition I've added in the private section of the TMdArrow class:

```
fArrowDblClick: TNotifyEvent;
```

In this case I've used the TNotifyEvent type, which has only a Sender parameter and is used by Delphi for many events, including OnClick and OnDblClick events. Using this field I've defined a very simple published property, with direct access to the field:

```
property OnArrowDblClick: TNotifyEvent
  read fArrowDblClick write fArrowDblClick;
```

Notice again the standard naming convention, with event names starting with *On*. The fArrowDblClick method pointer is activated (executing the corresponding function) inside the specific ArrowDblClick dynamic method. This happens only if an event handler has been specified in the program that uses the component:

```
procedure TMdArrow.ArrowDblClick;
begin
  if Assigned (FArrowDblClick) then
    FArrowDblClick (Self);
end;
```

This method is defined in the protected section of the type definition to allow future subclasses to both call and change it. Basically, the ArrowDblClick method is called by the handler of the wm_LButtonDblClk Windows message, but only if the double-click took place inside the arrow's point. To test this condition, we can use some of the Windows API's region functions.

NOTE A *region* is an area of the screen enclosed by any shape. For example, we can build a polygonal region using the three vertices of the arrow-point triangle. The only problem is that to fill the surface properly, we must define an array of TPoints in a clockwise direction (see the description of the CreatePolygonalRgn in the Windows API Help for the details of this strange approach). That's what I did in the ComputePoints method.

Once we have defined a region, we can test whether the point where the double-click occurred is inside the region by using the PtInRegion API call. You can see the complete source code of this procedure in the following listing:

```
procedure TMdArrow.WMLButtonDblClk (
  var Msg: TWMLButtonDblClk); // message wm_LButtonDblClk;
var
  HRegion: HRgn;
begin
  // perform default handling
  inherited;

  // compute the arrowhead region
  HRegion := CreatePolygonRgn (fArrowPoints, 3, WINDING);
  try // check whether the click took place in the region
    if PtInRegion (HRegion, Msg.XPos, Msg.YPos) then
      ArrowDblClick;
  finally
    DeleteObject (HRegion);
  end;
end;
```

Registering Property Categories

We've added to this component some custom properties and a new event. If you arrange the properties in the Object Inspector by category (a feature available since Delphi 5), all the new elements will show up in the generic Miscellaneous category. Of course, this is far from ideal, but we can easily register the new properties in one of the available categories.

We can register a property (or an event) in a category by calling one of the four overloaded versions of the RegisterPropertyInCategory function, defined in the new DesignIntf unit. When calling this function, you indicate the name of the category, and you can specify the property name, its type, or the property name and the component it belongs to. For example, we can add the following lines to the Register procedure of the unit to register the OnArrowDblClick event in the Input category and the Filled property in the Visual category:

```
uses
  DesignIntf;

procedure Register;
begin
  RegisterComponents('Md', [TMdArrow]);
  RegisterPropertyInCategory ('Input', TMdArrow, 'OnArrowDblClick');
  RegisterPropertyInCategory ('Visual', TMdArrow, 'Filled');
end;
```

In Delphi 5, the first parameter was a class indicating the category type; now the parameter is simply a string, a much simpler solution. This change also makes it straightforward to define new categories: you simply pass its name as the first parameter of the `RegisterPropertyInCategory` function, as in:

```
RegisterPropertyInCategory ('Arrow', TMdArrow, 'Direction');
RegisterPropertyInCategory ('Arrow', TMdArrow, 'ArrowHeight');
```

Creating a brand new category for the specific properties of our component can make it much simpler for a user to locate its specific features. Notice, though, that since we rely on the Design-Intf unit, you should compile the unit containing these registrations in a design-time package, not a run-time one (in fact, the required DesignIde unit cannot be distributed). For this reason, I've written this code in a separate unit than the one defining the component and added the new unit (MdArrReg) to the package MdDesPk, including all of the design-time-only units; this is discussed later, in the section "Installing the Property Editor."

WARNING   It's debatable whether using a category for the specific properties of a component is a good idea. On one side, a user of the component can easily spot specific properties. At the same time, some of the new properties might not pertain to any of the existing categories. On the other side, however, categories can be overused. If every component introduces new categories, users may get confused. You also face the risk of having as many categories as there are properties.

Notice that my code registers the `Filled` property in two different categories. This is not a problem, because the same property can show up multiple times in the Object Inspector under different groups, as you can see in Figure 11.9.

To test the arrow component I've written a very simple example program, ArrowDemo, which allows you to modify most of its properties at run time. This type of test, after you have written a component or while you are writing it, is very important.

NOTE   The *Localizable* property category has a special role, related to the use of the ITE (Integrated Translation Environment). When a property is part of this category, its value will be listed in the ITE as a property that can be translated into another language. (A complete discussion of the ITE is beyond the scope of this book.)

FIGURE 11.9:

The Arrow component
defines a custom property
category, *Arrow*, as you
can see in the Object
Inspector.

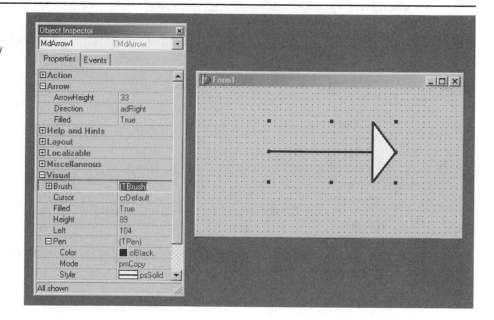

FIGURE 11.9:

The Arrow component
defines a custom property
category, *Arrow*, as you
can see in the Object
Inspector.

Customizing Windows Controls

One of the most common ways of customizing existing components is to add some predefined behavior to their event handlers. Every time you need to attach the same event handler
to components of different forms, you should consider adding the code of the event right
into a subclass of the component. An obvious example is that of edit boxes accepting only
numeric input. Instead of attaching to each of them a common OnChar event handler, we can
define a simple new component. This component, however, won't handle the event; events
are for component users only. Instead, the component can either handle the Windows message directly or override a method, as described in the next two sections.

Overriding Message Handlers: The Numeric Edit Box

To customize an edit box component to restrict the input it will accept, all you need to do is
handle the wm_Char Windows messages that occur when the user presses any but a few specific keys (namely, the numeric characters).

One way to respond to a message for a given window (whether it's a form or a component) is
to create a new *message-response* method that you declare using the message keyword. Delphi's
message-handling system makes sure that your message-response method has a chance to

respond to a given message before the form or component's default message handler does. You'll see in the next section that, instead of creating a new method (as we do here), you can override an existing virtual method that responds to a given message. Below is the code of the TMdNumEdit class:

```
type
  TMdNumEdit = class (TCustomEdit)
  private
    fInputError: TNotifyEvent;
  protected
    function GetValue: Integer;
    procedure SetValue (Value: Integer);
  public
    procedure WmChar (var Msg: TWmChar); message wm_Char;
    constructor Create (Owner: TComponent); override;
  published
    property OnInputError: TNotifyEvent read fInputError write fInputError;
    property Value: Integer read GetValue write SetValue default 0;
    property AutoSelect;
    property AutoSize;
    property BorderStyle;
    // and so on...
```

This component inherits from TCustomEdit instead of TEdit so that it can hide the Text property and surface the Integer Value property instead. Notice that I don't create a new field to store this value, because we can use the existing (but now unpublished) Text property. To do this, we'll simply convert the numeric value to and from a text string. The TCustomEdit class (or actually the Windows control it wraps) automatically paints the information from the Text property on the surface of the component:

```
function TMdNumEdit.GetValue: Integer;
begin
  // set to 0 in case of error
  Result := StrToIntDef (Text, 0);
end;

procedure TMdNumEdit.SetValue (Value: Integer);
begin
  Text := IntToStr (Value);
end;
```

The most important method is the response for the wm_Char message. In the body of this method, the component filters out all the nonnumeric characters and raises a specific event in case of an error:

```
procedure TMdNumEdit.WmChar (var Msg: TWmChar);
begin
```

```
    if not (Char (Msg.CharCode) in ['0'..'9']) and not (Msg.CharCode = 8) then
    begin
      if Assigned (fInputError) then
        fInputError (Self);
    end
    else
      inherited;
  end;
```

This method checks each character as the user enters it, testing for numerals and the Backspace key (which has an ASCII value of 8). The user should be able to use Backspace in addition to the system keys (the arrow keys and Del), so we need to check for that value. We don't have to check for the system keys, because they are surfaced by a different Windows message, wm_SysChar.

That's it. Now if you place this component on a form, you can type something in the edit box and see how it behaves. You might also want to attach a method to the OnInputError event to provide feedback to the user when a wrong key is typed.

A Numeric Edit with Thousands Separators

As a further extension to the example, when typing large numbers it would be nice for the thousands separators to automatically appear and update themselves as required by the user input. You can do this by overriding the internal Change method and formatting the number properly. There are only a couple of small problems to consider. The first is that to format the number you need to have one, but the text of the edit with the thousands separators (possibly misplaced) cannot be converted to a number directly. I've written a modified version of the StringToFloat function, called StringToFloatSkipping, to accomplish this.

The second small problem is that if you modify the text of the edit box the current position of the cursor will get lost. So you need to save the original cursor position, reformat the number, and then reapply the cursor position considering that if a separator has been added or removed, it should change accordingly. All these considerations are summarized by the following complete code of the TMdThousandEdit class:

```
type
  TMdThousandEdit = class (TMdNumEdit)
  public
    procedure Change; override;
  end;

function StringToFloatSkipping (s: string): Extended;
var
  s1: string;
  I: Integer;
```

```
begin
  // remove non-numbers, but keep the decimal separator
  s1 := '';
  for i := 1 to length (s) do
   if s[i] in ['0'..'9'] then
      s1 := s1 + s[i];
  Result := StrToFloat (s1);
end;

procedure TMdThousandEdit.Change;
var
  CursorPos, // original position of the cursor
  LengthDiff: Integer; // number of new separators (+ or -)
begin
  if Assigned (Parent) then
  begin
    CursorPos := SelStart;
    LengthDiff := Length (Text);
    Text := FormatFloat ('#,###',
      StringToFloatSkipping (Text));
    LengthDiff := Length (Text) - LengthDiff;
    // move the cursor to the proper position
    SelStart := CursorPos + LengthDiff;
  end;
  inherited;
end;
```

Overriding Dynamic Methods: The Sound Button

Our next component, TMdSoundButton, plays one sound when you press the button and
another sound when you release it. The user specifies each sound by modifying two String
properties that name the appropriate WAV files for the respective sounds. Once again, we
need to intercept and modify some system messages (wm_LButtonDown and wm_LButtonUp),
but instead of handling the messages by writing a new message-response method, we'll override the appropriate *second-level* handlers.

NOTE   When most VCL components handle a Windows message, they call a *second-level* message
handler (usually a dynamic method), instead of executing code directly in the message-
response method. This makes it simpler for you to customize the component in a derived class.
Typically, a second-level handler will do its own work and then call any event handler that the
component user has assigned.

Here is the code of the TMdSoundButton class, with the two protected methods that override the second-level handlers, and the two string properties that identify the sound files.

You'll notice that in the property declarations, we read and write the corresponding private fields without calling a get or set method, simply because we don't need to do anything special when the user makes changes to those properties.

```
type
  TMdSoundButton = class(TButton)
  private
    FSoundUp, FSoundDown: string;
  protected
    procedure MouseDown(Button: TMouseButton;
      Shift: TShiftState; X, Y: Integer); override;
    procedure MouseUp(Button: TMouseButton;
      Shift: TShiftState; X, Y: Integer); override;
  published
    property SoundUp: string read FSoundUp write FSoundUp;
    property SoundDown: string read FSoundDown write FSoundDown;
  end;
```

There are several reasons why overriding existing second-level handlers is generally a better approach than handling straight Windows messages. First, this technique is more sound from an object-oriented perspective. Instead of duplicating the message-response code from the base class and then customizing it, you're overriding a virtual method call that the VCL designers planned for you to override. Second, if someone needs to derive another class from one of your component classes, you'll want to make it as easy for them to customize as possible, and overriding second-level handlers is less likely to induce strange errors (if only because you're writing less code). Finally, this will make your component classes more consistent with VCL—and therefore easier for someone else to figure out. Here is the code of the two second-level handlers:

```
uses
  MMSystem;

procedure TMdSoundButton.MouseDown(Button: TMouseButton; Shift: TShiftState;
  X, Y: Integer);
begin
  inherited MouseDown (Button, Shift, X, Y);
  PlaySound (PChar (FSoundDown), 0, snd_Async);
end;

procedure TMdSoundButton.MouseUp(Button: TMouseButton; Shift: TShiftState;
  X, Y: Integer);
begin
  inherited MouseUp (Button, Shift, X, Y);
  PlaySound (PChar (FSoundUp), 0, snd_Async);
end;
```

In both cases, you'll notice that we call the inherited version of the methods *before* we do anything else. For most second-level handlers, this is a good practice, since it ensures that we execute the standard behavior before we execute any custom behavior.

Next, you'll notice that we call the PlaySound Win32 API function to play the sound. You can use this function (which is defined in the MmSystem unit to play either WAV files or system sounds, as the SoundB example demonstrates. Here is a textual description of the form of this sample program (from the DFM file):

```
object MdSoundButton1: TMdSoundButton
  Caption = 'Press'
  SoundUp = 'RestoreUp'
  SoundDown = 'RestoreDown'
end
```

NOTE   Selecting a proper value for these sound properties is far from simple. Later in this chapter, I'll show you how to add a property editor to the component to simplify the operation.

Handling Internal Messages: The Active Button

The Windows interface is evolving toward a new standard, including components that become highlighted as the mouse cursor moves over them. Delphi provides similar support in many of its built-in components, but what does it take to mimic this behavior for a simple button? This might seem a complex task to accomplish, but it is not.

The development of a component can become much simpler once you know which virtual function to override or which message to hook onto. The next component, the TMdActiveButton class, demonstrates this by handling some internal Delphi messages to accomplish its task in a very simple way. (For information about where these internal Delphi messages come from, see the sidebar "Component Messages and Notifications.")

The ActiveButton component handles the cm_MouseEnter and cm_MouseExit internal Delphi messages, which are received when the mouse cursor enters or leaves the area corresponding to the component:

```
type
  TMdActiveButton = class (TButton)
  protected
    procedure MouseEnter (var Msg: TMessage);
      message cm_mouseEnter;
    procedure MouseLeave (var Msg: TMessage);
      message cm_mouseLeave;
  end;
```

The code you write for these two methods can do whatever you want. For this example, I've decided to simply toggle the bold style of the font of the button itself. You can see the effect of moving the mouse over one of these components in Figure 11.10.

```
procedure TMdActiveButton.MouseEnter (var Msg: TMessage);
begin
  Font.Style := Font.Style + [fsBold];
end;

procedure TMdActiveButton.MouseLeave (var Msg: TMessage);
begin
  Font.Style := Font.Style - [fsBold];
end;
```

FIGURE 11.10:

An example of the use of the ActiveButton component

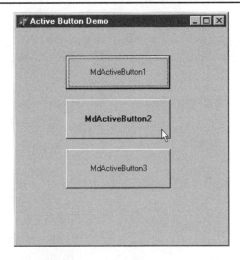

You can add other effects at will, including enlarging the font itself, making the button the default, or increasing its size a little. The best effects usually involve colors, but you should inherit from the TBitBtn class to have this support (TButton controls have a fixed color).

Component Messages and Notifications

To build the ActiveButton component, I've used two internal Delphi component messages, as indicated by their *cm* prefix. These messages can be quite interesting, as the example highlights, but they are almost completely undocumented by Borland. There is also a second group of internal Delphi messages, indicated as component notifications and distinguished by their *cn* prefix. I don't have enough space here to discuss each of them or provide a detailed analysis; browse the VCL source code if you want to learn more.

WARNING   As this is a rather advanced topic, feel free to skip this section if you are new to writing Delphi components. But component messages are not documented in the Delphi help file, so I felt it was important to at least *list* them here.

Component Messages

A Delphi component passes *component messages* to other components to indicate any change in its state that might affect those components. Most of these messages start as Windows messages, but some of them are more complex, higher-level translations and not simple remappings. Also, components send their own messages as well as forwarding those received from Windows. For example, changing a property value or some other characteristic of the component may necessitate telling one or more other components about the change.

We can group these messages into categories:

- Activation and input focus messages are sent to the component being activated or deactivated, receiving or losing the input focus:

cm_Activate	Corresponds to the OnActivate event of forms and of the application
cm_Deactivate	Corresponds to OnDeactivate
cm_Enter	Corresponds to OnEnter
cm_Exit	Corresponds to OnExit
cm_FocusChanged	Sent whenever the focus changes between components of the same form (later, we'll see an example using this message)
cm_GotFocus	Declared but not used
cm_LostFocus	Declared but not used

- Messages sent to child components when a property changes:

cm_BiDiModeChanged	cm_IconChanged
cm_BorderChanged	cm_ShowHintChanged
cm_ColorChanged	cm_ShowingChanged
cm_Ctl3DChanged	cm_SysFontChanged
cm_CursorChanged	cm_TabStopChanged
cm_EnabledChanged	cm_TextChanged
cm_FontChanged	cm_VisibleChanged

Monitoring these messages can help track changes in a property. You might need to respond to these messages in a new component, but it's not likely.

- Messages related to *ParentXxx* properties: cm_ParentFontChanged, cm_ParentColor-Changed, cm_ParentCtl3DChanged, cm_ParentBiDiModeChanged, and cm_Parent-ShowHintChanged. These are very similar to the messages of the previous group.

- Notifications of changes in the Windows system: cm_SysColorChange, cm_WinIniChange, cm_TimeChange, and cm_FontChange. Handling these messages is useful only in special components that need to keep track of system colors or fonts.

- Mouse messages: cm_Drag is sent many times during dragging operations. cm_MouseEnter and cm_MouseLeave are sent to the control when the cursor enters or leaves its surface, but these are sent by the Application object as low-priority messages. cm_MouseWheel corresponds to wheel-based operations.

  cm_Drag has a DragMessage parameter that indicates a sort of submessage, and the address of the TDragRec record that indicates the mouse position and the components involved in the dragging operation. The cm_Drag message isn't that important, because Delphi defines many drag events and drag methods you can override. However, you can respond to cm_Drag for a few things that don't generate an event or method call. This message is sent to find the target component (when the DragMessage field is dmFindTarget); to indicate that the cursor has reached a component (the dmDragEnter submessage), is being moved over it (dmDragMove), or has left it (dmDragLeave); when the drop operation is accepted (dmDragDrop); and when it is aborted (dmDragCancel).

- Application messages:

cm_AppKeyDown	Sent to the Application object to let it determine whether a key corresponds to a menu shortcut
cm_AppSysCommand	Corresponds to the wm_SysCommand message
cm_DialogHandle	Sent in a DLL to retrieve the value of the DialogHandle property (used by some dialog boxes not built with Delphi)
cm_InvokeHelp	Sent by code in a DLL to call the InvokeHelp method
cm_WindowHook	Sent in a DLL to call the HookMainWindow and UnhookMainWindow methods

You'll rarely need to use these messages yourself. There is also a cm_HintShowPause message, which is apparently never handled in VCL.

- Delphi internal messages:

`cm_CancelMode`	Terminates special operations, such as showing the pull-down list of a combo box
`cm_ControlChange`	Sent to each control before adding or removing a child control (handled by some common controls)
`cm_ControlListChange`	Sent to each control before adding or removing a child control (handled by the DBCtrlGrid component)
`cm_DesignHitTest`	Determines whether a mouse operation should go to the component or to the form designer
`cm_HintShow`	Sent to a control just before displaying its hint (only if the ShowHint property is True)
`cm_HitTest`	Sent to a control when a parent control is trying to locate a child control at a given mouse position (if any)
`cm_MenuChanged`	Sent after MDI or OLE menu-merging operations

- Messages related to special keys:

`cm_ChildKey`	Sent to the parent control to handle some special keys (in Delphi, this message is handled only by DBCtrlGrid components)
`cm_DialogChar`	Sent to a control to determine whether a given input key is its accelerator character
`cm_DialogKey`	Handled by modal forms and controls that need to perform special actions
`cm_IsShortCut`	I haven't yet figured out the exact role of this new message.
`cm_WantSpecialKey`	Handled by controls that interpret special keys in an unusual way (for example, using the Tab key for navigation, as some Grid components do)

- Messages for specific components:

cm_GetDataLink	Used by DBCtrlGrid controls (and discussed in Chapter 18)
cm_TabFontChanged	Used by the TabbedNotebook components
cm_ButtonPressed	Used by SpeedButtons to notify other sibling Speed-Button components (to enforce radio-button behavior)
cm_DeferLayout	Used by DBGrid components

- OLE container messages: cm_DocWindowActivate, cm_IsToolControl, cm_Release, cm_UIActivate, and cm_UIDeactivate.

- Dock-related messages, including cm_DockClient, cm_DockNotification, cmFloat, and cm_UndockClient.

- Method-implementation messages, such as cm_RecreateWnd, called inside the RecreateWnd method of TControl; cm_Invalidate, called inside TControl.Invalidate; cm_Changed, called inside TControl.Changed; and cm_AllChildrenFlipped, called in the DoFlipChildren methods of TWinControl and TScrollingWinControl. In the similar group fall two action list–related messages, cm_ActionUpdate and cm_ActionExecute.

Finally, there are messages defined and handled by specific components and declared in the respective units, such as cm_DeferLayout for DBGrid controls and a group of almost 10 messages for action bar components.

Component Notifications

Component notification messages are those sent from a parent form or component to its children. These notifications correspond to messages sent by Windows to the parent control's window, but logically intended for the control. For example, interaction with controls such as buttons, edit, or list boxes, causes Windows to send a wm_Command message to the parent of the control. When a Delphi program receives these messages, it forwards the message to the control itself, as a notification. The Delphi control can handle the message and eventually fire an event. Similar dispatching operations take place for many other commands.

The connection between Windows messages and component notification ones is so tight that you'll often recognize the name of the Windows message from the name of the notification message, simply replacing the initial *cn* with *wm*. There are several distinct groups of component notification messages:

- General keyboard messages: cn_Char, cn_KeyUp, cn_KeyDown, cn_SysChar, and cn_SysKeyDown.

- Special keyboard messages used only by list boxes with the `lbs_WantKeyboardInput` style: `cn_CharToItem` and `cn_VKeyToItem`.

- Messages related to the owner-draw technique: `cn_CompareItem`, `cn_DeleteItem`, `cn_DrawItem`, and `cn_MeasureItem`.

- Messages for scrolling, used only by scroll bar and track bar controls: `cn_HScroll` and `cn_VScroll`.

- General notification messages, used by most controls: `cn_Command`, `cn_Notify`, and `cn_ParentNotify`.

- Control color messages: `cn_CtlColorBtn`, `cn_CtlColorDlg`, `cn_CtlColorEdit`, `cn_Ctl-ColorListbox`, `cn_CtlColorMsgbox`, `cn_CtlColorScrollbar`, and `cn_CtlColorStatic`.

Some more control notifications are defined for common controls support (in the ComCtrls unit).

An Example of Component Messages

As a very simple example of the use of some component messages, I've written the CMNTest program. This program has a form with three edit boxes, and associated labels. The first message it handles, `cm_DialogKey`, allows it to treat the Enter key as if it were a Tab key. The code of this method for the Enter key's code and sends the same message, but passes the `vk_Tab` key code. To halt further processing of the Enter key, we set the result of the message to 1:

```
procedure TForm1.CMDialogKey(var Message: TCMDialogKey);
begin
  if (Message.CharCode = VK_RETURN) then
  begin
    Perform (CM_DialogKey, VK_TAB, 0);
    Message.Result := 1;
  end
  else
    inherited;
end;
```

The second message, `cm_DialogChar`, monitors accelerator keys. This can be useful to provide custom shortcuts without defining an extra menu for them. In this case, I'm simply logging the special keys in a label:

```
procedure TForm1.CMDialogChar(var Msg: TCMDialogChar);
begin
  Label1.Caption := Label1.Caption + Char (Msg.CharCode);
  inherited;
end;
```

Finally, the form handles the `cm_FocusChanged` message, to respond to focus changes without having to handle the `OnEnter` event of each of its components. Again, the simple action is to display a description of the focused component:

```
procedure TForm1.CmFocusChanged(var Msg: TCmFocusChanged);
begin
  Label5.Caption := 'Focus on ' + Msg.Sender.Name;
end;
```

The advantage of this approach is that it works independently of the type and number of components you add to the form, and it does so without any special action on your part. Again, this is a trivial example for such an advanced topic, but if you add to this the code of the ActiveButton component, you have at least a few reasons to look into these special, undocumented messages. At times, writing the same code without their support can become extremely complex.

A Nonvisual Dialog Component

The next component we'll examine is completely different from the ones we have seen up to now. After building window-based controls and simple graphic components, I'm now going to build a nonvisual component.

The basic idea is that forms are components. When you have built a form that might be particularly useful in multiple projects, you can add it to the Object Repository or make a component out of it. The second approach is more complex than the first, but it makes using the new form easier and allows you to distribute the form without its source code. As an example, I'll build a component based on a custom dialog box, trying to mimic as much as possible the behavior of standard Delphi dialog box components.

The first step in building a dialog box in a component is to write the code of the dialog box itself, using the standard Delphi approach. Just define a new form and work on it as usual. When a component is based on a form, you can almost visually design the component. Of course, once the dialog box has been built, you have to define a component around it in a nonvisual way.

The standard dialog box I want to build is based on a list box, because it is common to let a user choose a value from a list of strings. I've customized this common behavior in a dialog box and then used it to build a component. The simple `ListBoxForm` form I've built has a list box and the typical OK and Cancel buttons, as shown in its textual description:

```
object MdListBoxForm: TMdListBoxForm
  BorderStyle = bsDialog
  Caption = 'ListBoxForm'
  object ListBox1: TListBox
```

```
      OnDblClick = ListBox1DblClick
    end
    object BitBtn1: TBitBtn
      Kind = bkOK
    end
    object BitBtn2: TBitBtn
      Kind = bkCancel
    end
  end
```

The only method of this dialog box form relates to the double-click event of the list box, which closes the dialog box as though the user clicked the OK button, by setting the ModalResult property of the form to mrOk. Once the form works, we can start changing its source code, adding the definition of a component and removing the declaration of the global variable for the form.

NOTE   For components based on a form, you can use two Pascal source code files: one for the form and the other for the component encapsulating it. It is also possible to place both the component and the form in a single unit, as I've done for this example. In theory it would be even nicer to declare the form class in the implementation portion of this unit, hiding it from the users of the component. In practice this is not a good idea. To manipulate the form visually in the Form Designer, the form class declaration must appear in the interface section of the unit. The rationale behind this behavior of the Delphi IDE is that, among other things, this constraint minimizes the amount of code the module manager has to scan to find the form declaration—an operation that must be performed often to maintain the synchronization of the visual form with the form class definition.

The most important of these operations is the definition of the TMdListBoxDialog component. This component is defined as "nonvisual" because its immediate ancestor class is TComponent. The component has one public property and these three published properties:

- Lines is a TStrings object, which is accessed via two methods, GetLines and SetLines. This second method uses the Assign procedure to copy the new values to the private field corresponding to this property. This internal object is initialized in the Create constructor and destroyed in the Destroy method.

- Selected is an integer that directly accesses the corresponding private field. It stores the selected element of the list of strings.

- Title is a string used to change the title of the dialog box.

The public property is SelItem, a read-only property that automatically retrieves the selected element of the list of strings. Notice that this property has no storage and no data: it simply accesses other properties, providing a virtual representation of data:

```
type
  TMdListBoxDialog = class (TComponent)
```

```
private
  FLines: TStrings;
  FSelected: Integer;
  FTitle: string;
  function GetSelItem: string;
  procedure SetLines (Value: TStrings);
  function GetLines: TStrings;
public
  constructor Create(AOwner: TComponent); override;
  destructor Destroy; override;
  function Execute: Boolean;
  property SelItem: string read GetSelItem;
published
  property Lines: TStrings read GetLines write SetLines;
  property Selected: Integer read FSelected write FSelected;
  property Title: string read FTitle write FTitle;
end;
```

Most of the code of this example is in the Execute method, a function that returns True or False depending on the modal result of the dialog box. This is consistent with the Execute method of most standard Delphi dialog box components. The Execute function creates the form dynamically, sets some of its values using the component's properties, shows the dialog box, and if the result is correct, updates the current selection:

```
function TMdListBoxDialog.Execute: Boolean;
var
  ListBoxForm: TListBoxForm;
begin
  if FLines.Count = 0 then
    raise EStringListError.Create ('No items in the list');
  ListBoxForm := TListBoxForm.Create (Self);
  try
    ListBoxForm.ListBox1.Items := FLines;
    ListBoxForm.ListBox1.ItemIndex := FSelected;
    ListBoxForm.Caption := FTitle;
    if ListBoxForm.ShowModal = mrOk then
    begin
      Result := True;
      Selected := ListBoxForm.ListBox1.ItemIndex;
    end
    else
      Result := False;
  finally
    ListBoxForm.Free;
  end;
end;
```

Notice that the code is contained within a try/finally block, so if a run-time error occurs when the dialog box is displayed, the form will be destroyed anyway. I've also used exceptions to raise an error if the list is empty when a user runs it. This error is by design, and using an exception is a good technique to enforce it. The other methods of the component are quite straightforward. The constructor creates the FLines string list, which is deleted by the destructor; the GetLines and SetLines methods operate on the string list as a whole; and the GetSelItem function (listed below) returns the text of the selected item:

```
function TMdListBoxDialog.GetSelItem: string;
begin
  if (Selected >= 0) and (Selected < FLines.Count) then
    Result := FLines [Selected]
  else
    Result := '';
end;
```

Of course, since we are manually writing the code of the component and adding it to the source code of the original form, we have to remember to write the Register procedure.

Using the Nonvisual Component

Once you've done that and the component is ready, you must provide a bitmap. For nonvisual components, bitmaps are very important because they are used not only for the Component Palette, but also when you place the component on a form. After preparing the bitmap and installing the component, I've written a simple project to test it. The form of this test program has a button, an edit box, and the MdListDialog component. In the program, I've added only a few lines of code, corresponding to the OnClick event of the button:

```
procedure TForm1.Button1Click(Sender: TObject);
begin
  // select the text of the edit, if corresponding to one of the strings
  MdListDialog1.Selected := MdListDialog1.Lines.IndexOf (Edit1.Text);
  // run the dialog and get the result
  if MdListDialog1.Execute then
    Edit1.Text := MdListDialog1.SelItem;
end;
```

That's all you need to run the dialog box we have placed in the component, as you can see in Figure 11.11. As you've seen, this is an interesting approach to the development of some common dialog boxes.

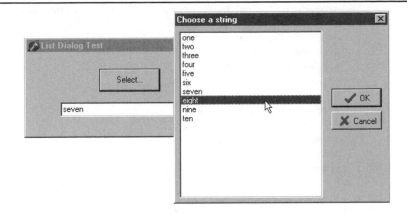

FIGURE 11.11:

The ListDialDemo example
shows the dialog box I've
encapsulated in the ListDial
component.

Defining Custom Actions

Besides defining custom components, you can define and register new standard actions, which will be made available in the Action Editor of the Action List component. Creating new actions is not complex. You have to inherit from the TAction class and override some of the methods of the base class.

There are basically three methods to override. The HandlesTarget function returns whether the action object wants to handle the operation for the current target, which is by default the control with the focus. The UpdateTarget procedure can set the user interface of the controls connected with the action, eventually disabling the action if the operation is currently not available. Finally, you can implement the ExecuteTarget method to determine the actual code to execute, so that the user can simply select the action and doesn't have to implement it.

To show you this approach in practice, I've implemented the three cut, copy, and paste actions for a list box, in a way similar to what VCL does for an edit box (although I've actually simplified the code a little). I've written a base class, which inherits from the generic TListControlAction class of the new ExtActns unit. This base class, TMdCustomListAction, adds some common code, shared by all the specific actions, and publishes a few action properties. The three derived classes have their own ExecuteTarget code, plus little more. Here are the four classes:

```
type
  TMdCustomListAction = class (TListControlAction)
  protected
    function TargetList (Target: TObject): TCustomListBox;
    function GetControl (Target: TObject): TCustomListControl;
  public
```

```
    procedure UpdateTarget (Target: TObject); override;
published
  property Caption;
  property Enabled;
  property HelpContext;
  property Hint;
  property ImageIndex;
  property ListControl;
  property ShortCut;
  property SecondaryShortCuts;
  property Visible;
  property OnHint;
end;

TMdListCutAction = class (TMdCustomListAction)
public
  procedure ExecuteTarget(Target: TObject); override;
end;

TMdListCopyAction = class (TMdCustomListAction)
public
  procedure ExecuteTarget(Target: TObject); override;
end;

TMdListPasteAction = class (TMdCustomListAction)
public
  procedure UpdateTarget (Target: TObject); override;
  procedure ExecuteTarget (Target: TObject); override;
end;
```

The HandlesTarget method, one of the three key methods of actions, is provided by the TListControlAction class, with this code:

```
function TListControlAction.HandlesTarget(Target: TObject): Boolean;
begin
  Result := ((ListControl <> nil) or
    (ListControl = nil) and (Target is TCustomListControl)) and
    TCustomListControl(Target).Focused;
end;
```

The UpdateTarget method, instead, has two different implementations. The default one is provided by the base class and used by the copy and cut actions. These actions are enabled only if the target list box has at least one item and an item is currently selected. The status of the paste action depends instead on the Clipboard status:

```
procedure TMdCustomListAction.UpdateTarget (Target: TObject);
begin
  Enabled := (TargetList (Target).Items.Count > 0)
```

```
      and (TargetList (Target).ItemIndex >= 0);
end;

function TMdCustomListAction.TargetList (Target: TObject): TCustomListBox;
begin
  Result := GetControl (Target) as TCustomListBox;
end;

function TMdCustomListAction.GetControl(Target: TObject): TCustomListControl;
begin
  Result := Target as TCustomListControl;
end;

procedure TMdListPasteAction.UpdateTarget (Target: TObject);
begin
  Enabled := Clipboard.HasFormat (CF_TEXT);
end;
```

The TargetList function uses the GetControl function of the TListControlAction class, which returns either the list box connected to the action at design time or the target control, the list box control with the input focus.

Finally, the three ExecuteTarget methods simply perform the corresponding actions on the target list box:

```
procedure TMdListCopyAction.ExecuteTarget (Target: TObject);
begin
  with TargetList (Target) do
    Clipboard.AsText := Items [ItemIndex];
end;

procedure TMdListCutAction.ExecuteTarget(Target: TObject);
begin
  with TargetList (Target) do
  begin
    Clipboard.AsText := Items [ItemIndex];
    Items.Delete (ItemIndex);
  end;
end;

procedure TMdListPasteAction.ExecuteTarget(Target: TObject);
begin
  (TargetList (Target)).Items.Add (Clipboard.AsText);
end;
```

Once you've written this code in a unit and added it to a package (in this case, the MdPack package), the final step is to register the new custom actions in a given category. This is indicated as the first parameter of the `RegisterActions` procedure, while the second is the list of action classes to register:

```
procedure Register;
begin
  RegisterActions ('List',
    [TMdListCutAction, TMdListCopyAction, TMdListPasteAction], nil);
end;
```

To test the use of these three custom actions, I've written the ListTest example on the companion CD. This program has two list boxes plus a toolbar that contains three buttons connected with the three custom actions and an edit box for entering new values. The program allows a user to cut, copy, and paste list box items. Nothing special, you might think, but the strange fact is that the program has absolutely no code!

Writing Property Editors

Writing components is certainly an effective way to customize Delphi, helping developers to build applications faster without requiring a detailed knowledge of low-level techniques. The Delphi environment is also quite open to extensions. In particular, you can extend the Object Inspector by writing custom property editors and to extend the Form Designer by adding component editors.

NOTE   Along with these techniques, Delphi offers some internal interfaces to add-on tool developers. Using these interfaces, known as OpenTools API, requires an advanced understanding of how the Delphi environment works and a fairly good knowledge of many advanced techniques that are not discussed in this book. You can find technical information and some examples of these techniques on my Web site, `www.marcocantu.com`, along with links to other sites where these techniques are presented.

Every property editor must be a subclass of the abstract `TPropertyEditor` class, which is defined in the DesignEditors unit of the ToolsApi and provides a standard implementation for the `IProperty` interface.

NOTE   The Tools API in Delphi 6 has changed considerably, also for consistency with Kylix. For example, the DsgnIntf unit of Delphi 5 has been split into the units DesignIntf, DesignEditors, and other specific units. Borland has also introduced interfaces to define the sets of methods of each kind of editor. However, most of the simpler examples, such as those presented in this book, compile almost unchanged. As this is not an in-depth analysis of the Tools API, I'm not providing a list of changes from Delphi 5 to Delphi 6, although they are substantial. For more information, you can study the extensive source code in the `\Source\ToolsApi` directory of Delphi 6.

Delphi already defines some specific property editors for strings (the `TStringProperty` class), integers (the `TIntegerProperty` class), characters (the `TCharProperty` class), enumerations (the `TEnumProperty` class), sets (the `TSetProperty` class), so you can actually inherit your property editor from the one of the type of property you are working with.

In any custom property editor, you have to redefine the `GetAttributes` function so it returns a set of values indicating the capabilities of the editor. The most important attributes are paValueList and paDialog. The paValueList attribute indicates that the Object Inspector will show a combo box with a list of values (eventually sorted if the paSortList attribute is set) provided by overriding the `GetValues` method. The paDialog attribute style activates an ellipsis button in the Object Inspector, which executes the `Edit` method of the editor.

An Editor for the Sound Properties

The sound button we built earlier had two sound-related properties: `SoundUp` and `SoundDown`. These were actually strings, so we were able to display them in the Object Inspector using a default property editor. However, requiring the user to type the name of a system sound or an external file is not very friendly, and it's a bit error-prone.

When you need to select a file for a string property, you can reuse an existing property editor, the `TMPFilenameProperty` class. All you have to do is register this editor for the property using the special `RegisterPropertyEditor` procedure, as in:

```
RegisterPropertyEditor (TypeInfo (string), TDdhSoundButton, 'SoundUp',
  TMPFileNameProperty);
```

This editor allows you to select a file for the sound, but we want to be able to choose the name of a system sound as well. (As described earlier, system sounds are predefined names of sounds connected with user operations, associated with actual sound files in the Sounds applet of the Windows Control Panel.) For this reason, instead of using this simple approach I'll build a more complex property editor. My editor for sound strings allows a user to either choose a value from a drop-down list or display a dialog box from which to load and test a sound (from a sound file or a system sound). For this reason, the property editor provides both `Edit` and `GetValues` methods:

```
type
  TSoundProperty = class (TStringProperty)
  public
    function GetAttributes: TPropertyAttributes; override;
    procedure GetValues(Proc: TGetStrProc); override;
    procedure Edit; override;
  end;
```

TIP   The default Delphi convention is to name a property editor class with a name ending with *Property* and all component editors with a name ending with *Editor*.

The GetAttributes function combines both the paValueList (for the drop-down list) and the paDialog attributes (for the custom edit box), and also sorts the lists and allows the selection of the property for multiple components:

```
function TSoundProperty.GetAttributes: TPropertyAttributes;
begin
  // editor, sorted list, multiple selection
  Result := [paDialog, paMultiSelect, paValueList, paSortList];
end;
```

The GetValues method simply calls the procedure it receives as parameter many times, once for each string it wants to add to the drop-down list (as you can see in Figure 11.12):

```
procedure TSoundProperty.GetValues(Proc: TGetStrProc);
begin
  // provide a list of system sounds
  Proc ('Maximize');
  Proc ('Minimize');
  Proc ('MenuCommand');
  Proc ('MenuPopup');
  Proc ('RestoreDown');
  Proc ('RestoreUp');
  Proc ('SystemAsterisk');
  Proc ('SystemDefault');
  Proc ('SystemExclamation');
  Proc ('SystemExit');
  Proc ('SystemHand');
  Proc ('SystemQuestion');
  Proc ('SystemStart');
  Proc ('AppGPFault');
end;
```

FIGURE 11.12:

The list of sounds provides a hint for the user, who can also type in the property value or double-click to activate the editor (shown later, in Figure 11.13).

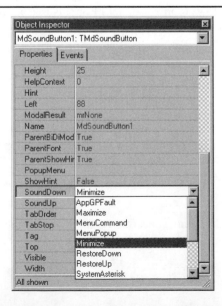

A better approach would be to extract these values from the Windows Registry, where all these names are listed. The `Edit` method is very straightforward, as it simply creates and displays a dialog box. You'll notice that we could have just displayed the Open dialog box directly, but we decided to add an intermediate step to allow the user to test the sound. This is similar to what Delphi does with graphic properties. You open the preview first, and load the file only after you've confirmed that it's correct. The most important step is to load the file and test it before you apply it to the property. Here is the code of the `Edit` method:

```
procedure TSoundProperty.Edit;
begin
  SoundForm := TSoundForm.Create (Application);
  try
    SoundForm.ComboBox1.Text := GetValue;
    // show the dialog box
    if SoundForm.ShowModal = mrOK then
      SetValue (SoundForm.ComboBox1.Text);
  finally
    SoundForm.Free;
  end;
end;
```

The `GetValue` and `SetValue` methods called above are defined by the base class, the string property editor. They simply read and write the value of the current component's property that we are editing. As an alternative, you can access the component you're editing by using the `GetComponent` method (which requires a parameter indicating which of the selected components you are working on—0 indicates the first component). When you access the component directly, you also need to call the `Modified` method of the `Designer` object (a property of the base class property editor). We don't need this `Modified` call in the example, as the base class `SetValue` method does this automatically for us.

The `Edit` method above displays a dialog box, a standard Delphi form that is built visually, as always, and added to the package hosting the design-time components. The form is quite simple; a ComboBox displays the values returned by the `GetValues` method, and four buttons allow you to open a file, test the sound, and terminate the dialog box by accepting the values or canceling. You can see an example of the dialog box in Figure 11.13. Providing a drop-down list of values *and* a dialog box for editing a property causes the Object Inspector to display only the arrow button that indicates a drop-down list and to omit the ellipsis button to indicate that a dialog box editor is available.

FIGURE 11.13:

The Sound Property Editor's form displays a list of available sounds and lets you load a file and hear the selected sound.

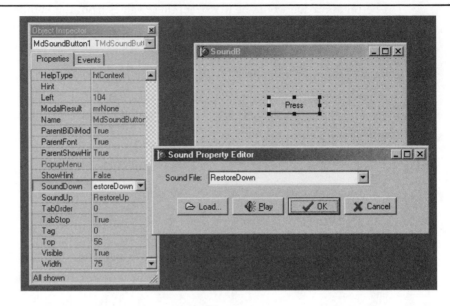

The first two buttons of the form each have a simple method assigned to their OnClick event:

```
procedure TSoundForm.btnLoadClick(Sender: TObject);
begin
  if OpenDialog1.Execute then
    ComboBox1.Text := OpenDialog1.FileName;
end;

procedure TSoundForm.btnPlayClick(Sender: TObject);
begin
  PlaySound (PChar (ComboBox1.Text), 0, snd_Async);
end;
```

Unfortunately, I haven't found a simple way to determine whether a sound is properly defined and is available. (Checking the file is possible, but the system sounds create a few issues.) The PlaySound function returns an error code when played synchronously, but only if it can't find the default system sound it attempts to play if it can't find the sound you asked for. If the requested sound is not available, it plays the default system sound and doesn't return the error code. PlaySound looks for the sound in the Registry first and, if it doesn't find the sound there, checks to see whether the specified sound file exists.

TIP   If you want to further extend this example, you might add graphics to the drop-down list displayed in the Object Inspector—if you can decide which graphics to attach to particular sounds.

Installing the Property Editor

After you've written this code, you can install the component and its property editor in Delphi. To accomplish this, you have to add the following statement to the Register procedure of the unit:

```
procedure Register;
begin
  RegisterPropertyEditor (TypeInfo(string), TMdSoundButton, 'SoundUp',
    TSoundProperty);
  RegisterPropertyEditor (TypeInfo(string), TMdSoundButton, 'SoundDown',
    TSoundProperty);
end;
```

This call registers the editor specified in the last parameter for use with properties of type string (the first parameter), but only for a specific component and for a property with a specific name. These last two values can be omitted to provide more general editors. Registering this editor allows the Object Inspector to show a list of values and the dialog box called by the Edit method.

To install this component we can simply add its source code file into an existing or new package. Instead of adding this unit and the others of this chapter to the MdPack package, I built a second package, containing all the add-ins built in this chapter. The package is named MdDesPk (which stands for "*Mastering Delphi* design package"). What's new about this package is that I've compiled it using the {$DESIGNONLY} compiler directive. This directive is used to mark packages that interact with the Delphi environment, installing components and editors, but are not required at run time by applications you've built.

> **NOTE**   The source code of all of the add-on tools is in the **MdDesPk** subdirectory, along with the code of the package used to install them. There are no examples demonstrating how to use these design-time tools, because all you have to do is select the corresponding components in the Delphi environment and see how they behave.

The property editor's unit uses the SoundB unit, which defines the TMdSoundButton component. For this reason the new package should refer to the existing package. Here is its initial code (I'll add other units to it later in this chapter):

```
package MdDesPk;

{$R *.RES}
{$ALIGN ON}
...
{$DESCRIPTION 'Mastering Delphi DesignTime Package'}
{$DESIGNONLY}
```

```
requires
  vcl,
  Mdpack;

contains
  PeSound in 'PeSound.pas',
  PeFSound in 'PeFSound.pas' {SoundForm};
```

Writing a Component Editor

Using property editors allows the developer to make a component more user-friendly. In fact, the Object Inspector represents one of the key pieces of the user interface of the Delphi environment, and Delphi developers use it quite often. However, there is a second approach you can adopt to customize how a component interacts with Delphi: write a custom component editor.

Just as property editors extend the Object Inspector, component editors extend the Form Designer. In fact, when you right-click within a form at design time, you see some default menu items, plus the items added by the component editor of the selected component. Examples of these menu items are those used to activate the Menu Designer, the Fields Editor, the Visual Query Builder, and other editors of the environment. At times, displaying these special editors becomes the default action of a component when it is double-clicked.

Common uses of component editors include adding an About box with information about the developer of the component, adding the component name, and providing specific wizards to set up its properties.

Subclassing the *TComponentEditor* Class

A component editor should generally inherit from the TComponentEditor class, which provides the base implementation of the IComponentEditor interface. The most important methods of this interface are:

- GetVerbCount returns the number of menu items to add to the local menu of the Form Designer when the component is selected.

- GetVerb is called once for each new menu item and should return the text that will go in the local menu for each.

- ExecuteVerb is called when one of the new menu items is selected. The number of the item is passed as the method's parameter.

- Edit is called when the user double-clicks the component in the Form Designer to activate the default action.

Once you get used to the idea that a "verb" is nothing but a new menu item with a corresponding action to execute, the names of the methods of this interface become quite intuitive. This interface is actually much simpler than those of property editors we've seen before.

NOTE Like property editors, component editors were modified extensively from Delphi 5 to Delphi 6, and are now defined in the DesignEditors and DesignIntf units. But, again, the simpler examples like this one keep compiling almost unchanged, so I won't delve into the differences.

A Component Editor for the ListDialog

Now that I've introduced the key ideas about writing component editors, we can look at an example, an editor for the ListDialog component built earlier. In my component editor, I simply want to be able to show an About box, add a copyright notice to the menu (an improper but very common use of component editors), and allow users to perform a special action—previewing the dialog box connected with the dialog component. I also want to change the default action to simply show the About box after a beep (which is not particularly useful but demonstrates the technique).

To implement this property editor, the program must override the four methods listed above:

```
uses
  DesignIntf;

type
  TMdListCompEditor = class (TComponentEditor)
    function GetVerbCount: Integer; override;
    function GetVerb(Index: Integer): string; override;
    procedure ExecuteVerb(Index: Integer); override;
    procedure Edit; override;
  end;
```

The first method simply returns the number of menu items I want to add to the local menu:

```
function TMdListCompEditor.GetVerbCount: Integer;
begin
  Result := 3;
end;
```

This method is called only once, before displaying the menu. The second method, instead, is called once for each menu item, so in this case it is called three times:

```
function TMdListCompEditor.GetVerb (Index: Integer): string;
begin
```

```
  case Index of
    0: Result := ' MdListDialog (©Cantù)';
    1: Result := '&About this component...';
    2: Result := '&Preview...';
  end;
end;
```

The effect of this code is to add the menu items to the local menu of the form, as you can see in Figure 11.14. Selecting any of these menu items just activates the ExecuteVerb method of the component editor:

```
procedure TMdListCompEditor.ExecuteVerb (Index: Integer);
begin
  case Index of
    0..1: MessageDlg ('This is a simple component editor'#13 +
      'built by Marco Cantù'#13 +
      'for the book "Mastering Delphi"', mtInformation, [mbOK], 0);
    2: with Component as TMdListDialog do
      Execute;
  end;
end;
```

FIGURE 11.14:

The custom menu items added by the property editor of the ListDialog component

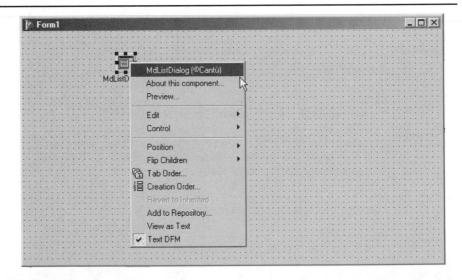

I decided to handle the first two items in a single branch of the case statement, although I could have skipped the code for the copyright notice item. The other command changes calls the Execute method of the component we are editing, determined using the Component property of the TComponentEditor class. Knowing the type of the component, we can easily access its methods after a dynamic type cast.

The last method refers to the default action of the component and is activated by double-clicking it in the Form Designer:

```
procedure.Edit;
begin
x
  Beep;
  ExecuteVerb (0);
end;
```

Registering the Component Editor

To make this editor available to the Delphi environment, we need to register it. Once more we can add to its unit a `Register` procedure and call a specific registration procedure for component editors:

```
procedure TMdListCompEditor.Edit;
begin
  // produce a beep and show the about box
  Beep;
  ExecuteVerb (0);
end;
```

I've added this unit to the MdDesPk package, which includes all of the design-time extensions of this chapter. After installing and activating this package you can create a new project, place a tabbed list component in it, and experiment with it.

What's Next?

In this chapter we have seen how to define various types of properties, how to add events, and how to define and override component methods. We have seen various examples of components, including simple changes to existing ones, new graphical components, and, in the final section, a dialog box inside a component. While building these components, we have faced some new Windows programming challenges. In general, programmers often need to use the Windows API directly when writing new Delphi components.

Writing components is a very handy technique for reusing software, but to make your components easier to use, you should try to integrate them as much as possible within the Delphi environment, writing property editors and component editors.

There are many more extensions of the Delphi IDE you can write, including custom wizards. I've personally built many Delphi extensions, some of which are available (with source code) on my Web site, www.marcocantu.com.

After discussing components and delving a little into the Delphi environment, the next chapter focuses on Delphi DLLs. We have already met DLLs in many previous chapters, and it is time for a detailed discussion of their role and how to build them. In the same chapter, I'll also further discuss the use of Delphi packages, which are a special type of DLL.

CHAPTER 12

Libraries and Packages

- DLLs in Windows 95, 98, and NT

- Building and using DLLs in Delphi

- Calling DLL functions at run time

- Sharing data in DLLs

- The structure of Delphi packages

- Placing forms in packages and DLLs

Windows executable files come in two flavors: *programs* and *dynamic link libraries* (DLLs). When you write a Delphi application, you typically generate a program file, an EXE. However, Delphi applications often use calls to functions stored in DLLs. Each time you call a Windows API function directly, you actually access a DLL. Delphi also allows programmers to use run-time DLLs for the component library. When you create a package, you basically create a DLL. Delphi can also generate plain dynamic link libraries. The New page of the Object Repository includes a DLL skeleton generator, which generates very few lines of source code.

It is very simple to generate a DLL in the Delphi environment. However, some problems arise from the nature of DLLs. Writing a DLL in Windows is not always as simple as it seems, because the DLL and the calling program need to agree on calling conventions, parameter types, and other details. This chapter covers the basics of DLL programming from the Delphi point of view and provides some simple examples of what you can place in a Delphi DLL. While discussing the examples, I'll also refer to other programming languages and environments, simply because one of the key reasons for writing a procedure in a DLL is to be able to call it from a program written in a different language.

The second part of the chapter will focus on a specific type of dynamic link library, the Delphi *package*. These packages are not as easy to use as they first seem, and it took Delphi programmers some time to figure out how to take advantage of them effectively. Here I'm going to share with you some of these interesting tips and techniques.

The Role of DLLs in Windows

Before delving into the development of DLLs in Delphi and other programming languages, I'll give you a short technical overview of DLLs in Windows, highlighting the key elements. We will start by looking at dynamic linking, then see how Windows uses DLLs, explore the differences between DLLs and executable files, and end with some general rules to follow when writing DLLs.

What Is Dynamic Linking?

First of all, you need to understand the difference between static and dynamic linking of functions or procedures. When a subroutine is not directly available in a source file, the compiler adds the subroutine to an internal table, which includes all external symbols. Of course, the compiler must have seen the declaration of the subroutine and know about its parameters and type, or it will issue an error.

After compilation of a normal—*static*—subroutine, the linker fetches the subroutine's compiled code from a Delphi compiled unit (or static library) and adds it to the executable. The resulting EXE file includes all the code of the program and of the units involved. The Delphi linker is smart enough to include only the minimum amount of code of the units used by the program and to link only the functions and methods that are actually used.

> **NOTE**   A notable exception to this rule is the inclusion of virtual methods. The compiler cannot determine in advance which virtual methods the program is going to call, so it has to include them all. For this reason, programs and libraries with too many virtual functions tend to generate larger executable files. While developing the VCL, the Borland developers had to balance the flexibility obtained with virtual functions against the reduced size of the executable files achieved by limiting the virtual functions.

In the case of dynamic linking, which occurs when your code calls a DLL-based function, the linker simply uses the information in the `external` declaration of the subroutine to set up some tables in the executable file. When Windows loads the executable file in memory, first it loads all the required DLLs, and then the program starts. During this loading process, Windows fills the program's internal tables with the addresses of the functions of the DLLs in memory. If for some reason the DLL is not found, the program won't even start, often complaining with nonsense error messages (such as the notorious "a device attached to your system is not functioning").

Each time the program calls an external function, it uses this internal table to forward the call to the DLL code (which is now located in the program's address space). Note that this scheme does not involve two different applications. The DLL becomes part of the running program and is loaded in the same address space. All the parameter passing takes place on the application's stack (because the DLL doesn't have a separate stack).

You can see a sketch of how the program calls statically or dynamically linked functions in Figure 12.1. Notice that I haven't yet discussed compilation of the DLL—because I wanted to focus on the two different linking mechanisms first.

> **NOTE**   The term *dynamic linking*, when referring to DLLs, has nothing to do with the late-binding feature of object-oriented programming languages. Virtual and dynamic methods in Object Pascal have nothing to do with DLLs. Unfortunately, the same term is used for both kinds of procedures and functions, which causes a lot of confusion. When I speak of dynamic linking in this chapter, I am referring not to polymorphism but to DLL functions.

FIGURE 12.1:

Static and dynamic linking in Windows

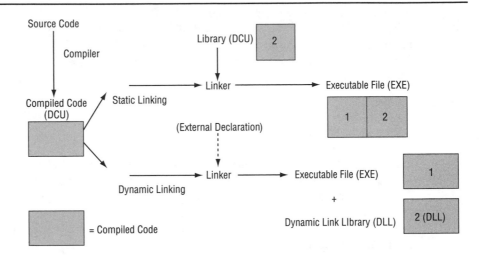

There is another approach to using DLLs, which is even more dynamic than the one we have just discussed. In fact, at run time, you can load a DLL in memory, search for a function (provided you know its name), and call the function by name. This approach requires more complex code and takes some extra time to locate the function. The execution of the function, however, has the same speed of the call of an implicitly loaded DLL. On the positive side, you don't need to have the DLL available to start the program. We will use this approach in the DynaCall example later in the chapter.

For the most part, the internal structure of a normal executable file (an EXE file) and a dynamic link library (a DLL, whatever its extension) is the same. They are both executable files. An important difference between programs and DLLs is that a DLL, even when loaded in memory, is not a running program. It is only a collection of procedures and functions that other programs can call. These procedures and functions use the stack of the calling program (the *calling thread*, to be precise). So another difference between a program and a library is that a library doesn't create its own stack—it uses the stack of the program calling it. In Win32, because a DLL is loaded into the application's address space, any memory allocations of the DLL or any global data it creates reside in the address space of the main process.

What Are DLLs For?

Now that you have a general idea of how DLLs work, we can focus on the reasons for using them in Windows:

- If different programs use the same DLL, the DLL is loaded in memory only once, thus saving system memory. DLLs are mapped into the private address space of each process (each running application), but their code is loaded in memory only once.

The operating system will try to load the DLL at the same address in each application's address space (using the preferred base address specified by the DLL). If that address is not available in a particular application's virtual address space, the DLL code image for that process will have to be relocated, an operation that is expensive in both performance and memory use. The reason is that the relocation happens on a per-process basis, not system-wide.

- You can provide a different version of a DLL, replacing the current one. If the subroutines in the DLL have the same parameters, you can run the program with the new version of the DLL without having to recompile it. If the DLL has new subroutines, it doesn't matter at all. Problems might arise only if a routine in the older version of the DLL is missing in the new one. Problems also arise if the new DLL does not implement the functions in a manner that is compatible with the operation of the old DLL.

These generic advantages apply in several cases. If you have a complex algorithm, or some complex forms required by several applications, you can store them in a DLL. This will let you reduce the executable's size and save some memory when you run several programs using those DLLs at the same time.

The second advantage is particularly applicable to complex applications. If you have a very big program that requires frequent updates and bug fixes, dividing it into several executables and DLLs allows you to distribute only the changed portions instead of one single large executable. This makes sense for Windows system libraries in particular: You generally don't need to recompile your code if Microsoft provides you an updated version of Windows system libraries—for example, in a new version of the operating system.

Another common technique is to use DLLs to store nothing except resources. You can build different versions of a DLL containing strings for different languages and then change the language at run time, or you can prepare a library of icons and bitmaps and then use them in different applications. The development of language-specific versions of a program is particularly important, and Delphi includes support for it through the Integrated Translation Environment (ITE) and the external environment, which are more advanced topics than I have room to go into.

Another key advantage is that DLLs are independent of the programming language. Most Windows programming environments, including most macro languages in end-user applications, allow a programmer to call a subroutine stored in a DLL. This means you can build a DLL in Delphi and call it from Visual Basic, Excel, and many other Windows applications.

Understanding System DLLs

The Windows system DLLs take advantage of all the key benefits of DLLs I've just highlighted. For this reason, it is worth examining them. First of all, Windows has many system DLLs. The three central portions of Windows—Kernel, User, and GDI—are implemented using DLLs (with 32-bit or 16-bit code depending on the OS version). Other system DLLs are operating-system extensions, such as the DLLs for common dialog boxes and controls, OLE, device drivers, fonts, ActiveX controls, and hundreds of others.

Dynamic system libraries are one of the technical foundations of the Windows operating systems. Since each application uses the system DLLs for anything from creating a window to producing output, every program is linked to those DLLs. When you change your printer, you do not need to rebuild your application or get a new version of the Windows GDI library, which manages the printer output. You only need to provide a specific driver, which is a DLL called by GDI to access your printer. Each printer type has its own driver DLL, which makes the system extremely flexible.

From a different point of view, version handling is important for the system itself. If you have an application compiled for Windows 95, you should be able to run it on Windows Me, Windows 2000, and (possibly) future versions of Windows, but the application might behave differently, as each version of Windows has different system code.

The system DLLs are also used as system-information archives. For example, the User DLL maintains a list of all the active windows in the system, and the GDI DLL holds the list of active pens, brushes, icons, bitmaps, and the like. The free memory area of these two system DLLs is usually called "free system resources," and the fact that it is limited plays a very important role in Windows versions still relying on 16-bit code, such as the Windows 9x family. On NT platforms, GDI and User resources are limited only by available system memory.

Rules for Delphi DLL Writers

In short, there are some rules for Delphi DLL programmers. A DLL function or procedure to be called by external programs must follow these guidelines:

- It has to be listed in the DLL's exports clause. This makes the routine visible to the outside world.

- Exported functions should also be declared as stdcall, to use the standard Win32 parameter-passing technique instead of the optimized register parameter-passing technique (which is the default in Delphi). The exception to this rule is if you want to use these libraries only from other Delphi applications.

- The types of the parameters of a DLL should be the default Windows types, at least if you want to be able to use the DLL within other development environments. There are further rules for exporting strings, as we'll see in the FirstDll example.

- A DLL can use global data that won't be shared by calling applications. Each time an application loads a DLL, it stores the DLL's global data in its own address space, as we will see in the DllMem example.

Using Existing DLLs

We have already used existing DLLs in examples in this book, when calling Windows API functions. As you might remember, all the API functions are declared in the system Windows unit. Functions are declared in the `interface` portion of the unit, as shown here:

```
function PlayMetaFile(DC: HDC; MF: HMETAFILE): BOOL; stdcall;
function PaintRgn(DC: HDC; RGN: HRGN): BOOL; stdcall;
function PolyPolygon(DC: HDC; var Points; var nPoints; p4: Integer):
  BOOL; stdcall;
function PtInRegion(RGN: HRGN; p2, p3: Integer): BOOL; stdcall;
```

Then, in the `implementation` portion, instead of providing each function's code, the unit refers to the external definition in a DLL:

```
const
  gdi32 = 'gdi32.dll';

function PlayMetaFile; external gdi32 name 'PlayMetaFile';
function PaintRgn; external gdi32 name 'PaintRgn';
function PolyPolygon; external gdi32 name 'PolyPolygon';
function PtInRegion; external gdi32 name 'PtInRegion';
```

NOTE In `Windows.PAS` there is a heavy use of the `{$EXTERNALSYM identifier}` directive. This has little to do with Delphi itself; it applies to C++Builder. This symbol prevents the corresponding Pascal symbol from appearing in the C++ translated header file. This helps keep the Delphi and C++ identifiers in synch, so that code can be shared between the two languages.

The external definition of these functions refers to the name of the DLL they use. The name of the DLL must include the .DLL extension, or the program will not work under Windows 2000 (even though it will work under Windows 9x). The other element is the name of the DLL function itself. The `name` directive is not necessary if the Pascal function (or procedure) name matches the DLL function name (which is case-sensitive).

To call a function that resides in a DLL, you can provide its declaration and external definition, as shown above, or you can merge the two in a single declaration. Once the function is properly defined, you can call it in the code of your Delphi application just like any other function.

Using a C++ DLL

As an example, I've written a very simple DLL in C++, with some trivial functions, just to show you how to call DLLs from a Delphi application. I won't explain the C++ code in detail (it's basically C code, anyway) but will focus instead on the calls between the Delphi application and the C++ DLL. In Delphi programming it is common to use DLLs written in C or C++.

Suppose you are given a DLL built in C or C++. You'll generally have in your hands a .DLL file (the compiled library itself), an .H file (the declaration of the functions inside the library), and a .LIB file (another version of the list of the exported functions for the C/C++ linker). This LIB file is totally useless in Delphi, while the DLL file is used as-is, and the H file has to be translated into a Pascal unit with the corresponding declarations.

In the following listing, you can see the declaration of the C++ functions I've used to build the CppDll library example. The complete source code and the compiled version of the C++ DLL and of the source code of the Delphi application using it are in the CppDll directory on the CD. You should be able to compile this code with any C++ compiler; I've tested it only with recent Borland C++ compilers. Here are the C++ declarations of the functions:

```
extern "C" __declspec(dllexport)
int WINAPI Double (int n);
extern "C" __declspec(dllexport)
int WINAPI Triple (int n);
__declspec(dllexport)
int WINAPI Add (int a, int b);
```

The three functions perform some basic calculations on the parameters and return the result. Notice that all the functions are defined with the WINAPI modifier, which sets the proper parameter-calling convention; and they are preceded by the __declspec(dllexport) declaration, which makes the functions available to the outside world.

Two of these C++ functions also use the C naming convention (indicated by the extern "C" statement), but the third one, Add, doesn't. This affects the way we call these functions in Delphi. In fact, the internal names of the three functions correspond to their names in the C++ source code file, except for the Add function. Since we didn't use the extern "C" clause for this function, the C++ compiler used *name mangling*. This is a technique used to include information about the number and type of parameters in the function name, which the C++ language requires in order to implement function overloading. The result when using the Borland C++ compiler is a funny function name: @Add$qqsii. This is actually the name we have to use in our Delphi example to call the Add DLL function (which explains why you'll generally avoid C++ name mangling in exported functions, and why you'll generally declare them all as extern "C"). The following are the declarations of the three functions in the Delphi CallCpp example:

```
function Add (A, B: Integer): Integer;
  stdcall; external 'CPPDLL.DLL' name '@Add$qqsii';
```

```
function Double (N: Integer): Integer;
  stdcall; external 'CPPDLL.DLL' name 'Double';
function Triple (N: Integer): Integer;
  stdcall; external 'CPPDLL.DLL';
```

As you can see, you can either provide or omit an alias for an external function. I've provided one for the first function (there was no alternative, because the exported DLL function name @Add$qqsii is not a valid Pascal identifier) and for the second, although in the second case it was unnecessary. If the two names match, in fact, you can omit the name directive, as I did for the third function above. If you are not sure of the actual names of the functions exported by the DLL, you can use the optional Windows viewer for executable files, with the QuickView command of Windows Explorer or Borland's TDump32 command-line program, available in the Delphi BIN folder.

Remember to add the stdcall directive to each definition, so that the caller module (the application) and the module being called (the DLL) use the same parameter-passing convention. If you fail to do so, you will get random values passed as parameters, a bug that is very hard to trace.

NOTE   When you have to convert a large C/C++ header file to the corresponding Pascal declarations, instead of doing a manual conversion you can use a tool to partially automate the process. One of these tools is HeadConv, written by Bob Swart. You'll find a copy on his Web site, **www.drbob42.com**. Notice, though, that automatic header translation from C/C++ to Pascal is not possible, because Pascal is more strongly typed than C/C++, so you have to use types more precisely.

To use this C++ DLL, I've built a Delphi example, named CallCpp. Its simple form has buttons to call the functions of the DLL and some visual components for input and output parameters (see Figure 12.2). The code of the button event handlers looks like:

```
procedure TForm1.BtnDoubleClick(Sender: TObject);
begin
  SpinEdit1.Value := Double (SpinEdit1.Value);
end;
```

FIGURE 12.2:

The output of the CallCpp example when you have pressed each of the buttons

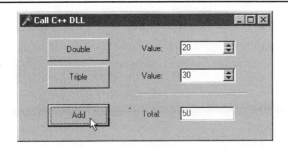

Notice that to run this application, you should have the DLL in the same directory as the project, in one of the directories on the path, or in the Windows or System directories. If you move the executable file to a new directory and try to run it, you'll get a run-time error indicating that the DLL is missing.

Creating a DLL in Delphi

Besides using DLLs written in other environments, you can use Delphi to build DLLs that can be used by Delphi programs or with any other development tool that supports DLLs. Building DLLs in Delphi is so easy that you might overuse this feature. In general, I suggest you try to build components and packages instead of plain DLLs. As I'll discuss later in this chapter, packages often contain components, but they can also include plain noncomponent classes, allowing you to write object-oriented code and to reuse it effectively.

Placing a collection of functions in a DLL is a more traditional approach to programming: DLLs cannot export classes and objects, at least unless you use Microsoft's COM technology or some other advanced techniques.

As I've already mentioned, building a DLL is useful when a portion of the code of a program is subject to frequent changes. In this case you can frequently replace the DLL, keeping the rest of the program unchanged. Similarly, when you need to write a program that provides different features to different groups of users, you can distribute different versions of a DLL to those users.

A Simple Delphi DLL

As a starting point in exploring the development of DLLs in Delphi, I'll show you a very simple library built in Delphi. The primary focus of this example will be to show the syntax you use to define a DLL in Delphi, but it will also illustrate a few considerations involved in passing string parameters. To start, select the File ➤ New command and choose the DLL option in the New page of the Object Repository. This creates a very simple source file that starts with the following definition:

```
library Project1;
```

The library statement indicates that we want to build a DLL instead of an executable file. Now we can add routines to the library and list them in an exports statement:

```
function Triple (N: Integer): Integer; stdcall;
begin
  Result := N * 3;
end;
```

```
function Double (N: Integer): Integer; stdcall;
begin
  Result := N * 2;
end;

exports
  Triple, Double;
```

In this basic version of the DLL, we don't need a uses statement; but in general, the main project file includes only the exports statement, while the function declarations are placed in a separate unit. In the final source code of the FirstDll example on the CD, I've actually changed the code slightly from the version listed above, to show a message each time a function is called. There are two ways to accomplish this. The simplest is to use the Dialogs unit and call the ShowMessage function.

The code requires Delphi to link a lot of VCL code into the application. If you statically link the VCL into this DLL, the resulting size will be about 375 KB. The reason is that the ShowMessage function displays a VCL form that contains VCL controls and uses VCL graphics classes; and those indirectly refer to things like the VCL streaming system and the VCL application and screen objects. For this simple case, a better alternative is to show the messages using direct API calls, using the Windows unit and calling the MessageBox function, so that the VCL code is not required. This change in code brings the size of the application down to only about 40 KB.

NOTE   This huge difference in size underlines the fact that you should not overuse DLLs in Delphi, to avoid compiling the code of the VCL in multiple executable files. Of course, you can reduce the size of a Delphi DLL by using run-time packages, as detailed later in this chapter.

If you run a test program like the CallFrst example (described later) using the API-based version of the DLL, its behavior won't be correct. In fact, you can click the buttons that call the DLL functions several times without first closing the message boxes displayed by the DLL. This happens because the first parameter of the MessageBox API call above is zero. Its value should instead be the handle of the program's main form or the application form, information I don't have at hand in the DLL itself.

Overloaded Functions in Delphi DLLs

When you create a DLL in C++, overloaded functions use name mangling to generate a different name for each function, including the type of the parameters right in the name, as we've seen in the CppDll example.

When you create a DLL in Delphi and use overloaded functions (that is, multiple functions using the same name and marked with the overload directive), Delphi allows you to export only one of the overloaded functions with the original name, indicating its parameters list in the exports clause. If you want to export multiple overloaded functions, you should specify different names in the exports clause to distinguish the overloads. This is demonstrated by this portion of the FirstDLL code:

```
function Triple (C: Char): Integer; stdcall; overload;
function Triple (N: Integer): Integer; stdcall; overload;

exports
  Triple (N: Integer),
  Triple (C: Char) name 'TripleChar';
```

NOTE   The reverse is possible as well: You can import a series of similar functions from a DLL and define them all as overloaded functions in the Pascal declaration. Delphi's OpenGL.PAS unit contains a series of examples of this technique.

Exporting Strings from a DLL

In general, functions in a DLL can use any type of parameter and return any type of value. There are two exceptions to this rule:

- If you plan to call the DLL from other programming languages, you should probably try using Windows native data types instead of Delphi-specific types. For example, to express color values, you should use integers or the Windows ColorRef type instead of the Delphi native TColor type, doing the appropriate conversions (as in the FormDLL example, described in the next section). Other Delphi types that, for compatibility, you should avoid using include objects, which cannot be used by other languages at all, and Pascal strings, which can be replaced by PChar strings. In other words, every Windows development environment must support the basic types of the API, and if you stick to them, your DLL will be usable with other development environments. Also, Pascal file variables (text files and binary file of record) should not be passed out of DLLs, but you can use Win32 file handles.

- Even if you plan to use the DLL only from a Delphi application, you cannot pass Delphi strings (and dynamic arrays) across the DLL boundary without taking some precautions. This is because of the way Delphi manages strings in memory—allocating, reallocating, and freeing them automatically. The solution to the problem is to include the ShareMem system unit both in the DLL and in the program using it. This unit must be included as the first unit of each of the projects.

Objects actually can be passed out of a DLL, if the objects are designed to be used like interfaces or pure abstract classes. All methods of these objects must be virtual, and objects must be created by the DLL. This is more or less what happens with COM objects, the approach you should use for multilanguage applications. For Delphi-only projects with libraries exporting objects, you should rather use packages, as we'll see later in this chapter.

In the FirstDLL example, I've actually included both approaches: One function receives and returns a Pascal string, and another one receives as parameter a PChar pointer, which is then filled by the function itself. The first function is very simple:

```
function DoubleString (S: string; Separator: Char): string; stdcall;
begin
  Result := S + Separator + S;
end;
```

The second one is quite complex because PChar strings don't have a simple + operator, and they are not directly compatible with characters; the separator must be turned into a string before adding it. Here is the complete code; it uses input and output PChar buffers, which are compatible with any Windows development environment:

```
function DoublePChar (BufferIn, BufferOut: PChar;
    BufferOutLen: Cardinal; Separator: Char): LongBool; stdcall;
var
  SepStr: array [0..1] of Char;
begin
  // if the buffer is large enough
  if BufferOutLen > StrLen (BufferIn) * 2 + 2 then
  begin
    // copy the input buffer in the output buffer
    StrCopy (BufferOut, BufferIn);
    // build the separator string (value plus null terminator)
    SepStr [0] := Separator;
    SepStr [1] := #0;
    // append the separator
    StrCat (BufferOut, SepStr);
    // append the input buffer once more
    StrCat (BufferOut, BufferIn);
    Result := True;
  end
  else
    // not enough space
    Result := False;
end;
```

This second version of the code is certainly more complex, but the first can be used only from Delphi. Moreover, the first version requires us to include the ShareMem unit in the DLL (and in the programs using it) and to deploy the file BorlndMM.DLL (the name stands for Borland Memory Manager) along with the program and the specific library.

Calling the Delphi DLL

How can we use the library we've just built? We can call it from within another Delphi project or from other environments. As an example, I've built the CallFrst project (stored in the FirstDLL directory).

To access the DLL functions, we must declare them as `external`, as we've done with the C++ DLL. This time, however, we can simply copy and paste the definition of the functions from the source code of the Delphi DLL, adding the `external` clause, as in:

```
function Double (N: Integer): Integer;
  stdcall; external 'FIRSTDLL.DLL';
```

This declaration is similar to those used to call the C++ DLL. This time, however, we have no problems with function names. The source code of the example is actually quite simple. Once they are redeclared as `external`, the functions of the DLL can simply be used as if they were local functions. Here are two examples, with calls to the string-related functions:

```
procedure TForm1.BtnDoubleStringClick(Sender: TObject);
begin
  // call the DLL function directly
  EditDouble.Text := DoubleString (EditSource.Text, ';');
end;

procedure TForm1.BtnDoublePCharClick(Sender: TObject);
var
  Buffer: string;
begin
  // make the buffer large enough
  SetLength (Buffer, 1000);
  // call the DLL function
  if DoublePChar (PChar (EditSource.Text), PChar (Buffer), 1000, '/') then
    EditDouble.Text := Buffer;
end;
```

Figure 12.3 shows the effect of this program's calls to the DLL.

FIGURE 12.3:

The output of the CallFrst example, which calls the DLL we've built in Delphi

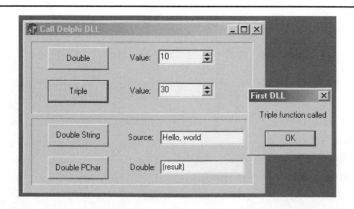

Project and Library Names in Delphi 6

For a library, as for a standard application, you end up with a library name matching a Delphi project filename. Following a similar technique introduced in Kylix for compatibility with standard Linux naming conventions for shared object libraries (the Linux equivalent of Windows DLLs), Delphi 6 introduced special compiler directives you can use in libraries to determine their executable filename. Some of these directives make more sense in the Linux world than on Windows, but they've all been added anyway.

- $LIBPREFIX is used to add something in front of the library name. Paralleling the Linux technique of adding *lib* in front of library names, this directive is used by Kylix to add *bpl* at the beginning of package names. This is due to the fact that Linux uses a single extension (.so) for libraries, while in Windows you can have different library extensions, something Borland uses for packages (.bpl).

- $LIBSUFFIX is used to add text after the library name and before the extension. This can be used to specify versioning information or other variations on the library name and can be quite useful also on Windows.

- $LIBVERSION is used to add a version number after the extension—something very common in Linux, but you should generally avoid this on Windows.

As an example, consider the following directives, which generate a library called MarcoNameTest60.dll:

```
library NameTest;
{$LIBPREFIX 'Marco'}
{$LIBSUFFIX '60'}
```

NOTE   Unlike past versions, Delphi 6 packages use the $LIBSUFFIX directive extensively. For this reason, the VCL package generates the VCL.DCP file and the VCL60.BPL file. The advantage of this approach is that you won't need to change the requires portions of your packages for every new version of Delphi. Of course, this will become handy to maintain Delphi 7– and Delphi 6–compatible packages, but isn't helpful now for Delphi 5 compatibility.

A Delphi Form in a DLL

Besides writing simple DLLs with functions and procedures, you can place a complete form built with Delphi into a DLL. This can be a dialog box or any other kind of form, and it can be used not only by other Delphi programs, but also by other development environments or macro languages.

To build the FormDLL example, I've built a simple form with three scroll bars you can use to select a color and two preview areas for the resulting pen and brush colors. The form also contains two bitmap buttons and has its BorderStyle property set to bsDialog. Aside from developing a form as usual, I've only added two new subroutines to the unit that defines the form. In the interface portion of the unit, I've added the following declarations:

```
function GetColor (Col: LongInt): LongInt; stdcall;
procedure ShowColor (Col: LongInt;
   FormHandle: THandle; MsgBack: Integer); stdcall;
```

In both subroutines the Col parameter is the initial color. Notice that I've passed it as a long integer, which corresponds to the Windows ColorRef data type. As mentioned before, using the TColor Delphi type might have caused problems with non-Delphi applications: Even though a TColor is very similar to a ColorRef, these types don't always correspond. When you write a DLL, I suggest you use only the Windows native data types (unless you are sure only Delphi programs will use the DLL).

The GetColor function returns the final color (which is the same as the initial color if the user clicks the Cancel button). The value is returned immediately because the function shows the form as a modal form. The ShowColor procedure, instead, simply displays the form (as a modeless form) and returns immediately. For this reason the form needs a way to communicate back to the calling form. In this case I've decided to pass as parameters the handle for the window of the calling form and the ID of the message to use to communicate back with it.

In the next sections, you'll see how to write the code of the two subroutines; and you'll also see what problems arise, particularly when you place a modeless form in a DLL. Of course, I'll also provide a few alternative fixes.

Using the DLL Form as Modal

When you want to place a Delphi component (such as a form) in a DLL, you can only provide functions that create, initialize, or run the component or access its properties and data. The simplest approach is to have a single function that sets the data, runs the component, and returns the result, as in the modal version. Here is the code of the function, added to the implementation portion of the unit that defines the form:

```
function GetColor (Col: LongInt): LongInt; stdcall;
var
  FormScroll: TFormScroll;
begin
  // default value
  Result := Col;
  try
    FormScroll := TFormScroll.Create (Application);
    try
```

```
      // initialize the data
      FormScroll.SelectedColor := Col;
      // show the form
      if FormScroll.ShowModal = mrOK then
        Result := FormScroll.SelectedColor;
    finally
      FormScroll.Free;
    end;
  except
    on E: Exception do
      MessageDlg ('Error in FormDLL: ' + E.Message, mtError, [mbOK], 0);
  end;
end;
```

An important element is the structure of the GetColor function. The code creates the form at the beginning, sets some initial values, and then runs the form, eventually extracting the final data. What makes this different from the code we generally write in a program is the use of exception handling:

- A try/except block protects the whole function, so that any exception generated by the function will be trapped, displaying a proper message. The reason for handling every possible exception is that the calling application might be written in any language, in particular one that doesn't know how to handle exceptions. Even when the caller is a Delphi program, it is sometimes useful to use the same protective approach.

- A try/finally block protects the operations on the form, ensuring that the form object will be properly destroyed, even when an exception is raised.

By checking the return value of the ShowModal method, the program determines the result of the function. I've set the default value before entering the try block to ensure that it will always be executed (and also to avoid the compiler warning indicating that the result of the function might be undefined).

Now that we have updated the form and written the code of the unit, we can move to the project source code, which (temporarily) becomes the following:

```
library FormDLL;

uses
  ScrollF in 'SCROLLF.PAS' {FormScroll};

exports
  GetColor;
end.
```

We can now use a Delphi program to test the form we have placed in the DLL. The UseCol example is in the same directory as the previous DLL, FormDLL (and both projects

are part of the FormDLL project group, the file `FormDll.BPG`). The form of the UseCol
example contains a button to call the `GetColor` function of the DLL. Here is the definition
of this function and the code of the `Button1Click` method:

```
function GetColor (Col: LongInt): LongInt; stdcall; external 'FormDLL.DLL';

procedure TForm1.Button1Click(Sender: TObject);
var
  Col: LongInt;
begin
  Col := ColorToRGB (Color);
  Color := GetColor (Col)
end;
```

Running this program (see Figure 12.4) displays the dialog box, using the current background color of the main form. If you change the color and click OK, the program uses the
new color as the background color for the main form.

FIGURE 12.4:

The execution of the
UseCol test program when
it calls the dialog box we
have placed in the FormDLL

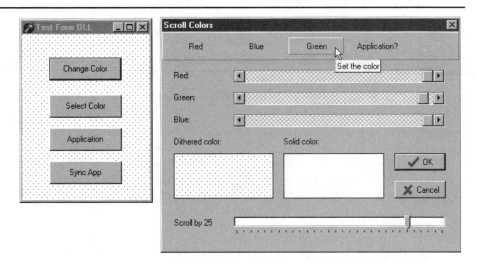

If you execute this as a modal dialog box, almost all the features of the form work fine. You
can see the tooltips, the flat speed buttons in the toolbar behave properly, and you get no
extra entry in the task bar. This might be obvious, but is not what will happen when we use
the form inside the DLL as a modeless form. Even with modal forms, however, I recommend
synchronizing the application objects of the DLL and the executable file, as described in the
next section.

A Modeless Form in a DLL

The second subroutine of the FormDLL example uses a different approach. As mentioned, it receives three parameters: the color, the handle of the main form, and the message number for notification when the color changes. These values are stored in the private data of the form:

```
procedure ShowColor (Col: LongInt;
  FormHandle: THandle; MsgBack: Integer); stdcall;
var
  FormScroll: TFormScroll;
begin
  FormScroll := TFormScroll.Create (Application);
  try
    // initialize the data
    FormScroll.FormHandle := FormHandle;
    FormScroll.MsgBack := MsgBack;
    FormScroll.SelectedColor := Col;
    // show the form
    FormScroll.Show;
  except
    on E: Exception do
    begin
      MessageDlg ('Error in FormDLL: ' + E.Message, mtError, [mbOK], 0);
      FormScroll.Free;
    end;
  end;
end;
```

When the form is activated, it checks to see if it was created as a modal form (simply testing the FormHandle field). In this case, the form changes the caption and the behavior of the OK button, as well as the overall style of the Cancel button (you can see the modified buttons in Figure 12.5):

```
procedure TFormScroll.FormActivate(Sender: TObject);
begin
  // change buttons for modeless form
  if FormHandle <> 0 then
  begin
    BitBtn1.Caption := 'Apply';
    BitBtn1.OnClick := ApplyClick;
    BitBtn2.Kind := bkClose;
  end;
end;
```

When the DLL-based form is used as a modeless form, its buttons are slightly modified (as you can see comparing this image with that of Figure 12.4).

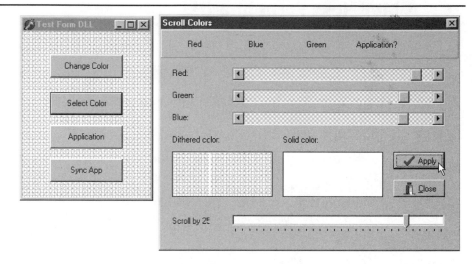

The ApplyClick method I've manually added to the form simply sends the notification message to the main form, using one of the parameters to send back the selected color:

```
SendMessage (FormHandle, MsgBack, SelectedColor, 0);
```

Finally, the form's OnClose event destroys the form object, by setting the Action parameter to caFree. Now let's move back to the demo program. The second button of the UseForm example's form has the following code:

```
procedure TForm1.BtnSelectClick(Sender: TObject);
var
  Col: LongInt;
begin
  Col := ColorToRGB (Color);
  ShowColor (Col, Handle, wm_user);
end;
```

The form also has a message-handling method, connected with the wm_user message. This method reads the value of the parameter corresponding to the color and sets it:

```
procedure TForm1.UserMessage(var Msg: TMessage);
begin
  Color := Msg.WParam;
end;
```

Running this program produces some strange effects. Basically, the modeless form and the main form are not synchronized, so they both show up in the Windows Taskbar; and when you minimize the main form, the other one remains on the screen. The two forms behave as if they were part of separate applications, because two Delphi programs (the DLL and the EXE) have two separate global Application objects, and only the Application object of the executable file has an associated window.

To test this situation, I've added a button to both the main form and the DLL form, showing the numeric value of the `Application` object's handle. Here is the code for one of them:

```
ShowMessage ('Application Handle: ' + IntToStr (Application.Handle));
```

For the form in the DLL, you'll invariably get the value 0, while for the form in the executable you get a numeric value determined each time by Windows.

To fix the problem we can add to the DLL an initialization function that passes the handle of the application window to the library. In practice, we copy the `Handle` of the executable's `Application` object to the same property of the DLL's `Application` object. This is enough to synchronize the two `Application` objects and make the two forms behave as in a simple Delphi program. Here is the code of the function in the DLL:

```
procedure SyncApp (AppHandle: THandle); stdcall;
begin
  Application.Handle := AppHandle;
end;
```

And here is the call to it in the executable file:

```
procedure TForm1.BtnSyncClick(Sender: TObject);
begin
  SyncApp (Application.Handle);
  BtnSync.Enabled := False;
end;
```

NOTE Assigning the handle of the application object of the DLL is not a work-around for a bug but a documented operation required by the VCL. The VCL `Application` object supports assignment to its **Handle** property (unlike most other **Handle** properties of the VCL) specifically to allow programmers to tie DLL-based forms into the environment of a host application.

I've connected this code to a button, instead of executing it automatically at startup, to let you test the behavior in the two different cases. Before you click the Sync App button, the secondary modeless form behaves oddly. If you close it, synchronize the applications, and then create another instance of the modeless form, it will behave almost correctly. The only visible problem is that the flat speed buttons of the modeless form won't be highlighted when the mouse moves over them. We'll see how to fix this problem using run-time packages at the end of the chapter.

NOTE Technically this behavior of the speed buttons depends on the fact that the controls in the DLL form don't receive the `cm_MouseEnter` and `cm_MouseLeave` messages, because the DLL's `Application.Idle` method is never called. The DLL's `Application` object, in fact, is not running the application's message loop. You can activate it by exporting from the DLL a function that calls the internal `Application.Idle` routine, and call that function from the host application when its message loop goes idle. As I've mentioned, however, all these problems (and a few others) can be better solved by using run-time packages.

Calling a Delphi DLL from Visual Basic for Applications

We can also display this color dialog box from other programming languages. Calling this DLL from C or C++ is easy. To link the application, you need to generate an import library (using the IMPLIB command-line utility) and add the resulting LIB file to the project. Since I've already used a C++ compiler in this chapter, this time I will write a similar example using Microsoft Word for Windows and Visual Basic for Applications instead.

To start, open Microsoft Word. Then open its Macro dialog box (with the Tools ➤ Macro menu item or a similar command, depending on your version of Word), type a new macro name, such as **DelphiColor**, and click the Create button. You can now write the BASIC code, which declares the function of our DLL and calls it. The BASIC macro uses the result of the DLL function in two ways. By calling Insert, it adds to the current document a description of the color with the amount of red, green, and blue; and by calling Print it displays the numeric value in the status bar:

```
Declare Function GetColor Lib "FormDLL"(Col As Long) As Long
Sub MAIN
  NewColor = GetColor(0)
  Print "The code of the color is " + Str$(NewColor)
  Insert "Red:" + Str$(NewColor Mod 256) + Chr$(13)
  Insert "Green:" + Str$(Int(NewColor / 256) Mod 256) + Chr$(13)
  Insert "Blue:" + Str$(Int(NewColor / (256 * 256))) + Chr$(13)
End Sub
```

Unfortunately, there is no easy way to use RGB colors in Word, since Word's color schemes are based on fixed color codes. Here is an example of the output of this macro:

```
Red: 141
Green: 109
Blue: 179
```

You can find the text of this macro in the file WORDCALL.TXT, in the directory containing this DLL. If you want to test it, remember to first copy the DLL file into one of the directories of the path or into the Windows system directory.

NOTE   A better way to integrate Delphi code with Office applications is to use OLE Automation, instead of writing custom DLLs and calling them from the macro language. We'll see examples of OLE Automation in Chapter 20.

Calling a DLL Function at Run Time

Up to now, we've always referenced in our code the functions exported by the libraries, so that the DLLs will be loaded along with the program. I mentioned earlier that we can also delay the loading of a DLL until the moment it is actually needed, so we'd be able to use the rest of the program in case the DLL is not available.

Dynamic loading of a DLL in Windows is accomplished by calling the LoadLibrary API function, which searches the DLL in the program folder, in the folders on the path, and in some system folders. If the DLL is not found, Windows will show an error message, something you can skip by calling Delphi's SafeLoadLibrary function. This function has the same effect as the API it encapsulates, but it suppresses the standard Windows error message and should be the preferred way to load libraries dynamically in Delphi.

If the library is found and loaded (something you know by checking the return value of LoadLibrary or SafeLoadLibrary), a program can call the GetProcAddress API function, which searches the DLL's exports table, looking for the name of the function passed as a parameter. If GetProcAddress finds a match, it returns a pointer to the requested procedure. Now we can simply cast this function pointer to the proper data type and call it.

Whichever loading functions you've used, don't forget to call FreeLibrary at the end, so that the DLL can be properly released from memory. In fact, the system uses a reference-counting technique for libraries, releasing them when each loading request has been followed by a freeing request.

The example I've built to show dynamic DLL loading is named DynaCall and uses the FirstDLL library we built earlier in this chapter (to make the program work, I've copied the DLL into the same folder as the DynaCall example). Instead of declaring the Double and Triple functions and using them directly, this example obtains the same effect with somewhat more complex code. The advantage, however, is that the program will run even without the DLL. Also, if new *compatible* functions are added to the DLL, we won't have to revise the program's source code and recompile it to access those new functions. Here is the core code of the program:

```
type
  TIntFunction = function (I: Integer): Integer; stdcall;

const
  DllName = 'Firstdll.dll';

procedure TForm1.Button1Click(Sender: TObject);
var
  HInst: THandle;
  FPointer: TFarProc;
  MyFunct: TIntFunction;
begin
  HInst := SafeLoadLibrary (DllName);
  if HInst > 0 then
  try
    FPointer := GetProcAddress (HInst,
      PChar (Edit1.Text));
```

```
    if FPointer <> nil then
    begin
      MyFunct := TIntFunction (FPointer);
      SpinEdit1.Value := MyFunct (SpinEdit1.Value);
    end
    else
      ShowMessage (Edit1.Text + ' DLL function not found');
  finally
    FreeLibrary (HInst);
  end
  else
    ShowMessage (DllName + ' library not found');
end;
```

How do you call a procedure in Delphi, once you have a pointer to it? One solution is to convert the pointer to a procedural type and then call the procedure using the procedural-type variable, as in the listing above. Notice that the procedural type you define must be compatible with the definition of the procedure in the DLL. This is the Achilles' heel of this method—there is no check of the parameter types.

What is the advantage of this approach? In theory, you can use it to access any function of any DLL at any time. In practice, it is useful when you have different DLLs with compatible functions or a single DLL with several compatible functions, as in our case. What we can do is to call the `Double` and `Triple` methods simply by entering their names in the edit box. Now, if someone gives us a DLL with a new function receiving an integer as a parameter and returning an integer, we can call it simply by entering its name in the edit box. We don't even need to recompile the application.

With this code, the compiler and the linker ignore the existence of the DLL. When the program is loaded, the DLL is not loaded immediately. We might make the program even more flexible and let the user enter the name of the DLL to use. In some cases, this is a great advantage. A program may switch DLLs at run time, something the direct approach does not allow. Note that this approach to loading DLL functions is common in macro languages and is used by many visual programming environments. Also, the code of the Word macro we saw earlier in this chapter uses this approach to load the DLL and to call the external function. Well, you don't want to recompile Word, do you?

Only a system based on a compiler and a linker, such as Delphi, can use the direct approach, which is generally more reliable and also a little bit faster. I think the indirect loading approach of the DynaCall example is useful only in special cases, but it can be extremely powerful.

A DLL in Memory: Code and Data

We can use this technique, based on the GetProcAddress API function, to test which memory address of the current process a function has been mapped to, with the following code:

```
procedure TForm1.Button3Click(Sender: TObject);
var
  HDLLInst: THandle;
begin
  HDLLInst := SafeLoadLibrary ('dllmem');
  Label1.Caption := Format ('Address: %p', [
    GetProcAddress (HDLLInst, 'SetData')]);
  FreeLibrary (HDLLInst);
end;
```

This code displays, in a label, the memory address of the function, within the address space of the calling application. If you run two programs using this code, they'll generally both show the same address. This demonstrates that the code is loaded only once at a common memory address.

> **NOTE**   The memory address will be different if the DLL had to be relocated in one of the processes, or if each process has relocated the DLL to a different base address. In these cases, the code is generally not shared in memory but actually loaded multiple times, because absolute address references in the code must be rewritten to refer to the proper new addresses. As the code is modified by the loader, it cannot be shared.

If the code of the DLL is loaded only once, what about the global data? Basically, each copy of the DLL has its own copy of the data, in the address space of the calling application. However, it is indeed possible to share global data between applications using a DLL. The most common technique for sharing data is to use memory-mapped files. I'll use this technique for a DLL, but it can also be used to share data directly among applications.

This example is called DllMem and uses a project group with the same name, as in the previous examples of this chapter. The DllMem project group includes the DllMem project (the DLL itself) and the UseMem project (the demo application). The DLL code has a simple project file, which exports four subroutines:

```
library dllmem;

uses
  SysUtils,
  DllMemU in 'DllMemU.pas';

exports
  SetData, GetData,
  GetShareData, SetShareData;
end.
```

The actual code is in the secondary unit (D11MemU.PAS), which has the code of the four routines that read or write two global memory locations. These hold an integer and a pointer to an integer. Here are the variable declarations and the two Set routines:

```
var
  PlainData: Integer = 0; // not shared
  ShareData: ^Integer; // shared

procedure SetData (I: Integer); stdcall;
begin
  PlainData := I;
end;

procedure SetShareData (I: Integer); stdcall;
begin
  ShareData^ := I;
end;
```

Sharing Data with Memory-Mapped Files

For the data that isn't shared, there isn't anything else to do. To access the shared data, however, the DLL has to create a memory-mapped file and then get a pointer to this memory area. These two operations require two Windows API calls:

- CreateFileMapping requires as parameters the filename (or $FFFFFFFF to use a virtual file in memory), some security and protection attributes, the size of the data, and an internal name (which must be the same to share the mapped file from multiple calling applications).

- MapViewOfFile requires as parameters the handle of the memory mapped file, some attributes and offsets, and the size of the data (again).

Here is the source code of the initialization section, executed every time the DLL is loaded into a new process space (that is, once for each application that uses the DLL):

```
var
  hMapFile: THandle;

const
  VirtualFileName = 'ShareD11Data';
  DataSize = sizeof (Integer);

initialization
  // create memory mapped file
  hMapFile := CreateFileMapping ($FFFFFFFF, nil,
    Page_ReadWrite, 0, DataSize, VirtualFileName);
  if hMapFile = 0 then
    raise Exception.Create ('Error creating memory-mapped file');
```

```
    // get the pointer to the actual data
    ShareData := MapViewOfFile (
      hMapFile, File_Map_Write, 0, 0, DataSize);
```

When the application terminates and the DLL is released, it has to free the pointer to the mapped file and the file mapping itself:

```
finalization
    UnmapViewOfFile (ShareData);
    CloseHandle (hMapFile);
```

The code of the program using this DLL, UseMem, is very simple. The form of this application has four edit boxes (two with an UpDown control connected), five buttons, and a label. The first button saves the value of the first edit box in the DLL data, getting the value from the connected UpDown control:

```
    SetData (UpDown1.Position);
```

If you click the second button, the program copies the DLL data to the second edit box:

```
    Edit2.Text := IntToStr(GetData);
```

The third button is used to display the memory address of a function, with the source code shown at the beginning of this section, and the last two buttons have basically the same code as the first two, but they call the SetShareData procedure and GetShareData function.

If you run two copies of this program, you can see that each copy has its own value for the plain global data of the DLL, while the value of the shared data is common. Set different values in the two programs and then get them in both, and you'll see what I mean. This situation is illustrated in Figure 12.6.

FIGURE 12.6:

If you run two copies of the UseMem program, you'll see that the global data in its DLL is not shared.

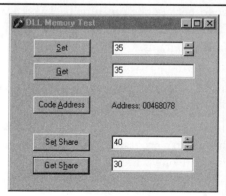

Memory-mapped files reserve a minimum of a 64 KB range of virtual addresses and consume physical memory in 4 KB pages. The example's use of 4-byte Integer data in shared memory is rather expensive, especially if you use the same approach for sharing multiple values. If you need to share several variables, you should place them all in a single shared memory area (accessing the different variables using pointers or building a record structure for all of them).

Using Delphi Packages

In Delphi, component packages are an important type of DLL. Packages allow you to bundle a group of components and then link the components either statically (adding their compiled code to the executable file of your application) or dynamically (keeping the component code in a DLL, the run-time package that you'll distribute along with your program). In the last chapter, you saw how to build a package. Now I want to underline some advantages and disadvantages of the two forms of linking for a package. There are many elements to keep in mind:

- Using a package as a DLL makes the executable files much smaller.

- Linking the package units into the program allows you to distribute only part of the package code. Generally, the size of the executable file of an application plus the size of the required package DLLs that it requires is much bigger than the size of the statically linked program. The linker includes only the code actually used by the program, whereas a package must link in all the functions and classes declared in the interface sections of all the units contained in the package.

- If you distribute several Delphi applications based on the same packages, you might end up distributing less code, because the run-time packages are shared. In other words, once the users of your application have the standard Delphi run-time packages, you can ship them very small programs.

- If you run several Delphi applications based on the same packages, you can save some memory space at run time; the code of the run-time packages is loaded in memory only once between the multiple Delphi applications.

- Don't worry too much about distributing a large executable file. Keep in mind that when you make minor changes to a program, you can use any of various tools to create a *patch file*, so that you distribute only a file containing the differences, not a complete copy of the files.

- If you place a few of your program's forms in a run-time package, you can share them among programs. When you modify these forms, however, you'll generally need to recompile the main program as well, and distribute both of them again to your users. The next section discusses this complex topic in detail.

Package Versioning

A very important and often misunderstood element is the distribution of updated packages. When you update a DLL, you can ship the new version, and the executable programs requiring this DLL will generally still work (unless you've removed existing exported functions or changed some of their parameters).

When you distribute a Delphi package, however, if you update the package and modify the interface portion of any unit of the package, you might need to recompile all the applications that use the package. This is required if you add methods or properties to a class, but not if you add new global symbols (or modify anything not used by client applications). There is no problem at all for changes affecting only the implementation section of the package's units.

A DCU file in Delphi has a version tag based on its timestamp and a checksum computed from the interface portion of the unit. When you change the interface portion of a unit, every other unit based on it should be recompiled. The compiler compares the timestamp and checksum of the unit of previous compilations with the new timestamp and checksum, and decides whether the dependent unit must be recompiled. This is why you have to recompile each unit when you get a new version of Delphi, which has modified system units.

A package is a collection of units. In Delphi 3, a checksum of the package, obtained from the checksum of the units it contains and the checksum of the packages it requires, was added as an extra entry function to the package library, so that any executable based on an older version of the package would fail at startup.

Delphi 4 and following versions have relaxed the run-time constraints of the package. The design-time constraints on DCU files remain identical, though. The checksum of the packages is not checked anymore, so you can directly modify the units that are part of a package and deploy a new version of the package to be used with the existing executable file. Since methods are referenced by name, you cannot remove any existing method. You cannot even change its parameters, because of name-mangling techniques specifically added to the packages to protect against changes in parameters.

Removing a method referenced from the calling program will stop the program during the loading process. If you make other changes, however, the program might fail unexpectedly during its execution. For example, if you replace a component placed on a form compiled in a package with a similar component, the calling program might still able to access the one in that memory location, although it is now a different component!

If you decide to follow this treacherous road of changing the interface of units in a package without recompiling all the programs that use it, you should at least limit your changes. When you add new properties or nonvirtual methods to the form, you should be able to maintain full compatibility with existing programs already using the package. Also, adding fields and virtual methods might affect the internal structure of the class, leading to problems with existing programs that expect a different class data and virtual method table (VMT) layout. Of course, this applies to the binary compatibility between the EXE and the BPL (Borland Package Library).

WARNING   Here I'm referring to the distribution on compiled programs divided between EXE and packages, not to the distribution of components to other Delphi developers. In this latter case the versioning rules are more stringent, and you must take extra care in package versioning.

Having said this, I recommend never changing the interface of any unit exported by your packages. To accomplish this, you can add to your package a unit with form-creation functions (as in the DLL with forms presented earlier) and use it to access another unit, which defines the form. Although there is no way to *hide* a unit that is linked into a package, if you never directly use the class defined in a unit, but use it only through other routines, you'll have more flexibility in modifying it. You can also use form inheritance to modify a form within a package without really affecting the original version.

The most stringent rule for packages is the following one used by component writers: For long-term deployment and maintenance of code in packages, plan on having a major release with minor maintenance releases. A major release of your package will require all client programs to be recompiled from source; the package file itself should be renamed with a new version number, and the interface sections of units can be modified. Maintenance releases of that package should be restricted to implementation changes to preserve full compatibility with existing executables and units.

Forms Inside Packages

We've already discussed (in Chapter 11, "Creating Components") the use of component packages in Delphi applications. As I'm discussing the use of packages and DLLs for partitioning an application, here I'll start discussing the development of packages holding forms. We've seen earlier in this chapter that you can use forms inside DLLs, but this sometimes causes a few problems. If you are building both the library and the executable file in Delphi, using packages results in a much better and cleaner solution.

At first sight, you might believe that Delphi packages are a way to distribute components to be installed in the environment. Instead, you can use packages as a way to structure your code but, unlike DLLs, retain the full power of Delphi's OOP. Consider this: A package is a collection of compiled units and your program uses several units. The units the program refers to will be compiled inside the executable file, unless you ask Delphi to place them inside a package.

So how do you set up an application so that its code is split among one or more packages and a main executable file? You only need to compile some of the units in a package and then set up the options of the main program to dynamically link this package. For example, I've made a copy of the "usual" color selection form and renamed its unit as PackScrollF, then I've created a new package and added the unit to it, as you can see in Figure 12.7.

FIGURE 12.7:

The structure of the package hosting a form in Delphi's Package Editor

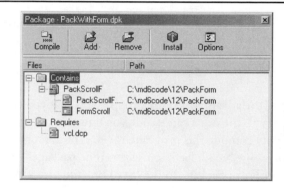

Before compiling this package, you should change its default output directories to refer to the current folder, not the standard /Projects/Bpl subfolder of Delphi. To do this, go to the Directories/Conditional page of the package Project Options, and set the current directory (a single dot, for short) for the Output directory (for the BPL) and DCP output directory. Then compile the package and do not install it in Delphi—there's no need to.

At this point, you can create a normal application and write the standard code you'll use in a program to show a secondary form, as in the following listing:

```
uses
  PackScrollF;

procedure TForm1.BtnChangeClick(Sender: TObject);
var
  FormScroll: TFormScroll;
begin
  FormScroll := TFormScroll.Create (Application);
  try
    // initialize the data
    FormScroll.SelectedColor := Color;
    // show the form
    if FormScroll.ShowModal = mrOK then
      Color := FormScroll.SelectedColor;
  finally
    FormScroll.Free;
  end;
end;
```

```
procedure TForm1.BtnSelectClick(Sender: TObject);
var
  FormScroll: TFormScroll;
begin
  FormScroll := TFormScroll.Create (Application);
  // initialize the data and UI
  FormScroll.SelectedColor := Color;
  FormScroll.BitBtn1.Caption := 'Apply';
  FormScroll.BitBtn1.OnClick := FormScroll.ApplyClick;
  FormScroll.BitBtn2.Kind := bkClose;
  // show the form
  FormScroll.Show;
end;
```

One of the advantages of this approach is that you can refer to a form compiled into a package with the exact same code you'll use for a form compiled in the program. In fact, if you simply compile this program, the unit of the form will actually be bound to it. To keep it in the package, you'll have to use run-time packages for the application and manually add the PackWithForm package to the list of run-time packages (this is not suggested by the Delphi IDE as we have not installed the package in the development environment).

Once you've done this step, compile the program and it will behave exactly as usual. But now the form is in a DLL package, and you can even modify the form in the package, recompile it, and simply run the application to see the effects. Notice, though, that for most changes affecting the interface portion of the units of the package (for example, adding a component or a method to the form), you should also recompile the executable program calling the package.

NOTE   You can find the package and the program testing it in the **PackForm** folder of the source code related to the current chapter. The code of the next example is in the same folder.

Loading Packages at Run Time

In the example above, I indicated that the PackWithForm package is a run-time package to be used by the application. This means that the package is required to run the application and is loaded when the program starts. Both aspects can be avoided by loading the package dynamically, as we've done with DLLs. The resulting program will be more flexible, start more quickly, and use less memory.

An important element to keep in mind is that you'll need to call the LoadPackage and UnloadPackage Delphi functions rather than the LoadLibrary and FreeLibrary Windows API functions. The difference is that the functions provided by Delphi load the packages, but also call their proper initialization and finalization code.

Besides this important element—easy to accomplish once you know about it—the program will require some extra code, as we cannot refer from the main program to the unit hosting the form. We cannot use the form class directly, nor access to its properties or components. At least not with the standard Delphi code. Both issues, however, can be solved using class references, class registration, and RTTI (run-time type information). Let me start with the first one. In the form unit, in the package, I've added this initialization code:

```
initialization
  RegisterClass (TFormScroll);
```

As the package is loaded, the main program can use Delphi's GetClass function to get the class reference of the registered class and then call the Create constructor for this class reference.

To solve the second problem, I've made the SelectedColor property of the form in the package a published property, so that it is accessible via RTTI. Then I've replaced the code accessing this property (FormScroll.Color) with the following:

```
SetPropValue (FormScroll, 'SelectedColor', Color);
```

Summing up all of these changes, here is the code used by the main program (the Dyna-PackForm application) to show the modal form from the dynamically loaded package:

```
procedure TForm1.BtnChangeClick(Sender: TObject);
var
  FormScroll: TForm;
  FormClass: TFormClass;
  HandlePack: HModule;
begin
  // try to load the package
  HandlePack := LoadPackage ('PackWithForm.bpl');
  if HandlePack > 0 then
  begin
    FormClass := TFormClass(GetClass ('TFormScroll'));
    if Assigned (FormClass) then
    begin
      FormScroll := FormClass.Create (Application);
      try
        // initialize the data
        SetPropValue (FormScroll, 'SelectedColor', Color);
        // show the form
        if FormScroll.ShowModal = mrOK then
          Color := GetPropValue (FormScroll, 'SelectedColor');
      finally
        FormScroll.Free;
      end;
    end;
  end
  else
    ShowMessage ('Form class not found');
```

```
    UnloadPackage (HandlePack);
  end
  else
    ShowMessage ('Package not found');
  end;
```

Notice that the program unloads the package as soon as it is done with it. This is not compulsory. I could have moved the UnloadPackage call in the OnDestroy handler of the form, and avoided reloading the package after the first time.

Now you can try running this program without the package available, and you'll see that it will start properly, only to complain it cannot find the package as you click the Change button. In this program, you don't need to use run-time packages to keep the unit outside of your executable file, as you are not referring to the unit in your code. Also, the PackWithForm package doesn't need to be listed in the run-time packages. However, you must use run-time packages, or else your program will include the VCL global variables (as the Application object) and the dynamically loaded package will include another version, because it will refer to the VCL packages anyway.

Using Interfaces in Packages

Accessing the classes of the forms by means of methods and properties is much simpler than using RTTI all over the place. To build a larger application, I definitely try to use interfaces and to have multiple forms, each implementing a few standard interfaces defined by the program. An example cannot really do justice to this type of architecture, which becomes relevant for a large program, but I've tried nonetheless to build a program to show how this idea can be applied in practice.

NOTE   If you don't know much about interfaces, I suggest you to refer to the related portion of Chapter 3 before reading this section.

To architect the IntfPack project, I've used three packages plus a demo application. Two of the three packages (called IntfFormPack and IntfFormPack2) define alternative forms used to select a color. The third package (called IntfPack) hosts a shared unit, used by both other packages. This unit basically includes the definition of the interface. I couldn't add it to both other packages because you cannot load two packages with a unit having the same name (even by run-time loading).

The only file of the IntfPack package is the IntfColSel unit, displayed in Listing 12.1. This unit defines the common interface (and you'll probably have a number of them in real-world application) plus a list of registered classes, which mimics Delphi's RegisterClass approach, but makes available the complete list so that you can easily scan it.

Listing 12.1:   The IntfColSel unit of the IntfPack package

```
unit IntfColSel;

interface

uses
  Graphics, Contnrs;

type
  IColorSelect = interface
  ['{3F961395-71F6-4822-BD02-3B475FF516D4}']
    function Display (Modal: Boolean = True): Boolean;
    procedure SetSelColor (Col: TColor);
    function GetSelColor: TColor;
    property SelColor: TColor
      read GetSelColor write SetSelColor;
  end;

procedure RegisterColorSelect (AClass: TClass);

var
  ClassesColorSelect: TClassList;

implementation

procedure RegisterColorSelect (AClass: TClass);
begin
  if ClassesColorSelect.IndexOf (AClass) < 0 then
    ClassesColorSelect.Add (AClass);
end;

initialization
  ClassesColorSelect := TClassList.Create;

finalization
  ClassesColorSelect.Free;

end.
```

Once we have this interface available, we can define forms that implement it, as in the following example, taken form the IntfFormPack:

```
type
  TFormSimpleColor = class(TForm, IColorSelect)
    ...
  private
    procedure SetSelColor (Col: TColor);
    function GetSelColor: TColor;
  public
    function Display (Modal: Boolean = True): Boolean;
```

The two access methods simply read and write the value of the color from some components of the form (a simple ColorGrid in this specific case), while the Display method internally calls either Show or ShoModal, depending on the parameter:

```
function TFormSimpleColor.Display(Modal: Boolean): Boolean;
begin
  Result := True; // default
  if Modal then
    Result := (ShowModal = mrOK)
  else
  begin
    BitBtn1.Caption := 'Apply';
    BitBtn1.OnClick := ApplyClick;
    BitBtn2.Kind := bkClose;
    Show;
  end;
end;
```

The form is structured like that of the last example, still available in the second package, and has an OK button that is turned into an Apply button. Finally, the unit has the registration code in the initialization section, so that it is executed when the package is dynamically loaded:

```
RegisterColorSelect (TFormSimpleColor);
```

With this architecture in place, we can build a rather elegant and flexible main program, which is based on a single form. When the form is created, it defines a list of packages (called HandlesPackages) and loads them all. I've hard-coded the package in the code of the example, but of course you can as well search for the packages of the current folder or use a configuration file to make the application structure more flexible. Finally, after loading the packages, the program shows the registered classes in a list box. This is the code of the LoadDynaPackage and FormCreate methods:

```
procedure TFormUseIntf.FormCreate(Sender: TObject);
var
  I: Integer;
begin
  // loads all runtime packages
  HandlesPackages := TList.Create;
  LoadDynaPackage ('IntfFormPack.bpl');
  LoadDynaPackage ('IntfFormPack2.bpl');

  // add class names and select the first
  for I := 0 to ClassesColorSelect.Count - 1 do
    lbClasses.Items.Add (ClassesColorSelect [I].ClassName);
  lbClasses.ItemIndex := 0;
end;
```

```
procedure TFormUseIntf.LoadDynaPackage(PackageName: string);
var
  Handle: HModule;
begin
  // try to load the package
  Handle := LoadPackage (PackageName);
  if Handle > 0 then
    // add to the list for later removal
    HandlesPackages.Add (Pointer(Handle))
  else
    ShowMessage ('Package ' + PackageName + ' not found');
end;
```

The main reason for keeping the list of package handles is to be able to unload them all when the program ends. In fact, we don't need these handles to access the forms defined in those packages. The run-time code used to create and show a form simply uses the corresponding component classes. This is a snippet of code used to display a modeless form (an option controlled by a check box):

```
var
  AComponent: TComponent;
  ColorSelect: IColorSelect;
begin
  AComponent := TComponentClass
    (ClassesColorSelect[LbClasses.ItemIndex]).Create (Application);
  ColorSelect := AComponent as IColorSelect;
  ColorSelect.SelColor := Color;
  ColorSelect.Display (False);
```

The program actually uses the Supports function to check that the form really does support the interface before using it, and also accounts for the modal version of the form, but its essence is properly depicted in the four statements above. By the way, notice that the code doesn't actually require a form. A nice exercise would be to add to the architecture a package with a component encapsulating the color selection dialog box or inheriting from it.

WARNING The main program refers to the unit hosting the interface definition but should not link this file in. Rather, it should use the run-time package containing this unit, as the dynamically loaded packages do. Otherwise the main program will use a different copy of the same code, including a different list of global classes. It is this list of global classes, not the use of the same interface, that should not be duplicated in memory.

Packages Versus DLLs

In the preceding section, we've seen that using packages is a fine alternative to using DLLs for sharing compiled code among multiple Delphi applications or splitting a large executable into multiple (and partially independent) modules. As a summary, here are a few of the differences between the two approaches:

- DLLs are collections of functions; packages can easily "export" classes and objects.

- Dynamically loading a DLL implies losing any safety in the function call, in case you pass the wrong parameters. Dynamically loading packages requires some extra coding as well, but is definitely simpler and safer, particularly if you use interfaces.

- Packages force you to use the VCL run-time package for the application, although even when using DLLs, run-time packages help solve quite a few difficulties (as we'll discuss shortly).

- DLLs can be used across programming languages and development environments, but packages are limited to Delphi and C++Builder. If you need libraries in a Delphi-only environment, packages are the native solution and should generally be preferred.

Using DLLs also accounts for a few extra troubles that you can partially solve by letting the DLLs share run-time packages. The following sections discuss the problem briefly, as this is not the recommended approach anyway.

Executables and DLLs Sharing the VCL Packages

In the FormDLL example, we faced a problem: When you place forms inside a DLL, you don't get the proper behavior for the flat buttons even if you synchronize the two application objects. Moreover, both the executable file and the DLL contain the compiled code of the VCL library, leading to useless duplication. As discussed earlier, the simplest solution to this issue is to use a package instead of a DLL.

Another solution is to keep the DLL in its format, but let it use run-time packages, so that no global objects will be duplicated between the executable and the library. In this case there will be only one `Application` object, shared by the program and the DLL, instead of two separate objects, so we don't need the synchronization code any more.

Another simplification to the program comes from the fact that the modeless form inside the DLL can communicate back to the main form by accessing the list of the forms (available to the shared global `Screen` object) or simply using the `Application.MainForm` property. This is what I've done in the FormDllP example on the CD.

With this approach, you face the risk of having the main form and the form in the DLL not synchronized at all, with two entries in the Taskbar; also, this code still has all the other problems of the first version of the FormDLL example. The problem lies in the fact that when you run the program, the DLL is initialized before the application, so it is the DLL that initializes the Forms unit of the VCL. Within a DLL, the VCL creates the `Application` object but doesn't create the corresponding window.

There are two radically different approaches to this initialization issue: One is to change the initialization order by loading the DLL dynamically after the application has started; the second is to add some extra initialization code in the program. None of these techniques provides a better solution than using packages altogether!

Dynamically Loading the DLL with Packages

The first solution is demonstrated by the FirstDLLD library and the UseDyna example, which dynamically loads the DLL built with run-time packages. The main program loads the DLL at startup, in the `OnCreate` event handler of the form:

```
procedure TForm1.FormCreate(Sender: TObject);
begin
  hInstDll := SafeLoadLibrary ('FormDllD.dll');
  if hInstDll <= 0 then
    raise Exception.Create ('FormDllD library not found');
end;
```

In the program I haven't declared the functions exported by the DLL, to avoid the implicit link of the library. Instead I've declared two procedure types:

```
type
  TGetColorProc = function (Col: LongInt): LongInt; stdcall;
  TShowColorProc = procedure (Col: LongInt); stdcall;
```

These types are used for converting the generic pointer returned by the `GetProcAddress` function, as we've already seen in the DynaCall example:

```
procedure TForm1.BtnChangeClick(Sender: TObject);
var
  Col: LongInt;
  GetColorProc: TGetColorProc;
  FPointer: TFarProc;
begin
  FPointer := GetProcAddress (hInstDll, 'GetColor');
  if FPointer = nil then
    raise Exception.Create ('GetColor DLL function not found');
  GetColorProc := TGetColorProc (FPointer);
  // original code
  Col := ColorToRGB (Color);
  Color := GetColorProc (Col);
end;
```

Using dynamic loading is the correct approach, officially supported by Delphi. Still, you have to call the functions dynamically, which requires a little extra coding.

Fixing the Initialization Code

An alternate solution is to keep the external functions defined in the main program, let the DLL start first and initialize the VCL, and let the VCL create the Application object without the connected window. In fact, we can add one line of code to the library to ask for the creation of the window of the Application object during the library initialization process (before the executable creates its own main objects). We accomplish this by writing the code in the initialization section of one of the units of the DLL:

```
initialization
  Application.CreateHandle;
```

Because this code is in the DLL, the application fails to load its icon. The solution is actually very simple. In the OnCreate event handler of the main form (in the main program), simply reload the current icon:

```
Application.Icon.Handle := LoadIcon (HInstance, 'MAINICON');
```

Exploring the Structure of a Package

You might wonder: is it possible to know whether a unit has been linked in the executable file or if it's part of a run-time package? Not only is this possible in Delphi, but you can also explore the overall structure of an application. A component can use the undocumented ModuleIsPackage global variable, declared in the SysInit unit. You should never need this, but it is technically possible for a component to have different code depending on whether it is packaged or not. The following code extracts the name of the run-time package hosting the component, if any:

```
var
  fPackName: string;
begin
  // get package name
  SetLength (fPackName, 100);
  if ModuleIsPackage then
  begin
    GetModuleFileName (HInstance, PChar (fPackName), Length (fPackName));
    fPackName := PChar (fPackName) // string length fixup
  end
  else
    fPackName := 'Not packaged';
```

Besides accessing package information from within a component (as in the code above), you can also do so from a special entry point of the package libraries, the GetPackageInfoTable function. This function returns some specific package information that Delphi stores as resources and includes in the package DLL. Fortunately, we don't need to use low-level techniques to access this information, since Delphi provides some high-level functions to manipulate it.

You can use two functions to access package information:

- GetPackageDescription returns a string that contains a description of the package. To call this function, you must supply the name of the module (the package library) as the only parameter.

- GetPackageInfo doesn't directly return information about the package. Instead, you pass it a function that it calls for every entry in the package's internal data structure. In practice, GetPackageInfo will call your function for every one of the package's contained units and required packages. In addition, GetPackageInfo sets several flags in an Integer variable.

These two function calls allow us to access internal information about a package, but how do we know which packages our application is using? You could determine this by looking at an executable file using low-level functions, but Delphi helps you again by supplying a simpler approach. The EnumModules function doesn't directly return information about an application's modules but allows you to pass it a function, which it calls for each module of the application, the main executable file, and for each of the packages the application relies on.

To demonstrate this approach, I've built a simple example program that displays the module and package information in a TreeView component. Each first-level node corresponds to a module, and within each module I've built a subtree that displays the contained and required packages for that module, as well as the package description and compiler flags (RunOnly and DesignOnly). You can see the output of this example in Figure 12.8.

In addition to the TreeView component, I've added several other components to the main form, but hidden them from view: a DBEdit, a Chart, and a FilterComboBox. I added these components simply to include more run-time packages in the application, beyond the ubiquitous VCL60.BPL. The only method of the form class is FormCreate, which calls the module enumeration function:

```
procedure TForm1.FormCreate(Sender: TObject);
begin
  EnumModules(ForEachModule, nil);
end;
```

FIGURE 12.8:

The output of the PackInfo
example, with the details of
the packages it uses

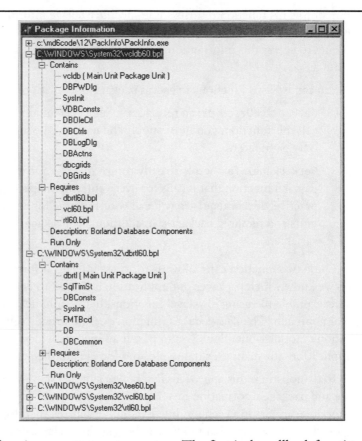

The EnumModules function accepts two parameters. The first is the callback function (in our case, ForEachModule), and the second is a pointer to a data structure that the callback function will use (in our case, nil, since we didn't need this). The callback function must accept two parameters—an HInstance value and an untyped pointer—and must return a Boolean value. The EnumModules function will, in turn, call our callback function for each module, passing the instance handle of each module as the first parameter and the data structure pointer (nil in our example) as the second.

```
function ForEachModule (HInstance: Longint;
  Data: Pointer): Boolean;
var
  Flags: Integer;
```

```
    ModuleName, ModuleDesc: string;
    ModuleNode: TTreeNode;
begin
  with Form1.TreeView1.Items do
  begin
    SetLength (ModuleName, 200);
    GetModuleFileName (HInstance,
      PChar (ModuleName), Length (ModuleName));
    ModuleName := PChar (ModuleName); // fixup
    ModuleNode := Add (nil, ModuleName);

    // get description and add fixed nodes
    ModuleDesc := GetPackageDescription (PChar (ModuleName));
    ContNode := AddChild (ModuleNode, 'Contains');
    ReqNode := AddChild (ModuleNode, 'Requires');

    // add information if the module is a package
    GetPackageInfo (HInstance, nil, Flags, ShowInfoProc);
    if ModuleDesc <> '' then
    begin
      AddChild (ModuleNode, 'Description: ' + ModuleDesc);
      if Flags and pfDesignOnly = pfDesignOnly then
        AddChild (ModuleNode, 'Design Only');
      if Flags and pfRunOnly = pfRunOnly then
        AddChild (ModuleNode, 'Run Only');
    end;
  end;
  Result := True;
end;
```

As you can see in the preceding code, the ForEachModule function begins by adding the module name as the main node of the tree (by calling the Add method of the TreeView1.Items object and passing nil as the first parameter). It then adds two fixed child nodes, which are stored in the ContNode and ReqNode variables declared in the implementation section of this unit.

Next, the program calls the GetPackageInfo function and passes it another callback function, ShowInfoProc, which I'll discuss shortly. The program adds the details for the main module (see Figure 12.9), simply because this will provide a list of the application's units. At the end of this function, we add more information if the module is a package, such as its description and compiler flags (we know it's a package if its description isn't an empty string).

FIGURE 12.9:

The PackInfo example also
lists the units that are part
of the current application.

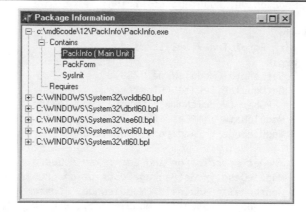

Earlier, I mentioned passing another callback function, the ShowInfoProc procedure, to the
GetPackageInfo function, which in turn calls our callback function for each contained or
required package of a module. This procedure creates a string that describes the package and
its main flags (added within parentheses), and then inserts that string under one of the two
nodes (ContNode and ReqNode), depending on the type of the module. We can determine the
module type by examining the NameType parameter. Here is the complete code of our second
callback function:

```
procedure ShowInfoProc (const Name: string; NameType: TNameType; Flags: Byte;
  Param: Pointer);
var
  FlagStr: string;
begin
  FlagStr := ' ';
  if Flags and ufMainUnit <> 0 then
    FlagStr := FlagStr + 'Main Unit ';
  if Flags and ufPackageUnit <> 0 then
    FlagStr := FlagStr + 'Package Unit ';
  if Flags and ufWeakUnit <> 0 then
    FlagStr := FlagStr + 'Weak Unit ';
  if FlagStr <> ' ' then
    FlagStr := ' (' + FlagStr + ')';
  with Form1.TreeView1.Items do
    case NameType of
      ntContainsUnit: AddChild (ContNode, Name + FlagStr);
      ntRequiresPackage: AddChild (ReqNode, Name);
    end;
end;
```

Here, you'll notice that the Flags parameter doesn't contain flag style information, as the
online help seems to imply. If you want to investigate this topic further, examine the SysUtils unit.

What's Next?

In this chapter we have seen how you can call functions that reside in DLLs, how to create DLLs using Delphi, and how to use strings and place Delphi forms inside a library. Another technique for placing Delphi forms and other classes in libraries is to use packages, special DLLs that the IDE uses for installing components, but that you can use for dividing an application into multiple executable files.

I will get back to the topics of libraries that expose objects and classes when I discuss COM and OLE in Chapters 19 and 20. For the moment, instead, we'll move to a totally different topic, the development of database-oriented and client/server applications with Delphi.

PART III

Database Programming

CHAPTER 13

Delphi's Database Architecture

- Delphi's database components

- Database access alternatives

- Using data-aware controls

- The DBGrid and multirecord objects

- Manipulating table fields

- Database applications with standard controls

Delphi's support for database applications is one of the key features of the programming environment. Many programmers spend most of their time writing data-access code, which needs to be the most robust portion of a database application. This chapter provides an overview of Delphi's extensive support for database programming.

What you won't find here is a discussion of the theory of database design. I'm assuming that you already know the fundamentals of database design and have already designed the structure of a database. I won't delve into database-specific problems; my goal is to help you understand how Delphi supports database access.

I'll begin with an explanation of the alternatives Delphi offers in terms of data access, and then I'll provide an overview of the database components that are available in Delphi. This chapter includes an overview of the TDataSet class, an in-depth analysis of the TField components, and the use of data-aware controls. The following chapters will provide information on more advanced database programming topics, such as client/server programming, the use of dbGo, dbExpress, and InterBase Express.

Accessing a Database: BDE, dbExpress, and Other Alternatives

In the first few versions of Delphi, the only available technology to access database data was to use the Borland Database Engine (BDE). Starting with Delphi 3, the portion of VCL related to Database access has been restructured to open it up to multiple database access solutions. Delphi 5 saw the introduction of specific sets of components supporting Microsoft's ActiveX Data Objects (ADO) and InterBase Express (IBX). Delphi 6 adds to the picture dbExpress, which is a brand-new cross-platform and database-independent data-access technology provided by Borland with Kylix on Linux and Delphi 6 on Windows.

With all these alternatives, it is easy to get confused on which approach to use. In the following sections I've provided a short description of the key elements of these data-access technologies available in Delphi, trying to suggest in which case you'll want to use each of them.

Borland Database Engine (BDE)

The BDE originated with Paradox, well before Delphi existed, and was extended by Borland to support other local databases and many SQL servers. The BDE has direct access to dBASE, Paradox, ASCII, FoxPro, and Access tables. A series of drivers (called SQL Links and available only in Delphi Enterprise) allows access to some SQL servers, including Oracle, Sybase, Microsoft, Informix, InterBase, and DB2 servers. If you need access to a different database, the BDE can also interface with ODBC drivers.

The advantage of using a common database engine is that your application will be portable among different servers of the same category (porting from a local database to an SQL server is generally much more complex). The specific advantages of using the BDE are that this technology is very well integrated in Delphi; its elements are very well documented; and it is the only viable solution for accessing local files such as Paradox and dBase tables.

The disadvantages of this solution: Borland has stopped developing it (there will be no further updates); you'll have to install and configure it on the client computers; it is quite a "heavyweight" engine, with large installation files and memory requirements; and it is available only on Windows. If you have existing Delphi BDE applications accessing local files, there is no hurry to convert them and get rid of the BDE, unless you want to move your applications to Linux. If you are using an SQL server, migrating to another data-access technology will probably be easier.

BDE is still a good solution, if you balance advantages and disadvantages, but its long-term viability is certainly in doubt. I'll keep using the BDE for the simpler examples of this chapter, but only for the sake of simplicity. In any case, I'll try to stress the elements common to all the dataset components rather than focus on specific features of BDE or Paradox.

The Delphi components related to the BDE are all hosted in the Data Access page of the Components palette. There are three dataset components, Table, Query, and StoredProc, plus the UpdateSQL used in connection with the Query component. The Database and Session components are used to set up the database connection. The BatchMove component is for copying data; the rarely used NestedTable component allows you to nest master-detail data in a sub-table; and the BDEClientDataSet component, introduced in Delphi 6, merges a ClientDataSet with a BDE-related data-access component.

ActiveX Data Objects (ADO)

ADO, which stands for ActiveX Data Objects, is Microsoft's high-level interface for database access. ADO is implemented on Microsoft's data-access OLE DB technology, which provides access to relational and non-relational databases as well as e-mail and file systems and custom business objects. ADO is an engine with features comparable to the BDE: database server independence supporting local and SQL servers alike, a really heavyweight engine, and a simplified configuration (because it is not centralized). Installation should in theory not be an issue, as the engine is part of recent versions of Windows. However, the limited compatibility among versions of ADO will force you to upgrade your users' computers to the same version you've used for developing the program—and the sheer size of the MDAC (Microsoft Data Access Components) installation, which updates large portions of the operating system, makes this operation far from simple.

ADO offers some definite advantages if you plan on using Access or SQL Server, as Microsoft's drivers for their own databases are of better quality than the average OLE DB providers. For Access databases, specifically, using Delphi's ADO components is a good solution. But if you plan using other SQL servers, first check the availability of a good quality driver, as you might have some surprises. ADO is very powerful, but you have to learn living with it, as it really stands in the way between your program and the database, providing services but occasionally also issuing different commands than you are expecting. On the negative side, do not even think of using ADO if you plan future cross-platform development: this Microsoft-specific technology is not available on Linux or other operating systems.

In short, use ADO if you plan working only on Windows, want to use Access or other Microsoft databases, or you find a good OLE DB provider for each of the database servers you plan working with (at the moment, for example, this excludes InterBase and many other SQL servers).

ADO components (part of a package Borland called ADO Express in Delphi 5 and now calls dbGo in Delphi 6) are all grouped in the ADO page of the Components palette. The three core components are ADOConnection (for database connection), ADOCommand (for executing SQL commands), and ADODataSet (for executing requests that return a result set). There are also three compatibility components—ADOTable, ADOQuery, and ADOStoredProc—which you can use for porting BDE-based applications to ADO. Finally, there is the RDSConnection component, for accessing data in remote multitier applications.

NOTE   Chapter 16, "ActiveX Data Objects," covers ADO and related technologies in great detail.

The dbExpress Library

One of the relevant new features of Delphi 6 is the introduction of the dbExpress database library for the Windows platform. I say "library" because, unlike BDE and ADO, dbExpress uses a lightweight approach; and I underline "Windows" because the same library is available also for Linux in Borland Kylix.

Being light and portable are actually the two key characteristics of dbExpress and the reasons it has been introduced by Borland, along with the development of the Kylix project. There are certainly other database libraries you could use in the past and can still use with Delphi, but this new offering is worth a thought. Consider also it requires basically no configuration on the user machines.

Compared to other powerhouses, dbExpress is really limited in its capabilities. It can access only SQL servers (no local files); it has no caching capabilities and provides only unidirectional access to the data; it can natively work only with SQL queries and is unable of generating the corresponding SQL update statements.

At first sight, you might think that these limitations make the library pretty useless. On the contrary, these are *features* that make it interesting. Unidirectional datasets with no direct update are the norm if you need to produce reporting, including generating HTML pages showing the content of a database. If you want to build a user interface to edit the data, instead, consider that Delphi includes specific components (the ClientDataSet and Provider, in particular) that provide caching and query resolution. These components allow your dbExpress-based application to have much more control than you can have with a separate (and monolithic) database engine, which does extra things for you but often does it the way it wants, not the way you would like.

Considering that Borland is pushing this library, and it is the only viable database-independent solution on Linux, I really urge you to consider it for new applications, and even to think about updating existing Delphi applications to this new architecture.

InterBase Express (IBX)

Delphi includes components for native access to Borland's own open-source (and free) Inter-Base server. Unlike BDE, ADO, and dbExpress, this is not a server-independent database engine, but a technology for accessing a specific database server. If you plan using only Inter-Base as your back-end RDBMS, using a specific set of components can give you more control of the server, provide the best performance, and allow you also to configure and maintain the server from within a custom client application.

NOTE   The use of InterBase Express highlights the case of database-specific custom datasets, which are available from third-party vendors for many servers (there are other dataset components for InterBase, as there are for Oracle, Access, dBase files, and many others).

In short, you can consider using InterBase Express (or other comparable sets of components) if you are sure you won't change your database and want to achieve best performance and control at the expense of flexibility and portability. The down side is that the extra performance and control you gain might be limited, and you'll have to learn how to use another set of components with a specific behavior, compared to learning how to use a generic engine and applying your knowledge to different situations.

The ClientDataSet Component

Finally, there is a component derived from TDataSet that has a peculiar behavior and can be combined with other data-access components. The ClientDataSet component, in fact, is a dataset accessing data kept in memory. The in-memory data can be totally temporary (lost as you exit the program), saved to a local file as a snapshot, and imported by another dataset using a Provider component. This last situation is certainly the most common: You can hook a ClientDataSet to any other local dataset, or use Borland's multitier support (discussed in

Chapter 17, "Multitier Database Applications with DataSnap") to retrieve data from a dataset hosted by a different application, possibly running on a separate computer.

The ClientDataSet component becomes particularly useful if the data-access components you are using provide limited or no caching. This is particularly true of the new dbExpress engine, but can equally help you when using the BDE or other native components. On the other hand, ADO already provides most of the services of the ClientDataSet component and using these two at the same time can be useful only in limited situations.

Classic BDE Components

Each of the database-access solutions discussed above has its own set of data-access, database connection, and extra utility components on a specific page of the Component palette. In Delphi 6, the classic BDE components have been moved to the new BDE page and include the Table, Query, and StoredProc components. The ADO, dbExpress, and InterBase Express components are each in specific pages, and all include specific dataset components and others that tend to mimic the BDE components, simplifying the porting of existing applications. The Data Access page of the Component palette in Delphi 6 includes only the Data Source component and others not specifically related with any single data access technology.

Besides the data-access component of your choice, a Delphi visual application generally uses some data-aware controls (in the Data Controls page) and the DataSource component. Data-aware controls are visual components used to view and edit the data in a form and are extensions of standard components such as edit and list boxes, radio buttons, images, and the grid. The DataSource component has the role of connector between the data-aware controls and a dataset component.

Tables and Queries

The simplest traditional way to specify data access in Delphi was to use the BDE Table component. A Table object simply refers to a database table. When you use a Table component, you need to indicate the name of the database you want to use in its DatabaseName property. You can enter an alias or the path of the directory with the table files. The Object Inspector lists the available names, which depend on the aliases installed in the BDE.

You also need to indicate a proper value in the TableName property. The Object Inspector lists the available tables of the current database (or directory), so you should generally select the DatabaseName property first.

Another classic dataset is the BDE Query component. A query requires a SQL language command. You can customize a query using SQL more easily than you can customize a table (as long as you know at least the basic elements of SQL, of course). The Query component has a DatabaseName property like the Table component, but it does not have a TableName property. The table is indicated in the SQL statement, stored in the SQL property.

For example, you can write a simple SQL statement like this:

```
select * from Country
```

where Country is the name of a table and the asterisk (*) indicates that you want to use all of the fields in the table.

The efficiency of a table or a query varies depending on the database you are using. In general, we can say that the Table component tends to be faster on local tables, while the Query component tends to be faster on SQL servers, although this is just a very general rule, and in many cases you might have the opposite effect. We'll see some efficiency issues while discussing client/server development in Chapter 14, "Client/Server Programming."

The third BDE dataset component is StoredProc, which refers to stored procedures of a SQL server database. You can run these procedures and get the results in the form of a database table. Stored procedures can only be used with SQL servers.

Specific Table Features

The BDE Table component has specific features not shared by all datasets. For example, it has filters, ranges, and specific techniques for locating records. A filter, set in the Filter property and activated by toggling the Filtered property, is available in each dataset, although its role changes depending on the underlying implementation. A range, instead, is specific to a Table and allows you to specify the two extreme values and consider only the record falling within that interval.

When using a Table, and particularly a local one, there are specific methods you can use to find a record, such as GotoKey, FindKey, GotoNearest, FindNearest, and Locate. The Locate method is shared by all datasets, and I'll discuss it later along with other general features of the TDataSet class. The other methods are specific of the TTable class and work in conjunction with the index set in the ndexFieldNames property of the component.

The simplest approach is to use the FindNearest method for the approximate search and the FindKey method to look for an exact match:

```
// goto
Table1.FindNearest ([EditName.Text]);

// go near
if not Table1.FindKey ([EditName.Text]) then
  MessageDlg ('Name not found', mtError, [mbOk], 0);
```

Both find methods use as parameters an array of constants. Each array element corresponds to one of the fields of the current index. You can also pass only the value for the initial field or fields of the index, so the following fields will not be considered.

NOTE   I won't discuss these features in details, showing complete examples, because some of them are limited to the BDE and makes sense only for local tables, not for SQL server–based tables. Actually if you set a filter or a range over a Table connected with a SQL server, the BDE will try to generate a proper select statement, avoiding fetching all the data and filtering it locally. The problem is that this isn't always possible and you lose most of your control, two good reasons to use the Query component when working with SQL servers.

A Query with Parameters

When you need slightly different versions of the same SQL query, instead of modifying the text of the Query (stored in the SQL property) each time, you can write a query with a parameter and simply change the value of the parameter. For example, if you decide to have a user choose the countries of a continent (using the Country table of the DBDEMOS database), you can write the following parametric query:

```
select *
from Country
where Continent = :Continent
```

In this SQL clause, :Continent is a parameter. We can set its data type and startup value, using the editor of the Params property collection of the Query component. When the Parameters collection editor is open, as shown in Figure 13.1, you see a list of the parameters defined in the SQL statement and set the data type and the initial value of these parameters.

FIGURE 13.1:

Editing the collection of parameters of a Query component

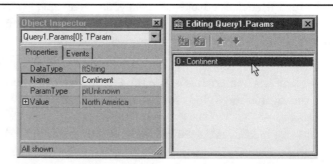

The form displayed by this program, called ParQuery and available on the companion CD, uses a list box to provide all the available values for the parameters. Instead of preparing the items of the list box at design time, we can extract the available continents from the same database table as the program starts. This is accomplished using a second query component, with this SQL statement:

```
select distinct Continent
from Country
```

After activating this query, the program scans its result set, extracting all the values and adding them to the list box:

```
procedure TQueryForm.FormCreate(Sender: TObject);
begin
  // get the list of continents
  Query2.Open;
  while not Query2.EOF do
  begin
    ListBox1.Items.Add (Query2.Fields [0].AsString);
    Query2.Next;
  end;
  ListBox1.ItemIndex := 0;

  // open the first query
  Query1.Params[0].Value := ListBox1.Items [0];
  Query1.Open;
end;
```

Before opening the query, the program selects as its parameter the first item of the list box, which is also activated by setting the ItemIndex property to 0. When the list box is selected, the program closes the query and changes the parameter:

```
procedure TQueryForm.ListBox1Click(Sender: TObject);
begin
  Query1.Close;
  Query1.Params[0].Value := ListBox1.Items [Listbox1.ItemIndex];
  Query1.Open;
end;
```

This displays the countries of the selected continent in the list box, as you can see in Figure 13.2. The final refinement is that when the user enters a record with a new continent, it is added automatically to the list box. Instead of refreshing the entire list, with the same code executed in the FormCreate method, we can do this by handling the BeforePost event and adding the continent to the list if it is not already there:

```
procedure TQueryForm.Query1BeforePost(DataSet: TDataSet);
var
  StrNewCont: string;
begin
  // add the continent, if not already in the list
  StrNewCont := Query1.FieldByName ('Continent').AsString;
  if ListBox1.Items.IndexOf (StrNewCont) < 0 then
    ListBox1.Items.Add (StrNewCont);
end;
```

We can add a little extra code to this program to take advantage of a specific feature of
parameterized queries. To react faster to a change in the parameters, these queries can be
optimized, or *prepared*. Simply call the Prepare method before the program first opens the
query (after setting the Active property of the Query component to False at design time)
and call Unprepare once the query won't be used anymore:

```
procedure TQueryForm.FormCreate(Sender: TObject);
begin
  ...
  // prepare and open the first query
  Query1.Prepare;
  Query1.Params[0].Value := ListBox1.Items [0];
  Query1.Open;
end;

procedure TQueryForm.FormDestroy(Sender: TObject);
begin
  Query1.Close;
  Query1.Unprepare;
end;
```

Prepared parameterized queries are very important when you work on a complex query. In
fact, the BDE or the SQL server must read the text of the query and determine how to process
it. If you use the same query (even if a parametric one) over and over, the engine doesn't need
to reprocess the query but already knows how to handle it.

Master/Detail Structures

Often you need to relate tables, which have a one-to-many relationship. This means that for
a single record of the master table, there are many detailed records in a secondary table. A
classic example is that of an invoice and the items of the invoice; another is a list of customers

and the orders each customer has made. This is very common situation in database programming, and Delphi provides explicit support for it with the master/detail structure. We'll see this structure for BDE Table and Query components, but the same technique applies to almost all of the datasets available in Delphi.

NOTE   The `TDataSet` class has a generic `DataSource` property for setting up a master data source, but the Table component, for example, uses a different property (`MasterSource`) to express the same concept.

Master/Detail with Tables

The simplest ways to create a master/detail structure in Delphi is to use the Database Form Wizard, selecting a master/detail form in the first page. To accomplish the same effect manually, place two table components in a form or data module, connect them with the same database, and connect each with a table. In the MastDet example, I've used the customer and orders tables of the DBDEMOS database, and I've used a data module. Now add a DataSource component for each table, and for the secondary table set a master source to the data source connected to the first table. Finally relate the secondary table to a field (called `MasterField`) of the main table, using the special property editor provided.

A Data Module for Data-Access Components

To build a Delphi database application, you can place data-access components and the data-aware controls in a form. This is handy for a simple program, but having the user interface and the data access and data model in a single, often large, unit is far from a good idea. For this reason, Delphi implements the idea of *data module*, a container of nonvisual components I already introduced in Chapter 1, "The Delphi 6 IDE."

At design time, a data module is similar to a form, but at run time it exists only in memory. The `TDataModule` class derives directly from `TComponent`, so it is completely unrelated to the Windows concept of a window (and is fully portable among different operating systems). Unlike a form, a data module has just a few properties and events. For this reason, it's useful to think of data modules as components and method containers.

Like a form or a frame, a data module has a designer. This means Delphi creates for a data module a specific Object Pascal unit for the definition of its class and a form definition file that lists its components and their properties.

There are several reasons to use data modules. The simplest one is to share data-access components among multiple forms, as I'll demonstrate at the beginning of the next chapter. This technique works in conjunction with visual form linking, the ability to access components of another form or data module at design time (with the File ➢ Use Unit command). The second

Continued on next page

reason is to separate the data from the user interface, improving the structure of an application. Data modules in Delphi even exist in versions specific for multitier applications (remote data modules) and server-side HTTP applications (Web data modules).

Finally, remember that you can use the Diagram page of the editor, introduced in Chapter 1, to see a graphical representation of the connections among the components of a data module, as you can see in this example for the MastDet application:

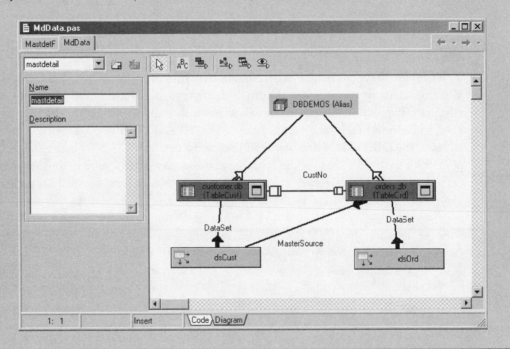

The following is the complete listing (only without the irrelevant positional properties) of the Data Module used by the MastDet program on the CD:

```
object DataModule1: TDataModule1
  OnCreate = DataModule1Create
  object TableCust: TTable
    DatabaseName = 'DBDEMOS'
    TableName = 'customer.db'
  end
  object TableOrd: TTable
    DatabaseName = 'DBDEMOS'
    IndexName = 'CustNo'
    MasterFields = 'CustNo'
```

```
        MasterSource = dsCust
        TableName = 'orders.db'
      end
    object dsCust: TDataSource
      DataSet = TableCust
    end
    object dsOrd: TDataSource
      DataSet = TableOrd
    end
  end
```

TIP   Starting with Delphi 5, you can also create a master/detail structure using the Data Diagram view of a data module.

In Figure 13.3 you can see an example of the main form of the MastDet program at run time. I've placed data-aware controls related to the master table in the upper portion, and I've placed a grid connected with the detail table in the lower portion of the form. This way, for every master record, you immediately see the list of the connected detail record, in this case all the orders by the current client. Each time you select a new customer, the grid below displays only the orders pertaining to that customer.

FIGURE 13.3:

The MastDet example at run time

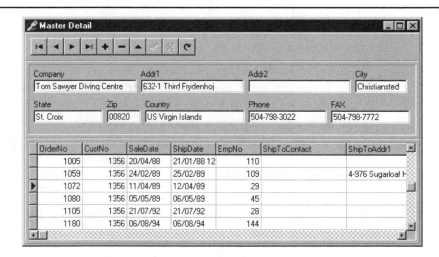

A Master/Detail Structure with Queries

The previous example used two tables to build a master/detail form. As an alternative, you can define this type of join using a SQL statement. After setting the master DataSource for the detailed query, you simply set up its SQL statement with a parameter having the same name of the field of the master dataset this data source refers to.

For this example (called Orders), I've joined the ORDERS.DB table with ITEMS.DB, which describes the items of each order. The two tables can be joined using the `OrderNo` field. When you generate the code, the program behaves exactly like the previous one, Mast-Det. This time, however, the trick is in the SQL statements of the second query object:

```
select OrderNo, ItemNo, PartNo, Qty
from items
where OrderNo = :OrderNo
```

As you can see, this SQL statement uses a parameter, `OrderNo`. This parameter is connected directly to the first query, because the `DataSource` property of `QueryItems` is set to `dsOrders`, which is connected to `QueryOrders`. In other words, the second query is considered to be a data control connected to the first data source. Each time the current record in the first data source changes, the `QueryItems` component is updated, just like any other component connected to `dsOrders`. The field used for the connection, in this case, is the field having the same name as the query parameter.

Other BDE Related Components

Along with Table, Query, StoredProc, and DataSource, other components are on the Data Access page of the Component palette, the BDE page. I'll cover these components in the next chapter, but here is a short summary:

- The Database component is used for transaction control, security, and connection control. It is generally used only to connect to remote databases in client/server applications or to avoid the overhead of connecting to the same database in several forms. The Database component is also used to set a local alias, one used only inside a program. Once this local alias is set to a given path, the Table and Query components of the application can refer to the local database alias. This is much better than replicating the hard-coded path in each DataSet component of the program.

TIP   The Borland Database Engine (BDE) uses an alias to refer to a database file or directory. You can define new aliases for databases by using the Database Explorer or the Database Engine Configuration utility. It is also possible to define them by writing code in Delphi that calls the `AddStandardAlias` and `AddAlias` methods of the `Session` global object, followed by a call to `SaveConfigFile` to make the alias persistent. The alternative is the low-level `DbiAddAlias` BDE function. In some of the program of this chapter I'll use the DBDEMOS database alias, which refers to Delphi's demo database, installed by default in the `C:\Program Files\Common Files\Borland Shared\Data` directory.

- The Session component provides global control over database connections for an application, including a list of existing databases and aliases and an event to customize database login.

- The BatchMove component is used to perform batch operations, such as copying, appending, updating, or deleting values, on one or more databases.

- The UpdateSQL component allows you to write SQL statements to perform various update operations on the dataset, when using a read-only query (that is, when working with a complex query). This component is used as the value of the UpdateObject property of tables or queries.

Using Data-Aware Controls

Once you've set up the proper data-access components, you can build a user interface to let a user view the data and eventually edit it. Delphi provides many components that resemble the usual Windows controls but are data-aware. For example, the DBEdit component is similar to the Edit component, and the DBCheckBox component corresponds to the CheckBox component. You can find all of these components in the Data Controls page of the Delphi Component palette.

All of these components are connected to a data source using the corresponding property, DataSource. Some of them relate to the entire dataset, such as the DBGrid and DBNavigator components, while the others refer to a specific field of the data source, as indicated by the DataField property. Once you select the DataSource property, the DataField property will have a list of values available in the drop-down combo box of the Object Inspector.

NOTE   In Chapter 18, "Writing Database Components," we'll discuss the technical details of these controls, as we'll see how to write custom data-aware components.

Notice that all the data-aware components are totally unrelated to the data-access technology, provided the data-access component inherits from TDataSet. This means that your investment on the user interface is totally preserved when you change the data-access technology. What is true, however, is that some of the lookup components and an extended use of the DBGrid, displaying a lot of data, only make more sense when working with local data, and should generally be avoided in a client/server situation, as we'll see in the next chapter.

Data in a Grid

The DBGrid is a grid capable of displaying a whole table at once. It allows scrolling and navigation, and you can edit the grid's contents. It is an extension of the other Delphi grid controls.

You can customize the DBGrid by setting the various flags of its Options property and modifying its Columns collection. The grid allows a user to navigate the data, using the scroll-bars, and perform all the mayor actions. A user can edit the data directly, insert a new record in a given position by pressing the Insert key, append a new record at the end by going to the last record and pressing the Down arrow key, and delete the current record by pressing Ctrl+Del.

The Columns property is a collection where you can choose the fields of the table you want to see in the grid and set column and title properties (color, font, width, alignment, caption, and so on) for each field. Some of the more advanced properties, such as ButtonStyle and DropDownRows, can be used to provide custom editors for the cells of a grid or a drop-down list of values (indicated in the PickList property of the column).

An alternative to the DBGrid is the DBCtrlGrid component, a multirecord grid that can host panels with other data-aware controls. These controls are duplicated in each panel for each record of the dataset. I'll discuss the DBCtrlGrid control at the end of this chapter.

DBNavigator and Dataset Actions

DBNavigator is a collection of buttons used to navigate and perform actions on the database. You can disable some of the buttons of the DBNavigator control, by removing some of the elements of the VisibleButtons set.

The buttons perform basic actions on the connected dataset, so you can easily replace them with your own toolbar, particularly if you use an ActionList component with the predefined database actions provided by Delphi. In this case, in fact, you get all the standard behaviors, but you'll also see the various buttons enabled only when their action is legitimate.

TIP   If you use the standard actions, you can avoid connecting them to a specific DataSource component, and the actions will be applied to the dataset connected to the visual control that currently has the input focus. This way a single toolbar can be used for multiple datasets displayed by a form.

Text-Based Data-Aware Controls

There are multiple text-oriented components:

- DBText displays the contents of a field that cannot be modified by the user. It is a data-aware Label graphical control. It can be very useful, but users might confuse this control with the plain labels that indicate the content of each field-based control.

- DBEdit lets the user edit a field (change the current value) using an Edit control. At times, you might want to disable editing and use a DBEdit as if it were a DBText, but highlighting the fact that this is data coming from the database.

- DBMemo lets the user see and modify a large text field, eventually stored in a memo or BLOB (binary large object) field. It resembles the Memo component and has full editing capabilities, but all the text is rendered in a single font.

- DBRichEdit is a component that lets the user edit a formatted text file; it is based on a RichEdit Windows common control and, in contrast to DBMemo, it allows text with multiple fonts and paragraph styles.

List-Based Data-Aware Controls

For letting a user choose a value in a predefined list (which reduces input errors), you can use many different components. DBListBox, DBComboBox, and DBRadioGroup are similar, providing a list of strings in the Items property, but they do have some differences:

- The DBListBox component allows selection of predefined items ("closed selection"), but not text input, and can be used to list many elements. Generally it's best to show only about six or seven items, to avoid using up too much space on the screen.

- The DBComboBox component can be used both for closed selection and for user input. The csDropDown style of the DBComboBox, in fact, allows a user to enter a new value, besides selecting one of the available ones. The component also uses a smaller area of the form because the drop-down list is usually displayed only on request.

- The DBRadioGroup component presents radio buttons (which permit only one selection), allows only closed selection, and should be used only for a limited number of alternatives. A nice features of this component is that the values displayed can be exactly those you want to insert in the database, but you can also choose to provide some sort of mapping. The values of the user interface (some descriptive strings stored in the Items property) will map to corresponding values stored in the database (some numeric or character-based codes listed in the Values property). For example, you can map some numeric codes indicating departments to a few descriptive strings:

```
object DBRadioGroup1: TDBRadioGroup
  Caption = 'Department'
  DataField = 'Department'
  DataSource = DataSource1
  Items.Strings = (
    'Sales'
    'Accounting'
    'Production'
    'Management')
```

```
Values.Strings = (
  '1'
  '2'
  '3'
  '4')
end
```

A slightly different component is the DBCheckBox, used to show and toggle an option, corresponding to a Boolean field. It is a limited list, because it has only two possible values, plus the undetermined state for fields with null values. You can determine which are the values to send back to the database by setting the ValueChecked and ValueUnchecked properties of this component.

The usage of a DBRadioGroup control, with the settings discussed above, and a DBCheckBox control is highlighted by the DbAware example.

Creating Local Tables with FieldDefs

The DbAware example would be a rather simple program if it didn't have an extra feature: It can create a new table for the DBDEMOS database. Delphi allows you to set the definition of the fields of a table—its internal structure—at design time, using the collection editor of the FieldDefs property. Once you've defined the fields, you can then right-click the table component at design time and select the Create Table command.

This list of field definitions is generally extracted from the database, but if you set the StoreDefs property of the table to True, it will be saved in the DFM file along with the other table properties. The effect of the StoreDefs property is more complex than it seems at first. If you right-click the form, you'll notice that its local menu offers an Update Table Definition option, along with the expected Delete Table and Rename Table. That is, you can store the field definitions locally, but if the structure of the physical table changes, you should update this definition as well. Until Delphi 4, the field definitions were invariably loaded from the database table at run time; now you can preload them, speeding up the table opening. However, if the local and the actual table definitions do not match, you can get in trouble.

In the DbAware example, I've used this technique to create a new database table, called Workers, which stores data about the employees of a company. This is the definition of the fields of the table, along with the other key properties:

```
object Table1: TTable
  DatabaseName = 'DBDEMOS'
  FieldDefs = <
    item
      Name = 'LastName'
      DataType = ftString
```

Continued on next page

```
                Size = 20
              end
              item
                Name = 'FirstName'
                DataType = ftString
                Size = 20
              end
              item
                Name = 'Department'
                DataType = ftSmallint
              end
              item
                Name = 'Branch'
                DataType = ftString
                Size = 20
              end
              item
                Name = 'Senior'
                DataType = ftBoolean
              end
              item
                Name = 'HireDate'
                DataType = ftDate
              end>
          StoreDefs = True
          TableName = 'Workers'
      end
```

Regardless of the fact you might have created the table at design time, the program must do so the first time it is executed on a different computer. In practice, when the program starts, it checks whether the table already exists and creates one if it doesn't:

```
procedure TForm1.FormCreate(Sender: TObject);
begin
  if not Table1.Exists then
    Table1.CreateTable;
  Table1.Open;
end;
```

Finally, the program has some code to fill in the table with random values. As this is kind of tedious but not too complex, I won't discuss the details here, but let you look at the source code of the DbAware example if you are interested. I'll use the table produced by this program in other examples in this book, so you might want to run it once and create the table anyway.

Using Lookup Controls

If the list of values is extracted from another dataset, then instead of the DBListBox and DBComboBox controls you should use the specific DBLookupListBox or DBLookupCombo-Box components. These components are used every time you want to select for a field a record of another dataset.

For example, if you build a standard form for taking orders, the orders dataset will generally have a field hosting a number indicating the customer who made the order. Working directly with the customer number is not the most natural way; most users will prefer to work with customer names. However, in the database, the names of the customers are stored in a different table, to avoid duplicating the customer data for each order by the same customer. To get around such a situation, with local databases or small lookup tables, you can use a DBLookupComboBox control. (This technique doesn't port very well to client/server architecture with large lookup tables, as discussed in the next chapter.)

The DBLookupComboBox component can be connected to two data sources at the same time, one source containing the actual data and a second containing the display data. Basically, I've built a standard form using the ORDERS.DB tables of the DBDEMOS database, with several DBEdit controls (you can as well use the Database Form Wizard to build this plain form). The example actually uses a Query component selecting most fields of the orders table.

At this point we want to remove the standard DBEdit component connected to the customer number and replace it with a DBLookupComboBox component (and a DBText component for understanding what exactly is going on). The lookup component (and the DBText) is connected with the DataSource for the order and with the CustNo field. To let the lookup component show the information extracted from another table, CUSTOMER.DB, we need to add another table component referring to it, and new data source connected to the table.

For the program to work, you need to set several properties of the DBLookupComboBox1 component. Here is a list of the relevant values:

```
object DBLookupComboBox1: TDBLookupComboBox
  DataField = 'CustNo'
  DataSource = DataSourceOrders
  KeyField = 'CustNo'
  ListField = 'Company;CustNo'
  ListSource = DataSourceCustomer
  DropDownWidth = 300
end
```

The first two properties determine the main connection, as usual. The other three properties determine the secondary source (ListSource), the field used for the join (KeyField), and the information to display (ListField). Besides entering the name of a single field, you can provide multiple fields, as I've done in the example. Only the first field is displayed as combo box text, but if you set a large value for the DropDownWidth property, the pull-down list of the combo box will include multiple columns of data. You can see this output in Figure 13.4.

FIGURE 13.4:

The output of the Cust-
Lookup example, with the
DBLookupComboBox
showing multiple fields in
its drop-down list

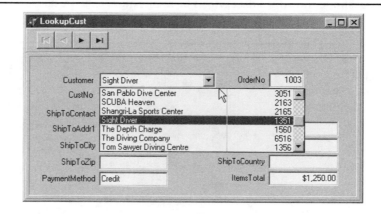

TIP   If you set the index of the table connected with the DBLookupComboBox to the Company field, the drop-down list will show the companies in alphabetical order instead of customer-number order. This is what I've done in the example.

What about the code of this program? Well, there is none. Everything works just by setting the correct properties. The three joined data sources do not need custom code. This demonstrates that using master/detail and lookup connections can be very fast to set up and very efficient. The only real drawback is that these techniques, particularly the lookup, cannot be used when the number of records becomes too large, particularly in a networked or client/server environment. Moving hundreds of thousands of records just to make a nice-looking lookup combo box probably won't be very effective.

NOTE   In Delphi 6, both the TDBLookupComboBox and TDBLookupListBox controls have a Null-ValueKey property, which indicates the shortcut that can be used to set the value to null, by calling the Clear method of the corresponding field.

Graphical Data-Aware Controls

Finally, Delphi includes two graphical data-aware controls:

- DBImage is an extension of an Image component that shows a picture stored in a BLOB field (provided the database uses a graphic format that the Image component supports, such as BMP and JPEG).

- DBChart is a data-aware business graphic component or the data-aware version of the TeeChart control built by David Berneda.

To demonstrate the use of the DBChart control, I've added this component to a simple example showing a data grid. The application, called ChartDB, shows a pie chart with the surface of each country of the COUNTRY.DB table, as you can see in Figure 13.5.

FIGURE 13.5:

The output of the ChartDB example, which is based on the TDbChart control

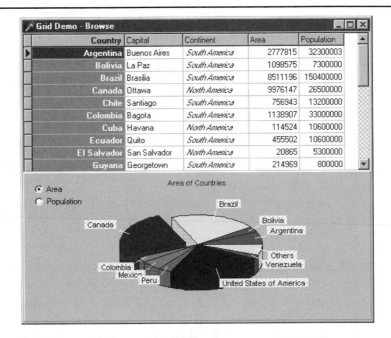

The program has almost no code, as all the settings can be done using the specific component editor, which has several options but is quite easy to use. Here are some of the key properties of the component, taken from the form description:

```
object DBChart1: TDBChart
  Legend.Visible = False
  Align = alClient
  object Series1: TPieSeries
    Marks.ArrowLength = 8
    Marks.Visible = True
    DataSource = Table1
    XLabelsSource = 'Name'
    ExplodeBiggest = 3
    OtherSlice.Style = poBelowPercent
    OtherSlice.Text = 'Others'
    OtherSlice.Value = 2
    PieValues.ValueSource = 'Area'
  end
end
```

What I've done is show the area field as the data source for the pie chart (the PieValues .ValueSource property of the series), use the name field for the labels (the XLabelsSource property of the series), and condense all the countries with a value below 2 percent in a single section indicated as Others (the OtherSlide subproperties).

As a minor addition to the code, I've added two radio buttons you can use to toggle between the area and the population. The code of the two radio buttons simply sets the source of the series, after casting it to the proper series type, as in:

```
procedure TForm1.RadioPopulationClick(Sender: TObject);
begin
  DBChart1.Title.Text [0] := 'Population of Countries';
  (DBChart1.Series [0] as TPieSeries).PieValues.ValueSource := 'Population';
end;
```

The DataSet Component

Instead of focusing right away on the use of a specific dataset, I prefer starting with a generic introduction of the features of the TDataSet class, which are shared by all inherited data-access classes. The DataSet component is a very complex one, so I won't list all of its capabilities but only discuss its core elements.

The idea behind this component is to provide access to a series of records that are read from some source of data, kept in internal buffers (for performance reasons), and eventually modified by a user, with the possibility of writing back changes to the persistent storage. This approach is generic enough to be applied to different types of data (even non-database data) but has a few rules. First, there can be only one active record at a time, so if you need to access data in multiple records, you must move to each of them, read the data, then move again, and so on. You'll find an example of this and related techniques in the section about navigation.

Second, you can edit only the active record: you cannot modify a set of records at the same time, as you can in a relational database. Moreover, you can modify data in the active buffer only after you explicitly declare you want to do so, by giving the Edit command to the dataset. You can also use the Insert command to create a new blank record, and close both operations (insert or edit) by giving a Post command.

Other interesting elements of a dataset I will explore in the following sections are its status (and the status change events), navigation and record positions, and the role of the field objects. As a summary of the capabilities of the DataSet component, I've included the public methods of its class in Listing 13.1 (the code has been edited and commented for clarity). Not all of these methods are directly used everyday, but I decided to keep them all in the listing. In

Chapter 18, I'll also discuss the virtual methods of the protected portion of the class, which we'll need to override to build custom dataset components.

Listing 13.1:   The public interface of the _TDataSet_ class (excerpted)

```
TDataSet = class(TComponent, IProviderSupport)
...
public
  // create and destroy, open and close
  constructor Create(AOwner: TComponent); override;
  destructor Destroy; override;
  procedure Open;
  procedure Close;
  property BeforeOpen: TDataSetNotifyEvent read FBeforeOpen write FBeforeOpen;
  property AfterOpen: TDataSetNotifyEvent read FAfterOpen write FAfterOpen;
  property BeforeClose: TDataSetNotifyEvent
    read FBeforeClose write FBeforeClose;
  property AfterClose: TDataSetNotifyEvent read FAfterClose write FAfterClose;

  // status information
  function IsEmpty: Boolean;
  property Active: Boolean read GetActive write SetActive default False;
  property State: TDataSetState read FState;
  function ActiveBuffer: PChar;
  property IsUniDirectional: Boolean
    read FIsUniDirectional write FIsUniDirectional default False;
  function UpdateStatus: TUpdateStatus; virtual;
  property RecordSize: Word read GetRecordSize;
  property ObjectView: Boolean read FObjectView write SetObjectView;
  property RecordCount: Integer read GetRecordCount;
  function IsSequenced: Boolean; virtual;
  function IsLinkedTo(DataSource: TDataSource): Boolean;

  // datasource
  property DataSource: TDataSource read GetDataSource;
  procedure DisableControls;
  procedure EnableControls;
  function ControlsDisabled: Boolean;

  // fields, including blobs, details, calculated, and more
  function FieldByName(const FieldName: string): TField;
  function FindField(const FieldName: string): TField;
  procedure GetFieldList(List: TList; const FieldNames: string);
  procedure GetFieldNames(List: TStrings);
  property FieldCount: Integer read GetFieldCount;
  property FieldDefs: TFieldDefs read FFieldDefs write SetFieldDefs;
  property FieldDefList: TFieldDefList read FFieldDefList;
  property Fields: TFields read FFields;
  property FieldList: TFieldList read FFieldList;
  property FieldValues[const FieldName: string]: Variant
```

```delphi
  read GetFieldValue write SetFieldValue; default;
property AggFields: TFields read FAggFields;
property DataSetField: TDataSetField
  read FDataSetField write SetDataSetField;
property DefaultFields: Boolean read FDefaultFields;
procedure ClearFields;
function GetBlobFieldData(FieldNo: Integer;
  var Buffer: TBlobByteData): Integer; virtual;
function CreateBlobStream(Field: TField;
  Mode: TBlobStreamMode): TStream; virtual;
function GetFieldData(Field: TField;
  Buffer: Pointer): Boolean; overload; virtual;
procedure GetDetailDataSets(List: TList); virtual;
procedure GetDetailLinkFields(MasterFields, DetailFields: TList); virtual;
function GetFieldData(FieldNo: Integer;
  Buffer: Pointer): Boolean; overload; virtual;
function GetFieldData(Field: TField; Buffer: Pointer; NativeFormat: Boolean):
  Boolean; overload; virtual;
property AutoCalcFields: Boolean
  read FAutoCalcFields write FAutoCalcFields default True;
property OnCalcFields: TDataSetNotifyEvent
  read FOnCalcFields write FOnCalcFields;

// position, movement
procedure CheckBrowseMode;
procedure First;
procedure Last;
procedure Next;
procedure Prior;
function MoveBy(Distance: Integer): Integer;
property RecNo: Integer read GetRecNo write SetRecNo;
property Bof: Boolean read FBOF;
property Eof: Boolean read FEOF;
procedure CursorPosChanged;
property BeforeScroll: TDataSetNotifyEvent
  read FBeforeScroll write FBeforeScroll;
property AfterScroll: TDataSetNotifyEvent
  read FAfterScroll write FAfterScroll;

// bookmarks
procedure FreeBookmark(Bookmark: TBookmark); virtual;
function GetBookmark: TBookmark; virtual;
function BookmarkValid(Bookmark: TBookmark): Boolean; virtual;
procedure GotoBookmark(Bookmark: TBookmark);
function CompareBookmarks(Bookmark1, Bookmark2: TBookmark): Integer; virtual;
property Bookmark: TBookmarkStr read GetBookmarkStr write SetBookmarkStr;

// find, locate
function FindFirst: Boolean;
function FindLast: Boolean;
function FindNext: Boolean;
```

```
function FindPrior: Boolean;
property Found: Boolean read GetFound;
function Locate(const KeyFields: string; const KeyValues: Variant;
  Options: TLocateOptions): Boolean; virtual;
function Lookup(const KeyFields: string; const KeyValues: Variant;
  const ResultFields: string): Variant; virtual;

// filtering
property Filter: string read FFilterText write SetFilterText;
property Filtered: Boolean read FFiltered write SetFiltered default False;
property FilterOptions: TFilterOptions
  read FFilterOptions write SetFilterOptions default [];
property OnFilterRecord: TFilterRecordEvent
  read FOnFilterRecord write SetOnFilterRecord;

// refreshing, updating
procedure Refresh;
property BeforeRefresh: TDataSetNotifyEvent
  read FBeforeRefresh write FBeforeRefresh;
property AfterRefresh: TDataSetNotifyEvent
  read FAfterRefresh write FAfterRefresh;
procedure UpdateCursorPos;
procedure UpdateRecord;
function GetCurrentRecord(Buffer: PChar): Boolean; virtual;
procedure Resync(Mode: TResyncMode); virtual;

// editing, inserting, posting, and deleting
property CanModify: Boolean read GetCanModify;
property Modified: Boolean read FModified;
procedure Append;
procedure Edit;
procedure Insert;
procedure Cancel; virtual;
procedure Delete;
procedure Post; virtual;
procedure AppendRecord(const Values: array of const);
procedure InsertRecord(const Values: array of const);
procedure SetFields(const Values: array of const);

// events related to editing, inserting, posting, and deleting
property BeforeInsert: TDataSetNotifyEvent
  read FBeforeInsert write FBeforeInsert;
property AfterInsert: TDataSetNotifyEvent
  read FAfterInsert write FAfterInsert;
property BeforeEdit: TDataSetNotifyEvent read FBeforeEdit write FBeforeEdit;
property AfterEdit: TDataSetNotifyEvent read FAfterEdit write FAfterEdit;
property BeforePost: TDataSetNotifyEvent read FBeforePost write FBeforePost;
property AfterPost: TDataSetNotifyEvent read FAfterPost write FAfterPost;
property BeforeCancel: TDataSetNotifyEvent
  read FBeforeCancel write FBeforeCancel;
property AfterCancel: TDataSetNotifyEvent
```

```
      read FAfterCancel write FAfterCancel;
   property BeforeDelete: TDataSetNotifyEvent
      read FBeforeDelete write FBeforeDelete;
   property AfterDelete: TDataSetNotifyEvent
      read FAfterDelete write FAfterDelete;
   property OnDeleteError: TDataSetErrorEvent
      read FOnDeleteError write FOnDeleteError;
   property OnEditError: TDataSetErrorEvent
      read FOnEditError write FOnEditError;
   property OnNewRecord: TDataSetNotifyEvent
      read FOnNewRecord write FOnNewRecord;
   property OnPostError: TDataSetErrorEvent
      read FOnPostError write FOnPostError;

   // support, utilities
   function Translate(Src, Dest: PChar;
      ToOem: Boolean): Integer; virtual;
   property Designer: TDataSetDesigner read FDesigner;
   property BlockReadSize: Integer read FBlockReadSize write SetBlockReadSize;
   property SparseArrays: Boolean read FSparseArrays write SetSparseArrays;
 end;
```

The Status of a Dataset

When you operate on a dataset in Delphi, you can work in different states, indicated by a specific State property, which can assume several different values:

dsBrowse   indicates that the dataset is in normal browse mode, used to look at the data and scan the records.

dsEdit   indicates that the dataset is in edit mode. A dataset enters this state when the program calls the Edit method or the DataSource has the AutoEdit property set to True, and the user starts editing a data-aware control, such as a DBGrid or DBEdit. When the changed record is posted, the dataset exits the dsEdit state.

dsInsert   indicates that a new record is being added to the dataset. Again, this might happen when calling the Insert method, moving to the last line of a DBGrid, or using the corresponding command of the DBNavigator component.

dsInactive   is the state of a closed dataset.

dsSetKey   indicates that we are preparing a search on the dataset. This is the state between a call to the SetKey method and a call to the GotoKey or GotoNearest methods (see the Search example later in this chapter).

dsCalcFields   is the state of a dataset while a field calculation is taking place; that is, during a call to an OnCalcFields event handler. Again, I'll show this in an example.

dsNewValue, dsOldValue, and dsCurValue   are the states of a dataset when an update of the cache is in progress.

dsFilter   is the state of a dataset while setting a filter; that is, during a call to an `OnFilter-Record` event handler.

In simple examples, the transitions between these states are handled automatically, but it is important to understand them because there are many events referring to the state transitions. For example, every dataset fires events before and after any state change. When a program requests an `Edit` operation, the component fires the `BeforeEdit` event just before entering in edit mode (an operation you can stop by raising an exception). Immediately after entering edit mode, the dataset receives the `AfterEdit` event. After the user has finished editing and requests to store the data, executing the `Post` command, the dataset fires a `BeforePost` event, which can be used to check the input before sending the data to the database, and an `AfterPost` event after the operation has been successfully completed.

Another more general state-change tracking technique is to handle the `OnStateChange` event of the DataSource component. As a very simple example you can show the current status with code like this:

```
procedure TForm1.DataSource1StateChange(Sender: TObject);
var
  strStatus: string;
begin
  case Table1.State of
    dsBrowse: strStatus := 'Browse';
    dsEdit: strStatus := 'Edit';
    dsInsert: strStatus := 'Insert';
  else
    strStatus := 'Other state';
  end;
  StatusBar.Panels[0].Text := strStatus;
end;
```

The code considers only the three most common states a dataset component, ignoring the inactive state and other special cases.

The Fields of a Dataset

I mentioned earlier that a dataset has only one record that is the current, or active, one. The record is stored in a buffer, and you can operate on it with some generic methods, but to access the data of the record you need to use the field objects of the dataset. This explains why field components (technically instances of class derived from the `TField` class) play a fundamental role in every Delphi database application. Data-aware controls are directly connected to these field objects, which correspond to database fields.

By default, Delphi automatically creates the TField components at run time, each time the program opens a dataset component. This is done after reading the metadata associated with the table or the query the dataset refers to. These field components are stored in the Fields array property of a dataset. You can access these values by number (accessing the array directly) or by name (using the FieldByName method). Each field can be used for reading or modifying the data of the current record, using its Value property or type-specific properties, like AsDate, AsString, AsInteger, and so on:

```
var
   strName: string;
begin
   strName := Table1.Fields[0].AsString
   strName := Table1.FieldByName('LastName').AsString
```

Value is a variant type property, so using the type-specific access properties is a little more efficient. The dataset component has also a shortcut property for accessing the variant-type value of a field, the default FieldValues property. Being a default property means you can omit it from the code by applying the square brackets directly to the dataset:

```
strName := Table1.FieldValues ['LastName'];
strName := Table1 ['LastName'];
```

Creating the field components each time a dataset is opened is only a default behavior. As an alternative, you can create the field components at design time, using the Fields editor (double-click a dataset to see the Fields editor in action, or activate its local menu and choose the Fields Editor command). After creating a field for the LastName column of a table, for example, you can refer to its value by applying one of the AsXxx methods to the proper field object:

```
strName := Table1LastName.AsString;
```

Besides being used to access the value of a field, each field object also has properties for controlling visualization and editing of its value, including range of values, edit masks, display format, constraints, and many others. These properties, of course, depend on the type of the field—that it is, on the specific class of the field object. If you create persistent fields you can set some properties at design time, instead of writing code at run time, maybe in the AfterOpen event of the dataset.

NOTE   Although the Fields editor is similar to the editors of the collections used by Delphi, fields are not part of a collection. They are components created at design time, listed in its published section of the form class, and available in the drop-down combo box at the top of the Object Inspector.

As you open the Fields editor for a dataset, it appears empty. You have to activate the local menu of this editor to access its capabilities. The simplest operation you can do is to select the Add command, which allows you to add any other fields in the dataset to the list of fields. Figure 13.6 shows the Add Fields dialog box, which lists all the fields that are available in a table. These are the database table fields that are not already present in the list of fields in the editor.

FIGURE 13.6:

The Fields editor with the Add Fields dialog box

The Define command of the Fields editor, instead, lets you define a new calculated field, lookup field, or field with a modified type. In this dialog box, you can enter a descriptive field name, which might include blank spaces. Delphi generates an internal name—the name of the field component—which you can further customize. Next, select a data type for the field. If this is a calculated field or a lookup field, and not just a copy of a field redefined to use a new data type, simply check the proper radio button. We'll see how to define a calculated field in the section "Adding a Calculated Field" and a lookup field in two following sections.

NOTE
A TField component has both a Name property and a FieldName property. The Name property is the usual component name. The FieldName property is either the name of the column in the database table or the name you define for the calculated field. It can be more descriptive than the Name, and it allows blank spaces. The FieldName property of the TField component is copied to the DisplayLabel property by default, but this field name can be changed to any suitable text. It is used, among other things, to search a field in the FieldByName method of the TDataSet class and when using the array notation.

All of the fields that you add or define are included in the Fields editor and can be used by data-aware controls or displayed in a database grid. If a field of the original database table is not in this list, it won't be accessible. When you use the Fields editor, Delphi adds the declaration of the available fields to the class of the form, as new components (much as the Menu Designer adds TMenuItem components to the form). The components of the TField class, or more specifically its subclasses, are fields of the form, and you can refer to these components directly in the code of your program to change their properties at run time or to get or set their value.

In the Fields editor, you can also drag the fields to change their order. Proper field ordering is particularly important when you define a grid, which arranges its columns using this order.

TIP   An even better feature of the Fields editor is that you can drag fields from this editor to the surface of a form and have Delphi automatically create a corresponding data-aware control (such as a DBEdit, a DBMemo, or a DBImage). The type of control created depends on the data type of the field. This is a very fast way to generate custom forms, and I suggest you try it out if you've never used it before. This is my preferred way to build database-related forms, much better than using the Database Form Wizard.

Using Field Objects

Before we look at an example, let's go over the use of the TField class. The importance of this component should not be underestimated. Although it is often used behind the scenes, its role in database applications is fundamental. As I already mentioned, even if you do not define specific objects of this kind, you can always access the fields of a table or a query using their Fields array property, the FieldValues indexed property, or the FieldByName method. Both the Fields property and the FieldByName function return an object of type TField, so you sometimes have to use the as operator to downcast their result to its actual type (like TFloatField or TDateField) before accessing specific properties of these subclasses.

The FieldAcc example is a simple extension of a form generated by the Database Form Wizard. I've added to it three speed buttons in the toolbar panel, accessing various field properties at run time. The first button changes the formatting of the population column of the grid. To do this, we have to access the DisplayFormat property, a specific property of the TFloatField class. For this reason we have to write:

```
procedure TForm2.SpeedButton1Click(Sender: TObject);
begin
  (Table1.FieldByName ('Population') as
    TFloatField).DisplayFormat := '###,###,###';
end;
```

When you set field properties related to data input or output, the change applies to every record in the table. When you set properties related to the value of the field, instead, you always refer to the current record only. For example, we can output the population of the current country in a message box by writing:

```
procedure TForm2.SpeedButton2Click(Sender: TObject);
begin
  ShowMessage (string (Table1 ['Name']) +': '+ string (Table1 ['Population']));
end;
```

When you access the value of a field, you can use a series of *As* properties to handle the current field value using a specific data type (if this is available; otherwise, an exception is raised):

```
AsBoolean: Boolean;
AsDateTime: TDateTime;
AsFloat: Double;
AsInteger: LongInt;
AsString: string;
AsVariant: Variant;
```

These properties can be used to read or change the value of the field. Changing the value of a field is possible only if the dataset is in edit mode. As an alternative to the *As* properties indicated above, you can access the value of a field by using its Value property, which is defined as a variant.

Most of the other properties of the TField component, such as Alignment, DisplayLabel, DisplayWidth, and Visible, reflect elements of the field's user interface and are used by the various data-aware controls, particularly DBGrid. In the FieldAcc example, clicking the third speed button changes the Alignment of every field:

```
procedure TForm2.SpeedButton3Click(Sender: TObject);
var
  I: Integer;
begin
  for I := 0 t7 Table1.FieldCount - 1 do
    Table1.Fields[I].Alignment := taCenter;
end;
```

This affects the output of the DBGrid, and of the DBEdit control I've added to the toolbar, which shows the name of the country. You can see this effect, along with the new display format, in Figure 13.7.

Name	Capital	Continent	Area	Population
Argentina	Buenos Aires	South America	2777815	32,300,003
Bolivia	La Paz	South America	1098575	7,300,000
Brazil	Brasilia	South America	8511196	150,400,000
Canada	Ottawa	North America	9976147	26,500,000
Chile	Santiago	South America	756943	13,200,000
Colombia	Bagota	South America	1138907	33,000,000
Cuba	Havana	North America	114524	10,600,000
Ecuador	Quito	South America	455502	10,600,000
El Salvador	San Salvador	North America	20865	5,300,000
Guyana	Georgetown	South America	214969	800,000

A Hierarchy of Field Classes

There are several field class types in VCL. Delphi automatically uses one of them depending on the data definition in the database, when you open a table at run time or when you use the Fields editor at design time. Table 13.1 shows the complete list of subclasses of the TField class.

TABLE 13.1: The Subclasses of TField

Subclass	Base Class	Definition
TADTField	TObjectField	An ADT (Abstract Data Type) field, corresponding to an object field in an object relational database.
TAggregateField	TField	An aggregate field represents a maintained aggregate. It is used in the ClientDataSet component and discussed in Chapter 14, "Client/Server Programming."
TArrayField	TObjectField	An array of objects in an object relational database.
TAutoIncField	TIntegerField	Whole positive number connected with a Paradox auto-increment field of a table, a special field automatically assigned a different value for each record. Note that Paradox AutoInc fields do not always work perfectly, as discussed in the next chapter.
TBCDField	TNumericField	Real numbers, with a fixed number of digits after the decimal point.
TBinaryField	TField	Generally not used directly. This is the base class of the next two classes.
TBlobField	TField	Binary data and no size limit (BLOB stands for binary large object). The theoretical maximum limit is 2 GB.
TBooleanField	TField	Boolean value.
TBytesField	TBinaryField	Arbitrary data with a large (up to 64 KB characters) but fixed size.
TCurrencyField	TFloatField	Currency values, with the same range as the new **Real** data type.
TDataSetField	TObjectField	An object corresponding to a separate table in an object relational database.
TDateField	TDateTimeField	Date value.
TDateTimeField	TField	Date and time value.
TFloatField	TNumericField	Floating-point numbers (8 byte).
TFMTBCDField	TNumericField	(New field type in Delphi 6) A true binary-coded decimal (BCD), as opposed to the existing **TBCDField** type, which converted BCD values to the Currency type. This field type is used automatically only by dbExpress datasets.
TGraphicField	TBlobField	Graphic of arbitrary length.
TGuidField	TStringField	A field representing a COM Globally Unique Identifier, part of the ADO support.

Continued on next page

TABLE 13.1 continued: The Subclasses of TField

Subclass	Base Class	Definition
TIDispatchField	TInterfaceField	A field representing pointers to **IDispatch** COM interfaces, part of the ADO support.
TIntegerField	TNumericField	Whole numbers in the range of long integers (32 bits).
TInterfacedField	TField	Generally not used directly. This is the base class of fields that contain pointers to interfaces (**IUnknown**) as data.
TLargeIntField	TIntegerField	Very large integers (64 bit).
TMemoField	TBlobField	Text of arbitrary length.
TNumericField	TField	Generally not used directly. This is the base class of all the numeric field classes.
TObjectField	TField	Generally not used directly. The base class for the fields providing support for object relational databases.
TReferenceField	TObjectField	A pointer to an object in an object relational database.
TSmallIntField	TIntegerField	Whole numbers in the range of integers (16 bits).
TSQLTimeStampField	TField	(New field type in Delphi 6) Supports the date/time representation used in dbExpress drivers
TStringField	TField	Text data of a fixed length (up to 8192 bytes).
TTimeField	TDateTimeField	Time value.
TVarBytesField	TBytesField	Arbitrary data, up to 64 KB characters. Very similar to the **TBytes-Field** base class.
TVariantField	TField	A field representing a variant data type, part of the ADO support.
TWideStringField	TStringField	A field representing a Unicode (16 bits per character) string.
TWordField	TIntegerField	Whole positive numbers in the range of words or unsigned integers (16 bits).

The availability of any particular field type, and the correspondence with the data definition, depends on the database in use. This is particularly true for the new field types that provide support for object relational databases.

Adding a Calculated Field

Now that you've been introduced to TField objects and seen an example of their run-time use, it is time to build a simple example based on the declaration of field objects at design time using the Fields editor. We can start again from the first example we built, GridDemo, and add a calculated field. The COUNTRY.DB database table we are accessing has both the population and the area of each country, so we can use this data to compute the population density.

To build the new example, named Calc, select the Table component in the form, and open the Fields editor. In this editor, choose the Add command, and select some of the fields. (I've decided to include them all.) Now select the Define command, and enter a proper name and data type (TFloatField) for the new calculated field, as you can see in Figure 13.8.

FIGURE 13.8:

The definition of a calculated field in the Calc example

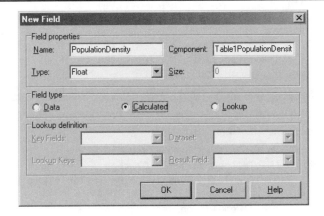

WARNING It is obvious that as you create some field components at design time using the Fields editor, the fields you skip won't get a corresponding object. What might not be obvious is that the fields you skip will not be available even at run time, with Fields or **FieldByName**. When a program opens a table at run time, if there are no design-time field components, Delphi creates field objects corresponding to the table definition. If there are some design-time fields, however, Delphi uses those fields without adding any extra ones.

Of course, we also need to provide a way to calculate the new field. This is accomplished in the OnCalcFields event of the Table component, which has the following code (at least in a first version):

```
procedure TForm2.Table1CalcFields(DataSet: TDataSet);
begin
  Table1PopulationDensity.Value := Table1Population.Value / Table1Area.Value;
end;
```

NOTE Calculated fields are computed for each record and recalculated each time the record is loaded in an internal buffer, invoking the **OnCalcFields** event over and over again. For this reason, a handler of this event should be extremely fast to execute, and cannot alter the status of the dataset, by accessing different records. A more time-efficient (but less memory-efficient) version of a calculated field is provided by the ClientDataSet component with "internally calculated" fields, which are evaluated only once, when they are loaded, with the result stored in memory for future requests.

Everything fine? Not at all! If you enter a new record and do not set the value of the population and area, or if you accidentally set the area to zero, the division will raise an exception, making it quite problematic to continue using the program. As an alternative, we could have handled every exception of the division expression and simply set the resulting value to zero:

```
try
  Table1PopulationDensity.Value := Table1Population.Value / Table1Area.Value;
except
  on Exception do
    Table1PopulationDensity.Value := 0;
end;
```

However, we can do even better. We can check if the value of the area is defined—if it is not null—and if it is not zero. It is better to avoid using exceptions when you can anticipate the possible error conditions:

```
if not Table1Area.IsNull and
    (Table1Area.Value <> 0) then
  Table1PopulationDensity.Value := Table1Population.Value / Table1Area.Value
else
    Table1PopulationDensity.Value := 0;
```

The code of the Table1CalcFields method above (in each of the three versions) accesses some fields directly. This is possible because I used the Fields editor, and it automatically created the corresponding field declarations, as you can see in this excerpt of the interface declaration of the form:

```
type
  TCalcForm = class(TForm)
    Table1: TTable;
    Table1PopulationDensity: TFloatField;
    Table1Area: TFloatField;
    Table1Population: TFloatField;
    Table1Name: TStringField;
    Table1Capital: TStringField;
    Table1Continent: TStringField;
    procedure Table1CalcFields(DataSet: TDataset);
    ...
```

Each time you add or remove fields in the Fields editor, you can see the effect of your action immediately in the grid present in the form. Of course, you won't see the values of a calculated field at design time; they are available only at run time, because they result from the execution of compiled Pascal code.

Since we have defined some components for the fields, we can use them to customize some of the visual elements of the grid. For example, to set a display format that adds a comma to separate thousands, we can use the Object Inspector to change the DisplayFormat property of some field components to "###,###,###". This change has an immediate effect on the grid at design time.

NOTE   The display format I've just mentioned (and used in the previous example) uses the Windows International Settings to format the output. When Delphi translates the numeric value of this field to text, the comma in the format string is replaced by the proper `ThousandSeparator` character. For this reason, the output of the program will automatically adapt itself to different International Settings. On computers that have the Italian configuration, for example, the comma is replaced by a period.

After working on the table components and the fields, I've customized the DBGrid using its `Columns` property editor. I've set the Population Density column to read-only and set its `ButtonStyle` property to cbsEllipsis, to provide a custom editor. When you set this value, a small button with an ellipsis is displayed when the user tries to edit the grid cell. Pressing the button invokes the `OnEditButtonClick` event of the DBGrid:

```
procedure TCalcForm.DBGrid1EditButtonClick(Sender: TObject);
begin
  MessageDlg (Format (
    'The population density (%.2n)'#13 +
    'is the Population (%.0n)'#13 +
    'divided by the Area (%.0n).'#13#13 +
    'Edit these two fields to change it.',
    [Table1PopulationDensity.AsFloat,
    Table1Population.AsFloat,
    Table1Area.AsFloat]),
    mtInformation, [mbOK], 0);
end;
```

Actually, I haven't provided a real editor, but rather a message describing the situation, as you can see in Figure 13.9, which shows the values of the calculated fields. To create an editor, you might build a secondary form to handle special data entries.

FIGURE 13.9:

The output of the Calc example. Notice the Population Density calculated column, the ellipsis button, and the message displayed when you select it.

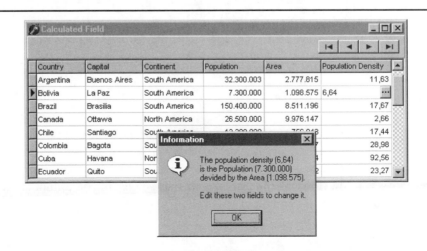

Lookup Fields

As an alternative to placing a DBLookupComboBox component in a form (discussed earlier in this chapter under "Using Lookup Controls"), we can also define a lookup field, which can be displayed with a drop-down lookup list inside a DBGrid component. We've seen that to add a fixed selection to a DBGrid, we can simply edit the PickList subproperty of the Columns property. To customize the grid with a live lookup, instead, we have to define a lookup field using the Fields editor.

As an example, I've built the FieldLookup program, which has a grid displaying orders with a lookup field to display the name of the employee who took the order, instead of the code number of this employee. To accomplish this, I added to the data module a Table component referring to the EMPLOYEE.DB table. Then I opened the Fields editor for the ORDERS table and added all the fields. I selected the EmpNo field and set its Visible property to False, to remove it from the grid (we cannot remove it altogether, because it is used to build the cross-reference with the corresponding field of the EMPLOYEE table).

Now it is time to define the lookup field. If you've followed the preceding steps, you can use the Fields editor of the ORDERS table and select the New Field command, obtaining the New Field dialog box. (As an alternative in Delphi 5, it's possible to use the Diagram page of the editor, drop the two tables there, and drag a lookup relation from the ORDERS table to the EMPLOYEE table, connecting the two in the resulting New Field dialog box. In Delphi 6, though, the lookup relation button is still part of the Diagram page but doesn't seem to be working at all.)

The values you specify in the New Lookup Field dialog box will affect the properties of a new TField added to the table, as demonstrated by the DFM description of the field:

```
object Table2Employee: TStringField
  FieldKind = fkLookup
  FieldName = 'Employee'
  LookupDataSet = Table2
  LookupKeyFields = 'EmpNo'
  LookupResultField = 'LastName'
  KeyFields = 'EmpNo'
  Size = 30
  Lookup = True
end
```

This is all that is needed to make the drop-down list work (see Figure 13.10) and to view the value of the cross-references field at design time, too. Notice that there is no need to customize the Columns property of the grid, because the drop-down button and the value of seven rows are taken by default. This doesn't mean you cannot use this property to further customize these and other visual elements of the grid.

FIGURE 13.10:

The output of the Field-Lookup example, with the drop-down list inside the grid displaying values taken from another database table

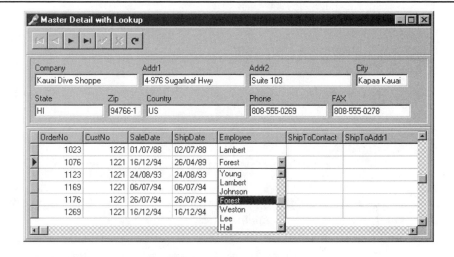

Handling Null Values with Field Events

Beyond a few interesting properties, the field objects have a few key events. The OnValidate event can be used to provide extended validation of the value of a field, and should be used whenever you need a complex rule that the ranges and constraints provided by the field cannot express. This event is triggered before the data is written to the record buffer, whereas the OnChange event is fired soon after the data has been written.

Two more events, OnGetText and OnSetText, can be used to customize the output of a field. These two events are extremely powerful: they allow you to use data-aware controls even when the representation of a field you want to display is different from the one Delphi will provide by default.

An example of the use of these events is the handling of null value. On SQL servers, storing an empty value or a null value for a field are two separate operations. The latter tends to be more correct, but Delphi by default uses empty values and displays the same output for an empty or a null field. Although this can be useful in general for strings and numbers, it becomes extremely important for dates, where it is hard to set a reasonable default value and where if the user blanks out the field you might have an invalid input.

The NullDates program displays a specific text for dates that have a null value and clears the field (setting it to the null value) when the user uses an empty string in input. Here is the relevant code of the two event handlers for the field:

```
procedure TForm1.Table1ShipDateGetText(Sender: TField;
  var Text: String; DisplayText: Boolean);
begin
```

```
  if Sender.IsNull then
    Text := '<undefined>'
  else
    Text := Sender.AsString;
end;


procedure TForm1.Table1ShipDateSetText(Sender: TField; const Text: String);
begin
  if Text = '' then
    Sender.Clear
  else
    Sender.AsString := Text;
end;
```

In Figure 13.11 you can see an example of the output of this program, with undefined (or null) values for some shipping dates.

FIGURE 13.11:

By handling the OnGet-Text and OnSetText events of a date field, the NullDates example displays a specific output for null values

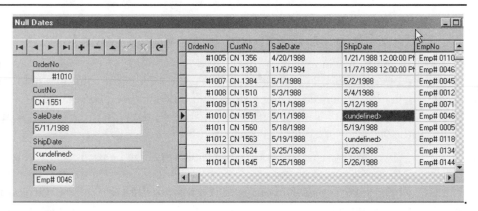

Navigating a Dataset

We've seen that a dataset has only one active record, and you can imagine that the active record changes often, in response of user actions or because of internal commands given to the dataset. To move around the dataset and change the active record, there are methods of the TDataSet class, as you can see in Listing 13.1, particularly in the section commented as "position, movement." You can move to the next or previous record, jump back and forth by a given number of records (with MoveBy), or go directly to the first or last record of the dataset. These operations of the dataset are generally available in the DBNavigator component or in the standard dataset actions, and they are not particularly complex to understand.

What is not obvious, though, is how a dataset handles the extreme positions. If you open any dataset with a navigator attached, you can see that as you move on record by record, the Next button remains enabled even when you've reached the last record. It's only when you try to move forward after the last record that the current record apparently doesn't change and the button is disabled. This is because the Eof test (end of file) succeeds only when the cursor has been moved to a special position after the last record. If you jump to the end with the Last button, instead, you'll immediately be at the very end. You'll see exactly the same behavior for the first record (and the Bof test). As we'll see in a while, this approach is very handy, as we can scan a dataset testing for Eof to be True and, at this point, we know we've also already processed the last record of the dataset.

NOTE   Handling this special record positions before the beginning and after the end of the dataset, which are called *cracks*, is very important (and quite confusing) when you write a custom dataset, as we'll see in Chapter 18.

Besides moving around record by record or by a given number of records, programs might need to jump to specific records or positions. Some datasets support the RecordCount property and allow movement to a record at a given position in the dataset using the RecNo property. These properties can be used only for datasets that support positions natively, which basically excludes all client/server architectures, unless you grab all of the records in a local cache (something you'll generally want to avoid) and then navigate on the cache. As we'll see in the next chapter, when you open a query on a SQL server you fetch only the records you are using, so Delphi doesn't know the record count, at least not in advance.

There are two alternatives you can use to refer to a record in a dataset, regardless of its type:

- You can save a reference to the current record and then jump back to it after moving around. This is accomplished by using bookmarks, either in the TBookmark or the more modern TBookmarkStr form. This approach is discussed in the upcoming section "Using Bookmarks."

- You can locate a record of the dataset matching given criteria, using the Locate method. This even works after you close and reopen the dataset, because you're working at a logical (and not physical) level. This approach is presented in the next section.

Locating Records in a Table

To show you an example of the use of the Locate method, I've built the Search example, which has a table connected to EMPLOYEE.DB. The form I've prepared has the data-aware edit boxes inside a scroll box aligned to the client area, so that a user can freely resize the form without any problems. When the form becomes too small, scroll bars will appear automatically in the area holding the edit boxes. Another feature is a toolbar with buttons connected to some of the predefined dataset actions available in the ActionList component plus two custom actions to host the search code.

The searching capabilities are activated by the two buttons connected to custom actions. The first button is connected to `ActionGoto`, used for an exact match, and the second to `ActionGoNear`, for a partial match. In both cases, we want to compare the text in the edit box with the `LastName` fields of the EMPLOYEE table. If the local table has an index on the field (as in the specific case) `Locate` will use it, but the method will work with or without indexes (only at a different speed).

If you've never used `Locate`, at first sight the help file won't be terribly clear. The idea is that you must provide a list of fields you want to search, and a list of values, one for each field. If you pass only one field, the value is passed directly, as in the case of the example:

```
procedure TSearchForm.ActionGotoExecute(Sender: TObject);
begin
  if not Table1.Locate ('LastName', EditName.Text, []) then
    MessageDlg ('"' + EditName.Text + '" not found', mtError, [mbOk], 0);
end;
```

If you search for multiple fields, you have to pass a variant array with the list of the values you want to match. The variant array can be created from a constant array with the `VarArrayOf` function or from scratch using the `VarArrayCreate` call. This is a code snippet from the example:

```
Table1.Locate ('LastName;FirstName', VarArrayOf (['Cook', 'Kevin']), [])
```

Finally, we can use the same method to look for a record even if we know only the initial portion of the field we are looking for. Simply add the `loPartialKey` flag to the `Options` parameter (the third) of the `Locate` call.

NOTE   Using `Locate` makes sense specifically for local tables, but doesn't port very well to client/server applications. In fact, on local tables this technique is rather optimized by letting the dataset read in only the records it is looking for, using local indexes. On a SQL server, instead, similar client-side techniques imply moving all the data to the client application first, which is generally a bad idea. Locating the data should be performed with restricted SQL statements. You can still call `Locate` after you're retrieved a limited dataset. For example, you can search a customer by name after you've selected all the customer of a given town or area, obtaining a result set of a limited size. There's more on this topic in the next chapter, which is devoted to client/server development.

The Total of a Table Column

So far in our examples, the user can view the current contents of a database table and manually edit the data or insert new records. Now we will see how we can change some data in the table through the program code. The idea behind this example is quite simple. The EMPLOYEE table we have been using has a Salary field. A manager of the company could indeed browse through the table and change the salary of a single employee. But what will be the total salary expense for the company? And what if the manager wants to give a 10 percent salary increase (or decrease) to everyone?

These are the two aims of the Total example, which is an extension of the previous program. The toolbar of this new example has some more buttons and actions. There are a few other minor changes from the previous example. I opened the Fields editor of the table and removed the Table1Salary field, which was defined as a TFloatField. Then I selected the New Field command and added the same field, with the same name, but using the TCurrencyField data type. This is not a calculated field; it's simply a field converted into a new (but equivalent) data type. Using this new field type the program will default to a new output format, suitable for currency values.

Now we can turn our attention to the code of this new program. First, let's look at the code of the total action. This action lets you calculate the sum of the salaries of all the employees, then edit some of the values, and compute a new total. Basically, we need to scan the table, reading the value of the Table1Salary field for each record:

```
var
  Total: Real;
begin
  Total := 0;
  Table1.First;
  while not Table1.EOF do
  begin
    Total := Total + Table1Salary.Value;
    Table1.Next;
  end;
  MessageDlg ('Sum of new salaries is ' +
    Format ('%m', [Total]), mtInformation, [mbOk], 0);
end
```

This code works, as you can see from the output in Figure 13.12, but it has some problems. One problem is that the record pointer is moved to the last record, so the previous position in the table is lost. Another is that the user interface is refreshed many times during the operation.

FIGURE 13.12:

The output of the Total
program, showing the total
salaries of the employees

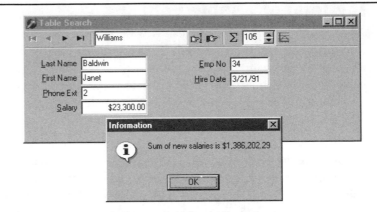

Using Bookmarks

To avoid these two problems, we need to disable updates and to store the current position of
the record pointer in the table and restore it at the end. This can be accomplished using a
table bookmark, a special variable storing the position of a record in a database table. Delphi's
traditional approach is to declare a variable of the TBookmark data type, and initialize it while
getting the current position from the table:

```
var
   Bookmark: TBookmark;
begin
   Bookmark := Table1.GetBookmark;
```

At the end of the ActionTotalExecute method, we can restore the position and delete the
bookmark with the following two statements:

```
Table1.GotoBookmark (Bookmark);
Table1.FreeBookmark (Bookmark);
```

As a better (and more up-to-date) alternative, we can use the Bookmark property of the
TDataset class, which refers to a bookmark that is disposed of automatically. (This is technically implemented as an *opaque string*, a structure subject to string lifetime management, but
it is not a string, so you're not supposed to look at what's inside it.) This is how you can modify the code above:

```
var
   Bookmark: TBookmarkStr;
begin
   Bookmark := Table1.Bookmark;
   ...
   Table1.Bookmark := Bookmark;
```

To avoid the other side effect of the program (we see the records scrolling while the routine browses through the data), we can temporarily disable the visual controls connected with the table. The table has a `DisableControls` method we can call before the `while` loop starts and an `EnableControls` method we can call at the end, after the record pointer is restored.

Disabling the data-aware controls connected with a table during long operations not only improves the user interface (since the output is not changing constantly), it also speeds up the program considerably. In fact, the time spent to update the user interface is much greater than the time spent performing the calculations. To test this, try commenting out the `DisableControls` and `EnableControls` methods of the Total example, and see the speed difference.

Finally, we face some dangers from errors in reading the table data, particularly if the program is reading the data from a server using a network. If any problem occurs while retrieving the data, an exception takes place, the controls remain disabled, and the program cannot resume its normal behavior. So we should use a `try/finally` block. Actually, if you want to make the program 100 percent error-proof, you should use two nested `try/finally` blocks. Including this change and the two discussed above, here is the resulting code:

```
procedure TSearchForm.ActionTotalExecute(Sender: TObject);
var
  Bookmark: TBookmarkStr;
  Total: Real;
begin
  Bookmark := Table1.Bookmark;
  try
    Table1.DisableControls;
    Total := 0;
    try
      Table1.First;
      while not Table1.EOF do
      begin
        Total := Total + Table1Salary.Value;
        Table1.Next;
      end;
    finally
      Table1.EnableControls;
    end
  finally
    Table1.Bookmark := Bookmark;
  end;
  MessageDlg ('Sum of new salaries is ' +
    Format ('%m', [Total]), mtInformation, [mbOK], 0);
end;
```

I've written this code to show you an example of a loop to browse the contents of a table, but keep in mind that there is an alternative approach based on the use of a SQL query returning the sum of the values of a field. When you use a SQL server, the speed advantage of a SQL call to compute the total can be very large, since you don't need to move all the data of each field from the server to the client computer. The server sends the client only the final result.

Editing a Table Column

The code of the increase action is similar to the one we have just seen. The `ActionIncrease-Execute` method also scans the table, computing the total of the salaries, as the previous method did. Although it has just two more statements, there is a key difference. When you increase the salary, you actually change the data in the table. The two key statements are within the `while` loop:

```
while not Table1.EOF do
begin
  Table1.Edit;
  Table1Salary.Value := Round (Table1Salary.Value * SpinEdit1.Value) / 100;
  Total := Total + Table1Salary.Value;
  Table1.Next;
end;
```

The first statement brings the table into edit mode, so that changes to the fields will have an immediate effect. The second statement computes the new salary, multiplying the old one by the value of the SpinEdit component (by default, 105) and dividing it by 100. That's a 5 percent increase, although the values are rounded to the nearest dollar. With this program, you can change salaries by any amount—even double the salary of each employee—with the click of a button.

Notice that the table enters the edit mode every time the `while` loop is executed. This is because in a dataset, edit operations can take place only one record at a time. You must finish the edit operation, calling **Post** or moving to a different record as in the code above. At that time, if you want to change another record, you have to enter edit mode once more.

Customizing a Database Grid

Unlike most other data-aware controls, which are quite simple to use, the DBGrid control has many options and is more powerful than you might think. The following sections explore some of the advanced operations you can do using a DBGrid control. A first example shows how to draw in a grid, a second one shows how to clone the behavior of a check box for a

Boolean selection inside a grid, and the final example shows how to use the multiple-selection feature of the grid.

Painting a DBGrid

There are many reasons you might want to customize the output of a grid. A good example is to highlight specific fields or records. Another is to provide some form of output for fields that usually don't show up in the grid, such as BLOB, graphic, and memo fields.

To thoroughly customize the drawing of a DBGrid control, you have to set its Default-Drawing property to False and handle its OnDrawColumnCell event. In fact, if you leave the value of DefaultDrawing set to True, the grid will display the default output before the method is called. This way, all you can do is add something to the default output of the grid, unless you decide to draw over it, which will take extra time and cause flickering.

The alternative approach is to call the DefaultDrawColumnCell method of the grid, perhaps after changing the current font or restricting the output rectangle. In this last case you can provide an extra drawing in a cell and let the grid fill the remaining area with the standard output. This is what I've done in the DrawData program.

The DBGrid control in this example, which is connected to the commonly used BIOLIFE table of the DBDEMOS database, has the following properties:

```
object DBGrid1: TDBGrid
  Align = alClient
  DataSource = DataSource1
  DefaultDrawing = False
  Font.Height = -16
  Font.Name = 'MS Sans Serif'
  Font.Style = [fsBold]
  TitleFont.Height = -11
  TitleFont.Name = 'MS Sans Serif'
  TitleFont.Style = []
  OnDrawColumnCell = DBGrid1DrawColumnCell
end
```

The OnDrawColumnCell event handler is called once for every cell of the grid and has several parameters, including the rectangle corresponding to the cell, the index of the column we have to draw, the column itself (with the field, its alignment, and other subproperties), and the status of the cell. How can we set the color of specific cells to red? We can simply change it in the special cases:

```
procedure TForm1.DBGrid1DrawColumnCell(Sender: TObject;
  const Rect: TRect; DataCol: Integer; Column: TColumn;
  State: TGridDrawState);
begin
```

```
    // red font color if length > 100
    if (Column.Field = Table1Lengthcm) and (Table1Lengthcm.AsInteger > 100) then
      DBGrid1.Canvas.Font.Color := clRed;

    // default drawing
    DBGrid1.DefaultDrawDataCell (Rect, Column.Field, State);
  end;
```

The next step is to draw the memo and the graphic fields. For the memo we can simply implement the memo field's OnGetText and OnSetText events. In fact, the grid will even allow editing on a memo field if its OnSetText event is not nil. Here is the code of the two event handlers. I've used Trim to remove trailing nonprinting characters, which make the text appear to be empty when editing:

```
procedure TForm1.Table1NotesGetText(Sender: TField;
  var Text: String; DisplayText: Boolean);
begin
  Text := Trim (Sender.AsString);
end;

procedure TForm1.Table1NotesSetText(Sender: TField; const Text: String);
begin
  Sender.AsString := Text;
end;
```

For the image, the simplest approach is to create a temporary TBitmap object, assign the graphics field to it, and paint the bitmap to the Canvas of the grid. As an alternative, I've removed the graphic field from the grid, by setting its Visible property to False, and added the image to the fish name, with the following extra code in the OnDrawColumnCell event handler:

```
var
  Bmp: TBitmap;
  OutRect: TRect;
  BmpWidth: Integer;
begin
  // default output rectangle
  OutRect := Rect;

  if Column.Field = Table1Common_Name then
  begin
    // draw the image
    Bmp := TBitmap.Create;
    try
      Bmp.Assign (Table1Graphic);
      BmpWidth := (Rect.Bottom - Rect.Top) * 2;
      OutRect.Right := Rect.Left + BmpWidth;
```

```
    DBGrid1.Canvas.StretchDraw (OutRect, Bmp);
  finally
    Bmp.Free;
  end;
  // reset output rectangle, leaving space for the graphic
  OutRect := Rect;
  OutRect.Left := OutRect.Left + BmpWidth;
end;

// red font color if length > 100 (omitted - see above)

// default drawing
DBGrid1.DefaultDrawDataCell (OutRect, Column.Field, State);
```

As you can see in the code above, the program shows the image in a small rectangle on the left of the grid cell and then changes the output rectangle to the remaining area before activating the default drawing. You can see the effect in Figure 13.13.

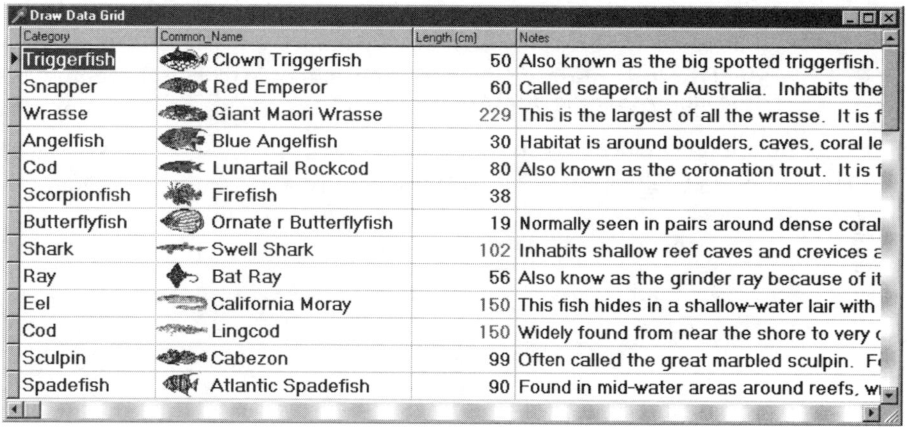

FIGURE 13.13:

The DrawData program displays a grid that includes the text of a memo field and the ubiquitous Borland fishes.

A Check Box Cell

Another common extension of the DBGrid control, found in many third-party components, is the use of check boxes to select the status of Boolean field values. A simple way to do this is to place a DBCheckBox control in front of the grid when the user selects the corresponding item. I've done this in the CheckDbg example, which uses the Workers table created in the DbAware example discussed earlier in this chapter.

The form displayed by the program contains only the grid and the check box. This is a summary of the textual description of the form:

```
object DbaForm: TDbaForm
  OnCreate = FormCreate
  object DBGrid1: TDBGrid
```

```
    Align = alClient
    DataSource = DataSource1
    OnColEnter = DBGrid1ColEnter
    OnDrawColumnCell = DBGrid1DrawColumnCell
    OnKeyPress = DBGrid1KeyPress
  end
  object DBCheckBox1: TDBCheckBox
    Caption = 'Senior'
    DataField = 'Senior'
    DataSource = DataSource1
    ValueChecked = 'True'
    ValueUnchecked = 'False'
    Visible = False
  end
  object Table1: TTable
    DatabaseName = 'DBDEMOS'
    TableName = 'Workers'
  end
end
```

Notice that the check box is initially hidden and that the program handles several events of the DBGrid control. The first is the OnDrawColumnCell event, which is not used to customize the drawing (the DefaultDrawing property is set to True), but only to compute the position of the check box when a cell of the corresponding field is selected:

```
procedure TDbaForm.DBGrid1DrawColumnCell(Sender: TObject;
  const Rect: TRect; DataCol: Integer; Column: TColumn;
  State: TGridDrawState);
begin
  if (gdFocused in State) and (Column.Field = Table1Senior) then
  begin
    DBCheckBox1.SetBounds (
      Rect.Left + DBGrid1.Left + 1,
      Rect.Top + DBGrid1.Top + 1,
      Rect.Right - Rect.Left + 1,
      Rect.Bottom - Rect.Top + 1);
  end;
end;
```

The check box itself is displayed or hidden as the user enters or exits the corresponding column, by the handler of the OnColEnter event. Note that we cannot refer to the column by position, since a user can move the columns:

```
procedure TDbaForm.DBGrid1ColEnter(Sender: TObject);
begin
  if DBGrid1.Columns [DBGrid1.SelectedIndex].Field = Table1Senior then
    DBCheckBox1.Visible := True
  else
    DBCheckBox1.Visible := False;
end;
```

Finally, as an extra extension, when the check box is visible (that is, when the user has activated the corresponding field), the program intercepts the keyboard input in the grid, toggling the selection of the check box instead of accepting the input:

```
procedure TDbaForm.DBGrid1KeyPress(Sender: TObject; var Key: Char);
begin
  if DBCheckBox1.Visible and (Ord (Key) > 31) then
  begin
    Key := #0;
    Table1.Edit;
    DBCheckBox1.Checked := not DBCheckBox1.Checked;
    DBCheckBox1.Field.AsBoolean := DBCheckBox1.Checked;
  end;
end;
```

To make this work we must not only toggle the status of the check box, but also go into edit mode and update the data of the field. You can see an example of the output of this program in Figure 13.14.

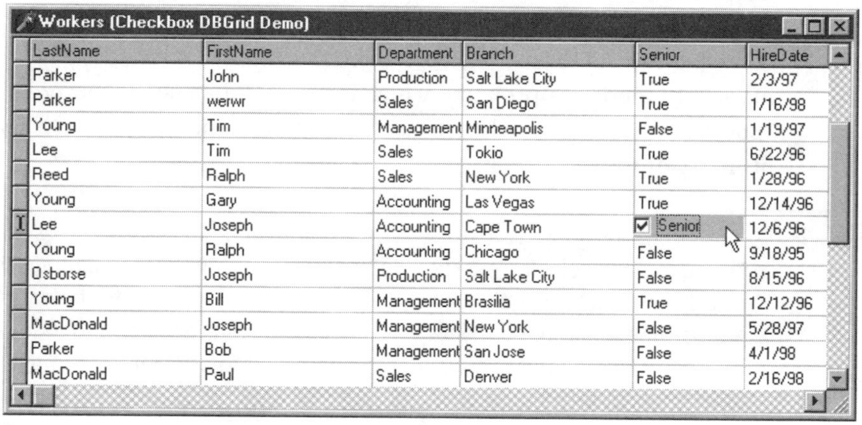

FIGURE 13.14:

The grid of the CheckDbg example uses a check box for selecting the value of a Boolean field.

LastName	FirstName	Department	Branch	Senior	HireDate
Parker	John	Production	Salt Lake City	True	2/3/97
Parker	werwr	Sales	San Diego	True	1/16/98
Young	Tim	Management	Minneapolis	False	1/19/97
Lee	Tim	Sales	Tokio	True	6/22/96
Reed	Ralph	Sales	New York	True	1/28/96
Young	Gary	Accounting	Las Vegas	True	12/14/96
Lee	Joseph	Accounting	Cape Town	☑ Senior	12/6/96
Young	Ralph	Accounting	Chicago	False	9/18/95
Osborse	Joseph	Production	Salt Lake City	False	8/15/96
Young	Bill	Management	Brasilia	True	12/12/96
MacDonald	Joseph	Management	New York	False	5/28/97
Parker	Bob	Management	San Jose	False	4/1/98
MacDonald	Paul	Sales	Denver	False	2/16/98

A Grid Allowing Multiple Selection

The third and last example of customizing the DBGrid control relates to multiple selection. You can set up the DBGrid so that a user can select multiple rows (that is, multiple records). This is very easy, since all you have to do is toggle the dgMultiSelect element of the Options property of the grid. Once you've selected this option, a user can keep the Ctrl key pressed and click with the mouse to select multiple rows of the grid, with the effect you can see in Figure 13.15.

FIGURE 13.15:

The MltGrid example has a DBGrid control that allows the selection of multiple rows.

Since the database table can have only one active record, what information is stored in the grid for the selected items? The grid simply keeps a list of bookmarks to the selected records. This list is available in the `SelectedRows` property, which is of type `TBookmarkList`. Besides accessing the number of objects in the list with the `Count` property, you can get to each bookmark with the `Items` property, which is the default array property. Each item of the list is on a `TBookmarkStr` type, which represents a bookmark pointer you can assign to the `Bookmark` property of the table.

NOTE   The `TBookmarkStr` is a string type for convenience, but its data should be considered "opaque" and volatile. You shouldn't rely on any particular structure to the data you may find if you peek at a bookmark's value, and you shouldn't hold on to the data too long or store it in a separate file. Bookmark data will vary with database driver and index configuration, and it may be rendered unusable when rows are added to or deleted from the dataset (by you or by other users of the database).

To summarize the steps, here is the code of the MltGrid example, activated by pressing the button to move the Name field of the selected records to the list box:

```
procedure TForm1.Button1Click(Sender: TObject);
var
  I: Integer;
  BookmarkList: TBookmarkList;
  Bookmark: TBookmarkStr;
begin
  // store the current position
  Bookmark := Table1.Bookmark;
  try
    // empty the list box
    ListBox1.Items.Clear;
```

```
      // get the selected rows of the grid
      BookmarkList := DbGrid1.SelectedRows;
      for I := 0 to BookmarkList.Count - 1 do
      begin
        // for each, move the table to that record
        Table1.Bookmark := BookmarkList[I];
        // add the name field to the listbox
        ListBox1.Items.Add (Table1.FieldByName ('Name').AsString);
      end;
    finally
      // go back to the initial record
      Table1.Bookmark := Bookmark;
    end;
  end;
```

Dragging to a Grid

Another interesting technique is to use dragging with grids. Dragging *from* a grid is not particularly difficult, as you know which are the current record and the column the user has selected. Dragging *to* a grid, instead, is apparently hard to program. You might remember that in Chapter 3, "The Object Pascal Language: Inheritance and Polymorphism," I mentioned the "protected hack;" this is the technique I'm going to use to implement dragging to a grid.

The example, called DragToGrid, has a grid connected to the COUNTRY.DB demo table, an edit where you can type the new value for a field, and a label you can drag over a cell of the grid to modify the related field. The real problem is how to determine this field. The code is only a few lines, as you can see below, but it is certainly cryptic, and requires some explanation:

```
type
  TDBGHack = class (TDbGrid)
  end;

procedure TFormDrag.DBGrid1DragDrop(Sender, Source: TObject; X, Y: Integer);
var
  gc: TGridCoord;
begin
  gc := TDBGHack (DbGrid1).MouseCoord (x, y);
  if (gc.y > 0) and (gc.x > 0) then
  begin
    DbGrid1.DataSource.DataSet.MoveBy (gc.y - TDBGHack(DbGrid1).Row);
    DbGrid1.DataSource.DataSet.Edit;
    DBGrid1.Columns.Items [gc.X - 1].Field.AsString := EditDrag.Text;
  end;
  DBGrid1.SetFocus;
end;
```

The first operation is to determine the cell over which the mouse was released. Starting with the X and Y mouse coordinates, we can call the protected MouseCoord method to access the row and column of the cell. Unless the drag target is the very first row (usually hosting the titles) or the first column (usually hosting the indicator), the program moves the current record by the difference between the requested row (gc.y) and the current active row (the protected Row property of the grid). The next step is to put the dataset into edit mode, grab the field of the target column (Columns.Items [gc.X - 1].Field), and change its text.

Database Applications with Standard Controls

Although it is generally faster to write Delphi applications based on data-aware controls, this is certainly not required. When you need to have very precise control over the user interface of a database application, you might want to customize the transfer of the data from the field objects to the visual controls. My personal view is that this is necessary only in very specific cases, as you can customize the data-aware controls extensively by setting the properties and handling the events of the field objects. However, trying to work without the data-aware controls should help you understand the default behavior of Delphi, and it will help me introduce some more database-related events (discussed in the sections "Database Events" and "Field Events").

The development of an application not based on data-aware controls can follow two different approaches. You can mimic the standard Delphi behavior in code, possibly departing from it in specific cases, or you can go for a much more customized approach. I'll demonstrate the first technique in the NonAware example and the latter in the SendToDb example.

Mimicking Delphi Data-Aware Controls

If you want to build an application that doesn't use data-aware controls but behaves like a standard Delphi application, you can simply write event handlers for the operations that would be performed automatically by data-aware controls. Basically you need to place the dataset in edit mode as the user changes the content of the visual controls, and update the field objects of the dataset as the user exits from the controls, moving the focus to another element.

TIP   This approach can be handy for integrating a control that's not data-aware into a standard application. A good example is the use of the DateTimePicker control for selecting a date, as demonstrated later in the section "Editing Dates with a Calendar."

The other element of the NonAware example is a list of buttons corresponding to some of those in the DBNavigator control and connected to five custom actions. I cannot use the standard dataset actions for this example simply because they automatically hook to the data source associated with the control having the focus, a mechanism that fails with the non–data-aware edit boxes of this example.

The program has several event handlers we've not used for past applications using data-aware controls. First of all, we have to show the data of the current record in the visual controls (as in Figure 13.16), by handling the OnDataChange event of the DataSource1 component:

```
procedure TForm1.DataSource1DataChange(Sender: TObject; Field: TField);
begin
  EditName.Text := Table1Name.AsString;
  EditCapital.Text := Table1Capital.AsString;
  ComboContinent.Text := Table1Continent.AsString;
  EditArea.Text := Table1Area.AsString;
  EditPopulation.Text := Table1Population.AsString;
end;
```

FIGURE 13.16:

The output of the Non-Aware example in Browse mode. The program manually fetches the data every time the current record changes.

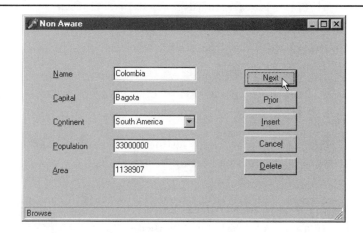

The handler of the OnStateChange event of the control displays the status of the table in a status bar control. As the user starts typing in one of the edit boxes or drops down the combo box list, the program sets the table in edit mode:

```
procedure TForm1.EditKeyPress(Sender: TObject; var Key: Char);
begin
  if not (Table1.State in [dsEdit, dsInsert]) then
    Table1.Edit;
end;
```

This method is connected with the OnKeyPress event of the five components and is similar to the OnDropDown event handler of the combo box. As the user leaves one of the visual controls, the handler of the OnExit event copies the data to the corresponding field, as in this case:

```
procedure TForm1.EditCapitalExit(Sender: TObject);
begin
  if (Table1.State in [dsEdit, dsInsert]) then
    Table1Capital.AsString := EditCapital.Text;
end;
```

The operation takes place only if the table is in edit mode; that is, only if the user has typed in this or another control. This is not really ideal, because extra operations are done even if the text of the edit box didn't change, but the extra steps happen fast enough not to be a concern. For the first edit box, we check the text before copying it, raising an exception if the edit box is empty:

```
procedure TForm1.EditNameExit(Sender: TObject);
begin
  if (Table1.State in [dsEdit, dsInsert])then
    if EditName.Text <> '' then
      Table1Name.AsString := EditName.Text
    else
    begin
      EditName.SetFocus;
      raise Exception.Create ('Undefined Country');
    end;
end;
```

An alternative approach for testing the value of a field is to handle the BeforePost event of the dataset. Keep in mind that in this example, the posting operation is not handled by a specific button but takes place as soon as a user moves to a new record or inserts a new one:

```
procedure TForm1.Table1BeforePost(DataSet: TDataSet);
begin
  if Table1Area.Value < 100 then
    raise Exception.Create ('Area too small');
end;
```

In each of these cases, an alternative to raising an exception is to set a default value. However, if a field has a default value it is better to set it up front, so that a user can see which value will be sent to the database. To accomplish this, you can handle the AfterInsert event of a dataset, which is fired immediately after a new record has been created (we could have used the OnNewRecord event, as well):

```
procedure TForm1.Table1AfterInsert(DataSet: TDataSet);
begin
  Table1Continent.Value := 'Asia';
end;
```

Sending Requests to the Database

You can further customize the user interface of your application if you decide not to handle the same sequence of editing operations as in standard Delphi data-aware controls. This allows you complete freedom, although there might be some side effects (such as limited ability to handle concurrency, something I'll discuss in the next chapter).

For this new example, I've replaced the first edit box with another combo box, and replaced all the buttons related to table operations (which corresponded to DBNavigator buttons) with two custom ones, used to get the data from the database and send an update to it. To underline the difference of this example, I've even removed the DataSource component.

The GetData method, connected with the corresponding button, simply gets the fields corresponding to the record indicated in the first combo box:

```
procedure TForm1.GetData;
begin
  Table1.FindNearest ([ComboName.Text]);
  ComboName.Text := Table1Name.AsString;
  EditCapital.Text := Table1Capital.AsString;
  ComboContinent.Text := Table1Continent.AsString;
  EditArea.Text := Table1Area.AsString;
  EditPopulation.Text := Table1Population.AsString;
end;
```

This method is called whenever the user presses the button, selects an item of the combo box, or presses the Enter key while in the combo box:

```
procedure TForm1.ComboNameClick(Sender: TObject);
begin
  GetData;
end;

procedure TForm1.ComboNameKeyPress(Sender: TObject; var Key: Char);
begin
  if Key = #13 then
    GetData;
end;
```

To make this example work smoothly, at start-up the combo box is filled with all the names of the countries of the table:

```
procedure TForm1.FormCreate(Sender: TObject);
begin
  // fill the list of names
  Table1.Open;
  while not Table1.Eof do
  begin
```

```
      ComboName.Items.Add (Table1Name.AsString);
      Table1.Next;
    end;
  end;
```

With this approach, the combo box becomes a sort of selector of the record, as you can see in Figure 13.17. Notice that thanks to this selection, the program doesn't need navigational buttons.

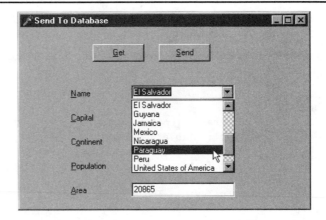

Finally, the user can change the values of the controls and click the Send button. The code to be executed depends on whether the operation is an update or an insert. We can determine this by looking at the name (although with this code, a wrong name cannot be modified any more):

```
procedure TForm1.SendData;
begin
  // raise an exception if there is no name
  if ComboName.Text = '' then
    raise Exception.Create ('Insert the name');

  // check if the record is already in the table
  if Table1.FindKey ([ComboName.Text]) then
  begin
    // modify found record
    Table1.Edit;
    Table1Capital.AsString := EditCapital.Text;
    Table1Continent.AsString := ComboContinent.Text;
    Table1Area.AsString := EditArea.Text;
    Table1Population.AsString := EditPopulation.Text;
    Table1.Post;
  end
  else
```

```
begin
  // insert new record
  Table1.InsertRecord ([ComboName.Text, EditCapital.Text,
    ComboContinent.Text, EditArea.Text, EditPopulation.Text]);
  // add to list
  ComboName.Items.Add (ComboName.Text)
end;
```

Before sending the data to the table, you can do any sort of validation test on the values. In this case, it doesn't make much sense to handle the events of the database components, because we have full control on when the update or insert operation is done.

Database Events

To further illustrate how you can use the events of a database application, I've written a simple program that logs all the events being fired. This program handles all of the events of a table and a data source component (although some of these events won't actually be executed, unless you add some extra code, as described later). For each event, I simply send its description to a list box, with the effect you can see in Figure 13.18.

FIGURE 13.18:

The output of the DbEvts program, which logs all the events related to database components

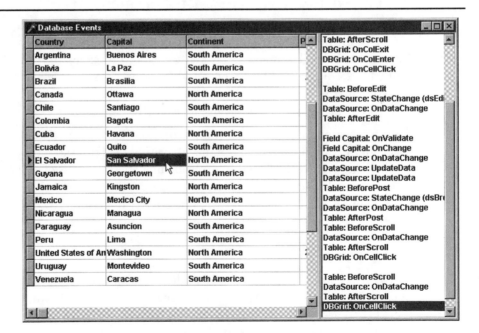

Most of the event handlers simply display the name of the component and that of the event, as in

```
procedure TForm1.Table1AfterEdit(DataSet: TDataset);
begin
  AddToList ('Table: AfterEdit');
end;
```

The field events are slightly more complex, but they use a single handler for the various field components:

```
procedure TForm1.FieldChange(Sender: TField);
begin
  AddToList ('Field ' + Sender.FieldName + ': OnChange');
end;
```

The form's AddToList method adds a new item to the list box and selects it, automatically scrolling the list if required:

```
procedure TForm1.AddToList(Str: string);
begin
  // add item and select it
  Listbox1.ItemIndex := Listbox1.Items.Add (Str);
end;
```

Finally, the program has a pop-up menu connected to the list box to clear the list or save the items to a file. The menu also has a command you can use to add a blank line, thus separating blocks of events. This operation is also done automatically by a timer, which adds a blank line to the list box unless the last item is already an empty string. This makes the output more readable, as you can see in Figure 13.18.

It is very important to study the output of this program as well as its code. You can try doing all the various operations on the table using the DBGrid, such as inserting, editing, and deleting records, and see the corresponding effect in terms of events fired by the VCL components. To see even more events, you can set the Filtered property of the table to True, define a calculated field, try to cause errors (for example, by duplicating the value of the name field), add a check box to open or close the table, and so forth.

Field Events

The DbEvts program shows the calls to the OnChange and OnValidate events of the field objects. Two other events, OnSetText and OnGetText, are not shown, because the handlers of these events are not simply called to indicate that an operation occurred. On the contrary, their event handlers must perform the operation of getting data from or setting it to the corresponding field objects.

These two events are quite special, and their use is not as simple as it might seem at first sight. For this reason, they require a separate example, named FldText. This is only a slight revision of the DbAware example described earlier in this chapter, replacing the DBRadioGroup control with a DBListbox control. The problem is that a DBListBox control directly connects with a string field, while I want to connect it with an integer field, with each value indicating an option. Of course, I don't want a user to see or select a number, so I have to map the numbers stored in the database to the strings visible on the screen. In the earlier example, the DBRadioGroup control provided that mapping. Now I have to use an alternative approach.

In the FldText example, the Department field has two handlers for the OnGetText and OnSetText events. In the OnGetText event handler, you can extract the numeric value of the Sender field and set the value of the Text reference parameter:

```
procedure TDbaForm.Table1DepartmentGetText(Sender: TField;
  var Text: String; DisplayText: Boolean);
begin
  case Sender.AsInteger of
    1: Text := 'Sales';
    2: Text := 'Accounting';
    3: Text := 'Production';
    4: Text := 'Management';
  else
    Text := '[Error]';
  end;
end;
```

WARNING In the code of the OnGetText event handler you cannot refer to the text of the field, for example, using the DisplayText property or the GetData method, since they would call the OnGetText event, in an infinite recursion.

In the OnSetText event handler, you can examine the string and decide the value of the field according to the conversion rule, in this case a simple mapping of values done with an if/then/else statement:

```
procedure TDbaForm.Table1DepartmentSetText(Sender: TField; const Text: String);
begin
  if Text = 'Sales' then
    Sender.Value := 1
  else if Text = 'Accounting' then
    Sender.Value := 2
  else if Text = 'Production' then
    Sender.Value := 3
  else if Text = 'Management' then
    Sender.Value := 4
  else
    raise Exception.Create ('Error in Department field conversion');
end;
```

The effect is that not only is the value visible in the DBListBox (as you can see in Figure 13.19), it also shows up in the DBGrid. By contrast, in the DbAware example, the grid displayed the numeric value.

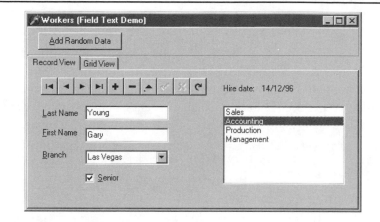

Editing Dates with a Calendar

As a final example of the use of non–data-aware controls, the DbDates application shows how to use a MonthCalendar component to handle dates with a nice graphical component instead of a plain edit box. This example is based on the Events table from the DBDEMOS database, which lists Olympic events. The example uses (for the first time) a DBImage control, with the following settings (whose effect is illustrated in Figure 13.20):

```
object DBImage1: TDBImage
  DataField = 'Event_Photo'
  DataSource = DataSource1
  Stretch = True
end
```

NOTE   Graphic, memo, and BLOB fields in Delphi are handled exactly like other fields. Just connect the proper editor or viewer, and most of the work is done behind the scenes by the system.

FIGURE 13.20:

The selection of a date with the monthly calendar

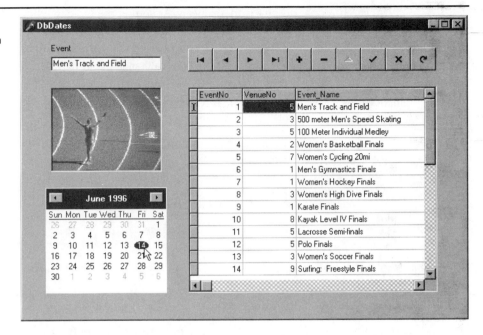

Although the DBImage control works with no extra effort on our part, we must connect the MonthCalendar control with the corresponding field by handling two events of the DataSource control:

```
procedure TForm1.DataSource1DataChange(Sender: TObject; Field: TField);
begin
  MonthCalendar1.Date := Table1Event_Date.Value;
end;
```

```
procedure TForm1.DataSource1UpdateData(Sender: TObject);
begin
  Table1Event_Date.Value := MonthCalendar1.Date;
end;
```

Besides copying the data back and forth, with the code listed above, the program must also put the table into edit mode as the user clicks the calendar control. The most obvious approach is to write a handler for the OnClick event of the control:

```
procedure TForm1.MonthCalendar1Click(Sender: TObject);
begin
  Table1.Edit;
end;
```

However, this code doesn't work properly. As you set the table in edit mode, the OnDataChange event is executed once more, resetting the selection in the calendar. The overall effect is that the user's first click doesn't change the selection. To avoid this problem we can set a flag in the OnClick event handler and test it in the OnDataChange event handler, or we can temporarily disconnect the second event handler. In the following code, I've taken the second approach:

```
procedure TForm1.MonthCalendar1Click(Sender: TObject);
begin
  // disconnect handler
  DataSource1.OnDataChange := nil;
  // set table in edit mode
  Table1.Edit;
  // reconnect handler
  DataSource1.OnDataChange := DataSource1DataChange;
end;
```

A Multirecord Grid

So far we have seen that you can either use a grid to display records of a database table or build a form with specific data-aware controls for the various fields, accessing the records one by one. There is a third alternative: use a multirecord object (a DBCtrlGrid), which allows you to place many data-aware controls in a small area of a form and automatically duplicate these controls for multiple records.

Here is what we can do to build the Multi1 example. Create a new blank form, place a Table component and a DataSource component in it, and connect them to the COUNTRY.DB table. Now place a DBCtrlGrid on the form, set its size and the number of rows and columns, and place two edit components connected with the Name and Capital fields of the table. To place these DBEdit components, you can also open the Fields editor and drag the two fields to the control grid. At design time, you simply work on the active portion of the grid (see Figure 13.21, on the right), and at run time, you can see these controls replicated multiple times (see Figure 13.21, on the left).

FIGURE 13.21:

The DBCtrlGrid of the Multi1 example at design time (on the right) and at run time (on the left)

You can simply set the number of columns and rows. Then each time you resize the control, the width and height of each panel are set accordingly. What is not available is a way to align the grid automatically to the client area of the form.

Moving Control Grid Panels

To improve the last example, we might resize the grid using the FormResize method. We could simply write the following code (in the Multi2 example):

```
procedure TForm1.FormResize(Sender: TObject);
begin
  DBCtrlGrid1.Height := ClientHeight - Panel1.Height;
  DBCtrlGrid1.Width := ClientWidth;
end;
```

This works, but it is not what I want. I'd like to increase the number of panels, not enlarge them. To accomplish this, we can define a minimum height for the panels and compute how many panels can fit in the available area each time the form is resized. For example, in Multi2, I've added one more statement to the FormResize method above, which now becomes

```
procedure TForm1.FormResize(Sender: TObject);
begin
  DBCtrlGrid1.RowCount := (ClientHeight - Panel1.Height) div 100;
  DBCtrlGrid1.Height := ClientHeight - Panel1.Height;
  DBCtrlGrid1.Width := ClientWidth;
end;
```

Instead of doing the same for the columns of the control grid component, I've added a TrackBar component to a panel. When the position of the trackbar changes (the range is from 2 to 10), the program sets the number of columns of the control grid and resizes it. In fact, if you simply set the number of columns, they'll have the same width as before. Here is the code of the trackbar's OnChange event handler:

```
procedure TForm1.TrackBar1Change(Sender: TObject);
begin
  LabelCols.Caption := Format ('%d Columns', [TrackBar1.Position]);
  DBCtrlGrid1.ColCount := TrackBar1.Position;
  DBCtrlGrid1.Width := ClientWidth;
end;
```

This code and the FormResize method above allow you to change the configuration of the control grid at run time in various ways. You can see an example of a crammed version of the form in Figure 13.22.

FIGURE 13.22:

The output of the Multi2 example, with an excessive number of columns

Handling Database Errors

Another important element of database programming is handling database errors in custom ways. Of course, you can let Delphi show an exception message each time a database error occurs, but you might want to try to correct the errors or simply show more details. There are basically three approaches you can use to handle database-related errors:

- You can wrap a try/except block around risky database operations, such as a call to the Open method of a Query or to the Post method of a dataset. This is not possible when the operation is generated by the interaction with a data-aware control.

- You can install a handler for the OnException event of the global Application object or use the ApplicationEvents component, as described in the next example.

- You can handle specific events of the datasets related to errors, as OnPostError, OnEditError, OnDeleteError, and OnUpdateError. These events will be discussed later in the example.

While most of the exception classes in Delphi simply deliver an error message, with database exceptions you see a list of errors, showing local BDE error codes and also the native error codes of the SQL server you are connected to. Besides the Message property, the EDBEngineError class has two more properties, ErrorCount and Errors. This last property is a list of errors:

```
property Errors[Index: Integer]: TDBError;
```

Each item within this list is an object of the class TDBError, which has the following properties:

```
type
  TDBError = class
    ...
  public
    property Category: Byte read GetCategory;
    property ErrorCode: DBIResult read FErrorCode;
    property SubCode: Byte read GetSubCode;
    property Message: string read FMessage;
    property NativeError: Longint read FNativeError;
  end;
```

I've used this information to build a simple database program showing the details of the errors in a memo component. To handle all of the errors, the DBError example installs a handler for the OnException event of an ApplicationEvents component. The event handler simply calls a specific method used to show the details of the database error, in case it is an EDBEngineError:

```
procedure TForm1.ApplicationEvents1Exception (Sender: TObject; E: Exception);
begin
  Beep;
  if E is EDBEngineError then
    ShowError (EDBEngineError (E))
  else
    ShowMessage (E.Message);
end;
```

I decided to separate the code used to show the error to make it easier for you to copy this code and use it in different contexts. Here is the code of the ShowError method, which outputs all of the available information to the Memo1 component that I've added to the form:

```
procedure TForm1.ShowError(E: EDBEngineError);
var
  I: Integer;
begin
```

```
Memo1.Lines.Add('');
Memo1.Lines.Add('Error: ' + (E.Message));
Memo1.Lines.Add('Number of errors: ' + IntToStr(E.ErrorCount));
// iterate through the Errors records
for I := 0 to E.ErrorCount - 1 do
begin
  Memo1.Lines.Add('Message: ' + E.Errors[I].Message);
  Memo1.Lines.Add('   Category: ' + IntToStr(E.Errors[I].Category));
  Memo1.Lines.Add('   Error Code: ' + IntToStr(E.Errors[I].ErrorCode));
  Memo1.Lines.Add('   SubCode: ' + IntToStr(E.Errors[I].SubCode));
  Memo1.Lines.Add('   Native Error: ' + IntToStr(E.Errors[I].NativeError));
  Memo1.Lines.Add('');
end;
end;
```

Besides this error-handling code, the program has a table and a query, along with the error-related event handlers. As already mentioned, you can install an event handler related to specific errors of a dataset. The three events OnPostError, OnDeleteError, and OnEditError have the same structure. Their handlers receive as parameters the dataset, the error itself, and an action you can request from the system; this can be set to daFail, daAbort, or daRetry:

```
procedure TForm1.Table1PostError(DataSet: TDataSet; E: EDatabaseError;
  var Action: TDataAction);
begin
  Memo1.Lines.Add (' -> Post Error: ' + E.Message);
end;
```

If you don't specify an action, as in the code above, the default daFail is used, and the exception reaches the global handler. Using daAbort stops the exception and can be used if your event handler already displays a message. Finally, if you have a way to determine the cause of the error and fix it, you can use the daRetry action.

NOTE   The fourth error event, OnUpdateError, has a different structure and is used along with cached updates as the information is sent back from the local cache to the database. This handler is important for handling update conflicts among different users as described in the next example.

The example has also a DBGrid connected with the table. You can use the DBGrid to perform some illegal operations, such as adding a new record with the same key as an existing one or trying to execute illegal SQL queries. Pressing the four buttons on the left of the memo generate errors, as you can see in Figure 13.23.

FIGURE 13.23:

The third button of the DBError form generates an exception with 17 database errors!

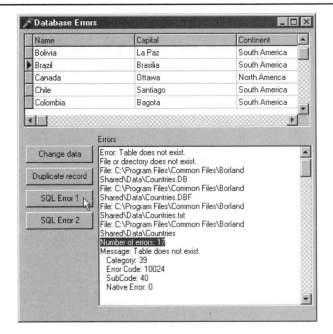

What's Next?

In this chapter, we have seen examples of database access from Delphi programs. I have covered the basic data-aware components as well as the development of database applications based on standard controls. We've explored the internal architecture of the TDataSet class and of field objects, and discussed many of the events and properties shared by all datasets and used by all database applications. Even though most of the demonstrations used BDE tables and queries, in the entire text there was little or no code specific to those components. Most of what I've described equally applies to client/server applications, built with BDE, dbExpress, IBX, ADO or other dataset components.

We've discussed calculated fields, lookup fields, customizations of the DBGrid control, and many rather advanced techniques. What we really haven't delved into is the database and data-access side of the picture, which depends on the actual type of database engine and server you plan using. The next chapter will start focusing in this topic, with an in-depth overview of client/server development. Following chapters will put the accent on specific data-access technologies and provide even more advanced information.

CHAPTER 14

Client/Server Programming

- Overview of client/server

- Porting local applications

- Elements of database design

- Client/server with BDE

- The dbExpress library

- Using the ClientDataSet component

- Local databases with MyBase

In the last chapter, we examined Delphi's support for database programming, using local files (particularly Paradox) in most of examples but not focusing on any specific database technology. This chapter moves on to the use of SQL server databases, focusing on client/server development with the BDE and the new dbExpress technology. A single chapter cannot cover this complex topic in detail, so I'll simply introduce it from the perspective of the Delphi developer and add some tips and hints. The next chapter extends our discussion of client/server programming, providing some real-world examples. I'll use InterBase in both chapters, because this is the RDBMS (relational database management system), or SQL server, that is included in the Enterprise edition of Delphi and because it is a free and open-source server.

In a rapid application development tool such as Delphi, you can indeed take the same components and code developed for a local database application and use them in a client/server environment. However, this handy feature may prove to be dangerous to beginners, as a standard technique that works well for local access might become extremely inefficient in a client/server application.

An Overview of Client/Server Programming

The database applications in previous chapters used the BDE to access data stored in files either on the local machine or on a networked computer. In both cases we used a file server, whose only role was to store the file on a hard disk, because the database engine (the BDE) was running exclusively on the computer that also hosted the application. In this configuration, when we query one of the tables, its data is first copied into a local cache of the BDE and then processed.

As an example, consider taking a table like EMPLOYEE (part of the InterBase sample database, which ships with Delphi), adding thousands of records to it, and placing it on a networked computer working as a file server. If we want to know the highest salary paid by the company, we can open a Table component (EmpTable) connected with the database table and run this code:

```
EmpTable.Open;
EmpTable.First;
MaxSalary := 0;
while not EmpTable.Eof do
begin
  if EmpTable.FieldByName ('Salary').AsCurrency > MaxSalary then
    MaxSalary := EmpTable.FieldByName ('Salary').AsCurrency;
  EmpTable.Next;
end;
```

The effect of this approach is to move all the data of the (large) table from the networked computer to the local machine, an operation that might take minutes. Because Delphi includes a Query component, you might think of using the following SQL code to compute this maximum value:

```
select Max(Salary) from Employee
```

In case of a local table, this query would be processed by the local SQL engine of the BDE, and the entire dataset of the table would still need to be moved from the networked computer to the local one, with similarly poor performance. But if you use InterBase and let the server execute the SQL code, only the result set—a single number—will need to be transferred to the local computer.

NOTE   The two code excerpts above are part of the GetMax example, which includes some code to time the two approaches. Using the Table component on the small EMPLOYEE table takes about ten times longer than using the query, even if the InterBase server is installed on the client computer.

If you want to store a large amount of data on a central computer and avoid moving the data to client computers for processing, the only solution is to let the central computer manipulate the data and send back to the client only a limited amount of information. This is the foundation of client/server programming.

In general, you'll use an existing program on the server (an RDBMS) and write a custom client application that connects to it. Sometimes, however, you might even want to write both a custom client and a custom server, as in three-tier applications. Delphi support for this type of program—what has been called the MIDAS architecture—is covered in Chapter 17, "Multitier Database Applications with DataSnap."

The *upsizing* of an application—that is, the transfer of data from local files to a SQL server database engine—is generally done for performance reasons and to allow for larger amounts of data. Going back to the previous example, in a client/server environment, the query used to select the maximum salary would be computed by the RDBMS, which would send back to the client computer only the final result, a single number! With a powerful server computer (such as a multiprocessor Sun SparcStation), the total time required to compute the result might be minimal.

However, there are also other reasons to choose a client/server architecture:

The amount of data   A Paradox table cannot exceed 2 GB, but even around 300 MB you might start having serious speed problems, and errors in the indexes become more frequent.

The need for concurrent access to the data   Paradox uses the Paradox.NET file to keep track of which user is accessing the various tables and records. The Paradox approach to handling multiple users is based on *pessimistic locking*. When a user starts an editing operation on a record, none of the other users can do the same (to avoid any update conflict), as we saw in the last chapter. In a system with tens of users, this might lead to serious problems, because a single user might block the work of many others. SQL server databases, by contrast, generally use *optimistic locking*, an approach that allows multiple users to work on the same data and delays the concurrency control until the time the users send back some updates.

Protection and security   An RDBMS usually has many more protection mechanisms than the simple password you can add to a Paradox table. When your application is based on files, a malicious or careless user might simply delete those vital files. When SQL servers are based on robust operating systems, instead, they provide multiple levels of protection, make backup easier, and often allow only the database administrator to modify the structure of the tables.

Programmability   An RDBMS database can host business rules, in the form of stored procedures, triggers, table views, and other techniques we'll discuss in this and the next chapter. Choosing how to divide the application code between the client and the server is one of the main issues of client/server programming.

Transaction control   Local files offer some support for transactions, but the transaction support provided by an RDBMS database is generally much greater. This is another important aspect of the overall robustness of the system.

From Local to Client/Server

Now we can start focusing on particular techniques useful for client/server programming. Keep in mind that the general goal is to distribute the workload properly between the client and the server and reduce the network bandwidth required to move information back and forth.

The foundation of this approach is good database design, which involves both table structure and appropriate data validation and constraints, or business rules. Enforcing the validation of the data on the server is important, as the integrity of the database is one of the key aims of any program. However, the client side should include data validation as well, to improve the user interface and make the input and the processing of the data more user-friendly. It makes little sense to let the user enter invalid data and then receive an error message from the server, when we can prevent the wrong input in the first place.

NOTE   If you use a CASE tool for the definition of the database, or import the definition in such a tool afterward, you can use Delphi's Case Wizard to generate a corresponding data dictionary and have the field objects created at design time automatically import the constraints specified on the server.

Unidirectional Cursors

In local databases, tables are sequential files whose order is either the physical order or is defined by an index. By contrast, SQL servers work on logical sets of data, not related to a physical order. A *relational* database server handles data according to the relational model, a mathematical model based on set theory.

What is important for the present discussion is that in a relational database, the records (sometimes called tuples) of a table are identified not by position but exclusively through a primary key, based on one or more fields. Once you've obtained a set of records, the server adds to each of them a reference to the following one, which makes it fast to move from a record to the following one but terribly slow to move back to the previous record. For this reason, it is common to say that an RDBMS uses a *unidirectional* cursor. Connecting such a table or query to a DBGrid control is practically impossible, as this would make it terribly slow when browsing the grid backward.

The BDE helps a lot to handle unidirectional cursors, as it keeps in a local cache the records already loaded in the table. Thus, when we move to following records, they are requested from the SQL server; but when we go back, the BDE jumps in and provides the data. In other words, the BDE makes these cursors fully bidirectional, although this might use quite a lot of memory. When using dbExpress, which doesn't provide a similar caching system, a program needs to keep in memory the records it has already accessed. This can be easily accomplished by means of the ClientDataSet component.

NOTE   The simple case of a DBGrid used to browse an entire table is common in local programs but should generally be avoided in a client/server environment. It's better to filter out only part of the records and only the fields you are interested in. Do you need to see a list of names? Return all those starting with the letter *A*, then those with *B*, and so on, or ask the user for the initial letter of the name.

If proceeding backward might result in problems, keep in mind that jumping to the last record of a table is even worse; usually this operation implies fetching all the records! A similar situation applies to the RecordCount property of datasets. Computing the number of records often implies moving them all to the client computer. This is the reason why the thumb of the vertical scrollbar of the DBGrid works for a local table but not for a remote one. If you need to know the number of records, run a separate query to let the server (and not the client) compute it. For example, you can see how many records will be selected from the EMPLOYEE table if you are interested in those records having a salary field higher than 50,000:

```
select count(*)
from Employee
where Salary > 50000
```

TIP   Using the SQL instruction `count(*)` is a handy way to compute the number of records returned by a query. Instead of the * wildcard, we could have used the name of a specific field, as in `count(First_Name)`, possibly combined with either `distinct` or `all`, to count only records with different values for the field or all the records having a non-`null` value.

Parametric Queries and Null Values

Parametric queries are a very useful technique. Essentially, they allow you to run multiple queries with different result sets while the server only needs to work out the access strategy for solving the query once.

You can force this initial preparation of the query access strategy by calling the `Prepare` method of a Query component. With this operation, the server receives the query, checks its syntax, and while compiling it determines how to use indexes and other access techniques. Multiple executions of the query will be faster because these initial operations have already been executed once for all. Of course, you should call `Prepare` again if you change the SQL text of the query. Also, remember to call `Unprepare` at the end, to free some BDE resources.

Note that some powerful SQL servers can do the same operation by caching the requests and automatically determining that you are sending the same request twice. If the server is smart enough, preparing the query might result in little or no performance gain.

NOTE   When you write parametric queries against a SQL server, you should consider `null` values with care. In fact, to test for a `null` value, you should not write a `field = null` test, but use the specific expression `field is null` instead.

Elements of Database Design

Although this is a book on Delphi programming and not on databases, I feel it's quite important to discuss a few elements of good (and modern) database design. The reason is simple: if your database design is incorrect or convoluted, you'll either have to write terribly complex SQL statements and server-side code, or write a lot of Delphi code to access your data, possibly even fighting against the design of the `TDataSet` class.

Entities and Relations

The *classic* relational database design approach, based on the entity–relation (E-R) model, involves having one table for every entity you need to represent in your database, with one field for each data element you need plus one field for every one-to-one or one-to-many relation to another entity (or table). For many-to-many relations, instead, you'll need a separate table.

As an example of a one-to-one relation, consider a table representing a university course. This would have a field for each relevant data element (name and description, room where it is held, and so on) plus a single field indicating the teacher. The data of the teacher, in fact, should not be stored within the course data, but in a separate table, as it might be referenced from elsewhere.

The schedule of each course can include an undefined number of hours in different days, so they cannot be added inside the same table describing the course. Instead, this information must be placed on a separate table, including all of the schedules, with a field referring to the class each schedule is for. In a one-to-many relation, such as this, "many" records of the schedule table point back to the same "one" record of the course table.

A more complex situation is required to store which student is taking which class. Students cannot be listed directly in the course table, as their number is not fixed, and the classes cannot be stored within the student's data for the same reason. In a similar many-to-many relation, the only approach is to have an extra table representing the relation, which lists references to students and courses.

Normalization Rules

The *classic* design principles include a series of so-called *normalization* rules. The goal of these rules is to avoid duplicating data in your database (not only for saving space, but mainly to avoid ending up with incongruous data). For example, you don't repeat all of the customer details in each order, but refer to a separate customer entity. This way you save memory, but when the customer details change (for example, because of a change of address) all of the orders of this customer will reflect the new data. Other tables that relate to the same customer will probably be automatically updated as well.

Normalization rules imply using codes for commonly repeated values. For example, if you have a few different shipment options, you won't use a string-based description for these options within the orders table, but would rather use a short numeric code, mapped to a description in a separate lookup table.

This last rule, which should not be taken to the extreme, is to avoid having to join a large number or table for every query. You can either account for some de-normalization (leaving a short shipment description within the orders table) or use the client program to provide the description, again ending up with a formally incorrect database design. This last option is practical only when you use a single development environment (let's say, Delphi) to access this database.

From Primary Keys to OIDs

In a relational database, records are not identified by a physical position (as in Paradox and other local databases) but only by the data within the record itself. Typically, you don't need the data of all of the fields to identify a record, but only a subset of the data, forming the so-called *primary key*. If the fields that are part of the primary key must identify an individual record, their value must be different for each possible record of the table.

NOTE   Technically, many database servers add internal record identifiers to the tables, but this happens only for internal optimizations and has little to do with the logical design of a relational database. Also, these internal identifiers work differently in different SQL servers and might even change among versions, a good reason not to rely on them.

The early incarnations of the relational theory dictated the use of *logical keys*, which means selecting one or more records that indicate an entity without risk of any confusion. This is often easier to say than to accomplish. For example, company names are not generally unique, and even the company name and its location don't provide a complete guarantee. Moreover, if a company changes its name (not an unlikely event, as Borland can teach us) or its location, and you have references to the company within other tables, you must change all those references as well, with the risk of ending up with dangling references.

For this reason, and also for efficiency (using strings for references implies using a lot of space in secondary tables, where references often occurs), logical keys have been invariably phased out for physical or surrogate keys. *Physical keys* refer to a single field of the table identifying an element in a unique way. For example, each person in the U.S. has a Social Security number (SSN), but almost every country has a tax ID or other government-assigned number that identifies each person. The same typically exists for companies. Although these ID numbers are guaranteed to be unique, they might change depending on the country (creating troubles for the database of a company also selling its goods abroad) or even within a single country (to account for new tax laws). They are also often inefficient, as they might be quite large (Italy, for example, uses a 16-character code, letters and numbers, to identify people).

Another common approach is to use *surrogate keys*, which are basically numbers identifying each record, in the form of client codes, order numbers, and so on. These surrogate keys are commonly used in database design. However, in many cases, these end up being some sort of *logical identifiers*, with client codes showing up all over the places, not a great idea overall.

WARNING   The situation becomes particularly troublesome when these surrogate keys also have a meaning and must follow specific rules. For example, companies must number invoices with unique and consecutive numbers, without leaving holes in the numbering sequence. This situation is extremely complex to handle programmatically, if you consider that only the database can determine these unique consecutive numbers when we send new data to it. At the same time, we need to identify the record before we send it to the database, otherwise we won't be able to fetch it again. Practical examples of how to solve this situation are discussed in the next chapter.

OIDs to the Extreme

An extension to the use of surrogate keys is the use of a unique identifier, also called object identifier (OID). An OID is a number, or a string with sequence of numbers and digits, added to each record of each table representing an entity (and at times even to records of tables representing relations). Differently from client codes, invoice numbers, SSN, or purchase order numbers, OIDs are totally random, without any sequencing rule, and never visible to the end user. This means you can still use surrogate keys (if your company is used to them) along with OIDs, but all the external references to the table will be based on OIDs.

Another common rules suggested by the promoters of this approach (which is part of the theories supporting object-relational mapping) is the use of system-wide unique identifiers. If you have a table of client companies and a table of employees, you might wonder why you should use a unique ID for such diverse data. The reason is that, if you do so, you'll be able to sell goods to an employee without having to duplicate the employee information into the customers table, but simply referring to the employee in your order and invoice. An order is placed by someone identified by an OID, and this OID can refer to many different tables (but of course not all of them).

NOTE   Using OIDs and the object-relational mapping is an advanced element of the design of Delphi database applications. My personal suggestion is to investigate this topic before embracing medium or large-size Delphi projects, as the benefit can be relevant (after some investment in studying this approach and building some basic support code).

External Keys and Referential Integrity

Getting back to the standard database design, the keys identifying a record (whichever their type) can be used as external keys in other tables, for example to represent the various types of relations discussed earlier. All SQL servers are capable of verifying these external references, so that you cannot refer to a nonexistent record of another table. These referential integrity constraints are expressed when you create a table.

Besides not being allowed to add references to nonexistent records, you're generally prevented from deleting a record if there are external references to it. Some SQL servers go one step further: As you delete a record, instead of simply denying the operation, they can automatically delete all records that refer to it from other tables.

More Constraints

Besides the uniqueness of primary keys and the referential constraints, you can generally use the database to impose more validity rules on the data. You can ask for specific columns (such as those referring to a tax ID or a purchase order number) to include only unique values. You can impose uniqueness of the values of multiple columns—for example, to indicate you cannot run two classes in the same room at the same time.

In general, simple rules can be expressed imposing constraints on a table, while more complex rules generally imply the execution of stored procedures activated by triggers (every time the data changes, for instance, or there is new data).

Again, there is much more to proper database design, but the simple elements discussed in this section can provide a starting point, or a good refresher.

NOTE   For more on the Data Definition Language and Data Manipulation Language of SQL, see the bonus chapter "Essential SQL" on the *Mastering Delphi* CD.

Client/Server with the BDE

Now let's consider how Delphi fits into the client/server picture. How does it help us build client/server applications? As I've mentioned, you can still use all the components and techniques discussed in the Chapter 13, "Delphi's Database Architecture," although in some cases alternate approaches will help you leverage the power of the RDBMS your application is dealing with.

As a starting point, let's cover a few considerations on Delphi client/server development using the BDE and its components. After this I'll move to dbExpress, which in Delphi 6 is the recommended general solution for client/server development.

NOTE   For a list of the alternative approaches Delphi 6 offers for database access, see the initial part of the preceding chapter.

SQL Links

The BDE doesn't know how to handle the RDBMS; it uses some further drivers, called SQL Links, to perform this operation. As an alternative, the BDE can also interact with ODBC drivers. Borland provides native BDE drivers for InterBase, Oracle, Informix, Microsoft SQL Server, Sybase, and DB2.

If the BDE is still required on the local machines, it can actually be very efficient. For example, when you use the pass-through mode for queries, the BDE doesn't try to interpret the SQL code but passes it directly to the RDBMS server. This allows you to use a server's specific SQL commands and also to speed up the execution. The pass-through mode is activated using the BDE Administrator utility.

Having the BDE between the client and the server can also help in building applications designed to work with multiple servers. In practice, however, it's not easy to do this and still obtain the best performance, because of differences in the SQL dialects understood by each SQL server. In particular, data types are handled differently by the various servers. If the same table were placed on two servers that have data type differences, Delphi would need to use two different TField objects (which creates a few headaches if you want to define the fields at design time).

The Database Component

In local BDE applications, programmers usually refer to the database by indicating the alias of the file path in the DatabaseName property of the Table and Query components. A better approach is to use the Database component to define a local alias and then let all the DataSet components refer to this local alias.

As an example, consider the components of the GetMax application mentioned at the beginning of this chapter:

```
object Database1: TDatabase
  AliasName = 'IBLOCAL'
  Connected = True
  DatabaseName = 'IB'
  LoginPrompt = False
  Params.Strings = (
    'USER NAME=SYSDBA'
    'PASSWORD=masterkey')
  SessionName = 'Default'
end
object EmpTable: TTable
  DatabaseName = 'IB'
  TableName = 'EMPLOYEE'
end
```

```
object EmpQuery: TQuery
  DatabaseName = 'IB'
  SQL.Strings = (
    'select Max(Salary) from Employee ')
end
```

In a client/server application, using the Database component is almost mandatory, as it is required to define connectivity and login parameters (the user name and password, as you can see in the Params property above) and to handle transactions.

Keep in mind that the Database component establishes a connection with the RDBMS, representing one of the clients of the system. As such, on most servers it requires a license, and your organization is typically paying for a fixed number of licenses. If the same application or the same computer uses multiple connections to the server, it can count as multiple clients! Fortunately, by setting the KeepConnection property of the Database component, you can specify whether to keep the database connection active even when there is no active DataSet component using the connection. If your program can fetch some data and then operate on it locally, disconnecting from the server might help you conserve licenses.

BDE Table and Query Components in Client/Server

In Delphi there are two BDE components you use to access an existing database table: Table and Query. When building client/server applications, programmers tend to use the Query component exclusively, but that is certainly not mandatory, and there are cases in which using the simpler Table component has no drawback. Here's a quick look at the pros and cons of both components:

- While the Table component should not be used to access a large table, it can work perfectly well with a small lookup table. By opening a Table component, you don't transfer the entire content of the table to the local machine; the data is moved only when you access specific records.

- Consider also that with the Table component, the BDE asks the server first for the table structure and then for the table data. These two steps are necessary for setting up the proper internal structures of the BDE, and they are not executed by the Query component. If you activate the BDE's Schema Caching feature, the logical structure of the table will be kept locally, saving this extra step. Of course, this might create problems if the logical structure of the table changes on the server.

- One problem with the Table component is that the BDE mimics a bidirectional cursor by caching the data locally. With a Query component, instead, you can specify whether you want this caching or not with the Unidirectional property.

- Another point to consider is that you can generally edit the result of a simple query, sending the data back to the SQL server. This is accomplished by setting the RequestLive property to True. For more complex queries, however, you'll need to use an UpdateSQL component, something we'll discuss later in this chapter.

- When trying to minimize the data moved between the server and the client, you need to consider the size of each record as well as the total number of them. When you select only a few fields with a query, only part of the data is considered. A Table component, instead, always entails transferring the entire record to the local machine, even if you've filtered out some fields using the Fields editor. The same problem takes place when you ask for a live query (by setting the RequestLive property). In this case, the BDE needs to see the entire record in order to send back the proper update commands. This means that selecting all the records of a table with a live query is equivalent to using the Table component.

- The Query component is not limited to select SQL statements; you can also use it to insert or delete records. When the Query component returns a dataset, you generally activate it with the Open method (or with the equivalent operation, setting the Active property to True). When the Query component is used to perform an operation on the server, you activate it by calling the ExecSQL method.

Using Table and Query Filters

One way to limit the amount of data returned by a table is to filter it. Using the Filter property of the Table component, you can specify a condition similar to the where clause of a query. When you work with local databases, the filter is applied by the BDE, but with a SQL server, the BDE passes the condition to the server in the query generated for the table. This makes filtered tables very portable between local and client/server applications.

WARNING   The situation is different if you filter the records in the Pascal code, using the OnFilterRecord event. In this case, all the records are sent to the client application, which does its own custom filtering.

If you use a filter with a Query component, the filtering operation will always be performed locally by the BDE, even when you are working with a SQL server. In this case, the BDE asks the server for the entire result set of the query. This would be reasonable only when the user of the application changes the filtering condition often. For a query, only the local filter will be modified, and the data in the local cache will be used. For a table, the BDE will generate an updated query to be executed.

Live Queries and Cached Updates

When working with local data, it is very common to use grids and other visual controls, edit the data, and send it back to the database. We've already seen that using a DBGrid might cause problems when working with an RDBMS, as moving on the grid might send numerous data requests to the server, creating a huge amount of network traffic.

When you use the Query component to connect to some data, you cannot edit the data unless its RequestLive property is set to True. If you are working with local tables, the query is always elaborated by the BDE with the Local SQL engine. The BDE will allow for a live query only if it is quite simple: All joins should be outer joins; there cannot be a distinct key; there can be no aggregation, no group by or having clause, no subqueries, and no order by unless supported by an index; and there are other rules you can find in Delphi's Help.

If you are working with a SQL server, setting a live query will put the BDE in control of the query, instead of the server. When connected to a SQL server, a live query behaves like a Table component. (So it makes sense to use the table anyway, in these cases.)

> **TIP**   Most SQL servers, including InterBase, allow you to define updateable views based on the result of a select statement that the Local SQL engine of the BDE won't consider updateable. Then you can simply hook a Table component to the view, letting the SQL server do the work and bypassing the Local SQL engine of the BDE.

If the BDE determines that the dataset cannot be updated, it sets the CanModify property to False. The DataSource component checks this value before allowing an editing operation. A solution to this problem is to avoid the use of data-aware controls, as discussed in the last chapter, and use specific SQL queries to update, insert, and delete records.

A better approach is to automate this process (retaining the capabilities of the data-aware controls) by using the UpdateSQL component together with the Query component. The UpdateSQL can be used only in conjunction with cached updates, a topic discussed in the last chapter. The basic idea is that the update operations are kept in a local cache until the program calls the ApplyUpdates method of the Query component. This operation corresponds to the execution of a series of update, insert, and delete SQL operations on the server, using the data in the cache. The required SQL commands are held by the UpdateSQL component, which has a design-time editor you can use to generate these SQL commands almost automatically.

Cached updates solve the live queries issue, reduce network traffic, define a standard way to solve updates conflicts, and reduce the server load, but they require more memory on the client computer.

A much better approach than using cached updates is to rely on the ClientDataSet component, which is extremely powerful and allows you to do similar things yet leaving you a lot more programmatic control.

The UpdateSQL Component

The role of the UpdateSQL component is to provide a query with the update statements required to make its result set editable. Its key properties are `DeleteSQL`, `InsertSQL`, and `ModifySQL`, but the most important element is the `UpdateObject` property of the related Query component. The update SQL statements are executed when you apply the cached updates, sending the changes to the server. Because cached updates maintain the information on the original records, the updates usually indicate which record to update by passing the original data. This is the only way we have to identify a record on a SQL server, and this technique also helps the server to track any updates on the same record done by other users.

All this setup might seem to imply a lot of work, but it is actually very simple. After you've written a query, you can connect the UpdateSQL component to it and activate the component editor, as shown in Figure 14.1.

FIGURE 14.1:

The UpdateSQL component editor in action

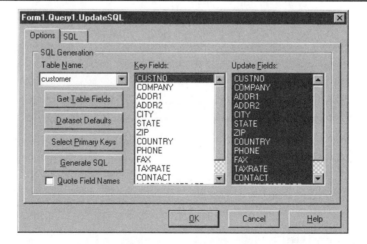

This component editor has two tabs. The first indicates the criteria used to generate the SQL statements for adding, deleting, or modifying records. With a join, you can select the table to update and the fields involved. When you've completed this step, click the Generate SQL button and the editor will move to the second tab, where you can inspect the generated SQL code for the three operations.

The UpdateSQL Example

To demonstrate the real power of the UpdateSQL component, I've built a complex example called UpdateSQL, based on the Employee, Department, and Job tables of the IBLocal database we've used in the past. Here is the textual description of the UpdateSQL component of the example:

```
object EmpUpdate: TUpdateSQL
  ModifySQL.Strings = (
    'update EMPLOYEE'
    'set'
    '  FIRST_NAME = :FIRST_NAME,'
    '  LAST_NAME = :LAST_NAME,'
    '  SALARY = :SALARY,'
    '  DEPT_NO = :DEPT_NO,'
    '  JOB_CODE = :JOB_CODE,'
    '  JOB_GRADE = :JOB_GRADE,'
    '  JOB_COUNTRY = :JOB_COUNTRY'
    'where'
    '  EMP_NO = :OLD_EMP_NO')
  InsertSQL.Strings = (
    'insert into EMPLOYEE'
    '  (FIRST_NAME, LAST_NAME, SALARY, DEPT_NO, JOB_CODE,'
    '  JOB_GRADE, JOB_COUNTRY)'
    'values'
    '  (:FIRST_NAME, :LAST_NAME, :SALARY, :DEPT_NO, :JOB_CODE, '
    '  :JOB_GRADE, :JOB_COUNTRY)')
  DeleteSQL.Strings = (
    'delete from EMPLOYEE'
    'where'
    '  EMP_NO = :OLD_EMP_NO')
end
```

To delete the employee records, the program uses a stored procedure, which is already available in the sample database and is connected to the following component:

```
object spDelEmployee: TStoredProc
  DatabaseName = 'AppDB'
  StoredProcName = 'DELETE_EMPLOYEE'
  ParamData = <
    item
      DataType = ftInteger
      Name = 'EMP_NUM'
      ParamType = ptInput
    end>
end
```

The OnUpdateRecord event of the Query component uses the stored procedure instead of the default UpdateSQL component for deleting records. Here is the code of the event handler:

```
procedure TdmData.qryEmployeeUpdateRecord(DataSet: TDataSet;
  UpdateKind: TUpdateKind; var UpdateAction: TUpdateAction);
begin
  // when deleting the record, use the stored procedure
  if UpdateKind = ukDelete then
  begin
    // assign emp_no value
    with dmData do
      spDelEmployee.Params[0].Value := qryEmployeeEMP_NO.OldValue;
    try
      // invoke stored procedure that tries to delete employee
      dmData.spDelEmployee.ExecProc;
      UpdateAction := uaApplied; // success
    except
      UpdateAction := uaFail;
    end;
  end
  else
  try
    // apply updates
    dmData.EmpUpdate.Apply(UpdateKind);
    UpdateAction := uaApplied;
  except
    UpdateAction := uaFail;
  end;
end;
```

Notice that because we perform the update operation directly, we must indicate in the UpdateAction parameter whether it succeeds or not. This code is part of the data module. The main form, visible at run time in Figure 14.2, has a couple of extra features. If the user closes the form with any updates pending, the OnCloseQuery event of the form displays a warning message, allowing the user to apply the updates or skip them:

```
procedure TMainForm.FormCloseQuery(Sender: TObject;
  var CanClose: Boolean);
var
  Res: Integer;
begin
  with dmData do
    if qryEmployee.UpdatesPending then
    begin
      Res := MessageDlg (CloseMsg, mtInformation, mbYesNoCancel, 0);
      if Res = mrYes then
        AppDB.ApplyUpdates ([qryEmployee]);
      CanClose := Res <> mrCancel;
    end;
end;
```

FIGURE 14.2:

The main form of the UpdateSql example along with a secondary form

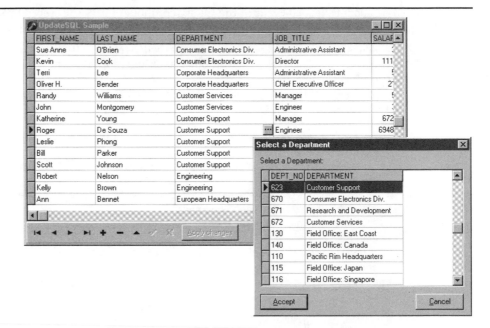

The second feature is the use of a secondary form to update the fields that are related to other tables—the fields involved in the joins. The program uses two secondary dialog boxes, which get the data from other two Query components. The dialog boxes are displayed when the user clicks the ellipsis button of the DBGrid control, in the OnEditButtonClick event. Here is the first part of this event handler, related to the selection of the department:

```
procedure TMainForm.DBGrid1EditButtonClick(Sender: TObject);
begin
  // check whether this is the department field
  if DBGrid1.SelectedField = dmData.qryEmployeeDEPARTMENT then
    with TfrmDepartments.Create(self) do
    try
      dmData.qryDepartment.Locate('DEPT_NO',
        dmData.qryEmployeeDEPT_NO.Value, []);
      if ShowModal = mrOk then
        with dmData do
        begin
          if not (qryEmployee.State in [dsEdit, dsInsert]) then
            qryEmployee.Edit;
          qryEmployeeDEPT_NO.Value := qryDepartment.Fields[0].Value;
          qryEmployeeDEPARTMENT.Value := qryDepartment.Fields[1].Value;
        end;
    finally
      Free;
    end
  else // similar code for the job fields...
```

Finally, the Apply button simply calls the `ApplyUpdates` method if there are pending updates and then refreshes the data of the query:

```
procedure TMainForm.btnApplyClick(Sender: TObject);
begin
  with dmData do
    if qryEmployee.UpdatesPending then
    begin
      AppDB.ApplyUpdates([qryEmployee]);
      // refresh the data
      qryEmployee.Close;
      qryEmployee.Open;
      btnApply.Enabled := False;
    end;
end;
```

If you run this program, you'll notice that even if the underlying query is read-only, you can change data directly in the DBGrid, as you would do with a regular Table component. The visual operations you do are temporarily stored in the cache; then, when you issue the update operation, the UpdateSQL and the StoredProc components provide the actual code. Also keep in mind that the Salary field has some constraints (defined in the sample database), so you have to change it carefully to avoid errors on the server when the changes are applied.

Update Conflicts

When you are working with local tables, using cached updates might cause concurrency problems. A plain edit operation usually places a lock on the table, so that the other users cannot modify the same record until the first user has posted the updates. The previous chapter covered locking and concurrency issues in detail.

When working with SQL servers, however, the default locking behavior is optimistic. Multiple users can update the same records, and only when the data is sent back does the server verify the original data of the record before updating it, potentially raising an error. More precisely, the update statement uses one or more original fields to locate the record you want to update. If you use all fields and another user has changed the record, then the server will not find the original record and will cause an update error.

You can manually control this behavior either in the code of the UpdateSQL component (indicating to include all the fields read in the query) or by using the UpdateMode property of the Table and Query components. The default value, upWhereAll, indicates that the update query will have a where clause with all the original fields of the record. In many cases, the fact that another user has modified a field different from those we have modified is not an error. We can set the upWhereChanged mode to let Delphi generate an exception and show an error message only if the current and the other user have both modified the same fields. The third alternative is to use the key field only to identify the record, which means that update conflicts will be ignored and that the last user posting the data will simply override any previous change. As you can imagine, this is generally an option to avoid in a client/server, multiuser environment.

Using Transactions

Whether you are working with a SQL server, you should use *transactions* to make your applications more robust. The idea of a transaction can be described as a series of operations to be considered as a single, "atomic" whole that cannot be split.

An example may help to clarify the concept. Suppose you have to raise the salary of each employee of a company by a fixed rate, as we did in the Total example of the preceding chapter. Now if during the operation an error occurs, you might want to undo the previous changes. If you consider the operation "raise the salary of each employee" as a single transaction, it should either be completely done or completely ignored. Or consider the analogy with financial transactions—if only part of the operation is performed, because of an error, you might end up with a missed credit or with some extra money!

Working with database operations as transactions serves a useful purpose. You can start a transaction and do several operations that should all be considered parts of a single larger operation; then, at the end, you can either commit the changes or *roll back* the transaction, discarding all the operations done up to now. Typically, you might want to roll back a transaction if an error occurred during its operations.

Handling transactions in Delphi is quite simple. By default, each edit/post operation is considered a single *implicit* transaction, but you can alter this behavior by handling them explicitly. Simply use the following three methods of the BDE Database component (other database connection components have similar methods):

StartTransaction   marks the beginning of a transaction.

Commit   confirms all the updates to the database done during the transaction.

Rollback   returns the database to its state prior to starting the transaction.

The Database component determines the transaction isolation level using the `Trans-Isolation` property. When one user starts a transaction and modifies data, should such changes be visible to other users? And what happens if the user rolls back the transaction? To such questions there isn't a universal answer; every programmer should try to answer them according to the requirements or business rules of the application. There are three alternative values for transaction isolation in the BDE:

tiDirtyRead   makes the updates of a transaction immediately visible to other transactions and users even before they are committed. This is the only possibility for local databases, which have very limited transaction support.

tiReadCommitted makes available to other transactions only the updates already committed.

tiRepeatableRead hides every other transaction started by other users after the current one. Following repeat calls within a transaction will always produce the same result, as if the database took a snapshot of the data when the current transaction started.

Most but not all SQL servers support only the most advanced levels. The default choice should be tiReadCommitted, which is quite powerful but not too heavy on the SQL server (as it adds very few internal locks).

As a general suggestion, transactions should involve only a minimal number of updates (only those strictly related and part of a single atomic operation) and should be kept short in time. You should avoid transactions that wait for user input to complete them, as the user might be temporarily gone and the transaction might remain active for a long time. Using update statements on multiple records and using cached updates can help us make the transactions small and fast.

To further inspect transactions and experiment with the update mode of the Table component, you can use the TranSample application. As you can see in Figure 14.3, you can simply use the radio buttons to choose the alternatives, and click the push buttons on the right of the toolbar to manually start, commit, and roll back a transaction. To get a real idea of the different effects, you should run multiple copies of the program (provided you have enough licenses on your InterBase server).

FIGURE 14.3:

The TranSample application allows you to test the transaction isolation of a database and the update modes of a table.

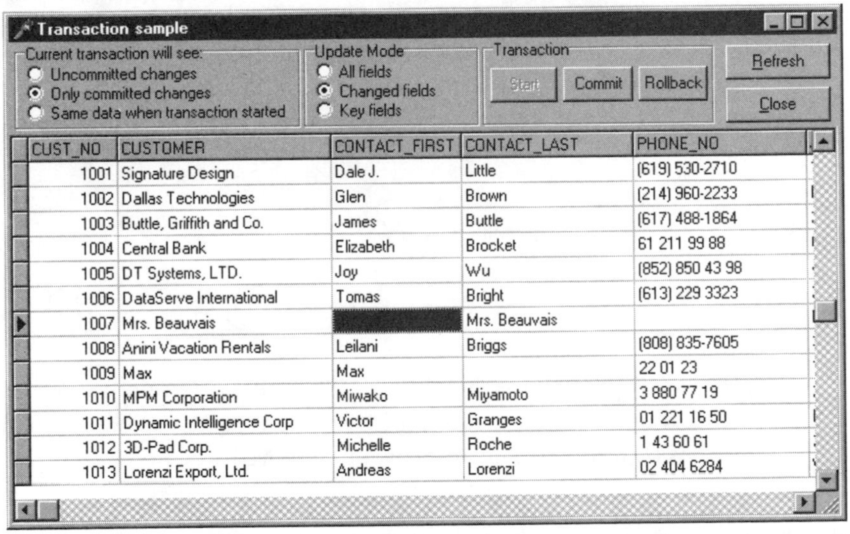

Using SQL Monitor

Just as you need a debugger to test a Delphi application, you need some tools to test how a client/server application behaves and to speed it up if possible. In particular, it is very important to look at the information moving from the client to the server (the explicit SQL requests our program does and those added by the BDE) and from the server to the client (the actual data). This is what the SQL Monitor tool included in Delphi Enterprise is for.

NOTE   Notice that the SQL Monitor tool is specific to the BDE. The dbExpress and InterBase Express component sets have similar monitoring capabilities, directly embedded inside specific components.

As you can see in Figure 14.4, the central window of SQL Monitor shows a list of the low-level commands sent to the server. The bottom portion of the window shows the selected line of the above list on multiple rows, which helps when the line is too long.

FIGURE 14.4:

The SQL Monitor running

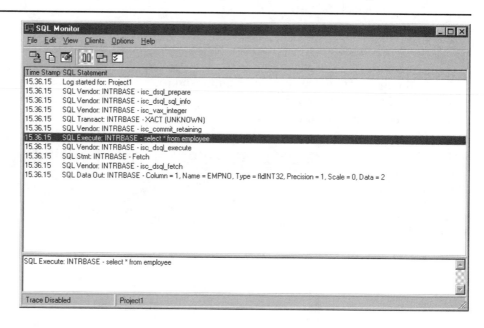

To use SQL Monitor, simply select the client program you want to inspect. Then set the proper trace options (by using the corresponding speed button or the Options ➢ Trace Options command). The available options are listed in Table 14.1.

TABLE 14.1: The Trace Options of the SQL Monitor

Trace Option	Meaning
Prepared Query Statement	Enables tracing of the SQL statements every time they are prepared.
Executed Query Statement	Traces all the SQL statements sent to the server.
Input Parameters	Shows input parameters as they become available. This is important for testing whether the parameters are correct.
Fetched Data	Shows the data sent by the server (a very slow operation).
Statement Operations	Shows the requests preceding the execution of a SQL statement, such as the allocation, preparation, and parsing of the input.
Connect/Disconnect	Shows the connection and disconnection events. This is an important test when the **KeepConnection** of the **Database** component is set to False, as the client won't maintain the connection with the server but will establish it only as needed (with the side effect of reducing the number of licenses required, in some cases). Looking at the frequency of these events might help you understand whether it is better to keep the connection active or not.
Transactions	Traces the transactions, including those activated automatically by the BDE if you don't use transactions directly.
Blob I/O	Shows the data about BLOB fields.
Miscellaneous	Traces other operations that don't fit any of the above categories.
Vendor Errors	Shows server error messages.
Vendor Calls	Shows client API calls.

SQL Monitor is useful for seeing if the SQL statements sent by the BDE to the server are correct, but it also helps you see how many operations are done behind the scenes. Along with the time-stamp information for each operation, the number of operations can give some clue about your application's speed (although you should remember that the presence of SQL Monitor slows down the connection quite a lot).

In other words, SQL Monitor should be your guide in determining how to speed up your client/server application, using some of the tricks described in this chapter. At the same time, however, it takes a lot of experience and a good understanding of SQL to interpret its output properly.

As an example of the use of SQL Monitor, we can test what happens when we use the Filter property of a Table component. In a new project, simply place a Table, a DataSource, and a DBGrid. Select a database and a table (for example, the EMPLOYEE table of IBLocal) and set the Filtered property to True and the Filter property to EmpNo>20. If you now run the program, SQL Monitor will show you that the select statement generated by the BDE has a where clause corresponding to the filter. You can see this situation in Figure 14.5.

FIGURE 14.5:

SQL Monitor showing SQL statements generated by a Table component

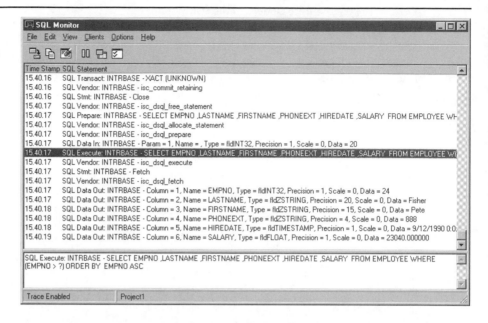

Performance Tuning

Besides using the SQL Monitor (or another monitoring technique) to determine the potential bottlenecks in your applications, you can do several things to speed up your client/server programs. The key element to keep in mind—as I've stressed many times in this chapter—is to reduce the network traffic, by reducing the result sets returned by the server both in the number of records and in the size of each.

Besides a good overall database design and a good Delphi implementation of it, there are many settings you can check. The following tips might come in handy, but they won't help as much as a better design!

- In InterBase, you can set an automatic sweep (or "garbage collection") interval. The operation is also automatically performed when you do a backup. Because a sweep slows down the database, it should not be done too frequently. However, if you never do it, the database will keep track of many leftover deleted records, reducing the overall performance and using extra memory.

- Use indexes on the fields used more often, particularly if you sort the result set on them. Keep in mind, though, that a good RDBMS will add at least temporary indexes for you. Using indexes can speed up queries quite a lot, particularly if the indexed fields are used to join two tables.

Continued on next page

- If you sort a field in descending order, a corresponding descending index might help.

- If you're an expert user, you might examine the *query plan*, the approach used by the server to perform a query, which is displayed (for example) when you use WISQL. The query plan will show you whether the SQL server is using indexes. In some cases, you might need to modify some complex queries to help the query optimizer built into the RDBMS.

- Check the server settings, including its cache, to obtain the best overall performance. The operating system cache on the server computer might help as well. In InterBase, if you want to perform all the updates physically, you can set the Forced Writes option in the Maintenance ➢ Database Properties menu of the InterBase Server Manager.

- Whenever possible, avoid an excessive use of transactions and try to keep them short and focused. Use a local cache instead of transactions (or together with them) to let the client computer do some more work for you, and skip some costly server operations.

- Handle transactions directly, disabling the auto-commit feature of the BDE; to do this, set SQLPASSTHRU MODE to SHARED NOAUTOCOMMIT. (You can set this and other BDE features described in this list with the BDE Administrator program.)

- If you have no licensing problems, set the KeepConnection property of the BDE Database component to True.

- With the BDE, set TRACE MODE to 0 when you are not debugging, to avoid having the drivers send trace strings to the debugger and slowing down the operations. Also the other monitoring services should be disabled when you're not debugging the application.

- In the BDE, enable schema caching (set ENABLE SCHEMA CACHE to TRUE). This setting reduces the time required to open a table, as the client doesn't need to ask for the metadata. You can also use the Delphi FieldDefs and StoreDefs properties of the Table component to store the metadata directly in the client program.

- With Microsoft and Sybase SQL Servers, try to set the PACKETSIZE parameter to a minimum of 4 KB, also modifying the corresponding value on the server. With these servers, also check that the DRIVER FLAGS parameter is set to 0. If it is 2048, queries will be executed in asynchronous mode and will be much slower.

- With ORACLE, DB/2, and ODBC drivers, try to fine-tune the ROWSET SIZE parameter until you obtain the best performance.

- With the InterBase driver, if you don't use explicit transactions, set the DRIVER FLAGS parameter to 4096. This value enables *soft commits*, meaning that after each commit or rollback operation the open cursors won't have to be refreshed.

The dbExpress Library

As I mentioned in Chapter 13, one of the most notable new features of Delphi 6 is the adoption of the dbExpress database access library, a new SQL server access layer introduced by Borland in its Kylix product for Linux, and now with Delphi 6 also for Windows. As I've already provided a general overview of dbExpress in the preceding chapter, let's focus right away on the technical details.

Working with Unidirectional Cursors

The motto of dbExpress could be "fetch but don't cache." The key difference between this library and BDE or ADO is that dbExpress can only execute SQL queries and fetch the results in a *unidirectional cursor*. In "unidirectional" database access, you can move from one record to the next, but you cannot get back to a previous record of the dataset. This is because the library doesn't store the data is has retrieved in a local cache, but only passes it from the database server to the calling application.

Using a unidirectional cursor might sound like a limitation, and it really is! Besides having problems with the navigation, you cannot connect a database grid to a dataset like this. So what is a unidirectional dataset good for?

- You can use a unidirectional dataset for reporting purposes. In a printed report, but also an HTML page or an XML transformation, you move from record to record, produce the output, and that's it. No need to get back to past records and, in general, no interaction of the user with the data. Unidirectional datasets are probably the best option for Web and multitier architectures.

- You can use a unidirectional dataset to feed a local cache, such as the one provided by a ClientDataSet component. At this point, you can connect visual components to the in-memory dataset and operate on it with all the standard techniques, including the use of visual grids. You can freely navigate and edit the data in the in-memory cache, but also control it far better than with the BDE or ADO.

The important thing to notice is that, in these circumstances, avoiding the caching of the database engine actually saves time and memory. The library doesn't have to use extra memory for the cache and doesn't need to waste time storing data, duplicating information. Over the last couple of years, many programmers moved from BDE-based cached updates to the ClientDataSet component, which provides more flexibility in managing the content of the data and update information they keep in memory. However, using a ClientDataSet on top of the BDE (or ADO) exposes you to the risk of having two separate caches, actually wasting a lot of memory.

Another advantage of using the ClientDataSet component is that its cache supports editing operations, and the updates stored in this cache can be applied to the original database server by the DatasetProvider component. This component can generate the proper SQL update statements, and can do so in a more flexible way than the BDE (although ADO is quite powerful in this respect). In general, the provider can also use a dataset for the updates, but this isn't directly possible with the dbExpress dataset components.

Platforms and Databases

A key element of the dbExpress library is its availability for both Windows and Linux, in contrast to all the other database engines available for Delphi (BDE and ADO), which are available only for Windows. Notice, though, that some of the database-specific components, such as InterBase Express, are also available on multiple platforms.

When you use dbExpress, you are provided with a common framework, which is independent from the actual SQL database server you are planning to use. dbExpress comes with drivers for MySQL, InterBase, Oracle, and IBM DB2. These drivers are available as separate DLLs you have to deploy along with your program or as compiled units you can link into the executable file.

NOTE   It is actually possible to write custom drivers for the dbExpress architecture. This is documented in details in the paper *dbExpress Draft Specification*, published on the Borland Community Web site. At the time of this writing, this document is at `http://community.borland.com/article/0,1410,22495,00.html`. You'll probably be able to find third-party drivers. For example, there is a free one (available also in Kylix), which bridges dbExpress and ODBC.

The dbExpress Components

The VCL components used to interface the dbExpress library encompass a group of dataset components plus a few ancillary ones. To differentiate these components from other database-access families, the components are prefixed with the letters *SQL*, underlining the fact that they are used for accessing RDBMS servers.

These components include a database connection component, a few dataset components (a generic one, three specific versions for tables, queries, and stored procedures, and one encapsulating a ClientDataSet component), and a monitor utility.

The SQLConnection Component

The TSQLConnection class inherits from the TCustomConnection component, and handles database connections, the same as its sibling classes (the Database, ADOConnection, and IBConnection components).

TIP   Unlike other component families, in dbExpress the connection is compulsory. In each of the dataset components, you cannot specify directly which database to use, but can only refer to a SQLConnection.

The connection component uses the information available in the `drivers.ini` and `connections.ini` files, which are the only two configuration files of dbExpress (these files are saved by default under `\Program Files\Common Files\Borland Shared\DBExpress`). The first, `drivers.ini`, lists the available dbExpress drivers, one for each supported database. For each driver, there is a set of default connection parameters. For example, the InterBase section reads as follows:

```
[Interbase]
GetDriverFunc=getSQLDriverINTERBASE
LibraryName=dbexpint.dll
VendorLib=GDS32.DLL
BlobSize=32
CommitRetain=True
Database=database.gdb
Password=masterkey
RoleName=RoleName
TransIsolation=ReadCommited
User_Name=sysdba
WaitOnLocks=True
```

The parameters indicate the dbExpress driver DLL (the `LibraryName` value), the entry function to use (`GetDriverFunc`), the vendor client library, and some more specific parameters that depend on the database. If you read the entire `drivers.ini` file, you'll see that the parameters are really database-specific. I have to say that some of these parameters don't make a lot of sense at the driver level, such as the database to connect to, but the list includes all the available parameters, regardless of their actual usage.

The `connections.ini` file provides the database specific description. This list resembles the aliases of the BDE, and you can enter multiple connection details for every database driver. The connection describes the physical database you want to connect to. As an example, this is the portion for the default `IBLocal` definition:

```
[IBLocal]
BlobSize=32
CommitRetain=True
Database=database.gdb
DriverName=Interbase
Password=masterkey
RoleName=RoleName
TransIsolation=ReadCommited
User_Name=sysdba
WaitOnLocks=True
```

As you can see by comparing the two listings, this is a subset of the parameters of the driver. When you create a new connection, the system will copy the default parameters from the driver; you can then edit them for the specific connection—for example, providing a proper database name. Each connection relates to the driver for its key attributes, as indicated by the DriverName property.

The important thing to notice is that these initialization files are used only at design time. In fact, when you select a driver or a connection at design time, the values of these files are copied to corresponding properties of the SQLConnection component, as in this example:

```
object SQLConnection1: TSQLConnection
  ConnectionName = 'IBLocal'
  DriverName = 'Interbase'
  GetDriverFunc = 'getSQLDriverINTERBASE'
  LibraryName = 'dbexpint.dll'
  LoginPrompt = False
  Params.Strings = (
    'BlobSize=-1'
    'CommitRetain=False'
    'Database=c:\program files\interbase corp\interbase6\examples\' +
      'database\employee.gdb'
    'DriverName=Interbase'
    'LocaleCode=0x0000'
    'Password=masterkey'
    'RoleName=RoleName'
    'ServerCharSet=ASCII'
    'SQLDialect=1'
    'Interbase TransIsolation=ReadCommited'
    'User_Name=sysdba'
    'WaitOnLocks=True')
  VendorLib = 'GDS32.DLL'
end
```

At run time, your program will rely on the properties to have all the required information, so you don't need to deploy the two INI files along with your programs. In theory, the files will be required if you want to change the DriverName or ConnectionName properties at run time. However, in case you want to connect your program to a new database, you can set directly the relevant properties.

When you add a new SQLConnection component to an application, you can proceed in different ways. You can set up a driver, using the list of values available for the DriverName property, and then select a predefined connection, by selecting one of the values available in the ConnectionName property. This second list is filtered according with the driver you've already selected. As an alternative, you can start by selecting directly the ConnectionName property, which in this case includes the entire list.

Instead of hooking up an existing connection, you can define a new one (or see the details of the existing connections) by double-clicking the SQLConnection component and launching the dbExpress Connection Editor (Figure 14.6). This editor lists, on the left side, all of the predefined connections, for a specific driver or all of them, and allows you to edit the connection properties using the grid on the right. You can use the toolbar buttons to add, delete, rename, and test connections, and to open the read-only dbExpress Drivers Settings window, shown in Figure 14.7.

FIGURE 14.6:

The dbExpress Connection Editor

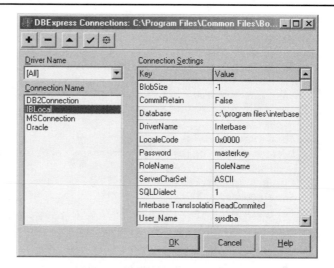

FIGURE 14.7:

The dbExpress Drivers Settings window of the dbExpress Connection Editor

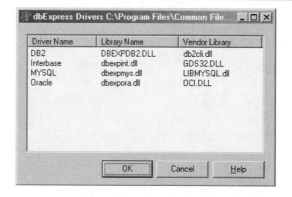

Besides editing the predefined connection settings, the dbExpress Connection Editor allows you also to select a connection for the SQLConnection component. This is what the OK button is for. Notice, in fact, that if you change some of the settings, the data is immediately written to the INI files: clicking the Cancel button doesn't revert your editing!

If you want to define access to a database, editing the connection properties is certainly the suggested approach. This way when you need to access the same database from another application, or another connection within the same application, all you need to do is to select the connection. However, since this operation copies the connection data, notice that updating the connection doesn't automatically refresh the values within other SQLConnection components referring to the same named connection: you have to reselect the connection these other components refer to. In this respect, the predefined connections are very different from the BDE aliases.

What really matters for the SQLConnection component is the value of its properties. Driver and vendor libraries are listed in properties you can freely change at design time (although you'll rarely want to do this), while the database and other database-specific connection settings are specified in the Params properties. This is a string list including information such as the database name, the user name and password, and so on. In practice, you could set up a SQL-Connection component by setting up the driver and then assigning the database name directly in the Params property, forgetting about the predefined connection. I'm not suggesting this as the best option, but it is certainly a possibility; the predefined connections are handy, but when the data changes, you still have to manually refresh every SQLConnection component.

Actually, to be complete, I have to mention that there is an alternative. You can set the LoadParamsOnConnect property to indicate that you want to refresh the component parameters from the initialization files every time you open the connection. In this case, a change in the predefined connections will be reloaded when you open the connection, at either design time or run time. At design time, this provides a handy technique (which has the same effect as reselecting the connection), but using it at run time means you'll also have to deploy the connections.ini file, which can be a good idea or an inconvenient one, depending on your deployment environment.

The only property of the SQLConnection component that is not related to the driver and database settings is LoginPrompt. Setting it to False allows you to provide a password skipping the login request, both at design time and run time. If this is very handy for development, it can reduce the security of your system. Of course this is also the option you'll want to use for unattended connections, for example on a Web server.

The dbExpress Dataset Components

The dbExpress component's family provides four different dataset components: a generic dataset, a table, a query, and a stored procedure. The latter three components are provided for compatibility with the equivalent BDE components and have similarly named properties. If you don't have to port existing code, you should tend to use the general SQLDataSet component, which can be used to execute a query but also to access a table or a stored procedure.

The first important thing to notice is that all of these datasets inherit from a new special base class, TCustomSQLDataSet. This class and its derived classes represent unidirectional datasets, with the key features I've already described. In practice, this means that the browse operations are limited to calling First and Next, while Prior, Last, Locate, the use of bookmarks, and all other navigational features are disabled.

NOTE   Technically, some of the moving operations call the CheckBiDirectional internal function and eventually raise an exception. CheckBiDirectional refers to the public IsUnidirectional property of the TDataSet class, which you can eventually use in your own code to disable operations that are illegal on unidirectional datasets.

Besides having limited navigational capabilities, these datasets have no editing support, so a lot of methods and events common to other datasets are not available. For example, there is no AfterEdit or BeforePost event.

As I mentioned earlier, of the four dataset components for dbExpress, the fundamental one is TSQLDataSet, which can be used both to retrieve a dataset and to execute a command. The two alternatives are activated by calling the Open method (or setting the Active property to True) and by calling the ExecSQL method.

The SQLDataSet component can retrieve an entire table, or use a SQL query or a stored procedure for reading a dataset or issuing a command. The CommandType property determines one of the three access modes. The possible values are ctQuery, ctStoredProc, and ctTable, which determine the value of the CommandText property (and also the behavior of the related property editor in the Object Inspector). For a table or stored procedure, the CommandText property indicates the name of the related element of the database, and the editor provides a drop-down list with the possible values. For a query, the CommandText property stores the text of the SQL command, and the editor provides a little help in building the SQL query (in case it is a select statement). You can see the editor in Figure 14.8.

When you use a table, the component will generate a SQL query for you, as dbExpress targets only SQL databases. The generated query will include all the fields of the table, and if you specify the SortFieldNames property, it will include a sort by directive.

FIGURE 14.8:

The CommandText Editor used by the SQLDataSet component for queries

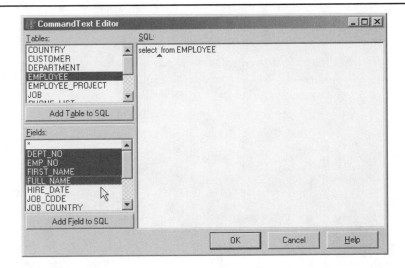

The three *specific* dataset components offer a similar behavior, but you specify the SQL query in the SQL string list property, the stored procedure in the StoredProcName property, and the table name in the TableName property, as in the three corresponding BDE components.

The SQLClientDataSet Component

The SQLClientDataSet is a combination of three components: the SQLDataSet component, a (hidden) provider, and the ClientDataSet. The idea is to be a helper, as you need only one component instead of three, which must also be connected. However, it doesn't surface all of the properties and events of the underlying components, so in complex situations, it's better to use the various components it stands for. I'll cover this and other variations of the Client-DataSet component later in this chapter, after I discuss the ClientDataSet itself in detail.

The SQLMonitor Component

The final component of the dbExpress group is the SQLMonitor, used to log the requests sent from dbExpress to the database server. This monitor provides capabilities similar to the stand-alone SQL Monitor application, which is bound to the BDE and cannot be used with the dbExpress library (and the analogous IBXMonitor component of the InterBase Express family, as we'll see in the next chapter).

The TimeStamp Field Type

Along with dbExpress, Delphi 6 introduces the `TSQLTimeStampField` field type, mapped to the timestamp data type that many SQL servers have (InterBase included). This data type is now available also in Delphi and is called `TSQLTimeStamp`. A time stamp is a simple record-based representation of a date or time, quite different from the floating-point representation used by the `TDateTime` data type. A time stamp is defined as:

```
TSQLTimeStamp = packed record
  Year : SmallInt;
  Month : Word;
  Day : Word;
  Hour : Word;
  Minute : Word;
  Second : Word;
  Fractions : LongWord;
end;
```

A time stamp field can automatically covert standard date and time values using the `AsDate-Time` property (as opposed to the native `AsSQLTimeStamp` property). You can also do custom conversions and further manipulation of time stamps by using the routines provided by the Sql-TimSt unit, including functions like `DateTimeToSQLTimeStamp`, `SQLTimeStampToStr`, and `VarSQLTimeStampCreate`.

A Simple dbExpress Demo

After that introduction, let's have a look at an actual demonstration, highlighting the key features of these components and showing how to use the ClientDataSet to provide caching and editing support for the unidirectional datasets. In another example, later on, I'll show you an example of native use of the unidirectional query, with no caching and editing support required.

The standard visual application based on dbExpress uses this series of components:

- The SQLConnection component provides the connection with the database and the proper dbExpress driver.

- The SQLDataSet component, which is hooked to the connection (via the `SQLConnection` property), indicates which SQL query to execute or table to open (using the `CommandType` and `CommandText` properties discussed earlier).

- The DataSetProvider component, connected with the dataset, extracts the data from the SQLDataSet and can generate the proper SQL update statements.

- The ClientDataSet component reads from the data provider and stores all the data (if its PacketRecords property is set to –1) in memory. This component has a lot of extra features and provides the actual data to the application, with full navigation and editing capabilities. You'll need at least to call its ApplyUpdates method to send the actual updates back to the database server (through the provider).

- The DataSource component allows you to surface the data from the ClientDataSet to the visual data-aware controls.

As I mentioned earlier, the picture can be simplified by using the SQLClientDataSet, which replaces the two datasets and the provider. The SQLClientDataSet combines most of the properties of the components it replaces. For a simple example, you'll have to set the DBConnection property for connecting to the proper database, the CommandType and CommandText properties to specify which data to fetch, and the PacketRecords property to indicate how many records to retrieve in each block. You'll also need to call to the ApplyUpdates method to send the actual updates back to the database.

These are the key properties of the core components of the DbxSingle example:

```
object SQLConnection1: TSQLConnection
  ConnectionName = 'IBLocal'
  LoginPrompt = False
end
object SQLClientDataSet1: TSQLClientDataSet
  CommandText = 'EMPLOYEE'
  CommandType = ctTable
  DBConnection = SQLConnection1
end
```

As an alternative, the DbxMulti example uses the entire sequence of components:

```
object SQLConnection1: TSQLConnection
  ConnectionName = 'IBLocal'
  LoginPrompt = False
end
object SQLDataSet1: TSQLDataSet
  SQLConnection = SQLConnection1
  CommandText = 'select * from EMPLOYEE'
end
object DataSetProvider1: TDataSetProvider
  DataSet = SQLDataSet1
end
object ClientDataSet1: TClientDataSet
  ProviderName = 'DataSetProvider1'
end
object DataSource1: TDataSource
  DataSet = ClientDataSet1
end
```

Both examples also have some visual controls: a grid and a toolbar based on the action manager architecture.

Applying Updates

What is important to do in every example based on a local cache, like the one provided by the ClientDataSet and SQLClientDataSet components, is to write the local changes back to the database server. This is typically accomplished by calling the ApplyUpdates method. But when should you call it? You can either keep the changes in the local cache for a while and then apply a bunch of updates at once, or post each change right away. In these two simple examples, I've gone for the latter approach, attaching the following event handler to the AfterPost (fired after an edit or an insert operation) and AfterDelete events of the ClientDataSet components:

```
procedure TForm1.DoUpdate(DataSet: TDataSet);
begin
  // immediately apply local changes to the database
  SQLClientDataSet1.ApplyUpdates(0);
end;
```

If you want to apply all the updates in a single batch, you can either do this when the form is closed or the program ends, or let a user do the update operation by selecting a specific command. We'll explore some of these alternatives when discussing the ClientDataSet component in more detail.

Monitoring the Connection

Another feature, which I've added only to the DbxSingle example, is the monitoring capability offered by the SQLMonitor component. In the example, the component is activated as the program starts.

Every time there is a tracing string available, the component fires the OnTrace event to let you choose whether to include the string in the log. If the LogTrace parameter of this event is True (the default value), the component logs the message in the TraceList string list and fires the OnLogTrace event to indicate that a new string has been added to the log.

The component can also automatically store the log into the file indicated by its FileName property, but I haven't used this feature in the example. All I've done is to handle the OnLogTrace event, adding the last message to a memo component with the following code (and the output of Figure 14.9):

```
procedure TForm1.SQLMonitor1LogTrace(Sender: TObject;
  CBInfo: pSQLTRACEDesc);
begin
  MemoLog.Lines.Add (CBInfo.pszTrace);
end;
```

FIGURE 14.9:

A sample log obtained by
the SQLMonitor in the
DbxSingle example.

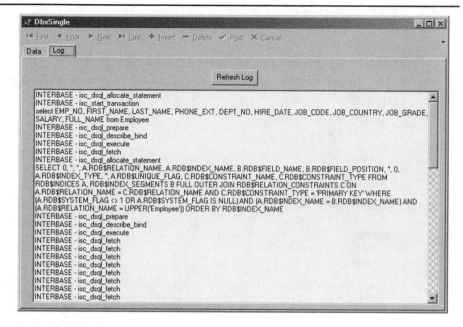

Also, a button allows a user to refresh the memo with the entire content of the trace list:

```
procedure TForm1.Button1Click(Sender: TObject);
begin
  MemoLog.Lines := SQLMonitor1.TraceList;
end;
```

Controlling the SQL Update Code

If you run the DbxSingle program and change, for example, the telephone number of an
employee, the monitor will log this update operation:

```
update EMPLOYEE  set
  PHONE_EXT = ?
where
  EMP_NO = ? and
  FIRST_NAME = ? and
  LAST_NAME = ? and
  PHONE_EXT = ? and
  HIRE_DATE = ? and
  DEPT_NO = ? and
  JOB_CODE = ? and
  JOB_GRADE = ? and
  JOB_COUNTRY = ? and
  SALARY = ? and
  FULL_NAME = ?
```

The structure of the `update` statement depends on the `UpdateMode` property of the SQL-ClientDataSet component. Trying to use upWhereChanged or upWhereKeyOnly, however, causes an error, as the component is unable to determine which are the key records, and the provider doesn't generate a correct `update` statement. In fact, it simply tries to update the update the record based on the specific field changed, without including the key field in the `where` statement:

```
update EMPLOYEE set
   PHONE_EXT = ?
where
   PHONE_EXT = ?
```

The `update` statement should rather be:

```
update EMPLOYEE set
   PHONE_EXT = ?
where
   EMP_NO = ? and
   PHONE_EXT = ?
```

How can we obtain the proper `update` call? Considering we cannot directly attach a component like the UpdateSQL (which is a BDE-only component), a simple solution would be to force the inclusion of the key field. This can be accomplished in the ClientDataSet architecture by turning on the pfInKey flag of the `ProviderOptions` property of the source field.

This can easily be accomplished in the DbxMulti example, after adding persistent fields for the SQLDataSet component, but the problem is that the database library should locate the key fields automatically. In the DbxSingle example, we have no control on the source dataset and its fields, so the only solution is to write the `update` statements in a totally custom way, with quite some effort.

NOTE   We'll be able to discuss this type of problem again as we get into the details of the ClientDataSet component, the Provider, the Resolver, and other technical details later in this chapter and in Chapter 17.

Accessing Database Metadata with *SetSchemaInfo*

All RDBMS systems use special-purpose tables (generally called *system tables*) for storing metadata, such as the list of the tables, their fields, indexes, and constraints, and any other system information. As dbExpress provides a unified API for working with different SQL servers, it provides also a common way for accessing metadata. The TSQLDataSet component has a method, SetSchemaInfo, which fills the dataset with system information. This SetSchemaInfo method has three parameters:

SchemaType   indicates the type of information requested and includes stTables, stSysTables, stProcedures, stColumns, and stProcedureParams.

SchemaObject   indicates the object you are referring to, such as the name of the table for which you are requesting the columns.

SchemaPattern   is a filter, so that you can limit your request to tables, columns, or procedures starting with the given letters. This is very handy if you use prefixes to identify groups of elements.

For example, in the SchemaTest program, a button reads into the dataset all of the tables of the connected database:

```
ClientDataSet1.Close;
SQLDataSet1.SetSchemaInfo (stTables, '', '');
ClientDataSet1.Open;
```

The program uses the usual group of dataset provider, client dataset and data source component to display the resulting data in a grid, as you can see in Figure 14.10. After you're retrieved the tables, you can select a row of the grid and press the second button to see a list of the fields of this table:

```
SQLDataSet1.SetSchemaInfo (stColumns, ClientDataSet1['Table_Name'], '');
ClientDataSet1.Close;
ClientDataSet1.Open;
```

FIGURE 14.10:

The SchemaTest example allows you to see the tables of a database and the columns of a given table.

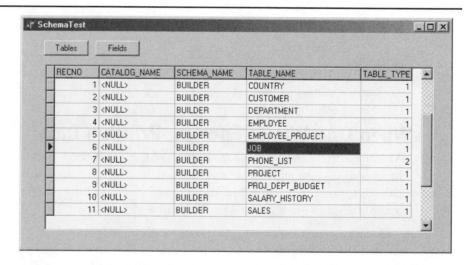

Besides accessing database metadata, dbExpress provides a way to access to its own configuration information, including the installed drivers and the configured connections. The unit DbConnAdmin defines a TConnectionAdmin class for this purpose, but the aim of this support is probably limited to dbExpress add-on utilities for developers, as letting end users access multiple databases in a totally dynamic way is not very common.

TIP The DbxExplorer demo included in Delphi 6 shows how to access both dbExpress administration files and schema information. Also check the help file under "The structure of metadata datasets" within the section "Developing database applications."

A Round-Up on dbExpress

After we've delved a little more into the dbExpress architecture and SQL components, I can try to add a few comments about this solution and its alternatives. On the whole, dbExpress provides a much neater architecture, compared to the BDE. In particular, I like it a lot when a database engine does things for me but lets me control what's going on and fine-tune every element. Ready-to-use defaults, such as those provided by the SQLClientDataSet component, are nice, but it is important for me in real-world applications to be able to take full control and write the exact SQL code I want my system to execute.

NOTE Another complaint I have is that I don't really like the architecture used for the specific Client-DataSet components bound to the various technologies (BDE, ADO, dbExpress and so on). In Chapter 19, "COM Programming," I'll discuss an alternate approach. In particular, I dislike the fact that you cannot code for a generic base component, but have to tune your code to the specific version of the ClientDataSet. Moreover, this architecture isn't extensible: you'll have to write a new specific component for each data access class you want to use (or to write). This seems really contrary to the spirit of OOP and to the overall architecture of VCL. My suggestion is simply to avoid using these all-in-one components and get used to dropping the DataSet–Provider–ClientDataSet triad every time you need to (or build a custom compound component for them).

When One-Way Is Enough: Printing Data

We have seen that one of the key elements of the dbExpress library is that it returns unidirectional datasets and that we can use the ClientDataSet component (in one of its incarnations) to store the records in a local cache. Now it is interesting to discuss at least a simple example where a unidirectional dataset is all we need.

This is common in *reporting*, that is, to produce information for each record in sequence without needing any further access to the data. This broad category includes producing printed reports (via a set of reporting components or using the printer directly), sending data to other applications like Microsoft Excel or Word, saving data to files (including HTML and XML formats), and more.

As I don't want to delve into HTML and XML right now, and we still haven't discussed COM-based automation, I'll go ahead with an example of printing—nothing fancy and nothing based on reporting components, but a simple way to produce a draft report on your video and printer. For this reason, I'm going to use Delphi's simplest technique to produce a printout: assigning a file to the printer with the `AssignPrn` RTL procedure.

The example, called UniPrint, has a unidirectional SQLDataSet component, hooked to an InterBase connection and based on the following SQL statement, which joins the employee table with the department table to display the name of the department where each employee works:

```
select d.DEPARTMENT, e.FULL_NAME, e.JOB_COUNTRY, e.HIRE_DATE
from EMPLOYEE e
inner join DEPARTMENT d on d.DEPT_NO = e.DEPT_NO
```

To handle printing, I've written a somewhat generic routine, requiring as parameters the data to print, a progress bar for status information, the output font, and the maximum format size of each field. The entire routine, listed below, uses file-print support and the graphic objects recall technique, and formats each field in a fixed-size, left-aligned string, to produce a columnar type of report. The call to the `Format` function has a parametric format string, built dynamically using the size of the field.

Here is the code, which uses three nested `try/finally` blocks to release all the resources properly:

```
procedure PrintOutDataSet (data: TDataSet;
  progress: TProgressBar; Font: TFont; maxSize: Integer = 30);
var
  PrintFile: TextFile;
  I: Integer;
  sizeStr: string;
  oldFont: TFontRecall;
begin
  // assign the printer to a file
  AssignPrn (PrintFile);
  Rewrite (PrintFile);

  // set the font and keep the original one
  oldFont := TFontRecall.Create (Printer.Canvas.Font);
  try
    Printer.Canvas.Font := Font;
    try
      data.Open;
      try
        // print header (field names) in bold
        Printer.Canvas.Font.Style := [fsBold];
        for I := 0 to data.FieldCount - 1 do
        begin
          sizeStr := IntToStr (min (data.Fields[i].DisplayWidth, maxSize));
          Write (PrintFile, Format ('%-' + sizeStr + 's',
```

```
            [data.Fields[i].FieldName]));
        end;
        Writeln (PrintFile);

        // for each record of the dataset
        Printer.Canvas.Font.Style := [];
        while not data.EOF do
        begin
          // print out each field of the record
          for I := 0 to data.FieldCount - 1 do
          begin
            sizeStr := IntToStr (min (data.Fields[i].DisplayWidth, maxSize));
            Write (PrintFile, Format ('%-' + sizeStr + 's',
              [data.Fields[i].AsString]));
          end;
          Writeln (PrintFile);
          // advance ProgressBar
          progress.Position := progress.Position + 1;
          data.Next;
        end;
      finally
        // close the dataset
        data.Close;
      end;
    finally
      // reassign the original printer font
      oldFont.Free;
    end;
  finally
    // close the printer/file
    System.CloseFile (PrintFile);
  end;
end;
```

The program invokes this routine when the Print All button is clicked. The program executes a separate query, which returns the number of records of the employee table to set up the progress bar (the unidirectional dataset, in fact, has no way to know how many records it is going to retrieve until it has reached the last one). Then it sets the output font, possibly using a fixed-width font, and calls the PrintOutDataSet routine.

```
procedure TNavigator.PrintAllButtonClick(Sender: TObject);
var
  Font: TFont;
begin
  // set ProgressBar range
  EmplCountData.Open;
  try
```

```
    ProgressBar1.Max := EmplCountData.Fields[0].AsInteger;
  finally
    EmplCountData.Close;
  end;

  Font := TFont.Create;
  try
    Font.Name := 'Courier New';
    Font.Size := 9;
    PrintOutDataSet (EmplData, ProgressBar1, Font);
  finally
    Font.Free;
  end;
end;
```

ClientDataSet and MyBase

The general idea of a client/server application implies that the computation workload is shared between two separate programs, the RDBMS and a client application. Although it is very hard to strike a precise line between the two sides, it is certainly useful to do operations on the client. Most database engines (BDE, as we've seen in this chapter, and ADO, as we'll see in Chapter 16, "ActiveX Data Objects") can manipulate client-side data stored in a cache. Using the ClientDataSet component, you can do the same regardless of the database engine you are using, which makes your program more flexible, particularly if you want to use dbExpress, which doesn't provide a similar feature natively.

A practical example will underline what I mean: Suppose you've written a SQL query to retrieve a rather large dataset, and a user wants to see the same data in a different order. You can certainly run a new query, with the proper order by clause, but this implies sending the same (possibly large) dataset once more from the server to the client. Since the client already has the data in memory, it would be more practical and generally faster to re-sort the data in memory and present the same data to the user with a different ordering.

The ClientDataSet component allows you to do this: Attaching the code to sort the data by assigning a proper field name to the IndexFieldNames property. This is often accomplished when the user clicks the field title in a DBGrid component (firing the OnTitleClick event):

```
procedure TForm1.DBGrid1TitleClick(Column: TColumn);
begin
  ClientDataSet1.IndexFieldNames := Column.Field.FieldName;
end;
```

TIP
Unlike local databases, a ClientDataSet can have dynamic indexes, as they are computed in memory anyway. The component also supports indexes based on a calculated field, specifically an *internally calculated* field, a type of field available only for this dataset. Unlike ordinary calculated fields, which are computed every time the record is used, values of internally calculated fields are kept in memory. This is why indexes consider them as plain fields.

Indexing is not all the ClientDataSet has to offer. When you have an index, you can define groups based on it, possibly with multiple levels of grouping. There is even specific support for determining the position of a record within a group (first, last, or middle position). Over groups or entire tables, you can define aggregates; that is, you can compute the sum or average value of a column for the entire table or the current group on-the-fly. The data doesn't need to be posted to a physical server, because these aggregate operations take place in memory. You can even define new aggregate fields, to which you can directly connect data-aware controls. I'll explore these capabilities in the next section.

Another very interesting area of the ClientDataSet component is its ability to handle the updates log, undoing changes, looking at their list before committing them, and so on. I'll explore this next.

The ClientDataSet component supports many features, only some of which are related to the three-tier architecture (covered in Chapter 17). This component represents a database completely mapped in memory and can also be made persistent to a local file. Borland marketing has introduced the name MyBase to describe this feature of the ClientDataSet component, which was formerly called the briefcase model.

The important thing to keep in mind is that all of these features are available to any client/server and even local applications. The ClientDataSet component, in fact, can get its data from a remote connection, from a local dataset (as you must do with dbExpress), or from a local MyBase file. This is another huge area to explore, so I'll simply show you a couple of examples highlighting key features.

WARNING The use of the ClientDataSet component, in each of its incarnations, requires either the deployment of the `Midas.dll` library or the inclusion in the project of the MidasLib unit (available in compiled format only). The core code of this component, in fact, is not directly part of the library and is not available in source code format. This is unfortunate, as many Delphi developers are accustomed to debugging into the source code and using it as the ultimate reference. It is noteworthy, though, the inclusion in Delphi 6 of the DCU version of the library, obtained from a C-language source code. This allows you to avoid deploying the actual library along with your program.

The Packets and the Cache

The ClientDataSet component reads data in packets made of the number of records indicated by the `PacketRecords` property. The default value of this property is –1, which means that the provider will pull all the records at once (this is reasonable only for a small dataset). Alternatively, you can set this value to zero to ask the server for only the field descriptors and no actual data or use any positive value to specify an actual number.

If you retrieve only a partial dataset, as you browse past the end of local cache, if `FetchOn-Demand` property is set to True (the default value), the ClientDataSet component will get more records from its source. This same property also controls whether BLOB fields and nested datasets of the current records are fetched automatically (these values might not be already part of the data packet, depending on the value of the `Options` of the dataset provider).

If you turn off this property, you'll need to manually fetch more records, by calling the `GetNextPacket` method, until the method returns zero. (You'll call `FetchBlobs` and `Fetch-Details` for these other elements.)

> **WARNING** Notice, by the way, that before you set a index for the data, you should retrieve the entire dataset (either by going to its last record or by setting the `PacketRecords` property to –1). Otherwise you'll have an odd index based on partial data.

Filtering

As with any other dataset, you can use the `Filter` property to specify the inclusion in the dataset of portions of the data the component is bound to. When manipulating a large table, of course, you should use a proper query so that you don't retrieve a large dataset from a SQL server. Filtering up-front in the server should generally be your first choice.

However, local filtering in the ClientDataSet can be quite useful, particularly because the filter expressions you can use are much more extensive than those you can use with other datasets. In particular, you can use the standard comparison and logical operators (`Population > 1000 and Area < 1000`) and arithmetic operators (`Population / Area < 10`), but also string functions (`Substring(Last_Name), 1, 2 = 'Ca'`), date and time functions (`Year (Invoice_Date) = 2002`), and others, including a `Like` function, wildcards, and an `In` operator.

These filtering capabilities are fully documented in the VCL Help file. Notice that the documentation was already there for Delphi 5, but most of these features didn't actually work. Now they do.

Grouping and Aggregates

We've already seen that a ClientDataSet can have an index different than the order in which it received the data. Once you've defined an index, you can group the data by that index. In practice, a group is defined as a list of consecutive records (according to the index) for which the value of the indexed field doesn't change. For example, if you have an index by state, all the addresses within that state will fall in the group.

Grouping

The CdsCalcs example has a ClientDataSet component that extracts its data from the Country table of the familiar DBDEMOS database. This operation is performed using a DataSetProvider component to the form, connecting the three components as follows:

```
object Table1: TTable
  Active = True
  DatabaseName = 'DBDEMOS'
  TableName = 'COUNTRY.DB'
end
object DataSetProvider1: TDataSetProvider
  DataSet = Table1
end
object ClientDataSet1: TClientDataSet
  ProviderName = 'DataSetProvider1'
end
```

I could have also used the specific BDEClientDataSet component, as I'll discuss later. Now we can focus on the definition of the group. This is obtained, along with the definition of an index, by specifying a grouping level for the index itself:

```
object ClientDataSet1: TClientDataSet
  IndexDefs = <
    item
      Name = 'ClientDataSet1Index1'
      Fields = 'Continent'
      GroupingLevel = 1
    end>
  IndexName = 'ClientDataSet1Index1'
```

When you have a group active, you can make this obvious to the user by displaying the grouping structure in the DBGrid, as shown in Figure 14.11. Simply handle the OnGetText event for the grouped field (the Continent field in the example), and show the text only if the record is the first of the group:

```
procedure TForm1.ClientDataSet1ContinentGetText(Sender: TField;
  var Text: String; DisplayText: Boolean);
begin
```

```
    if gbFirst in ClientDataSet1.GetGroupState (1) then
      Text := Sender.AsString
    else
      Text := '';
  end;
```

FIGURE 14.11:

The CdsCalcs example demonstrates that by writing a little code, you can have the DBGrid control visually show the grouping defined in the ClientDataSet.

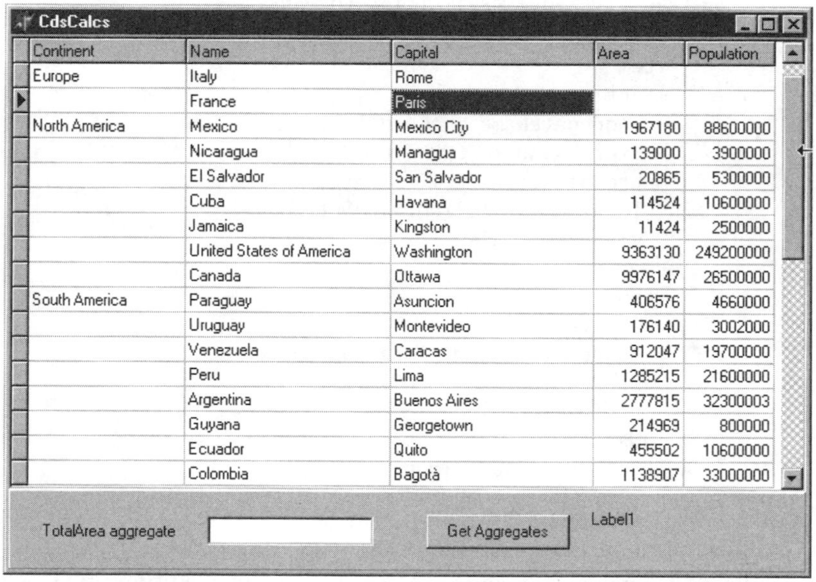

Defining Aggregates

Another feature of the ClientDataSet component is support for *aggregates*. An aggregate is a calculated value based on multiple records, such as the sum or the average value of a field for the entire table or a group of records (defined with the grouping logic I've just discussed). Aggregates are *maintained*; that is, they are recalculated immediately if one of the records changes. For example, the total of an invoice can be maintained automatically while the user types in the invoice items.

NOTE   Aggregates are maintained incrementally, not by recalculating all the values every time one value changes. Aggregate updates take advantage of the deltas tracked by the ClientDataSet. For example, to update a sum when a field is changed, the ClientDataSet subtracts the old value from the aggregate and adds the new value. Only two calculations are needed, even if there are thousands of rows in that aggregate group. For this reason, aggregate updates are instantaneous.

There are two ways to define aggregates. You can use the `Aggregates` property of the ClientDataSet, which is a collection, or you can define aggregate fields using the Fields editor. In both cases, you define the aggregate expression, give it a name, and connect it to an index and a grouping level (unless you want to apply it to the entire table). Here is the `Aggregates` collection of the CdsCalcs example:

```
object ClientDataSet1: TClientDataSet
  Aggregates = <
    item
      Active = True
      AggregateName = 'Count'
      Expression = 'COUNT (NAME)'
      GroupingLevel = 1
      IndexName = 'ClientDataSet1Index1'
      Visible = False
    end
    item
      Active = True
      AggregateName = 'TotalPopulation'
      Expression = 'SUM (POPULATION)'
      Visible = False
    end>
  AggregatesActive = True
```

Notice in the last line above that you must activate the support for aggregates, in addition to activating each specific aggregate you want to use. Disabling aggregates is important, because having too many of them can slow down a program. The alternative approach, as I mentioned, is to use the Fields editor, select the New Field command of its shortcut menu, and choose the Aggregate option (available, along with the InternalCalc option, only in a ClientDataSet). This is the definition of an aggregate field:

```
object ClientDataSet1: TClientDataSet
  object ClientDataSet1TotalArea: TAggregateField
    FieldName = 'TotalArea'
    ReadOnly = True
    Visible = True
    Active = True
    DisplayFormat = '###,###,###'
    Expression = 'SUM(AREA)'
    GroupingLevel = 1
    IndexName = 'ClientDataSet1Index1'
  end
```

The aggregate fields are displayed in the Fields editor in a separate group, as you can see in Figure 14.12. The advantage of using an aggregate field, compared to a plain aggregate, is that you can define the display format and hook the field directly to a data-aware control, such as a DBEdit in the CdsCalcs example. Because the aggregate is connected to a group, as soon as you select a record of a different group, the output will be automatically updated. Also, if you change the data, the total will immediately show the new value.

To use plain aggregates, instead, you have to write a little code, as in the following example (notice that the Value of the aggregate is a variant):

```
procedure TForm1.Button1Click(Sender: TObject);
begin
  Label1.Caption :=
    'Area: ' + ClientDataSet1TotalArea.DisplayText + #13'Population : '
    + FormatFloat ('###,###,###', ClientDataSet1.Aggregates [1].Value) +
    #13'Number : ' + IntToStr (ClientDataSet1.Aggregates [0].Value);
end;
```

Manipulating Updates

One of the core ideas behind the ClientDataSet component is that it is used as a local cache to collect some input from a user and then send a batch of update requests to the database. The component has both a list of the changes to apply to the database server, stored in the same format used by the ClientDataSet (accessible though the Delta property), and a complete updates log that you can manipulate with a few methods (including an Undo capability).

The Status of the Records

The component lets us monitor what's going on within the data packets. The UpdateStatus method returns one of the following indicators for the current record:

```
type TUpdateStatus = (usUnmodified, usModified, usInserted, usDeleted);
```

To check the status of every record in the client dataset easily, you can add a string-type calculated field to the dataset (I've called it ClientDataSet1Status) and compute its value with the following OnCalcFields event handler:

```
procedure TForm1.ClientDataSet1CalcFields(DataSet: TDataSet);
begin
  ClientDataSet1Status.AsString := GetEnumName (TypeInfo(TUpdateStatus),
    Integer (ClientDataSet1.UpdateStatus));
end;
```

This method (based on the RTTI GetEnumName function) converts the current value of the TUpdateStatus enumeration to a string, with the effect you can see in Figure 14.13.

FIGURE 14.13:

The CdsDelta program displays the status of each record of a ClientDataSet.

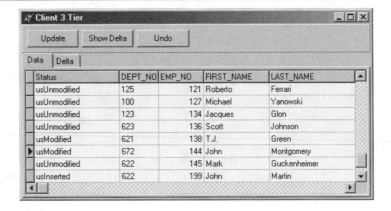

Accessing the Delta

Beyond examining the status of each record, the best way to understand which changes have occurred in a given ClientDataSet (but haven't been uploaded to the server) is to look at the delta, the list of changes waiting to be applied to the server. This property is defined as follows:

```
property Delta: OleVariant;
```

The format used by the Delta property is the same as that used to transmit the data from the client to the server. What we can do, then, is add another ClientDataSet component to an application and connect it to the data in the Delta property of the first client dataset:

```
if ClientDataSet1.ChangeCount > 0 then
begin
  ClientDataSet2.Data := ClientDataSet1.Delta;
  ClientDataSet2.Open;
```

In the CdsDelta example, I've added a data module with the two ClientDataSet components and an actual source of data, a SQLDataSet mapped to InterBase's EMPLOYEE demo table. Both client datasets have the extra status calculated field, with a slightly more generic version than the code discussed earlier, because the event handler is shared between them.

> **TIP** To create persistent fields for the ClientDataSet hooked to the delta (at run time), I've temporarily connected it, at design time, to the same provider of the main ClientDataSet. The structure of the delta, in fact, is the same of the dataset it refers to. After creating the persistent fields, I've removed the connection.

The form of this application has a page control with two pages, each with a DBGrid, one for the actual data and one for the delta. Some code hides or shows the second tab depending on the existence of data in the change log, as returned by the ChangeCount method, and updates the delta when the corresponding tab is selected. The core of the code used to handle the delta is very similar to the last code snippet above, and you can study the example source code on the CD to see more details.

You can see the change log of the CdsDelta application in Figure 14.14. Notice that the delta dataset has two entries for each modified record: the original values and the modified fields, unless this is a new or deleted record, as indicated by its status.

FIGURE 14.14:

The CdsDelta example allows you to see the temporary update requests stored in the Delta property of the ClientDataSet.

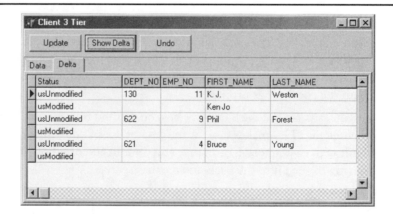

> **TIP** You can also filter the delta dataset (or any other ClientDataSet) depending on its update status, using the StatusFilter property. This allows you to show new, updated, and deleted records in separate grids or in a grid filtered by selecting an option in a TabControl.

Undo and *SavePoint*

Because the update data is stored in the local memory (in the delta), besides applying the updates and sending them to the application server, we can reject them, removing entries from the delta. The ClientDataSet component has a specific UndoLastChange method to accomplish this. The parameter of this method allows you to *follow* the undo operation (the name of this parameter is FollowChange). This means the client dataset will move to the record that has been restored by the undo operation.

Here is the code connected to the Undo button of the CdsDelta example:

```
procedure TForm1.ButtonUndoClick(Sender: TObject);
begin
  DmCds.cdsEmployee.UndoLastChange (True);
end;
```

An extension of the undo support is the possibility to save a sort of bookmark of the change log position (the current status) and to restore it later by undoing all successive changes. The SavePoint property can be used either to save the number of changes in the log or to reset the log to a past situation. Notice, anyway, that you can only remove records from the change log, not reinsert changes. In other words, the ChangeLog refers to a position in a log, so it can only go back to a position in which there were fewer records! This position is just a number of changes, so if you undo some changes and then do more edits, that number of changes will become meaningless.

Enabling and Disabling Logging

Keeping track of changes makes sense if you need to send the updated data back to a server database. In local applications with data stored to a MyBase file, keeping this log around can become useless and consumes memory. For this reason, you can disable logging altogether with the LogChanges property.

You can also call the MergeChangesLog method to remove all current editing from the change log. This makes sense if the dataset doesn't directly originate by a provider but was built with custom code, or in case you want to add or edit the data programmatically, without having to send it to the back-end database server.

TIP   The ClientDataSet in Delphi 6 has a new property, DisableStringTrim, which allows you to keep trailing spaces in field values. In past versions, in fact, string fields were invariably trimmed, which creates trouble with some databases.

Updating the Data

Now that we have a better understanding of what goes on during local updates, we can try to make this program work by sending the local update (stored in the delta) back to the database server. To apply all the updates from a dataset at once, pass -1 to the ApplyUpdates method.

If the provider (or actually the Resolver component inside it) has trouble applying an update, it triggers the OnReconcileError event. This can take place because of a concurrent update by two different people. As we tend to use optimistic locking in client/server applications, this should be regarded as a normal situation.

The OnReconcileError event allows you to modify the Action parameter (passed by reference), which determines how the server should behave:

```
procedure TForm1.ClientDataSet1ReconcileError(DataSet: TClientDataSet;
  E: EReconcileError; UpdateKind: TUpdateKind; var Action: TReconcileAction);
```

This method has three parameters: the client dataset component (in case more than one client application is interacting with the application server), the exception that caused the error (with the error message), and the kind of operation that failed (ukModify, ukInsert, or ukDelete). The return value, which you'll store in the Action parameter, can be any one of the following:

```
type TReconcileAction = (raSkip, raAbort, raMerge, raCorrect, raCancel,
  raRefresh);
```

- The raSkip value specifies that the server should skip the conflicting record, leaving it in the delta (this is the default value).

- The raAbort value tells the server to abort the entire update operation and not even try to apply the remaining changes listed in the delta.

- The raMerge value tells the server to merge the data of the client with the data on the server, applying only the modified fields of this client (and keeping the other fields modified by other clients).

- The raCorrect value tells the server to replace its data with the current client data, overriding all field changes already done by other clients.

- The raCancel value cancels the update request, removing the entry from the delta and restoring the values originally fetched from the database (thus ignoring changes done by other clients).

- The raRefresh value tells the server to dump the updates in the client delta and to replace them with the values currently on the server (thus keeping the changes done by other clients).

If you want to test a collision, you can simply launch two copies of the client application, change the same record in both clients, and then post the updates from both. We'll do this later to generate an error, but let's first see how to handle the OnReconcileError event.

This is actually a simple thing to accomplish, but only because we'll receive a little help. Since building a specific form to handle an OnReconcileError event is very common, Delphi already provides such a form in the Object Repository. Simply go to the Dialogs page and select the Reconcile Error Dialog item. This unit exports a function you can directly use to initialize and display the dialog box, as I've done in the CdsDelta example:

```
procedure TDmCds.cdsEmployeeReconcileError (DataSet: TCustomClientDataSet;
  E: EReconcileError; UpdateKind: TUpdateKind; var Action: TReconcileAction);
begin
  Action := HandleReconcileError(DataSet, UpdateKind, E);
end;
```

WARNING As the source code of the Reconcile Error Dialog unit suggests, you should use the Project Options dialog to remove this form from the list of automatically created forms (if you don't, an error will occur when you compile the project). Of course, you need to do this only if you haven't set up Delphi to skip the automatic form creation.

The HandleReconcileError function simply creates the form of the dialog box and shows it, as you can see in the code provided by Borland:

```
function HandleReconcileError(DataSet: TDataSet; UpdateKind: TUpdateKind;
  ReconcileError: EReconcileError): TReconcileAction;
var
  UpdateForm: TReconcileErrorForm;
begin
  UpdateForm := TReconcileErrorForm.CreateForm(DataSet, UpdateKind,
    ReconcileError);
  with UpdateForm do
  try
    if ShowModal = mrOK then
    begin
      Result := TReconcileAction(ActionGroup.Items.Objects[
        ActionGroup.ItemIndex]);
      if Result = raCorrect then
        SetFieldValues(DataSet);
    end
    else
      Result := raAbort;
  finally
    Free;
  end;
end;
```

The Reconc unit, which hosts the Reconcile Error dialog, contains over 350 lines of code, so we can't describe it in detail. However, you should be able to understand the source code by studying it carefully. Alternatively, you can simply use it without caring about how everything works.

The dialog box will appear in case of an error, reporting the requested change that caused the conflict and allowing the user to choose one of the possible TReconcileAction values. You can see an example in Figure 14.15.

FIGURE 14.15:

The Reconcile Error dialog provided by Delphi in the Object Repository and used by the CdsDelta example

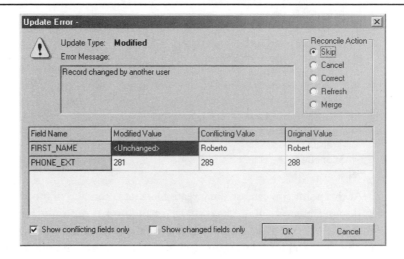

When you call ApplyUpdates, you start a rather complex update sequence, discussed in more detail in Chapter 17 for multitier architectures. In short, the delta is sent to the provider, which fires the OnUpdateData event and then receives a BeforeUpdateRecord event for every record to update. These are two chances you have to take a look at the changes and force specific operations on the database server.

MyBase (or the Briefcase Model)

The last capability of the ClientDataSet component I want to discuss in this chapter is its support for mapping memory data to local files, building stand-alone applications. The same technique can be applied in multitier applications to use the client program even when you're not physically connected to the application server. In this case, you can save all the data you expect to need in a local file for travel with a laptop (perhaps visiting client sites). You'll use the client program to access the local version of the data, edit the data normally, and when you reconnect, apply all the updates you've performed while disconnected.

To map a ClientDataSet to a local file you only need to set its FileName property, which requires an absolute pathname. To build a minimal MyBase program (called MyBase1), all you need is a ClientDataSet component hooked to a file and with a few fields defined (in the FieldDefs property):

```
object ClientDataSet1: TClientDataSet
  FileName = 'C:\md6code\14\MyBase1\test'
  FieldDefs = <
    item
      Name = 'one'
      DataType = ftString
      Size = 20
    end
    item
      Name = 'two'
      DataType = ftSmallint
    end>
  StoreDefs = True
end
```

At this point you can use the Create DataSet command of the local menu of the ClientDataSet at design time, or call its CreateDataSet method at run time, to physically create the file for the table. As you make changes and close the application, the data will be automatically saved to the file. (You might want to disable the change log, though, to reduce the size of this data.) The dataset, in any case, also has a SaveToFile method and a LoadFromFile method you can use in your code.

MyBase1, my example program, shown in Figure 14.16, doesn't require any database server or database connection to work. It needs only your own program and the Midas.dll file, but you can even get rid of it by including the MidasLib unit in the project. And the program doesn't require any actual Pascal code, either.

FIGURE 14.16:

The MyBase1 example, which saves data directly to a MyBase file

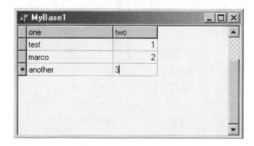

> **TIP** MyBase generally saves the datasets in XML format, although the internal CDS format is still available. I'll explore this format in detail when I discuss XML in Chapter 23, "XML and SOAP." For the moment, suffice to say this is a text-based format (so it is less space-efficient than the internal format), which can be manipulated programmatically but immediately makes some sense even if you try reading it.

The MyBase support in Delphi 6 also includes the possibility of extracting the XML representation of a memory dataset by using the XMLData property. In Delphi 5, you could obtain the same by saving the ClientDataSet in XML format in a memory stream.

Abstract Data Types in MyBase

The ClientDataSet component supports most data types provided by Delphi, including nested data types and abstract data types, the case I want to investigate with this second MyBase example. In the FieldDefs property editor of a ClientDataSet component you can and select the ftADT value for the DataType property of one of fields. Now move to the ChildDefs property and define the child fields. This is the field definition of the AdtDemo example:

```
FieldDefs = <
  item
    Name = 'ID'
    DataType = ftInteger
  end
  item
    Name = 'Name'
    ChildDefs = <
      item
        Name = 'LastName'
        DataType = ftString
        Size = 20
      end
      item
        Name = 'FirstName'
        DataType = ftString
        Size = 20
      end>
    DataType = ftADT
    Size = 2
  end>
```

At this point, provide the FileName, create the dataset, and you are ready to compile and run the application. If you use a DBGrid to view the resulting dataset, it will allow you to expand or collapse the subfields of the ADT field, as you can see in Figure 14.17. The *condensed* value of the field is defined in the AdtDemo program by handling the OnGetText event of the ADT field:

```
procedure TForm1.ClientDataSet1NameGetText(Sender: TField;
  var Text: String; DisplayText: Boolean);
begin
  Text := ClientDataSet1NameFirstName.AsString + ' ' +
    ClientDataSet1NameLastName.AsString;
end;
```

FIGURE 14.17:

The AdtDemo example
shows the support for
expanding or collapsing the
definition of an ADT field.

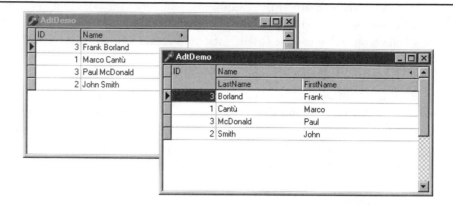

Indexing for ADT Fields

We've seen how easily you can set up an index as the user selects the title of a DBGrid. In ADT fields, the situation becomes a little more complex. The AdtDemo program, in fact, uses the FullName property of the field (not the FieldName property) because of the ADT definition. For the LastName child field, in fact, the index should be based on Name.LastName, not simply on LastName. Also, the ADT field cannot itself be indexed, so if it is selected, the program uses as index the LastName subfield. Here is the code:

```
procedure TForm1.DBGrid1TitleClick(Column: TColumn);
begin
  if Column.Field.FullName = 'Name' then
    ClientDataSet1.IndexFieldNames := 'Name.LastName'
  else
    ClientDataSet1.IndexFieldNames := Column.Field.FullName;
end;
```

What's Next?

This chapter has presented a somewhat detailed introduction to client/server programming with Delphi. We saw what the key issues are and delved a little into some interesting areas of client/server programming. After a general introduction, I discussed the use of the dbExpress database library Borland is introducing in Delphi 6 and of the ClientDataSet component and MyBase technology.

There is certainly more we can say about client/server programming in Delphi, and in the next chapter I'll discuss some real-world examples, after introducing InterBase and the IBX components. Chapter 16 will then focus on Microsoft's ADO database engine.

CHAPTER 15

InterBase and IBX

- Getting started with InterBase 6

- Server-side programming: views, stored procedures, and triggers

- Using InterBase Express

- Pieces for a real-world example

Client/server programming requires two sides: a client application that you probably want to build with Delphi, and a relational database management system (RDBMS), usually a "SQL server." In this chapter, I focus on one specific SQL server, InterBase. There are many reasons for this choice. InterBase is the SQL server developed by Borland; it is an open source project and can be obtained for free; and it has traditionally been bound with Delphi, which has specific dataset components for it.

For all of these reasons, InterBase should be a good choice for your Delphi client/server development, although there are many other equally powerful alternatives. I'll discuss Inter-Base from the Delphi perspective, without delving in to its internal architecture. A lot of the information presented also applies to other SQL servers, so even if you've decided not to use InterBase, you might still find it valuable.

Getting Started with InterBase 6

After installing InterBase 6, you'll be able to activate the server from the Windows Start menu, but if you plan on using it frequently, you should install it as a Windows service (of course, only if you have Windows NT/2000, as Windows 9x/Me doesn't have support for services). When the server is active, you'll see a corresponding icon in the Tray Icon area of the Windows Taskbar (unless you start it as a service). The menu connected with this icon allows you to see status information (see Figure 15.1) and do some very limited configuration.

FIGURE 15.1:

The status information displayed by InterBase when you double-click its tray icon

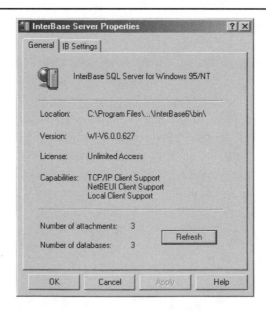

Inside InterBase

Even though it has a limited market share, InterBase is a very powerful RDBMS. In this section I'll introduce the key technical features of InterBase, without getting into too much detail. This is a book on Delphi programming, in fact. Unfortunately, there is currently very little published about InterBase, although there are some ongoing efforts for an InterBase book and there is a wealth of information in the documentation accompanying the product and on a few Web sites devoted to the product.

InterBase was built from the beginning with a very modern and robust architecture. Its original author, Jim Starkey, invented an architecture for handling concurrency and transactions without imposing physical locks on portions of the tables, something other well-known database servers can hardly do even today. InterBase architecture is called Multi-Generational Architecture (MGA), and it handles concurrent access to the same data by multiple users, who can modify records without affecting what other concurrent users see in the database.

This approach naturally maps to the *Repeatable Read* transaction isolation mode, in which a user within a transaction keeps seeing the same data, regardless of changes done and committed by other users. Technically, the server handles this by maintaining a different version of each accessed record for each open transaction. Even if this approach (also called *versioning*) can lead to larger memory consumption, it avoids almost any physical lock on the tables and makes the system much more robust in case of a crash. Also, MGA pushes toward a very clear programming model—Repeatable Read—which other well-known SQL servers don't even support without losing most of their performance.

If Multi-Generational Architecture is at the heart of InterBase, the server has many other technical advantages:

- A limited footprint, which makes InterBase the ideal candidate for running directly on client computers, including portables. The disk space required by InterBase for a minimal installation is well below 10 MB, and its memory requirements are also incredibly limited.

- Good performance on large amounts of data.

- Availability on many different platforms (including 32-bit Windows, Solaris, and Linux), with totally compatible versions, which makes the server scalable from very small to huge systems without notable differences.

- A very good track record, as InterBase has been in use for 15 years with very few problems.

- A language very close to the SQL standard.

- Advanced programming capabilities, with positional triggers, selectable stored procedures, updateable views, exceptions, events, generators, and more.
- Simple installation and management, with limited administration headaches.

A Short History of InterBase

Jim Starkey wrote InterBase for his own Groton Database Systems company (hence the `.gds` extension still in use for InterBase files). The company was later bought by Ashton-Tate, which was then acquired by Borland. Borland handled InterBase directly for a while, then created an InterBase subsidiary, which was later re-absorbed into the parent company.

Starting with Delphi 1, an evaluation copy of InterBase has been distributed along with the development tool, spreading the database server among developers. Although it doesn't have a large piece of the RDBMS market, which is dominated by a handful of players, InterBase has been chosen by a few very relevant organizations, from Ericsson to the U.S. Department of Defense, from stock exchanges to home banking systems.

More recent events include the announcement of InterBase 6 as an open source database (December 1999), the effective release of source code to the community (July 2000), and the release of the officially certified version of InterBase 6 by Borland (March 2001).

In between these events, there were announcements of the spin-off of a separate company to run the consulting and support business on top of the open source database. Contacts with a group of former InterBase developers and managers (who had left Borland) didn't lead to an agreement, but the group decided to go ahead even without Borland's help and formed IBPhoenix (`www.ibphoenix.com`) with the plan of supporting InterBase users.

At the same time, independent groups of InterBase experts formed the InterBase Developer Initiative (IBDI; `www.interbase2000.org`) and started the Firebird open source project to further extend InterBase. For this reason, SourceForge currently hosts two different versions of the project, InterBase itself run by Borland and the Firebird project run by this independent group. You see that the picture is rather complex, but this certainly isn't a problem for InterBase, as there are currently many organizations pushing it, along with Borland.

IBConsole

In past versions of InterBase, there were two main tools you could use to interact directly with the program: the Server Manager application, which could be used to administer both a local and a remote server; and Windows Interactive SQL (WISQL). Version 6 includes a much more powerful front-end application, called IBConsole. This is a full-fledged Windows program (built with Delphi) that allows you to administer, configure, test, and query an InterBase server, whether local or remote.

IBConsole is a simple and complete system for managing InterBase servers and their databases. You can use it to look into the details of the database structure, modify it, query the data (which can be useful to develop the queries you want to embed in your program), back up and restore the database, and perform all the other administrative tasks.

As you can see in Figure 15.2, IBConsole allows you to manage multiple servers and databases, all listed in a single, handy configuration tree. You can ask for general information about the database and list its entities (tables, domains, stored procedures, triggers, and everything else), accessing the details of each. You can also create new databases and configure them, back up the files, update the definitions, check what's going on and who is currently connected, and so on.

FIGURE 15.2:

IBConsole allows you to manage, from a single computer, InterBase databases hosted by multiple servers.

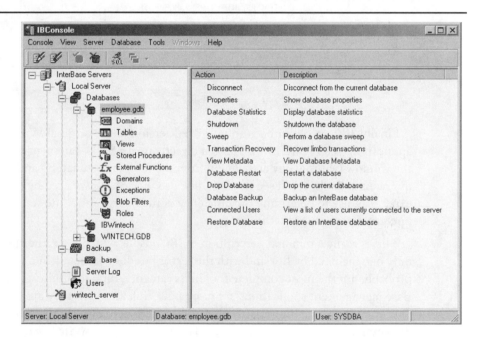

The IBConsole application allows you to open multiple windows to look at detailed information, such as the tables window depicted in Figure 15.3. In this window, you can see lists of the key properties of each table (columns, triggers, constraints, and indexes), see the raw metadata (the SQL definition of the table), access permissions, have a look at the actual data, modify it, and study the dependencies of the table. Similar windows are available for each of the other entities you can define in a database.

FIGURE 15.3:

IBConsole can open separate windows to show you the details of each entity—in this case, a table.

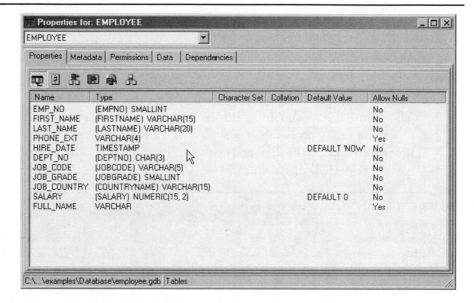

Finally, IBConsole embeds an improved version of the original Windows Interactive SQL application (see Figure 15.4). You can directly type a SQL statement in the upper portion of the window (without any actual help from the tool, unfortunately) and then execute the SQL query. As a result, you'll see the data, but also the access *plan* used by the database (which an expert can use to determine the efficiency of the query) and some statistics on the actual operation performed by the server.

This is really a minimal description of IBConsole, which is a rather powerful tool and the only one included by Borland with the server besides command-line tools. IBConsole is probably not the most complete tool in its category, though. Quite a few third-party Inter-Base management applications are more powerful, although they are not all very stable or user-friendly. Some InterBase tools are shareware programs, while others are totally free. Two examples, out of many, are InterBase Workbench (www.interbaseworkbench.com) and IB_WISQL (done with and part of InterBase Objects, www.ibobjects.com).

FIGURE 15.4:

The Interactive SQL window of IBConsole allows you to try out in advance the queries you plan to include in your Delphi programs.

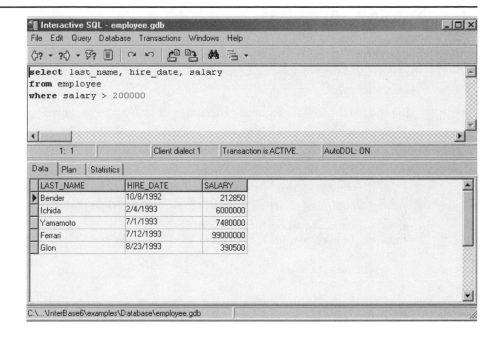

TIP   To find the latest third-party InterBase tools, have a look at www.interbase2000.org/tools, which hosts an up-to-date list.

Server-Side Programming

At the beginning of the previous chapter, I underlined the fact that one of the objectives of client/server programming—and one of its problems—is the division of the workload between the computers involved. When you activate SQL statements from the client, the burden falls on the server to do most of the work. However, you should try to use `select` statements that return a large result set, to avoid jamming the network.

Besides accepting DDL and DML requests, most RDBMS servers allow you to create routines directly on the server using the standard SQL commands plus their own server-specific extensions (which are generally not portable). These routines typically come in two forms, stored procedures and triggers.

Stored Procedures

Stored procedures are like the global functions of a Delphi unit and must be explicitly called by the client side. Stored procedures are generally used to define routines for data maintenance, to group sequences of operations you need in different circumstances, or to hold complex select statements.

Like Pascal procedures, stored procedures can have one or more typed parameters. Unlike Pascal procedures, they can have more than one return value. As an alternative to returning a value, a stored procedure can also return a result set, the result of an internal select statement or a custom fabricated one.

The following is a stored procedure written for InterBase; it receives a date in input and computes the highest salary among the employees hired on that date:

```
create procedure maxsaloftheday(ofday date)
returns (maxsal decimal(8,2)) as
begin
  select max(salary)
  from employee
  where hiredate = :ofday
  into :maxsal;
end
```

Notice the use of the into clause, which tells the server to store the result of the select statement in the maxsal return value. To modify or delete a stored procedure, you can later use the alter procedure and drop procedure commands.

Looking at this stored procedure, you might wonder what its advantage is compared to the execution of a similar query activated from the client. The difference between the two approaches is not in the result you obtain but in its speed. A stored procedure is compiled on the server in an intermediate and faster notation when it is created, and the server determines at that time the strategy it will use to access the data. By contrast, a query is compiled every time the request is sent to the server. For this reason, a stored procedure can replace a very complex query, provided it doesn't change too often!

From Delphi you can activate a stored procedure returning a result set by using either a Query or a StoredProc component. With a Query, you can use the following SQL code:

```
select *
from MaxSalOfTheDay ('01/01/1990')
```

Triggers (and Generators)

Triggers behave more or less like Delphi events and are automatically activated when a given *event* occurs. Triggers can have specific code or call stored procedures; in both cases, the execution is done completely on the server. Triggers are used to keep data consistent, checking new data in more complex ways than a check constraint allows, and to automate the side effects of some input operations (such as creating a log of previous salary changes when the current salary is modified).

Triggers can be fired by the three basic data update operations: insert, update, and delete. When you create a trigger, you indicate whether it should fire before or after one of these three actions.

As an example of a trigger, we can use a generator to create a unique index in a table. Many tables use a unique index as primary key. InterBase doesn't have an AutoInc field, unlike Paradox and other local databases. Because multiple clients cannot generate unique identifiers, we can rely on the server to do this. Almost all SQL servers offer a counter you can call to ask for a new ID, which you should later use for the table. InterBase calls these automatic counters *generators*, while Oracle calls them *sequences*. Here is the sample InterBase code:

```
create generator cust_no_gen;
...
gen_id (cust_no_gen, 1);
```

The gen_id function then extracts the new unique value of the generator passed as first parameter, with the second parameter indicating how much to increase (in this case, by one).

At this point you can add a trigger to a table, an automatic handler for one of the table's events. A trigger is similar to the event handler of the Table component, but you write it in SQL and execute it on the server, not on the client. Here is an example:

```
create trigger set_cust_no for customers
before insert position 0 as
begin
  new.cust_no = gen_id (cust_no_gen, 1);
end
```

This trigger is defined for the Customer table and is activated each time a new record is inserted. The new symbol indicates the new record we are inserting. The position option indicates the order of execution of multiple triggers connected to the same event. Triggers with the lowest values will be executed first.

Inside a trigger, you can write DML statements that also update other tables, but watch out for updates that end up reactivating the trigger, creating an endless recursion. You can later modify or disable a trigger by calling the alter trigger statement or drop trigger.

TIP   Triggers fire automatically for specified events. If you have to make many changes in the database using batch operations, the presence of a trigger might slow down the process. If the input data has already been checked for consistency, you can temporarily deactivate the trigger. These batch operations are often coded in stored procedures, but stored procedures generally cannot issue DDL statements, like those required for deactivating and reactivating the trigger. In this situation, you can define a view based on a simple `select * from table` command, thus creating an alias for the table. Then you can let the stored procedure do the batch processing on the table and apply the trigger to the view (which should also be used by the client program).

Using InterBase Express

The examples built in the last chapter either still used the BDE or were done with the new dbExpress database engine. Using this server-independent engine could allow you to switch the database server used by your application, although in practice this is often far from simple. You might decide that an application you are building will invariably use a given database server, possibly the internal server of the company you are working for. In this case, you can decide to skip any database engine or library as well and write programs that are tied directly to the API of the specific database server, which will make your program intrinsically nonportable to other SQL servers.

Of course, you won't generally use similar APIs directly, but rather base your development on some native or third-party dataset components, which wrap these APIs and naturally fit into Delphi and the architecture of its class library. An example of such a family of components is InterBase Express (IBX). Applications built using these components should work better and faster (even if only marginally), giving you more control over the specific features of the server. For example, IBX provides you a set of administrative components specifically built for InterBase 6.

NOTE   I'll examine the IBX components because they are tied to InterBase (the database server discussed in this chapter) and because that set is the only one available in the standard Delphi installation. Other similar sets of components (for InterBase, Oracle, and other database servers) are equally powerful and well-regarded in the Delphi programmers' community. A good example (and an alternative to IBX) is InterBase Objects, `www.ibobjects.com`.

IBX Dataset Components

The IBX components include custom dataset components and a few others. The dataset components inherit from the base `TDataSet` class, can use all the common Delphi data-aware controls, provide a field editor and all the usual design-time features, and can be used in the Data Module Designer, but they don't require the BDE.

You can actually choose among multiple dataset components. Three datasets of IBX have a role and a set of properties similar to their BDE counterparts:

- IBTable resembles the Table component and allows you to access a single table or view.

- IBQuery resembles the Query component and allows you to execute a SQL query, returning a result set. The IBQuery component can be used together with the IBUpdateSQL component to obtain a live (or editable) dataset.

- IBStoredProc resembles the StoredProc component and allows you to execute a stored procedure.

For new applications, you should generally use the IBDataSet component, which allows you to work with a live result set obtained by executing a `select` query. It basically merges IBQuery with IBUpdateSQL in a single component. The three components above, in fact, are provided mainly for compatibility with Delphi BDE applications.

Many other components in InterBase Express don't belong to the dataset category, but are still used in applications that need to access to a database:

- IBDatabase mimics the BDE Database component and is used to set up the database connection. The BDE also uses the specific Session component to perform some global tasks done by the IBDatabase component.

- IBTransaction allows complete control over transactions. It is important in InterBase to use transactions explicitly and isolate each transaction properly, using the Snapshot isolation level for reports and the Read Committed level for interactive forms. Each dataset explicitly refers to a given transaction, so you can have multiple concurrent transactions against the same database, choosing which datasets take part in which transaction.

- IBSQL lets you execute SQL statements that don't return a dataset (for example, DDL requests, or update and delete statements) without the overhead of a dataset component.

- IBDatabaseInfo is used for querying the database structure and status.

- IBSQLMonitor is used for debugging the system, since the SQL Monitor debugger provided by Delphi is a BDE-specific tool.

- IBEvents receives events posted by the server.

This group of components provides greater control over the database server than you can have with the BDE. For example, having a specific transaction component allows you to manage multiple concurrent transactions over one or multiple databases, as well as a single transaction spanning multiple databases. The IBDatabase component allows you to create databases, test the connection, and generally access system data, something the Database and Session BDE components don't fully provide.

TIP   A feature of the IBX datasets that is new in Delphi 6 is the ability to set up the automatic behavior of a generator as a sort of auto-incremental field. This is accomplished by setting the `GeneratorField` property using its specific property editor. An example of this is discussed later in this chapter in the section "Generators and IDs."

IBX Administrative Components

A new page of Delphi 6 Component palette, InterBase Admin, hosts InterBase 6 administrative components. Although your aim is probably not to build a full InterBase console application, including some administrative features (such as backup handling or user monitoring) can make sense in applications meant for power users.

Most of these components have self-explanatory names. They are IBConfigService, IBBackupService, IBRestoreService, IBValidationService, IBStatisticalService, IBLogService, IBSecurityService, IBServerProperties, IBInstall, and IBUninstall. I won't build any advanced examples of the use of these components, as they are more focused towards the development of server management applications than that of client programs. I'll only embed a couple of them in a simple example, later in this chapter.

From BDE to IBX

To demonstrate how simple it can be to move from the use of the BDE to the use of IBX, I've built a trivial application, using the Database Form Wizard (which is strictly bound to the BDE). The application, on the companion CD, is called IbEmp and shows only a few fields of the *usual* Employee table of the corresponding InterBase demo database.

All of the features of the IbEmp example are summarized by the properties of its Query component:

```
object Query1: TQuery
  DatabaseName = 'IBLocal'
  RequestLive = True
  SQL.Strings = (
    'SELECT * '
    'FROM EMPLOYEE')
end
```

I could have extended the structure of this example generated by Delphi, adding a Database component to handle the connection, but I decided this was useless, as my intention was only to port the example to the use of the IBX components. The interesting example, in fact, is IbEmp2, which I started by copying all of the source code files of the version generated by the wizard. (The previous example is available on the companion CD just so you can try this type of porting, as the example by itself is not particularly interesting.)

After replacing the Query component with an IBQuery, I had to add two more components: IBTransaction and IBDatabase. Any IBX application requires at least an instance of each of these two components. You cannot set database connections in a dataset (as you can do with a plain Query), and at least a transaction object is required even to read the result of a query.

Here are the key properties of these components in the IbEmp2 example:

```
object IBTransaction1: TIBTransaction
  Active = False
  DefaultDatabase = IBDatabase1
end
object IBQuery1: TIBQuery
  Database = IBDatabase1
  Transaction = IBTransaction1
  CachedUpdates = False
  SQL.Strings = (
    'SELECT * FROM EMPLOYEE')
end
object IBDatabase1: TIBDatabase
  DatabaseName = 'C:\Program Files\InterBase ' +
    'Corp\InterBase6\examples\Database\employee.gdb'
  Params.Strings = (
    'user_name=SYSDBA'
    'password=masterkey')
  LoginPrompt = False
  IdleTimer = 0
  SQLDialect = 1
  TraceFlags = []
end
```

The changes don't take too much time to perform, and if you are accessing the same database table as in the BDE-based program, you won't need to change the data-aware components at all, but only hook the DataSource component to IBQuery1. Because I'm not using the BDE, I had to type in the pathname of the InterBase database. However, not everyone in the world has the Program Files folder, which depends on the local version of Windows, and of course the InterBase sample data files could have been installed in any other location of the disk. We'll try to solve these problems in the next example.

WARNING Notice that I've embedded the password in the code, a very naïve approach to security. Not only can anyone run the program, but someone could even extract the password by looking at the hexadecimal code of the executable file. I used this approach so I wouldn't need to keep typing in my password while testing a program, but in a real application you should require your users to do so if they care about the security of their data.

Building a Live Query

The IbEmp2 example has a query that doesn't allow editing. To activate editing, you need to use an IBTable component or add to the query an IBUpdateSQL component, even if the query is very simple. Usually the BDE does the behind-the-scenes work that lets you edit the result set of a simple query, but we are not using the BDE now.

The relationship between the IBQuery and IBUpdateSQL components is the same as between the Query and UpdateSQL components. To highlight this, I've taken the main form of the UpdateSql example discussed in the last chapter and ported it to the InterBase Express components, building the UpdSql2 example. I've simply copied the two components from the original example, pasted them into an editor, changed the type of the object, and copied the resulting text into a new form. The properties are so similar that I had only to ignore a couple of missing ones (the DatabaseName and the UpdateMode properties).

At this point, I simply added an IBDatabase and an IBTransaction component, a data source and a grid, and my program was up and running. The key element of these components, in fact, is their SQL code, which is attached to the SQL property of the query and the ModifySQL, DeleteSQL, and InsertSQL properties of the update component.

However, this time I've made the reference to the database a little more flexible. Instead of typing in the database name at design time, I've extracted the InterBase folder from the Windows Registry (where Borland saves it while installing the programs). This is the code executed when the program starts:

```
uses
  Registry;

procedure TForm1.FormCreate(Sender: TObject);
var
  Reg: TRegistry;
begin
  Reg := TRegistry.Create;
  try
    Reg.RootKey := HKEY_LOCAL_MACHINE;
    Reg.OpenKey('\Software\Borland\InterBase\CurrentVersion', False);
    IBDatabase1.DatabaseName := Reg.ReadString('RootDirectory') +
```

```
        'examples\database\employee.gdb';
    finally
      Reg.CloseKey;
      Reg.Free;
    end;
    EmpDS.DataSet.Open;
  end;
```

The source code actually contains alternate code for using the database installed in the Data subfolder of the Borland Shared folder, used for Delphi sample databases. Notice also that InterBase 6 places the sample databases in a different subfolder than InterBase 5 did.

NOTE   For more information about the Windows Registry and INI files, see the related sidebar in Chapter 10, "The Architecture of Delphi Applications."

The new feature of this example, compared to the last version, is the presence of a transaction component. As I've already said, the InterBase Express components make the use of a transaction component compulsory, explicitly following a requirement of InterBase. Simply adding a couple of buttons to the form to commit or roll back the transaction would be enough, because a transaction starts automatically as you edit any dataset attached to it.

I've also improved the program a little by adding an ActionList component to it. This includes all the standard database actions and adds two custom actions for transaction support, Commit and Rollback. Both actions are enabled when the transaction is active:

```
procedure TForm1.ActionUpdateTransactions(Sender: TObject);
begin
  acCommit.Enabled := IBTransaction1.InTransaction;
  acRollback.Enabled := acCommit.Enabled;
end;
```

When executed, they perform the main operation but also need to reopen the dataset in a new transaction (which can also be done by "retaining" the transaction context). Actually, CommitRetaining doesn't reopen a new transaction, but it allows the current transaction to remain open. This way, you can keep using your datasets, which won't be refreshed (so you won't see edits already committed by other users) but will keep showing the data you've modified. This is the code:

```
procedure TForm1.acCommitExecute(Sender: TObject);
begin
  IBTransaction1.CommitRetaining;
end;

procedure TForm1.acRollbackExecute(Sender: TObject);
begin
  IBTransaction1.Rollback;
```

```
    // reopen the dataset in a new transaction
    IBTransaction1.StartTransaction;
    EmpDS.DataSet.Open;
end;
```

WARNING   Be aware that InterBase closes any opened cursors when a transaction ends, which means you have to reopen them and refetch the data even if you haven't made any changes. When committing data, instead, you can ask InterBase to retain the "transaction context"—not to close open datasets—by issuing a `CommitRetaining` command, as mentioned before. The reason for this behavior of InterBase depends on the fact that a transaction corresponds to a snapshot of the data. Once a transaction is finished, you are supposed to read the data again to refetch records that may have been modified by other users. Version 6.0 of InterBase includes also a `RollbackRetaining` command, which I've decided not to use, because in a rollback operation, the program should refresh the dataset data to show the original values on screen, not the updates you've discarded.

The last operation refers to a generic dataset and not a specific one because I'm going to add a second alternate dataset to the program. The actions are connected to a text-only toolbar, as you can see in Figure 15.5. The program opens the dataset at startup and automatically closes the current transaction on exit, after asking the user what to do, with the following `OnClose` event handler:

```
procedure TForm1.FormClose(Sender: TObject; var Action: TCloseAction);
var
  nCode: Word;
begin
  if IBTransaction1.InTransaction then
  begin
    nCode := MessageDlg ('Commit Transaction? (No to rollback)',
      mtConfirmation, mbYesNoCancel, 0);
    case nCode of
      mrYes: IBTransaction1.Commit;
      mrNo: IBTransaction1.Rollback;
      mrCancel: Action := caNone; // don't close
    end;
  end;
end;
```

An alternative to using the IBQuery and IBUpdateSQL components is to use the IBDataSet component, which combines the two. An InterBase dataset, in fact, is a live query with a complete set of SQL statements for all the main operations. The differences between using the two components and the single one are minimal. Using IBQuery and IBUpdateSQL is probably better when porting an existing application based on the two equivalent BDE components, even if porting the program directly to the IBDataSet component doesn't really require a lot of extra work.

FIGURE 15.5:

The output of the UpdSql2 example

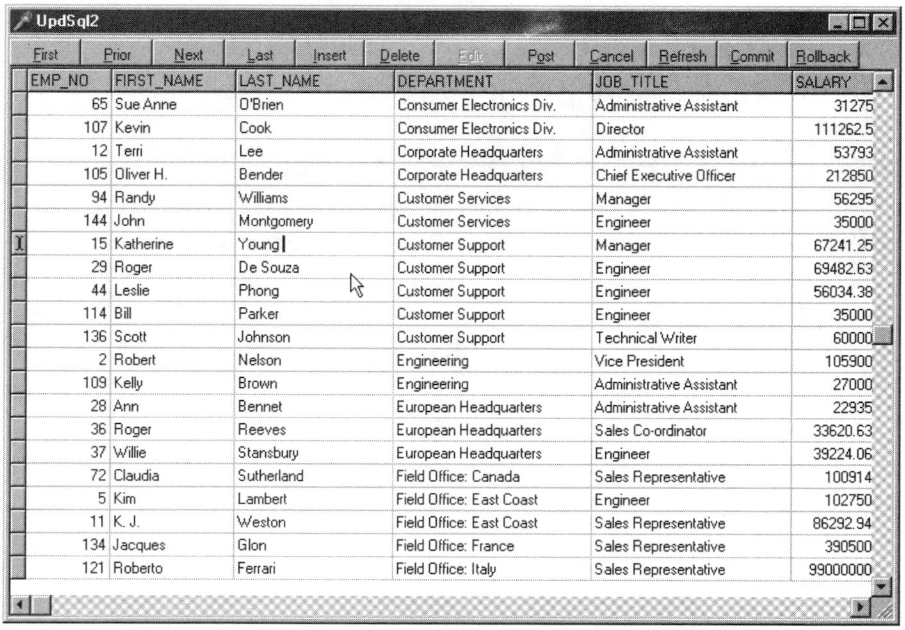

EMP_NO	FIRST_NAME	LAST_NAME	DEPARTMENT	JOB_TITLE	SALARY
65	Sue Anne	O'Brien	Consumer Electronics Div.	Administrative Assistant	31275
107	Kevin	Cook	Consumer Electronics Div.	Director	111262.5
12	Terri	Lee	Corporate Headquarters	Administrative Assistant	53793
105	Oliver H.	Bender	Corporate Headquarters	Chief Executive Officer	212850
94	Randy	Williams	Customer Services	Manager	56295
144	John	Montgomery	Customer Services	Engineer	35000
15	Katherine	Young	Customer Support	Manager	67241.25
29	Roger	De Souza	Customer Support	Engineer	69482.63
44	Leslie	Phong	Customer Support	Engineer	56034.38
114	Bill	Parker	Customer Support	Engineer	35000
136	Scott	Johnson	Customer Support	Technical Writer	60000
2	Robert	Nelson	Engineering	Vice President	105900
109	Kelly	Brown	Engineering	Administrative Assistant	27000
28	Ann	Bennet	European Headquarters	Administrative Assistant	22935
36	Roger	Reeves	European Headquarters	Sales Co-ordinator	33620.63
37	Willie	Stansbury	European Headquarters	Engineer	39224.06
72	Claudia	Sutherland	Field Office: Canada	Sales Representative	100914
5	Kim	Lambert	Field Office: East Coast	Engineer	102750
11	K. J.	Weston	Field Office: East Coast	Sales Representative	86292.94
134	Jacques	Glon	Field Office: France	Sales Representative	390500
121	Roberto	Ferrari	Field Office: Italy	Sales Representative	99000000

In the UpdSql2 example, I've provided both alternatives, so that you can test the differences yourself. Here is part of the DFM description of the dataset component:

```
object IBDataSet1: TIBDataSet
  Database = IBDatabase1
  Transaction = IBTransaction1
  CachedUpdates = False
  BufferChunks = 32
  DeleteSQL.Strings = (
    'delete from EMPLOYEE'
    'where EMP_NO = :OLD_EMP_NO')
  InsertSQL.Strings = (
    'insert into EMPLOYEE'
    '  (FIRST_NAME, LAST_NAME, SALARY, DEPT_NO, JOB_CODE, JOB_GRADE, ' +
    '  JOB_COUNTRY)'
    'values'
```

```
  '  (:FIRST_NAME, :LAST_NAME, :SALARY, :DEPT_NO, :JOB_CODE, ' +
  '  :JOB_GRADE, :JOB_COUNTRY)')
SelectSQL.Strings = (...)
UpdateRecordTypes = [cusUnmodified, cusModified, cusInserted]
ModifySQL.Strings = (...)
end
```

If you connect the IBQuery1 or the IBDataSet1 components to the data source and run the program, you'll see that the behavior is identical. Not only do the components have a similar effect; the available properties and events are also very similar.

Monitoring InterBase Express

SQL Monitor works by using a hook into the BDE architecture. For this reason, you cannot use it with applications based on the InterBase Express components. Instead, you can simply embed in your application a copy of the IBSQLMonitor component and produce a custom log.

You can even write a more generic monitoring application, as I've done in the IbxMon example. I've placed in its form a monitoring component and a RichEdit control, and written the following handler for the OnSQL event:

```
procedure TForm1.IBSQLMonitor1SQL(EventText: String);
begin
  if Assigned (RichEdit1) then
    RichEdit1.Lines.Add (TimeToStr (Now) + ': ' + EventText);
end;
```

The if Assigned test can be useful when receiving a message during shutdown, and it is required when you add this code directly inside the application you are monitoring.

To receive the messages from other applications (or from the current one), you have to turn on the tracing options of the IBDatabase component. In the UpdSql2 example (discussed earlier, in the section "Building a Live Query"), I turned them all on:

```
object IBDatabase1: TIBDatabase
  ...
  TraceFlags = [tfQPrepare, tfQExecute, tfQFetch, tfError, tfStmt,
                tfConnect, tfTransact, tfBlob, tfService, tfMisc]
```

If you run the two examples at the same time, the output of the IbxMon program will list the details about the UpdSql2 program's interaction with InterBase, as you can see in Figure 15.6.

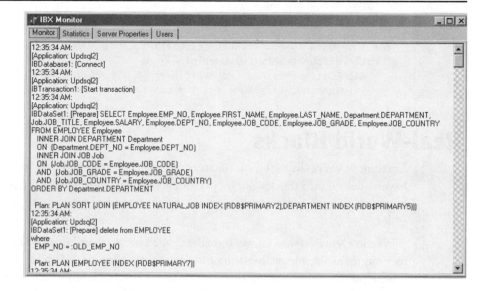

FIGURE 15.6:

The output of the IbxMon example, based on the IBMonitor component

Getting More System Data

The IbxMon example doesn't only monitor the InterBase connection, but it allows you also to query some settings to the server using the various tabs of its page control. The example embeds a few IBX administrative components, showing server statistics, a few server properties, and all connected users. You can see an example of server properties in Figure 15.7 and the code for extracting the users in the following code fragment.

FIGURE 15.7:

The assorted server information displayed by the IbxMon application

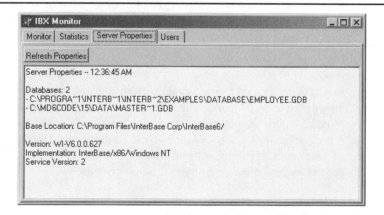

```
// grab the users data
IBSecurityService1.DisplayUsers;
// display the name of each user
for i := 0 to IBSecurityService1.UserInfoCount - 1 do
  with IBSecurityService1.UserInfo[i] do
    RichEdit4.Lines.Add (Format ('User: %s, Full Name: %s, Id: %d',
      [UserName, FirstName + ' ' + LastName, UserId]));
```

Real-World Blocks

Up to now, we've discussed specific techniques related to InterBase programming, but we haven't delved into the development of an actual application, with the problems this presents in practice. In the following subsections, I'll discuss a few practical techniques, with no specific order.

Nando Dessena (who knows InterBase much better than I do) and I have used all of these techniques in a seminar discussing the porting of an internal Paradox application to InterBase. The application discussed in that circumstance was much larger and more complex, and I've trimmed it down to only a few tables to make it fit into the space I have for this chapter.

TIP The database discussed in this section is called `mastering.gdb` and is hosted on the companion CD inside the **data** subfolder of the folder for this chapter. You can examine it using InterBase Console, possibly after making a copy to a writable drive so that you can fully interact with it.

Generators and IDs

I've mentioned in the last chapter that I'm quite a fan of an extensive use of IDs to identify the records in each table of a database.

NOTE I even tend to use a single sequence of IDs for an entire system, something often indicated as an Object ID (OID). The advantage is that I can place a series of related objects in different tables, depending on their internal structure, one of the possible approaches for implementing inheritance using relational tables. In such a circumstance, however, the IDs of the two tables must be unique. As you might not know in advance which objects could be used in place of others, adopting a global OID allows more freedom later. The drawback is that, if you have lots of data, using an integer as the ID (that is, having only 4 billion objects) might not be enough. For this reason, InterBase 6 supports 64-bit generators.

How do you generate the unique values for these IDs when multiple clients are running? Keeping a table with a *latest* value is going to create troubles, as multiple concurrent transactions (from different users) will see the same values. If you don't use tables, you can use a database-independent mechanism, including the rather large Windows GUIDs or the so-called high-low technique (the assignment of a base number to each client at startup—the high number—that is combined with a consecutive number—the low number—determined by the client).

Another approach, bound to the database, is the use of internal mechanisms for sequences, indicated with different names in each SQL server. In InterBase they are called *generators*. The characteristic of these sequences is that they operate and are incremented outside of transactions, so that they provide unique numbers even to concurrent users (remember that InterBase forces you to open a transaction even to read data).

We've already seen how to create a generator. Here is the definition for the one in my demo database, followed by the definition of the view you can use to query for a new value:

```
create generator g_master;

create view v_next_id (
  next_id
  ) as
select gen_id(g_master, 1) from rdb$database
;
```

Inside the RWBlocks application, I've added to a data module an IBQuery component (as I don't need it to be an editable dataset) with the following SQL:

```
select next_id from v_next_id;
```

The advantage, compared to using the direct statement, is that this is easier to write and maintain, even if the underlying generator changes (or in case you switch to a different approach behind the scenes). Moreover, in the same data module I've added a function, which returns a new value for the generator:

```
function TDmMain.GetNewId: Integer;
begin
  // return the next value of the generator
  QueryId.Open;
  try
    Result := QueryId.Fields[0].AsInteger;
  finally
    QueryId.Close;
  end;
end;
```

This method can be called in the AfterInsert event of any dataset, to fill in the value for the ID:

```
mydataset.FieldByName ('ID').AsInteger := data.GetNewId;
```

As I've mentioned, the IBX datasets in Delphi 6 can be tied directly to a generator, simplifying the overall picture quite a lot. Thanks to the specific property editor (shown in Figure 15.8), in fact, connecting a field of the dataset to the generator becomes trivial.

FIGURE 15.8:

The editor of the `GeneratorField` property of the IBX datasets in Delphi 6

Notice that both these approaches are much better than the one, based on a server-side trigger, discussed earlier in this chapter. In that case, in fact, the Delphi application didn't know the ID of the record sent to the database and so was unable to refresh it. Not having the record ID (which is also the only key field) on the Delphi side implies it is almost impossible to insert such a value directly inside a DBGrid. If you try, you'll see that the value you insert apparently gets lost right away, only to reappear in case of a full refresh.

Using client-side techniques instead, based on the manual code or the `GeneratorField` property, causes no trouble, as the Delphi application knows the ID, the record key, before posting it, so it can easily place it in a grid and refresh it properly.

Case-Insensitive Searches

An interesting issue with SQL servers in general, not specifically InterBase, has to do with case-insensitive searches. Suppose you don't want to show a large amount of data inside a grid (which is rather a bad idea for a client/server application). You instead choose to let the user type the initial portion of a name and then filter a query on this input, displaying only the smaller resulting record set in a grid. I've done this for a table of companies.

This search by company name is going to be executed quite frequently and will probably take place on a large table. However, if we simply search using the `starting with` or `like` operators, the search will be case sensitive, as in the following SQL statement:

```
select * from companies
where name starting with 'win';
```

To make a case-insensitive search, you can use the `upper` function on both sides of the comparison to test the uppercase values of each string, but a similar query would be very slow, as it won't be based on an index. On the other hand, saving the company names (or any other name) in uppercase letters would be rather silly, because when you have to print out those names, the result will be quite unnatural (even if very common in old information systems).

If we can trade off some disk space and memory for the extra speed, we can use a trick: add an extra field to the table, to store the uppercase value of the company name, using a server-side trigger to generate it and update it. We can then ask the database to maintain an index on the uppercase version of the name, to speed our search operation even further.

In practice, the table definition will look like this:

```
create domain d_uid as integer;
create table companies
(
  id          d_uid not null,
  name        varchar(50),
  tax_code    varchar(16),
  name_upper  varchar(50),
constraint companies_pk primary key (id)
);
```

To copy the uppercase name of each company into the related field, we cannot rely on client-side code, as an inconsistency would cause problems. In a case like this, it is better to use a trigger on the server, so that each time the company name changes, its uppercase version is updated accordingly. Another trigger will be used for the insertion of a new company:

```
create trigger companies_bi for companies
active before insert position 0
as
begin
  new.name_upper = upper(new.name);
end;

create trigger companies_bu for companies
active before update position 0
as
begin
  if (new.name <> old.name) then
    new.name_upper = upper(new.name);
end;
```

Finally, I've added an index to the table with this DDL statement:

```
create index i_companies_name_upper on companies(name_upper);
```

With this structure behind the scenes, we can now select all the companies starting with the text of an edit box (edSearch) by writing the following code in a Delphi application:

```
dm.DataCompanies.Close;
dm.DataCompanies.SelectSQL.Text :=
  'select c.id, c.name, c.tax_code,' +
```

```
  ' from companies c ' +
  ' where name_upper starting with ''' +
 UpperCase (edSearch.Text) + '''';
dm.DataCompanies.Open;
```

TIP   Using a prepared parametric query, we might be able to make this code even faster.

As an alternative, we could have created a server-side calculated field in the table definition, but this would have prevented us from having an index on the field, which speeds up our queries considerably:

```
name_upper  varchar(50) computed by (upper(name))
```

Handling Locations and People

You might notice that the table describing companies is quite bare. In fact, it has no company address, nor any contact information. The reason is simple: I want to be able to handle companies that have multiple offices (or locations) and list contact information about multiple employees of those companies.

Every location is bound to a company. Notice, though, that I've decided not to use a location identifier related to the company (such as a progressive location number for each company) but a global ID for all of the locations. This way I can refer to a location ID (let's say, for shipping goods) without having to refer also to the company ID. This is the definition of the table storing company locations:

```
create table locations
(
  id          d_uid not null,
  id_company  d_uid not null,
  address     varchar(40),
  town        varchar(30),
  zip         varchar(10),
  state       varchar(4),
  phone       varchar(15),
  fax         varchar(15),
constraint locations_pk primary key (id),
constraint locations_uc unique (id_company, id)
);

alter table locations add constraint locations_fk_companies
  foreign key (id_company) references companies (id)
  on update no action on delete no action;
```

The final definition of a foreign key relates the id_company field of the locations table with the ID field of the companies table. The other table lists names and contact information for people at specific company locations. To follow the database normalization rules, I should have added to this table only a reference to the location, as each location relates to a company. However, to make it simpler to change the location of a person within a company and to make my queries much more efficient (avoiding an extra step), I've added to the people table both a reference to the location and to the company.

The table also has another unusual feature: One of the people working for a company can be set as the key contact. This is obtained with a Boolean field (defined with a domain, as the Boolean type is not supported by InterBase) and by adding triggers to the table so that only one employee of each company can have this flag active:

```
create domain d_boolean as char(1)
  default 'F'
  check (value in ('T', 'F')) not null

create table people
(
  id            d_uid not null,
  id_company    d_uid not null,
  id_location   d_uid not null,
  name          varchar(50) not null,
  phone         varchar(15),
  fax           varchar(15),
  email         varchar(50),
  key_contact   d_boolean,
constraint people_pk primary key (id),
constraint people_uc unique (id_company, name)
);

alter table people add constraint people_fk_companies
  foreign key (id_company) references companies (id)
  on update no action on delete cascade;
alter table people add constraint people_fk_locations
  foreign key (id_company, id_location)
  references locations (id_company, id);

create trigger people_ai for people
active after insert position 0
as
begin
  /* if a person is the key contact, remove the
     flag from all others (of the same company) */
  if (new.key_contact = 'T') then
    update people
    set key_contact = 'F'
    where id_company = new.id_company
    and id <> new.id;
end;
```

```
create trigger people_au for people
active after update position 0
as
begin
  /* if a person is the key contact, remove the
     flag from all others (of the same company) */
  if (new.key_contact = 'T' and old.key_contact = 'F') then
    update people
    set key_contact = 'F'
    where id_company = new.id_company
    and id <> new.id;
end;
```

Building a User Interface

The three tables we have discussed so far have a clear master/detail relation. For this reason, the RWBlocks example uses three IBDataSet components for accessing the data, hooking up the two secondary tables to the main one. The code for the master/detail support is that of a standard database example based on queries, so I won't discuss it further (but I suggest you study the source code of the example).

Each of the datasets has a full set of SQL statements, to make the data editable. Whenever you enter a new detail element, the program hooks it to its master tables, as in the two following methods:

```
procedure TDmCompanies.DataLocationsAfterInsert(DataSet: TDataSet);
begin
  // initialize the data of the detail record
  // with a reference to the master record
  DataLocationsID_COMPANY.AsInteger := DataCompaniesID.AsInteger;
end;

procedure TDmCompanies.DataPeopleAfterInsert(DataSet: TDataSet);
begin
  // initialize the data of the detail record
  // with a reference to the master record
  DataPeopleID_COMPANY.AsInteger := DataCompaniesID.AsInteger;
  // the suggested location is the active one, if available
  if not DataLocations.IsEmpty then
    DataPeopleID_LOCATION.AsInteger := DataLocationsID.AsInteger;
  // the first person added becomes the key contact
  // (checks whether the filtered dataset of people is empty)
  DataPeopleKEY_CONTACT.AsBoolean := DataPeople.IsEmpty;
end;
```

As this code suggests, a data module hosts the dataset components. Actually, the program has a data module for every form (hooked up dynamically, as you can create multiple instances of each form). Each of these data modules has a separate transaction, so that the various operations done in different pages are totally independent. The database connection, instead, is centralized. A main data module hosts the corresponding component, which is referenced by all the datasets. Each of the data modules is created dynamically by the form referring to it, and its value is stored in the dm private field of the form:

```
procedure TFormCompanies.FormCreate(Sender: TObject);
begin
  dm := TDmCompanies.Create (Self);
  dsCompanies.Dataset := dm.DataCompanies;
  dsLocations.Dataset := dm.DataLocations;
  dsPeople.Dataset := dm.DataPeople;
end;
```

This way we can easily create multiple instances of a form, with an instance of the data module connected to each of them. The form connected to the data module has three DBGrid controls, each tied to a data module and one of the corresponding datasets. You can see this form at run time, with some actual data, in Figure 15.9.

FIGURE 15.9:

A form showing companies, office locations, and people (part of the RWBlocks example)

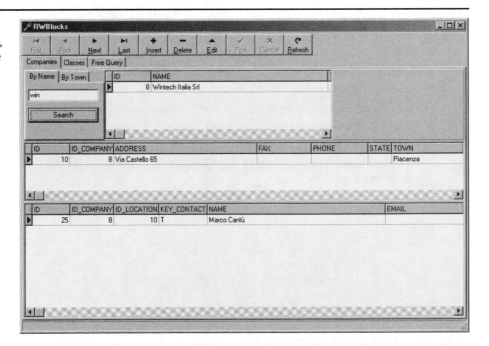

The form is actually hosted by a main form, which in turn is based on a page control, with the other forms embedded. Only the form connected with the first page is created when the program starts. The ShowForm method I've written takes care of parenting the form to the tab sheet of the page control, after removing the form border:

```
procedure TFormMain.FormCreate(Sender: TObject);
begin
  ShortDateFormat := 'dd/mm/yyyy';
  ShowForm (TFormCompanies.Create (self), TabCompanies);
end;

procedure TFormMain.ShowForm (Form: TForm; Tab: TTabSheet);
begin
  Form.BorderStyle := bsNone;
  Form.Align := alClient;
  Form.Parent := Tab;
  Form.Show;
end;
```

The other two pages, instead, are populated at runtime:

```
procedure TFormMain.PageControl1Change(Sender: TObject);
begin
  if PageControl1.ActivePage.ControlCount = 0 then
    if PageControl1.ActivePage = TabFreeQ then
      ShowForm (TFormFreeQuery.Create (self), TabFreeQ)
    else if PageControl1.ActivePage = TabClasses then
      ShowForm (TFormClasses.Create (self), TabClasses);
end;
```

The companies form hosts the search by company name we've already discussed in the last section, plus a search by location. You enter the name of a town and get back a list of companies having an office in that town:

```
procedure TFormCompanies.btnTownClick(Sender: TObject);
begin
  with dm.DataCompanies do
  begin
    Close;
    SelectSQL.Text :=
      'select c.id, c.name, c.tax_code' +
      ' from companies c ' +
      ' where exists (select loc.id from locations loc ' +
      ' where loc.id_company = c.id and upper(loc.town) = ''' +
      UpperCase(edTown.Text) + ''' )';
    Open;
    dm.DataLocations.Open;
    dm.DataPeople.Open;
  end;
end;
```

If you look at the source code of the form, you'll find a lot more code. Some of it is related to closing permission (as a user cannot close the form while there are pending edits not posted to the database), while a good amount relates to the use of the form as a lookup dialog, as described later.

Booking Classes

Another portion of the program and of the database involves booking training classes and courses. (Needless to say, although I built this program as a showcase, it also helps me run my own business.) In the database is a classes table listing all the training courses, each with a title and the planned date. Another table hosts registration by company, including the classes registered for, the ID of the company, and some notes. Finally, a third table has a list of people who've signed up, each hooked to a registration for his or her company, with the amount paid.

The rationale behind this company-based registration is that invoices are sent out to companies, which book the classes for their programmers and can receive specific discounts. This is a case in which the database is a little more normalized, as the people registration doesn't refer directly to a class, but only to the company registration for that class. Here is the definition of the tables involved (I've omitted foreign key constraints and other elements):

```
create table classes
(
  id           d_uid not null,
  description  varchar(50),
  starts_on    timestamp not null,
constraint classes_pk primary key (id)
);
create table classes_reg
(
  id           d_uid not null,
  id_company   d_uid not null,
  id_class     d_uid not null,
  notes        varchar(255),
constraint classes_reg_pk primary key (id),
constraint classes_reg_uc unique (id_company, id_class)
);
create domain d_amount as numeric(15, 2);
create table people_reg
(
  id               d_uid not null,
  id_classes_reg   d_uid not null,
  id_person        d_uid not null,
  amount           d_amount,
constraint people_reg_pk primary key (id)
);
```

The data module for this group of tables uses a master/detail/detail relationship, and has code to set the connection with the active master record when a new detail record is created. Each dataset has a generator field for its ID, and each has the proper update and insert SQL statements. These statements have been generated by the corresponding component editor using only the ID field to identify existing records and updating only the fields of the original table. In fact, each of the two secondary datasets retrieves data from a lookup table, either the list of companies or the list of people. Finally, I had to edit manually the RefreshSQL statements to repeat the proper inner join. Here is an example:

```
object IBClassReg: TIBDataSet
  Database = DmMain.IBDatabase1
  Transaction = IBTransaction1
  AfterInsert = IBClassRegAfterInsert
  DeleteSQL.Strings = (
    'delete from classes_reg'
    'where id = :old_id')
  InsertSQL.Strings = (
    'insert into classes_reg (id, id_class, id_company, notes)'
    'values (:id, :id_class, :id_company, :notes)')
  RefreshSQL.Strings = (
    'select reg.id, reg.id_class, reg.id_company, reg.notes, c.name '
    'from classes_reg reg'
    'join companies c on reg.id_company = c.id'
    'where id = :id')
  SelectSQL.Strings = (
    'select reg.id, reg.id_class, reg.id_company, reg.notes, c.name '
    'from classes_reg reg'
    'join companies c on reg.id_company = c.id'
    'where id_class = :id')
  ModifySQL.Strings = (
    'update classes_reg'
    'set'
    '  id = :id,'
    '  id_class = :id_class,'
    '  id_company = :id_company,'
    '  notes = :notes'
    'where id = :old_id')
  GeneratorField.Field = 'id'
  GeneratorField.Generator = 'g_master'
  DataSource = dsClasses
end
```

To complete the discussion of IBClassReg, here is its only event handler:

```
procedure TDmClasses.IBClassRegAfterInsert(DataSet: TDataSet);
begin
  IBClassReg.FieldByName ('id_class').AsString :=
    IBClasses.FieldByName ('id').AsString;
end;
```

The IBPeopleReg dataset has similar settings, but the IBClasses dataset is simpler, at design time. At run time, the SQL code of this dataset is dynamically modified, using three alternatives to display scheduled classes (whenever the date is after today's date), classes already started or finished in the current year, and classes of past years. A user selects one of the three groups of records for the table with a tab control, which hosts the DBGrid for the main table (see Figure 15.10).

FIGURE 15.10:

The form for class registrations of the RWBlocks example

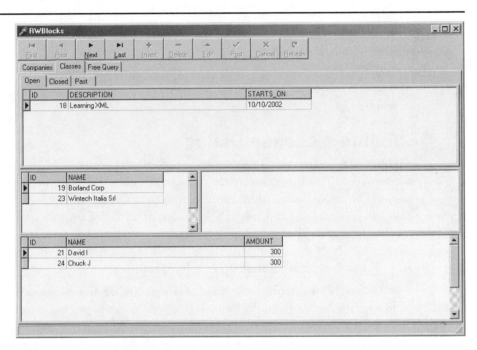

The three alternative SQL statements are created when the program starts, or actually when the class registrations form is created and displayed. The program stores the final portion of the three alternative instructions (the where clause) in a string list, and selects one of the strings when the tab changes:

```
procedure TFormClasses.FormCreate(Sender: TObject);
begin
  dm := TDmClasses.Create (Self);
  // connect the datasets to the data sources
  dsClasses.Dataset := dm.IBClasses;
  dsClassReg.DataSet := dm.IBClassReg;
  dsPeopleReg.DataSet := dm.IBPeopleReg;
  // open the datasets
  dm.IBClasses.Active := True;
  dm.IBClassReg.Active := True;
  dm.IBPeopleReg.Active := True;
```

```
  // prepare the SQL for the three tabs
  SqlCommands := TStringList.Create;
  SqlCommands.Add (' where Starts_On > ''now''');
  SqlCommands.Add (' where Starts_On <= ''now'' and ' +
    ' extract (year from Starts_On ) >= extract(year from current_timestamp)');
  SqlCommands.Add (' where extract (year from Starts_On) < ' +
    ' extract(year from current_timestamp)');
end;
procedure TFormClasses.TabChange(Sender: TObject);
begin
  dm.IBClasses.Active := False;
  dm.IBClasses.SelectSQL [1] := SqlCommands [Tab.TabIndex];
  dm.IBClasses.Active := True;
end;
```

Building a Lookup Dialog

The two detail datasets of this class registration form display some lookup fields. Instead of showing the ID of the company that booked the class, for example, it shows the company name. This is obtained with an inner join in the SQL statement and by configuring the DBGrid columns not to display the company ID. In a local application, or one with a limited amount of data, we could have used a lookup field. However, copying the entire lookup dataset locally or opening it for browsing should be limited to tables with about a hundred records at most, embedding some search capabilities.

If you have a large table, like a table of companies, an alternative solution can be to use a secondary dialog box to do the lookup selection. For example, we can choose a company using the form we've already built and taking advantage of its search capabilities. To display this form as a dialog box, the program creates a new instance of it, shows some hidden buttons already there at design time, and lets the user select a company to refer to from the other table.

To simplify the use of this lookup, which can happen multiple times in a large program, I've added to the companies form a class function, having as output parameters the name and ID of the selected company. An initial ID can be passed to the function to determine its initial selection. Here is the complete code of this class function, which creates an object of its class, selects the initial record if requested, shows the dialog box, and finally extracts the return values:

```
class function TFormCompanies.SelectCompany (
  var CompanyName: string; var CompanyId: Integer): Boolean;
var
  FormComp: TFormCompanies;
begin
```

```
    Result := False;
    FormComp := TFormCompanies.Create (Application);
    FormComp.Caption := 'Select Company';
    try
      // activate dialog buttons
      FormComp.btnCancel.Visible := True;
      FormComp.btnOK.Visible := True;
      // select company
      if CompanyId > 0 then
        FormComp.dm.DataCompanies.SelectSQL.Text :=
          'select c.id, c.name, c.tax_code' +
          ' from companies c ' +
          ' where c.id = ' + IntToStr (CompanyId)
      else
        FormComp.dm.DataCompanies.SelectSQL.Text :=
          'select c.id, c.name, c.tax_code' +
          ' from companies c ' +
          ' where name_upper starting with ''a''';
      FormComp.dm.DataCompanies.Open;
      FormComp.dm.DataLocations.Open;
      FormComp.dm.DataPeople.Open;

      if FormComp.ShowModal = mrOK then
      begin
        Result := True;
        CompanyId := FormComp.dm.DataCompanies.FieldByName ('id').AsInteger;
        CompanyName := FormComp.dm.DataCompanies.FieldByName ('name').AsString;
      end;
    finally
      FormComp.Free;
    end;
  end;
```

Another slightly more complex class function (available within the example's source code, but not listed here) allows the selection of a person of a given company to register people for classes. In this case, the form is displayed after disallowing searching another company or changing it.

In both cases, the lookup is triggered by adding an ellipsis button to the column of the DBGrid—for example, the grid column listing the names of companies registered for classes. When this button is pressed, the program calls the class function to display the dialog box and uses its result for updating the hidden ID field and the visible name field:

```
procedure TFormClasses.DBGridClassRegEditButtonClick(Sender: TObject);
var
  CompanyName: string;
```

```
    CompanyId: Integer;
begin
  CompanyId := dm.IBClassReg.FieldByName ('id_Company').AsInteger;
  if TFormCompanies.SelectCompany (CompanyName, CompanyId) then
  begin
    dm.IBClassReg.Edit;
    dm.IBClassReg.FieldByName ('Name').AsString := CompanyName;
    dm.IBClassReg.FieldByName ('id_Company').AsInteger := CompanyId;
  end;
end;
```

Adding a Free Query Form

The final feature of the program is a form where a user can directly type in a SQL statement and run it. As a helper, the form lists in a combo box the available tables of the database, obtained when the form is created by calling:

```
DmMain.IBDatabase1.GetTableNames (ComboTables.Items);
```

Selecting an item of the combo box generates a simple SQL query:

```
MemoSql.Lines.Text := 'select * from ' + ComboTables.Text;
```

The user, if an expert, can then edit the SQL, possibly introducing restrictive clauses, and then run the query:

```
procedure TFormFreeQuery.ButtonRunClick(Sender: TObject);
begin
  QueryFree.Close;
  QueryFree.SQL := MemoSql.Lines;
  QueryFree.Open;
end;
```

You can see this third form of the RWBlocks program in Figure 15.11. Of course, I'm not suggesting that you add SQL editing to programs intended for all of your users. This feature is intended for power users, maybe programmers. I basically wrote it for myself!

FIGURE 15.11:

The free query form of the RWBlocks example is intended for power users.

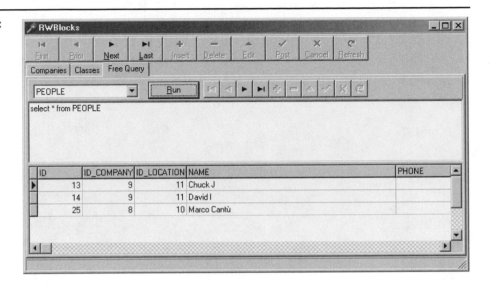

What's Next?

After looking at other, more general, database access technologies Delphi provides (such as the BDE and dbExpress), in this chapter I've introduced the InterBase database and the IBX family of components. The last part of the chapter presented a complete real-world application, discussing a series of general-purpose techniques you can probably apply even to completely different InterBase applications.

Now we are ready to focus on another data access alternative, Microsoft's own ADO technology, which Delphi fully supports with a specific set of dataset components since version 5. In subsequent chapters, we'll continue to explore database development, with multitier architectures and the development of database-oriented Delphi components.

CHAPTER 16

ActiveX Data Objects

- Microsoft Data Access Components (MDAC)

- dbGo

- Data link files

- Getting schema information

- Using the Jet engine

- Transaction processing

- Disconnected and persistent recordsets

- The briefcase model and deploying MDAC

I wish to acknowledge and thank Guy Smith-Ferrier for writing this chapter. Guy is a programmer, author, and speaker. He is the author of several commercial software products and countless internal systems for independent and blue-chip companies alike. He has written many articles for *The Delphi Magazine* and for others on topics beyond Delphi, and he has spoken at numerous conferences in North America and Europe. Guy lives in England with his wife, his son, and his cat.

Since the mid-1980s, database programmers have been on a quest for the "holy grail" of *database independence*. The idea is to use a single API that applications can use to interact with many different sources of data. The use of such an API would release developers from a dependence upon a single database engine and allow them to adapt to the world's changing demands. Vendors have produced many solutions to this goal, the two most notable early solutions being Microsoft's Open Database Connectivity (ODBC) and Borland's Independent Database Application Programming Interface (IDAPI), more commonly known as the Borland Database Engine (BDE).

Microsoft started to replace ODBC with OLE DB in the mid-1990s with the success of COM. However, OLE DB is what Microsoft would class a *system-level* interface and is intended to be used by system-level programmers. It is very large and complex and unforgiving. It makes greater demands on the programmer and requires a higher level of knowledge in return for lower productivity. ActiveX Data Objects (ADO) is a layer on top of OLE DB and is referred to as an *application-level* interface. It is considerably simpler than OLE DB and more forgiving. In short, it is designed for use by application programmers.

ADO has great similarities with the BDE. They are, after all, designed to solve very similar problems. Both support navigation of datasets, manipulation of datasets, transaction processing, and cached updates (called *batch updates* in ADO), so the concepts and issues involved in using ADO are similar to those of the BDE. However, there are also differences. ADO is a more recent technology. This gives it an advantage over the BDE because it is better suited to today's needs and doesn't need to carry so much deadwood around with it. Perhaps more importantly, ADO has a wider interpretation of "data." The BDE is used for accessing "rectangular" data—that is, data in rows and columns. This is ideal for accessing data from databases. ADO can be used for accessing this data but can also be used for accessing non-rectangular data, including directory structures, documents, Web sites, and e-mail.

In this chapter we will look at ADO and *dbGo*. (This set of Delphi components was called ADOExpress but has been renamed dbGo in Delphi 6, because Microsoft has objected to the use of the term *ADO* in product names.) It is possible to use ADO in Delphi without using dbGo. By importing the ADO type library, you can gain direct access to the ADO interfaces; this is, indeed, how Delphi programmers used ADO before the release of Delphi 5. However, this path bypasses Delphi's database infrastructure and ensures that you are unable to make use of other Delphi technologies such as DataSnap. Alternatively, you can turn to Delphi's active third-party market for other ADO component suites such as Adonis, AdoSolutio, Diamond ADO, and Kamiak.

This chapter uses dbGo for all of its examples, not only because it is readily available and supported but also because it is a very viable solution. Regardless of your final choice, you will find the information here useful.

Microsoft Data Access Components (MDAC)

ADO is part of a bigger picture called Microsoft Data Access Components (MDAC). MDAC is an umbrella for Microsoft's database technologies and includes ADO, OLE DB, ODBC, and RDS (Remote Data Services). Often you will hear people use the terms MDAC and ADO interchangeably (but incorrectly) because their version numbers and releases are now aligned. As ADO is only distributed as part of MDAC, we talk in terms of MDAC releases. The major releases of MDAC have been versions 1.5, 2.0, 2.1, 2.5, and 2.6. Microsoft releases MDAC independently and makes it available for free download and virtually free distribution (there are distribution requirements, but almost all Delphi developers will not have trouble meeting these requirements). MDAC is also distributed with most Microsoft products that have some kind of database content. This includes Windows 98, Windows 2000, Windows Millennium Edition, Microsoft Office, Internet Explorer, and SQL Server. In addition, Delphi 6 Enterprise ships with MDAC 2.5, and Delphi 5 Enterprise ships with MDAC 2.1.

There are two consequences of this level of availability. First, it is highly likely that your users will already have MDAC installed on their machines. Second, whatever version your users have, or you upgrade them to, it is also virtually certain that someone, either you, your users, or other application software, will upgrade their existing MDAC to whatever the current release of MDAC is. There is no way you will be able to prevent this, as MDAC is installed with such commonly used software as Internet Explorer. Add to this the fact that Microsoft supports only the current release of MDAC and the release before it, and you are forced to arrive at a conclusion:

> Your applications must be designed to work with the current release of MDAC or the release before it.

If you chart the releases of MDAC, you can expect to see a new version of MDAC every 10 months on average (Delphi itself has a new release every 14 months on average).

As an ADO developer, you should regularly check the MDAC pages on Microsoft's site at www.microsoft.com/data. From there you can download the latest version of MDAC for free. At the time of writing, this is MDAC 2.6, which you can download from www.microsoft.com/data/download_260rtm.htm (5.2 MB), but you should check for a more recent version first.

While you are on this Web site, you should take the opportunity to download the MDAC SDK (13 MB) if you do not already have it or the Platform SDK (the MDAC SDK is part of the Platform SDK). The MDAC SDK is your bible. Download it and consult it regularly and use it to answer your ADO questions. You should treat this as your first port of call when you need MDAC information. Beyond this, you should read the README files that come with MDAC. Look in `\Program Files\Common Files\System\ADO` for all of the files ending `README.TXT`.

Finally, in getting ready for using ADO in your Delphi applications, you should check for dbGo/ADOExpress updates on Borland's excellent community site (`http://community .borland.com`). Informal patches are released here that are often a must-have. For example, there is a show-stopping problem when using MDAC 2.6 and Delphi 5's ADOExpress, which requires a patch.

OLE DB Providers

OLE DB providers enable access to a source of data. They are ADO's equivalent to the BDE's drivers. However, although the BDE's Driver SDK has been available for many years, there are no third-party BDE drivers. This is not the case for OLE DB providers. MDAC includes many providers that I'll discuss, but many more are available from Microsoft and, more prolifically, the third-party market. It is no longer possible to reliably list all available OLE DB providers, because the list is so large and ever-changing, but here are some of the main vendors of these drivers:

Company	Web Site	OLE DB Provider
B2 Systems	www.b2systems.com	SQL Server, Oracle, Sybase, Informix, RDB, DB2, flat files
ISG	www.isgsoft.com	ISG Navigator (ISAM, DB2, IMS, Informix, Jasmine, Open Ingres, Oracle, SQL Server, Sybase, Adabas, RDB, RMS, VSAM)
Merant	www.merant.com	DB2, Informix, Lotus Notes, SQL Server, Ingres, Oracle, Sybase

You should add to this list almost all database vendors, as the majority now supply their own OLE DB providers. For example, Oracle supplies the ORAOLEDB provider. Notable omissions include InterBase; at the time of writing, Borland doesn't plan to write an OLE DB provider for InterBase. Your only solutions are to access InterBase either using the ODBC Driver, or through Jason Wharton's InterBase provider (`www.ibobjects.com`, although this is still in development) or Dmitry Kovalenko's IBProvider (www.lcpi.lipetsk.ru/prog/eng/index.html).

TIP Jason Wharton's OLE DB Provider is additionally interesting because it is written using Binh Ly's OLE DB Provider Development Toolkit (www.techvanguards.com/products/optk/install.htm). If you want to write your own OLE DB provider, this is an easier way than most.

MDAC OLE DB Providers

When you install MDAC, you automatically install the OLE DB providers shown in Table 16.1:

TABLE 16.1: OLE DB Providers Included with MDAC

Driver	Provider	Description
MSDASQL	ODBC Drivers	ODBC drivers (default)
Microsoft.Jet.OLEDB.3.5	Jet 3.5	MS Access 97 databases only
Microsoft.Jet.OLEDB.4.0	Jet 4.0	MS Access databases et al.
SQLOLEDB	SQL Server	MS SQL Server databases
MSDAORA	Oracle	Oracle databases
MSOLAP	OLAP Services	Online Analytical Processing
SampProv	Sample provider	Example of an OLE DB provider for CSV files
MSDAOSP	Simple provider	For creating your own providers for simple text data

If you do not specify which OLE DB provider you are using, OLE DB defaults to the ODBC OLE DB Provider, which is used for backward compatibility with ODBC. As you learn more about ADO, you will discover the limitations of this provider. It's probable that you will eventually tire of these limitations, and I recommend that you look from the beginning for an OLE DB provider that is specific to your database rather than struggle with the ODBC OLE DB Provider.

The Jet OLE DB Providers support MS Access and other "desktop" databases. We will return to these providers later.

The SQL Server Provider supports SQL Server 7, SQL Server 2000, and Microsoft Database Engine (MSDE). MSDE is worth taking a moment's thought over. MSDE is SQL Server with most of the tools removed and some code added to deliberately degrade performance when there are more than 5 active connections. MSDE is important for two reasons. First, it is free. You can download it from Microsoft's Web site and, with very few restrictions, distribute it with your application. Second, MSDE is SQL Server. Of course you don't get the

SQL Server tools, and it does deliberately degrade performance, but it is SQL Server. This means that it is perfect for use with low numbers of users. When the number of users increases and performance starts to suffer, your upgrade path to SQL Server is just a question of paying for SQL Server. Compatibility is virtually assured. You use the same OLE DB provider, and you use it in exactly the same way with exactly the same names and parameters. This is because MSDE is SQL Server. Because of these reasons and because Microsoft is moving their emphasis away from Access, MSDE is worth considering for future developments.

The OLE DB Provider For OLAP can be used directly but is more often used by ADO Multi-Dimensional (ADOMD). ADOMD is an additional ADO technology designed to provide Online Analytical Processing (OLAP). If you have used Delphi's Decision Cube, or Excel's Pivot Tables, or Access's Cross Tabs, then you have used some form of OLAP.

In addition to these MDAC OLE DB providers, Microsoft supplies other OLE DB providers with other products or with downloadable SDKs. The Active Directory Services OLE DB Provider is included with the ADSI SDK; the AS/400 And VSAM OLE DB Provider is included with SNA Server; and the Exchange OLE DB Provider is included with Microsoft Exchange 2000.

The OLE DB Provider For Indexing Service provides access to (and is part of) Microsoft Indexing Service, a Windows NT and 2000 mechanism that speeds up file searches by building catalogs of file information. Indexing Service is integrated into IIS and, consequently, is often used for indexing Web sites. Microsoft Indexing Service is also available for Windows NT 4 as part of the NT 4 Option Pack.

The OLE DB Provider For Internet Publishing is included with Internet Explorer 5, Windows 2000, and Office 2000 and allows developers to manipulate directories and files using HTTP. This is useful for maintaining Web sites that support either FrontPage Web Extender (WEC) or Web Distributed Authoring and Versioning (WebDAV).

Still more OLE DB providers come in the form of *service providers*. As their name implies, OLE DB service providers provide a service to other OLE DB providers. Often these service providers will go unnoticed because they are invoked automatically as needed without programmer intervention. The Cursor Service, for example, is invoked when you create a client-side cursor, and the Persisted Recordset provider is invoked to save data locally.

dbGo

The set of components that make up dbGo (Table 16.2) should be easily recognizable by programmers familiar with the BDE, dbExpress, or IBExpress.

TABLE 16.2: dbGo Components

dbGo Component	Description	BDE Equivalent Component
TADOConnection	Connection to a database	TDatabase
TADOCommand	Executes an action SQL command	No equivalent
TADODataSet	All-purpose TDataSet	No equivalent
TADOTable	Encapsulation of a table	TTable
TADOQuery	Encapsulation of SQL SELECT	TQuery
TADOStoredProc	Encapsulation of a stored procedure	TStoredProc
TRDSConnection	Remote Data Services connection	No equivalent

The four dataset components (TADODataSet, TADOTable, TADOQuery, TADOStored-Proc) are implemented almost entirely by their immediate ancestor TCustomADODataSet. This component provides the majority of dataset functionality, and its descendants are mostly thin wrappers that expose different features of the same component. As such, the components have a lot in common. In general, however, TADOTable, TADOQuery, and TADOStoredProc are viewed as "compatibility" components and are used to aid the transition of knowledge and code from their BDE counterparts. Be warned, though: These compatibility components are similar to their counterparts but not exactly the same. You will find differences in any application except the most trivial. TADODataSet is the component of choice partly because of its versatility but also because it is closer in appearance to the ADO Recordset interface upon which it is based. Throughout this chapter, we will use all of the TDataSet components to give you the experience of using each.

Enough theory. Let's see some action. Drop a TADOTable onto a form. Look in the Object Inspector and you will not see any DatabaseName or AliasName properties. ADO doesn't use aliases, so there are no alias-related properties. Instead ADO runs on *connection strings*. Connection strings are the lifeblood of ADO, and you should take time out to master this subject. You can type in a connection string by hand if you know what you are doing, but only programmers who think that VI is a great editor of our time enjoy doing this. For the rest of us, there is the connection string editor. In the Object Inspector, click the ellipses in the ConnectionString property. This invokes Delphi's connection string editor (Figure 16.1).

FIGURE 16.1:

Delphi's connection string
editor

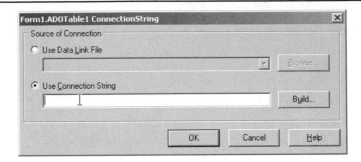

This editor adds little value to the process of entering a connection string, so you can click Build to go straight to Microsoft's connection string editor (Figure 16.2).

FIGURE 16.2:

Microsoft's connection
string editor

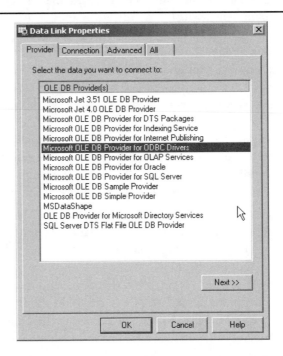

This is a tool you will come to know and love—or maybe just to know. The first tab shows the OLE DB providers and service providers installed on your computer. The list will vary according to the version of MDAC and other software installed on your computer. You can see that the OLE DB Provider for ODBC Drivers is selected by default. In our first example, we will open the infamous MS Access Northwind database using the Jet 4.0 OLE DB Provider. Northwind is the Microsoft equivalent of DBDEMOS; it is the test data used in many examples on ADO because it is so widely available. The exact location of Northwind and its name are not fixed, but you should search your hard disk for Northwind.mdb or NWind.mdb. Microsoft SQL Server comes with a very similar version of the same database, also called Northwind.

Double-click the Jet 4.0 OLE DB Provider and you will be presented with the Connection tab. This page varies according to the provider you select, but for Jet it simply asks you for the name of the database and your login details. If you have Microsoft Office installed on your computer, then the database name will probably be

```
c:\program files\microsoft office\office\samples\northwind.mdb
```

Click the Test Connection button to test the validity of your selections.

The Advanced tab handles access control to the database, and this is where you would specify exclusive or read-only access to the database.

The All tab lists all the parameters in the connection string. The list is specific to the OLE DB provider you selected on the first page. You should make a mental note of this page, because it contains many parameters that are the answers to many problems. Click OK to close the Microsoft connection string editor, click OK again to close the Borland connection string editor, and the value will be returned to the ConnectionString property, which will now be set to

```
Provider=Microsoft.Jet.OLEDB.4.0;Data Source=c:\program files\microsoft office\
    office\samples\northwind.mdb;Persist Security Info=False
```

So connection strings are just a string with many parameters delimited by semicolons. If you want to add, edit, or delete any of these parameter values programmatically, you must write your own routines to find the parameter in the list and amend it appropriately.

Now that we have set the connection string, we can select a table. Drop down the list of tables using the TableName property in the Object Inspector. Select the Customers table and set Active to True. Add a TDataSource and a TDBGrid and connect them all together, and you are now using ADO.

Incidentally, if you are going to use dbGo on a permanent basis, you might benefit from a simple tip. If you followed along with the last example, you will have noticed that you had to flip back and forth between the Data Access page and the ADO page to drop a TDataSource component onto the form. If you use dbGo exclusively, then the TDataSource component is the only component you will ever need on the Data Access page. Delphi's IDE prevents you from adding the same component to multiple pages, but you can move components. To move the TDataSource component from the Data Access page to the ADO page, right-click the palette, select Properties, and drag TDataSource onto the ADO page. If, however, you use both ADO and another database technology such as the BDE, then you can simulate installing

TDataSource on multiple pages by creating a Component Template for a TDataSource and installing it on the ADO page. This is a more elegant solution than creating a TADODataSource descendant, because the component that is dropped onto the form is still a genuine TDataSource and not some other component.

TADOConnection

When a TADOTable component is used in this way, it creates its own connection component behind the scenes in the same way that the BDE components create their temporary TDatabase component. You do not have to accept the default connection it creates, and you should not accept it. Instead, you should create your own connection in the form of a TADOConnection component.

The TADOConnection component is used for many of the same purposes as the BDE's TDatabase component. It allows you to customize the login procedure, control transactions, execute action commands directly, and reduce the number of connections in an application. Using a TADOConnection is easy. Place one on a form and set its `ConnectionString` property in the same way as for the TADOTable. Alternatively, you can double-click a TADO-Connection to invoke the connection string editor directly. With the `ConnectionString` set to `Northwind.mdb`, you can disable the login dialog box by setting `LoginPrompt` to False. To make use of the new connection, set `ADOTable1`'s `Connection` property to `ADOConnection1`. You will see `ADOTable1`'s `ConnectionString` property reset because `Connection` and `ConnectionString` are mutually exclusive. One of the benefits of using a TADOConnection is that the connection string is centralized instead of scattered throughout many components. Another, more important, benefit is that all of the components that share the TADOConnection share a single connection. Without your own TADOConnection, each ADO dataset uses its own connection.

Data Link Files

So a TADOConnection allows us to centralize the definition of a connection string within a form or data module. However, even though this is a worthwhile step forward from scattering the same connection string throughout all ADO datasets, it still suffers from a fundamental flaw: If you use a database engine that defines the database in terms of a filename, then the path to the database file(s) is hard-coded in the EXE. This makes for a very fragile application. The BDE uses aliases to overcome this problem; ADO uses Data Link files. A Data Link file is a connection string in an INI file. The following is an example of a Data Link file:

```
[oledb]
; Everything after this line is an OLE DB initstring
Provider=Microsoft.Jet.OLEDB.4.0;Data Source=c:\program files\microsoft office\
    office\samples\northwind.mdb;Persist Security Info=False
```

Although you can give a Data Link file any extension, the recommended extension is .UDL. You can create a Data Link using any text editor, or you can right-click Windows Explorer, select New, then Text Document, rename the file with a UDL extension, and then double-click the file to invoke the Microsoft connection string editor.

To use the Data Link file, set the TADOConnection's ConnectionString to:

```
File Name=TEST.UDL
```

assuming that the file is called TEST.UDL and it is in the same directory as the EXE. You can place your Data Link files anywhere on the hard disk, but if you are looking for a common, shared location, then you can use the DataLinkDir function in ADODB.PAS:

```
ShowMessage('The Data Link directory is ' + DataLinkDir);
```

If you haven't altered MDAC's defaults, DataLinkDir will return

```
C:\Program Files\Common Files\System\OLE DB\Data Links
```

Delphi 5's ADOExpress suffers from a flaw when using data link files, which is fixed in Delphi 6's dbGo. In 5, set the Connected property of the TADOConnection to True and watch the ConnectionString property. The ConnectionString becomes the actual connection string that is in use (i.e., the one from the data link file). The problem is that when the property is streamed to the form when the application is saved, it is the active connection string that is saved. The reference to the data link file is permanently forgotten. If you change the data link file, you will not see any change to your application.

If you want to use data link files and you don't want to suffer from this problem, use the following TADOConnectionX component instead of TADOConnection:

```
TADOConnectionX = class(TADOConnection)
private
  FUDLFile: string;
protected
  procedure DoConnect; override;
published
  property UDLFile: string read FUDLFile write FUDLFile;
end;
```

The component has a UDLFile property where the UDL filename is permanently stored (you must manually set this property yourself). The class has a single method, DoConnect, which ensures that the UDL file is always read each time the connection is opened:

```
procedure TADOConnectionX.DoConnect;
begin
  if FUDLFile <> '' then
    ConnectionString:= 'File Name=' + FUDLFile;
  inherited;
end;
```

Dynamic Properties

Imagine that you are responsible for designing a new database middleware architecture. You have to reconcile two opposing goals of a single API for all databases and access to database-specific features. You could take the approach of designing an interface that is the sum of all of the features of every database ever created. Each class would have every property and method imaginable, but it would only use the properties and methods it had support for. It doesn't take much discussion to realize that this isn't a good solution. ADO has to solve these apparently mutually exclusive goals, and it does so using *dynamic properties*. Almost all ADO interfaces, and their corresponding dbGo components, have a property called Properties that is a collection of database-specific properties. These properties can be accessed by their ordinal position, like this:

```
ShowMessage(ADOTable1.Properties[1].Value);
```

But they are more usually accessed by name like this:

```
ShowMessage(ADOConnection1.Properties['DBMS Name'].Value);
```

It would be tedious to list all of the different dynamic properties for all of the different classes for all of the different OLE DB providers for all of the situations in which they are used, but to give you an idea of their importance, a typical ADO Connection or Recordset has approximately 100 dynamic properties. As we will see throughout this chapter, the answers to many ADO questions lie in dynamic properties, so keep your eyes and ears open for the ones that solve your problems. An important event, OnRecordsetCreate, was planned to be added to TCustomADODataSet in Delphi 6, which you may need to be aware of when using dynamic properties. (This event was not yet included as this book went to press.) OnRecordsetCreate is called immediately after the recordset has been created but has not been opened. This is useful when setting some dynamic properties as certain properties can only be set when the recordset is closed.

Getting Schema Information

One of the BDE components for which there is no apparent ADO alternative is TSession. TSession is used for several purposes, but a common use is to retrieve schema information (information about the structure of the database and its contents). In ADO this information can be retrieved using TADOConnection's OpenSchema method. This method accepts four parameters. The first, and most interesting, is the kind of data that OpenSchema should return. It is a TSchemaInfo value, which is a set of 40 values including those for retrieving a list of tables, indexes, columns, views, and stored procedures. The second parameter is a filter to place on the data before it is returned. We will see an example of this parameter in a moment.

The third parameter is a GUID for a provider-specific query and is only used if the first parameter is siProviderSpecific. The fourth and final parameter is a TADODataSet into which the data is returned. This last parameter illustrates a common theme in ADO: any method that needs to return more than a small amount of data will return its data as a Recordset, or in dbGo terms, a TADODataSet.

To use TADOConnection.OpenSchema, you need an open a TADOConnection. The following example retrieves a list of primary keys for every table into a TADODataSet:

```
ADOConnection1.OpenSchema(siPrimaryKeys, EmptyParam, EmptyParam, ADODataSet1);
```

Each field in a primary key has a single row in the result set. So a table with a composite key of two fields has two rows. The two EmptyParam values indicate that these parameters are given empty values and are ignored.

When EmptyParam is passed as the second parameter, the result set includes all information of the requested type for the entire database. For many kinds of information, you will want to filter the result set. You can, of course, apply a traditional Delphi filter to the result set using the Filter and Filtered properties or the OnFilterRecord event. However, this applies the filter on the client side in this example. Using the second parameter, we can apply a more efficient filter at the source of the schema information. The filter is specified as an array of values. Each element of the array has a specific meaning relevant to the kind of data being returned. For example, the filter array for primary keys has three elements: the first is the catalog (*catalog* is ANSI-speak for the database), the second is the schema, and the third is the table name. This example returns a list of primary keys for the Customers table:

```
var
  Filter: OLEVariant;
begin
  Filter := VarArrayCreate([0, 2], varVariant);
  Filter[2] := 'CUSTOMERS';
  ADOConnection1.OpenSchema(
  siPrimaryKeys, Filter, EmptyParam, ADODataSet1);
end;
```

You can retrieve the same information using ADOX, and this warrants a brief comparison between OpenSchema and ADOX. ADOX is an additional ADO technology that allows you to retrieve and update schema information. It is ADO's equivalent to SQL's Data Definition Language (DDL, i.e., CREATE, ALTER, DROP) and Data Control Language (DCL, i.e., GRANT, REVOKE). ADOX is not directly supported in dbGo, but you can easily import the ADOX type library and use it successfully in Delphi applications. Unfortunately, ADOX is not as universally implemented as OpenSchema, so there are greater gaps. If you just want to retrieve information and not to update it, then OpenSchema is usually a better choice.

Using the Jet Engine

Now that you have some of the MDAC and ADO basics under your belt, we can take a moment out to look at the Jet engine. This engine is of great interest to some and of no interest to others. If you're interested in Access, Paradox, dBase, text, Excel, Lotus 1-2-3, or HTML, then this section is for you. If you have no interest in any of these formats, you can safely skip this section.

The Jet database engine is usually associated with Microsoft Access databases, and this is, indeed, its forte. However, the Jet engine is also an all-purpose desktop database engine, and this lesser-known attribute is where much of its strength lies. Since using the Jet engine with Access is its default mode and is straightforward, this section mostly covers use of non-Access formats, which are not so obvious.

Before we look at these formats, we should discuss the availability of the Jet engine. It was included with MDAC from v1.5c until, and including, v2.5. From MDAC v2.6, the Jet engine was dropped from MDAC (which accounts for the reduction in download size from 7.5 MB to 5.2 MB). You can download a distributable version of the Jet engine from www.microsoft.com/ data/download.htm. Of course, if you have installed MDAC prior to v2.6, or Microsoft Access, Office, Excel, Visual Basic, or Visual C++ on your user's machine, then your user will already have the Jet engine.

There are two Jet OLE DB providers: the Jet 3.51 OLE DB Provider and the Jet 4.0 OLE DB Provider. The Jet 3.51 OLE DB Provider uses the Jet 3.51 engine and supports Access 97 databases only. If you intend to use Access 97 and not Access 2000, then you will get better performance using this OLE DB provider in most situations than using the Jet 4.0 OLE DB Provider. The Jet 4.0 OLE DB Provider supports Access 97, Access 2000, and Installable Indexed Sequential Access Method (IISAM) drivers. Installable ISAM drivers are those written specifically for the Jet engine to support access to ISAM formats such as Paradox, dBase, and text, and it is this facility that makes the Jet engine so useful and versatile. The complete list of ISAM drivers installed on your machine depends on what software you have installed on your machine. You can find this list by looking in the registry at

```
HKEY_LOCAL_MACHINE\Software\Microsoft\Jet\4.0\ISAM Formats
```

However, the Jet engine includes drivers for Paradox, dBase, Excel, text, and HTML.

Paradox

The Jet engine, naturally, expects to be used with Access databases. To use it with any database other than Access, you need to tell it which IISAM driver to use. This is a painless process that involves setting the Extended Properties connection string argument in the connection string editor. We'll do a quick example. Add a TADOTable to a form and invoke the connection string editor. Select the Jet 4.0 OLE DB Provider. Select the All page, locate the Extended Properties property, and double-click it to show the dialog box illustrated in Figure 16.3.

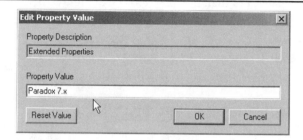

Enter **Paradox 7.x** in the Property Value as shown and click OK. Now go back to the Connection tab and enter the name of the directory containing the Paradox tables. For example you can enter

```
c:\program files\common files\borland shared\data
```

which contains Delphi's DBDEMOS Paradox tables. Unfortunately, the Browse button showing the ellipses does not react to the Extended Properties value and always expects to select a file and not a directory, and so it has little value when used with Paradox databases. Click OK on both dialog boxes and select a table in the TADOTable's TableName. Set Active to True and you are now using Paradox through ADO.

Sadly, I have some bad news for Paradox users. Under certain circumstances, you will need to install the BDE in addition to the Jet engine. It is bizarre that in a chapter dedicated to ADO we are talking about the need to install the BDE in addition to MDAC, but depending on your application this may be true. Jet 4.0 requires the BDE in order to be able to update Paradox tables, but it doesn't require the BDE just to read them. The same is true for most releases of the Paradox ODBC Driver. As disastrous as this sounds, all is not lost. Microsoft has received justified criticism on this point and has made a new Paradox IISAM available that does not require the BDE. You can get these updated drivers from Microsoft Technical Support.

NOTE   As you learn more and more about ADO, you will discover how much of ADO depends on the OLE DB provider and the DBMS (database management system) in question. You will see how the desktop databases such as Paradox and dBase have more restrictions and fewer functional features. If you are using Paradox simply because it is free, then you would be well advised to use another free database such as Access or MSDE. Alternatively, if leaving Paradox is not an option, then you should closely compare the BDE's support for Paradox with ADO's support for Paradox. In some cases, you will find the BDE's support better.

Excel

Excel is easily accessed using the Jet OLE DB Provider. Once again, we use the Extended Properties property and set it to Excel 8.0. Assume that we have an Excel spreadsheet called ABCCompany.xls that, in Excel, looks like Figure 16.4.

FIGURE 16.4:

ABCCompany.xls in Excel

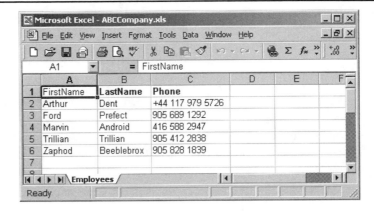

Notice that the sheet is called Employees. Our mission is to open and read this file using Delphi. You can, of course, solve this problem by automating Excel with only a small knowledge of COM. However, the ADO solution is considerably easier to implement.

Ensure that your spreadsheet is not open in Excel. Add a TADODataSet to a form. Set ConnectionString to use the Jet 4.0 OLE DB Provider and set Extended Properties to Excel 8.0. In the Connection tab, set the database name to the full file and path specification of the Excel spreadsheet. Close the connection string editor. The TADODataSet component works by opening or executing a value in its CommandText property. This value might be the name of a table or an SQL statement or a stored procedure or the name of a file. You specify how this value is interpreted by setting the CommandType property. Set CommandType to cmdTableDirect to indicate that the value in CommandText is the name of a table and that all columns should be returned from this table. Select CommandText in the Object Inspector and you will see a drop-down arrow. Drop down the arrow and a single "table" will be displayed: Employees$. (Excel workbooks are suffixed with a $.) Set Active to True, add a TDataSource and a TDB-Grid and connect them altogether, and you will see the Excel spreadsheet. It will be a little difficult to view in the grid because each column has a width of 255 characters. You can change this either by adding columns to the grid and changing their Width properties, or by adding persistent fields and changing their Size or DisplayWidth properties. After a little rearranging, you should see something like Figure 16.5.

FIGURE 16.5:
ABCCompany.xls in Delphi

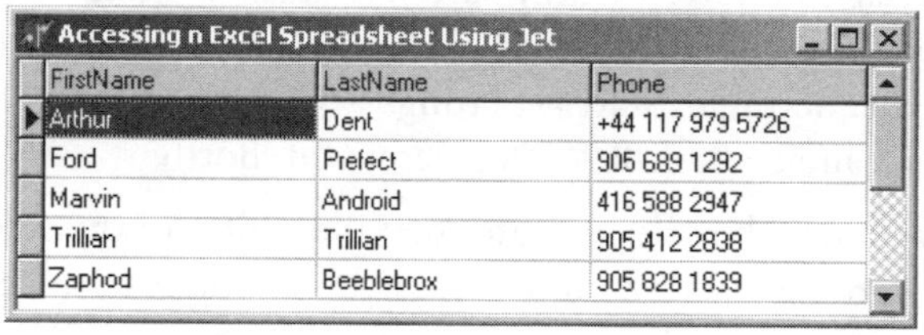

FirstName	LastName	Phone
Arthur	Dent	+44 117 979 5726
Ford	Prefect	905 689 1292
Marvin	Android	416 588 2947
Trillian	Trillian	905 412 2838
Zaphod	Beeblebrox	905 828 1839

Now save your application. If you run it from the IDE, you will discover the first of the limitations of the Excel IISAM: the XLS file is opened exclusively. To run the application, you will first need to close the application that is open in the IDE and then run it from Windows Explorer. When you run the program, you will notice another limitation of this IISAM driver: you can add new rows and edit existing rows, but you cannot delete rows.

Incidentally, you could have used either TADOTable or TADOQuery, instead of TADODataSet, but you need to be aware of how ADO treats symbols in things like table names and field names. If you were to use a TADOTable and drop down the list of tables, you would see the Employees$ table as you would expect. Unfortunately if you attempt to open the table, you will receive an error. The same is true for `SELECT * FROM Employees$` in a `TADOQuery`. The problem lies with the dollar sign in the table name. If you use characters such as dollars, dots, or, more importantly, spaces in table names or field names, then you must enclose the name in square brackets (e.g., `[Employees$]`).

Text Files

One of the very useful IISAM drivers that comes with the Jet engine is the Text IISAM. This driver allows you to read and update text files of almost any structured format. We will start with a simple text file to get up and running and then cover the variations later. Assume we have a simple text file called `NightShift.TXT` that contains the following text:

```
CrewPerson ,HomeTown
Neo        ,Cincinnati
Trinity    ,London
Morpheus   ,Milan
```

Add a TADOTable to a form, set its `ConnectionString` to use the Jet 4.0 OLE DB Provider, and set Extended Properties to Text. The Text IISAM considers a directory a database, so you need to enter the directory that contains the `NightShift.TXT` file as the database name. Back in the Object Inspector, drop down the list of tables in the `TableName` property. The "database" consists of all of the text files in this directory. You will notice that the dot in the filename has been converted to a hash, as in `NightShift#TXT`. Set `Active` to True, add a TDataSource and a TDBGrid and connect them altogether, and you will see the contents of the text file in a grid.

If your computer's settings are such that the decimal separator is a comma instead of a period (so that 1,000.00 is displayed as 1.000,00), then you will need to either change your Regional Settings (Start ➤ Settings ➤ Control Panel ➤ Regional Settings ➤ Numbers) or take advantage of SCHEMA.INI, described shortly.

Of course, the grid indicates that the widths of the columns are 255 characters. You can change these just as we did in Excel by adding persistent fields or columns to the grid and then setting the relevant width property. Alternatively you can define the structure of the text file more specifically using SCHEMA.INI.

Text files come in all shapes and sizes. Often you do not need to worry about the format of a text file because the Text IISAM takes a peek at the first 25 rows to see whether it can determine the format for itself. It uses this information and some additional information in the Registry to decide how to interpret the file and how to behave. If you have a file that doesn't match a regular format the Text IISAM can determine, then you can provide this information in the shape of SCHEMA.INI. SCHEMA.INI is an INI file located in the same directory as the text files to which it refers. It contains *schema* information, also called metadata, about any or all of the text files in the same directory. Each text file is given its own section, identified by the name of the text file, such as [NightShift.TXT].

Thereafter you can specify the format of the file, the names, types, and sizes of columns, any special character sets to use, and any special column formats (e.g., date/time, currency). Let's assume that we change our NightShift.TXT file to the following format:

```
Neo          |Cincinnati
Trinity      |London
Morpheus     |Milan
```

In this example, the column names are not included in the text file and the delimiter is a vertical bar. An associated SCHEMA.INI file might look something like the following:

```
[NightShift.TXT]
Format=Delimited(|)
ColNameHeader=False
Col1=CrewPerson Char Width 10
Col2=HomeTown Char Width 30
```

Regardless of whether or not you use a SCHEMA.INI file, you will encounter two limitations of the Text IISAM: rows cannot be deleted, and rows cannot be edited.

Importing and Exporting

The Jet engine is particularly adept at importing and exporting data. The process of exporting data is the same for each export format and consists of executing a SELECT statement with a special syntax. Let's start with an example of exporting data from the Northwind

Access database to a Paradox table. You will need an active TADOConnection, called ADO-Connection1 in our example, that uses the Jet 4.0 OLE DB Provider to open the Northwind.mdb Access database. The following code exports the Customers table to a Paradox Customers.db file:

```
ADOConnection1.Execute('SELECT * INTO Customers ' +
    'IN "C:\Temp" "Paradox 7.x;" FROM CUSTOMERS');
```

Let's look at the pieces of this SELECT statement. The INTO clause specifies the new table that will be created by the SELECT statement; this table must not already exist. The IN clause specifies the database to which the new table is added; in Paradox, this is a directory that already exists. The clause immediately following the database is the name of the IISAM driver to be used to perform the export. *You must include the trailing semicolon at the end of the driver name.* The FROM clause is a regular part of any SELECT statement.

All export statements follow these same basic clauses, but you will find that some IISAM drivers have differing interpretations of what a database is. I'll do another couple of examples to demonstrate the differences. Here, we export the same data to Excel:

```
ADOConnection1.Execute('SELECT * INTO Customers ' +
    'IN "Northwind.xls" "Excel 8.0;" FROM CUSTOMERS');
```

A new Excel file called Northwind.xls is created in the application's current directory. A workbook called Customers is added, containing all of the data of the Customers table in Northwind.mdb. You can also export data to Excel by automating Excel, but if you have ever done this you will know that this ADO solution is simpler by far.

This next example exports the same data to HTML:

```
ADOConnection1.Execute('SELECT * INTO [Customers.htm] ' +
    'IN "C:\Temp" "HTML Export;" FROM CUSTOMERS');
```

In this example, the database is the directory, as it was for Paradox but not for Excel. The table name must include the .htm extension and, therefore, it must be enclosed in square brackets. Notice that the name of the IISAM driver is "HTML Export", not just "HTML", because this driver can only be used for exporting to HTML.

The last IISAM driver we'll look at in this investigation of the Jet engine is the sister to HTML Export: HTML Import. Add a TADOTable to a form, set its ConnectionString to use the Jet 4.0 OLE DB Provider and Extended Properties to HTML Import. Set the database name to the name of the HTML file created by the export a few moments ago—that is, C:\Temp\Customers.htm. Close the connection string editors and set the TableName to Customers. Open the table and you have just imported the HTML file! Bear in mind, though, that the name of this IISAM driver is "HTML Import", not just "HTML". If you attempt to update the data in any way, you'll receive an error because this driver is intended for import only. Finally, if you create your own HTML files containing tables and want to open these tables using this driver, then remember that the name of the table is the value of the CAPTION tag of the HTML TABLE.

Cursor Locations and Cursor Types

There are two properties of ADO datasets that have a fundamental impact on your application and are inextricably linked with each other: `CursorLocation` and `CursorType`. The key to a successful application and to understanding your dataset's behavior and capabilities and the performance of your application lies in understanding these two properties.

The `CursorLocation`, of type `TCursorLocation`, allows you to specify what is in control of the retrieval and update of your data. You have two choices: client (`clUseClient`) or server (`clUseServer`). Your choice affects your dataset's functionality, performance, and scalability.

A client cursor is managed by the ADO Cursor Engine. This engine is an excellent example of an OLE DB service provider: it provides a service to other OLE DB providers. The ADO Cursor Engine manages the data from the client side of the application. All data in the result set is retrieved from the server to the client when the dataset is opened. Thereafter, the data is held in memory and updates and manipulation are managed by the ADO Cursor Engine. One benefit is that manipulation of the data, after the initial retrieval, is considerably faster. Furthermore, as the manipulation is performed in memory, the ADO Cursor Engine is more versatile than most server-side cursors and offers facilities that cannot be reproduced by server-side cursors. I'll examine these benefits later, as well as other technologies that depend on client-side cursors such as disconnected and persistent recordsets.

A server-side cursor is managed by the DBMS. In a client/server database such as SQL Server, Oracle, or InterBase, this means that the cursor is managed physically on the server. In a desktop database such as Access or Paradox, the "server" location is simply a logical location, as the database is running on the desktop. Server-side cursors are often faster to load than client-side cursors because not all of the data is transferred to the client when the dataset is opened. This also makes them more suitable for very large result sets where the client has insufficient memory to hold the entire result set in memory. Often you can determine what kinds of features will be available to you with each cursor location by thinking through how the cursor works. A good example of how features determine cursor type is locking, which I will cover in more detail later. To place a lock on a record requires a server-side cursor, because there must be a conversation between the application and the DBMS.

Another issue that will affect your choice of cursor location is scalability. Server-side cursors are managed by the DBMS; in a client/server database, this will be located on the server. As more and more users use your application, the load on the server increases with each server-side cursor. A greater workload on the server means that the DBMS becomes a bottleneck faster, so the application is less scalable. You can achieve better scalability by using client-side cursors. The initial hit on opening the cursor is often heavier, because all the data is transferred to the client, but the maintenance of the open cursor can be lower. As you can see, many conflicting issues are involved in choosing the correct cursor location for your datasets.

Your choice of cursor location directly affects your choice of cursor type. To all intents and purposes there are four cursor types, but I will digress for a moment to explain why there is one unused value. There is a cursor type that means "unspecified." Many values in ADO signify an unspecified value, and I will cover them all here and explain why you won't have much to do with them. They exist in Delphi because they exist in ADO. ADO was mostly designed for Visual Basic and C programmers. In these languages, you use the objects directly without any of the assistance that dbGo provides. As such, you can create and open *recordsets*, as they are called in ADO-speak, without having to specify every value for every property. The properties for which a value has not been specified have an unspecified value. However, in dbGo we use components. These components have constructors, and these constructors initialize the properties of the components. So from the moment you create a dbGo component, it will usually have a value for each and every property. The consequence is that we have little need for the unspecified values in many enumerated types.

Back to the cursor types. Cursor types, of type TCursorType, affect how your data is read and updated. There are four choices: forward-only, static, keyset, and dynamic. Before we get too involved in all of the permutations of cursor locations and cursor types, you should be aware that there is only one cursor type available for client-side cursors: the static cursor. All other cursor types are only available to server-side cursors. I'll return to the subject of cursor type availability after we have looked at the various cursor types, in increasing order of expensiveness.

The least expensive cursor type, and therefore the type with the best possible performance, is the forward-only cursor, which, as the name implies, will let you navigate forward. The cursor reads the number of records specified by CacheSize (default of 1) and each time it runs out of records, it reads another CacheSize set. Any attempt to navigate backward through the result set beyond the number of records in the cache will result in an error.

Knowing how a forward-only cursor works should help you to understand why they do not support bookmarks. A bookmark normally allows your dataset to navigate by jumping to a selected row. Because you can only travel forward through a forward-only cursor and any bookmark placed will be behind the current cursor position, bookmarks are not supported. As such a forward-only cursor is not suitable for use in the user interface where the user can control the direction through the result set. However, it is eminently suitable for batch operations and reports, because these situations start at the top of the result set and work progressively toward the end, then the result set is closed.

A static cursor works by reading the complete result set and providing a window of CacheSize records into the result set. As the complete result set has been retrieved by the server, you can navigate both forward and backward through the result set. However, in exchange for this facility, the data is static—that is, updates, insertions, and deletions made by other users cannot be seen because the cursor's data has already been read.

A keyset cursor is best understood by breaking *keyset* down into its two words *key* and *set*. Key, in this context, refers to an identifier for each row. Often this will be a primary key. A keyset cursor, therefore, is a set of keys. When the result set is opened, the complete list of keys for the result set is read. If, for example, the dataset was a query like SELECT * FROM CUSTOMERS, then the list of keys would be built from SELECT CUSTID FROM CUSTOMERS. This set of keys is held until the cursor is closed. When the application requests data, the OLE DB provider reads the rows using the keys in the set of keys. Consequently, the data is always up to date. If another user changes a row in the result set, then the changes will be seen when the data is reread. However, the set of keys, itself, is static; it is read only when the result set is first opened. So if another user adds new records, these additions will not be seen. Deleted records become inaccessible, and changes to primary keys (you don't let your users change primary keys, do you?) are also inaccessible.

The last, and most expensive, cursor type is dynamic. A dynamic cursor is almost identical to a keyset cursor. The sole difference is that the set of keys is reread when the application requests data that is not in the cache. As the default for TADODataSet.CacheSize is 1, this is very frequent. You can imagine the additional load this places on the DBMS and the network and why this is the most expensive cursor. However, the result set can see and respond to the additions and deletions made by other users.

Ask and Ye Shall Not Receive

Now that we know all about cursor locations and cursor types, a word of warning: not all combinations of cursor location and cursor type are possible. Usually, this is a limitation imposed by the DBMS and/or the OLE DB provider as a result of the functionality and architecture of the DBMS. For example, client cursors always force the cursor type to static. You can see this for yourself. Add a TADODataSet to a form, set its ConnectionString to any database, set ClientLocation to clUseCursor and CursorType to ctDynamic. Now set Active to True and keep your eye on the CursorType; it changes to ctStatic. We learn an important lesson from this example:

> What you ask for is not necessarily what you get.

Always check your properties after opening a dataset for what you think you "know" is true.

Each OLE DB provider will make different changes according to different requests and circumstances, but to give you a rough idea of what you can expect here are a few examples. The Jet 4.0 OLE DB Provider changes most cursor types to keyset. The SQL Server OLE DB Provider often changes keyset and static to dynamic. The Oracle OLE DB Provider changes all cursor types to forward-only. The ODBC OLE DB Provider makes various changes according to the ODBC driver in use.

RecordCount = –1

Armed with all of this knowledge about cursors, we can explain why ADO datasets sometimes return –1 for their RecordCount. A forward-only cursor cannot know how many records are in the result set until it reaches the end, so it returns –1 for the RecordCount. A static cursor always knows how many records are in the result set, because it reads the entire set when it is opened, so it returns the number of records in its result set. A keyset cursor also knows how many records are in the result set, because it has to retrieve a fixed set of keys when the result set is opened, so it also returns a useful value for RecordCount. A dynamic cursor does not reliably know how many records are in the result set, because it is regularly rereading the set of keys, so it returns –1. You could, of course, avoid using RecordCount altogether and execute SELECT COUNT(*) FROM tablename, but this will be an accurate reflection of the number of records in the database, which is not necessarily the same as the number of records in the dataset.

Client Indexes

One of the many benefits of client-side cursors is the ability to create local, or *client*, indexes. You can try this out for yourself. Assuming that you have an ADO client-side dataset for the Northwind's Customer table, which has a grid attached to it, set the dataset's IndexFieldNames property to CompanyName. Immediately the grid will show that the data is in CompanyName order. There is an important point to make here: In order to index the data, ADO did not have to reread the data from its source. The index was created from the data in memory. This means not only is the creation of the index just about as fast as it could possibly be, but the network and the DBMS are not overloaded with transferring the same data over and over in different orders. The IndexFieldNames property has more potential. Set it to Country;CompanyName and you will see the data ordered first by country and then, within country, in company name order. Now set IndexFieldNames to CompanyName DESC. Be sure to write DESC in capitals and not "desc" or "Desc". I'm sure you won't be surprised to see that the data is now sorted in descending order.

This simple but powerful feature allows us to solve one of the great bugbears of database developers. From time to time users seem to ask the inevitable, and quite reasonable, question, "Can I click the columns of the grid to sort my data?" There are three traditional answers to this question:

- "Yes. I can replace all of my grids with non–data-aware controls such as `TListView` that have the sorting built into the control. Of course, I lose all of the benefits of data-aware controls with this solution."

- "Yes. I can trap the TDBGrid's `OnTitleClick` event and rebuild the SQL SELECT statement to include an appropriate ORDER BY clause and then reissue the SELECT statement. Of course, this will mean requerying exactly the same data as I already have just to get it in a different order, but the user is always right."

- "No. I admit that this would be a cool feature, but the extra load on the DBMS and the network is antisocial to other users."

Sadly, none of the above are acceptable answers. Client indexes to the rescue! Add the following `OnTitleClick` event to the grid:

```
procedure TForm1.DBGrid1TitleClick(Column: TColumn);
begin
  if ADODataSet1.IndexFieldNames = Column.Field.FieldName then
    ADODataSet1.IndexFieldNames := Column.Field.FieldName + ' DESC'
  else
    ADODataSet1.IndexFieldNames := Column.Field.FieldName
end;
```

This simple event checks to see whether the current index is built on the same field as the column. If it is, then a new index is built on the column but in descending order. If not, then a new index is built on the column. When the user clicks the column for the first time, it is sorted in ascending order, and when it is clicked for the second time, it is sorted in descending order. You could extend this to allow the user to Ctrl-click several column titles to build up more complicated indexes. Of course, all of this can be achieved using TClientDataSet, but that solution is not as elegant for two reasons: descending indexes must be built from scratch (because TClientDataSet does not support the DESC keyword) and existing ascending indexes cannot be changed to descending indexes (they must be deleted and rebuilt).

Cloning

ADO is crammed full of features. You can argue that "feature-rich" can translate into "footprint-rich," but it also translates into more powerful and reliable applications. One such powerful feature is cloning. A cloned recordset is a new recordset that has all of the same properties as the original from which it is cloned. First, I'll explain how you can create and use a clone, and then I'll explain why they are so useful.

You can clone a recordset, or, in dbGo-speak, a dataset, using the Clone method. You can clone any ADO dataset, but we will use TADOTable in this example. Add a TADOTable to a form and set its ConnectionString to use any OLE DB provider that returns rectangular data (e.g., the Jet or SQL Server OLE DB providers). Set its TableName to any table and open the table. Add a TDataSource and a TDBGrid to allow you to view the table. Now add a second TADOTable and a button with the following code:

```
ADOTable2.Clone(ADOTable1);
```

This line clones ADOTable1 and assigns the clone to ADOTable2. If you add another TData-Source and TDBGrid to show ADOTable2, you will see a second view of the data. The two datasets have their own record pointers and other status information, so the clone does not interfere with its original copy.

This behavior makes them ideal for *black box programming*. This term comes from an old story, in which you could ask the black box any question at all and it would guarantee to provide an answer. You couldn't see inside the black box and you didn't know how it worked, just that it did. The black box did what it was supposed to and no more. It is this last part that is so essential to programming: functions and procedures do *no more than they are supposed to*. Sometimes this is also referred to as having "zero side effects." So in this example, the CountSelected function attempts to count all of the rows where the Selected field is True:

```
function CountSelected(
ADODataSet: TCustomADODataSet): integer;
var
  Bookmark: TBookmark;
begin
  Result := 0;
  Bookmark := ADODataSet.GetBookmark;
  try
    ADODataSet.First;
    while not ADODataSet.EOF do
    begin
      if ADODataSet.FieldByName('Selected').AsBoolean then
        Inc(Result);
      ADODataSet.Next;
    end;
    ADODataSet.GoToBookmark(Bookmark);
  finally
    ADODataSet.FreeBookmark(Bookmark);
  end;
end;
```

At first sight, this function appears to be a black box function. It dutifully saves the current row position of the dataset using a bookmark and restores the position before returning, so that the net effect of moving the row position is zero. This is a standard approach to black box programming: if you change something in your routine that you are not supposed to change, then you must restore it again afterward.

Sadly, this routine is not black box. The movement of the row pointer will be observed by any data-aware controls, and the user interface will be updated by every row movement. A better solution to this problem is to use cloning:

```
function CountSelected(ADODataSet: TCustomADODataSet): integer;
var
  Clone: TADODataSet;
begin
  Result := 0;
  Clone := TADODataSet.Create(nil);
  try
    Clone.Clone(ADODataSet);
    Clone.First;
    while not Clone.EOF do
    begin
      if Clone.FieldByName('Selected').AsBoolean then
        Inc(Result);
      Clone.Next;
    end;
    Clone.Close;
  finally
    Clone.Free;
  end;
end;
```

The new clone will not interfere with its original in any way, making it ideal for black box programming. In particular, note that the closing of the clone does not close the original or other clones. In fact, not even the closing of the original closes its clones. I will use cloning later in this chapter, but before we close this subject, there are two points worth mentioning.

WARNING   A recordset must support bookmarks in order to be cloned, so forward-only and dynamic cursors cannot be cloned. You can determine whether a recordset supports bookmarks using the `Supports` method (e.g., `ADOTable1.Supports([coBookMark])`).

TIP   One of the useful side effects of clones is that the bookmarks created by one clone are usable by all other clones.

Transaction Processing

Transaction processing allows developers to group together individual updates to a database into a single logical unit of work. The benefit is that a database engine can be told to accept or reject the complete unit of work as a single entity. The facility is present in nearly all of today's DBMSs, because it's essential for maintaining the integrity of the database. The classic example used to illustrate the need for transaction processing is the transfer of money to and from a bank account. The movement of money from one account into another consists of two steps: the removal of money from one account and the addition of the same money into another account. The entire transaction must either wholly succeed or wholly fail in order for integrity to be maintained. If only one half of the transaction succeeds, the money will either have been created (by adding money to one account while failing to remove it from the other) or destroyed (by removing money from one account while failing to add it to the other). Database programming is full of examples that require transaction processing, and in this section we will see how ADO handles this subject.

ADO's transaction processing support is controlled using a TADOConnection. The following list summarizes the relevant methods:

TADOConnection Method	Description	TDatabase Equivalent
BeginTrans	Begins a transaction	StartTransaction
CommitTrans	Commits a transaction	Commit
RollbackTrans	Rolls back a transaction	Rollback

To investigate ADO's transaction processing support, we will build a simple test program. We will use this test program to investigate the different levels of transaction processing support offered by different OLE DB providers and different databases.

Create a new application and add a TADOConnection. Set the ConnectionString to use the ODBC OLE DB Provider and the DBDEMOS Paradox data supplied with Delphi. You might find it easier to first create an ODBC Data Source, say DBDEMOS, and refer to that. Set the LoginPrompt to False and Connected to True. Add a TADOTable, set Connection to ADOConnection1, TableName to Customers, and Active to True. Add a TDataSource and a TDBGrid and connect them so that the Customers table is shown in the grid. Add three buttons to the top of the form to execute each of the following commands:

```
ADOConnection1.BeginTrans;
ADOConnection1.CommitTrans;
ADOConnection1.RollbackTrans;
```

The running application should look something like Figure 16.6.

FIGURE 16.6:

ADO transaction processing

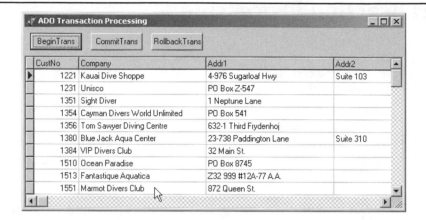

Click the BeginTrans button and you will receive an error indicating that the DBMS or the OLE DB provider is not capable of beginning a transaction. The problem lies with the Paradox ODBC Driver, which simply doesn't support transaction processing. You can find out what level of transaction processing support you have using the connection's Transaction DDL dynamic property—for example,

```
if ADOConnection1.Properties['Transaction DDL'].Value > DBPROPVAL_TC_NONE then
   ADOConnection1.BeginTrans;
```

The DBPROPVAL_TC_NONE constant comes from OLEDB.PAS along with several others like it. The related constants indicate that transaction support is available for Data Manipulation Language (DML) statements, meaning that SQL UPDATE, INSERT, and DELETE statements will all be included in transactions. ADO updates databases using SQL, so all of the dbGo components' DML methods (e.g., Append, Post, Delete) are also included in this list. The difference between the DBPROPVAL_TC constants is the level of support for Data Definition Language (DDL) commands included in a transaction. DDL is the set of SQL commands that alter the structure of the database and allow developers to perform actions such as adding and deleting columns and adding new tables. Given the nature of these commands, it is unlikely that you would want to mix DDL commands in a transaction with DML commands, so your interest in the Transaction DDL dynamic property might not extend beyond the DBPROPVAL_TC_NONE constant. If you do intend to include DDL commands in a transaction, you should check the other constants to see how the DDL will be treated by the DBMS. Some DBMSs will ignore the DDL, some will generate an exception if it is included in a transaction, some will cause certain DDL commands to lock a table, and others will automatically commit a transaction when the DDL is executed.

Let's get back to our test application. Change the TADOConnection's ConnectionString to use the Jet 4.0 OLE DB Provider and set its Extended Properties (in the All tab) to

Paradox 7.x. Set the database name to Delphi's DBDEMOS directory (c:\program files\ common files\borland shared\data). Save the connection string and reopen the TADOTable. You should see no difference from the previous example. Now run the application and click the BeginTrans button. Success? Unfortunately, no. This is a cruel, cruel trick on the part of the Jet 4.0 OLE DB Provider. Make a few changes and click the RollbackTrans button; close the application down and restart it. You will see that the changes that you made were permanent and your act of rolling them back made no difference at all. As I said, it is a cruel trick, because transactions on a Paradox database cannot be rolled back, and this makes them rather useless. If you read through the section in this chapter on the Jet engine and, in particular, the section on Paradox, you will recall that I mentioned that the support for Paradox is lower than most developers would like. Transaction processing is one such example.

Now let's look at how Access handles transaction processing. Create an ODBC System Data Source Name using the ODBC Manager. Call it Northwind DSN, use the Microsoft Access ODBC driver, and set the database to Northwind.mdb. In Delphi, change the TADO-Connection to use the ODBC OLE DB Provider and the new Northwind DSN. Now save the connection string, change the TADOTable's TableName from Customer to Customers, and open it. Run the application and click the BeginTrans button. At last, transaction processing that works. You can make changes to the Northwind database and roll back the changes, and they will be rolled back! However, something you cannot do is start a transaction within a transaction. Try clicking the BeginTrans button twice and you get a "Cannot start more trans-actions on this session" error. This is a limitation of ODBC and not the Jet engine and is a useful example of why you should always try to locate an OLE DB provider for your DBMS instead of an ODBC driver.

Nested Transactions

If you try the same test again but use the Jet 4.0 OLE DB Provider, you will see that you can click the BeginTrans button five times before receiving an error on the sixth attempt. Jet supports *nested transactions*, which are transactions that exist within the context of another transaction. The nested or *inner* transaction can be committed or rolled back without affecting the outcome of the *outer* transaction. Let's work through a sequence of steps to be sure of how this works:

1. Begin a transaction.

2. Change the ContactName of the Around The Horn record from Thomas Hardy to Dick Solomon.

3. Begin a nested transaction.

4. Change the `ContactName` of the Bottom-Dollar Markets record from Elizabeth Lincoln to Sally Solomon.

5. Roll back the inner transaction.

6. Commit the outermost transaction.

The net effect is that only the change to the Around The Horn record is permanent. If, however, the inner transaction had been committed and the outer transaction rolled back, then the net effect would be that *none* of the changes were permanent (even the changes in the inner transaction). Although we are using Access to illustrate this behavior, the behavior is the same for all OLE DB providers that support nested transactions. This, of course, leads us to an ongoing theme in our ADO exploration: The ADO documentation simply states how any given feature is supposed to work when it is fully implemented by the OLE DB provider and the DBMS, but it does not necessarily follow that it *is* implemented for all OLE DB providers and all DBMSs. In the example of nested transactions, we have seen that ODBC does not support them and that the Jet OLE DB Provider supports up to five levels of nested transactions. The SQL Server OLE DB Provider supports nesting, but this depends on the version of SQL Server being used. In SQL Server 7.0 and 2000, full nested transaction support is provided. In SQL Server 6.5, only "fake nesting" is supported, where all inner-transaction instructions are ignored. You can commit and roll back inner transactions without any effect. It is only the outermost transaction that decides whether the complete sum of all of the work is committed or rolled back.

There is another issue that you should consider if you intend to use nested transactions. TADOConnection has a property called `Attributes`, which determines how the connection should behave when a transaction is committed or rolled back. It is a set of `TXActAttributes` that, by default, is empty. There are only two values in `TXActAttributes`: xaCommitRetaining and xaAbortRetaining (this value is often mistakenly written as xaRollbackRetaining because this would have been a more logical name for it). When xaCommitRetaining is included in `Attributes` and a transaction is committed, a new transaction is automatically started. When xaAbortRetaining is included in `Attributes` and a transaction is rolled back, a new transaction is automatically started. This means that if you include these values in `Attributes`, a transaction will always be in progress, because when you end one transaction another will always be started. Most programmers prefer to be in greater control of their transactions than allowing them to be automatically started, so these values are not commonly used. However, they have a special relevance to nested transactions. If you nest a transaction and set `Attributes` to [xaCommitRetaining, xaAbortRetaining], then the outermost transaction can never be ended. Consider the sequence of events:

1. An outer transaction is started.

2. An inner transaction is started.

3. The inner transaction is committed or rolled back.

4. A new inner transaction is automatically started as a consequence of the `Attributes` property.

The outermost transaction can never be ended because a new inner transaction will also be started when one ends. The conclusion is that the use of the `Attributes` property and the use of nested transactions should be considered mutually exclusive.

Lock Types

ADO supports four different approaches to locking your data for update. In this section I will provide an overview of the four approaches, and in subsequent sections we will take a closer look. The four approaches are made available to you through the dataset's `LockType` property, of type `TLockType`, and can be ltReadOnly, ltPessimistic, ltOptimistic, or ltBatchOptimistic (there is, of course, an ltUnspecified but, for the reasons mentioned earlier, we are ignoring "unspecified" values).

The ltReadOnly value specifies that the data is read-only and cannot be updated. As such, there is effectively no locking control required because the data cannot be updated.

The ltPessimistic and ltOptimistic values offer the same "pessimistic" and "optimistic" locking control that the BDE offers. One important benefit that ADO offers over the BDE in this respect is that the choice of locking control remains yours. If you use the BDE, the decision to use pessimistic or optimistic locking is made for you by the BDE driver you use. If you use a desktop database such as dBase or Paradox, then the BDE driver uses pessimistic locking; if you use a client/server database such as InterBase, SQL Server, or Oracle, the BDE driver uses optimistic locking.

Pessimistic Locking

The words *pessimistic* and *optimistic* in this context refer to the developer's expectations of conflict between user updates. Pessimistic locking assumes that there is a high probability that users will attempt to update the same records at the same time and that a conflict is likely. In order to prevent such a conflict, the record is locked when the edit begins. The record lock is maintained until the update is completed or cancelled. A second user who attempts to edit the same record at the same time will fail in their attempt to place their record lock and will receive a "Could not update; currently locked" exception.

This approach to locking will be familiar to developers who have worked with desktop databases such as dBase and Paradox. The benefit is that the user knows that if they can begin editing a record, then they will succeed in saving their update. The disadvantage of pessimistic locking is that the user is in control of when the lock is placed and when it is removed. If the user is skilled with the application, then this could be as short as a couple of seconds. However, in database terms a couple of seconds is an eternity. At the worst end of the scale, the user can begin an edit and go to lunch, and the record could be locked until the user returns. As a consequence of this, most proponents of pessimistic locking guard against this eventuality by using a TTimer or other such device to time out any locks after a certain amount of keyboard and mouse inactivity.

Another problem with pessimistic locking is that it requires a server-side cursor. Earlier we looked at cursor locations and saw that they have an impact on the availability of the different cursor types. Now we can see that cursor locations also have an impact on locking types. Later in this chapter we will see more benefits of client-side cursors, and if you choose to take advantage of these benefits, then you'll be unable to use pessimistic locking.

Pessimistic locking is one of the areas of ADOExpress/dbGo that changed in Delphi 6. This section describes the way pessimistic locking works in version 6 (which is now the same as for ADO). Create a new application and add a TADODataSet. Set its ConnectionString to use either the Jet or SQL Server Northwind database. Set its CommandType to cmdTable and CommandText to Customers. As we will be using pessimistic locking, we must set the Cursor-Location to clUseServer and LockType to ltPessimistic. Finally, set Active to True. Add a TDataSource and a TDBGrid, connect them altogether, and ensure that the grid is aligned to client.

Now for the test. Run the application and begin editing a record. Using Windows Explorer, run a second copy of the same application and attempt to edit the same record; you will fail because the record is locked by another user.

If you were using ADOExpress in Delphi 5, the attempt to edit the same record at the same time would have succeeded, because ADOExpress in version 5 did not lock the record at the beginning of the edit. The work-around for this problem in Delphi 5 involved creating a clone of the original recordset and forcing a record lock in the clone before an edit, and releasing the record lock before the actual post or when the edit was cancelled.

Jet Page and Row Locking

This section demystifies some of the issues surrounding locking in Microsoft's Jet engine. If you have no interest in Access as a database, you can safely skip over this section.

The Jet 4.0 OLE DB Provider, which you will recall is used primarily for Access 2000 databases although it can also be used with Access 97 databases, supports both page-level and row-level locking. The Jet 3.5 OLE DB Provider, which is used solely for Access 97 databases, supports page-level locking only. A *page* is a length of data. The page in question completely contains the record for which the lock is required. In Jet 3.5, a page is 2 KB in length, and in Jet 4.0 it is 4 KB. It is unlikely that a record is exactly 2 KB or 4 KB, so the locking of a single record usually includes the locking of one or more subsequent records. Clearly this locks additional records unnecessarily, which is a disadvantage of page locking and is the main reason why Jet 4.0 offers a choice of page or row locking.

Row locking, sometimes referred to as Alcatraz in the Jet engine, allows a single row to be locked individually with no additional space locked. As such, this solution provides the least lock contention. The path to understanding locking in Jet lies in Jet's dynamic properties. Most of your control over Jet locking is provided by the ADO Connection object's dynamic properties. The first and most important dynamic property is Jet OLEDB:Database Locking Mode, which can be revealed in a TADOConnection as follows:

```
ShowMessage(ADOConnection1.Properties[
  'Jet OLEDB:Database Locking Mode'].Value);
```

By default this value is 1, which means that the connection will allow recordsets to choose between row locking and page locking. The only alternative value is 0, which forces page locking. However, in order to ensure that all users use the same locking mechanism, the first user who opens the database dictates the locking mode used by all users. This mode remains in force until all users have disconnected from the database.

The second part of the locking jigsaw is the recordset. The recordset itself can specify its locking mode, using the Jet OLEDB:Locking Granularity dynamic property. By default this value is 2, which indicates that it should use row-level locking. Setting this value to 1 indicates that the recordset should use page locking. The Jet OLEDB:Locking Granularity dynamic property is ignored if the connection's Jet OLEDB:Database Locking Mode is not 1. You will have to use the OnRecordsetCreate event added in Delphi 6 to set the dynamic property, because it can only be set when the recordset is created but closed. (OnRecordsetCreate was not yet functional as this book went to press. Also, if you are using ADOExpress in Delphi 5, you will have to modify the source code of TCustomADODataSet.OpenCursor to add in your own OnRecordsetCreate event immediately after the recordset is created.) Thus, so far, Jet 4.0 uses row-level locking by default. This is true but there is an extra twist to add to this tale.

Row-level locking is only the default for recordsets. It is not the default for SQL you execute directly, or what BDE developers refer to as "non-passthrough SQL." For SQL statements you write yourself and execute directly, the default locking mode is still page locking, even using Jet 4.0.

Having gone through these trials and tribulations you will be pleased to learn that Jet provides a significant level of control over its locking facilities. Once again, this control is offered by dynamic properties and is available through TADOConnection. The following list shows the relevant dynamic properties:

Property	Description
Jet OLEDB:Lock Delay	Milliseconds to wait before attempting to reacquire a lock (default is 0)
Jet OLEDB:Lock Retry	Number of times to retry a failed lock (default is 0)
Jet OLEDB:Max Locks Per File	Maximum number of locks that Jet can place on a database (default is 9500)
Jet OLEDB:Page Locks To Table	Number of page locks before Jet promotes to a table lock (default is 0)

Updating JOINs

One of the reasons why people used to turn to cached updates in the BDE and, more recently, TClientDataSet, is to make an SQL JOIN updatable. Consider the following SQL equi-join:

```
SELECT * FROM Products, Suppliers
WHERE Products.SupplierID=Suppliers.SupplierID
```

This statement provides a list of products and the details of the suppliers of those products. The BDE considers any SQL JOIN to be read-only because inserting, updating, and deleting rows in a join is ambiguous. For example, should the insert of a row into the above join result in a new product and also a new supplier or just a new product?

The BDE supports cached updates, which allow the developer to resolve this ambiguity by specifying exactly what the developer wants to happen. Although the BDE's cached updates implementation is often flawed, and cached updates are now discouraged in favor of the more reliable TClientDataSet, the concept is sound.

ADO supports an equivalent to cached updates, called batch updates, which are very similar. In the next section we will take a closer look at ADO's batch updates, what they can offer you, and why they are so important. However, in this section they will not be needed to solve the problem of updating a join for a very simple reason: in ADO, joins are naturally updatable. Place a TADOQuery on a form and set its connection string to use a Northwind database. Enter the SQL join above in its SQL property and set `Active` to True. Add a TDataSource and a TDBGrid and connect them altogether and run the program. Now edit one of the Product's fields and save the changes (by moving off the record). No error occurs because the update has been applied successfully. ADO has taken a more practical approach to the problem: it has made some intelligent guesses. In an ADO join, each field object knows which underlying table it belongs to. If you update a field of the Products table and post the change, then a SQL UPDATE statement is generated to update the field in the Products table. If you change a field in the Products table and a field in the Suppliers table, then two SQL UPDATE statements are generated, one for each table.

The inserting of a row into a join follows a similar behavior. If you insert a row and enter values for the Products table only, then a SQL INSERT statement is generated for the Products table. If you enter values for both tables, two SQL INSERT statements are generated, one for each table. The order in which the statements are executed is important, because the new product might relate to the new supplier, so the new supplier is inserted first.

The biggest problem with ADO's solution can be seen when a row in a join is deleted. The deletion attempt will appear to fail. The exact message you see depends on the version of ADO you are using and the DBMS, but it will be along the lines that you cannot delete the row because other records relate to it. The error message can be confusing. In our scenario, the error message implies that a product cannot be deleted because there are records that relate to the product. The error occurs whether the product has any related records or not. The explanation can be found by following through the same logic for deletions as for insertions. Two SQL DELETE statements are generated: one for the Suppliers table and then another for the Products table. Contrary to appearances, the DELETE statement for the Product table succeeds. It is the DELETE statement for the Suppliers table that fails, because the Supplier cannot be deleted while it still has dependent records.

If you are curious about the SQL statements that get generated and you use SQL Server, you can see these statements using SQL Server Profiler.

Despite understanding how this works, a better way of looking at this problem is through the user's eyes. From their point of view, when they delete a row in the grid, do they intend to delete just the product or both the product and the supplier? I would wager that 99% of users expect the former and not the latter. Fortunately you can achieve exactly this with our old friend, the dynamic property—in this case, the Unique Table dynamic property. You can specify that deletes refer to just the Products table and not to Suppliers using the following line of code:

```
ADOQuery1.Properties['Unique Table'].Value := 'Products';
```

As this value cannot be assigned at design time, the next best alternative is to place this line in the form's OnCreate event.

For me, updatable joins are just one of many examples of how the designers of ADO have replaced traditional problems with elegant solutions.

Batch Updates

Batch updates are ADO's equivalent to the BDE's cached updates; they are similar in functionality, syntax, and, to some extent, implementation, with the all-important difference being that their implementation is not fundamentally flawed. The idea is the same for both database technologies: By using batch/cached updates, any changes you make to your records can be made in memory and then later the entire "batch" of changes can be submitted as one operation. There are some performance benefits to this approach, but there are more practical reasons why this technology is a necessity: the user might not be connected to the database at the time they make their updates. This would be the case in the infamous "briefcase" application, which we will return to later, but this can also be the case in Web applications that use another ADO technology, Remote Data Services (RDS).

You can enable batch updates in any ADO dataset by setting LockType to ltBatchOptimistic before the dataset is opened. In addition, you will need to set the CursorLocation to clUse-Client, as batch updates are managed by ADO's cursor engine. Hereafter, changes are all made to a "delta" (i.e., a list of changes). The dataset looks to all intents and purposes as if the data has changed, but the changes have only been made in memory; they have not been applied to the database. To make the changes permanent, use UpdateBatch (equivalent to cached updates' ApplyUpdates):

```
ADODataSet1.UpdateBatch;
```

(Fortunately, there is no equivalent to the cached update's CommitUpdates method, because the successful changes are automatically removed from the batch.) To reject the entire batch of updates, use either CancelBatch or CancelUpdates. There are many similarities in method and property names between ADO's batch updates and BDE's cached updates and TClient-DataSet. UpdateStatus, for example, can be used in exactly the same way as for cached updates to identify records according to whether they have been inserted, updated, deleted, or unmodified. This is particularly useful for highlighting records in different colors in a grid or showing their status on a status bar. Some differences between the syntaxes are slight, such as changing RevertRecord to CancelBatch(arCurrent). Others require more effort.

One useful cached update feature that is not present in ADO batch updates is the dataset's UpdatesPending property. This property is true if changes have been made but not yet applied. This is particularly useful in a form's OnCloseQuery event:

```
procedure TForm1.FormCloseQuery(
Sender: TObject; var CanClose: Boolean);
begin
  CanClose := True;
  if ADODataSet1.UpdatesPending then
    CanClose := (MessageDlg('Updates are still pending' #13 +
      'Close anyway?', mtConfirmation, [mbYes, mbNo], 0) = mrYes);
end;
```

However, with a little knowledge and a little ingenuity we can implement a suitable ADOUpdatesPending function. The little knowledge is that ADO datasets have a property called FilterGroup, which is a kind of filter. Unlike a dataset's Filter property, which filters the data based on a comparison of the data against a condition, FilterGroup filters based on the status of the record. One such status is fgPendingRecords, which includes all records that have been modified but not yet applied. So to allow the user to look through all of the changes they have made so far, you need only execute two lines:

```
ADODataSet1.FilterGroup := fgPendingRecords;
ADODataSet1.Filtered := True;
```

Naturally, the result set will now include the records that have been deleted. If you try this yourself, the effect that you will see will depend on the version of dbGo you have and the patches you have applied to it. In early versions of ADOExpress, the deleted record showed the fields of the previous record. This either was confusing (if there was a previous record) or resulted in a fatal error (if there wasn't). In later versions, the fields are just left blank, which also is not very helpful because you don't know what record has been deleted.

Back to the UpdatesPending problem. The "little ingenuity" is the knowledge of clones, discussed earlier. The idea of the ADOUpdatesPending function is that it will set the FilterGroup to restrict the dataset to only those changes that have not yet been applied. All we need to do is to see whether there are any records in the dataset once the FilterGroup has been applied. If there are, then some updates are pending. However, if we do this with the actual dataset, then the setting of the FilterGroup will move the record pointer and the user interface will be updated. The best solution is to use a clone.

```
function ADOUpdatesPending(ADODataSet: TCustomADODataSet): boolean;
var
  Clone: TADODataSet;
begin
  Clone := TADODataSet.Create(nil);
  try
    Clone.Clone(ADODataSet);
```

```
      Clone.FilterGroup := fgPendingRecords;
      Clone.Filtered    := True;
      Result := not (Clone.BOF and Clone.EOF);
      Clone.Close;
    finally
      Clone.Free;
    end;
  end;
```

In this function we clone the original dataset, set the `FilterGroup`, and check to see whether the dataset is at both beginning of file and also end of file. If it is, then no records are pending.

Optimistic Locking

Earlier we looked at the `LockType` property and saw how pessimistic locking worked. In this section, we'll look at optimistic locking, not only because it is the preferred locking type for medium- to high-throughput transactions but also because it is the locking scheme employed by batch updates.

Optimistic locking assumes that there is a low probability that users will attempt to update the same records at the same time and that a conflict is unlikely. As such, the attitude is that all users can edit any record at any time, and we deal with the consequences of conflicts between different users' updates to the same records when the changes are saved. Thus, conflicts are considered an exception to the rule. This means that there are no controls to prevent two users from editing the same record at the same time. The first user to save their changes will succeed. The second user's attempt to update the same record might fail. This behavior is essential for briefcase applications and Web applications, where there is no permanent connection to the database and, therefore, no way to implement pessimistic locking. In contrast with pessimistic locking, optimistic locking has the additional considerable benefit that resources are consumed only momentarily and, therefore, the average resource usage is much lower, making the database more scalable.

Let's consider an example. Assume that we have a TADODataSet connected to the Customers table of Northwind, that `LockType` is set to ltBatchOptimistic, and the contents are displayed in a grid. Assume that we also have a button to call `UpdateBatch`. Run the program twice and begin editing a record in the first copy of the program. Although for the sake of simplicity we will be demonstrating a conflict using just a single machine, the scenario and subsequent events are unchanged when using multiple machines. In this example I will choose the Bottom-Dollar Markets company in Canada and change the name to Bottom-Franc Markets. Save the change, move off the record to post it, and click the button to update the batch. Now, in the second copy of the program, locate the same record and change the company name to Bottom-Pound Markets. Move off the record and click the button to update the batch. It will fail. As with many ADO error messages, the exact message you receive will depend not only on the version of ADO you are using but also on how closely you followed the example. In ADO 2.6, the error message is "Row cannot be located for updating. Some values may have been changed since it was last read." This is the nature of optimistic locking. The update to the record is performed by executing the following SQL statement:

```
UPDATE CUSTOMERS SET CompanyName="Bottom-Pound Markets"
WHERE CustomerID="BOTTM" AND CompanyName="Bottom-Dollar Markets"
```

The number of records affected by this update statement is expected to be 1, because it locates the original record using the primary key and the contents of the CompanyName field as it was when the record was first read. In our example, however, the number of records affected by the UPDATE statement is 0. This can only occur if the record has been deleted, or the record's primary key has changed, or the field that we are changing was changed by someone else. Hence, the update fails.

If our "second user" had changed the ContactName field and not the CompanyName field, then the UPDATE statement would have looked like this:

```
UPDATE CUSTOMERS SET ContactName="Liz Lincoln"
WHERE CustomerID="BOTTM" AND ContactName="Elizabeth Lincoln"
```

In our scenario, this statement would have succeeded because the other user didn't change the primary key or the contact name.

This behavior differs from the BDE's behavior in the same scenario. In this example, using the BDE the attempt to update the contact name would have failed because, by default, the BDE includes every field in the WHERE clause. The consequence of this is that any change to the record will fail if any other user has already changed any field, regardless of whether the changed fields are the same fields or different fields. Fortunately, both the BDE and ADO allow you to specify how you want to locate the original record: in the BDE you use the UpdateMode property, and in ADO the Update Criteria dynamic property of a dataset. The following list shows the possible values that can be assigned to this dynamic property:

Constant	Locate Records By
adCriteriaKey	Primary key columns only
adCriteriaAllCols	All columns
adCriteriaUpdCols	Primary key columns and changed columns only
adCriteriaTimeStamp	Primary key columns and a timestamp column only

The reason why the BDE and ADO differ in their behavior is that their defaults differ. The BDE's default behavior is equivalent to ADO's adCriteriaAllCols, whereas ADO's default is adCriteriaUpdCols. Don't fall into the trap of thinking that one of these settings is better than another for your whole application. In practice, your choice of setting will be influenced by the contents of each table. Say that the Customers table has just `CustomerID`, `Name`, and `City` fields. In this case, the update of any one of these fields is logically not mutually exclusive with the update of any of the other fields, so a good choice for this table would be adCriteriaUpdCols (i.e., the default). If, however, the Customers table included a `PostalCode` field, then the update of a `PostalCode` field would be mutually exclusive with the update of the `City` field by another user (because if the city changes, then surely so should the postal code, and possibly vice versa). In this case, you could argue that adCriteriaAllCols would be a safer solution.

Another issue to be aware of is how ADO deals with errors during the update of multiple records. Using the BDE's cached updates and TClientDataSet, you can use the `OnUpdateError` event to handle each update error as the error occurs and resolve the problem before moving on to the next record. In ADO, you cannot establish such a dialog. You can monitor the progress and success or failure of the updating of the batch using the dataset's `OnWillChangeRecord` and `OnRecordChangeComplete`, but you cannot revise the record and resubmit it during this process as you can with the BDE and TClientDataSet. There's more: if an error occurs during the update process, the updating does not stop. It continues to the end until all updates have been applied or have failed. This can produce a rather unhelpful and blatantly incorrect error message. If more than one record cannot be updated, or the single record that failed is not the last record to be applied, then the error message in ADO 2.6 is "Multiple-step OLE DB operation generated errors. Check each OLE DB status value, if available. No work was done." The last sentence is the problem; it states that "No work was done," but this is incorrect. It is true that no work was done on the record that failed, but other records were successfully applied and their updates stand.

Resolving Update Conflicts

As a consequence of the nature of applying updates, the approach that you need to take to update the batch is to update the batch, let the individual records fail, and then deal with the failed records once the process is over. You can determine which records have failed by setting the dataset's `FilterGroup` to fgConflictingRecords:

```
ADODataSet1.FilterGroup := fgConflictingRecords;
ADODataSet1.Filtered := True;
```

For each failed record, you can inform the user of three critical pieces of information about each field using the following `TField` properties:

Property	Description
NewValue	The value this user changed it to
CurValue	The new value from the database
OldValue	The value when first read from the database

Users of TClientDataSet will be aware of the very handy TReconcileErrorForm dialog, which wraps up the process of showing the user the old and new records and allows them to specify what action to take. Unfortunately, there is no ADO equivalent to this form, and TReconcileErrorForm has been written with TClientDataSet so much in mind that it is difficult to convert it for use with ADO datasets.

One last gotcha to point out when using these TField properties: They are taken straight from the underlying ADO Field objects to which they refer. This means, as is common in ADO, that you are at the mercy of your chosen OLE DB provider to support the features you hope to use. All is well for most providers, but the Jet OLE DB Provider returns the same value for CurValue as it does for OldValue. In other words, if you use Jet, you cannot determine what the other user changed the field to unless you resort to your own measures.

Disconnected Recordsets

All this knowledge of batch updates allows us to take advantage of our next ADO feature: disconnected recordsets. A disconnected recordset is a recordset that has been disconnected from its connection. What is impressive about this feature is that the user cannot tell the difference between a regular recordset and a disconnected one; their feature sets and behavior are almost identical. To disconnect a recordset from its connection, the CursorType must be set to clUseClient and the LockType must be set to ltBatchOptimistic. You then simply tell the dataset that it no longer has a connection:

```
ADODataSet1.Connection := nil;
```

Hereafter, the recordset will continue to contain the same data, support the same navigational features, and allow records to be added, edited, and deleted. The only relevant difference is that you cannot update the batch because you need to be connected to the server to update the server. To reconnect the connection (and use UpdateBatch):

```
ADODataSet1.Connection := ADOConnection1;
```

This same feature is available to the BDE and other database technologies by switching over to TClientDataSets, but the beauty of the ADO solution is that you can build your entire application using dbGo dataset components and be unaware of disconnected recordsets. At the point that you discover this feature and want to take advantage of it, you can continue to use the same components that you always used.

So why would you want to disconnect your recordsets? For two reasons:

- To keep the total number of connections lower
- To create a briefcase application

I'll cover keeping down the number of connections here and return to briefcase applications later. Most regular client/server business applications open tables and maintain a permanent connection to their database while the table is open. However, there are usually only two reasons why you want to be connected to the database: to retrieve data and to update data. If you change your regular client/server application so that, after the table is opened and the data retrieved, then the dataset is disconnected from the connection and the connection dropped, your user will be none the wiser and the application will not need to maintain an open database connection. The following code shows the two steps:

```
ADODataSet1.Connection := nil;
ADOConnection1.Connected := False;
```

The only other point at which a connection is required is when the batch of updates needs to be applied, so the update code would look like this:

```
ADOConnection1.Connected := True;
ADODataSet1.Connection := ADOConnection1;
try
  ADODataSet1.UpdateBatch;
finally
  ADODataSet1.Connection := nil;
  ADOConnection1.Connected := False;
end;
```

If this approach were followed throughout the application, the average number of open connections at any one time would be minimal because the connections would only be open for the small amount of time that they are required. The consequence of this change is scalability; The application will be able to cope with significantly more simultaneous users than one that maintains an open connection. The downside, of course, is that the reopening of the connection can be a lengthy process on some, but not all, database engines, so the application will be slower to update the batch.

Connection Pooling

All of this talk of dropping connections and reopening them brings us to the subject of connection pooling. Connection pooling, not to be confused with session pooling, allows connections to a database to be reused once they have been finished with. This happens automatically and, if your OLE DB provider supports it and it is enabled, you need take no action to take advantage of connection pooling. There is a single reason why you would want to pool your connections: performance. The problem with database connections is that it can take time to establish a connection. In a desktop database such as Access, this is typically a small amount of time. In a client/server database such as Oracle used on a network, this time could be measured in seconds. Given such an expensive (in performance terms) resource, it makes sense to promote its reuse. With ADO's connection pooling enabled, ADO Connection objects are placed in a pool when the application "destroys" them. Subsequent attempts to create an ADO connection will automatically search the connection pool for a connection with the same connection string. If a suitable connection is found, it is reused; otherwise, a new connection is created. The connections themselves stay in the pool until they are reused, the application closes, or they time out. By default, connections will time out after 60 seconds, but from MDAC 2.5 onward you can set this using the HKEY_CLASSES_ROOT\CLSID\<ProviderCLSID>\SPTimeout registry key. The connection pooling process occurs seamlessly, without the intervention or knowledge of the developer. This process is similar to the BDE's database pooling under Microsoft Transaction Server (MTS) and COM+, with the important exception that ADO performs its own connection pooling without the aid of MTS or COM+.

By default, connection pooling is enabled on all of the MDAC OLE DB providers for relational databases (including SQL Server and Oracle) with the notable exception of the Jet OLE DB Provider. If you use ODBC you should choose between ODBC's connection pooling and ADO's connection pooling, but you should not use both. From MDAC 2.1 on, ADO's connection pooling is enabled and ODBC's is disabled.

NOTE Connection pooling does not occur on Windows 95 regardless of the OLE DB provider.

To be truly comfortable with connection pooling, you will need to see the connections getting pooled and timed out. Unfortunately, there are no adequate ADO connection pool spying tools available at the time of writing, so we will use SQL Server's Performance Monitor as it can accurately spy on SQL Server database connections. Figure 16.7 is a look at SQL Server's Performance Monitor with all of the "counters" deleted except User Connections. This allows us to concentrate of the subject of connection pooling.

The Last field under the graph shows us the number of active connections to the database.

To see how connection pooling works, you can set up a very simple test. Create a new application and add a TADOConnection to the form. Set the ConnectionString to use the SQL Server OLE DB Provider and the Northwind database but leave Connected as False. Now add a check box with the following OnClick event:

```
procedure TForm1.CheckBox1Click(Sender: TObject);
begin
  ADOConnection1.Connected := CheckBox1.Checked;
end;
```

FIGURE 16.7:

SQL Server's Performance Monitor

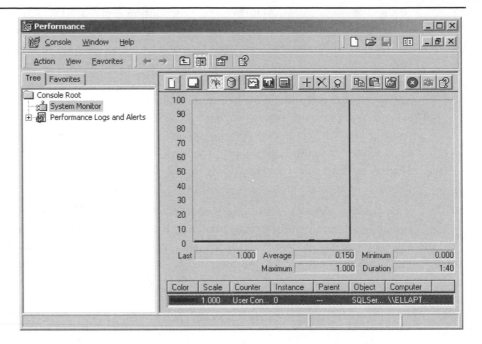

Run the program and make sure that you can see the Performance Monitor at the same time. Now click the check box to open the connection. In the Performance Monitor, you will see the connection count increase by one. Now close the application and the count immediately decreases by one, because the connection pool is destroyed with the application. Now rerun the program, check the check box, and check it a second time to close the connection. You will see that the connection count does not decrease by one. Observe Performance Monitor for a further 60 seconds, and the connection count will then decrease by one when the pooled connection times out.

You can enable or disable connection pooling either in the Registry or in the connection string. The key in the Registry is OLEDB_SERVICES and can be found at HKEY_CLASSES_ROOT\ CLSID\<ProviderCLSID>. It is a bit array that allows you to disable several OLE DB services, including connection pooling, transaction enlistment, and the cursor engine. To disable connection pooling using the connection string, include ";OLE DB Services=-2" at the end of the connection string. To enable connection pooling for the Jet OLE DB Provider, you can include ";OLE DB Services=-1" at the end of the connection string, which enables all OLE DB services.

Persistent Recordsets

One of the very useful features that contributes to the briefcase model is persistent record-sets. These allow you to save the contents of any recordset to a local file, which can be loaded later. Apart from aiding with the briefcase model, this feature allows developers to create true single-tier applications. It means that you can deploy a database application without having to deploy a database. This makes for a very small footprint on your client's machine.

You can "persist" your datasets using the SaveToFile method:

```
ADODataSet1.SaveToFile('Local.ADTG');
```

This will save the data and its delta in a file on your hard disk. You can reload this file using the LoadFromFile method, which accepts a single parameter indicating the file to load. The format of the file is Advanced Data Table Gram (ADTG), which is a proprietary Microsoft format. It does, however, have the advantage of being very efficient. If you prefer, you can save the file as XML by passing a second parameter to SaveToFile:

```
ADODataSet1.SaveToFile('Local.XML', pfXML);
```

However, ADO does not have its own built-in XML parser (as TClientDataSet does), so it must use the MSXML parser. Your user must either install Internet Explorer 5 or later or download the MSXML parser from the Microsoft Web site. If you intend to persist your files locally in XML format, be aware of a few disadvantages. First, the saving and loading of XML files is slower than the saving and loading of ADTG files. Second, ADO's XML files (and XML files in general) are significantly larger than their ADTG counterparts (XML files are typically twice as large as their ADTG counterparts). Third, ADO's XML format is specific to Microsoft, as most companies' XML implementations are. This means that the XML generated in ADO is not readable by Borland's TClientDataSet and vice versa. In fact, it's worse than that, because the XML generated in ADO 2.1 is incompatible with the XML in ADO 2.5. Fortunately this last problem can be overcome using Delphi 6's new TXML-Transform component, which can be used to translate between different XML structures.

If you intend to use these features solely for single-tier applications and not as part of the briefcase model, then you can save yourself a little effort by using a TADODataSet and setting its CommandType to cmdFile and its CommandText to the name of the file. This will save you the effort of having to call LoadFromFile manually. You will, however, still have to call SaveToFile. In a briefcase application, however, this approach is too limiting, as the dataset can be used in two different modes.

The Briefcase Model

Our new-found knowledge of batch updates, disconnected recordsets, and persistent record-sets allows us to take advantage of the "briefcase model." The idea behind the briefcase model is that your users want to be able to use your application while they are out on the road. They want to take the same application that they use on the desktops in the office and use it on their laptops while on their clients' sites. The problem with this scenario traditionally is that when your users are at their clients' sites, they are not connected to their database server, because their database server is running on their network back at their office. Consequently, there is no data on their laptop, and the data cannot be updated anyway.

This is where that new-found knowledge comes in. Assume that the application has already been written; the user has requested this new briefcase enhancement, and you have to retrofit it into your existing application. You need to add a new option for your users to allow them to "prepare" the briefcase application. This simply consists of executing SaveToFile for each and every table in the database. The result is a collection of ADTG or XML files that mirror the contents of the database. These files are then copied to the laptop where a copy of the application has previously been installed.

The application needs to be sensitive to whether it is running locally or connected to the network. You can decide this either by attempting to connect to the database and seeing whether it fails, by detecting the presence of a local "briefcase" file, or by creating some flag of your own design. If the application decides it is running in briefcase mode, then it needs to use LoadFromFile for each table instead of setting Connected to True for the TADOConnections and Active to True for the ADO datasets. Thereafter, the briefcase application needs to use SaveToFile instead of UpdateBatch whenever data is saved. Upon return to the office, there needs to be an update process where each table is loaded from its local file, the dataset is connected to the database, and the changes are applied using UpdateBatch. Voilà, the briefcase model.

Deploying MDAC

MDAC, and therefore ADO, can be almost freely distributed. There are some conditions on its distribution, but these are to protect Microsoft from unreasonable behavior and it is unlikely that regular application developers will fall afoul of them. To distribute MDAC, you distribute and execute MDAC_TYP.EXE. You may not distribute and install MDAC components individually. If you use InstallShield Express For Delphi, then you will have to run MDAC_TYP.EXE separately from your regular InstallShield Setup program, because InstallShield Express For Delphi cannot shell out to an external program—i.e., MDAC_TYP.EXE. If you use an installation program that can shell out to another program, you might want to be aware of some of the parameters you can pass to `MDAC_TYP.EXE`. The various parameters affect whether the user has to specifically accept the end user license, whether the file copy dialog is shown, whether there is an automatic reboot on completion (or the user decides to reboot or there is no reboot), and, finally, whether `MDACSET.LOG` is a summary log file or a full log file. The /Q parameter is a quiet, but not completely silent, setup. A truly silent setup can be achieved with `/Q:A /C:"setup /QNT"` parameters. See the Platform SDK for a complete list of setup parameters. Although I have not tested installing every version of MDAC on top of every other version of MDAC, my experience is that, despite the progress bar indicating the successful progress of the installation, an earlier version of MDAC does not overwrite a later version of MDAC.

In addition to installing MDAC, you will also need to install DCOM if the target is Windows 95.

One invaluable tool that you should add to your toolbox is Component Checker. This is available for free download from `www.microsoft.com/data/download.htm`. Component Checker is the most accurate method of determining which version of MDAC is installed on a machine. It scans for all ADO, OLE DB, and ODBC files and gets their version numbers. It can compare all of these version numbers against its own internal database of correct version numbers for each release of MDAC. At the end of its analysis, it reveals the version of MDAC that most closely matches the files installed on a machine. It is also useful as a kind of "REGEDIT For MDAC," as it reports on all of the MDAC registry information using a considerably more relevant user interface than REGEDIT. Finally, it is the only safe way of removing MDAC from a machine.

ADO.NET

ADO.NET is part of Microsoft's new dotNet (or ".NET") architecture—their redesign of application development tools to better suit the needs of Web development. At the time of writing, Visual Studio.NET was in beta, so this section has been included solely as a means to give you an idea of where ADO is heading.

ADO.NET is a revolution of ADO. It looks at the problems of Web development and addresses shortcomings of ADO's solution. The problem with ADO's solution is that it is based on COM. For one- and two-tier applications, COM imposes few problems, but in the world of Web development it is unacceptable as a transport mechanism. COM suffers from three main problems for use in Web development: it (mostly) runs only on Windows; the transmission of recordsets from one process requires COM marshalling; and COM calls cannot penetrate corporate firewalls. ADO.NET's solution to all of these problems is to use XML.

Continued on next page

Some other redesign issues focus around breaking up the ADO recordset into separate classes. The resulting classes are adept at solving a single problem instead of multiple problems. For example, the ADO.NET class currently called `DataSetReader` is very similar to a read-only, forward-only server-side recordset and, as such, is best suited to reading a result set very quickly. A `DataTable` is most like a disconnected, client-side recordset. A `DataRelation` has similarities with the MSDataShape OLE DB Provider. So you can see that your knowledge of how ADO works is of great benefit in understanding the basic principles of ADO.NET.

If you wish to experiment with ADO.NET in Delphi before direct support is added to Delphi, then you will need to give Delphi access to the ADO.NET classes, which are called "managed" classes and are based on a new run-time environment called the Common Language Runtime (CLR). These classes are not COM classes and, as such, Delphi cannot normally access them. However, Visual Studio.NET includes a utility called `REGASM.EXE`, which takes any "assembly" (library of managed classes) and creates a COM type library interface to the managed classes. As Delphi can easily access COM classes, simply import the resulting type library into Delphi and use the classes as if they were COM classes.

What's Next?

This chapter described ActiveX Data Objects (ADO) and dbGo, the set of Delphi components for accessing the ADO interfaces. You've seen how to take advantage of Microsoft Data Access Components (MDAC) and various server engines, and I've described some of the benefits and hurdles you'll encounter in using ADO.

The next chapter will take you into the world of Delphi's DataSnap architecture, for developing custom client and server applications in a three-tier environment.

CHAPTER 17

Multitier Database Applications with DataSnap

- Logical three-tier architecture

- The technical foundation of DataSnap

- The connection protocols and the data packets

- Delphi's support components (client-side and server-side)

- The connections broker and other new Delphi 6 features

Large companies often have broader needs than applications using local database and SQL servers can meet. In the past few years, Borland Software Corporation has been addressing the needs of large corporations, and it even temporarily changed its own name to Inprise to underline this new enterprise focus. The name was changed back to Borland, but the focus on enterprise development remains.

Delphi is targeting many different technologies: three-tier architectures based on Windows NT and DCOM, CORBA architectures based on NT and Unix servers, TCP/IP and socket applications, and—most of all—SOAP- and XML-based Web services. This chapter focuses on database-oriented multitier architectures, while XML-oriented solutions will be discussed in Chapter 23, "XML and SOAP."

Even though I haven't yet discussed COM and sockets (covered in Chapters 19 to 21), in this chapter we'll build multitier architectures based on those technologies. As we'll use high-level Delphi support, not knowing the details of some of the foundations should not create any problem. I'll concentrate more on the programming aspects of these architectures than on installation and configuration (the latter aspects are subject to change across different operating systems and are too complex to cover thoroughly).

Before proceeding, I should emphasize two important elements. First, the tools to support this kind of development are available only in the Enterprise version of Delphi; and second, you'll have to pay a license fee to Borland in order to deploy the necessary server-side software for DataSnap. This second requirement makes this architecture cost-effective mainly for large systems (that is, servers connected to dozens or even hundreds of clients). The license fee is only required for deployment of the server application and is a flat fee for each server you deploy to (regardless of the number of clients that will connect). The license fee is not required for development or evaluation purposes.

NOTE   You spend money on the DataSnap license, but you might save on the SQL server client licenses. When SQL server licenses were based on the number of connections, companies have saved tens of thousands of dollars in those licenses by connecting the hundreds of clients to a few instances of the DataSnap server, using few connections with the SQL server. Nowadays, the licenses for most SQL servers are based on the number of users who connect to the database, not the number of connections active at each time, so this kind of savings doesn't always apply.

One, Two, Three Levels

Initially, database PC applications were client-only solutions: the program and the database files were on the same computer. From there, adventuresome programmers moved the database files onto a network file server. The client computers still hosted the application software and the entire database engine, but the database files were now accessible to several users at the same time. You can still use this type of configuration with a Delphi application and Paradox files (or, of course, Paradox itself), but the approach was much more widespread just few years ago.

The next big transition was to client/server development, embraced by Delphi since its first version. In the client/server world, the client computer requests the data from a server computer, which hosts both the database files and a database engine to access them. This architecture downplays the role of the client, but it also reduces its requirements for processing power on the client machine. Depending on how the programmers implement client/server, the server can do most (if not all) of the data processing. In this way, a powerful server can provide data services to several less powerful clients.

Naturally, there are many other reasons for using centralized database servers, such as the concern for data security and integrity, simpler backup strategies, central management of data constraints, and so on. The database server is often called a SQL server, because SQL is the language most commonly used for making queries into the data, but it may also be called a DBMS (database management system), reflecting the fact that the server provides tools for managing the data, such as support for backup and replication.

Of course, some applications you build may not need the benefits of a full DBMS, so a simple client-only solution might be sufficient. On the other hand, you might need some of the robustness of a DBMS system, but on a single, isolated computer. In this case, you can use a local version of a SQL server, such as InterBase. Traditional client/server development is done with a two-tier architecture. However, if the DBMS is primarily performing data storage instead of data- and number-crunching, the client might contain both user interface code (formatting the output and input with customized reports, data-entry forms, query screens, and so on) and code related to managing the data (also known as *business rules*). In this case, it's generally a good idea to try to separate these two sections of the program and build a logical three-tier architecture. The term *logical* here means that there are still just two computers (that is, two physical tiers), but we've now partitioned the application into three distinct elements.

Delphi 2 introduced support for a logical three-tier architecture with data modules. As you'll recall, a *data module* is a nonvisual container for the data access components of an application, but it often includes several handlers for database-related events. You can share a single data module among several different forms and provide different user interfaces for the same data; there might be one or more data-input forms, reports, master/detail forms, and various charting or dynamic output forms.

The logical three-tier approach solves many problems, but it also has a few drawbacks. First, you must replicate the data-management portion of the program on different client computers, which might hamper performance, but a bigger issue is the complexity this adds to code maintenance. Second, when multiple clients modify the same data, there's no simple way to handle the resulting update conflicts. Finally, for logical three-tier Delphi applications, you must install and configure the database engine (if any) and SQL server client library on every client computer.

The next logical step up from client/server is to move the data-module portion of the application to a separate server computer and design all the client programs to interact with it. This is exactly the purpose of remote data modules, which were introduced in Delphi 3. Remote data modules run on a server computer—generally called the application server. The application server in turn communicates with the DBMS (which can run on the application server or on another dedicated computer). Therefore, the client machines don't connect to the SQL server directly, but indirectly via the application server.

At this point there is a fundamental question: Do we still need to install the database access software? The traditional Delphi client/server architecture (even with three logical tiers) requires you to install the database access on each client, something quite troublesome when you must configure and maintain hundreds of machines. In the physical three-tier architecture, you need to install and configure the database access only on the application server, not on the client computers. Since the client programs have only user interface code and are extremely simple to install, they now fall into the category of so-called *thin clients*. To use marketing-speak, we might even call this a *zero-configuration thin-client architecture*. But let us focus on technical issues instead of marketing terminology.

The Technical Foundation of DataSnap

When Borland introduced this physical multitier architecture in Delphi, it was called MIDAS (Middle-tier Distributed Application Services). For example, Delphi 5 included the third version of this technology, MIDAS 3. Now Delphi 6 renames this technology as *DataSnap* and extends its capabilities.

DataSnap requires the installation of specific libraries on the server (actually the middle-tier computer), which provides your client computers with the data extracted from the SQL server database or other data sources. DataSnap does not require a SQL server for data storage. DataSnap can serve up data from a wide variety of sources, including SQL, CORBA, other DataSnap servers, or just data computed on the fly.

As you would expect, the client side of DataSnap is extremely thin and easy to deploy. The only file you need is `Midas.dll`, a small (260 KB) DLL that implements the `ClientDataSet` and `RemoteServer` components and provides the connection to the application server. As we've seen in Chapter 14, "Client/Server Programming," this DLL is basically a small, stand-alone database engine. It caches data from a remote data module and enforces the rules requested by the Constraint Broker.

The application server uses the same DLL to handle the datasets (called *deltas*) returned from the clients when they post updated or new records. However, the server also requires several other libraries, all of which are installed by DataSnap.

The *IAppServer* Interface

Starting with Delphi 5, the two sides of a DataSnap application communicate using the `IAppServer` interface.

> **NOTE** In Delphi 5 (and 6), the `IAppServer` interface supersedes Delphi 4's `IProvider` interface. The main reason for this change was support for stateless objects. With `IProvider`, the server stored status information about the client program—for example, which records had already been passed to the client. This made it difficult to adapt the server-side objects to stateless connection layers, like CORBA message queues and MTS, and also to move toward HTTP and Web-based support. Other reasons for moving to this new architecture were to make the system more dynamic (providers are now exported by setting a property, not by changing the type library) and to reduce the number of calls, or *round-trips*, which can affect performance. DataSnap makes fewer calls but delivers more data each time.

The `IAppServer` interface has the following methods:

```
AS_ApplyUpdates
AS_GetRecords
AS_DataRequest
AS_GetProviderNames
AS_GetParams
AS_RowRequest
AS_Execute
```

You'll seldom need to call them directly, anyway, because there are Delphi components to be used on the client and server sides of the application that embed these calls, making them easier (and at times even hiding them completely). In practice, the server will make available to the client objects implementing this interface, possibly along with other custom interfaces.

> **NOTE** A DataSnap server exposes an interface using a COM type library, a technology I'll discuss in Chapter 20, "Automation, ActiveX, and Other COM Technologies."

The Connection Protocol

DataSnap defines only the higher-level architecture and can use different technologies for moving the data from the middle tier to the client side. DataSnap supports most of the leading standards, including the following:

Distributed COM (DCOM) and Stateless COM (MTS or COM+)   DCOM is directly available in Windows NT/2000 and 98/Me, and it requires no additional run-time applications on the server. You still have to install it on Windows 95 machines. DCOM is basically an extension of COM technology (discussed in Chapter 19, "COM Programming," and Chapter 20) that allows a client application to use server objects that exist and execute on a separate computer. The DCOM infrastructure allows you to use stateless COM objects, available in the COM+ and in the older MTS (Microsoft Transaction Server) architectures. Both COM+ and MTS provide features such as security, component management, and database transactions, and are available in Windows NT/2000 and in Windows 98/Me.

Due to the complexity of DCOM configuration and of its problems in passing through firewalls, even Microsoft is abandoning DCOM in favor of SOAP-based solutions.

TCP/IP sockets   These are available on most systems. Using TCP/IP you might distribute clients over the Web, where DCOM cannot be taken for granted, and have many fewer configuration headaches. To use sockets, the middle-tier computer must run the ScktSrvr.exe application provided by Borland, a single program that can run either as an application or as a service. This program receives the client requests and forwards them to the remote data module (executing on the same server) using COM. Sockets provide no protection against failure on the client side, as the server is not informed and might not release resources when a client unexpectedly shuts down.

HTTP and SOAP   The use of HTTP as a transport protocol over the Internet simplifies connections through firewalls or proxy servers (which generally don't like custom TCP/IP sockets). You need a specific Web server application, httpsrvr.dll, which accepts client requests and creates the proper remote data modules using COM. These Web connections can use SSL security but must register themselves by adding a call to EnableWebTransport in the UpdateRegistry method. Finally, Web connections based on HTTP transport can use DataSnap object-pooling support.

NOTE   The DataSnap HTTP transport can use XML as the data packet format, enabling any platform or tool that can read XML to participate in a DataSnap architecture. This is an extension of the original DataSnap data packet format, which is also platform-independent. The use of XML over HTTP is also the foundation of SOAP. There's more on XML in Chapter 23.

CORBA   Common Object Request Broker Architecture is an official standard for object management available on most operating systems. Compared to DCOM, the advantage is that your client and server applications can be also written with Java and other products. The Borland implementation of CORBA, VisiBroker, is available with Delphi Enterprise. CORBA provides many benefits, including location transparency, load balancing, and fail-over from the ORB run-time software. (An in-depth discussion of CORBA is certainly beyond the scope of this book, and in practice only a limited number of Delphi programmers use CORBA.)

Internet Express   As an extension to this architecture, you can transform the data packets into XML and deliver them to a Web browser. In this case, you basically have one extra tier: the Web server gets the data from the middle tier and delivers it to the client. I'll discuss this new architecture, called Internet Express, in Chapter 23. The DLL can also be folded into the executable file by using the MidasLib unit.

Providing Data Packets

The entire Delphi multitier data-access architecture centers around the idea of *data packets*. In this context, a data packet is a block of data that moves from the application server to the client or from the client back to the server. Technically, a data packet is a sort of subset of a dataset. It describes the data it contains (usually a few records of data), and it lists the names and types of the data fields. Even more important, a data packet includes the constraints—that is, the rules to be applied to the dataset. You'll typically set these constraints in the application server, and the server sends them to the client applications along with the data.

All communication between the client and the server occurs by exchanging data packets. The provider component on the server manages the transmission of several data packets within a big dataset, with the goal of responding faster to the user. As the client receives a data packet, in a ClientDataSet component, the user can edit the records it contains. As mentioned earlier, during this process the client also receives and checks the constraints, which are applied during the editing operations.

When the client has updated the records and sends a data packet back, that packet is known as a *delta*. The delta packet tracks the difference between the original records and the updated ones, recording all the changes the client requested from the server. When the client asks to apply the updates to the server, it sends the delta to the server, and the server tries to apply each of the changes. I say *tries* because if a server is connected to several clients, the data might have changed already, and the update request might fail.

Since the delta packet includes the original data, the server can quickly determine if another client has already changed it. If so, the server fires an OnReconcileError event, which is one of the vital elements for thin-client applications. In other words, the three-tier architecture uses an update mechanism similar to the one Delphi uses for cached updates. As we have seen in Chapter 14, "Client/Server Programming Techniques," the ClientDataSet manages data in a memory cache, and it typically reads only a subset of the records available on the server side, loading more elements only as they're needed. When the client updates records or inserts new ones, it stores these pending changes in another local cache on the client, the *delta cache*.

The client can also save the data packets to disk and work off-line, thanks to the MyBase support discussed in Chapter 13, "Delphi's Database Architecture." Even error information and other data moves using the data packet protocol, so it is truly one of the foundation elements of this architecture.

NOTE   It's important to remember that data packets are protocol-independent. A data packet is merely a sequence of bytes, so anywhere you can move a series of bytes, you can move a data packet. This was done to make the architecture suitable for multiple transport protocols (including DCOM, CORBA, HTTP, and TCP/IP) and for multiple platforms.

Delphi Support Components (Client-Side)

Now that we've examined the general foundations of Delphi's three-tier architecture, we can focus on the components that support it. For developing client applications, Delphi provides the ClientDataSet component, which provides all the standard dataset capabilities and embeds the client side of the IAppServer interface. In this case, the data is delivered through the remote connection.

The connection to the server application is made via another component you'll also need in the client application. You should use one of the four specific connection components (available in the DataSnap page):

- The DCOMConnection component can be used on the client side to connect to a DCOM and MTS server, located either on the current computer or in another one indicated by the ComputerName property. The connection is with a registered object having a given ServerGUID or ServerName.

- The CorbaConnection component can be used to hook with a CORBA server. You indicate the HostName (the name or IP address) to indicate the server computer, the RepositoryID to request a specific data module on the server, and optionally the ObjectName property if the data module exports multiple objects.

- The SocketConnection component can be used to connect to the server via a TCP/IP socket. You should indicate the IP address or the host name, and the GUID of the server object (in the InterceptGUID property). In Delphi 5, this connection component has an extra property, SupportCallbacks, which you can disable if you are not using callbacks and want to deploy your program on Windows 95 computers that don't have Winsock 2 installed.

NOTE   In the WebServices page, you can also find the SoapConnection component, which requires a specific type of server and will be discussed in Chapter 23.

- The WebConnection component is used to handle an HTTP connection that can easily get through a firewall. You should indicate the URL where your copy of httpsrvr.dll is located and the name or GUID of the remote object on the server.

Delphi 6 adds new client-side components to the DataSnap architecture, mainly for managing connections:

- The ConnectionBroker component can be used as an alias of an actual connection component, something useful when you have a single application with multiple client datasets. In fact, to change the physical connection of each of the datasets, you only need to change the Connection property of the ConnectionBroker. You can also use the events of this virtual connection component in place of those of the actual connections, so you don't have to change any code if you change the data transport technology. For the same reason, you can refer to the AppServer object of the ConnectionBroker instead of the corresponding property of a physical connection.

- The SharedConnection component can be used to connect to a secondary (or child) data module of a remote application, piggy-backing on an existing physical connection to the main data module. In other words, an application can connect to multiple data modules of the server with a single, shared connection.

- The LocalConnection component can be used to target a local dataset provider as the source of the data packet. The same effect can be obtained by hooking the ClientDataSet directory to the provider. However, using the LocalConnection, you can write a local application with the same code as a complete multitier application, using the IAppServer interface of the "fake" connection. This will make the program easier to scale up, compared to a program with a direct connection.

A few other components of the DataSnap page relate to the transformation of the DataSnap data packet into custom XML formats. These components (XMLTransform, XMLTransform-Provider, and XMLTransformClient) will be discussed in Chapter 23.

Delphi Support Components (Server-Side)

On the server side (or actually the middle tier), you'll need to create an application or a library that embeds a remote data module, a special version of the TDataModule class. There are actually specialized remote data modules for transactional COM and CORBA support. In the Multitier page of the New Items dialog box (obtained with the File ➢ New ➢ Others menu) are specific wizards to create remote data modules of each of these types.

The only specific component you need on the server side is the DataSetProvider. You need one of these components for every table or query you want to make available to the client applications, which will then use a separate ClientDataSet component for every exported dataset. The DataSetProvider was already introduced in Chapter 14.

NOTE   The DataSetProvider component of Delphi 5 and 6 supersedes the stand-alone Provider component of Delphi 4 and the internal Provider object, which was embedded in the TBDEDataSet subclasses.

Building a Sample Application

Now we're ready to build a sample program. This will allow us to observe some of the components I've just described in action, and it will also allow us to focus on some other problems, shedding light on other pieces of the Delphi multitier puzzle. I'll build the client and application server portions of a three-tier application in two steps. The first step will simply test the technology using a bare minimum of elements. These programs will be very simple.

From that point, we'll add more power to the client and the application server. In each of the examples, we'll display data from local Paradox tables, and we'll set up everything to allow you to test the programs on a stand-alone computer. I won't cover the steps you have to follow to install the examples on multiple computers with various technologies—that would be the subject of at least one other book.

The First Application Server

The server side of our basic example is very easy to build. Simply create a new application and add a remote data module to it using the corresponding icon in the Multitier page of the Object Repository. The simple Remote Data Module Wizard (see Figure 17.1) will ask you for a class name and the instancing style. As you enter a class name, such as AppServerOne, and click the OK button, Delphi will add a data module to the program. This data module will have the usual properties and events, but its class will have the following Pascal declaration:

```
type
  TAppServerOne = class(TRemoteDataModule, IAppServerOne)
  private
```

```
        end
    end
```

What about the main form of this program? Well, it's almost useless, so we can simply add a label to it indicating that it's the form of the server application. When you've built the server, you should compile it and run it once. This operation will automatically register it as an Automation server on your system, making it available to client applications. Of course, you should register the server on the computer where you want it to run, either the client or the middle tier.

The First Thin Client

Now that we have a working server, we can build a client that will connect to it. We'll again start with a standard Delphi application and add a DCOMConnection component to it (or the proper component for the specific type of connection you want to test). This component defines a ComputerName property that you'll use to specify the computer that hosts the application server. If you want to test the client and application server from the same computer, you can leave this blank.

Once you've selected an application server computer, you can simply display the ServerName property's combo-box list to view the available DataSnap servers. This combo box shows the servers' registered names, by default the name of the executable file of the server followed by the name of the remote data module class, as in AppServ1.AppServerOne. Alternatively, you can type the GUID of the server object in the ServerGUID property. Delphi will automatically fill this property as you set the ServerName property, determining the GUID by looking it up in the Registry.

At this point, if you set the DCOMConnection component's Connected property to True, the server form will appear, indicating that the client has activated the server. You don't usually need to perform this operation, because the ClientDataSet component typically activates the RemoteServer component for you. I've suggested this simply to emphasize what's happening behind the scenes.

TIP   You should generally leave the DCOMConnection component's Connected property set to False at design time, to be able to open the project in Delphi even on a computer where the DataSnap server is not already registered.

As you might expect, the next step is to add a ClientDataSet component to the form. You must connect the ClientDataSet to the DCOMConnection1 component via the RemoteServer property, and thereby to one of the providers it exports. You can see the list of available providers in the ProviderName property, via the usual combo box. In this example, you'll be able to select only DataSetProvider1, as this is the only provider available in the server we've just built. This operation connects the dataset in the client's memory with the dbExpress dataset on the server. If you activate the client dataset and add a few data-aware controls (or a DBGrid), you'll immediately see the server data appear in them, as illustrated in Figure 17.2.

FIGURE 17.2:

When you activate a ClientDataSet component connected to a remote data module at design time, the data from the server becomes visible as usual.

DEPT_NO	EMP_NO	FIRST_NAME	FULL_NAME	HIRE
600	2	Robert	Nelson, Robert	12/28
621	4	Bruce	Young, Bruce	12/28
130	5	Kim	Lambert, Kim	2/6/1
180	8	Leslie	Johnson, Leslie	4/5/1
622	9	Phil	Forest, Phil	4/17/
130	11	K. J.	Weston, K. J.	1/17/
000	12	Terri	Lee, Terri	5/1/1
900	14	Stewart	Hall, Stewart	6/4/1
623	15	Katherine	Young, Katherine	6/14/
671	20	Chris	Papadopoulos, Chris	1/1/1
671	24	Pete	Fisher, Pete	9/12/
120	28	Ann	Bennet, Ann	2/1/1
623	29	Roger	De Souza, Roger	2/18/
110	34	Janet	Baldwin, Janet	3/21/

Here is the DFM file for our minimal client application, ThinCli1:

```
object Form1: TForm1
  Caption = 'ThinClient1'
  object DBGrid1: TDBGrid
    Align = alClient
    DataSource = DataSource1
  end
  object DCOMConnection1: TDCOMConnection
    ServerGUID = '{09E11D63-4A55-11D3-B9F1-00000100A27B}'
    ServerName = 'AppServ1.AppServerOne'
  end
  object ClientDataSet1: TClientDataSet
    Aggregates = <>
    Params = <>
    ProviderName = 'DataSetProvider1'
    RemoteServer = DCOMConnection1
  end
  object DataSource1: TDataSource
    DataSet = ClientDataSet1
  end
end
```

Obviously, the programs of our first three-tier application are quite simple, but they demonstrate how to create a dataset viewer that splits the work between two different executable files. At this point, our client is only a viewer. If you edit the data on the client, it won't be updated on the server. To accomplish this, you'll need to add some more code to the client. However, before we do that, let's add some features to the server.

Adding Constraints to the Server

When you write a traditional data module in Delphi, you can easily add some of the application logic, or business rules, by handling the dataset events, and by setting field object properties and handling their events. You should avoid doing this work on the client application; instead, write your business rules on the middle tier.

In the DataSnap architecture, you can send some constraints from the server to the client and let the client program impose those constraints during the user input. You can also send field properties (such as minimum and maximum values and the display and edit masks) to the client and (using some of the data access technologies) process updates through the dataset used to access the data (or a companion UpdateSql object).

Field and Table Constraints

When the provider interface creates data packets to send to the client, it includes the field definitions, the table and field constraints, and one or more records (as requested by the ClientDataSet component). This implies that you can customize the middle tier and build distributed application logic by using SQL-based constraints.

The constraints you create using SQL expressions can be assigned to an entire dataset or to specific fields. The provider sends the constraints to the client along with the data, and the client applies them before sending updates back to the server. This reduces network traffic, compared to having the client send updates back to the application server and eventually up to the SQL server, only to find that the data is invalid. Another advantage of coding the constraints on the server side is that if the business rules change, you need to update the single server application and not the many clients on multiple computers.

But how do you write constraints? There are several properties you can use:

- BDE datasets have a `Constraints` property, which is a collection of `TCheckConstraint` objects. Every object has a few properties, including the expression and the error message.

- Each field object defines the `CustomConstraint` and `ConstraintErroMessage` properties. There is also an `ImportedConstraint` property for constraints imported from the SQL server.

- Each field object has also a `DefaultExpression` property, which can be used locally or passed to the ClientDataSet. This is not an actual constraint, only a suggestion to the end user.

Our next example, AppServ2, adds a few constraints to a remote data module connected to the sample EMPLOYEE InterBase database. After connecting the table to the database and creating the field objects for it, you can set the following special properties:

```
object SQLDataSet1: TSQLDataSet
  ...
  object SQLDataSet1EMP_NO: TSmallintField
    CustomConstraint = 'x > 0 and x < 10000'
    ConstraintErrorMessage =
      'Employee number must be a positive integer below 10000'
    FieldName = 'EMP_NO'
  end
  object SQLDataSet1FIRST_NAME: TStringField
    CustomConstraint = 'x <> '#39#39
    ConstraintErrorMessage = 'The first name is required'
    FieldName = 'FIRST_NAME'
    Size = 15
  end
  object SQLDataSet1LAST_NAME: TStringField
    CustomConstraint = 'not x is null'
    ConstraintErrorMessage = 'The last name is required'
    FieldName = 'LAST_NAME'
  end
end
```

NOTE   The expression 'x <> '#39#39 is the DFM transposition of the string x <> '', indicating that we don't want to have an empty string. The final constraint, not x is null, instead allows empty strings but not null values.

Including Field Properties

You can control whether the properties of the field objects on the middle tier are sent to the ClientDataSet (and copied into the corresponding field objects of the client side), by using the poIncFieldProps value of the Options property of the DataSetProvider. This flag controls the download of the field properties Alignment, DisplayLabel, DisplayWidth, Visible, DisplayFormat, EditFormat, MaxValue, MinValue, Currency, EditMask, and DisplayValues, if they are available in the field. Here is an example of another field of the AppServ2 example with some custom properties:

```
object SQLDataSet1SALARY: TBCDField
  DefaultExpression = '10000'
  FieldName = 'SALARY'
  DisplayFormat = '#,###'
  EditFormat = '####'
  Precision = 15
  Size = 2
end
```

With this setting, you can simply write your middle tier the way you usually set the fields of a standard client/server application. This approach also makes it faster to move existing applications from a client/server to a multitier architecture. The main drawback of sending fields to the client is that transmitting all the extra information takes time. Turning off `poIncFieldProps` can dramatically improve network performance of datasets with many columns.

A server can generally filter the fields returned to the client; it does this by declaring persistent field objects with the Fields editor and omitting some of the fields. Because a field you're filtering out might be required to identify the record for future updates (if the field is part of the primary key), you can also use the field's `ProviderFlags` property on the server to send the field value to the client but make it unavailable to the ClientDataSet component (this provides some extra security, compared to sending the field to the client and hiding it there).

Field and Table Events

You can write middle-tier dataset and field event handlers as usual and let the dataset process the updates received by the client in the traditional way. This means that updates are considered to be operations on the dataset, exactly as when a user is directly editing, inserting, or deleting fields locally.

This is accomplished by setting the `ResolveToDataSet` property of the `TDatasetProvider` component, again connecting either the dataset used for input or a second one used for the updates. This approach is possible with datasets supporting editing operations. These includes BDE, ADO, and InterBase Express datasets, but not those of the new dbExpress architecture.

With this technique, the updates are performed by the dataset, which implies a lot of control (the standard events are being triggered) but generally slower performance. Flexibility is much greater, as you can use standard coding practices. Also, porting existing local or client/ server database applications, which use dataset and field events, is much more straightforward with this model. However, keep in mind that the user of the client program will receive your error messages only when the local cache (the delta) is sent back to the middle tier. Saying to the user that some data prepared half an hour ago is not valid might be a little awkward. If you follow this approach, you'll probably need to apply the updates in the cache at every `AfterPost` event on the client side.

Finally, if you decide to let the dataset and not the provider do the updates, Delphi helps you a lot in handling possible exceptions. Any exceptions raised by the middle-tier update events (for example, `OnBeforePost`) are automatically transformed by Delphi into update errors, which activate the `OnReconcileError` event on the client side (more on this event later in this chapter). No exception is shown on the middle tier, but the error travels back to the client.

Adding Features to the Client

After adding some constraints and field properties to the server, we can now return our attention to the client application. The first version was very simple, but now there are several features we can add to it to make it work well. In the ThinCli2 example, I've embedded support for checking the record status and accessing the delta information (the updates to be sent back to the server), using some of the ClientDataSet techniques already discussed in Chapter 13. The program also handles reconcile errors and supports the briefcase model.

Keep in mind that while you're using this client to edit the data locally, you'll be reminded of any failure to match the business rules of the application, set up on the server side using constraints. The server will also provide us with a default value for the Salary field of a new record and pass along the value of its DisplayFormat property. In Figure 17.3 you can see one of the error messages this client application can display, which it receives from the server. This message is displayed while editing the data locally, not when you send it back to the server.

FIGURE 17.3:

The error message
displayed by the ThinCli2
example when the
employee ID is too large

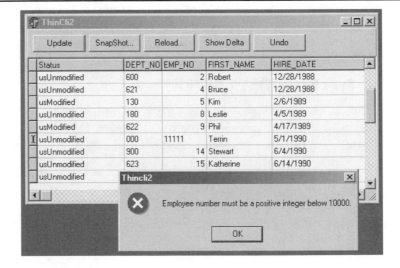

The Update Sequence

This client program also includes a button to Apply the updates to the server and a standard reconcile dialog. Here is a summary of the complete sequence of operations related to an update request and the possible error events:

1. The client program calls the ApplyUpdates method of a ClientDataSet.

2. The delta is sent to the provider on the middle tier. The provider fires the OnUpdateData event, where you have a chance to look at the requested changes before they reach the

database server. At this point you can modify the delta, which is passed in a format compatible with the data of a ClientDataSet.

3. The provider (technically, a part of the provider called the "resolver") applies each row of the delta to the database server. Before applying each update, the provider receives a BeforeUpdateRecord event. If you've set the ResolveToDataSet flag, this update will eventually fire local events of the dataset in the middle tier.

4. In case of a server error, the provider fires the OnUpdateError event (on the middle tier) and the program has a chance of fixing the error at that level.

5. If the middle-tier program doesn't fix the error, the corresponding update request remains in the delta. The error is returned to the client side at this point or after a given number of errors have been collected, depending on the value of the MaxErrors parameter of the ApplyUpdates call.

6. Finally, the delta packet with the remaining updates is sent back to the client, firing the OnReconcileError event of the ClientDataSet for each remaining update. In this event handler, the client program can try to fix the problem (possibly prompting the user for help), modifying the update in the delta, and later reissuing it.

Refreshing Data

You can obtain an updated version of the data, which other users might have modified, by calling the Refresh method of the ClientDataSet. However, this operation can be done only if there are no pending update operations in the cache, as calling Refresh raises an exception when the change log is not empty:

```
if cds.ChangeCount = 0 then
  cds.Refresh;
```

If only some records have been changed, you can refresh the others by calling RefreshRecords. This method refreshes only the current record, but it should be used only if the user hasn't modified the current record. In this case, in fact, RefreshRecords leaves the unapplied changes in the change log. As an example, you can refresh a record every time it becomes the active one, unless it has been modified and the changes have not yet been posted to the server:

```
procedure TForm1.cdsAfterScroll(DataSet: TDataSet);
begin
  if cds.UpdateStatus = usUnModified then
    cds.RefreshRecord;
end;
```

When the data is subject to frequent changes by many users and each user should see changes right away, you should generally apply any change immediately in the AfterPost and `AfterDelete` methods, and call `RefreshRecords` for the active record (as shown above) or each of the records visible inside a grid. This code is actually part of the ClientRefresh example, connected to the AppServ2 server. For debugging purposes, the program also logs the EMP_NO field for each record it refreshes, as you can see in Figure 17.4.

FIGURE 17.4:

The form of the ClientRefresh example, which automatically refreshes the active record and allows more extensive updates by pressing the buttons

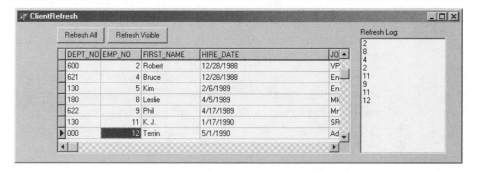

I've done this by adding a button to the ClientRefresh example. The handler of this button moves from the current record to the first visible record of the grid and then to the last visible record. This is accomplished by noting that there are `RowCount - 1` rows visible, assuming that the first row is the fixed one hosting the field names. The program doesn't call `RefreshRecord` every time, as each movement will trigger an `AfterScroll` event with the code shown above. This is the code to refresh the visible rows, which might even be triggered by a timer:

```
var
  i: Integer;
  bm: TBookmarkStr;
begin
  // refresh visible rows
  cds.DisableControls;
  // start with the current row
  i := TMyGrid(DbGrid1).Row;
  bm := cds.Bookmark;
  try
    // get back to the first visible record
    while i > 1 do
    begin
      cds.Prior;
      Dec (i);
    end;
    // return to the current record
    i := TMyGrid(DbGrid1).Row;
    cds.Bookmark := bm;
    // go ahead until the grid is complete
```

```
      while i < TMyGrid(DbGrid1).RowCount do
      begin
        cds.Next;
        Inc (i);
      end;
    finally
      // set back everything and refresh
      cds.Bookmark := bm;
      cds.EnableControls;
    end;
```

This approach generates a huge amount of network traffic, so you might want to trigger updates only when there are actual changes. This can be implemented by adding a callback technology to the server, so that it can inform all connected clients that a given record has changed. The client can determine whether it is interested in the change and eventually trigger the update request.

Advanced DataSnap Features

There are many more features in DataSnap than I've covered up to now. Here is a quick tour of some of the more advanced features of the architecture, partially demonstrated by the AppSPlus and ThinPlus examples. Unfortunately, demonstrating every single idea would turn this chapter into an entire book (and not every Delphi programmer is interested in and can afford DataSnap), so I'll limit myself to an overview.

Besides the features discussed in the following sections, the AppSPlus and ThinPlus examples demonstrate the use of a socket connection, limited logging of events and updates on the server side, and direct fetching of a record on the client side. The last feature is accomplished with this call:

```
procedure TClientForm.ButtonFetchClick(Sender: TObject);
begin
  ButtonFetch.Caption := IntToStr (cds.GetNextPacket);
end;
```

This allows you to get more records than are actually required by the client user interface (the DBGrid). In other words, you can fetch records directly, without waiting for the user to scroll down in the grid. I suggest you study the details of these complex examples after reading the rest of this section.

Parametric Queries

If you want to use parameters in a query or stored procedure, then instead of building a custom solution (with a custom method call to the server), you can let Delphi help you. First define the query on the middle tier with a parameter, such as:

```
select * from customer where Country = :Country
```

Use the Params property to set the type and default value of the parameter. On the client side, you can use the Fetch Params command of the ClientDataSet's shortcut menu, after connecting it to the proper provider. At run time, you can call the equivalent FetchParams method of the ClientDataSet component.

Now you can provide a local default value to the parameter by acting on the Params property. This will be sent to the middle tier when you fetch the data. The ThinPlus example refreshes the parameter with the following code:

```
procedure TFormQuery.btnParamClick(Sender: TObject);
begin
  cdsQuery.Close;
  cdsQuery.Params[0].AsString := EditParam.Text;
  cdsQuery.Open;
end;
```

You can see the secondary form of this example, which shows the result of the parametric query in a grid, in Figure 17.5. In the figure you can also see some custom data sent by the server, as explained in the section "Customizing the Data Packets."

FIGURE 17.5:

The secondary form of the ThinPlus example, showing the data of a parametric query

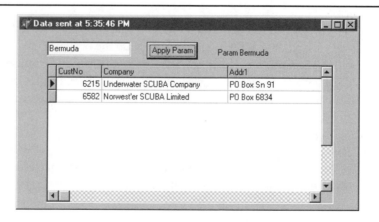

Custom Method Calls

Since the server has a normal COM interface, we can add more methods or properties to it and call them from the client. Simply open the type library editor of the server and use it as with any other COM server. In the AppSPlus example, I've added a custom Login method with the following implementation:

```
procedure TAppServerPlus.Login(const Name, Password: WideString);
begin
  // TODO: add actual login code...
  if Password <> Name then
    raise Exception.Create ('Wrong name/password combination received')
  else
    Query.Active := True;
  ServerForm.Add ('Login:' + Name + '/' + Password);
end;
```

The program makes a simple test, instead of checking the name/password combination against a list of authorizations as a real application should do. Also, disabling the Query doesn't really work, as it can be activated by the provider. Disabling the DataSetProvider is actually a more robust approach. The client has a simple way to access the server, the AppServer property of the remote connection component. Here is a sample call from the ThinPlus example, which takes place in the AfterConnect event of the connection component:

```
procedure TClientForm.ConnectionAfterConnect(Sender: TObject);
begin
  Connection.AppServer.Login (Edit2.Text, Edit3.Text);
end;
```

Note that you can call extra methods of the COM interface through DCOM and also using a socket-based or HTTP connection. Because the program uses the safecall calling convention, the exception raised on the server is automatically forwarded and displayed on the client side. This way, when a user selects the Connect check box, the event handler used to enable the client datasets is interrupted, and a user with the wrong password won't be able to see the data.

NOTE   Besides direct method calls from the client to the server, you can also implement callbacks from the server to the client. This can be used, for example, to notify every client of specific events. COM events are one way to do this. As an alternative, you can add a new interface, implemented by the client, which passes the implementation object to the server. This way, the server can call the method on the client computer. Callbacks are not possible with HTTP connections, though.

Master/Detail Relations

If your middle-tier application exports multiple datasets, you can retrieve them using multiple ClientDataSet components on the client side and connect them locally to form a master/detail structure. This will create quite a few problems for the detail dataset unless you retrieve all of the records locally.

This solution also makes it quite complex to apply the updates; you cannot usually cancel a master record until all related detail records have been removed, and you cannot add detail records until the new master record is properly in place. (Actually, different servers handle this differently, but in most cases where a foreign key is used, this is the standard behavior.) What you can do to solve this problem is to write complex code on the client side to update the records of the two tables according to the specific rules.

A completely different approach is to retrieve a single dataset that already includes the detail as a dataset field, a field of type TDatasetField. To accomplish this, you need to set up the master/detail relation on the server application:

```
object TableCustomer: TTable
  DatabaseName = 'DBDEMOS'
  TableName = 'customer.db'
end
object TableOrders: TTable
  DatabaseName = 'DBDEMOS'
  MasterFields = 'CustNo'
  MasterSource = DataSourceCust
  TableName = 'ORDERS.DB'
end
object DataSourceCust: TDataSource
  DataSet = TableCustomer
end
object ProviderCustomer: TDataSetProvider
  DataSet = TableCustomer
end
```

On the client side, the detail table will show up as an extra field of the ClientDataSet, and the DBGrid control will display it as an extra column with an ellipsis button. Clicking the button will display a secondary form with a grid presenting the detail table (see Figure 17.6). If you need to build a flexible user interface on the client, you can then add a secondary Client-DataSet connected to the dataset field of the master dataset, using the DataSetField property. Simply create persistent fields for the main ClientDataSet and then hook up the property:

```
object cdsDet: TClientDataSet
  DataSetField = cdsTableOrders
end
```

With this setting you can show the detail dataset in a separate DBGrid placed as usual in the form (the bottom grid of Figure 17.6) or in any other way you like. Note that with this structure, the updates relate only to the master table, and the server should handle the proper update sequence even in complex situations.

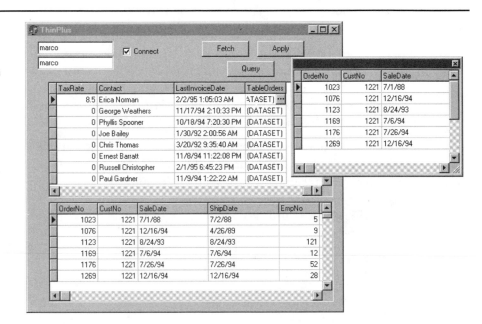

FIGURE 17.6:

The ThinPlus example shows how a dataset field can either be displayed in a grid in a floating window or extracted by a Client-DataSet and displayed in a second form. You'll generally do one of the two things, not both!

Using the Connection Broker

I've already mentioned that the ConnectionBroker component can be helpful in case you might want to change the physical connection used by many ClientDataSet components of a single program. In fact, by hooking each ClientDataSet to the ConnectionBroker, you can change the physical connection of them all simply by updating the physical connection of the broker.

These are the settings used by the ThinPlus example:

```
object Connection: TSocketConnection
  ServerName = 'AppSPlus.AppServerPlus'
  AfterConnect = ConnectionAfterConnect
  Address = '127.0.0.1'
end
object ConnectionBroker1: TConnectionBroker
  Connection = Connection
end
```

```
object cds: TClientDataSet
  ConnectionBroker = ConnectionBroker1
end
// in the secondary form
object cdsQuery: TClientDataSet
  ConnectionBroker = ClientForm.ConnectionBroker1
end
```

That's basically all you have to do. To change the physical connection, drop a new DataSnap connection component to the main form and set the Connection property of the broker to it.

WARNING   There are some glitches with the ConnectionBroker, even in the shipping version of Delphi 6. If you experience unusual errors in a program that uses this component, try removing it. Of course, this note applies only until Borland provides a patch to fix this behavior.

More Provider Options

I've already mentioned the Options property of the DataSetProvider component, noting that it can be used to add the field properties to the data packet. There are several other options you can use to customize the data packet and the behavior of the client program. Here is a short list:

- You can minimize downloading BLOB data with poFetchBlobsOnDemand option. In this case, the client application can download BLOBs by specifying the FetchOnDemand property of the ClientDataSet to True or by calling the FetchBlobs method for specific records. Similarly, you can disable the automatic downloading of detail records by setting the poFetchDetailsOnDemand option. Again, the client can use the FetchOnDemand property or call the FetchDetails method.

- When you are using a master/detail relation, you can control cascades with either of two options. The poCascadeDeletes flag controls whether the provider should delete detail records before deleting a master record. You can set this option if the database server performs cascaded deletes for you as part of its referential integrity support. Similarly, you can set the poCascadeUpdates option when the update of key values of a master/detail relation can be performed automatically by the server.

- You can limit the operations on the client side. The most restrictive option, poReadOnly, disables any update. If you want to give the user a limited editing capability, use poDisableInserts, poDisableEdits, or poDisableDeletes.

- You can resend to the client a copy of the records the client has modified with poAutoRefresh, which is useful in case other users have simultaneously made other, nonconflicting changes. You can also send back to the client changes done in the BeforeUpdateRecord or `AfterUpdateRecord` event handlers by specifying the poPropogateChanges option. This option is also handy when you are using autoincrement fields, triggers, and other techniques that modify data on the server or middle tier beyond the changes requested from the client tier.

- Finally, if you want the client to drive the operations, you can enable the poAllow-CommandText option. This lets you set the SQL query or table name of the middle tier from the client, using the `GetRecords` or `Execute` methods.

The Simple Object Broker

The SimpleObjectBroker component provides an easy way to locate a server application among several server computers. You simply provide a list of available computers, and the client will try each of them in order until it finds one that is available.

Moreover, if you enable the `LoadBalanced` property, the component will randomly choose one of the servers; when many clients use the same configuration, the connections will be automatically distributed among the multiple servers. If this seems like a "poor man's" object broker, consider that some highly expensive load-balancing systems don't actually offer much more than this.

Object Pooling

When multiple clients connect to your server at the same time, you have two options. The first is to create a remote data module object for each of them and let each request be processed in sequence (the default behavior for a COM server with the ciMultiInstance style). Alternatively, you can let the system create a different instance of the application for every client (ciSingleInstance). This requires more resources and more SQL server connections (and licenses), potentially overloading the BDE (as it cannot handle more than a set number of threads or processes).

An alternative approach is offered by the support in DataSnap for object pooling. All you need to do to request this feature is add a call to `RegisterPooled` in the overridden `UpdateRegistry` method. Combined with the stateless support built into this architecture, the pooling capability allows you to share some middle-tier objects among a much larger number of clients.

The users on the client computers will spend most of their time reading data and typing in updates, and they generally don't continue asking for data and sending updates. When the client is not calling a method of the middle-tier object, this can be used for another client. Being stateless, in fact, every request reaches the middle tier as a brand-new operation, even when a server is dedicated to a specific client.

Pooling mechanisms are built into MTS and CORBA, but DataSnap makes it available also for HTTP and socket-based connections, and for the Internet Express Web client.

Customizing the Data Packets

There are many ways to include custom information within the data packet handled by the IAppServer interface. The simplest is probably to handle the OnGetDataSetProperties event of the provider itself. This event has a Sender parameter, a dataset parameter indicating where the data is coming from, and an OleVariant array Properties parameter, in which you can place the extra information. You need to define one variant array for each extra property and include the name of the extra property, its value, and whether you want the data to return to the server along with the update delta (the IncludeInDelta parameter).

Of course, you can pass properties of the related dataset component, but you can also pass any other value (extra fake properties). In the AppSPlus example, I pass to the client the time the query was executed and its parameters:

```
procedure TAppServerPlus.ProviderQueryGetDataSetProperties(
  Sender: TObject; DataSet: TDataSet; out Properties: OleVariant);
begin
  Properties := VarArrayCreate([0,1], varVariant);
  Properties[0] := VarArrayOf(['Time', Now, True]);
  Properties[1] := VarArrayOf(['Param', Query.Params[0].AsString, False]);
end;
```

On the client side, the ClientDataSet component has a GetOptionalParameter method to retrieve the value of the extra property with the given name. The ClientDataSet also has the SetOptionalParameter method to add more properties to the dataset. These values will be saved to disk (in the briefcase model) and eventually sent back to the middle tier (by setting the IncludeInDelta member of the variant array to True). Here is a simple example of the retrieval of the dataset in the code above:

```
Caption := 'Data sent at ' + TimeToStr (TDateTime (
  cdsQuery.GetOptionalParam('Time')));
Label1.Caption := 'Param ' + cdsQuery.GetOptionalParam('Param');
```

The effect of this code was visible in Figure 17.5. An alternative and more powerful approach for customizing the data packet sent to the client is to handle the OnGetData event of the provider, which receives the outgoing data packet in the form of a client dataset. Using the methods of this client dataset, you can edit data before it is sent to the client. For example, you might encode some of the data or filter out sensitive records.

What's Next?

Borland originally introduced its multitier technology in Delphi 3 and has kept extending it from version to version. In addition to further updates and the change of the MIDAS name to DataSnap, Delphi 6 sees the introduction of XML and SOAP support, introducing an alternate and extended architecture for multitier applications. We'll fully explore this topic in Chapter 23.

For the moment, we'll continue with database programming, discussing data-aware controls and custom datasets. In the next part of the book we'll explore COM, sockets, and Internet programming, getting to XML and SOAP at the end of the book, after we've discussed a lot of foundation material.

CHAPTER 18

Writing Database Components

- Data-aware components: the data link

- Field-oriented data-aware controls

- Data-aware TrackBar and ProgressBar

- Record-oriented data-aware controls

- A record viewer

- Building custom datasets

- Saving a dataset to a local stream

In Chapter 11, "Creating Components," we explored the development of Delphi components in depth. Now that I've discussed database programming, we can get back to the earlier topic and focus on the development of database-related components.

There are basically two families of such components. There are data-aware controls you can use to present the data of a field or an entire record to the users of a program. There are dataset components you can define to provide data to existing data-aware controls, reading it from a database or any other data source. In this chapter, I'll cover both topics.

The Data Link

When you write a Delphi database program, you generally connect some data-aware controls to a DataSource component, and then connect the DataSource component to a dataset. The connection between the data-aware control to the DataSource is called a *data link* and is represented by an object of class TDataLink. The data-aware control creates and manages this object and represents its only connection to the data. From a more practical perspective, to make a component data-aware, you need to add a data link to it and surface some of the properties of this internal object, such as the DataSource and DataField properties.

Delphi uses the DataSource and DataLink objects for bidirectional communication. The dataset uses the connection to notify the data-aware controls that new data is available (because the dataset has been activated, or the current record has changed, and so on). Data-aware controls use the connection to ask for the current value of a field or to update it, notifying the dataset of this event.

The relations among all these components are complicated by the fact that some of the connections can be one-to-many. For example, you can connect multiple data sources to the same dataset, and you generally have multiple data links to the same data source, simply because you need one link for every data-aware component, and in most cases you connect multiple data-aware controls to each data source.

The *TDataLink* Class

We'll work for much of this chapter with TDataLink and its derived classes, which are defined in the DB unit. This class has a set of protected virtual methods, which have a role similar to events. They are "almost-do-nothing" methods you can override in a specific subclass to intercept user operations and other data-source events. Here is a list, extracted from the source code of the class:

```
type
  TDataLink = class(TPersistent)
  protected
    procedure ActiveChanged; virtual;
```

```
procedure CheckBrowseMode; virtual;
procedure DataSetChanged; virtual;
procedure DataSetScrolled(Distance: Integer); virtual;
procedure FocusControl(Field: TFieldRef); virtual;
procedure EditingChanged; virtual;
procedure LayoutChanged; virtual;
procedure RecordChanged(Field: TField); virtual;
procedure UpdateData; virtual;
```

All of these virtual methods are called by the DataEvent private method, a sort of window procedure for a data source, a procedure triggered by several data events (see the TDataEvent enumeration). These events originate in the dataset, fields, or data source, and are generally applied to a dataset. The DataEvent method of the dataset component dispatches the events to the connected data sources. Each data source calls the NotifyDataLinks method to forward the event to each connected data link, and then the data source triggers either its own OnDataChange or OnUpdateData event.

Derived DataLink Classes

The TDataLink class is not technically an abstract class, but you'll seldom use it directly. When you need to create data-aware controls, you'll need to use one of its derived classes or derive a new one yourself. The most important class derived from TDataLink is the TFieldDataLink class, which is used by data-aware controls that relate to a single field of the dataset. Most data-aware controls fall into this category, and the TFieldDataLink class solves the most common problems of this type of component.

All of the table- or record-oriented data-aware controls define specific subclasses of TDataLink, as we'll do later on. The TFieldDataLink class has a list of events corresponding to the virtual methods of the base class it overrides. This makes the class simpler to customize, as you can use event handlers instead of having to inherit a new class from it. Here's an example of an overridden method, which fires the corresponding event, if available:

```
procedure TFieldDataLink.ActiveChanged;
begin
  UpdateField;
  if Assigned(FOnActiveChange) then FOnActiveChange(Self);
end;
```

The TFieldDataLink class contains also the Field and FieldName properties that let you connect the data-aware control to a specific field of the dataset. The link keeps also a reference to the current visual component, using the Control property.

Writing Field-Oriented Data-Aware Controls

Now that you understand the theory of how the data link classes work, I can start building some data-aware controls. The first two examples I'll build are data-aware versions of the ProgressBar and TrackBar common controls. We can use the first to display a numeric value, such as a percentage, in a visual way. We can use the second to allow a user to change the numeric value as well.

A Read-Only ProgressBar

A data-aware version of the ProgressBar control is a relatively simple case of a data-aware control, because it is a read-only control. This component is derived from the version that's not data-aware and adds a few properties of the data link object it encapsulates:

```
type
  TMdDbProgress = class(TProgressBar)
  private
    FDataLink: TFieldDataLink;
    function GetDataField: string;
    procedure SetDataField (Value: string);
    function GetDataSource: TDataSource;
    procedure SetDataSource (Value: TDataSource);
    function GetField: TField;
  protected
    // data link event handler
    procedure DataChange (Sender: TObject);
  public
    constructor Create (AOwner: TComponent); override;
    destructor Destroy; override;
    property Field: TField read GetField;
  published
    property DataField: string read GetDataField write SetDataField;
    property DataSource: TDataSource read GetDataSource write SetDataSource;
  end;
```

As with every data-aware component that connects to a single field, this control makes available the DataSource and DataField properties. There is very little code to write here; simply export the properties from the internal data link object, as follows:

```
function TMdDbProgress.GetDataField: string;
begin
  Result := FDataLink.FieldName;
end;


procedure TMdDbProgress.SetDataField (Value: string);
begin
```

```
    FDataLink.FieldName := Value;
  end;

  function TMdDbProgress.GetDataSource: TDataSource;
  begin
    Result := FDataLink.DataSource;
  end;

  procedure TMdDbProgress.SetDataSource (Value: TDataSource);
  begin
    FDataLink.DataSource := Value;
  end;

  function TMdDbProgress.GetField: TField;
  begin
    Result := FDataLink.Field;
  end;
```

Of course, to make this component work, you must create and destroy the data link when the component itself is created or destroyed:

```
  constructor TMdDbProgress.Create (AOwner: TComponent);
  begin
    inherited Create (AOwner);
    FDataLink := TFieldDataLink.Create;
    FDataLink.Control := self;
    FDataLink.OnDataChange := DataChange;
  end;

  destructor TMdDbProgress.Destroy;
  begin
    FDataLink.Free;
    FDataLink := nil;
    inherited Destroy;
  end;
```

In the preceding constructor, notice that the component installs one of its own methods as an event handler for the data link. This is where the most important code of the component resides. Every time the data changes, we modify the output of the progress bar to reflect the values of the current field:

```
  procedure TMdDbProgress.DataChange (Sender: TObject);
  begin
    if (FDataLink.Field <> nil) and (FDataLink.Field is TNumericField) then
      Position := FDataLink.Field.AsInteger
    else
      Position := Min;
  end;
```

Following the convention of the VCL data-aware controls, if the field type is invalid, the component doesn't display an error message—it simply disables the output. Alternatively, you might want to check the field type when `SetDataField` method assigns it to the control.

In Figure 18.1 you can see an example of the DbProgr application's output, which uses both a label and a progress bar to display an order's quantity information. Thanks to this visual clue, you can step through the records and easily spot orders for many items. One obvious benefit to this component is that the application contains almost no code, since all the important code is in the component itself.

FIGURE 18.1:

The data-aware ProgressBar in action in the DbProgr example

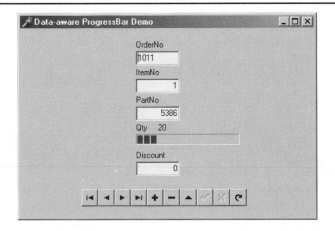

As you've seen, a read-only data-aware component is not too difficult to write. It gets extremely complex, on the other hand, to use such a component inside a DBCtrlGrid container.

NOTE   If you remember the discussion of the `Notification` method in Chapter 11, you might wonder what happens if the data source referenced by the data-aware control is destroyed. The good news is that the data source has a destructor that removes itself from its own data links. So there is no need for a `Notification` method for data-aware controls, even though you'll see books and articles suggesting it, and VCL has plenty of this extra useless code.

Replicable Data-Aware Controls

Extending a data-aware control to support its use inside a DBCtrlGrid component is rather complex and not well documented. You can find a complete "replicable" version of the progress bar in the MdDataPack package and an example of its use in the **RepProgr** folder, along with an HTML file describing its development. The DBCtrlGrid component has a peculiar behavior, as it displays on screen multiple versions of the same physical control, using some

Continued on next page

"smoke and mirrors." The grid can attach the control to a data buffer other than the current record and redirects the control paint operations to another portion of the monitor.

In short, to appear in the DBCtrlGrid, a component must have its csReplicatable control style set, a flag merely indicating that your component actually supports being hosted by a control grid. First, the component must respond to the `cm_GetDataLink` Delphi message and return a pointer to the data link, so that the control grid can use and change it. Second, it needs a custom `Paint` method to draw the output in the appropriate canvas object, which is provided in a parameter of the `wm_Paint` message in case the csPaintCopy flag of the `ControlState` property is set.

The actual code of the example is rather complex, and the DBCtrlGrid component is not heavily used, so I decided not to give you full details here, but you can find the full code and some more information in the source code on the companion CD. Here's the output of a test program that uses this component:

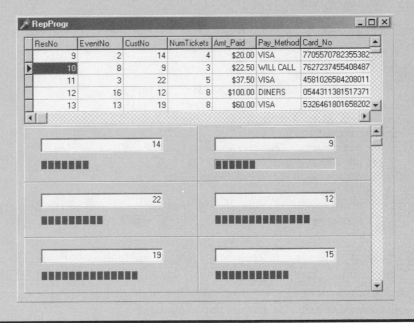

A Read-Write TrackBar

The next step is to write a component that allows a user to modify the data in a database, not just browse it. The overall structure of this type of component isn't very different from the previous version, but there are a few extra elements. In particular, when the user starts interacting with the component, the code should put the dataset into edit mode and then notify the dataset that the data has changed. The dataset will then use an event handler of the FieldDataLink to ask for the updated value.

To demonstrate how you can create a data-aware component that modifies the data, I've decided to extend the TrackBar control. This probably isn't the simplest example, but it demonstrates several important techniques.

Here's the definition of the component's class:

```
type
  TMdDbTrack = class(TTrackBar)
  private
    FDataLink: TFieldDataLink;
    function GetDataField: string;
    procedure SetDataField (Value: string);
    function GetDataSource: TDataSource;
    procedure SetDataSource (Value: TDataSource);
    function GetField: TField;
    procedure CNHScroll(var Message: TWMHScroll); message CN_HSCROLL;
    procedure CNVScroll(var Message: TWMVScroll); message CN_VSCROLL;
    procedure CMExit(var Message: TCMExit); message CM_EXIT;
  protected
    // data link event handlers
    procedure DataChange (Sender: TObject);
    procedure UpdateData (Sender: TObject);
    procedure ActiveChange (Sender: TObject);
  public
    constructor Create (AOwner: TComponent); override;
    destructor Destroy; override;
    property Field: TField read GetField;
  published
    property DataField: string read GetDataField write SetDataField;
    property DataSource: TDataSource read GetDataSource write SetDataSource;
  end;
```

Compared to the read-only data-aware control built earlier, this class is a bit more complex, because it has three message handlers, including component notification handlers, and two new event handlers for the data link. The component installs these event handlers in the constructor, which also disables the component:

```
constructor TMdDbTrack.Create (AOwner: TComponent);
begin
  inherited Create (AOwner);
  FDataLink := TFieldDataLink.Create;
  FDataLink.Control := self;
  FDataLink.OnDataChange := DataChange;
  FDataLink.OnUpdateData := UpdateData;
  FDataLink.OnActiveChange := ActiveChange;
  Enabled := False;
end;
```

All of the get and set methods and the DataChange event handler are very similar to those in the TMdDbProgress component. The only difference is that whenever the data source or data field changes, the component checks the current status to see whether it should enable itself:

```
procedure TMdDbTrack.SetDataSource (Value: TDataSource);
begin
  FDataLink.DataSource := Value;
  Enabled := FDataLink.Active and (FDataLink.Field <> nil) and
    not FDataLink.Field.ReadOnly;
end;
```

This code tests three conditions: the data link should be active, the link should refer to an actual field, and the field shouldn't be read-only. When the user changes the field, the component should also consider that the field name might be invalid; to test for this condition, the component should rather use a try/finally block:

```
procedure TMdDbTrack.SetDataField (Value: string);
begin
  try
    FDataLink.FieldName := Value;
  finally
    Enabled := FDataLink.Active and (FDataLink.Field <> nil) and
      not FDataLink.Field.ReadOnly;
  end;
end;
```

The control executes the same test when the dataset is enabled or disabled:

```
procedure TMdDbTrack.ActiveChange (Sender: TObject);
begin
  Enabled := FDataLink.Active and (FDataLink.Field <> nil) and
    not FDataLink.Field.ReadOnly;
end;
```

The most interesting portion of this component's code is related to its user interface. When a user starts moving the scroll thumb, the component should do the following: put the dataset into edit mode, let the base class update the thumb position, and alert the data link (and therefore the data source) that the data has changed. Here's the code:

```
procedure TMdDbTrack.CNHScroll(var Message: TWMHScroll);
begin
  // enter edit mode
  FDataLink.Edit;
  // update data
  inherited;
  // let the system know
  FDataLink.Modified;
end;
```

```
procedure TMdDbTrack.CNVScroll(var Message: TWMVScroll);
begin
  // enter edit mode
  FDataLink.Edit;
  // update data
  inherited;
  // let the system know
  FDataLink.Modified;
end;
```

When the dataset needs new data—for example, to perform a Post operation—it simply requests it from the component via the TFieldDataLink class's OnUpdateData event:

```
procedure TMdDbTrack.UpdateData (Sender: TObject);
begin
  if (FDataLink.Field <> nil) and (FDataLink.Field is TNumericField) then
    FDataLink.Field.AsInteger := Position;
end;
```

If the proper conditions are met, the component simply updates the data in the proper table field. Finally, if the component loses the input focus, it should force a data update (if the data has changed) so that any other data-aware components showing the value of that field will display the correct value as soon as the user moves to a different field. If the data hasn't changed, the component won't bother updating the data in the table. This is the standard CmExit code for components used by VCL and borrowed for our component as well:

```
procedure TMdDbTrack.CmExit(var Message: TCmExit);
begin
  try
    FDataLink.UpdateRecord;
  except
    SetFocus;
    raise;
  end;
  inherited;
end;
```

Again, there is a demo program for testing this component; you can see its output in Figure 18.2. The DbTrack program contains a check box to enable and disable the table, the visual components, and a couple of buttons you can use to detach the vertical TrackBar component from the field it relates to. Again, I placed these on the form to test enabling and disabling the track bar.

FIGURE 18.2:

The DbTrack example has a couple of track bars you can use to enter data in a database table. The check box and buttons are used to test the enabled status of the components.

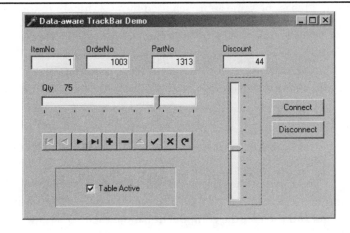

Creating Custom Data Links

The data-aware controls I've built up to this point all referred to specific fields of the dataset, so I was able to use a TFieldDataLink object to establish the connection with a data source. Now I want to build a data-aware component that works with a dataset as a whole, a simple record viewer.

Delphi's database grid shows the value of several fields and several records simultaneously. In my record viewer component, I want to list all the fields of the current record, using a customized grid. This example will show you how to build a customized grid control, and a custom data link to go with it.

A Record Viewer Component

In Delphi there are no data-aware components that manipulate multiple fields of a single record, without displaying other records. In fact, the only component that displays multiple fields from the same table is the DBGrid, which displays multiple fields and multiple records.

The record viewer component I'm going to describe in this section is based on a two-column grid; the first column displays the table's field names, while the second column displays the corresponding field values. The number of rows in the grid will correspond to the number of fields, with a vertical scroll bar in case they can't fit in the visible area.

The data link we need in order to build this component is a simple class, connected only to the record viewer component, and declared directly in the implementation portion of its unit. This is the same approach used by VCL for some specific data links. Here's the definition of the new class:

```
type
  TMdRecordLink = class (TDataLink)
  private
    RView: TMdRecordView;
  public
    constructor Create (View: TMdRecordView);
    procedure ActiveChanged; override;
    procedure RecordChanged (Field: TField); override;
  end;
```

As you can see, the class overrides the methods related to the principal event, in this case simply the activation and data (or record) change. Alternatively, I could have exported some events and then let the component handle them. That's what the TFieldDataLink does, but the approach I've taken makes more sense for a data link class, because you'll want to use it with different data-aware components. The constructor requires the associated component as its only parameter:

```
constructor TMdRecordLink.Create (View: TMdRecordView);
begin
  inherited Create;
  RView := View;
end;
```

After storing a reference to the associated component, the other methods can operate on it directly:

```
procedure TMdRecordLink.ActiveChanged;
var
  I: Integer;
begin
  // set number of rows
  RView.RowCount := DataSet.FieldCount;
  // repaint all...
  RView.Invalidate;
end;

procedure TMdRecordLink.RecordChanged;
begin
  inherited;
  // repaint all...
  RView.Invalidate;
end;
```

As you've seen, the record link code is very simple. Most of the difficulties in building this example depend on the use of a grid. To avoid dealing with useless properties, I've derived the record viewer grid from the TCustomGrid class. This class incorporates much of the code for grids, but most of its properties, events, and methods are protected. For this reason, the class declaration is quite long, because it needs to publish many existing properties. Here is an excerpt (excluding the base class properties):

```
type
  TMdRecordView = class(TCustomGrid)
  private
    // data-aware support
    FDataLink: TDataLink;
    function GetDataSource: TDataSource;
    procedure SetDataSource (Value: TDataSource);
  protected
    // redefined TCustomGrid methods
    procedure DrawCell (ACol, ARow: Longint; ARect: TRect;
      AState: TGridDrawState); override;
    procedure ColWidthsChanged; override;
    procedure RowHeightsChanged; override;
  public
    constructor Create (AOwner: TComponent); override;
    destructor Destroy; override;
    procedure SetBounds (ALeft, ATop, AWidth, AHeight: Integer); override;
    procedure DefineProperties (Filer: TFiler); override;
    // public parent properties (omitted...)
  published
    // data-aware properties
    property DataSource: TDataSource read GetDataSource write SetDataSource;
    // published parent properties (omitted...)
  end;
```

Besides redeclaring the properties to publish them, the component defines a data link object and the DataSource property. There's no DataField property for this component, because it refers to an entire record. The component's constructor is very important. It sets the values of many unpublished properties, including the grid options:

```
constructor TMdRecordView.Create (AOwner: TComponent);
begin
  inherited Create (AOwner);
  FDataLink := TMdRecordLink.Create (self);
  // set numbers of cells and fixed cells
  RowCount := 2; // default
  ColCount := 2;
  FixedCols := 1;
  FixedRows := 0;
  Options := [goFixedVertLine, goFixedHorzLine,
    goVertLine, goHorzLine, goRowSizing];
  DefaultDrawing := False;
  ScrollBars := ssVertical;
  FSaveCellExtents := False;
end;
```

The grid has two columns, one of them fixed, and no fixed rows. The fixed column is used for resizing each row of the grid. Unfortunately, a user cannot drag the fixed row to resize the columns, because you can't resize fixed elements, and the grid already has a fixed column.

NOTE   An alternative approach could be to have an extra empty column, as the DBGrid control does. You'd be able to resize the two other columns after adding a fixed row. Overall, though, I prefer my implementation.

I've used an alternative approach to resize the columns. The first column (holding the field names) can be resized either using programming code or visually at design time, and the second column (holding the values of the fields) will be resized to use the remaining area of the component, leaving space for the borders, lines, and vertical scrollbar:

```
procedure TMdRecordView.SetBounds (ALeft, ATop, AWidth, AHeight: Integer);
begin
  inherited;
  ColWidths [1] := Width - ColWidths [0] - GridLineWidth * 3 -
    GetSystemMetrics (sm_CXVScroll) - 2; // border
end;
```

This takes place when the component size changes and when either of the columns change. With this code, the DefaultColWidth property of the component becomes, in practice, the fixed width of the first column.

After everything has been set up, the key method of the component is the overridden DrawCell method, detailed in Listing 18.1. This is where the control displays the information about the fields and their values. There are three things it needs to draw. If the data link is not connected to a data source, the grid displays an "empty element" sign (*[]*). When drawing the first column, the record viewer shows the DisplayName of the field, which is the same value used by the DBGrid for the heading. When drawing the second column, the component accesses the textual representation of the field value, extracted with the DisplayText property (or with the AsString property for memo fields).

Listing 18.1:   **The DrawCell method of the custom RecordView component**

```
procedure TMdRecordView.DrawCell(ACol, ARow: Longint; ARect: TRect;
  AState: TGridDrawState);
var
  Text: string;
  CurrField: TField;
  Bmp: TBitmap;
begin
  CurrField := nil;
  Text := '[]'; // default
  // paint background
```

```
  if (ACol = 0) then
    Canvas.Brush.Color := FixedColor
  else
    Canvas.Brush.Color := Color;
  Canvas.FillRect (ARect);
  // leave small border
  InflateRect (ARect, -2, -2);
  if (FDataLink.DataSource <> nil) and FDataLink.Active then
  begin
    CurrField := FDataLink.DataSet.Fields[ARow];
    if ACol = 0 then
      Text := CurrField.DisplayName
    else if CurrField is TMemoField then
      Text := TMemoField (CurrField).AsString
    else
      Text := CurrField.DisplayText;
  end;
  if (ACol = 1) and (CurrField is TGraphicField) then
  begin
    Bmp := TBitmap.Create;
    try
      Bmp.Assign (CurrField);
      Canvas.StretchDraw (ARect, Bmp);
    finally
      Bmp.Free;
    end;
  end
  else if (ACol = 1) and (CurrField is TMemoField) then
  begin
    DrawText (Canvas.Handle, PChar (Text), Length (Text), ARect,
      dt_WordBreak or dt_NoPrefix)
  end
  else // draw single line vertically centered
    DrawText (Canvas.Handle, PChar (Text), Length (Text), ARect,
      dt_vcenter or dt_SingleLine or dt_NoPrefix);
  if gdFocused in AState then
    Canvas.DrawFocusRect (ARect);
end;
```

The final portion of the method is where the component considers memo and graphic fields. If the field is a TMemoField, the DrawText function call doesn't specify the dt_SingleLine flag, but uses dt_WordBreak flag to wrap the words when there's no more room. For a graphic field, of course, the component uses a completely different approach, assigning the field image to a temporary bitmap, and then stretching it to fill the surface of the cell.

Notice also that the component sets the DefaultDrawing property to False, so that it's also responsible for drawing the background and the focus rectangle, as it does in the DrawCell method. The component also calls the InflateRect API function to leave a small area between the cell border and the output text. The actual output is produced by calling another Windows API function, DrawText, which centers the text vertically in its cell.

This drawing code works both at run time, as you can see in Figure 18.3, and at design time. The output may not be perfect, but this component can certainly be very useful in many cases. If you want to display the data for a single record, instead of building a custom form with labels and data-aware controls, you can easily use this record viewer grid. Of course, it's important to remember that the record viewer is a read-only component: it's certainly possible to extend it to add editing capabilities (they're already part of the TCustomGrid class). However, instead of adding this support, we've decided to make the component more complete by adding support for displaying BLOB fields.

FIGURE 18.3:

The ViewGrid example demonstrates the output of the RecordView component, using Borland's sample BioLife database table.

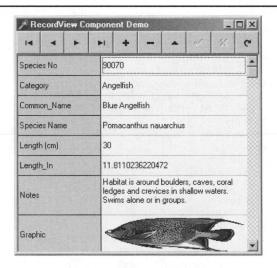

To improve the graphical output, the control makes the lines for those fields twice as high as those for plain text fields. This operation is accomplished when the dataset connected to the data-aware control is activated. The ActiveChanged method of the data link is triggered also by the RowHeightsChanged methods, connected to the DefaultRowHeight property of the base class:

```
procedure TMdRecordLink.ActiveChanged;
var
  I: Integer;
begin
  // set number of rows
  RView.RowCount := DataSet.FieldCount;
  // double the height of memo and graphics
  for I := 0 to DataSet.FieldCount - 1 do
    if DataSet.Fields [I] is TBlobField then
```

```
        RView.RowHeights [I] := RView.DefaultRowHeight * 2;
      // repaint all...
      RView.Invalidate;
    end;
```

At this point, we stumble into a minor problem. In the DefineProperties method, the TCustomGrid class saves the values of the RowHeights and ColHeights properties. We could disable this streaming by overriding the method and not calling inherited (which is generally a bad technique to use), but it is also possible to toggle the FSaveCellExtents protected field to disable this feature.

Customizing the DBGrid Component

Besides writing brand-new custom data-aware components, it's common for Delphi programmers to customize the DBGrid control. The goal for the next component is to enhance the DBGrid with the same kind of custom output I've used for the RecordView component, directly displaying graphic and memo fields. To do this, the grid needs to make the row height resizable, to allow space for a reasonable amount of text and big enough for graphics. You can see an example of this grid at design time in Figure 18.4.

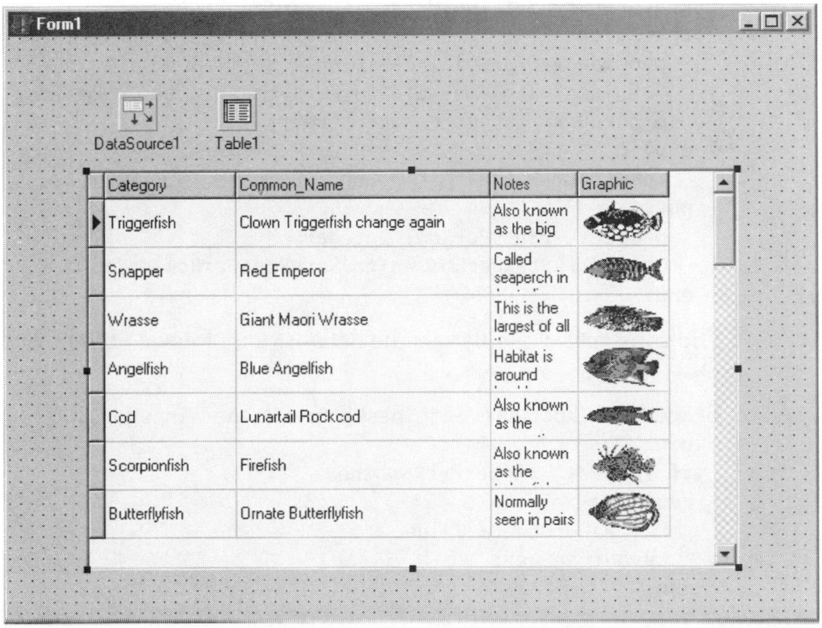

FIGURE 18.4:

An example of the MdDbGrid component at design time. Notice the output of the graphics and memo fields.

While creating the output was a simple matter of adapting the code used in the record viewer component, setting the height of the grid cells ended up being a very difficult problem to solve. The lines of code you'll see for that operation may be few, but they cost me hours of work!

NOTE   Unlike the generic grid we've used above, a DBGrid is a virtual view on the dataset—there is no relation between the number of rows shown on the screen and the number of rows of data in the dataset. When you scroll up and down through the data records of the dataset, you are not scrolling up and down through the rows of the DBGrid; the rows are stationary while the data moves from one row to the next to give the appearance of movement. For this reason, the program doesn't try to set the height of an individual row to suit its data, but it sets the height of all the data rows to a multiline height value.

This time the control doesn't have to create a custom data link, because it is deriving from a component that already has a complex connection with the data. The new class has a new property to specify the number of lines of text for each row and overrides a few virtual methods:

```
type
  TMdDbGrid = class(TDbGrid)
  private
    FLinesPerRow: Integer;
    procedure SetLinesPerRow (Value: Integer);
  protected
    procedure DrawColumnCell(const Rect: TRect; DataCol: Integer;
      Column: TColumn; State: TGridDrawState); override;
    procedure  LayoutChanged; override;
  public
    constructor Create (AOwner: TComponent); override;
  published
    property LinesPerRow: Integer
      read FLinesPerRow write SetLinesPerRow default 1;
  end;
```

The constructor simply sets the default value for the FLinesPerRow field. Here is the set method for the property:

```
procedure TMdDbGrid.SetLinesPerRow(Value: Integer);
begin
  if Value <> FLinesPerRow then
  begin
    FLinesPerRow := Value;
    LayoutChanged;
  end;
end;
```

The side effect of changing the number of lines is a call to the LayoutChanged virtual method. The system calls this method frequently when one of the many output parameters changes. In the code of this method, the component first calls the inherited version and then sets the height of each row. As a basis for this computation it uses the same formula of the TCustomDBGrid class: the text height is calculated using the sample word *Wg* in the current font (this text is used because it includes both a full-height uppercase character and a lower-case letter with a descender). Here's the code:

```
procedure TMdDbGrid.LayOutChanged;
var
  PixelsPerRow, PixelsTitle, I: Integer;
begin
  inherited LayOutChanged;

  Canvas.Font := Font;
  PixelsPerRow := Canvas.TextHeight('Wg') + 3;
  if dgRowLines in Options then
    Inc (PixelsPerRow, GridLineWidth);

  Canvas.Font := TitleFont;
  PixelsTitle := Canvas.TextHeight('Wg') + 4;
  if dgRowLines in Options then
    Inc (PixelsTitle, GridLineWidth);

  // set number of rows
  RowCount := 1 + (Height - PixelsTitle) div (PixelsPerRow * FLinesPerRow);

  // set the height of each row
  DefaultRowHeight := PixelsPerRow * FLinesPerRow;
  RowHeights [0] := PixelsTitle;
  for I := 1 to RowCount - 1 do
    RowHeights [I] := PixelsPerRow * FLinesPerRow;
end;
```

WARNING   Font and TitleFont are the grid defaults that can be overridden by properties of the individual DBGrid column objects. This component would currently ignore those settings.

The difficult part here was to get the last four statements correct. You can simply set the DefaultRowHeight property, but in that case the title row will probably be too high. At first, I tried setting the DefaultRowHeight and then the height of the first row, but this complicated the code used to compute the number of visible rows in the grid (the read-only VisibleRowCount property). If you specify the number of rows (in order to avoid having rows hidden beneath the lower edge of the grid), the base class keeps recomputing them.

Finally, here's the code used to draw the data, ported from the RecordView component and adapted slightly for the grid:

```
procedure TMdDbGrid.DrawColumnCell (const Rect: TRect; DataCol: Integer;
  Column: TColumn; State: TGridDrawState);
var
  Bmp: TBitmap;
  OutRect: TRect;
begin
  if FLinesPerRow = 1 then
    inherited DrawColumnCell(Rect, DataCol, Column, State)
  else
  begin
    // clear area
    Canvas.FillRect (Rect);
    // copy the rectangle
    OutRect := Rect;
    // restrict output
    InflateRect (OutRect, -2, -2);
    // output field data
    if Column.Field is TGraphicField then
    begin
      Bmp := TBitmap.Create;
      try
        Bmp.Assign (Column.Field);
        Canvas.StretchDraw (OutRect, Bmp);
      finally
        Bmp.Free;
      end;
    end
    else if Column.Field is TMemoField then
    begin
      DrawText (Canvas.Handle, PChar (Column.Field.AsString),
        Length (Column.Field.AsString), OutRect, dt_WordBreak or dt_NoPrefix)
    end
    else // draw single line vertically centered
      DrawText (Canvas.Handle, PChar (Column.Field.DisplayText),
        Length (Column.Field.DisplayText), OutRect,
        dt_vcenter or dt_SingleLine or dt_NoPrefix);
  end;
end;
```

In the code above you can see that if the user displays just a single line, the grid uses the standard drawing technique with no output for memo and graphic fields. However, as soon as you increase the line count, you'll see a better output.

To see this code in action, run the GridDemo example. This program has two buttons you can use to increase or decrease the row height of the grid, and two more buttons to change the font. This is an important test because the height in pixels of each cell is the height of the font multiplied by the number of lines.

Building Custom Datasets

When discussing the TDataSet class and the alternative families of dataset components available in Delphi, in Chapter 13, "Delphi's Database Architecture," I mentioned the possibility of writing a custom dataset class. Now it's time to have a look at an actual example. The reasons for writing a custom dataset relate to the fact that you won't need to deploy a database engine but you'll still be able to take full advantage of Delphi's database architecture, including things like persistent database fields and data-aware controls.

Writing a custom dataset is one of the most complex task for a component developer, so this is one of the most advanced areas (as far as low-level coding practices, including tons of pointers) of the entire book. Moreover, Borland hasn't released any official documentation on writing custom datasets. If you are early in your experience with Delphi, you might want to skip the rest of this chapter and come back here later.

The TDataSet class is an abstract class, which declares several virtual abstract methods—23 to be precise. Every subclass of TDataSet must override all of those methods.

Before discussing the development of a custom dataset, we need to explore a few technical elements of the TDataSet class, in particular record buffering. The class maintains a list of buffers, which store the values of different records. These buffers store the actual data, but they also usually store further information for the dataset to use when managing the records. These buffers don't have a predefined structure, and each custom dataset must allocate the buffers, fill them, and destroy them. The custom dataset must also copy the data from the record buffers to the various fields of the dataset, and vice versa. In other words, the custom dataset is entirely responsible for handling these buffers.

In addition to managing the data buffers, the component is also responsible for navigating among the records, managing the bookmarks, defining the structure of the dataset, and creating the proper data fields. The TDataSet class is nothing more than a framework; you must fill it with the appropriate code. Fortunately, most of the code follows a standard structure, which the TDataSet-derived VCL classes use. Once you've grasped the key ideas, you'll be able to build multiple custom datasets borrowing quite a lot of code.

To simplify this type of reuse, I've collected the common features required by any custom dataset in a TMDCustomDataSet class. However, I'm not going to discuss the base class first and the specific implementation later, because that would probably be rather complex to understand. Instead, I'll detail the code required by a dataset, presenting methods of the generic and specific classes at the same time, according to a logical flow.

The Definition of the Classes

The starting point, as usual, is the declaration of the two classes discussed in this section, the generic custom dataset I've written and the specific component storing data in a stream. These declaration of these classes is available in Listing 18.2. Besides virtual methods, the classes contain a series of protected fields used to manage the buffers, track the current position and record count, and handle many other features. You should also notice another record declaration at the beginning, a structure used to store the extra data for every data record we place in a buffer. The dataset places this information in each record buffer, following the actual data.

Listing 18.2: **The declaration of** TMdCustomDataSet **and** TMdDataSetStream

```
// in the unit MdDsCustom
type
  EMdDataSetError = class (Exception);

  TMdRecInfo = record
    Bookmark: Longint;
    BookmarkFlag: TBookmarkFlag;
  end;
  PMdRecInfo = ^TMdRecInfo;

  TMdCustomDataSet = class(TDataSet)
  protected
    // status
    FIsTableOpen: Boolean;
    // record data
    FRecordSize,          // the size of the actual data
    FRecordBufferSize,    // data + housekeeping (TRecInfo)
    FCurrentRecord,       // current record (0 to FRecordCount - 1)
    BofCrack,             // before the first record (crack)
    EofCrack: Integer;    // after the last record (crack)
    // create, close, and so on
    procedure InternalOpen; override;
    procedure InternalClose; override;
    function IsCursorOpen: Boolean; override;
    // custom functions
    function InternalRecordCount: Integer; virtual; abstract;
    procedure InternalPreOpen; virtual;
    procedure InternalAfterOpen; virtual;
    procedure InternalLoadCurrentRecord(Buffer: PChar); virtual; abstract;
    // memory management
```

```
  function AllocRecordBuffer: PChar; override;
  procedure InternalInitRecord(Buffer: PChar); override;
  procedure FreeRecordBuffer(var Buffer: PChar); override;
  function GetRecordSize: Word; override;
  // movement and optional navigation (used by grids)
  function GetRecord(Buffer: PChar; GetMode: TGetMode; DoCheck: Boolean):
    TGetResult; override;
  procedure InternalFirst; override;
  procedure InternalLast; override;
  function GetRecNo: Longint; override;
  function GetRecordCount: Longint; override;
  procedure SetRecNo(Value: Integer); override;
  // bookmarks
  procedure InternalGotoBookmark(Bookmark: Pointer); override;
  procedure InternalSetToRecord(Buffer: PChar); override;
  procedure SetBookmarkData(Buffer: PChar; Data: Pointer); override;
  procedure GetBookmarkData(Buffer: PChar; Data: Pointer); override;
  procedure SetBookmarkFlag(Buffer: PChar; Value: TBookmarkFlag); override;
  function GetBookmarkFlag(Buffer: PChar): TBookmarkFlag; override;
  // editing (dummy vesions)
  procedure InternalDelete; override;
  procedure InternalAddRecord(Buffer: Pointer; Append: Boolean); override;
  procedure InternalPost; override;
  procedure InternalInsert; override;
  // other
  procedure InternalHandleException; override;
published
  // redeclared dataset properties
  property Active;
  property BeforeOpen;
  property AfterOpen;
  property BeforeClose;
  property AfterClose;
  property BeforeInsert;
  property AfterInsert;
  property BeforeEdit;
  property AfterEdit;
  property BeforePost;
  property AfterPost;
  property BeforeCancel;
  property AfterCancel;
  property BeforeDelete;
  property AfterDelete;
  property BeforeScroll;
  property AfterScroll;
  property OnCalcFields;
  property OnDeleteError;
  property OnEditError;
  property OnFilterRecord;
  property OnNewRecord;
  property OnPostError;
```

```
    end;

// in the unit MdDsStream
type
  TMdDataFileHeader = record
    VersionNumber: Integer;
    RecordSize: Integer;
    RecordCount: Integer;
  end;

  TMdDataSetStream = class(TMdCustomDataSet)
  private
    procedure SetTableName(const Value: string);
  protected
    FDataFileHeader: TMdDataFileHeader;
    FDataFileHeaderSize,    // optional file header size
    FRecordCount: Integer;  // current number of records
    FStream: TStream;       // the physical table
    FTableName: string;     // table path and file name
    FFieldOffset: TList;    // field offsets in the buffer
  protected
    // open and close
    procedure InternalPreOpen; override;
    procedure InternalAfterOpen; override;
    procedure InternalClose; override;
    procedure InternalInitFieldDefs; override;
    // edit support
    procedure InternalAddRecord(Buffer: Pointer; Append: Boolean); override;
    procedure InternalPost; override;
    procedure InternalInsert; override;
    // fields
    procedure SetFieldData(Field: TField; Buffer: Pointer); override;
    // custom dataset virutal methods
    function InternalRecordCount: Integer; override;
    procedure InternalLoadCurrentRecord(Buffer: PChar); override;
  public
    procedure CreateTable;
    function GetFieldData(Field: TField; Buffer: Pointer): Boolean; override;
  published
    property TableName: string read FTableName write SetTableName;
  end;
```

In dividing the methods into sections (as you can see by looking at the source code files), I've marked each one with a roman number. You'll see those numbers in a comment describing the method, so that while browsing this long listing you'll immediately know which of the three sections you are in.

Section I: Initialization, Opening, and Closing

The first methods I'll examine are responsible for initializing the dataset, and for opening and closing the file stream we'll use to store the data. In addition to initializing the component's internal data, these methods are responsible for initializing and connecting the proper TFields objects to the dataset component. To make this work, all we need to do is to initialize the FieldsDef property with the definitions of the fields for our dataset, then call a few standard methods to generate and bind the TField objects. This is the general InternalOpen method:

```
procedure TMDCustomDataSet.InternalOpen;
begin
  InternalPreOpen; // custom method for subclasses

  // initialize the field definitions
  InternalInitFieldDefs;

  // if there are no persistent field objects, create the fields dynamically
  if DefaultFields then
    CreateFields;
  // connect the TField objects with the actual fields
  BindFields (True);

  InternalAfterOpen; // custom method for subclasses

  // sets cracks and record position and size
  BofCrack := -1;
  EofCrack := InternalRecordCount;
  FCurrentRecord := BofCrack;
  FRecordBufferSize := FRecordSize + sizeof (TMdRecInfo);
  BookmarkSize := sizeOf (Integer);

  // everything OK: table is now open
  FIsTableOpen := True;
end;
```

You'll notice that the method sets most of the local fields of the class, and also the BookmarkSize field of the base TDataSet class. Within this method, I call two custom methods I introduced in my custom dataset hierarchy: InternalPreOpen and InternalAfterOpen. The first, InternalPreOpen, is used for operations required at the very beginning, such as checking whether the dataset can actually be opened and reading the header information from the file. The code checks an internal version number for consistency with the value saved when the table is first created, as you'll see later on. By raising an exception in this method, we can eventually stop the open operation.

Here is the code for the to methods in the derived stream-based dataset:

```
const
  HeaderVersion = 10;

procedure TMdDataSetStream.InternalPreOpen;
begin
  // the size of the header
  FDataFileHeaderSize := sizeOf (TMdDataFileHeader);

  // check if the file exists
  if not FileExists (FTableName) then
    raise EMdDataSetError.Create ('Open: Table file not found');

  // create a stream for the file
  FStream := TFileStream.Create (FTableName, fmOpenReadWrite);

  // initialize local data (loading the header)
  FStream.ReadBuffer (FDataFileHeader, FDataFileHeaderSize);
  if FDataFileHeader.VersionNumber <> HeaderVersion then
    raise EMdDataSetError.Create ('Illegal File Version');
  // let's read this, double check later
  FRecordCount := FDataFileHeader.RecordCount;
end;

procedure TMdDataSetStream.InternalAfterOpen;
begin
  // check the record size
  if FDataFileHeader.RecordSize <> FRecordSize then
    raise EMdDataSetError.Create ('File record size mismatch');
  // check the number of records against the file size
  if (FDataFileHeaderSize + FRecordCount * FRecordSize) <> FStream.Size then
    raise EMdDataSetError.Create ('InternalOpen: Invalid Record Size');
end;
```

The second method, InternalAfterOpen, is used for operations required after the field definitions have been set and is followed by code that compares the record size read from the file against the value computed in the InternalInitFieldDefs method. The code checks also that the number of records read from the header is compatible with the actual size of the file. This test might fail if the dataset wasn't closed properly: you might want to modify this code to let the dataset refresh the record size in the header anyway.

The InternalOpen method of the custom dataset class is specifically responsible for calling InternalInitFieldDefs, which determines the field definitions (at either design time or run time). For this example, I've decided to base the field definitions on an external file, a simple INI file that provides a section for every field. Each section contains the name and data type of the field, as well as its size if it is string data. Listing 18.3 is the Contrib.INI file that we'll use in the component's demo application:

Listing 18.3: The Contrib.INI **file for the demo application**

```
[Fields]
Number = 6

[Field1]
Type = ftString
Name = Name
Size = 30

[Field2]
Type = ftInteger
Name = Level

[Field3]
Type = ftDate
Name = BirthDate

[Field4]
Type = ftCurrency
Name = Stipend

[Field5]
Type = ftString
Name = Email
Size = 50

[Field6]
Type = ftBoolean
Name = Editor
```

This file, or a similar one, must use the same name as the table file and must be in the same directory. The InternalInitFieldDefs method (shown in Listing 18.4) will read it, using the values it finds to set up the field definitions and determine the size of each record. The method also initializes an internal TList object that stores the offset of every field inside the record. We'll use this TList to access fields' data within the record buffer, as you can see in the code listing.

Listing 18.4: The InternalInitFieldDefs **method of the stream-based dataset**

```
procedure TMdDataSetStream.InternalInitFieldDefs;
var
  IniFileName, FieldName: string;
  IniFile: TIniFile;
```

```
    nFields, I, TmpFieldOffset, nSize: Integer;
    FieldType: TFieldType;
begin
  FFieldOffset := TList.Create;
  FieldDefs.Clear;
  TmpFieldOffset := 0;
  IniFilename := ChangeFileExt(FTableName, '.ini');
  Inifile := TIniFile.Create (IniFilename);
  // protect INI file
  try
    nFields := IniFile.ReadInteger (' Fields', 'Number', 0);
    if nFields = 0 then
      raise EDataSetOneError.Create (' InitFieldsDefs: 0 fields?');
    for I := 1 to nFields do
    begin
      // create the field
      FieldType := TFieldType (GetEnumValue (TypeInfo (TFieldType),
        IniFile.ReadString ('Field' + IntToStr (I), 'Type', '')));
      FieldName := IniFile.ReadString ('Field' + IntToStr (I), 'Name', '');
      if FieldName = ''   then
        raise EDataSetOneError.Create (
          'InitFieldsDefs: No name for field ' + IntToStr (I));
      nSize := IniFile.ReadInteger ('Field' + IntToStr (I), 'Size', 0);
      FieldDefs.Add (FieldName, FieldType, nSize, False);
      // save offset and compute size
      FFieldOffset.Add (Pointer (TmpFieldOffset));
      case FieldType of
        ftString:                     Inc (TmpFieldOffset, nSize + 1);
        ftBoolean, ftSmallInt, ftWord:  Inc (TmpFieldOffset, 2);
        ftInteger, ftDate, ftTime:    Inc (TmpFieldOffset, 4);
        ftFloat, ftCurrency, ftDateTime:  Inc (TmpFieldOffset, 8);
      else
        raise EDataSetOneError.Create (
          'InitFieldsDefs: Unsupported field type');
      end;
    end; // for
  finally
    IniFile.Free;
  end;
  FRecordSize := TmpFieldOffset;
end;
```

Closing the table is simply a matter of disconnecting the fields (using some standard calls). Each class must dispose the data it allocated and update the file header, the first time records are added and each time the record count has changed:

```
procedure TMDCustomDataSet.InternalClose;
begin
  // disconnect field objects
  BindFields (False);
```

```
  // destroy field object (if not persistent)
  if DefaultFields then
    DestroyFields;
  // close the file
  FIsTableOpen := False;
end;

procedure TMdDataSetStream.InternalClose;
begin
  // if required, save updated header
  if (FDataFileHeader.RecordCount <> FRecordCount) or
    (FDataFileHeader.RecordSize = 0) then
  begin
    FDataFileHeader.RecordSize := FRecordSize;
    FDataFileHeader.RecordCount := FRecordCount;
    if Assigned (FStream) then
    begin
      FStream.Seek (0, soFromBeginning);
      FStream.WriteBuffer (FDataFileHeader, FDataFileHeaderSize);
    end;
  end;
  // free the internal list field offsets and the stream
  FFieldOffset.Free;
  FStream.Free;
  inherited InternalClose;
end;
```

Another related function is used to test whether the dataset is open, something we can solve using the corresponding local field:

```
function TMDCustomDataSet.IsCursorOpen: Boolean;
begin
  Result := FIsTableOpen;
end;
```

These are the opening and closing methods you need to implement in any custom dataset. However, most of the time, you'll also add a method to create the table. In this example, the CreateTable method creates an empty file and inserts information in the header: a fixed version number, a dummy record size (we don't know the size until we initialize the fields), and the record count (which is zero to start):

```
procedure TMdDataSetStream.CreateTable;
begin
  CheckInactive;
  InternalInitFieldDefs;

  // create the new file
  if FileExists (FTableName) then
```

```
   raise EMdDataSetError.Create ('File ' + FTableName + ' already exists');
FStream := TFileStream.Create (FTableName, fmCreate or fmShareExclusive);
try
  // save the header
  FDataFileHeader.VersionNumber := HeaderVersion;
  FDataFileHeader.RecordSize := 0;    // used later
  FDataFileHeader.RecordCount := 0;   // empty
  FStream.WriteBuffer (FDataFileHeader, FDataFileHeaderSize);
finally
  // close the file
  FStream.Free;
end;
end;
```

Section II: Movement and Bookmark Management

As mentioned earlier, one of the things every dataset must implement is *bookmark management*, which is necessary for navigating through the dataset. Logically, a bookmark is a reference to a specific record of the dataset, something that uniquely identifies the record so that a dataset can access it and compare it to other records. Technically, bookmarks are pointers. You can implement them as pointers to specific data structures that store record information, or you can implement them as simple record numbers. For simplicity, I'll use the latter approach.

Given a bookmark, you should be able to find the corresponding record, but given a record buffer, you should also be able to retrieve the corresponding bookmark. This is the reason for appending the TMdRecInfo structure to the record data in each record buffer. This data structure stores the bookmark for the record in the buffer, as well as some bookmark flags defined as:

```
type
  TBookmarkFlag = (bfCurrent, bfBOF, bfEOF, bfInserted);
```

The system will request us to store these flags in each record buffer, and will later ask us to retrieve the flags for a given record buffer.

To summarize, the structure of a record buffer stores the data of the record, the bookmark, and the bookmark flags, as you can see in Figure 18.5.

FIGURE 18.5:

The structure of each buffer of the custom dataset, along with the various local fields referring to its sub-portions

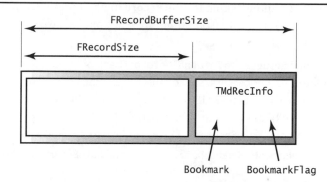

To access the bookmark and flags, we can simply use as an offset the size of the actual data, casting the value to the PMdRecInfo pointer type, and then access the proper field of the TMdRecInfo structure via the pointer. The two methods used to set and get the bookmark flags demonstrate this technique:

```
procedure TMDCustomDataSet.SetBookmarkFlag (Buffer: PChar;
  Value: TBookmarkFlag);
begin
  PMdRecInfo(Buffer + FRecordSize).BookmarkFlag := Value;
end;


function TMDCustomDataSet.GetBookmarkFlag (Buffer: PChar): TBookmarkFlag;
begin
  Result := PMdRecInfo(Buffer + FRecordSize).BookmarkFlag;
end;
```

The methods we use to set and get the current bookmark of a record are similar to the previous two, but they add some complexity because we receive a pointer to the bookmark in the Data parameter. Casting this pointer as an integer pointer (PInteger) and dereferencing it, we obtain the bookmark value:

```
procedure TMDCustomDataSet.GetBookmarkData (Buffer: PChar; Data: Pointer);
begin
  PInteger(Data)^ := PMdRecInfo(Buffer + FRecordSize).Bookmark;
end;


procedure TMDCustomDataSet.SetBookmarkData (Buffer: PChar; Data: Pointer);
begin
  PMdRecInfo(Buffer + FRecordSize).Bookmark := PInteger(Data)^;
end;
```

The key bookmark management method is InternalGotoBookmark, which your dataset uses to make a given record the current one. You'll notice that this isn't the standard navigation technique, since it's much more common to move to the next or previous record (something we can accomplish using the GetRecord method presented in the next section), or to move to the first or last record (something we'll accomplish using the InternalFirst and InternalLast methods described shortly).

Oddly enough, the InternalGotoBookmark method doesn't expect a bookmark parameter, but a pointer to a bookmark, so we must dereference it to determine the bookmark value. The following method, InternalSetToRecord, is what you use to jump to a given bookmark, but it must extract the bookmark from the record buffer passed as a parameter. Then, InternalSetToRecord calls InternalGotoBookmark. Here are the two methods:

```
procedure TMDCustomDataSet.InternalGotoBookmark (Bookmark: Pointer);
var
  ReqBookmark: Integer;
begin
  ReqBookmark := PInteger (Bookmark)^;
  if (ReqBookmark >= 0) and (ReqBookmark < InternalRecordCount) then
    FCurrentRecord := ReqBookmark
  else
    raise EMdDataSetError.Create ('Bookmark ' +
      IntToStr (ReqBookmark) + ' not found');
end;

procedure TMDCustomDataSet.InternalSetToRecord (Buffer: PChar);
var
  ReqBookmark: Integer;
begin
  ReqBookmark := PMdRecInfo(Buffer + FRecordSize).Bookmark;
  InternalGotoBookmark (@ReqBookmark);
end;
```

In addition to the bookmark management methods just described, there are several other navigation methods we use to move to specific positions within the dataset, such as the first or last record. Actually, these two methods don't move the current record pointer to the first or last record, but move it to one of two special locations before the first record and after the last one. These are not actual records; Borland calls them *cracks*. The beginning-of-file crack, or BofCrack, has the value –1 (set in the InternalOpen method), since the position of the first record is zero. The end-of-file crack, or EofCrack, has the value of the number of records, since the last record has the position FRecordCount - 1. We've used two local fields, called EofCrack and BofCrack, to make this code easier to read:

```
procedure TMDCustomDataSet.InternalFirst;
begin
  FCurrentRecord := BofCrack;
end;

procedure TMDCustomDataSet.InternalLast;
```

```
begin
  EofCrack := InternalRecordCount;
  FCurrentRecord := EofCrack;
end;
```

The InternalRecordCount method is a virtual method introduced in my TMDCustomDataSet class, as different datasets can either have a local field for this value (as in case of the stream-based dataset, which has an FRecordCount field) or compute it on-the-fly.

Another group of optional methods is used to get the current record number (used by the DBGrid component to show a proportional vertical scroll bar), set the current record number, or determine the number of records. These methods are quite easy to understand, if you recall that the range of the internal FCurrentRecord field is from 0 to the number of records minus 1. In contrast, the record number reported to the system ranges from 1 to the number of records:

```
function TMDCustomDataSet.GetRecordCount: Longint;
begin
  CheckActive;
  Result := InternalRecordCount;
end;

function TMDCustomDataSet.GetRecNo: Longint;
begin
  UpdateCursorPos;
  if FCurrentRecord < 0 then
    Result := 1
  else
    Result := FCurrentRecord + 1;
end;

procedure TMDCustomDataSet.SetRecNo(Value: Integer);
begin
  CheckBrowseMode;
  if (Value > 1) and (Value <= FRecordCount) then
  begin
    FCurrentRecord := Value - 1;
    Resync([]);
  end;
end;
```

Notice that it is the generic custom dataset class that implements all the methods of this section. The derived stream-based dataset doesn't need to modify any of them.

Section III: Record Buffers and Field Management

Now that we've covered all the support methods, we can examine the core of a custom dataset. Besides opening and creating records and moving around between them, the component really needs to move the data from the stream (the persistent file) to the record buffers, and from the record buffers to the TField objects that are connected to the data-aware controls. The management of record buffers is quite complex, because each dataset also needs to allocate, empty, and free the memory it requires:

```
function TMDCustomDataSet.AllocRecordBuffer: PChar;
begin
  GetMem (Result, FRecordBufferSize);
end;

procedure TMDCustomDataSet.FreeRecordBuffer (var Buffer: PChar);
begin
  FreeMem (Buffer);
end;
```

The reason for allocating memory this way is that a dataset generally adds more information to the record buffer, so the system has no way of knowing how much memory to allocate. You'll notice that in the AllocRecordBuffer method, the component allocates the memory for the record buffer, including both the database data and the record information. In fact, in the InternalOpen method I wrote

```
FRecordBufferSize := InternalRecordSize + sizeof (TMdRecInfo);
```

The component also needs to implement a function to reset the buffer, InternalInitRecord, usually filling it with numeric zeros or spaces.

Oddly enough, we must also implement a method that returns the size of each record, but only the data portion—not the entire record buffer. This method is necessary for implementing the read-only RecordSize property, used only in a couple of peculiar cases in the entire VCL source code. In the generic custom dataset, the GetRecordSize method returns the value of the FRecordSize field.

Now we've actually reached the core of our custom dataset component. The methods of this group are GetRecord, which reads data from the file, InternalPost and InternalAddRecord, which update or add new data to the file, and InternalDelete, which removes data and is not implemented in my sample dataset.

The most complex method of this group is probably GetRecord, which serves multiple purposes. In fact, this method is used by the system to retrieve the data for the current record, fill a buffer passed as a parameter, and retrieve the data of the next or previous records. The GetMode parameter determines its action:

```
type
  TGetMode = (gmCurrent, gmNext, gmPrior);
```

Of course, a previous or next record might not exist. Even the current record might not exist; for example, when the table is empty (or in case of an internal error). In these cases we don't retrieve the data but return an error code. Therefore, this method's result can be one of the following values:

```
type
  TGetResult = (grOK, grBOF, grEOF, grError);
```

Checking to see if the requested record exists is slightly different than you might expect. We don't have to determine if the current record is in the proper range, only if the requested one is. For example, in the gmCurrent branch of the case statement, we use the standard expression CurrentRecord>=InternalRecourdCount. To fully understand the various cases, you might want to read the code a couple of times.

It took me some trial and error (and system crashes caused by recursive calls) to get it straight when I wrote my first custom dataset a few years back. To test it, consider that if you use a DBGrid, the system will perform a series of GetRecord calls, until either the grid is full or GetRecord return grEOF. Here's the entire code of the GetRecord method:

```
// III: Retrieve data for current, previous, or next record
// (moving to it if necessary) and return the status
function TMdCustomDataSet.GetRecord(Buffer: PChar;
  GetMode: TGetMode; DoCheck: Boolean): TGetResult;
begin
  Result := grOK; // default
  case GetMode of
    gmNext: // move on
      if FCurrentRecord < InternalRecordCount - 1 then
        Inc (FCurrentRecord)
      else
        Result := grEOF; // end of file
    gmPrior: // move back
      if FCurrentRecord > 0 then
        Dec (FCurrentRecord)
      else
        Result := grBOF; // begin of file
    gmCurrent: // check if empty
      if FCurrentRecord >= InternalRecordCount then
        Result := grError;
  end;
  // load the data
  if Result = grOK then
    InternalLoadCurrentRecord (Buffer)
  else if (Result = grError) and DoCheck then
    raise EMdDataSetError.Create ('GetRecord: Invalid record');
end;
```

If there's an error and the DoCheck parameter was True, GetRecord raises an exception. If everything goes fine during record selection, the component loads the data from the stream, moving to the position of the current record (given by the record size multiplied by the record number). In addition, we need to initialize the buffer with the proper bookmark flag and bookmark (or record number) value. This is accomplished by another virtual method I introduced, so that derived classes will only need to implement this portion of the code, while the complex GetRecord method remains unchanged:

```
procedure TMdDataSetStream.InternalLoadCurrentRecord (Buffer: PChar);
begin
  FStream.Position := FDataFileHeaderSize + FRecordSize * FCurrentRecord;
  FStream.ReadBuffer (Buffer^, FRecordSize);
  with PMdRecInfo(Buffer + FRecordSize)^ do
  begin
    BookmarkFlag := bfCurrent;
    Bookmark := FCurrentRecord;
  end;
end;
```

We move data to the file in two different cases: when you modify the current record (that is, a post after an edit) or when you add a new record (a post after an insert or append). We use the InternalPost method in both cases, but we can check the dataset's State property to determine which type of post we're performing. In both cases we don't receive a record buffer as a parameter, so we must use the ActiveRecord property of TDataSet, which points to the buffer for the current record:

```
procedure TMdDataSetStream.InternalPost;
begin
  CheckActive;
  if State = dsEdit then
  begin
    // replace data with new data
    FStream.Position := FDataFileHeaderSize + FRecordSize * FCurrentRecord;
    FStream.WriteBuffer (ActiveBuffer^, FRecordSize);
  end
  else
  begin
    // always append
    InternalLast;
    FStream.Seek (0, soFromEnd);
    FStream.WriteBuffer (ActiveBuffer^, FRecordSize);
    Inc (FRecordCount);
  end;
end;
```

In addition, there's another related method, InternalAddRecord. This method is called by the AddRecord method, which in turn is called by InsertRecord and AppendRecord. These last two are public methods a user can call. This is an alternative to inserting or appending a new record to the dataset, editing the values of the various fields, and then posting the data, since the InsertRecord and AppendRecord calls receive the values of the fields as parameters. All we must do at that point is replicate the code used to add a new record in the InternalPost method:

```
procedure TMdDataSetOne.InternalAddRecord(Buffer: Pointer; Append: Boolean);
begin
  // always append at the end
  InternalLast;
  FStream.Seek (0, soFromEnd);
  FStream.WriteBuffer (ActiveBuffer^, FRecordSize);
  Inc (FRecordCount);
end;
```

The last file operation I should have implemented is one that removes the current record. This operation is common, but it is actually quite complex. If we take a simple approach, such as creating an empty spot in the file, then we'll need to keep track of that spot and make the code for reading or writing a specific record work around that spot. An alternate solution is to make a copy of the entire file, without the given record, and then replace the original file with the copy. Given these choices, I felt that for this example I could forgo supporting record deletion.

Section IV: From Buffers to Fields

In the last few methods, we've seen how datasets move data from the data file to the memory buffer. However, there's little Delphi can do with this record buffer, because it doesn't yet know how to interpret the data in the buffer. We need to provide two more methods: GetData, which copies the data from the record buffer to the field objects of the dataset, and SetData, which moves the data back from the fields to the record buffer. What Delphi will do automatically for us is move the data from the field objects to the data-aware controls, and back.

The code for these two methods isn't very complex, primarily because we saved the field offsets inside the record data in a TList object called FFieldOffset. By simply incrementing the pointer to the initial position in the record buffer of the current field's offset, we'll be able to get the specific data, which takes Field.DataSize bytes.

A confusing element of these two methods is that they both accept a Field parameter and a Buffer parameter. At first, one might think that the buffer passed as parameter is the record buffer. Actually, I found out that the Buffer is a pointer to the field object's raw data. If you use one of the field object's methods to move that data, it will call the dataset's GetData or

SetData methods, probably causing an infinite recursion. Instead, you should use the Active-Buffer pointer to access the record buffer, use the proper offset to get to the data for the current field in the record buffer, and then use the provided Buffer to access the field data. The only difference between the two methods is the direction we're moving the data:

```
function TMdDataSetOne.GetFieldData (Field: TField; Buffer: Pointer): Boolean;
var
  FieldOffset: Integer;
  Ptr: PChar;
begin
  Result := False;
  if not IsEmpty and (Field.FieldNo > 0) then
  begin
    FieldOffset := Integer (FFieldOffset [Field.FieldNo - 1]);
    Ptr := ActiveBuffer;
    Inc (Ptr, FieldOffset);
    if Assigned (Buffer) then
      Move (Ptr^, Buffer^, Field.DataSize);
    Result := True;
    if (Field is TDateTimeField) and (PInteger(Ptr)^ = 0) then
      Result := False;
  end;
end;

procedure TMdDataSetOne.SetFieldData(Field: TField; Buffer: Pointer);
var
  FieldOffset: Integer;
  Ptr: PChar;
begin
  if Field.FieldNo >= 0 then
  begin
    FieldOffset := Integer (FFieldOffset [Field.FieldNo - 1]);
    Ptr := ActiveBuffer;
    Inc (Ptr, FieldOffset);
    if Assigned (Buffer) then
      Move (Buffer^, Ptr^, Field.DataSize)
    else
      raise Exception.Create (
        'Very bad error in TMdDataSetStream.SetField data');
    DataEvent (deFieldChange, Longint(Field));
  end;
end;
```

The GetField method should return True or False to indicate whether the field contains data or is empty. However, unless you use a special marker for blank fields, it's very difficult to determine this, since we're storing values of different data types. For example, a test such as `Ptr^<>#0` makes sense only if you are using a string representation for all of the fields. If you use this test, zero integer values and empty strings will show as null values (the data-aware controls will be empty), which may be what you want. The problem is that Boolean False values won't show up. Even worse, floating-point values with no decimals and few digits won't be displayed, because the exponent portion of their representation will be zero! However, to make this example work in Delphi 6, I had to consider as empty each date/time field with an initial zero. Without this code, Delphi tries to convert the illegal *internal* zero date (internally, date fields don't use a `TDateTime` data type but a different representation) raising an exception. The code used to work with past versions of Delphi.

WARNING   While trying to fix this problem, I also found out that if you call `IsNull` for a field, this request is resolved by calling `GetFieldData` without passing any buffer to fill but looking only for the result of the function call. This is the reason for the `if Assigned (Buffer)` test within the code.

There's one final method, which doesn't fall into any category: `InternalHandleException`. Generally, this method silences the exception, as it is activated only at design time.

Testing the Stream-Based DataSet

After all this work, we're finally ready to test an application example of the custom dataset component, installed in the component's package for this chapter. The form displayed by the StreamDSDemo program is quite simple, as you can see in Figure 18.6. It has a panel with two buttons, a check box, and a navigator component, plus a DBGrid filling its client area.

FIGURE 18.6:

The form of the StreamDS-Demo example. The custom dataset has been activated, so we can already see the data at design time.

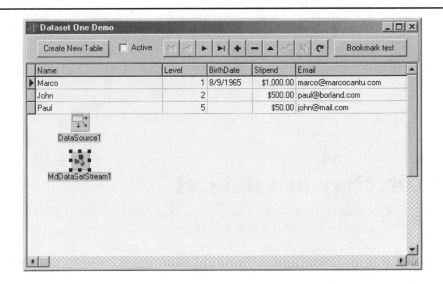

Figure 18.6 shows the form of the example at design time, but we've activated the custom dataset so that its data is already visible. Of course we'd already prepared the INI file with the table definition (it's the file we already listed when discussing the dataset initialization), and we executed the program to add some data to the file.

It's also possible to modify the form using Delphi's Fields editor and set the properties of the various field objects. Everything works as it does with one of the standard dataset controls! However, to make this work you'll need to enter the name of the custom dataset's file in the TableName property, using the complete path.

WARNING   As the demo program defines the absolute path of the table file at design time, you'll need to fix it if you copy the examples to a different drive or directory. In the example, the TableName property is used only at design time. At run time, in fact, the program looks for the table in the current directory.

The code of the example is rather simple, especially compared to the code of the custom dataset. If the table doesn't exist yet, you can click the Create button:

```
procedure TForm1.Button1Click(Sender: TObject);
begin
  MdDataSetStream1.CreateTable;
  MdDataSetStream1.Open;
  CheckBox1.Checked := MdDataSetStream1.Active;
end;
```

You'll notice that we create the file first, open and close it, and then open the table. This is the same behavior as the TTable component (which accomplishes this using the CreateTable method). To simply open or close the table, you can click the check box:

```
procedure TForm1.CheckBox1Click(Sender: TObject);
begin
  MdDataSetStream1.Active := CheckBox1.Checked;
end;
```

Finally, I've created a method that tests custom dataset's bookmark management code and seems to work.

A Directory in a Dataset

An important idea related to datasets in Delphi is that they simply represent a set of data, regardless where this data comes from. An SQL server or a local file are examples of traditional datasets, but you can use the same technology to show a list of users of a system, a list of files of a folder, the properties of some objects, some XML-based data, and so on.

As an example, the second (and last) dataset presented in this chapter is a list of files. This is based once more on a generic approach. I've built a generic dataset based on a list of objects in memory (using a TObjectList), then derived a version in which the objects correspond to the files of a folder. The actual example is simplified by the fact it is a read-only dataset, so you might even find it simpler than the previous dataset I presented.

NOTE Some of the ideas presented here were discussed in an article I wrote for the Borland Community Web site, `http://community.borland.com`, published in June 2000.

A List as a Dataset

The generic list-based dataset is called TMdListDataSet and contains the list of objects, created when you open the dataset and freed when you close it. This dataset doesn't store the actual record data within the buffer; rather, it saves in the buffer only the position in the list of the entry corresponding to the record's data. This is the class definition:

```
type
  TMdListDataSet = class (TMdCustomDataSet)
  protected
    // the list holding the data
    FList: TObjectList;
    // dataset virtual methods
    procedure InternalPreOpen; override;
    procedure InternalClose; override;
    // custom dataset virtual methods
    function InternalRecordCount: Integer; override;
    procedure InternalLoadCurrentRecord (Buffer: PChar); override;
  end;
```

You can see that by writing a generic custom data class, we can override few virtual methods of the TDataSet class and of this custom dataset class, and have a working dataset (although this is still an abstract class, which requires extra code from subclasses to work). When the dataset is opened, we have to create the list and set the record size, to indicate we're simply saving the list index in the buffer:

```
procedure TMdListDataSet.InternalPreOpen;
begin
  FList := TObjectList.Create (True); // owns the objects
  FRecordSize := 4; // an integer, the list item id
end;
```

Further subclasses at this point should also fill the list with actual objects.

Tip   Similarly to the ClientDataSet, my list dataset keeps all of its data in memory. However, using some smart techniques, you can also create a list of "fake" objects, and then load the actual objects only when you are accessing them.

Closing is simply a matter of freeing the list, which has a record count corresponding to the list size:

```
function TMdListDataSet.InternalRecordCount: Integer;
begin
  Result := fList.Count;
end;
```

The only other method is used to save the data of the current record in the record buffer, including the bookmark information. The core data is simply the position of the current record, which matches the list index (and also the bookmark):

```
procedure TMdListDataSet.InternalLoadCurrentRecord (Buffer: PChar);
begin
  PInteger (Buffer)^ := fCurrentRecord;
  with PMdRecInfo(Buffer + FRecordSize)^ do
  begin
    BookmarkFlag := bfCurrent;
    Bookmark := fCurrentRecord;
  end;
end;
```

Directory Data

The derived directory dataset class has to provide a way to load the objects in memory when the dataset is opened, to define the proper fields, and to read and write the value of those fields. Of course, it has also a property indicating the directory to work on, or to be more precise, the directory plus the file mask used for filtering the files (as in c:\docs*.txt):

```
type
  TMdDirDataset = class(TMdListDataSet)
  private
    FDirectory: string;
    procedure SetDirectory(const NewDirectory: string);
  protected
    // TDataSet virtual methdos
    procedure InternalInitFieldDefs; override;
    procedure SetFieldData(Field: TField; Buffer: Pointer); override;
    function GetCanModify: Boolean; override;
    // custom dataset virtual methods
    procedure InternalAfterOpen; override;
  public
```

```
    function GetFieldData(Field: TField; Buffer: Pointer): Boolean; override;
  published
    property Directory: string read FDirectory write SetDirectory;
  end;
```

The GetCanModify function is another virtual method of TDataSet, used to determine if the dataset is read-only. In this case, it simply returns False. Also, we won't have to write any code for the SetFieldData procedure, but we have to define it because it is an abstract virtual method.

As I am dealing with a list of objects, the unit includes also a class for those objects. In this case, I am working with file data extracted by a TSearchRec buffer by the TFileData class constructor:

```
type
  TFileData = class
  public
    ShortFileName: string;
    Time: TDateTime;
    Size: Integer;
    Attr: Integer;
    constructor Create (var FileInfo: TSearchRec);
  end;

constructor TFileData.Create (var FileInfo: TSearchRec);
begin
  ShortFileName := FileInfo.Name;
  Time := FileDateToDateTime (FileInfo.Time);
  Size := FileInfo.Size;
  Attr := FileInfo.Attr;
end;
```

This constructor is called for each folder while opening the dataset:

```
procedure TMdDirDataset.InternalAfterOpen;
var
  Attr: Integer;
  FileInfo: TSearchRec;
  FileData: TFileData;
begin
  // scan all files
  Attr := faAnyFile;
  FList.Clear;
  if SysUtils.FindFirst(fDirectory, Attr, FileInfo) = 0 then
  repeat
    FileData := TFileData.Create (FileInfo);
    FList.Add (FileData);
  until SysUtils.FindNext(FileInfo) <> 0;
  SysUtils.FindClose(FileInfo);
end;
```

The next step is to define the fields of the dataset, which in this case are fixed and depend on the available directory data:

```
procedure TMdDirDataset.InternalInitFieldDefs;
begin
  if fDirectory = '' then
    raise EMdDataSetError.Create ('Missing directory');

  // field definitions
  FieldDefs.Clear;
  FieldDefs.Add ('FileName', ftString, 40, True);
  FieldDefs.Add ('TimeStamp', ftDateTime);
  FieldDefs.Add ('Size', ftInteger);
  FieldDefs.Add ('Attributes', ftString, 3);
  FieldDefs.Add ('Folder', ftBoolean);
end;
```

Finally, the component has to move the data from the object of the list referenced by the current record buffer (the ActiveBuffer value) to each field of the dataset, as requested by the GetFieldData method. This function uses either Move or StrCopy, depending on the data type and does some conversions for the attributes codes (*H* for hidden, *R* for read-only, and *S* for system) extracted from the related flags and used also to determine whether a file is actually a folder. Here is the code:

```
function TMdDirDataset.GetFieldData (Field: TField; Buffer: Pointer): Boolean;
var
  FileData: TFileData;
  Bool1: WordBool;
  strAttr: string;
  t: TDateTimeRec;
begin
  FileData := fList [PInteger(ActiveBuffer)^] as TFileData;
  case Field.Index of
    0: // filename
      StrCopy (Buffer, pchar(FileData.ShortFileName));
    1: // timestamp
    begin
      t := DateTimeToNative (ftdatetime, FileData.Time);
      Move (t, Buffer^, sizeof (TDateTime));
    end;
    2: // size
      Move (FileData.Size, Buffer^, sizeof (Integer));
    3: // attributes
    begin
      strAttr := '   ';
      if (FileData.Attr and SysUtils.faReadOnly) > 0 then
        strAttr [1] := 'R';
```

```
    if (FileData.Attr and SysUtils.faSysFile) > 0 then
      strAttr [2] := 'S';
    if (FileData.Attr and SysUtils.faHidden) > 0 then
      strAttr [3] := 'H';
    StrCopy (Buffer, pchar(strAttr));
  end;
  4: // folder
  begin
    Bool1 := FileData.Attr and SysUtils.faDirectory > 0;
    Move (Bool1, Buffer^, sizeof (WordBool));
  end;
  end; // case
  Result := True;
end;
```

The tricky part in writing this code was figuring out the internal format of dates stored within date/time fields. This is not the common TDateTime format used by Delphi, and not even the internal TTimeStamp, but what is called the internally called the "native" date time format. I've written a conversion function cloning one I've found in the VCL code for the date/time fields:

```
function DateTimeToNative(DataType: TFieldType; Data: TDateTime): TDateTimeRec;
var
  TimeStamp: TTimeStamp;
begin
  TimeStamp := DateTimeToTimeStamp(Data);
  case DataType of
    ftDate: Result.Date := TimeStamp.Date;
    ftTime: Result.Time := TimeStamp.Time;
  else
    Result.DateTime := TimeStampToMSecs(TimeStamp);
  end;
end;
```

With this dataset available, building the demo program (shown in Figure 18.7) was simply a matter of connecting a DBGrid component to it and adding a folder-selection component, Delphi 6's ShellTreeView control. This control is set up to work only on files, by setting its Root property to C:\. When the user selects a new folder, the OnChange event handler of the ShellTreeView control refreshes the dataset.

FIGURE 18.7:

The output of the DirDemo example, which uses a rather unusual dataset, showing directory data.

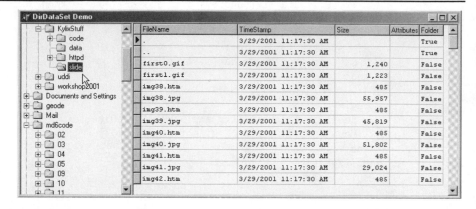

```
procedure TForm1.ShellTreeView1Change(Sender: TObject; Node: TTreeNode);
begin
  MdDirDataset1.Close;
  MdDirDataset1.Directory := ShellTreeView1.Path + '\*.*';
  MdDirDataset1.Open;
end;
```

What's Next?

In this chapter we've delved inside Delphi's database architecture, by first examining the development of data-aware controls and then studying the internals of the TDataSet class to write a couple of custom dataset components. With this information, and all the other ideas presented in this part devoted to database programming, you should probably be able to choose the architecture of your database applications, depending on your needs.

NOTE I've actually extended the list-based dataset to build an object-based version, hosting the business logic of an application and mapped to a relational database. Refer to my Web site (www.marcocantu.com) or contact me for the availability of this code.

Database programming is certainly a core element of Delphi, the reason for devoting several chapters of the book to this topic. We'll get back to this topic when focusing on presenting database data over the Web, in Chapters 21 and 22.

For the moment, though, we have to introduce another important element of Windows applications, COM and OLE Automation, covered in the next two chapters.

PART IV

Beyond Delphi: Connecting with the World

- Chapter 19: COM Programming
- Chapter 20: From Automation to COM+
- Chapter 21: Internet Programming: Sockets and Indy Components
- Chapter 22: Web Programming with WebBroker and WebSnap
- Chapter 23: XML and SOAP

COM Programming

- What are OLE and COM?

- COM, GUIDs, and class factories

- Delphi interfaces and COM

- The VCL COM-support classes

- Windows shell interfaces

For about 10 years, starting soon after the release of Windows 3.0, Microsoft has kept promising that its operating system and their API would be based on a real object model instead of functions. According to the speculations, Windows 95 (and later Windows 2000) should have been based on this revolutionary approach. Nothing like this happened, but Microsoft kept pushing COM (Component Object Model), built the Windows 95 shell on top of it, pushed applications integration with COM and derivative technologies (such as Automation), and reached the peak by introducing COM+ with Windows 2000.

Now, soon after the release of the complete foundation required for high-level COM programming, Microsoft has decided to switch to a new core technology, part of the dotNet (or .Net, if you prefer) initiative. My impression is that COM wasn't really suited for the integration of fine-grained objects, though it succeeded in providing an architecture for integrating applications or large objects.

NOTE   dotNet is a mix of interesting new technologies and pure marketing hype, and this book doesn't discuss it in detail. Even if it were possible to predict how dotNet will affect programmers using Microsoft development tools, it is far from clear how it will affect Delphi programmers. dotNet, in fact, is based on a class library very similar to Delphi's VCL, and it is unclear what the advantage will be of switching to it. If Borland could bundle the VCL with an operating system, along with its core run-time packages, you'd have a situation very similar to dotNet, as far as the library is concerned. Instead, if you are looking for a virtual machine and portable code, you can certainly consider Java and the portability between Windows and Linux possible with the CLX library of Delphi 6 and Kylix. Having said this, I'm not underestimating dotNet, but this is a book on Delphi programming. In any case, we'll get back to many core elements of dotNet in the final chapters, discussing XML and SOAP. Finally, the system can expose dotNet objects as COM objects, so after you learn COM you'll also have a chance to interact with dotNet.

In this chapter, we'll build our first COM object and integrate COM objects with the Windows shell. Type libraries, Automation, and other topics will be covered in the next chapter. I will stick to the basic elements to let you understand the role of this technology without delving heavily into the details. I'll bear in mind the clouds on the future of COM, declared obsolete by Microsoft after the announcement of dotNet but still heavily used by the same company inside their applications and operating systems.

A Short History of OLE and COM

Part of the confusion related to COM technology comes from the fact that Microsoft has used different names for it for marketing reasons. Everything started with Object Linking and Embedding (OLE, for short), which was an extension of the DDE (Dynamic Data Exchange) model. Using the Clipboard allows you to copy some raw data, and using DDE allows you to connect parts of two documents. OLE allows you to copy data from a server application to a client application, along with information regarding the server or a reference to information stored in the Windows Registry. The raw data might be copied along with the link (object embedding) or kept in the original file (object linking). OLE Documents are now called *Active Documents*.

Microsoft updated OLE to OLE 2 and started adding new features, such as OLE Automation and OLE Controls. The next step was to build the Windows 95 shell using OLE technology and interfaces and then to rename the OLE Controls (previously known also as OCX) as ActiveX controls, changing the specification to allow for lightweight controls suitable for distribution over the Internet. For a while, Microsoft promoted ActiveX controls as suitable for the Internet, but the idea was never fully accepted by the development community, certainly not as "suitable" for Internet development.

As this technology was extended and became increasingly important to the Windows platform, Microsoft changed the name to OLE, and then to COM, and now to COM+ for Windows 2000. These changes in naming are only partially related to technological changes and are driven to a large extent by marketing purposes.

What, then, is COM? Basically, the Component Object Model, or COM, is a technology that defines a standard way for a client module and a server module to communicate through a specific interface. Here, "module" indicates an application or a library (a DLL); the two modules may execute on the same computer or on different machines connected via a network. Many interfaces are possible, depending on the role of the client and server, and you can add new interfaces for specific purposes. These interfaces are implemented by server objects. A server object usually implements more than one interface, and all the server objects have a few common capabilities, because they must all implement the IUnknown interface.

The good news is that Delphi is fully compliant with COM. When you look at the source code, Object Pascal seems to be easier to use than C++ or other languages for writing COM objects. This simplicity mainly derives from the incorporation of interface types into the Object Pascal language. By the way, interfaces are also similarly used to integrate Java with COM on the Windows platform.

The purpose of COM interfaces is to communicate between two software modules, two executable files, or one executable file and a DLL. Implementing COM objects in DLLs is generally simpler, because in Win32, a program and the DLL it uses reside in the same memory address space. This means that if the program passes a memory address to the DLL, the address remains valid. When you use two executable files, COM has a lot of work to do behind the scenes to let the two applications communicate. This mechanism is called *marshaling*. Note that a DLL implementing COM objects is described as an *in-process* server, whereas when the server is a separate executable, it is called an *out-of-process* server. However, when DLLs are executing on another machine (DCOM) or inside a host environment (MTS), they are also out-of-process.

Implementing *IUnknown*

Before we start looking to an example of COM development, I would like to introduce a few COM basics. The first is that every COM object must implement the IUnknown interface, also dubbed IInterface in Delphi 6 for non-COM usage of interfaces (as we saw in Chapter 3, "The Object Pascal Language: Inheritance and Polymorphism"). This is the base interface from which every Delphi interface inherits, and Delphi provides a couple of different classes with ready-to-use implementations of IUnknown/IInterface, including TInterfacedObject and TComObject. The first can be used to have an internal object unrelated with COM, while the second is used to create objects that can be exported by servers. As I'll discuss in Chapter 20, "From Automation to COM+," several other classes inherit from TComObject and provide support for more interfaces, which are required by Automation servers or ActiveX controls.

As mentioned in Chapter 3, the IUnknown interface has three methods: _AddRef, _Release, and QueryInterface. Here is the definition of the IUnknown interface (extracted from the System unit):

```
type
  IUnknown = interface
  ['{00000000-0000-0000-C000-000000000046}']
    function QueryInterface(const IID: TGUID;
      out Obj): Integer; stdcall;
    function _AddRef: Integer; stdcall;
    function _Release: Integer; stdcall;
  end;
```

The _AddRef and _Release methods are used to implement reference counting. The QueryInterface method handles the type information and type compatibility of the objects.

NOTE   In the code above, you can see an example of an **out** parameter, a parameter passed back from the method to the calling program but without an initial value passed by the calling program to the method. The **out** parameters have been added to Delphi's Object Pascal language specifically to support COM. It's also important to note that although Delphi's language definition for the interface type is designed for compatibility with COM, Delphi interfaces do not require COM. This was already highlighted in Chapter 3, where I built a complex interface-based example with no COM support whatsoever.

You don't usually need to implement these methods, as you can inherit from one of the Delphi classes already supporting them. The most important class is TComObject, defined in the ComObj unit. When you build a COM server, you'll generally inherit from this class. Because TComObject is a complex class, this excerpt shows only its key elements:

```
type
  TComObject = class(TObject, IUnknown, ISupportErrorInfo)
  private
    FNonCountedObject: Boolean;
    FRefCount: Integer;
  protected
    { IUnknown }
    function IUnknown.QueryInterface = ObjQueryInterface;
    function IUnknown._AddRef = ObjAddRef;
    function IUnknown._Release = ObjRelease;
    { ISupportErrorInfo }
    function InterfaceSupportsErrorInfo(const iid: TIID): HResult; stdcall;
  public
    constructor Create;
    destructor Destroy; override;
    procedure Initialize; virtual;
    function ObjAddRef: Integer; virtual; stdcall;
    function ObjQueryInterface(const IID: TGUID; out Obj): HResult;
      virtual; stdcall;
    function ObjRelease: Integer; virtual; stdcall;
    property RefCount: Integer read FRefCount;
  end;
```

This class implements the IUnknown interface (using the ObjAddRef, ObjQueryInterface, and ObjRelease methods, as indicated by the method-mapping statements in the protected portion of the class) and the ISupportErrorInfo interface (through the InterfaceSupportsError-Info method). The implementation of reference counting for the TComObject class has been extended to support threading. Instead of using Inc and Dec, the code uses the thread-safe InterlockedIncrement and InterlockedDecrement API functions, as you can see in the source code of the class:

```
function TComObject.ObjAddRef: Integer;
begin
  Result := InterlockedIncrement(FRefCount);
end;

function TComObject.ObjRelease: Integer;
begin
  Result := InterlockedDecrement(FRefCount);
  if Result = 0 then Destroy;
end;
```

As you can see, the implementation of `Release` destroys the object when there are no more references to it. At first sight, the need to call this method each time you operate on an object seems like a lot of work. However, you might remember from Chapter 3 that when you're using interface variables to refer to objects, Delphi automatically adds the reference-counting calls to the compiled code, which automatically destroys unreferenced objects. This labor-saving feature makes Delphi a convenient tool for COM development.

The most complex method is `QueryInterface`, which in Delphi is actually implemented through the `GetInterface` method of the `TObject` class:

```
function TComObject.ObjQueryInterface(const IID: TGUID; out Obj): HResult;
begin
  if GetInterface(IID, Obj) then
    Result := S_OK
  else
    Result := E_NOINTERFACE;
end;
```

The role of the `QueryInterface` method is twofold:

- `QueryInterface` is used for type checking. The program can ask an object the following questions: Are you of the type I'm interested in? Do you implement the interface I want to call? And the specific methods? If the answer is no, the program can look for another object, maybe asking another server.

- If the answer is yes, `QueryInterface` usually returns a pointer to the object, using its reference output parameter (`out`).

To understand the role of the `QueryInterface` method, it is important to keep in mind that a COM object can implement multiple interfaces, as the event `TComObject` does. When you call `QueryInterface`, you might ask for one of the possible interfaces of the object, using the `TGUID` parameter.

Globally Unique Identifiers

The `QueryInterface` method has a special parameter of the `TGUID` type. This is an ID that identifies any COM server class and any interface in the system. When you want to know whether an object supports a specific interface, you ask the object whether it implements the interface that has a given ID (which for the default OLE interfaces is determined by Microsoft).

Another ID is used to indicate a specific class, a specific server. The Windows Registry stores this ID, with indications of the related DLL or executable file. The developers of an OLE server define the class identifier.

Both of these IDs are known as GUIDs, or *globally unique identifiers*. If each developer uses a number to indicate its own OLE servers, how can we be sure that these values are not duplicated? The short answer is that we cannot. The real answer is that a GUID is such a long number (with 16 bytes, or 128 bits, or a number with 38 digits!) that it is almost impossible to come up with two random numbers having the same value. Moreover, programmers should use the specific API call CoCreateGuid (directly or through their development environment) to come up with a valid GUID that reflects some system information.

In fact, GUIDs created on machines with network cards are guaranteed to be unique, because network cards contain unique serial numbers that form a base for the GUID creation. GUIDs created on machines with CPU IDs (such as the Pentium III) should also be guaranteed unique, even without a network card. With no unique hardware identifier, GUIDs are unlikely to ever duplicate.

WARNING   Besides being careful not to copy the GUID from someone else's program (which can result in two completely different COM objects using the same GUID), you should never make up your own ID by entering a casual sequence of numbers. Windows checks the IDs, and using a casual sequence won't generate a valid ID. An OLE server with an invalid ID is not recognized, and you won't get an error message! Windows also won't include an API or technique to validate a GUID. The risk with creating class or interface IDs by hand is that you could coincidentally duplicate a GUID that is already in use somewhere else in the system. However, to avoid this problem, simply press Ctrl+Shift+G in the Delphi editor, and you will get a new, properly defined, unique GUID.

Delphi defines a TGUID data type (in the System unit) to hold these numbers:

```
type
  TGUID = record
    D1: Integer;
    D2: Word;
    D3: Word;
    D4: array [0..7] of Byte;
  end;
```

This structure is actually quite odd but is required by Windows. You can assign a value to a GUID using the standard hexadecimal notation stored inside a string, as in this code fragment:

```
const
  Class_ActiveForm1: TGUID = '{1AFA6D61-7B89-11D0-98D0-444553540000}';
```

If you need to generate a GUID manually and not in the Delphi environment, you can simply call the CoCreateGuid Windows API function, as demonstrated by the NewGuid example (see Figure 19.1). This example is so simple that I've decided not to list its code.

(You can find the source code for this application, along with the chapter's other examples, in the folder for Chapter 19 on the companion CD.)

FIGURE 19.1:

An example of the GUIDs generated by the NewGuid example. Values depend on my computer and the time I run this program.

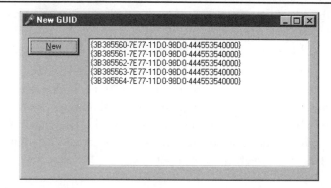

To handle GUIDs, Delphi provides the `GUIDToString` function and the opposite `String-ToGUID` function. You can also use the corresponding Windows API functions, such as `StringFromGuid2`, but in this case, you must use the WideString type instead of the string type. Any time OLE is involved, you have to use the WideString type, unless you use Delphi functions that automatically do the required conversion for you. Actually, OLE API functions use the `PWChar` type (pointer to null-terminated arrays of wide characters), but simply casting a WideString to `PWChar` does the trick.

Tip   Keep in mind that GUIDs come in different flavors. The two most important types are interface IDs (or IID), which refer to an interface, and class IDs (or CLSID), which refer to a specific object in a server. These two kinds of IDs both use the GUID style.

The Role of Class Factories

When we register the GUID of a COM object in the Registry, we can use a specific API function to create the object, such as the `CreateComObject` API:

```
function CreateComObject (const ClassID: TGUID): IUnknown;
```

This API function will look into the Registry, find the server registering the object with the given GUID, load it, and, if the server is a DLL, call the `DLLGetClassObject` method of the DLL. This is a function every in-process server must provide and export:

```
function DllGetClassObject (const CLSID, IID: TGUID;
  var Obj): HResult; stdcall;
```

This API function receives as parameters the requested class and interface, and it returns an object in its reference parameter. The object returned by this function is a *class factory*.

Now, what is a class factory? As the name suggests, a class factory is an object capable of creating other objects. Each server can have multiple objects. The server exposes the class factory, and the class factory can create one of these various objects. Each object, then, can have multiple interfaces. One of the many advantages of the Delphi simplified approach to COM development is that the system can provide a class factory for us. For this reason, I'm not going to add a class factory to our simple example.

The call to the `CreateComObject` API doesn't stop at the creation of the class factory, however. After retrieving the class factory, `CreateComObject` calls the `CreateInstance` method of the `IClassFactory` interface. This method creates the requested object and returns it. If no error occurs, this object becomes the return value of the `CreateComObject` API.

By setting up this mechanism (including the class factory and the `DLLGetClassObject` call), you make it very simple to create objects. `CreateComObject` is just a simple function call with a complex behavior behind the scenes. What's great in Delphi is that the complex mechanism is handled for you by the run-time system. So it's time to start looking in detail at how Delphi makes COM really easy to master.

Class Factories and Other Delphi COM Classes

Besides the `TComObject` class, Delphi includes several other predefined COM classes. We'll use them in the following sections, but here is a list of the most important COM classes of the Delphi VCL:

- `TInterfacedObject`, defined in the System unit, inherits from `TObject` and implements the `IUnknown` interface. It is used only for internal objects.

- `TComObject`, defined in the ComObj unit, inherits from `TObject` and implements both the `IUnknown` interface and the `ISupportErrorInfo` interface. Unlike `TInterfacedObject`, this class also has a related class factory.

- `TTypedComObject`, defined in the ComObj unit, inherits from `TComObject` and implements the `IProvideClassInfo` interface (in addition to the `IUnknown` and `ISupportErrorInfo` interfaces already implemented by the base class, `TComObject`).

- `TAutoObject`, defined in the ComObj unit, inherits from `TTypedComObject` and implements also the `IDispatch` interface.

- `TActiveXControl`, defined in the AxCtrls unit, inherits from `TAutoObject` and implements several interfaces (`IPersistStreamInit`, `IPersistStorage`, `IOleObject`, and `IOleControl`, to name just a few).

For each of these classes, Delphi also defines a class factory. The class factory classes form another hierarchy, with the same structure. Their names are `TComObjectFactory`, `TTypedComObjectFactory`, `TAutoObjectFactory`, and `TActiveXControlFactory`. Class factories are important, and every COM server requires them. Usually we simply use class factories by creating an object in the initialization section of the unit defining the corresponding server object class.

A First COM Server

There is no better way to understand COM than to build a simple COM server hosted by a DLL. A library hosting a COM object is indicated in Delphi as an ActiveX library. For this reason we can start the development of this project by selecting File ➤ New ➤ Other, moving to the ActiveX page, and selecting the ActiveX Library option. This generates a project file I've saved as FirstCom on the companion CD. This is the complete source code:

```
library FirstCom;

uses
  ComServ;

exports
  DllGetClassObject,
  DllCanUnloadNow,
  DllRegisterServer,
  DllUnregisterServer;

{$R *.RES}

begin
end.
```

The four functions exported by the DLL are required for COM compliance and are used by the system as follows:

- To access the class library (DllGetClassObject)

- To check whether the server has destroyed all its objects and can be unloaded from memory (DllCanUnloadNow)

- To add or remove information about the server in the Windows Registry (DllRegisterServer and DllUnregisterServer)

You generally don't have to implement these functions, because Delphi provides a default implementation in the ComServ unit. For this reason, in the code of our server, we only need to export them.

COM Interfaces and Objects

Now that we have the structure of our COM server in place, we can start developing it. The first step is to write the code of the interface we want to implement in the server. The interface can be very similar to the code of an abstract class, listing all the methods we want to make available from our server. (I have already discussed Object Pascal interfaces in Chapter 3.) Here is the code of a simple interface, which you should add to a separate unit (called NumIntf in the example):

```
type
  INumber = interface
    ['{B4131140-7C2F-11D0-98D0-444553540000}']
    function GetValue: Integer; stdcall;
    procedure SetValue (New: Integer); stdcall;
    procedure Increase; stdcall;
  end;
```

The IID was added to the code by pressing the Ctrl+Shift+G key combination.

After declaring the custom interface, we can add the actual object to the server. To accomplish this, we can use the COM Object Wizard (available in the ActiveX page of the File ➤ New ➤ Other dialog box). You can see this wizard's dialog box in Figure 19.2. Here you should enter the name of the class of the server, the interface you want to implement, and a description. I've disabled the generation of the type library to avoid introducing too many topics at once. You should also choose an instancing and a threading model, as described in the related sidebar.

FIGURE 19.2:

The COM Object Wizard

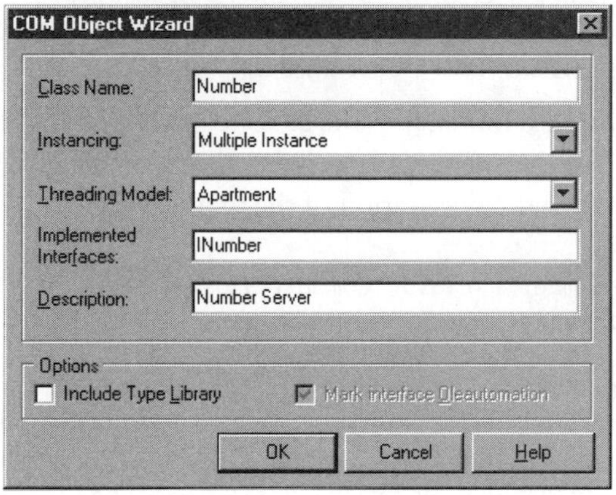

The code generated by the COM Object Wizard is actually quite simple. The interface contains the definition of the class to fill with methods and data:

```
type
  TNumber = class(TComObject, INumber)
    protected
      {Declare INumber methods here}
    end;
```

The server class inherits from the TComObject class, which I discussed in the last section. In the code generated by the wizard, after the server class comes the definition of the GUID for the server:

```
const
  Class_Number: TGUID = '{5B2EF181-3AAE-11D3-B9F1-00000100A27B}';
```

Finally, there is some code in the initialization section (which uses most of the options we've set up in the wizard's dialog box):

```
initialization
  TComObjectFactory.Create(ComServer, TNumber, Class_Number, 'Number',
    'Number Server', ciMultiInstance, tmApartment);
```

This code creates an object of the TComObjectFactory class, passing as parameters the global ComServer object, a class reference to the class we've just defined, the GUID for the class, the server name, the server description, and the instancing and threading models we want to use.

The global ComServer object, defined in the ComServ unit, is a manager of the class factories available in the server library. It uses its own ForEachFactory method to look for the class supporting a given COM object request, and it keeps track of the number of allocated objects. As we've already seen, in fact, the ComServ unit implements the functions required by the DLL to be a COM library.

Having examined the source code generated by the wizard, we can now complete it by adding to the TNumber class the methods required for implementing the INumber interface. First, write the declaration of the methods:

```
type
  TNumber = class(TComObject, INumber)
  private
    fValue: Integer;
  public
    function GetValue: Integer; virtual; stdcall;
    procedure SetValue (New: Integer); virtual; stdcall;
    procedure Increase; virtual; stdcall;
  end;
```

At this point, simply activate class completion by pressing Shift+Ctrl+C and fill the methods with the proper code. This is so straightforward that I'm not going to list it here; you can find the source code on the companion CD.

COM Instancing and Threading Models

When you create a COM server, you should choose a proper instancing and threading model, which can significantly affect the behavior of the COM server.

Instancing affects only out-of-process servers (any COM server in a separate executable file, rather than a DLL) and can assume three values:

Multiple   indicates that when several client applications require the COM object, the system starts multiple instances of the server.

Single   indicates that, even when several client applications require the COM object, there is only one instance of the server application; it creates multiple internal objects to service the requests.

Internal   indicates that the object can only be created inside the server; client applications cannot ask for one.

The second decision relates to the thread support of the COM object, which is valid for in-process servers only (DLLs). The threading model is a joint decision of the client and the server application: if both sides agree on one model, it is used for the connection. If no agreement is found, COM can still set up a connection using marshaling, which can slow down the operations. And keep in mind that a server must not only publish its threading model in the Registry (as a result of setting the option in the wizard); it must also follow the rules for that threading model in the code. Here are the key highlights of the various threading models:

The Single model   indicates no real support for threads. The requests reaching the COM server are serialized, so that the client can perform one operation at a time.

The Apartment model, or "single-threaded Apartment"   indicates that only the thread that created the object can call its methods. This means that the requests for each server object are serialized, but other objects of the same server can receive requests at the same time. For this reason, the server object must take extra care only to access global data of the server (using critical sections, mutexes, or some other synchronization techniques). This is the threading model generally used for ActiveX controls inside Internet Explorer.

The Free model, or "multi-threaded Apartment"   indicates that the client has no restrictions, which means that multiple threads can use the same object at the same time. For this reason, every method of every object must protect itself and the nonlocal data it uses against multiple simultaneous calls. This threading model is more complex for a

Continued on next page

> server to support than the Single and Apartment models, because even access to the object's own instance data must be handled with thread-safe care.
>
> **The fourth option, Both** indicates that the server object supports both the Apartment model and the Free model.
>
> **The final option, Neutral** was introduced in Windows 2000 and is available only under COM+. It indicates that multiple clients can call the object on different threads at the same time, but COM guarantees you that the same method is not invoked twice at the same time. Guarding for concurrent access to the data of the objet is required. Under COM, it is mapped to the Apartment model.

Initializing the COM Object

If you look back at the definition of the TComObject class, you will notice it has a nonvirtual constructor. (Actually, it has multiple nonvirtual constructors, which I've omitted from the listing.) Each TComObject constructor calls the virtual Initialize method. For this reason, if you want to customize the creation of an object and then initialize it, you should not define a new constructor (which will never be called). What you should do is override its Initialize method, as I've done in the TNumber class. Here is the final version of this class:

```
type
  TNumber = class(TComObject, INumber)
  private
    fValue: Integer;
  public
    function GetValue: Integer; virtual; stdcall;
    procedure SetValue (New: Integer); virtual; stdcall;
    procedure Increase; virtual; stdcall;
    procedure Initialize; override;
    destructor Destroy; override;
  end;
```

As you can see, I've also overridden the destructor of the class, because I wanted to test the automatic destruction of the COM objects provided by Delphi. Here is the code for this pseudoconstructor and the destructor:

```
procedure TNumber.Initialize;
begin
  inherited;
  fValue := 10;
end;
```

```
destructor TNumber.Destroy;
begin
  inherited;
  MessageBox (0, 'Object Destroyed', 'TDLLNumber', mb_OK); // API call
end;
```

In the first method, calling the inherited version is good practice, even though the TComObject.Initialize method has no code in this version of Delphi. The destructor, instead, must call the base class version. This is the code required to make our COM object work properly and to let us know when an object is actually destroyed.

Testing the COM Server

Now that we've finished writing our COM server object, we can register and use it. Simply compile its code and then use the Run ➤ Register ActiveX Server menu command in Delphi. You do this to register the server on your own machine, with the results you can see in Figure 19.3.

FIGURE 19.3:

The new registered server in Windows RegEdit

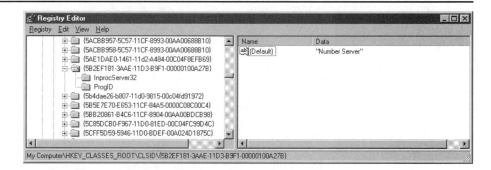

When you distribute this server, you should install it on the client computers. To accomplish this, you can write a REG file to install the server in the Registry. However, this is not really the best approach, because the server already includes a function you can activate to register the server. This function can be activated by the Delphi environment, as we've seen, or in a few other ways:

- You can pass the COM server DLL as a command-line parameter to Microsoft's RegSvr32.exe program, found in the \Windows\System directory.

- You can use the similar TRegSvr.exe demo program that ships with Delphi. (The compiled version is in the \Bin directory, and its source code is in the \Demos\ActiveX directory.)

- You can let an installation builder program call the registration function of the server.

Having registered the server, we can now turn to the client side of our example. This time, the example is called TestCom and is stored in a separate directory. In fact, the program loads the server DLL through the OLE/COM mechanism, thanks to the server information present in the Registry, so it's not necessary for the client to know which directory the server resides in.

The form displayed by this program is very similar to the one we've used to test the object inside the DLL. In the client program, you must include the source code file with the interface and redeclare the COM server GUID. Of course, the code of the program's `FormCreate` method should be updated to create the required COM objects. The program starts with all the buttons disabled (at design time), and it enables them only after an object has been created. This way, if an exception is raised while creating one of the objects, the buttons related to the object won't be enabled:

```
procedure TForm1.FormCreate(Sender: TObject);
begin
  // create first object
  Num1 := CreateComObject (Class_Number) as INumber;
  Num1.SetValue (SpinEdit1.Value);
  Label1.Caption := 'Num1: ' + IntToStr (Num1.GetValue);
  Button1.Enabled := True;
  Button2.Enabled := True;

  // create second object
  Num2 := CreateComObject (Class_Number) as INumber;
  Label2.Caption := 'Num2: ' + IntToStr (Num2.GetValue);
  Button3.Enabled := True;
  Button4.Enabled := True;
end;
```

Notice in particular the call to `CreateComObject` and the following as cast. The API call starts the COM object-construction mechanism I've already described in detail. This call also dynamically loads the server DLL. The return value is an `IUnknown` object. This object must be converted to the proper interface type before assigning it to the `Num1` and `Num2` fields, which now have the interface type `INumber` as their data type:

```
type
  TForm1 = class(TForm)
    ...
  private
    Num1, Num2 : INumber;
```

WARNING   To downcast an interface to the actual type, *always* use the **as** cast, which for interfaces performs a `QueryInterface` call behind the scenes. This provides some protection, because it raises an exception if the interface you are casting to is not supported by the given object. In the case of interfaces, the **as** cast is the only way to *extract* an interface from another interface. If you write a plain cast of the form `INumber(CreateComObject(Class_Number))`, the program will crash, even if the cast seems to make sense, as in the case above. Casting an interface pointer to another interface pointer is an error. Period. Never do it.

In Figure 19.4, you can see the output of this test program, which is very similar to the previous version. Notice that this time, Num2 shows the initial value of the object at start-up, as set up in its Initialize method. Notice also that I've added one more button, which creates a third temporary COM object:

```
procedure TForm1.Button5Click(Sender: TObject);
var
  Num3: INumber;
begin
  // create a new temporary COM object
  Num3 := CreateComObject (Class_Number) as INumber;
  Num3.SetValue (100);
  Num3.Increase;
  ShowMessage ('Num3: ' + IntToStr (Num3.GetValue));
end;
```

FIGURE 19.4:

The output of the TestCom example, a COM client

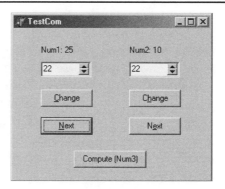

Pressing this button, you simply get the value of the number following 100. To see why I added this method to the example, you need to press the button a second time, after the message showing the result. Now you get a second message, indicating that the object has been destroyed. This demonstrates that simply letting an interface object go out of scope automatically calls the object's Release method, decreases the object's reference count, and destroys the object if its reference count reaches zero. Chapter 3 described this reference-counting mechanism in more detail.

The same happens to the other two objects as soon as the program terminates. Even if the program doesn't explicitly destroy the two objects in the FormDestroy method, they are indeed destroyed, as the message shown by their Destroy destructor clearly demonstrates. This happens because they were declared to be of an interface type, and Delphi is going to use reference counting for them.

Using Interface Properties

As a further small step, we can extend the example by adding a property to the INumber interface. When you add a property to an interface, you indicate the data type and then the read and write directives. You can have read-only or write-only properties, but the read and write clauses must always refer to a method because interfaces don't hold anything else but methods.

Here is the updated interface, which is part of the PropCom example:

```
type
  INumberProp = interface
    ['{B36C5800-8E59-11D0-98D0-444553540000}']
    function GetValue: Integer; stdcall;
    procedure SetValue (New: Integer); stdcall;
    property Value: Integer read GetValue write SetValue;
    procedure Increase; stdcall;
  end;
```

I've given this interface a new name and, what's even more important, a new interface ID. I could have inherited the new interface type from the previous one, but this would have provided no real advantage. COM by itself doesn't really support inheritance, and from the perspective of COM, all interfaces are different simply because they have different interface IDs. Needless to say, in Delphi we can use inheritance to improve the structure of the code of the interfaces and of the server objects implementing them.

In the PropCom example, I've updated the server class declaration simply by writing:

```
type
  TDllNumber = class (TComObject, INumberProp)
  ...
```

This class also has a new server object ID. The client program, also on the CD, can now simply use the Value property instead of the SetValue and GetValue methods. Here is a small excerpt from the FormCreate method:

```
Num1 := CreateComObject (Class_NumPropServer) as INumberProp;
Num1.Value := SpinEdit1.Value;
Label1.Caption := 'Num1: ' + IntToStr (Num1.Value);
```

The difference between using methods and properties for an interface is only syntactical, because interface properties cannot access private data as class properties can. By using properties, we can make the code a little more readable.

Calling Virtual Methods

We've built a couple of examples based on COM, but you might still feel uncomfortable with the idea of a program calling methods of objects that are created within a DLL. How is this possible if those methods are not exported by the DLL? The COM server, the DLL, creates an object and returns it to the calling application. By doing this, the DLL creates an object with a *virtual method table* (VMT). (Remember that all the interface methods are virtual by default.)

Because every object embeds a pointer to its VMT, the main program receives an object, and also a way to work on it, by calling its virtual methods. The main program doesn't need to know the memory address of those methods, because the objects know it, exactly as they do with a polymorphic call. But COM is even more powerful than this: you don't even have to know which programming language was used to create the object, provided its VMT follows the standard dictated by COM.

TIP   The COM-compatible VMT implies also a strange effect. The method names are not important, provided their address is in the proper position in the VMT. This is why you can map a method of an interface to an actual function implementing it.

To sum things up, we can say that COM provides a language-independent binary standard for objects. The objects you share among modules are compiled, and their VMT has a particular structure, determined by COM and not by the development environment you've used.

Windows Shell Programming

In the last section, we built a fully standard COM object, packaged it as an in-process server, and used it from a standard client. However, the COM interface we implemented was a custom interface we'd built. Now we can try to build clients and servers related to the Windows shell interfaces, which are all based on COM. The original Windows API was basically a collection of functions, but all the most recent APIs are generally based on COM.

The following sections use some existing servers that are part of the Windows shell; we'll write a client application and use the COM servers provided by the system. This case illustrates the difference from the traditional use of the Windows API calls. I'm also going to write some COM servers to be used by the Windows system, particularly the Explorer. This case illustrates the difference from the traditional development of a callback function invoked by the system.

Creating Shortcuts

One of the simplest shell interfaces we can use in a client application is the IShellLink interface. This interface relates to Windows shortcuts and allows programmers to access the information of an existing shortcut or to create a new one. In the ShCut example on the CD-ROM, I'm going to create various types of shortcuts, all referring to the program itself. Of course, once you understand how to do this, you can easily extend the example and create shortcuts for any program or file.

The example has an edit box for the name of the shortcut, a few check boxes, and two buttons. When the Create button is pressed, the text in the edit box is used as the name of a new shortcut, which is placed in the current directory, on the desktop, or in the Start menu. These options are not exclusive; a user can create multiple shortcuts at once.

The most important code is at the very beginning of this method. The CreateComObject call creates a system object, as indicated by the GUID passed as a parameter. The result of this call (which is an IUnknown interface) is converted both to an IShellLink interface and to an IPersistFile interface:

```
uses
  ComObj, ActiveX, ShlObj, Registry;

procedure TForm1.Button1Click(Sender: TObject);
var
  AnObj: IUnknown;
  ShLink: IShellLink;
  PFile: IPersistFile;
  FileName: string;
  WFileName: WideString;
  Reg: TRegIniFile;
begin
  // access the two interfaces of the object
  AnObj := CreateComObject (CLSID_ShellLink);
  ShLink := AnObj as IShellLink;
  PFile := AnObj as IPersistFile;
```

Actually, we could have written the last three lines of code above using this shorter notation:

```
ShLink := CreateComObject (CLSID_ShellLink) as IShellLink;
PFile := ShLink as IPersistFile;
```

If you look at similar examples built in other languages, you'll notice that to access the IPersistFile interface, the programs use custom calls to the QueryInterface method. The two as expressions basically call QueryInterface for us.

Once we have the IShellLink interface, we can call some of its methods, such as SetPath and SetWorkingDirectory:

```
// get the name of the application file
FileName := ParamStr (0);
// set the link properties
ShLink.SetPath (PChar (FileName));
ShLink.SetWorkingDirectory (PChar (ExtractFilePath (FileName)));
```

Once we've set up the shell link object, we have to save it, depending on the status of the three check boxes, calling the Save method of the IPersistFile interface of the object. The simplest version is the one used to save the link in the current directory:

```
// save the file in the current dir
if cbDir.Checked then
begin
  // using a WideString
  WFileName := ExtractFilePath (FileName) + EditName.Text + '.lnk';
  PFile.Save (PWChar (WFileName), False);
end;
```

The call to the Save method (which creates the physical LNK file) requires a "pointer to wide char" parameter. The simplest way to obtain this is to declare a long string and then cast it to a PWChar. Do not try casting a plain string to PWChar—the compiler will emit a warning and the program won't work!

To create the shortcut on the desktop or in the Start menu, we should first determine the corresponding system folder by looking up the proper value in the Registry. By writing the program this way, we ensure it will work on different versions of Windows and on localized versions as well. Here is the source code for the last two check boxes:

```
// save on the desktop
if cbDesktop.Checked then
begin
  Reg := TRegIniFile.Create(
    'Software\MicroSoft\Windows\CurrentVersion\Explorer');
  WFileName := Reg.ReadString ('Shell Folders', 'Desktop', '') +
    '\' + EditName.Text + '.lnk';
  Reg.Free;
  PFile.Save (PWChar (WFileName), False);
end;
// save in the Start Menu
if cbStartMenu.Checked then
begin
```

```
    Reg := TRegIniFile.Create(
      'Software\MicroSoft\Windows\CurrentVersion\Explorer');
    WFileName := Reg.ReadString ('Shell Folders', 'Start Menu', '') +
      '\' + EditName.Text + '.lnk';
    Reg.Free;
    PFile.Save (PWChar (WFileName), False);
  end;
```

To look up the information in the Registry, I've used the `TRegIniFile` class, although there are other related classes in the VCL, such as the `TRegistry` class. The effect of running this program and pressing the button is that Windows will add a new link in the directory of the project, on the desktop, or in the Start menu. You can see an example of the program in Figure 19.5.

FIGURE 19.5:

The simple user interface of the ShCut example, and two shortcuts created with it in the project folder and on the desktop

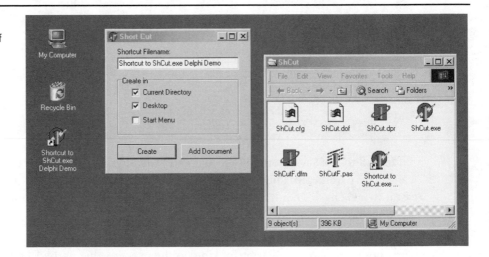

Using Shell APIs and Objects

As an extra feature, the program can also add a new document to the list of recently used ones, calling the `SHAddToRecentDocs` method:

```
procedure TForm1.Button2Click(Sender: TObject);
var
  ProjectFile: string;
begin
  ProjectFile := ChangeFileExt (ParamStr (0), '.dpr');
  SHAddToRecentDocs (SHARD_PATH, PChar(ProjectFile));
end;
```

This has very little to do with COM, and I've added it to the example only to highlight that there is a very large number of shell-related APIs, available in the ShlObj unit, besides the original and more limited ShellApi unit.

Another example, available in the source code for this chapter and called FindFolders, highlights the use of another *plain* (non-COM) shell function, SHBrowseForFolder. In the example you can see the following code:

```
procedure TForm1.btnBrowseClick(Sender: TObject);
var
  bi: TBrowseInfo;
  pidl: pItemIdList;
  strpath, displayname: string;
begin
  SetLength (displayname, 100);

  bi.hwndOwner := Handle;
  bi.pidlRoot := nil;
  bi.pszDisplayName := pChar (displayname);
  bi.lpszTitle := 'Select a folder';
  bi.ulFlags := bif_StatusText;
  bi.lpfn := nil;
  bi.lParam := 0;

  pidl := SHBrowseForFolder (bi);

  SetLength (strPath, 100);
  SHGetPathFromIdList (pidl, PChar(strPath));
  Edit1.Text := strPath;
end;
```

The FindFolders example even shows some Delphi-specific APIs to interact with files and folders (available also on Linux) including SelectDirectory, which has the same effect of SHBrowseForFolder but a different user interface. The example also uses the DirectoryExists and ForceDirectories functions, available in the FileCtrl unit. You can see how they are used by looking in the source code of the example.

NOTE   Notice that in Delphi 6, some of the Shell API is also encapsulated in the sample ShellListView, ShellTreeView, and ShellComboBox controls. I've used these controls in a few examples throughout the book, including the DirDemo example of Chapter 18, "Writing Database Components."

The "To-Do File" Application

As a second example of integrating a Delphi program with the system shell, I've tried to write a simple real-world application that uses file dragging and a context menu handler. I'll start with the file dragging first, because this will actually introduce some of the techniques used by the context menu handler.

As I mentioned, this application is actually useful; you can use it to create a sort of "to-do list." It is based on a Paradox table that stores filenames and notes about the files. The form of the application has a DBGrid component showing only a single column containing the filenames and a memo control hosting the notes related to the current file. You can see this form at design time in Figure 19.6.

FIGURE 19.6:

The form of the ToDoFile example at design time

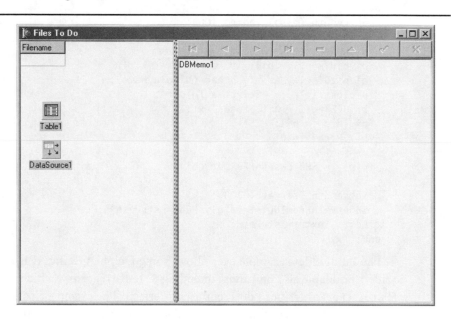

Notice that the navigator component has no "New Record" button, and the DBGrid is set up as a read-only component. In fact, users should not be able to create new records except by dragging a file onto the form, and they're not allowed to change the filename field in any way (except by deleting it). All the user can do is edit the notes field, entering a description of the operations to be done on the file.

Creating the Database

To create the database table for this example, I've used the `FieldDefs` property to define the structure and set the `StoreDefs` property to True to save the table definition along with the form DFM file. The table has two fields, a string field called Filename and a memo field called Notes. Of course, you can also create the table at design time, using the table component's local menu. The program, however, calls the `CreateTable` method in the `OnCreate` event handler, unless this has already been done:

```
procedure TToDoFileForm.FormCreate(Sender: TObject);
begin
  // eventually create the table
  if not Table1.Exists then
    Table1.CreateTable;
  // activate the table
  Table1.Activate;
  // accept dragging to the form
  DragAcceptFiles (Handle, True);
end;
```

Dragging Files to the Form

As you can see in the listing above, the form initialization code also registers the window with the system as a file-dragging target, by calling the `DragAcceptFiles` Windows API function. As a result, the application's cursor changes to the typical "drag accept" icon when a file is dragged over it. You can see an example of this cursor in Figure 19.7.

FIGURE 19.7:

The drag-accept cursor displayed by the ToDoFile application as a user drags a file over it

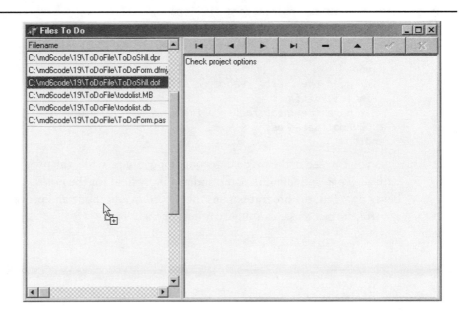

When a file-dragging operation is performed, the system sends the window a wm_DropFiles message. This message passes (among its other parameters) a handle to a file-drop structure from which you can extract information by using the DragQueryFile API function. When this API function is called with the $FFFFFFFF parameter, it returns the number of files dragged to the window; when it is called with a numeric parameter, it fills a buffer with the name of that file. For this reason, the code of a wm_DropFiles message handler gets the number of files first and then loops for each of the files, as the following listing demonstrates:

```
procedure TToDoFileForm.DropFiles(var Msg: TWmDropFiles);
var
  nFiles, I: Integer;
  Filename: string;
begin
  // get the number of dropped files
  nFiles := DragQueryFile (Msg.Drop, $FFFFFFFF, nil, 0);
  // for each file
  try
    for I := 0 to nFiles - 1 do
    begin
      // allocate memory
      SetLength (Filename, 80);
      // read the file name
      DragQueryFile (Msg.Drop, I, PChar (Filename), 80);
      // normalize file
      Filename := PChar (Filename);
      // add a new record
      Table1.InsertRecord ([Filename, '']);
    end;
  finally
    DragFinish (Msg.Drop);
  end;
  // open the (last) record in edit mode
  Table1.Edit;
  // move the input focus to the memo
  DBMemo1.SetFocus;
end;
```

As you can see in the preceding code, for every new file, the program inserts a new record with the corresponding filename and an empty field for the notes. Then, for the last file being dragged, the program opens the record in edit mode and moves the focus to the memo control, so that a user can fill the notes for the file.

Creating a Context-Menu Handler

Now that we have the base program running, we can add a shell extension to the system to let the user simply select a file and "send" it to the application without having to do the dragging operation, which is not always handy when there are many programs running. A context-menu extension is one of the available Windows shell extensions and is activated every time a user right-clicks a file in the Windows Explorer.

Technically, a context menu is a COM server exposing an internal object that is going to be created and used by the system. A context-menu COM object must implement two different interfaces, IContextMenu and IShellExtInit. The first interface defines specific actions for the context menu, such as defining the number of menu items to add and their text, while the second interface defines a way to access the file or files the user is operating on. This is the resulting definition of the COM server object class:

```
type
  TToDoMenu = class(TComObject, IUnknown, IContextMenu, IShellExtInit)
  private
    fFileName: string;
  protected
    {Declare IContextMenu methods here}
    function QueryContextMenu(Menu: HMENU; indexMenu,
      idCmdFirst, idCmdLast, uFlags: UINT): HResult; stdcall;
    function InvokeCommand(
      var lpici: TCMInvokeCommandInfo): HResult; stdcall;
    function GetCommandString(idCmd, uType: UINT; pwReserved: PUINT;
      pszName: LPSTR; cchMax: UINT): HResult; stdcall;
    {Declare IShellExtInit methods here}
    function IShellExtInit.Initialize = InitShellExt;
    function InitShellExt (pidlFolder: PItemIDList;
      lpdobj: IDataObject; hKeyProgID: HKEY): HResult; stdcall;
  end;
```

Notice that the class implements the Initialize method of the IShellExtInit interface with a differently named method, InitShellExt. The reason is that I wanted to avoid confusion with the Initialize method of the TComObject base class, which is the hook we have to initialize the object, as described earlier in this chapter. Let's examine the InitShellExt method first; it is definitely the most complex one:

```
function TToDoMenu.InitShellExt(pidlFolder: PItemIDList;
  lpdobj: IDataObject; hKeyProgID: HKEY): HResult; stdcall;
var
  medium: TStgMedium;
  fe: TFormatEtc;
begin
  Result := E_FAIL;
```

```
// check if the lpdobj pointer is nil
if Assigned (lpdobj) then
begin
  with fe do
  begin
    cfFormat := CF_HDROP;
    ptd := nil;
    dwAspect := DVASPECT_CONTENT;
    lindex := -1;
    tymed := TYMED_HGLOBAL;
  end;
  // transform the lpdobj data to a storage medium structure
  Result := lpdobj.GetData(fe, medium);
  if not Failed (Result) then
  begin
    // check if only one file is selected
    if DragQueryFile (medium.hGlobal, $FFFFFFFF, nil, 0) = 1 then
    begin
      SetLength (fFileName, 1000);
      DragQueryFile (medium.hGlobal, 0, PChar (fFileName), 1000);
      // realign string
      fFileName := PChar (fFileName);
      Result := NOERROR;
    end
    else
      Result := E_FAIL;
  end;
  ReleaseStgMedium(medium);
  end;
end;
```

The initial portion of the method transforms the pointer to the IDataObject interface, which we receive as a parameter, into the same data structure used in a file drop operation, so that we can read the file information by using the DragQueryFile function again. This complex way of coding is actually the simplest one you can use! At the end of this operation, we have the value of the filename. Any selection of multiple files is not accepted.

We can now look at the methods of the IContextMenu interface. The first, QueryContextMenu, is used to add new items to the local menu of the file. In this case, we add a new menu item (calling the InsertMenu API function) only if the ToDoFile application is running. We can determine this by searching for a window corresponding to the TToDoFileForm class, which should be unique in the system. The result of the function is the number of items added to the menu:

```
function TToDoMenu.QueryContextMenu(Menu: HMENU;
  indexMenu, idCmdFirst, idCmdLast, uFlags: UINT): HResult;
begin
```

```
      // add entry only if the program is running
      if FindWindow ('TToDoFileForm', nil) <> 0 then
      begin
        // add a new item to context menu
        InsertMenu (Menu, indexMenu, MF_STRING or MF_BYPOSITION, idCmdFirst,
          'Send to ToDoFile');
        // return the number of menu items added
        Result := 1;
      end
      else
        Result := 0;
    end;
```

Now that items have been added to the menu, a user can select them. While he or she moves over the items, a descriptive message is displayed in the status bar of the Windows Explorer. The menu ID (idCmd) we receive in the GetCommandString method is simply the relative number, starting with zero, of the items we have added to the menu. When the cursor is over an item, we simply copy a string with its description to the buffer provided by the system:

```
    function TToDoMenu.GetCommandString(idCmd, uType: UINT;
      pwReserved: PUINT; pszName: LPSTR; cchMax: UINT): HRESULT;
    begin
      if idCmd = 0 then
      begin
        // return help string for menu item
        strCopy (pszName, 'Add file to the ToDoFile database');
        Result := NOERROR;
      end
      else
        Result := E_INVALIDARG;
    end;
```

The final step is the operation to do once a menu item is actually selected. The InvokeCommand method receives a pointer to a structure holding the request. This method follows a standard pattern of first checking that the request is valid by looking at the two 16-bit words of the lpici.lpVerb value. After these preliminary (but required) steps, we check the value to see which menu item was activated; or, if the context menu has only one item, as in this case, we simply test for a value of zero. The following is the skeleton of the code, before we add the specific action:

```
    function TToDoMenu.InvokeCommand (var lpici: TCMInvokeCommandInfo): HResult;
    begin
      Result := NOERROR;
      // make sure we are not being called by an application
      if HiWord(Integer(lpici.lpVerb)) <> 0 then
      begin
        Result := E_FAIL;
        Exit;
```

```
  end;
  // make sure we aren't being passed an invalid argument number
  if LoWord(lpici.lpVerb) > 0 then
  begin
    Result := E_INVALIDARG;
    Exit;
  end;
  // execute the command specified by lpici.lpVerb
  if LoWord(lpici.lpVerb) = 0 then
  begin
    // actual code still missing here
  end
end;
```

Sending Data to Another Application with *wm_CopyData*

Because we have the filename the user is operating on, all we have to do in the context-menu handler is send this name to the main form of the ToDoFile application. The problem is that the context-menu handler DLL runs in the Windows Explorer process, so it cannot send the value of a memory pointer to another process. This would simply be useless; as in Win32, different applications have separate memory address spaces.

We saw in the last chapter that one way to share data among applications is to use a memory-mapped file. Another technique, which is actually better in this case, is to use the wm_CopyData message. This is a special Windows message, which can be used to send a memory buffer to another application: Windows will resolve all the memory conversion problems for us. A program basically fills the CopyDataStruct data structure with the data and indicates its length, and then must use the SendMessage API to forward it to a destination window. For this reason we need to use FindWindow again to get the handle of the main window of the ToDoFile application. Here is the rest of the code of the InvokeCommand method:

```
var
  hwnd: THandle;
  cds: CopyDataStruct;
begin
  ...
  if LoWord(lpici.lpVerb) = 0 then
  begin
    // get the handle of the window
    hwnd := FindWindow ('TToDoFileForm', nil);
    if hwnd <> 0 then
    begin
      // prepare the data to copy
      cds.dwData := 0;
      cds.cbData := length (fFileName);
      cds.lpData := PChar (fFileName);
```

```
    // activate the destination window
    SetForegroundWindow (hwnd);
    // send the data
    SendMessage (hwnd, wm_CopyData, lpici.hWnd, Integer (@cds));
  end;
end;
```

Before sending the data, we must activate the destination window by calling the Set-ForegroundWindow API. This is necessary because we are going to activate a window that was created by another thread, something Windows doesn't normally do. Notice also that if you write this call in the ToDoFile application as it receives the wm_CopyData message, it will produce no effect at all.

As the context-menu handler sends data to it, the application has to be extended to handle the wm_CopyData message. In this event handler, we receive the same structure we sent for the other side, although between the send operation done by the context-menu handler and the receive operation done by the application. Windows takes care of mapping the data properly to the other address space. As a result, extracting the filename is actually very simple, but keep in mind that this is so only because Windows does a lot of work behind the scenes. Using a plain Windows message other than wm_CopyData will never work!

Here is the code I've added to the form of the ToDoFile application. It does several things: It restores the application if it was minimized, retrieves the name of the file, inserts a new record in the database table, copies the filename, and moves the focus to the memo control once more.

```
procedure TToDoFileForm.CopyData(var Msg: TWmCopyData);
var
  Filename: string;
begin
  // restore the window if minimized
  if IsIconic (Application.Handle) then
    Application.Restore;

  // extract the filename from the data
  Filename := PChar (Msg.CopyDataStruct.lpData);
  // insert a new record
  Table1.Insert;
  // set up the file name
  Table1.FieldByName ('Filename').AsString := Filename;
  // move the input focus to the memo
  DBMemo1.SetFocus;
end;
```

Registering the Shell Extension

After writing this shell extension, we must register it. With the usual Run ➤ Register ActiveX Server command, we can register the server in the system, but we still have to provide some extra information to register it as a shell extension, in this case for any type of file. There are several approaches: you can edit the Registry manually, you can write a REG file, or you can add registration information right into the COM server library, which is my preferred approach. In a Delphi COM server, the default registration takes place in the TComObjectFactory class, when the UpdateRegistry method is executed. We can modify the default registration by inheriting a class from the standard class factory class and overriding this method:

```
type
  TToDoMenuFactory = class (TComObjectFactory)
  public
    procedure UpdateRegistry (Register: Boolean); override;
  end;
```

In this method, we should either add the entry in the Registry or delete it, depending on the value of the Boolean parameter:

```
procedure TToDoMenuFactory.UpdateRegistry(Register: Boolean);
var
  Reg: TRegistry;
begin
  inherited UpdateRegistry (Register);

  Reg := TRegistry.Create;
  Reg.RootKey := HKEY_CLASSES_ROOT;
  try
    if Register then
      if Reg.OpenKey('\*\ShellEx\ContextMenuHandlers\ToDo', True) then
        Reg.WriteString('', GUIDToString(Class_ToDoMenuMenu))
    else
      if Reg.OpenKey('\*\ShellEx\ContextMenuHandlers\ToDo', False) then
        Reg.DeleteKey ('\*\ShellEx\ContextMenuHandlers\ToDo');
  finally
    Reg.CloseKey;
    Reg.Free;
  end;
end;
```

WARNING   I've checked this code under Windows 2000, but I'm not completely sure it works also on Windows 98/Me, as the shell portion of the registry has been subject to subtle changes among different versions of Windows.

In the initialization section of the COM object unit, we also need to create a new global object of this class instead of the base class factory class:

```
initialization
  TToDoMenuFactory.Create (ComServer, TToDoMenu, Class_ToDoMenuMenu,
    'ToDoMenu', 'ToDoMenu Shell Extension', ciMultiInstance, tmApartment);
```

Now you can simply register the server and set it up as a context-menu handler by using the Delphi Run ➤ Register ActiveX Server menu command, the RegSrv32 application, or most of the tools used to create installation programs.

What's Next?

In this chapter I have discussed the foundations of Microsoft's COM technology. We've seen how Delphi supports COM and built a few simple servers. In the second part of the chapter, we've spend some time discussing the COM-based Shell API and the development of a shell extension.

The next chapter opens up COM to its higher-level techniques, covering Automation, Documents, and ActiveX Controls. Now that we know the foundations, exploring these COM-technologies will definitely be simpler, although we won't delve into the low-level details of these technologies.

CHAPTER 20

From Automation to COM+

- OLE Automation

- Creating and using Automation servers

- Using type libraries

- Automating office programs

- The OLE Container component

- Building an ActiveX and an ActiveForm

- Introducing COM+

After the last chapter, which was devoted to the foundations of Microsoft's COM architecture, it is time to look into some of the actual high-level Windows programming techniques based on COM. We'll start by discussing Automation and the role of type libraries. Also, we'll see how to work properly with Delphi data types in Automation servers and clients.

Later, we'll focus on the use of the Automation support provided by Microsoft Office applications, made simple thanks to the ready-to-use components that embed Office server programs and documents. In the final part of the chapter, we'll explore the use of embedded objects, with the OleContainer component, and the development of OLE controls or ActiveX controls.

I'll also introduce stateless COM (MTS and COM+) technologies and a few other advanced ideas. But let's begin with more foundational material.

OLE Automation

In the last chapter, we saw that you can use COM to let an executable file and a library share objects, and that this can be used to interact with the Windows shell. Most of the time, however, users want applications that can talk to each other. One of the approaches you can use for this goal is OLE Automation. After presenting a couple of examples that use custom interfaces based on type libraries, I'll cover the development of Word and Excel OLE controllers, showing how to transfer database information to those applications.

NOTE   The current Microsoft documentation uses the term *Automation* instead of *OLE Automation*, and uses the terms *active document* and *compound document* instead of *OLE Document*. This book uses this new terminology along with the older "OLE" terminology incorporated into many Delphi component names and other identifiers.

In Windows, applications don't live in separate worlds; users often want them to interact. The Clipboard and DDE offer a simple way for applications to interact, as users can copy and paste data between applications. However, more and more programs offer an OLE Automation interface to let other programs drive them. Beyond the obvious advantage of programmed automation compared to manual user operations, these interfaces are completely language-neutral, so you can use Delphi, C++, Visual Basic, or a macro language to drive an OLE Automation server regardless of the programming language used to write it.

OLE Automation is quite straightforward to implement in Delphi, thanks to the extensive work by the compiler and VCL to shield developers from its intricacies. To support OLE Automation, Delphi provides a wizard and a powerful type-library editor, and it supports dual interfaces.

When you use an in-process DLL, the client application can use the server and call its methods directly, because they are in the same address space. When you use OLE Automation, the situation is more complex. The client (called the *controller*) and the server are two separate applications running in different address spaces. For this reason, the system must dispatch the method calls using a complex mechanism called *marshaling* (something I won't cover in detail). What is important to know is that there are two ways a controller can call the methods exposed by a server:

- It can ask for the execution of a method, passing its name in a string, in a way similar to the dynamic call to a DLL. This is what Delphi does when you use a variant to call the OLE Automation server. This technique is very easy to use, but it is rather slow and provides very little compiler type-checking.

- It can import the definition of a Delphi interface for the object on the server and call its methods in a more direct way (simply dispatching a number). This technique, based on interfaces, allows the compiler to check the types of the parameters and produces faster code, but it requires a little more effort from the programmer. Also, you end up binding your controller application to a specific version of the server. A variation of this technique involves the use of dispatch interfaces, based on the definition of the interfaces.

In the following examples, we'll use all these techniques and compare them a little further.

Introducing Type Libraries

The most important difference between the two approaches is that the second generally requires a *type library*, one of the foundations of OLE and COM. A type library is basically a collection of type information. This collection generally describes all of the elements (the objects, the interfaces, and other type information) made available by a server. The key difference between a type library and other descriptions of these elements (such as some C or Pascal code) is that a type library is language-independent. The type elements are defined by OLE as a subset of the standard elements of programming languages, and any development tool can use them. Why do we need this information?

As mentioned before, an OLE Automation controller can use variants and have no type information about the server it is using. This means that, behind the scenes, every function call has to be dispatched to the server using the `Invoke` method of `IDispatch`, passing the function name as a string parameter and hoping the name corresponds to an existing function of the server.

Although this sounds difficult, a small code fragment using the old Automation interface of Microsoft Word, registered as `Word.Basic`, illustrates how simple it is for a programmer:

```
var
  VarW: Variant;
begin
  VarW := CreateOleObject ('Word.Basic');
  VarW.FileNew;
  VarW.Insert ('Mastering Delphi by Marco Cantù');
```

NOTE   As we'll see later, recent versions of Word still register the `Word.Basic` interface, which corresponds to the internal WordBasic macro language, but it also registers the new interface `Word.Application`, which corresponds to the VBA macro language. We'll also see that Delphi provides some components that simplify the connection with Microsoft Office applications.

These three lines of code start Word (unless it was already running), create a new document, and add a few words to it. You can see the effect of this code in Figure 20.1. The code uses a variant, which is a *type-variant* data type. A variant can assume as its value different data types, including a COM object supporting the `IDispatch` interface. Variants are type-checked at run time; this is why the compiler can compile the code even if it doesn't know about the methods of the OLE Automation server.

FIGURE 20.1:

This Word document is being created and composed by a Delphi application, WordTest.

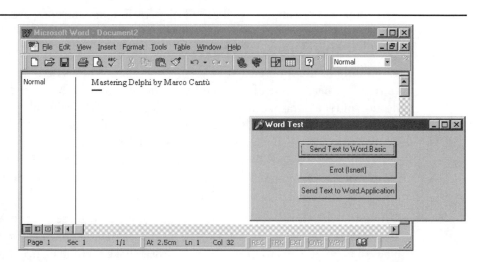

Unfortunately, the Delphi compiler has no way to check whether the methods exist. Doing all the type checks at run time is risky, because if you make even a minor spelling error in a function name, you get no warning whatsoever of your error until you run the program and reach that line of code. For example, if you type `VarW.Isnert`, the compiler will not complain about the misspelling at all, but at run time, you'll get an error. Because it doesn't recognize the name, Word assumes the method does not exist.

Although the OLE `IDispatch` interface supports the approach we've just seen, it is also possible—and safer—for a server to export the description of its interfaces and objects using a type library. This type library can then be converted by a specific tool (such as Delphi) into definitions written in the language you want to use to write your client or controller program (such as Object Pascal). This makes it possible for a compiler to check whether the code is correct.

Once the compiler has done its checks, it can use either of two different techniques to send the request to the server. It can use a plain VTable (that is, an entry in an interface type declaration), or it can use a `dispinterface` (dispatch interface). We used an interface type declaration in the last chapter, so it should be familiar. A `dispinterface` is basically a way to map each entry in an interface to a number. Calls to the server can then be dispatched by number. We can consider this an intermediate technique, in between dispatching by function name and using a direct call in the VTable.

> **NOTE**   The term *dispinterface* is actually a keyword. A `dispinterface` is automatically generated by the type-library editor for every interface. Along with `dispinterface`, Delphi uses other related keywords: `dispid` indicates the number to associate with each element; `readonly` and `writeonly` are optional specifiers for properties.

The term used to describe this ability to connect to a server in two different ways, using a more dynamic or a more static approach, is *dual interfaces*. This means that in writing an OLE controller, you can choose to access the methods of a server in two ways: you can use late binding and the mechanism provided by the `dispinterface`, or you can use early binding and the mechanism based on the VTables, the interface types.

It is important to keep in mind that (along with other considerations) different techniques result in faster or slower execution. Looking up a function by name (and doing the type checking at run time) is the slowest approach, using a `dispinterface` is much faster, and using the direct VTable call is the fastest approach. We'll do this kind of test in the TlibCli example, later in this chapter.

Writing an OLE Automation Server

We'll start by writing an OLE Automation server. To create an OLE Automation object, you can use Delphi's Automation Object Wizard. Start with a new application, open the Object Repository by selecting File ➤ New, move to the ActiveX page, and choose Automation Object. In the resulting Automation Object Wizard (shown in Figure 20.2), enter the name of the class (without the initial *T*, because this will be added automatically for you) and click OK. Delphi will now open the type-library editor.

FIGURE 20.2:

Delphi's Automation
Object Wizard

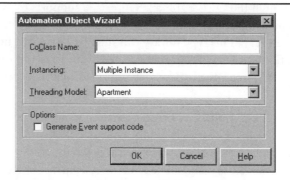

As you can see in Figure 20.2, Delphi can generate OLE Automation servers that also export events. Select the corresponding check box of the Wizard, and Delphi will add the proper entries in the type library and in the source code it generates.

The Type-Library Editor

The type-library editor is the tool you can use to define a type library in Delphi. Figure 20.3 shows its window after I've added some elements to it. The type-library editor allows you to add methods and properties to the OLE Automation server object we've just created. Once this is done, it can generate both the type library (TLB) file and the corresponding Object Pascal source code.

FIGURE 20.3:

The type-library editor, showing the details of an interface

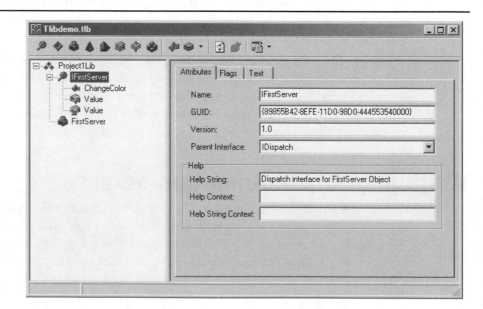

To build a first example, we can add to the server a property and a method. In the editor, we actually add these two elements to the interface, which should be called IFirstServer. Select it, and then click the Method button of the toolbar. (The names of these buttons can be displayed by using the shortcut menu of the toolbar.) Now you have to give it a name, such as ChangeColor. You can type the name either in the Tree View control on the left side of the window or in the Name edit box on the right side. Delphi automatically defines the new method as a function in the Invoke Kind box and (as you'll see on the Parameters page) assigns it an HRESULT return value and no parameters. This corresponds to the Pascal definition:

```
procedure ChangeColor; safecall;
```

There are two reasons for this difference in the type of method. The first is that in the IDL language used by COM, all methods are indicated as functions (following the C language style); the second is that Delphi handles the HRESULT error codes automatically in every method that uses the safecall calling convention.

NOTE The methods contained in OLE Automation interfaces in Delphi generally use the safecall calling convention. This wraps a try/except block around each method and provides a default return value indicating error or success.

Now we can add a property to the interface by clicking the Property button of the type-library editor's toolbar. Again, we can type a name for it, such as Value, and select a data type in the Type combo box. Besides selecting one of the many types already listed, you can also enter other types directly, particularly interfaces of other objects. Keep in mind, however, that OLE Automation supports only a subset of Delphi types. In this example, we can select the long type, which corresponds to Delphi's Integer type.

If you look again in the Parameters page for this example (see Figure 20.4), you can see that both the Set and Get (actually called Put and Get in the COM jargon) methods have the HRESULT return value. You can also see that while the Put method uses the property's data type as its parameter (as with Delphi properties), the Get method uses a pointer to the type as its out parameter. This definition corresponds to the following elements of the Pascal interface:

```
function Get_Value: Integer; safecall;
procedure Set_Value(Value: Integer); safecall;
property Value: Integer read Get_Value write Set_Value;
```

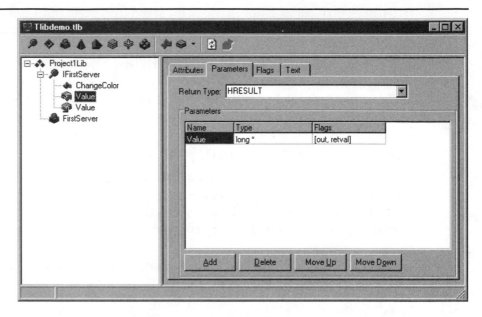

Clicking the Refresh button on the type-library editor toolbar generates the Pascal version of the interface. We'll examine it shortly, but first I want you to focus on the Text page of the editor, which includes the definition we've just created, written in the IDL language:

```
interface IFirstServer: IDispatch
{
  [id(0x00000001)]
  HRESULT _stdcall ChangeColor( void );
  [propget, id(0x00000002)]
  HRESULT _stdcall Value([out, retval] long * Value );
  [propput, id(0x00000002)]
  HRESULT _stdcall Value([in] long Value );
};
```

Fortunately, Delphi's type-library editor saves you from writing similar code by hand, and the Delphi environment options (in the Type Library page) include a radio button to select Pascal or IDL in the text displayed by the type-library editor.

The Code of the Server

Now we can close the type-library editor and save the changes. This operation adds three items to the project: the type library file, a corresponding Pascal definition, and the declaration of the server object. The type library is connected to the project using a resource-inclusion statement, added to the source code of the project file:

```
{$R *.TLB}
```

You can always reopen the type-library editor by using the View ➤ Type Library command or by selecting the proper TLB file in the normal File Open dialog box of Delphi.

As mentioned earlier, the type library is also converted into an interface definition and added to a new Pascal unit. This unit is quite long, so I've listed in the book only its key elements. The most important part is the new interface declaration:

```
type
  IFirstServer = interface(IDispatch)
    ['{89855B42-8EFE-11D0-98D0-444553540000}']
    procedure ChangeColor; safecall;
    function Get_Value: Integer; safecall;
    procedure Set_Value(Value: Integer); safecall;
    property Value: Integer read Get_Value write Set_Value;
  end;
```

Then comes the dispinterface, which associates a number with each element of the IFirstServer interface:

```
type
  IFirstServerDisp = dispinterface
    ['{89855B42-8EFE-11D0-98D0-444553540000}']
    procedure ChangeColor; dispid 1;
    property Value: Integer dispid 2;
  end;
```

The last portion of the file includes the so-called CoClass (also shown in the type-library editor), a class used to create an object on the server (and for this reason used on the client side of the application, not on the server side):

```
type
  CoFirstServer = class
    class function Create: IFirstServer;
    class function CreateRemote(const MachineName: string): IFirstServer;
  end;
```

All the declarations of this file (I've skipped some others) can be considered an internal, hidden implementation support. You don't need to understand them fully in order to write most OLE Automation applications.

Finally, Delphi generates a file with the declaration of the actual object. This unit is added to the application and is the one we'll work on to finish the program. This unit declares the class of the server object, which must implement the interface we've just defined:

```
type
  TFirstServer = class(TAutoObject, IFirstServer)
  protected
    function Get_Value: Integer; safecall;
    procedure ChangeColor; safecall;
    procedure Set_Value(Value: Integer); safecall;
  end;
```

Delphi already provides us with the skeleton code of the methods, so you only need to fill the lines in between. This is the final code of the server object methods of the TLibDemo example from the companion CD:

```
function TFirstServer.Get_Value: Integer;
begin
  Result := ServerForm.Value;
end;

procedure TFirstServer.ChangeColor;
begin
  ServerForm.ChangeColor;
end;

procedure TFirstServer.Set_Value(Value: Integer);
begin
  ServerForm.Value := Value;
end;
```

In this case, the three methods refer to a property and two methods I've added to the form. In general, you should not add code related to the user interface inside the class of the server object. It is better to refer to a user interface element, such as a form class, and let it perform the actions.

I've added a property to the form because I want to change the Value property and have a side effect (displaying the value in an edit box). The server object, in this example, exposes some properties and methods of the application. Here is the part of the declaration of the TServerForm class I've edited manually:

```
type
  TServerForm = class(TForm)
    ...
  private
    CurrentValue: Integer;
  protected
    procedure SetValue (NewValue: Integer);
  public
    property Value: Integer read CurrentValue write SetValue;
    procedure ChangeColor;
  end;
```

The implementation of these methods is quite straightforward, and you can easily guess what their code looks like. What's important is the SetValue method, which might produce a side effect:

```
procedure TServerForm.SetValue (NewValue: Integer);
begin
  if NewValue <> CurrentValue then
```

```
begin
  CurrentValue := NewValue;
  UpDown1.Position := CurrentValue;
  end;
 end;
```

The form of this example has an edit box with an associated UpDown component as well as a couple of buttons to show the current value and change the color. You can see this form at design time in Figure 20.5.

FIGURE 20.5:

The form of the TLibDemo example at design time

Registering the Automation Server

The unit containing the server object has one more statement, added by Delphi to the `initialization` section:

```
initialization
  TAutoObjectFactory.Create(ComServer, TFirstServer, Class_FirstServer,
    ciMultiInstance);
end.
```

> **NOTE**   In this case, I've selected multiple instancing. For the various instancing styles possible in COM, see the sidebar "COM Instancing and Threading Models" in Chapter 19, "COM Programming."

This is not very different from the creation of class factories we saw in the examples of the last chapter. Combined with the call to the `Initialize` method of the `Application` object, which Delphi adds by default to the project source code of any program, the `initialization` code above makes the registration of this server straightforward.

You can add the server information to the Windows Registry by running this application on the target machine (the computer where you want to install the OLE Automation server), passing to it the `/regserver` parameter on the command line. You can do this by selecting Start ➤ Run, by using the Explorer or File Manager, or by running the program within

Delphi after you've entered a command-line parameter (using the Run ➤ Parameters command). Another command-line parameter, /unregserver, is used to remove this server from the Registry.

Writing a Client for Our Server

Now that we have built a server, we can prepare a client program to test it. This client can connect to the server either by using variants or by using the new type library. This second approach can be implemented manually or by using the techniques introduced in Delphi 5 for wrapping components around Automation servers. We'll actually try out all of these approaches.

Create a new application—I've called it TLibCli—and then open the type library file of the server, after (optionally) copying it to the project's directory. Save the type library file, using Delphi's File ➤ Save menu command, and a new version of the interface declarations will be generated for you. Of course, in this case you could have grabbed the Pascal declarations from the server source code, but I'm trying to follow a more general approach, which also applies when you haven't written the server yet. In fact, you can usually extract the type library directly from the executable file of the server or from a DLL shipped with the program.

WARNING   Do not add the type library to the client application, though, because we are writing the OLE Automation controller, not a server. The Delphi project of a controller should not include the type library of the server it connects to.

You can refer to the Pascal file generated by the type-library editor in the code of the main form:

```
uses
  TlibdemoLib_TLB;
```

I've already mentioned that one of the elements of this unit generated by the type library is the *creation* class, or CoClass, a special class with two class functions you can use to create a server object locally or remotely (using DCOM). I've already shown you the interface of this class, but here is the implementation:

```
class function CoFirstServer.Create: IFirstServer;
begin
  Result := CreateComObject(Class_FirstServer) as IFirstServer;
end;

class function CoFirstServer.CreateRemote(
  const MachineName: string): IFirstServer;
begin
  Result := CreateRemoteComObject(MachineName, Class_FirstServer)
    as IFirstServer;
end;
```

You can use the first of these two functions, `Create`, to create a server object (and possibly start the server application) on the same computer. You can use the second function, `CreateRemote`, to create the server on a different computer, as long as your version of the operating system supports DCOM.

The two functions are a shortcut of the `CreateComObject` call, which allows you to create an instance of a COM object if you know its GUID. As an alternative, you can also use the `CreateOleObject` function, which requires as a parameter the registered name of the server. There is another difference between these two creation functions: `CreateComObject` returns an object of the `IUnknown` type, whereas `CreateOleObject` returns an object of the `IDispatch` type.

In my example, I'm going to use the `CoFirstServer.Create` shorthand. When you create the server object, you get as return value an `IFirstServer` interface. You can use it directly or store it in a variant variable. Here is an example of the first approach:

```
var
   MyServer: Variant;
begin
   MyServer := CoFirstServer.Create;
   MyServer.ChangeColor;
```

This code, based on variants, is not very different from that of the first controller we built in this chapter (the one that used Microsoft Word). Here is the alternative code, which has exactly the same effect:

```
var
   IMyServer: IFirstServer;
begin
   IMyServer := CoFirstServer.Create;
   IMyServer.ChangeColor;
```

Interfaces, Variants, and Dispatch Interfaces: Testing the Speed Difference

As I mentioned in the section introducing type libraries, one of the differences between these approaches is speed. It is actually quite complex to assess the exact performance of each technique because there are many factors involved. I've added a simple test to the TLibCli example on the companion CD, just to give you an idea. Here is the code of the test, a loop that accesses the `Value` of the server. The total value is displayed only to fool the optimizer, which might otherwise remove some of the code. The real output of the program relates to the timing, which is determined by calling the `GetTickCount` API function before and after executing the loop. (Two alternatives are to use Delphi's own time functions, which are slightly less precise,

or to use the very precise timing functions of the multimedia support unit, MMSystem.)
Here is the code of one of the methods; they are quite similar:

```
procedure TClientForm.BtnIntfClick(Sender: TObject);
var
  I, K: Integer;
  Ticks: Cardinal;
begin
  Screen.Cursor := crHourglass;
  try
    Ticks := GetTickCount;
    K := 0;
    for I := 1 to 100 do
      K := K + IMyServer.Value;
    Ticks := GetTickCount - Ticks;
    ListResult.items.Add (Format (
      'Interface: %d - Seconds %.3f', [K, Ticks / 1000]));
  finally
    Screen.Cursor := crDefault;
  end;
end;
```

With this program, you can compare the output obtained by calling this method based on
an interface, the corresponding version based on a variant, and even a third version based on a
dispatch interface. An example of the output (which is added to a list box so you can do several
tests and compare the results) is shown in Figure 20.6. Obviously, the timing depends on the
speed of your computer, and you can also alter the results by increasing or decreasing the
maximum value of the loop counter.

FIGURE 20.6:

The TLibCli OLE Automation
controller can access the
server in different ways,
with different performance
results. Notice the server
window in the background.

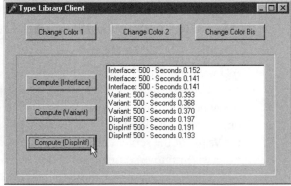

We've already seen how you can use the interface and the variant. What about the dispatch interface? You can declare a variable of the dispatch interface type, in this case:

```
var
  DMyServer: IFirstServerDisp;
```

Then you can use it to call the methods as usual, after you've assigned an object to it by casting the object returned by the CoClass:

```
DMyServer := CoFirstServer.Create as IFirstServerDisp;
```

Looking at the timing and at the internal code of the example, there is apparently very little difference between the use of the interface and of the dispatch interface, because the two are actually connected. In other words, we can say that dispatch interfaces are a technique in between variants and interfaces, but they deliver almost all of the speed of interfaces.

The Scope of Automation Objects

Another important element to keep in mind is the *scope* of the automation objects. Variants and interface objects use reference-counting techniques, so if a variable that is related to an interface object is declared locally in a method, at the end of the method the object will be destroyed and the server may terminate (if all the objects created by the server have been destroyed). For example, writing a method with this code produces very little effect:

```
procedure TClientForm.ChangeColor;
var
  IMyServer: IFirstServer;
begin
  IMyServer := CoFirstServer.Create;
  IMyServer.ChangeColor;
end;
```

Unless the server is already active, a copy of the program is created, and the color is changed, but then the server is immediately closed as the interface-typed object goes out of scope. The alternative approach I've used in the TLibCli example is to declare the object as a field of the form and create the COM objects at start-up, as in this procedure:

```
procedure TClientForm.FormCreate(Sender: TObject);
begin
  IMyServer := CoFirstServer.Create;
end;
```

With this code, as the client program starts, the server program is immediately activated. At the program termination, the form field is destroyed and the server closes. A further alternative is to declare the object in the form, but then create it only when it is used, as in these two code fragments:

```
// MyServerBis: Variant;
if varType (MyServerBis) = varEmpty then
  MyServerBis := CoFirstServer.Create;
MyServerBis.ChangeColor;

// IMyServerBis: IFirstServer;
if not Assigned (IMyServerBis) then
  IMyServerBis := CoFirstServer.Create;
IMyServerBis.ChangeColor;
```

NOTE   A variant is initialized to the `varEmpty` type when it is created. If you instead assign the value null to the variant, its type becomes `varNull`. Both `varEmpty` and `varNull` represent variants with no value assigned, but they behave differently in expression evaluation. The `varNull` value always propagates through an expression (making it a null expression), while the `varEmpty` value quietly disappears.

The Server in a Component

When creating a client program for our server or any other Automation server, we can use a better approach, namely, wrapping a Delphi component around the COM server. Actually, if you look at the final portion of the TlibdemoLib_TLB file, you can find the following declaration:

```
// OLE Server Proxy class declaration
TFirstServer = class(TOleServer)
private
  FIntf: IFirstServer;
  FProps: TFirstServerProperties;
  function GetServerProperties: TFirstServerProperties;
  function GetDefaultInterface: IFirstServer;
protected
  procedure InitServerData; override;
  function Get_Value: Integer;
  procedure Set_Value(Value: Integer);
public
  constructor Create(AOwner: TComponent); override;
  destructor  Destroy; override;
  procedure Connect; override;
  procedure ConnectTo(svrIntf: IFirstServer);
  procedure Disconnect; override;
  procedure ChangeColor;
  property  DefaultInterface: IFirstServer read GetDefaultInterface;
  property  Value: Integer read Get_Value write Set_Value;
published
  property  Server: TFirstServerProperties read GetServerProperties;
end;
```

This is a new component, derived from T0leServer, that the system registers in the Register procedure, which is part of the unit. If you add this unit to a package, the new server component will become available on the Delphi Component Palette. You can also import the type library of the new server (with the Project ≻ Import Type Library menu command), add the server to the list (by clicking the Add button and selecting the server's executable file), and install it in a new or existing package. The component will be placed in the Servers page of the Palette. The Import Type Library dialog box indicating these operations is visible in Figure 20.7.

FIGURE 20.7:

The Import Type Library dialog box can be used to import an Automation server object as a new Delphi component.

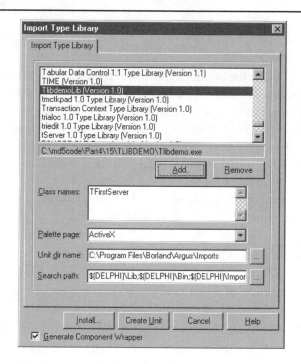

I've created a new package, PackAuto, available in the directory of the TlibDemo project. In this package, I've added the directive LIVE_SERVER_AT_DESIGN_TIME in the Directories/ Conditionals page of the Project Options dialog box of the package. This enables an extra feature that you don't get by default: at design time, the server component will have an extra property that lists as subitems all the properties of the Automation server. You can see an example in Figure 20.8, taken from the TLibComp example at design time.

WARNING The LIVE_SERVER_AT_DESIGN_TIME directive should be used with care with the most complex Automation servers (including programs such as Word, Excel, PowerPoint, and Visio). In fact, this setting requires the application to be in a particular mode before you can use some properties of their automation interfaces. For example, you'll get exceptions if you touch the Word server before a document has been opened in Word. That's why this feature is not active by default in Delphi—it's problematic at design time for many servers.

FIGURE 20.8:

A server component, with
the live properties at design
time

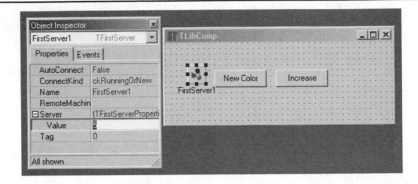

As you can see in the Object Inspector, the component has few properties. AutoConnection indicates when to start up the server component at design time and as soon as the client program starts. As an alternative, the Automation server is started the first time one of its methods is called. Another property, ConnectKind, indicates how to establish the connection with the server. It can always start a new instance (ckNewInstance), use the running instance (ckRunningInstance, which causes an access violation if the server is not already running), or select the current instance or start a new one if none is available (ckRunningOrNew). Finally, you can ask for a remote server with ckRemote and directly attach a server in the code after a manual connection with ckAttachToInterface.

OLE Data Types

OLE and COM do not support all of the data types available in Delphi. This is particularly important for OLE Automation, because the client and the server are often executed in different address spaces, and the system must move the data from one side to the other. Also keep in mind that OLE interfaces should be accessible by programs written in any language.

COM data types include basic data types such as Integer, SmallInt, Byte, Single, Double, WideString, Variant, and WordBool (but not Boolean). Table 20.1 presents the mapping of some basic data types, available in the type-library editor, to the corresponding Delphi types.

TABLE 20.1: OLE and Delphi Data Types

OLE Type	Delphi Type
BSTR	WideString
byte	ShortInt
CURRENCY	Currency
DATE	TDateTime
DECIMAL	TDecimal

Continued on next page

TABLE 20.1 continued: OLE and Delphi Data Types

OLE Type	Delphi Type
double	Double
float	Single
GUID	GUID
int	SYSINT
long	Integer
LPSTR	PChar
LPWSTR	PWideChar
short	SmallInt
unsigned char	Byte
unsigned int	SYSUINT
unsigned long	UINT
unsigned short	Word
VARIANT	OleVariant

Notice that SYSINT is currently defined as an Integer, so don't worry about the apparently strange type definition. Besides the basic data types, you can also use OLE types for complex elements such as fonts, string lists, and bitmaps, using the IFontDisp, IStrings, and IPictureDisp interfaces. The following sections describe the details of a server that provides a list of strings and a font to a client.

Exposing Strings Lists and Fonts

The ListServ example is a practical demonstration of how you can expose two complex types, such as a list of strings and a font, from an OLE Automation server written in Delphi. I've chosen these two specific types simply because they are both supported by Delphi.

The IFontDisp interface is actually provided by Windows and is available in the ActiveX unit. The AxCtrls Delphi unit extends this support by providing conversion methods like GetOleFont and SetOleFont. The IStrings interface is provided by Delphi in the StdVCL unit, and the AxCtrls unit provides conversion functions for this type (along with a third type I'm not going to use, TPicture).

WARNING   To run this and similar applications, the StdVCL library must be installed and registered on the client computer. On your computer, it is registered during Delphi's installation.

The server we are building has a plain form containing a list-box component. It includes an Automation object built around the following interface:

```
type
  IListServer = interface (IDispatch)
    ['{323C4A84-E400-11D1-B9F1-004845400FAA}']
    function Get_Items: IStrings; safecall;
    procedure Set_Items(const Value: IStrings); safecall;
    function Get_Font: IFontDisp; safecall;
    procedure Set_Font(const Value: IFontDisp); safecall;
    property Items: IStrings read Get_Items write Set_Items;
    property Font: IFontDisp read Get_Font write Set_Font;
  end;
```

The server object has the same four methods listed in its interface as well as some private data storing the status, the initialization function, and the destructor:

```
type
  TListServer = class (TAutoObject, IListServer)
  private
    fItems: TStrings;
    fFont: TFont;
  protected
    function Get_Font: IFontDisp; safecall;
    function Get_Items: IStrings; safecall;
    procedure Set_Font(const Value: IFontDisp); safecall;
    procedure Set_Items(const Value: IStrings); safecall;
  public
    destructor Destroy; override;
    procedure Initialize; override;
  end;
```

The code of the methods is limited to few statements. The pseudoconstructor creates the internal objects, and the destructor destroys them. Here is the first of the two:

```
procedure TListServer.Initialize;
begin
  inherited Initialize;
  fItems := TStringList.Create;
  fFont := TFont.Create;
end;
```

The Set and Get methods copy information from the OLE interfaces to the local data and then from this to the form and vice versa. The two methods of the strings, for example, do this by calling the GetOleStrings and SetOleStrings Delphi functions.

After we've compiled and registered the server, we can turn our attention to the client application. This embeds the Pascal translation of the type library of the server, as in the previous example, and then implements an object that uses the interface. Instead of creating the server when the object starts, the client program creates it when it is required. I've described this technique earlier, but the problem is that because there are several buttons a user can click, and we don't want to impose an order, every event should have a handler like this:

```
if not Assigned (ListServ) then
  ListServ := CoListServer.Create;
```

This kind of code duplication is quite dangerous, so I've decided to use an alternative approach. I've defined a property corresponding to the interface of the server and defined a read method for it. The property is mapped to some internal data I've defined with a different name to avoid the error of using it directly. Here are the definitions added to the form class:

```
private
  fInternalListServ: IListServer;
  function GetListSrv: IListServer;
public
  property ListSrv: IListServer read GetListSrv;
```

The implementation of the Get method can check whether the object already exists. This code is going to be repeated often, but that should not slow down the application noticeably:

```
function TListCliForm.GetListSrv: IListServer;
begin
  // eventually create the server
  if not Assigned (fInternalListServ) then
    fInternalListServ := CoListServer.Create;
  Result := fInternalListServ;
end;
```

You can see an example of the client application running (along with the server) in Figure 20.9.

FIGURE 20.9:

The ListCli and ListServ applications share complex data, namely fonts and lists of strings.

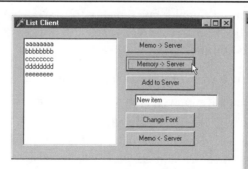
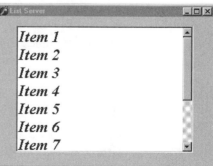

This is an example of the selection of a font, which is then sent to the server:

```
procedure TListCliForm.btnFontClick(Sender: TObject);
var
  NewFont: IFontDisp;
```

```
begin
  // select a font and apply it
  if FontDialog1.Execute then
  begin
    GetOleFont (FontDialog1.Font, NewFont);
    ListSrv.Font := NewFont;
  end;
end;
```

There are also several methods related to the strings, which you can see by looking at the source code of the program.

Using Office Programs

So far, we've built both the client and the server side of the OLE Automation connection. If your aim is just to let two applications you've built cooperate, this is certainly a useful technique, although it is not the only one. We've seen some alternative data-sharing approaches in the last two chapters (using memory-mapped files and the wm_CopyData message). The real value of OLE Automation is that it is a standard, so you can use it to integrate your Delphi programs with other applications your users own. A typical example is the integration of a program with office applications, such as Microsoft Word and Microsoft Excel, or even with stand-alone applications, such as AutoCAD.

Integration with these applications provides a two-fold advantage:

- You can let your users work in an environment they know—for example, generating reports and memos from database data in a format they can easily manipulate.

- You can avoid implementing complex functionality from scratch, such as writing your own word-processing code inside a program. Instead of just reusing components, you can reuse complex applications.

There are also some drawbacks with this approach, which are certainly worth mentioning:

- The user must own the application you plan to integrate with, and they may also need a recent version of it to support all the features you are using in your program.

- You have to learn a new programming language and programming structure, often with limited documentation at hand. It is true, of course, that you are still using Pascal, but the code you write depends on the OLE data types, the types introduced by the server, and in particular, a collection of interrelated classes that are often difficult to understand.

- You might end up with a program that works only with a specific version of the server application, particularly if you try to optimize the calls by using interfaces instead of variants. In particular, Microsoft does not attempt to maintain script compatibility between major releases of Word or other Office applications.

We've already seen a small source code excerpt from the WordTest example, but now I want to complete the coverage of this limited but interesting test program by providing a few extra features.

Sending Data to Microsoft Word

Delphi simplifies the use of Microsoft Office applications by preinstalling some ready-to-use components that wrap the Automation interface of these servers. These components, available in the Servers page of the Palette, have been installed using the same technique I demonstrated in the last section.

> **NOTE** What I want to underline here is that the real plus of Delphi lies in this technique of creating components to wrap existing Automation servers, rather than in the availability of some predefined server components.

Technically, it is possible to use variants to interact with Automation servers, as we've seen in the section "Introducing Type Libraries." Using interfaces and the type libraries is certainly better, because the compiler helps you catch errors in the source code and produces faster code. Thanks to the new server component, this process is also quite straightforward.

I've written a program, called DBOffice, which uses predefined server components to send a table to Word and to Excel. In both cases, you can use the application object, the document/worksheet object, or a combination of the two. There are other specialized components, for tasks such as handling Excel charts, but this example will suffice to introduce use of the built-in Office components.

> **NOTE** The DBOffice program was tested with Office 97. I'm currently using StarOffice more often than the Microsoft suite, so I never feel compelled to give Microsoft more money by upgrading to their newer offerings.

In case of Microsoft Word, I use only a document object with default settings. The code used to send the table to Word starts by adding some text to a document:

```
procedure TFormOff.BtnWordClick(Sender: TObject);
begin
  WordDocument1.Activate;
  // insert title
  WordDocument1.Range.Text := 'American Capitals from ' + Table1.TableName;
  WordDocument1.Range.Font.Size := 14;
```

This code follows the typical `while` loop, which scans the database table and has the following code inside:

```
while not Table1.EOF do
begin
  // send the two fields
```

```
    WordDocument1.Range.InsertParagraphAfter;
    WordDocument1.Paragraphs.Last.Range.Text :=
      Table1.FieldByName ('Name').AsString + #9 +
      Table1.FieldByName ('Capital').AsString;
    Table1.Next;
  end;
```

The final part of the code gets a little more complex. It works on a selection and on a row of the table, respectively stored in two variables of the Range and Row types defined by Word and available in the Word97 unit (the program will have to be updated if you choose the Office 2000 version of the server component while installing Delphi).

```
procedure TFormOff.BtnWordClick(Sender: TObject);
var
  RangeW: Word97.Range;
  v1: Variant;
  ov1: OleVariant;
  Row1: Word97.Row;
begin
  // code above...
  RangeW := WordDocument1.Content;
  v1 := RangeW;
  v1.ConvertToTable (#9, 19, 2);
  Row1 := WordDocument1.Tables.Item(1).Rows.Get_First;
  Row1.Range.Bold := 1;
  Row1.Range.Font.Size := 30;
  Row1.Range.InsertParagraphAfter;
  ov1 := ' ';
  Row1.ConvertToText (ov1);
end;
```

As you can see in the last statement above, in order to pass a parameter, you must first save it in an OleVariant variable, because many parameters are passed by reference, so you cannot pass a constant value. This implies that if there are many parameters, you must still define some, even if you are fine with the default values. An often-useful alternative is to use a temporarily variant variable and apply the method to it, because variants don't require strict type-checking on the parameters. This technique is used in the code above to call the ConvertToTable method, which has more than 10 parameters.

Building an Excel Table

In the case of Excel, I've used a slightly different approach and worked with the application object. The code creates a new Excel spreadsheet, fills it with a database table, and formats the result. It uses an Excel internal object, Range, which is not to be confused with a similar type available in Word (the reason this type is prefixed with the name of the unit defining the Excel type library). Here is the complete code:

```pascal
procedure TFormOff.BtnExcelClick(Sender: TObject);
var
  RangeE: Excel97.Range;
  I, Row: Integer;
  Bookmark: TBookmarkStr;
begin
  // create and show
  ExcelApplication1.Visible [0] := True;
  ExcelApplication1.Workbooks.Add (NULL, 0);
  // fill is the first row with field titles
  RangeE := ExcelApplication1.ActiveCell;
  for I := 0 to Table1.Fields.Count - 1 do
  begin
    RangeE.Value := Table1.Fields [I].DisplayLabel;
    RangeE := RangeE.Next;
  end;
  // add field data in following rows
  Table1.DisableControls;
  try
    Bookmark := Table1.Bookmark;
    try
      Table1.First;
      Row := 2;
      while not Table1.EOF do
      begin
        RangeE := ExcelApplication1.Range ['A' + IntToStr (Row),
          'A' + IntToStr (Row)];
        for I := 0 to Table1.Fields.Count - 1 do
        begin
          RangeE.Value := Table1.Fields [I].AsString;
          RangeE := RangeE.Next;
        end;
        Table1.Next;
        Inc (Row);
      end;
    finally
      Table1.Bookmark := Bookmark;
    end;
  finally
    Table1.EnableControls;
  end;
  // format the section
  RangeE := ExcelApplication1.Range ['A1', 'E' + IntToStr (Row - 1)];
  RangeE.AutoFormat (3, NULL, NULL, NULL, NULL, NULL, NULL);
end;
```

You can see the effect of this code in Figure 20.10. Notice that in the code I don't handle any events of the Office applications, but many are available. Handling these events was quite complex in the past, but they now become as simple to handle as events of native Delphi components. The presence of these events is a reason to have specific objects for documents and other specific elements: you might want to know when the user closes a document, and that therefore this is an event of the document object, not of the application object.

FIGURE 20.10:

The Excel spreadsheet \generated by the DBOffice application

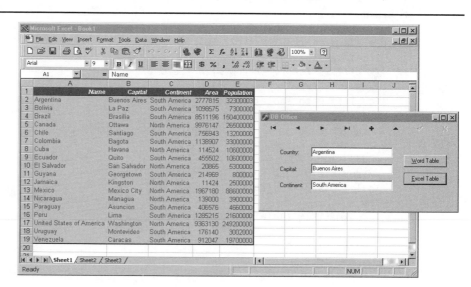

NOTE   When using the Office server components, one of the key problems is the lack of adequate documentation. Although Microsoft distributes some of it with the high-end version of the Office suite, this is certainly not Delphi friendly. A totally alternative approach to solve the problem is to use OfficePartner, a set of components from TurboPower Software (**www.turbopower.com**). These components map the Office servers, like those available in Delphi, but they also provide extensive property editors that allow you to work visually with the internal structure of these servers. With these property editors, you can create documents, paragraphs, tables, and all the other internal objects even at design time! From my experience, this can really save a lot of time.

Using Compound Documents

Compound documents, or active documents, are Microsoft's names for the technology that allows in-place editing of a document within another one (for example, a picture in a Word document). This is the technology that originated the term OLE, but although it is still in use, its role is definitely more limited than Microsoft envisioned when it was introduced in the early 1990s. Compound documents actually have two different capabilities, *object linking* and *embedding* (hence the term OLE):

- Embedding an object in a compound document corresponds to a smart version of the copy and paste operations you make with the Clipboard. The key difference is that when you copy an OLE object from a server application and paste it into a container application, you copy both the data and some information about the server (its GUID). This allows you to activate the server application from within the container to edit the data.

- Linking an object to a compound document instead copies only a reference to the data and the information about the server. You generally activate object linking by using the Clipboard and making a Paste Link operation. When editing the data in the container application, you'll actually modify the original data, which is stored in a separate file.

Because the server program refers to an entire file (only part of which might be linked in the client document), the server will be activated in a stand-alone window, and it will act upon the entire original file, not just the data you've copied. When you have an embedded object, instead, the container might support visual (or *in-place*) editing, which means that you can modify the object in context, inside the container's main window. The server and container application windows, their menus, and their toolbars are merged automatically, allowing the user to work within a single window on several different object types—and therefore with several different OLE servers—without leaving the window of the container application.

Another key difference between embedding and linking is that the data of an embedded object is stored and managed by the container application. The container saves the embedded object in its own files. By contrast, a linked object physically resides in a separate file, which is handled by the server exclusively, even if the link refers only to a small portion of the file.

In both cases, the container application doesn't have to know how to handle the object and its data—not even how to display it—without the help of the server. Accordingly, the server application has a lot of work to do, even when you are not editing the data. Container applications often make a copy of the image of an OLE object and use the bitmap to represent the data, which speeds up some operations with the object itself. The drawback of this approach is that many commercial OLE applications end up with bloated files (because two copies of the same data are saved). If you consider this problem along with the relative slowness of OLE and the amount of work necessary to develop OLE servers, you can understand why the use of this powerful approach is still somewhat limited, compared with what Microsoft envisioned a few years ago.

Compound document containers can support OLE in varying degrees. You can place an object in a container by inserting a new object, by pasting or *paste-linking* one from the Clipboard, by dragging one from another application, and so on.

Once the object is placed inside the container, you can then perform operations on it, using the server's available *verbs*, or actions. Usually the *edit verb* is the default action—the action performed when you double-click on the object. For other objects, such as video or sound clips, *play* is defined as the default action. You can typically see the list of actions supported by the current contained object by right-clicking it. The same information is available in many programs via the Edit ➢ Object menu item, which has a submenu that lists the available verbs for the current object.

NOTE   Delphi provides no *visual* support for building compound document servers. You can always write a server implementing the proper interfaces. Compound document container support, instead, is easily available through the OleContainer component.

The OLE Container Component

To create an OLE container application in Delphi, place an OleContainer component in a form. Then select the component and right-click to activate its shortcut menu, which will have an Insert Object command. When you select this command, Delphi displays the standard OLE Insert Object dialog box. This dialog box allows you to choose from one of the server applications registered on the computer.

Once the OLE object is inserted in the container, the shortcut menu of the control container component will have several more custom menu items. The new menu items include commands to change the properties of the OLE object, insert another one, copy the existing object, or remove it. The list also includes the verbs, or actions, of the object (such as Edit, Open, or Play). Once you have inserted an OLE object in the container, the corresponding server will launch to let you edit the new object. As soon as you close the server application, Delphi updates the object in the container and displays it at design time in the form of the Delphi application you are developing.

If you look at the textual description of a form containing a component with an object inside, you'll notice a Data property, which contains the actual data of the OLE object. Although the client program stores the data of the object, it doesn't know how to handle and show that without the help of the proper server (which must be available on the computer where you run the program). This means that the OLE object is *embedded*.

To fully support compound documents, a program should provide a menu and a toolbar or panel. These extra components are important because in-place editing implies a merging of the user interface of the client and that of the server program. When the OLE object is activated in place, some of the pull-down menus of the server application's menu bar are added to the menu bar of the container application.

OLE menu merging is handled almost automatically by Delphi. You only need to set the proper indexes for the menu items of the container, using the GroupIndex property. Any menu item with an odd index number is replaced by the corresponding element of the active OLE object. More specifically, the File (0) and Window (4) pull-down menus belong to the container application. The Edit (1), View (3), and Help (5) pull-down menus (or the groups of pull-down menus with those indexes) are taken by the OLE server. A sixth group, named Object and indicated with the index 2, can be used by the container to display another pull-down menu between the Edit and View groups, even when the OLE object is active. The OleCont demo program I've written to demonstrate these features allows a user to create a new object by calling the InsertObjectDialog method of the TOleContainer class.

The InsertObjectDialog method shows a system dialog box, but it doesn't automatically activate the OLE object:

```
procedure TForm1.New1Click(Sender: TObject);
begin
  if OleContainer1.InsertObjectDialog then
    OleContainer1.DoVerb (OleContainer1.PrimaryVerb);
end;
```

Once a new object has been created, you can execute its primary verb using the DoVerb method. The program also displays a small toolbar with some bitmap buttons. I placed some TWinControl components in the form to let the user select them and thus disable the Ole-Container. To keep this toolbar/panel visible while in-place editing is occurring, you should set its Locked property to True. This forces the panel to remain present in the application and not be replaced by a toolbar of the server.

To show what happens when you don't use this approach, I've added to the program a second panel, with some more buttons. Because I haven't set its Locked property, this new toolbar will be replaced with that of the active OLE server. When in-place editing launches a server application that displays a toolbar, that server's toolbar replaces the container's toolbar, as you can see in the lower part of Figure 20.11.

TIP   To make all the automatic resizing operations work smoothly, you should place the OLE container component in a panel component and align both of them to the client area of the form.

Another way to create an OLE object is to use the PasteSpecialDialog method, called in the PasteSpecial1Click event handler of the example. Another standard OLE dialog box, wrapped in a Delphi function, is the one showing the properties of the object, which is activated with the Object Properties item in the Edit pull-down menu by calling the ObjectPropertiesDialog method of the OleContainer component.

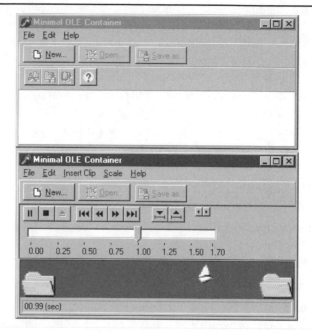

You can see an example of the resulting standard OLE dialog box in Figure 20.12. Obviously, this dialog box changes depending on the nature of the active OLE object in the container. The last feature of the OleCont program is support for files; this is actually one of the simplest additions we can make, because the OLE container component already provides file support.

Using the Internal Object

In the preceding program, the user determined the type of the internal object created by the program. In this case, there is little you can do to interact with the internal objects. Suppose, instead, that you want to embed a Word document in a Delphi application and then modify it by code. You can do this by using OLE Automation with the embedded object, as demonstrated by the WordCont example (the name stands for *Word container*).

In the form of this example, I've added an OleContainer component, set its AutoActivate property to aaManual (so that the only possible interaction is with our code), and added a toolbar with a couple of buttons. The code for the two buttons is quite straightforward, once you know that the embedded object corresponds to a Word document:

```
procedure TForm1.Button1Click(Sender: TObject);
var
  Document: Variant;
begin
  // activates if not running
  if not (OleContainer1.State = osRunning) then
    OleContainer1.Run;
  // get the document
  Document := OleContainer1.OleObject;
  // first paragraph to bold
  Document.Paragraphs.Item(1).Range.Bold := 1;
end;

procedure TForm1.Button3Click(Sender: TObject);
var
  Document, Paragraph: Variant;
begin
  // activate if not running
  if not (OleContainer1.State = osRunning) then
    OleContainer1.Run;
  // get the document
  Document := OleContainer1.OleObject;
  // add paragraphs, getting the last one
  Document.Paragraphs.Add;
  Paragraph := Document.Paragraphs.Add;
  // add text to the paragraph, using random font size
```

```
    Paragraph.Range.Font.Size := 10 + Random (20);
    Paragraph.Range.Text := 'New text (' +
      IntToStr (Paragraph.Range.Font.Size) + ')'#13;
  end;
```

You can see the effect of this code in Figure 20.13. The code is not terribly powerful, but it does show how you can merge the usage of OLE Containers and OLE Automation techniques.

FIGURE 20.13:

The WordCont example shows how to use OLE Automation with an embedded object.

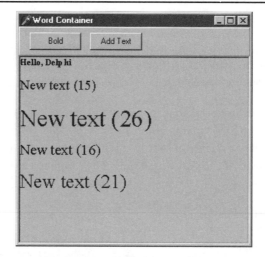

Introducing ActiveX Controls

Microsoft's Visual Basic was the first program development environment to introduce the idea of supplying software components to the mass market. Actually, the concept of reusable software components is older than Visual Basic—it's well rooted in the theories of object-oriented programming (OOP). But OOP languages never delivered the reusability they promised, probably more because of marketing and standardization problems than for any other reason. Although Visual Basic does not fully exploit OOP, it applies the component concept through its standard way of building and distributing new controls that developers can integrate into the environment.

The first technical standard promoted by Visual Basic was *VBX*, a 16-bit specification that was fully available in the 16-bit version of Delphi. In moving to the 32-bit platforms, Microsoft replaced the VBX standard with the more powerful and more open *ActiveX* controls.

NOTE ActiveX controls used to be called OLE controls (or OCX). The name change reflects a new marketing strategy from Microsoft rather than a technical innovation. Technically, ActiveX can be considered a minor extension to the OCX technology. Not surprisingly, then, ActiveX controls are usually saved in files with the `.ocx` extension.

From a general perspective, an ActiveX control is not very different from a Windows, Delphi, or Visual Basic control. A control in any of these languages is always a window, with its associated code defining its behavior. The key difference between various families of controls is in the *interface* of the control—the interaction between the control and the rest of the application. Typical Windows controls use a message-based interface; VBX controls use properties and events; OLE Automation objects use properties and methods; and ActiveX controls use properties, methods, and events. These three elements of properties, methods, and events are also found in Delphi's own components.

Using OLE jargon, an ActiveX control is a "compound document object which is implemented as an in-process server DLL and supports OLE Automation, visual editing, and inside-out activation." Perfectly clear, right? Let's see what this definition actually means. An ActiveX control uses the same approach as OLE server objects, which are the objects you can insert into an OLE Document, as we saw in the last chapter. The difference between a generic OLE server and an ActiveX control is that, whereas ActiveX controls can only be implemented in one way, OLE servers can be implemented in three different ways:

- As stand-alone applications (for example, Microsoft Excel)

- As out-of-process servers—that is, executables files that cannot be run by themselves and can only be invoked by a server (for example, Microsoft Graph and similar applications)

- As in-process servers, such as DLLs loaded into the same memory space as the program using them

ActiveX controls can only be implemented using the last technique, which is also the fastest: as in-process servers. Furthermore, ActiveX controls are OLE Automation servers. This means you can access properties of these objects and call their methods. You can see an ActiveX control in the application that is using it and interact with it directly in the container application window. This is the meaning of the term *visual editing*, or *in-place activation*. A single click activates the control rather than the double-click used by OLE Documents, and the control is active whenever it is visible (which is what the term *inside-out activation* means), without having to double-click it.

As I've mentioned before, an ActiveX control has properties, methods, and events. Properties can identify states, but they can also activate methods. (This is particularly true for ActiveX controls that are *updated* VBX controls, because in a VBX there *was* no other way to activate a method than by setting a property.) Properties can refer to aggregate values, arrays, subobjects, and so on. Properties can also be dynamic (or read-only, to use the Delphi term).

In an ActiveX control, properties are divided into different groups: stock properties that most controls need to implement; ambient properties that offer information about the container (similar to the `ParentColor` or `ParentFont` properties in Delphi); extended properties managed by the container, such as the position of the object; and custom properties, which can be anything.

Events and methods are, well, events and methods. *Events* relate to a mouse click, a key press, the activation of a component, and other specific user actions. *Methods* are functions and procedures related to the control. There is no major difference between the ActiveX and Delphi concepts of events and methods.

ActiveX Controls Versus Delphi Components

Before I show you how to use and write ActiveX controls in Delphi, let's go over some of the technical differences between the two kinds of controls. ActiveX controls are DLL-based. This means that when you use them, you need to distribute their code (the OCX file) along with the application using them. In Delphi, the code of the components can be statically linked to the executable file or dynamically linked to it using a run-time package, so you can always choose.

Having a separate file allows you to share code among different applications, as DLLs usually do. If two applications use the same control (or run-time package), you need only one copy of it on the hard disk and a single copy in memory. The drawback, however, is that if the two programs have to use two different versions (or builds) of the ActiveX control, some compatibility problems might arise. An advantage of having a self-contained executable file is that you will also have fewer installation problems.

Now, what is the drawback of using Delphi components? The real problem is not that there are fewer Delphi components than ActiveX controls, but that if you buy a Delphi component, you'll only be able to use it in Delphi and Borland C++Builder. If you buy an ActiveX control, on the other hand, you'll be able to use it in multiple development environments from multiple vendors. Even so, if you develop mainly in Delphi and find two similar components based on the two technologies, I suggest you buy the Delphi one—it will be more integrated with your environment, and therefore easier for you to use. Also, the native Delphi component will probably be better documented (from the Pascal perspective), and it will take advantage of Delphi and Object Pascal features not available in the general ActiveX interface, which is traditionally based on C and C++.

Using ActiveX Controls in Delphi

Delphi comes with some preinstalled ActiveX controls, and you can buy and install more third-party ActiveX controls easily. After this description of how ActiveX controls work in general, I'll demonstrate one in an example.

The Delphi installation process is very simple. Select Component ➢ Import ActiveX Control in the Delphi menu. This opens the Import ActiveX dialog box, where you can see the list of ActiveX control libraries registered in Windows. If you choose one, Delphi will read its type library, list its controls, and suggest a filename for its unit. If the information is correct, click the Create Unit button to view the Pascal source code file created by Delphi as a *wrapper* for the ActiveX control. Click the Install button to add this new unit to a Delphi package and to the Component Palette.

Using the WebBrowser Control

To build my example, I've used a preinstalled ActiveX control available in Delphi. Unlike the third-party controls, this is not available in the ActiveX page of the palette, but in the Internet page. The control, called WebBrowser, is a wrapper around Microsoft's Internet Explorer engine. The example is a very limited Web browser.

The WebBrows program on the CD-ROM has a TWebBrowser ActiveX control covering its client area and a control bar at the top and a status bar at the bottom. To move to a given Web page, a user can type in the combo box of the toolbar, select one of the visited URLs (saved in the combo box), or click on the Open File button to select a local file.

The actual implementation of the code used to select a Web or local HTML file is in the GotoPage method:

```
procedure TForm1.GotoPage(ReqUrl: string);
begin
  WebBrowser1.Navigate (ReqUrl, EmptyParam, EmptyParam, EmptyParam,
    EmptyParam);
end;
```

EmptyParam is a predefined OleVariant you can use whenever you want to pass a default value as a reference parameter. This is a handy shortcut you can use to avoid creating an empty OleVariant each time you need a similar parameter. This method is called for by a file, when the user clicks on the Enter key in the combo box, or by selecting the Go button, as you can see in the source code on the companion CD.

FIGURE 20.14:

The WebDemo program at
startup: it fully supports
graphics and all other Web
extensions, as it is based on
the Internet Explorer
engine.

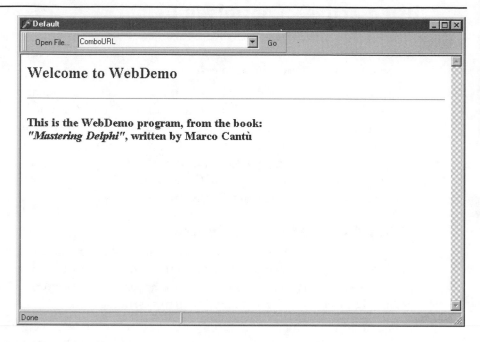

The program also handles four events of the WebBrowser control. When the download
operations start and end, the program updates the text of the status bar and also the drop-
down list of the combo box:

```
procedure TForm1.WebBrowser1DownloadBegin(Sender: TObject);
begin
  StatusBar1.Panels[0].Text := 'Downloading ' +
    WebBrowser1.LocationURL + '...';
end;

procedure TForm1.WebBrowser1DownloadComplete(Sender: TObject);
var
  NewUrl: string;
begin
  StatusBar1.Panels[0].Text := 'Done';
  // add URL to combobox
  NewUrl := WebBrowser1.LocationURL;
  if (NewUrl <> '') and (ComboURL.Items.IndexOf (NewUrl) < 0) then
    ComboURL.Items.Add (NewUrl);
end;
```

Two other useful events are the OnTitleChange, used to update the caption with the title of the
HTML document, and the OnStatusTextChange event, used to update the second part of the
status bar. This code basically duplicates the information displayed in the first part of the status
bar by the previous two event handlers.

Writing ActiveX Controls

Besides using existing ActiveX controls in Delphi, you can easily develop new ones. Although you can write the code of a new ActiveX control yourself, implementing all the required OLE interfaces (and there are many), it's much easier to use one of the techniques directly supported by Delphi:

- You can use the ActiveX Control Wizard to turn a VCL control into an ActiveX control. You start from an existing VCL component, which must be a `TWinControl` descendant, and Delphi wraps an ActiveX around it. During this step, Delphi adds a type library to the control. (Wrapping an ActiveX control around a Delphi component is exactly the opposite of what we did to use an ActiveX inside Delphi.)

- You can create an ActiveForm, place several controls inside it, and ship the entire form (without borders) as an ActiveX control. This second technique is the same one used by Visual Basic and is generally aimed at building Internet applications. However, it is also a very good alternative for the construction of an ActiveX control based on multiple Delphi controls or on Delphi components that do not descend from `TWinControl`.

An optional step you can take in both cases is to prepare a property page for the control, to use as a sort of property editor for setting the initial value of the properties of the control in any development environment—a kind of alternative to the Object Inspector in Delphi. Because most development environments allow only limited editing, it is more important to write a property page than it is to write a component or a property editor for a Delphi control.

Building an ActiveX Arrow

As an example of the development of an ActiveX control, I've decided to take the Arrow component we developed in Chapter 11, "Creating Components," and turn it into an ActiveX. We cannot use that component directly, because it was a graphical control, a subclass of `TGraphicControl`. However, turning a graphical control into a window-based control is usually a straightforward operation.

In this case, I've just changed the base class name to `TCustomControl` (and changed the name of the class of the control, as well, to avoid a name clash):

```
type
  TMdWArrow = class(TCustomControl)
  ...
```

The `TWinControl` class has very minimal support for graphical output. Its `TCustomControl` subclass, however, has basically the same capabilities as the `TGraphicControl` class. The key difference is that a `TCustomControl` object has a window handle.

After installing this new component in Delphi, we are ready to start developing the new example. To create a new ActiveX library, select File ➤ New, move to the ActiveX page, and choose ActiveX library. Delphi creates the bare skeleton of a DLL, as we saw at the beginning of this chapter. I've saved this library as XArrow, in a directory with the same name, as usual.

Now it is time to use the ActiveX Control Wizard, available in the ActiveX page of the Object Repository—Delphi's New dialog box. In this wizard (shown in Figure 20.15), you select the VCL class you are interested in, customize the names shown in the edit boxes, and click OK; Delphi then builds the complete source code of an ActiveX control for you.

FIGURE 20.15:

Delphi's ActiveX Control Wizard

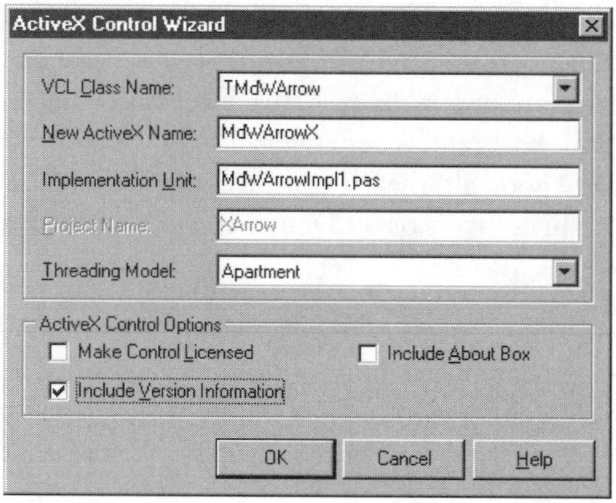

The use of the three check boxes at the bottom of the ActiveX Control Wizard window may not be obvious. If you include design-time license support, the user of the control won't be able to use it in a design environment without the proper *license key* for the control. The second check box allows you to include version information for the ActiveX, in the OCX file. If the third check box is selected, the ActiveX Control Wizard automatically adds an About box to the control.

Take a look at the code the ActiveX Control Wizard generates. The key element of this wizard is the generation of a type library. You can see the library generated for our arrow control in Delphi's type-library editor in Figure 20.16. From the type library information, the Wizard also generates an import file with the definition of an interface, the dispinterface, and other types and constants.

FIGURE 20.16:

The type-library editor
with the type library of
the demo ActiveX control
I've created

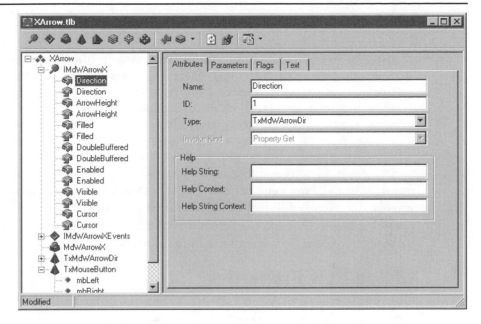

In this example, the import file is named XArrow_TLB.PAS. The first part of this file includes
a couple of GUIDs, one for the library as a whole and one for the control, and other constants
for the definition of values corresponding to the OLE enumerated types used by properties of
the Delphi control, for example:

```
type
  TxMdWArrowDir = TOleEnum;
const
  adUp = $00000000;
  adLeft = $00000001;
  adDown = $00000002;
  adRight = $00000003;
```

The real meat is the declaration of the IMdWArrowX interface, which I suggest you look at in
the source code. Notice that the final part of the import unit includes the declaration of the
TMdWArrowX class. This is a TOleControl-derived class you can use to install the control in Delphi,
as we've seen in the first part of this chapter. You don't need this class to build the ActiveX control; you need it to install the ActiveX control in Delphi. The class used by the ActiveX server has
the same class name but a different implementation.

The rest of the code, and the code you'll customize, is in the main unit, which in my example
is called MdWArrowImpl1. This unit has the declaration of the ActiveX server object,
TMdWArrowX, which inherits from TActiveXControl and implements the specific IMdWArrowX
interface.

NOTE   The TActiveXControl class does most of the work for providing ActiveX support in Delphi. This class implements interfaces required by every ActiveX control: IConnectionPointContainer, IDataObject, IObjectSafety, IOleControl, IOleInPlaceActiveObject, IOleInPlaceObject, IOleObject, IPerPropertyBrowsing, IPersistPropertyBag, IPersistStorage, IPersistStreamInit, IQuickActivate, ISimpleFrameSite, ISpecifyPropertyPages, IViewObject, and IViewObject2. Just the declaration of the TActiveXControl class takes more than 250 lines of code, and its implementation code is responsible for a good part of the 4,000 lines of code of the AxCtrls unit.

Before we customize this control in any way, let's see how it works. You should first compile the ActiveX library and then register it using Delphi's Run ➤ Register ActiveX Server menu command. Now you can install the ActiveX control as we've done in the past, except you have to specify a different name for the new class to avoid a name clash. If you use this control, it doesn't look much different from the original VCL control, but the advantage is that the same component can now be installed also in other development environments.

Adding New Properties

Once you've created an ActiveX control, adding new properties, events, or methods to it is—surprisingly—simpler than doing the same operation for a VCL component. Delphi, in fact, provides specific visual support for the former, not for the latter.

You can open the Pascal unit with the implementation of the ActiveX control, and choose Edit ➤ Add To Interface. As an alternative, you can use the same command from the shortcut menu of the editor. Delphi opens the Add To Interface dialog box (see Figure 20.17). In the combo box of this dialog box, you can choose between a new property, method, or event. In this example, the first selection will affect the IMdWArrowX interface and the second the IMdWArrowXEvents interface.

FIGURE 20.17:

The Add To Interface dialog box, with the syntax helper in action

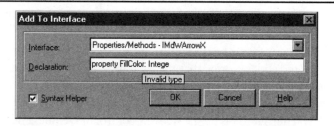

In the edit box, you can then type the declaration of this new interface element. If the Syntax Helper check box is activated, you'll get hints describing what you should type next and highlighting any errors. You can see the syntax helper in action in Figure 20.17. When you define a new ActiveX interface element, keep in mind that you are restricted to OLE data types. In the XArrow example, I've added two properties to the ActiveX control. Because the Pen and the Brush properties of the original Delphi components are not accessible, I've made their color available. These are examples of what you can write in the edit box of the Add To Interface dialog (executing it twice):

```
property FillColor: Integer;
property PenColor: Integer;
```

NOTE   Since a TColor is a specific Delphi definition, it is not legal to use it. TColor is an Integer subrange that defaults to Integer size, so I've used the standard Integer type directly.

The declarations you enter in the Add To Interface dialog box are automatically added to the control's type library (TLB) file, to its import library unit, and to its implementation unit:

```
type
  IMdWArrowX = interface(IDispatch)
    function Get_FillColor: Integer; safecall;
    procedure Set_FillColor(Value: Integer); safecall;
    function Get_PenColor: Integer; safecall;
    procedure Set_PenColor(Value: Integer); safecall;
    ...
    property FillColor: Integer read Get_FillColor write Set_FillColor;
    property PenColor: Integer read Get_PenColor write Set_PenColor;
```

All you have to do to finish the ActiveX control is fill in the Get and Set methods of the implementation. Here is the code of the first property:

```
function TMdWArrowX.Get_FillColor: Integer;
begin
  Result := ColorToRGB (FDelphiControl.Brush.Color);
end;

procedure TMdWArrowX.Set_FillColor(Value: Integer);
begin
  FDelphiControl.Brush.Color := Value;
end;
```

If you now install this ActiveX control in Delphi once more, the two new properties will appear. The only problem with this property is that Delphi uses a plain integer editor, making it quite difficult to enter the value of a new color by hand. A program, by contrast, can easily use the RGB function to create the proper color value.

Adding a Property Page

As it stands, other development environments can do very little with our component, because we've prepared no property page—no property editor. A property page is fundamental so that programmers using the control can edit its attributes. However, adding a property page is not as simple as adding a form with a few controls. The property page, in fact, will integrate with the host development environment. The property page for our control will show up inside a property page dialog of the host environment, which will provide the OK, Cancel, and Apply buttons, and the tabs for showing multiple property pages (some of which might be provided by the host environment).

The nice thing is that support for property pages is built into Delphi, so adding one takes little time. You open an ActiveX project, then open the usual New Items dialog box, move to the ActiveX page, and choose Property Page. What you get is not very different from a form. In fact, the TPropertyPage1 class (created by default) inherits from the TPropertyPage class of VCL, which in turn inherits from TCustomForm.

In the property page, you can add controls as in a normal Delphi form, and you can write code to let the controls interact. I've added to the property page a combo box with the possible values of the Direction property, a check box for the Filled property, an edit box with an UpDown control to set the ArrowHeight property, and two shapes with corresponding buttons for the colors. The only code added to the form relates to the two buttons used to change the color of the two shape components, which offer a preview of the colors of the actual ActiveX control. The OnClick event of the button uses a ColorDialog component, as usual:

```
procedure TPropertyPage1.ButtonPenClick(Sender: TObject);
begin
  with ColorDialog1 do
  begin
    Color := ShapePen.Brush.Color;
    if Execute then
    begin
      ShapePen.Brush.Color := Color;
      Modified; // enable Apply button!
    end;
  end;
end;
```

What is important to notice in this code is the call to the Modified method of the TPropertyPage class. This call is required to let the property page dialog box know we've modified one of the values and to enable the Apply button. When a user interacts with one of the other controls of this form, this call is made automatically. For the two buttons, however, we need to add this line ourselves.

TIP Another tip relates to the **Caption** of the property page form. This will be used in the property dialog box of the host environment as the caption of the tab corresponding to the property page.

The next step is to associate the controls of the property page with the actual properties of the ActiveX control. The property page class automatically has two methods for this: **UpdateOleObject** and **UpdatePropertyPage**. As their names suggest, these two methods copy data from the property page to the ActiveX control and vice versa. Here is the code for my example:

```
procedure TPropertyPage1.UpdatePropertyPage;
begin
  { Update your controls from the OleObject }
  ComboDir.ItemIndex := OleObject.Direction;
  CheckFilled.Checked := OleObject.Filled;
  EditHeight.Text := IntToStr (OleObject.ArrowHeight);
  ShapePen.Brush.Color := OleObject.PenColor;
  ShapePoint.Brush.Color := OleObject.FillColor;
end;

procedure TPropertyPage1.UpdateObject;
begin
  { Update the OleObject from your controls }
  OleObject.Direction := ComboDir.ItemIndex;
  OleObject.Filled := CheckFilled.Checked;
  OleObject.ArrowHeight := UpDownHeight.Position;
  OleObject.PenColor := ColorToRGB (ShapePen.Brush.Color);
  OleObject.FillColor := ColorToRGB (ShapePoint.Brush.Color);
end;
```

The final step is to connect the property page itself to the ActiveX control. When the control was created, the Delphi ActiveX Control Wizard automatically added a declaration for the **DefinePropertyPages** method to the implementation unit. In this method, we call the **DefinePropertyPage** method (this time the method name is singular) for each property page we want to add to the ActiveX. This method has as its parameter the GUID of the property page, something you can find in the corresponding unit. (Of course, you'll need to add a **uses** statement referring to that unit.) Here is the code of my example:

```
procedure TMdWArrowX.DefinePropertyPages(
  DefinePropertyPage: TDefinePropertyPage);
begin
  DefinePropertyPage(Class_PropertyPage1);
end;
```

NOTE The connection between the ActiveX control and its property page takes place using a GUID. This is possible because the property page object can be created through a class factory, and its GUID is stored in the Windows Registry when you register the ActiveX control library. To see what's going on, look at the `initialization` section of the property page unit, which calls `TActiveXPropertyPageFactory.Create`.

Now that we've finished developing the property page, and after recompiling and reregistering the ActiveX library, we can install the ActiveX control inside a host development environment (including Delphi itself) and see how it looks. Figure 20.18 shows an example. (If you've already installed the ActiveX control in Delphi, you should uninstall it prior to rebuilding it. This process might also require closing and reopening Delphi itself.)

FIGURE 20.18:

The XArrow ActiveX control and its property page, hosted by the Delphi environment

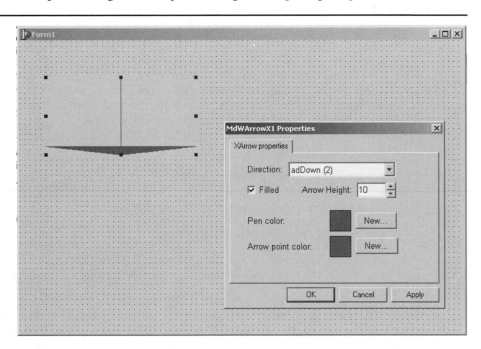

ActiveForms

As I've mentioned, Delphi provides an alternative to the use of the ActiveX Control Wizard to generate an ActiveX control. You can use an ActiveForm, which is an ActiveX control that is based on a form and can host one or more Delphi components. This is exactly the technique used in Visual Basic to build new controls, and it makes sense when you want to create a compound component.

For example, to create an ActiveX clock, we can place on an ActiveForm a label (a graphic control that cannot be used as a starting point for an ActiveX control) and a timer, and connect the two with a little code. The form/control becomes basically a container of other controls, which makes it very easy to build compound components (easier than for a VCL compound component).

To build such a control, close the current project, and select the ActiveForm icon in the ActiveX page of the File ➣ New dialog box. Delphi asks you for some information in the following ActiveForm Wizard dialog box, similar to the ActiveX Control Wizard dialog box.

ActiveForm Internals

Before we continue with the example, let's look at the code generated by the ActiveForm Wizard. The key difference from a plain Delphi form is in the declaration of the new form class, which inherits from the TActiveForm class and implements a specific ActiveForm interface:

```
type
  TAXForm1 = class(TActiveForm, IAXForm1)
```

As usual, the IAXForm interface is declared in the type library and in a corresponding Pascal file generated by Delphi. Here is a small excerpt of the IAXForm1 interface from the XF1Lib.pas file, with some comments I've added:

```
type
  IAXForm1 = interface(IDispatch)
    ['{51661AA1-9468-11D0-98D0-444553540000}']
    // Get and Set methods for TForm properties
    function Get_Caption: WideString; safecall;
    procedure Set_Caption(const Value: WideString); safecall;
    ...
    // TForm methods redeclared
    procedure Close; safecall;
    ...
    // TForm properties
    property Caption: WideString read Get_Caption write Set_Caption;
```

The code generated for the TAXForm1 class implements all the Set and Get methods, which change or return the corresponding properties of the form, and it implements the events, which again are the events of the form. Here is a small excerpt:

```
private
  procedure ActivateEvent(Sender: TObject);
protected
  procedure Initialize; override;
  function Get_Caption: WideString; safecall;
  procedure Close; safecall;
  procedure Set_Caption(const Value: WideString); safecall;
```

Let's look at the implementation of properties first:

```
function TAXForm1.Get_Caption: WideString;
```

```
begin
  Result := WideString(Caption);
end;

procedure TAXForm1.Set_Caption(const Value: WideString);
begin
  Caption := TCaption(Value);
end;
```

The TForm events are set to the internal methods when the form is created:

```
procedure TAXForm1.Initialize;
begin
  OnActivate := ActivateEvent;
  ...
end;
```

Each event then maps itself to the external ActiveX event, as in the following two methods:

```
procedure TAXForm1.ActivateEvent(Sender: TObject);
begin
  if FEvents <> nil then FEvents.OnActivate;
end;
```

Because of this mapping, you should not handle the events of the form directly. Instead, you can either add some code to these default handlers or override the TForm methods that end up calling the events. (This is exactly the approach you use when building a Delphi component.) Keep in mind that the interface properties of an ActiveForm are meant for developers using it as a control, not for final users of the ActiveForm on the Web. This mapping problem refers only to the events of the form itself, not to the events of the components of the form. You can continue to handle the events of the components as usual.

The XClock ActiveX Control

Now that we've looked at the code generated by Delphi, we can return to the development of the XClock example. Place on the form a label with a large font and centered text, aligned to the client area and a timer. Then write an event handler for its OnTimer event, so that the control updates the output of the label with the current time every second:

```
procedure TXClock.Timer1Timer(Sender: TObject);
begin
  Label1.Caption := TimeToStr (Time);
end;
```

Now compile this library, register it, and install it in a package to test it in the Delphi environment. You can see an example of its use in Figure 20.19. Notice in this figure the effect of the sunken border. This is controlled by the AxBorderStyle property of the active form, one of the few properties of active forms that is not available for a plain form.

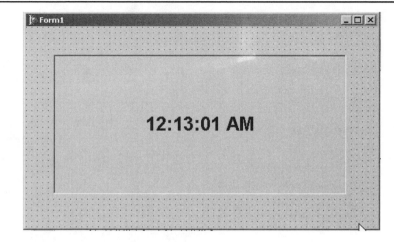

ActiveForms are usually considered as a technique to deploy a Delphi application via the Internet. However, the ActiveX and ActiveForm support provided by Delphi represent to different ways to build ActiveX controls, which can be used both on a Web page and in another development environment.

ActiveX in Web Pages

In the last example, we used Delphi's ActiveForm technology to create a new ActiveX control. In fact, an ActiveForm is an ActiveX control based on a form. Borland documentation often implies that ActiveForms should be used in HTML pages, but you can use any ActiveX control on a Web page.

NOTE   Microsoft once promoted ActiveX as an Internet technology for delivering interactive content. Due to complexities and security problems inherent in downloading executable code, the market never really bought into this. Microsoft has since dropped ActiveX from its Internet technologies list. Still, this technology might have a value in an intranet to let you deliver small applications to users of your local area network, as you can relax the security settings when accessing local Web sites.

Basically, each time you create an ActiveX library, Delphi enables the Project ➤ Web Deployment Options and Project ➤ Web Deploy menu items. The first allows you to specify how and where to deliver the proper files. As shown in Figure 20.20, in this dialog box you can set the server directory for deploying the ActiveX component, the URL of this directory, and the server directory for deploying the HTML file (which will have a reference to the ActiveX library using the URL you provide).

FIGURE 20.20:

The Web Deployment
Options dialog box

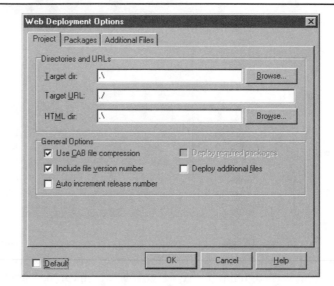

You can also specify the use of a compressed CAB file, which can store the OCX file and other auxiliary files, such as packages, making it easier and faster to deliver the application to the user. A compressed file, in fact, means a faster download. Using the options shown in Figure 20.20, Delphi generates the HTML file and CAB file for the XClock project in the same directory. Opening this HTML file in Internet Explorer produces the output shown in Figure 20.21.

WARNING   At times, when you load an HTML page referring to an ActiveX, all you get is a red *X* marker indicating a failure to download the control. There are various possible explanations for this problem. First, Internet Explorer must be set up properly, allowing the download of controls and (if the control is not signed) lowering the security level. Second, other problems might arise when the control requires a DLL or a package that is not part of the downloaded CAB file. Third, you might get the red slash marker when there is a mismatch in the version number—*or* you might see an older version of the control in action.

FIGURE 20.21:

The XClock control in the
sample HTML page

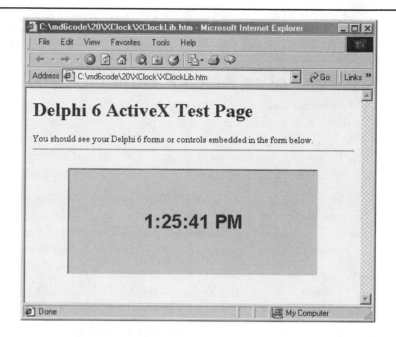

Besides showing you how to deploy the XClock control on a Web page, I've created the XForm1 example to demonstrate the problems with event handlers of ActiveForms mentioned in the previous section "ActiveForm Internals." Because the form events are exported as events of the control, you should not handle the events of the form directly but add some code to the default handlers provided by the Active Form. For example, if you add a handler for the OnPaint event of the form and write the following code, it will never be executed:

```
procedure TFormX1.FormPaint(Sender: TObject);
begin
  Canvas.Brush.Color := clYellow;
  Canvas.Ellipse(0, 0, Width, Height);
end;
```

If you want to paint something on the form's background, instead, you have to modify the corresponding handler installed by the ActiveForm Wizard:

```
procedure TFormX1.PaintEvent(Sender: TObject);
begin
  Canvas.Brush.Color := clBlue;
  Canvas.Rectangle (20, 20, ClientWidth - 20, ClientHeight - 20);
  if FEvents <> nil then FEvents.OnPaint;
end;
```

As an alternative, you can place a frame, a panel, or another component on the surface of the form, and handle *its* events. In the XForm1 example, I've added a PaintBox component, with a bevel component behind it to make the area of the PaintBox visible.

The Role of an ActiveX Form on a Web Page

Before we look at another example, it is important to stop for a second to consider the role of an ActiveX form placed inside a Web page. Basically, placing a form in a Web page corresponds to letting a user download and execute a custom Windows application. There is little else happening. You download an executable file and start it. This is one of the reasons the ActiveX technology raises so many concerns about security.

The XFUser example highlights the situation. It calls the GetUserName Windows API function and shows the user name on the screen. Its effect is certainly not astonishing, as the name of the user will be displayed in a label. However, this example highlights a couple of important points (which apply both to ActiveForms and ActiveX controls in general):

- In an ActiveX control or form, you can call any Windows API function (which means the user viewing the Web page must have Windows on his or her computer) or certain Windows API–compatible libraries.

- An ActiveX can access the system information of the computer, such as the user name, the directory structure, and so on. This is why, before downloading an ActiveX, Web browsers check whether the ActiveX has a proper authentication, or signature. (You should note that this signature identifies the author of the control and that the module has not been corrupted or tampered with since the author published it; it doesn't prove in any way that the control is safe.)

Well, I could continue, but I think my point is clear. ActiveX controls and ActiveForms inside Web pages have problems, and even Microsoft has slowly abandoned this technology. For this reason, I'm going to show you only one more example, which is instructive on how external environments can interact with an ActiveX control.

Setting Properties for the XArrow

An ActiveForm has a few properties you can set when you use it inside a development environment, and a plain ActiveX control has even more. For example, if you want to set properties in the HTML file hosting the control, you can use a special param tag, but the control must support a special interface known as IPersistPropertyBag.

Starting with Delphi 4, the IPersistPropertyBag support is built in, providing support for all of the properties of the ActiveX control or ActiveForm. As an example, I've used the Web Deploy options on the XArrow control. Then, I've modified the automatically generated HTML file with three param tags:

```
<object classid="clsid:482B2145-4133-11D3-B9F1-00000100A27B"
    codebase="./XArrow.cab" width="350" height="250" align="center"
    hspace="0" vspace="0">
    <param name="ArrowHeight" value="100">
    <param name="Filled" value="-1">
    <param name="FillColor" value="111829">
</object>
```

You can compare the default and customized output of the control in Figure 20.22.

FIGURE 20.22:

By using the param tag, we can set values for the properties of an ActiveX control in the HTML file hosting it. The two copies of the program show the default and the customized output.

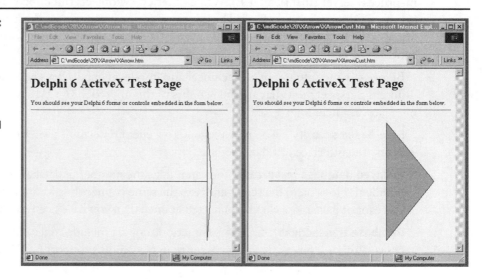

Introducing COM+

In addition to plain COM servers, Delphi also allows you to create enhanced COM objects, including stateless objects and transaction support. This type of COM object was first introduced by Microsoft with the MTS (Microsoft Transaction Server) acronym, and later renamed as COM+ in Windows 2000.

Delphi 6 supports building both standard stateless objects and DataSnap remote data modules based on stateless objects. In both cases you'll start the development by using one of the available Delphi wizards, using the New Items dialog box and selecting the Transactional Object icon of the ActiveX page or the Transactional Data Module icon of the Multitier page. You must add these objects to an ActiveX library project, not to a plain application. Another icon, COM+ Event Object, is used to support COM+ events.

MTS is an operating-system service you can install on Windows NT and 98; it was renamed as COM+ in Windows 2000, so I'll call it COM+ but this actually refers to both. This system service provides a run-time environment supporting database transaction services, security, resource pooling, and an overall improvement in robustness for DCOM applications. The run-time environment manages objects called *COM+ components*. These are COM objects stored in an in-process server (that is, a DLL). While other COM objects run directly in the client application, COM+ objects are handled by this run-time environment, in which you install the COM+ libraries. COM+ objects must support specific COM interfaces, starting with IObjectControl, which is the base interface (like IUnknown for a COM object).

Before getting into too many technical and low-level details, let's consider COM+ from a different perspective. What are the benefits of this approach? COM+ provides a few interesting features, including:

Role-based security   The role assigned to a client determines whether it has the right to access the interface of a data module.

Reduced database resources   You can reduce the number of database connections, as the middle tier logs on to the server and uses the same connections for multiple clients (although you cannot have more clients connected at once than you have licenses for the server).

Database transactions   COM+ transaction support includes operations on multiple databases, although few SQL servers other than Microsoft's support COM+ transactions.

Creating a COM+ Component

The starting point for creating a COM+ component is the creation of an ActiveX library project. After this step you can select a new Transactional Object in the ActiveX page of the New Items dialog box. In the resulting dialog box (see Figure 20.23), enter the name of the new component (*ComPlus1Object* in my ComPlus1 example).

FIGURE 20.23:

Delphi's New Transactional
Object dialog box, used to
create a COM+ object

The New Transactional Object dialog box allows you to enter a name for the class of the COM+ object, the threading model (because COM+ serializes all the requests, Single or Apartment will generally do), and a transactional model:

Requires A Transaction indicates that each call from the client to the server is considered to be a transaction (unless the caller supplies an existing transaction context).

Requires A New Transaction indicates that each call is considered a new transaction.

Supports Transactions indicates that the client must explicitly provide a transaction context.

Does Not Support Transaction (the default choice, and the one I've used) indicates that the remote data module won't be involved in any transaction.

As you close this dialog, Delphi adds a type library and an implementation unit to the project and opens the type-library editor, where you can define the interface of your new COM object. For this example I've added a Value integer property, an Increase method having as parameter an amount, and an AsText method returning a WideString with the formatted value. As you accept the edits in the type-library editor (clicking the Refresh button or closing the window), Delphi shows the Implementation File Update Wizard, if the corresponding IDE option is set. This wizard will ask for your confirmation before adding four methods to the class, including the get and set methods of the property. You can now write some code for the COM object, which for my example was quite trivial.

As you've compiled an ActiveX library, or COM library, which hosts a COM+ component, you can use the Component Services administrative tool (shown in the Microsoft Management Console, or MMC) to install and configure the COM+ component. Even better, you can use the Delphi IDE to install the COM+ component using the Run ➢ Install COM+ Object menu command. In the subsequent dialog box, you'll be able to select the component to install (as a library can host multiple components), and choose the COM+ application where to install the component.

A COM+ application is nothing more than a way to group COM+ components; it is not an actual program or anything like one (why they call it application is not fully clear to me). So in the Install COM+ Object dialog, you can select an existing application/group, choose the Install Into New Application page, and enter a name and description for it.

I've called the COM+ application *Mastering Delphi Demo*, as you can see in Figure 20.24 in the Component Services administration. This is the front end you can use to fine-tune the behavior of your COM+ components, setting their activation model (just-in-time activation, object pooling, and so on), their transaction support, and the security and concurrency models you want to use. You can also use this console to monitor the objects and the actual method calls (in case these take a long time to execute). In Figure 20.24, you can see that there are currently two active objects.

FIGURE 20.24:

The newly installed COM+ component inside a custom COM+ application (as shown by Microsoft's Component Services tool)

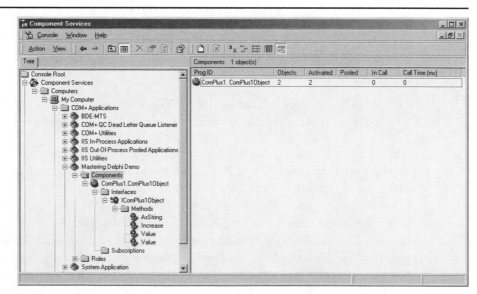

TIP   Because you've created one or more objects, the COM library remains loaded in the COM+ environment and some of the objects might be kept in cache, even if there are no clients connected to them. For this reason, you cannot generally recompile the COM library after using it, unless you use the MMC to shut it down.

I've actually created a client program for the COM+ object, but this is exactly like any other Delphi COM client. After importing the type library, which is automatically registered while installing the component, I created an interface-type variable referring to it and called its methods as usual. You can find the example on the CD accompanying this book.

Transactional Data Modules

The same types of features are available when creating a *transactional data module*—that is, a remote data module within a COM+ component. Once you've created a transactional data module, you can build a Delphi DataSnap application as we've done in Chapter 17, "Multi-tier Database Applications with DataSnap." You can add one or more dataset components, add one or more providers, and export the provider(s). You can also add custom methods to the data module type library by editing the type library or using the Add To Interface command.

Within a COM+ component or transactional data module, you can also use the `GetObject-Context` method, which returns the `IObjectContext` interface of the COM+ object. The `IObjectContext` interface provides support for transactions:

- You can use `SetComplete` to tell the COM+ environment that the object has finished working and can be deactivated, so that the transaction can be committed.

- You can call `EnableCommit` to indicate that the object hasn't finished but the transaction should be committed.

- You can call `DisableCommit` to stop the commit operation, even if the method is done, disabling the object deactivation between method calls.

- You can call `SetAbort` to say that the object has finished and can be activated but the transaction cannot be committed.

- You can call `IsInTransaction` to check whether the object is part of a transaction.

Other methods of the `IContextObject` interface include `CreateInstance`, which creates another COM+ object in the same context and within the current transaction, `IsCallerInRole`, which checks if the object's caller is in a particular "security" role, and `IsSecurityEnabled` (whose name is self-explanatory).

Once you've built a transactional data module within a server library, you can install it as I've shown above for a plain COM+ object. After the transactional data module has been installed, it will be directly available to other applications and visible in the management console.

An important feature of COM+ is that it becomes much easier to configure DCOM support using this environment. In fact, the COM+ environment of a client computer can grab information from the COM+ environment of a server computer, including registration information for the COM+ object you want to be able to call over a network. The same network configuration is way more complex if done with plain DCOM, without MTS or COM+.

TIP   Even though COM+ configuration is much better than DCOM configuration, still you are limited to computers with a recent version of the Windows operating system. Considering that even Microsoft is moving away from DCOM technology, before you build a large system based on this technology you should at least evaluate the alternative provided by SOAP (discussed in Chapter 23, "XML and SOAP").

COM+ Events

Client applications that use traditional COM objects and Automation servers can call methods of those servers, but this is not an efficient way to check whether the server has updated data for the client. For this reason, it is possible for a client to define a COM object that implements a *callback* interface, pass this object to the server, and let the server call it. Traditional COM events (which use the IConnectionPoint interface) are simplified by Delphi for Automation objects, but are still quite complex to handle.

COM+ introduces a simplified event model, in which the events are COM+ components and the COM+ environment manages the connections. In traditional COM callbacks, the server object doesn't have to keep track of the multiple clients it has to notify to, which is one of the reasons for the complexity of its code. In COM+, the server calls into a single event interface, and the COM+ environment will forward the event to all clients that have expressed interest for it. This way, the client and the server are less coupled, making it possible for a client to receive notification from different servers, without any change in its code.

NOTE   Some critics say that Microsoft introduced this model only because it was very complex to handle COM events in the traditional way for Visual Basic developers. Windows 2000 actually provides a few operating-system features specifically intended for VB developers.

To create a COM+ event, you should create a COM library (or ActiveX library) and use the COM+ Event Object wizard. The resulting project will contain a type library with the definition of the interface used to fire the events, plus some *fake* implementation code. The actual server that will receive the notification of the events, in fact, will provide the actual implementation of the interface. The fake code is there only to support Delphi's COM registration system.

While building the MdComEvents library, I added to the type library a single method with two parameters, resulting in the following code (in the interface definition file):

```
type
  IMdInform = interface(IDispatch)
    ['{202D2CC8-8E6C-4E96-9C14-1FAAE3920ECC}']
    procedure Informs(Code: Integer; const Message: WideString); safecall;
  end;
```

The main unit includes the fake COM object and its class factory, to let the server register itself. The code looks like this (notice that the method is abstract, and it has no implementation):

```
type
  // fake abstract class
  TMdInform = class (TAutoObject, IMdInform)
  protected
    procedure Informs(Code: Integer; const Message: WideString);
      virtual; safecall; abstract;
  end;

begin
  TAutoObjectFactory.Create(ComServer, TMdInform, Class_MdInform,
    ciMultiInstance, tmApartment);
end.
```

At this point, you can compile the library and install it in the COM+ environment. Again, after selecting a COM+ application (that is, a group of COM+ components), use the shortcut menu of its Components folder to add a new component to it. In the COM Component Install Wizard, click the Install New Event Class button and select the library you've just compiled. Your COM+ event definition will be automatically installed.

To test whether it works, you'll have to build an actual implementation of this event interface and a client invoking it. The implementation can be added to another ActiveX library, hosting a plain COM object. Within Delphi's COM Object Wizard you can select the interface to implement, choosing it in the list that appears when you select the List button. An example of this rather long list, dubbed Interface Selection Wizard, is shown in Figure 20.25.

FIGURE 20.25:

Delphi 6's new Interface
Selection Wizard, used in
this case to select an event
interface

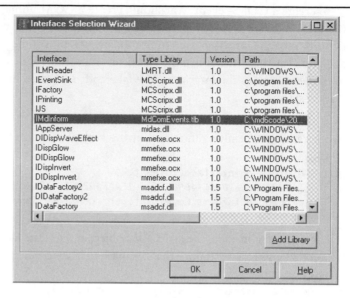

The resulting library, which in my example is called EvtSubscriber, exposes an Automation object, a COM object implementing the IDispatch interface (which is mandatory for COM+ Events). In my example, the object has the following definition and code:

```
type
  TInformSubscriber = class(TAutoObject, IMdInform)
  protected
    procedure Informs(Code: Integer; const Message: WideString); safecall;
  end;

procedure TInformSubscriber.Informs(Code: Integer; const Message: WideString);
begin
  ShowMessage ('Message <' + IntToStr (Code) + '>: ' + Message);
end;
```

After compiling this library, you can first install it into the COM+ environment, then you have to bind it to the event. This second step is accomplished in the Component Services management console by selecting the Subscriptions folder under the event object registration, and using the New ➢ Subscription shortcut menu. In the resulting wizard, you can choose the interface to implement (but there is probably only one interface in your COM+ event library), then you'll see a list of COM+ components that implement this interface. Selecting one or more of them you'll set up the subscription binding, which is listed under the Subscriptions folder. You can see an example of my configuration while building this example in Figure 20.26.

FIGURE 20.26:

A COM+ Event with two subscriptions in the Component Services management console.

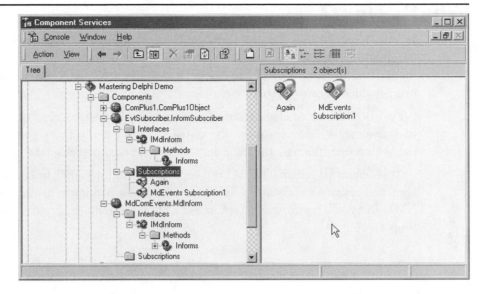

Finally, we can focus on the application that fires the event, which I've called Publisher, as it publishes the information other COM objects are interested in. This is actually the simplest step of this process, as it is a plain COM client that uses the event server. After importing the COM+ event type library, you can add to the publisher code like this:

```
var
  Inform: IMdInform;
begin
  Inform := CoMdInform.Create;
  Inform.Informs (20, Edit1.Text);
```

My example actually creates the COM object in the FormCreate method to keep the reference around, but the effect is the same. Now the client program thinks it is calling the COM+ event object, but this object, provided by the COM+ environment, actually calls the method for each of the active subscribers. In this case you'll end up seeing a message box. To make things a little more interesting, you can actually subscribe twice the same server to the event interface. The net effect is, without touching your client code, you'll get two message boxes, one for each of the subscribed servers.

Obviously this effect becomes interesting when you have multiple different COM components that can handle the event, as you can easily enable and disable each of them in the management console, changing the COM+ environment without modifying the code of any program.

What's Next?

In this chapter, I have discussed applications of Microsoft's COM technology, covering automation, documents, controls, and more. We've seen how Delphi makes the development of Automation servers and clients, and ActiveX controls, reasonably simple. Delphi even enables us to wrap components around Automation servers, such as Word and Excel.

I've also introduced elements of COM+ provided by Delphi 6 and discussed briefly the use of ActiveForms inside a browser. I've stated this is not really a very good approach to Internet Web programming—the topic discussed in the next two chapters.

As I mentioned earlier, if COM has a key role in Windows 2000, future versions of Microsoft's operating systems will downplay its role to push the dotNet infrastructure including SOAP and XML. But you'll have to *wait* until Chapter 23 to see a complete discussion of Delphi 6 XML support.

CHAPTER 21

Internet Programming: Sockets and Indy Components

- Using sockets

- The WinInet API

- Standard Internet actions

- The Internet Direct (Indy) components

- Mail and HTTP

In this chapter I'll provide an introduction to Internet programming in Delphi, using some of the components available in the IDE. With the advent of the Internet era, writing programs based on Internet protocols has become commonplace, so I've devoted three chapters to this topic. This chapter focuses on low-level socket programming and Internet protocols; the next chapter is devoted to server-side Web programming; and the final chapter of the book covers Web services, XML, and SOAP.

We'll start by looking at the use of Delphi socket components, then we'll move to the use of the Internet Direct (Indy) components supporting the most common Internet protocols. I will introduce some elements of HTTP programming, leading up to building HTML files out of database data.

Although you probably just want to use a high-level protocol, our discussion of Internet programming starts from the core concepts and low-level applications. The reason is that understanding TCP/IP and sockets will help you grasp most of the other concepts more easily.

Specifically, I'm going to focus on the use of the connectivity provided by Delphi socket components, which are based on TCP/IP and the low-level Windows sockets. Before we look into the foundations of sockets, let me list a couple of alternative approaches you can use for Internet programming, which I'll cover in more detail in later sections:

- The Delphi socket components provide a good interface for direct use of the Windows sockets API, implementing some custom protocols of your own.

- For standard protocols, you can also use the Indy components, included in Delphi 6.

Foundations of Socket Programming

To understand the description of the socket components in the Delphi Help file, and also to read along with the description of the examples in the book, you need to be confident with several terms related to the Internet in general and with sockets in particular.

The heart of the Internet is the Transmission Control Protocol/Internet Protocol (TCP/IP for short), a combination of two separate protocols that work together to provide connection over the Internet (and can also provide connection over a private intranet). In brief, IP is responsible for defining and routing the *datagrams* (Internet transmission units) and specifying the addressing scheme. TCP is responsible for higher-level transport services.

Configuring a Local Network: IP Addresses

If you have a local network available, you'll be able to test the following programs on it; otherwise, you can simply use the same computer as client and server. In this case, as I've done in the examples, use the address 127.0.0.1 (or *localhost*), which is invariably the address of the current computer. If your network is complex, ask your network administrator to set up proper IP addresses for you. If you want to set up a simple network with a couple of spare computers, you can simply set up the IP address yourself, a 32-bit number usually represented with each of its four components (called *octets*) separated by dots. These numbers have a complex logic underneath them, with the first octet indicating the class of the address.

Specific IP addresses are actually reserved for unregistered internal networks. Internet routers will ignore these address ranges, so you can freely do your tests without interfering with an actual network. For example, the "free" IP address range 192.168.0.0 through 192.168.0.255 can be used for experiments on a network of fewer than 255 machines.

Local Domain Names

How does the IP address map to a name? On the Internet, the client program looks up the values on a domain name server. But it is also possible to have a local *hosts* file, a text file that you can easily edit to provide nice local mappings. You can take a look at the HOSTS.SAM file (installed in a subdirectory of the Windows directory) to see a sample and then eventually rename the file as HOSTS, without the extension, to activate local host mapping.

Should you use an IP or a hostname in your programs? Hostnames are easier to remember and won't require a change if the IP address changes (for whatever reason). On the other hand, IP addresses don't require any resolution, while hostnames must be resolved (a time-consuming operation if the lookup takes place on the Web).

TCP Ports

Each TCP connection takes place though a *port*, which is represented by a 16-bit number. The IP address and the TCP port together specify an Internet connection, or a *socket* (to use a more precise term). Different processes running on the same machine cannot use the same socket—the same port.

Some TCP ports have a standard usage for specific high-level protocols and services. In other words, you should use those port numbers when implementing those services and stay away from them in any other case. Here is a short list:

Protocol	Port
HTTP (Hypertext Transfer Protocol)	80
FTP (File Transfer Protocol)	21
SMTP (Simple Mail Transfer Protocol)	25
POP3 (Post Office Protocol, version 3)	110
Telnet	23

The Services file (another text file similar to the Hosts file) lists the standard ports used by services. You can add your own entry to the list, giving your service a name of your own choosing. Client sockets always specify the port number or the service name of the server socket to which they want to connect.

High-Level Protocols

I've used the term *protocol* many times now, but what does it mean exactly? A protocol is a set of rules the client and server agree upon to determine the communication flow. The low-level Internet protocols, such as TCP/IP, are usually implemented by an operating system. But the term *protocol* is also used for high-level Internet standard protocols (such as HTTP, FTP, or SMTP). These protocols are defined in standard documents available on the Web on the site of the Internet Engineering Task Force (www.ietf.org).

If you want to implement a custom communication, you can define your own (possibly simple) protocol, a set of rules determining which request the client can send to the server and how the server can respond to the various possible requests. We'll see an example of a custom protocol later on. Transfer protocols are at a higher level than transmission protocols, because they abstract from the transport mechanism provided by TCP/IP. This makes the protocols independent not only from the operating system and the hardware but also from the physical network.

Socket Connections

How do you start communication through a socket? The server program starts running first, but it simply waits for a request from a client. The client program requests a connection indicating the server it wishes to connect to. When the client sends the request, the server can accept the connection, starting a specific server-side socket, which connects to the client-side socket.

To support this model, there are three different types of socket connections:

- *Client connections* are initiated by the client and connect a local client socket with a remote server socket. Client sockets must describe the server they want to connect to, by providing either its hostname or IP address and its port.

- *Listening connections* are passive server sockets waiting for a client. Once a client makes a new request, the server spawns a new socket devoted to that specific connection and then gets back to listening. Listening server sockets must indicate the port that represents the service they provide. (In fact, the client is going to connect through that port.)

- *Server connections* are the connections activated by servers, as they accept a request from a client.

These different types of connections are important only for establishing the link from the client to the server. Once the link is established, both sides are free to make requests and to send data to the other side.

Delphi Socket Components

Delphi 6 ships with three sets of socket components you can use to read and write information over a TCP/IP connection. The Internet page of the palette hosts the ClientSocket and Server-Socket components (already available in Delphi 5) plus the new TcpClient and TcpServer components (also available in Kylix). To these *native* Borland sockets, the Indy components add the IdTCPClient and the IdTCPServer components. These three sets of components have very similar features, which depend on the underlying protocol. There are technical differences, of course, and platform issues, which can determine your choice.

Host and Port

To use a socket component, you must provide a host and a service. On the server side the host is the address of the current computer; on the client side you can indicate either a domain name or an IP address. The ClientSocket component uses two different properties for these settings (Host and Address), while the TcpClient component and the IdTCPClient component use a single string property and can determine whether it is a hostname or an address by looking at its content (the property is called RemoteHost and Host, respectively).

Similarly the service is indicated with the Port property or the Service property, in a ClientSocket, and with the single RemotePort string in a TcpClient and with the single numeric Port in an IdTCPClient. The respective servers determine their listening port using analogous properties (called Port, LocalPort, and DefaultPort in the three components).

NOTE   The Indy server sockets allow binding to multiple IP addresses and/or ports, using the Bindings collection.

Blocking, Nonblocking, and Multithreaded Connections

When working with sockets in Windows, multiple approaches are possible. Reading data from a socket or writing to it can happen asynchronously, so that it does not block the execution of other code in your network application. This is called a *nonblocking connection*. Nonblocking connections read and write asynchronously: the Windows socket support basically sends a message when data is available. Using the ClientSocket and ServerSocket components, for example, the system fires the OnRead or OnWrite events of the client, and the

OnClientRead or OnClientWrite events of servers inform your socket when the other end of the connection tries to read or write some data.

As an alternative to the asynchronous approach, you can also use *blocking connections*, where your application waits for the reading or writing to be completed before executing the next line of code. In this case, you have to write the code in sequence on both sides, because otherwise the events won't be triggered. When using a blocking connection, you must use a thread on the server, and you'll generally use a thread also on the client.

The Indy components use an in-between approach. They use blocking connections exclusively, and you can either place their code in a thread or use a special helper component (IdAntiFreeze). Using blocking connections for implementing a protocol has the advantage of simplifying the program logic, because you don't have to use the state-machine approach of nonblocking connections, as exemplified later.

Finally, when writing threaded code with the ServerSocket components working on a blocking connection, you can use the TWinSocketStream class to do the actual reading and writing operations. You can use the WaitForData method of the TWinSocketStream class to wait until the socket on the other end is ready to write. You can also create the socket stream class and specify a timeout value, so that if the connection is lost, it won't hang forever.

Using Sockets

After all that theory, let's take a look at a couple of examples. The first is the Sock1 program on the companion CD and is made of the Server1 and Client1 applications, built with the ClientSocket and ServerSocket components in nonblocking mode. The server has a form with the following component:

```
object ServerSocket1: TServerSocket
  Active = True
  Port = 50
  ServerType = stNonBlocking
  OnClientConnect = ServerSocket1ClientConnect
  OnClientDisconnect = ServerSocket1ClientDisconnect
  OnClientRead = ServerSocket1ClientRead
end
```

All the code of the application relates to the events of this component, as the program provides no specific interaction with the user. However, the server has three list boxes for outputting the status, the messages sent from the client, and a log of the events. For example, as a client connects, the server adds the client address to the log:

```
procedure TForm1.ServerSocket1ClientConnect(Sender: TObject;
  Socket: TCustomWinSocket);
begin
```

```
    lbLog.Items.Add ('Connected: ' + Socket.RemoteHost + ' (' +
      Socket.RemoteAddress + ')' );
    PostMessage (Handle, wm_RefreshClients, 0, 0);
  end;
```

Notice that the OnClientConnect event indicates the first occasion for the server to
know about the connected client. Using the Socket property, which refers to the low-level
TCustomWinSocket, the server can track who is trying to connect. At the end of this and
other events, I want to update the list of the connections, using the ActiveConnections
property of the server. However, in the OnClientConnect event handler, this list is still not
updated, so I post a message to the form to delay the operation:

```
const
  wm_RefreshClients = wm_User;

procedure TForm1.RefreshClients; // message wm_RefreshClients
var
  I: Integer;
begin
  lbClients.Clear;
  for I := 0 to ServerSocket1.Socket.ActiveConnections - 1 do
    with ServerSocket1.Socket.Connections [I] do
      lbClients.Items.Add (RemoteAddress + ' (' + RemoteHost + ')');
end;
```

Similar code is executed as the client disconnects from the server:

```
procedure TForm1.ServerSocket1ClientDisconnect(Sender: TObject;
  Socket: TCustomWinSocket);
begin
  lbLog.Items.Add ('Disconnected: ' + Socket.RemoteHost + ' (' +
    Socket.RemoteAddress + ')' );
  PostMessage (Handle, wm_RefreshClients, 0, 0);
end;
```

Finally, as the client sends some information to the server (writes to the socket), the server
can read the message by calling the ReceiveText function. You should do this read operation
only when there is some data available—that is, when the OnClientRead event is fired. Notice
also that this is a *destructive* read: the information extracted from the stream is removed from
it. Here is the code:

```
procedure TForm1.ServerSocket1ClientRead(Sender: TObject;
  Socket: TCustomWinSocket);
begin
  // read from the client
```

```
    lbMsg.Items.Add (Socket.RemoteHost + ': ' + Socket.ReceiveText);
  end;
```

Now we can move to the client side of the application, which has a form hosting a client-socket component with the following properties:

```
object ClientSocket1: TClientSocket
  Active = False
  Address = '127.0.0.1'
  ClientType = ctNonBlocking
  Port = 50
  OnConnect = ClientSocket1Connect
  OnDisconnect = ClientSocket1Disconnect
end
```

The client form is more interactive. It has two edit boxes and a check box. In the first edit box, you can type the address of the server you want to connect to (to replace the default value listed above), using the check box to activate or deactivate the socket connection:

```
procedure TForm1.cbActivateClick(Sender: TObject);
begin
  if not ClientSocket1.Active then
    ClientSocket1.Address := EditServer.Text;
  ClientSocket1.Active := cbActivate.Checked;
end;
```

As you connect or disconnect, the program simply updates the caption of the form. In the second edit box, you can type a message to send to the server and a button you can press to send the message:

```
procedure TForm1.btnSendClick(Sender: TObject);
begin
  ClientSocket1.Socket.SendText (EditMsg.Text);
end;
```

Notice that this example program doesn't check whether the connection is active before using it, which can result in errors. In Figure 21.1, you can see an example of the client and the server. As the server indicates, a second copy of the client application is running on another computer and is connected to it.

FIGURE 21.1:

The client and server applications of the Sock1 example, demonstrating the use of the socket components

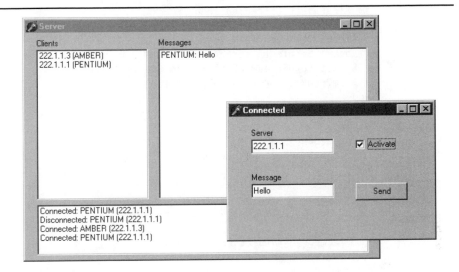

Using Sockets with a Custom Protocol

Unless you want to send and receive only simple text messages, you might want to define some communication rules between the client and the server. A set of communication rules is generally indicated as a protocol. Basically, the server can receive different requests and, depending on the type of request and whether it can be accomplished, reply to the client.

The server program of the Sock2 example accepts four types of requests: the listing of a directory, a bitmap file, a text file, and the execution of a program on the server. When the server sends back a file, its reply should indicate both what it is going to send back and the actual information. The only method modified from the Sock1 example is the `Server-Socket1ClientRead` procedure, which starts by extracting the five initial characters of the text received by the client that host the command:

```
strCommand := Socket.ReceiveText;
lbLog.Items.Add ('Client: ' + Socket.RemoteAddress + ': ' + strCommand);
// extract the file name (all commands have 5 characters)
strFile := Copy (strCommand, 6, Length (strCommand) - 5);
```

The actual code depends on the initial command defined by the protocol (in this case either *EXEC!* to execute a file on the server, *TEXT!* to return a text file, *BITM!* to retrieve a bitmap file, or *LIST!* to return a directory listing). Here is the code for two of these four alternatives:

```
// send back a text file
if Pos ('TEXT!', strCommand) = 1 then
begin
```

```
if FileExists (strFile) then
begin
  strFeedback := 'TEXT!';
  Socket.SendText (strFeedback);
  Socket.SendStream (TFileStream.Create (strFile,
    fmOpenRead or fmShareDenyWrite));
end
else
begin
  strFeedback := 'ERROR' + strFile + ' not found';
  Socket.SendText (strFeedback);
end;
end
// send back a directory listing
else if Pos ('LIST!', strCommand) = 1 then
begin
  if DirectoryExists (strFile) then
  begin
    strFeedback := 'LIST!';
    Socket.SendText (strFeedback);
    FileListBox1.Directory := strFile;
    Socket.SendText (FileListBox1.Items.Text);
  end
  else
  begin
    strFeedback := 'ERROR' + strFile + ' not found';
    Socket.SendText (strFeedback);
  end;
end
else
begin
  strFeedback := 'ERROR' + 'Undefined command: ' + strCommand;
  Socket.SendText (strFeedback);
end;
```

For the directory listings, I've used an invisible FileListBox component. For sending back the text file, I've used the SendStream method, creating a new stream on the fly. The advantage is that there is no need to destroy the temporary stream, as the SendStream method becomes the owner of the stream and destroys it when it is done.

The program sends back multiple pieces of information one after the other. This will create a few problems on the client side, as all the information is received in a single stream. However, the server responds with a five-character header that we can use to determine the content of the rest of the stream. After receiving these headers, the client application sets a status field so that it knows which type of information is coming next. In other words, in the client program, we implement a very simple finite-state machine, a typical technique for socket programming. The client application has five possible states, listed in an enumerated type:

```
type
  TCliStatus = (csIdle, csList, csBitmap, csText, csError);
```

This type is used for the CliStatus field of the form. The form has two edit boxes referring to a directory or a file a user can request from the server. When the user presses the Get Dir button, the client program passes to the server the name of the directory indicated by the first edit box. The server will return a list of files, which the client program saves in a list box. At this point, the user can select one of the files from the list box, and the client program will copy it, along with the complete path, into the second edit box. The text of this second edit box is used by the other three buttons—Exec, Bitmap, and Text—which send further requests to the server. In Figure 21.2, you can see an example of the main form of the client program after a directory has been retrieved.

FIGURE 21.2:

The form of the Client2 program after the server has returned the list of the files of a directory

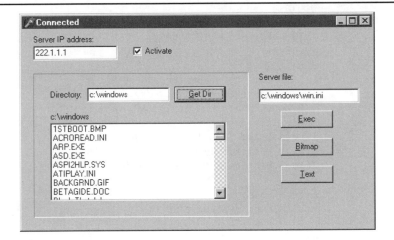

The core of the program is in the ClientSocket1Read method, triggered by the socket when there is data to read. The method is first used to get the header indicating which type of data is reaching the program and to set the client program to the proper status:

```
case CliStatus of
  // look for data to receive
  csIdle:
  begin
    Socket.ReceiveBuf (Buffer, 5);
    strIn := Copy (Buffer, 1, 5);
    if strIn = 'TEXT!' then
      CliStatus := csText
    else if strIn = 'BITM!' then
      CliStatus := csBitmap
    // .. and so on
```

Since we don't retrieve all the data, the event is triggered again soon afterward, and this time we are ready to get the actual data. Here are two more branches of the case statement:

```
// get a directory listing
csList:
  begin
    ListFiles.Items.Text := Socket.ReceiveText;
    cliStatus := csIdle;
  end;
// read a bitmap file
csBitmap:
  with TFormBmp.Create (Application) do
  begin
    Stream := TMemoryStream.Create;
    Screen.Cursor := crHourglass;
    try
      while True do
      begin
        nReceived := Socket.ReceiveBuf (Buffer, sizeof (Buffer));
        if nReceived <= 0 then
          Break
        else
          Stream.Write (Buffer, nReceived);
        // delay (200 milliseconds)
        Sleep (200);
      end;
      // reset and load the temporary file
      Stream.Position := 0;
      Image1.Picture.Bitmap.LoadFromStream (Stream);
    finally
      Stream.Free;
      Screen.Cursor := crDefault;
    end;
    Show;
    cliStatus := csIdle;
  end;
```

For loading the bitmap, I simply move the data to a Buffer (declared as array [0..9999] of Char) and then from the buffer to a memory stream, which is later loaded in the Image component of the secondary form. Because the data flow can slow down, the program has a hard-coded delay of 200 milliseconds every time some data is read. Unlike file-reading operations, the loop doesn't stop when the data read is less than the data requested, but only when *no* data is read. (In case of error, the value returned by the ReceiveBuff method is –1.)

Sending Database Data over a Socket Connection

Using the techniques we've seen so far, we can write an application that moves database records over a socket. The idea will be to write a front end for data input and a back end for data storage. The client application will have a simple data-entry form and use a database table with string fields for Company, Address, State, Country, Email, and Contact, and a floating-point field for the company ID (called CompID).

> **NOTE**   Moving database records over a socket is exactly what you can do with DataSnap and a socket connection component, or with the SOAP support built into Delphi 6 and discussed in Chapter 23, "XML and SOAP."

The client program I've come up with works on a table with this structure saved in the current directory. (You can see the related code in the OnCreate event handler.) The core method on the client side is the handler of the OnClick event of the Send All button, which sends all the new records to the server. The new records are determined by looking to see whether the record has a valid value for the CompID field. This field, in fact, is not set up by the user but is determined by the server application when the data is sent.

For all new records, the client program packages the field information in a string list, using the structure *FieldName=FieldValue*, obtained using the Values property of the string list. The string corresponding to the entire list is then sent to the server. At this point, the program stops in an apparently infinite loop:

```
// save database data in a string list
Data := TStringList.Create;
table1.First;
while not Table1.Eof do
begin
  // if the record is still not logged
  if Table1CompID.IsNull or (Table1CompId.AsInteger = 0) then
  begin
    lbLog.Items.Add ('Sending ' + Table1Company.AsString);
    Data.Clear;
    // create strings with structure "FieldName=Value"
    for I := 0 to Table1.FieldCount - 1 do
      Data.Values [Table1.Fields[I].FieldName] := Table1.Fields [I].AsString;
    // send the record
    ClientSocket1.Socket.SendText (Data.Text);
    // wait for response
    fWaiting := True;
    while fWaiting do
      Application.ProcessMessages;
  end;
  Table1.Next;
end;
```

The program waits forever ... or until the handler of another message sets the fWaiting field of the form to False. This happens when the server sends some feedback indicating that the record was received or when the user presses the Stop button. The btnSendAllClick method automatically connects to the server at the beginning and disconnects at the end.

Now let us look at the server. This program has a database table, again stored in the local directory, with two new fields added to the client application's table: LoggedBy, a string field; and LoggedOn, a data field. The values of the two extra fields are determined automatically by the server as it receives data, along with the value of the CompID field. All these operations are done in the ServerSocket1ClientRead method after unpacking the data received by the client:

```
// read from the client
strCommand := Socket.ReceiveText;
// reassemble the data
Data := TStringList.Create;
try
  Data.Text := strCommand;
  // new record
  Table1.Insert;
  // set the fields using the strings
  for I := 0 to Table1.FieldCount - 1 do
    Table1.Fields [I].AsString := Data.Values [Table1.Fields[I].FieldName];
  // complete with random ID, sender, and date
  Table1CompID.AsInteger := GetTickCount;
  Table1LoggedBy.AsString := Socket.RemoteAddress;
  Table1LoggetOn.AsDateTime := Date;
  Table1.Post;
  // get the value to return
  strFeedback := Table1CompID.AsString;
  // send results back
  lbLog.Items.Add (strFeedback);
  Socket.SendText (strFeedback);
finally
  Data.Free;
end;
```

Except for the fact that some data might be lost, there is no problem when fields have a different order and if they do not match, because the data is stored in the *FieldName=Field-Value* structure. After receiving all the data and posting it to the local table, the server sends back the company ID to the client. The client program, after sending the record, goes into *waiting mode*, a situation modified by receiving feedback from the server:

```
procedure TForm1.ClientSocket1Read(Sender: TObject;
  Socket: TCustomWinSocket);
begin
  if fWaiting then
  begin
    Table1.Edit;
```

```
    Table1CompId.AsString := Socket.ReceiveText;
    Table1.Post;
    lbLog.Items.Add (Table1Company.AsString + ' logged as ' +
      Table1CompId.AsString);
    fWaiting := False;
  end;
end;
```

When receiving feedback, the client program saves the company ID, which marks the record as sent. If the user modifies the record, there is no way to send an update to the server. To accomplish this, you might add a modified field to the client database table and make the server check to see if it is receiving a new field or a modified field. With a modified field, the server should not add a new record but update the existing one.

This is one of the many additions you can make to the program, to make it usable in a real-world environment. The existing code of the program and the previous examples on sockets should provide all you need to complete a similar task. I've limited myself to this version of the application, as shown in Figure 21.3. Notice that the server program has two pages, one with the usual log and the other with a DBGrid showing the current data of the server database table.

FIGURE 21.3:

The client and server programs of the database socket example (DbSock)

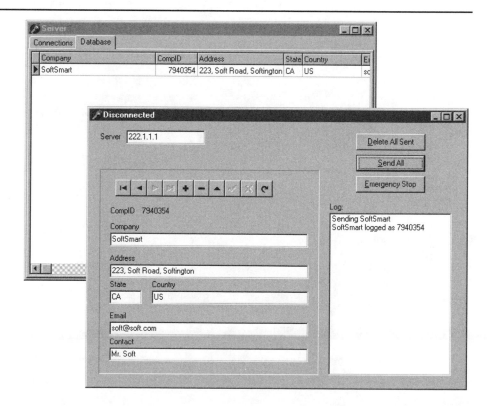

Working with Blocking Sockets and Threads

A program like the one I've just built is nice, but it won't really scale up on a large system, because the server uses a blocking connection and the requests are processed in sequence. Now, even if making the database-related code multithreading wouldn't be easy, I'll take the excuse of this example to show you how to build a program based on blocking sockets and threads. (If you don't know much about threads, read the sidebar "Working with Threads" before proceeding.)

Working with Threads

Win32 has an API to allow two procedures or methods execute at the same time. Delphi provides a TThread class that will let us create and control threads. The first thing to know about the TThread class is that you never use it directly, because it is an abstract class—a class with a virtual abstract method. To use threads, you always subclass TThread (optionally starting with the Thread Object of the New Items dialog box (File ➤ New ➤ Other) and use the features of this base class.

The TThread class has a constructor with a single parameter (CreateSuspended) that lets you choose whether to start the thread immediately or suspend it until later. There are also some public synchronization methods:

```
procedure Resume;
procedure Suspend;
function Terminate: Integer;
function WaitFor: Integer;
```

The published properties include Priority, Suspended, and two read-only, low-level values: Handle and ThreadID. The class also provides a protected interface, which includes two key methods for your thread subclasses:

```
procedure Execute; virtual; abstract;
procedure Synchronize(Method: TThreadMethod);
```

The Execute method, declared as a virtual abstract procedure, must be redefined by each thread class. It contains the main code of the thread, the code you would typically place in a *thread function* when using the Windows API.

The Synchronize method is used to avoid concurrent access to VCL components. The VCL code runs inside the main thread of the program, and you need to synchronize access to VCL to avoid reentry problems (errors from reentering a function before a previous call is completed) and concurrent access to shared resources. The only parameter of Synchronize is a method that accepts no parameters, typically a method of the same thread class. As you cannot pass parameters to this method, it is common to save some values within the data of the thread object in the Execute method and use those values in the *synchronized* methods.

Continued on next page

> Another way to avoid conflicts is to use the synchronization techniques offered by the operating system. The SyncObjs unit defines VCL classes for some of these low-level synchronization objects: events (with the `TEvent` class and the `TSingleEvent` class) and critical sections (with the `TCriticalSection` class).

In the server program (see the SockDbThread example on the companion CD), the socket component now has a thread-blocking type and has handlers for many events, including in particular `OnGetThread`. No methods are hooked to the read and write events, as they won't be triggered anymore (they are used exclusively by message-based nonblocking sockets):

```
object ServerSocket1: TServerSocket
  Active = True
  Port = 51
  ServerType = stThreadBlocking
  OnAccept = ServerSocket1Accept
  OnGetThread = ServerSocket1GetThread
  OnClientConnect = ServerSocket1ClientConnect
  OnClientDisconnect = ServerSocket1ClientDisconnect
end
```

The `OnAccept`, `OnClientConnect`, and `OnClientDisconnect` event handlers are used only for logging information to the screen, while the `OnGetThread` event handler has a key role of creating the server-side thread object:

```
procedure TForm1.ServerSocket1GetThread(Sender: TObject; ClientSocket:
  TServerClientWinSocket; var SocketThread: TServerClientThread);
begin
  lbLog.Items.Add('GetThread: ' + ClientSocket.RemoteHost + ' (' +
    ClientSocket.RemoteAddress + ')' );
  SocketThread := TDbServerThread.Create(False, ClientSocket);
end;
```

This must be an object of a class inherited by the specific `TServerClientThread` class (not the generic Delphi `TThread` class) and with its core code placed in an overridden `ClientExecute` method (not the generic `Execute` method):

```
type
  TDbServerThread = class(TServerClientThread)
  private
    strCommand: string;
    strFeedback: string;
  public
    procedure ClientExecute; override;
    procedure Log;
    procedure LogFeedback;
```

```pascal
    procedure AddRecord;
  end;

procedure TDbServerThread.ClientExecute;
var
  Stream: TWinSocketStream;
  Buffer, strIn: string;
  nRead: Integer;
begin
  // keep going
  Stream := TWinSocketStream.Create(ClientSocket, 5000);
  try
    while not Terminated and ClientSocket.Connected do
    begin
      // initialize (thread might be reused)
      Buffer := '';
      strIn := '';
      SetLength(Buffer, 64);
      repeat
        nRead := Stream.Read(Buffer[1], 64);
        if nRead = 0 then
        begin
          ClientSocket.Close;
          Break;
        end;
        SetLength (Buffer, nRead);
        StrIn := StrIn + Buffer;
      until (Pos(#10#13'.'#10#13, Buffer) > 0);

      if strIn = '' then
        Continue // keep going
      else
      begin
        // handle the request, if anything arrived
        StrCommand := Copy (strIn, 1, Pos (#10#13'.'#10#13, strIn) -1);
        Synchronize(Log);
        Synchronize(AddRecord);
        // send results back
        Synchronize(LogFeedback);
        Stream.Write(strFeedback[1], Length (strFeedback));
      end;
    end;
  finally
    Stream.Free;
  end;
end;
```

The server reads data from the client and sends the feedback using a `TWinSocketStream`, a compulsory approach for blocking servers. The thread is kept active, as it can be reused for subsequent calls, and reads from a buffer until it find a specific separator (in this case, a dot between two line separators, exactly as occurs in the SMTP protocol). When the data is received, the server does a *synchronized* call to the `AddRecord` method, which is similar to the code of the previous version of the example.

WARNING This approach is far from perfect, as all database accesses are serialized, but you could solve the problem by moving the database access component within the thread and adding a Session object in case of a BDE application. Not all databases like multithreaded access, though, so serializing the calls is not always a bad idea.

This is the multithreaded server application. The client program, instead, uses a standard thread class, derived from `TThread`. The class creates a client server object internally, so that multiple threads could spawn multiple socket connections in parallel (something the program doesn't really use) and receives a table to work on as parameter in the constructor:

```
type
  TLogEvent = procedure(Sender: TObject; LogMsg: String) of object;

  TSendThread = class(TThread)
  private
    ClientSocket: TClientSocket;
    FTable: TTable;
    FOnLog: TLogEvent;
    FLogMsg: String;
    procedure SetOnLog(const Value: TLogEvent);
  protected
    procedure Execute; override;
    procedure DoLog;
  public
    constructor Create(ATable: TTable);
    property OnLog: TLogEvent read FOnLog write SetOnLog;
  end;
```

On the client side, the finite-state machine logic (send, set the wait flag, receive another event, disable the flag, get the next record) is now replaced by a continual and more logical flow of operations, all part of the `Execute` method of the thread. You need to add some code to let the program wait until the server sends a reply. Again, the blocking socket of the client is not used directly but via a `TWinSocketStream` object:

```
procedure TSendThread.Execute;
var
  I: Integer;
  Data: TStringList;
```

```
    Stream: TWinSocketStream;
    Buf: String;
begin
  try
    Data := TStringList.Create;
    ClientSocket := TClientSocket.Create (nil);
    Stream := nil;
    try
      ClientSocket.Address := EditServer.Text;
      ClientSocket.ClientType := ctBlocking;
      ClientSocket.Port := 51;
      ClientSocket.Active := True;
      Stream := TWinSocketStream.Create(ClientSocket.Socket, 30000);

      FTable.First;
      while not FTable.Eof do
      begin
        // if the record is still not logged
        if FTable.FieldByName('CompID').IsNull or
          (FTable.FieldByName('CompID').AsInteger = 0) then
        begin
          FLogMsg := 'Sending ' + Table.FieldByName('Company').AsString;
          Synchronize(DoLog);
          Data.Clear;
          // create strings with structure "FieldName=Value"
          for I := 0 to FTable.FieldCount - 1 do
            Data.Values [FTable.Fields[I].FieldName] :=
              FTable.Fields [I].AsString;
          // send the record followed by separator
          Buf := Data.Text + #10#13'.'#10#13;
          ClientSocket.Socket.SendText(Buf);
          // wait for reponse
          if Stream.WaitForData(30000) then
          begin
            FTable.Edit;
            SetLength(Buf, 256);
            SetLength(Buf, Stream.Read(Buf[1], Length(Buf)));
            FTable.FieldByName('CompID').AsString := Buf;
            FTable.Post;
            FLogMsg := FTable.FieldByName('Company').AsString +
                ' logged as ' + FTable.FieldByName('CompID').AsString;
          end
          else
            FlogMsg := 'No response for ' +
                FTable.FieldByName('Company').AsString;
          Synchronize(DoLog);
        end;
```

```
        FTable.Next;
      end;
    finally
      ClientSocket.Active := False;
      ClientSocket.Free;
      Stream.Free;
      Data.Free;
    end;
  except
    // trap exceptions
  end;
end;
```

The thread also has an event handler to let the forms using it define the effect of the OnLog operation, in the synchronized DoLog method. Finally, this is how the thread starts, when the user clicks a button in the form:

```
procedure TForm1.Button2Click(Sender: TObject);
var
  SendThread: TSendThread;
begin
  SendThread := TSendThread.Create(Table1);
  SendThread.OnLog := OnLog;
  SendThread.Resume;
end;
```

Internet Protocols

After discussing the low-level socket components, we are ready to delve into the core topic of this chapter, the use of higher-level Internet protocols.

As already mentioned, Delphi 6 now ships with a collection of open-source Internet components called Internet Direct, or Indy for short. The Indy components, previously called WinShoes (a pun on the term WinSockets), are built by a group of developers led by Chad Hower and are available also in Kylix. You can find more information and possibly updated versions of the actual components at www.nevrona.com/indy.

The Indy components are available within the Delphi IDE, but they are not the only set of Internet components. Delphi 6 Component Palette also has another page of Internet protocol components, the FastNet page. These are available for compatibility with Delphi 5 and earlier versions. Third-party solutions, both freely available or for sale, also provide implementations of Internet protocols.

Here and in the next chapter, I'm going to focus exclusively on the Indy components. This chapter focuses on the use of Internet protocols within Windows applications, while the next shows examples of the use of these protocols within Web server applications.

Sending and Receiving Mail

Probably the most common operation you do on the Internet is to send and receive e-mail. There is generally very little need to write a complete application to handle e-mail, as some of the existing programs are actually rather complete. For this reason, I have no intention of writing a general-purpose mail program here. You can find some examples of those among Delphi Internet demos.

Other than creating a general-purpose mail application, what else can one do with the mail components and protocols? There are many possibilities, which I've tried to group in two areas:

Automatic generation of mail messages   An application you've written can have an About box for sending a registration message back to your marketing department or a specific menu item for sending a request to your tech support. You might even decide to enable a tech-support connection whenever an exception occurs. Another related task would be automating the dispatching of a message to a list of people or generating an automatic message from your Web site, an example I'll show you toward the end of this chapter.

Use of mail protocols for communication with users who are only occasionally online When you must move data between users who are not always online, you can write an application on a server to synchronize among them, and you can give each user a specialized client application for interacting with the server. An alternative is to use an existing server application, such as a mail server, and write the two specialized programs based on the mail protocols. The data sent over this connection will generally be formatted in special ways, so you'll want to use a specific e-mail addresses for these messages (not your primary e-mail address). As an example, you could rewrite the earlier DbSock example to dispatch mail messages instead of using a custom socket connection. This will give you the advantage of being firewall-friendly and allowing the server to be temporarily offline, as the requests would be kept on the mail server.

Sending Messages with Your Mail Program

The simplest technique for automating the generation of an e-mail message is to use your existing mail application, adding a message to its outbox. Using the ShellExecute API function, you can easily send a message to the default mail program registered on the computer.

To test this technique, I've prepared a simple form with two edit boxes and a memo for the input. Pressing a button creates a string with all the information about the message and then sends it, simply executing the string with the *mailto:* prefix. Here is the code of the Send button of the MailGen example from the companion CD:

```
uses
  ShellApi;

procedure TForm1.BtnSendClick(Sender: TObject);
var
  strMsg: string;
  I: Integer;
begin
  // set the basic information
  strMsg := 'mailto:' + EditAddress.Text + '?Subject=' + EditSubject.Text +
    '&Body=';
  // add first line
  if Memo1.Lines.Count > 0 then
    strMsg := strMsg + Memo1.Lines [0];
  // add subsequent lines separated by the newline symbol
  for I := 1 to Memo1.Lines.Count - 1 do
    strMsg := strMsg + '%0D%0A' + Memo1.Lines [I];
  // send the message
  ShellExecute (Handle, 'open', pChar (strMsg), '', '', SW_SHOW);
end;
```

To show the body of the message on multiple lines, you can separate each line with the carriage return and line feed characters (usually indicated in Delphi as #13 and #10). These values should be explicitly added to the string in hexadecimal format and prefixed by the % sign, as required by a URL. You can actually obtain this encoding automatically by using the NMURL component.

NOTE   You can also send mail with the TSendMail predefined action, which is based on the MAPI standard.

Mail In and Out

To showcase the development of simple e-mail management programs, I could build an example of how you can send and receive mail. The Indy components, though, include a rather complete set of examples, and I don't see any reason to duplicate those, as using the mail protocols means placing a message component (IdMessage) in your application, filling it with data, and then using the IdSMTP component to send the mail message. To *retrieve* a mail message from your mailbox, use the IdPop3 component, which will return you an IdMessage object.

Just to give you an idea of how this works, I've written a program for sending mail to multiple people at once, using a list stored in an ASCII file. I originally used this program myself for sending mail to people who sign up on my Web site, but later I extended the program by adding database support and reading subscriber logs automatically. The original version of the program is still a good introduction to the use of the SMTP component of Indy.

The SendList program keeps a list of names and e-mail addresses in a local file, which is displayed in a list box. A few buttons allow you to add and remove items, or modify them by removing the item, editing it, and then adding the item again. When the program closes, the updated list is automatically saved. Now let's get to the interesting portion of the program. The top-most panel, shown in Figure 21.4, allows you to enter the subject, the sender address, and the information used to connect to the mail server (hostname, username, and eventually a password).

FIGURE 21.4:

The SendList program in action

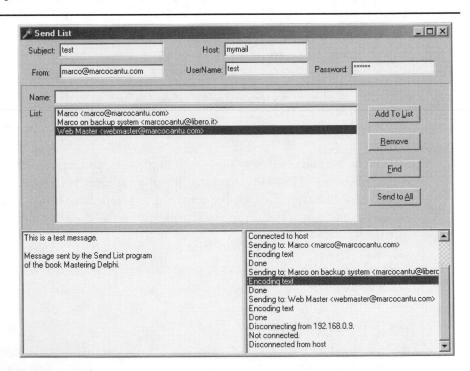

You'll probably want to make the value of these edit boxes persistent, possibly in an INI file. I haven't done this, only because I don't really want you to see my mail connection details! The value of these edit boxes, along with the list of addressee, allows you to send the series of mail messages, after customizing each of them, with the following code:

```
procedure TMainForm.BtnSendAllClick(Sender: TObject);
var
  nItem: Integer;
  Res: Word;
begin
  Res := MessageDlg ('Start sending from item ' +
    IntToStr (ListAddr.ItemIndex) + ' (' +
    ListAddr.Items [ListAddr.ItemIndex] + ')?'#13 +
    '(No starts from 0)', mtConfirmation, [mbYes, mbNo, mbCancel], 0);
  if Res = mrCancel then
    Exit;
  if Res = mrYes then
    nItem := ListAddr.ItemIndex
  else
    nItem := 0;
  // connect
  Mail.Host := eServer.Text;
  Mail.UserID := eUserName.Text;
  if ePassword.Text <> '' then
  begin
    Mail.Password := ePassword.Text;
    Mail.AuthenticationType := atLogin;
  end;
  Mail.Connect;
  // send the messages, one by one, prepending a custom message
  try
    // set the fixed part of the header
    MailMessage.From.Name := eFrom.Text;
    MailMessage.Subject := eSubject.Text;
    MailMessage.Body.SetText (reMessageText.Lines.GetText);
    MailMessage.Body.Insert (0, 'Hello');
    while nItem < ListAddr.Items.Count do
    begin
      // show the current selection
      Application.ProcessMessages;
      ListAddr.ItemIndex := nItem;
      MailMessage.Body [0] := 'Hello ' + ListAddr.Items [nItem];
      MailMessage.Recipients.EMailAddresses := ListAddr.Items [nItem];
      Mail.Send(MailMessage);
      Inc (nItem);
    end;
  finally // we're done
    Mail.Disconnect;
  end;
end;
```

Another interesting example of the use of the mail is to notify developers of problems within applications, something you might want to use more in an internal application than in one you'll distribute widely. You can obtain this effect by modifying the ErrorLog example of Chapter 4, "The Run-Time Library," and sending mail when an exception (or one of a given type only) occurs.

Working with HTTP

Handling mail messages is certainly interesting, and mail protocols are probably still the most widespread Internet protocols. The other popular protocol is HTTP, the one used by Web servers and Web browsers. This is the protocol to which we'll devote the rest of this chapter and all of the following.

On the client side of the Web, the main activity is browsing—reading HTML files. Besides building a custom browser, you can embed the Internet Express ActiveX control within your program (as I've done in WebDemo example in Chapter 20, "From Automation to COM+"). You can also directly activate the browser installed on the computer of the user, for example, opening an HTML page by calling the ShellExecute method (defined in the ShellApi unit):

```
ShellExecute (Handle, 'open', FileName, '', '', sw_ShowNormal);
```

Using ShellExecute, we can simply execute a document, such as a file. Windows will start the program associated with the HTM extension, using the action passed as the parameter (in this case, *open*). You can use a similar call to view a Web site, by using a string like *'http://www.example.com'* instead of a filename. In this case, the system recognizes the *http* section of the request as requiring a Web browser and launches it.

On the server side, you generate and make available the HTML pages. At times, it may be enough to have a way to produce static pages, occasionally extracting new data from a database table to update the HTML files as needed. In other cases, you'll need to generate pages dynamically based on a request from a user.

As a starting point, I'll discuss HTTP by building a simple but complete client and server, then we'll move on to discussing HTML producer components and introducing the Web server extension technologies (CGI and ISAPI). In the next chapter, we'll move from this "core technology" level to the RAD development style for the Web supported by Delphi 6, discussing the WebBroker and WebSnap architectures.

Grabbing HTTP Content

As an example of the use of the HTTP protocols, I've decided to write a very specific search application. The program simply hooks onto the Google Web site, searches for a keyword, and retrieves the first hundred sites found. Instead of showing the resulting HTML file, the program parses it to extract only the URLs of the related sites to a list box. The description of these sites is kept in a separate string list and is displayed as you click a list-box item. So the program demonstrates two techniques at once: retrieving a Web page and parsing its HTML code.

To demonstrate how you should work with blocking connections, such as those used by Indy, I've implemented the program using a background thread for the actual processing. (See the sidebar "Working with Threads," earlier in this chapter, for a very short introduction to this topic.) This approach also gives the advantage of being able to start multiple searches at once. The thread class used by the WebFind application receives as input a URL to look for, strUrl.

The class has two output procedures, AddToList and ShowStatus, to be called inside the Synchronize method. The code of these two methods sends some results or some feedback to the main form, respectively adding a line to the listbox and changing the status bar SimpleText property. The key method of the thread is the Execute method. Before we look at it, however, let me show you how the thread is activated by the main form:

```
const
  strSearch = 'http://www.google.com/search?as_q=';

procedure TForm1.BtnFindClick(Sender: TObject);
var
  FindThread: TFindWebThread;
begin
  // create suspended, set initial values, and start
  FindThread := TFindWebThread.Create (True);
  FindThread.FreeOnTerminate := True;
  // grab the first 100 entries
  FindThread.strUrl := strSearch + EditSearch.Text + '&num=100';
  FindThread.Resume;
end;
```

The URL string is made of the main address of the search engine, followed by some parameters. The first, as_q, indicates the words you are looking for. The second, num=100, indicates the number of sites to retrieve; you cannot use numbers at will but are limited to few alternatives, with 100 being the largest possible value.

WARNING The WebFind program works with the server on the Google Web site at the time this book was written and tested. The custom software on the site can change any day, however, which might prevent WebFind from operating correctly.

The Execute method of the thread, activated by the Resume call, simply calls the two methods actually doing the work and shown in Listing 21.1. In the first, GrabHtml, the program connects to the HTTP server using a dynamically created IdHttp component, and reads the HTML with the result of the search. The second method, HtmlToList, extracts the URLs referring to other Web sites from the result, the strRead string.

Listing 21.1:   **The *TFindWebThread* class (of the WebFind program)**

```
unit FindTh;

interface

uses
  Classes, IdComponent, SysUtils, IdHTTP;

type
  TFindWebThread = class(TThread)
  protected
    Addr, Text, Status: string;
    procedure Execute; override;
    procedure AddToList;
    procedure ShowStatus;
    procedure GrabHtml;
    procedure HtmlToList;
    procedure HttpWork (Sender: TObject; AWorkMode: TWorkMode;
      const AWorkCount: Integer);
  public
    strUrl: string;
    strRead: string;
  end;

implementation

{ TFindWebThread }

uses
  WebFindF;

procedure TFindWebThread.AddToList;
begin
  if Form1.ListBox1.Items.IndexOf (Addr) < 0 then
  begin
    Form1.ListBox1.Items.Add (Addr);
    Form1.DetailsList.Add (Text);
  end;
end;

procedure TFindWebThread.Execute;
begin
```

```pascal
    GrabHtml;
    HtmlToList;
    Status := 'Done with ' + StrUrl;
    Synchronize (ShowStatus);
end;

procedure TFindWebThread.GrabHtml;
var
  Http1: TIdHTTP;
begin
  Status := 'Sending query: ' + StrUrl;
  Synchronize (ShowStatus);
  Http1 := TIdHTTP.Create (nil);
  try
    Http1.OnWork := HttpWork;
    strRead := Http1.Get (StrUrl);
  finally
    Http1.Free;
  end;
end;

procedure TFindWebThread.HtmlToList;
var
  strAddr, strText: string;
  nText: integer;
  nBegin, nEnd: Integer;
begin
  Status := 'Elaborating data for: ' + StrUrl;
  Synchronize (ShowStatus);
  strRead := LowerCase (strRead);
  repeat
    // find the initial part HTTP reference
    nBegin := Pos ('href=http', strRead);
    if nBegin <> 0 then
    begin
      // get the remaining part of the string, starting with 'http'
      strRead := Copy (strRead, nBegin + 5, 1000000);
      // find the end of the HTTP reference
      nEnd := Pos ('>', strRead);
      strAddr := Copy (strRead, 1, nEnd - 1);
      // move on
      strRead := Copy (strRead, nEnd + 1, 1000000);
      // add the URL if 'google' is not in it
      if Pos ('google', strAddr) = 0 then
      begin
        nText := Pos ('</a>', strRead);
        strText := copy (strRead, 1, nText - 1);
        // remove cached references and duplicates
        if (Pos ('cached', strText) = 0) then
        begin
          Addr := strAddr;
```

```
            Text := strText;
            AddToList;
          end;
        end;
      end;
    until nBegin = 0;
end;

procedure TFindWebThread.HttpWork(Sender: TObject; AWorkMode: TWorkMode;
  const AWorkCount: Integer);
begin
  Status := 'Received ' + IntToStr (AWorkCount) + ' for ' + strUrl;
  Synchronize (ShowStatus);
end;

procedure TFindWebThread.ShowStatus;
begin
  Form1.StatusBar1.SimpleText := Status;
end;

end.
```

The program looks for subsequent occurrences of the href="http substring, copying the text up to the closing > character. If the found string contains the word *google*, or its target text includes the word *cached*, it is omitted from the result. You can see the effect of this code in the output of Figure 21.5. Notice that I've already gotten the result of a request, but the program is currently retrieving another page, as indicated in the status bar. You can start multiple searches at the same time, but be aware that the results will all be added to the same memo component.

FIGURE 21.5:

The WebFind application can be used to search for a list of sites on the Google search engine.

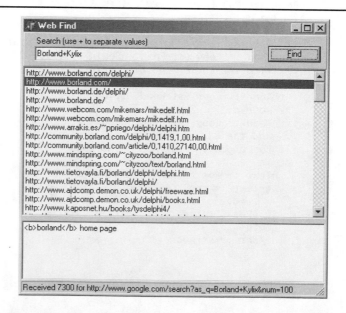

The WinInet API

When you need to use the FTP and HTTP protocols, as alternatives to using particular VCL components, you can use a specific API provided by Microsoft in the WinInet DLL. This library is part of the core operating system and implements the FTP and HTTP protocols on top of the Windows sockets API.

With just three calls—InternetOpen, InternetOpenURL, and InternetReadFile—you can retrieve a file corresponding to any URL and store a local copy or analyze it. Other simple methods can be used for FTP; I suggest you look for the source code of the Delphi unit, listing all the functions, and for the specific Help file for the DLL, which is not part of the SDK Help shipping with Delphi.

The InternetOpen function establishes a generic connection and returns a handle you can use in the InternetOpenURL call. This second call returns a handle to the URL that you can pass to the InternetReadFile function in order to read blocks of data. In the following sample code, the data is stored in a local string. When all the data has been read, the program closes the connection to the URL and the Internet session by calling the InternetCloseHandle function twice.

```
var
  hHttpSession, hReqUrl: HInternet;
  Buffer: array [0..1023] of Char;
  nRead: Cardinal;
  strRead: string;
  nBegin, nEnd: Integer;
begin
  strRead := '';
  hHttpSession := InternetOpen ('FindWeb', INTERNET_OPEN_TYPE_PRECONFIG,
    nil, nil, 0);
  try
    hReqUrl := InternetOpenURL (hHttpSession, PChar(StrUrl), nil, 0,0,0);
    try // read all the data
      repeat
        InternetReadFile (hReqUrl, @Buffer, sizeof (Buffer), nRead);
        strRead := strRead + string (Buffer);
      until nRead = 0;
    finally
      InternetCloseHandle (hReqUrl);
    end;
  finally
    InternetCloseHandle (hHttpSession);
  end;
end;
```

Browsing on Your Own

Although I doubt you are interested in writing a new Web browser, it might be interesting anyway to see how you can grab an HTML file from the Internet and display it locally, using the HTML viewer available in CLX (the TextBrowser control). Connecting this control to an Indy HTTP client, you can come up with a simplistic text-only browser with limited navigation in minutes. The core is to write

```
TextBrowser1.Text := IdHttp1.Get (NewUrl);
```

where `NewUrl` is complete location of the Web resource you want to access to. In the Browse-Fast example on the CD-ROM, this URL is entered in a combo box, which keeps track of recent requests. The effect of a similar call is to return the textual portion of a Web page (see Figure 21.6), as grabbing the graphic content requires much more complex coding. The TextBrowser control, in fact, is better defined as a local file viewer than as a browser.

FIGURE 21.6:

The output of the Browse-Fast text-only browser

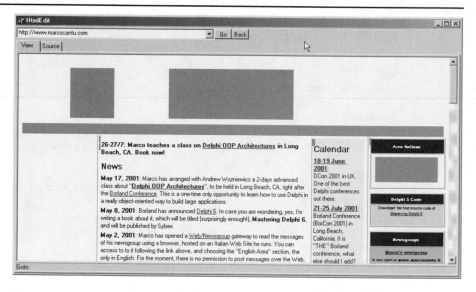

In any case, I've added to the program only very limited support for hyperlinks. When a user moves the mouse over a link, its link text is copied to a local variable (`NewRequest`), which is then used in case of a click on the control to compute the new HTTP request to forward. Merging the current address (`LastUrl`) with the request, though, is far from trivial, even with the help of the `IdUrl` class provided by Indy. Here is the code I've come up with, which handles only the simplest cases:

```
procedure TForm1.TextBrowser1Click(Sender: TObject);
var
  Uri: TIdUri;
```

```
begin
  if NewRequest <> '' then
  begin
    Uri := TIdUri.Create (LastUrl);
    if Pos ('http:', NewRequest) > 0 then
      GoToUrl (NewRequest)
    else if NewRequest [1] = '/' then
      GoToUrl ('http://' + Uri.Host + NewRequest)
    else
      GoToUrl ('http://' + Uri.Host + Uri.Path + NewRequest);
  end;
end;
```

Again, this example is really trivial and is far from usable, but building a browser involves a *little* more than the ability to connect via HTTP and display HTML files.

A Simple HTTP Server

The situation with the development of an HTTP server is quite different. Building a server to deliver static pages based on HTML files is far from simple, although one of the Indy demos provides a rather good starting point for this. A custom HTTP server, instead, might be interesting when building a totally dynamic site, something I'll focus on in more detail in the next chapter.

To show you how you can start the development of a custom HTTP server, I've built the HttpServ example. This program has a form with a list box used for logging requests and an IdHTTPServer component, with these settings:

```
object IdHTTPServer1: TIdHTTPServer
  Active = True
  DefaultPort = 8080
  OnCommandGet = IdHTTPServer1CommandGet
end
```

The server uses the port 8080 instead of the standard port 80, so that you can run it alongside another Web server. All of the custom code is in the OnCommandGet event handler, which simply returns a fixed page plus some information about the request itself:

```
procedure TForm1.IdHTTPServer1CommandGet(AThread: TIdPeerThread;
  RequestInfo: TIdHTTPRequestInfo; ResponseInfo: TIdHTTPResponseInfo);
var
  HtmlResult: String;
begin
  // log
  Listbox1.Items.Add (RequestInfo.Document);
  // respond
  HtmlResult := '<h1>HttpServ Demo</h1>' +
```

```
      '<p>This is the only page you''ll get from this example.</p><hr>' +
      '<p>Request: ' + RequestInfo.Document + '</p>' +
      '<p>Host: ' + RequestInfo.Host + '</p>' +
      '<p>Params: ' + RequestInfo.UnparsedParams + '</p>' +
      '<p>The headers of the request follow: <br>' +
    RequestInfo.Headers.Text + '</p>';
  ResponseInfo.ContentText := HtmlResult;
end;
```

By passing a path and some parameters in the command line of the browser, you'll see them reinterpreted and displayed. For example, Figure 21.7 shows the effect of the command line:

```
http://localhost:8080/test?user=marco
```

FIGURE 21.7:

The page displayed by connecting a browser to the custom HttpServ program

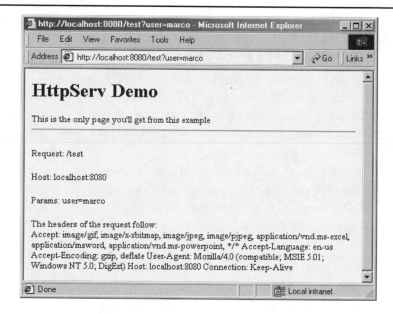

If this example seems too trivial, you'll see a slightly more interesting version in the next section, as I discuss the generation of HTML with Delphi's producer components.

NOTE   If you plan building an advanced Web server or other Internet servers with Delphi, then as an alternative to the Indy components, have a look at the DXSock components from Brain Patchwork DX (www.dxsock.com).

Generating HTML

The Hypertext Markup Language, better known by its acronym HTML, is the most widespread format for content on the Web. HTML is the format Web browsers typically read; it is a standard defined by the W3C, the World Wide Web Consortium, which is one of the bodies controlling the Internet. The current standard is represented by HTML 4, although not all browsers fully support that. When building a Web site, you always need to choose a lowest-common-denominator approach to support most of the browsers in use—that is, unless you are targeting a specific group of users whom you ask to adopt a specific browser (as happens in intranet situations). If you don't know much about the tags included in HTML files, you may want to read the sidebar "The Format of HTML Files" for a fast introduction.

The Format of HTML Files

If you have a little familiarity with HTML but don't work with it often enough to have all the basic elements "down cold," here's a quick summary.

HTML files are basically ASCII text files. Besides plain text, an HTML file contains many tags, which might determine the style of the font, the type of paragraph, or a link to another HTML file or an image, among other things.

Most tags are paired as opening tags and closing tags (the closing tag is usually the same as the opening tag but is preceded by a slash, /) to indicate where the style or content begins and ends. For example, you write `<b>important</b>` to set the word *important* in bold, and you write `<title>Document Title</title>` to define the title of a document as *Document Title*. (A few elements, such as `<br>` for a line break and `<img>` for a graphic or "image," stand alone and do not use a matching closing tag.)

An HTML document begins with the `<html>` tag and is divided into two parts, marked as `<head>` and `<body>`. Each of these three tags requires the corresponding terminator. In the head portion of the HTML file, you'll generally write the title (often displayed in the title bar of the browser) and a few other generic elements.

In the body, you write the contents of the file, generally starting with its visible title. You can use headings with different levels, marked with the `<hX>` tag, where you'd replace X with a number from 1 to 6. These are followed by plain paragraphs (`<p>`), preformatted paragraphs (`<pre>`, a style generally used for program listings), various types of lists, and many other elements. The text will often have links to other pages or other parts of the current page, using the `<a>` ("anchor") tag.

Another relevant element of HTML is tables. The `<table>` and `</table>` tags indicate the beginning and the end of the table, and its optional `border` attribute displays borders with a given width. The `<tr>` and `</tr>` tags introduce and close each row, and the tags

Continued on next page

<th>...</th> and <td>...</td> indicate a table header cell and a table data cell, respectively. The number of columns depends on the items in each row. Different rows, in fact, can have different numbers of items.

HTML was recently refined by the W3C to be more consistent, flexible, and interoperable with advanced systems such as XML; the new version is named XHTML (Extensible HTML). HTML and XHTML are the subject of many books, and you can find dozens of tutorials on them just by browsing the Web. A good, complete source on the topic is *Mastering XHTML* by Tittel et al. (Sybex, 2001).

Delphi's HTML Producer Components

If your version of Delphi includes the HTML producer components (available on the Internet page of the Component Palette), you can use them to generate the HTML files and particularly to turn a database table into an HTML table. Many developers believe that the use of these components makes sense only when writing a Web server extension. Although they were introduced for this purpose and are part of the WebBroker technology, you can still use three out of the four producer components in any application in which you must generate a static HTML file.

Before looking at the HtmlProd example, which demonstrates the use of these HTML producer components, let me summarize their role:

- The simplest of the HTML producer components is the PageProducer, which manipulates an HTML file in which you've embedded special tags. The advantage of this approach is that you can generate such a file using the HTML editor you prefer. At run time, the PageProducer converts the special tags to actual HTML code, giving you a straightforward method for modifying sections of an HTML document. The special tags have the basic format <#tagname>, but you can also supply named parameters within the tag. You'll process the tags in the OnTag event handler of the PageProducer.

- The DataSetPageProducer extends the PageProducer by automatically replacing tags corresponding to field names of a connected data source.

- The DataSetTableProducer component is generally useful for displaying the contents of a table, query, or other dataset. The idea is to produce an HTML table from a dataset, in a simple yet flexible way. The component has a very nice preview, so you can see how the HTML output will look in a browser directly at design time.

- The QueryTableProducer is similar to the previous one (it is actually a subclass), but it's specifically tailored for building parametric queries based on input from an HTML search form. For this reason, I'll delay the coverage of this component to the next chapter.

Producing HTML Pages

A very simple example of using tags is creating an HTML file that displays fields with the current date or a date computed relative to the current date, such as an expiration date. If you examine the HtmlProd example, you'll find the following component in the main form:

```
object PageProducer1: TPageProducer
  HTMLDoc.Strings = (...)
  OnHTMLTag = PageProducer1HTMLTag
end
```

The source HTML can be specified using an external file (with the advantage that you can edit it without having to recompile the application using it) or a string list, stored in the HTMLDoc property. This is a plain HTML file that might contain a few special tags introduced by the # symbol:

```
<html>
<head>
<title>Producer Demo</title>
</head>
<body>
<h1>Producer Demo</h1>
<p>This is a demo of the page produced by the <b><#appname></b> application on
<b><#date></b>.</p>
<hr>
<p>The prices in this catalog are valid until <b><#expiration
days=21></b>.</p>
</body>
</html>
```

WARNING   If you prepare this file with an HTML editor (something I suggest you do), it might automatically place quotes around tag parameters, as in days="21", because this is required by HTML 4 and XHTML 1. The PageProducer component has a **StripParamQuotes** property, which can be activated to remove those extra quotes when the component parses the code (before calling the OnHTMLTag event handler).

The Demo Page button simply copies the PageProducer component's output to the Text of a Memo with the statement

```
Memo1.Text := PageProducer1.Content;
```

As you call the Content function of the PageProducer component, it reads the input HTML code, parses it, and triggers the OnTag event handler for every special tag. In this method, we check the value of the tag (passed in the `TagString` parameter) and return a different HTML text (in the `ReplaceText` reference parameter), producing the output of Figure 21.8.

FIGURE 21.8:

The output of the HtmlProd example, a simple demonstration of the Page-Producer component, when the user clicks the Demo Page button

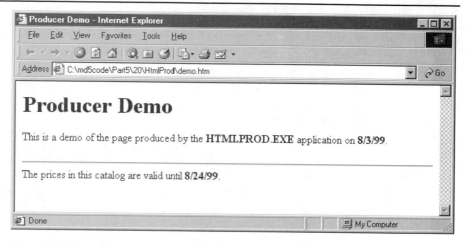

```
procedure TFormProd.PageProducer1HTMLTag(Sender: TObject;
  Tag: TTag; const TagString: String; TagParams: TStrings;
  var ReplaceText: String);
var
  nDays: Integer;
begin
  if TagString = 'date' then
    ReplaceText := DateToStr (Now)
  else if TagString = 'appname' then
    ReplaceText := ExtractFilename (Forms.Application.Exename)
  else if TagString = 'expiration' then
  begin
    nDays := StrToIntDef (TagParams.Values['days'], 0);
    if nDays <> 0 then
      ReplaceText := DateToStr (Now + nDays)
    else
      ReplaceText := '<i>{expiration tag error}</i>';
  end;
end;
```

Notice, in particular, the code we've written to convert the last tag, #expiration, which requires a parameter. The PageProducer places the entire text of the tag parameter (in this case, *days=21*) in a string that's part of the `TagParams` list. To extract the value portion of this string (the portion after the equal sign), you can use the `Values` property of the `TagParams` string list and search for the proper entry at the same time. If it can't locate the parameter or if its value isn't an integer, the DLL displays an error message.

TIP The PageProducer component supports user-defined tags, which can be any string you like, but you should first review the special tags defined by the **TTags** enumeration. The possible values include tgLink (for the `link` tag), tgImage (for the `img` tag), tgTable (for the `table` tag), and a few others. If you create a custom tag, as in the PageProd example, the value of the **Tag** parameter to the HTMLTag handler will be tgCustom.

Producing Pages of Data

The HtmlProd example also has a DataSetPageProducer component, with the following settings and HTML source code:

```
object DataSetPageProducer1: TDataSetPageProducer
  HTMLDoc.Strings = (
    '<html><head>'
    '<title>Data for <#name></title>'
    '</head><body>'
    '<h1><center>Data for <#name></center></h1>'
    '<p>Capital: <#capital></p>'
    '<p>Continent: <#continent></p>'
    '<p>Area: <#area></p>'
    '<p>Population: <#population></p>'
    '<hr>'
    '<p>Last updated on <#date><br>'
    'HTML file produced by the program <#program>.</p>'
    '</body></html>')
  OnHTMLTag = DataSetPageProducer1HTMLTag
  DataSet = Table1
end
```

Simply by using tags with the names of the fields of the connected dataset (the usual COUNTRY.DB database table), the program automatically gets the value of the fields of the current record and replaces it automatically. This produces the output of Figure 21.9, which shows a browser connected to the HtmlProd example working as an HTTP server, as I'll discuss later. In the source code of the program related to this component, in fact, there is no reference to the database data:

```
procedure TFormProd.BtnLineClick(Sender: TObject);
begin
  Memo1.Clear;
  Memo1.Text := DataSetPageProducer1.Content;
  BtnSave.Enabled := True;
end;

procedure TFormProd.DataSetPageProducer1HTMLTag(Sender: TObject; Tag: TTag;
  const TagString: String; TagParams: TStrings; var ReplaceText: String);
```

```
begin
  if TagString = 'program' then
    ReplaceText := ExtractFilename (Forms.Application.Exename)
  else if TagString = 'date' then
    ReplaceText := DateToStr (Date);
end;
```

FIGURE 21.9:

The output of the HtmlProd example for the Print Line button

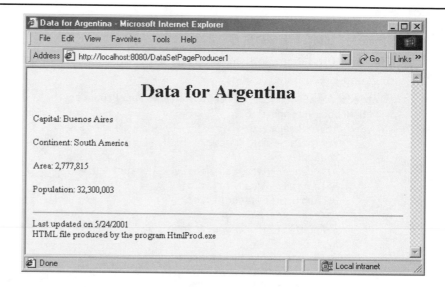

Producing HTML Tables

The last button of the HtmlProd example is Print Table. This button is connected to a DataSetTableProducer component, again calling its Content function and copying its result to the Text of the Memo. By simply connecting the DataSet property of the DataSetTable-Producer to Table1, you can produce a standard HTML table. Actually, the component by default generates only 20 rows, as indicated by the MaxRows property. If you want to get all the records of the table, you can set this property to -1, a simple but undocumented setting.

TIP   The DataSetTableProducer component starts from the current record rather than from the first one. This means that the second time you press the Print Table button, you'll see no records in the output. Adding a call to the First method of the table before calling the Content method of the producer component fixes the problem.

To make the output of this producer component more complete, you can do two different operations. The first is to provide some Header and Footer information, to generate the HTML heading and closing elements, and add a Caption to the HTML table. The second is to customize the table itself, by using the setting specified by the RowAttributes, TableAttributes, and Columns properties. The property editor of the columns, which is also the default component editor, allows you to set most of these properties, providing at the same time a very nice preview of the output, as you can see in Figure 21.10. Before using this editor, you can set up properties for fields of the table, using the Fields editor. This is how, for example, you can format the output of the population and area fields to use thousands separators.

FIGURE 21.10:

The editor of the Columns property of the DataSetTableProducer component provides you with a preview of the final HTML table (if the database table is active).

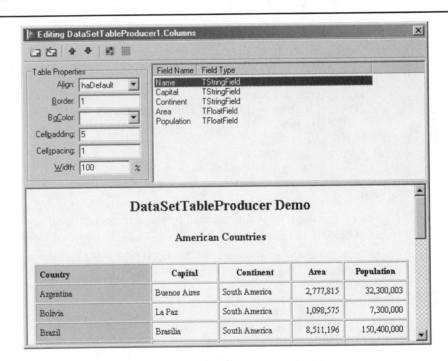

There are three techniques you can use to customize the HTML table, and it's worth reviewing each of them:

- You can use the table producer component's Column property to set properties, such as the text and color of the title, or the color and the alignment for the cells in the rest of the column.

- You can use the TField properties, particularly those related to output. In the example, I've set the DisplayFormat property of the Table1Continent field object to ###,###,###. This is the approach to use if you want to determine the actual output of each field. You might go even further and embed HTML tags in the output of a field.

- You can handle the DataSetTableProducer component's OnFormatCell event to customize the output further. In this event, you can set the various column attributes uniquely for a given cell, but you can also customize the output string (stored in the CellData parameter) and embed HTML tags. This is something you can't do using the Columns property.

In the HtmlProd example, I've used a handler for this event to turn the text of the Population and Area columns to bold font and to a red background for large values (unless it is the header row). Here is the code:

```
procedure TFormProd.DataSetTableProducer1FormatCell(
  Sender: TObject; CellRow, CellColumn: Integer;
  var BgColor: THTMLBgColor; var Align: THTMLAlign;
  var VAlign: THTMLVAlign; var CustomAttrs, CellData: String);
begin
  if (CellRow > 0) and
    ((((CellColumn = 3) and (Length (CellData) > 8)) or
    ((CellColumn = 4) and (Length (CellData) > 9))) then
  begin
    BgColor := 'red';
    CellData := '<b>' + CellData + '</b>';
  end;
end;
```

The rest of the code is summarized by the settings of the table producer component (formatted slightly to make it more readable and take less space):

```
object DataSetTableProducer1: TDataSetTableProducer
  Caption = '<h2>American Countries</h2>'
  Columns = <
    item FieldName = 'Name'
      BgColor = 'silver'
      Title.Align = haLeft
      Title.BgColor = 'silver'
      Title.Caption = 'Country'
    end
    item FieldName = 'Capital'...
    item FieldName = 'Continent'...
    item FieldName = 'Area'
      Align = haRight
    end
    item FieldName = 'Population'
      Align = haRight
    end>
  Footer.Strings = ('<hr><i>Produced by HtmlProd</i></body></html>')
  Header.Strings = (<html><head><title>DataSetTableProducer Demo</title>'
    '</head><body><h1><center>DataSetTableProducer Demo</center></h1>')
  MaxRows = -1
  DataSet = Table1
```

```
        TableAttributes.Border = 1
        TableAttributes.CellPadding = 5
        OnFormatCell = DataSetTableProducer1FormatCell
    end
```

You can see the output of this program in Figure 21.11. I suggest you study the source code of the HTML file this program generates so that you can see the richness of its output and therefore the advantage of using this component.

FIGURE 21.11:

The output of the Print All button of the HtmlProd example, which is based on the DataSetTableProducer component

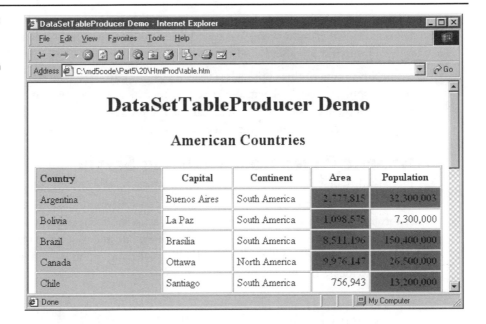

Using Style Sheets

The latest incarnations of HTML include a very powerful mechanism for separating content from presentation: Cascading Style Sheets (CSS). Using a style sheet, you can separate the formatting of the HTML (colors, fonts, font sizes, and so on) from the actual text displayed (the content of the page). This approach makes your code more flexible and your Web site easier to update. In addition, you can separate the task of making the site graphically appealing (the work of a Web designer) from automatic content generation (the work of a programmer). Style sheets are a rather complex technique, in which you give formatting values to the main types of HTML sections and to special "classes" (which have nothing to do with OOP). Again, see an HTML reference for the details.

How can we update table generation in the HtmlProd example to include style sheets? Simply enough, we can provide a link to the style sheet to use in the Header property of a second DataSetTableProducer component, with the line

```
<link rel="stylesheet" type="text/css" href="test.css">
```

We can then update the code of the OnFormatCell event handler with the following action (instead of the two lines changing the color and adding the bold font tag):

```
CustomAttrs := 'class="highlight"';
```

The style sheet I've provided (test.css, available in the source code of the example) defines a *highlight* style, which has exactly the bold font and red background that were hard-coded in the first DataSetTableProducer component.

The advantage of this approach is that now a graphic artist can modify the CSS file and give our table a nicer look without touching its code. When you want to provide many formatting elements, using a style sheet can also reduce the total size of the HTML file. This is an important element that can reduce download time.

Dynamic Pages from a Custom Server

The HtmlProd component can be used to generate static HTML files, but doubles as a Web server, using an approach similar to what I've demonstrated in the HttpServ example, but in a more realistic context. The program, in fact, accesses the request of one of the possible page producers, simply passing the name of the component in a request. This is a portion of the OnCommandGet event handler of its IdHTTPServer component, which uses the FindComponent method to locate the proper producer component:

```
var
  Req, Html: String;
  Comp: TComponent;
begin
  Req := RequestInfo.Document;
  if Req [1] = '/' then
    Req := Copy (Req, 2, 1000); // skip '/'
  Comp := FindComponent (Req);
  if (Req <> '') and Assigned (Comp) and
    (Comp is TCustomContentProducer) then
  begin
    Table1.First;
    Html := TCustomContentProducer (Comp).Content;
  end;
  ResponseInfo.ContentText := Html;
end;
```

In case the parameter is not there (or is not valid), the server responds with an HTML-based menu of the available components:

```
Html := '<h1>Html Proc Menu<h1><p><ul>';
for I := 0 to ComponentCount - 1 do
  if Components [i] is TCustomContentProducer then
    Html := Html + '<li><a href="/' + Components [i].Name + '">' +
      Components [i].Name + '</a></li>';
Html := Html + '</ul></p>';
```

Finally, if the program returns a table that uses CSS, the browser will request the CSS file from the server, so I've added some specific code to return it. With the proper generalizations, this code shows how a server can respond, returning files, and also how to indicate the MIME type of the response (ContentType):

```
if Pos ('test.css', Req) > 0 then
begin
  CssTest := TStringList.Create;
  try
    CssTest.LoadFromFile(ExtractFilePath(Application.ExeName) + 'test.css');
    ResponseInfo.ContentText := CssTest.Text;
    ResponseInfo.ContentType := 'text/css';
  finally
    CssTest.Free;
  end;
  Exit;
end;
```

Publishing Static Databases on the Web

Once you know how to produce files, you can simply add links from one to another and produce a series of cross-linked HTML files, representing a portion of a Web site. There are circumstances in which writing a program that examines a database and produces files is the best approach for publishing database data on a Web site. You can use a similar technique if the following conditions apply:

If the data doesn't change very often A catalogue updated monthly or weekly is a good example. Even if you can update the site automatically every night, this is still a possible technique. (For real-time information, of course, this is certainly not a good approach!)

If the amount of data is limited and available space not is an issue This seems obvious, but the formatted HTML output might take much more space than the original database files. If you use a server-side program (such as those I'll be discussing in the next chapter) to generate the HTML from the database data on the fly, you might need less disk space on the Web site. Keep in mind that preparing all the HTML files beforehand usually results in much better performance (faster server response time to Web requests, and lower memory overhead to process the requests) than generating the data on the fly.

If the number of ways to navigate is limited   If there are three or four obvious paths of navigation (a main one and two or three cross-references), you can generate all of them statically. Otherwise, the cross-referencing HTML files will be much larger than the files with the actual data, and the time required to generate them may become excessive.

Even if only parts of these conditions apply to your specific needs, you can consider using a mixed approach. You can have a portion of the data and of the navigational files generated periodically and have a CGI and ISAPI application on the site, as well as let users do free searches and follow other less frequent paths.

NOTE   On the companion CD you can find an example, called DbCross, that generates hundreds of HTML files out of a master/detail database structure. The program also collects other data about the records, while generating the files, and produces a complete cross-reference. At the end, you can navigate by customers–orders by each customer–details of the order or by sale parts–orders where each part appears–details of each order. The code is quite complex, but I've tried to comment it in some detail, so you should be able to follow it.

What's Next?

In this chapter, we've focused on some core Internet technologies, including the use of sockets and core Internet protocols. I've discussed the main idea and shown a few examples of the use of the mail and HTTP protocols. You can find many more examples of the use of the Indy components in the demos done by their developers.

After this introduction to the world of the Internet, we are now ready to delve into two key areas, the present and the future. The present is represented by the development of Web applications, and we'll explore the development of dynamic Web sites in the next chapter, focusing first on the *old* WebBroker technology and then moving to the new WebSnap architecture. The future is represented by the development of Web services and the use of XML and related technology, which will be discussed in Chapter 23.

CHAPTER 22

Web Programming with WebBroker and WebSnap

- Dynamic Web pages

- CGI, ISAPI, and Apache modules

- The WebBroker architecture

- The Web App debugger

- The new WebSnap architecture

- Adapters and server-side scripting

If the Internet has a growing role in the world, a good part of it depends on the success of the World Wide Web, based on the HTTP protocol. We've already discussed, in the preceding chapter, HTTP and the development of client- and server-side applications based on it. With the availability of several high-performance, scalable, and flexible Web servers, you'll rarely want to create your own. Dynamic Web server applications, in fact, are generally built by integrating scripting or compiled programs within Web servers, rather then replacing them with custom software.

This chapter is entirely focused on the development of server-side applications, which extend existing Web servers. We have already introduced the dynamic generation of HTML pages toward the end of the last chapter. Now we have to see how to integrate this dynamic generation within a server. This chapter is a logical continuation of the last one but won't complete the coverage of Internet programming, as the next chapter is further devoted to this topic, covering specifically XML and Web services.

WARNING   To test some of the examples in this chapter, you'll need access to a Web server. The simplest solution is probably to use the version of Microsoft's IIS or Personal Web Server already installed on your computer. My personal preference, however, is to use the free and open-source Apache Web Server, available (along with extensive documentation) at `www.apache.org`. In any case, I won't spend much time giving you details on the configuration of your Web server to enable the use of applications; refer to its documentation for this.

Dynamic Web Pages

When you browse a Web site, you generally download static pages—HTML-format text files—from the Web server to your client computer. As a Web developer, you can create these pages manually, but for most businesses, it makes more sense to build the static pages from information in a database of some type (a SQL server, a series of files, and so on). Using this approach, you're basically generating a snapshot of the data in HTML format, which is quite reasonable if the data isn't subject to frequent changes. This approach was discussed in Chapter 21, "Internet Programming: Sockets and Indy Components."

As an alternative to static HTML pages, you can build dynamic ones. To do this, you extract information directly from a database in response to the browser's request, so that the HTML sent by your application displays current data, not an old snapshot of the data. This approach makes sense if the data changes frequently.

As mentioned earlier, there are a couple of ways you can program custom behavior at the Web server, and these are ideal ways for you to generate HTML pages dynamically. The two most common protocols for programming Web servers are CGI (the Common Gateway Interface) and the Web server APIs. Another technique, Active Server Pages (ASP), is quite popular in the Microsoft world, and I'll discuss it briefly because Delphi includes specific support for it.

NOTE Keep in mind that Delphi's WebBroker technology (available in both the Enterprise and Professional editions) flattens the differences between CGI, WinCGI, and ISAPI by providing a common class framework. This way, you can easily turn a CGI application into a WinCGI one, upgrade it to use the ISAPI model, or integrate it into Apache.

An Overview of CGI

CGI is a standard protocol for communication between the client browser and the Web server. It's not a particularly efficient protocol, but it is widely used and is not platform specific. This protocol allows the browser both to ask for and to send data, and it is based on the standard command-line input and output of an application (usually a console application). When the server detects a page request for the CGI application, it launches the application, passes command-line data from the page request to the application, and then sends the standard output of the application back to the client computer.

There are many tools and languages you can use to write CGI applications, and Delphi is only one of them. Given the obvious limitation that your Web server must be an Intel-based Windows or Linux system, you can build some fairly sophisticated CGI programs in Delphi and Kylix. Despite the fact that it's called a standard, there are actually different flavors of CGI. Traditional CGI uses the standard command-line input and output, along with environment variables. WinCGI uses an INI file passed as a command-line parameter to the application (instead of environment variables) and specific input and output files (instead of using command-line input/output). Server vendors developed WinCGI primarily for Visual Basic programmers, who cannot access environment variables. Another new variation, called FastCGI, is supposed to make the entire process of calling a CGI application much faster, but it's not widely supported yet.

To build a CGI program without using any support class, you can simply create a Delphi console application, remove the typical project source code, and replace it with the following statements:

```
program CgiDate;
{$APPTYPE CONSOLE}

uses SysUtils;

begin
```

```
writeln ('content-type: text/html');
writeln;
writeln ('<html><head>');
writeln ('<title>Time at this site</title>');
writeln ('</head><body>');
writeln ('<h1>Time at this site</h1>');
writeln ('<hr>');
writeln ('<h3>');
writeln (FormatDateTime('"Today is " dddd, mmmm d, yyyy,' +
    '"<br> and the time is" hh:mm:ss AM/PM', Now));
writeln ('</h3>');
writeln ('<hr>');
writeln ('<i>Page generated by CgiDate.exe</i>');
writeln ('</body></html>');
end.
```

CGI programs produce a header followed by the HTML text using the standard output. If you execute this program directly, you'll see the text in a terminal window. If you run it instead from a Web server and send the output to a browser, the formatted HTML text will appear, as shown in Figure 22.1.

FIGURE 22.1:

The output of the CgiDate application, as seen in a browser

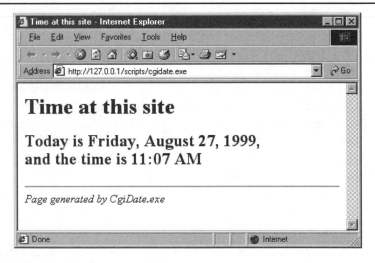

Building advanced and complex applications with plain CGI requires a lot of work. For example, to extract status information on the HTTP request, you need to access to the relevant environment variables, as in:

```
// get the pathname
GetEnvironmentVariable ('PATH_INFO', PathName, sizeof (PathName));
```

An Overview of ISAPI/NSAPI

A completely different approach is the use of the Web server APIs, the popular ISAPI (Internet Server API, introduced by Microsoft) and the less common NSAPI (Netscape Server API). These APIs allow you to write a DLL that the server loads into its own address space and usually keeps in memory for some time. Once it loads the DLL, the server can execute individual requests via threads within the main process, instead of launching a new EXE for every request (as it must in CGI applications).

When the server receives a page request, it loads the DLL (if it hasn't done so already) and executes the appropriate code, which may launch a new thread or use an existing one to process the page request (the IIS Web server offers thread pooling support to avoid creating a new thread for each request). The DLL code then sends the appropriate data back to the client that requested the page. Because this communication generally occurs in memory, this type of application is much faster than CGI, and a given system will be able to support more simultaneous page requests this way.

The main drawback to server API DLLs is that their tight integration with the server is an Achilles' heel; if the DLL crashes or produces memory leaks, the entire Web server can crash. However, the most recent releases of Microsoft's IIS Web server fix the problem by running the DLL in a *protected* space. Another problem is that when the DLL is in memory, you cannot compile an updated version; you need to unload the DLL first or momentarily stop the Web server (an operation you can do only on a test-bed computer).

Technically, ISAPI DLLs are not very different from plain Windows DLLs. They must export a couple of specific functions that the Web server will call: `GetExtensionVersion` and `HttpExtensionProc`. The server calls the first function when it loads the DLL for the first time and the second function for every following request. The parameters of these functions are complex data structures holding input data and server methods you can call to produce the result. Here is a sample of this function (taken from the IsapiDem example), which uses the `lpszPathInfo` field and the `WriteClient` function:

```
function HttpExtensionProc(var ECB: TEXTENSION_CONTROL_BLOCK): DWORD; stdcall;
var
  OutStr: string;
  StrLength: Cardinal;
begin
  with ECB do
  begin
    OutStr :=
      '<html><head><title>First Isapi Demo</title></head><body>' +
      '<h2><center>First Isapi Demo</center></h2>' +
      '<p>Hello Mastering Delphi Readers...</p><hr>' +
      '<p><b>Activated by ' + PChar(@lpszPathInfo[1]) + '</b></p>' +
```

```
    '<p><i>From IsapiDLL on ' + DateToStr(Now) + ' at ' + TimeToStr(Now) +
    '</i></p></body></html>';
  StrLength := Length(OutStr);
  WriteClient(ConnID, PChar (OutStr), StrLength, 0);
 end;
 Result := HSE_STATUS_SUCCESS;
end;
```

The program doesn't simply use the lpszPathInfo parameter but uses the substring starting with the second character, to get rid of the initial slash. To be more precise, the expression PChar(@lpszPathInfo[1]) takes the string starting at the memory address of the second character of the path (a zero-based characters array).

Apache Modules

Similarly to Microsoft's IIS, the Apache server of the Apache Foundation (www.apache.org) allows server-side extensions by means of CGI or with specific extension libraries. In case of Apache, these libraries are called *modules*, or dynamic modules. In the Apache configuration, you can list the modules you are interested in and eventually connect them to a virtual directory.

Needless to say, you can program Apache modules in a similar low-level way to what I've just done for ISAPI, but I won't show you an example. I'll do it later using the Apache support added to the WebBroker architecture in Delphi 6.

Delphi's WebBroker Technology

The CGI and ISAPI code snippets I've shown you so far demonstrate the plain, direct approach to the protocol and API. Extending these examples at that level is certainly possible, but what is interesting in Delphi is to use the WebBroker technology. This comprises a class hierarchy within VCL and CLX, built to simplify server-side development on the Web, and a specific type of data modules, called WebModules. Both the Enterprise and Professional editions of Delphi 5 include this framework (differently from the more advanced and newer WebSnap framework, which is available only in the Enterprise version of Delphi 6).

Using the WebBroker technology, you can begin developing an ISAPI or CGI application or an Apache module very easily. On the first page (*New*) of the New Items dialog box, select the Web Server Application icon. The subsequent dialog box will offer you options (two more than in Delphi 5). As you can see in Figure 22.2, you can choose ISAPI, CGI, WinCGI, Apache module, and the Web App Debugger.

FIGURE 22.2:

The alternative options for building a Web server application in Delphi

TIP
As a starting point for your server-side application, you can also use the DB Web Application Wizard, available in the Business page of the New Items dialog box. This wizard generates a program with a BDE table or query connected to a DataSetTableProducer. It can be helpful, but the generated code is really very limited and there is no support for Apache and the Web App Debugger.

For example, if you select the first option, Delphi will generate the basic structure of an ISAPI application for you. The application that Delphi generates (no matter which type you choose) is based on the TWebModule class, a container very similar to a data module. The WebModule code is similar to that of a data module, as we'll see in a moment, but the code of the library is worth looking at:

```
library Project1;

uses
  WebBroker,
  ISAPIThreadPool,
  ISAPIApp,
  Unit1 in 'Unit1.pas' {WebModule1: TWebModule};

{$R *.RES}

exports
  GetExtensionVersion,
  HttpExtensionProc,
  TerminateExtension;

begin
  Application.Initialize;
  Application.CreateForm(TWebModule1, WebModule1);
  Application.Run;
end.
```

WARNING   This code changes slightly between Delphi versions. If you have older code around, you'll need to refer to the WebBroker unit instead of the previous HTTPApp unit. Delphi 6 adds the reference to the ISAPIThreadPool unit, which provides support for pooling threads under ISAPI (with a couple of classes not documented in the Help file).

Although this is a library that exports the ISAPI functions, the code looks similar to that of an application. However, it uses a trick—the Application object used by this program is not the typical global object of class TApplication but an object of a new class. This new Application object is of class TISAPIApplication (or TCGIApplication if you've built that type of application), which derives from TWebApplication.

Although these application classes provide the foundations, you won't use them very often (just as you don't use the Application object very often in a form-based Delphi application). The most important operations take place in the WebModule. This component derives from TCustomWebDispatcher, which provides support for all the input and output of our programs.

In fact, the TCustomWebDispatcher class defines Request and Response properties, which store the client request and the response we're going to send back to the client. Each of these properties is defined using a base abstract class (TWebRequest and TWebResponse), but an application initializes them using a specific object (such as the TISAPIRequest and TISAPIResponse subclasses). These classes make available all the information passed to the server, so you have a single, simple approach to accessing all the information. The same is true of a response, which is very easy to manipulate. One advantage to this approach is that an ISAPI DLL written with this framework is very similar to a CGI application; in fact, they are frequently identical in the source code you write.

If this is the structure of Delphi's framework, how do you write the application code? Well, in the WebModule, you can use the Actions editor (shown in Figure 22.3) to define a series of actions (stored in the Actions array property) depending on the *pathname* of the request. This pathname is a portion of the CGI or ISAPI application's URL, which comes after the program name and before the parameters, such as path1 in the following URL:

```
http://www.example.com/scripts/cgitest.exe/path1?param1=date
```

By providing different actions, your application can easily respond to requests with different pathnames, and you can assign a different producer component or call a different OnAction event handler for every possible pathname. Of course, you can omit the pathname to handle a generic request. Consider also that, instead of basing your application on a WebModule, you can use a plain data module and add a WebDispatcher component to it. This is a good approach if you want to turn an existing Delphi application into a Web server extension.

FIGURE 22.3:

The Actions property editor of the WebModule, along with the properties of one of the actions in the Object Inspector

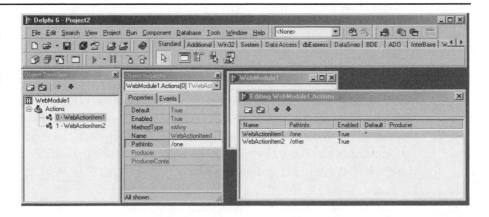

WARNING The WebModule incorporates the WebDispatcher and doesn't require it as a separate component. Unlike WebSnap applications, in fact, WebBroker programs cannot have multiple dispatchers or multiple Web modules. Notice also that the actions of the WebDispatcher have absolutely nothing to do with the actions stored in a `TActionList` component.

When you define the accompanying HTML pages that launch the application, the links will make page requests to the URLs for each of those paths. Having one single ISAPI DLL that can perform different operations depending on a parameter (in this case, the pathname) allows the server to keep a copy of this DLL in memory and respond much faster to user requests. The same is partially true for a CGI application: The server has to run several instances but can cache the file and make it available faster.

The `OnAction` event is where you put the code to specify the *response* to a given *request*, the two main parameters passed to the event handler. Here is a simple example:

```
procedure TWebModule1.WebModule1WebActionItem1Action(Sender: TObject;
  Request: TWebRequest; Response: TWebResponse; var Handled: Boolean);
begin
  Response.Content :=
    '<html><head><title>Hello Page</title></head><body>' +
    '<h1>Hello</h1>' +
    '<hr><p><i>Page generated by Marco</i></p></body></html>';
end;
```

The `Content` property of the `Response` parameter is where you enter the HTML code that you want users to see. The only drawback of this code is that the output in a browser will be correctly displayed on multiple lines, but looking at the HTML source code, you'll see a single line corresponding with the entire string. To make the HTML source code more readable, by splitting it up onto multiple lines, you can insert the #13 newline character.

To let other actions handle this request, you'll set the last parameter, Handled, to False. Otherwise, the default value is True, and once you've handled the request with your action, the WebModule assumes you're finished. Most of an ISAPI application's code will be in the OnAction event handlers for the actions defined in the WebModule container. These actions receive a request from the client and return a response using the Request and Response parameters.

When using the producer components, your OnAction event often returns, as Response.Content, the Content of the producer component, with a simple assignment. You can shortcut this code by assigning a producer component to the Producer property of the action itself, with no need to write these simple event handlers anymore (but don't do both things, as that might get you into trouble).

TIP   As an alternative to the Producer property, you can use the ProducerContent property introduced in Delphi 6. This new property allows you to connect custom producer classes that don't inherit from the TCustomContentProducer class but implement the IProduceContent interface. The ProducerContent property is *almost* an interface property: It behaves in the same way, but thanks to its property editor and not based on the new support for interfaced properties of Delphi 6.

Building a Multipurpose WebModule

To demonstrate how easily you can build a feature-rich server-side application using Delphi's support, I've created the BrokDemo example. This example can be compiled as a CGI or an ISAPI application, simply by choosing the proper project file. The WebModule is shared by the two projects, without any difference in the source code, a practical proof that, using the WebBroker framework, you can move from ISAPI to CGI, from Apache to the Web App Debugger (although this last step requires a little extra tweaking in the source code). In the past, I tended to test programs with CGI (to avoid having to stop the server to free the library and recompile it) and then deploy them with ISAPI. Now I tend to test with the Web App Debugger and then deploy under Apache.

A key element is the list of actions we're going to support with this application. The actions can be managed in the Actions editor or directly in the Object TreeView, as we've already seen in Figure 22.3. Actions are also visible in the Designer page of the editor, so you can graphically see their relationship with database objects, as shown for the BrokDemo in Figure 22.4. If you examine the figure or the source code, you'll notice that I've given a specific name to every action. I've also given meaningful names to the OnAction event handlers. For instance, TimeAction as a method name should be much more understandable than the WebModule1WebActionItem1Action name automatically generated by Delphi.

FIGURE 22.4:

The structure of the
BrokDemo example, as
shown by the Designer

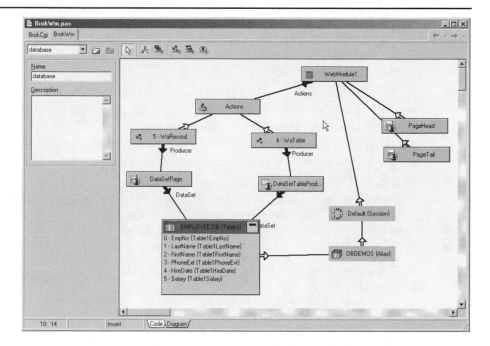

Every action has a different pathname, with one of them marked as default and executed even if no pathname is specified. The first interesting idea in this program is the use of two PageProducer components, used for the initial and final portion of every page, PageHead and PageTail. Centralizing this code makes it easier to modify it, particularly if it is based on external HTML files. The HTML produced by these components is added at the beginning and the end of the resulting HTML in the OnAfterDispatch event handler of the Web module:

```
procedure TWebModule1.WebModule1AfterDispatch(Sender: TObject;
  Request: TWebRequest; Response: TWebResponse; var Handled: Boolean);
begin
  Response.Content := PageHead.Content + Response.Content + PageTail.Content;
end;
```

I'm adding the initial and final HTML at the end of the page generation simply because this allows the components to produce the HTML as if they were making all of it. Starting with some HTML in the OnBeforeDispatch event means that you cannot directly assign the producer components to the actions, or the producer component will override the Content you've already provided in the response. The PageTail component includes a custom tag for the script name, replaced by the following code, which uses the current request object available within the Web module:

```
procedure TWebModule1.PageTailHTMLTag(Sender: TObject; Tag: TTag;
```

```
  const TagString: String; TagParams: TStrings; var ReplaceText: String);
begin
  if TagString = 'script' then
    ReplaceText := Request.ScriptName;
end;
```

This code is activated to expand the <#script> tag of the PageTail component's HTMLDoc property. The code of the time and date actions is straightforward. The really interesting part begins with the Menu path, which is the default action. In its OnAction event handler, the application uses a for loop to build a list of the available actions (using their names without the first two letters, which are always Wa in my example), providing a link to each of them with an anchor (an <a> tag):

```
procedure TWebModule1.MenuAction(Sender: TObject; Request: TWebRequest;
  Response: TWebResponse; var Handled: Boolean);
var
  I: Integer;
begin
  Response.Content := '<h3>Menu</h3><ul>'#13;
  for I := 0 to Actions.Count - 1 do
    Response.Content := Response.Content + '<li> <a href="' +
      Request.ScriptName + Action[I].PathInfo + '"> ' +
      Copy (Action[I].Name, 3, 1000) + '</a>'#13;
  Response.Content := Response.Content + '</ul>';
end;
```

Another action of the BrokDemo example provides users with a list of the system settings related to the request, something that is quite useful for debugging. It is also instructive to learn how much information, and exactly what information, the HTTP protocol transfers from a browser to a Web server and vice versa. To produce this list, the program looks for the value of each property of the TWebRequest class, as this initial snippet demonstrates:

```
procedure TWebModule1.StatusAction(Sender: TObject; Request: TWebRequest;
  Response: TWebResponse; var Handled: Boolean);
var
  I: Integer;
begin
  Response.Content := '<h3>Status</h3>'#13 +
    'Method: ' + Request.Method + '<br>'#13 +
    'ProtocolVersion: ' + Request.ProtocolVersion + '<br>'#13 +
    'URL: ' + Request.URL + '<br>'#13 +
    'Query: ' + Request.Query + '<br>'#13 + ...
```

Dynamic Database Reporting

The BrokDemo example defines two more actions, indicated by the /table and /record pathnames. For these two last actions, our program produces a main list of names and then displays the details of one record, using a DataSetTableProducer component to format the entire table and a DataSetPageProducer component to build the record view. Here are the properties of these two components:

```
object DataSetTableProducer1: TDataSetTableProducer
  DataSet = Table1
  OnFormatCell = DataSetTableProducer1FormatCell
end
object DataSetPage: TDataSetPageProducer
  HTMLDoc.Strings = (
    '<h3>Employee: <#LastName></h3>'
    '<ul><li> Employee ID: <#EmpNo>'
    '<li> Name: <#FirstName> <#LastName>'
    '<li> Phone: <#PhoneExt>'
    '<li> Hired On: <#HireDate>'
    '<li> Salary: <#Salary></ul>')
  OnHTMLTag = PageTailHTMLTag
  DataSet = Table1
end
```

To produce the entire table, we simply connect the DataSetTableProducer to the Producer property of the corresponding actions, without providing any specific event handler. The table is made more powerful by adding internal links to the specific records. The following code is executed for each cell of the table but activated only for the first column or the first row (the one with the title):

```
procedure TWebModule1.DataSetTableProducer1FormatCell(Sender: TObject;
  CellRow, CellColumn: Integer; var BgColor: THTMLBgColor;
  var Align: THTMLAlign; var VAlign: THTMLVAlign;
  var CustomAttrs, CellData: String);
begin
  if (CellColumn = 0) and (CellRow <> 0) then
    CellData := '<a href="' + ScriptName + '/record?LastName=' +
      Table1['LastName'] + '&FirstName=' + Table1 ['FirstName'] + '"> ' +
      CellData + ' </a>';
end;
```

You can see the result of this action in Figure 22.5. When the user selects one of the links, the program is called again, and it can check the QueryFields string list and extract the parameters from the URL. It then uses the values corresponding to the table fields used for the record search (which is based on the FindNearest call).

FIGURE 22.5:

The output corresponding to the *table* path of the BrokDemo example, which produces an HTML table with internal

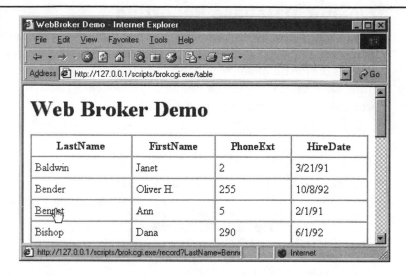

```pascal
procedure TWebModule1.RecordAction(Sender: TObject; Request: TWebRequest;
  Response: TWebResponse; var Handled: Boolean);
begin
  Table1.Open;
  // go to the requested record
  Table1.FindNearest ([Request.QueryFields.Values['LastName'],
    Request.QueryFields.Values['FirstName']]);
  // get the output
  Response.Content := Response.Content + DataSetPage.Content;
end;
```

NOTE   The example we've just built accesses a Paradox table via the BDE. The CGI version executes once for every request and will actually load and unload the BDE each time it runs. As alternatives, you can consider three different approaches: using ISAPI instead of CGI (to keep the application and the BDE loaded in memory), accessing the data from a plain file (or avoid the BDE with some other data access technology), or running another BDE application on the server (so that the BDE will remain loaded in memory). When using the BDE in an ISAPI application, though, you need to add a Session component to avoid concurrent access by multiple threads to the same BDE session.

Of Queries and Forms

The previous example used some of the HTML producer components introduced earlier in this chapter. There is another component of this group we haven't used yet, the QueryTableProducer. As we'll see in a moment, this component makes building even complex database programs a breeze. Suppose you want to search for some customers in a database. You might construct the following HTML form (embedded in an HTML table for better formatting):

```
<h4>Customer QueryProducer Search Form</h4>
<form action="/scripts/CustQueP.dll/search" method="POST">
<table>
<tr><td>State:</td>
  <td><input type="text" name="State"></td></tr>
<tr><td>Country:</td>
  <td><input type="text" name="Country"></td></tr>
<tr><td></td>
  <td><center><input type="Submit"></center></td></tr>
</table></form>
```

NOTE   As in Delphi, an HTML form hosts a series of controls (typically, things like input fields). There are visual tools to help you design these forms, or you can manually enter the proper HTML code. The available controls include buttons, input text (or edit boxes), selections (or combo boxes), and radio buttons (or input buttons). You can define buttons as specific types, such as Submit or Reset, which imply standard behaviors. An important element of forms is the *request method,* which can be either POST (data is passed behind the scenes, and you receive it in the `ContentFields` property) or GET (data is passed as part of the URL, and you extract it from the `QueryFields` property).

There is a very important element to notice in the form: the names of the input components (*State* and *Country*), which should match the parameters of a Query component:

```
select
  Company, State, Country
from
  CUSTOMER.DB
where
  State = :State or Country = :Country
```

This code is used in the CustQueP (customer query producer) example. To build it, I've placed a Query component inside the WebModule and generated the field objects for it. In the same WebModule, I've added a QueryTableProducer component connected to the `Producer` property of the `/search` action. The program will generate the proper response. How does this work? When we activate the QueryTableProducer component by calling its `Content` function, it initializes the Query component by obtaining the parameters from the HTTP request. The component can automatically examine the request method and then use either the `QueryFields` property (if the request is a GET) or the `ContentFields` property (if the request is a POST).

One problem with using a static HTML form as we did before is that it doesn't tell us which states and countries we can search for. To address this, we can use a selection control instead of an edit control in the HTML form. However, if the user adds new records to the database table, we'll need to update the element list automatically. As a final solution, we can design the ISAPI DLL to produce a form on-the-fly, and we can fill the selection controls with the available elements.

We'll generate the HTML for this page in the /form action, which we've connected to a PageProducer component. The PageProducer contains the following HTML text, which embeds two special tags:

```
<h4>Customer QueryProducer Search Form</h4>
<form action="CustQueP.dll/search" method="POST">
<table>
<tr><td>State:</td>
  <td><select name="State"><#State></select></td></tr>
<tr><td>Country:</td>
  <td><select name="Country"><option> </option><#Country></select></td></tr>
<tr><td></td>
  <td><center><input type="Submit"></center></td></tr>
</table></form>
```

You'll notice that the tags have the same name as some of the table's fields. When the PageProducer encounters one of these tags, it adds an <option> HTML tag for every distinct value of the corresponding field. Here's the OnTag event handler's code, which is quite generic and reusable:

```
procedure TWebModule1.PageProducer1HTMLTag(Sender: TObject; Tag: TTag;
  const TagString: String; TagParams: TStrings; var ReplaceText: String);
begin
  ReplaceText := '';
  Query2.SQL.Clear;
  Query2.SQL.Add ('select distinct ' + TagString + ' from customer');
  try
    Query2.Open;
    try
      Query2.First;
      while not Query2.EOF do
      begin
        ReplaceText := ReplaceText +
          '<option>' + Query2.Fields[0].AsString + '</option>'#13;
        Query2.Next;
      end;
    finally
      Query2.Close;
    end;
  except
    ReplaceText := '{wrong field: ' + TagString + '}';
  end;
end;
```

This method used a second Query component, which I manually placed on the form and connected to the DBDEMOS database, and it produces the output shown in Figure 22.6.

FIGURE 22.6:

The form action of the CustQueP example produces an HTML form with a selection component dynamically updated to reflect the current status of the database.

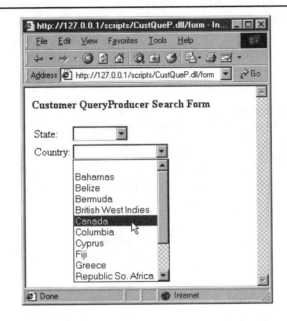

Finally, this Web server extension, like many others we've built, allows the user to view the details of a specific record. As in the last example, we can accomplish this by customizing the output of the first column (column zero), which is generated by the QueryTableProducer component:

```
procedure TWebModule1.QueryTableProducer1FormatCell(
  Sender: TObject; CellRow, CellColumn: Integer;
  var BgColor: THTMLBgColor; var Align: THTMLAlign;
  var VAlign: THTMLVAlign; var CustomAttrs, CellData: String);
begin
  if (CellColumn = 0) and (CellRow <> 0) then
    CellData := '<a href="' + Request.ScriptName + '/record?' + CellData +
      '">' + CellData + '</a>'#13;
  if CellData = '' then
    CellData := ' ';
end;
```

TIP   When you have an empty cell in an HTML table, most browsers render it without the border. For this reason, I've added a "nonbreaking space" symbol (** **) into each empty cell. This is something you'll have to do in each HTML table generated with Delphi's table producers.

The action for this link is /record, and we'll pass a specific element after the ? parameter (without the parameter name, which is slightly nonstandard). The code we use to produce the HTML tables for the records doesn't use the producer components as we've been doing; instead, it is very similar to the code of an early ISAPI example:

```
procedure TWebModule1.RecordAction(Sender: TObject; Request: TWebRequest;
  Response: TWebResponse; var Handled: Boolean);
var
  I: Integer;
begin
  if Request.QueryFields.Count = 0 then
    Response.Content := 'Record not found'
  else
  begin
    Query2.SQL.Clear;
    Query2.SQL.Add ('select * from customer ' +
      'where Company="' + Request.QueryFields[0] + '"');
    Query2.Open;
    Response.Content :=
      '<html><head><title>Customer Record</title></head><body>'#13 +
      '<h1>Customer Record: ' + Request.QueryFields[0] + '</h1>'#13 +
      '<table border>'#13;
    for I := 1 to Query2.FieldCount - 1 do
      Response.Content := Response.Content +
        '<tr><td>' + Query2.Fields [I].FieldName + '</td>'#13'<td>' +
        Query2.Fields [I].AsString + '</td></tr>'#13;
    Response.Content := Response.Content + '</table><hr>'#13 +
      // pointer to the query form
      '<a href="' + Request.ScriptName + '/form">' +
      ' Next Query </a>'#13 + '</body></html>'#13;
  end;
end;
```

Debugging with the Web App Debugger

Debugging Web applications written in Delphi is often quite difficult. In fact, you cannot simply run the program and set breakpoints in it, but should convince the Web server to run your CGI program or library within the Delphi debugger. This can be accomplished by indicating a Host application in Delphi's Run Parameters dialog box, but it implies letting Delphi run the Web server (which is often a Windows service, not a stand-alone program).

To solve all of these issues, Borland has added to Delphi 6 a specific Web App Debugger program. This tool, activated by the corresponding item of the Tools menu, is a Web server, which waits for requests on a port you can set up (1024 by default). When a request arrives, the program can forward it to a stand-alone executable, using COM-based techniques. This means you can run the Web server application from within the Delphi IDE, set all the breakpoints you need, and then (when the program is activated through the Web App Debugger) debug the program as you'll do for a plain executable file.

The Web App Debugger does also a good job in logging all the received requests and the actual responses returned to the browser, as you can see in Figure 22.7. The program also has a Statistics page, which interestingly tracks the time required for each response, allowing you to test the efficiency of an application in different conditions.

FIGURE 22.7:

The log of the Web App Debugger with its LogDetail window

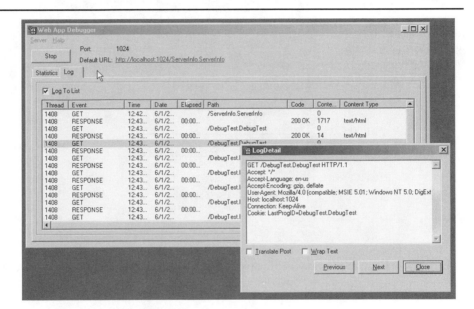

By using the corresponding option of the New Web Server Application dialog, you can easily create a new application compatible with the debugger. This defines a standard project, which creates both a main form and a data module. The (useless) form includes code for registering the application as an OLE automation server, as:

```
const
  CLASS_ComWebApp: TGUID = '{33A4D4F0-E082-4723-9165-5D8F95AF1577}';

initialization
  TWebAppAutoObjectFactory.Create(Class_ComWebApp, 'FirstDemo',
    'FirstDemo Object');
```

The information is used by the Web App Debugger to get a list of the available programs. This is done when you use the default URL for the debugger, indicated in the form as a link, as you can see (for example) in Figure 22.8. The list includes all of the registered servers, not only those running. In fact, the use of COM Automation accounts for the automatic activation of a server. Not that this is a good idea, though, as running and terminating the program each time will make the process much slower. Again, the idea is to run the program within the Delphi IDE, to be able to debug it easily. Notice, though that the list can be expanded with the detailed view, which includes a list of the actual executable files and many other details.

FIGURE 22.8:

A list of applications registered with the Web App Debugger is displayed when you hook to its *home* page.

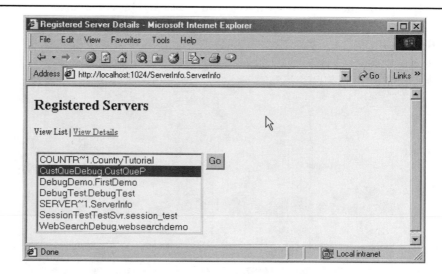

The data module for this type of project has some initialization code as well:

```
uses WebReq;

initialization
    WebRequestHandler.WebModuleClass := TWebModule2;
```

This approach should be used only for debugging. To deploy the actual application you should then use one of the other options. What you can do is create the project files for another type of Web server program and add to the project the same Web module of the debug application. The presence of the extra initialization line won't create a problem.

The reverse is slightly more complex. To debug an existing application, you have to create a program of this type, remove the Web module, add the existing one, and patch it by adding a line to set the WebModuleClass of the WebRequestHandler, like the one in the preceding code snippet. To account for possible missing initialization of the WebRequestHandler object, you might want to change this type of code into:

```
if WebRequestHandler <> nil then
    WebRequestHandler.WebModuleClass := ... // Web module class
```

WARNING By doing this for the CustQueP example (it is the CustQueDebug project), I realized that some of the Web request settings are different. So instead of using the `ScriptName` property of the request (set to empty for a Web debug application), you have to use the `InternalScript-Name` property.

There are other two interesting elements in the use of the Web App Debugger. The first is that you can test your programs without having a Web server installed and without having to tweak its settings. In other words, you don't have to deploy your programs to test them—you simply try them out right away. Another advantage is that, contrary to doing early development of the applications as CGI, you can start experimenting with a multithreaded architecture right away, without having to deal with the loading and unloading of libraries, which often implies shutting down the Web server and possibly even the computer.

NOTE If your aim is to build an ISAPI application, you can also use a specific ISAPI DLL debugging tool. One such tool, called IntraBob, has been built by Bob Swart and is available on his Web site (`www.drbob42.com`) as freeware.

Working with Apache

If you plan on using Apache instead of IIS or another Web server, you can certainly take advantage of the common CGI technology to deploy your applications on almost any Web server. However, using CGI means some reduced speed and some trouble handling state information (as you cannot keep any data in memory). This is a good reason for writing an ISAPI application or a dynamic Apache module. Using Delphi's WebBroker technology, you can also easily compile the same code for both technologies, so that moving your program to a different Web platform becomes much simpler. Finally, you can also recompile a CGI program or a dynamic Apache module with Kylix and deploy it on a Linux server.

As I've mentioned, Apache can run traditional CGI applications but has also a specific technology for keeping the server extension program loaded in memory at all times for faster response. To build such a program in Delphi 6, you can simply use the Apache Shared Module option of the New Web Server Application dialog box. You end up with a library having this type of source code for its project:

```
library Apache1;

uses
  WebBroker,
  ApacheApp,
  ApacheWm in 'ApacheWm.pas' {WebModule1: TWebModule};
```

```
{$R *.res}

exports
  apache_module name 'apache1_module';

begin
  Application.Initialize;
  Application.CreateForm(TWebModule1, WebModule1);
  Application.Run;
end.
```

Notice in particular the exports clause, which indicates the name used by Apache configuration files to reference the dynamic module. In the project source code, you can add two more definitions, the module name and the content type, in the following way:

```
ModuleName := 'Apache1_module';
ContentType:= 'Apache1-handler';
```

If you don't set them, Delphi will assign them some default values, which are built adding the *_module* and *-handler* strings to the project name, ending up with the two names I've used above.

An Apache module is generally not deployed within a script folder, but within the modules subfolder of the server itself (by default, c:\Program Files\Apache\modules). Then you have to edit the http.conf file, adding a line to load the module, as:

```
LoadModule apache1_module modules/apache1.dll
```

Finally, you have to indicate when the module is invoked. The handler defined by the module can be associated with a given file extension (so that your module will process all of the files having a given extension) or with a physical or virtual folder. In the latter case, the folder doesn't exist, but Apache pretends it is there. This is how you can set up a virtual folder for the simple Apache1 module:

```
<Location /Apache1>SetHandler Apache1-handler</Location>
```

As Apache is inherently case sensitive (because of its Linux heritage), you might also want to add a second, lowercase virtual folder:

```
<Location /apache1>SetHandler Apache1-handler</Location>
```

Now you can invoke the sample application with the URL http://localhost/Apache1. A great advantage of using virtual folder in Apache is that a user doesn't really distinguish between the physical and dynamic portions of your site, as we'll better see in the next example.

Because the development of Apache modules with WebBroker is almost identical to the development of other types of programs, instead of building an actual application (besides the over-simplistic Apache1 example) I've created a new version of the BrokDemo example, already available as a CGI or ISAPI program. To do this, I've taken the project file of an

Apache module from that example, added the local Web modules to it, and modified the project source code to reflect the proper module name and handler. I've actually defined them differently than the default, as the following code excerpt demonstrates:

```
library BrokApache;

exports apache_module name 'brokdemo_module';

begin
  ContentType:= 'brokdemo-handler';
```

After compiling the module and editing the http.conf file as explained above, the program was ready to be used in two different ways, CGI and dynamic module. An obvious difference between the two types of invocation is their URLs:

```
http://localhost/scripts/brokcgi.exe/table
http://localhost/brokdemo/table
```

Not only is the latter URL simpler, but it hides the fact that we are running an application with a /table parameter. In fact, it seems we are accessing a specific folder of the server. Actually, the Apache configuration file can be modified to also invoke CGI applications through virtual folders, which explains why CGI applications have a path-like command prefixing the request. Another related explanation is that Linux CGI applications, like any other executable file, have no extension whatsoever, so their names still seem to be part of a path.

Practical Examples

After this general introduction to the core idea of the development of server-side applications with WebBroker, let me end this part of the chapter with two simple practical examples. The first is a classic Web counter. The second is an extension of the WebFind program presented in the preceding chapter to produce a dynamic page instead of filling a list box.

A Web Hit Counter

The server-side applications we've built up to now were based only on text. Of course, you can easily add references to existing graphics files. What's more interesting, however, is to build server-side programs capable of generating graphics that change over time.

A typical example is a *page hit counter*. To write a Web counter, we save the current number of hits to a file and then read and increase the value every time the counter program is called. How do we return this information? If all we need is some HTML text with the number of hits, the code is straightforward:

```
procedure TWebModule1.WebModule1WebActionItem1Action(Sender: TObject;
  Request: TWebRequest; Response: TWebResponse; var Handled: Boolean);
```

```
var
  nHit: Integer;
  LogFile: Text;
  LogFileName: string;
begin
  LogFileName := 'WebCont.log';
  System.Assign (LogFile, LogFileName);
  try
    // read if the file exists
    if FileExists (LogFileName) then
    begin
      Reset (LogFile);
      Readln (LogFile, nHit);
      Inc (nHit);
    end
    else
      nHit := 0;
    // saves the new data
    Rewrite (LogFile);
    Writeln (LogFile, nHit);
  finally
    Close (LogFile);
  end;
  Response.Content := IntToStr (nHit);
end;
```

WARNING This simple file handling does not scale. When multiple visitors hit the page at the same time, this code may return false results or fail with a file I/O error because a request in another thread has the file open for reading while this thread tries to open the file for writing. To support a similar scenario, you'll need to use a mutex (or a critical section in a multithreaded program) to let each subsequent thread wait until the thread currently using the file has completed its task.

What's a little more interesting is to create a graphical counter that can be easily embedded into any HTML page. There are basically two approaches for building a graphical counter: you can prepare a bitmap for each digit up front and then combine them in the program, or you can simply let the program draw over a memory bitmap to produce the graphic you want to return. In the WebCount program, I've chosen this second approach.

Basically, we can create an Image component that holds a memory bitmap, which we can paint on with the usual methods of the TCanvas class. Then we can attach this bitmap to a TJpegImage object. Accessing the bitmap through the JpegImage component converts the image to the JPEG format. At this point, we can save the JPEG data to a stream and return it. As you can see, there are many steps, but the code is not really complex:

```
// create a bitmap in memory
Bitmap := TBitmap.Create;
try
  Bitmap.Width := 120;
  Bitmap.Height := 25;
  // draw the digits
  Bitmap.Canvas.Font.Name := 'Arial';
  Bitmap.Canvas.Font.Size := 14;
  Bitmap.Canvas.Font.Color := RGB (255, 127, 0);
  Bitmap.Canvas.Font.Style := [fsBold];
  Bitmap.Canvas.TextOut (1, 1, 'Hits: ' +
    FormatFloat ('###,###,###', Int (nHit)));
  // convert to JPEG and output
  Jpeg1 := TJpegImage.Create;
  try
    Jpeg1.CompressionQuality := 50;
    Jpeg1.Assign(Bitmap);
    Stream := TMemoryStream.Create;
    Jpeg1.SaveToStream (Stream);
    Stream.Position := 0;
    Response.ContentStream := Stream;
    Response.ContentType := 'image/jpeg';
    Response.SendResponse;
    // the response object will free the stream
  finally
    Jpeg1.Free;
  end;
finally
  Bitmap.Free;
end;
```

The three statements responsible for returning the JPEG image are the two that set the ContentStream and ContentType properties of the Response and the final call to SendResponse. The content type must match one of the possible MIME types accepted by the browser, and the order of these three statements is relevant. There is also a SendStream method in the Response object, but it should be called only after sending the type of the data with a separate call.

You can see the effect of this program in Figure 22.9. To obtain it, I've added the following code to an HTML page:

```
<img src="http://localhost/scripts/webcount.exe" border=0 alt="hit counter">
```

FIGURE 22.9:

The graphical Web hit counter in action

Searching with a Web Search Engine

In Chapter 21, I discussed the use of the Indy HTTP client component to retrieve the result of a search on the Google Web site. Now I'm going to extend the example a little, turning it into a server-side application. The WebSearch program on the companion CD, available as a CGI application or a Web App Debugger executable, has an action that simply returns the HTML retrieved by the search engine and a second action that fills a client data set component, then hooked to a table page producer. This is the code of this second action:

```
const
  strSearch = 'http://www.google.com/search?as_q=borland+delphi&num=100';

procedure TWebModule1.WebModule1WebActionItem1Action(Sender: TObject;
  Request: TWebRequest; Response: TWebResponse; var Handled: Boolean);
var
  I: integer;
begin
  if not cds.Active then
    cds.CreateDataSet
  else
    cds.EmptyDataSet;
  for i := 0 to 5 do // how many pages?
  begin
    // get the data form the search site
    GrabHtml (strSearch + '&start=' + IntToStr (i*100));
    // scan it to fill the cds
    HtmlStringToCds;
  end;
  cds.First;
  // return producer content
  Response.Content := DataSetTableProducer1.Content;
end;
```

The `GrabHtml` method is identical to the WebFind example, while the `HtmlStringToCds` method is similar to corresponding method (which adds the items to a list box) and adds the addresses and their textual descriptions by calling:

```
cds.InsertRecord ([0, strAddr, strText]);
```

The ClientDataSet component, in fact, is set up with three fields: the two strings plus a line counter. This extra empty field is used to have the extra column in the table producer. The code fills the column in the cell-formatting event, which also adds the hyperlink:

```
procedure TWebModule1.DataSetTableProducer1FormatCell(Sender: TObject; CellRow,
  CellColumn: Integer; var BgColor: THTMLBgColor; var Align: THTMLAlign;
  var VAlign: THTMLVAlign; var CustomAttrs, CellData: String);
begin
  if CellRow <> 0 then
  case CellColumn of
    0: CellData := IntToStr (CellRow);
    1: CellData := '<a href="' + CellData + '">' + SplitLong(CellData) + '</a>';
    2: CellData := SplitLong (CellData);
  end;
end;
```

The call to `SplitLong` is used to add some extra spaces within the output text, to avoid having grid columns that are too large, as the browser won't split the text on multiple lines unless it contains spaces or other special characters. The result of this program is a rather slow application (because of the multiple HTTP requests it must forward) producing output like Figure 22.10.

FIGURE 22.10:

The WebSearch program shows the result of the multiple searches done on Google.

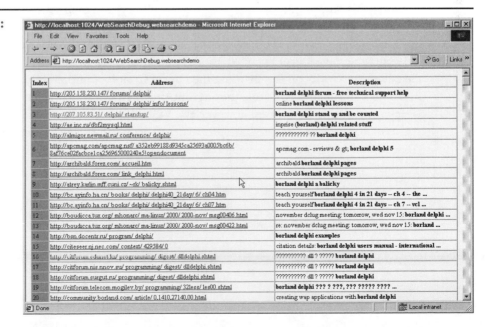

Active Server Pages

Another approach to the development of server-side applications is the use of scripting. Before looking at the scripting technology embedded in the WebSnap framework, let me shortly discuss Microsoft's Active Server Pages (ASP) technology and how you can use Delphi to support it. The idea behind ASP is to add scripts to the HTML code, so that part of the text on a Web page is directly available while other information can be added at run time on the server. The client receives a plain HTML file. The difference between this approach and ISAPI is that you don't need to recompile a program on the server to see a change; you simply update the script. ASP offers a complex model, where you can attach persistent data to a session (for example, a user moving from page to page of a section of your Web site) and to the entire application (the section of the Web site, regardless of the user).

ASP is quite a complex technology, and here I can only discuss it in relation to Delphi programming. One of the features of ASP is that it allows you to create COM objects within a script, and you can write those COM objects in Delphi. The Delphi IDE even provides specific support classes and a wizard to help you build ASP objects. Compared to ISAPI or CGI, one of the advantages is that your ASP object built in Delphi can get access to session and application information, exactly as an ASP script does. This means we automatically get extra features such as persistent user data built into our server-side object. By building a compiled ASP object, we can also increase the speed of complex server-side code. (ASP scripts are not always the best solution in term of performance.) But, again, I don't want to discuss ASP in detail, only focus on Delphi support.

To try this out, simply create a new ActiveX library, and then start the Active Server Object Wizard (from the ActiveX page of the File ≻ New dialog box). As you can see in Figure 22.11, the wizard has a couple of options. You can build an object integrated with the ASP script by selecting the Page-Level Event Methods radio button, or an internal object (which can be installed as an MTS object) by using the Object Context option. Only in the first case does the object automatically handle the OnStartPage method, which receives as parameter the *scripting context*. In both cases, however, the VCL classes you inherit from (TASPObject and TASPMTSObject, respectively) have properties to access the Request, Response, Session, Server, and Application ASP objects.

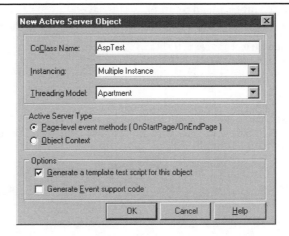

Once you've created the ASP object with the wizard (I've used the Page-Level Event Methods option for the AspTest example), Delphi will bring up the Type Library editor, where you can prepare a list of properties and methods for your ASP object. Simply add the features you need, and then write their code. For example, you can write the following simple test method:

```
procedure Tasptest.ShowData;
begin
   Response.Write ('<h3>Delphi wrote this text</h3>');
end;
```

and activate it from the following ASP script (only slightly modified from the demo script the Delphi wizard will generate for you):

```
<h4>Message</h4>
<% Set DelphiASPObj = Server.CreateObject("asptest1.asptest")
   DelphiASPObj.showData
%>
```

The interesting element is that the same script (or another ASP script of the same application) can also set global values our Delphi object can access. Similarly, multiple objects can communicate, setting global variables for the application and session variables for the specific user. For example, we can add the following text to the ASP page:

```
<h4>hello</h4>
<%
   Session.Value("UserName") = "Marco"
   DelphiASPObj.Hello
%>
```

I've written the code used to set the property and the method invocation one after the other, but they can even be in different pages. This new *dynamic* property (Microsoft's term for these values added to an object) is saved in the session, so it depends on the current user. The Hello method can use the username to welcome them:

```
procedure Tasptest.Hello;
var
  strName: string;
begin
  strName := Session ['UserName'];
  Response.Write ('<h3>Hello, ' + strName + '</h3>');
  Response.Write ('<p>Page started at ' + TimeToStr (StartTime) + '</p>');
end;
```

You can see the result of this and the previous method combined in Figure 22.12. The last line of the method uses a variable that's set when the page is first loaded, in the OnStartPage method (despite the name, this is not an event handler, but a method the ASP engine will call as the page containing the object is activated):

FIGURE 22.12:

The Web page generated by the AspTest object I've built with Delphi

```
procedure Tasptest.OnStartPage(const AScriptingContext: IUnknown);
begin
  inherited OnStartPage(AScriptingContext);
  StartTime := Now;
end;
```

Technically, this method retrieves the scripting context. The TASPObject base class uses the method to initialize all the ASP objects (including the two, Response and Session, I use in the code), surfacing them as properties.

To generate more complex HTML from the Delphi ASP object, you can use Producer components, optionally connecting them to a dataset. In the AspTest example, I've added a Table component and a DataSetTableProducer, connected them as usual, and written the following code to activate it:

```
procedure Tasptest.ShowTable;
begin
  DataModule1 := TDataModule1.Create (nil);
  try
    Response.Write (DataModule1.DataSetTableProducer1.Content)
  finally
    DataModule1.Free;
  end;
end;
```

It will actually make more sense to create the data module when the COM object is created and destroyed (overriding Initialize and Destroy) or when the page is loaded and unloaded (with OnStartPage and OnEndPage).

WebSnap

After this lengthy introduction of the core elements of the development of Web server applications with Delphi, we can finally focus on some of the new related technologies introduced in Delphi 6. There were two good reasons for not jumping right into this topic from the beginning of this chapter. The first is that WebSnap builds on the foundation offered by WebBroker, so that you cannot learn how to use the new features if you don't know the core ones. For example, a WebSnap application is technically a CGI or WinCGI program, or an ISAPI or Apache module. The second reason is that since WebSnap is included only in the Enterprise version of Delphi, not all Delphi programmers have the chance to use it (needing to limit their expense to the Professional version of Delphi 6, which includes WebBroker).

WebSnap has a few definitive advantages over the plain WebBroker, such as allowing for multiple pages, integrating server-side scripting, and XSL and Delphi 5 Internet Express technology (these last two elements will be covered in the next chapter). Moreover, there are many ready-to-use components for handling common tasks, such as users' login, session management, and so on. Instead of listing all the features of WebSnap right away, though, I've decided to cover them in a sequence of simple and focused applications. All of these applications have been built using the Web App Debugger, for testing purposes, but you'll be able to easily deploy them using one of the other available technologies.

The starting point of the development of a WebSnap application is a dialog box that you can invoke either in the WebSnap page of the New items dialog box (File ➤ New ➤ Other) or using the new Internet toolbar of the IDE. The resulting dialog box, shown in Figure 22.13, allows you to choose the type of application (like in a WebBroker application) and to customize the initial application components (but you'll be able to add more later on). The bottom portion of the dialog determines the behavior of the first page, usually the default or home page of the program. A similar dialog box is displayed also for subsequent pages.

FIGURE 22.13:

The options offered by the New WebSnap Application dialog box include the type of server and a button for the selection of the core application components.

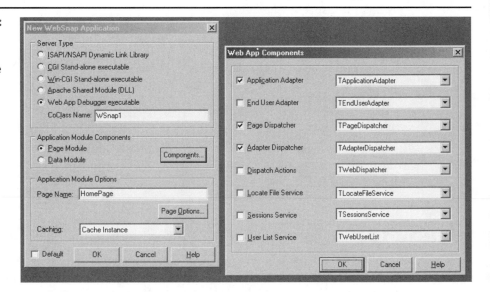

If you go ahead, choosing the defaults and typing in a name for the home page, the dialog box will create a project and open up a `TWebAppPageModule` for you. This module contains the components you've chosen, by default:

- A WebAppComponents component is a container of all of the centralized services of the WebSnap application, such as the user list, core dispatcher, session services, and so on. Not all of its properties must be available, as an application might not need all of the available services.

- One of these core services is offered by the PageDispatcher component, which (automatically) holds a list of the available pages of the application and defines the default one.

- Another core service is given by the AdapterDispatcher component, which handles HTML form submissions and image requests.

- The ApplicationAdapter is the first component we encounter of the *adapters* family. These components offer fields and actions to the server-side scripts evaluated by the program. Specifically, the ApplicationAdapter is a fields adapter that exposes the value of its own `ApplicationTitle` property. By entering a value for this property, it will be made available to the scripts.

- Finally, the module hosts a PageProducer that includes the HTML code of the page—in this case, the default page of the program. Unlike WebBroker applications, the HTML for this component is not stored inside its `HTMLDoc` string list property or referenced by its `HTMLFile` property. The HTML file is an external file, stored by default in the folder hosting the source code of the project and referenced from the application using a statement similar to a resource include statement: `{*.html}`.

Because the HTML file included by the PageProducer is kept as a separate file (the LocateFileService component will eventually help you for its deployment), you can edit it to change the output of a page of your program without having to recompile the application. These possible changes relate not only to the fixed portion of the HTML file but also to some of its dynamic content, thanks to the support for server-side scripting. The default HTML file, based on a standard template, actually already has some scripting in it.

The HTML file is visible within the Delphi editor with reasonably good syntax highlighting, simply by selecting the corresponding lower tab, such as WSnapDM.html in my simple example, shown in Figure 22.14. The editor also has other pages for a WebSnap module, including by default an HTML Result page, where you can see the HTML generated after evaluating the scripts, and a Preview page hosting what a user will see inside a browser.

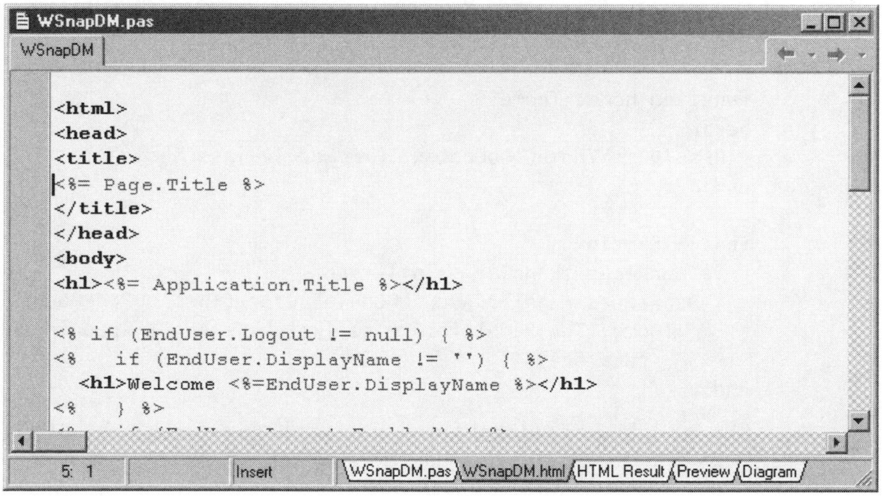

FIGURE 22.14:

The Delphi 6 editor for a WebSnap module includes a simple HTML editor and a preview of its output.

TIP   If you prefer editing the HTML of your Web application with another more sophisticated editor, you can set up your choice in the Internet page of the Environment Options dialog box. Within this page, you can see a list of file extensions. Selecting the Edit button for one of these groups of extensions, you can choose an external editor to use for these files. At this point, the External Editor button of the Internet toolbar will become active.

The standard HTML template used by WebSnap adds to any page of the program its title and the application title, using simple script lines such as:

```
<h1><%= Application.Title %></h1>
<h2><%= Page.Title %></h2>
```

We'll get back to the scripting in a while. But let me start the development of the WSnap1 example by simply creating a program with multiple pages. Before I do this, let me finish this overview by showing you the extra source code of a sample Web page module:

```
type
  Thome = class(TWebAppPageModule)
    ...
  end;

function home: Thome;

implementation

{$R *.dfm}   {*.html}

uses WebReq, WebCntxt, WebFact, Variants;

function home: Thome;
begin
  Result := Thome(WebContext.FindModuleClass(Thome));
end;

initialization
  if WebRequestHandler <> nil then
    WebRequestHandler.AddWebModuleFactory(TWebAppPageModuleFactory.Create(
      Thome, TWebPageInfo.Create([wpPublished {, wpLoginRequired}], '.html'),
        caCache));
end.
```

The module uses a global function instead of a typical global object of forms to support caching of the pages. This Web App Debugger application also has some extra code in the initialization section, particularly some registration code, to let the application know the role of the page and its behavior.

Managing Multiple Pages

The first notable difference between WebSnap and WebBroker is that, instead of having a single data module with multiple actions eventually connected to producer components, WebSnap has multiple data modules, each corresponding to an action and having a producer component with an HTML file attached to it. Actually, you can still add multiple actions to a page/module, but the idea is that you structure applications around pages and not around actions. Like actions, the name of the page is indicated in the request path.

As an example, I've added to the WebSnap application, built with default settings, two more pages. For the first, in the New WebSnap Page Module dialog (see Figure 22.15), I've chosen a standard page producer and given to it the name *date*. For the second, I've gone with a DataSetPageProducer and given it the name *country*. After saving the files, you can start testing the application. Thanks to some of the scripting I'll discuss later, each page lists all of the available pages (unless you've unchecked the Published check box in the New Web-Snap Page Module dialog).

FIGURE 22.15:

The New WebSnap Page Module dialog box

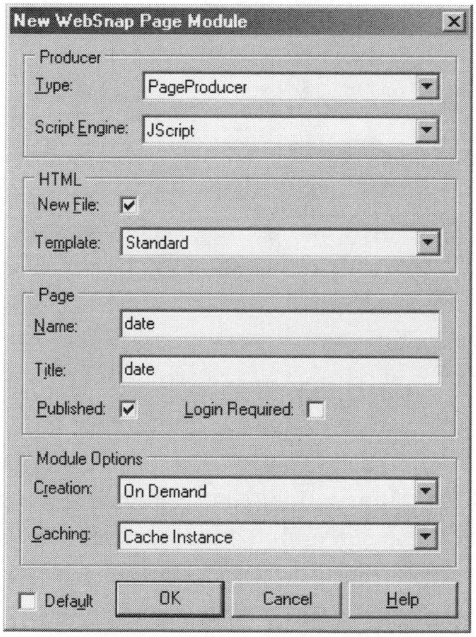

All of the pages will be rather empty, but at least we have the structure in place. To complete the home page, I've simply edited its linked HTML file directly. For the date page, I've employed the same approach as a WebBroker application. I've added to the HTML text some custom tags, as in:

```
<p>The time at this site is <#time>.</p>
```

and I've added some code to the `OnTag` event handler of the producer component to replace this tag with the current time.

For the third page, the country page, I've modified the HTML to include tags for the various fields of the country table, as in:

```
<h3>Country: <#name></h3>
```

Then I've attached the table to the page producer (and I've also added a session component to account for concurrent requests in multiple threads):

```
object DataSetPageProducer: TDataSetPageProducer
  DataSet = Table1
end
object Table1: TTable
  DatabaseName = 'DBDEMOS'
  SessionName = 'Session1_2'
  TableName = 'country.db'
end
object Session1: TSession
  Active = True
  AutoSessionName = True
end
```

To open this table when the page is first created and reset it to the first record in further invocations, I've handled the `OnBeforeDispatchPage` event of the Web page module, adding this code to it:

```
Table1.Open;
Table1.First;
```

The fact that a WebSnap page can be very similar to a portion of a WebBroker application (basically an action tied to a producer) is quite important, in case you want to port existing Web-Broker code to this new architecture. You can even port your existing DataSetTableProducer components to the new architecture. Technically, you can generate a new page, remove its producer component, replace it with a DataSetTableProducer, and hook this component to the `PageProducer` property of the Web page module. In practice, this approach would cut out the HTML file of the page and its scripts.

In the WSnap1 program, I've used a better technique. I've added a custom tag (`<#htmltable>`) to the HTML file and used the `OnTag` event of the page producer to add to the HTML the result of the data set table:

```
if TagString = 'htmltable' then
  ReplaceText := DataSetTableProducer1.Content;
```

Server-Side Scripts

If having multiple pages in a server-side program, each associated with a different page module, changes the way you write a program, having the server-side scripts at hand offers an even more powerful approach. For example, the standard scripts of the WSnap1 example account for the application and page titles, and for the index of the pages. This is generated by an enumerator, the technique used to scan a list from within a WebSnap script code. Let's have a look at it:

```
<table cellspacing="0" cellpadding="0"><td>
<%  e = new Enumerator(Pages)
    s = ''
    c = 0
    for (; !e.atEnd(); e.moveNext())
    {
      if (e.item().Published)
      {
        if (c > 0) s += ' | '
        if (Page.Name != e.item().Name)
          s += '<a href="' + e.item().HREF + '">' + e.item().Title + '</a>'
        else
          s += e.item().Title
        c++
      }
    }
    if (c>1) Response.Write(s)
%>
</td></table>
```

> **NOTE**   Typically, WebSnap scripts are written in JavaScript, an object-based language very common for Internet programming because it is the only scripting language generally available in browsers (on the client side). JavaScript, technically indicated as ECMAScript, borrows the core syntax of the C language and has almost nothing to do with Java. Actually, WebSnap uses Microsoft's ActiveScripting engine, which supports both JScript (a variation of JavaScript) and VBScript.

Inside the single cell of this table (which, oddly enough, has no rows), the script outputs a string with the `Reponse.Write` command. This string is built with a `for` loop over an enumerator of the pages of the application, stored in the `Pages` global entity. The title of each page is added to the string, only if the page is published and using an hyperlink only for pages different than the current one. Having this code in a script, instead of hard-coded into a Delphi component, allows you to pass it over to a good Web designer to turn it into something a little more visually appealing.

TIP To publish or unpublish a page, don't look for a property in the Web page module. This status is controlled by a flag of the `AddWebModuleFactory` method called in the Web page module initialization code. Simply comment or uncomment this flag to obtain the desired effect.

As a sample of what you can do with scripting, I've added to the WSnap2 example (an extension of the WSnap1 example) a *demoscript* page. The script of this page can generate a full table of multiplied values with the following scripting code (see Figure 22.16 for its output):

```
<table border=1 cellspacing=0>
<tr>
  <th> </th>
  <% for (j=1;j<=5;j++) { %>
  <th>Column <%=j %></th>
  <% } %>
</tr>
<% for (i=1;i<=5;i++) { %>
<tr>
  <td>Line <%=i %></td>
  <% for (j=1;j<=5;j++) { %>
  <td>Value= <%=i*j %></td>
  <% } %>
</tr>
<% } %>
</table>
```

FIGURE 22.16:

The WSnap2 example has a custom menu stored in an included file reference by each page.

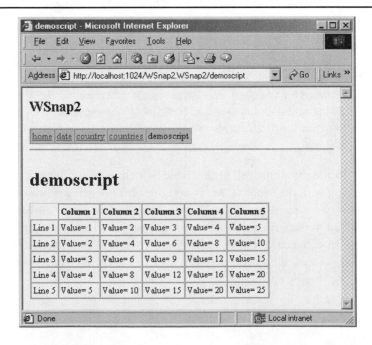

In this script, the <%= symbol replaces the longer Response.Write command. Another important feature of server-side scripting is the inclusion of pages within other pages. For example, if you plan on modifying the menu, you can include the related HTML and script in a single file, instead of changing it and maintaining it in multiple pages. File inclusion is generally done with a statement like:

```
<!-- #include file="menu.html" -->
```

In Listing 22.1, you can find the complete source code of the include file for the menu, referenced by all the other HTML files of the project. In Figure 22.16, you can see an example of this menu, across the top of the page with the table generation script mentioned earlier.

Listing 22.1:   The *menu.html* file included in each page of the WSnap2 example

```
<html>
<head>
<title><%= Page.Title %></title>
</head>
<body>
<h2><%= Application.Title %></h2>
<table cellspacing="0" cellpadding="2" border="1" bgcolor="#c0c0c0">
<tr>
<%   e = new Enumerator(Pages)
     for (; !e.atEnd(); e.moveNext())
     {
       if (e.item().Published)
       {
         if (Page.Name != e.item().Name)
           Response.Write ('<td><a href="' + e.item().HREF + '">' +
             e.item().Title + '</a></td>')
         else
           Response.Write ('<td>' + e.item().Title + '</td>')
       }
     }
%>
</tr>
</table>
<hr>
<h1><%= Page.Title %></h1>
<p>
```

This script for the menu uses the Pages list and the Page and Application global scripting objects. WebSnap makes available a few other global objects, including EndUser and Session objects (in case you add the corresponding adapters to the application), the Modules object, and the Producer object, which allows access to the Producer component of the Web page module. The script also has available the Response and Request objects of the Web module.

Adapters

Besides these global objects, within a script you can access all the adapters available in the corresponding Web page module. (Adapters in other modules, including shared Web data modules, must be referenced by prefixing their name with the Modules object and the corresponding module.) The idea is that adapters allow you to pass information from your compiled Delphi code to the interpreted script, providing a scriptable interface to your Delphi application. Adapters contain fields that represent data and host actions that represent commands. The server-side scripts can access these values and issue these commands, passing specific parameters to them.

> **NOTE** Technically, adapters implement an IDispatch interface that can be accessed by the script through an Active Scripting engine language, such as JavaScript. The page producer component is responsible for invoking the Active Scripting engine and has a property indicating the language of the script. Because of this, you'll have to register two type libraries (and deploy the corresponding DLLs) to make this work on a machine where Delphi is not installed: WebBrokerScript.tlb and stdvcl140.dll. As the first is a type library, it must be installed with Delphi's TRegSvr utility (available in the **bin** subfolder) rather than Microsoft's RegSvr32 program. Of course, the server computer must also have Microsoft Active Scripting Engine installed in order to work.

Adapter Fields

For simple customizations, you can simply add new fields to the specific adapters. For instance, in the WSnap2 example, I've added a custom field to the application adapter. After selecting this component, you can either open up its Fields editor (accessible via its local menu) or simply work within the Object TreeView. After adding a new field (called Count in the example), you can assign a value to it in its OnGetValue event. As I want to count the hits (or requests) on any page of the Web application, I've also handled the OnBeforePageDispatch event of the *global* PageDispatcher component. Here is the code of the two methods:

```
procedure Thome.PageDispatcherBeforeDispatchPage(Sender: TObject;
  const PageName: String; var Handled: Boolean);
begin
  Inc (HitCount);
end;

procedure Thome.CountGetValue(Sender: TObject; var Value: Variant);
begin
  Value := HitCount;
end;
```

Of course, I could have used the page name to also count hits on each specific page (and I could have added some support for persistency, as the count is reset every time you run a new instance of the application). Now that I've added a custom field to an existing adapter (corresponding to the Application script object), I can access it from within any script, like this:

```
<p>Application hits since last activation:
<%= Application.Count.Value %></p>
```

Adapter Components

In the same way, you can also add custom adapters to specific pages. If you need to pass along a few fields, use the generic Adapter component. Other custom adapters (besides the global ApplicationAdapter we've already used) include these:

- The PagedAdapter component has built-in support for showing its content over multiple pages.

- The DataSetAdapter component is used to access a Delphi dataset from a script and is covered in the next section.

- The StringValuesList holds a list of name/value pairs, like a string list, and can be used directly or to provide a list of values to an adapter field. The inherited DataSetValues-List adapter has the same role but grabs the list of name/value pairs from a dataset, providing support for lookups and other selections.

- User-related adapters, such as the EndUser, EndUserSession, and LoginForm adapters, are used to access user and session information and to build a login form for the application, automatically tied to the users list. I'll cover these adapters in the section "Sessions, Users, and Permissions" later in this chapter.

Using the AdapterPageProducer

Most of these components are used in conjunction with an AdapterPageProducer component. The AdapterPageProducer, in fact, can generate portions of script after you visually design the desired result. As an example, I've added to the WSnap2 application the *inout* page, which has an adapter with two fields, one standard and one Boolean:

```
object Adapter1: TAdapter
  OnBeforeExecuteAction = Adapter1BeforeExecuteAction
  object TAdapterActions
    object AddPlus: TAdapterAction
      OnExecute = AddPlusExecute
    end
    object Post: TAdapterAction
      OnExecute = PostExecute
    end
  end
```

```
  object TAdapterFields
    object Text: TAdapterField
      OnGetValue = TextGetValue
    end
    object Auto: TAdapterBooleanField
      OnGetValue = AutoGetValue
    end
  end
end
```

The adapter has also a couple of actions, used to post the current user input and to add a plus sign to the text. The same plus sign is added anyway when the Auto field is enabled. Developing the user interface for this form, and the related scripting, would take some time using plain HTML. But the AdapterPageProducer component (used in this page) has an integrated HTML designer, which Borland calls Web Surface Designer. Using this tool, you can visually add a form to the HTML page and add an AdapterFieldGroup to it. Connect this field group to the adapter to have editors for the two fields automatically displayed. Then you can add an AdapterCommandGroup and connect it to the AdapterFieldGroup, to have buttons for all of the actions of the adapter. You can see an example of this designer in Figure 22.17.

FIGURE 22.17:

The Web Surface Designer of Delphi 6 for the *inout* page of the WSnap2 example, at design time

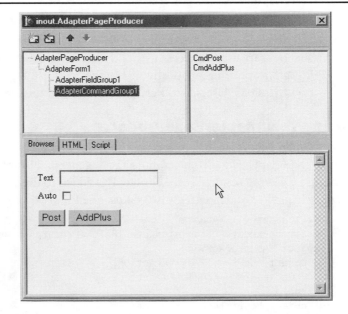

To be more precise, the fields and buttons are automatically displayed if the AddDefault-Fields and AddDefaultCommands properties of the field group and command group are set. The effect of the visual operations I've done to build this form are summarized in the following DFM snippet:

```
object AdapterPageProducer: TAdapterPageProducer
  object AdapterForm1: TAdapterForm
    object AdapterFieldGroup1: TAdapterFieldGroup
      Adapter = Adapter1
      object FldText: TAdapterDisplayField
        FieldName = 'Text'
      end
      object FldAuto: TAdapterDisplayField
        FieldName = 'Auto'
      end
    end
    object AdapterCommandGroup1: TAdapterCommandGroup
      DisplayComponent = AdapterFieldGroup1
      object CmdPost: TAdapterActionButton
        ActionName = 'Post'
      end
      object CmdAddPlus: TAdapterActionButton
        ActionName = 'AddPlus'
      end
    end
  end
end
```

Now that we have an HTML page with some scripts to move data back and forth and issue commands, we can have a look at the source code required to make this work. First, you'll have to add to the class two local fields to store the adapter fields and manipulate them, and you need to implement the OnGetValue event for both, returning the field values. When each of the buttons is pressed, we have to retrieve the text passed by the user, which is not automatically copied into the corresponding adapter field. You can obtain this effect by looking at the ActionValue property of these fields, which is set only if something was entered (for this reason, when nothing is entered we set the Boolean field to False). To avoid repeating this code for both actions, I've placed it in the OnBeforeExecuteAction event of the Web page module:

```
procedure Tinout.Adapter1BeforeExecuteAction(Sender, Action: TObject;
  Params: TStrings; var Handled: Boolean);
begin
  if Assigned (Text.ActionValue) then
    fText := Text.ActionValue.Values [0];
  fAuto := Assigned (Auto.ActionValue);
end;
```

Notice that each action can have multiple values (in case of components allowing multiple selections); but this is not the case, so we can simply grab the first element. Finally, I've written the code for the OnExecute events of the two actions:

```
procedure TInout.AddPlusExecute(Sender: TObject; Params: TStrings);
begin
  fText := fText + '+';
end;

procedure TInout.PostExecute(Sender: TObject; Params: TStrings);
begin
  if fAuto then
    AddPlusExecute (Self, nil);
end;
```

As an alternative, adapter fields have a public EchoActionFieldValue property that you can set to get the value entered by the user and place it again in the resulting form. This technique is typically used in case of errors, to let the user change the input starting with the values already entered.

> **NOTE**   The AdapterPageProducer component has specific support for cascading style sheets (CSS). You can define the CSS for a page using either the **StylesFile** property or **Styles** string list. Any element of the editor of the items of the producer, at this point, can define a specific style or choose one of the styles of the attached CSS. This last operation (which is the suggested approach) is accomplished using the **StyleRule** property.

Scripts Rather Than Code?

Even this simple example of the combined use of an adapter and an adapter page producer, with its visual designer, shows the power of this architecture. However, this approach also has a big drawback. By letting the components generate the script (in the HTML, you have only the <#SERVERSCRIPT> tag), you save a lot of development time, but at the same time you end up mixing the script with the code, so that changes to the user interface will require updating the program. The division of responsibilities between the Delphi application developer and the HTML/script designer is lost. And, ironically, we end up having to run a script to accomplish something the Delphi program could have done right away, possibly even much faster!

So my opinion is that this is a very powerful architecture and a huge step forward from WebBroker, but it has to be used with some care, to avoid misusing some of these technologies just because they are simple and powerful (and they are indeed). For example, it might be worth using the designer of the AdapterPageProducer to generate the first version of a page, then grabbing the generated script and copying to the HTML of a plain PageProducer, so that a Web designer can modify the script with a specific tool.

For nontrivial applications, I tend to prefer the possibilities offered by XML and XSL, which are available within this architecture even if they don't have a central role. More on this specific topic in the next chapter.

WebSnap and Databases

One of the areas where Delphi has always shined is database programming. For this reason, it is not surprising to see a lot of support for handling datasets within the WebSnap framework. Specifically, you can use the DataSetAdapter component to connect to a dataset and display its values in a form or a table using the visual editor of the AdapterPageProducer component.

A WebSnap Data Module

As an example, I've built a new WebSnap application (called WSnapTable) with an Adapter-PageProducer as its main page to display a table in a grid and another AdapterPageProducer in a secondary page to show a form with a single record. I've also added to the application a WebSnap Data Module, as a container of the dataset components. The data module has a ClientDataSet wired to a dbExpress dataset through a provider and based on an InterBase connection, as shown here:

```
object ClientDataSet1: TClientDataSet
  Active = True
  ProviderName = 'DataSetProvider1'
end
object SQLConnection1: TSQLConnection
  Connected = True
  ConnectionName = 'IBLocal'
  LoginPrompt = False
end
object SQLDataSet1: TSQLDataSet
  SQLConnection = SQLConnection1
  CommandText =
    'select CUST_NO, CUSTOMER, ADDRESS_LINE1, CITY, STATE_PROVINCE, ' +
    '  COUNTRY from CUSTOMER'
end
object DataSetProvider1: TDataSetProvider
  DataSet = SQLDataSet1
end
```

The DataSetAdapter

Now that we have a dataset available, we can add a DataSetAdapter to the first page, and connect it to the ClientDataSet of the Web module. The adapter automatically makes available all of the fields of the dataset and several predefined actions for operating on it (such as

Delete, Edit, and Apply). You can add them explicitly to the Actions and Fields collections to exclude some of them and customize their behavior, but this is not always required.

Like the PagedAdapter, the DataSetAdapter has a PageSize property where you can indicate the number of elements to display in each page. The component also has commands that you can use to navigate among pages. This approach is particularly suitable when you want to display a large dataset in a grid. These are the adapter settings for the main page of the WSnapTable example:

```
object DataSetAdapter1: TDataSetAdapter
  DataSet = WebDataModule1.ClientDataSet1
  PageSize = 6
end
```

The corresponding page producer has a form containing two command groups and a grid. The first command group (displayed above the gird) has the predefined commands for handling pages: CmdPrevPage, CmdNextPage, and CmdGotoPage. This last command generates a list of numbers for the pages, so that a user can jump to each of them directly. The AdapterGrid component has the default columns plus an extra one hosting a couple of commands, Edit and Delete. The bottom command group has a button used to create a new record. You can see an example of the output of the table in Figure 22.18 and the complete settings of the AdapterPageProducer in Listing 22.2.

FIGURE 22.18:

The page shown by the WSnapTable example at start up includes the initial portion of a *paged* table.

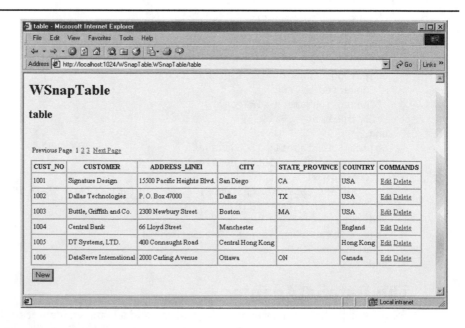

Listing 22.2: **AdapterPageProducer settings for the WSnapTable main page**

```
object AdapterPageProducer: TAdapterPageProducer
  object AdapterForm1: TAdapterForm
```

```
    object AdapterCommandGroup1: TAdapterCommandGroup
      DisplayComponent = AdapterGrid1
      object CmdPrevPage: TAdapterActionButton
        ActionName = 'PrevPage'
        Caption = 'Previous Page'
      end
      object CmdGotoPage: TAdapterActionButton
        ActionName = 'GotoPage'
      end
      object CmdNextPage: TAdapterActionButton
        ActionName = 'NextPage'
        Caption = 'Next Page'
      end
    end
    object AdapterGrid1: TAdapterGrid
      TableAttributes.CellSpacing = 0
      TableAttributes.CellPadding = 3
      Adapter = DataSetAdapter1
      AdapterMode = 'Browse'
      object ColCUST_NO: TAdapterDisplayColumn
        FieldName = 'CUST_NO'
      end
      object ColCUSTOMER: TAdapterDisplayColumn
        FieldName = 'CUSTOMER'
      end
      object ColADDRESS_LINE1: TAdapterDisplayColumn
        FieldName = 'ADDRESS_LINE1'
      end
      object ColCITY: TAdapterDisplayColumn
        FieldName = 'CITY'
      end
      object ColSTATE_PROVINCE: TAdapterDisplayColumn
        FieldName = 'STATE_PROVINCE'
      end
      object ColCOUNTRY: TAdapterDisplayColumn
        FieldName = 'COUNTRY'
      end
      object AdapterCommandColumn1: TAdapterCommandColumn
        Caption = 'COMMANDS'
        object CmdEditRow: TAdapterActionButton
          ActionName = 'EditRow'
          Caption = 'Edit'
          PageName = 'formview'
          DisplayType = ctAnchor
        end
        object CmdDeleteRow: TAdapterActionButton
          ActionName = 'DeleteRow'
          Caption = 'Delete'
          DisplayType = ctAnchor
        end
      end
```

```
        end
      object AdapterCommandGroup2: TAdapterCommandGroup
        DisplayComponent = AdapterGrid1
        object CmdNewRow: TAdapterActionButton
          ActionName = 'NewRow'
          Caption = 'New'
          PageName = 'formview'
        end
      end
    end
  end
```

In this rather long listing, there are a few things to notice. First, the grid has the Adapter-Mode property set to Browse, other possibilities being Edit, Insert, and Query. This dataset display mode for adapters determines the type of user interface (text or edit boxes and other input controls) and the visibility of other buttons (for example, Apply and Cancel buttons are only present in the edit view, the opposite for the Edit command).

NOTE   The adapter mode can also be modified using server-side script and accessing Adapter.Mode.

Second, I've modified the display of the commands inside the grid, using the ctAnchor value for the DisplayType property instead of the default button style. Similar properties are available in most components of this architecture to tweak the HTML code they produce.

Editing the Data in a Form

Finally, some of the commands are connected to a different page, the page that is going to be displayed after the commands are invoked. For example, the edit command has its PageName property set to formview. This second page of the application has an AdapterPageProducer with components hooked to the same DataSetAdapter of the other table, so that all of the request will be automatically synchronized. Selecting the edit command, in fact, the program will open the secondary page displaying the data of the record corresponding to the command.

Listing 22.3 shows the details of the page producer of the second page of the program. Again, building the HTML form visually using the Delphi specific designer (see Figure 22.19) was a very fast operation.

FIGURE 22.19:

The formview page shown by the WSnapTable example at design time, in the Web Surface Designer (or AdapterPageProducer editor)

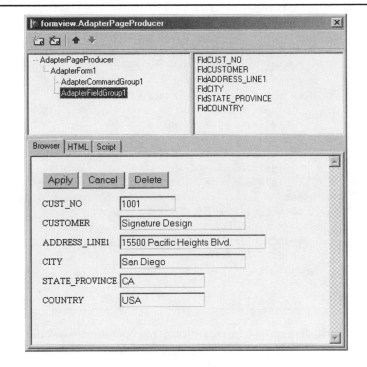

Listing 22.3:   **AdapterPageProducer settings for the formview page**

```
object AdapterPageProducer: TAdapterPageProducer
  object AdapterForm1: TAdapterForm
    object AdapterErrorList1: TAdapterErrorList
      Adapter = table.DataSetAdapter1
    end
    object AdapterCommandGroup1: TAdapterCommandGroup
      DisplayComponent = AdapterFieldGroup1
      object CmdApply: TAdapterActionButton
        ActionName = 'Apply'
        PageName = 'table'
      end
      object CmdCancel: TAdapterActionButton
        ActionName = 'Cancel'
        PageName = 'table'
      end
      object CmdDeleteRow: TAdapterActionButton
        ActionName = 'DeleteRow'
        Caption = 'Delete'
```

```
          PageName = 'table'
        end
      end
      object AdapterFieldGroup1: TAdapterFieldGroup
        Adapter = table.DataSetAdapter1
        AdapterMode = 'Edit'
        object FldCUST_NO: TAdapterDisplayField
          DisplayWidth = 10
          FieldName = 'CUST_NO'
        end
        object FldCUSTOMER: TAdapterDisplayField
          DisplayWidth = 27
          FieldName = 'CUSTOMER'
        end
        object FldADDRESS_LINE1...
        object FldCITY...
        object FldSTATE_PROVINCE...
        object FldCOUNTRY...
      end
    end
  end
```

In the listing, you can see that all the operations send the user back the main page and that the AdapterMode is set to Edit, unless there are update errors or conflicts. In this case, the same page is displayed again, with a description of the errors obtained by adding an Adapter-ErrorList component at the top of the form.

The second page is not published, because selecting it without referring to a specific record would make very little sense. To unpublish the page, I've simply commented the corresponding flag in the initialization code. Finally, to make the changes to the database persistent, you can call the ApplyUdpates method in the OnAfterPost and OnAfterDelete events of the ClientDataSet component hosted by the data module. Another problem (which I haven't fixed) relates to the fact that the SQL server assigns the ID of each customer, so that when you enter a new record, the data in the ClientDataSet and in the actual database are not aligned any more. This can cause Record Not Found errors, a problem I've not fixed in the example.

Master/Detail in WebSnap

The DataSetAdapter component has specific support for master/detail relationships between datasets. After you've created the relationship among the datasets, as usual, define an adapter for each dataset and then connect the MasterAdapter property of the adapter of the detail dataset. Setting up the master/detail relationship between the adapters makes them work in a more seamless way. For example, when you change the work mode of the master, or enter new records, the detail automatically enters into Edit mode or is refreshed.

In the WSnapMD example, I've defined such a relationship using two SQLClientDataSet components connected with an InterBase database via dbExpress. All these components and the related adapters are in a Web data module, which has the structure displayed in the design view in Figure 22.20. I haven't provided a complete listing of the details of these components, as it shouldn't be too difficult for you to rebuild it after looking at the example itself.

FIGURE 22.20:

The design view of the Web data module of the WSnapMD example. Both the datasets and the adapters have a master/detail relationship.

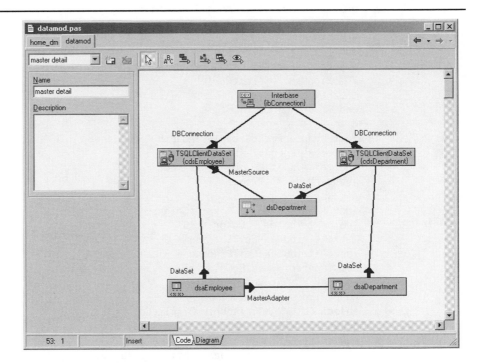

The only page of this WebSnap application has an AdapterPageProducer component hooked to both dataset adapters. The form of this page, in fact, has both a field group hooked to the master and a grid connected with the detail. Unlike other examples, I've tried to improve the user interface by adding custom attributes for the various elements, as you can see in the following detailed excerpt:

```
object AdapterPageProducer: TAdapterPageProducer
  object AdapterForm1: TAdapterForm
    Custom = 'Border="1" CellSpacing="0" CellPadding="10" ' +
      'BgColor="Silver" align="center"'
    object AdapterCommandGroup1: TAdapterCommandGroup
      DisplayComponent = AdapterFieldGroup1
```

```
        Custom = 'Align="Center"'
        object CmdFirstRow: TAdapterActionButton
          ActionName = 'FirstRow'
          Caption = '   First   '
        end
        object CmdPrevRow: TAdapterActionButton
          ActionName = 'PrevRow'
          Caption = ' Previous '
        end
        object CmdNextRow: TAdapterActionButton
          ActionName = 'NextRow'
          Caption = '   Next   '
        end
        object CmdLastRow: TAdapterActionButton
          ActionName = 'LastRow'
          Caption = '   Last   '
        end
      end
      object AdapterFieldGroup1: TAdapterFieldGroup
        Custom = 'BgColor="Silver"'
        Adapter = WDataMod.dsaDepartment
        AdapterMode = 'Browse'
      end
      object AdapterGrid1: TAdapterGrid
        TableAttributes.BgColor = 'Silver'
        TableAttributes.CellSpacing = 0
        TableAttributes.CellPadding = 3
        HeadingAttributes.BgColor = 'Gray'
        Adapter = WDataMod.dsaEmployee
        AdapterMode = 'Browse'
        object ColEMP_NO: TAdapterDisplayColumn...
        object ColFIRST_NAME: TAdapterDisplayColumn...
        object ColLAST_NAME: TAdapterDisplayColumn...
        object ColDEPT_NO: TAdapterDisplayColumn...
        object ColJOB_CODE: TAdapterDisplayColumn...
        object ColJOB_COUNTRY: TAdapterDisplayColumn...
        object ColSALARY: TAdapterDisplayColumn...
      end
    end
  end
```

I've used a gray background, displayed some of the grid borders (HTML grids are used very often by the Web surface designer), centered most of the elements, and added some spacing. Notice that I've added some extra spaces to the button captions, to avoid them being too small. The effect of these settings (and the master/detail structure) is visible at run time in Figure 22.21.

FIGURE 22.21:

The WSnapMD example shows a master/detail structure and has some customized output.

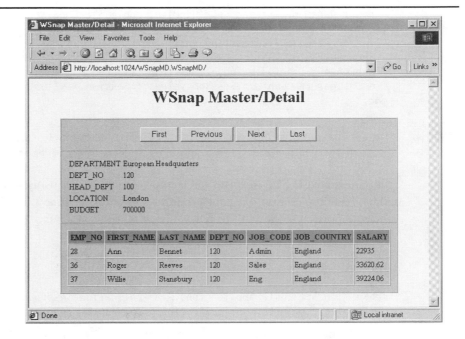

Sessions, Users, and Permissions

Another very interesting area of the WebSnap architecture is its support for sessions and users. Sessions are supported using a classic approach: temporary cookies. These cookies are sent to the browser, so that following requests from the same user can be acknowledged by the system. By adding data to a session instead of an application adapter, you can have data that depends on the specific session or user (although a user can possibly run multiple sessions by opening multiple browser windows on the same computer). For supporting sessions, the application keeps data in memory, so this feature is not available in case of CGI programs.

Using Sessions

To underline the importance of this type of support, I've built a WebSnap application with a single page showing both the total number of hits and the total number of hits for each session. The program has a SessionService component with default values for its MaxSessions and DefaultTimeout properties. For every new request, the program increases both an nHits private field of the page module and the SessionHits value of the current session:

```
procedure TSessionDemo.WebAppPageModuleBeforeDispatchPage(Sender: TObject;
```

```
  const PageName: String; var Handled: Boolean);
begin
  // increase application and session hits
  Inc (nHits);
  WebContext.Session.Values ['SessionHits'] :=
    Integer (WebContext.Session.Values ['SessionHits']) + 1;
end;
```

NOTE   The WebContext object (of type TWebContext) is a thread variable, created by WebSnap for each request, which provides thread-safe access to other global variables used by program.

The associated HTML displays status information both by using some custom tags evaluated by the OnTag event of the page producer and some script, evaluated by the engine. Here is the core portion of the HTML file:

```
<h3>Plain Tags</h3>
<p>Session id: <#SessionID>
<br>Session hits: <#SessionHits></p>
<h3>Script</h3>
<p>Session hits (via application): <%=Application.SessionHits.Value%>
<br>Application hits: <%=Application.Hits.Value%></p>
```

The parameters of the output are provided by the OnTag event handler and the OnGetValue events of the fields:

```
procedure TSessionDemo.PageProducerHTMLTag(Sender: TObject; Tag: TTag;
  const TagString: String; TagParams: TStrings; var ReplaceText: String);
begin
  if TagString = 'SessionID' then
    ReplaceText := WebContext.Session.SessionID
  else if TagString = 'SessionHits' then
    ReplaceText := WebContext.Session.Values ['SessionHits']
end;

procedure TSessionDemo.HitsGetValue(Sender: TObject; var Value: Variant);
begin
  Value := nHits;
end;

procedure TSessionDemo.SessionHitsGetValue(Sender: TObject; var Value: Variant);
begin
  Value := Integer (WebContext.Session.Values ['SessionHits']);
end;
```

The effect of this program is visible in Figure 22.22, where I've activated two sessions in two different copies of Internet Explorer.

FIGURE 22.22:

Two instances of the
browser operate on two
different sessions of the
same WebSnap application.

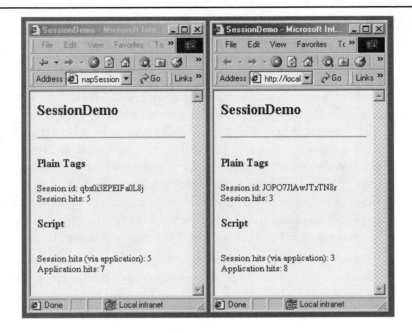

TIP   In this example, I've voluntarily used both the traditional WebBroker tag replacement and the newer WebSnap adapter fields and scripting, so that you can compare the two approaches and keep in mind that they are both available in a WebSnap application.

Requesting Login

Besides generic sessions, WebSnap also has specific support for users and login-based authorized sessions. You can add to an application a list of users (with the WebUserList component), each with a name and a password. My impression is that this component is rather rudimentary in the data it can store. Instead of filling it with your list of users, however, you can keep the list in a database table (or in some other proprietary format) and use the events of the WebUserList component to retrieve your custom users data and check the user passwords.

You'll generally also add to the application the SessionService and EndUserSession-Adapter components. At this point, you can ask the users to log in, indicating for each page whether it can be viewed by everyone or only by logged-in users. This is accomplished by setting the wpLoginRequired flag in the constructor of the TWebPageModuleFactory and TWebAppPageModuleFactory classes in the initialization code of the Web page unit.

The reason for having rights and publication information in the factory rather than in the Web-PageModule, is that the program can check the access rights and list the pages even without loading the module.

When a user tries to see a page that requires the user identification, the login page indicated in the EndUserSessionAdapter component is displayed. You can create such a page rather easily by creating a new Web page module based on an AdapterPageProducer and adding to it the LoginFormAdapter. In the editor of the page, add a field group within a form, connect the field group to the LoginFormAdapter, and add a command group with the default Login button. The resulting login form will have fields for the username and its password, but also for the requested page. This last value is automatically filled with the requested page, in case this page required authorization and the user wasn't already logged in. This is done so that a user can immediately reach the requested page without being bounced back to a generic menu.

The login form is typically not published, because the corresponding Login command is already available when the user isn't logged into the system; when the user logs in, it is replaced by a Logout command. This is obtained by the standard script of the Web Page Module, and particularly:

```
<% if (EndUser.Logout != null) { %>
<%   if (EndUser.DisplayName != '') { %>
  <h1>Welcome <%=EndUser.DisplayName %></h1>
<%   } %>
<%   if (EndUser.Logout.Enabled) { %>
  <a href="<%=EndUser.Logout.AsHREF%>">Logout</a>
<%   } %>
<%   if (EndUser.LoginForm.Enabled) { %>
  <a href=<%=EndUser.LoginForm.AsHREF%>>Login</a>
<%   } %>
<% } %>
```

There isn't much else to say about the WSnapUsers application, as it has almost no custom code and settings. The access to the users data is demonstrated by the script of the standard template shown above.

Single Page Access Rights

Besides having pages that require a login for access, you can give specific users the right to see more pages than others. Any user, in fact, has a set of rights separated by semicolons or commas. The user must have all of the rights defined for the requested page generally listed in the ViewAccess and ModifyAccess properties of the adapters, which indicate respectively whether the user can see the given elements while browsing or can even edit them. These settings are very granular, and can be applied to entire adapters or some specific adapter fields (notice I'm referring to the adapter fields, not the user interface components within the designer). For example, you can hide some of the columns of a table to given users by hiding the corresponding fields (and also in other cases, as specified by the HideOptions property).

The global PageDispatcher component also has the OnCanViewPage and OnPageAccessDenied events that can also be used to control the access to the various pages of the program within the program code, allowing for even greater control.

What's Next?

In this chapter, I've covered Web server applications, using multiple techniques (CGI, ISAPI, Apache dynamic modules) and two different frameworks of the Delphi class library: Web-Broker and WebSnap. This wasn't certainly an in-depth presentation, as one could write an entire book on this topic alone. It was intended as a starting point, and (as usual) I've tried to make the core concepts clear rather than building very complex examples.

If you want to learn more details of the WebSnap framework and see different examples in actions, refer to the extensive Delphi demos for this area, in the \Demos\WebSnap folder. Some of the other available options, relating to XML, XSL, and client-side scripts, will be examined in the next chapter, where I'll also discuss Web services as a powerful alternative to HTTP/HTML-based distributed applications.

CHAPTER 23

XML and SOAP

- Introducing XML, Extensible Markup Language

- Working with XML: DOM and SAX

- Delphi 6 and XML: interfaces and mapping

- Internet Express

- Using XSTL

- Web services

- SOAP and WSDL

Building applications for the Internet means using protocols and creating browser-based user interfaces, as we've done in the preceding two chapters, but also opens up the opportunity of exchanging business documents electronically. The emerging standards for this type of activity all center around the XML document format and include the SOAP transmission protocol, XML schemas for the validation of documents, and XSL for rendering them as HTML.

In this chapter, I'll discuss all of these technologies and the extensive support Delphi 6 offers for them, a series of features collectively known as BizSnap. Since you might not know XML and related technologies, I'll provide a little introduction about each of them, but you should refer to books specifically devoted to each subject to know more. What I won't try to do is to cover *why* this is a revolution for running the IT side of a business and what it opens up. In the conclusion of the chapter, I'll point you to some initiatives you might be interested in tracking.

Introducing XML

XML, or Extensible Markup Language, is a simplified version of SGML and is getting a lot of attention in the IT world. XML is a *markup language*, meaning it uses symbols to describe its own content—in this case, *tags* consisting of specially defined text enclosed in angle brackets. It is named *extensible* because it allows for free markers (in contrast, for example, to HTML, which has predefined markers). The XML language is a standard promoted by the World Wide Web Consortium (better known as W3C, www.w3.org).

TIP The XML Recommendation is at www.w3.org/TR/REC-xml.

XML has been touted as the ASCII of year 2000, to indicate a simple and widespread technology, and also to indicate that XML document is actually a plain text file (optionally with Unicode characters instead of plain ACSII text). The important element of XML is that it is descriptive, as every tag has an almost human-readable name. Here is a small example, in case you've never seen an XML document:

```
<book>
  <title>Mastering Delphi 6</title>
  <author>Cantu</author>
  <publisher>Sybex</publisher>
</book>
```

XML has also a few disadvantages I want to underline from the beginning. The biggest is that without a formal description, a document is worth very little. If you want to exchange documents with another company, you have to agree on what each tag means and also on the semantic meaning of the content. (For example, when you have a quantity, you have to agree on the measurement system or include it in the document.) Another disadvantage is that XML documents are much larger than other formats; using strings for numbers, for example, is far from efficient, and the repeated opening and closing tags eat up a lot of space. The good news is that XML compresses quite well, exactly for the same reasons.

Core XML Syntax

There are a few technical elements of XML that are worth knowing before discussing its usage within Delphi. Here is a short summary of the key elements of the XML syntax:

- White space (including the space character, carriage return, line feed, and tabs) is generally ignored (as in an HTML document). It is important to format an XML document to make it readable by a human being, but your programs won't care much.

- You can add comments within <!-- and --> markers, which are basically ignored by any XML processor. There are also directives and processing instructions, enclosed within <? and ?> markers.

- There a few special or reserved characters you cannot use in the text. The only two symbols you can *never* use are the less-than character (or "left angle bracket," used to delimit a marker) replaced by < and the ampersand character replaced by &. Other optional special characters are > for the greater-than symbol (right angle bracket), ' for the single quote, and " for the double quote.

- To add non-XML content (for example, binary information or a script), you can use a CDATA section, enclosed within <![CDATA[and]]>.

- All markers are enclosed by angle brackets, < and >. Markers are case sensitive (in contrast to HTML).

- For each opening marker, you must have a matching closing marker, denoted by an initial slash character, as in:

    ```
    <node>value</node>
    ```

- Markers must not overlap—they must be *properly nested*, as in the first line below (the second line is not correct):

    ```
    <node>xx <nested> yy</nested> </node>  // OK
    <node>xx <nested> yy</node> </nested>  // WRONG
    ```

- If a marker has no content (but its presence is important anyway), you can replace the opening and closing markers with an single marker that includes a final or "trailing" slash: `<node/>`.

- Markers can also have attributes, using multiple attribute names followed by a value enclosed within quotes: `<node attrib1="aaa">`.

- Any XML node can have multiple attributes, multiple embedded tags, and only one block of text, representing the value of the node. If it's technically possible, it is common practice for XML nodes to have either a textual value or embedded tags, and not both. Here is an example of the full syntax of a node:

```
<node attrib1="aaa" attrib2="bbb">
  value1
  <child1>
    value2
  </child1>
</node>
```

- A node can have multiple child nodes with the same tag (tags need not be unique). Attribute names are unique for each node.

Well-Formed XML

If the elements discussed in the previous section define the syntax of an XML document, they are not enough. A XML document is considered syntactically correct, or *well formed*, if it follows a few extra rules. Notice that this type of check doesn't guarantee that the content of the document is meaningful, but only the tags are properly laid out.

One of the rules is that each document should have a prologue, indicating that is it indeed an XML document, which version of XML it complies with, and the possibly the type of character encoding. Here is an example:

```
<?xml version="1.0" encoding="UTF-8"?>
```

Possible encodings include various Unicode character sets (such as UTF-8, UTF-16, and UTF-32) or some ISO encodings (such as ISO-10646-xxx or ISO-8859-xxx). The prologue can also include external declarations, the schema used to validate the document, namespace declarations, an associated XSL file, and some internal entity declarations. Refer to XML documentation or books for more information on these topics.

An XML document is well formed if it has a prologue, has a proper syntax (see the rules in the previous section), and has a tree of nodes with a single root. Most tools (including Internet Explorer) check whether a document is well formed when loading it.

NOTE   As you can see, XML is more formal and precise than HTML. The W3C is coming along with an XHTML standard that will make HTML documents XML-compliant, for better processing with XML tools. This implies many changes in a typical HTML document, such as avoiding attributes with no values, adding all the closing markers (as `</p>` and `</li>`), adding the slash to stand-alone markers (as `<hr/>` and `<br/>`), proper nesting, and more. An HTML-to-XHTML converter, called HTML Tidy, is hosted by the W3C Web site at `www.w3.org/People/Raggett/tidy/`.

Working with XML

To get acquainted with the format of XML, you can use one of the existing XML editors available on the market. You can also simply type your XML code into Notepad and then try to load it into Internet Explorer to see whether it is correct. In this case, you'll see it within the browser in a tree-like structure.

To speed up this type of operation, I've build the simplest XML editor I could come up with—basically Notepad with some XML syntax-checking and a browser attached to it. The XmlEditOne example has a PageControl with three pages. The first page, Settings, hosts a couple of components where you can insert the path and the name of the file and you want to work with. (The reason for not using a standard dialog will become clear when I show you an extension of the program.) The edit box hosting the complete filename is automatically updated with the path and filename, provided the AutoUpdate check box is selected.

The second page hosts a Memo control, with the text of the XML file, loaded and saved by clicking the two toolbar buttons. As soon as you load the file, or each time you modify its text, its content is loaded into a DOM to let a parser check for its correctness (something that would be quite complex to do with your own code). To parse the code, I've used the XMLDocument component available in Delphi 6, which is basically a wrapper around a DOM available on the computer and indicated by its `DOMVendor` property. I'll discuss the use of this component in a little more detail in the next section. For the moment, suffice to say you can assign a string list to its `XML` property and activate it to let it parse the XML text and eventually report an error with an exception.

For this specific example, though, this behavior is far from good, because while typing the XML code you'll have temporarily incorrect XML. Still, I prefer not to ask the user to click a button to do the validation, but let it run continuously. As it is not possible to disable the parse exception raised by the XMLDocument component, I had to work at a lower level, extracting the `DOMPersist` property (referring to the persistency interface of the DOM) after extracting the `IXMLDocumentAccess` interface from the XMLDocument component (called `XmlDoc` in this code). At this point, I can also extract the `IDOMParseError` interface from the document component, to display any error message in the status bar:

```
procedure TFormXmlEdit.MemoXmlChange(Sender: TObject);
var
  eParse: IDOMParseError;
begin
  XmlDoc.Active := True;
  xmlBar.Panels[1].Text := 'OK';
  xmlBar.Panels[2].Text := '';
  (XmlDoc as IXMLDocumentAccess).DOMPersist.loadxml(MemoXml.Text);
  eParse := (XmlDoc.DOMDocument as IDOMParseError);
  if eParse.errorCode <> 0 then
    with eParse do
    begin
      xmlBar.Panels[1].Text := 'Error in: ' + IntToStr (Line) + '.' +
        IntToStr (LinePos);
      xmlBar.Panels[2].Text := SrcText + ': ' + Reason;
    end;
end;
```

You can see an example of the output of the program in Figure 23.1, alongside the XML tree view provided by the third page (for a correct document). The third page of the program is built using the WebBrowser component, which embeds the ActiveX control of Internet Explorer. Unfortunately, there is no direct way to assign a string with the XML text to this control, so you'll have to save the file first and then move to its page to trigger the loading of the XML in the browser (or manually click the Refresh button).

FIGURE 23.1:

The XmlEditOne example allows you to enter XML text in a memo, indicating errors as you type, and shows the result in the embedded browser.

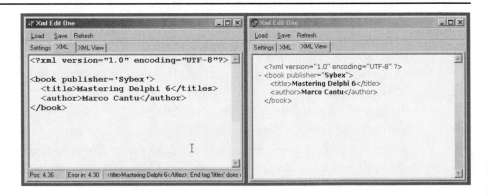

Unicode support in Internet Explorer 5 is quite limited, even on Windows 2000 (which has, in general, rather good Unicode support). If you change the final letter in my last name to an accented letter, as it should be, you won't see any problem when checking the document with the DOM, but you'll see an error when viewing it in the browser. The same happens if you change the format to UTF-16.

Managing XML Documents

Now that you know the core elements of XML, we can start discussing how to manage XML documents in Delphi programs (or in programs in general, as some of the techniques discussed here go beyond the language used). There are two typical techniques for manipulating XML documents, using a Document Object Model (DOM) interface or using the Simple API for XML (SAX). The two approaches are quite different:

- The DOM loads the entire document into a hierarchical tree of nodes, allowing you to read them and manipulate them to change the document. For this reason, the DOM is suited when you want to navigate the XML structure in memory and edit it, or even for creating new documents from scratch.

- The SAX parses the document firing an event for each element of the document, without building any structure in memory. Once parsed by the SAX, the document is lost, but this operation is generally much faster than the construction of the DOM tree. Using the SAX is good for reading a document once, possibly looking for portion of its data.

There is a third classic way to manipulate (and specifically create) XML documents: string management. Creating a document by adding strings is certainly the fastest operation, particularly if you can do a single pass (and don't need to modify nodes already generated). Even reading documents by means of string functions is very fast, but this can become quite difficult for complex structures.

Finally, Delphi 6 provides two more techniques you should consider. The first is the definition of interfaces mapping the document structure and used to access the document instead of the generic DOM interface. As we'll see, this approach makes for faster coding and more robust applications. Another technique is the development of transformations that allow you to read a generic XML document into a ClientDataSet component or save the dataset into an XML file of a given structure (not the specific XML structure natively supported by the ClientDataSet, or MyBase).

I won't try to fully assess which option is better suited for each type of document and manipulation, but I will try to highlight some of the advantages and disadvantages while discussing examples of each approach in the next sections.

Programming with the DOM

Since an XML document has a tree-like structure, loading an XML document into a tree in memory is quite a natural fit. This is what the Document Object Model does. The DOM is a standard interface, so that when you have written code that uses a DOM, you can switch DOM implementations without changing your source code (at least, if you haven't used any non-custom extensions).

In Delphi, you can install several DOM implementations, available as COM servers, and use their interfaces. One of the most commonly used DOMs on Windows is the one provided by Microsoft as part of the MSXML SDK. That DOM is also used by Internet Explorer (even if generally in an older version), but the SDK contains some rather detailed documentation, which will probably help you. Other frequently used DOMs are available from IBM and Apache (this one is called Xerces).

TIP   There are also a couple of native Object Pascal DOM components. One is the open source OpenXML, available at www.philo.de/xml. Another native Delphi DOM is offered by Turbo-Power. The advantage of these solutions is that they don't require an external library for the program to execute, because the DOM component gets compiled into your application.

Delphi 6 embeds the DOM implementations into a wrapper component, called XMLDocument. I've just used this component in the preceding example, but here I want to examine its role in a more general way. The idea behind using this component is that, instead of the actual DOM interface, you remain even more independent from the implementations and can work with some simplified methods, or helpers.

The DOM interface, in fact, is quite complex to use. A document is a collection of nodes, each having a name, a text element, a collection of attributes, and a collection of child nodes. Each collection of nodes allows accessing elements by position or searching them by name. Notice that the text within the tags of a node, if any, is rendered as a child of the node and listed in its collection of child nodes. The root node has some extra methods for creating new nodes, values, or attributes.

With Delphi's XMLDocument, you can actually work at two different levels:

- At a lower level, you can use the DOMDocument property (of the IDOMDocument interface type) to access a standard W3C Document Object Model interface. The official DOM is defined in the xmldom unit, and includes interfaces like IDOMNode, IDOMNodeList,

`IDOMAttr`, `IDOMElement`, and `IDOMText`. With the official DOM interfaces, Delphi supports a lower-level but standard programming model. Notice that the actual DOM implementation will be the one indicated by the XMLDocument component.

- As a higher-level alternative, the XMLDocument component implements also the `IXMLDocument` interface. This is a custom DOM-like interface defined by Borland in the XMLIntf unit and comprising interfaces like `IXMLNode`, `IXMLNodeList`, and `IXMLNodeCollection`. This Borland interface simplifies some of the DOM operations by replacing multiple method calls, which are repeated quite often in sequence, with a single property or method.

In the following examples (particularly the DomCreate demo), I'll use both approaches so you can have a better idea of the practical differences among the two approaches.

An XML Document in a TreeView

The starting point is generally loading a document from a file or creating it from a string, but you can also start with a brand new document. As a first example of the use of the DOM, I've built a program that can load an XML document into a DOM and show its structure in a TreeView control. I've also added to the program, called XmlDomTree on the companion CD, a few buttons with sample code used to access to the elements of a sample file, as an example of accessing the DOM data. Loading the document is actually quite simple, while showing it in a tree requires a recursive function that navigates the nodes and subnodes. Here is the code of the two methods:

```
procedure TFormXmlTree.btnLoadClick(Sender: TObject);
begin
  OpenDialog1.InitialDir := ExtractFilePath (Application.ExeName);
  if OpenDialog1.Execute then
  begin
    XMLDocument1.LoadFromFile(OpenDialog1.FileName);
    Treeview1.Items.Clear;
    DomToTree (XMLDocument1.DocumentElement, nil);
    TreeView1.FullExpand;
  end;
end;

procedure TFormXmlTree.DomToTree (XmlNode: IXMLNode; TreeNode: TTreeNode);
var
  I: Integer;
  NewTreeNode: TTreeNode;
  NodeText: string;
  AttrNode: IXMLNode;
begin
  // skip text nodes and other special cases
```

```
if not (XmlNode.NodeType = ntElement) then
  Exit;
// add the node itself
NodeText := XmlNode.NodeName;
if XmlNode.IsTextElement then
  NodeText := NodeText + ' = ' + XmlNode.NodeValue;
NewTreeNode := TreeView1.Items.AddChild(TreeNode, NodeText);
// add attributes
for I := 0 to xmlNode.AttributeNodes.Count - 1 do
begin
  AttrNode := xmlNode.AttributeNodes.Nodes[I];
  TreeView1.Items.AddChild(NewTreeNode,
    '[' + AttrNode.NodeName + ' = "' + AttrNode.Text + '"]');
end;
// add each child node
if XmlNode.HasChildNodes then
  for I := 0 to xmlNode.ChildNodes.Count - 1 do
    DomToTree (xmlNode.ChildNodes.Nodes [I], NewTreeNode);
end;
```

This code is quite interesting, as it highlights some of the operations you can do with a DOM. First of all, each node has a NodeType property that you can use to determine whether the node is an element, attribute, text node, or special entity (such as CDATA and others). Another aspect is that you cannot access the textual representation of the node, its NodeValue, unless it has a text element (notice that the text node will be skipped, as per the initial test). After displaying the name of the item, and then the text value if available, the program (Figure 23.2) shows the content of each attribute directly and of each subnode calling the DomToTree method recursively.

FIGURE 23.2:

The XmlDomTree example can open a generic XML document and show it inside a TreeView common control.

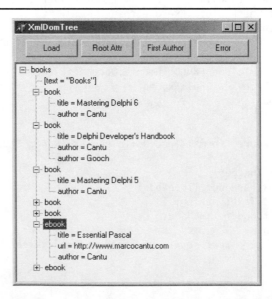

Once you have loaded the sample document that accompanies the XmlDomTree program (and shown in Listing 23.1) into the XMLDocument component, you can use the various methods to access generic nodes, as in tree-building code above, or fetch specific elements. For example, you can grab the value of the attribute *text* of the root node by writing:

```
XMLDocument1.DocumentElement.Attributes ['text']
```

Notice that if there is no attribute called *text*, the call will fail with a rather generic error message, "Invalid variant type conversion," which helps neither you nor the end user to understand what's wrong. If you need to access to the first attribute of the root without knowing its name, you can use the following more generic code:

```
XMLDocument1.DocumentElement.AttributeNodes.Nodes[0].NodeValue
```

To access the actual nodes, you use a similar technique, possibly taking advantage of the ChildValues array. This is a Delphi extension to the DOM, which allows you to pass as parameter either the name of the element or its numeric position:

```
XMLDocument1.DocumentElement.ChildNodes.Nodes[1].ChildValues['author']
```

This code gets the (first) author of the second book. I cannot use the ChildValues['book'] expression, as there are multiple nodes with the same name under the root node.

Listing 23.1: The sample XML document used by examples in this chapter

```xml
<?xml version="1.0" encoding="UTF-8"?>
<books text="Books">
  <book>
    <title>Mastering Delphi 6</title>
    <author>Cantu</author>
  </book>
  <book>
    <title>Delphi Developer's Handbook</title>
    <author>Cantu</author>
    <author>Gooch</author>
  </book>
  <book>
    <title>Mastering Delphi 5</title>
    <author>Cantu</author>
  </book>
  <book>
    <title>Delphi COM Programming</title>
    <author>Harmon</author>
  </book>
  <book>
    <title>Thinking in C++</title>
    <author>Eckel</author>
  </book>
  <ebook>
    <title>Essential Pascal</title>
```

```
      <url>http://www.marcocantu.com</url>
      <author>Cantu</author>
   </ebook>
   <ebook>
      <title>Thinking in Java</title>
      <url>http://www.mindview.com</url>
      <author>Eckel</author>
   </ebook>
</books>
```

Creating Documents Using the DOM

Although I mentioned earlier that you can create an XML document by chaining together some strings, this is far from a robust technique. Using a DOM to create a document ensures that the XML will be well formed. Also, if the DOM has a schema definition attached, you can validate the structure of the document while adding data to it.

To highlight different cases of document creation, I've built the DomCreate example (a program I originally created with the Xerces DOM from the Apache group and changed slightly for supporting Delphi's XMLDocument). This program can create XML documents within the DOM, showing the text of them on a memo and optionally in a TreeView.

> **TIP**
>
> The XMLDocument component uses the **doAutoIndent** option to improve the output of the XML text to the memo by formatting the XML in a slightly better way. You can choose the type of indentation by setting the **NodeIndentStr** property. For formatting a generic XML text, you can also use the global **FormatXMLData** function using the default setting (2 spaces) as indentation. Oddly, there doesn't seem a way to pass a different parameter to the function.

The first button of the form, Simple, creates some simple XML text using the low-level, official DOM interfaces. The program calls the `createElement` method of the document for each node, adding them as children of other nodes:

```
procedure TForm1.btnSimpleClick(Sender: TObject);
var
  iXml: IDOMDocument;
  iRoot, iNode, iNode2, iChild, iAttribute: IDOMNode;
begin
  // empty the document
  XMLDoc.Active := False;
  XMLDoc.XML.Text := '';
  XMLDoc.Active := True;

  // root
  iXml := XmlDoc.DOMDocument;
  iRoot := iXml.appendChild (iXml.createElement ('xml'));
  // node "test"
  iNode := iRoot.appendChild (iXml.createElement ('test'));
```

```
  iNode.appendChild (iXml.createElement ('test2'));
  iChild := iNode.appendChild (iXml.createElement ('test3'));
  iChild.appendChild (iXml.createTextNode('simple value'));
  iNode.insertBefore (iXml.createElement ('test4'), iChild);

  // node replication
  iNode2 := iNode.cloneNode (True);
  iRoot.appendChild (iNode2);

  // add an attribute
  iAttribute := iXml.createAttribute ('color');
  iAttribute.nodeValue := 'red';
  iNode2.attributes.setNamedItem (iAttribute);

  // show XML in memo
  Memo1.Lines.Text := FormatXMLData (XMLDoc.XML.Text);
end;
```

Notice that text nodes are added explicitly, attributes are created with a specific create call, and that the code uses cloneNode to replicate an entire branch of the tree. Overall, the code is quite cumbersome to write, but after a while you might get used to this style. The effect of the program is visible (formatted in the memo and in the tree) in Figure 23.3.

FIGURE 23.3:

The DomCreate example can generate various types of XML documents using a DOM.

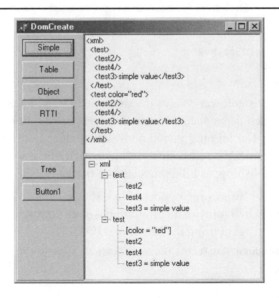

The second example of DOM creation relates to a dataset. I've added to the form a BDE Table component (but any other dataset would have done) and added to a button the call to my custom DataSetToDOM procedure, like this:

```
DataSetToDOM ('customers', 'customer', XMLDoc, Table1);
```

The `DataSetToDOM` procedure creates a root node with the text of the first parameter, then grabs each record of the dataset, defines a node with the second parameter, and adds a subnode for each field of the record, all using extremely generic code:

```
procedure DataSetToDOM (RootName, RecordName: string; XMLDoc: TXMLDocument;
  DataSet: TDataSet);
var
  iNode, iChild: IXMLNode;
  i: Integer;
begin
  DataSet.Open;
  DataSet.First;
  // root
  XMLDoc.DocumentElement := XMLDoc.CreateNode (RootName);

  // add table data
  while not DataSet.EOF do
  begin
    // add a node for each record
    iNode := XMLDoc.DocumentElement.AddChild (RecordName);
    for I := 0 to DataSet.FieldCount - 1 do
    begin
      // add an element for each field
      iChild := iNode.AddChild (DataSet.Fields[i].FieldName);
      iChild.Text := DataSet.Fields[i].AsString;
    end;
    DataSet.Next;
  end;
end;
```

The preceding code uses the simplified DOM access interfaces provided by Borland, which include an `AddChild` node that creates the subnode, and the direct access to the `Text` property for defining a child node with textual content. This apparently simple routine extracts an XML representation of your dataset, also opening up a lot of opportunities for Web publishing, as I'll discuss later in the section on XSL.

Another interesting opportunity is the generation of XML documents describing Delphi objects. The DomCreate program has a button used to describe a few selected properties of an object, again using the low-level DOM:

```
procedure AddAttr (iNode: IDOMNode; Name, Value: string);
var
  iAttr: IDOMNode;
begin
  iAttr := iNode.ownerDocument.createAttribute (name);
  iAttr.nodeValue := Value;
  iNode.attributes.setNamedItem (iAttr);
end;
```

```
procedure TForm1.btnObjectClick(Sender: TObject);
var
  iXml: IDOMDocument;
  iRoot: IDOMNode;
begin
  // empty the document
  XMLDoc.Active := False;
  XMLDoc.XML.Text := '';
  XMLDoc.Active := True;

  // root
  iXml := XmlDoc.DOMDocument;
  iRoot := iXml.appendChild (iXml.createElement ('Button1'));

  // a few properties as attributes (might also be nodes)
  AddAttr (iRoot, 'Name', Button1.Name);
  AddAttr (iRoot, 'Caption', Button1.Caption);
  AddAttr (iRoot, 'Font.Name', Button1.Font.Name);
  AddAttr (iRoot, 'Left', IntToStr (Button1.Left));
  AddAttr (iRoot, 'Hint', Button1.Hint);

  // show XML in memo
  Memo1.Lines := XmlDoc.XML;
end;
```

Of course, it is more interesting to have a generic technique capable of saving the properties of each Delphi component (or persistent object, to be more precise), recursing on persistent subobjects and indicating the names of referenced components. This is what I've done in the ComponentToDOM procedure, which uses the low-level RTTI information provided by the TypInfo unit, including the extraction of the list of the properties of a component. Once more, the program uses the simplified Delphi XML interfaces:

```
procedure ComponentToDOM (iNode: IXmlNode; Comp: TPersistent);
var
  nProps, i: Integer;
  PropList: PPropList;
  Value: Variant;
  newNode: IXmlNode;
begin
  // get list of properties
  nProps := GetTypeData (Comp.ClassInfo)^.PropCount;
  GetMem (PropList, nProps * SizeOf(Pointer));
  try
    GetPropInfos (Comp.ClassInfo, PropList);
    for i := 0 to nProps - 1 do
    begin
      Value := GetPropValue (Comp, PropList [i].Name);
      NewNode := iNode.AddChild(PropList [i].Name);
```

```
        NewNode.Text := Value;
        if (PropList [i].PropType^.Kind = tkClass) and (Value <> 0) then
          if TObject (Integer(Value)) is TComponent then
            NewNode.Text := TComponent (Integer(Value)).Name
          else
            // TPersistent but not TComponent: recurse
            ComponentToDOM (newNode, TObject (Integer(Value)) as TPersistent);
    end;
  finally
    FreeMem (PropList);
  end;
end;
```

These two lines of code, in this case, trigger the creation of the XML document (visible in Figure 23.4):

```
XMLDoc.DocumentElement := XMLDoc.CreateNode(self.ClassName);
ComponentToDOM (XMLDoc.DocumentElement, self);
```

FIGURE 23.4:

The XML generated to describe the form of the DomCreate program. Notice (in the tree and in the memo text) that properties of class types are further expanded.

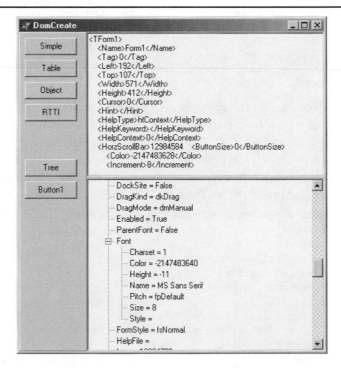

XML Data Binding Interfaces

We have seen that working with the DOM to access or generate a document is rather tedious, because you must use positional information and not logical access to the data. Also, handling series of repeated nodes of different possible types (as in the XML sample of Listing 23.1, describing books) is far from simple. Moreover, using a DOM, you can create any well-formed document, but (unless you use a validating DOM) you can add any subnode to any node, coming up with almost useless documents, as no one else will be able to manage them.

To solve these issues, Borland has added to Delphi 6 an XML Data Binding Wizard, which can examine an XML document or a document definition (a schema, a DTD, or another type of definition) and generate a set of interfaces for manipulating the document. These interfaces are specific to the document and its structure, and allow you to have more readable code, but are certainly less generic as far as the types of documents you can handle with them (and this is far more positive than it might sound at first).

You can activate the XML Data Binding Wizard by using the corresponding icon in the first page of the New Items dialog box of the IDE or by double-clicking directly on the XMLDocument component. (What is quite odd is that the corresponding command is not in the local menu of the component.)

After a first page where you can select a input file, this wizard shows you the structure of the document graphically, as you can see in Figure 23.5 for the sample XML file from Listing 23.1. In this page, you can give a name to each entity of the generated interfaces, in case you don't like the defaults suggested by the wizard. You can actually also change the rules used by the wizard to generate the names, an extended flexibility I'd like to have in other areas of the Delphi IDE. The final page gives you a preview of the generated interfaces and offers options for generating schemas and other definition files.

FIGURE 23.5:

Delphi's XML Data Binding Wizard can examine the structure of a document or a schema (or another document definition) to create a set of interfaces for simplified and direct access to the DOM data.

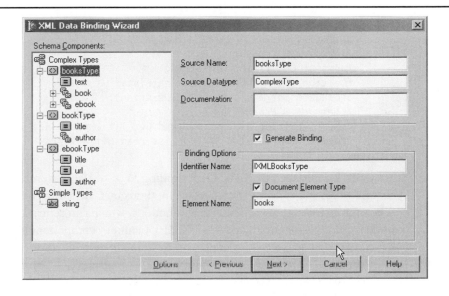

For the sample XML file with the author names, the XML Data Binding Wizard generates an interface of the root node, and four interfaces for the two lists of different elements and the actual elements (books and e-books). These are a few excerpts of the generated code, available in the XmlIntfDefinition unit of the XmlInterface example:

```
type
  IXMLBooksType = interface(IXMLNode)
    ['{C9A9FB63-47ED-4F27-8ABA-E71F30BA7F11}']
    { Property Accessors }
    function Get_Text: WideString;
    function Get_Book: IXMLBookTypeList;
    function Get_Ebook: IXMLEbookTypeList;
    procedure Set_Text(Value: WideString);
    { Methods & Properties }
    property Text: WideString read Get_Text write Set_Text;
    property Book: IXMLBookTypeList read Get_Book;
    property Ebook: IXMLEbookTypeList read Get_Ebook;
  end;

  IXMLBookTypeList = interface(IXMLNodeCollection)
    ['{3449E8C4-3222-47B8-B2B2-38EE504790B6}']
    { Methods & Properties }
    function Add: IXMLBookType;
    function Insert(const Index: Integer): IXMLBookType;
    function Get_Item(Index: Integer): IXMLBookType;
    property Items[Index: Integer]: IXMLBookType read Get_Item; default;
  end;

  IXMLBookType = interface(IXMLNode)
    ['{26BF5C51-9247-4D1A-8584-24AE68969935}']
    { Property Accessors }
    function Get_Title: WideString;
    function Get_Author: IXMLString_List;
    procedure Set_Title(Value: WideString);
    { Methods & Properties }
    property Title: WideString read Get_Title write Set_Title;
    property Author: IXMLString_List read Get_Author;
  end;
```

For each interface, the XML Data Binding Wizard also generates an implementation class that provides the code for the interface methods by translating the requests into DOM calls. The unit includes three initialization functions, which can return the interface of the root node from a document loaded in an XMLDocument component (or a component providing a generic IXMLDocument interface), or return one from a file, or create a brand new DOM:

```
function Getbooks(Doc: IXMLDocument): IXMLBooksType;
function Loadbooks(const FileName: WideString): IXMLBooksType;
function Newbooks: IXMLBooksType;
```

After generating these interfaces using the wizard, in the XmlInterface example, I've repeated XML document access code similar to the XmlDomTree example, but much simpler to write (and to read). For example, you can get the attribute of the root node by writing:

```
procedure TForm1.btnAttrClick(Sender: TObject);
var
  Books: IXMLBooksType;
begin
  Books := Getbooks (XmlDocument1);
  ShowMessage (Books.Text);
end;
```

Simple, isn't it? It is even simpler if you recall that while typing this code, Delphi's code insight can help by listing the available properties of each node, thanks to the fact that the parser can read in the interface definitions (while it cannot understand the format of a generic XML document). Accessing a node of one of the sublists is a matter of writing one of the following statements (possibly the second with the default array property):

```
Books.Book.Items[1].Title   // full
Books.Book[1].Title          // further simplified
```

Similarly simplified code can be used to generate new documents or add new elements, also thanks to the customized Add method is available in each list-based interface. Again, if you don't have a predefined structure for the XML document, as in the dataset-based and RTTI-based examples of the previous demonstration, you won't be able to use this approach.

Validation and Schemas in Short

The XML Data Binding Wizard can work from existing schemas or generate one for an XML document (and eventually save it in a file with the .XDB extension). But what is a schema for, and what does it look like? An XML document describes some data, but to exchange this data among companies it has to stick to some agreed structure. A schema is a document definition, against which a document can be checked for correctness, an operation usually indicated with the term *validation*.

The first—and still very widespread—type of validation available for XML was *document type definitions (DTDs)*. These documents describe the structure of the XML but cannot really define the possible content of each node. Also, DTDs are not XML document themselves but use a different, very awkward notation.

At the end of year 2000, the W3C approved the first official draft of XML *schemas* (already available in an incompatible version called XML-Data within Microsoft's DOM). An XML schema is itself a XML document, one that can validate both the structure of the XML tree and the content of the node. A schema is based on the use and definition of simple and complex data types, similar to what happens in an OOP programming language.

A schema defines complex types, indicating for each the possible nodes, their optional sequence (sequence, all), the number of occurrences for each subnode (minOccurs, maxOccurs), and the data type of each specific element. Here is the schema defined by the XML Data Binding Wizard for the usual sample books file:

```xml
<?xml version="1.0"?>
<xs:schema xmlns:xs="http://www.w3.org/2001/XMLSchema"
  xmlns:xdb="http://www.borland.com/schemas/delphi/6.0/XMLDataBinding">
  <xs:element name="books" type="booksType"/>
  <xs:complexType name="booksType">
    <xs:annotation>
      <xs:appinfo xdb:docElement="books"/>
    </xs:annotation>
    <xs:sequence>
      <xs:element name="book" type="bookType" maxOccurs="unbounded"/>
      <xs:element name="ebook" type="ebookType" maxOccurs="unbounded"/>
    </xs:sequence>
    <xs:attribute name="text" type="xs:string"/>
  </xs:complexType>
  <xs:complexType name="bookType">
    <xs:annotation>
      <xs:appinfo xdb:repeated="True"/>
    </xs:annotation>
    <xs:sequence>
      <xs:element name="title" type="xs:string"/>
      <xs:element name="author" type="xs:string" maxOccurs="unbounded"/>
    </xs:sequence>
  </xs:complexType>
  <xs:complexType name="ebookType">
    <xs:annotation>
      <xs:appinfo xdb:repeated="True"/>
    </xs:annotation>
    <xs:sequence>
      <xs:element name="title" type="xs:string"/>
      <xs:element name="url" type="xs:string"/>
      <xs:element name="author" type="xs:string"/>
    </xs:sequence>
  </xs:complexType>
</xs:schema>
```

NOTE   As I write, there are still very few DOM implementations that can be used to validate a document against an XML schema. Apache Xerces DOM has good support for schemas. Another tool I've used for validation is XSV (XML Schema Validator), an open source attempt at a conformant schema-aware processor, which can be used either directly via the Web or after downloading a command-line executable.

Using the SAX API

The Simple API for XML, or SAX, doesn't create a tree for the XML nodes, but simply parses the node-firing events for each node, attribute, value, and so on. Because it doesn't keep the document in memory, using the SAX allows managing much larger documents. Its approach is also very useful for one-time examination of a document, or retrieval of specific information. This is a list of events fired by the SAX:

- `StartDocument` and `EndDocument` for the entire document
- `StartElement` and `EndElement` for each node
- `Characters` for the text within the nodes

It is quite common to use a stack to handle the current path within the nodes tree, and push and pop elements to and from the stack for every `StartElement` and `EndElement` event.

Delphi 6 does not include specific support for the SAX interface, but this can be easily obtained by importing Microsoft's XML support (the MSXML library). In particular for the SaxDemo1 example I've used version 2 of MSXML: the Pascal version of its type library is available within the source code of the program, but you must have the COM library registered on your computer to run the program successfully.

To use the SAX, you have to install a SAX event handler within a SAX reader, then load a file and parse it. I've used the SAX reader interface provided by MSXML for VB programmers. In fact, the official (C++) interface had a few errors in its type library that prevented Delphi from importing it properly (the newer MSXML 3 might have fixed this issue by the time you read this).

In the main form of the SaxDemo1 example, I've declared:

```
sax: IVBSAXXMLReader;
```

In the `FormCreate` method, this is initialized with the actual COM object:

```
sax := CreateComObject (CLASS_SAXXMLReader) as IVBSAXXMLReader;
sax.ErrorHandler := TMySaxErrorHandler.Create;
```

The code also sets an error handler, which is a class implementing a specific interface, IVB-SAXErrorHandler, with three methods that are called depending on the severity of the problem: `error`, `fatalError`, and `ignorableWarning`.

Simplifying the code a little, the SAX parser is activated by calling the `parseURL` method after assigning a content handler to it:

```
sax.ContentHandler := TMySaxHandler.Create;
sax.parseURL (filename)
```

So the code ultimately resides in the TMySaxHandler class, which has the SAX events. Because I have multiple SAX content handlers in this example, I've written a base class with the core code and a few specialized versions for specific processing; this is the code of the base class, which implements both the IDispatch and IVBSAXContentHandler interfaces:

```
type
  TMySaxHandler = class (TInterfacedObject, IVBSAXContentHandler)
  protected
    stack: TStringList;
  public
    constructor Create;
    destructor Destroy; override;
    // IDispatch
    function GetTypeInfoCount(out Count: Integer): HResult; stdcall;
    function GetTypeInfo(Index, LocaleID: Integer; out TypeInfo):
      HResult; stdcall;
    function GetIDsOfNames(const IID: TGUID; Names: Pointer;
      NameCount, LocaleID: Integer; DispIDs: Pointer): HResult; stdcall;
    function Invoke(DispID: Integer; const IID: TGUID; LocaleID: Integer;
      Flags: Word; var Params; VarResult, ExcepInfo, ArgErr: Pointer):
      HResult; stdcall;
    // IVBSAXContentHandler
    procedure Set_documentLocator(const Param1: IVBSAXLocator);
      virtual; safecall;
    procedure startDocument; virtual; safecall;
    procedure endDocument; virtual; safecall;
    procedure startPrefixMapping(var strPrefix: WideString;
      var strURI: WideString); virtual; safecall;
    procedure endPrefixMapping(var strPrefix: WideString); virtual; safecall;
    procedure startElement(var strNamespaceURI: WideString;
      var strLocalName: WideString; var strQName: WideString;
      const oAttributes: IVBSAXAttributes); virtual; safecall;
    procedure endElement(var strNamespaceURI: WideString;
      var strLocalName: WideString; var strQName: WideString);
      virtual; safecall;
    procedure characters(var strChars: WideString); virtual; safecall;
    procedure ignorableWhitespace(var strChars: WideString);
      virtual; safecall;
    procedure processingInstruction(var strTarget: WideString;
      var strData: WideString); virtual; safecall;
    procedure skippedEntity(var strName: WideString); virtual; safecall;
  end;
```

The most interesting portion, of course, is the final list of SAX events. All this base class does is emit information to a log when the parser starts (startDocument) and finishes (endDocument) and keep track of the current node and all of its parent nodes with a stack:

```
// TMySaxHandler.startElement
stack.Add (strLocalName);
// TMySaxHandler.endElement
```

```
      stack.Delete (stack.Count - 1);
```

An actual implementation is provided by the `TMySimpleSaxHandler` class, which overrides the `startElement` event triggered for any new node to output the current position in the tree with the statement:

```
   Log.Add (strLocalName + '(' + stack.CommaText + ')');
```

The second method of the class is the `characters` event, triggered when a node value (or a test node) is encountered, to output its content:

```
procedure TMySimpleSaxHandler.characters(var strChars: WideString);
var
   str: WideString;
begin
   inherited;
   str := RemoveWhites (strChars);
   if (str <> '') then
      Log.Add ('Text: ' + str);
end;
```

The two methods produce the combined effect of Figure 23.6.

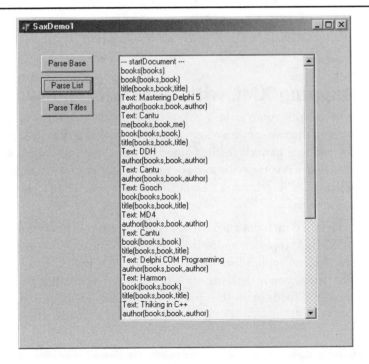

This is still a generic parsing operation affecting the entire XML file. The second derived SAX content handler class, instead, refers to the specific structure of the XML document, extracting only nodes of a give type. In particular, the program looks for nodes of the *title* type. When a node has this type (in startElement), the class sets the isbook Boolean variable. The text value of the node is considered only right after a node of this type is encountered:

```
procedure TMyBooksListSaxHandler.startElement(var strNamespaceURI,
  strLocalName, strQName: WideString; const oAttributes: IVBSAXAttributes);
begin
  inherited;
  isbook := (strLocalName = 'title');
end;

procedure TMyBooksListSaxHandler.characters(var strChars: WideString);
var
  str: string;
begin
  inherited;
  if isbook then
  begin
    str := RemoveWhites (strChars);
    if (str <> '') then
      Log.Add (stack.CommaText + ': ' + str);
  end;
end;
```

Mapping XML with Transformations

There is one more technique you can use in Delphi 6 to handle at least some XML documents. You can create a *transformation* to translate the XML of a generic document into the format used natively by the ClientDataSet component when saving data to a MyBase XML file. In the reverse direction, another transformation can turn a dataset available within a ClientDataSet (through a DataSetProvider component) into a XML file of a required format (or schema).

Delphi 6 includes a wizard to generate such transformations. Called XML Mapping Tool, or XML Mapper for short, it is invokable from the Tools menu of the IDE or executed as a stand-alone application. The XML Mapper, visible in Figure 23.7, is a design-time helper that assists you in defining transformation rules between the nodes of a generic XML document and fields of the data packet of the ClientDataSet.

FIGURE 23.7:

The XML Mapper shows the two sides of a transformation to define a mapping among them (with the rules indicated in the central portion).

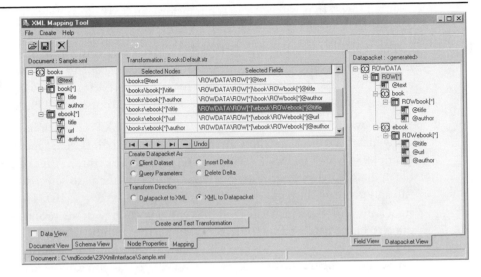

The XML Mapper windows has three areas:

- On the left is the XML document section, which displays information about the structure of the XML document (and eventually its data, if the related check box is active) in the Document View or an XML schema in the Schema View, depending on the selected tab.

- On the right is the data packet section, which displays information about the metadata in the data packet, either in the Field View indicating the dataset structure or in the Datapacket View reporting the XML structure. Notice, in fact, that the XML Mapper can also open files in the native ClientDataSet format.

- The central portion of the windows is used by the mapping section. This contains two pages as well: one for Mapping, where you can see the correspondences between selected elements of the two sides that will be part of the mapping, and one for Node Properties, where you can modify the data types and other details of each of the possible mappings.

The Mapping page of the central pane also hosts the local menu used to generate the transformation, while each other pane and view has specific local menus you can use to perform the various actions (beside the few commands in the main menu).

You can use XML Mapper to map an existing schema (or extract it from a document) to a brand new data packet, an existing data packet to a new schema or document, or an existing data packet into an existing XML document (if a match is reasonable). Besides converting the data of an XML file into a data packet, you can also convert to a delta packet of the ClientDataSet. This is useful for merging a document to an existing table, as if a user had inserted them. In particular, you can transform an XML document into a delta packet for records to be modified, deleted, or inserted.

The result of using the XML Mapper is one or more transformation files, each representing a one-way conversion (so you need at least two transformation files to convert data back and forth). These transformation files are then used at design time and at run time by the XMLTransform, XMLTransformProvider, and XMLTransformClient components.

As an example, I've tried opening the usual "books" XML, which has a structure that doesn't easily match a table, since there are two lists of values of different types (I've skipped easier examples in which the XML has a plain rectangular structure). After opening the Sample.XML file in the XML Document section, I've used its local menu to select all of its elements (Select All) and to create the data packet (Create Datapacket From XML). This automatically fills the right pane with the data packet and the central portion with the proposed transformation. You can also immediately view its effect in a sample program by selecting the Create And Test Transformation button. This opens a generic application that can load a document into the dataset using the transformation you've just created, as you can see in Figure 23.8.

FIGURE 23.8:

The Create and Test Transformation button of the XML Mapper tool allows you to immediately verify the effect of the transformations you are building

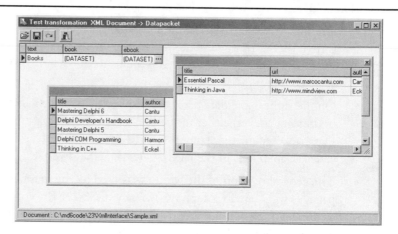

In this specific case, you can see that the XML Mapper generates a table with two dataset fields, one of each possible list of subelements. This was the only possible standard solution, as the two sublists have different structures, and is the only solution that allows you to edit the data in a DBGrid attached to the ClientDataSet and save it back to a complete XML file, as demonstrated by the XmlMapping example. This program is basically a Windows-based editor of a complex XML document.

It uses a TransformProvider component, with two transformation files attached, to read in an XML document and make it available to a ClientDataSet. As the name suggests, in fact, this component is a dataset provider. To build the user interface, I haven't connected the

ClientDataSet directly to a grid, as it has a single record with a text field plus two detailed datasets. For this reason, I've added to the program two more ClientDataSet components, attached to the dataset fields and connected to two DBGrid controls. This is probably easier to understand by looking at its DFM source code in the following excerpt and at its output in Figure 23.9.

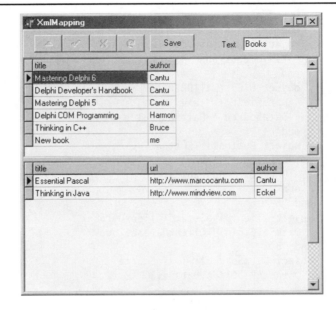

```
object Form1: TForm1
  Caption = 'XmlMapping'
  object XMLTransformProvider1: TXMLTransformProvider
    TransformRead.TransformationFile = 'BooksDefault.xtr'
    TransformWrite.TransformationFile = 'BooksDefaultToXml.xtr'
    XMLDataFile = 'Sample.xml'
  end
  object ClientDataSet1: TClientDataSet
    ProviderName = 'XMLTransformProvider1'
    object ClientDataSet1text: TStringField
      FieldName = 'text'
      Size = 5
    end
    object ClientDataSet1book: TDataSetField
      FieldName = 'book'
    end
    object ClientDataSet1ebook: TDataSetField
      FieldName = 'ebook'
    end
  end
end
```

```
        object DataSource1: TDataSource
          DataSet = ClientDataSet1
        end
        object Panel1: TPanel
          Align = alTop
          object Label2: TLabel
            Caption = 'Text'
            FocusControl = DBEdit2
          end
          object DBNavigator1: TDBNavigator
            VisibleButtons = [nbEdit, nbPost, nbCancel, nbRefresh]
          end
          object DBEdit2: TDBEdit
            DataField = 'text'
            DataSource = DataSource1
          end
          object Button1: TButton
            Caption = 'Save'
            OnClick = Button1Click
          end
        end
        object ClientDataSet2: TClientDataSet
          DataSetField = ClientDataSet1book
        end
        object DataSource2: TDataSource
          DataSet = ClientDataSet2
        end
        object DBGrid1: TDBGrid
          Align = alTop
          DataSource = DataSource2
        end
        object Splitter1: TSplitter
          Cursor = crVSplit
          Align = alTop
        end
        object ClientDataSet3: TClientDataSet
          DataSetField = ClientDataSet1ebook
        end
        object DataSource3: TDataSource
          DataSet = ClientDataSet3
          Left = 232
          Top = 224
        end
        object DBGrid2: TDBGrid
          Align = alClient
          DataSource = DataSource3
        end
      end
```

This program allows you to edit the data of the various sublists of nodes, within the grids, modifying them but also adding or deleting records. As you apply the changes to the dataset (clicking the Save button, which calls `ApplyUdpates`), the transform provider saves an updated version of the file to disk.

As an alternative approach, you can also create transformations that map only portions of the XML document into a dataset. As an example, see the `BooksOnly.xtr` file in the folder of the XmlMapping example. This can be useful for viewing the data, but the modified XML document you'll generate will have a different structure and content from the original, including only the portion you've selected. So this can be useful for viewing the data, but not for editing it.

NOTE   It is not surprising that the transformation files are themselves XML documents, as you can see by opening one in the editor. This XML document uses a custom format.

At the opposite side, we can see how a transformation can be used to take a database table or the result of a query and produce an XML file with a more readable format than the one provided by default by the ClientDataSet persistence mechanism. To build the MapTable example, I've placed a table component on a form and attached a DataSetProvider to it and a ClientDataSet to the provider. After opening the table and the client dataset, I saved its content to an XML file.

At that point, I opened the XML Mapper, loaded the data packet file into it, selected all of the data packet nodes (with the Select All command of its local menu) and invoked the Create XML From Datapacket command. In the following dialog box, I accepted the default name mappings for fields and only changed the suggested name for record nodes (*ROW*) into something more readable (*Customer*). If you now test the transformation, the XML Mapper will display the contents of the resulting XML document in a custom tree view, as you can see in Figure 23.10.

After saving the transformation file, I was ready to resume developing the program, adding to it another provider that takes the data from the ClientDataSet (as a user might edit in on an attached DBGrid before transforming it) and makes it available to an XMLTransform-Client component. This component has the transformation file connected to it, but not an XML file. In fact, clicking the button shows the XML document within a memo (after a formatting it) instead of saving it to a file, something you can do by calling the `GetDataAsXml` method (even if the Help file is far from clear about this):

```
procedure TForm1.btnMapClick(Sender: TObject);
begin
  Memo1.Lines.Text := FormatXmlData(XMLTransformClient1.GetDataAsXml(''));
end;
```

FIGURE 23.10:

When you convert from a data packet to an XML document, the XML Mapper can preview the document in a tree structure.

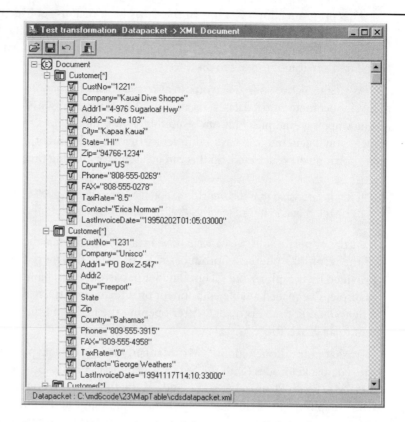

FIGURE 23.10:

When you convert from a data packet to an XML document, the XML Mapper can preview the document in a tree structure.

This is the only code of the program visible at run time in Figure 23.11. The application has much simpler code than the DomCreate example I used to generate a similar XML document, but requires the design-time definition of the transformation. The DomCreate example, instead, could work on any dataset at run time, without any connection to a specific table, as it had some rather generic code. In theory, it is possible to produce similar dynamic mappings by using the events of the generic XMLTransform component, but I find it much easier to use the DOM-based approach discussed earlier. Notice also that the `FormatXmlData` call produces much nicer output but slows down the program, because it involves loading the XML into a DOM.

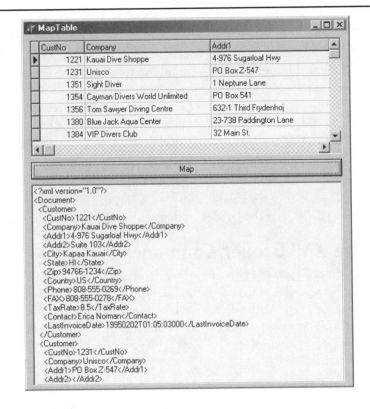

FIGURE 23.11:

The MapTable example can generate an XML document from a database table using a custom transformation file. You can see the original dataset in the DBGrid above and the resulting XML document in the memo control below

XML and Internet Express

Once you have defined the structure of an XML document, you might want to let users see and edit the data in a Windows application or over the Web. This second case is rather interesting, as Delphi provides specific support for it. Delphi 5 already included an architecture called Internet Express, which is now available in Delphi 6 as part of the WebSnap platform. WebSnap offers also support for XSL, which I'll discuss later.

In Chapter 17, "Multitier Database Applications with DataSnap," I discussed the development of DataSnap applications (formerly known as Midas applications). Internet Express provides a client component for this architecture, called XMLBroker, which can be used in place of a client dataset to retrieve data from a middle-tier DataSnap program and make it available to a specific type of page producer, called InetXpageProducer. You can use these components in a standard WebBroker application or in a WebSnap program. The idea behind Internet Express is that you write a Web server extension (CGI or ISAPI or Apache modules, as discussed in the preceding chapter), which in turn produces Web pages hooked to your DataSnap server. Your custom application acts as a DataSnap client and produces pages for a browser client. Internet Express offers the services required to build this custom application easily.

I know this sounds confusing, but Internet Express is a four-tier architecture: SQL server, application server (the DataSnap server), Web server with a custom application, and finally Web browser. Of course, you can place the database access components within the same application handling the HTTP request and generating the resulting HTML, as in a client/server solution. You can even access a local database or an XML file, in a single-tier structure.

In other words, Internet Express is a technology for building clients based on a browser, which lets you send the entire dataset to the client computer along with the HTML and some JavaScript for manipulating the XML and showing it into the user interface defined by the HTML. It is the JavaScript that enables the browser to show the data and manipulate it.

The XMLBroker Component

Internet Express uses multiple technologies to accomplish this. The DataSnap data packets are converted into the XML format, to let the program embed this data right into the HTML page for Web client-side manipulation. Actually, the Delta data packet is also represented in XML. These operations are performed by the XMLBroker component, which can handle XML and provide data to the new JavaScript components. Like the ClientDataSet, the XML-Broker has

- A MaxRecords property indicating the number of records to add to a single page

- A Params property hosting the parameters that components will forward to the remote query through the provider

- A WebDispatch property indicating the update request the broker responds to

The InetXPageProducer allows you to generate HTML forms from datasets, in a visual way similar to the development of an AdapterPageProducer user interface. Actually, the Internet Express architecture, the interfaces it uses internally, and some of its IDE editor can together be considered the parent of the WebSnap architecture. With the notable difference of generating scripts to be executed on the server side and on the client side, they both provide an editor for placing visual components and generating such scripts. A notable difference I'm personally not terribly happy about, though, is that the older Internet Express is more XML-oriented than newer WebSnap.

TIP   Another common feature of the InetXPageProducer and the AdapterPageProducer is the support for Cascading Style Sheets (CSS). These components have the two alternative Style and StylesFile properties for defining the CSS, and each visual element has a StyleRule property where you can select the style name.

JavaScript Support

To make the editing operations on the client side powerful, the InetXPageProducer uses special JavaScript components and code. Delphi embeds a rather large JavaScript library, which the browser will have to download. This might seem a nuisance, but it is the only way the browser interface (which is based on dynamic HTML) can be rich enough to support field constraints and other business rules with the browser. This is really impossible with plain HTML. The JavaScript files provided by Borland, and that you should make available on the Web site hosting the application, are the following:

File	Description
Xmldom.js	DOM-compatible XML parser (for browsers lacking native XML DOM support)
Xmldb.js	JavaScript classes for the HTML controls
Xmldisp.js	JavaScript classes for binding XML data with the HTML controls
Xmlerrdisp.js	Classes for reconciling errors
XmlShow.js	JavaScript functions to display data and delta packets (for debugging purposes)

HTML pages generated by Internet Express usually include references to these JavaScript files, such as:

```
<script language=Javascript type="text/javascript"
  src="IncludePathURL/xmldb.js"></script>
```

You can customize the JavaScript by adding code directly into the HTML pages or by creating a new Delphi components, written to fit with the Internet Express architecture that "emits" JavaScript code (possibly along with HTML). As an example, the sample TPrompt-QueryButton class of INetXCustom generates the following HTML and JavaScript code:

```
<script language=javascript type="text/javascript">
  function PromptSetField(input, msg) {
    var v = prompt(msg);
    if (v == null || v == "")
      return false;
    input.value = v
    return true;
  }
  var QueryForm3 = document.forms['QueryForm3'];
</script>
<input type=button value="Prompt..."
  onclick="if (PromptSetField(PromptResult, 'Enter some text\n'))
    QueryForm3.submit();">
```

TIP If you plan on using Internet Express, have a look at the INetXCustom extra demo components, available in the `\Demos\Midas\InternetExpress\INetXCustom` folder. Follow the detailed instructions in the `readme.txt` file for the installation of these components, which are provided by Borland with no support but allow you to add many more features to your Internet Express applications with little extra effort.

Of course, to deploy this architecture you don't need anything special on the client side, as any browser up to the HTML 4 standard can be used, on any operating system. The Web server, instead, must be a Win32 server (we're waiting for this technology to be available in Kylix) and you must deploy the DataSnap libraries on it (after paying the proper license fee to Borland, still not disclosed at this time).

Building a First Example

To better understand what I'm talking about, and as a way to cover some more technical details, let me try out a simple demo, called IeFirst. To avoid configuration issues, this is a CGI application accessing a dataset directly—in this case, a local table retrieved via the BDE. Later I'll show you how to turn an existing DataSnap Windows client to a browser-based interface. To build IeFirst, I've created a new CGI application and added to its data module a Table and a DataSetProvider. The next step is to add an XMLBroker component and connect it to the provider:

```
object Table1: TTable
  DatabaseName = 'DBDEMOS'
  TableName = 'employee.db'
end
object DataSetProvider1: TDataSetProvider
  DataSet = Table1
end
object XMLBroker1: TXMLBroker
  ProviderName = 'DataSetProvider1'
  WebDispatch.MethodType = mtAny
  WebDispatch.PathInfo = 'XMLBroker1'
  ReconcileProducer = PageProducer1
  OnGetResponse = XMLBroker1GetResponse
end
```

The `ReconcileProducer` property is required to show a proper error message in case of an update conflict. As we'll see later, one of the Delphi demos includes some custom code, but in this simple example I've simply connected a traditional PageProducer component with a generic HTML error message. After setting up the XML broker, you can add an InetXPage-Producer to the Web data module. This component has a standard HTML skeleton; I've customized to add a title to it, without touching the special tags:

```
<HTML><HEAD>
  <title>IeFirst</title>
</HEAD><BODY>
  <h1>Internet Express First Demo (IeFirst.exe)</h1>
  <#INCLUDES><#STYLES><#WARNINGS><#FORMS><#SCRIPT>
</BODY>
```

The special tags are automatically expanded using the JavaScript files of the directory specified by the IncludePathURL property. You *must* set this property to refer to the Web server directory where these files reside. You can find them in the \Delphi6\Source\WebMidas directory. The five tags have the following effect:

Tag	Effect
<#INCLUDES>	Generates the instructions to include the JavaScript libraries
<#STYLES>	Adds the embedded style sheet definition
<#WARNINGS>	Used at design time to show errors in the InetXPageProducer editor
<#FORMS>	Generates the HTML code produced by the components of the Web page
<#SCRIPT>	Adds a JavaScript block used to start up the client-side script

NOTE   The InetXPageProducer component handles also a few more internal tags. <#BODYELEMENTS> corresponds to all of the five tags of the predefined template. <#COMPONENT Name=WebComponent-Name> is part of the generated HTML code used to declare the components generated visually. <#DATAPACKET XMLBroker=BrokerName> is replaced with the actual XML of the data packet.

To customize the resulting HTML of the InetXPageProducer, you can use its editor, which again is similar to the one for WebSnap server-side scripting. Just double-click the InetXPage-Producer component, and Delphi opens up a window like the one in Figure 23.12 (with the final settings of the example). In this editor, you can create complex structures, starting with a query form, data form, or generic layout group. In the data form of my simple example, I've added a DataGrid and a DataNavigator component, without customizing them any further (an operation you do by adding child buttons, columns, and other objects, which fully replace the default ones).

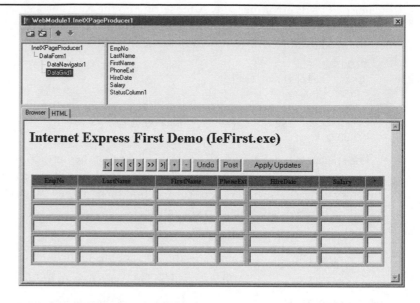

The DFM code for the InetXPageProducer and its internal components in my example is the following, where you can seen the core settings plus some limited graphical customizations:

```
object InetXPageProducer1: TInetXPageProducer
  IncludePathURL = '/jssource/'
  HTMLDoc.Strings = (...)
  object DataForm1: TDataForm
    object DataNavigator1: TDataNavigator
      XMLComponent = DataGrid1
      Custom = 'align="center"'
    end
    object DataGrid1: TDataGrid
      XMLBroker = XMLBroker1
      DisplayRows = 5
      TableAttributes.BgColor = 'Silver'
      TableAttributes.CellSpacing = 0
      TableAttributes.CellPadding = 2
      HeadingAttributes.BgColor = 'Aqua'
      object EmpNo: TTextColumn...
      object LastName: TTextColumn...
      object FirstName: TTextColumn...
      object PhoneExt: TTextColumn...
      object HireDate: TTextColumn...
      object Salary: TTextColumn...
      object StatusColumn1: TStatusColumn...
    end
  end
end
```

But the value of these components is in the HTML (and JavaScript) code they generate, which you can preview by selecting the HTML tab of the InetXPageProducer editor. Here are a few portions of the definitions in the HTML, for the buttons, the data grid heading, and one if its cells:

```
// buttons
<table align="center">
  <tr><td colspan="2">
    <input type="button" value="|<"
      onclick='if (xml_ready) DataGrid1_Disp.first();'>
    <input type="button" value="<<"
      onclick='if (xml_ready) DataGrid1_Disp.pgup();'>
...
// data grid heading
<table cellspacing="0" cellpadding="2" border="1" bgcolor="silver">
  <tr bgcolor="aqua">
    <th>EmpNo</th>
    <th>LastName</th>
  ...
  </tr>
  <tr>
    // a data cell
    <td><div>
      <input type="text" name="EmpNo" size="10"
        onfocus='if(xml_ready)DataGrid1_Disp.xfocus(this);'
        onkeydown='if(xml_ready)DataGrid1_Disp.keys(this);'>
  </div></td>...
```

When the HTML generator is set up, you can go back to the Web data module, add an action to it, and connect the action with the InetXPageProducer via the Producer property. This should be enough to make the program work through a browser, as you can see in Figure 23.13.

If you look at the HTML file received by the browser, you'll find the table mentioned in the preceding definition, some JavaScript code here and there, and the database data in the data packet XML format. This data is assembled by the XML broker and passed to the producer component to be embedded in the HTML file. Notice that the number of records sent to the client depends on the XMLBroker, not on the number of lines in the grid. Once the XML data is sent to the browser, in fact, you can use the buttons of the navigator component to move around in the data without requiring further access to the server to fetch more. This is quite different from the paging behavior of WebSnap. Not that one is better than the other; this depends on the specific application you are building.

FIGURE 23.13:

The IeFirst application sends to the browser some HTML components, an entire XML document, and the JavaScript code to show the data in the visual components.

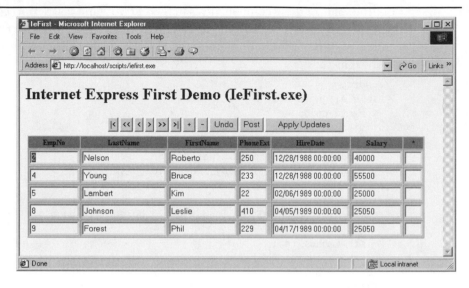

At the same time, the JavaScript classes in the system allow the user to type in new data, following the rules imposed by the JavaScript code hooked to dynamic HTML events. Notice that the grid, by default, has an extra asterisk column, indicating which records have been modified. The update data is collected in an XML data packet in the browser, and sent back to the server when the user clicks the Apply Updates button. At this point, the browser activates the action specified by the `WebDispath.PathInfo` property of the XMLBroker. There is no need to export this action from the Web data module, as this operation is automatic (although you can disable it by setting `WebDispath.Enable` to False).

The XMLBroker applies the changes to the server, returning the content of the provider connected to the `ReconcileProvider` property (or raising an exception if this is not defined). When everything works fine, the XMLBroker redirects the control to the main page that contains the data. However, I've experienced some problems with this technique, so the IeFirst example handles the `OnGetReponse`, indicating this is an update view:

```
procedure TWebModule1.XMLBroker1GetResponse(Sender: TObject;
  Request: TWebRequest; Response: TWebResponse; var Handled: Boolean);
begin
  Response.Content := '<h1>Updated</h1><p>' + InetXPageProducer1.Content;
  Handled := True;
end;
```

Master/Detail in Internet Express

My second Internet Express example goes a little beyond the basics by providing a master/detail data packet for Web browsing obtained through a DataSnap connection. The program uses the AppPlus server of Chapter 17, which defines the master/detail relationship between two tables. The dataset field embedded in the table will be transformed into a nested XML structure, delivering the same information.

The program uses a combination of XMLBroker, InetXPageProducer, and DCOMConnection. This time, I've customized the Web components, by adding a LayoutGroup component to obtain multiple columns, and I've also created fields to select the information to display. In Listing 23.2 are some snippets of the DFM file of this Web module: I've removed a lot of extra information, but I think it is worth looking at it.

Listing 23.2:   Portions of the DFM file for the IeMd example's Web module

```
object DCOMConnection1: TDCOMConnection
  Connected = False
  ServerName = 'AppSPlus.AppServerPlus'
end
object XMLBroker1: TXMLBroker
  ProviderName = 'ProviderCustomer'
  RemoteServer = DCOMConnection1
  WebDispatch.PathInfo = 'XMLBroker1'
end
object InetXPageProducer1: TInetXPageProducer
  IncludePathURL = '/jssource/'
  object DataForm1: TDataForm
    object LayoutGroup1: TLayoutGroup
      DisplayColumns = 2
      object DataNavigator1: TDataNavigator
        XMLComponent = FieldGroup1
        object FirstButton1: TFirstButton
          XMLComponent = FieldGroup1
          Caption = '|<'
        end
        object PriorButton1: TPriorButton
          XMLComponent = FieldGroup1
          Caption = '<'
        end
        object NextButton1: TNextButton
          XMLComponent = FieldGroup1
          Caption = '>'
        end
        ...
        object ApplyUpdatesButton1: TApplyUpdatesButton
          Caption = 'Apply Updates'
          XMLBroker = XMLBroker1
          XMLUseParent = True
        end
      end
      object FieldGroup1: TFieldGroup
        XMLBroker = XMLBroker1
```

```
              object CustNo: TFieldText
                DisplayWidth = 10
                Caption = 'CustNo'
                FieldName = 'CustNo'
              end
              object Company: TFieldText
                DisplayWidth = 30
                Caption = 'Company'
                FieldName = 'Company'
              end
              ...
            end
            object DataNavigator2: TDataNavigator
              XMLComponent = DataGrid1
              object FirstButton2: TFirstButton
                XMLComponent = DataGrid1
                Caption = '|<'
              end
              object PriorPageButton1: TPriorPageButton
                XMLComponent = DataGrid1
                Caption = '<<'
              end
              ...
            end
            object DataGrid1: TDataGrid
              XMLBroker = XMLBroker1
              XMLDataSetField = 'TableOrders'
              DisplayRows = 8
              object OrderNo: TTextColumn
                DisplayWidth = 10
                Caption = 'OrderNo'
                FieldName = 'OrderNo'
              end
              object SaleDate: TTextColumn
                DisplayWidth = 18
                Caption = 'SaleDate'
                FieldName = 'SaleDate'
              end
              ...
            end
          end
        end
      end
    end
```

Once the structure is set up, you can deploy the CGI executable on the Web server and see the effect illustrated in Figure 23.14 directly in a browser. Notice that the HTML you receive is rather large, as it includes the entire master/detail structure. Once you've received it, however, you can browse the master table and the detail grid without having to ask the server for any more data.

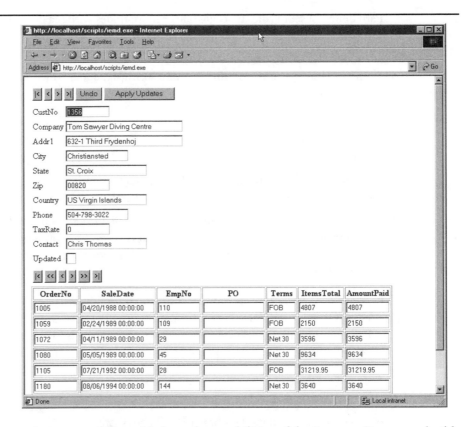

Obviously, much more could be said about the capabilities of the Internet Express to build a Web front end for a DataSnap server, as a possible alternative to the server-side scripting offered by WebSnap. Server-side scripting certainly allows for wider support of browsers, although most browsers have the minimal JavaScript required by Internet Express. Also, you should consider cases in which you prefer to have immediate feedback on the server for every action of the user or when you prefer to let the user prepare a large delta packet, even working in a disconnected situation, and then receive the entire batch of updates at once.

Using XSLT

Another approach for generating HTML starting from an XML document is the use of the Extensible Stylesheet Language (XSL) or, to be more precise, its XSL Transformations (XSLT) subset. XSLT uses other XML technologies, notably XPath and XPointer to identify portions of documents.

XPath defines a set of rules to locate one or more nodes within a document. The rules are based on a path-lie structure of the node within the XML tree, so that /books/book identifies any *book* node under the *books* document root. XPath uses a few special symbols to identify nodes:

- An asterisk (*) stands for any node; for example, book/* indicates any subnode under a *book* node.

- A dot (.) stands for the current node.

- The pipe symbol (|) indicates alternatives, as in book|ebook.

- A double slash (//) stands for any path, so that //title indicates all of the title nodes, whatever their parent nodes, and books//author indicates any author node under a books node regardless of the nodes in between.

- The at sign (@) indicates an attribute instead of a node, as in the hypothetical author/@lastname. A similar notation can be used to choose only nodes having a given value for an attribute—for example, all authors with a given first name: author[@name="marco"].

There are many other cases, but this short introduction to the rules of XPath should at least get you started and help you understand the following examples. An XSTL document is an XML document that works on the structure of a source XML document and generates in output another XML document, possibly an XHTML document you can view within a Web browser.

NOTE   Commonly used XSLT processors include MS-XML, Xalan from the Apache XML project (xml.apache.org), and the Java-based Xt of James Clarke.

The structure of an XSL file is quite simple, although its content can become extremely complex to understand. At the root should be a node like:

```
<xsl:stylesheet version="1.0" xmlns:xsl="...">
```

This node is followed by some of the base commands, such as the definition of a template to operate on a given type of nodes (xsl:template match), the activation of a template for a given node (xsl:apply-templates select), or the extraction of a value from an XML document (xsl:value-of select). There are also specific instructions you can use, including xsl:for-each, xsl:if, xsl:choose, xsl:sort (not available in MSXML the last time I checked), and xsl:number.

XSTL in Practice

After this short and probably unclear explanation, let me discuss a couple of examples. As a starting point, you should study XSL by itself, and then focus on its activation from within a Delphi application.

For your initial tests, you can connect an XSL file directly into an XML file. As you load the XML file in Internet Explorer, this will show you the resulting transformation, usually the HTML. The connection is indicated in the heading of the XML document with a command like:

```
<?xml-stylesheet type="text/xsl" href="sample1embedded.xsl"?>
```

This is what I've done in the `sample1embedded.xml` file available in the XslEmbed project. The related XSL embeds various XSL snippets that I cannot discuss in detail. For example, it grabs the entire list of authors or filters a specific group of them with this code:

```
<h2>All Authors</h2>
<ul>
  <xsl:for-each select="books//author">
    <li><xsl:value-of select="."/></li>
  </xsl:for-each>
</ul>
<h3>E-Authors</h3>
<ul>
  <xsl:for-each select="books/ebook/author">
    <li><xsl:value-of select="."/></li>
  </xsl:for-each>
</ul>
```

Some rather more complex code is used to extract nodes only when a specific value is present in a subnode or attribute, regardless of the higher-level nodes. This final XSL snippet also has an `if` statement and produces an attribute in the resulting node, as a way to build an `href` hyperlink in the HTML:

```
<h3>Marco's works (books + ebooks)</h3>
<ul>
  <xsl:for-each select="books/*[author = 'Cantu']">
    <li> <xsl:value-of select="title"/>
        <xsl:if test="url">
          (<a><xsl:attribute name="href"><xsl:value-of select="url"/>
              </xsl:attribute>Jump to document</a>)
        </xsl:if>
    </li>
  </xsl:for-each>
</ul>
```

Again, I suggest you get some more documentation on the topic, but these examples should at least get you started.

XSLT with WebSnap

Within the code of a program, you can execute the TransformNode method of a DOM node, passing to it another DOM hosting the XSL document. Instead of using this low-level approach, however, we can let WebSnap help us to create an XSL-based example. In fact, you can create a new WebSnap application (I've built a CGI program called XslCust in this case) and choose an XSLPageProducer component for its main page, to let Delphi help you start with the application code. Actually, Delphi also includes a skeleton XSL file for manipulating a ClientDataSet data packet and adds to the editor many new views. The XSL Text replaces the HTML file; the XML Tree shows the data, if any; the XSL tree shows the XSL within the Internet Explorer ActiveX; the HTML result shows the code produced by the transformation; and (finally) the Preview page shows what a user will see in a browser.

To make this actually work, you must provide some data to the XSLPageProducer component, via its XMLData property. This property can be hooked up to an XMLDocument but also directly to an XMLBroker component, as I've done in this case. The broker takes its data from a provider connected to a local table, attached to the Customers table of the classic DBDEMOS.

The effect is that, with the following Delphi-generated XSL, you get (even at design time) the output of Figure 23.15.

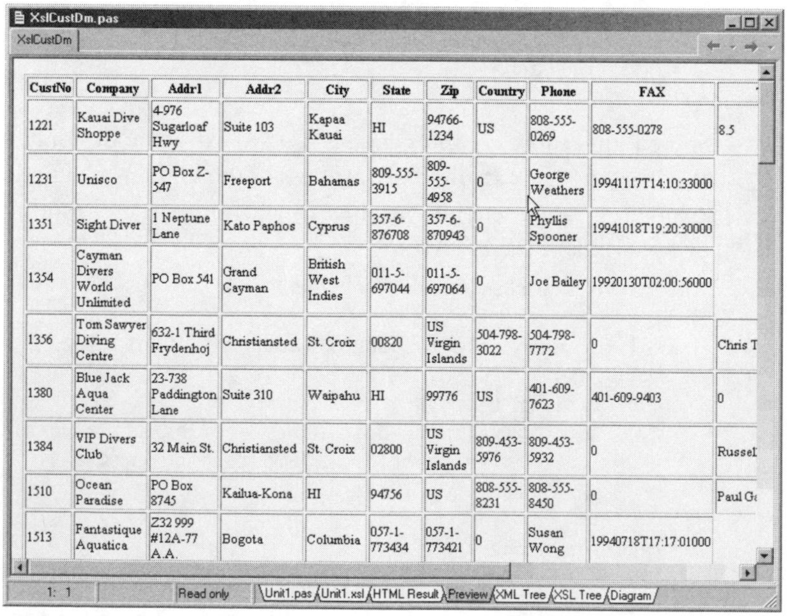

FIGURE 23.15:

The result of an XSTL transformation generated (even at design time) by the XSLPageProducer component in the XslCust example

```
<?xml version="1.0"?>
<xsl:stylesheet xmlns:xsl="http://www.w3.org/TR/WD-xsl">
  <xsl:template match="/">
    <html><body>
      <xsl:apply-templates/>
    </body></html>
  </xsl:template>

  <xsl:template match="DATAPACKET">
    <table border="1">
    <xsl:apply-templates select="METADATA/FIELDS"/>
    <xsl:apply-templates select="ROWDATA/ROW"/>
    </table>
  </xsl:template>

  <xsl:template match="FIELDS">
    <tr><xsl:apply-templates/></tr>
  </xsl:template>

  <xsl:template match="FIELD">
    <th><xsl:value-of select="@attrname"/></th>
  </xsl:template>

  <xsl:template match="ROWDATA/ROW">
    <tr><xsl:for-each select="@*">
      <td><xsl:value-of/></td>
    </xsl:for-each></tr>
  </xsl:template>
</xsl:stylesheet>
```

This code, based heavily on XSL templates, generates an HTML table made of the expansion of field metadata and row data. The fields are used to generate the table heading, with a <th> cell for each entry in a single row. The row data is used to fill in the other rows of the table with the value of each attribute (select="@*"). At this point, you should be able to modify this XSL file and change the output of the program.

Direct XSL Transformations with the DOM

Using the XSLPageProducer can certainly be handy, but generating multiple pages based on the same data just to handle different possible XSL styles with WebSnap doesn't seem to be the best approach. I've rather built a plain CGI application, called CdsXstl, that can transform a ClientDataSet data packet into different types of HTML, depending on the name of the XSL file passed as parameter to it. The advantage is that I can not only modify but even add new XSL files to the system without having to recompile the program.

To obtain the XSL transformation, the program loads both the XML and the XSL files into two XMLDocument components, called xmlDom and XslDom. Then it invokes the transformNode method of the XML document, passing the XSL document as parameter and filling in a third XMLDocument component, called HtmlDom:

```
procedure TWebModule1.WebModule1WebActionItem1Action(Sender: TObject;
  Request: TWebRequest; Response: TWebResponse; var Handled: Boolean);
var
  xslfile: string;
  attr: IDOMAttr;
begin
  // open the client dataset and load its XML in a DOM
  ClientDataSet1.Open;
  XmlDom.Xml.Text := ClientDataSet1.XMLData;
  XmlDom.Active := True;
  // load the requested xsl file
  xslfile := Request.QueryFields.Values ['style'];
  if xslfile = '' then
    xslfile := 'customer.xsl';
  xslDom.LoadFromFile ('c:\websites\xsl\' + xslfile);
  XSLDom.Active := True;
  if xslfile = 'single.xsl' then
  begin
    attr := xslDom.DOMDocument.createAttribute('select');
    attr.value := '//ROW[@CustNo="' + Request.QueryFields.Values ['id'] + '"]';
    xslDom.DOMDocument.getElementsByTagName ('xsl:apply-templates').
      item[0].attributes.setNamedItem(attr);
  end;
  // do the transformation
  HTMLDom.Active := True;
  xmlDom.DocumentElement.transformNode (xslDom.DocumentElement, HTMLDom);
  Response.Content := HTMLDom.XML.Text;
end;
```

The code uses the DOM to modify the XSL document for displaying a single record, adding the XPath statement for selecting the record indicated by the id query field. This id is added to the hyperlink by the XSL with the list of records, but here I'd rather skip listing more XSL files. You can study them, as they are available in the XSL subfolder of the folder for this example.

WARNING To run this program, the XSL files should be deployed to the folder c:\websites\xsl\, or anywhere you like after fixing the source code accordingly.

Web Services

Of all of the new features of Delphi 6, one stands out quite clearly: the support for Web services built into the product. The fact I'm discussing it at the end of the book has nothing to do with its importance, but only with the logical flow of the text, and with the fact that this is indeed not the starting point to learn Delphi programming.

But what is a Web service? It is a rapidly emerging technology that has the potential to change the way the Internet works for businesses. Browsing Web pages to enter your orders is fine for individuals (so-called B2C or business-to-consumer applications) but not for companies (so-called B2B or business-to-business applications). If you want to buy a few books, going to a book vendor Web site and punching in your requests is probably fine. But if you run a bookstore and want to place hundreds of orders a day, this is far from a good approach, particularly if you have a program that helps you track your sales and determine reorders. Grabbing the output of this program and reentering it into another application is really ridiculous.

The idea of Web services is to solve this issue: The program used to track sales can automatically create a request and send it to a Web service, which can immediately return information about the order. The next step might be to ask for a tracking number for the shipment. At this point, your program can use another Web service to track the shipment until it is at its destination, so you can tell your customers how long they have to wait. As the shipment arrives, your program can send a reminder via SMS or pager to the people with pending orders, issue a payment with a bank Web service, and … I could continue but I think I've given you an idea. Web services are for computer interoperability as much as the Web and email let people interact.

SOAP and WSDL

If the idea of Web services should be clear by now, what makes them possible is the Simple Object Access Protocol (SOAP). SOAP is built over standard HTTP, so that a Web server can handle the SOAP requests and the related data packets can pass though firewalls. SOAP defines an XML-based notation for requesting the execution of a method by an object on the server, passing parameters to it, and a notation to define the format of a response.

NOTE   SOAP was originally developed by DevelopMentor (the training company of COM expert Don Box) and Microsoft, to overcome weaknesses of using DCOM inside Web servers. Submitted to the W3C for standardization, it is being embraced by many companies, with a particular push from IBM. It is too early to see whether there will be a real standardization to let software programs from Microsoft, IBM, Sun, Oracle, and many others truly interoperate or whether some of these vendors will try to push a private version of the standard. In any case, SOAP is a cornerstone of Microsoft's dotNet architecture but also of the current proposals by Sun and Oracle.

SOAP is going to replace COM invocation, at least between different types of computers. Similarly, the definition of a SOAP service in the Web Services Description Language (WSDL) format is going to replace the IDL and type libraries used by COM and COM+. WSDL documents are another type of XML document that provides the metadata definition of a SOAP request. As you get a file in this format (generally published to define a service), you'll be able to create a program to call it.

Specifically, Delphi 6 provides a bidirectional mapping between WSDL and interfaces. This means you can grab a WSDL file and generate an interface for it. At this point, you can create a client program embedding SOAP requests via these interfaces and use a special Delphi component that allows you to convert your local interface requests into SOAP calls (as I doubt you want to manually generate the XML required for a SOAP request).

The other way around, you can define an interface (or use an existing one) and let a Delphi component generate a WSDL description for it. Another component provides you with a SOAP-to-Pascal mapping, so that by embedding this component and an object implementing the interface within a server-side program, you can have your Web service up and running in matter of minutes.

BabelFish Translations

As a first example of the use of Web service, I'm going to build a simple client for the BabelFish translation service offered by AltaVista. Because this is an experimental service, like most others, there is no guarantee that the service will be working by the time you read this. You can find this and other services for experiments on the XMethods Web site (www.xmethods.com) and also look for sample Web services provided by my own site (www.marcocantu.com).

After downloading the WSDL description of this service from XMethods (also available on the CD-ROM), I invoked Delphi's Web Services Importer in the Web Services page of the New items dialog box and selected the file. Delphi generated an Object Pascal interface for the Web service, as follows:

```
unit babelintf;

interface

uses
  Types, XSBuiltIns;

type
  BabelFishPortType = interface(IInvokable)
    ['{DF96B8F8-DD8E-43A1-9276-4F821D9EA3FA}']
    function BabelFish(const translationmode: String;
      const sourcedata: String): String; stdcall;
```

```
    end;

implementation

uses InvokeRegistry;

initialization
    InvRegistry.RegisterInterface(TypeInfo(BabelFishPortType), '', '');
end.
```

Notice first that the interface inherits from the IInvokable interface. This doesn't add anything in terms of methods to the IInterface base interface of Delphi, but is compiled with the flag used to enable RTTI generation, {$M+}, like the TPersistent class. In this code, you can also see that the interface is registered in the global invocation registry (or InvRegistry), passing the type information reference of the interface type.

NOTE   Having RTTI information for interfaces is actually the most important technological advance underlying SOAP invocation. Not that SOAP-to-Pascal mapping isn't important, as it is crucial to simplify the process, but having RTTI for an interface is what makes the entire architecture powerful and robust.

Once you have converted a WSDL definition into an easy-to-use interface, you need a component translating from interface call to SOAP call, and also handling the response and possible errors. This role can be played by the HTTPRio component, which implements the idea of a Remote Invocation Object (RIO) over HTTP. Delphi 6 was built opening up the road for SOAP, but also keeping it open for other remote invocation mechanisms.

In the BabelFish example, the HTTPRio component has the following settings, obtained by choosing the WSDL file first and then selecting the only available service and port from it, directly in the drop-down lists of the Object Inspector:

```
object HTTPRIO1: THTTPRIO
    WSDLLocation = 'C:\md6code\23\BabelFish\BabelFishService.xml'
    Service = 'BabelFish'
    Port = 'BabelFishPort'
    HTTPWebNode.Agent = 'Borland SOAP 1.1'
    Converter.Options = [soSendMultiRefObj, soTryAllSchema]
end
```

At this point, there is very little left to do. We have information about the service that can be used for its invocation, and we know the parameters required by the only available method. The two elements are merged by extracting the interface you want to call directly from the HTTPRio component, with an expression like HTTPRIO1 as BabelFishPortType. It might seem rather astonishing at first, but it is also outrageously simple. This is the Web service call done by the example:

```
EditTarget.Text := (HTTPRIO1 as BabelFishPortType).
    BabelFish(ComboBoxType.Text, EditSource.Text);
```

The resulting output of the program, depicted in Figure 23.16, allows you to learn foreign languages (although the teacher here has its shortcomings!). I haven't replicated the same example with stock options, currencies, weather forecasts, and the many other services available, as they would look much the same.

FIGURE 23.16:

An example of a translation from English to German obtained by AltaVista's BabelFish via a Web service

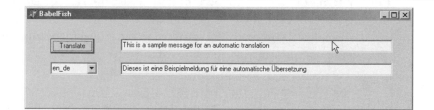

Building a Web Service

If calling a Web service in Delphi 6 is very straightforward, the same can be said of the development of an actual service. If you go into the Web Services page of the New items dialog box, you can see the SOAP Server Application option. Selecting it, Delphi presents you a list quite similar to selection of a WebBroker application. A Web service, in fact, is typically hosted by a Web server, using one of the available Web server extension technologies (CGI, ISAPI, Apache modules, etc.). After completing this step, Delphi will add three components to the resulting Web module, which is just a plain Web module, with no special additions:

- The HTTPSoapDispatcher component has the role of receiving the Web request, as any other HTTP dispatcher does.

- The HTTPSoapPascalInvoker component does the reverse operation of the HTTPRio component, as it can translate SOAP requests into calls of Pascal interfaces (instead of shifting interface method calls into SOAP requests).

- The WSDLHTMLPublish component can be used to extract the WSDL definition of the service from the interfaces it support, and performs the opposite role of the Web Services Importer Wizard. Technically, this is another HTTP dispatcher.

Once this framework is in place—something you can also do by adding the three components above to an existing Web module—we can start writing a service. As an example I've taken the euro conversion example of Chapter 4, "The Run-Time Library," and transformed it into a Web service called ConvertService. First of all, I've added to the program a unit defining the interface of the service, as follows:

```
type
  IConvert = interface(IInvokable)
  ['{FF1EAA45-0B94-4630-9A18-E768A91A78E2}']
    function ConvertCurrency (Source, Dest: string; Amount: Double): Double;
      stdcall;
    function ToEuro (Source: string; Amount: Double): Double; stdcall;
    function FromEuro (Dest: string; Amount: Double): Double; stdcall;
    function TypesList: string; stdcall;
  end;
```

Defining an interface directly in code, without having to use a tool such as the Type Library Editor, provides a great advantage. Notice that I've given a GUID to the interface, as usual, and used the stdcall calling convention, as the SOAP converter does not support the default register calling convention.

In the same unit defining the interface of the service, we should also register it, an operation which will be useful on both the client and server sides of the program, as we will be able to include this interface definition unit in both.

```
uses InvokeRegistry;

initialization
  InvRegistry.RegisterInterface(TypeInfo(IConvert));
```

Now that we have an interface we can expose to the public, we have to provide an implementation for it, again by means of the standard Pascal code (and with the help of the predefined TInvokableClass class:

```
type
  TConvert = class (TInvokableClass, IConvert)
  protected
    function ConvertCurrency (Source, Dest: string; Amount: Double): Double;
      stdcall;
    function ToEuro (Source: string; Amount: Double): Double; stdcall;
    function FromEuro (Dest: string; Amount: Double): Double; stdcall;
    function TypesList: string; stdcall;
  end;
```

The implementation of these functions, which call in the code of the euro conversion system of Chapter 4, is not discussed here as it has little to do with the development of the service itself. What is important to notice, instead, is that this implementation unit also has a registration call in its initialization section:

```
InvRegistry.RegisterInvokableClass (TConvert);
```

This is basically all. By registering the interface, we'll make it possible for the program to generate a WSDL description, as you can see in Figure 23.17, where I've used a browser to connect to the *wsdl* action of the service, implemented by the WSDLHTMLPublish component.

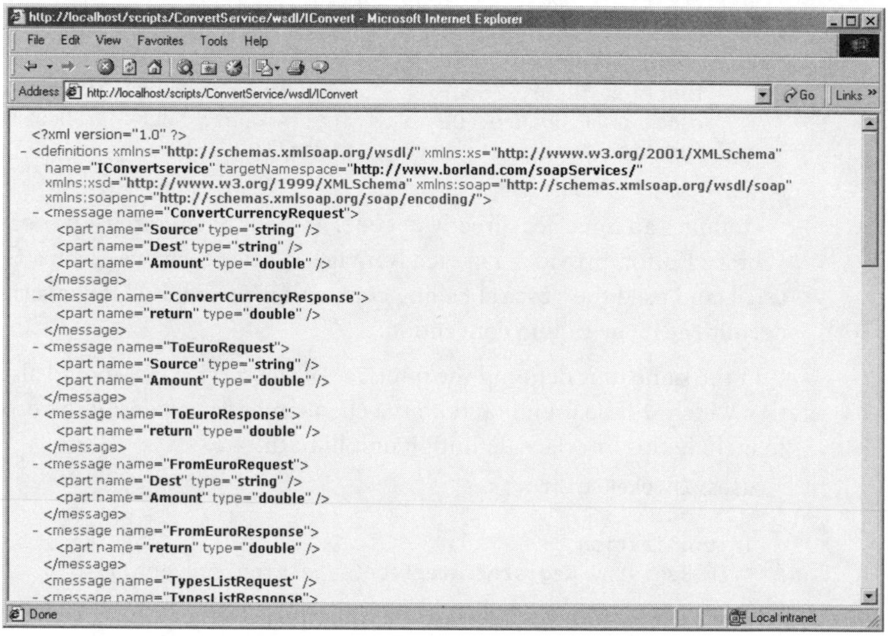

FIGURE 23.17:

The WSDL file generated automatically from the interface published by the ConvertService program

Of course, you cannot call the service from a browser, as the role of a Web service is not to display data on the Web but rather to let applications interoperate (still, you can reasonably have a Web application calling a service). Before I discuss the client application, though, let me cover another interesting element. For debugging purposes, I've added to the Web module an actual action, connected with code to generate information about the registered interfaces and servers:

```
Response.Content :=
  '<h3>GetMethExternalName - ToEuro</h3><p>' +
  InvRegistry.GetMethExternalName(TypeInfo(IConvert), 'ToEuro</p>') +
  '<h3>GetInterfaceExternalName - IConvert</h3><p>' +
  InvRegistry.GetInterfaceExternalName(TypeInfo(IConvert)) + '</p>' +
  '<h3>GetNamespaceByGUID - IConvert</h3><p>' +
  InvRegistry.GetNamespaceByGUID (IConvert) + '</p>';
```

The first call verifies whether a given method is properly registered and really exists, by calling the GetMethExternalName of the invocation registry. The result, unsurprisingly, is the same string passed as parameter, ToEuro. The second call, GetInterfaceExternalName, should return the external name of the interface, but I haven't been able to make it work properly (I left it in anyway, as it is supposed to work). The last call, GetNamespaceByGUID, returns the XML namespace of the interface, urn:ConvertIntf-IConvert. There are other similar calls you can make against the registry, which are quite interesting and demonstrate the power of this approach and of RTTI for interfaces.

Having said this, let me move to the client application, calling the service. This time I don't really need to start from the WSDL file, as I already have the Pascal interface. This time the form doesn't even have the HTTPRio component, which is created in code:

```
private
  Invoker: THTTPRio;

procedure TForm1.FormCreate(Sender: TObject);
begin
  Invoker := THTTPRio.Create(nil);
  Invoker.URL := 'http://localhost/scripts/ConvertService.exe/soap/iconvert';
  ConvIntf := Invoker as IConvert;
end;
```

As an alternative to using a WSDL file, the SOAP invoker component can be associated with an URL. Once this association has been done and the required interface has been extracted from the component, you can start writing straight Pascal code to invoke the service, as we saw earlier.

A user can fill the two combo boxes, calling the TypesList method, which returns a list of available currencies within a string (separated by semicolons). This list is extracted by replacing any semicolon with a line break and then assigning the multiline string directly to the combo items:

```
procedure TForm1.Button2Click(Sender: TObject);
var
  TypeNames: string;
begin
  TypeNames := ConvIntf.TypesList;
  ComboBoxFrom.Items.Text := StringReplace (TypeNames, ';', sLineBreak,
    [rfReplaceAll]);
  ComboBoxTo.Items := ComboBoxFrom.Items;
end;
```

At this point, after selecting two currencies, you can perform the conversion, with this code and the result of Figure 23.18:

```
procedure TForm1.Button1Click(Sender: TObject);
begin
  LabelResult.Caption := Format ('%n', [(ConvIntf.ConvertCurrency(
    ComboBoxFrom.Text, ComboBoxTo.Text, StrToFloat(EditAmount.Text)))]);
end;
```

DataSnap over SOAP

Now that we have a reasonably good idea of how to build a SOAP server and a SOAP client, we can have a look at how to use this technology in building a multitier DataSnap application. We'll use a Soap Server Data Module to create the new Web service and the SoapConnection component to connect a client application to it.

Let's look at the server side first. You have to move to the Web Services page of the New Items dialog box and use the Soap Server Application icon first to create a new Web service, and then use the Soap Server Data Module icon to add a DataSnap server-side data module to the SOAP server. This is what I've done in the SoapDataServer example (which uses the Web App Debugger architecture for testing purposes). From this point on, all you do is write a *normal* DataSnap server (or actually a middle-tier DataSnap application) as discussed in Chapter 17. In this specific case, I've added to the program InterBase access by means of dbExpress, resulting in the following structure:

```
object SoapTestDm: TSoapTestDm
  object SQLConnection1: TSQLConnection
    ConnectionName = 'IBLocal'
  end
  object SQLDataSet1: TSQLDataSet
    SQLConnection = SQLConnection1
    CommandText = 'select * from EMPLOYEE'
  end
  object DataSetProvider1: TDataSetProvider
    DataSet = SQLDataSet1
  end
end
```

The data module built for a SOAP-based DataSnap server defines a custom interface (so you can add methods to it) inheriting from IAppServer, which is now defined as a published interface (even though it doesn't inherit from IInvokable). The implementation class, TSoapTestDm, is the data module itself, as in other DataSnap types of servers. This is the code Delphi generated for me:

```
type
  ISoapTestDm = interface(IAppServer)
    ['{1F109687-6D8B-4F85-9BF5-EFFC87A9F10F}']
  end;

  TSoapTestDm = class(TSoapDataModule, ISoapTestDm, IAppServer)
    DataSetProvider1: TDataSetProvider;
    SQLConnection1: TSQLConnection;
    SQLDataSet1: TSQLDataSet;
  end;
```

The base TSoapDataModule doesn't inherit from TInvokableClass. This is not a problem as long as you provide an extra procedure to create the object (which is what TInvokableClass does for you) and add it to the registration code:

```
procedure TSoapTestDmCreateInstance(out obj: TObject);
begin
  obj := TSoapTestDm.Create(nil);
end;

initialization
  InvRegistry.RegisterInvokableClass(TSoapTestDm, TSoapTestDmCreateInstance);
  InvRegistry.RegisterInterface(TypeInfo(ISoapTestDm));
```

The server application actually also publishes the IAppServer interface, thanks to the only line of code in the SOAPMidas unit.

WARNING   Web service applications should not include more than one SOAP Data Module, as the registration cannot distinguish between multiple implementations of the same IAppServer interface.

To build the client application, called SoapDataClient, I've started with a plain program and added a SoapConnection component to it (from the Web Services page of the palette), hooking it to the URL of the DataSnap Web service, referring to the specific interface we are looking for:

```
object SoapConnection1: TSoapConnection
  Agent = 'Borland SOAP 1.1'
  URL = 'http://localhost:1024/SoapDataServer.SoapDataServer/Soap/ISoapTestDm'
end
```

From this point on, I've proceeded as usual, adding a ClientDataSet component, a Data-Source, and a DBGrid to the program, choosing the only available provider for the client dataset, and hooking the rest as usual. Not surprisingly, for this simple example, the client application has little custom code: a single call to open the connection when a button is clicked (to avoid startup errors) and an `ApplyUpdates` call to send changes back to the database.

Regardless of the apparent similarity of this program to all of the other DataSnap client and server programs built in Chapter 17, there is a very important difference worth underlining: The SoapDataServer and SoapDataClient programs do not use COM for exposing or calling the `IAppServer` interface. Quite the opposite—the socket- and HTTP-based connections of DataSnap still rely on local COM objects and a registration of the server in the Windows Registry. The native SOAP-based support provided by Delphi 6, instead, allows for a totally custom solution independent from COM and with many more chances to be ported to other operating systems (Linux being certainly the first, with a future release of Kylix).

What's Next?

In this final chapter of the book, I've covered XML and related technologies, including XSLT, SOAP, WSDL, XML schemas, XPath, and a few more. We've seen how Delphi 6 provides simplified DOM programming, XML access using interfaces, and XML transformations. I've also covered Internet Express and the development of Web services.

Besides tracking what goes on in the area of SOAP and WSDL, particularly in terms of standards conformance by the major players, there are a few interesting initiatives you should probably keep track of if you're interested in the development in business-to-business services. One of them is the UDDI proposal (`www.uddi.org`), pushed by Microsoft, IBM, Ariba, and many other companies, to create a universal registry of services. Another is ebXML (`www.ebxml.org`), a proposal by the U.N. office that defined the EDI standards for an XML-based global business exchange.

Of course, I don't want to delve too much into these nontechnical issues, but I thought it was worth mentioning them at the end of this book, as I try to give a few hints at a sort of "what's next" for Delphi programmers. Delphi is indeed a strong player in both the Windows and Linux client markets, in the client/server and enterprise application markets, and now takes a bold step in the areas of Web development and Web services.

Just as Borland wants to provide the best tools to developers, I hope this book has helped you master Delphi, the most successful tool Borland has brought to the market in the last few years. Remember to check from time to time the reference, foundations, and advanced material I've collected on my Web site (`www.marcocantu.com`). Check my site also for eventual updates and integration of the material in the book, and feel free to use the newsgroups hosted there for your questions about the book and about Delphi in general. Much of this material could not be included in the book, simply because of space constraints. Some of this extra material is actually already available on the companion CD, where you can continue reading about other aspects of Delphi programming.

INDEX

Note to the Reader: Throughout this index **boldfaced** page numbers indicate primary discussions of a topic. *Italicized* page numbers indicate illustrations.

B

C

G

I

S

T

V

W

X

Z

Visit Marco's Delphi Developer Web Site

This book's author, Marco Cantù, has created a site specifically for Delphi developers, at www.marcocantu.com. It's a great resource for all of your Delphi programming needs.

The site includes:

- The source code of the book (also available on the companion CD)
- Extra examples and tips
- Delphi components, wizards, and tools built by the author
- The online book *Essential Pascal* and the preliminary version of *Essential Delphi*
- Papers the author has written about Delphi, C++, and Java
- Extensive links to Delphi-related Web sites and documents
- Other material related to the author's books, the conferences he speaks at, and his training seminars

The site also hosts a newsgroup, which has a specific section devoted to the author's books, so that readers can discuss the book content with him and among themselves. Other sections of the newsgroup discuss Delphi programming and general topics. The newsgroup can also be accessed from a Web interface.